Social Problems:
Divergent Perspectives

CRITICAL READERS:

Douglas Degher,
Northern Arizona University

Michael Gordon,
The University of Connecticut

Jerry C. Jolley,
Lewis-Clark State College

Robert Lilly,
Northern Kentucky State College

Peter Manning,
Michigan State University

Charlotte O'Kelly,
Providence College

Howard Robboy,
Trenton State College

John R. Stratton,
University of Iowa

Ellis Williamson,
Florida Jr. College

Social Problems:
Divergent Perspectives

THOMAS J. SULLIVAN
Northern Michigan University

KENRICK S. THOMPSON
Northern Michigan University

RICHARD D. WRIGHT
Northern Michigan University

GEORGE R. GROSS
Northern Michigan University

DALE R. SPADY
Northern Michigan University

JOHN WILEY & SONS
New York · Chichester · Brisbane · Toronto

Library of Congress Cataloging in Publication Data

Main entry under title:

Social problems.
Includes index.
1. United States — Social conditions — 1960-
2. Social problems.   3. Sociology.   I. Sullivan,
Thomas J., 1944-
HN65.S575   309.1'73'092   79-20676
ISBN 0-471-02932-7

Printed in the United States of America

10 9 8 7 6 5 4 3

To Nancy, Chris, Dolores, Patti, and Carol

Foreword

Most nations trumpet their progress — the growth of industrial production, improvements in housing, the completion of massive construction projects, the extension of superhighways, and achievements in the arts and sciences. The United States — a country that is so prosperous and technologically advanced that it is the object of either uncritical idealization or bilious hostility — heralds its deficits and failures. Our mass media are continuously glutted with the reporting of one crime or tragedy after another; radio and television stations fill each broadcasting day via the news, soap operas, exposés, and documentaries with every imaginable pathological deviation or catastrophe. Details of problem-oriented news stories are available morning, noon, and night in the press or over the airwaves. A potential meltdown of a nuclear reactor competes for space in the media with anxieties about skyrocketing inflation, city bankruptcies, energy shortages, carcinogenic food additives, ghetto disturbances, prison riots, unconscionably high black teenage unemployment, school levy failures, strikes, high divorce rates, the increasing number of single-parent families, a massacre at a utopian commune in Guyana, and an unlimited number of other shams and scams.

Many Americans who are exposed to this overload of crises hour by hour and who are bombarded daily by routine warnings about protecting themselves and their property from an endless list of dangers have grave doubts that American society will survive the century. Philosophers and social scientists have compared the American condition to ancient Roman civilization and are predicting a similar demise for our republic. The American belief in progress, a major hallmark of the United States for most of the last century, has steadily given way to a deep depression about our flawed society during this period. More than ever before,

Americans flee their apprehensions about the present and the future by endorsing "end of the world" scenarios, space and other escape odysseys, and quests for lost continents. Our social problems are so seemingly insolvable that many of us have joined the "me" generation or are "laid back" or "into something" — from jogging to primal screaming. There are pop therapies still looking for pathologies to cure, and alternate lifestyles awaiting the experientially courageous.

For some, this world may seem well on its way to becoming unglued. Nearly everything is possible since hardly anything seems to be true. Traditional belief systems and conventional social arrangements have atrophied. Interpersonal networks, once routinized by geographic stability, are now formed, then abandoned, and reformed continually. Personal goals are often vague, transitory, and unsatisfying — even when achieved. On the broader scene, a president of the United States, in order to muster support for a faltering administration, invokes a quaint and frightening appeal slogan: "the moral equivalent of war." In truth, the United States and other Western societies are searching for a new consensus — new meanings, social institutions, overseeing goals — to replace those that emerged in the traumatic and chaotic period following the transformation from traditional preindustrial society to urban, mass culture and organization. We continue to grope for a new consensus on values and lifestyles — on the boundaries of what should be permissible and what is to be encouraged — in our postindustrial, technical age. This awkward flailing, more reminiscent of a drowning person trying desperately to stay afloat than of a super-technological and sophisticated social order, may be a sign of the search for what Kuhn, when he talks about stages and epochs in science, calls a new "paradigm." (Newtonian concepts giving way to relativity theory immediately comes to mind as a recent instance of the emergence of a new and exciting paradigm.)

Chaos, in search of a theory, describes the status of our social problems at the beginning of the eighth decade of the twentieth century. Although it does considerably more, *Social Problems: Divergent Perspectives* presents a reasoned, data-based, cool and incisive sociology of our modern society and its discontents. Each of the chapters is written by the coauthor whose area of expertise constitutes the substance of the chapter. Surprisingly, although the book is a joint enterprise involving many hands, there is a unity of approach and style throughout. Remove the listing of authors, and the reader would have difficulty discerning that there are five contributors.

Apart from the unity of the text, *Social Problems: Divergent Perspectives* is well organized and readable. The issues are current and cogent. As the authors point out in their introduction, the material is presented in the same way in each chapter. This approach provides for a logical and systematic presentation.

Three organizing principles are used: a functionalist perspective, conflict theory, and an interactionist approach. It is unfortunate that social problems cannot be understood adequately from just one approach and that these three perspectives are not equally useful to the understanding of each

of the problems. This is the bane of the field, however—we suffer from the lack of one unifying model. Within this constraint, imposed on all who work in the area, the authors present a balanced view of the issues from the three theoretical perspectives, and of the alternatives that follow from these approaches. Altogether, the book is a nice package in a complex area of inquiry.

We began this introduction by contrasting the seeming apathy and variation of peoples around the world toward their social problems with the active involvement of Americans in seeking solutions. The question is *why?* The answer, provided in *Social Problems: Divergent Perspectives,* lies in the authors' definition of a social problem: an *awareness* that a social condition threatens *group values* and can be remedied by *collective action.* Ours remains an active and involved society. We are intolerant of the distance between the real and the ideal, and we are addicted to the proposition that with good will, sacrifice, and social engineering, we can overcome all deficits. Naive? For sure. But most refreshing in a world that accepts ineptitude, inequality, and injustice as the stuff of humanity. Although the prospect for a quick fix to our problems is bleak, passive acceptance leads only to the perpetuation of social ills. This is the message of *Social Problems: Divergent Perspectives,* and it is a theme, going back to the earliest American sociologists, that we heartily endorse.

SIMON DINITZ
ALFRED C. CLARKE
The Ohio State University
RUSSELL R. DYNES
Executive Officer
American Sociological Association

Preface

Authors of textbooks on social problems have certain things in common: a concern about the major social problems that confront American society today, a desire to communicate with others about these problems and ways of alleviating them, and a plan by which they can accomplish these things. Each of the authors of this text has been teaching social problems courses at the college level for many years. Using this forum, each has attempted to communicate with others about the state of American society and what might be done about its problems. Collectively, we now embark on an effort to cast our net more broadly—to communicate with a much larger audience through the written medium. From the very beginning of this project, our plan has been to write a cogent, informative textbook on social problems that is both scholarly and readable. We do not presume to have written a comprehensive treatise providing all the answers for all of America's social problems; any such claim by an author would have to be viewed with great skepticism. We have, however, attempted to present the student reader with the most current information on social problems. We have tried to help the student analyze information about social problems. And we have suggested possible alternative solutions to some of these problems for the reader's consideration.

A problem that all authors face is which of the many topics to select for treatment in the text. There are a far greater number of socially problematic issues in America today than could possibly be covered effectively in one volume. We have selected the social problems that we and many other sociologists consider most pressing today. However, we have also chosen a few issues for discussion, such as problems of work and leisure, that we feel are growing in significance and that will be viewed as prominent social problems by the Ameri-

can public in the near future. We have included these topics to encourage students to look ahead and become sensitized to how the changing nature of American society may be creating new and important social problems.

Almost all social problems textbooks claim to integrate the many issues discussed by utilizing some theoretical framework. Each book is somewhat unique in this respect. However, most social problems textbooks have been criticized for their failure to achieve this integration. The more frequent criticisms include assertions that the treatment of theoretical perspectives is superficial and "thrown in"; that too many theories are considered so that coverage of each is inadequate; that some theories receive more coverage than others; and that there is no uniformity of coverage of the theoretical perspectives from one chapter to the next.

In this text, we have been concerned to avoid these objections by employing what we consider the most useful and important perspectives in sociology: functionalism, conflict, and interactionism. These serve as a vehicle for integrating the materials covered in each chapter. We present the major assumptions and concepts of each perspective in the first chapter, and then (with the exception of chapter 2, which concerns science and research methods) we employ the perspectives uniformly and integrate them into the treatment of every issue. We have used this strategy because we are convinced that there are "divergent perspectives" that should be used to analyze any social problem. To claim that one single viewpoint will suffice is deceptively oversimple and limits our horizons to only one dimension of a very complex and multifaceted social reality. We encourage the student to view these three perspectives as "tools" that can be used to understand social problems more completely. Thus, the student should come away from this text both furnished with information about specific social problems *and* equipped with the sociological tools to analyze any social problems.

Some books seem to be written for the instructor. Others purport to be geared to the student. We have attempted to write a book that will be instructive to the student *and* beneficial to the instructor. Throughout the text we have provided a number of aids to students—glossary terms, suggested readings, and ample tabular material—that are designed to augment information and views on the issues. In the Instructor's Manual for this text, we have provided materials to assist the instructor in helping the student understand complex social problems.

A course in social problems can be an exciting voyage of discovery. The excitement is enhanced if students, instructor, and textbook bring a sufficient amount of interest, enthusiasm, and energy to the task. We believe that this textbook has fulfilled its obligation in this respect.

Acknowledgments

A textbook often appears to be the simple product of its authors' labors. Nothing could be further from the truth. Any book is necessarily also the product of the interaction between its authors and a multitude of other people, and this text has benefited significantly from such interchanges. We are grateful for the helpful hints, suggestions, and guidance of George G. Thompson during the early stages of this project. As novices in the business of writing textbooks, we gained much from his experience. For their comments on parts of the manuscript, we thank Michael Loukinen, Duane Monette, Michael Sullivan, and Emil Vajda. We are extremely grateful for the support that we received from Northern Michigan University throughout the project. In particular, Dr. Robert B. Glenn and Mr. Cornell R. DeJong provided encouragement and support. The project would have been a longer and much more grueling experience without the patience, expertise, and dedication of our university's reference librarians, in particular Richard H. Swain and Roberta M. Henderson. We especially thank Dolores Wright and Mary Hanchek, whose persistence, willingness to work, and caustic wit not only helped us complete the project but also made it a more enjoyable experience. A manuscript's quality also depends on accurate typing. We are grateful to Christina F. Thompson for her careful typing and proofing of copy.

We should like to thank Simon Dinitz, Alfred C. Clarke, and Russell R. Dynes for their contribution in writing the foreword to our book. For their invaluable assistance in making this a better book, we are grateful to the following people at John Wiley & Sons: Richard Baker, Thomas Gay, Arthur Vergara, Ed Sandow, Carol Luitjens, Stella Kupferberg, Rafael Hernandez, and Rose Mary Hirsch. The authors, of course, take final responsibility for their text.

When five people set out to write a textbook, there are many family members to thank. We are grateful to all those wonderful people who gave their love, patience, and support that helped keep us together in both body and spirit for the duration of this project.

Contents

1.
THE STUDY OF SOCIAL PROBLEMS 3

A HISTORICAL PERSPECTIVE ON
THE STUDY OF SOCIAL PROBLEMS 3

The Beginnings of the Sociological Study of
   Social Problems   6
The Study of Social Problems in America   7
Social Problems: Divergent Perspectives   9

WHAT IS A SOCIAL PROBLEM? 9

Who Defines?   9
Basis for Defining   9
Personal Troubles, Public Issues?   10
Social Problem: A Definition   10

SOCIAL PROBLEMS IN AMERICAN
SOCIETY 12

Values and Norms   12
Power and Authority   13
Interest Groups and Vested Interests   15
Diversity and Subcultures in America   16
Ethnocentrism and Social Problems   17
Social Problems in a Democratic Society   17

SOCIOLOGICAL PERSPECTIVES ON
SOCIAL PROBLEMS 19

The Functionalist Perspective   19
The Conflict Perspective   23
The Interactionist Perspective   25
Multiple Definitions: Divergent Perspectives   29

DIFFICULTIES IN SOLVING SOCIAL
PROBLEMS 29

Is It a Social Problem?   29
Can It Be Solved?   30
Are We Willing to Solve It?   30
Should We Attempt a Solution?   31
Will We Accept the Costs?   31

ORGANIZATION OF THE BOOK 31

2.
THE USES AND MISUSES OF DATA 37

WAYS OF "KNOWING" 38

Traditional Knowledge   39
Charismatic Knowledge   40
Experiential Knowledge   41
Scientific Knowledge   42
Interest Groups and Scientific Objectivity   44

THE RESEARCH PROCESS 45

Stages in the Research Process   46
Major Issues in the Research Process   48

THE PRESENTATION OF DATA:
STRENGTHS AND PITFALLS 52

Statistical Presentation   52
Visual Presentation: Graphs and Charts   55

PROPAGANDA AND DISTORTION 56

CONCLUSION 59

3.
SOCIAL PROBLEMS IN OUR CITIES 65

URBAN LIFE IN AMERICA: A BRIEF
HISTORY 66

Immigration   66
Urban Migration   67
Urban Transportation   68
Urban Education   68

THE CITY AS A SOCIAL PROBLEM 69

The Functionalist Perspective   69
The Conflict Perspective   70
The Interactionist Perspective   71

WHAT IS A CITY? 71

Complexity and Specialization   72

Individualism and Social Diversity 72
Impersonality 73

ECONOMIC PROBLEMS OF THE
CENTRAL CITY 73

Decentralization 73
Decentralization and Business 75
The Flight of the Middle Class 75
The Case of New York City 76

RACIAL PROBLEMS IN CITIES 77

EDUCATION AND THE INNER CITY 78

The Educational Trap 79
School Financing 80
School Desegregation and Busing 81
Education and Social Problems 83

HOUSING 83

The Ghetto 84
Federal Housing Policy 85
The Dynamics of Land Use 87

TRANSPORTATION AND THE CITY 88

Modes of Transportation 88

FUTURE PROSPECTS: THE POLITICS
OF URBAN LIFE 91

Federal Programs 91
Regional Planning and Cooperation 92
Should We Save Our Cities? 95

CONCLUSION 95

4.
POPULATION PROBLEMS 101

WORLD POPULATION GROWTH: A
BRIEF HISTORY 102

Population Growth in Preindustrial
Societies 103
Industrialization and the Demographic
Transition 105

POPULATION AS A SOCIAL PROBLEM 106

The Functionalist Perspective 106
The Conflict Perspective 108

The Interactionist Perspective 109

POPULATION DYNAMICS 109

Mortality in the Modern World 110
Fertility 112
Migration 114

THE CONSEQUENCES OF
OVER-POPULATION 115

Crowding 115
Depletion of Mineral Resources 116
Food Shortages 117
The Fight for Survival 124
"And the Poor Get Children" 125

FUTURE PROSPECTS 125

Migration 125
Mortality 126
Fertility 126
Zero Population Growth 131

CONCLUSION 131

5.
PROBLEMS OF THE ENVIRONMENT 137

ENVIRONMENTAL PROBLEMS IN
HISTORICAL PERSPECTIVE 139

The American Indian 139
The Coming of Western Man 139
The Twentieth Century: Progress and Prob-
lems 141

ENVIRONMENTAL CONDITIONS AS
SOCIAL PROBLEMS 143

The Functionalist Perspective 143
The Conflict Perspective 143
The Interactionist Perspective 144

INTEREST GROUPS AND THE
ENVIRONMENT 145

Business and the Environment 145
The Environmental Movement 146
The Modern Environmental Controversy:
Economic Growth vs. an Unchanging En-
vironment 148

The Modern Dilemma   153

CASE STUDY: KEPONE   155

The Trouble Begins   156
Genesis of a Chemical   158
Telltale Signs   158
Missed Signals and Oversights   159
The Judgment   160
Counting the Costs   161
The Way Out   162

FUTURE PROSPECTS   163

Public Action on Environmental Problems   163
Interest Groups in the Solution of Environmental Problems   165
A Strategy for Environmental Solutions   169

CONCLUSION   170

6.
WEALTH AND POWER IN THE CORPORATE STATE   177

CORPORATE AND GOVERNMENTAL POWER—A BRIEF HISTORY   178

Corporate Growth   178
The Federal Government   179

CORPORATIONS AND GOVERNMENT AS SOCIAL PROBLEMS   180

The Functionalist Perspective   180
The Conflict Perspective   181
The Interactionist Perspective   183

THE CORPORATION IN MODERN SOCIETY   183

Power and Wealth   184
Corporate Power and the Individual Consumer   187
Multinational Corporations   189

GOVERNMENT   192

The Federal Government   192
The Interstate Commerce Commission   193
Federal Government Expansion   195
The Government and the Military   195

WHO HAS POWER IN AMERICAN SOCIETY?   199

The Power Elite   199
Pluralism: An Alternate View of National Power   202
Evaluation of the Models   204
The Power Elite and Democratic Society   204

FUTURE PROSPECTS   205

Government Reform   206
Citizens' Groups and Peoples' Lobbies   207

CONCLUSION   209

7.
THE FAMILY   217

THE FAMILY: PAST AND PRESENT   219

The Family in a Preindustrial Society   219
The Family and the Industrial Revolution   221
The Family in a Postindustrial Society   224

THE FAMILY AS A SOCIAL PROBLEM   224

The Functionalist Perspective   224
The Conflict Perspective   225
The Interactionist Perspective   226
What is the Family?   227

CHANGING PATTERNS OF MARRIAGE AND FAMILY LIFE   229

The Marital Bond   233
Oral Contraception and the Family   233

DIVORCE   233

The Divorce Rate   234
Divorce and Social Class   235
Divorce and the Law   235
The Future of Divorce   236

ALTERNATIVE FAMILY FORMS   237

Open Marriage   242
Single Parenthood/The One-Parent Family   243
Group Marriage   244
Serial Polygamy   246
Communes   246
Parenthood: New Possibilities   248

Alternative Family Forms and the Three
Theoretical Perspectives — 248

THE FAMILY IN SEARCH OF A FUTURE 249

The Ideal and the Real — 249
The Pluralistic Family — 250

CONCLUSION 252

8.
HEALTH CARE 259

HEALTH CARE IN AMERICA: A HISTORICAL OVERVIEW 260

Early American Medicine — 260
Emergence of Modern Medicine — 261
The Modern Scourge: Chronic Disease — 263
The State of Health in America — 264

HEALTH CARE AS A SOCIAL PROBLEM 264

The Functionalist Perspective — 265
The Conflict Perspective — 265
The Interactionist Perspective — 266

SOCIAL FACTORS IN HEALTH AND ILLNESS 266

Social Class — 267
Sex Roles — 271
Occupational Status — 271
Education — 272

MENTAL ILLNESS 273

The Nature of Mental Illness — 273
The Treatment of Mental Illness — 277

PROBLEMS IN THE HEALTH CARE DELIVERY SYSTEM 279

Bureaucracy and Dehumanization — 279
The High Cost of Health Care — 281

FUTURE PROSPECTS: THE POLITICS OF HEALTH CARE 283

New Programs and Health Practitioners — 283
The Financing of Health Care — 285
Interest Groups in the Health Field — 289

CONCLUSION 290

9.
WORK AND LEISURE 297

WORK AND LEISURE: A BRIEF HISTORY 299

The Emergence of a Leisure Class — 299
The Emergence of the Protestant Ethic — 299
The Protestant Ethic and American Values — 300
Work and Leisure in Industrial Society — 300

WORK AND LEISURE AS SOCIAL PROBLEMS 302

The Functionalist Perspective — 302
The Conflict Perspective — 303
The Interactionist Perspective — 304
What Are Work and Leisure? — 305

WORK 306

The Multiple Dimensions of Work — 307
The Decline of the Work Ethic — 312

LEISURE 314

Reduced Work and Increased Leisure — 315
Block Leisure Time — 316
Difficulties in Using Leisure Time — 318
For Whom is Leisure a Problem? — 319

THE FUTURE OF WORK AND LEISURE 322

The Decline of Individualism — 323
The Reorganization of Work — 324
Leisure As Consumption — 326
Scenarios of the Future — 327

CONCLUSION 328

10.
AGING 335

THE AGED IN HISTORICAL AND CROSS-CULTURAL PERSPECTIVE 336

The Aged in Other Cultures — 336
The Role of the Aged — 338
The Aged in American History — 338

AGING AS A SOCIAL PROBLEM 340

The Functionalist Perspective — 340

The Conflict Perspective 341
The Interactionist Perspective 342

PROBLEMS OF THE AGED IN CONTEMPORARY AMERICAN SOCIETY 342

Work and Retirement 342
Finances 346
Social Participation and the Elderly 347
Aging and Health 350
Deviance and Aging 353
Institutionalization and the Aged 353

THE FUTURE OF THE AGED IN AMERICA 356

Providing for the Elderly 356
Communities for the Elderly 358
The Institutionalization of Death 362
Political Action, Interest Groups, and the Elderly 364

CONCLUSION 365

11.
POVERTY 371

POVERTY IN AMERICA: A BRIEF HISTORY 373

Industrialization and Poverty 373
The Poor in America 374
The Development of Modern Poverty Programs 375

POVERTY AS A SOCIAL PROBLEM 376

The Functionalist Perspective 376
The Conflict Perspective 377
The Interactionist Perspective 378
What is Poverty? 378

THE MANY FACES OF POVERTY 380

The Welfare Poor 380
The Marginal Poor 381
The Displaced Homemaker 381
The Working Poor 382

WHO ARE THE POOR? 383

Race 383

Rural Dwellers 385
The Elderly 386
The Young 387

CAUSES OF POVERTY 387

Functionalism and the "Inevitability of Poverty" 389
Poverty and Conflict 391
Blocked Opportunity 391
The Culture of Poverty 392
Interactionism, Societal Reaction, and Poverty 392
Welfare and Poverty 393

POVERTY IN AMERICA: PROSPECTS FOR THE FUTURE 396

Interpersonal Involvement and Individual Worth 396
A New War On Poverty 399
Full Employment 400
Training the Poor—A Functionalist Approach 401
Self-Help and Community Organization 402

CONCLUSION 403

12.
RACE AND ETHNIC RELATIONS 409

RACE AND ETHNIC RELATIONS 410
Race
Ethnicity 411
Minority Group 412

A HISTORY OF MINORITY GROUPS IN AMERICA 413

Blacks 413
Hispanic Americans 415
Native Americans 417

INTERGROUP RELATIONS AS A SOCIAL PROBLEM 419

The Functionalist Perspective 419
The Conflict Perspective 420
The Interactionist Perspective 420

THE STATUS OF MINORITIES IN THE
UNITED STATES TODAY 421

Blacks 421
Hispanic Americans 423
Native Americans 425
The Costs of Racism 426

REACTIONS TO PREJUDICE AND
DISCRIMINATION 427

Black Reactions 428
Mexican American Reactions 429
Native American Reactions 431
Intergroup Relations 431

SOURCES OF PREJUDICE AND
DISCRIMINATION 432

Psychological Sources 432
Prejudice and Discrimination as Learned 434
Prejudice, Discrimination, and the Social
Order 434

PROSPECTS FOR THE FUTURE 437

Programs to Reduce Individual Discrimination 437
Programs to Reduce Institutionalized Discrimination 438
The Politics of Equality 441

CONCLUSION 441

13.
SEX ROLES 449

THE HISTORY OF SEX ROLES 450

Hunting and Gathering Societies 450
Preindustrial America 451
Industrial America 451
The Women's Rights Movement: The Early
Days 452
The Women's Rights Movement: A Re-
surgence 454

SEX ROLES AS A SOCIAL PROBLEM 455

The Functionalist Perspective 455
The Conflict Perspective 456

The Interactionist Perspective 457

MASCULINITY AND FEMININITY 458

Gender Versus Sex Role 458
Growing Up Male 460
Growing Up Female 462

DISCRIMINATION AND INEQUALITY 464

Economic Discrimination 465
Other Types of Discrimination 468

THE CHANGING MALE SEX ROLE 469

Men and Masculinity 469
Men's Liberation 471
Some Dimensions of the "Liberation" 473

FUTURE PROSPECTS 474

Masculine, Feminine, or Human? 474
The New Women's Movement and the
Quest for Human Rights 474
Recent Developments 477

CONCLUSION 479

14.
INTERGROUP CONFLICT, VIOLENCE, AND WAR 487

THE HISTORY OF VIOLENCE IN
AMERICA 488

Civil Disorder 488
Political Violence 492
War 494

CONFLICT AND VIOLENCE AS SOCIAL
PROBLEMS 495

The Functionalist Perspective 495
The Conflict Perspective 495
The Interactionist Perspective 496

SOURCES OF INTERGROUP CONFLICT 496

Biological Sources of Violence 496
Frustration, Deprivation, and Violence 499
Violence as Learned Behavior 500
Social Sources of Violence 502

THE CONSEQUENCES OF INTERGROUP CONFLICT AND VIOLENCE 504

The Social Functions of Conflict   504
The Consequences of War: The Impact on American Society   505

CONTROLLING VIOLENCE: PROSPECTS FOR THE FUTURE 509

Controlling Violence   510
Preventing Conflict and Violence   512
Preventing War   514

CONCLUSION   516

VIOLENCE IN THE FAMILY 548

Child Abuse   549
Spouse Abuse   550

ABORTION 551

The Legal Status of Abortion   551
The Abortion Controversy   553

SUICIDE 554

Explanations of Suicide   554
The Extent of Suicide   555
Suicide Prevention   557

CONCLUSION   557

15.
DEVIANT BEHAVIOR 525

DEVIANCE IN AMERICAN HISTORY 526

Absolutist   527
Legalist   527
Relativist   528

DEVIANT BEHAVIOR AS A SOCIAL PROBLEM 529

The Functionalist Perspective   529
The Conflict Perspective   531
The Interactionist Perspective   531

SOURCES OF DEVIANT BEHAVIOR 532

Deviance and Social Structure   532
Deviance and Differential Association   534
Deviance and Labeling   535

HOMOSEXUALITY 537

Theories of Homosexuality   537
Patterns of Homosexuality   539
Homosexuality as a Social Problem   541

PROSTITUTION 543

The Extent of Prostitution   543
Becoming a Prostitute   543
Functions of Prostitution   544
Problems and Exploitation   544

PORNOGRAPHY 546

Pornography and the Law   546
The Scientific Evidence   547

16.
CRIME AND DELINQUENCY 567

CRIME AND PUNISHMENT: A BRIEF HISTORY 569

Crime and Punishment in America   569
From Reform to Incarceration   571

CRIME AND DELINQUENCY AS SOCIAL PROBLEMS 572

The Functionalist Perspective   572
The Conflict Perspective   573
The Interactionist Perspective

CRIME AND CRIMINALS IN THE UNITED STATES 574

Measuring Crime   574
Characteristics of Criminals   578

PATTERNS OF CRIMINAL BEHAVIOR 580

Criminal Assault and Homicide   580
Theft   581
Organized Crime   582
White Collar Crime   585
Sex Offenses   586
Victimless Crimes   587

THE SYSTEM OF CRIMINAL JUSTICE 588

Processing the Alleged Criminal   588

JUVENILE DELINQUENCY 594

Measuring Delinquency	596
The Characteristics of Delinquents	596

CRIME AND DELINQUENCY: FUTURE PROSPECTS 599

Punishment	599
Better Law Enforcement	600
Compensation of Victims	601
Bail Reform	601
Decriminalization and Legalization	601
Reforming the Offender	602
Reforming Juvenile Justice	602

CONCLUSION 604

17.
DRUGS AND ALCOHOL 611

ALCOHOL AND DRUG USE IN HISTORY 613

Drug Use: An Ancient Practice	613
Drugs and Alcohol in America	614

DRUGS AND ALCOHOL AS SOCIAL PROBLEMS 618

The Functionalist Perspective	618
The Conflict Perspective	618
The Interactionist Perspective	619

DRUGS, DRUG ABUSE, AND DRUG ADDICTION 619

Psychoactive Drugs	619
Drug Abuse	622
Drug Addiction	623

STIMULANTS 624

Tobacco	624
Cocaine	625
Amphetamines	626

DEPRESSANTS 628

Barbiturates	628
Tranquilizers	629

HALLUCINOGENS 630

PCP	630

MARIJUANA 631

Who Uses Marijuana?	631
Marijuana as a Social Problem	631

NARCOTICS 634

Who Uses Heroin?	634
Heroin as a Social Problem	635

ALCOHOL 636

Patterns of Alcohol Use	637
Theories of Alcoholism	639

FUTURE PROSPECTS: DRUG USE IN AMERICA 640

The Treatment of Heroin Addiction	640
The Treatment of Alcoholism	643

CONCLUSION 645

18.
SOCIAL MOVEMENTS IN A CHANGING AMERICA 653

SOCIAL MOVEMENTS IN AMERICAN HISTORY 655

Youth as a Subculture	655
Religious and Communal Movements	657

SOCIAL MOVEMENTS AS A SOCIAL PROBLEM 660

The Functionalist Perspective	660
The Conflict Perspective	661
The Interactionist Perspective	661

SOCIAL MOVEMENTS AS A RESPONSE TO SOCIAL PROBLEMS 662

Social Movements and Social Change	663
Social Change in America	664

THE YOUTH MOVEMENT AND THE COUNTERCULTURE 668

The Beliefs of the Youth Counterculture	668
Origins of the Youth Counterculture	670
Who Joins the Youth Movement?	672
The Youth Movement as a Social Problem	672

THE RISE OF UNCONVENTIONAL RELIGIOUS MOVEMENTS 672

Krishna Consciousness   673
The Jesus Movement   674
The Unification Church   674
Who Joins Unconventional Religious
   Groups?   675
The Unconventional Religions as a Social
   Problem   677

COMMUNES IN AMERICAN SOCIETY 678

Modern-Day Communes   678
The Ideology of Communes   678
Who Joins Communes?   681
Communes as a Social Problem   681

FUTURE PROSPECTS 682

The Counterculture   682
The Unconventional Religions   683
Communes   683

CONCLUSION 685
PHOTO CREDITS 707
NAME INDEX 709
SUBJECT INDEX 719

Social Problems:
Divergent Perspectives

PART 1

Understanding Social Problems

CHAPTER 1

The Study of Social Problems

A HISTORICAL PERSPECTIVE ON THE STUDY OF
SOCIAL PROBLEMS

The Beginnings of the Sociological Study of Social
Problems. The Study of Social Problems in America.
Sociology, Public Interest, and Social Problems Today.
Social Problems: Divergent Perspectives.

WHAT IS A SOCIAL PROBLEM?

Who Defines? Basis for Defining. Personal Troubles,
Public Issues? Social Problem: A Definition.

SOCIAL PROBLEMS IN AMERICAN SOCIETY

Values and Norms. Power and Authority. Interest Groups
and Vested Interests. Diversity and Subcultures in
America. Ethnocentrism and Social Problems. Social
Problems in a Democratic Society.

SOCIOLOGICAL PERSPECTIVES ON SOCIAL
PROBLEMS

The Functionalist Perspective. The Conflict Perspective.
The Interactionist Perspective. Multiple Definitions:
Divergent Perspectives.

DIFFICULTIES IN SOLVING SOCIAL PROBLEMS

ORGANIZATION OF THE BOOK

During the middle 1970s, the unemployment rate in the United States reached its all-time high since the Great Depression of the 1930s: 9 percent. This means that more than 8.3 million people were jobless. To this figure should be added at least another million people who had become so discouraged over the dismal prospects of finding a job that they stopped looking. AFL-CIO president George Meany observed that the situation was equivalent to all of the employed people in sixteen states suddenly finding themselves without work. For many of these people, unemployment meant suffering the consequences of poverty—a marginal existence in an affluent society, a lack of work in a society that places great value on productive activity, and dreams of a comfortable life for oneself and one's children shattered by the reality that not all Americans share in that affluence. In addition to the unemployed, there were many other Americans who faced the bleak consequences of poverty—children in welfare families, elderly on fixed incomes, and those devastated by catastrophic health care expenses. This situation, while unacceptable to many people, may not improve significantly in the near future. Economists have estimated that even a 5 percent unemployment rate is unlikely in the near future; the elderly are a growing proportion of our population; and health care costs continue to skyrocket.

Conditions of poverty and unemployment are generally considered, by both social scientists and the general public, to be social problems that merit our concern. At first glance, you may not be impressed by, or particularly concerned about, these issues—at least not yet. If you have never been exposed to the difficulties and degradations of poverty, or even of unemployment, it may be hard for you to view them as significant social problems. However, try to imagine what it would be like to be unemployed and poor. What if the college you are now attending were to close its doors to you, and you were unable to find gainful employment? Think, for a moment, about trying to live on meager welfare or unemployment benefits. Further, consider the possibility that this bleak prospect showed no promise of improvement in the future. If you were personally affected in this way—as millions of your fellow Americans are today—you

A bread line in Pittsburgh, 1915. Unemployment has long been considered a social problem. Both social scientists and the general public have been concerned about its amelioration.

would probably view poverty and unemployment as important social problems warranting national attention.

However, sociologists do not define conditions as social problems simply because they personally affect some people. When should conditions, such as poverty and unemployment, be considered social problems? It is important to remember that the extent to which one defines a condition as a problem depends on what groups one is a member of. For example, some groups in American society are more adversely affected by unemployment, and the poverty that often accompanies it, than are other groups. Even in what is considered by many to be a healthy economy, certain groups—such as black teenagers—remain heavily unemployed (see Table 1.1).

TABLE 1.1

Unemployment Rates by Sex, Race, and Age[a]

	MAY 1975	APRIL 1978
National	9.2	6.0
Females	9.1	7.0
Males	7.8	5.2
White teenagers	19.8	14.6
Black teenagers	35.4	35.3

[a] The rates are seasonally adjusted

SOURCE. U.S. Department of Labor, *Employment and Earnings* 21 (June 1975) and 25 (May 1978).

Yet, among these groups for whom this condition is not a direct threat, need there be any concern? Before attempting to answer this question, the student should realize that there are complex interrelationships between various social conditions and social problems (see Fig. 1.1). For example, all

Figure 1.1 Interrelationships between Various Social Conditions and Social Problems. Adapted from Jerome G. Manis, "Assessing the Seriousness of Social Problems," *Social Problems* 22 (October 1974), p. 10. Copyright by the Society for the Study of Social Problems.

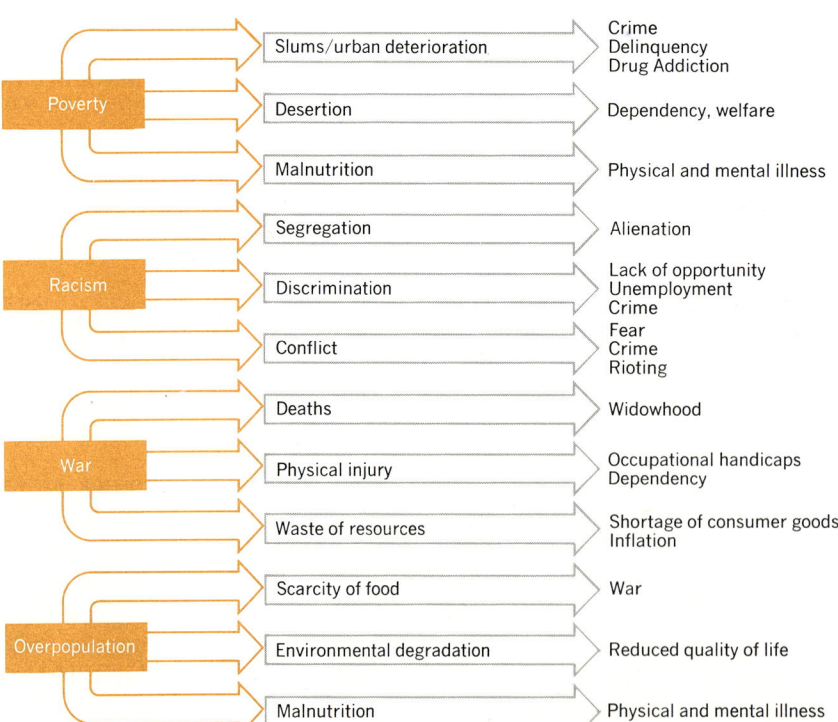

This classic Depression-era photo by Margaret Bourke-White, showing people in Louisville lining up for relief after a flood, powerfully expresses the irony of black need in the land of white plenty.

Americans are affected, at least indirectly, by high levels of poverty and unemployment. Taxes are funneled into welfare programs and unemployment benefits; crime rates are associated with both poverty and unemployment; large groups of dissatisfied and disgruntled poor can threaten social stability through rioting and other disruptive actions. So, while some conditions may have a direct impact only on certain isolated groups, the consequences of these conditions are often widespread. With such complex relationships between social conditions, few are unaffected. Therefore, in deciding whether a particular social condition should be defined as a social problem, we must look at all the consequences—both direct and indirect—that result from given social conditions.

Although many people view concern over social problems as a recent development, sociology has, from its very beginnings, been directly concerned with understanding social problems and finding solutions for them. Before presenting the sociological definitions of, and approaches to, social prob-

lems to be employed in this book, it will be useful to acquaint the student with the way in which some earlier sociologists dealt with social problems. An awareness of this history will illustrate how the approach used in this text grows out of a long tradition of interest in such issues.

A HISTORICAL PERSPECTIVE ON THE STUDY OF SOCIAL PROBLEMS

The Beginnings of the Sociological Study of Social Problems

During the 1800s, Europe experienced recurrent episodes of rioting, burning, and general social disruption. This disorder resulted from sweeping changes that were transforming European society — industrialization and urbanization were bringing about significant changes in the foundation of the social order, while political changes, such as those ushered in by the French Revolution, shifted political and economic power to new groups in society.

The earliest sociologists lived and wrote during this period; their concern over the extensive conflict and turmoil moved them to study the basis of social stability and order. They developed a scientific approach to the study of society that became the beginning of the sociological study of social problems.

Auguste Comte

French sociologist Auguste Comte (1798–1857), often referred to as the "father of sociology," had suffered the sacrifices, sorrows, and fears that inevitably accompany conflict and war. As a result, he was concerned with attacking the social conditions that he felt threatened the stability of French society. While still a young man, he began developing a science of society—which he labeled *sociology*—that would provide insight into his country's problems.[1] Comte believed that sociologists could facilitate social progress—and thereby solve social problems—by educating people to an *awareness* of the sources of social problems. For him, the most serious problems in French society were the conflict and violence that accompanied social change and the declining importance of central social institutions, such as the family and the church.

Emile Durkheim

Another French sociologist of the nineteenth century, Emile Durkheim (1855–1917), contributed to the study of social problems by conducting a ground-breaking study of the causes of suicide.[2] Like Comte, Durkheim was concerned with those factors that contributed to social stability. He argued that suicide was a social condition that resulted from identifiable social forces. He showed that suicide can be one extreme consequence of the lack of social stability—without group involvement, a person is more likely to commit suicide. He was also the first sociologist to apply statistical procedures to the scientific analysis of social problems.

Karl Marx

The German social thinker Karl Marx (1818–1883) approached the problems of his age from a dif-

ferent perspective than Comte or Durkheim. Marx was sensitive to the position of the underdog in society. He looked around himself and saw the brutal consequences industrialization had on many people, especially the working and lower classes. While Comte and Durkheim valued stability and social order, Marx realized that social stability, while beneficial to some, often rests on the poverty, misfortune, and exploitation of less fortunate groups in society.[3] For Marx, one of the major problems of the day was inequality and the suffering and degradation that accompanied it. Through scientific analysis, he hoped to determine the sources of social inequality, so that it might be eliminated. It was Marx's belief that, once the basic problems of inequality and the maldistribution of wealth and power had been solved, other problems (such as poverty and crime) would also be substantially relieved.

The Study of Social Problems in America

While the sociological study of social problems arose out of European social conditions, it had become firmly rooted in American soil by the end of the nineteenth century. This was a period of widespread change in America—urbanization and industrialization in the North, the recent demise of slavery in the South, foreign immigrants crowding into cities—and many American scholars were attracted to the new scientific discipline of sociology as a valuable tool with which to attack the many problems resulting from these changes.

Lester Frank Ward

Many early American sociologists, like Lester Frank Ward (1841–1913), were more reform-oriented in their thinking than were their European counterparts. Ward believed in social progress and in the ability of people to shape the direction of social change.[1] In Ward's thinking, sociologists could work toward the solution of social problems in the same way that physical scientists had identified and attempted to rectify undesirable conditions, such as disease. Much of Ward's concern was directed at the same conditions of poverty and inequality that attracted Marx's attention. However, while Marx found the solution in basic reorganization of the structure of society, Ward felt that the same problems could be alleviated through improved educational and occupational opportunities for all people. He favored social programs, such as free public education and strong child-labor laws, to acheive these ends.

Sociology, Public Interest, and Social Problems Today

The interest of American sociologists in the study of social problems has increased enormously since Ward's time. Although modern sociology has probably paid more attention to *understanding* than to *solving* these problems, sociologists have frequently been instrumental in proposing and implementing concrete solutions. The specific conditions defined by sociologists as social problems over the past four decades have shown considerable variation (see Table 1.2). Some topics, such as crime and delinquency, have always been a central concern. With other conditions, such as unemployment and war, interest has fluctuated considerably. Certain conditions, such as the state of the environment, have only recently attracted the attention of sociologists studying social problems.

The issues that grab the interest of the public as significant problems sometimes do not coincide with the central concerns of sociologists. For example, population problems, one of the most frequently discussed issues in textbooks on social problems, has been mentioned little, if at all, by the public in surveys of opinion over the past forty years. On the other hand, problems of war and peace—among those mentioned most frequently by the public—are among the least frequently discussed topics in social problems textbooks.[5] This brings us back to the central concern of this chapter: how do we define a social problem? Is something a social problem because sociologists say it is? Does it become a social problem when a large proportion of the public believes that it is? The answers to these questions are complex and will be discussed at length in the remainder of this chapter.

TABLE 1.2
Social Problems as Identified by Textbooks, 1934–1975

Problem	Number of Times Each Problem Is Analyzed					
	1934-39 (N=5)[a]	1940-49 (N=4)	1950-59 (N=6)	1960-69 (N=8)	1970-75 (N=11)	Total (N=34)
1. Crime and delinquency	4	4	6	7	9	30
2. Marriage and the family	3	4	6	6	8	27
3. Population (including migration and immigration)	4	2	6	5	9	26
4. Race and ethnic relations	3	2	4	7	10	26
5. Poverty	3	3	2	5	9	22
6. Health, mental and physical	3	4	5	4	6	22
7. Labor and working conditions	3	1	4	2	6	16
8. Urban problems	1	1	3	7	4	16
9. Personal pathologies: alcoholism, suicide, drugs	2	2	2	2	6	14
10. Unemployment (as separate issue from poverty)	2	2	4	0	3	11
11. Ecology	1	1	2	1	5	10
12. War and peace	1	1	3	3	2	10

[a] *N* refers to the *number* of textbooks consulted.

SOURCE. Robert H. Lauer, "Defining Social Problems: Public and Professional Perspectives," *Social Problems* 24 (October 1976), p. 127. Copyright by the Society for the Study of Social Problems.

Social Problems: Divergent Perspectives

All of the sociologists whom we have discussed helped to develop an orientation toward the study of social problems that is fundamental to the approach that the present book takes to these issues. This orientation is based on three assumptions. First, it is possible for society to move toward more desirable social arrangements. We *can intervene* in the solution of social problems. Second, sociology can provide the *scientific understanding* that makes possible informed human intervention in the solution of social problems. Uninformed meddling in social problems will likely create more severe problems for society. Third, there is not merely one sociological perspective on social problems, but rather there are *divergent perspectives* — different approaches, partially competing and partially complementary, to the understanding of social problems. By utilizing these divergent perspectives rather than clinging to one narrow view, we shall achieve a more complete comprehension of current social problems and their implications for American society.

Now we can move on to the essential task of defining a social problem. In the next section, we will present a general definition of the circumstances under which a social condition may be considered a social problem. Later in this chapter, we will present three sociological approaches to social problems that will provide greater insight concerning the issues discussed in succeeding chapters.

WHAT IS A SOCIAL PROBLEM?

We have observed that there is considerable agreement among the members of society that certain issues are social problems; with other issues, there is far less consensus. There is also disagreement concerning how to *define* social problems. It is easy to say, "That's a problem" but more difficult to specify *what characteristics all social problems have in common*. Let us examine some considerations that go into defining social problems.

Who Defines?

First we must ask, *who* **is doing the defining?** Do these people represent the opinion of the majority on the issue? Or, are they instead a group with some particular interest? Sometimes a social problem, while adverse to some groups, is beneficial to certain others in society. Imagine for a moment the consequences if many of the activities currently classified as crimes, such as prostitution, gambling, and drug use, were suddenly legalized. We would need considerably fewer policemen and a smaller number of jails and prisons. Many people in the criminal justice system — from policemen to prison guards, from counselors to bail bondsmen — would find themselves without a job. In other words, these people benefit from the existence of crime, and it is to their advantage to define many behaviors as crimes, to define crimes as a social problem, and to argue that an extensive criminal justice system is necessary to protect society against this menace.

This points up an important stand that sociologists must take to the study of social problems. They must engage in what sociologist Peter Berger has defined as "debunking" — that is, the sociologist must attempt to "unmask the pretensions and the propaganda by which men cloak their actions with each other."[6] For example, those in the criminal justice system would not agree with our previous assessment of how crime is actually beneficial to them. They would claim to be unequivocally committed to ending all types of crime. Yet we cannot accept their statement as a reflection of total reality. When we engage in debunking, influential groups may feel threatened by newly discovered sociological knowledge, and what we learn will often be unpleasant. Yet, a full comprehension of social problems can be based only on a free, open, and thorough analysis of social conditions — with no special consideration given to important groups or long-held values.

Basis for Defining

In addition to the above concern, we must ask, **what criteria do particular groups use to define certain conditions as social prob-**

lems? Central to understanding how people define conditions as social problems is the concept of *values.* This concept is discussed at more length in the next section, but for now we can say that values refer to the general preferences and priorities of a group. For example, in American society we place value on a high standard of living, including material well-being and affluence; we also value individual achievement and success, efficiency and practicality, and equality. While these are well-established values in American life, the extent to which our behavior is consistent with these values is highly variable. We value equality, yet many groups are treated in a discriminatory fashion.

One reason for this divergence between values and behavior is that some values will inevitably conflict with one another and some will be deemed more important than others. For example, in a context in which two groups might compete for the same profitable occupation, would you expect members of those groups to place equality above their own success by ensuring that all people have an equal opportunity to compete for the position? Or would the chance for success take on such priority that each group ignored its value of equality by placing whatever barriers it could against the other group's chance to acquire the position? This is an example of *value conflict,* a resolution of which depends on how we order our values. The priority given to different values is an important determinant of what conditions will be defined by a particular group as a social problem.

Personal Troubles, Public Issues?

A third question that we must ask, as proposed by the noted sociologist C. Wright Mills, is, **does the situation involved represent a personal trouble or a public issue?**[7] When unemployment strikes a particular family, that is a personal trouble because the values and goals of only that family are threatened, and this is seen as primarily the problem of that family. On the other hand, when the United States has an unemployment rate of 9 percent, we are dealing with a public issue because the values of a large group are threatened, the issues are publicly debated, and some collective solutions are proposed. Mills recognized the importance of values in the identification of social problems: "No problem can be adequately formulated unless the values involved and the apparent threat to them are stated. These values and their imperilment constitute the terms of the problem itself."[8]

Considered broadly in the public forum (in a national television newscast or in a presidential address), unemployment may be regarded as a public issue. At the same time, however, it may also represent a private or personal trouble. Thus, in terms of the values, interests, and feelings of various groups, there may be dramatic differences between "social problems." The sociologist must, in Mills's words, "make clear the values that are really threatened in the troubles and issues involved, who accepts them as values, and by whom or by what are they threatened."[9] As a public issue, unemployment may over time be regarded as more or less of a social problem. Predictably, during periods of high national unemployment more attention is paid to this issue than when the rate is low. As a personal trouble, however, unemployment takes on a number of social aspects, each one of which the sociologist must attempt to understand and interpret in order to assess the broader social issue most effectively.

Social Problem: A Definition

From our analysis of the preceding questions, we can now formulate the following general definition that will serve as a guide to our study of social problems: **A social problem may be said to exist when an influential group is aware of a social condition that threatens its values and that may be remedied by collective action.** Let us examine separately the four key elements in this definition.

1. **An influential group.**

   Any definition of the term *influence* is likely to be controversial, but for our purposes an influential group is a group that can have significant impact on public debate or social policy at the national level. For a condition to be defined as a social problem, it must be considered as such not just by *any* group, but by some group with influence. For example, in recent years, groups concerned about the pollution of our environment have been able to make their concerns heard through their influence in the voting booth. In the purchase or boycott of products, by mobilizing their organizations for demonstrations and marches, and by pursuing their objectives in the courts. As a consequence, environmental pollution is now considered a social problem. However, such groups as the Anti-Vivisection Society—which is devoted to the humane treatment of laboratory animals—have no such influence; and, unless they can interest some influential group in their concern, the issue about which they are concerned will not be defined as a social problem.

2. **Awareness of a social condition.**

Today, environmental pollution is widely recognized as a social problem. However, during the late nineteenth century, at the height of the Industrial Revolution, few people viewed emissions from factories as a problem. The spewing of pollutants into the environment was largely accepted as a fact of life that society must tolerate in order to reap the benefits of industrialization and technology. Today, measures are taken by such public agencies as the Environmental Protection Agency to eliminate sources of pollution—sometimes at the expense of factory efficiency. So the simple existence of a condition does not make it a problem; someone must be aware of it as an undesirable condition.

3. **Threatened values.**

As we have observed, any group's values will necessarily be ranked in order of priority—that is, how important is that threatened value in relation to other values? In 1900, most groups placed greater value on increased industrial production than on environmental cleanliness. Furthermore, the values of many people concerning the desirability of clean air may have been threatened in 1900, but the threat was perceived only by isolated individuals rather than by influential groups.

Although some nineteenth-century writers, like Charles Dickens, viewed environmental pollution as a problem, most people of the time did not.

'Coketown was a triumph of fact... It was a town of red brick, or of brick that would have been red if the smoke and ashes had allowed it... It was a town of machinery and tall chimneys, out of which interminable serpents of smoke trailed themselves for ever and ever, and never got uncoiled.' (CHARLES DICKENS, *Hard Times.*)

4. **Remedied by collective action.**
Social conditions that cannot be improved through collective action may be threatening to the values of influential groups, but they are not considered social problems. During much of our history, poverty was seen as inevitable, and the poor were viewed as lazy and unmotivated. Poverty was not considered a social problem because nothing could be done about it. Today, many influential people feel that poverty can be reduced or eliminated through proper social intervention, and it is thus considered a social problem. Whether collective action is possible depends on whether influential groups participate in developing the strategies and solutions to attack it. If these groups agree that poverty or environmental pollution should not be tolerated, there is more likely to be a collective effort toward its solution.

The general definition that we have just examined will assist us in understanding how a condition comes to be defined as a social problem. In order to more fully comprehend the intricacies of this process, we turn to the modern sociological study of social problems, particularly as it applies to American society.

SOCIAL PROBLEMS IN AMERICAN SOCIETY

We have framed a general definition of social problems and discussed some of the major difficulties and pitfalls to be avoided. It is clear, however, that **social problems arise within the context of a particular society.** How does a problem get to be a social problem in America? What do we need to know about our society in order to understand its problems? In this section, we will present an outline of some of the societal structures and processes that are important for an understanding of social problems. The concepts and processes discussed, which derive from a sociological analysis of society, provide a unique approach to the study of social problems and the understanding of human social behavior.

Values and Norms

In the sociological study of social problems, two basic concepts are values and norms. **Values are standards shared by members of groups that specify desirable needs, wants, and attitudes.** For example, a widely held value among members of the middle class in America is that obtaining a formal education is highly desirable. Furthermore, most groups in America place great value on success and material comfort. **Norms are expected ways of thinking, feeling, and behaving that some group defines as appropriate.** For example, it is expected in most groups that one will achieve success in certain socially approved ways, such as working hard at legitimate business enterprises, rather than through illegal means, such as robbery. Norms constitute the "thou shalts" and "thou shalt nots," the prescriptions and proscriptions, of the group.

Values and norms are important in the study of social problems, for they greatly influence people's behavior and the way in which they react to such problems. Consider the problem of poverty. Most would agree today that poverty is a social problem. Yet in *The Other America,* social critic Michael Harrington pointed out that for some people in society—principally those of the middle and upper-middle classes—poverty is an "invisible land."[10] Since they do not see it and have no first-hand experience with it, it is not for them a problem. Since these people place great value on individual initiative and achievement, they feel that the poor could improve their condition if they only tried hard enough. Some of these people may even believe that the extent of poverty has been deliberately exaggerated and overemphasized by those who benefit from the welfare system, such as social workers, the unemployed, and the poor.

So, in order for people to understand or behave in a situation, they develop a *definition of the situation*—a perception and interpretation of what is happening, why people behave the way they do, and what behavior is appropriate for themselves.[11] This definition is very important because, if people define a situation in a certain way, then that, for them, is reality, and they will behave as if it were. In other words, social reality is *subjective*—it is based on the meanings and interpretations that we attach to things and events, and these meanings and interpretations are based, at least in part, on the values that we hold. For example, if a person is convinced that only lazy people are poor and that it is their laziness that accounts for their poverty, then this definition of the situation will determine that person's response to the situation. Objectively, of course, a variety of social factors are important in causing poverty: lack of education, racial and ethnic discrimination, social class, and the like.

Social conditions and experiences shape people's values. For example, Harrington and others have noted that freeway systems in urban centers of America strategically and conveniently avoid the poverty-stricken areas.[12] How many middle- and upper-middle-class people really know what it is like to live in poverty? Most of them have never been poor, nor have they viewed a poverty area firsthand. Without such experience, it is hard to imagine the enormous difficulties that face poor people and the way in which poverty can grind a person down so that any initiative that might have once existed is gone. It is easy, from a very comfortable middle-class position, to believe that individual effort will be rewarded by success. So the values of such people concerning poverty are shaped by their lack of personal experience. It is easy to see that norms and values are crucial to our understanding of social problems. It is also important to keep in mind that these norms and values will vary from culture to culture and from one subculture to another.

Power and Authority

Most social problems encountered in America are related in some way to the exercise of power and the use of authority—either as forces that exacerbate problems or as necessary elements in their alleviation.

What is Power?

Power exists in many forms. As sociologist Robert Bierstedt has observed:

Society . . . is shot through with power relations—the power a father exercises over his child, a master over his slave, a teacher over his pupils, the victor over the vanquished, the blackmailer over his victim, the warden over his prisoners, the judge over his convicted defendant, an employer over his employee, a general over his lieutenants, a captain over his crew, a creditor over his debtor, and so on through an impressively large number of social relationships.[13]

This pervasive character of power clearly illustrates that power is a central social process. But what is power? There are many definitions of power, and they all have their flaws. However, for our purposes, *power* **may be defined as the opportunity existing within a social relationship that permits one person to carry out his will, even against the resistance of others.** In other words, you are powerful to the extent that you can have your own way, even when others resist you.

Sources of Power

In general terms, there are three sources of power. The first is the *strength of numbers*. If a group has access to large numbers of people—especially a numerical majority—then it is more likely to gain its way since many opposition groups would be outnumbered. The second source of power is *organization*—the ability to effectively coordinate the actions of people toward a goal. It is possible for a small but well-organized group to exercise power over an unorganized but larger group. As an example, consider the group of New York City residents who protested the landing of the supersonic Concorde jetliner at a nearby airport in 1977. Approximately 100 protesters used their automobiles to slow down traffic on the expressway leading to the airport. The resulting traffic jam involved thousands of motorists and caused significant delays in departing aircraft. The third source of power is *access to resources* that can be used to persuade or force others to conform to one's wishes. Resources come in many forms (see Table 1.3). The group that possesses the greatest resources will, other things being equal, have the most power.[14]

TABLE 1.3

Examples of Resources That Can Provide Power

ECONOMIC	POLITICAL	SOCIAL STATUS
Income	Force (military-police)	Prestige
Wealth	Influence	Access to the powerful in political and economic sectors
Access to credit	Incumbency of office	
Control over employment conditions	Prestige of office	Access to the media
Control over wages and prices	Creation of law	

What is Authority?

Authority and power are closely related. In fact, *authority* **can be defined as institutionalized power.** The term *institutionalized* refers to a frequently repeated pattern of behavior that is considered crucial to a group's welfare. Institutionalized behavior becomes invested with a sense of legitimacy — people accept it as the right and proper way to behave. In fact, authority is sometimes referred to as legitimate power; it is supported by the values of the group or society. For example, leadership in our society has become institutionalized in the form of an elected government; education of the young is institutionalized in our school systems; our religious beliefs have become institutionalized in the major established churches.

So power, if it is exercised by a particular group over a period of time, may become institutionalized, in which case it is authority — the ability to direct or to give orders, where those being ordered believe that the orders are legitimate and that the person giving them has the right to do so.

Sources of Authority

In general, there are three types of authority.[15] One type is *traditional authority,* which is based on the belief that **what is customary and habitual is also right and proper.** The traditions of the group, which usually go back far beyond the memory of the current generation, must be maintained.

The people who enforce those traditions are perceived as having the legitimate right to do so. For example, in our society, parents have almost total control over their children. This is authority — legitimate and institutionalized power — that is based on our religious and legal traditions, which have taught us that it is right and proper for parents to have such control over their children.

A second type of authority is *legal-rational authority,* which is based on a belief in **those practices that achieve goals most efficiently.** Contemporary man views this type of authority as legitimate because it is consistent with modern faith in rationality. For example, Americans tend to believe that, through the application of human reason, any problem can be understood and solved. Many people refuse to believe that there is a serious energy crisis. They think that, if sufficient money is spent and if our scientists work diligently on the problem, the energy shortage can be eliminated through technological advances. Because of this faith in the application of reason to problem solving, we sometimes accept forms of organization, such as bureaucracies or assembly lines, that are based on rational procedures as the most efficient means of achieving a goal.

A third type of authority is *charismatic authority,* which is based on **a person's ability to show — through revelation, magical power, or personal attractiveness — that he possesses some unique quality or force of command.** This type of authority is based on the conviction that tradition or law is less important than the charisma possessed by the individual. There are many illustrations throughout history of persons whose authority was based at least partly on charisma — Jesus, Hitler, and John F. Kennedy are the most commonly cited examples. Each had some special qualities that motivated others to accord him the legitimate right to command them. However, usually the great person's "message" must become traditionalized or rationalized, or both, if the charismatic leader's authority is to survive his or her death.

All social life involves to some extent the exercise of power and authority. Our understanding of the various social problems we'investigate will be enhanced to the extent that we can identify the manner in which power and authority play a role in the emergence and solution of social problems.

Interest Groups and Vested Interests

In a complex society such as our own, people have a wide variety of interests and values, and the interests and values of some groups will inevitably be incompatible with those of other groups. For example, a professional naturalist would be expected to place preservation of our wilderness areas above the expansion of our suburbs. A land developer, on the other hand, would probably feel that retaining natural beauty is secondary to the construction of housing for all people. The environmentalist and the land developer are members of different interest groups. **An *interest group* is any group that is organized to support the distinctive and joint concerns of its members.** In our diverse society, there exists a bewildering array of interest groups—the John Birch Society, the Socialist Workers Party, the Anti-Vivisection Society, the Humane Society, the National Association for the Advancement of Colored People, and thousands of others. The members of each have joined together to pursue their common interests.

One type of interest group is a *vested interest group*—that is, **a group that benefits in some fashion from the status quo.** It generally opposes social change that might eliminate its privileges and promotes change that will enhance its interests. For example, the physician-members of the American Medical Association generally benefit from privately financed medicine and have opposed governmentally funded health care and many other changes in health care organization in the United States. The National Rifle Association lobbies in the political arena for the vested interests of its members—to preserve the privilege of gun ownership for its members through the exertion of powerful political pressure against gun control legislation.

The impact of interest groups and vested interests on the development of social problems can be

The school busing issue illustrates how different interest groups may disagree on what constitutes a social problem.

illustrated by the events leading to the enactment (and subsequent repeal) of the Eighteenth Amendment to the United States Constitution, popularly known as Prohibition.[16] During the 1800s in the United States, there was growing concern among certain groups regarding the consumption of alcohol. (The student should compare this state of affairs with our general definition of social problems and consider whether alcohol use would have been considered a social problem according to that definition.) Urban, native, middle-class Americans were concerned about alcohol consumption among immigrants and marginal laborers. Christian groups opposed consumption of alcohol because it contradicted some of their religious beliefs and because they viewed it as a threat to their religious dominance. Although there were many groups involved, a particularly influential one, the Women's Christian Temperance Union (WCTU), was formed in 1874. It was composed primarily of rural and small-town, middle-class Protestants, and it worked for the total prohibition of alcohol. The WCTU believed that economic and social success derived from moral virtue; for them alcohol reform was a means of helping the underdog achieve success by abstaining from alcohol and leading a morally virtuous life based on Christian ethics.

Because of the social position of its members and the numbers of people who supported it, the WCTU was able to form a coalition with other groups that would in return support their temperance goals. For example, they supported the right of newly developed labor unions to organize and strike, in return for which the unions advocated abstinence and formed temperance societies. The WCTU also supported Prohibitionist candidates for office and during the 1890s formed an alliance with the Populist Party. Largely due to the strategies and tactics of the WCTU and other such interest groups, the Eighteenth Amendment was ratified as a part of the Constitution in 1919. Despite the popularity of alcohol among many groups in the United States, antialcohol interest groups were able to create the public definition of alcohol consumption as a social problem and exercise their power to institute their own solution. The success of the WCTU was particularly due to its ability to mobilize large numbers of people and to gain allies among other groups. In 1933, the Twenty-first Amendment to the Constitution repealed the prohibition of alcohol. As an interest group, the WCTU had lost credibility, membership, and power.

Diversity and Subcultures in America

In America prior to the Industrial Revolution, society was basically *homogeneous*—**people held very similar norms, values, and beliefs.** Common cultural meanings were shared by most people. There was little question about what was the proper way to lead one's life. As American society industrialized and urbanized, it also become more *heterogeneous*. **A *heterogenous society* is one in which individuals and groups possess a wide range of different characteristics, beliefs, norms, and traditions.** There is greater diversification and more social differentiation—differences between people and groups that develop out of social interaction. Today, we have a seemingly endless array of religions, ethnic groups, social classes, races, occupations, political preferences—to name only a few of the most prominent areas in which Americans differ from one another.

This heterogeneity and social differentiation raises serious questions that have relevance for the study of social problems: what is the proper way to lead one's life? How do you view those who have chosen a quite different lifestyle? In any culture, there will be norms that are binding on every member. However, in a complex social order like the United States, we find a great diversity of norms, all deriving from the nature of the groups that compose society. In such a situation, *subcultures* often form, which are **groups with some norms, beliefs, and values that are distinct from those of the wider culture.** A subculture is a kind of "culture within a culture."

In American society, there are many subcultures; each has a distinct set of norms and values concerning appropriate behavior, and what is important in life. Modern sociologists speak, for example, of delinquent subcultures, a subculture of violence, and subcultures among adolescents, students, the elderly, police, prison inmates, the disabled, drug addicts, homosexuals—to name just a few. Each subculture has some distinctive values, norms, and perspectives that set it apart from the others. For example, members of a drug subculture often live and work in the wider culture, but at the same time they possess a distinct set of norms and values that legitimates the use of drugs. They probably all agree that the experience that results from drugs is superior to that of alcohol, and that all people would choose to use drugs if only they had an opportunity to enjoy them. A distinct terminology (*stash, joint, fix, dime bag, "feel a Jones coming on"*) provides a sense of uniqueness and cohesion and makes it difficult for nonmembers to understand what they are saying. The members of the subculture share similar experiences and problems—such as how to obtain drugs and avoid arrest—and their unique norms and values grow out of their interaction based on these similarities. Although subcultures are in some ways unique, they also share much in common with the larger culture of which they are a part.

Subcultures not only add interesting and colorful diversity to American society but also constitute a very real dynamic factor that must be taken into account when we study social problems. The norms, values, and beliefs of a subculture will differ, often with strong impact and repercussion, from those of the wider society and other subcultures. In fact, subcultural lifestyles often reflect those issues that are regarded by the larger society as social problems. It is easy to say that one lifestyle or set of values is "better" than another. One might believe that values stressing law, order, and stability in a police subculture are superior to the radical youth subculture's concern with freedom of expression and fear of a police state (to cite two extreme examples). Yet such personal opinion can be very misleading when attempting to understand a complex social order.

Ethnocentrism and Social Problems

People often have strong reactions to, and feelings about, the diverse subcultures in America, and these reactions and feelings can complicate the study of social problems. Sociologists use the term *cultural relativity* to refer to **the realization that no custom or convention is good or bad by itself but must be viewed in terms of the whole culture within which it exists.** The opposite stance is referred to as *ethnocentrism,* or **the tendency to view one's own culture and customs as "right" and "best," and to judge other cultures by one's own standards.** To illustrate this, let us consider the custom, found among some African peoples, of enlarging the lips, lengthening the neck, and encouraging female breasts to sag through the use of metal rings and weights. To Americans, these practices seem senseless and even brutal, and the results ugly; but in the view of Africans who embrace these practices, the effect has great value and beauty. However, even when we know why some Africans do this, we still compare them to our own cultural standards for beauty and find the practices repugnant. Of course, to the African, *our* physical appearance and perceptions of beauty might seem equally unattractive.

In terms of social problems, we can readily grasp the significance of ethnocentrism. What is consid-

ered a social problem in one culture or subculture may not be so considered in another. For example, many become concerned when young men shave their heads and young women put on dhotis and join an Eastern religious movement, such as the Krishna Consciousness. Americans generally find such lifestyles puzzling and upsetting, and many would consider such unusual religious groups as social problems. However, in India, such religious beliefs and behavior would not be viewed as a problem; on the contrary, it would be considered desirable to find young people turning to such traditional religious ways.

Within our own society, there is a tendency to evaluate the lifestyles of others from the point of view of our own subculture. Many regard a middle-class, affluent lifestyle as the "best," refer to divorce as a problem, and see deviant sexual lifestyles as abhorrent. These and their like are all functions of ethnocentrism. In studying the issues that will be considered in this book, continually ask yourself, "Is this really a problem?" From whose point of view? In this way, you will be reminded of the ethnocentric basis of what is often regarded as a social problem. For sociologists, the stance of cultural relativism results in greater understanding of social conditions and social problems.

Social Problems in a Democratic Society

We have seen that many of the social problems to be considered in this book are partly attributable to the nature of our modern society. In addition, the manner in which we react to, and attempt to solve these problems has fundamental implications for the nature of our social order, including our democratic institutions. Classical statements of democracy—"of, by, and for the people," "the majority rules," etc.—imply that, through the democratic process, the greatest good is provided to the greatest number of people because decision making is based on the "will of the people." Yet the turmoil of the past two decades has taught us that the decision-making process in our society does not always resemble this democratic ideal.

One problem is, who constitutes the "majority" today? Who makes military decisions; who makes the laws; who decides when justice is done; *who defines social problems?* It is important to bear in mind that, unless they are simplified, the complexities of the social order are almost impossible for the public to understand. But in simplification there is danger of distortion. The simplification process often occurs in the mass media: television, radio, magazines, and newspapers help the public to understand our economy, political structure, legal system, and the like by simplifying the complexity of events and social processes. However, this simplification is sometimes achieved by not reporting certain information or events that are complex and confusing. When they do this, the media essentially serve as gatekeepers of information. *Gatekeeping* refers to **the ability of the mass media (sometimes through agreement with the government) to withhold information from the public or to channel and control what the public sees and hears.**

This points to a second, and related, problem in our democratic system: how do we ensure that the public is reasonably informed so that it can participate in democratic decision making? Do we know everything, for example, about the Watergate affair? It is evident that the Federal Bureau of Investigation withheld information regarding the Kennedy assassinations. If the public cannot be sure that the government is telling the truth, and if at the same time it lacks confidence in the media, how can the public reasonably expect to make informed decisions about issues?

These concerns are critical in the study of social problems in a democratic society. Our democratic institutions are founded on the belief that the only guarantee against corruption and tyranny is freedom of information. Yet, because some groups engage in gatekeeping and the public is poorly informed, it is debatable whether many people approach the study of social problems with anything resembling complete information. Do we really have sufficient information concerning such social problems as poverty or crime to allow us to attempt solutions? If the public is poorly informed

A democracy is supposed to represent the will of, and provide the greatest good for, the people. However, the busing issue illustrates how difficult it is to determine a common 'good.'

about such issues, the likelihood is increased that some powerful interest group will be able to initiate policies that benefit their narrow interests but that are of little help to most other groups in society. To preserve our democratic institutions, it is essential to guard against the possibility that some groups will gain undue influence over the political process while other groups are systematically denied a voice in political decision making.

So, whether we achieve our political and social ideals will rest in part on the manner in which we solve the social problems discussed in the following chapters. As we confront each of these problems, we shall need to keep before us a number of questions:

1. Who is responsible for certain issues being defined as social problems?
2. Who benefits from the existence of social problems?
3. Who speaks for the "majority"?
4. Which groups are effectively represented by powerful decision makers in society, and which are not so represented?
5. What is the relationship between social problems, so-called democratic principles, and the "majority"?
6. If the "majority" rules, then what becomes of the welfare of the "minority"? In fact, what happens to "minority" opinion?

SOCIOLOGICAL PERSPECTIVES ON SOCIAL PROBLEMS

In order to understand social problems, it is crucial to have an awareness of the nature and operation of society. In other words, we must understand how the concepts and processes discussed in the previous section fit together in the actual daily operation of society. Sociologists, as scientists, use theories as a tool in achieving this understanding. **A *theory* is a statement about the relationship between two or more conditions.** For example, a theory might state that juvenile delinquency is associated with certain types of home life, such as broken homes. Theories are useful in the study of social problems for a number of reasons. First, a theory is an *explanation*—it tells us *why* something happened. What is it about broken homes that leads to juvenile delinquency? Facts do not speak for themselves. They must be placed within a theoretical framework that helps explain them. Second, a theory serves to *focus our attention* on specific types of phenomena. If we are interested in juvenile delinquency, where might we begin? We could look at biological, psychological, or a host of other possible factors. Sociological theories focus on social behavior and the impact of social institutions on individual behavior. Third, a theory points out what we should look for to *expand our knowledge*. As information is organized into a

theory, we begin to see gaps in knowledge that might be filled through further investigation. Last, and often most important, a theory enables us to *predict future events*. A theory, if it is to be considered anything better than a guess, has to be something that can be tested through observation. Do the predictions of the theory actually occur?

There are many theories in sociology that attempt to explain specific conditions, such as juvenile delinquency, suicide, and homosexuality. We will be discussing some of these theories throughout this book. However, there is no general "theory of society" that is accepted by all sociologists, and thus there is no one orientation to social problems that is utilized by all sociologists. Rather, sociology contains a number of *theoretical perspectives:* **general orientations toward the nature and operation of society, each emphasizing the importance of particular social processes.** They are neither true nor false; rather they are tools that sensitize us to certain aspects of "reality."

There are three major theoretical perspectives that have been developed by social scientists in their attempt to understand the workings of society: *functionalism, conflict,* and *interactionism.* Each has been applied to the study of social problems, and, although they contain some fundamental differences, all have proved useful. By utilizing all three perspectives in the analysis of social problems, we shall gain a more complete understanding of the problems and potential solutions. The basic assumptions of each of the three perspectives are outlined in Table 1.4.

The Functionalist Perspective

The functionalist school of thought is the oldest in sociology, and it is found in most of the social sciences. Its roots in sociology can be traced back well over a century to Comte and Durkheim. The basic assumption of this perspective is that **society is a *system* composed of interrelated and interdependent parts.** Each part makes a contribution to the operation of the system, whereby the entire system is enabled to function.[17] A simple way to picture this is to use the analogy of a biological organism. A human being, for example, is a biological organism composed of many parts, each one of which has a specific role to play. The heart pumps blood, the lungs draw oxygen into the body and expel carbon dioxide, and the brain coordinates the activities of the various parts. Each of these separate parts is related in very complex ways to the others and is also dependent on them. Each performs an essential function without which the entire system might collapse, as in the case of heart failure. Biological organisms, of course, have certain characteristics that societies do not have, and

TABLE 1.4

Sociological Perspectives: Models of Man, Society, and Social Problems

	FUNCTIONALISM	CONFLICT	INTERACTIONISM
HUMAN NATURE	Self-seeking, but molded by society. Man as a "cog" who performs important functions.	Non-Marxian: inherently self-seeking; must be restrained by society. Marxian: inherently good and altruistic; corrupted by alienating social institutions.	Tabula rasa; molded through interaction and communication with others in social relationships.
SOCIETY	An organism: a system made up of interrelated and interdependent parts; held together by consensus and mutual dependence.	An arena: a setting in which groups struggle over scarce, valued resources; held together through coercion and the formation of temporary, shifting alliances through which people pursue their own interests.	A jam session: society is continually created and recreated through social interaction; held together by mutually accepted definitions of social reality
SOCIAL PROBLEMS	Objective conditions that emerge from certain social arrangements and threaten the smooth functioning of society.	Non-Marxian: objective conditions that result from a conflict-ridden society that reflects the self-seeking nature of human beings; subjective conditions that flow from man's insatiable desires. Marxian: objective conditions that emerge from inherent flaws in noncommunist societies.	Subjectively defined conditions that emerge from shared definitions of social reality.
EFFICACY OF HUMAN INTERVENTION	Can be alleviated through human intervention, but not ultimately solvable because all systems suffer flaws.	Non-Marxian: can be alleviated by human intervention but not ultimately solvable. Marxian: can be solved through radical restructuring of society and creation of a utopia.	Can be alleviated by human intervention but not ultimately solvable because new shared definitions can always emerge.

although this oversimplified example cannot be applied directly to the operation of society, some of the general principles are similar.[18]

Functional Prerequisites

According to the functionalist perspective, if society is to continue, certain essential tasks must be accomplished. If they are not, society may disintegrate or change its form substantially. The functionalists refer to such essential tasks as *functional prerequisites:* **things that must be accomplished in some fashion by every society.** Some of these are: (1) adaptation to the physical environment; (2) provision for the sexual reproduction of the members of society; (3) allocation of essential roles to people (for example, in our society we need people to fill roles as physicians, carpenters, homemakers, and many other roles); (4) communication between members (a common language); (5) agreement on basic meanings, such as how long a centimeter is, what love is, what money means; (6) a shared set of goals toward which groups strive; (7) norms to regulate how these goals will be reached; (8) regulation of emotional expression (expressing emotions in a nondisruptive fashion); (9) socialization of new members into the ways of society; and (10) effective controls over disruptive behavior.[19]

Each society must create some agents or institutions that meet the needs of these functional prerequisites. For example, the family as an institution functions to ensure the sexual reproduction of society's members and to socialize new members into the life patterns of society. The police and legal systems are mechanisms to control disruptive behavior that might threaten the stability of the social order. Religion is a provider of values and goals for members of society and education a provider of training for the essential roles that must be filled. However, the functionalists point out that there are *functional alternatives:* **different institutions or social arrangements that might develop to perform the same function.**[20] For example, some functions previously performed by the family, such as education, are now performed by other institutions. Other instances could be cited, but the

point to be made is that **any society must develop some social arrangements to perform the basic functions essential for survival.**

Some of the complex issues in the study of social problems can be better appreciated if we make the distinction between manifest and latent functions. **A** *manifest function* **is an intended consequence of some event or institution.** In other words, when we do something, we expect certain results from our actions. **A** *latent function* **is a consequence that was unexpected or unintended.** For example, one of the *manifest* functions of a college is to provide people with specialized training necessary to hold important positions in society. Some *latent* functions of college, which were certainly not intended by the founders, include providing the opportunity of deferring adult responsibilities, serving as a recreational center for young adults (who party, go to athletic events, have panty raids, and the like), and functioning as a marriage market where people go to find an acceptable spouse. These latent functions are just as much a part of the operation of the system of higher education as are its intended purposes.

Equilibrium and Social Change

According to the functionalist perspective, all social systems exhibit a tendency toward *equilibrium* — **maintenance of a particular balance, or steady state, in which the parts of the system remain in the same relationship to one another.** The system tends to resist social change; change is seen as disruptive unless it occurs at a slow pace. Since society is made up of interconnected and interdependent parts, a change in one part of the system will lead to changes in at least some of the other parts. For example, the establishment of compulsory education for children provoked very significant changes in other parts of American society. It removed children from the labor force, thus making more jobs available for adults. Since children were no longer working, they made no economic contributions to the family, and the economic functions of the family declined. It also resulted in a group of people in society who were biologically mature but not accorded full adult status.

The Functionalist Perspective and Social Problems

Functionalism views society as an organized, stable, and integrated system in which there is agreement over values and goals and cooperation among members. This emphasis is reflected in the functionalist approach to social problems. From the functionalist perspective, *a social problem may be said to exist when some condition disrupts the smooth functioning of the system and threatens the existence or effective operation of society.* In this framework, members of a society might not be aware of the existence of a problem even though sociologists could predict that the system would be threatened if some condition persisted. For example, in the late 1700s, few people conceived of a world "population problem" even though a few astute observers, such as Thomas Malthus, predicted precisely this based on existing conditions. Furthermore, there may be disagreement among groups within society over what conditions are social problems. Some may see disruption of the existing system as desirable whereas others may wish to preserve the status quo. However, the existence of a social problem from the *functionalist* point of view does not depend on awareness of the problem by the members of society (although they may be aware of it); rather it depends on whether the condition threatens the existence or effective operation of society. We can illustrate this approach to social problems through a brief discussion of some problems dealt with in greater detail in later chapters.

Sex Roles

According to the functionalist perspective, some sex role differentiation is vital to the effective functioning of the social order. Sex roles, like other features of society, are viewed in terms of their contribution to order and stability. Sex role learning helps to ensure that young boys and girls are socialized to perform tasks essential to society. For example, a sufficient number of females must want to have children so that population does not decline; men and women must cooperate in some fashion in the family to ensure that children are raised and

There is great controversy about the roles of women and men in contemporary society. How social scientists analyze such issues depends on the theoretical perspective employed.

learn acceptable goals and values; and people must learn who are appropriate sexual partners so that sexual competition does not become disruptive. If sex role conflict becomes extreme—there is little consensus about the proper place of each sex—it may threaten the equilibrium of society because these essential tasks will not be properly performed. Sex role conflict would then constitute a social problem.

Divorce

Divorce is another phenomenon that is viewed as potentially disruptive by functionalists. Divorce represents the breaking up of the most crucial institution in society—the family. The functionalist might ask: what would be the consequence if divorce were to become extremely widespread? Would the ultimate result be the dissolution of the family? Divorce might then be considered a social problem, since the important functions performed by the family—sexual reproduction, socialization of the young, emotional support of its members—would be hindered and the smooth operation of the society threatened.

Drug Use

From the functionalist perspective, drug use can be defined as a social problem if its use interferes with the ability of people in society to contribute to the accomplishment of necessary tasks and the achievement of desired goals. A technologically complex society, such as America, requires that many people be able to carry out tasks calling for either considerable manual dexterity or ample intellectual acumen. We must be clear-headed, rational, and able to coordinate our behavior with that of others. The heavy use of drugs, such as alcohol or amphetamines, can interfere with these skills and abilities. This is very costly for society in terms of automobile accidents, inefficiency at work, and injuries or drug-related health impairments. So the extent to which drug use is a social problem for a particular society depends on the degree to which it interferes with the achievement of essential tasks and goals.

The Conflict Perspective

Many sociologists have strong objections to a strict functional analysis of society because it overemphasizes the orderliness and stability of society while ignoring the importance and extent of conflict and change.[21] These dissenters, of whom Karl Marx was one, contend that if all parts of society were well-integrated and functional, there would be near-perfect balance and little conflict or social change. However, we need only look around to see that conflict and change are always present in society. For example, in recent years women have been demanding the opportunity to compete for jobs traditionally held only by men. Many women are no longer satisfied with secretarial and clerical positions that have little authority and reap few rewards. Since desirable jobs are in short supply, the result is conflict between men and women over these positions. As the women's rights movement has progressed, competition and conflict has spilled over into many arenas. It has even reached the point that an amendment to the Constitution—the Equal Rights Amendment—has been proposed as a means for making further headway in women's struggle over those resources traditionally controlled by men. This situation hardly reflects the consensus, cooperation, and stability that functionalists argue is the foundation of social order. To account for the ever-present reality of conflict and change, the conflict perspective is an alternative to the functionalist scheme.

Scarcity and Conflict

The conflict perspective rests on an important assumption: **there are certain things that members of society value highly, and most of these valued things are in scarce supply.** In American society, we might consider wealth, power, beauty, and prestige to be among these scarce resources. **Because of their scarcity, people—either individually or in groups—struggle with one another to attain them.** From this perspective, society is an arena for the struggle over scarce resources. Furthermore, each group in society has certain interests—there are things that are beneficial to it—and what is in the interest of one group may be to the disadvantage of another. Thus, society is characterized by a clash of interests, and groups pursue those things that are to their own advantage.

Struggle and conflict, which are central to this perspective, can take many forms. If they always (or even frequently) involved violence, then we would have a war of all against all, and society would be impossible. As one means of controlling the amount of violence, norms emerge that determine what types of conflict are allowable for which groups. For example, conflict can take the form of competition and disagreements. Thus, robbery is not an acceptable means of acquiring greater wealth; however, participating in a labor strike or acquiring more education than others is an approved way of competing for the limited money available.

The conflict perspective points to another important process in society: groups use the legal system in society to improve or maintain their position and to pursue their own interests. For example, the labor strike was not always an acceptable action for workers. At one time, employers had the legal and legitimate right to use violence against workers who interfered with the operation of their business. Workers had no such right. After a long struggle based on the resources available to labor unions (the large masses of workers they could command as well as the support of other groups), unions forced the passage of laws legitimizing the strike as a bargaining tool. This does not mean that the conflict is over—only that is has taken the different, nonviolent form of periodic labor negotiations. However, management and unions still use whatever resources they have available to maintain their position and increase their share of valued resources. They may temporarily cooperate to reach their individual goals with little or no violence, but they cooperate only if they feel that it is in their own interest to do so.

Conflict and Social Change

From the conflict perspective, conflict is an inevitable part of all societies because of the scarcity of valued objects. From this struggle, a certain degree of social change will emerge. In this view, social change is mainly the reordering of the distribution of scarce goods among groups. Out of struggle, new winners emerge or new uneasy truces are established. Unlike the functionalist, who views change as potentially disruptive, the conflict theorist views change as potentially beneficial—it can lead to advancements, improvements, and the emergence of new groups as dominant forces in society. Without it, society would become stagnant.

Within the conflict school, there are many points of view. Karl Marx believed that, given certain political and economic arrangements, conflict was inevitable and that violent revolution was the tool that would bring about the ultimate resolution of this struggle.[22] Marx saw the final result of conflict much as Charles Darwin viewed the evolution of life—namely, that matters would move to a more adaptive state of existence. For Marx, violent revolution would lead to an ultimate state of communistic utopia, in which scarcity and conflict would no longer exist.

Few theorists share Marx's optimistic view of progress. Most conflict theorists today, such as Ralf Dahrendorf, believe that *conflict and change are inevitable under any social arrangement,* and that *conflict yields no final result.*[23] Rather, *continuous conflict leads simply to a succession of different (not necessarily better) structural arrangements in society.* These conflict theorists see change as being without *necessary* utility to society as a whole. **Change merely results in new arrangements for controlling the scarcities of society, and these arrangements are not permanent.** But whichever view we take (Marx or Dahrendorf), they all agree on one point—**the source of conflict in society is the struggle over scarce, valued items.**

The Conflict Perspective and Social Problems

Since, from the conflict perspective, conflict and strife are inevitable, these conditions are not necessarily seen as a social problem for society. From the conflict perspective, *a social problem may be said to exist when a group with some power believes that its values and interests are not being served or that it is not getting its share of scarce resources.* Whereas the functionalist definition specified that social problems affect *society as a whole,* the conflict definition holds that only a *group* or a mere *portion of society may be affected.* In addition, this definition requires the awareness of a condition by some group with a degree of power and the group's definition of it as a problem. The oppression and deprivation of minority groups in the United States has been with us for some time; however, until those subordinate groups gained access to some resources that provide power, the conditions were not defined as social problems. Through demonstrations and rioting, these minority groups threatened the interests of the dominant groups in society, who then began to define these conditions as problems about which something ought to be done.

Sex Roles

For the conflict theorist, some degree of role conflict is a normal part of the social order. There is never complete consensus between the sexes about what each expects from the other, and "sexual bargaining" inevitably ensues: the attempt by each sex to gain what it wants from the other at least cost. So interaction between the sexes involves bargaining or exchange, a form of conflict. Yet such conditions are not necessarily a social problem. Sex role interaction becomes a social problem, as it is today, when an awareness emerges among groups of women that they are not receiving the share of valued resources (such as prestigious occupations and high incomes) to which they feel they are entitled and when these groups have the power to make sex role discrimination a public concern.

Divorce

In somewhat the same fashion, divorce is viewed as normal or necessary from the conflict perspective. This is not to say that conflict theorists deny or ignore the disruptive effects of divorce; yet there are marital unions that generate dissension and hostility, and divorce is one mechanism through which such conflict may be handled. When does divorce become a social problem? Divorce is a threat to the family, a fundamental and cherished institution. When this institution is threatened by widespread divorce, some groups view their ability to lead a desirable lifestyle as threatened. Whether the dissolution of the traditional family is perceived as a problem depends on which groups are threatened. For a number of reasons, poor black families in the United States have often been single-parent families, usually headed by women. Yet since this affected a relatively small and powerless group of people, it had not been defined as a social problem. Today, when divorce threatens the families of more affluent and influential groups, divorce is considered a social problem. So, from the conflict perspective, divorce emerges as a social problem when particular groups with some power feel that their interests are threatened by that condition.

Drug Use

From the conflict perspective, drug use becomes a social problem when some group feels that the use of drugs interferes with its ability to compete for scarce resources and achieve its goals. Drugs can be a mechanism used to pacify subordinate groups such that they are not motivated to change the status quo. This is beneficial to the dominant groups but leaves the subordinate group at a disadvantage in the struggle for resources. Thus, many minority groups have viewed drug use as detrimental to the advancement of their group because it saps energies and resources that might be used to promote group goals. In addition, the extent to which drug use is defined as a social problem depends on which groups are affected. When drug use was limited to poor people and marginal groups (minority groups, musicians, beatniks), few considered it a serious problem. As drug use has spread to more influential groups, it became defined as a problem by these groups.

The Interactionist Perspective

The interactionist perspective focuses on individuals and the process of everyday social interaction between them rather than on larger structures of society, such as religion,

the economy, or education. In dealing with social life at the individual level, the interactionist places importance on human symbolic processes.[24] A well-known social psychologist, Herbert Blumer, has commented:

> The term "symbolic interaction" refers . . . to the peculiar and distinctive character of interaction as it takes place between human beings. The peculiarity consists in the fact that human beings interpret or "define" each other's actions instead of merely reacting to each other's actions. . . . Thus, human interaction is mediated by the use of symbols, by interpretation, or by ascertaining the meaning of another's actions.[25]

To understand the full import of Blumer's remarks, we must discuss some basic social processes as seen from the interactionist perspective.

The Looking-Glass Self

A central concept in the interactionist perspective is the notion of *self* (or self-concept). **The *self* refers to those thoughts and feelings that people have about themselves.** It is the view we hold of who or what we are. Do you consider yourself brave, likable, generous, attractive? These might be parts of your self-concept, along with your awareness of yourself as a student, employee, musician, or tennis player. An important issue for the interactionist is to determine the manner in which a person develops a particular self-concept. There are certain things that we can learn about ourselves without the aid of others. For example, we need little help from others to learn how tall we are—we can measure that. We do not need others to learn the color of our eyes—we can see that for ourselves in a mirror. These examples deal with qualities that have a certain "objective" character, for we can observe and measure them independently of what others might think of them. However, how do you determine whether you are a "likable," "easy-going," or "beautiful" person? These are much more subjective qualities that depend on the judgments of others and that are difficult to observe and measure.

Charles Horton Cooley proposed that such qualities become incorporated into a person's self through a process he called *the looking-glass self,* in which **we learn what kind of person we are by seeing and hearing how others react to us.**[26] Cooley described three stages in the development of the self, each of which was dependent on interaction with other people. The first stage of the process is *how we imagine we appear to others.* Do we give the impression of being witty, humorous, or helpful? As a part of social interaction, we continually manage impressions in the presence of others so that they will view us in a certain fashion. The second stage is *how we imagine others react to our appearance.* Did the person frown and shake his head, thus indicating disapproval, or did he smile, indicating that he accepted and approved of the self we have presented? In this way, we build up in our minds a conception of the other person's reaction to, and assessment of, ourselves. The third stage is *how we react to what we take to be the feelings of others about us.* We might feel a sense of shame or anxiety if we believe the other's reaction was negative; or we might feel a sense of pride and satisfaction following a positive reaction. By putting together our evaluations of such interchanges, we construct a picture of who we are. Furthermore, the daily reactions of others serve to affirm and reaffirm our conceptions of ourselves. We continue to see ourselves as desirable and likable because in our everyday interaction people treat us as if we were desirable and likable.

Social Reality and Shared Expectations

As this process of self-concept development illustrates, the interactionist perspective places great importance on face-to-face social interaction; it is out of such interaction that we gain much of our knowledge and understanding of the world.[27] From this point of view, social reality cannot be understood as a purely objective phenomenon. Rather, **social reality is what a particular group agrees it is.** Something is real if people treat it as real. If you think you are handsome or beautiful, this definition of the situation will shape your approach toward members of the opposite sex you meet on campus. If you think you are intelligent and capable, this will influence your decision to continue in college or apply to graduate school. To some extent irrespective of objective reality, your definition of reality will influence your behavior.

However, social reality and definitions of situations must be shared and reaffirmed through social interaction. After the tenth refusal for a date or a string of low grades on your transcript, it becomes more difficult for you to retain the concept of yourself as physically attractive or intelligent. Your interpretation of objects and events must be reasonably consistent with others' interpretations; otherwise, social interaction is impossible. As members of particular groups, we learn common social and cultural meanings that help us construct a reality from what is happening around us. Our definitions of particular situations are strongly influenced by the expectations we share with others. **From the interactionist perspective, the social structure of society rests on a set of shared expectations that make human interaction possible.** Because we share expectations about the definition of situations and about how people ought to behave, social interaction is relatively predictable and orderly.

To illustrate the manner in which social reality is constructed from shared expectations, it is useful to think of society as analogous to a *jam session*. A jam session is an informal gathering of jazz musicians each of whom plays for his own satisfaction and for the enjoyment of his fellow musicians. A jam session is a patterned form of social interaction in that each player enters the session with shared expectations for his own and others' behavior; each musician understands the social norms that are supposed to govern the encounter. A jam session is further patterned in the sense that the participants are expected to focus on central themes (tunes), attempt to keep rhythm, and stay on key. However, every jam session is truly unique. Each musician enters the situation with his own idiom or style based on his personality, his instrument, his training and experience, and his creativity. The pattern that emerges in each jam session is a unique, one-time blending of the improvisations of each of the participants around a central theme. Although the outcome is patterned, *relatively* predictable, and well-coordinated, it is different from anything produced by any other group of musicians (or by the same musicians at any other time). Each session is the unique product of the interaction of the participants.

Society is like a jam session in that shared expectations of the various groups and individuals in society provide the framework that gives coherence to social interaction. Because group members define social reality similarly, coordinated and predictable patterns of social interaction emerge. However, each interaction has its novel aspects because every person and group has its own distinctive personality, values, and interests, all of which leave their mark on each interaction situation.

Symbols are the principal vehicles through which expectations are conveyed from one person to another. A symbol is any object, word, or event that stands for, represents, or takes the place of something else. Symbols have certain characteristics. First, the meaning of symbols derives from social consensus—the group's agreement that one thing will represent something else. A flag represents love of country or patriotism; a green light means *go*, not *stop*; a frown stands for displeasure. Second, the relationship between the symbol and what it represents is arbitrary—there is no inherent connection. There is nothing about the color green that compels us to use that, rather than red, as a symbol for *go*; a flag is in reality a piece of cloth for which we could substitute anything, as long as we agreed that it stood for country. Finally, symbols need not be tied to physical reality. We can use symbols to represent things with no physical existence, such as justice, mercy, or God, or to stand for things that do not exist at all, such as unicorns.

Human beings respond to reality that is mediated through a set of symbols. In a sense, the world we inhabit is one that we construct through the meanings that we agree to attach to symbols. We respond to symbolic reality, not physical reality. We all participate in constructing this symbolic or social reality through our acceptance of the meanings that others attach to objects and events. When a traffic policeman blows his whistle or holds up his hand, he means something by those gestures, and you understand them in much the same way he does. Through those gestures, he communicates certain expectations to you. When you respond appropriately, showing that you understand and accept the meanings, you in effect reaffirm the social reality to which both of you are responding. If this agreement does not occur, then social interaction may collapse and some redefinition is called for.

The Interactionist Perspective and Social Problems

From the interactionist perspective, a social problem is a subjective phenomenon that may not necessarily arise from any "objective" conditions. A social problem emerges from shared meanings and definitions about the world. From this perspective, *a social problem may be said to exist when a condition is defined by a major group in society as a problem and the group behaves as though the condition were a problem.* This definition may seem somewhat general, but the generality derives from the assumptions of this perspective. For the interactionist, social life is rooted in symbols, shared expectations, and commonly agreed-upon definitions of reality. As a result, *interpretation* of reality is the key element in defining social problems. A group perceives a condition as a problem within the context of its own shared meanings, social definitions, and values.

Sex Roles

The interactionist perspective directs our attention to how members of different groups define a particular behavior and how shared expectations concerning appropriate behavior change over time. In preindustrial America, appropriate sex role behavior was clearly defined for both males and females, and there were widely shared expectations about how men and women should behave. People knew, for the most part, what was expected of them. Today, traditional sex role definitions are changing,

and many people find themselves in a situation in which they are unclear about what is expected of them or in which their sex role expectations clash with the expectations held by others. Many of these groups have defined sex roles as a social problem because this lack of consensus makes coordinated behavior difficult, if not impossible.

Divorce

There have also been important changes in attitudes about divorce. While divorce has become more common today, it is also subject to less stigmatization than in the past; it is increasingly viewed as an acceptable option for couples. However, these changes in attitudes about divorce clash with some of the social meanings we attach to institutions such as marriage and the family. We still view these institutions as central to our culture and (at least ideally) as permanent bonds between people. They are so important to us that we are reluctant to condone the widespread collapse of them. So, divorce, which has been around for some time, is currently defined as a social problem because it seems to contradict the shared meanings and definitions we hold concerning related institutions.

Drug Use

From the interactionist perspective, social interaction is based on shared consensus concerning social meanings and values. Drug use can threaten that consensus in a number of ways. The lack of predictability induced by many drugs can lead people to define them as a social problem. In other cases, the use of drugs may be perceived as interfering with the development and maintenance of this consensus. For many affluent groups, the use of drugs such as marijuana and LSD leads to the emergence of drug subcultures that do not seem to share the dominant cultural values (such as hard work and respect for one's parents) that underlie the lifestyle of the dominant group. Parents fear that their children will become immersed in such subcultures and reject the values they hope to pass on to them.

Multiple Definitions: Divergent Perspectives

The definitions of social problems that we have presented are many and varied. Each rests on a different theoretical perspective. It is our contention that no single definition by itself provides a sufficient understanding of social problems. Rather, each complements the others. However, there are some important overriding similarities and differences that should be highlighted.

An important similarity between the **conflict** and **interactionist** definitions is that **they both emphasize the "subjective": there must be an awareness or perception by some group that a condition is undesirable for it to be a social problem.** The **functionalist** definition differs from the others in that **it emphasizes the "objective": a condition is a social problem if it threatens the smooth functioning of society regardless of whether people are aware of the threat.**

The general definition of social problems first presented will enable us tentatively to identify which conditions seem to constitute social problems. Then, we can use the theoretically based definitions to point up possibilities that our general definition did not include—such as the possibility that a condition might pose a problem although no member of society was aware of it. These more specific definitions also help us state more clearly why a certain condition is a social problem, for whom it is a social problem, the dimensions of the problem, and the feasible solutions of the problem. We can see, then, the importance of viewing social problems from some theoretical base. Even though most sociological definitions of social problems are grounded on different groups' perceptions of certain conditions as social problems, we have nevertheless observed that there is often an inconsistency between what sociologists define as social problems and what the public views as social problems. We avoid this contradiction through the use of the three theoretical perspectives discussed previously; as a result, we obtain a more comprehensive and useful definition of social problems.

Through the conflict and interactionist perspectives, we retain *group perception and definition* as important elements (the "subjective"). Through the inclusion of the functionalist perspective, however, we may conclude that some *conditions unrecognized by any group* might be important social problems (the "objective"). Thus, given important group values and goals, the sociologist might recognize certain conditions as threatening to the group even though the group itself did not recognize them as such. So our general definition should be used only as an initial perspective in identifying some conditions as a problem. **Once a problem has been identified, the concepts and processes of each theoretical perspective should be applied to provide a detailed basis for understanding and possibly solving the problem.**

DIFFICULTIES IN SOLVING SOCIAL PROBLEMS

While the primary focus of sociology has been on the understanding of social problems, we are nevertheless concerned about solutions to problems and will indicate throughout this book some possible steps toward coming to grips with them. Yet one should not become overly optimistic about our ability to solve the problems of our society. Some cautions must be kept in mind.

Is It A Social Problem?

In solving social problems, the first, and most critical, factor is that an influential group must be aware that a condition exists. Even though a social problem might exist from the functionalist perspective without such public awareness, it certainly would not be solved until such awareness arose. For example, awareness of poverty as a social problem has fluctuated over time. During the Great Depression, when poverty was visible and extensive, there was great concern about it and pressure for government programs to alleviate it. As economic conditions improved, public interest waned.

Some sociologists question whether the problem of unemployment can, in fact, be completely solved.

By the 1950s, little public interest was being expressed, and almost no attention was focused on the plight of the poor in society. As a result, little was done to contend with the problems of the impoverished other than to mount simple welfare efforts by local public authorities.

Can It Be Solved?

The public not only has to acknowledge the existence of an issue, but it must also feel that the condition is capable of solution by human intervention. For example, many people would consider the winter weather of Alaska as posing serious problems for the people of that state. But is weather, as such, something we can do anything about? We consider it, at our current level of technology, a condition of nature that people must simply endure. Consequently, we do not think of Alaska's weather as being a *social* problem.

Likewise, in terms of social conditions, we must ask, do we have the necessary knowledge needed to solve certain undesirable conditions? The social sciences have developed a considerable understanding of human social behavior, but to what extent can we control social forces as a chemist might manipulate physical elements? Do we know enough about the complex intertwining of various social forces to be able substantially to reduce the amount of crime in society? We must keep this issue before us as we discuss each social problem.

Are We Willing To Solve It?

Once an issue has been recognized as a social problem capable of solution, we must ask whether society is willing to solve it. If televised violence is shown to have adverse effects on children, and we know that we can solve the problem by banning violent programs from the screen, will we do it? From what we see today, the answer is possibly that we will not. If we knew that we could substantially reduce environmental pollution by reducing the level of affluence to which most Americans have become accustomed, would we do it? Again, possibly not. Some "problem" areas are only problems for a minority, and the majority may thus be content to continue things as they are.

Should We Attempt A Solution?

Some of the complex problems that arise in solving social problems can be appreciated if we refer back to the concepts of *manifest* and *latent functions*. When we consider solutions to social problems, we must realize that we do not always know what the latent functions of a social problem are. If we outlaw gambling, prostitution, and other vices, what will happen? Will people who were supported by these vices suddenly turn up on welfare? Will the clientele of prostitutes turn to homosexuality or rape as substitutes? By attempting premature solutions based on a lack of complete information, we may create more serious problems than those we solve. Prohibition is one example of this. The attempt to halt the consumption of alcohol resulted in the rise of an illegal liquor industry that in turn gave birth to large-scale organized crime in the United States. The "cure" to one problem turned out to be worse than the "disease."

Will We Accept The Costs?

Are we financially willing to attempt the solution of various social problems? Cost, while it might seem callous to consider, is an important factor in doing battle with social ills. At this moment, we are capable of cleaning up both our water and our air. The technology to achieve this is known. But at what cost? There are, as we all know, finite economic resources available in our society. We can use those resources however we see fit, but what shall be our priorities? Will we sacrifice our material standard of living to obtain a clean environment? Turning to unemployment: will we provide training and jobs for the jobless millions regardless of what it costs us *personally?* Choices must be made.

Unhappily, there are limits to what we can do to alleviate human suffering. Despite our concern, empathy, or good intentions, there are limits to our capacities, and this can have painful consequences. For example, one of the tragedies of the war on poverty of the 1960s was that broad promises were made to many people, who then expected the elimination of poverty and the advent of the good life for all; but the promises born of enthusiasm and a sincere commitment were not enough.

"Today's problems should have been solved in the 1950's, but in the 50's we were solving the problems of the 20's, in the 20's we were solving the problems of the 1890's..."

So the solution of social problems will not be easy and must be approached with great caution. Some of the proposed solutions to be examined in this book are not new. We have been aware of many of these social problems for decades, and the fact that they are still with us attests to the difficulties in solving them. However, solutions are closer at hand if we possess a thorough understanding of the nature of social problems. The major purpose of this book is to help provide such an understanding.

ORGANIZATION OF THE BOOK

This book has been divided into five parts. In Part 1, "Understanding Social Problems" (including the introductory chapter and a chapter on the uses of data in the study of social problems), the student is introduced to the way in which sociologists approach the study of social problems. In Part 2, "Problems for the Nation and the World" (including chapters on problems in our cities, population problems, environmental problems, and the growth of corporations and government), the focus of attention is on problems that confront American society but that are also worldwide problems and with important implications for the interdependence of the nations of the world.

In Part 3, "Social Institutions and the Life Cycle" (including chapters on the family, health care, work and leisure, and problems of the aged), our concern is with some of the problems confronting major social institutions in American society and problems that a person confronts at different stages of life. In Part 4, "Conflict and Social Inequality" (including chapters on poverty, race and minority-group relations, problems caused by changing sex roles, and intergroup conflict and war), the emphasis is on those conditions in American society that result from social inequality and generate social conflict. In Part 5, "Deviant Behavior" (including chapters on various forms of deviant behavior, crime and delinquency, drugs and substance abuse, and various types of social movements), the focus of concern is on some of the major forms of deviant or disruptive behavior in American society and their implications for the quality of American life. Although there are other ways that the topics might have been organized, the authors find this organization to be the most meaningful in terms of the natural interrelationships between problems.

However, each chapter has been written in a fashion that is understandable to the student provided this introductory chapter has been mastered. In that way, should an alternative sequence of reading the chapters be decided upon, the student should encounter no problems in understanding the material.

Within each chapter, an organization has been used that will enhance the student's understanding of the social problem under consideration and the social processes relevant to the solution of that problem. (The first two chapters, because they deal with introductory material, are organized somewhat differently.) First, each chapter begins with a brief introduction to the nature of the problem. Second, the student is presented with a historical view of the problem in order to understand how the problem, as it exists today, emerged from recent history. Such an understanding, it is believed, will enhance our ability to evaluate the feasibility of solutions and alternatives. Third, each problem is examined utilizing the three theoretical perspectives presented in the first chapter. In this way, the relevant social factors influencing the problem will be before us as we review the dimensions of the problem in American society. Fourth, an in-depth consideration of the problem itself is presented, with discussions of its dimensions and ramifications for American society. Fifth, we discuss the prospects for the future of each problem. In this context, potential solutions to the problem are presented and evaluated.

GLOSSARY TERMS

Authority	Heterogeneous	Power
Conflict perspective	Homogeneous	Social differentiation
Cultural relativity	Interactionist perspective	Social problem
Definition of the situation	Interest group	Subculture
Ethnocentrism	Latent function	Theory
Functionalist perspective	Manifest function	Values
Gatekeeping	Norm	Vested interest group

REFERENCES

[1] Auguste Comte, *System of Positive Philosophy*, J. H. Bridges and F. Harrison, trans. (London: Longmans, Green, 1875–1877; original French edition, 1851–1854).

[2] Emile Durkheim, *Suicide: A Study in Sociology*, John Spaulding and George Simpson, trans. (New York: The Free Press, 1951).

[3] Karl Marx, *Selected Writings in Sociology and Social Philosophy*, T. B. Bottomore, trans. (London: McGraw-Hill, 1964).

[4] Lester Ward, *Applied Sociology* (New York: Ginn and Co., 1906).

[5] Robert H. Lauer, "Defining Social Problems: Public and Professional Perspectives," *Social Problems* 24 (October 1976), pp. 122–130.

[6] Peter L. Berger, *Invitation to Sociology* (New York: Doubleday-Anchor, 1963), p. 38.

[7] C. Wright Mills, *The Sociological Imagination* (New York: Oxford University Press, 1959), pp. 129–130.

[8] Ibid.

[9] Ibid., p. 130.

[10] Michael Harrington, *The Other America: Poverty in the United States* (New York: Penguin Books, 1962).

[11] William I. Thomas and Dorothy S. Thomas, *The Child in America* (New York: Alfred A. Knopf, 1932), p. 572.

[12] Harrington, *The Other America*.

[13] Robert Bierstedt, *Power and Progress: Essays in Sociological Theory* (New York: McGraw-Hill, 1974), p. 221.

[14] Ibid.

[15] See Max Weber, *The Theory of Social and Economic Organization*, Talcott Parsons, ed. (New York: The Free Press, 1947), and Robert A. Nisbet, *The Sociological Tradition* (New York: Basic Books, 1966).

[16] See Joseph R. Gusfield, *Symbolic Crusade: Status Politics and The American Temperance Movement* (Urbana, Ill.: University of Illinois Press, 1963).

[17] See Talcott Parsons, *The Social System* (New York: The Free Press, 1951), and Robert K. Merton, *Social Theory and Social Structure*, 2d ed. (New York: The Free Press, 1968).

[18] For a discussion of these issues, see Jonathan H. Turner, *The Structure of Sociological Theory* (Homewood, Ill.: Dorsey Press, 1974).

[19] See D. F. Aberle et. al., "The Functional Prerequisites of Society," *Ethics* 60 (January 1950), pp. 100–111.

[20] Merton, *Social Theory and Social Structure*.

[21] See Lewis Coser, *Continuities in the Study of Social Conflict* (New York: The Free Press, 1967), and Randall Collins, *Conflict Sociology* (New York: Academic Press, 1975).

[22] Marx, *Selected Writings*.

[23] Ralf Dahrendorf, *Class and Class Conflict in Industrial Society* (Stanford, Calif.: Stanford University Press, 1959).

[24] See George Herbert Mead, *Mind, Self, and Society From the Standpoint of a Social Behaviorist*, Charles W. Morris, ed. (Chicago: University of Chicago Press, 1934), and Charles Horton Cooley, *Human Nature and the Social Order* (Glencoe, Ill.: The Free Press, 1956).

[25] Herbert G. Blumer, "Society as Symbolic Interaction," in Arnold M. Rose, ed., *Human Behavior and Social Processes* (Boston: Houghton Mifflin, 1962), p. 180.

[26] Cooley, *Human Nature and the Social Order*.

[27] Peter L. Berger and Thomas Luckmann, *The Social Construction of Reality* (Garden City, N.Y.: Doubleday, 1966).

SUGGESTED READINGS

Berger, Peter. *Invitation to Sociology*. New York: Doubleday, Anchor Books, 1963.
One of the most effective brief introductions to the science of sociology. Berger's easy-to-read style makes this book ideal for students taking their first or second course in sociology.

Davis, Kingsley, and Moore, Wilbert E. "Some Principles of Stratification." *American Sociological Review*, April 1945, pp. 242–249.
This article illustrates functionalism by using the example of the purpose behind the existence of social classes.

Etzioni, Amitai. *Social Problems*. Englewood Cliffs, N.J.: Prentice-Hall, 1976.

Etzioni provides an excellent overview of the study of social problems. Of particular interest is his discussion of the different techniques used by sociologists in order to investigate and understand problematic issues in our society.

Goffman, Erving. *Presentation of Self in Everyday Life*. Garden City, N.Y.: Doubleday, 1959.
This book introduces the interactionist process as it is used in day-to-day activities. It is a general and nontechnical treatment of the perspective.

Marx, Karl. *Manifesto of the Communist Party*. Chicago: Charles H. Kerr, 1888.
This brief work is one of the foundations on which the

conflict perspective is built. It illustrates the nature of conflict based on an analysis of economic life in industrial societies.

Mills, C. Wright. *The Sociological Imagination.* New York: Oxford University Press, 1959.

Despite the heavy emphasis on conflict theory in all of Mills's writings, *The Sociological Imagination* provides a good, general overview of how sociology can be used to understand social issues.

Questions for Discussion

1. Discuss the history of social problems, including a consideration of how early sociologists in Europe and America approached these issues. How were the problems confronting people in preindustrial America similar to and different from those we face today?

2. What is a social problem? Discuss each of the important considerations in identifying one. How is a social problem defined according to the authors of your text?

3. What are the important dimensions of social problems in American society? Discuss how factors like values, norms, the subjective nature of reality, power, authority, interest groups, subcultures, ethnocentrism, gatekeeping, and democracy affect our consideration of social problems.

4. Why are theories necessary in studying social problems? Do you think one of the three perspectives discussed is better suited for approaching social problems than the other two? Which one? Why do you feel it is the most effective?

5. From the functionalist perspective, society is a system, and as with most systems, certain things must exist to keep it operating (functional prerequisites). Is it possible to have a society that does not have all of the prerequisites mentioned in the chapter? Describe a society that is missing one or more of the functional prerequisites.

6. The conflict perspective rests on the assumption that people will struggle over certain scarce resources that are highly valued. Would the conflict perspective still be valid in an automated society that could provide everything that people wanted?

7. The interactionist perspective relies on our subjective interpretations of situations and experiences. Describe how two separate groups might interpret an issue differently so that only one group viewed it as a social problem.

CHAPTER 2

The Uses and Misuses of Data

WAYS OF "KNOWING"

Traditional Knowledge. Charismatic Knowledge.
Experiential Knowledge. Scientific Knowledge. Interest
Groups and Scientific Objectivity.

THE RESEARCH PROCESS

Stages in the Research Process. Major Issues in the
Research Process.

THE PRESENTATION OF DATA: STRENGTHS AND
PITFALLS

Statistical Presentation. Visual Presentation: Graphs and
Charts.

PROPAGANDA AND DISTORTION

CONCLUSION

Today, people are bombarded from all sides with information and facts—much of it inaccurate and misleading—that clamor for attention and recognition. Through television, newspapers, and advertising, we are continually being implored to want this, to believe that, to buy something else. "Honest Don" wants to give us a "square deal—fair deal" on one of his used cars. Headlines blare out the high incidence of crime. One politician tells us that welfare leads to increases in unemployment because it discourages people from using their own initiative. Another blames crime on leniency in the criminal justice system and proposes long prison sentences as a solution. Opinion polling agencies claim to know what the American public believes on the basis of talking to 1500 people out of a population of 200,000,000! Out of this barrage of information, what is one to accept?

The ability to analyze information accurately is a central concern in the study of social problems because public policies designed to solve these problems are often based on the acceptance of certain information or facts. More and bigger prisons are built to solve the crime problem. Welfare payments are kept low in order to motivate people to look for jobs. National health insurance is proposed as a solution for rising health care costs. All such policies are based on someone's understanding and interpretation of information. Especially in a democratic society, it is critical that citizens have adequate information with which to make decisions that are in the long-term interests of their community and society.

However, as noted sociologist C. Wright Mills pointed out, information alone is not enough to allow people to participate rationally in the decisions that affect their lives:

It is not only information that [people] need—in this Age of Fact, information often dominates their attention and overwhelms their capacities to assimilate it. It is not only the skills of reason that they need—although their struggles to acquire these often exhaust their limited moral energy.

What they need, and what they feel they need, is a quality of mind that will help them to use information and to develop reason in order to achieve lucid summations of what is going on in the world and of what may be happening within themselves.[1]

Citizens of democratic societies need not only information and the skills with which to assimilate it into their lives in a meaningful fashion; they also need the intellectual "tools" with which to evaluate the accuracy of information.

How does one raise the veil of distortion that shrouds so much information in the world today? The principal strategy employed by sociologists to achieve this end is the scientific method. The recent development of sophisticated methodological and statistical techniques in the social sciences has made possible tremendous advances in our ability to analyze and understand social problems. In this chapter, we will introduce the student to the scientific method and some elementary methodological and statistical techniques used by sociologists in the study of social problems. However, **any information can be *misused*—facts can be distorted or misinterpreted and the truth concealed if it is to the advantage of some particular group to do so.** Therefore, a further objective of this chapter is to acquaint the student with some of the ways in which information (or *data,* as it is called in the scientific literature) can be distorted to give a misleading picture of reality. However, not all information is to be mistrusted. This chapter will provide the student with some tools with which to separate appropriate uses of data from its misuses.

WAYS OF "KNOWING"

People rarely question how they know what they know. On what basis do we accept something as "real" or "true?" How do facts become established? Consider the following facts. Night follows day, which follows night—in endless succession. Summer is associated with hot weather, winter with cold. Professional baseball players who hit well are generally paid well. Children from single-parent families are more likely to be brought before juvenile courts for delinquent acts than are children with both parents in the home.

These are all facts. A *fact* is something that has been observed to occur in the world. A fact might be descriptive (there are 220 million people in the United States) or refer to an association (the relationship just mentioned between single-parent families and delinquency). However, despite the common refrain "just give me the facts," facts do not speak for themselves. They must be interpreted by answering the question, why did this occur? So, how does one establish and interpret facts?

Sociology is a science, which means that it uses a particular method—the scientific method—for acquiring knowledge about the world. However, the scientific method is only one of the means commonly accepted in our society of acquiring knowledge or "truth." Other ways of knowing include knowledge through tradition, charisma, and personal experience. These other ways deserve discussion because opinions about, and policies to deal with, social problems are often based on them, and the conclusions people arrive at through these ways of knowing often diverge sharply from scientific conclusions regarding the same problem.

Traditional Knowledge

Traditional truth **is based on a belief in the validity of custom and traditional authority.** Something is considered true because it is a taken-for-granted "fact" that has been passed down over generations. A fact is accepted or explained "because that's the way it has always been." It is considered true because the group's elders, in their wisdom, say it is so. For example, a technique for making arrows that, at the time of its discovery, was viewed by a group as only one of several ways of accomplishing the job, over time can come to be defined as the *only* proper way of doing the job. What was originally a purely utilitarian way of accomplishing something can, if practiced repeatedly over generations, become invested with tradition and become a sacred rite. This type of knowledge is highly subjective in nature because its validity is assumed rather than directly tested.

Traditional knowledge has important implications for how people think about social problems. Conditions that may come to be viewed by some groups as social problems can emerge and continue to exist because they are supported by traditional truths. For example, social inequality is sometimes perpetuated because of traditional religious teachings and practices. Until recently, blacks held a subordinate position in the Mormon church to the extent that entrance into the lay priesthood was denied them. This practice was based on early teachings of the church and had become a part of its tradition. The recent change in policy resulted from a religious revelation that the Church President claimed to receive. The lack of access by women to many positions in our society has also been justified on the basis of biblical and other religious teachings. In traditional Judeo-Christian teachings, woman is subordinate to man (made from his rib), and reproduction is viewed as a very important activity for people to engage in. These teachings have been used to justify male dominance over women and the view that woman's primary function is to have children. On the basis of such beliefs, many groups have clung to the traditional definition of the role of women and thus perpetuated the unequal treatment of women in our society.

Throughout history, explanations of the causes of physical and mental illness have relied on traditional sources of knowledge. For example, many religious traditions have defined disease as the result of some sort of divine intervention or divine punishment. The Babylonians in Mesopotamia believed that epidemics were a punishment wrought by God when people were wicked or sinful. The ancient Hebrews, in addition to believing that disease was a divine punishment, also believed that cleanliness was a sign of moral purity. Because of this belief, they engaged in some sound preventive health practices, such as dumping their garbage outside the city—but these customs were based on traditional rather than scientific knowledge.[2]

Because traditional truth is backed by custom and authority, it is extremely difficult to challenge effectively. People cling to it tenaciously, and distortions and inaccuracies concerning social problems that result from traditional knowledge can severely hamper efforts to solve those prob-

Charismatic leaders have the ability to attract devoted followers
and to incite them to action.

lems. An example of a challenge to traditional truth is that of Galileo, who advocated the theory that the earth moves around the sun, and not vice versa, as the biblical interpretation of his time held. He was forced to recant this view before the elders of the medieval Church on pain of death. (However, his last words were reported to have been: "It [the earth] nevertheless moves.") Traditional truth has an enormous impact on the beliefs of the people of any society.

Charismatic Knowledge

***Charismatic truth* is knowledge allegedly possessed by someone with special powers.** These powers derive from the person's charisma or "gift," such as the powers of clairvoyance, special visions, or even direct revelations from the deities. Charismatic leaders are believed to possess some type of extraordinary (supernormal) power. It is the possession of these special powers that legitimates their claim to having access to information that

others do not have. "Because I believe in it and I tell it to you, then it must be true" is the hallmark of the charismatic leader. People accept facts and their explanation by saying, "because our leader says it is so."

Charismatic knowledge can be an extremely potent force in the emergence and development of social problems because it can incite people to engage in actions or follow lifestyles that others consider to be social problems. Evangelical religious cults and many political movements are examples of groups whose claim to the "truth" is based on charismatic knowledge. For example, Jesus of Nazareth claimed to be the son of God; Hitler claimed to have a special insight regarding the destiny of the German people; modern gurus, such as the Rev. Sun Myung Moon of the Unification Church and the child-God Maharaj-Ji of the Divine Light Mission, claim to know some ultimate truths whereby people can save themselves from a corrupt and alienating society; and charismatic faith healers in modern times have convinced many peo-

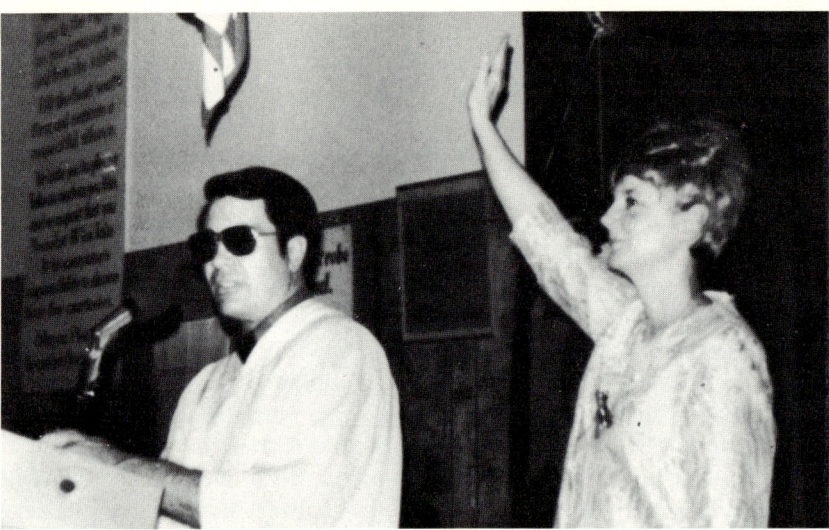

Charismatic leaders like the Reverend Jim Jones are often able to convince followers to adopt unconventional lifestyles and even to engage in bizarre behavior, such as the mass suicide at the People's Temple compound in Guyana.

ple that their diseases could be cured through faith. In all these cases, charismatic leaders and their truths brought about profound changes in their followers and sometimes in the society of which they were a part.

Experiential Knowledge

Experiential truth **is knowledge based on personal observation and on first-hand experience.** Proponents of experiential knowledge believe that a single, direct observation of something leads to truth and that facts can be readily understood if directly observed. This type of knowledge has always been considered important in our society. In the late 1960s, many people reacted against what they perceived to be the alienating consequences of runaway technology based on an inherently corrupt method of obtaining knowledge — science. They placed great validity on experiential knowledge, as exemplified by such statements as "I've seen it" or "I've actually done it; therefore, I know it is true." They are convinced that, because of their unique position as observers, they know the truth.

A faith in experiential knowledge has important consequences for our understanding of social problems and our choice of solutions to those problems. People who have some direct experience with a particular problem — whether as perpetrators, victims, or people trying to alleviate the problem — claim to be the only ones who can really understand it and recommend feasible solutions. People without such experience are disparagingly dismissed as naive, impractical, or mere theoreticians. For example, welfare workers who see their clients doing little during the day, drinking, and living in squalid tenements may conclude, on the basis of these observations, that all welfare recipients are lazy, stupid, and dissolute, and that they could improve their lives if they cleaned themselves up and engaged in more morally responsible activities. Thus, these welfare workers might come to see the poverty problem as the result of individual inadequacies rather than as the consequences of certain characteristics of society. Likewise, police officers and prison guards, because of their first-hand contact with crime, often believe that they are in a unique position to know the truth about crime. Because they see the same people committing crimes and returning to prison repeatedly

—despite the best efforts of the criminal justice system to rehabilitate them—they conclude that these people commit crimes because they are especially evil or have some personality flaw. Again, social causes of behavior that lie outside the individual tend to be ignored.

There are important shortcomings inherent in experiential knowledge. First, it assumes that one must experience something directly in order to understand it. Yet, is this always true? Must one have died in order to understand the problems associated with death? Must one have fought in a war to understand the causes of war? Must one have undergone an operation in order to be a surgeon? Clearly, the direct experiencing of something does not always (although it may in some cases) put a person in a better position to understand the causes of that phenomenon. Second, those with direct experience of something are commonly those people who have a vested interest in viewing that thing in a particular way. It is to the advantage of the police and prison guards to view crime as the result of individual inadequacies for at least two reasons. First, it is a simple explanation that offers an important role to the criminal justice system in reducing crime. Second, it absolves the criminal justice system of any responsibility in perpetuating crime. Given this vested interest, those with direct experience often have a biased view concerning what they observe. So, as a basis for understanding social problems, experiential knowledge has some basic flaws that scientific knowledge attempts to overcome.

Scientific Knowledge

How does the scientific method overcome the limitations of these other ways of knowing, so that we can develop a more accurate and comprehensive understanding of social problems? *Science* **refers to the general method (or set of characteristic methods) by which knowledge is obtained through systematic observations.**[3] It is essentially a set of rules and procedures, shared by members of the scientfic community, for obtaining knowledge about the world. The aims of science are discovery, explanation, and prediction. That is, science seeks answers to these questions: what is happening? how and why is it happening? under what circumstances is it likely to happen again? In order to answer these questions, science must interweave facts and theory. Facts without theories are useless because they lack interpretation; theories explain facts. Theories that are not supported by facts are merely unsubstantiated speculations. There are five central characteristics of science that distinguish it from the ways of knowing already discussed.

First, science is based on *observation*. Scientific truth finally rests on the scientist's demonstrating to his or her colleagues that proposed facts or relationships can be found in the world. Science assumes that there is order in the universe—that phenomena are sufficiently patterned to permit generalizations based on observation. There are some questions that are beyond the scope of current scientific methods, such as, is there a God? Beliefs regarding the existence of God are matters of faith—one either believes, has doubts, or disbelieves. There is no type of observation that we know of that can settle this question; so there is no scientific truth one way or the other on this issue.

Second, scientific observation is *systematic*—it follows rules accepted by other scientists; it is done publicly and thus is capable of being repeated by others. For example, based on years of personal observation (the experiential method), a welfare worker might conclude that most welfare recipients are lazy cheats who receive government aid fraudulently. Irrespective of whether these observations are accurate, they are not scientific. They are merely anecdotal and represent only one welfare worker's experience. The welfare worker has not specified who was observed, under what conditions, in what manner, and for how long—all matters of great concern to scientists because the conditions of observation can greatly affect the observations themselves. Other scientists must be able to repeat the research in order to check on the biases or misinterpretations of the observer. Unlike the experiential method, science *does not* assume that one direct observation leads to truth and that facts can be readily understood if directly observed.

Third, science studies and seeks to understand *cause-and-effect-relationships*. Science assumes that all events are caused and that this makes the universe an orderly and predictable place. Clearly, if events had no cause and were thus unpredictable, human intervention in the study of social problems would be difficult, if not impossible.

Fourth, all scientific knowledge is *provisional*—**there are no ultimate scientific truths.** For the scientist, every fact and theory is subject to further testing, reinterpretation, correction, and refutation. Nothing is accepted as a definitive fact, as the ultimate truth, or as the final solution to a problem.

Fifth, science is (or attempts to be) *objective*—**that is, the scientist tries, as much as possible, to prevent his or her own values and interests from influencing the outcome of research.** Any question tht can be answered by the scientific method is an appropriate subject for scientific inquiry— regardless how threatening the topic may be to traditional beliefs, commonsense assumptions, or vested interests. For example, studies of religious beliefs and customs, sexual preferences and practices, and the backgrounds and attitudes of convicted murderers are all within the purview of scientific observation and analysis.

The scientific method, with these unique characteristics, is quite different from the other ways of knowing. Furthermore, it is especially valuable for the study of social problems because it is more likely than the others to result in an accurate understanding of problems and their solutions. With the other ways of knowing, people are more likely to cling to outmoded, inaccurate, and possibly damaging, conceptions of human behavior. This can be illustrated in the area of criminal behavior. There have been numerous scientific theories to explain criminal behavior. For example, Cesare Lombroso (1835–1909) theorized that most criminals are "born criminals"—they are genetically inferior types whose physical, social, and emotional characteristics are throwbacks to a more primitive human type.[4] He made observations of criminals that supported his theory and reported the results to his scientific colleagues. His theory was accepted as an accurate interpretation of the "facts" about criminals by many scholars and penologists prior to the 1930s.

However, because all scientific truths are *provisional,* scientists continually questioned and tested the extent to which Lombroso's theory fit both old and new facts. His theory did not hold up in the face of these *repeated observations.* Other studies showed that the vast majority of the people with characteristics of Lombroso's "primitive" type were not criminal, and most criminals were found to be quite "normal." Furthermore, some of Lombroso's fellow scientists pointed out that his conclusions were based on data taken from prisoners. Since many, if not most, criminals are not imprisoned for their crimes, Lombroso's sample of criminals did not represent all people who commit crimes but rather the select few who end up in prison. Finally, many social scientists observed that criminal acts seem to be highly situational—they occur under circumstances that the criminal defines as involving provocation or the opportunity to commit a crime. Based on these *systematic observations* of the facts and their relationship to Lombroso's theory, scholars began to search for other theories to explain crime.

Edwin Sutherland (1883–1950) proposed a theory that seriously challenged the validity of Lombroso's theory.[5] Sutherland argued that criminal behavior is learned in interaction with other people. People come to engage in criminal behavior because they define it as acceptable and appropriate under certain circumstances, and this they do because those people who are important to them act in such a way that crime appears to be an acceptable behavior. They learn criminal motives and attitudes in interaction with others.

Today, most social scientists believe with Sutherland that crime is primarily a learned behavior and that Lombroso's conclusions are invalid. However, the student can see that, if the study of social problems relied on traditional, charismatic, or even experiential knowledge, we might still be clinging to outmoded ideas such as the genetic basis of criminal behavior. Science generates an intellectual caution based on the provisional nature of scientific knowledge and the reliance on repeated observations. In addition, even though it may be in the scientist's interests to accept one theory, he must nonetheless be *objective*— evaluate information in such a way that his own values and interests do not influence the outcome. For these reasons,

"ACCORDING TO THIS THEORY, IT'S STRONGLY IMPROBABLE THAT ANYTHING SHOULD EVER HAPPEN ANYTIME, ANYWHERE."

scientific knowledge is more useful and accurate in the study of social problems than the other ways of knowing. The student should be cautious about pronouncements or policies based on these other types of knowledge. Yet, the student should also be skeptical of pronouncements based on science, because scientific findings can be misused and misrepresented.

Interest Groups and Scientific Objectivity

The problem of scientific objectivity is so important in the study of social problems that a few cautionary remarks are in order. Science is a tool for gaining knowledge about the world. As such, it can be used by any group to further its own ends, and the outcome may or may not be beneficial to other groups in society. **Pressure groups are interest groups that actively seek to enhance their own interests through legal means such as economic and political pressure and by persuading the public of the justice of their cause.** They are often well organized and powerful, possessing such resources as money and access to politicians and the media. Pressure groups are frequently in a position to manipulate data, even scientific data, so as to provide the public with biased, distorted and misleading impressions of events. Their purpose is to persuade people to align themselves with ideas, products, or programs that fit the interests of the pressure group but not necessarily the best interests of the general public or those who eventually identify with their cause.

Because science enjoys a great deal of legitimacy in the United States as a means of knowing, pressure groups have often tried to use "scientific" data to support their values and interests. For example, the English philosopher Herbert Spencer and other so-called Social Darwinists believed in the evolutionary principle of "survival of the fittest"—that people with desirable and necessary characteristics will (and should) survive and prosper because they were the most "fit" of the species. Thus, they believed that those who prospered did so because they had beneficial qualities. The poor, as evidenced by their lack of success, obviously did not have such qualities. The Social Darwinists were courted by influential industrialists in nineteenth-century England and America. Andrew Carnegie, the steel magnate, sponsored a lecture tour in the United States for Spencer, whom he called the "prophet of progress." The scientific theories of the Social Darwinists—that those who were at the top of society were there because of "natural superiority"—fit the values and interests of such capitalists as Carnegie because it explained their success in a positive and self-flattering way while it provided a justification for their power in society.

The problem of maintaining scientific objectivity is especially difficult for scientists who are closely associated with interest groups. By working closely with an interest group, the scientist may become so much a part of the group under study that he or she completely loses objectivity as a scientist. This problem is illustrated in the case of a professor in

In American society interest groups exert competing political pressure, complicating the public solution of social problems.

the criminology department at a major state university who at the same time is a member of the police department serving a large city.[6] Since working part-time as a policeman, this professor, according to his own admission, has taken on the world-view of the "cop" at his own. He also receives a large income from making films on the problems of police work, which are sold to criminal justice programs in universities and police academies. Such training programs have tended to have a conservative, experiential-knowledge bias, to which this professor's orientation and products cater. When any person has such a vested interest in perpetuating the traditional police view of the nature of crime, one must immediately be wary how objective that person's observations are.

In conclusion, although science can be a powerful tool for the acquisition of knowledge, the student should be wary of people using the label "scientific" to legitimate their data. These self-proclaimed labels can be used to mislead and distort in the same way that other techniques are used. A thing is not scientific simply because someone proclaims it so but rather because it fits the characteristics of science that we have described. In order to equip the student with information needed to understand the misleading uses of scientific data, the remainder of this chapter is devoted to social research and the presentation of data — how it should be done and how it can be manipulated to distort reality.

THE RESEARCH PROCESS

There are a number of clearly defined steps or stages in the process of conducting scientific research. For example, let us suppose that we are interested in the social problem of juvenile delinquency. Where do we start? What causes juvenile delinquency? Is it due to slum living? poverty? personality maladjustment? or broken homes? How do we acquire scientific answers to these questions? The following steps in the research process serve as a guide for the scientific investigator.[7] Not all researchers would follow them in precisely this order, but all must be included in some fashion during the research process.

Stages in The Research Process

Defining the Problem

Defining the problem is the crucial first step in the research process. If the problem itself is poorly defined, then the data gathered in the study will be rather meaningless, and thus feasible solutions will be nearly impossible to formulate. The problem must not be defined so broadly that a research effort could never provide an answer. The general problem we are concerned with might be juvenile delinquency, but we cannot analyze all the possible causes of delinquency in one study. So we will limit ourselves to one achieveable goal: to study the nature of the relationship between broken homes and juvenile delinquency.

Reviewing the Literature

After initially defining the research problem, the scientist becomes familiar with existing ideas and research on the subject by reviewing relevant papers, articles, books, and the like. This is done in order to learn from the experience and investigations of others who have previously dealt with the problem. The scientist then attempts to extend, revise, or perhaps refute the work of his or her predecessors. After reviewing the literature, the researcher may conclude that the problem has been poorly defined and must be reformulated.

Formulating a Hypothesis

Next, the scientist will formulate a *hypothesis* **—a tentative statement relating the variables (or their characteristics) to each other. A** *variable* **is a property or characteristic whose value or form can vary.** Examples of important social variables are: age (which can range over the whole age scale), sex (which can take the obvious two forms), religious affiliation (which might be Protestant, Buddhist, or any of a host of other forms), and social class (which can range from the lowest class position to the highest).

It is the hypothesis whose truth the scientist wishes to determine in the course of the investigation. In our case, the hypothesis might state: children from broken homes are more likely to become juvenile delinquents. However, this is not yet sufficiently precise to enable us to test it. What do we mean by *broken homes? juvenile delinquents?* The researcher must next construct **indicators**—devices that state in observable terms precisely how differences or changes in the variables under study will be measured. Indicators allow scientists to measure variables in the same way each time they are measured, which in turn makes it possible to duplicate studies and to determine the comparability of different studies. For example, we might use the absence of one parent from the home as our indicator of broken homes and referrals to juvenile court as our indicator of juvenile delinquency.

Choosing a Research Design

One of the most critical decisions a scientist must make is the choice of *research design*—a plan of how to conduct research and collect data. Although a variety of techniques are available for conducting sociological research, two general types have dominated social science research—quantitative and qualitative methods.[8] ***Quantitative methods* are based on the assumption that social phenomena are numerical in nature, or can be put in numerical form.** When employing quantitative methods, the researcher might utilize questionnaires, surveys, or existing data sources such as census records. Statistical procedures are used to determine the existence and strength of relationships between variables. Quantitative methods are more useful in studying observable and quantifiable things, such as sex or social class; they are less useful for the study of the subjective experiences of people. For our study of juvenile delinquency, we might use juvenile court records, or interviews with delinquents and their families.

***Qualitative methods* are based on the assumption either that social phenomena are**

not numerical in nature, or that information is lost or distorted by putting it in numerical form. When employing qualitative methods, the researcher might utilize participant observation, open-ended interviews, case studies, or personal documents. Qualitative methods place more emphasis on the importance of understanding the world as individuals perceive it and in their own words. In our juvenile delinquency study, we might interview at length one or two delinquents in order to understand what they perceive as influencing their behavior. We might determine whether or not a home is broken by asking the juveniles for their perceptions of, or feelings about, their parents' relationship and their home life. Another qualitative approach would be to spend time with a juvenile gang to observe first-hand the sequence of events that leads to a delinquent act and the subsequent arrest. The goal of such research is not statistically to prove that some association exists, but rather to understand how an individual experiences and reacts to what happens to him or her.

It is important to note that quantitative and qualitative research methods are not mutually exclusive; a single research project might employ both types. Each taps into a different order of reality and can teach us different things about social problems. The choice of research design should depend on the nature of the problem under study and the resources available to the researcher.

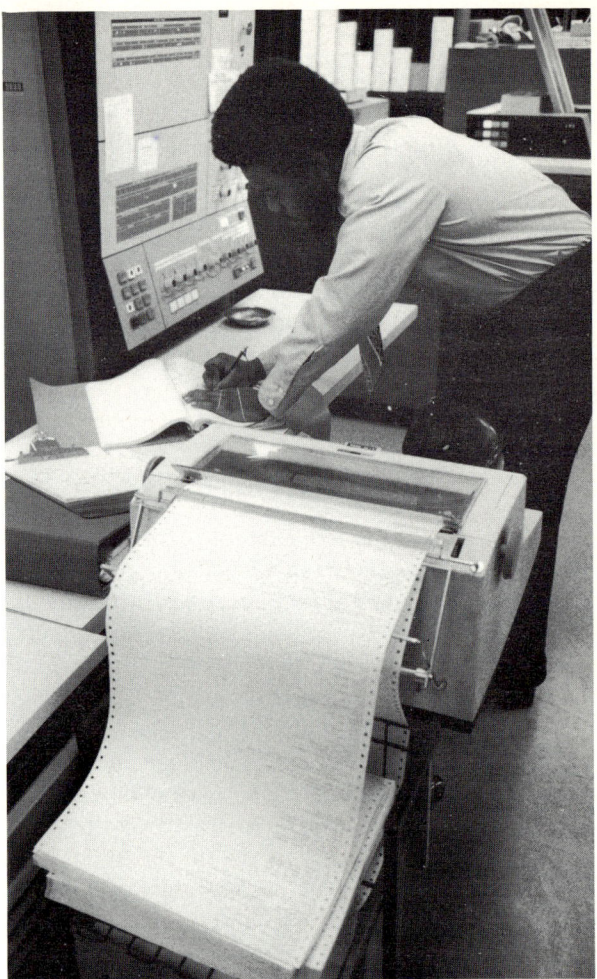

Research on modern social problems usually involves the use of high-speed computers and sophisticated statistical procedures to analyze information.

Collecting the Data

Next, the investigator collects and records data in a manner consistent with the chosen research design. For example, the frequency of referrals to the juvenile court of children from single-parent families might be compared with that of young people from families with both parents present.

Analyzing the Results and Drawing a Conclusion

After collecting and organizing the data, the researcher will arrange the information in an orderly fashion, interpret the findings, and confirm, reject, or modify the hypothesis. This is a very complex process involving the meticulous interweaving of research methodology and theory. The final phase of the research process is for the scientist to write a report (in the form of a scholarly paper, an oral presentation, an article for a scientific journal, or a book) in which the research is described and the scientist's conclusions presented. The researcher is ethically obliged to share these findings—including all of the errors in the project—with colleagues in the discipline and with anyone else interested in the topic.

Major Issues in the Research Process

The final stage of the research process just described—analyzing the results and drawing a conclusion—is an extremely complex and important stage and warrants further attention by the student of social problems. It is at this stage in the research process that the student must be especially wary of *how* and *on what basis* conclusions are drawn and recommendations made. It is here that misuses and distortion of the data are most often introduced. We will point up some of the major problems to watch for at this stage.

Association or Correlation versus Cause

Suppose we found that 75 percent of the youngsters referred to juvenile court in a particular community were from single-parent families. Does this association (or correlation) prove or confirm our hypothesis that children from broken homes are more likely to become juvenile delinquents? Do broken homes cause juvenile delinquency? The answer is no—not necessarily! Why not? Because any association between two variables, no matter how strong and consistent, does not by itself prove that one variable caused the other.

Statements about causality are always an inference or an assumption; causality is never directly observed. A little thought should make clear that, given an association between two variables, there are four logically possible relationships between them (see Fig. 2.1). So, while an association does not necessarily mean that the variables are causally related, the existence of such an association certainly *suggests* that there might be a causal relationship. The scientist must then look further to determine whether it exists and what its precise nature might be. How can we reasonably infer that one variable causes another? For us to be able to infer a causal relationship, the following four criteria must be met.[9]

1. *Statistical correlation*. There must be a statistical correlation between the variables. **A statistical correlation expresses the strength of a relationship between two (or more)**

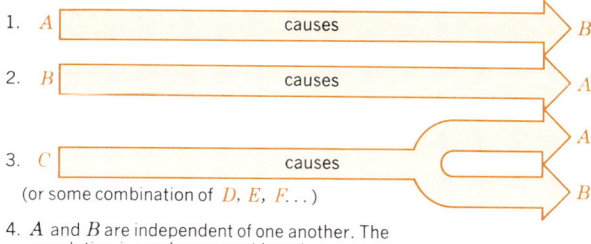

Figure 2.1   Logically Possible Relationships between Two Variables That Are Associated or Correlated. Adapted from Carlo L. Lastrucci. *The Scientific Approach* (Cambridge, Mass: Schenkman Publishing Co., 1967), p. 187.

variables in mathematical terms, usually as a number called a *correlation coefficient*. If, for example, broken homes and juvenile delinquency are associated with one another in 75 percent of the cases, then the correlation coefficient for that association would be high, indicating a strong relationship between broken homes and juvenile delinquency. When two variables have absolutely no consistent relationship to one another, the correlation coefficient is zero. When the presence of one variable is always associated with the absence of the other variable, the correlation is -1.0. Correlations of 0.3 or 0.4 indicate a weak relationship between the variables. Correlations of about 0.6 and above indicate a stronger relationship between the variables.

Assuming that we find a statistical correlation, any of the four logical possibilities in Figure 2.1 might account for it. We are a step closer to inferring causality, but we must probe further. The next question we must ask is, can the relationship between broken homes and juvenile delinquency be explained by some third variable, such as social class, that accounts for the association between the first two?

2. *Lack of spuriousness*. The correlation must not be *spurious*—that is, it must not be explainable by some third variable (*C*) that causes both *A* and *B* (see Figure 2.2).[10] For example, there is a high positive correlation between the number of fire engines at a

SPURIOUS RELATIONSHIP

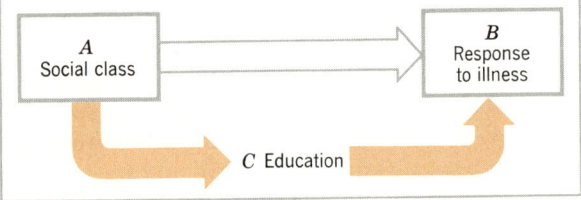

INTERVENING VARIABLE RELATIONSHIP

Figure 2.2 Spurious and Intervening Variable Relationships. Adapted from Kenneth D. Bailey, *Methods of Social Research* (New York: The Free Press, 1978), p. 42. Reprinted with permission of Macmillan Publishing Co., Inc. Copyright © 1978 by the Free Press, a division of Macmillan Publishing Co., Inc.

fire (*A*) and the amount of damage (*B*) associated with the blaze. Why? Because the size of the blaze (*C*) results in both more fire engines being called into service and greater fire damage. To infer that *A* causes *B* and to propose that fewer fire engines be sent to a blaze in order to reduce fire damage is clearly absurd.

Spurious correlations can be a source of bewilderment and misinterpretation when dealing with social problems. For example, the rates of ice cream consumption and juvenile delinquency tend to be regularly associated. Does this mean that eating ice cream predisposes one to delinquent behavior? Should we ban ice cream? Obviously, there is no causal link between the two. Both are associated with the third factor, summer weather. When the weather is warm and school is out, young people are more likely to eat ice cream and they also have more free time and opportunity to engage in delinquent acts.

To understand the real causes of social problems, it is essential to consider the possibility that a relationship is spurious. One way to do

this is the use of *controls — **methods for excluding the likelihood that other variables might be influencing the relationship.*** For example, a third variable that might be controlled for in our study is poverty. It is possible that poverty causes both broken homes and juvenile delinquency. Thus, the latter two variables may be correlated because they are each separately related to the third variable, poverty. The scientist would control for poverty by looking at the relationship between broken homes and delinquency separately among the poor and among the nonpoor. If, in each of those two groups, the correlation between broken homes and delinquency still occurs, then the relationship is not spurious.

If we determine that the relationship between delinquency and broken homes is not spurious, can we infer that the latter causes the former? Not yet. We must ask a further question. Were the children referred to the juvenile court before, or after, the family became a one-parent unit?

3. *Prior occurrence.* The assumed causal variable must occur prior to the assumed effect variable. The broken home must exist before the young people embark on their delinquent careers. For it is possible that juvenile delinquency causes broken homes — that is, perhaps minors who commit delinquent acts behave in ways that serve to break up their own families. Or possibly the tensions and burdens placed on the parents because of the delinquent acts (blaming one another, court appearances, and the like) lead to family deterioration. Without establishing the temporal sequence, it is logically possible that either variable might have caused the other (*see* Fig. 2.1).

How can the researcher test the time sequence? One means is to determine which occurs first in the majority of cases. If, for example, the researcher finds that the family was a one-parent unit for several months prior to the child's engaging in delinquent acts in, say, 80 or 90 percent of the cases, then it is reasonable to assume that broken homes cause delinquency in the vast majority of cases. So, in the study of social problems, it is often difficult, but nonetheless important, to know which factors occurred first in order to determine the causal sequence. There is one final criterion to be considered in the determination of causality.

4. *Nonrandom and nonaccidental.* The correlation between the variables must not be random or accidental. Because there are so many phenomena in the universe, and because time and space are finite, some things may be associated with one another without being causally linked. There may be a statistical association but no causal relationship. This is one reason why scientists place great emphasis on replication of studies. If we find a statistical association between juvenile delinquency and broken homes in our community, the association may be purely random or accidental—there may be no causal relationship between the variables. This is why scientists are very tentative about conclusions based on one study only. If we repeat the study, or if similar studies are conducted elsewhere, and the results are the same, then we can more completely infer a causal relationship. Thus, replication is an important check for purely random or accidental associations.

Intervening Variable Relationships

Once we have inferred a causal relationship between two variables, we must then consider the possibility that the relationship is more complex than was originally thought. There might be, for example, more than two factors involved in the relationship. One way to check for this is to search for *intervening variables*—**variables that come between, or intervene between, the original two variables in a causal sequence** (see Fig. 2.2). That is, *A* and *B* may be correlated because *A* causes *C* which in turn causes *B*. This is quite distinct from a spurious relationship in which there is no actual relationship between *A* and *B*. In the intervening variable relationship, *A* still is a cause of *B* but the causation is indirect—it operates through other variables.[11]

In the area of physical health and illness, it has long been known, for example, that social class influences a person's response to illness—that is, there is a strong correlation between the two.[12] Lower-class people are less likely to seek the help of a physician when sick; they put off seeking professional help longer, and they are less likely to practice preventive health measures (such as going to a physician for a checkup or receiving immunization against disease). However, when other variables are introduced, the effects of social class are reduced considerably. For instance, irrespective of social class, those with less education are more likely to delay seeking health care and tend not be engaged in preventive health practices. A lower-class person, of course, is more likely to have less education than others, and it is education that directly affects one's response to illness. Thus, the relationship is more complex than simply a direct causal one between social class and response to illness (see Fig. 2.2).

Sampling and Bias

It is normally impossible for a social scientist to collect data from all the people to whom his hypotheses refer. For example, there are simply too many juvenile delinquents in a city or the nation to interview all of them. The researcher must therefore choose a sample—part of that group about which he is concerned to serve as the source of data. However, if the sample is not chosen properly, it can lead to distorted and inaccurate conclusions.

An important characteristic of a sample is that it be free of biases that would affect the outcome of the research. **A *bias* is a feature of the sampling procedure that introduces another variable (or variables) that influences the relationship between the assumed cause and effect variables.** Biased sampling can substantially distort our understanding of social problems and lead us to totally inappropriate solutions. For example, homosexuality traditionally has been considered outside the normal psychological range of human sexuality. Many people have assumed that it is the result of some personality defect or disturbance. Because of this, homosexuality has sometimes been treated as a form of mental illness, with heterosexuality being treated as normal. These conclusions resulted from a number of studies conducted by practicing psychologists. The studies typically were based on samples of homosexuals drawn from the patients of psychotherapists. Beginning with Evelyn Hooker in 1957, critics of these studies have suspected that the samples were biased because all of the homosexuals studied either were or had been receiving treatment for psychological disorders. Such samples might overestimate the degree of psychological disturbance among *all homosexuals,* those who have never had therapy as well as those in therapy.[13]

To check this, Hooker took a sample of thirty homosexuals who were not in treatment and thirty heterosexuals also not in treatment and gave the groups a battery of psychological tests that are used to uncover psychological abnormalities. She took the results to a panel of judges, who were supposedly experts at interpreting these tests, and asked them to identify which test results were by homosexuals and which by heterosexuals. The judges were unable to separate the groups. The conclusion that Hooker drew from the experiment was that homosexuality is not associated with the types of psychological abnormalities that her tests could detect. Recent comprehensive comparisons of homosexuals and heterosexuals have supported Hooker's conclusion that sexual preference, by itself, is not a strong determinant of psychological adjustment, social stability, or happiness.[14]

This illustration points to an important characteristic of a sample, its representativeness. **A *representative sample* is one in which people with the various characteristics important to the study are included in the sample in the same proportions as they are found in the population to which one wishes to generalize.** If you wish to make a statement about *all* homosexuals, then your sample must truly represent all homosexuals.

How might we detect biases due to unrepresentative samples in our study of the relationship be-

tween broken homes and delinquency? If we choose our sample of delinquents from those referred to juvenile court, are they representative of all the young people who commit delinquent acts, including those who have not been caught and officially processed as delinquent? There is good reason to suspect that they are not. We may find, for example, that police are more likely to refer to the court youngsters from single-parent families than those from families in which both parents are present—even though they commit the same kinds of acts, with the same frequency. Police and school officials may do this because they believe that two-parent families can handle their children's delinquency without the intervention of the juvenile court, whereas single-parent families are in need of such assistance. So the rate of delinquency may not vary according to the type of familiy the child comes from, but the rate of referral to juvenile court may be affected by family background.

There are other sources of bias that can lead to an unrepresentative sample, but the point is clear. Unless we devise a means of eliminating sampling bias, we will not be able properly to test our hypothesis and make generalizations. In evaluating conclusions regarding social problems, we must be vitally concerned whether the data on which the conclusions rest were drawn from a properly constructed sample.

Validity and Reliability

A final aspect of the research process that has implications for the study of social problems concerns the *indicators* of variables. Are these indicators valid and reliable? **A *valid indicator* measures what it claims to measure.** A yardstick is a valid indicator of length but an invalid indicator of temperature. The student might ask, for example, whether the single-parent family really represents what we understand by the term "broken home." Aren't there other types of home situations that are as "broken" or detrimental to the child's well-being as living in a home with only one parent? Although we could argue the issue, the point is that the choice of indicators can have a crucial effect on the conclusions drawn. If we had chosen a different indicator of broken homes (for example, the existence of a behavioral problem of alcoholism among one of the parents), then our conclusions concerning the causes of juvenile delinquency might be substantially altered.

A *reliable indicator* measures (whatever it does measure) consistently over time and from one situation to the next. For example, juvenile court data may not be the same from one community to another or perhaps even between courts within the same area. If one court is especially concerned about truancy violations, it may officially label the violators as delinquent while another court deals with these problems informally. In this case, juvenile court records would not be a reliable indicator of delinquency because the records did not consistently measure the same thing.

In evaluating data concerning social problems, it is important to consider issues of validity and reliability because such measurement problems can drastically influence whether a person would conclude from the data that a particular solution was feasible. If a researcher's indicators are invalid or unreliable, then the study has not adequately tested its hypotheses, and the accuracy of the findings must be viewed with skepticism.

THE PRESENTATION OF DATA: STRENGTHS AND PITFALLS

When care is taken in evaluating the research process as we have described, one is in a better position to accept or reject the conclusions drawn by the researchers. But the student of social problems is not yet out of the woods of distortion and misinformation. The manner in which the researcher *presents* data to the public can either clarify or distort the reality that the data purport to describe. The retort "You can prove anything with statistics" is true only for those unfamiliar with statistical presentation. We will discuss some of the major ways in which social problems data are presented to the public and point up some ways in which this presentation can be distorted. Thus informed, the student will be better able critically to evaluate any data presented.

Statistical Presentation

Statistics can be a useful tool in the research process by presenting masses of numerical data in a clear, concise, and meaningful manner. However, if improperly presented or interpreted, statistics can be very misleading.

Statistics are numerical data.[15] There are two main types of statistical analysis: *descriptive statistics* and *statistical inference*. **Descriptive statistics attempts to condense and summarize numerical data in a clear and convenient form; it includes all of the cases in the population under analysis.** For example, incomes of families in a community may be summarized by calculating the *average income* or by indicating the *range of incomes* from the lowest to the highest. This summary would be a *description* of the data without any attempt to derive broader generalizations. **Statistical inference is concerned with making generalizations based on a limited sample of cases drawn from some population.** An attempt to estimate the birthrate in the entire United States from a sample of 10,000 families drawn from various educational and income levels, religious backgrounds, and regions of the country would be an example of statistical inference. In the study of social problems, the student is most likely to encounter descriptive statistics, so we will describe some of the most common types and the major ways in which they can be misleading.

Descriptive Statistics

The term *average* is not a clearly defined concept. It is used to mean different things because there are several different kinds of averages. What the "average" means may be very different depending on which average is used. When someone refers to *average income,* it is crucial to know *to which type of average* that person is referring. There are three "averages" that are used to summarize numerical data in the social sciences — the mean (or arithmetic average), the median, and the mode.

Arithmetic Mean

The *arithmetic mean* is the most widely used average. It is calculated by dividing the sum

of all values of a variable by the number of cases.** For example, in a hypothetical firm with ten executives, the mean income would be $26,800 (see Table 2.1). A serious weakness of the arithmetic mean, however, is that it is affected by extreme cases. If we look at the mean incomes for each race, whites have a substantially higher mean income than nonwhites. However, this is largely due to the one very high income of $85,000 among the whites. If this were replaced with a lower income, say $29,000, the mean of both races would be the same. (The student should calculate this for himself to be sure of the accuracy of this assertion.)

TABLE 2.1
Hypothetical Distribution of Incomes, by Race, among Executives of a Firm

	ALL EXECUTIVES	WHITES	NONWHITES
	$17,000		$17,000
	17,000	$17,000	
	17,000		17,000
	18,000	18,000	
	19,000	19,000	
	20,000		20,000
	23,000	23,000	
	25,000		25,000
	27,000		27,000
	85,000	85,000	
Mean =	$26,800	$32,400	$21,200
Median =	19,500	19,000	20,000
Mode =	17,000	none	17,000

Median

The *median* is the second most widely used average; it is the midpoint—there are just as many cases wth values below the median as there are above the median. The median income of our ten executives is $19,500. (Note that if there are an equal number of cases, as there are here, then the median is the midpoint of the gap between the middle values. Our two middle values are the fifth and sixth on the list—$19,000 and $20,000 —the midpoint of which is $19,500.) Unlike the mean, the median is not greatly affected by extreme values. In our example, the median income for whites and nonwhites is quite similar, and it varies little from the median of all races combined.

Mode

The *mode* is used less frequently than either the mean or the median, but it is an appropriate average in some instances. The mode is the most frequently occurring value. In our case, the modal income of all races combined is $17,000. If every value occurs an equal number of times, then there is no mode, as is the case among the whites in our sample. If two or more values occur an equal number of times, then there would be two or more modes.

Now let us turn to some examples of how these "averages" can affect the study of social problems. If we were concerned that nonwhites were being discriminated against in terms of salaries in our hypothetical firm, we might approach the problem by comparing average incomes. But which "average?" If we use the mean, then surely we would conclude that discrimination is occurring. The mean shows that whites make an average income that is $10,000 greater than that of non-whites. However, the one large salary among whites accounts for this. If we use the median income, then our data show that nonwhites make slightly more than whites do. Because the mean is so drastically affected by extreme cases, the median is a more useful average for data such as these. Our choice of which average to use to present our data would drastically affect our conclusion concerning the existence of discriminatory practices in salaries. So, averages are certainly useful in formulating policy guidelines. However, which average one uses is crucial, and exceptional cases must be taken into consideration.

Ratios, Proportions, and Rates

A *ratio* shows the relation in size between two numbers. A ratio that is commonly used in the social sciences is the *sex ratio*—the number of males in a population per 100 females. If a certain neighborhood of 5 families consists of 2 men and 3 women heads of households, the sex ratio for family heads is 2:3 or 67/100. **A *proportion* is a special type of ratio, in which the denominator is the entire group.** For example, if there are 1 Native American, 2 white, and 2 black families in the neighborhood, the proportion of whites is 2/5 or 40 percent. **A** *rate* **is a special type of ratio in which the numerator is the number of times a specified kind of event occurs during a particular time period and the denominator is the whole number of times that it might have occurred.** For example, the general fertility rate (one type of birthrate) is presented in terms of the number of live births per 1000 females of child-bearing age — 15 to 44 years of age inclusive. If in a social problems class with 5 students whose scores were 17, 23, 70, 70, and 95, the cutoff for a passing grade on the exam is 60, the failure rate is 2/5 or 0.4.

Rates are an important and frequently used descriptive statistic. However, the type and source of the data that comprise the denominator and numerator of any rate can influence the conclusions that we draw. One frequently cited rate is the divorce rate. Increases in the divorce rate have created consternation among many people and have led to numerous programs to cope with the problem. However, the manner in which we calculate the divorce rate has an important impact. In Table 2.2, we have presented two hypothetical societies. Each society has the same population size and the same number of divorces. Yet the denominator we choose in calculating the divorce rate can drastically change our impression of each society. If we use the whole population in calculating the divorce rate — a common practice — then both societies have the same divorce rate. However, many of the people in the population — those who are not married — could not possibly become divorced, so it is somewhat of a distortion to include them in the calculation. If we use only the number of married people in the denominator, then Society *B,* which has twice as many married people, has half the divorce rate of Society *A.*

Another rate that has important policy implications is the unemployment rate, which is generally calculated by dividing the number of people over sixteen years of age who are looking for work by the number of people who are employed. Billions of dollars in federal funds are distributed to states and municipalities on the basis of the unemployment rate. However, there is much controversy concerning how it is calculated.[16] For example, the denominator in the unemployment rate as currently calculated does not include people in the military. Some experts have argued that, especially since the discontinuance of the military draft, military jobs should be considered like any others for purposes of calculating the unemployment rate because these people choose the military as a job and are in fact being paid for their work. If this were done, the unemployment rate would be lower than it is, especially in certain locations. Others have pointed to the problem of calculating the rate in terms of individuals employed rather than households employed. Currently, if a man loses his job, he is included in the unemployment figures even though his wife may have a very lucrative job that provides the household with a satisfactory income. If unemployment rates were calculated on the basis of households, many people currently considered unemployed would not be included in the unemployment statistics. Thus the unemployment rate would be lower.

So one must take great care in evaluating the importance of rates because the manner in which they are constructed can drastically affect any conclusions that might be drawn. Rates are constructed for certain purposes to reflect reality in a certain way. Which way of calculating a rate is appropriate depends to some extent on the researcher's purposes.

Statistical Inference

Statistical inference **is concerned with making decisions about whether to accept or reject a hypothesis.** The rules for making such decisions are specified in advance by scientists, and, although they do not guarantee that the decision will always be correct, they do allow any two scientists to make the same decisions concerning a

TABLE 2.2
Divorce Rates in Two Hypothetical Societies

	SOCIETY *A*	SOCIETY *B*
Population size	100	100
Number of married people	20	40
Number of divorces	2	2
"Crude" divorce rate	2/100 or 2%	2/100 or 2%
"Refined" divorce rate	2/20 or 10%	2/40 or 5%

particular case. Also, the probability of making an incorrect decision is known in advance.

Returning to our juvenile delinquency example, let us hypothesize that children from broken homes are as likely to commit delinquent acts as are children from unbroken homes. To test this hypothesis, we might interview all the children in a particular city, determine whether they have engaged in delinquent acts, and look at their home life. We would then have data on the entire population with which we are concerned, and our hypothesis could be tested directly, without the need to make any inferences. However, such studies of a whole population are extremely costly and time-consuming and normally exceed the resources available to a sociologist.

In order to test our hypothesis, then, it is necessary to draw a representative sample of children from the population. Suppose in our sample we find that all of the delinquents come from broken homes and all of the nondelinquents come from unbroken homes. What does this finding tell us? Can we be sure that all, or even most, of the delinquents in the whole city come from broken homes? We cannot be completely sure because there is the possibility (although it is a small one) that, in a population in which there is no relationship between delinquency and broken homes, our sample would, purely by chance, show such a relationship. What, then, can we infer? Using methods that need not concern us here, mathematicians can determine the probability that a sample as unusual as this one might be drawn from a given population. Suppose that such an unusual sample could be expected to occur twice in 1000 times. This means that 2 times out of 1000 times we would draw a sample that showed such a strong relationship between delinquency and broken homes even though in the whole population of children there was no such relationship.

Where does this leave us? We must now make a decision whether to infer the existence of such a relationship among all children. Before beginning this study, we establish a *significance level* — **a technical means of determining the probability that our findings might occur by chance.** If we had chosen a significance level of 0.01 (a fairly common level), then we would be willing to reject the hypothesis that there is no difference if the differences in our sample could have occurred once out of 100 times by chance. Since our findings could have occurred only 2 times out of 1000, we would reject the hypothesis that there is no relationship between broken homes and delinquency and infer that there was an association between the two variables. However, this is an inference. We might be wrong. It is not until subsequent studies replicating a previous approach produce the same conclusion that we can feel comfortable about inferring a relationship. As we have emphasized repeatedly in this study, a single finding is viewed with great caution by scientists.

This decision based on statistical inference is an important one for the scientist studying social problems. What are the consequences of rejecting the hypothesis concerning delinquency and broken homes although it is actually true? Programs may be developed and funds dispersed to attack the problem of broken homes, which is thought to be the source of delinquency. If there is actually no relationship, then we will be wasting both energy and funds and delaying attempts to deal with the real source of the problem. So statistical inference is a vitally important part of the study of social problems. What is the likelihood of making errors when we infer something from our data? What are the consequences when our inferences are incorrect? These are often difficult decisions to make, but they are nonetheless at the core of the scientific study of social problems.

Visual Presentation: Graphs and Charts

Masses of statistical data can be summarized in a visual fashion through the use of charts, graphs, and tables. Social scientists make considerable use of these devices to communicate information clearly and concisely. However, graphic materials, if improperly utilized, can be very misleading.[17] People with a vested interest in a particular interpretation of the data can construct charts and graphs in such a way that they seem to say what they want them to say. We will illustrate some of the ways in which this can be done.

Many graphic presentations utilize two perpendicular lines, each representing a variable of concern (see Fig. 2.3). The purpose is to show visually how changes in one variable are associated with changes in the other. In our illustration, we are attempting to illustrate how suicide rates vary with age. The intervals between units along each line should represent degrees of difference between the cases (or categories) on each variable in a way that accurately portrays their social importance.

Suppose you were interested in the social problem of high suicide rates and how they might be reduced. Since your resources are limited, you want to focus your attention where you can do the most good—possibly with age groups in which the suicide rate seems to increase the most dramatically. You begin your search for information. In Figure 2.3, we can see that suicide rates increase at a relatively substantial rate as age increases, and this is the interpretation of the data that most researchers in this field accept. However, if for some reason, one wanted to portray, with the exact same data, the suicide rate as increasing gradually with age, then all one need do is "shrink" the units on the vertical line, as we have done in Figure 2.4. In this "elastic" graph, one gets the impression that age does not have the dramatic impact on suicide rates that Figure 2.3 suggests. By constructing a graph in this fashion, one can either deliberately or inadvertently give an erroneous impression concerning the relationship between age and suicide rates. It should be kept in mind that the data in both cases are the same. What changes is the impression that is given to the reader by the graph.

Another graphing problem results from the use of uneven intervals. The researcher may use intervals on one of the lines that do not represent equivalent differences on the variables. In Figure 2.5, the age variable is divided into ten-year intervals. However, the spacings between the age categories on the graph *increase* as age increases. This gives the distorted impression that the suicide rate increases substantially slower between the ages of 15 and 74 than it does either before or after those ages. A comparison with Figure 2.3 and Figure 2.4 will show that neither figure gives the impression in this regard that Figure 2.5 gives.

Other illustrations could be presented, but the point should be clear. Data concerning social prob-

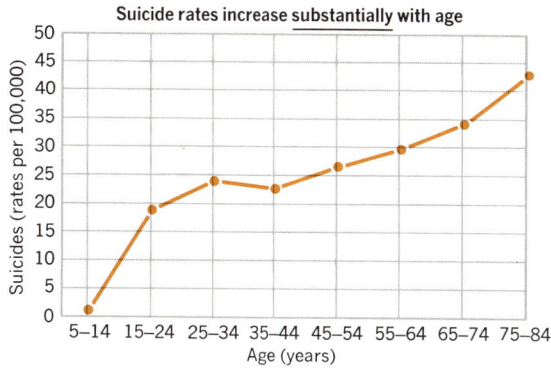

Figure 2.3 Suicide Rates, by Age, among U.S. Males, 1976. National Center for Health Statistics, *Facts of Life and Death*, DHEW Publication No. (PHS) 79-1222 (Washington, D.C.: U.S. Government Printing Office, 1978), p. 46.

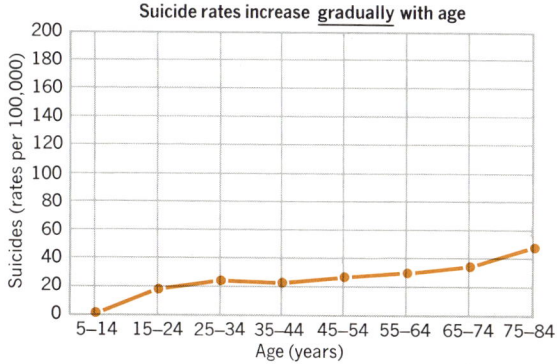

Figure 2.4 Suicide Rates, by Age, among U.S. Males, 1976. National Center for Health Statistics, *Facts of Life and Death*, DHEW Publication No. (PHS) 79-1222 (Washington, D.C.: U.S. Government Printing Office, 1978), p. 46.

lems can be presented in visual form in such a fashion that, while the information is accurate, the general impression is misleading. The student of social problems should inspect visually presented information very carefully to ensure that the impression given is an accurate one.

PROPAGANDA AND DISTORTION

Despite the repeated cautions presented in this chapter and the knowledge with which the student is now armed concerning the ways in which infor-

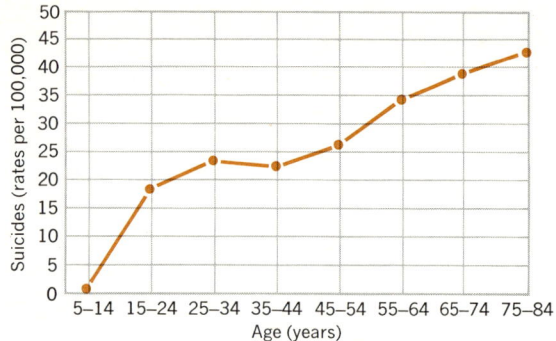

Figure 2.5 Suicide Rates, by Age, among U.S. Males, 1976. National Center for Health Statistics, *Facts of Life and Death*, DHEW Publication No. (PHS) 79-1222 (Washington, D.C.: U.S. Government Printing Office, 1978), p. 46.

mation can be distorted, there will still be many situations when the student is confronted with data the accuracy of which he or she is unable to evaluate. The data may look very impressive and the source unimpeachably reliable. Should it be accepted or rejected? There is no simple answer to this question, but there are a number of clues that should lead the student to regard the information as suspect.

First, does the person presenting the information have a vested interest in a particular interpretation of the data or in a particular research conclusion? We have emphasized repeatedly the role that interests can play in the distortion of social research. The student should be cautious whenever the person presenting the information benefits from the acceptance by others of his or her interpretation of the data.

Second, can the data or conclusions be traced to a readily identifiable source? If something is repeated often enough, by people with considerable prestige or credibility, there is a tendency for others to accept it as true. Newspapers often report that "reliable sources say," "experts report," or "official estimates are"—without indicating who the experts and officials are or what the data are that serve as a basis for their reports.[18] For example, in 1977, *Newsweek* reported (concerning San Francisco) that "Officials reckon that 28% of the city's voters

are homosexual." Diligent search has been unable to turn up the officials who made such a claim or the basis on which the estimate might have been made. Yet the *Newsweek* report has now become a major source for providing information about the size of the homosexual population of San Francisco.

There has been much speculation about how widespread organized crime is in the United States. Over the years, many have ventured guesses concerning the extent of its annual revenues.[19] In 1969, *Time* magazine estimated that they were "well over $30 billion." The same year that President Nixon told Congress that the figure was "anywhere from $20 billion to $50 billion," Attorney General John Mitchell reported that $50 billion was the minimum revenue of organized crime. There were numerous other estimates, but throughout the 1970s the figure settled on by most of the press and public was Mitchell's $50 billion.

The curious thing is that nowhere can one find out where any of these figures comes from. We assume that Nixon and Mitchell had access to government studies from which they derived their information; but we do not know this. This is not to imply that these men were deliberately misleading the public. The point is that if some statement or figure is repeated often enough—by public figures, the press, and others in influential positions—it takes on a life of its own, and people begin to assume that it must be true or else it would not be constantly repeated. However, the student of social problems should be wary of data if there is no readily identifiable source to which one can turn and from which one can learn how the data were gathered.

Third, is the information presented in a propagandistic fashion? It is important to differentiate between *propaganda* and *education*.[20] ***Propaganda* is information designed to persuade people to adopt a particular viewpoint in order to further the interests of the propagandist(s). *Education* is the systematic and formalized transmission of knowledge, skills, and values; its aim is to provide all sides of an issue in order that the person may make his or her own decision.**

Propagandists commonly use several rather simple methods to persuade the public.[21] All of the propaganda techniques have one element in common: an appeal to the values, prejudices, biases, and preconceptions of their audience.

Bandwagon is a method in which the propagandist attempts to build support of a particular product, person, or idea by creating the impression that everyone else is lending his or her support—the implication being that if you don't "jump on the bandwagon" too, you will be left out. An example of this is the motto, "join the Pepsi generation"—implying that if you don't drink Pepsi, you're not really "with it."

Card stacking is a technique in which facts are selected and arranged in such a way that the only conclusion that seems logical is the one that supports the propagandist's point of view. Facts damaging to that point of view are ignored. This technique is commonly used in commercial and political advertisements. For example, many breakfast cereals contain a high proportion of sugar, which is the major nutritional ingredient. However, advertisements emphasize the vitamins and minerals in the product and not the sugar and preservatives it also contains.

Glittering generalities is a method of surrounding a candidate, product, or policy with attractive and commonly accepted, but rather vague and meaningless, words or slogans such as "freedom," "democracy," and "the American way." "Law and order" is a glittering generality often used by political candidates to convince voters to support them. Yet these candidates often know little about the causes of crime or how to reduce it.

Name calling is a technique in which the propagandist attempts to attach an unfavorable label to something that he or she opposes. A political candidate might, for example, claim that an opponent's programs will lead to more "creeping socialism" or even that they are "communist inspired." For example, the American Medical Association (AMA) has referred to government-sponsored prepaid medical care by using the pejorative term "socialized medicine" as a means of opposing such legislation.

Plain folks is a method of identifying the propagandist's product or ideas with the "common person." For example, a political candidate might ask people to refer to him by his first name or some form of endearment such as "Uncle Charlie" in order to convince them that he is just "plain folks" like themselves.

Testimonial is the technique of using famous and respected people to make public statements favoring or opposing something. For example, celebrities such as movie stars and athletes are used by commercial advertisers to sell products and by political candidates to lend credibility and glamour to their campaigns. For instance, the well-known movie and television actor, William Conrad, used this technique in an advertisement for the Bonanza Steak Houses. Conrad said, "You know me, William Conrad, I tell it like it is. . . ."

Transfer is a method of seeking approval for something by associating it with something else that the audience views favorably. For example, cigarette commercials often attempt to associate cigarette

Much of television advertising uses the propaganda technique known as the *testimonial*—the use of famous or respected people to endorse a product.

smoking with youth, vigor, and sexual attractiveness by the models they choose to do the advertisements and by the activities the actors are portrayed as engaged in. Ronald Reagan has had a successful career in politics related, at least in part, to the positive, wholesome, and straightforward image that he portrayed in his movie and television career.

These propaganda techniques are used by pressure groups to distort information so as to present their viewpoint on an issue in the best possible light. The student of social problems must be wary of any data which are presented in propagandistic fashion.

CONCLUSION

Social problems are highly controversial issues that affect the values and interests of many groups in society. Accurate information is essential in order to understand social problems and to make decisions and implement measures to deal with them effectively. Science provides the best means of arriving at valid and reliable information to be used toward these ends. However, scientific conclusions may be rejected by groups that find other sources of knowledge more consistent with their values and more useful in convincing other people of their point of view. On the other hand, because of the considerable credibility attached to scientific data, pressure groups frequently try to use "scientific" evidence to support their interests. More often than not, these pressure groups try to influence the scientist's findings and conclusions so that they are interpreted in a manner consistent with their way of thinking. Information on social problems—even that supplied by some members of the scientific community—should be viewed with some degree of skepticism since biases may affect their methods of data collection and their conclusions.

In this chapter we have compared the scientific method with other ways of knowing. The goal has been to sensitize the student to the difference between them and to provide a means for evaluating the methods by which data on social problems are generated. In addition, we have considered some of the more common errors committed in scientific studies on social problems. This should provide the student with a means of separating truly scientific information from "pseudoscience," which is really propaganda. These tools will be useful in assessing and evaluating the ideas and data presented in the chapters that follow and the information concerning social problems provided in the media.

GLOSSARY TERMS

Arithmetic mean	Mode	Research design
Charismatic truth	Pressure group	Sampling bias
Controls	Propaganda	Science
Descriptive statistics	Proportion	Spuriousness
Experiential truth	Qualitative methods	Statistical correlation
Fact	Quantitative methods	Statistical inference
Hypothesis	Rate	Traditional truth
Indicator	Ratio	Validity
Intervening variables	Reliability	Variable
Median	Representative sample	

REFERENCES

[1] C. Wright Mills, *The Sociological Imagination* (New York: Oxford University Press, 1959), p. 5.

[2] Rodney Coe, *The Sociology of Medicine*, 2d ed. (New York: McGraw-Hill, 1978).

[3] See Morris R. Cohen and Ernest Nagel, *An Introduction to Logic and Scientific Method* (New York: Harcourt Brace & World, 1962), and Julian L. Simon, *Basic Research Methods in Social Sciences*, 2d ed. (New York: Random House, 1978), pp. 500–514.

[4] Cesare Lombroso, *Crime: Its Causes and Remedies* (Boston: Little, Brown, 1911). For a discussion of Lombroso's theory and the controversy surrounding it, see Hermann Mannheim, *Comparative Criminology* (Boston: Houghton Mifflin, 1965).

[5] Edwin H. Sutherland, *Principles of Criminology*, 4th ed. (Philadelphia: Lippincott, 1947). See also Edwin H. Sutherland and Donald R. Cressey, *Criminology*, 10th ed. (Philadelphia: Lippincott, 1978), pp. 77–97. Sutherland's theory is discussed in more detail in Chapter 15.

[6] The issues in the case discussed here can be found in George L. Kirkham, *Signal Zero* (Philadelphia: Lippincott, 1976), and Peter K. Manning, "Review of *Signal Zero* by George L. Kirkham," *Criminology* 16 (May 1978), pp. 133–136.

[7] Alan Orenstein and William R. F. Phillips, *Understanding Social Research: An Introduction* (Boston: Allyn and Bacon, 1978).

[8] Kenneth D. Bailey, *Methods of Social Research* (New York: The Free Press, 1978), pp. 51–52.

[9] For a more lengthy discussion, see Travis Hirschi and Hanan C. Selvin, *Delinquency Research* (New York: The Free Press, 1967), and Simon, *Basic Research Methods*, pp. 385–390.

[10] Earl R. Babbie, *The Practice of Social Research* (Belmont, Cal.: Wadsworth, 1975).

[11] Bailey, *Methods of Social Research*, p. 42.

[12] Robert L. Kane, et al., *The Health Gap: Medical Service and the Poor* (New York: Springer, 1976).

[13] See Evelyn Hooker, "The Adjustment of the Male Overt Homosexual," *Journal of Projective Techniques* 21 (1957), pp. 18–31, and Alan P. Bell and Martin S. Weinberg, *Homosexualities: A Study of Diversity Among Men and Women* (New York: Simon and Schuster, 1978).

[14] Ibid.

[15] Judith D. Handel, *Introductory Statistics for Sociology* (Englewood Cliffs, N.J.: Prentice-Hall, 1978).

[16] See Philip Shabecoff, "Overhaul Is Urgent in Jobless Figures," *New York Times* (July 16, 1978), p. 19.

[17] Thad R. Harshbarger, *Introductory Statistics: A Decision Map* (New York: Macmillan, 1977).

[18] Martin Plissner, "Figure It This Way: Figures Can Be Unreliable," *The Milwaukee Journal* (March 27, 1978), p. 1.

[19] Ibid.

[20] See George N. Gordon, *Persuasion: The Theory and Practice of Manipulative Communication* (New York: Hastings House, 1971), pp. 152–170.

[21] Alfred McClung Lee and Elizabeth Briant Lee, *The Fine Art of Propaganda* (New York: Harcourt, Brace & World, 1939).

SUGGESTED READINGS

Bailey, Kenneth D. *Methods of Social Research.* New York: The Free Press, 1978.
A good recent text on social research that is quite readable and that provides an overview of the basic issues in data analysis.

Dornbusch, Sanford M., and Schmid, Calvin F. *A Primer of Social Statistics.* New York: McGraw-Hill, 1955.
A classic that helps the student appreciate statistics as a universal language and a fundamental and essential tool for solving problems.

Hastings, William A. *How to Think about Social Problems: A Primer for Citizens.* New York: Oxford University Press, 1979.

A short and breezy little book in which the first couple of chapters are devoted to a discussion of the misuses of statistical information.

Huff, Darrell. *How to Lie with Statistics.* New York: W. W. Norton, 1954.
Standard reading for the serious student of social problems. It is short, concise, and easy to read, with numerous examples of how statistical information has been distorted.

Zeisal, Hans. *Say It with Figures.* 5th rev. ed. New York: Harper & Row, 1968.
A little book that discusses in simple and straightforward fashion the problems associated with the visual presentation of data and alternative solutions to these problems.

Questions
for Discussion

1. The scientific method is an important means for gathering facts about social problems. However, it represents only one way of knowing. What are the three other types of knowledge? Discuss why the scientific method is the best means for studying social problems.

2. Pressure groups seek to persuade the public that their point of view is the most accurate and righteous. Discuss some of the pressures placed on scientists by interest groups.

3. A statistical correlation or association between two variables, no matter how strong or consistent, does not by itself prove that one variable causes the other. What four criteria must be met before a person can reasonably infer that one variable caused another?

4. A biased sample can distort our understanding of social problems and lead us to use inappropriate means to try to deal with them. What is a representative sample? Discuss why representative samples are crucial to the scientific study of social problems.

5. If we are to have accurate information on social problems, it is essential that we have valid and reliable indicators of them. What is a valid indicator? A reliable indicator?

6. There are different types of averages that are used in studying social problems. Identify the three averages discussed in the text and discuss their advantages and disadvantages as means of summarizing facts.

7. Why are graphs and charts useful to the student of social problems? How can they be used to distort information?

8. What is the difference between education and propaganda? How can one recognize propaganda? Why does propaganda appeal to many people?

PART TWO

Problems for the Nation and the World

CHAPTER 3

Social Problems in the Cities

URBAN LIFE IN AMERICA: A BRIEF HISTORY

Immigration. Urban Migration. Urban Transportation. Urban Education.

THE CITY AS A SOCIAL PROBLEM

The Functionalist Perspective. The Conflict Perspective. The Interactionist Perspective.

WHAT IS A CITY?

Complexity and Specialization. Individualism and Social Diversity. Impersonality.

ECONOMIC PROBLEMS OF THE CENTRAL CITY

Decentralization. Decentralization and Business. The Flight of the Middle Class. The Case of New York City.

RACIAL PROBLEMS IN CITIES

EDUCATION AND THE INNER CITY

The Educational Trap. School Financing. School Desegregation and Busing. Education and Social Problems.

HOUSING

The Ghetto. Federal Housing Policy. The Dynamics of Land Use.

TRANSPORTATION AND THE CITY

Modes of Transportation.

FUTURE PROSPECTS: THE POLITICS OF URBAN LIFE

Federal Programs. Regional Planning and Cooperation. Should We Save Our Cities?

CONCLUSION

During the 1960s, many of our major cities were plagued with chaotic disruptions; burning, rioting, and looting became commonplace events. The entire nation was stunned by this eruption of urban violence at a level seldom seen in recent decades. Today, urban residents see headlines proclaiming the high rate of crime in cities. Many citydwellers are afraid to venture into some parts of the city at night—and are terrified of some neighborhoods even in the daytime. Double locks, dead bolts, and property-marking equipment are now considered necessities in many urban households. A substantial number of citizens have bought firearms to protect themselves against the dangers of city life.

In addition to crime and violence, modern American cities are plagued by other very serious and complex problems. In 1975, New York City was on the brink of economic collapse, and it is still struggling to solve its financial problems. In other cities, more welfare money was paid out than ever before. Schools in the suburbs cut back on athletic programs owing to a shortage of funds. Inner-city schools despair of ever being able to provide opportunities for their students equal to those available to students in more affluent schools. A shortage of good teachers, decent facilities, and modern (or in some cases simply usable) equipment handicaps the inner-city school in its efforts to provide a high-quality education.

The list of woes that plague American cities seems endless. Although the riots of the 1960s have subsided, urban social conditions have not improved, and some experts would say that they have deteriorated further. Unless these serious problems of the cities are alleviated, we may be faced in the near future with a recurrence of severe social disorders, possibly involving greater destruction than did those of the past. Why have our cities experienced such problems? How did these conditions come about and—what is most important—what can be done about them? These are some of the questions that we will investigate in this chapter. Finding answers to them is important because one striking fact of life in the United States is that we are an urban people. Over 73 percent of our population is officially classified as urban (see Fig. 3.1). **The official definition of an** *urban*

place **is an area with 2500 or more people, so obviously not all of these people live in our major cities. Nevertheless,** *it is in our cities that many of our most serious social problems emerge, intensify, and occasionally reach crisis proportions.*

It is fitting, then, that we begin our study of American social problems by looking at the conditions of our cities today. In order to understand the roots of urban problems, their dimensions and feasible solutions, it will be useful to see how these problems emerged as American cities developed.

URBAN LIFE IN AMERICA: A BRIEF HISTORY

The growth of cities in the United States did not reach major proportions until after the Civil War (see Fig. 3.1). Prior to 1860, American cities were relatively small and primarily nonindustrial, centering on mercantile activity in support of the surrounding rural population.[1] With the growth of cities, there were a number of significant developments in America that have contributed to the emergence of the social problems facing our cities today. We will discuss a few of these developments to illustrate how urban problems emerge over a period of time.

Immigration

Between 1840 and 1920, large numbers of immigrants, primarily from Europe, came to the United States searching for a better way of life. Wave upon wave of Italians, Irish, Scandinavians, and others spread out into American cities in search of work and a decent life. In 1905 more than 1,000,000 immigrants entered the United States, and in 1914 the figure topped 1,200,000.[2]

The vast majority of the immigrants were unskilled workers. They served as an important source of labor in the burgeoning industrial and manufacturing cities. However, they also contributed to many of the urban problems that are still with us today. There were occasional periods of high unemployment in the cities when there were more immigrants than jobs. Poverty and crime were com-

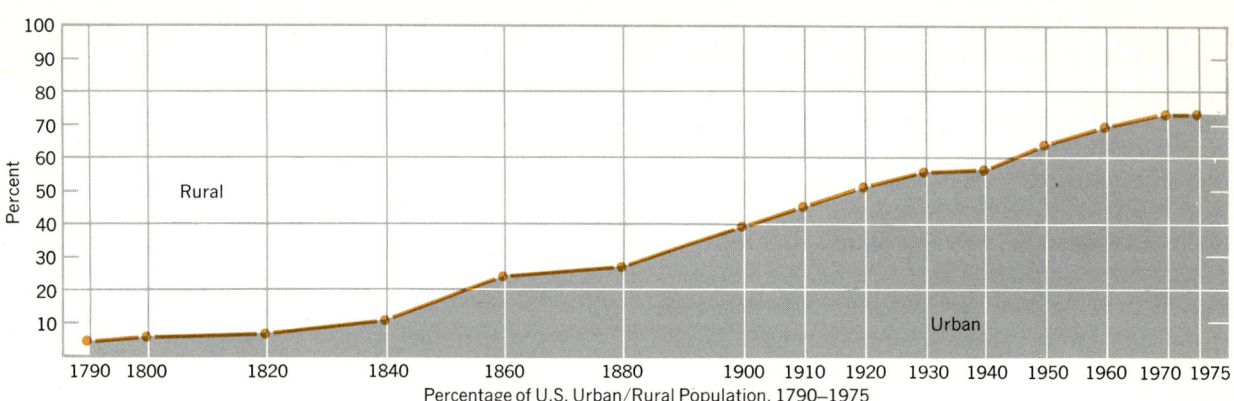

Figure 3.1 Percentage of U.S. Urban/Rural Population, 1790–1975. U.S. Bureau of the Census, *Historical Statistics of the United States, Colonial Times to 1970* (Washington, D.C.: U.S. Government Printing Office, 1975), pp. 11–12; and U.S. Bureau of the Census, *Statistical Abstract of the United States, 1977* (Washington, D.C.: U.S. Government Printing Office, 1977), p. 17.

mon; crowding and congestion were rampant—the streets of New York and other cities were filled to overflowing; decent housing was scarce; the crowding and poor living conditions resulted in many health problems. It was during this period that the slums of our major cities took on their modern form. Settlement houses—one part of that period's welfare effort—were established by affluent philanthropists to attack some of these problems. Many of the urban problems we are still grappling with—crowding, poverty, congestion, crime, and the like—can be traced back to this period.

Urban Migration

In addition to the surge of new immigrants to our shores, there was also some very significant migration of groups from rural areas of America to cities during this period, particularly from the South into northern and western cities. The effect of this migration on cities can be illustrated by the migration of blacks from the South. Between 1915 and 1920, 500,000 blacks left the rural South, with 75 percent of those going to the large cities of the north and west.[3] The stage for discrimination and racial conflict was set when large numbers of blacks moved

into neighborhoods that were previously white. One early incident occurred

in the grimly industrial city of East St. Louis, Illinois, on July 1, 1917. On that grisly day a mob of whites, its feigned fury masking careful deliberation, set fire to Negro residences, then coolly shot the fleeing occupants. Other mobs beat and hanged blacks.[4]

Since that time, it has not taken much for underlying racial prejudice to precipitate violent clashes in American cities.

Black migrants to urban areas encountered other serious problems. They had higher rates of divorce, desertion, juvenile delinquency, illegitimacy, and unemployment than did the rest of the population. One reason why blacks experienced these problems to such a degree was that the agricultural skills they brought from the South were of little value in industrial cities, and thus they found it difficult to find work. However, they might have overcome this problem, as the European immigrants were eventually able to do, if the black migrants had not faced another very serious and practically insurmountable barrier: racial prejudice and discrimination. Blacks in the growing cities were limited to the most menial and low-paying occupations. In 1910, nearly one-half of the black males in Chicago were porters, servants, waiters, or janitors.[5] Institutionalized discrimination prevented blacks from getting jobs in skilled occupations with higher status and greater rewards. It is no wonder, then, that blacks experienced very serious social problems. American cities today still feel the effects of this early heritage—through families living in poverty generation after generation, increased crime rates, and lingering racial hostilities.

Urban Transportation

In the early 1800s, most urban residents moved about American cities on foot, and this was a feasible mode of transportation since distances were usually short. During the 1830s, the *omnibus* was introduced as a means of transportation. The omnibus was a horsedrawn vehicle that seated approximately twelve people. By 1833, eighty omnibuses were licensed to operate on the streets of New York, and by 1853 the number had increased to 683.[6] However, the fare on these omnibuses was so high that it was out of the reach of most laborers. Fares ranged from six to twelve cents, which was prohibitively expensive for a person who earned approximately one dollar per day. Thus, this was hardly *mass* transit—it was primarily for the more affluent urbanites. Because transportation was limited, the population of these early cities was concentrated in fairly small, and often quite crowded, areas.

In the 1850s, *horsecars*—horsedrawn railroad cars—began to replace the omnibus as the primary mode of urban transportation. In Boston in 1840, for example, the omnibuses carried approximately 1 million passengers, but by 1860 the horsecars were hauling over 13 million in Boston and nearly 45 million in New York. Despite the increasing scale of public transportation, the cost was still beyond the reach of many poor urbanites.[7]

The advent of the automobile did little to ameliorate the plight of the poor citydweller. In fact, one of the effects of expanded automobile ownership was to threaten the economic viability of some public transit systems by drawing off many paying customers. Between 1915 and 1929, the number of automobile registrations leaped from 2,332,426 to 23,120,897.[8] Following World War II, the spread of automobile ownership increased. Since automobiles in these years were bought almost exclusively by members of the middle class, who also provided the main support for public transportation, a direct threat was posed to the ability of public transit companies to survive and expand. This led to a dramatic increase in fares in order to pay for the cost of operating a system with fewer riders. Thus the poor, who could not afford automobiles, were forced to pay higher fares for a less efficient transit system. While some cities were able to provide inexpensive urban transit, others were left without truly effective public transportation.[9] Our growing reliance on the automobile as the primary mode of transportation has contributed to the decentralization of our cities and to traffic congestion, which are primary problems in American cities today.

Urban Education

The public school movement in the United States began essentially as an attempt at solving an emerging urban crisis—the increasing numbers of poor people, many of them immigrants, who had flocked to cities in the 1800s. In Boston, for example, the public school system was built up between 1800 and 1860 as a means of promoting social order during a period of seeming disorganization and as an effort to Americanize immigrants. During this period, Boston found the ranks of its poor swollen first by Americans fleeing from economically depressed rural areas into the city, and then by immigrants from abroad. Crime, drunkenness, and vagrancy increased, and there was a fear that these impoverished Bostonians would become a permanent poor urban class, passing their poverty on through the generations.[10]

In response to this, the citizens of Boston turned to education. "In nineteenth-century Boston, therefore, to a greater extent than in most other cities, citizens heralded public education as the most vital institutional answer to poverty and its related social problems."[11] In one program, special permits were issued to children over the age of seven who were unqualified to attend school. In another program, intermediate school classrooms were opened in lower-class neighborhoods to teach children who were not prepared to enter the grammar schools. Before long, these intermediate schools were populated solely by the poor, and the school system had become segregated along social class lines. Then, as today, schools generated social problems, such as segregation, at the same time that they were viewed by many as solutions to social problems.

We have seen that some of the problems in American cities are not new; they have been developing for a long period. This makes them more difficult to ameliorate because their sources are deeply embedded in our society. However, it also means that it is crucial that we attempt to solve them before they become even more intractable.

THE CITY AS A SOCIAL PROBLEM

The Functionalist Perspective

In order to understand the problems of urban areas, it is essential to comprehend the place of cities in American life. The world today is fundamentally an urban world. While not all people live in cities, almost all are dependent on them to maintain their way of life. According to the functionalist perspective, a city is a delicately balanced social network in which goods are produced and distributed, economic and social transactions occur, and groups strive to achieve goals that are important to them. It is the concentration of people and economic resources in a compact area that makes possible the production of goods and services to support our affluent, technologically based lifestyle. In a sense, it is cities that make possible our civilization.

However, this complex social network can be easily disrupted. In an urban society, people are completely dependent on a large number of other people for the necessities of life—food, shelter, clothing, and the like. Because of the complexity of this interdependence, disruptions having widespread ramifications can result from a variety of small and relatively localized conditions. For example, the blackout in New York City in 1977—a power failure—resulted in widespread looting and disruption, with $150 million to $300 million in direct losses to store merchants. The consequences are still being felt by the city. In some areas, stores that closed following the looting have still not opened for business, which has had a depressing effect on economic conditions in their neighborhoods. In this fashion, high crime rates may lead those able to do so to abandon their neighborhoods rather than live in fear and danger. As a result, the tax base of the city declines, leaving it less able to provide satisfactory services, such as transportation and education. Declines in these services may motivate others to move to locales where such problems do not exist. The declining quality of education may also leave many city residents without the skills to secure satisfactory employment. This in turn forces people into the ranks of the unemployed and welfare recipients, becoming nonproductive dependents who further strain the resources of the city.

From the functionalist perspective, then, the conditions of the city become social problems when they disrupt the smooth functioning of the city and threaten the achievement of an acceptable lifestyle. However, the city is not simply a self-contained system; it is also part of a larger system, for cities play a critical role in the life of the nation of which they are a part. Cities are the centers of finance, commerce, industry, and culture. Even those people who do not live in cities depend on them for goods, services, and information. Conditions that interfere with the functioning of cities can have a ripple effect across the nation. If life in our major cities is so unpleasant that people leave, they must go somewhere. Rural farmlands are regularly torn up to build new suburbs. The problems that were once limited to the cities often emerge in new communities growing rapidly because of the influx of former urban residents.

Thus the cities cannot be considered in isolation. **From the functionalist perspective, the problems that beset them must be viewed as a result of both the strains and imbalances**

Chicago, Illinois—one of America's largest cities and replete with
a full array of urban problems.

created within cities themselves and the changes and pressures from the larger social network of which the city is a part.

The Conflict Perspective

From the conflict perspective, society is an arena in which groups compete and struggle over scarce and valued resources. In this view, urban areas can be seen as made up of a large number of interest groups competing with one another. This struggle takes many forms. Labor groups demand higher salaries and improved working conditions. If dissatisfied, they may go on strike, disrupting transportation or industry. During the 1960s, the urban struggle took an especially violent form in the ghetto riots that raked many large and small cities. These riots were, on one level, an attempt by poor people to gain, through looting and burning, the food, clothing, and other items they could not afford. On another level, the riots were a consequence of the oppression and frustration of an urban minority

group. On yet another level, the riots were an effort by a previously powerless minority group to exert some influence on the political process of the city and the nation in order to achieve its goals.

From the conflict perspective, then, urban conditions are considered social problems when groups with some power feel that these conditions impede their efforts to attain valued goals and resources. The extent to which crime, housing, or educational conditions are viewed as social problems depends on which groups are affected and whether these groups perceive them as a hindrance.

The struggle for resources pits many groups against one another. For example, merchants in the central business district (who may work, but not live, in the city) make efforts to divert government funds into projects to beautify the shopping districts. This is to their advantage because a pleasant atmosphere invites more shoppers to their stores. However, since funds are always limited, the beautification project will draw funds away from other projects that might benefit other groups—low-cost housing for the poor, senior-citizen recreational centers, or improved local transportation. Whether dilapidated housing or poor schools is defined as a social problem depends on which groups are affected and on what power they have to make the issue a public issue.

Cities can also play an important role in the conflict between groups by generating an awareness that members of a particular group share a problem and that collective action might alleviate the problem. This awareness of a commonly shared problem is similar to Marx's notion of class consciousness.[12] Because of the concentration of people in cities, there is greater likelihood of becoming aware that others share a problem, and the possibility of organizing many people around a particular issue is much greater. This awareness and communication is enhanced when people with similar characteristics are concentrated in the same neighborhood. Without such communication, people are unlikely to become aware of common interests, and they are unlikely to have the power to make their concerns felt.

The Interactionist Perspective

The interactionist perspective, focusing as it does on the importance of subjective perception of social reality, provides us with some unique insight into the issues defined as social problems in cities. The noted urban analyst Edward Banfield contends that many of the popularly conceived problems of the city are only problems in a relative sense.[13] If we compare present conditions in our cities to those of yesteryear, we must conclude that the lives of urban dwellers, even the most poor, have vastly improved over the past fifty years. Whereas private bathroom facilities were once considered a luxury in urban housing, we now consider dwelling units without them to be substandard. Urban schools today, even with all their problems, are technological and educational marvels compared to the schools of the past.

Despite the objective improvements in urban conditions, people have grown to expect more than they did in the past. Conditions that in the past would have been accepted as one of life's unpleasant but inevitable burdens are now considered problems that warrant our concern and collective action. If the urban poor believe they are deprived because they do not own a car or a color television set, then this is the reality to which they will respond. These feelings of deprivation may result in frustration that could burst out in violent ways. While they may not be deprived of the means of life (food, clothing, and shelter) they do suffer from *relative deprivation*—the feeling that they are deprived relative to what others have acquired and to what they expect. To some extent, it is urban life that has created, or at least intensified, this sense of relative deprivation. By concentrating people in relatively small areas, urban dwellers are more aware of the lifestyle of others. The "have-nots" are more aware of what the "haves" possess. This relative deprivation is also intensified by advertising, which creates the impression that all people should aspire toward affluence.

The interactionist perspective also focuses on the importance of shared expectations as the foundation for social order. In an urban society, with a diverse and heterogeneous population, the emergence of shared expectations and commonly agreed upon definitions of reality becomes more problematic. The city draws people from differing life circumstances, with differences in material possessions, social status, and lifestyles. With such variation, people are less likely to share common goals and values, and thus concerted action toward some end is more difficult.

WHAT IS A CITY?

At first glance, the answer to the question, what is a city?, seems obvious. It is the land, buildings, traffic, noise, and crowds that we see before us. However, from a sociological perspective, a city is also a complex set of social relationships that makes it distinct from rural areas. In order to understand the social problems of cities, it is useful to comprehend the type of social relationships that emerge in such settings.

To grasp the special qualities of a city, think for a moment about your own upbringing. Were you brought up in a city or a small town? If in an urban area, what do you imagine are the differences between that and small town or rural life? What people commonly say is: in a small town, everyone knows who you are and what you do—in a city, you can do pretty much what you want; people look you in the eye in a small town—it seems like noboby looks at you at all in big cities; everybody is rushing and hurrying in the cities—in a small town, people are more relaxed and have more time to spend with you. These commonsense reactions point to some of the sociological differences between urban and rural life.

" I FIND THAT AS LONG AS YOU AVOID EYE CONTACT, YOU HARDLY REALIZE THERE IS A CROWD."

Complexity and Specialization

One important characteristic of urban life is its complex and extensive *division of labor,* in which people take on a variety of highly specialized tasks.[14] As a consequence, individuality and independence are encouraged, and people tend to be formal, businesslike, and impersonal in their relationships with others. For example, people in small communities commonly experience substantial overlap in their work, leisure, and family relationships. They probably know the grocery store owner and call him by name, they play baseball or go bowling with the local gas station owner, or they attend church with the chief of police. In the city, on the other hand, this blending of social relationships is less common. Our contacts with people tend to be very limited and specialized. Social contacts tend to be brief, impersonal, and utilitarian.

Individualism and Social Diversity

While many people believe that rural life is conducive to individualism and independence, it is actually city life that permits a freedom not possible in small towns. In small communities, people are constantly under the scrutiny of others, and there are strong pressures to conform to community expectations. Nonconformity is viewed as threatening to the community, to be attacked rather than condoned or fostered. In the city, on the other hand, there is considerably less restriction on one's lifestyle. The anonymity of the city makes it easier for people to engage in nonconforming behavior.[15]

In addition, cities attract a wide variety of people. Men and women of different social class positions, racial and ethnic backgrounds, and varying religious identifications are a part of the cultural mosaic that characterizes our cities. These differences produce conflicts that are not as often present in rural areas. In a city, it is possible for a completely different and distinct subculture to develop in one geographic location. Old Town in Chicago, the Bowery and Harlem in New York, and Chinatown in San Francisco are all good examples of this. Furthermore, every city has its ethnic enclaves—sections heavily populated by Greeks, Italians, Jews,

Chicanos, blacks, etc. With such diversity in the city, it is possible for a person to choose from among a variety of lifestyles and find a part of the city in which such a lifestyle will be accepted, or at least not rejected.

Impersonality

One characteristic of cities that has intrigued many observers is the apparent impersonality, rudeness, and unwillingness of urbanites to help others. This aspect of cities was dramatized for the nation a few years ago when a young woman in New York named Kitty Genovese was attacked and murdered on the street in front of her apartment. Although thirty-eight of her neighbors heard her screams and watched the attack, which lasted over ten minutes, none lifted a finger to help her—not even to the extent of calling the police. How could people be so seemingly callous and indifferent to the suffering of another person?

In his classic essay on mental life in the metropolis, German sociologist Georg Simmel observed that citydwellers become more intellectual and rational in reaction to the complexities of urban life—they respond with their head instead of their heart.[16]

In a crowded and dense urban environment, a person is in danger of being overwhelmed by stimuli—requests and demands for his time, interest, and emotional involvement. There is so much going on that a person could not possibly pay attention to it all. People respond to this sensory overload by shutting out much of what is happening and attending only to what is directly important—family, friends, and work. This selective attention then becomes a normal, everyday reaction—urbanites shut out many things, such as another person in danger, even though such callousness seems to clash with humanitarian values. Much research on this topic has shown that people justify such behavior by claiming that they are not responsible for helping the other person. Such a claim is especially easy to make if there are others present who might assume the responsibility.[17] So, as Simmel pointed out, urbanites are more likely to react to situations with their head (calculate the personal costs of ac-

tion and rationalize inactivity) than with their heart (act on the basis of feelings about and empathy toward another human being). This is not to say that people in cities do not often act with kindness, thoughtfulness, and responsibility, or that people in rural communities are never rude and callous. Rather, the research suggests that urban social conditions increase the likelihood that a person will exhibit impersonality or refuse to help another.

The foregoing characteristics—specialization, diversity, and impersonality—are central characteristics that make our cities what they are. They contribute to the emergence of social problems and affect their potential solutions. Given this complexity and diversity, problems that arise in cities are absent, or are found in a different form, in rural areas. For example, problems in education discussed in this chapter emerge at least in part because the urban educational system must meet the needs of a whole array of subcultures, lifestyles, and personal values. Any proposed solutions must take into account this complexity if they are to be acceptable to the many affected groups. So, as we discuss the problems in our cities, the student should understand that underlying these problems and their solutions are the unique characteristics that make the city what it is.

ECONOMIC PROBLEMS OF THE CENTRAL CITY

American cities have never been clean and safe garden playgrounds. Decaying buildings, overcrowded tenement houses, impoverished neighborhoods, and high crime rates were more common in the cities of the early 1900s than they are today.[18] However, certain economic factors that confront the central cities today have exacerbated these conditions and introduce new and pressing elements into the picture.

Decentralization

In American cities of the early 1900s, the central business district emerged in part because it was easily accessible to the residents of the city. Limited transportation forced the citydweller to remain close to the center of the city, where jobs and services were located. The central business district served as the commercial and cultural core of the city. As long as this residential pattern continued, the central business district was able to retain a monopoly of accessibility, and was therefore capable of maintaining economic stability and growth. However, by the end of World War II, urban residential patterns began to undergo a fundamental shift that was to signal economic difficulties for the central city.[19]

After a lengthy period of growth in the central areas of the city, a process of *decentralization* began — people, businesses, and industries began to move away from the center of the city and out beyond its political boundaries. Two important factors involved in this decentralization were changes in transportation and the policies of the Federal Housing Administration.[20]

The role of changes in transportation is relatively straightforward. If you were dependent on limited public transportation to get to work or places to shop, then it was desirable to live near work or shopping centers or along transportation lines. This encouraged the concentration of residences near these locations, and urban areas remained fairly centralized. However, after the turn of the century, as the automobile became a more common possession, these limitations were removed, and urban areas began to spread to a much greater extent than before. While the upper classes previously had some residential flexibility, the popularity of the au-

tomobile made this a possibility for many others. One could now live far from work and from shopping centers without a great loss of accessibility.

These developments in transportation made outward expansion possible, but it remained for the Federal Housing Administration (FHA), created in 1933, to provide the final outward push. After World War II, the FHA developed programs to facilitate the purchase of new houses by providing federally guaranteed mortgage loans for the purchase of new homes. Since most land within cities was already used for either commercial or residential purposes, most new construction occurred outside the city. The flight from the city had begun. Farms were subdivided into homesites, and small communities began to blossom around the cities. Large tracts of uniformly constructed houses emerged with exotic or manorial names, such as Tropicana Estates, Cherryblossom Village, or Westlake Heights — all intended to give the impression of wide-open spaces, exclusivity, and affluence.

The decentralization of our cities has continued, as is vividly illustrated in Table 3.1 by the decline, sometimes substantial, in the populations of some of our major cities. In order to understand how urban problems emerge (and how they might be solved), it is crucial to keep in mind the forces that have brought about this shift. It did not occur simply because people were searching for a more enjoyable place to live. Rather, the primary factors were the emergence of new technologies in transportation and the development of new housing policies. These were not intended to lead to the downfall of the city, but it makes us aware of the

TABLE 3.1
Population Decline in Selected American Cities, 1950–1975

CITY	1950	1960	1970	1975
New York	7,891,957	7,781,984	7,895,563	7,481,613
Chicago	3,620,962	3,550,404	3,369,357	3,099,391
Philadelphia	2,071,605	2,002,512	1,949,996	1,815,808
Detroit	1,849,568	1,670,144	1,514,063	1,335,085
Washington, D.C.	802,178	763,956	756,668	711,518
San Francisco	775,357	740,316	715,674	664,520
Cleveland	914,808	876,050	750,879	638,793
Boston	801,444	697,197	641,071	636,725

SOURCE. U.S. Bureau of the Census, *Statistical Abstract of the United States,* 1977 (Washington, D.C.: U.S. Government Printing Office, 1977), pp. 22–24.

functionalist strictures concerning the extreme interdependence of urban areas. When policies or technologies are developed, it is important to investigate both their *manifest* and their *latent* consequences. In this case, the latent consequences for our cities have been dramatic and often very negative. Furthermore, solutions to problems of the cities must take into account the impact of technological and political developments in the future.

Decentralization and Business

As the populations of our cities became decentralized, especially during the 1950s and 1960s, the central business district lost its monopoly of accessibility. Suburban communities made repeated efforts to attract businesses in the hopes that their communities would lure more residents and have a solid economic base. Huge shopping centers were built with automobile transportation in mind—near highways and with large (and free) parking lots. This made them more convenient to suburban residents. In addition, the suburban shopping centers were new, clean, spacious, and carried products that were keyed to the affluent middle-class lifestyle of the suburbanite. As a consequence, consumer dollars that previously would have been spent in downtown businesses were being diverted to stores in outlying regions.

As the number of customers declined, many downtown merchants faced serious problems. Income declined while taxes, rents, and other costs of doing business continued to rise. It became harder to make ends meet. Owners often could not afford necessary maintenance or improvements for their buildings, which might have attracted more customers. In many cases, rather than resist the trend, they moved to the suburbs to regain the patrons that they had lost. The end result for the city was that the deterioration of many downtown areas proceeded rapidly. While some city neighborhoods were able to avoid the worst of this trend, for others the decline seemed inexorable.

This evacuation of retail businesses to the suburbs was accompanied by the relocation of industries in the outer fringes of the city. For industries, there were many attractions pulling them to the suburbs—land was cheap, taxes were generally lower than in the city, and the many skilled employees and management personnel living in the suburbs formed a ready source of labor. Many suburban communities encouraged this trend through various policies, such as tax breaks for relocated businesses. For the central city, however, the consequence was economic decline at an ever increasing pace.[21]

The Flight of the Middle Class

One of the most important ingredients in the decline of the city has been the movement of the affluent out of the city. The vast majority of the people migrating to the suburbs have been those residents who were financially well-to-do. At first, the people who left the city were mostly middle-class, white-collar employees. Before long, however, they were joined by working-class people who could afford to live in the suburbs. These affluent groups were able to buy new houses and pay the high cost of transportation to and from work.

Thus, it was precisely those groups who had the most to offer financially and economically to the city that abandoned it.[22] The income, sales, and property taxes that they would have paid as city-dwellers, and the purchases that they would have made from city businesses were being funneled into suburban coffers. The poor remaining in the city used more city services, and at the same time paid less to the city in taxes compared to the former middle-class residents. Abandoned businesses pay no taxes. So, the tax base of the cities declined as people and industry moved out. At the same time, suburbanites still use the cities for a variety of services, both economic and cultural. Some feel that suburban residents might even be considered parasites on the city—deriving enjoyment and vitality from what the city has to offer but providing little in the way of financial support for those services. Because of these changes, cities were faced with less income at the same time that their costs of operation were increasing. How were cities to continue providing all the services that people had come to expect—police and fire protection, education programs, parks, and the like? They were faced with the dilemma of what services to reduce or eliminate. For example, in 1976, when the crime index in Detroit was at an all-time high, the city government felt compelled to lay off over 300 police officers because it did not have the funds to pay their salaries. Such a decline in services often exacerbates urban problems by motivating even more city residents to flee to the suburbs.

The Case of New York City

The situation of many cities has become so desperate that some find themselves in severe financial straits. It is hard to imagine a bustling city going broke, but this is precisely the specter faced by some of them today. In 1975, the largest city in America, New York, announced that it was prepared to declare bankruptcy. The city leaders claimed that New York was no longer able to pay employees' salaries, daily operating expenses, and the debts it had incurred through the sale of bonds. The situation became so severe that New York State intervened and created an Emergency Financial Control Board (EFCB) to assume responsibility for the city's budget. Despite widespread controversy concerning the legal authority of the EFCB, the step was taken because of the exceptional nature of the crisis and the enormous ramifications should New York City go bankrupt.[23]

Why did New York find itself in such dire circumstances? There is considerable controversy concerning the causes of New York's unprecedented crisis, but several key factors have been identified.[24] In the first place, New York City had experimented with decentralizing municipal government into a number of separate agencies, and this had increased operating costs because separate management systems were required.

Second, some of the blame for the economic crisis has been placed on the shoulders of the political leadership of New York City. For example, during Mayor Lindsay's term of office, the welfare bureaucracy of the city was expanded to appease political groups in the city's ghettos. In addition, the public service unions in the city had acquired tremendous power, so that politicians seldom challenged their demands. When the unions demanded lucrative contracts, it was easier for political leaders to get another loan, increase taxes, or just let the city go a little more deeply in debt than it was for them to oppose these powerful interest groups who could bring the city to a halt through a strike by the garbage collectors or transit drivers.

Third, New York's problems were complicated by a traditional commitment of the city to provide quality services for its people—education, health services, mass transit, and cultural events. For example, the city had for many years provided a tuition-free college education to any city resident. Because of its liberal tradition, the city also had a commitment to aiding the poor through an expensive welfare program. The consequence of all of this was that New York City budget expenditures per resident were three times higher than the average expenditures per resident of the ten largest cities in the United States, and eight times higher than the average for all American cities.

Fourth, New York, like all cities, is a part of the national economy, and the recession of the 1970s along with high national inflation rates exacerbated its problems. The rise in municipal costs exceeded the increase in revenue. New York, like many other cities, has a flexible tax base—it generates a substantial part of its revenue from business and sales taxes, which are vulnerable to economic downturns (during which business and sales drop off) but which are beneficial during prosperous times. Property taxes are a more stable and less flexible form of revenue because the value of property is less drastically affected by economic slumps. When the national economy receded, New York's flexible tax base was in the worst possible position. In a sense, by their choice of a flexible rather than more stable tax base, the leaders of New York had gambled that the economic health of the nation would remain solid but lost the bet when the recession occurred.

Not all cities are in the dire circumstances in which New York finds itself. However, the New York experience illustrates exactly how vulnerable our cities are. A complex web of factors—often only vaguely understood by those who run our cities—can bring a thriving city to the brink of disaster. Furthermore, because the whole nation is dependent on these centers of commerce and industry, their downfall would have ramifications all across the nation. Because of this, the federal government, against much opposition, has agreed to provide loan guarantees so that New York can continue to borrow money in order to pay its debts and avoid bankruptcy. However, the loan guarantees are contingent on reforms in the fiscal policies of the city.

RACIAL PROBLEMS IN THE CITIES

One aspect of urban life that permeates and intensifies many social problems is the racial composition of American cities. Increasingly, a larger and larger proportion of the populace of American cities are members of minority groups. Table 3.2 illustrates this in relation to blacks. The extent to which blacks are overrepresented in cities becomes evident when one considers that blacks constitute only 11.4 percent of the population of the United States.[25] While blacks are the largest minority group in the United States, there are other sizable racial groups. In 1978, there were 12 million people of Hispanic extraction in the United States—about 5.5 percent of the population.[26] Most lived in metropolitan areas—77 percent of the Mexican Americans, 97 percent of the Puerto Ricans, and 91 percent of the others of Spanish descent.

There are other racial minorities crowded in our cities—Indians, Chinese, Filipinos, to name only a few—but their numbers are considerably smaller than those of blacks and Spanish-speaking Americans. Furthermore, although each minority group has some unique problems of its own, many of the problems of minority groups are similar. There are a number of reasons for this concentration of minority groups in our cities. As we have seen, many of them migrated to the cities in the early part of this century looking for employment. Once in the cities, they found it difficult to leave because, on the one hand, they could not afford housing in the suburbs, and on the other hand, there was blatant discrimination that made it practically impossible for them to purchase suburban housing even if they could afford it. The decentralization of cities also contributed to the changing racial composition. The affluent groups that moved to the suburbs were primarily white, leaving the cities to the poor and

TABLE 3.2
Percentage of City Population Classified Black

CITY	1950	1960	1970
Atlanta	36.6	38.3	51.3
Baltimore	23.8	35.0	46.4
Chicago	14.1	23.6	32.7
Cleveland	16.3	28.9	38.3
Detroit	16.4	29.2	43.7
New Orleans	32.0	37.4	45.0
Newark	17.2	34.4	54.2
Philadelphia	18.3	26.7	33.6
Richmond	31.7	42.0	42.0
St. Louis	18.0	28.8	40.9
Trenton	11.4	22.6	38.0
Washington	35.4	54.8	71.1

SOURCE: U.S. Bureau of the Census, *U.S. Census of Population: 1950, 1960, 1970* (Washington, D.C.: U.S. Government Printing Office).

the less affluent minority groups.

The concentration of minority groups in the cities is not a problem in itself. However, it does contribute to urban social problems in a number of ways. First, such concentration has promoted the development of "two Americas"—two separate social worlds that have little contact and little in common. One America belongs to the affluent suburbanite, mostly white, who, while certainly not wealthy, has a decent job, a comfortable home, and can look forward to a bright future. The other America consists of the poor urbanite, many of whom (but not all) belong to racial minorities, who derive their support from menial jobs or welfare payments, live in crowded and dangerous ghettos, and cannot look forward to sharing in the American dream.

The greater the separation between these two groups, the less understanding and sympathy they have for each other. The suburbanite sees the decay, crime, and poverty of the city and finds it easy to blame them on the minority-group member. If only, the suburbanite believes, they would work harder and lead a more respectable life as I have done, they could improve their lot in life. It is difficult to empathize with the problems confronting the poor without some contact with them. On the other hand, the minority-group member views the suburban whites as wealthy and powerful. It is their greed and callousness, says this poor per-

Members of urban minority groups often find themselves isolated in poorly maintained and depressing corners of the city. These people are among those most adversely affected by modern urban problems.

istics of the minority groups who make up a sizable part of the urban population. People do not see a criminal, but rather a *black* criminal; not a welfare recipient, but a *Mexican American* welfare recipient. Members of racial minorities come to be perceived as particularly lazy or prone to commit crimes. Thus, the behavior is defined as biologically caused rather than socially produced.

However, what many middle-class people define in racial and biological terms is in reality a problem of economics and social class.[27] These problems are the result of poverty, not biology. Because members of minority groups are overrepresented among the ranks of the poor, they are also more likely to commit crimes. In 1970, for example, 9 percent of the white population of the United States was classified as poor, whereas the corresponding figure among blacks was 24 percent! (See ch. 11.) Yet as long as many people believe that these problems are caused by race and not by poverty, progress toward effective solutions will be slow. Historically, poverty has been related to the problems of urban America. At the turn of the century, when Irish immigrants were the bulk of the American poor, they were the main perpetrators of crime, had the highest rates of alcoholism, and filled the unemployment roles. Today, the minority groups are the more recent immigrants to the city, have the highest rates of poverty, and, as a result, contribute most to many other urban social problems — crime, rioting, and unemployment.

Thus the racial composition of our cities is an important factor contributing to urban social problems. However, race itself is not the problem. The core difficulty is poverty, prejudice, and discrimination, which keep minority groups in such a powerless and deprived status. Furthermore, as long as the trends discussed continue, the problem will loom larger in the future and become more difficult to solve.

EDUCATION AND THE INNER CITY

We have seen that the tax base of most of our large cities is shrinking, which means that cities can no longer provide the same high level of services to

son, that stops me from sharing in their affluence. Mutual distrust and suspicion are the products of such a situation; and as long as a separation of this nature continues, the understanding of urban social problems and cooperative action to solve them will be impeded.

A second way in which the concentration of minority-group members in cities contributes to urban social problems is that it leads to a misunderstanding concerning what the source of certain problems is. Many members of the white middle class believe that the problems in our cities are caused by the inborn character-

city residents. One service that has been drastically affected by these difficulties is education. Furthermore, since education has a critical impact on many other problems, such as racial conflict and crime, it is a central concern for those interested in the problems of the city.

Historically, Americans have turned to the school systems for aid in solving numerous problems caused by social dislocations, and for the most part, the schools have responded well. Certainly the school system played the major role in Americanizing millions of immigrants and training them for absorption into a pluralistic society. Yet in the most severe crisis of the last one hundred years, the social strain created by urban problems, the schools have been slow to respond, and their responses so far have been futile.[28]

If the schools fail in their historically appointed tasks, the implications for urban life will be severe.

Many people feel that the schools should be our first weapon against the problem of poverty—the urban poor should use education as a tool, much as earlier immigrants did, to escape from poverty. However, because of the shrinking tax base, funds are limited in most cities. With less money available, school budgets do not keep pace with needs, and in most cases the urban educational system becomes inadequate as a means of upward social mobility. In contrast with most suburban schools, the inner-city school struggles with old and often dangerous buildings, less (and older) equipment, archaic educational technology, higher rates of teacher turnover, a lower quality of instructors, low staff morale, and obsolete texts.[29] There is also frequent conflict over the control of local schools. Many believe that the schools are not responsive to the specific needs of the children in the communities served by the school. There are tremendous pressures on schools to provide programs demanded by particular interest groups—remedial education programs, black studies programs, sex education, adult education, and the like.

An educational system confronted with these problems and conflicts will find it difficult to provide the motivation and training necessary for its students to become upwardly mobile. While such upward mobility is not impossible in this context—it certainly does occur—the poor student in such schools is at a tremendous disadvantage when competing for jobs or positions in universities against students who have graduated from more affluent schools. According to estimates of the United States Office of Education, 23 million adult Americans are functionally illiterate—they lack the basic reading and writing skills that are practically essential for achievement in our complex society.[30] So the escape from poverty made by earlier immigrant groups of urban poor is hampered by the shortcomings of today's inner-city schools and by the fact that upward mobility today requires more complex intellectual skills than it did seventy-five years ago. What has emerged for many students is an educational trap—a vicious circle that may perpetuate poverty.

The Educational Trap

Although education is intended to help people climb out of poverty, it sometimes has the opposite effect—the educational system helps to perpetuate conditions of poverty. This happens in a number of ways. In some cases, inner-city schools are unable, or unwilling, to accept the student's cultural background and build on those characteristics. Teachers, with middle-class backgrounds and values, expect inner-city students to show the same enthusiasm for learning and the same obedient behavior as they generally find among middle-class students. If the students do not meet the teacher's expectations—as they often do not—they may be neglected, labeled troublemakers, or sent to a special class for "slow learners." In these remedial classes, there is some effort to improve the students' educational performance, but because of a lack of money or properly trained teachers, many of these classes consist of simple custodial care during school hours.

In such a situation, one often finds a self-fulfilling prophecy—the teachers do not expect lower-class students to perform well academically, they do not encourage the students to excel in these areas, and as a consequence, the students perform at a rather low level. The students live up to the expectations

Conditions in inner-city schools often breed apathy and failure. Often, a self-fulfilling prophecy operates—urban schools expect little and the students may live up to that expectation.

inner city.[32] In order to prepare them for placement in urban schools, it has been suggested that teachers be trained much like Peace Corps volunteers, where a great deal of instruction is concentrated on learning the languages and cultural practices of the people among whom they will be working. Using this technique, school teachers would learn to understand the slang used by students. In many cases, slang comprises the bulk of their vocabulary and is important in educating them. Furthermore, teachers would take courses on inner-city subcultures to help them understand the lives of their students and how these lives affect their school performance. Such techniques might help teachers more effectively impart the verbal and vocational skills necessary for the students' successful adaptation to American culture, at the same time removing the teachers themselves from being a contributory factor to student inability to perform. In this way, the student might have a better opportunity to climb out of the cycle of poverty.

School Financing

Until recently, the major source of funds for public education has been the property tax. In poor districts, the tax base is low because the property tends to be old and dilapidated. As a consequence, poor districts have typically had less tax money available than the more affluent districts have had. Since many of the problems confronting inner-city schools stem from lack of adequate funds, one solution is to change the basis for funding education so that the amounts received by various school districts are more equitable and uniform. During the past decade, a number of state supreme courts have ruled that the use of property tax to support education is a discriminatory practice because it places the poor at a disadvantage and violates the equal protection clauses in most state constitutions. This has forced state legislatures to develop school funding plans that are more equitable. For example, California developed a program that provides every school district with monetary aid for every child in average daily attendance. In this program, a state-operated foundation guarantees that a minimum of $400 per student will be available if

the teachers and others have for them. For example, in one study, those high school students placed in noncollege preparatory programs were labeled as inferior students by both teachers and fellow students. In addition, the students in the program themselves accepted those labels.[31] Presumably, from the students' point of view, if the teachers say you are stupid, it must be true; and the student, believing this, often stops trying. Such beliefs on the part of students seem to lead to high rates of failure, uninvolvement in school activities, delinquency, and general misbehavior. Thus, the school system, through the expectations of the teachers, contributes to the failure of lower-class students in inner-city schools.

Some educational experts believe that some of these problems are due to the training most teachers receive which is inadequate for teaching in the

the taxes in a district do not equal that amount. If property taxes provide only $300, the state provides the additional $100. In addition, the state grants each district $125 per student.[33]

Through programs such as this, many of the negative effects of the use of the property tax are avoided. However, not all problems are solved. In the California program, involving as it does a state-supported minimum amount for each student and an additional flat payment per student by the state, the outcome is somewhat problematic. The $125 flat grant from the state is treated as part of the locally raised money. If a poor district raises $200 from local taxes, the flat grant is added to that before the state foundation makes up the difference between that amount and $400 (in this case, another $75; thus the district would have available a total of $400 per student). A wealthy district that can raise $400 per student from local taxes still receives the flat grant and thus has available $525 per student. So the wealthy district retains its advantage. New Jersey developed a program of using income tax revenues to improve education in low-income school districts. However, a report on that program showed that school districts of moderate wealth were receiving two-thirds of the new funds, while the poor districts in the state were receiving only 12 percent of the funds.[34] These examples from California and New Jersey illustrate that, while such financing reforms are certainly desirable, they have not eliminated the gap between rich and poor schools.

What is in store for the financing of our schools? For the immediate future, there will probably be new programs taking shape out of the clash of the many interest groups that have a stake in the outcome. Court litigation will undoubtedly continue for years concerning what types of funding are constitutional. One evaluation of various programs for alternative funding strategies showed that differences in spending between rich and poor districts have narrowed somewhat, that the poor school districts use the added funds effectively for new educational services—such as counselors, teaching aids, and the like—and that they hire new teachers to reduce class size. However, the overall effect on educational quality is as yet unknown. Nevertheless,

states have been made acutely aware that some equitable means of school financing must be developed.

School Desegregation and Busing

A condition that has existed for a substantial period, but that only in the past few decades has come to be viewed as a social problem, is segregation in our schools. School segregation is seen as having a number of serious implications. First, as was established by the Supreme Court in 1954, segregated schools are inherently unequal, and thus minority-group students would, by the very fact of being segregated, receive an inferior education. Second, minority-group schools, because they are poor and have little political clout, receive comparatively small amounts of money with which to run educational programs, and thus the educational deficiencies already mentioned are intensified. Third, segregated schools perpetuate racist attitudes that are anathema to a society that places great value on equality. To overcome these problems, school busing programs were established—the practice of busing children to schools outside their neighborhood in order to achieve some racial balance.

The Consequence of School Segregation

The busing policy was born of a study of educational opportunity in the United States mandated by Congress and undertaken by a team of social analysts headed by sociologist James S. Coleman. The report of the findings of this study became popularly known as the "Coleman Report" and has served as a basis for much social policy since then.[35] Coleman found that racial segregation in American public schools was extensive. Nearly 80 percent of all white students in the first and twelfth grades attended schools that were between 90 and 100 percent white. More than 65 percent of all black pupils in the first grade attended schools that were between 90 and 100 percent black. Furthermore, the report concluded that in every category, black students were attending schools that were educationally inferior to those attended by whites. In addition, black students were not achieving academically at the same level as other racial and ethnic groups in the public schools. Finally, the report concluded that the achievement of black students was more severely affected by poor school facilities and curricula and by badly trained teachers than was the achievement of white students. They also found that the educational background and aspirations of the other students in the school and family support for educational achievement were much more influential in the achievement of minority-group students than that of white students.[36]

School Integration and Its Consequences

Based partially on the Coleman Report, the courts began to require many American cities to integrate their schools, and in many cases busing programs were the only means of achieving this goal. In city after city, the reaction against busing has been loud and vociferous. The burning of school buses, minor rioting, demonstrations of protest, and police guarding of schools became commonplace. The busing program, which was to advance social goals of integration, conflicted with what many groups perceived to be their own individual interest. Many felt that their children's access to high-quality educational programs was being threatened. Existing racial antagonism also served to compound the conflict. From the conflict perspective, the outcome was almost inevitable. Groups formed to oppose busing and maintain the status quo in education because the educational system, as it existed, was to their benefit.

Beyond the conflict that it generated, has busing achieved its goal of improving the educational achievement of students from minority group backgrounds? Unfortunately, evaluations of the effectiveness of busing, and of integrated educational programs in general, have not been encouraging. After reviewing data from numerous studies on the subject, David Armor concludes that "None of the studies were able to demonstrate conclusively that integration has had an effect on academic achievement as measured by standardized tests."[37] In a study of the Boston busing program, Armor found that there were no increases in educational or occupational aspiration levels for bused students. In

fact, there was a *decline* in the proportion of those bused students who planned to attend college.

In addition to the lack of educational impact from busing programs, James Coleman has expressed a new concern—that desegregation programs have provided the incentive for whites to leave the city in ever larger numbers. He concludes that the end result will be a larger regional pattern of segregation between city and suburb. Some studies support his assertion. One study in Boston showed that, between 1973 and 1977, 45 percent of the white students left the rolls of the Boston Public Schools.[38] Other studies, however, see busing as having little impact on the continuing white flight. For example, one study, after controlling for other causes of white flight, concludes that there is an "implementation year effect"—white flight does increase during the first year busing is implemented—but that busing has little or no long-range impact.[39]

What are we to conclude concerning desegregation and busing? One observer comments:

Few social gains would be more significant, would better justify drastic and initially unpopular measures, than a solution, or a substantial contribution to a solution, of the nation's race or race-related problems. It does not appear, however, that compulsory integration has achieved or promises to achieve a solution. It appears, on the contrary, that the Court's attempt to compel integration is more likely to exacerbate than to ameliorate America's racial problems.[40]

This conclusion may be premature, since not all of the evidence on the issue has been gathered and evaluated. It is possible that the beneficial effects of school integration through busing will surface only after the program has been in operation for a long time. Nonetheless, the findings to date do not support the proponents of the position that school integration achieved through compulsory busing programs will significantly alleviate the educational problems of members of minority groups. In addition, school integration through busing may intensify other problems that already confront our cities —racial conflict and the flight of the affluent from the city. As the functionalist perspective makes us aware, a complex and interdependent system such as a city will be seriously shaken by a practice such as busing that has an effect on so many aspects of our lives. Whether such a disruption of the system has more beneficial than detrimental consequences remains to be seen. But it is naive to believe that such a program can be introduced without substantially changing the fabric—often in unexpected ways—of our urban areas.

Education and Social Problems

We began the discussion of education by pointing out that the historical role of schools in America has been to solve problems resulting from social disorganization. However, the extent to which one accepts this statement—and also the way one responds to the problems in urban education—depends to some extent on how one perceives education as an institution fitting into the modern world. From the functionalist perspective, schools play an important role in maintaining the social order. They are a major mechanism of socialization; they inculcate values and norms into the members of society. The schools also integrate individuals into the social order by providing them with the skills necessary to function in our society—whether these be specific vocational skills that enable one to perform important work, or social skills, such as learning how to get along with others, and how to survive in a bureaucratic society.

From this perspective, such programs as busing are to be evaluated in terms of the degree to which they enhance the achievement of these functions. Segregated schools fail at this, at least in terms of minority-group school children. On the other hand, as we have seen, it is not clear that busing has changed this situation. Nevertheless, schools and their problems are viewed, from this perspective, in terms of their effect on the integration of people into society. For many immigrant groups, schools performed this function admirably, providing them with language and vocational skills that made it possible for them to fully participate in society. However, because of a combination of factors—the severe problems of inner-city schools today and the

fact that racial prejudice is now a component of the situation—schools today seem less able to perform that function.

From the conflict perspective, schools have a quite different place in society—they are a mechanism that serves to support the status quo and those groups that benefit from existing conditions. Education is one of the primary means of social mobility today. It is the key to prestigious and high-paying jobs. Since good schools are scarce—our society is not yet willing to pay the cost of making all of our schools excellent—each group wants to ensure that its children have access to the best educational institutions. In an earlier era (and to some extent today), the wealthy were able to send their children to high-quality private schools that few could afford. This gave their children an enormous advantage in competing for jobs. In some cases, discrimination limited the access of some groups to good schools. Subordinate groups, such as blacks or Chicanos, find it difficult to enroll their children in the better schools, whether because their offspring cannot score sufficiently high on culturally biased intelligence tests or because their community does not have a tax base adequate to support quality schools. Whether intended or not, the outcome is that the middle class has access to considerably more educational resources than do the poor, so their children receive a superior education and retain their competitive advantage.

Thus, from the conflict perspective, the educational system excludes groups from effective participation in society as much as it integrates them. Whether a particular group is excluded or integrated depends on the amount of power they can bring to bear on the struggle. School integration, by busing or other means, is, then, an effort by a previously excluded group to obtain some of the rewards that can be had from the educational process. Whether it is an effective effort, remains to be seen.

HOUSING

Shelter from the elements is one of our more basic needs—and one that is becoming harder for people in urban areas to satisfy. The basic problem is how to provide *affordable* housing that meets our society's standards of acceptability, and it is a problem that affects the poor and minority groups most severely.

The quality of housing has improved for people of all income levels since World War II, and this has been accomplished without a major increase in that proportion of their income that people spend on housing.[41] However, our definitions of what is acceptable housing have changed substantially, and, by today's standards, the housing situation is still considered a severe problem. For example, when central heating and indoor plumbing were less common, lack of either was not considered a serious drawback. Today, we view such amenities as essential, and housing without them is considered substandard. If we define houses without such amenities as substandard, then in urban areas in 1970, 4.3 percent of the white population lived in substandard housing, whereas 15.2 percent of the dwellings of the black population would be so classified.[42] Much of the housing problem in urban areas is concentrated in slums or ghettos, and it is with these that we will begin our discussion.

The Ghetto

When we think about the worst social and physical conditions that exist in a city, we almost automatically think of the slum or ghetto. The term ghetto was originally used to designate that part of European cities to which Jews were restricted. Today, *ghetto* is used more broadly to refer to any part of a city in which the members of some ethnic or racial group live or are restricted; most often it is a poor and isolated area inhabited predominantly by the minority groups of the city. In the early 1900s in America, the Jews and Italians were among the dominant ghetto residents; today, blacks and Spanish-speaking Americans are predominant.

Why do slums exist in our cities? One reason was given by an angry slum resident to a group of politicians and civic leaders viewing abandoned buildings in a slum in New York:

You want to know who caused this? . . . Ask the goddam landlords who cut down maintenance and ser-

vices as soon as the first blacks and Puerto Ricans moved into the neighborhood. Ask the owners who let their buildings go to hell while putting every penny of the rent money into their pockets or the stock market. Ask the city officials who don't give a shit, who let the owners collect their rents and milk the buildings till there was nothing left to squeeze out of them.[43]

On the other side of this issue, a representative of the landlords had this explanation of the reason for the deterioration and abandonment of buildings in the slum:

That's right, put it all on the landlord. . . . Never mind that rent control in this city doesn't give landlords enough income to keep up their buildings. Never mind that some of these families break the place up and you have to go through hell and high water to evict them — and meanwhile you're getting hit with violations because of the damage they do. Never mind that you can drop dead begging and you still won't get a bank loan to fix up a building in a neighborhood like this. My friend, you don't *begin* to know why these buildings have been abandoned.[44]

This confrontation illustrates the complex nature of the problem of inner-city housing. Whatever its causes, all would agree that the abandonment of buildings in the inner city is a fairly common occurrence and a very serious problem. It has been estimated that between 1960 and 1969 in New York City alone more than 105,000 housing units were abandoned.[45] The tragedy is that housing, especially low-cost housing, is in dangerously short supply. The Department of Housing and Urban Development (HUD) presently holds title to 250,000 houses obtained when their owners defaulted on FHA loans.[46] These abandoned dwelling units, if refurbished and put back into use, might serve as an important source of housing, especially given that the population of the United States is expected to grow to nearly 300 million by the year 2025. Should this increase occur, and there is little reason to believe that it will not, we shall have to build the equivalent of 75 cities of 1 million population capacity to house these people. This would mean building about 25 cities the size of Chicago or 75 cities the size of Baltimore—a task of monumental proportions. In the next section, we will discuss a number of federal programs that have been developed to cope with the related problems of providing sufficient housing and replacing substandard housing.

Federal Housing Policy

Insured Mortgage Loans

As we mentioned earlier, one of the earliest housing policies was the National Housing Act of 1937, which encouraged the construction of new housing by providing federal insurance for mortgages on new homes. While this increased the number of housing units available to people, it did not deal with the problem of deteriorating inner-city housing, and in fact it exacerbated that problem. Since the program worked through private mortgage lenders, the housing constructed was the type for which they preferred to lend money—new, single-family dwellings, rather than the renovation of existing dwellings. They also preferred to lend to young middle-class people rather than to the old or the poor. The impact of the policy was to finance the construction of new houses in outlying residential areas of cities or in the suburbs and to ignore the inner city. In addition, the policy inadvertently encouraged increasing segregation in urban areas because the lenders preferred white customers and these white borrowers preferred to move to segregated neighborhoods.[47]

Urban Renewal

Urban renewal was initiated by the Housing Act of 1949. Its major purpose was to rehabilitate slum areas and provide low-cost housing for the inner-city poor. Urban renewal agencies were established to purchase slum properties, destroy the buildings on them, and then sell the property to private developers. In many cases, the private developers simply constructed the most financially rewarding buildings on the property—office buildings and luxury apartment houses. This intensified the housing problem of the poor since deteriorating buildings were torn down but replaced with nothing that the

poor could afford. In fact, during its first twenty years of existence, urban renewal tore down over twice as many housing units as it constructed.[48]

In those cases in which new housing for the poor was actually constructed, the consequences were often disastrous. Huge "projects" were constructed that housed dense concentrations of people, all of whom were poor. The "projects" were highly visible and very much stigmatized. People who had the resources to live elsewhere did so, and thus the people who filled the projects were those with the most serious social and personal problems, the fewest resources of any sort, and a history of living in poverty. Since neither the residents nor the project managers had the motivation or the resources to maintain the property, these projects deteriorated rapidly.

One project that illustrates the sad results of these problems was the Pruitt-Igoe complex in St. Louis, completed in 1955. Designed to house low-income families in suitable quarters, it soon became a "vertical ghetto" consisting of thirty-three eleven-story buildings. In addition to the problems just mentioned, Pruitt-Igoe had design and organizational problems that doomed it to failure. Garbage disposal was available only on the first floor. Elevators stopped on every third floor, necessitating for most residents a walk down dark stairs and hallways to reach their apartment. The hallways became a haven for criminals, and there was a high incidence of rapes, muggings, and assaults. The residents saw the projects as demeaning and dehumanizing. Needless to say, anyone who was able to do so left Pruitt-Igoe as quickly as possible. In 1972, the situation had deteriorated so badly that the housing authority dynamited the two worst buildings and removed the top seven stories of all the others, hoping to make them more manageable. This explosive surgery was ineffective, and the remainder of Pruitt-Igoe was demolished in 1973.[49]

With the failure of Pruitt-Igoe and other similar projects, the thrust of urban renewal has changed. Rather than attempting to provide low-cost housing for the poor, the effort today is toward rebuilding the central city so that it is an attractive and enjoyable place to be. Downtown commercial districts are being beautified; mall areas with

The Pruitt-Igoe public housing project in St. Louis was an example of the government's attempt to provide low-cost housing. Problems of crime and violence were rampant in the project, and in 1971, most of its 35 buildings were vacant.

Problems in the Pruitt-Igoe project were so severe that selective demolition was ordered in 1972 to improve conditions, with little success.

trees and fountains—pleasant places to shop and lounge—are being constructed. However, none of these programs has solved the problems of housing for the poor. On the contrary, urban renewal has resulted in a reduction in the number of housing units available to the poor in the United States.

Government Aid in Housing

We have observed that the Department of Housing and Urban Development holds title to 250,000 housing units. While this figure is small compared to our future needs, it is still significant. Some communities have developed programs to utilize these and other abandoned housing units. **Urban Homesteading refers to programs that make housing available to the poor at little or no cost with the provision that they live in, and make certain specified improvements on, the property.** The government takes possession of a house or building (usually due to nonpayment of mortgage or property taxes), and the house is listed in a public notice. Persons of low income who wish to own their own home may apply for possession, and the owner is determined through a drawing. The new owner, who typically pays one dollar for the house, is required to live in the building for a specified period and to make improvements required by the local building code.

This type of program involves two goals: it offers an opportunity for low-income people to own a home, and it preserves existing homes and neighborhoods. In many cases, the Urban Homesteading program has been successful in achieving these goals. A recent HUD report concludes that it will prove to be a promising tool for providing housing for the poor and rehabilitating urban neighborhoods.[50] However, in some cities, the program has failed in part due to a banking practice called redlining.[51] **Redlining refers to the identification of a neighborhood by a bank as a high-risk area and the refusal of the bank to lend money for purposes of buying or improving a building in that area (a red line drawn around the district on a map gave birth to the term).** Where redlining has been practiced, the new owners of housing have not been able to bor-

row the necessary funds to make improvements on their property. Because funds are not available, the neighborhoods are not maintained, and deterioration continues. Banks justify the practice as a business necessity because, they argue, experience has taught them that concentrations of minority groups and the poor in old residential neighborhoods result in high risks and unpaid loans. Some states are now attempting to enact legislation outlawing such procedures on the grounds that they unfairly discriminate against property owners in redlined neighborhoods who are capable of paying off a loan.

The Dynamics of Land Use

As with education, it is helpful in understanding the urban housing situation to view it from our three theoretical perspectives. In this way, some of the issues associated with these problems and the programs to solve them can be highlighted. From the functionalist perspective, urban land should be used for that purpose for which it is best suited. One central element of any land use decision must be economic considerations. Land in or near the center of the city is expensive and should be used by those persons or for those activities that can use it most intensively and productively.[52] The functionalist perspective would view this as a normal outcome of the nature of the social system. High-revenue-producing activities would have access to the most desirable locations because they could afford the high cost of operating in those areas. In addition, this economic competition for land would result in such areas being put to a use that is beneficial to society, such as providing jobs and services.

From the conflict perspective, on the other hand, land use results from the clash of interest groups over control of desirable pieces of property. The outcome, while attractive to some groups, may not be beneficial to society as a whole. For example, people living in a purely residential area may wage a stiff battle against the establishment of a business in their neighborhood. This conflict may result from a number of concerns such as the impact the business may have on the quality of life in the area or the effect it may have on property values. The resulting conflict between the residents and business representatives can be viewed as a struggle over a desirable yet scarce commodity—attractive land—and the group with the greatest resources will undoubtedly prevail. For example, when the University of Chicago decided to expand its facilities into the low-income residential area called Woodlawn, the neighborhood residents resisted the expansion and called on the services of Saul Alinsky, an experienced and well-known community organizer. After a long and bitter struggle, the university relented, and the neighborhood residents retained their control over the use of the land. In this case, the neighbors' power to make this large and prestigious university back down derived from very effective organization and very capable leadership by Alinsky.[53]

The functionalist and conflict perspectives tend to emphasize economic concerns, but there is more to land use than this. The interactionist perspective sensitizes us further to a consideration of the impact of symbols and sentiment.[54] Land takes on a symbolic importance and meaning for certain groups, which can dictate the uses to which it will be put. For example, in the heart of downtown Boston is the Boston Common—a 48-acre area with historical significance to the city. The fondness of Bostonians for this otherwise prime economic site has ruled out its commercial development and exploitation. In other words, our emotional attachment to the symbolic importance of land can override any logic dictated by purely economic considerations.

TRANSPORTATION AND THE CITY

Anyone who lives in an urban area is reminded daily of the extent to which cities are dependent on adequate transportation. Traffic congestion is a fact of life in almost all cities. The older industrial cities of the east and midwest were simply not built to carry large amounts of traffic on their streets, and the streets cannot be widened in most cases because all available land is occupied by buildings and sidewalks. As a consequence, there is much

heavier dependence on public transit in these cities. The newer cities of the south and west have wider streets and lower population density, but their spread-out nature makes them even more dependent on the private automobile, so that congestion on freeways and city streets is still quite common (see Table 3.3).

TABLE 3.3

Transportation by Workers in American Cities

I. Number of people using various types of transportation to get to work in urban areas

TYPE	NUMBER OF PEOPLE	PERCENTAGE OF TOTAL
Automobile	44,835,000	77
Bus/streetcar	4,116,000	7
Subway/elevated train	1,762,000	3
Railroad	473,000	less than 1
Taxicab	278,000	less than 1
Walk	4,505,000	8
Other Means	1,117,000	2
(Worked at home)	1,082,000	2

II. Percentage of workers using public transit in selected cities, 1970

CITY	PERCENTAGE
New York	61.8
Boston	39.3
Chicago	36.2
Minneapolis	19
Los Angeles	9.3
Houston	7.8
San Diego	5.5

SOURCE. U.S. Bureau of the Census, *Statistical Abstract of the United States: 1977* (Washington, D.C.: U.S. Government Printing Office, 1977), pp. 644–646.

Modes of Transportation

One major issue in the problem of urban transportation is which mode of transportation is effective and appropriate for urban areas. The major controversy is between the automobile and some form of mass transit. The issue is not over which should be eliminated, but rather what combination can meet the needs of a particular city.

The Automobile

The automobile has many very positive qualities: it is private, it is fast (barring traffic jams), and it is flexible (not limited to a specific, predetermined route). The automobile is also generally more comfortable and convenient, and the driver is not limited by the schedules of mass transit. Today, most travel in American cities is accomplished by private automobile. For example, 77 percent of all trips from home to work are made by car (see Table 3.3). Our dependence on the automobile can be underscored by the fact that, while we constitute only 6 percent of the world's population, we own over 50 percent of the world's cars.[55]

Despite its advantages, our use of the automobile is very costly in several respects. One cost is economic. Expressway construction, for example, costs over $3 million per mile for four lanes in the open countryside, and in the urban areas the figure is $5 million per mile *per lane*. Between 1947 and 1970, the total expenditures on highway construction by federal, state, and local governments was $249 billion. Another cost, of which we are becoming increasingly aware, is energy use. The automobile is very inefficient—approximately 80 percent of a car's energy intake is blown out the exhaust pipe.[56] A third cost is related to the vertical expansion of cities. As multistoried skyscrapers are

built with thousands of employees, enormous numbers of automobiles must converge on the city—creating congestion and raising noise levels—in order for people to get to work.

Mass Transportation

Public transportation has not fared well in the United States against the onslaught of the automobile. While some cities have high rates of public transit usage, in many other cities it is quite low (see Table 3.3). In 1950, there were 1406 public transit systems in operation in the United States. By 1976, this had dwindled to 955.[57] However, in the last decade, there has been substantial new construction of rail rapid transit. The BART system in San Francisco and the METRO system in Washington, D.C. are now in operation, and new systems are currently under construction in Atlanta, Baltimore, and Dade County (Miami), Florida. With increasing problems of congestion, pollution, and the energy shortage, there has been a renewed interest in different forms of mass transit.

Although most people still cling to the automobile as their major means of transportation, there is evidence that mass transportation is more

The Bay Area Rapid Transit System in San Francisco is often considered a model for new mass transportation systems. Despite its presence, many residents still prefer to travel by automobile, and traffic congestion and pollution persist as environmental problems.

economical. The costs of transportation can be viewed from either an individual or a collective point of view. For individuals, mass transit involves an immediate expense each time it is used—you have to reach into your pocket or purse each time you board the subway or bus. The visibility of that payment makes it seem costly, especially when gasoline is a once-a-week expense that may well involve the use of a credit card rather than cash. The car almost seems free to operate. But when one considers depreciation (several hundred dollars per year), fuel costs (which are rising each year), insurance, and maintenance, the cost of that private mode of transportation is considerable. In 1977, the average cost to operate an automobile was 31 cents per mile.[58] For the individual, then, most mass transit competes favorably if all costs are carefully taken into account. From a collective perspective, mass transit is also relatively economical. A single set of rapid transit tracks can carry 60,000 passengers per hour. It would require twenty lanes of freeway to carry an equal amount of people and, given the cost of highway construction, would be much more expensive. The BART system costs 19.5 cents per mile per passenger to operate, and this includes both the cost of operation and the payment of construction debts. With rising costs of energy, mass transit also makes economic sense. One rapid transit car can produce up to 640 passenger miles on the electrical equivalent of one gallon of diesel fuel. So in terms of the cost to society as a whole, mass transit is presently more economical than the automobile.[59]

Public Transportation and Public Needs

Most existing public transportation systems operated by local municipalities do not satisfy the needs of many urban residents. In most urban areas of the United States, 20 percent of the families do not own cars. They are completely dependent on public transportation to move them around the city, and the majority of these families comprise racial minorities, the elderly, and the handicapped.[60] In many cities, the needs of these people are not adequately served. Most public transportation falls into two patterns. The first is the bus

system, which circulates through the central business district; it it used by people moving around within this district. The second pattern runs from the downtown area to residential neighborhoods and sometimes the suburbs. However, in many cities this latter system is not very comprehensive, and the poor, who must rely on it, are forced to wait a long time for buses and to put up with lengthy rides to their destination. In addition, there is often little or no public transportation to locations in the suburbs where jobs are available. If a person does not have a car, those suburban jobs are largely out of reach.

Why have the needs of the poor been ignored? The conflict perspective can provide insight here. Much of the political pressure for mass transit comes from the merchants of the central business district. They would like to see their monopoly of accessibility restored, along with the accompanying revenue, by running mass transit lines from the affluent residential suburbs to the central business district. They have the resources and organization to be heard, and they usually succeed in their efforts. The poor, who need public transit systems, are ignored because they have few resources and limited access to the political system.[61]

The need for improved public transportation is critical if our cities are to remain desirable places to live and work. The government has responded to this need through programs to encourage cities to develop mass transit systems. Between 1965 and 1974, federal funding for mass transit increased 1700 percent, but this represents only a small part of federal transportation expenditures. In 1979, the federal government spent about $9 billion for highway construction and maintenance. Urban transit, on the other hand, received $2.8 billion in federal funds, plus $660 million for Amtrak.[62] However, the cost of building new systems is high, and it takes much time before a new system can be put into operation. For example, it cost over $25 million per mile to build the BART system in San Francisco, and it took more than 10 years to begin operation of the system. Some critics have argued that urban planners are pushing rail rapid transit in situations where other systems, such as buses, would be more desirable. These critics argue that cities become enamored with elaborate technology and space-age hardware and ignore simpler and less expensive alternatives.[63]

The critical problem for any public transportation system is to convince people to leave their cars home and to use mass transportation. For many people, the automobile still has many advantages that make it a more desirable form of transportation. When BART was being planned, motorists were asked if they supported the creation of a new mass transit system. The drivers responded with an enthusiastic yes, but when asked if they would use it, they tended to say no. Some implied that what they wanted was to get all the other drivers off the freeway so that they could have it to themselves. In the final analysis, transportation is a consumer commodity that must have the features that will make it acceptable to those who might patronize it.

FUTURE PROSPECTS: THE POLITICS OF URBAN LIFE

It should be clear to the student of urban problems that solutions are not easy to find, because the problems are so complex. In addition, there are numerous competing interest groups that perceive their goals as achievable through some programs and threatened by others. Nonetheless, there are a number of efforts under way to attack some of the problems that we have discussed. We can divide these programs into those initiated by the federal government and those that focus on regional planning (although federal funds may still be used).

Federal Programs

We have observed that certain economic difficulties lie at the core of many urban problems and that one important source of these economic problems is the flight of people and industries to the suburbs. To contend with these problems, many cities have turned to the federal government for assistance. We have already seen that urban renewal programs had as their goal the luring of middle-class people and the revenue they represent back into the city. City governments have sought increased funds for educational programs, job training, and other areas. City politicians have turned to Washington to provide solutions for their growing problems. In addition to the programs already discussed, two current efforts will illustrate the kind of aid that the federal government is providing to alleviate social problems in cities.

Community Development Block Grant Program

In 1974, the block grant program for community development (CDBG) was established.[64] It combined a number of previously established federal assistance programs: urban renewal, model cities, water and sewer facilities, open spaces, neighborhood facilities, rehabilitation loans, and public facility loans. The CDBG provides cities with a block of funds with relatively few strings attached. The goals of the program, which are extremely broad, include:

1. Elimination of slums
2. Conservation of our nation's neighborhoods and houses
3. Expansion and improvement of community services
4. Reduction of the isolation of low income groups
5. Provision of housing opportunities for the poor in more parts of urban areas
6. Restoration and preservation of properties of special value
7. Expansion of economic opportunities for low- and moderate-income groups

In order to obtain CDBG funds, a city must submit an application, including a three-year community development plan. Funds are then allocated on the basis of a complex formula that takes into account population size, the amount of poverty, and the extent of overcrowded housing. There is tremendous competition for these funds—by cities in dire need as well as those of substantial affluence. Under the criteria mentioned, a city with no overcrowded housing would still qualify for funds if it had a population of more than 50,000. While it seems ludicrous to provide federal funds for cities that do not have the problems the program is intended to solve, compromises were made during the legislative process to gain support to pass the programs. By broadening the criteria so that more cities, even those without serious problems, would benefit, the chance of congressional approval of the program was increased. The feeling seemed to be that a poor program was better than none.

The CDBG is no panacea. Because the funds are spread around in this fashion, the size of the grant in many cities is probably inadequate to realize the goals of the program. For example, in 1980, Hartford, Connecticut will receive $3.3 million and Jackson, Mississippi $4 million. While something positive will undoubtedly emerge from the funds in these communities, they will not be able to *solve* the problems they face.

Nonetheless, the CDBG program is an improvement over past efforts. It does channel some funds into cities with serious problems. It gives each city great flexibility in determining what its most serious problems are and how it will use its funds. It encourages citizen participation in the development of urban programs, and the CDBG funds have served as a lever by which some cities have been able to secure private funds or other federal funds. Furthermore, both the Ford and the Carter administrations have made proposals to change the allocation formula to ensure that cities with the greatest need will receive a larger proportion of the funds allocated.

Revenue Sharing

Revenue sharing is a program established by the federal government in 1972 to return to states and cities some of the tax dollars collected by the federal government. From January 1977 to September 1980 revenue sharing averaged $6.8 billion per year, but amounts received by different states vary. For example, in 1977 Mississippi received $42.86 per person ($100.5 million) while Florida received $24.43 per person ($204.1 million). Funds to cities also vary greatly, with New York City receiving $37.95 per person compared to San Diego's $10.99 per person.[65] The amount allocated is based on a formula that takes into account levels of personal income in a community and the relative weight of the local tax burden.

Just how effective the revenue sharing program

is remains to be seen. At present, a number of problems in the program have led some people to become disillusioned. To date, most of the spending under the revenue sharing program has been for public safety and public transportation programs. This emphasis is due to a number of restrictions that were written into the initial legislation. For example, cities were prohibited from using any revenue sharing funds for education. In 1977, Congress amended the program, removing all restrictions on the way funds could be spent by the cities. In some cities, rather than supplementing existing urban improvement programs, revenue sharing funds have been used to replace them. So the extent to which revenue sharing money is used as an additional resource to attack serious social problems is unknown.

Regional Planning and Cooperation

Most cities have recognized the need for planning in order to cope with the problems of our urban environment. The concept of urban planning is not new. However the widespread use of planning in the United States has emerged only in the past few decades, and it is fraught with so many difficulties that its benefits at this point have been modest.

Urban Planning

Most planning is designed to avoid the mistakes of past growth and to make the city a more pleasant place to live. Planners usually seek to avoid: the continuous development of land stretching from one community to the next without a break; the location of industry, with its pollution and noise, near residential neighborhoods; the glut of automobile traffic, which chokes many of our streets; and the separation of income groups within the city, which makes us strangers and sometimes enemies to each other. Some planners go so far as to assert that, through careful design, they can eliminate most of the crime, poverty, and human suffering that exist in our cities today—an ambitious claim and a goal probably unattainable by urban planning alone.

It is possible for urban planning to inadvertently benefit one group to the detriment of others. Urban planners tend to represent a specific group—

namely, the middle class—in their approach to urban design. Many planners see the less attractive working class districts of many of our older cities as undesirable environments. Often, a viable neighborhood will be classified as a slum when in fact it serves needed purposes, such as providing livable low-cost housing, shops that cater to a less affluent clientele, and recreational opportunities for children in the form of an abundant supply of vacant lots. As a result, urban designs should be examined to ensure that the interests of *all* urban residents are taken into account and not just those of some special interest group.

There are some planning concepts used in recent years that show considerable promise for the future. Let us consider two such programs.

New Towns

Some planners have proposed that we should plan totally new communities that anticipate human needs and desires rather than allow our existing cities to grow in an imperfectly controlled fashion. The *new towns* concept has been employed in Europe since the turn of the century, but it has only been in the last two decades that this plan has been considered in the United States. Perhaps the best-known example of the new town in the United States is Columbia, Maryland, located between Baltimore and Washington, D.C.

Planning for Columbia took eighteen months. During that time, a basic plan was created and the future of the community was determined. Construction began in 1966, and by 1978 the population had reached 43,000. By 1981, the total population of 110,000, which the plan provided for, may be reached.[66]

When it is completed, Columbia will consist of a complex of seven separate villages. Each village will contain three to four neighborhoods with a combined population of about 15,000 residents. Each village will contain stores, elementary schools, a high school, and recreational facilities. The community is unified by a central district containing offices, movie theaters, a hospital, restaurants, a shopping center, and a community college. Employment is provided by two industrial parks located on one edge of the community.

One drawback to Columbia is that its residents are uniformly affluent and middle class. While this new community does provide a sense of the "good life" for its inhabitants, the poor are left behind in the central city, and the division between the poor and the well-to-do is retained. This new town has not solved any of the basic problems of urban life but has simply insulated a few people from their effects. As Irving Lewis Allen commented,

Ideally, new towns should be relatively small, manageable, and workable microcosms of the metropolitan community with all its age, class, ethnic, and racial heterogeneity and, yes, its share of responsibility for the attendant social problems. But almost all commercial new town proposals, because of high housing costs and also because of the perceived tastes of prospective house buyers, cater to homogeneous segments of the population, middle-class people in the child-bearing and rearing years. The sense of community that is so dear to the planners is a result of this homogeneity. In this and other ways new town developers promote those amenities that are wrought by homogeneity, not pluralism.[67]

Allen believes that the commercial new town is an attempt to redeem the Suburban Dream, which has gone sour. Perhaps this is true, but the European experience with new towns has been more promising. One factor separating the American and European new town programs is sponsorship. American new towns are supported by private capital—they are ventures designed to profit the developer. The risks that might aid in the achievement of social goals are seldom taken, and the result is stable, affluent communities. In Europe, on the other hand, new towns are typically governmental endeavors, where profit is not the primary concern. As such, they have provided a broad economic mix, and if there is any complaint to be made it is that the new towns, especially in England, are overly represented by the working class.

Metropolitan Government

A report from the National Research Council concludes that:

The present system of local governments fails to answer the needs of a clearly metropolitan society.

Fragmented and overlapping government in metropolitan areas (1) aggravates the mismatch between resources and social needs, (2) makes the solution of metropolitan social problems more difficult, and (3) inhibits efficient administration of services.[68]

Some of the problems of our large metropolitan areas are the result of a highly fragmented governmental structure. In the New York metropolitan area alone there are over 1500 separate governmental units, consisting of city governments, county governments, fire protection districts, school districts, police jurisdictions, and the like. Since these units tend to operate independently and duplicate services, they cost a great deal to maintain, and they operate with decreased efficiency. Furthermore, there is no central body that can make decisions that are in the interests of the whole metropolitan area. Some have proposed the development of *metropolitan government* — a political institution that has jurisdiction over the whole metropolitan area and that consolidates competing and overlapping government services. If the suburbs, with their high tax base, and the city, with its other resources, joined to provide one overall unit of metropolitan areawide government, better and cheaper services would result. Why, then, is this not being done?

Linking government units in a metropolitan area is not easily accomplished. Most residents of the suburbs live there by choice; they wanted to escape from the city and its problems, and they believe they have been successful. The suburbanite is reluctant to join efforts with the city owing to the fear that the city will take over. Many central cities that were once in favor of metropolitan government are now also coming out in opposition to it, but for different reasons than those of the suburbanites. Minority groups, which have been in a largely powerless position for decades, are now becoming an influential segment of the urban population. With their increasing numbers has come an increase in their power in city government. The emergence of this new urban power base has been accompanied by the fear that if a metropolitan government were formed, the more affluent white suburbanites would dilute the power of minorities over urban political institutions resulting in a loss of influence for the minority populations.[69] With both the city and the suburbs opposed to a broader metropolitan government, is any effort in this direction likely to emerge? Let us look at two possibilities.

One form of metropolitan government that has been proposed is the *metropolitan federation*, modeled after the structure of the federal and state governments. One governmental body would make legislation in areas that affected the whole region, while smaller governmental units (e.g. existing cities and towns) would have jurisdiction over issues of local concern. This has seldom been considered seriously because few existing political units are willing to give some of their sovereignty to another group.

An alternative model for metropolitan government is sometimes referred to as *metropolitan cooperation*. This system consists of a council made up of representatives from the various governmental units in the metropolitan area (see Table 3.4); it meets to discuss common problems and possible solutions. This procedure has been more popular than the metropolitan federation because there is no change in local government — local units retain their autonomy and are not obliged to follow any decisions made by the council. If a decision is determined to be harmful to the interests of one of the units, that unit need not cooperate. As a result, this form of metropolitan government cannot provide the kind of careful planning and financial organization that is needed, but at least it provides a forum to discuss mutual problems, and some progress is possible.

TABLE 3.4
Metropolitan Areas in Which Some Form of Metropolitan Cooperation Is Functioning

Indianapolis/Marion County (Ind.)
Miami/Dade County (Fla.)
Jacksonville/Duval County (Fla.)
Nashville/Davidson County (Tenn.)
Portland/Multnomah County (Oreg.)
Seattle/King County (Wash.)

SOURCE. Leon Sager, "UNIGOV — Piecing Together City Government," *Mainliner* (June 1974), pp. 27–29.

If some sort of effective regional cooperation were developed, it might increase the likelihood that workable solutions to some urban social problems could be established. Because the interests of each government unit so often compete with one another, policies that are beneficial to one unit are sometimes detrimental to another. Each unit tends to look out for its own interests rather than the overall interests of the metropolitan area. For example, the flight of industry and middle-class people to the suburbs might be slowed if some metropolitan government, through *regional* zoning laws or property tax rates, had the authority to control where, and to what extent, industry or new housing could develop. If such flight were controlled, the deterioration of the central cities might be halted. However, until some sort of metropolitan cooperation emerges, our urban areas will remain a series of competing groups, each looking out for its own interests, with no coordinated plan of urban growth.

Should We Save Our Cities?

In looking at the many problems of the city, some people feel that the city—as the hub of commerce, industry, and culture—has outlived its usefulness and that extensive efforts to retain it as the center of such activities should be abandoned. Such a policy has many implications. Enormous amounts of money and other resources were utilized in the construction of our cities, and to duplicate that effort to provide small towns, shopping districts, residential areas, and industrial places of work in other locations would be beyond the ability of any nation—if the goal were to accomplish the change within a reasonable time period.

Our cities are also relatively efficient users of our dwindling energy resources. By creating high-density areas, we have reduced the need to expend large amounts of energy in transportation over large distances to get people together. Because of the high concentration of people, it is only in cities that certain economically marginal, but nonetheless essential, facilities can be supported— museums, opera houses, art galleries, symphony halls, and medical research centers find more resources available in cities. At present, few if any suburbs or small towns have the means to support such activities. Nonetheless, the student should consider the possibility that the role performed by our cities may be somewhat different in the future. While cities will undoubtedly remain important, they will also, without doubt, find themselves competing with suburban areas, new towns, and rural communities for their share of the occupational and cultural attractions provided by our society.

CONCLUSION

The problems that confront our cities today— crime, congestion, financial decline, and the like— at times appear so massive and overpowering that it is tempting to despair of ever finding adequate solutions. In fact, some have responded by abandoning the city rather than searching for workable solutions. Others are trying to rekindle pride in their cities in an effort to stop or reverse the flow of people from the city to the suburbs. Which group (if either) will eventually prove to have the workable solution we will not know for some time. Nonetheless, it is useful to return to the three theoretical perspectives in order to evaluate some of these future possibilities.

For the functionalist, interrelationships and interdependence are the central social processes with which we must concern ourselves. Conditions become social problems when they disrupt, or threaten to disrupt, the fragile network of urban life. Solutions to social problems must also take into account this interrelated character of social life. Thus, we noted some of the problems that exist in education in urban areas: poorly trained teachers, outmoded equipment, and a lack of financial resources. In addition, racial segregation in urban schools creates numerous difficulties. It would seem reasonable, then, to make resources available to inner-city schools and to eliminate the segregation which has detrimental effects. Yet, we saw that busing, as a means of reducing segregation, may create other problems. This illustrates the extent to which any major change has ramifications for other parts of the system.

The conflict perspective provides a very different view of urban problems and their solutions. Since the basic social process is the struggle over scarce resources and the exercise of power, conflict and tension are quite normal. What happens in urban areas depends on which groups have sufficient resources to ensure that their policies are enacted into law. Solutions to social problems must then be evaluated in terms of the feasibility of bringing them to fruition. If powerful interest groups oppose some alternative, then it is probably not realistic to consider it unless equally powerful groups are in favor of it. Furthermore, the likelihood of enacting some solution would be enhanced if influential groups came to perceive it as in their own interests and could be encouraged to support it. For example, the revitalization of the inner city may come about if influential people are convinced to move back into the city. This is actually happening in some cities where, through programs such as urban homesteading, young and affluent people are finding it desirable once again to live in the city. This return of affluent young professionals to the city has been called the "gentrification" of the city. When they return to the city, it is in their interest to support programs that benefit the inner city: better schools, better transportation, and the like. Furthermore, these middle-class groups have the political skills and economic resources to struggle successfully with other groups, whereas the poor and minority groups who had been left in the city by the flight to the suburbs have few such skills and resources. Thus we may see an alliance between these two very different groups who now find themselves equally affected by the ills that confront our urban areas.

When we adopt the interactionist perspective, we begin to realize that some urban problems are problems only in a relative sense—they are problems compared to the standards of acceptability that people establish. Conditions have improved substantially in our cities over the past century: schools, housing, and the like are far superior to what they once were. Yet, people compare their situation not to how things were in the past but rather to how they fare relative to what is possible today. Our standards of acceptability in housing and schools are much higher than in the past—and this is one sign of progress. However, it also makes us aware that urban conditions are likely to continue to be defined as a social problem if they lag behind the rising expectations of urban residents.

GLOSSARY TERMS

Class consciousness
Decentralization
Division of labor
Ghetto
Metropolitan cooperation

Metropolitan federation
Metropolitan government
Redlining
Relative deprivation

Revenue sharing
Urban homesteading
Urban place
Urban renewal

REFERENCES

[1] Amos Hawley, *Urban Society* (New York: Ronald Press, 1971).

[2] William H. Wilson. *Coming of Age: Urban America 1915–1945* (New York: John Wiley & Sons, 1974).

[3] Ibid.

[4] Ibid., p. 9.

[5] Ibid., p. 12.

[6] George Rogers Taylor, "The Beginnings of Mass Transportation in Urban America," *The Smithsonian Journal of History* 1 (Summer 1966), pp. 35–50.

[7] Ibid.

[8] Wilson, *Coming of Age,* p. 49.

[9] Glen E. Holt, "The Changing Perception of Urban Pathology," in Kenneth T. Jackson and Stanley K. Schultz, eds., *Cities in American History* (New York: Alfred A. Knopf, 1972), pp. 324–343.

[10] Stanley K. Schultz, "Breaking the Chains of Poverty: Public Education in Boston, 1800–1860," in Jackson and Schultz, eds., *Cities in American History,* pp. 306–323.

[11] Ibid., p. 307.

[12] See Karl Marx, *Manifesto of the Communist Party* (Chicago: Charles H. Kerr, 1888).

[13] Edward C. Banfield, *The Unheavenly City Revisited* (Boston: Little, Brown, 1974).

[14] See Emile Durkheim, *The Division of Labor in Society,* George Simpson, trans. (New York: The Free Press, 1933); and Louis Wirth, "Urbanism as a Way of Life," *American Journal of Sociology* 44 (July 1938), pp. 1–24.

[15] Wirth, "Urbanism as a Way of Life"; and Georg Simmel, "The Metropolis and Mental Life," in Kurt H. Wolff, ed., *The Sociology of Georg Simmel* (New York: The Free Press, 1950), pp. 635–640.

[16] Simmel, "The Metropolis and Mental Life," pp. 635–640.

[17] See James W. Vander Zanden, *Social Psychology* (New York: Random House, 1977), pp. 325–330.

[18] Banfield, *The Unheavenly City Revisited.*

[19] Hawley, *Urban Society.*

[20] Banfield, *The Unheavenly City Revisited.*

[21] J. John Palen, *The Urban World* (New York: McGraw-Hill, 1975).

[22] Karen Gerard, "The Locally Inspired Fiscal Crisis," *Society* 13 (May/June 1976), pp. 33–35.

[23] Joel E. Cohen, "The Limits of State Intervention in a Municipal Fiscal Crisis," *Fordham Urban Law Journal* 4 (1976), pp. 545–563.

[24] See Roger Frieland, Frances Fox Piven, and Robert R. Alford, *Comparing Public Policy: New Approaches and Methods* (Beverly Hills, Calif.: Sage Publications, 1977); Susan S. Fainstein and Norman I. Fainstein, "The Federally Inspired Fiscal Crisis," *Society* 13 (May/June 1976), pp. 27–32; Gerard, "The Locally Inspired Fiscal Crisis," pp. 33–35; and Terry Clark and Lorna Ferguson, "Fiscal Strain and Fiscal Health in American Cities" (paper presented at the Annual Meetings of the American Sociological Association, Chicago, 1977).

[25] U.S. Bureau of the Census, *Current Population Reports,* Series P-25 (Washington, D.C.: U.S. Government Printing Office, 1977).

[26] U.S. Bureau of the Census, *Statistical Abstract of the United States, 1977* (Washington, D.C.: U.S. Government Printing Office, 1977), p. 30; and "Its Your Turn in the Sun," *Time,* (October 16, 1978), p. 48.

[27] Banfield, *The Unheavenly City Revisited.*

[28] Daniel U. Levin, "The Crisis in Urban Education," in Melvin I. Urofsky, ed., *Perspectives on Urban America* (Garden City, N.Y.: Anchor Books, 1973), p. 187.

[29] See Sheila Klatzky, *School District Resources, Professional Qualifications, and Salary Competition* (Madison, Wis.: University of Wisconsin Institute for Research on Poverty, 1975).

[30] Edward B. Fiske, "A Graduate Who Says He Can't Read," *New York Times* (February 20, 1977), p. 1.

[31] Walter E. Schafer, Carol Olexa, and Kenneth Polk, "Programmed for Social Class: Tracking in High School," *Transaction* 7 (October 1970), pp. 39–46.

[32] Anthony J. LaGreca, "Critical Urban Problems," in Kent P. Schwirian, ed., *Contemporary Topics in Urban Sociology* (Morristown, N.J.: General Learning Press, 1977), pp. 339–401.

[33] John E. Coons, "The Law of School Finance," in Roger Demont, Larry Hillman, and Gerald Mansergh, eds., *Busing, Taxes, and Desegregation* (Detroit: Metropolitan Detroit Bureau of School Studies, Inc., 1973), pp. 1–28.

[34] Pranay Gupte, "Challenges to District Property Tax System Spread as More State Courts Order Alternative Methods," *New York Times* (June 25, 1978), p. 37.

[35] James S. Coleman, *Equality of Educational Opportunity* (Washington, D.C.: U.S. Government Printing Office, 1966).

[36] Ibid., pp. 3–22.

[37] David J. Armor, "The Evidence on Busing," *The Public Interest* 28 (Summer 1972), p. 99.

[38] Walter Goodman, "Integration, Yes; Busing, No." *New York Times Magazine* (August 24, 1975), p. 10 ff.; Michael Knight, "Scholars in New Rift over 'White Flight,' " *New York Times* (June 11, 1978), p. 27; and Diane Ravitch, "The 'White Flight' Controversy," *The Public Interest* 51 (Spring 1978), pp. 135–149. See also Jan Blakeslee, " 'White Flight' to the Suburbs: A Demographic Approach," *Focus: Institute for Research on Poverty Newsletter* 3 (Winter 1978–79), pp. 1–4.

[39] See Christine H. Rossell and Michael Giles, "School Desegregation and White Flight" (paper presented at the Annual Meetings of the American Sociological Association, New York, 1976).

[40] Lino A. Graglia, *Disaster by Decree* (Ithaca, N.Y.: Cornell University Press, 1976), p. 270.

[41] Frank deLeuw, Anne B. Schnare, and Raymond J. Struyk, *The Urban Predicament* (Washington, D.C.: The Urban Institute, 1976).

[42] Homer C. Hawkins, "Urban Housing and the Black Family," *Pylon* 37 (March 1976), pp. 73–84.

[43] Joseph P. Fried, *Housing Crisis, U.S.A.* (New York: Frederick A. Praeger, 1971), p. 4.

[44] Fried, *Housing Crisis, U.S.A.,* pp. 4–5.

[45] Palen, *The Urban World.*

[46] Mark T. Zimmerman, "Urban Homesteading: Maybe the Best Deal in Town," *The Nation* 223 (November 13, 1976), pp. 498–500.

[47] See Scott Greer, "Problems of Housing and Renewal of Cities," in Howard S. Becker, ed., *Social Problems* (New York: John Wiley & Sons, 1966), p. 532.

[48] U.S. Department of Health, Education, and Welfare,

Toward a Social Report (Washington, D.C.: U.S. Government Printing Office, 1969), p. 35.

[49] See Lee Rainwater, "A World of Trouble: The Pruitt-Igoe Housing Project," *The Public Interest* 8 (Summer 1977), pp. 116–126; and Palen, *The Urban World*, p. 259.

[50] U.S. Department of Housing and Urban Development, *Evaluation of the Urban Homesteading Demonstration Program* (Washington, D.C.: U.S. Government Printing Office, 1977).

[51] "A Plan for Punishing Banks That Redline," *Business Week* (April 10, 1978), pp. 34–35.

[52] Ernest W. Burgess, "The Growth of the City," *Publications of the American Sociological Society* 18 (1924), pp. 85–97.

[53] See Saul Alinsky, *Rules for Radicals: A Practical Primer for Realistic Radicals* (New York: Random House, 1971); and Palen, *The Urban World*.

[54] Walter Firey, "Sentiment and Symbolism as Ecological Variables," *American Sociological Review* 10 (April 1945), pp. 140–148.

[55] James J. Flink, *The Car Culture* (Cambridge, Mass.: The MIT Press, 1975).

[56] Ibid.

[57] U.S. Bureau of the Census, *Statistical Abstract of the United States, 1977* (Washington, D.C.: U.S. Government Printing Office, 1977), p. 645.

[58] American Automobile Association, *Your Driving Costs, 1977 Edition* (Falls Church, Va.: The American Automobile Association, 1977).

[59] See John B. Ray, *The Road and Car in American Life* (Cambridge, Mass.: The MIT Press, 1971), p. 271; and "Urban Transit at the Crossroads," *The American City and County* 92 (December 1977), pp. 31–34.

[60] James V. Cornehls and Delbert A. Tacbel, "The Outsiders and Urban Transportation," *Social Science Journal* 13 (April 1976), pp. 61–73.

[61] Ibid.

[62] Helen Leavitt, "Back to the Trolley: Shifting Gears in Urban Transportation," *New Leader* 61 (March 13, 1978), pp. 12–13.

[63] See Andrew Marshall Hamer, *The Selling of Rail Rapid Transit* (Lexington, Mass.: D. C. Heath, 1976).

[64] See Victor Bach, "The New Federalism in Community Development," *Social Policy* 7 (January/February 1977), pp. 32–38, and Richard P. Nathan, Paul R. Dommel, Sarah F. Liebschutz, and Milton D. Morris, "Monitoring the Block Grant Program for Community Development," *Political Science Quarterly* 92 (Summer 1977), pp. 219–244.

[65] "Carving Up a $26 Billion Revenue Sharing Melon," *U.S. News and World Report* 81 (October 11, 1976), pp. 85–87.

[66] Population information from the Greater Howard County Chamber of Commerce, Columbia, Md. See also Richard Oliver Brooks, *New Towns and Communal Values* (New York: Frederick A. Praeger, 1974).

[67] Irving Lewis Allen, *New Towns and the Suburban Dream* (Port Washington, N.Y.: Kennikat Press, 1977), p. 14.

[68] National Research Council, *Toward An Understanding of Metropolitan America* (San Francisco: Canfield Press, 1975), p. 105.

[69] Francis Friskin, "The Metropolis and the Central City: Can One Government Unite Them?" *Urban Affairs Quarterly* 8 (June 1973), pp. 395–422.

SUGGESTED READINGS

Allen, Irving Lewis. *New Towns and the Suburban Dream.* Port Washington, N.Y.: Kennikat Press, 1977.
A view of the problems that must be faced in the development of new towns. Allen also proposes some solutions for new towns.

Caputo, David A. *Urban America: The Policy Alternatives.* San Francisco: W. H. Freeman and Co., 1976.
An overview of some urban social problems, focusing on policies that might be developed to solve them.

Fried, Joseph P. *Housing Crisis U.S.A.* Baltimore: Penguin Books, 1971.
A general overview of the impact of government, business, and organized labor on the housing problem in the United States. Special attention is given to the housing problems faced by the poor.

Hammer, Andrew Marshall. *The Selling of Rail Rapid Transit.* Lexington, Mass.: D. C. Heath, 1976.
A detailed investigation of the benefits and disadvantages of various modes of public transportation. The major concentration is on the costs and effectiveness of subway and other rail systems compared to more common modes such as bus systems.

National Research Council. *Toward an Understanding of Metropolitan America.* San Francisco: Canfield Press, 1974.
A description of the problems encountered in governing large urban areas. Recommendations are given for dealing with governing metropolitan regions.

Questions for Discussion

1. Many people believe that the quality of life is better in a small town than in a large city. Today, we are experiencing major population shifts from the cities to smaller communities. Why are these moves taking place? Do *you* believe the quality of life is better in small towns? Why?

2. According to this chapter, what is the nature of the racial "problem" in our larger cities? What additional suggestions do you propose to cope with this problem? If we are unsuccessful in locating an effective solution, what will our society be like in twenty-five years?

3. School busing, designed to promote desegregation, *may* result in contributing to "white flight" from cities. If this is in fact the case, would it be best to abandon the policy of busing students? Are there any other methods that could reduce school segregation?

4. Locating and affording acceptable housing is a problem for most Americans, but one that especially affects the poor. Which of the various programs mentioned in the chapter do you think is the best approach to solving the housing problem? How would poor people be affected if middle-class families were to move into the cities in order to rehabilitate deteriorating neighborhoods?

5. Private automobiles are clearly an inefficient form of transportation for large cities. Do you believe that urban Americans will abandon the car? Which form of public transportation do you think is the most sensible? Why?

6. Two general styles of metropolitan government have been discussed in this chapter — metropolitan federation and metropolitan cooperation. While metropolitan federation appears to be the most effective, there has been considerable resistance to that form of government. Try to imagine some type of intermediate system that would be *both* effective and acceptable. What might be the consequences of not developing a metropolitan government system?

7. New towns represent a planning effort to create towns in which many of the problems presently faced by cities would be avoided. What characteristics would you incorporate in a new town so that it could be a heterogeneous community? How effective do you believe urban design can be in eliminating the social problems of our cities?

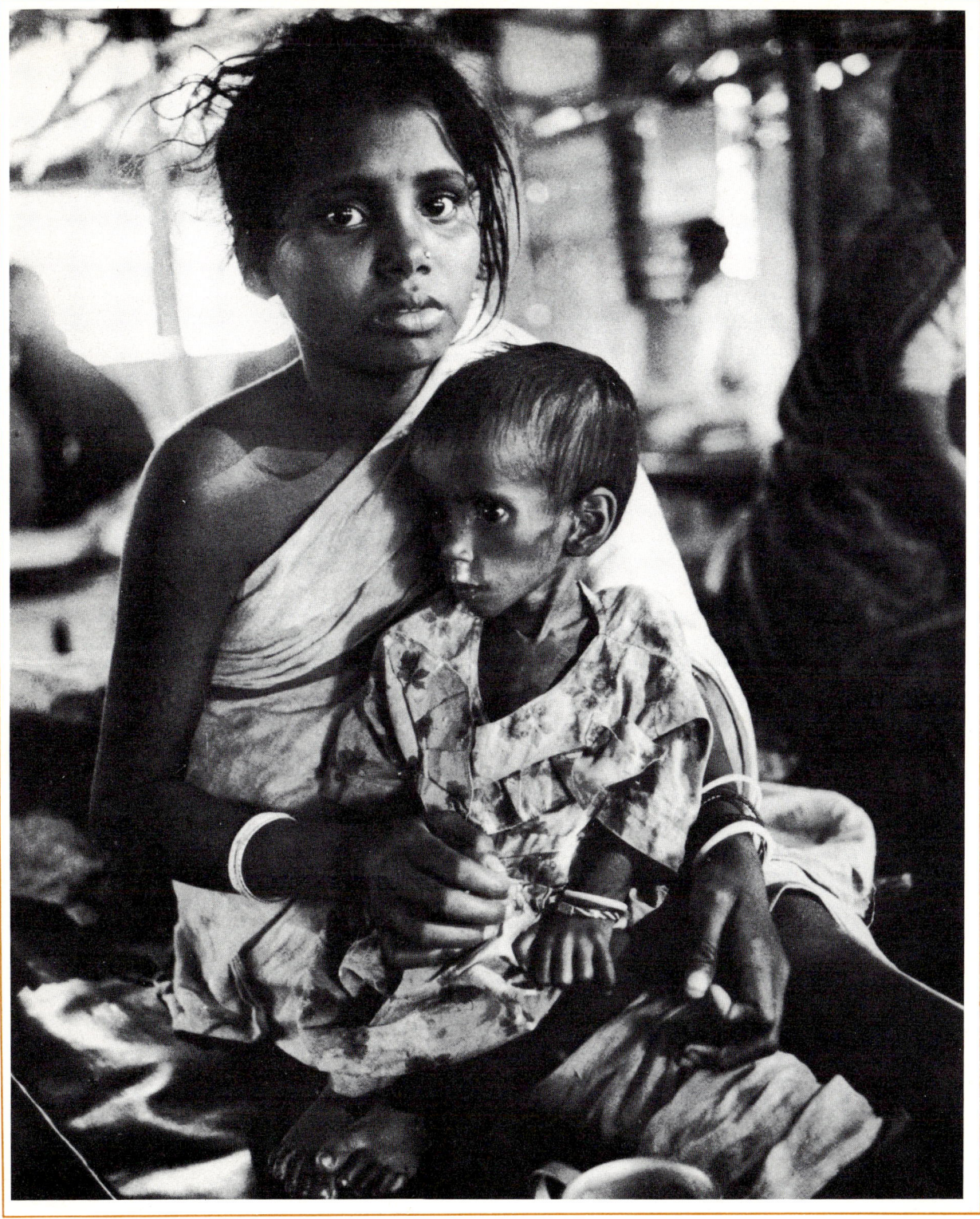

CHAPTER 4

Population Problems

WORLD POPULATION GROWTH: A BRIEF HISTORY

Population Growth in Preindustrial Societies.
Industrialization and the Demographic Transition.

POPULATION AS A SOCIAL PROBLEM

The Functionalist Perspective. The Conflict Perspective.
The Interactionist Perspective.

POPULATION DYNAMICS

Mortality in the Modern World. Fertility. Migration.

THE CONSEQUENCES OF OVERPOPULATION

Crowding. Depletion of Mineral Resources. Food
Shortages. The Fight for Survival. "And the Poor Get
Children."

FUTURE PROSPECTS

Migration. Mortality. Fertility. Zero Population Growth.

CONCLUSION

Imagine reading in the morning newspaper that both houses of the state legislature had passed a bill requiring compulsory sterilization.

> Under the new law, [the news article reports] which has had its title changed from "compulsory sterilization" bill to "family size limitation" bill, men up to age 55 and women up to age 45 must be sterilized within 180 days of the birth of their third living child. The first obligation rests on the man, and affects the woman only "if a vasectomy would endanger her husband's life." Prison terms of up to two years are provided for those who fail to comply with the measure. In practice, however . . . offenders would be sterilized and paroled. . . . [the state's] leading exponent of compulsory sterilization said that one million men would become eligible for vasectomies as soon as the law became effective, and declared his willingness to stake his reputation on the state's ability to sterilize more than a million a year. "Society," he said in an . . . interview, "has a duty to act against 'people pollution' just as it removes latrines built on a river used by people."[1]

This is not fiction, nor is it an imaginary projection of some frightening future. It is now. Our "news report" is an actual quotation describing actions taken by the legislature of the state of Maharashtra in India in 1976; the official quoted is Dr. D. N. Pai, that nation's "leading exponent of compulsory sterilization." While the law was rescinded with the fall of Prime Minister Indira Gandhi's government, it illustrates the extreme lengths to which people will go in efforts to alleviate the pressures of unwanted population growth. Although most people believe that such extreme measures would never intrude on their lives, the citizens of India probably felt similarly reassured a few decades ago. As we discuss the population problem in this chapter, the student should consider whether conditions may ever become so serious that some equally ghastly measures might become a fact of our everyday lives.

A *population* is the total number of human beings inhabiting a country, town or other area at a given time.[2] There is substantial controversy over which characteristics of a particular population constitute a social problem. Do populations of a certain size, density, or composition pose a social problem? What criteria are to be used in determining which aspects of a population entail a social problem? We will be considering these issues in this chapter. We will also discuss the consequences of overpopulation—compulsory sterilization, famine, disease, and the like. To help our analysis of solutions to population problems, we will examine the factors that contribute to population growth—fertility and mortality, economic development, and religious and cultural values.

Many people feel that some regions, such as the United States, do not have either too many or too few people; nevertheless, population must be viewed as a worldwide issue because of the interdependence of nations. For that reason, we shall concentrate on population in a worldwide context, although population problems at certain national and regional levels will be discussed in order to illustrate particular issues. Since the source and magnitude of population problems vary in different regions, we will investigate some reasons for that variation. In order to begin to understand some of these issues, it is helpful to look at how populations have grown throughout history and in different regions of the world.

WORLD POPULATION GROWTH: A BRIEF HISTORY

How many people are there in the world? How much will world population increase during your lifetime? Figure 4.1 shows world population growth from the beginning of the Christian Era to the present and projected to the year 2010; it also indicates the time interval for each successive doubling of the population. We can see that, prior to 1750, world population was relatively small and growth was slow. After 1750, world population began to increase at a more rapid rate, and it continues even more rapidly today. In 1978, world population was about 4.2 billion.[3] Should the current rate of increase remain unchanged, world population will reach approximately 8 billion by 2010! Not only is the population *increasing,* but in the recent past the *rate of increase* has been accelerating.

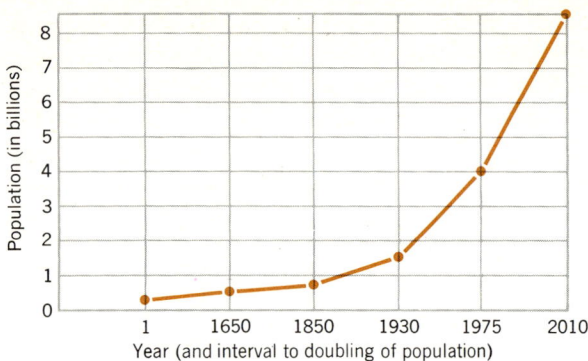

Figure 4.1 Estimated Population of the World, A.D. 1 to 1975, Projected to 2010. William Petersen, *Population*, 3rd ed. (New York: Macmillan, 1975), p. 9, and Harold F. Dorn, "World Population Growth," in Philip M. Hauser (ed.), *The Population Dilemma* (Englewood Cliffs, N.J.: Prentice-Hall, 1963), p. 10.

However, at least one recent study has found that the rate of increase of the world population between 1970 and 1975 has declined. While this is a hopeful sign, one must be cautious about inferring a permanent decline in the rate of increase, owing to the relatively short time interval involved.[4]

While the actual population figures themselves are impressive, their impact can be more clearly understood by looking at the number of years required for the population to double in size. From the beginning of the Christian Era, it took 1650 years for the world population to double. By comparison, if current growth rates continue, it will take only 35 years for today's world population to double. These figures begin to suggest the magnitude of the problem. How did this situation occur? We shall examine briefly some of the major influences on population growth—or the lack of it—throughout history.

Population Growth in Preindustrial Societies

The primary reason for the low rate of population growth in the world prior to 1750 was the extremely high death rate among almost all societies. Societies during this preindustrial period did not have the means to lower the death rate and thus increase life expectancy. For ex-

ample, until the seventeenth century, the average life expectancy in European countries was probably no more than 35 years, compared with well over 70 years today. **The most important factor in this high death rate was the extremely high infant mortality rate.** In any given year, as many as one-half of the infants born would die within their first year of life.[5] The causes of this high death rate were complex, but the two most important factors were disease and famine. By examining mortality experiences of preindustrial societies, we will have a better understanding of the population problem that confronts the world today.

Disease

Disease has accounted for more deaths in the Western world than any other factor, and this has been the case throughout history. Examination of Egyptian mummies and Greek medical records of the pre-Christian era indicates that diseases resembling smallpox, syphilis, and other modern afflictions caused disability and death during those ancient times.[6] In many instances it is not possible to pinpoint a single disease as the sole or primary cause of death. For example, the Crusaders during the thirteenth century suffered from a number of infectious diseases, such as typhus and plague, but they also suffered from scurvy, and affliction that only much later was recognized as due to a nutritional deficiency.[7]

Of all the diseases that have afflicted man, none was so devastating in terms of suffering, death, and social disruption as Bubonic Plague, or the Black Death—a disease transmitted to man primarily by rats carrying infected fleas.[8] In 1347, the Black Death appeared in Constantinople; from there it spread across Europe reaching the British Isles by 1349 and Russia by the spring of 1353. The first onslaught of plague was devastating, but it did not end there—it recurred numerous times, killing even more people. For example, in England, it first occurred between 1348 and 1350; and repeated onslaughts occurred in 1360, 1369, and 1375, remaining endemic for approximately eighty years. It is impossible to make a completely accurate estimate of the total number of deaths caused by this disease. However, a conservative estimate for Europe is that up to 25 percent of the population died in the first outbreak, perhaps 40 percent during the course of the century. As population scholar Kingsley Davis has observed, "Only one disease, the plague, seems to have been lethal enough to destroy population faster than humanity could restore it in the late ancient and medieval period."[9]

The plague, while possibly the most frightening and destructive disease, was not the only one in Europe during this period. Less devastating diseases (e.g. typhus, malaria, tuberculosis, and smallpox) were also major causes of mortality. The fatalities resulting from these diseases were far greater than would occur today, for a number of reasons. First, the medical knowledge to treat or prevent the diseases did not exist. Second, because of poor nutrition and occasional famines, people during this preindustrial period were less healthy and more susceptible to disease than are people today and were thus less likely to survive if they contracted a disease. Third, because of poor sanitation and the absence of other advances made possible by technology, diseases spread much more rapidly than they would today. Given this complex of factors, it is not surprising that population grew slowly, if at all, during this preindustrial period. Life was sometimes short and often filled with the misery of pain or disfigurement resulting from disease. In some cases, the wonder is that population grew at all!

Famine

> Oh, the praties they are
> small-
> Over here, over here
> Oh, the praties they are small
> When we dig em in the fall,
> and we eat em, coats and all,
> Full of fear, full of fear.
> (Irish famine song, 1846–1847)[10]

The "pratie" of this ditty is the potato, the mainstay of the Irish agricultural economy of the nineteenth century and a major part of the diet of the average Irish family. Between 1846 and 1851, po-

tato blight caused a massive famine in Ireland. Such famines have been fairly common in human history, showing the extent to which hunger and the possibility of starvation have been man's constant companions throughout history. In fact, until the advent of agriculture and the domestication of animals about six thousand years ago, the threat of death by starvation was a daily concern. The development of agricultural technology allowed for a fairly stable food supply throughout the year and made possible a surplus that could be stored in anticipation of lean times. However, agricultural surpluses have been scattered and unpredictable, and starvation has been an important check on population growth for many preindustrial societies.

The last major European famine was the potato famine in Ireland, in which it is estimated that one-eighth of the population died or emigrated to another country.[11] While food shortages have been a significant factor in the death rates of Europe throughout recorded history, they have not affected mortality to the extent that disease has.

While food shortages in Europe were regional and sporadic, in Asia there has been a near-constant presence of famine. Probably because Asia has a less predictable climate and rainfall, Asian famines have been far more severe than those in Europe. For example, China experienced 1828 famines between 108 B.C. and A.D. 1911 – almost one per year. While many of these famines were localized, each province or region had several famines within each generation. When famine occurs frequently during the lifetime of the average person, it is certainly understandable that it would be considered a normal and inevitable part of the human condition. One such severe famine occurred in China in 1877–78 and affected the four northern provinces. Even though this was only a century ago, communications were so ineffective that it took a year for news of the disaster to reach the Chinese capital. In the famine region, cannibalism was common, and local magistrates were ordered to "connive at the evasion of the law prohibiting the sale of children, so as to enable parents to buy a few days' food."[12] The dead were buried in holes, sometimes containing up to 10,000 people; between 9 million and 13 million people died from hunger, violence, or disease.

In summary, there were a number of important factors that contributed to a high death rate and a relatively low population growth in preindustrial societies. However, humankind was not destined to this bleak fate. With the Industrial Revolution, cataclysmic changes were set in motion that would moderate the impact of these factors for people in some societies. Yet these very same changes would usher in severe, and some feel intractable, population problems that still face us today.

Industrialization and the Demographic Transition

The *Industrial Revolution* refers to the changes in social and economic organization that resulted when human societies changed from using hand tools as the primary mode of economic production to using machine and power tools. It was the beginning of large-scale industrial production. In England and Europe, it began during the eighteenth century, in other societies at different times. The Industrial Revolution had a tremendous, although not immediate, impact on population growth. The *demographic transition* is a description of the changing patterns of birth and death rates brought about by industrialization. It is usually divided into three stages: a *preindustrial* **stage,** a *transitional* **stage,** and an *industrial* **stage.**[13] (See Fig. 4.2.)

The preindustrial stage occurs prior to the onset of industrialization, ending somewhere between 1750 and 1850 for most Western nations. During this stage, both crude birth rates and crude death rates are high, and the society experiences little population growth. The *crude birth rate* is the number of births occurring in a society in a given year for each 1000 people of that society:

Crude Birth Rate =
$$\frac{\text{number of births in a year}}{\text{midyear population}} \times 1000$$

The *crude death rate* is calculated in precisely the same way:

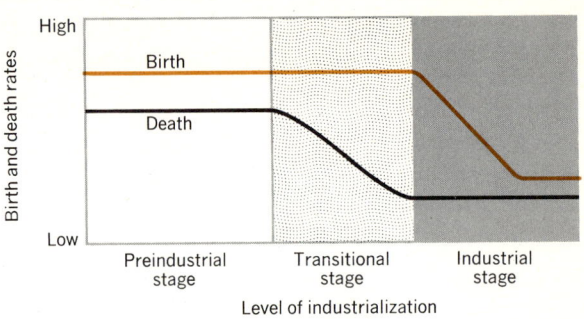

Figure 4.2   The Demographic Transition

Crude Death Rate =
$$\frac{\text{number of deaths in a year}}{\text{midyear population}} \times 1000$$

Since birth and death rates are nearly equal during the preindustrial stage, there is little natural increase. The *rate of natural increase* is the difference between the crude birth rate and the crude death rate. (Thus, if the crude birth rate is 30 per 1000, and crude death rate is 10 per 1000, then the rate of natural increase is 20 per 1000, or 2 percent.)

The onset of the *transitional stage* coincides with the beginning of industrialization. Industrialization brings about many advances in agriculture, sanitation, health care, and other areas, which result in *declining death rates*. Since birth rates are still high, the transitional period is characterized by *explosive population growth* due to a high rate of natural increase.

The *industrial stage* is characterized by a continual *decline in the crude death rate*; in addition, industrialization is accompanied by changes in cultural values (such as a desire for smaller families) that culminate in a *declining birth rate*. Since the difference between birth and death rates is diminishing during this stage, there is a *decline in the rate of natural increase*.

The demographic transition is characteristic of population growth patterns in most Western nations, such as the United States, that began industrializing between 1750 and 1850. In the early 1800s, the United States was a typical preindustrial society, characterized by high fertility and high

The large family—this one is soon to have 17 members—is common in preindustrial and transitional societies.

mortality. It was primarily an agricultural, nonurban society. The United States of this period could be defined as an underdeveloped country by today's standards. Changes in birth and death rates occurred over a relatively long period of time. Estimates place the crude birth rate for 1810 at about 55 births per 1000 people. By 1880, this rate had declined to 40 births per 1000 people, and by 1940 it was down to 20. After World War II, the birth rate climbed to 26 in 1947 and remained in the range of 24 to 25 for the next decade. By the 1960s, the rate had begun to decline again, and it is presently at a historic low of 15. During this period, there were correspondingly slow declines in mortality.[14]

The United States experience is typical of that of industrial societies in that declines in both mortality and fertility occurred over a long period of time and were due to the social changes accompanying industrialization. However, the situation confronting the newly developing nations today is radically different from this, and the demographic transition may not be applicable to them. Since this difference constitutes a major aspect of world population problems today, we will return to it in our later discussion of population growth in the modern world. Before examining this, however, we will consider the way in which population is considered to be a social problem from our three theoretical perspectives.

POPULATION AS A SOCIAL PROBLEM

The Functionalist Perspective

From the functionalist perspective, society is a system made up of interdependent and interconnected parts. A change in one part of the system may have potential consequences for all other parts of the system. One important component of society is the size of its population. Any change in the size of that population does not occur in isolation; rather it occurs against a backdrop of complex social factors—

Small families are common in societies that have reached the
industrial stage of the Demographic Transition.

the level of technology in a society, the type of economic organization, and societal values and goals. Changes in population, if they are substantial and occur rapidly, can disrupt the balance between these factors. However, if the system has sufficient time to adjust to the changes, such as through the emergence of new technologies to support larger populations, then such disruption need not occur. **From the functionalist perspective, then, population growth becomes a social problem when it occurs under conditions that make it difficult for the system to adjust without serious distortions that threaten the ability of the system to function smoothly.**

The Malthusian View

Thomas Robert Malthus (1766–1834) was an early proponent of the functionalist position, although he did not call it that. Malthus was an English clergyman and student of history and political economics.

He wrote prolifically on the principles of population growth between 1798 and 1834. Malthus believed that he had discovered a natural law — in this case, a divine law. This law was based on the belief that humankind was guilty of original sin and as such was destined to suffer throughout the ages. Two natural characteristics decreed by God are responsible for this continuous suffering: (1) an immutable passion between the sexes and (2) a limited ability to produce food. These two characteristics in turn yield the consequence that "Population, when unchecked, increases in a geometrical ratio. Subsistence increases only in an arithmetical ratio."[15] A geometrical ratio (e.g. 1, 2, 4, 8, 16 . . .) involves a continual doubling every generation, while an arithmetical ratio (e.g. 1, 2, 3, 4, 5 . . .) involves a much slower growth rate. In other words, population, if left unchecked, must eventually outstrip the food supply.

Malthusians (those who accept the basic position that Malthus stated) accept the func-

tionalist proposition that the different parts of the social system exist in a state of equilibrium which, if disturbed, will result in social change. Thus they believe that resources are limited and that population growth must be controlled or resources will be exhausted; the adjustments the system must make to accommodate such a depletion of resources may be undesirable—increased death rates. According to Malthus, there were two kinds of controls on population growth—*positive checks* and *preventative checks.* By *positive checks* Malthus refers to such factors as war, disease, and famine, which cause death and so reduce the existing population. (It is clear that Malthus's theological training influenced his view of population. His positive checks closely resemble three of the Four Horsemen of the Apocalypse described in the Book of Revelations in the New Testament.) The *preventative checks* are such factors as late marriage and celibacy, which reduce the birth rate and hence check population growth. However, Malthus, apparently on moral grounds, did not consider artificial means of birth control to be one of the preventative checks.[16]

For the functionalist like Malthus, then, the key to population as a social problem is that resources are limited and that uncontrolled population growth will threaten the exhaustion of available resources. If we ignore these basic principles, say the functionalists, the system may adjust to increased population size in ways we would consider undesirable, such as starvation or war. Furthermore, if we interfere with the checks on population growth, we may be laying the groundwork for more serious problems in the future because population will grow at an even more rapid rate and intensify problems of starvation and resource depletion.

The Conflict Perspective

The conflict perspective on population problems is quite at variance with that of Malthus and the functionalists. Whereas the functionalist perspective relies heavily on the view that *society is a system,* the conflict perspective emphasizes *power* and the *struggle over scarce resources* associated with the acquisition and maintenance of power. From the conflict perspective, population size becomes a social problem when some influential group defines it as threatening to its own interests. Thus, a large number of people *or a* small number of people might be defined as a social problem from this perspective. Some groups might benefit from a large and growing population, while others see it to their advantage to have a small and stable population. Likewise, a scarcity of resources such as food might be beneficial to some groups while detrimental to others. In short, from the conflict perspective, population size is not a problem for society as a whole, although it might be defined as a problem by particular groups.

The Marxian View

One variant of the conflict perspective is the view propounded by Karl Marx. While Marx did not have a specific theory of population problems, followers of Marx have derived a Marxian position on population from Marx's social and economic theories.[17] In this Marxian view, population tends to outstrip resources because of the specific characteristics of a particular society and not because of any natural law making this inevitable. In particular, Marx believed that a capitalist economic system (such as in England and the United States) is inherently inefficient since its productive output is influenced by the need to maintain a profit margin. Profits are a product of *economic demand,* which is not necessarily related to *human need. Economic demand refers to the amount of a product—such as food—that can be sold, rather than the amount that is required to satisfy the needs of a population.* Thus, if people are starving but have no money, then according to this definition there is no *demand* for food. Profits increase when there is greater economic demand, and demand rises when the supply of a product is scarce. In other words, a capitalist may limit the supply of needed products in order to increase the economic demand and enhance his profits—even though there is a pressing human need for these products.

Thus for Marxians, population is a social problem only because a particular economic system artificially limits the resources available in order to benefit one group. Conflict theorists like Marx believe that population exceeds resources only when an inequitable and inefficient economic system results in a maldistribution of resources.

For Marxians, the solution is not to reduce the number of people but rather to change the system of production and distribution. They argue that, since the wealthy and powerful would not willingly give up their favored status, it will have to be wrested from them through conflict. A variation on this argument is popular today with the political leaders of some developing nations. They argue that high rates of world population growth are not the problem. Rather, the problem is that resources are very unevenly distributed among the nations of the world. They contend that, if the affluent industrial nations would share their wealth, rapidly growing populations in the developing nations could be supported at a comfortable standard of living.

The Interactionist Perspective

From the interactionist perspective, population problems are a matter of *social definition.* A society may be overpopulated in terms of its current resources, but unless influential groups define this condition as a social problem, it will not be considered one. Thus, people vary in terms of what they consider a desirable population size and standard of living. Some view a growing population as a source of strength and place great value on large families. They believe that somehow these growing numbers will be provided for. Others look aghast at an increasingly crowded world in which there are fewer resources to be spread around and fewer places of relatively low population in which to live. Whereas the functionalist perspective places emphasis on the objective existence of resources to support a population, the interactionist perspective points out that people respond to the *quality of life* made possible by the resources that are available. You might define the current population level in the United States as a problem because you must travel farther afield in order to find a pristine wilderness in which to reflect on the affairs of the day. A person in Hong Kong, on the other hand, might not consider America as having a population problem because there is, in comparison to Hong Kong, so much open space and such a high standard of living.

Does the world have a population problem? For the interactionist, that depends on one's viewpoint. Some leaders in the developing countries today believe that there is no world population problem because there is so much open space remaining in the world; furthermore, they feel that industrialization will bring the same quality of life to the developing nations that it did to those nations that experienced the demographic transition a few centuries ago. As the interactionist perspective makes clear, if people define a situation as real, it is real in its consequence. Some of these leaders are acting on their definition of reality and doing little to stem the explosive population growth in their countries.

Thus, different versions of reality lead to radically different conclusions in terms of population policy. The issues in dispute nevertheless are very important to our analysis of population problems. In Figure 4.3, some basic information on population size, rate of growth, and per capita gross national product is presented. From these data, the student will undoubtedly draw his or her own conclusion about the seriousness of population problems as well as their source. However, according to the interactionist perspective, positions on issues are only *partially* the result of objective information. In addition, that information must be interpreted and understood in terms of the values and goals of a particular group. Thus different people might come to very divergent conclusions based on the same "objective" information.

POPULATION DYNAMICS

Any analysis of the problem of overpopulation must be based on a comprehension of *population dynamics* — the factors that influence population size. They are: mortality, fertility, and migration.

NATION		Population estimate 1978 (millions)	Rate of natural increase 1978 (annual percent)	Per Capita Gross National Product 1976 (U.S. $)
DEVELOPED	Australia	14.3	0.8	6,100
	Canada	23.6	0.9	7,510
	Sweden	8.3	0.1	8,670
	United States	218.4	0.6	7,890
	West Germany	61.3	−0.2	7,380
DEVELOPING	Colombia	25.8	2.4	630
	India	634.7	2.0	150
	Mexico	66.9	3.4	1,090
	Sri Lanka	14.2	1.7	200
	Thailand	45.1	2.3	380
	Togo	2.4	2.8	260
	Uganda	12.7	3.0	240

Figure 4.3 Population, Natural Increase, and Per Capita Gross National Product for Selected Developed and Developing Nations. Population Reference Bureau, *1977 World Population Data Sheet* (Washington, D.C.: Population Reference Bureau, 1978).

In our discussion of world population growth throughout history, we briefly considered the effects of mortality. Here we will analyze all three factors, particularly as they relate to the modern world.

Mortality in the Modern World

Industrial Nations

We have observed that death rates, which have been very high throughout much of human history, have declined substantially in modern industrial nations. Malthus's "positive checks" on population—disease, famine, and war—no longer take the enormous toll they once did. Life expectancy was probably no more than 35 years for the white populations of Europe and North America around 1700 and had increased very little during the previous

four centuries. (These figures are limited to whites because comparable data from earlier periods are not available for nonwhites.) By 1950, the white population of the United States had a life expectancy of 69 years. Nearly all of the countries of western and central Europe had similar gains in life expectancy.[18]

According to demographer Harold Dorn, four factors have contributed to this decline in mortality rates:

(a) the opening up of new continents, which provided additional sources of food, precious metals, and raw materials as well as an outlet for an increasing population; (b) the expansion of commerce, which made possible the transportation of food and capital goods over long distances; (c) technological changes in agriculture, together with the development of modern industry; and (d) increased control of disease by means of improved housing, better food and water supplies, adoption of sanitary measures, the growth of knowledge of preventative medicine, and discoveries in pharmacology and chemotherapy, particularly antibiotics and insecticides.[19]

The decline in mortality in the Western world was not an isolated event, but rather was a part of fundamental structural changes that were occurring in these societies; they were modernizing, urbanizing, and industrializing, and these changes had many effects, including declines in both mortality and, eventually, fertility. While all age groups experienced a decline in mortality, it was among infants that it was especially dramatic. In fact, much of the overall decline in mortality has been due to the substantial decline in infant mortality (deaths of persons under one year of age). This resulted not so much from medical advances as from the improved prenatal environment made possible by better sanitation and nutrition.

Developing Nations

While some of the factors relevant to the declines in mortality in the West also apply to the mortality experiences of the developing nations today, there are some important differences. For most of today's developing nations, preindustrial conditions of high birth rates and high death rates continued to prevail until well into the twentieth century. Just prior to World War II, Western technology and health practices that have been important in reducing mortality were introduced into the developing nations. For example, insecticides, such as DDT, were introduced; improvements were made in the transportation of food; more efficient agricultural practices were used in the developing nations; and modern health practices, such as innoculations against infectious disease, were made available.

As a consequence, societies which were, by virtually every standard, preindustrial now began to experience the low death rates of nations beginning to industrialize. In Ceylon (now called Sri Lanka), for example, the 1945 crude death rate was 22 deaths per 1000 people, while by 1949 deaths had declined to 12 per 1000 — that is, in a five-year period the death rate declined by nearly half. In the one-year period from 1946 to 1947, life expectancy increased from 43 to 52 years (an increase that had required approximately a half-century in the West). By the 1950s, Ceylon was experiencing a decline in its standard of living because of the rapid rate of population increase. By 1970, the rate of natural increase was 2.4 percent; at this rate, the population of Ceylon could *double* in 29 years. By 1977, the rate of natural increase had declined to 2.0.[20]

Whereas the Western decline in mortality occurred because of technological developments and changes in society (modernization, industrialization, and the like) that would eventually also lead to declines in fertility, the decline in mortality in the non-Western nations has been primarily a function of the introduction of Western technology and methods without the corresponding social and economic changes that might lead to a concomitant decline in birth rates. The effect has been death control without corresponding birth control and thus an explosive growth in population (see Fig. 4.4).

Thus, in the developing nations mortality has declined dramatically and life expectancy has increased at a rate many times faster than that in the West. Since infant mortality is still relatively high, there is great potential for additional decreases in overall mortality through reductions in infant mortality. The result of these changes has been a much more rapid rate of population increase among the developing nations than was experienced in the West. For example, the population of Europe has grown from 120 million in 1650 to 944 million today — an eightfold increase in 300 years. The population of the non-Western nations was about 1 billion in 1900, whereas, if projections hold, it will total approximately 5.5 billion by the end of this century — a sixfold increase in only 100 years.[21]

Today we confront a cruel irony. Historically, it has been *mortality* — principally in the form of the Malthusian positive checks — that has kept population growth at manageable levels. But the efforts of the Western nations to alleviate suffering and death through the introduction of modern technology has, as Malthus predicted, often led to additional suffering as a result of rapid population increase.

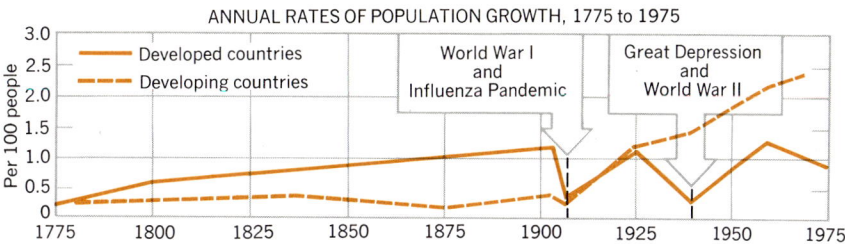

Figure 4.4 **Annual Rates of Population Growth, 1775–1975.**
From Ansley J. Coale, "The History of Human Population,"
Scientific American, **September 1974. Copyright © 1974 by**
Scientific American, Inc. All rights reserved.

Are the positive checks of war, disease, and famine the fate of human societies in the future? Will our attempt to alleviate starvation simply postpone it? Or are there alternative solutions to overpopulation? Since increasing mortality to slow down population growth contradicts most cherished human values, we must see what we can learn about the other factors that determine population size—fertility and migration.

Fertility

Fertility **refers to the number of children born. This is different from the biological potential for children—the biological maximum number of children that a given population can produce—which is referred to as** *fecundity*. (People often confuse the two terms and use *fertility* to refer to this potential.) As we have seen, prior to the eighteenth century, human societies generally experienced high rates of fertility. We know that fertility was high since there is adequate evidence of high mortality, and obviously a population with high mortality could not long survive unless it also had high fertility.

We have seen that mortality results from conditions, such as the "positive checks," over which people have only recently gained some degree of control. Thus, for most societies, mortality is high in spite of, rather than because of, the desires of its people. Once the means of bringing about lower mortality become available, it is only necessary to implement them. However, fertility is influenced by very different processes. Unlike mortality, the level of fertility has always been, at least in part, within the realm of human intervention. People can choose not to have children, and some people have done so in almost all societies throughout history. However, fertility is not controlled simply because people have the ability to do so. Levels of fertility are also dependent on a number of social institutions and cultural beliefs, together with certain physical and environmental factors. We will discuss the most important of these.

Family Structure

One major element that influences the level of fertility in a society is the family structure. In general, the type of family that exists in many preindustrial societies encourages high fertility.[22] For example, in traditional India, many people lived in what is called a *joint family*—a type of extended family in which a number of related adults live in one household and share responsibility for the economic support of the family and the raising of children. This type of family contributed to high fertility because couples were able to marry at a very young age and have children without worrying about how they would support their family. The responsibility for that support was spread over all adult members of the joint family. Such early marriage permitted them to make the fullest use of those years when reproduction is possible. Early marriage was also encouraged by the fact that marriages were arranged by the elders, and the young had little choice but to accede to their parents' wishes.

Just as the family structure in a society can contribute to high fertility, it can also be an important factor in a low fertility rate. In traditional Irish society, for instance, a man could not marry until he had sufficient property to support a family. In such an agrarian society, this meant that most men would not marry until their parents had reached a sufficiently advanced age to turn their land over to them. This transition was usually postponed as long as possible since, when control of the land passed into the son's hands, the father relinquished all authority over his son. If an irrevocable conflict developed between the parents and the son, it was the parents, not the son and his wife, who were required to leave. In practice, this type of family meant that both men and women married relatively late in life, which left fewer years during which reproduction was possible. Thus, in such situations, fertility is generally lower than in societies with a joint family such as in traditional India.[23]

In industrialized nations, the family is most often a *nuclear family*, consisting only of the parents and children (or, in some cases, only one parent and children). While it is possible to have many children in a nuclear family, such a family structure does not encourage this possibility since there is no one with whom to share the burden of childrearing. A large family is also an economic burden. With many children, one parent must spend much time in childrearing, which leaves only one parent to work full-time for the economic support of the family. It is much easier to provide for a nuclear family with few children.

The Status of Women

The status of women in a particular society can also make an important contribution to the level of fertility. In traditional India, for example, women had relatively low status. It was generally believed that women should be good mothers and wives and little else. A woman's worth was defined almost solely in terms of the number of children (especially sons) she bore. In fact, a daughter who remained single beyond the age at which she was expected to marry was regarded as a distinct liability by her family.[24]

Modern Indian women are less willing to accept this restricted lifestyle, which may prove important in India's efforts to lower its fertility. If women come to accept a lifestyle other than motherhood as satisfying and self-fulfilling, many of them may choose to have few or no children.[25] This has certainly been a factor in the low fertility rates in Western nations. Although American women still feel considerable pressure to have children, it is not the only means of self-fulfillment open to them. Women can find a place in society through work, hobbies, or creative endeavors.

Institutional Supports

In preindustrial societies, the family provides support for a person during times of hardship and in old age. In a large family, one could feel more secure about such support with many sons and daughters to be of assistance. There were no alternative institutions to provide that support—no retirement income or old-age homes to take care of you as you grew old, no health insurance to take care of you when you were sick, and no unemployment benefits or welfare to help you through hard times. In developing nations today, these institutional supports also do not exist, and thus, from the individual's point of view, a large family is important in filling this void. The family offers social and economic security during times of want. In industrial societies, these alternative institutions have emerged, thus making large families less essential.

Beliefs and Values

Another factor supporting high fertility in many societies is the culturally derived beliefs and values about family size, conception, and the other conditions related to fertility. An example of this is what Latin Americans call *machismo:* the belief in assertive masculinity, characterized by virility, courage, and aggressiveness. Such a belief affects fertility because the number of offspring a man fathers is believed to be a sign of his virility. While this idea is usually associated with Latin peoples, it is not restricted to them. One authority on population contends that it is found among many poor or disadvantaged groups because this belief serves as a defense mechanism against others perceived as superior.[26] In an attempt to deal with this problem of machismo in Italy, comic books are being published depicting the virile man as a skillful lover who knows how to *prevent* conception.[27]

Religion

Religious beliefs and practices also have an important, although sometimes indirect, effect on fertility. Nearly all of the world's major religions have traditionally advocated high fertility. The biblical injunction "Be fruitful and multiply" illustrates this, as do the Hindu incantation "Make the bride the mother of good and lucky children, bless her to get ten children and make the husband the eleventh one" and the prohibition in the *Koran* "Do not slay your children for fear of poverty. We give them sustenance and yourselves, too."[28] Through their teachings these religions encourage people to place great value on having children and to view efforts to reduce family size as wrong.

However, not all religious teachings encourage high fertility; in some cases, they have the opposite effect. For example, a study of Latin American fertility found that among Roman Catholics (the dominant religious group in Latin countries) the birth rate was high among married women; however, religious proscription of premarital sexual relations resulted in a low birth rate among unmarried women (that is, few illegitimate births).[29] In this case, certain religious beliefs encourage high fertility in one group of Catholics, while other beliefs encourage low fertility in a different group of Catholics.

Socioeconomic Factors

There are a number of related socioeconomic factors—income, education, residence, and age—that affect fertility. Low income and low education are usually associated with high fertility. People in rural areas also commonly have higher rates of fertility than people in urban areas. In addition, societies with a greater proportion of young adults have higher fertility. This latter relationship is especially disturbing because the developing countries today have a very young population—over 40 percent of their populations are under 15 years of age—so there is potential for continued high rates of fertility in the future because these young people have their fertility experience still ahead of them.

The relationship between these socioeconomic factors and overpopulation is complex. The socioeconomic factors tend to encourage high fertility and thus overpopulation. At the same time, overpopulation affects these socioeconomic factors. A rapidly growing population places a strain on educational and economic resources—the society finds it difficult to educate and provide for its growing population. Thus, with a rapidly growing populace, there are more poorly educated and low-income people—conditions that promote high fertility and therefore overpopulation. In other words, a *vicious circle* may emerge: overpopulation leads to more poverty and low educational levels, which in turn intensify overpopulation. The two factors—socioeconomic conditions and overpopulation can mutually reinforce one another.

With this review of some of the major factors that affect fertility, it is clear that we face a considerably different problem in trying to reduce fertility than in trying to reduce mortality. Reductions in mortality are usually supported by the values existing in society, and so the major problem is to develop or make available the appropriate technology to achieve that end. Reductions in fertility, on the other hand, may not be supported by basic institutions, such as the family and religion, and may run counter to important beliefs and values. Far from being simply a technological problem, fertility reduction is an extremely complex task involving changes in basic social institutions and values.

Migration

Migration has been an important factor in determining *population distribution*, but it may not have the effect on *population growth* desired by those concerned about the population problem. Malthus argued that, when Europeans reach sparsely inhabited areas, there might be *increased* population growth:

It has been universally remarked that all new colonies settled in healthy countries, where there was plenty of room and food, have constantly increased with astonishing rapidity in their population.[30]

Migration, particularly emigration (leaving an area or nation), is a frequently proposed solution to overcrowding in some of the world's more densely populated nations. However, one must realize that the major historical role of migration has been to redistribute people, especially into less densely populated areas. This has often led, as Malthus predicted, to overall net increases in world population — providing a short-range solution but contributing to the long-range problem of worldwide overpopulation.

THE CONSEQUENCES OF OVERPOPULATION

We have all been treated to the horror stories about what is happening, or will happen, as a result of our growing world population — starvation, strife, and misery play important parts in many of these scenarios. However, if we are truly to understand the problem and find feasible solutions, we must have a clear understanding — without sensationalism — of what the results of overpopulation, today and in the immediate future, are likely to be. In this section we will consider some of the undesirable consequences of overpopulation: crowding, limited resources, the scarcity of food, and the potential for conflict over ever more limited resources. Although you may feel that these conditions are of little relevance to the lives of comfortable, affluent Americans, we shall nevertheless suffer their adverse effects along with the rest of the world. This is so because all human societies constitute a system in which all parts are dependent on one another to some degree.

Crowding

World population is growing at a rate unparalleled in human history. In a number of regions, such as Latin America and Africa, this growth has led to significant increases in population density with resultant crowding, especially in urban areas. If this trend continues, crowding will become more intense in these areas and will involve other regions of the world as well. What is crowding? It used to be said that the frontiersman who could see the smoke of his neighbor's chimney felt hemmed in, whereas a life-long urban resident living in an apartment building housing several hundred people may feel he has adequate space. It is clear that crowding is not a simple matter of actual population density; it is also a matter of social definition. **Crowding** is a subjective phenomenon — it is a person's perception that he has insufficient space. **Density** is an objective phenomenon — it is measured by the number of people in a given space. *The effects of crowding must be seen as responses to relative conditions based on the individual's past experience*.

Most research on crowding is suggestive rather than conclusive. Probably the best-known studies of the effects of crowding are psychologist John B. Calhoun's experiments with rats.[31] Calhoun placed rats in pens and allowed them to breed until population density rose to a level far beyond that found in their natural environment. As a result of this overcrowding, a number of behavioral changes took place. For example, many females were unable to conceive, and others were unable to carry their unborn young to full term; some to whom offspring were born could not adequately care for their young.

While this research is suggestive, it is not necessarily directly applicable to man. While rats respond directly to physical conditions, people respond to a social reality that is mediated through culture. That is, human beings use symbols to communicate with one another and to interpret reality. Research on human beings living in crowded environments is inconsistent concerning the effects of crowding. Some studies show that certain bodily processes are affected by crowding, and some nervous disorders related to an excess of sensory stimuli are associated with high density. In other studies, child abuse, incest, and suicide appear to be more prevalent in areas of greater density.[32] Still, scientific opinion on the effects of crowding is not unanimous. For example, psychologist Jonathan

Freedman argues that crowding is not in itself undesirable; rather, the undesirable behavior usually associated with crowding is actually the result of other conditions, such as poverty and urban living.[33] Thus, a food riot in Bombay or a race riot in an American city both occur in crowded urban environments; but they also occur under conditions of poverty, which we know can, even in sparsely populated areas, be a factor in such disruptive behavior. The extent to which crowding alone is the culprit in such episodes is simply unknown at this point.[34]

Not only is there little consensus regarding the effects of crowding, but it is important to keep in mind that human beings define a situation as crowded on the basis of their group's values and past experience. However, while perceptions of crowding will vary depending on the circumstances, it is likely that more nations will experience additional crowding in the future, if present population trends continue, and whatever adverse effects crowding has will be intensified.

Depletion of Mineral Resources

While we might argue about the impact of crowding, there is little debate over the effect of population increase on resources. In fact, population can be defined as a social problem when the number of people exceeds the resources available to support them at a standard of living that they define as acceptable. While the complete exhaustion of resources can threaten human survival, problems arise long before that stage is reached. **Therefore, it is useful to think about resources in terms of *relative deprivation*: people feel deprived when available resources cannot support a socially acceptable lifestyle.** To maintain the standard of living acceptable to Americans and Western Europeans, a large supply of certain mineral resources is essential. Many of these minerals exist in a finite, limited supply; they are not readily renewable, and there are no ready substitutes.

In 1972, a group of concerned persons calling themselves The Club of Rome published the results of a major effort to determine the future supply of mineral resources in the world.[35] They used computer techniques to determine the available supplies of various resources in the future, based on estimates of current supplies of resources and the various rates of use of those resources. They developed a **static index,** which shows in how many years a given resource will be exhausted if there is meanwhile *no increase* in consumption. They also calculated an **exponential index,** which shows the estimated depletion time based on projected increases in the rate of consumption. At best these figures are estimates that the researchers themselves recognize as needing qualification. Increasing rates of consumption of resources are based on both population growth and rising per capita consumption. In other words, even if population levels were to remain constant, a rise in the standard of living of any country would result in an increase in the per capita use of resources and their potential depletion.

Lest the student feel that we could easily get along without some of these dwindling resources, consider what they are used for. Aluminum is widely used in American society, primarily in making aircraft, automobiles, kitchenware, and in electrical conductors. Yet, aluminum will be depleted in 100 years, according to the optimistic (static) estimates, and in only 31 years if the rates of usage increase. The loss of petroleum would have a devastating effect on the standard of living to which most Americans are accustomed. Yet the most optimistic figure that The Club of Rome could offer is 50 years until world supplies are depleted. Natural gas, in addition to being a heating fuel, is also a critical raw material in the production of nitrogen fertilizer, which is crucial to our food production. Yet The Club of Rome's most optimistic estimate is that natural gas will be depleted in 38 years. Some resources, such as chromium (used in stainless steel, automobile trim, and other products) and petroleum, may be harder to obtain in the future than they are today because of political disagreements between the United States and those nations holding large reserves of them. (We have already experienced some of these difficulties in our relations with the oil-producing nations.) Some feel that The Club of Rome report is far too pessimistic and that advances in technology will make available additional resources. There are so many factors affecting this picture that it is too early to predict whether the optimists or the pessimists will prove to be correct in the end.

In 1974, The Club of Rome published its second report, focusing primarily on the impact of anticipated shortages of resources.[36] The report points out that industrial nations, such as the United States, are becoming increasingly dependent on other nations for many metals (see Fig. 4.5). Given this international trade in mineral resources. The Club of Rome feels that the nations of the world are bound together in a complex relationship that makes each dependent on the others. Thus the problems of the developing nations can no longer be ignored by the industrialized nations such as the United States, because we depend on their resources to maintain our lifestyle. Since the developing nations wish to improve their standard of living, we must be concerned because any population with a relatively low standard of living, even if there is no population growth, requires additional resources to upgrade that standard. This means that the developing nations, to improve their standard of living, must dip into the already meager stockpile of resources in the world. Yet discouraging these nations from improving their standard of living is no solution either, because a low standard of living is linked to high fertility, which brings about more overpopulation. So, whether the developing nations improve their standard of living or remain at their current level with its associated high population growth, there will be an increased drain on the resources of the world. To understand both the implications of growth and the need for development in various nations, consider the information in Figure 4.6.

Food Shortages

Food shortages, including actual famines, are not recent developments. As we have seen, they have been among the major factors determining high mortality throughout human history. Today, however, the impact of food shortages is quite different from what it was in previous eras. One reason for this difference is that today the world is tied together by a vast communication and transportation network that provides instant information concerning events around the globe and that makes possible the rapid dissemination of food to most parts of the world. No longer would it take, as it did in nineteenth-century China, almost a year for the news of a famine to reach the capital.[37] In previous eras, authorities often did not learn about a famine quickly enough to do anything about it. Today, we learn of famines at once — in fact, we can sometimes predict their occurrence — and we can transport vast quantities of food to stricken areas.

A second reason why the impact of famines is different today is that those suffering from food shortages are aware that other nations possess a food surplus. Today, starving or malnourished people are commonly well aware of the abundance of food in other countries. This awareness, combined with the growing political influence of emerging nations, makes such people very unlikely to accept their fate quietly. When faced with widespread famine, they well may use what resources they have, such as withholding minerals important to us, to force us to share our surpluses. So, over and above humanitarian concerns, there are very convincing practical reasons why the affluent nations should seek solutions to food shortages wherever they occur.

A third reason why the impact of food shortages is different today than it was in previous eras is that the nature of the food shortages themselves has changed. In the past, most famines were **distribution famines — food shortages would exist in particular provinces or regions despite the presence of sufficient food elsewhere.** These famines were more often the result of inadequate transportation or the unwillingness of others to share food rather than of an absolute shortage of food. There are indications that the kinds of food shortages and potential famines that certain parts of the world may experience in the future will result from an absolute deficit in food supply rather than an uneven distribution. **A *deficit famine* is a food shortage in which there are no food supplies elsewhere to make up for local shortages.** Although it is difficult for those of us in the developed nations to accept the reality of a deficit famine, projections regarding the world food supply make it soberingly clear that such famines are possible.

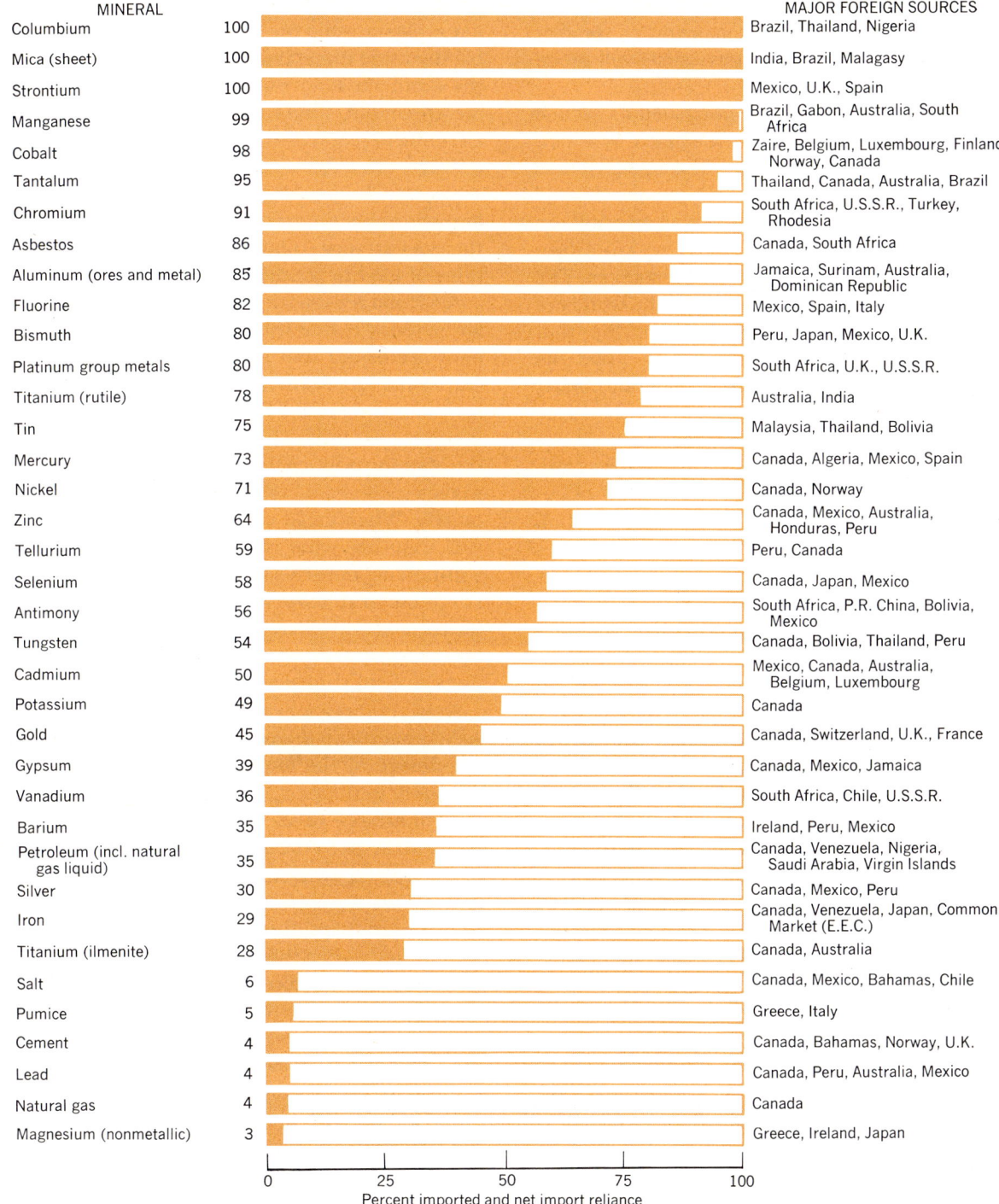

MINERAL		MAJOR FOREIGN SOURCES
Columbium	100	Brazil, Thailand, Nigeria
Mica (sheet)	100	India, Brazil, Malagasy
Strontium	100	Mexico, U.K., Spain
Manganese	99	Brazil, Gabon, Australia, South Africa
Cobalt	98	Zaire, Belgium, Luxembourg, Finland, Norway, Canada
Tantalum	95	Thailand, Canada, Australia, Brazil
Chromium	91	South Africa, U.S.S.R., Turkey, Rhodesia
Asbestos	86	Canada, South Africa
Aluminum (ores and metal)	85	Jamaica, Surinam, Australia, Dominican Republic
Fluorine	82	Mexico, Spain, Italy
Bismuth	80	Peru, Japan, Mexico, U.K.
Platinum group metals	80	South Africa, U.K., U.S.S.R.
Titanium (rutile)	78	Australia, India
Tin	75	Malaysia, Thailand, Bolivia
Mercury	73	Canada, Algeria, Mexico, Spain
Nickel	71	Canada, Norway
Zinc	64	Canada, Mexico, Australia, Honduras, Peru
Tellurium	59	Peru, Canada
Selenium	58	Canada, Japan, Mexico
Antimony	56	South Africa, P.R. China, Bolivia, Mexico
Tungsten	54	Canada, Bolivia, Thailand, Peru
Cadmium	50	Mexico, Canada, Australia, Belgium, Luxembourg
Potassium	49	Canada
Gold	45	Canada, Switzerland, U.K., France
Gypsum	39	Canada, Mexico, Jamaica
Vanadium	36	South Africa, Chile, U.S.S.R.
Barium	35	Ireland, Peru, Mexico
Petroleum (incl. natural gas liquid)	35	Canada, Venezuela, Nigeria, Saudi Arabia, Virgin Islands
Silver	30	Canada, Mexico, Peru
Iron	29	Canada, Venezuela, Japan, Common Market (E.E.C.)
Titanium (ilmenite)	28	Canada, Australia
Salt	6	Canada, Mexico, Bahamas, Chile
Pumice	5	Greece, Italy
Cement	4	Canada, Bahamas, Norway, U.K.
Lead	4	Canada, Peru, Australia, Mexico
Natural gas	4	Canada
Magnesium (nonmetallic)	3	Greece, Ireland, Japan

Percent imported and net import reliance

Figure 4.5 **Imports as a Percentage of Total U.S. Consumption, 1975. U.S. Council on Environmental Quality, *Environmental Quality—1977* (Washington, D.C.: U.S. Government Printing Office, 1977), p. 298.**

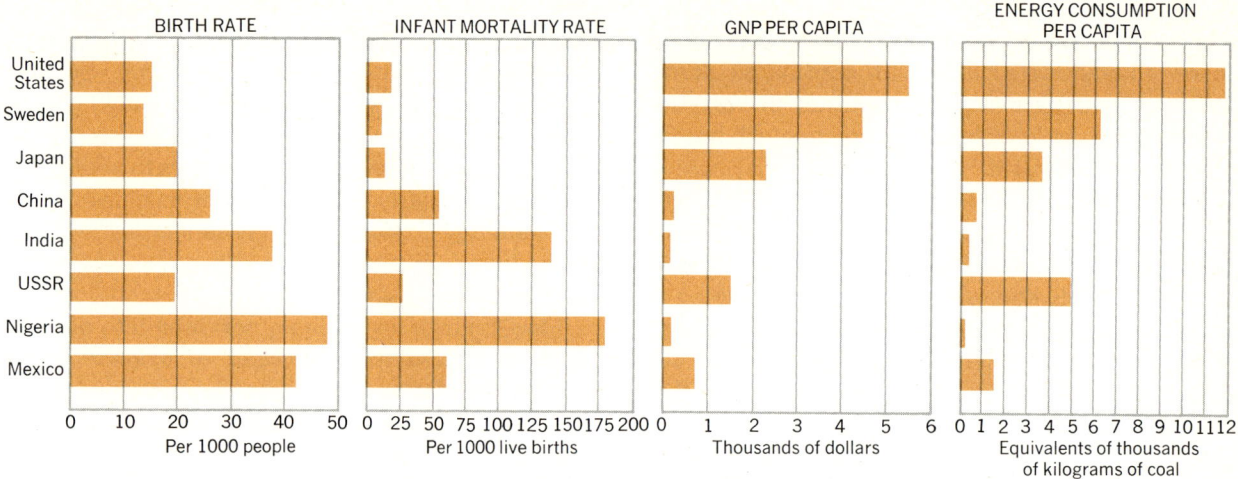

Figure 4.6 **The Development Gap, 1975. Population Reference Bureau, Inc. Washington, D.C., 1976.**

Over the past 10,000 years, food supplies have expanded tremendously. However, this has been accompanied by increases in population, so that much of the world still experiences occasional malnutrition or even famine despite increasing food supplies. In addition, since World War II there has been considerable variation among the different regions of the world in their ability to produce sufficient food to support their populations. This has been partly due to changes in weather and the willingness to adopt new agricultural technology. For example, most Latin American nations that were food exporters before the war are now food importers, while the United States, Canada, and to a lesser extent Australia have continually produced food surpluses. By 1973, the United States was exporting approximately three-fourths of its soybean production. Had it not been for the decision of the United States to use its food reserves to avert famine wherever possible, death from starvation would have been much more frequent. During the 1960s and early 1970s, the United States increased exports by bringing most of its 50 million fallow acres of farmland into production and by decreasing its grain reserves (and, to a limited extent, by increasing yields per acre).[38]

While there are ways of further increasing our exports, there are limits to American agricultural ca-

pabilities. Furthermore, as the President's Science Advisory Committee reported in 1966 (the last such report to be issued), the exportation of food by the United States may not be a long-term solution to the world food problem and may actually aggravate it by discouraging local authorities from increasing food production.[39] If food from the United States has limited potential for saving the world, what about other potential sources of food?

New Land

The earth is a huge planet with seemingly immense areas of unused land. Why not bring some of this under cultivation to supplement the world's food supply? Since this land is often of marginal value for agricultural uses, the results usually prove unsatisfactory. Some marginal land turns into desert or is destroyed by erosion when attempts are made to farm it. The data presented in Figure 4.7 illustrate the magnitude of this problem of increasing **desertification** (the transition of new land to deserts) in the world today. For example, this occurred in the Soviet Union when a massive project was undertaken to plow and cultivate 100 million acres of virgin land. Only after much of the land was plowed was it discovered that the region lacked sufficient rainfall to support crops. In other areas, such as western India, attempts at agriculture have resulted in turning marginal land into desert.[40] Although there is uncultivated land with some agricultural potential in certain regions, such as the tropics, present levels of knowledge and technology are inadequate to exploit it.

If such marginal land requires irrigation or intensive fertilization, these alterations of the natural environment may promote disease, mineralization of the water supply due to evaporation, or clogging of the irrigation systems with silt. Further, the extensive use of synthetic fertilizers may have other undesirable consequences. For example, the runoff of chemical fertilizers has led to the eutrophication of streams and ponds. *Eutrophication* **is the increase of nutrients in the water so that abnormal plant growth is promoted, which has an adverse effect on fish populations.** In areas such as the Philippines, where fish is an important source of protein, this attempt to alleviate food shortages has actually contributed further to the problem of malnutrition.

The use of insecticides to increase food production may also have undesirable side effects. First, concentrations of insecticides that are dangerous to human health may build up in the food chain and eventually be ingested by human beings. Second, insects, through selective survival, may, over a period of generations, become immune to the insecticide, requiring increased dosages to avoid crop damage. Similarly, because the insecticide may kill the natural predators of insects dangerous to crops, these insects may actually increase in numbers and become a more serious threat.

One strategy for bringing new land into production is to desalinate seawater to irrigate desert areas. *Desalinization* **is the removal of salts and other minerals from seawater.** While a number of nations have considered this possibility, it has usually been abandoned because of the high cost.

Farming the Seas

Since there seem to be limits to our ability to produce sufficient food from land-based agriculture, some have proposed that we turn to the sea as an important and unlimited source of new food. Yet the decline, beginning in 1969, in world fisheries

The plight of these citizens in Bangladesh may be the fate of millions of other human beings in the event of a deficit famine.

suggests not only that there are limits to this resource, but that these limits may have already been reached. While organisms other than fish (such as plankton and algae) can be, and are being, harvested from the oceans, these constitute part of an elaborate ecosystem. In an *ecosystem,* the various forms of life depend on one another so that a substantial change in the numbers of one organism may eventually affect the others. Therefore, large-scale use of plankton and algae may lead to declines in other oceanic resources, such as fish.[41]

The Green Revolution

Since the development of *new land* has proved to be less than successful, an alternative for increas-

Figure 4.7 **The Earth's Spreading Deserts.** *The New York Times,* **August 28, 1977, p. 43.**

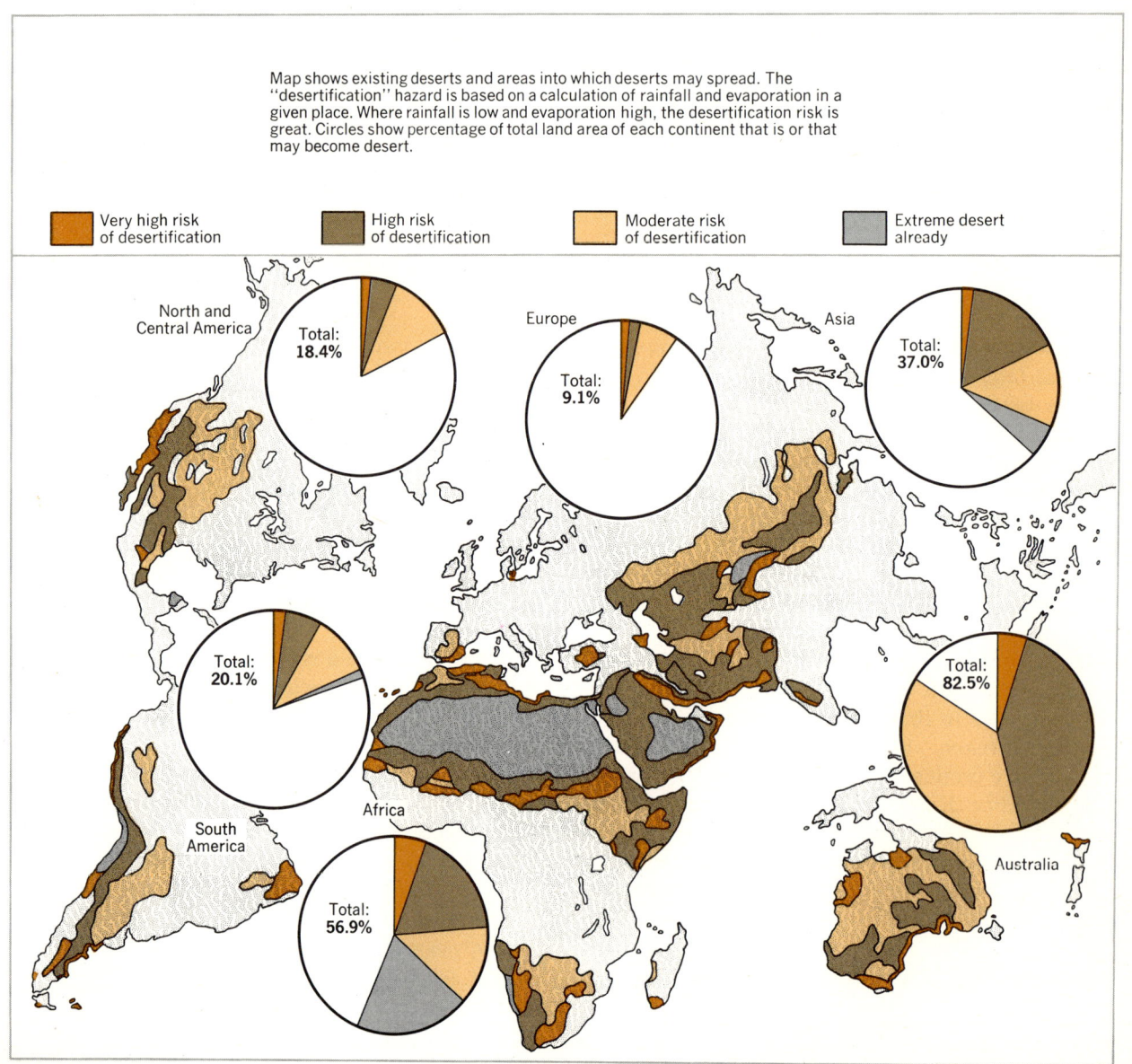

Map shows existing deserts and areas into which deserts may spread. The "desertification" hazard is based on a calculation of rainfall and evaporation in a given place. Where rainfall is low and evaporation high, the desertification risk is great. Circles show percentage of total land area of each continent that is or that may become desert.

Very high risk of desertification

High risk of desertification

Moderate risk of desertification

Extreme desert already

North and Central America — Total: 18.4%

Europe — Total: 9.1%

Asia — Total: 37.0%

South America — Total: 20.1%

Africa — Total: 56.9%

Australia — Total: 82.5%

Experimental varieties of rice have been well received in India. The high-yield strains have helped significantly in increasing food production in order to avoid famine.

ing food production has been to use *existing agricultural land* more efficiently.[42] In fact, man has been doing this for some time. For example, during the late nineteenth and early twentieth centuries, Japan substantially increased yields per acre through the use of fertilizers and intensive cultivation practices. By the middle of this century, the Japanese, in response to population pressures, were producing some of the highest yields per acre ever attained. Yet the plant strains and production techniques were not necessarily exportable. A rice strain that did well in Japan, for example, might not grow well in India.

In response to this situation, intensive research was undertaken. In Mexico, high-yield wheat strains were produced. In the Philippines, the International Rice Research Institute developed new strains of rice that had many of the advantages of the new wheat strains produced in Mexico. These grains can, under proper conditions, give far higher yields than the local varieties. Furthermore, unlike the native grains, they respond well to increased use of chemical fertilizers. Since they ripen earlier,

it is often possible to plant an additional crop during each year.

These technological developments and the resulting increase in agricultural production came to be called the **Green Revolution.** The results were remarkable. For example, in India grain production increased from 11 million tons in 1965 to 27 million in 1972 – a feat unparalleled in history. In the Philippines food independence was achieved. In fact, success in the early phases of the Green Revolution was so dramatic that some even suggested that the food problem would not be a shortage, but rather how to dispose of surpluses!

However, recent developments have caused this optimism to wane. Because of bad weather and shortages of fertilizer due to the skyrocketing cost of petroleum, both India and the Philippines were again importing food by the mid-1970s. Thus, some of the gains attributed to the Green Revolution were actually a function of unusually good weather over a period of several years.

Many new and unforeseen problems were created by the use of new seed strains. First, while some large landowners prospered, brought ruin to many small marginal farmers. In the Philippines, for instance, many small landholders were driven from their land because they could not get credit to buy the fertilizers necessary for growing the new grains. Many undoubtedly became poor migrants to the slums of Manila or joined the guerrilla movement. A second problem was (and still is) that much of the acreage devoted to the new grains was land taken out of the production of pulses (peas and beans), which constitute a major source of protein for many poor people. This resulted in malnutrition —that is, receiving insufficient nutrients to maintain health. Third, the new grains required extensive use of fertilizers, insecticides, and water—all of which may be, and often are, in short supply or available only in certain areas. With the increases in petroleum prices since 1973, the cost of fertilizer has greatly increased. Fourth, even where crops are abundant, large quantities are often lost because of inadequate transportation, storage, or marketing facilities. Fifth, while high-yield wheat and rice grains have been developed, relatively little progress has been made in other nutritionally important crops, such as corn and soybeans. Last, if the new strains prove susceptible to some disease or infestation, the result could be a massive crop failure of unparalleled proportions. While the amount of acreage devoted to high-yield grains has largely stabilized in the past decade, it still constitutes a significant part of world food production. In certain areas of Asia, for instance, the new grains have almost completely replaced traditional rice varieties (see Table 4.1). Prior to the introduction of the new rice, some fifteen to twenty varieties were grown, so that any particular disease or pest usually affected only a few of them.

Thus while such efforts to increase the yield of agricultural lands are important, the original optimism has been considerably tempered by developments. Many exotic alternatives to increase the food supply have been proposed. For example, progress has been made in *aquaculture*—the rearing of fish and other aquatic food sources under artificial conditions. However, while these efforts may eventually lead to a considerable increase in food,

TABLE 4.1

Acreage Planted in High-Yield Strains of Wheat and Rice in Asia

YEAR	ACRES
1965	200
1966	41,000
1967	4,047,000
1968	16,660,000
1969	31,319,000
1970	43,914,000
1971	50,549,000

SOURCE. Lester R. Brown, ''Population and Affluence: Growing Pressures on World Food Resources,'' *Population Bulletin*, vol. 29, no. 2 (1973) p. 9. Reprinted courtesy of Population Reference Bureau, Washington, D.C.

the returns are at present small, and we cannot rest on the faith that some novel technology will eventually be found to remove us from the Malthusian predicament we seem to be in.

The Next Two Decades

Assuming that all current food sources are used and that the world's ecosystem is strained to its limit, can we produce adequate food within a limited time to avert massive starvation? The world population may double by A.D. 2010; the population of the underdeveloped countries may double by 2000. A doubling of the population does not simply mean that we must double the amount of food available, since some people living today are not receiving a sufficient amount of food. Approximately a half-billion people today are undernourished—that is, slowly starving—while another billion are malnourished. Thus, when the population doubles, we must not only feed all the new faces, but also try to increase the meager amount of food some of the old faces have been receiving. As the Food Panel of the President's Advisory Council pointed out in 1966, the next two decades are critical. If a solution is not found by 1985, many nations will have reached a point at which the only likely outcome will be massive famine, and 1985 is rapidly approaching.[43]

Even if the supply of food were to keep pace with population growth, three related factors would remain crucial in avoiding starvation: (1) the willingness of those with a food surplus to make it available to groups in need; (2) the ability to transport these surpluses to areas of scarcity; and (3) the acceptance of available nutritional materials as food by those in need.

Willingness to Share

First, the fact that a nation possesses a food surplus does not necessarily mean that it is willing to share that surplus with those in need. A reluctance to share may be based on, among other things, political, military, or economic considerations. Thus, some nations would prefer to sell their surplus for a profit rather than share it for humanitarian reasons. After attempting to assist underdeveloped nations by giving them some of its grain surplus, the United States was sharply criticized by a number of grain-exporting nations for "dumping" its grain surplus on the world market, thus reducing overall world *economic demand* for their own exports. Also, a nation may be unwilling to share its surplus because to do so may reduce the incentive of the receiving nation to produce food.

Ability to Distribute

When food is available and parties with a surplus are willing to share, it may still prove difficult to get the food to those who need it. One reason for this is inadequate shipping facilities. For example, it would have required the equivalent of all American merchant shipping in 1965 to transport needed surpluses to the underdeveloped nations.[44] This, of course, would have left no ships for other imports and exports. Other difficulties in distribution include inadequate ports and storage facilities in the receiving countries, primitive internal transportation systems, and the diversion of surpluses back onto the open market as a means of enriching a few corrupt officials.

Definitions of Food

A third consideration involves cultural definitions of food. Simply because a substance can be ingested and is nutritional does not automatically make it *food* to those who share a particular culture. The polar Eskimo traditionally lived on meat and fish;

the Apache regarded fish as being unfit for human consumption; many Hindus are vegetarians and refuse to eat either fish or meat. Each culture defines which substances will be viewed as acceptable food. You may feel that extreme hunger would eliminate cultural barriers to the consumption of such items. It seems incongruous for Hindus to starve while cattle roam freely through the country. Yet how hungry would *you* have to be to dine on dog, cat, or insect larvae? Instances where potential food goes unused are numerous. For example, in many places, the residual cake from seed oil production (soybeans, etc.) is often not used for food even though it is very nutritious (and even constitutes a disposal problem).[45]

In summary, it is clear that a substantial portion of the world's population may well experience, in the immediate future, a severe food shortage of a type and scope unparalleled in world history. It is also clear that overpopulation and food scarcity involve more than mere numbers. Technology, international relations, cultural influences, and a host of other factors must be taken into account if we are to have any hope of coming to grips with the problem.

The Fight For Survival

If we do not find workable solutions to these problems, there may be consequences beyond the inevitable increase in death rates. Worldwide famine and starvation will create social disorder, pestilence, and possible international conflict. Traditionally, famine and its consequences were confined to some limited area. Today, however, they will be less localized. We have seen that the United States is part of a worldwide system that makes us increasingly dependent on other nations for certain resources. In the event of major food shortages, it is clear that great pressure will be brought to bear on the United States and other nations with a food surplus to export more food even at the risk of domestic shortages. For example, at the 1974 Conference on Food held in Rome, the United States was urged to make much more food available even though most of our surplus was already being exported.

In other words, the underdeveloped nations will

use whatever means are available to them in order to share in our surpluses. For example, developing nations will withhold whatever resources they have that we need in order to force us to part with those of our resources (such as food) that are in short supply in their countries. Since the energy crisis of the early 1970s, the Oil Producing and Exporting Countries have been using their vast oil reserves — which we need to maintain our standard of living — in precisely this fashion. Other nations, when facing a food shortage, will undoubtedly use the same strategy with the resources that they possess. Nations with no material resources that we need might turn to acts of sabotage, political terrorism, or even war. Would you be willing to accept a lower standard of living or less abundant food supplies in order to avert famine in other countries? Or, would you rather expand our military capability in order to counter such international pressure to share our agricultural resources?

In any future international crisis, the proliferation of nuclear technology adds an especially ominous dimension. In 1945, the United States was the only nation possessing the technology to build nuclear weapons. By 1949, we were joined by the Soviet Union. Since then, Britain, France, China, India, and possibly other nations have developed the capability to produce nuclear weapons. The number of nations with this ability will no doubt continue to increase. Even a mild food shortage, let alone a major famine, could generate the kind of political pressure that might tempt underdeveloped nations to threaten the use of nuclear weapons as a means of obtaining a larger share of the world's food supply. It is well known that those who are starving are ripe for demagoguery; if a leader promises them food, they are likely to listen regardless of the plan. The potential for war under such circumstances would be enormous. The war might be local, but even localized conflicts often have global consequences since the major powers tend to become involved either by accident or by design.

"And the Poor Get Children"[46]

We cannot complete our discussion of the consequences of overpopulation without returning to a brief mention of what is possibly the most tragic result. In our discussion of the effect of socioeconomic factors on fertility, we pointed to the potential existence of a vicious circle involving rapid population growth and fertility. When population growth is slow, as was the case in the United States, there is time to develop sufficient resources to maintain or improve the standard of living. However, when population increases rapidly, it places an increasing strain on society's ability to feed and clothe its growing masses. In the developing nations today, population is growing so rapidly that it increasingly taxes the resources available to them. As a consequence, rapid population growth increases the extent of poverty in these nations. The tragic aspect is that poverty is one cause of high fertility, which in turn can lead to overpopulation in a situation where death rates are not correspondingly high. Thus, there is a circular process: rapid population growth strains resources, which leads to poverty; and poverty causes high fertility, which leads to further population growth.

The consequences of overpopulation are many and varied. Nearly all of these results, however, have one thing in common — they are *undesirable*. To come to grips with the problem, we must investigate the steps that can be taken to reduce the threat of overpopulation.

FUTURE PROSPECTS

We now have before us the outline of the population problem, and we gave also seen that the problem has grown more acute. Can this trend be reversed? Are there actions that can be taken to alter future prospects? In searching for courses of action, we must examine those factors that have contributed to the problem — migration, mortality, and fertility.

Migration

Migration has often been proposed as a way of coping with overpopulation. Yet, for a number of reasons, this approach has limited possibilities in the late twentieth century. Where might one possibly migrate to? For *emigration* (**out-migration**) to have any appreciable effect, large numbers of people would have to leave an overcrowded area. Since we now lack the technical capability or the financial resources to send people to other habitable planets, we must find space on earth. While there are large areas of sparsely populated land on earth, few are readily adaptable to human habitation. For example, with present technology, the Arctic and Antarctic, the great deserts, the tropical rain forests, and the mountainous regions are incapable of supporting large populations. Furthermore, sparsely populated nations usually discourage *immigration* (**movement of people into an area or nation),** especially if those potential immigrants are culturally or racially different from their own people. For example, Indonesia, a nation with a relatively large amount of unused and potentially arable land, has been adamantly opposed to the immigration of Chinese, and presumably of Indians, Pakistanis, or others if large numbers tried to enter the country.[47] In fact, those countries with the highest population densities have found that other nations have erected barriers to immigration by their citizens.

At the time when Europe and the United States were experiencing their highest rate of population growth (1750–1870), it was still possible for people to move from one part of the world to another with relative freedom. While migration did drain off some European population during this period, it is not clear that this actually affected the net size of the population in Europe in the long run. Today, many nations, particularly the totalitarian states, have restrictions on emigration, and nearly all nations restrict immigration. To more fully appreciate how unimportant migration is as a factor influencing the populations of modern nations, consider the information in Table 4.2. In evaluating this information, compare the gain or loss in population due to migration with the total populations of the regions. The migration figures are quite small compared to the total population.

Another consideration is that where habitable lands *are* available, migration would probably involve some degree of conflict, possibly war. In this sense, the conflict perspective has implications for our evaluation of a potential, but questionable, solution to the problem. Even if the scarce resources of land were available, the cost of conflict would probably make extensive migration unfeasi-

TABLE 4.2
Net Migration Balances for Major World Regions, 1946–1957 and 1960–1970

REGION	1946–1957	1960–1970
Africa	+500,000[a]	−1,600,000
Asia	−500,000	−1,200,000
Europe	−5,400,000	−300,000
Latin America	+900,000	−1,900,000
Northern America	+3,400,000	+4,100,000
Oceania	+1,000,000	+900,000

[a] + = a gain in population due to migration during the time period; − = a loss in population due to migration during the time period.

SOURCE. United Nations, *International Migration Trends, 1950–1970.* Conference Background Paper. May 22, 1974.

ble. Finally, even if the difficulties of migration could be overcome, it is likely that any gain in the standard of living resulting from the smaller population due to emigration would lead to a decline in mortality and, hence, to an increasing population.

Mortality

High rates of mortality have played an important role in controlling population growth. Indeed, Malthus believed that mortality, in the form of the positive checks, would continue to be an important factor when the preventative checks were not utilized. We have already predicted that mortality, especially through famine, may prove to be an important control on population in the immediate future. However, this will be despite, rather than because of, human effort. While we recognize the effects of mortality, we can hardly advocate this factor as a solution. Such high mortality is simply not consistent with the values in most cultures. In fact, as was suggested earlier, any such solution could prove devastating for humanity and the world because inherent in it is a considerable potential for war.

Fertility

Since migration is not an effective, long-range solution to overpopulation, and since mortality is not an alternative that is acceptable to most people, we must turn to fertility as the primary focus of our efforts to control population growth. We have observed the many factors that promote high fertility.

Because of the complexity of these factors, there is no simple solution to the problem of high fertility. There are many current programs to attack some part of the problem, although they vary in effectiveness and the amount of time required to actually reduce population growth.

Contraception

One seemingly straightforward approach to lowering fertility is to prevent conception. **Some experts take the view that easy-to-use and effective contraceptives are the key to lowering fertility and reducing population growth.** In the United States, for example, the relatively high fertility in the years following World War II declined precipitously during the 1960s, and the widespread use of effective contraceptives certainly contributed to this decline. In West Germany, approximately one-third of the fertile women use oral contraceptives, and in 1976 the crude birth rate was 10 — the lowest in the world. Although German women use other contraceptive devices, the oral contraceptive pill is one of the more popular. In 1976, there were fewer births than deaths in Germany, and thus there was a declining population. Germans refer to this outcome of the widespread use of contraceptive pills as *Der Pillenknick* ("the pill pinch").[48]

Communist nations, such as the Soviet Union and China, had originally held to a Marxian view of population problems — the problem was not too many people, they argued, but rather a maldistribution of resources. Thus they did not promote contraception and in some cases did promote large families. However, their policies have changed in recent decades, and both now promote contraception. The Soviet Union has placed great emphasis on the manufacture and distribution of intrauterine devices (IUDs). This method has been favored by the government because of its effectiveness and the lack of side effects.[49]

In China, oral contraceptives are widely used along with — to a lesser extent — sterilization. The Chinese have supported extensive research on oral contraceptives, partly because they view sterilization as a crude and rather undesirable method of preventing conception. One form of oral contraceptive in China is the so-called "paper pill" — a very thin, postage-stamp-size piece of rice paper impregnated with a contraceptive compound. When swallowed, the rice paper dissolves. This is a much less expensive way to manufacture contraceptives than the pills popular in other countries. The Chinese have also experimented with other forms of oral contraceptives — once-a-month pills, contraceptive injections, and visiting-husband pills (intended for couples who work in different regions, they are taken only when the couple is together, and they provide protection for a few days) — but the effectiveness of these innovations is unknown.[50]

There is wide variation in the effectiveness of contraceptive methods (see Table 4.3). **Oral contraceptives and the IUD are by far the most effective methods. Sterilization has also proved both effective and increasingly popular.** In fact, use of the contraceptive pill has declined slightly in the United States (from 25 percent of all fertile couples in 1973 to 22 percent in 1976), while sterilization has become more popular. In 1976, 30 percent of the couples with wives of childbearing age were physically unable to have children, which is a 6 percent increase since 1973. Most of this sterilization is the result of surgical procedures.[51] The decline in popularity of the pill is at least partially accounted for by recent evidence associating the use of the pill with increased incidence of some diseases such as blood clots and strokes.

Despite the existence of very effective modern methods of contraception, many older methods still flourish. For example, in one survey in Japan in 1975, 78 percent of the respondents reported that they sometimes use the condom, while 30 percent said that they also use the rhythm method. However, Japan has achieved a dramatic decline in the birth rate since the 1940s, largely due to government-subsidized abortion programs.[52]

Given the effectiveness of contraception in reducing fertility, why not simply blanket the world with the whole gamut of contraceptive devices available so that people can use them when they desire? While it may be feasible, such an approach treats conception as a purely biological phenomenon and

TABLE 4.3
Accidental Pregnancy Rates per 100 Years of Exposure, by Method of Contraception

TYPE OF CONTRACEPTION	VARIOUS STUDIES	METROPOLITAN AMERICAN FAMILIES	COMPOSITE FROM SIX STUDIES
Oral progestin-estrogen	0.1–1.1	—	—
Intrauterine devices	0.9–8.5	—	—
Condom		13.8	14
Diaphragm and spermicide		14.4	12
Withdrawal		16.8	18
Spermicide alone		—	20
Rhythm·		38.5	24
Douche		40.5	31
Others		30.3	—
No contraception, with lactation	50		
No contraception, no lactation	63		

SOURCE: William Petersen, *Population*, 3d ed. (New York: Macmillan Publishing Co., Inc. 1975), p. 211. Copyright © 1975 by William Petersen. Reprinted with permission of Macmillan Publishing Co., Inc.

the prevention of conception as merely a technological feat. Yet they are much more than that—conception is a social event and the prevention of it is a decision that people must make. **Truly effective programs to reduce fertility must focus on those social and cultural factors that result in a couple's decision to have children.**

Family Planning

Family planning **programs encourage couples to have children when and if they are desired. It is an effort to encourage people to decide how many children they want, when they want them, and to use the contraceptive techniques available to achieve that end.** Strictly speaking, with family planning, a couple might decide to have a very large family, and if many couples so chose, high fertility would remain a problem. However, most family planning programs encourage people to want fewer children and thus work to lower fertility. So family planning programs in effect encourage people to use the contraceptive technology that is available.

There is considerable variation among the nations of the world in the acceptance of family planning programs. They are quite popular in the United States and, in fact, a U.S. Commission on Population Growth and the Future has recom-

mended that such services be expanded with the goal of planning for a stable population in the future.[53] Yet there is still opposition by some in America to certain aspects of family planning. Many groups are opposed to abortion as a device to lower fertility. Other groups are incensed by efforts to make contraceptive information available to high school students, among whom there is an alarming problem of illegitimate pregnancies. Still, most Americans have embraced the value of a small family and a stable population and view family planning as one means of achieving this.

In other parts of the world, such consensus does not always exist. Some Catholic nations in Latin America have generally been opposed to any form of family planning on religious grounds, although there appears to be a shift in that position recently toward more acceptance of such programs. India, on the other hand, has long stressed family planning as a means of reducing its explosive population growth. In fact, the zeal of the Indians reached such a point that several Indian states proposed mandatory sterilization programs for certain parts of the male population. Although these laws were rescinded when Indira Ghandi lost power in 1977, they illustrate the acceptance of family planning among some groups of Indians. A recent report showed that in approximately 12 percent of the married couples in India one partner, usually the

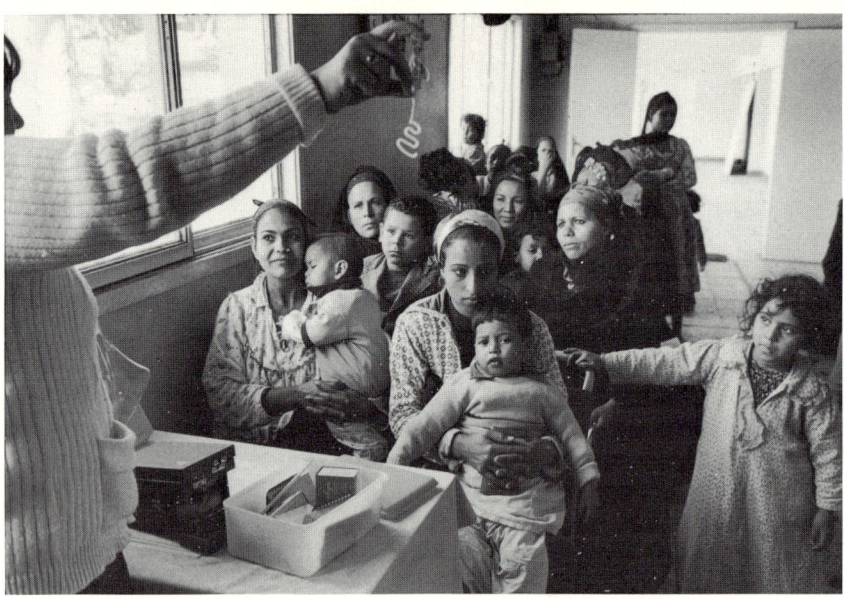

The intrauterine device, one of the more effective methods of contraception, is distributed by family planning agencies in developing nations like Egypt.

male, had been sterilized. Yet large families are still viewed by the vast majority of rural and poor Indians as most desirable.[54]

In countries where intensive family planning programs have been carried out, dramatic declines in fertility sometimes result. In Puerto Rico, a territory of the United States, intensive family planning programs have been established, and as can be seen in Figure 4.8, the result has been a substantial reduction in the age-specific birth rate between 1960 and 1974. **The *age-specific birth rate* is the number of births per 1000 women in a specific age category.** In Venezuela, on the other hand, relatively little energy has been expended on family planning programs, and the outcome, in comparison with Puerto Rico, is obvious.

The most effective approach to family planning appears to be the promotion of a combination of methods to lower fertility. Some methods are more consistent with the values of a particular culture. Contraceptive pills and IUDs account for about two-thirds of contraceptive use in the developing countries, with sterilization increasing rapidly.

However, we have seen that China finds sterilization to be a less than desirable contraceptive technique. In other nations, abortion is viewed with revulsion. In some instances, government programs on a national scale have promoted whatever methods are deemed acceptable and effective. In Bangladesh in 1976, for example, 12,000 welfare workers and 28,000 volunteers made efforts to contact all 15 million couples of childbearing age—a truly monumental family planning effort. They extolled the virtues of family planning, distributed condoms and pills, and indicated the locations of clinics where IUDs could be inserted or tubal ligation and vasectomies performed. In Pakistan, there is a national family planning network that distributed 4.6 million sets of contraceptive pills, each set protecting the woman from pregnancy for a month, and 83 million condoms in 1976.[55]

Thus family planning on a worldwide scale is now a massive undertaking that has already had a significant impact on fertility rates. In addition, research continues into more effective and more varied contraceptive devices, such as the male oral

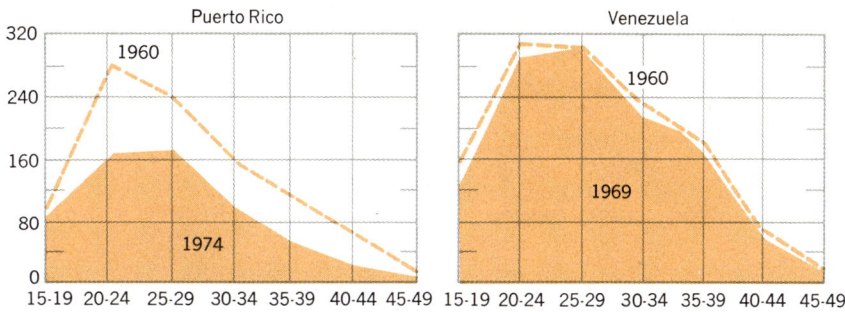

Figure 4.8 Age-Specific Birth Rates for Puerto Rico and Venezuela. U.S. Bureau of the Census, *World Fertility Patterns,* prepared for the Office of Population, U.S. Agency for International Development, October 1975.

contraceptive. It is estimated that about one-third of the world's people now have access to some family planning program.[56] But, is it adequate? Will these efforts to control population growth achieve their goals before the burgeoning world population, perhaps in combination with a catastrophic famine, results in widespread starvation? This question is the core of the issue, and we do not yet have an answer to it.

Economic Development

While we may applaud those who emphasize family planning and recognize the contribution that they have made to alleviating the world population problem, **it is important to recall that historically it has been** *economic development* **that has substantially lowered birth rates.** Recall the demographic transition and the role of industrialization in reducing birth rates. In fact, those nations actively involved in programs to control population growth have placed a major emphasis on economic development. While they recognize the need for family planning, these nations argue that no program of population control can be completely effective unless it is part of a more general program of economic development.

Proponents of economic development argue that long-term declines in fertility are only one part of a whole series of social and economic changes that occur together and mutually influence one another. Because of those changes related to economic develop- **ment, couples come to desire smaller families.** Many have argued that contraceptives are only a means to an end, and that the key to lower fertility is that people must want smaller families.[57] Thus, unless economic development, increasing education, and the other changes occur, people in the developing countries will continue to value large families, and family planning by itself will have only a limited impact on the population problem.

If we compare the decline in fertility in the United States with the situation that confronts the developing nations today, there is some reason for pessimism. There are two factors in the decline in birth rates in the United States that are somewhat different from conditions faced by the developing nations. First, in the United States there was a steady decline in birth rates over a period of one hundred years. The developing nations today do not have the luxury of that much time. At current birth rates, their populations are quickly growing so large that there may not be sufficient food to support them. Second, the decline in the birth rate in the United States was not due to intensive family planning programs nor to the use of contraceptives. Prior to 1920, few people were informed about effective contraceptive measures, and contraceptive devices were not widespread. Yet America was still able to achieve substantial reductions in fertility during this period.

The key to America's ability to reduce its birth rate was that people came to desire small families. As a result of urbanization, the increasing education of most couples, and the movement of women into positions other than those of mother and housewife, couples came to view large families of eight to ten children as a burden that hindered their ability to achieve a style of life acceptable to them. In an urban setting, large families are terribly expensive; and since the passage of child-labor laws, children have not been an economic resource for the urban family. At the same time, women came to perceive themselves as able to do more than have children. While most women still want children, a large family interferes with the mother's opportunity to develop a career, talents, or a hobby. For these reasons, people began to view small families as more desirable and, even without effective contraceptives, were able to lower the birth rate substantially.

Thus the simple existence of effective contraceptives is useless unless people genuinely want to have fewer children. Without that desire, the contraceptives will go unused, as happens in many developing countries today. This is not to say that contraceptives are irrelevant. The very low birth rates in the United States in the past two decades are certainly attributable to the development of two very effective contraceptive methods—the pill and the IUD. Still, these methods will be used only if the desire for small families exists; and, the proponents of economic growth argue, that desire emerges as a result of economic development and the social changes associated with it.

If the developing countries do not have the time to achieve low birth rates through economic development, is there no alternative? Are we doomed to catastrophic world population growth? Because the countries with low birth rates today achieved them through economic development does not necessarily mean that that route is the only possible one. It may be that a stable population can be achieved in other ways. The proponents of family planning make precisely this argument. Through extensive family planning counseling and education programs, the desire to have fewer children can be nourished. Then effective contraceptive technology can be made available. So even in the absence of economic development, birth rates might be lowered.

Will it work? The evidence of lowering birth rates in most countries today suggests that this strategy is working. Whether it can reduce birth rates to the low levels of the industrialized nations is as yet unknown. There are still many incentives for couples in developing countries to have a large family. The student should review the causes of high fertility (such as religious beliefs and the lack of institutional supports for small families) to determine the extent to which they still exist in developing countries and might attenuate the impact of family planning efforts. Nevertheless, there is room for optimism that current programs will, if not totally solve, at least alleviate the problem of overpopulation.

Zero Population Growth

With the publication in 1968 of Paul Ehrlich's popular book *The Population Bomb,* the term *zero population growth* (ZPG) became a household word.[58] **In popular usage, the term means that the birth rate is equal to the death rate, and thus the population is simply replacing itself and not growing.** Actually, ZPG is somewhat more complex than that. Technically, it means that the number of girls born just replaces the number of mothers, and that this situation must continue for at least fifty years before the population would actually stop growing. This condition is difficult to achieve over the long run because the number of women in their reproductive years varies considerably during different periods.

Nevertheless, many students of population problems have adopted the banner of zero population growth, in its more popular usage, because it stands as a symbol of a particular attitude toward population control—the belief that it is important to stop world population growth. So even though ZPG in its technical sense is unlikely to be achieved, it can still serve as a useful symbol to rally people to the cause of world population control.[59]

CONCLUSION

Our review of the problem of population growth is in many respects discouraging because the problems seem so complex, immediate, and difficult to solve. There is considerable disagreement between nations concerning how serious the problem is and what might be done about it. No single nation holds the key to solving the problem. We can conclude our discussion of this problem by using our three theoretical perspectives to sort out some of the basic issues surrounding population problems.

For the functionalist, population becomes a social problem when it grows so large that it interferes with the ability of society to support itself at an acceptable level. However, given the interdependence of nations, we cannot consider the population of one nation separately from that of the world as a whole. Although the United States may not have a population problem (in that we have adequate food and land to support our populace), food shortages due to overpopulation in other parts of the world may have an impact on us: these countries may demand some of our food supply, they may withhold some mineral resources that we need, or they may even be willing to wage war if they believe this might alleviate their problem. In any event, we are dependent on other nations, and their population problem is, to some extent, our population problem.

In evaluating solutions to population problems, the functionalist perspective makes us sensitive to the interrelationships between social institutions. We have emphasized that solutions to the population problem will undoubtedly focus on fertility — efforts to reduce the birth rate. This will mean smaller families around the globe. Still, a large family can be functional in many societies. In a preindustrial society, a large family is economically productive as an agricultural unit, and it also serves as a source of support for people in their old age. If we reduce the birth rate and thus bring about smaller families, we need to consider the impact this will have on the lives of people in these preindustrial societies. Industrial nations such as America reduced their family size over a long period of time, which provided the opportunity for the emergence of institutions that would take over some of the functions served by the large family. If today's developing nations reduce their family size quickly (which is the hope of family planners), there needs to be consideration given to what will replace the large family in the lives of these people. Thus solutions to the population problem begin to impact on many areas of our lives.

From the conflict perspective, population size (large or small) becomes defined as a social problem because an influential group defines it as threatening to its interests. This means that population problems may not be resolved simply by lowering the birth rate. Some nations, as we have seen, might resist this because they perceive a growing population as in their own interests. These nations argue that the problem of overpopulation is a smokescreen used by the affluent nations to protect their own interests by keeping the populations of other nations small. Thus even with changes in the birth rate, including an actual decline in the world population, there might still be groups who would argue that a problem exists because a declining population threatens their interests.

As we noted earlier, the interactionist perspective, to a much greater extent than the others, emphasizes people's perceptions of the quality of their life. If we expect a certain standard of living (in terms of material goods, food supplies, freedom of movement, and the like), then population size is a problem to the extent that it interferes with our ability to achieve it. Thus, people's definition of population problems is likely to vary in the future. If conditions improve, people will probably come to expect even more from their lives.

GLOSSARY TERMS

Age-specific birth rate
Aquaculture
Crowding
Crude birth rate
Crude death rate
Deficit famine
Demographic transition
Density
Desalinization

Desertification
Distribution famine
Emigration
Eutrophication
Family planning
Fecundity
Fertility
Green Revolution
Immigration

Industrial Revolution
Population
Population dynamics
Positive checks
Preventative checks
Rate of natural increase
Relative deprivation
Zero population growth

REFERENCES

[1] "Maharashtra Passes Family Size Limitation Measure," *Intercom 9* (September 1976), p. 5.

[2] For an analysis of the concept of population, see William Petersen, *Population,* 3d ed. (New York: Macmillan, 1975), and Julius Gould and William Kolb, eds., *A Dictionary of the Social Sciences* (New York: The Free Press, 1964), p. 518.

[3] Population Reference Bureau, *1977 World Population Data Sheet* (Washington, D.C.: Population Reference Bureau, 1978).

[4] George Washington University Medical Center, *Population Reports,* Series E, no. 5, January 1978.

[5] See Aaron Antonovsky, "Social Class, Life Expectancy, and Overall Mortality," in E. Gartly Jaco, ed., *Patients, Physicians, and Illness,* 2d ed. (New York: The Free Press, 1972), pp. 5–30; and Petersen, *Population,* p. 580.

[6] Hans Zinsser, *Rats, Lice, and History* (Boston: Little, Brown, 1935).

[7] Ralph Thomlinson, *Population Dynamics: Causes and Consequences of World Demographic Change* (New York: Random House, 1965).

[8] Petersen, *Population.*

[9] Kingsley Davis, *The Population of India and Pakistan* (New York: Russell and Russell, 1951), p. 45.

[10] In John Bartlett, *The Shorter Bartlett's Familiar Quotations* (New York: Permabooks, 1953), p. 440.

[11] Philip M. Hauser, ed., *The Population Dilemma* (Englewood Cliffs, N.J.: Prentice-Hall, 1963).

[12] Petersen, *Population,* p. 420.

[13] See Petersen, *Population,* pp. 10–15, and Warren S. Thompson and David T. Lewis, *Population Problems,* 5th ed. (New York: McGraw-Hill, 1965).

[14] Conrad Taeuber and Irene B. Taeuber, *The Changing Population of the United States* (New York: John Wiley & Sons, 1958), pp. 249–250, and United States Bureau of the Census, *Statistical Abstract of the United States, 1975* (Washington, D.C.: U.S. Government Printing Office, 1975), pp. 51–57.

[15] Thomas Robert Malthus, *On Population,* Gertrude Himmelfarb, ed. (New York: Modern Library, 1960), pp. 13–14. (Original edition, in 1798.)

[16] See Thompson and Lewis, *Population Problems,* pp. 14–35.

[17] See Karl Marx, *Das Kapital,* Eden Paul and Cedar Paul, trans. (New York: International Publishers, 1929), pp. 697–698, and Thompson and Lewis, *Population Problems,* pp. 48–50.

[18] See Antonovsky, "Social Class, Life Expectancy, and Overall Mortality," pp. 5–30, and Hauser, *The Population Dilemma,* p. 8.

[19] Harold F. Dorn, "World Population Growth," in Hauser, *The Population Dilemma,* pp. 8–9.

[20] See Population Reference Bureau, *1977 World Population Data Sheet,* and Petersen, *Population,* p. 595.

[21] Hauser, *The Population Dilemma,* p. 9.

[22] See Petersen, *Population,* p. 413; Kingsley Davis and Judith Blake, "Social Structure and Fertility: An Analytic Framework," *Economic Development and Cultural Change* 4 (April 1956), pp. 211–235, and Kenneth C. Kammeyer, ed., *Population Studies: Selected Essays and Research* (Chicago: Rand McNally, 1969), p. 317.

[23] Davis and Blake, "Social Structure and Fertility," pp. 211–235.

[24] Ibid.

[25] "The Delhi Dilemma," *Intercom* 5 (May 1976), p. 4.

[26] Petersen, *Population,* p. 196.

[27] "Italian Comic Books Teach Birth Control," *Intercom* 6 (June 1975), p. 5.

[28] See T. J. Samuel, "Culture and Human Fertility in India," in Kammeyer, *Population Studies,* p. 355, and Petersen, *Population,* p. 616.

[29] Phillips Cutright, Michael Hout, and David R. Johnson, "Structural Determinants of Fertility in Latin America: 1800–1970," *American Sociological Review* 41 (June 1976), pp. 511–526.

[30] Malthus, *On Population*, p. 39.

[31] John B. Calhoun, "Population Density and Social Pathology," *Scientific American* 206 (February 1962), pp. 139–148.

[32] Judd Marmor, "Marital Health and Overpopulation," in Sue Titus Reid and David L. Lyon, eds., *Population Crisis: An Interdisciplinary Perspective* (Glenview, Illinois: Scott, Foresman and Co., 1972), pp. 130–133.

[33] Jonathan L. Freedman, *Crowding and Behavior* (San Francisco: W. H. Freeman and Co., 1975).

[34] Nathan Keyfitz, "Population Density and the Style of Social Life," *BioScience* 16 (December 1966), pp. 868–873.

[35] Donella H. Meadows, Dennis L. Meadows, Jorgen Randers, and William V. Behrens III, *The Limits to Growth* (New York: Universe Books, 1972).

[36] Mihajlo Mesarovic and Eduard Pestel, *Mankind at the Turning Point: The Second Report to The Club of Rome* (New York: E. P. Dutton, 1974), p. 23.

[37] Petersen, *Population*, p. 420.

[38] Lester R. Brown, "Population and Affluence: Growing Pressures on Food Resources," *Population Bulletin*, vol. 29, no. 2, 1973.

[39] H. F. Robinson, "Dimensions of the World Food Crisis," *BioScience* 19 (January 1969), pp. 24–29.

[40] Brown, "Population and Affluence."

[41] Ibid.

[42] This discussion relies on Brown, "Population and Affluence."

[43] Tadd Fisher, "The Many-Faceted Food Problem," in Reid and Lyon, *Population Crisis*, pp. 87–92.

[44] Paul R. Ehrlich and John P. Holdren, "Population and Panaceas: A Technological Perspective," *Bio-Science* 19 (December 1969), pp. 1065–1071.

[45] Alan Berg, "Nutrition, Development, and Population Growth." **Population Bulletin,** vol. 29, no. 1, 1973.

[46] This is taken from the title of a book by Lee Rainwater, *And the Poor Get Children* (Chicago: Quadrangle Books, 1960).

[47] Thompson and Lewis, *Population Problems*, pp. 562–564.

[48] *"Der Pillenknick* in Germany," *Intercom* 4 (June 1976), p. 3.

[49] See Henry P. David, *Family Planning and Abortion in the Socialist Countries of Central and Eastern Europe* (New York: American Institute for Research, 1970), and Population Reference Bureau, *1978 World Population Data Sheet* (Washington, D.C.: Population Reference Bureau, 1978).

[50] See "Family Planning in the People's Republic," *Intercom* 4 (May 1976), pp. 2–3, and "Chinese See 'Attitude' as Birth Control Key," *Intercom* 5 (November 1977), pp. 1, 12.

[51] "Surgery on Rise in Birth Control," *The Detroit Free Press* (August 23, 1978), p. 1b.

[52] "Condoms, Two Children Population in Japan," *Intercom* 3 (October 1975), p. 12.

[53] Commission on Population Growth and the American Future, *Population and the American Future* (Washington, D.C.: U.S. Government Printing Office, 1972).

[54] See "Family Planning Progress in Pro-Natalist Paraguay," *Intercom* 8 (August/September 1975), p. 5, "The Delhi Dilemma," *Intercom* 4 (May 1976), p. 4, and Robert Cassen, "Welfare and Population: Notes on Rural India Since 1960," *Population and Development Review* 1 (September 1975), pp. 33–70.

[55] See "World Contraceptive Use Rising, Latest PRB Bulletin Reports," *Intercom* 5 (August 1977), p. 7, and "Contraceptive Inundation Planned for Pakistan," *Intercom* 4 (June 1976), p. 13.

[56] See "Volunteers Testing Male Steroid Pill," *Intercom* 4 (February 1976), p. 13, and "World Contraceptive Use Rising," *Intercom*, p. 7.

[57] Judith Blake and Prithwis Das Gupta, "Reproductive Motivation Versus Contraceptive Technology: Is Recent American Experience An Exception?" *Population and Development Review* 1 (December 1975), pp. 229–249.

[58] Paul Ehrlich, *The Population Bomb* (New York: Ballatine Books, 1968).

[59] Leon F. Bouvier, "U.S. Population in 2000: Zero Growth or Not?" *Population Bulletin*, vol. 30, no. 5, 1975.

SUGGESTED READINGS

Duncan, E. R. ed. *Dimensions of World Food Problems.* Ames, Iowa: Iowa State University Press, 1977.
A compendium of problems concerning food production. The book is a useful introduction for anyone wishing to become better informed concerning this issue. Food problems are shown to be highly complex.

Malthus, Thomas Robert. *An Essay on the Principle of Population.* 7th ed. London: Reeves & Turner, 1872.
This essay was the first book to pull together in a meaningful way the various influences on population. It demonstrates the significance of mortality in determining population size and shows in passing that migration is not a long-term solution.

McNeill, William H. *Plagues and Peoples.* Garden City, N.Y.: Doubleday, Anchor Books, 1976.
A detailed and well-documented history of epidemics throughout the world. Attention is given to the effects of disease on history. The first major work of this type since the publication of Hans Zinsser's *Rats, Lice and History* in the 1930s.

Meadows, Donella H. et al. *The Limits to Growth.* New York: Universe Books, 1972.
First of the controversial books published under the auspices of the Club of Rome. This volume contains a large number of computer projections showing the rate at which various resources will be exhausted under different sets of assumptions.

Petersen, William. *Population.* 3d ed. New York: Macmillan, 1975.
A very complete population text designed for use in undergraduate courses. The book is a good introduction for students interested in the field of population study.

Rainwater, Lee. *And the Poor Get Children.* Chicago: Quadrangle Books, 1960.
An excellent short description of the problems facing the urban poor in the area of family planning. Demonstrates that attitudes, self-conception, and role behavior are as important as contraceptive knowledge.

Reid, Sue Titus, and Lyon, David L. *The Population Crisis: An Interdisciplinary Perspective.* Glenview, Ill.: Scott-Foresman, 1972.
A collection of readings covering both biological and social aspects of the population problem. Readings of a historical nature are included.

Taeuber, Conrad, and Taeuber, Irene B. *The Changing Population of the United States.* New York: John Wiley & Sons, 1958.
A general description of the characteristics of, and changes in, the American population from colonial times through the 1950s. This is an extremely useful source for anyone interested in the background of the American population as it exists today.

Questions
for Discussion

1. It is difficult to understand population problems in the world today without considering the historical developments in this area. What does this history teach us concerning population growth? How did the development of industrial technology contribute to change in patterns of population growth?

2. The functional perspective on population is similar to the Malthusian view. How would a functionalist and/or a Malthusian define population as a problem?

3. The Marxian view of population problems is one variation of the conflict perspective. Discuss the problematic nature of population, first from a Marxian perspective, and second from a general conflict perspective.

4. Is the interactionist perspective useful in defining or understanding problems associated with population in view of the subjective nature of reality? If yes, why?

5. The three population dynamics, fertility, mortality and migration, have interacted to produce population problems in the world today. How does this interaction function and how has it changed over time?

6. Overpopulation leads to certain undesirable social conditions. Enumerate these results and indicate how they relate to one another. Can their effects be negated and if so, how?

7. Can we cope with the problem of overpopulation effectively? Discuss some of the means for coping and their relative merits.

8. If, in coping with overpopulation, the peoples of the world were to agree to some form of family planning, what kinds of related issues must be faced? Is this likely to be an effective solution? What is the likelihood that the United States or other countries will achieve zero population growth in the forseeable future?

CHAPTER 5

Problems of the Environment

ENVIRONMENTAL PROBLEMS IN HISTORICAL
PERSPECTIVE

The American Indian. The Coming of Western Man. The
Twentieth Century: Progress and Problems.

ENVIRONMENTAL CONDITIONS AS SOCIAL
PROBLEMS

The Functionalist Perspective. The Conflict Perspective.
The Interactionist Perspective.

INTEREST GROUPS AND THE ENVIRONMENT

Business and the Environment. The Environmental
Movement. The Modern Environmental Controversy:
Economic Growth v. an Unchanging Environment. The
Modern Dilemma.

CASE STUDY: KEPONE

The Trouble Begins. Genesis of a Chemical. Telltale Signs.
Missed Signals and Oversights. The Judgment. Counting
the Costs. The Way Out.

FUTURE PROSPECTS

Public Action on Environmental Problems. Interest Groups
in the Solution of Environmental Problems. A Strategy for
Environmental Solutions.

CONCLUSION

One patient twice has attempted suicide—once by taking an overdose of his medication, and another time by attempting to leap from an MCV [Medical College of Virginia] window. Another patient spent two weeks in a private mental hospital. Still another, said to have been calm and easygoing before his exposure, threw a hammer through his car window.

What Kepone does, metabolically, is circulate through the body in the blood stream, gathering in the brain, liver and spleen, but also seeking out the fatty tissue as a threatening storage bank—threatening because even if Kepone in the blood could be filtered out, more is bound to seep back from the fat.[1]

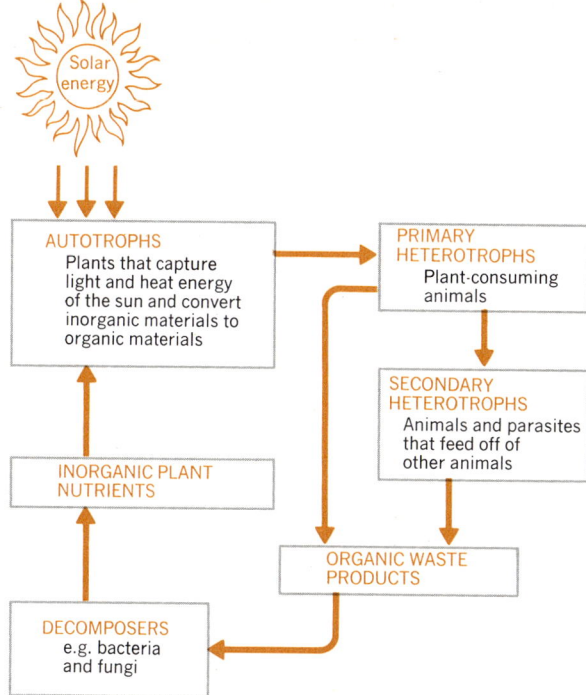

Figure 5.1   Basic Components of an Ecosystem.

This grim news account is unfortunately not uncommon in late twentieth-century America, for it describes one of the many instances where human activity has produced an undesirable effect on the environment that we all share. Prior to the 1950s, the American public was largely unconcerned about environmental issues. There have been, of course, those people throughout our history who were interested in the uses to which our environment was put and who were distressed over threats to it. However, any general feeling of concern about our ecological balance was undeveloped before the 1950s.

Today, the situation is quite different. Practically everyone living in the 1970s and 1980s has been sensitized to the impact of human activities on our environment.

The term *environment* **refers to all the conditions and circumstances that surround and affect an organism or group of organisms.** It is important to think of our environment as an *ecosystem*—**an area in which living organisms and nonliving substances interact with one another to produce an exchange of materials between the living and nonliving parts.**[2] In Figure 5.1, a very simplified version of an ecosystem is presented. **The key to an ecosystem—and central to our understanding of environmental problems—is the fact that all the parts of the environment are in dynamic interaction with one another. Each part is dependent on the others, and in changes one part may lead to changes in the other parts.**

Our environment consists of the natural world and all the processes essential for human survival and the maintenance of a socially acceptable standard of living. Environmental problems threaten not only a society's standard of living but also its very survival. Environmental problems come into being when human activity interferes with natural processes in an ecosystem resulting in changes that threaten health or survival. As our population grows and as our technology becomes more complex, the potential for such interference with nature usually increases. In this chapter, we examine some of these human activities and the hazards to the environment that have resulted. We will explore how an awareness of environmental problems has developed and how groups have organized to solve the problems. It will become clear that environmental problems are complex and that any effective action to resolve them will necessarily be equally complex. Since our population will continue to grow at least for the near future and technology will undoubtedly increase in complexity, it is essential that we come to grips with these problems before they are beyond solution.

ENVIRONMENTAL PROBLEMS IN HISTORICAL PERSPECTIVE

Environmental problems are not new. For as long as humanity has existed on the earth it has interfered to some degree with the natural processes of the ecosystem. However, such interference has not always been defined as a social problem. We can best begin our investigation of environmental problems by an examination of how people have perceived and related to their environment during earlier periods in American history.

The American Indian

I am a savage and I do not understand any other way. I have seen a thousand rotting buffalos on the prairie, left by the white man who shot them from a passing train. I am a savage and I do not understand how the smoking iron horse can be more important than the buffalo that we kill only to stay alive.

What is man without the beasts? If all the beasts were gone, men would die from a great loneliness of spirit. For whatever happens to the beasts, soon happens to man. All things are connected. (Chief Seattle, 1854)[3]

Like most societies throughout history, Native American groups were forced to adapt to conditions over which they had little control. However, to picture them as possessing an *environmental ethic* that placed great value on preserving the natural order is a romantic exaggeration.[4] No such ethic existed, at least on a conscious level, because there was no need for it; Native Americans used the environment to survive. That these people were able to exist in a relatively stable environment over a long period without damaging it significantly was due to the absence of technology (e.g. the steel-bladed ax) or population size that might have brought about such degradation. Many of the practices of the Native Americans prior to the migration of Europeans to the American continent would, on a larger scale, have been environmentally destructive. However, with the arrival of the Europeans, a technology appeared on the American scene that permitted radical alterations of the environment.

The Coming of Western Man

Unlike the American Indian, the Europeans who settled North America during the seventeenth century *did* possess an environmental ethic, although they were probably not aware of it.[5] Europe experienced a long history of settlement with scarce resources and limited space, and its people learned to live with these conditions. Houses, for instance, were usually designed to last for hundreds of years and were passed on through family inheritance. Land was also used quite efficiently, given the rather primitive technology of the times. When people of this kind suddenly find themselves in what appears to be an endless untamed wilderness, they are likely to react by viewing their earlier environmental ethic as irrelevant. There is no point in using land and resources cautiously if they appear to exist in an inexhaustable quantity. A new orientation toward the environment develops that emphasizes modifying the environment as necessary to maintain an acceptable lifestyle.

In the early years of migration to America, the new settlers altered the environment in order to survive, but as pathfinders such as Daniel Boone explored the country and blazed trails west of the Appalachians, *conquering* the land became an obsession.[6] The environment, in its wild and pristine state, seemed almost to stand in the way of the achievement of ever greater affluence and abundance. Survival was no longer sufficient; now it seemed necessary to wrest from the environment *all* of its seemingly unlimited value. Those who prevailed over the disposition of this new land were not the environmentalists of the east, such as Emerson and Thoreau, but rather the trailblazers, the farmers, the land developers, and those who profited from the sale of land and the exploitation of available resources. These groups had a vested interest in viewing the environment as a limitless thing to be used and exploited rather than as a fragile object to be protected and nurtured. These interest groups believed in — and for a time even seemed to prove the validity of — what Stewart Udall has called *the Myth of Superabundance:* "According to the myth, our resources were inexhaustible. It was an assumption that made wise management of the land and provident husbandry superfluous."[7] From the viewpoint of the early settler, the problem, if any, was not a shortage of resources but rather a shortage of people and a lack of technology adequate to exploit resources. Many Americans of this era believed that what was needed was a growing population of Americans to settle the land, defeat the indigenous Native Americans, and exploit the vast available resources.

The exploitation of resources as justified by the myth of superabundance was well established on the American scene long before the Civil War. However, the opportunities for exploitation were still somewhat limited by the relatively small population and the simple technology available. By the time of the Civil War, a steadily increasing population was beginning to make environmental exploitation a more serious concern. As Table 5.1 illustrates, population grew at an exceedingly rapid rate between 1790 and 1870, and it has continued to expand. In addition, most of the territory that is presently part of our nation had already been acquired.

The requirements of the Civil War itself also led to a considerable expansion of industry as well as to the encouragement of economic innovation. The results of all this were to be felt throughout the nineteenth and into the twentieth century: concentration of industry in the northern states and the development of a political system favoring those special economic interest groups whose activities degraded the natural environment. During this period, much of our timber was cut, and overgrazing began to be a serious problem in some of the western states. The lengths to which this wasteful

TABLE 5.1
Land Area, Population, and Rate of Increase, 1790–1970

	RESIDENT POPULATION			
CENSUS DATE	NUMBER	PER SQ. MILE OF LAND AREA	INCREASE OVER PRECEDING CENSUS (PERCENT)	AREA-LAND (SQ. MILE)
1790	3,929,214	4.5	(x)	864,746
1800	5,308,483	6.1	35.1	864,746
1810	7,239,881	4.3	36.4	1,681,828
1820	9,638,453	5.5	33.1	1,749,462
1830	12,866,020	7.4	33.5	1,749,462
1840	17,069,453	9.8	32.7	1,749,462
1850	23,191,876	7.9	35.9	2,940,042
1860	31,443,321	10.9	35.6	2,969,640
1870	39,818,449	13.4	26.6	2,969,640
1880	50,155,783	16.9	26.0	2,969, 640
1890	62,947,714	21.2	25.5	2,969,640
1900	75,994,575	25.6	20.7	2,969,834
1910	91,972,266	31.0	21.0	2,969,565
1920	105,710,620	35.6	14.9	2,969,451
1930	122,775,046	41.2	16.1	2,977,128
1940	131,669,275	44.2	7.2	2,977,128
1950	151,325,798	42.6	14.5	3,552,206
1960	179,323,175	50.5	18.5	3,540,911
1970	203,211,926	57.5	13.3	3,536,855

SOURCE. U. S. Bureau of the Census, *Statistical Abstract of the United States, 1973* (Washington, D.C.: U.S. Government Printing Office, 1973), p. 5.

exploitation of natural resources and disregard for the environment might go are illustrated by the wholesale slaughter of buffalo for their hides and humps or merely for sport.

We should not conclude from this that economic growth is necessarily undesirable or that all the practices of the nineteenth century entrepreneurs were evil. Most Americans have cherished an affluent lifestyle based on material consumption. Certainly, without the economic growth and concentration of the late nineteenth and early twentieth centuries, the United States would have found it more difficult to provide its present population with a high standard of living. In fact, one of the dimensions of the environmental problem is the balancing of the benefits against the disadvantages in particular types of activities. Nevertheless, the kind of economic growth that our ancestors experienced during the nineteenth century had its price: in this case, the price was not only the massive use of land and the occasional waste of large quantities of resources, but also the reinforcement of the myth of superabundance.

The Twentieth Century: Progress and Problems

Industrialization, which refers to the development and use of technology in a factory system, had become a fact of American life by 1900. During the current century, our industrial economy has had serious and far-reaching consequences for the environment. When compared to the adaptive strategy of the Native American with his limited technology, or the efforts at conquest of the early American settler, or even the get-rich-quick activities of the purveyors of the myth of superabundance, the environmental changes brought about by twentieth-century industry are enormously more serious and widespread.

A good example of the effect of modern industry can be found in the automobile industry. The efficiencies made possible by the factory system enable the production of vast quantities of cars, making them available at a cost that most people can afford. The production and operation of these motor vehicles requires enormous quantities of such products as steel, rubber, and petroleum that are produced by other industries. Many of these resources are in limited supply and thus their use in automobiles reduces the world supply of such materials and precludes their use elsewhere. The automobile (and of course trucks, buses, and the like) contributes significantly to air and noise pollution, and the concentration of automobiles in urban areas creates a number of health hazards, such as increases in respiratory illness and in the amount of lead in people's bodies (see Table 5.2). Finally, the possession of private cars by the majority of American families leads to alterations in our lifestyle that have environmental implications. For example, it is in part the automobile which brought about the mushrooming of suburban communities, and these suburban developments affect the environment by reducing the amount of farm or forest land avail-

TABLE 5.2
Body Lead Levels of Children Living Near Los Angeles Freeways and in Rural Lancaster, Cal.

MEASUREMENT	SEX	STUDY AREA	
		LOS ANGELES	LANCASTER
Blood lead, milligrams of lead per 100 ml	M	24	11
	F	17	10
Lead in long scalp hair, milligrams of lead per gram	M	59	21
	F	77	17
Lead in short scalp hair, milligrams of lead per gram	M	107	17
	F	70	12
Urine lead, milligrams of lead per liter	M	18	10
	F	16	14

SOURCE. U.S. Council on Evironmental Quality, *Environmental Quality — 1976* (Washington, D.C.: U.S. Government Printing Office, September 1976), p. 10.

One effect of the automobile has been to elevate the level of air pollution—sometimes to unsafe levels. Some residents of naturally beautiful places like Denver, Colorado, have found that the quality of life in their area has diminished.

able, wasting resources through the building of inefficient, single-family dwellings, and the destruction of wetlands and other animal habitats.

So, the immense productivity of an industrial economy far outstrips other, more simple technologies in its ability to adversely affect the environment. In addition to those already mentioned, some of the costs that Americans have had to bear to gain the benefits of an industrial economy include increased crime and delinquency (especially in the growing cities), a deterioration of the quality of our air and water, a growing shortage of virgin land, a decrease in the quantity of wildlife and the near or complete extinction of some species, and an increase in the amount of land marred by mining and other activities.

We now know that technology and increased numbers of people are two significant factors in determining resource use and in bringing about changes in the environment. Consumption of resources naturally increases as a population grows. However, to this must be added another development during the twentieth century: consumption of resources has risen at a more rapid rate than the rate at which the population has grown. In other words, as each year passes, industrialization and increasing technology result in *each person* consuming a *larger share* of resources than that person had consumed in the previous year. *This changing pattern of consumption can be illustrated by the fact that energy consumption in the United States grew by 100 percent between 1800 and 1900, grew 250 percent more between 1900 and 1950, and is expected to increase by nearly 400 percent between 1950 and 2000.* The same increasing rate of consumption has occurred in other areas. For example, the quantity of most metals and mineral fuels used in the United States since World War I exceeds the total used throughout the world in all history preceding 1914.[8]

By the middle of the twentieth century, then, the United States, along with other industrialized nations, had achieved a level of industrial technology enabling an unprecedented exploitation of the environment. In order to understand the problems that this creates and the reactions of people to these problems, we will utilize the three theoretical perspectives to see the conditions under which environmental conditions become social problems.

ENVIRONMENTAL CONDITIONS AS SOCIAL PROBLEMS

The Functionalist Perspective

One of the major features of the functionalist perspective is that it views society as a system composed of numerous integrated and interdependent parts. Systems exhibit a tendency toward equilibrium in which the various parts of the system maintain the same relationship to one another. Any change in one part of the system can have effects, even potentially disastrous ones, on other parts of the system. For the functionalist, interdependence and stability are crucial for the smooth functioning, and even the survival, of society. If changes occur in one part of the system, other parts may be altered so that vital functions are not accomplished and the functioning of the whole system is threatened. **From the functionalist perspective, then, environmental changes become social problems when they disrupt the smooth functioning of the system and threaten the existence or effective operation of society.**

All components of our environment—land, air, water, people, resources, and the like—can be considered a system. This ecosystem involves a delicate relationship in which each part contributes to the level of functioning of the complete environment in such a way that human life at a given standard of living is possible. In fact, one well-known environmentalist has used the expression *spaceship earth* to portray the fact that the earth, like a spaceship, is a closed system with finite resources that, if depleted or destroyed, cannot be replaced.[9] In this conception, we must get along with what we have since there is no way to replenish our supplies. If any major irreparable alteration of the environment occurs, we may be unable to continue our journey through space in the style to which we have become accustomed. Thus, pollution of the air or water, the destruction of arable land, or the

release of harmful chemicals into the environment may upset the balance between the parts of the system and have wide-ranging ramifications for the quality of human life. **In this context, one must be sensitive to both the *manifest* and the *latent* consequences of our actions on the environment.** What may seem like a harmless action performed for the best of reasons—e.g. the use of nitrogen fertilizers to increase the yield of farmland—may have long-range but unintended consequences that are highly destructive to the environment—such as the destruction of rivers and lakes by nitrogen fertilizers washed from farmland.

The Conflict Perspective

The conflict perspective does not represent a unified point of view on all issues. Rather, it consists of a range of views, representing different emphases and interpretations. Nevertheless, conflict theorists generally define society as an arena in which groups with varying amounts of power compete for scarce and valued resources. **From this point of view, environmental problems are not due to the limited amount of resources in the world (although these may in fact be limited) but are rather the result of the distribution of the resources available. The problem, then, is not how much is available, but more importantly who gets what share of what is available.** Various interest groups compete over available resources. Decisions that affect the environment are not made on the basis of maintaining some balance in a national or world system but rather result from the ability of some interest group to impose its will on others.

Another dimension of environmental problems, from the conflict perspective, is the *use* that will be made of available resources. For example, will a redwood forest be harvested for the wood products that can be produced, or will it be retained in its pristine state to be enjoyed for its natural beauty and serenity? The resolution of such conflicts involves not only the scarcity of a given resource, but also the choices that people make in terms of what end result they view as valuable and desirable. Is a slightly increased rate of cancer acceptable if the pesticides and insecticides that cause the cancer also make available an abundance of food that we could not otherwise grow? Since any choice by its very nature involves forgoing alternatives, there will always be groups who feel that their interests have not been served, and they will thus define certain environmental conditions as social problems.

A common but frustrating example of this involves industrial pollution. An environmentalist might wish to close a factory responsible for serious air or water pollution. Yet, an employee of the factory who might lose his job were the factory to close would probably prefer to ignore such assaults on the environment. Whichever alternative is chosen, some group will feel that its interests have not been served. This irreconcilable nature of many environmental problems makes feasible solutions extremely difficult to achieve.

The Interactionist Perspective

Interactionists place considerable emphasis on the subjective nature of social reality. People respond not to objective reality, but to reality as they perceive and interpret it. Society is not an objectifiable "thing" but is rather what people agree that it is at any given time. **From this perspective, environmental conditions can be considered social problems if some influential group defines them as such and behaves toward them as if they were problems. The condition need not actually threaten the system, as the functionalist perspective envisions.**

Because the definition of social reality will vary from one group to another, the condtiions that are considered social problems will also be different. For this reason there is often a lack of consensus about which environmental conditions are social problems. Some groups, for example, place great value on the material products that are produced by our industrial economy and seek to exploit the future potentialities of technology in terms of its ability to further enhance our material existence. They are certain, or nearly so, that the supply of resources, including water and air, are adequate for present and future needs and that human beings are (and will continue to be) capable of solving environmental problems. We may have to give up something, these people feel, such as air totally free of pollution, but what we receive in return from the unhindered application of technology is far more valuable and well worth the price of some degree of environmental degradation. For these people, some degree of environmental pollution or destruction is acceptable and not defined as a social problem.

On the other side of the issue, opposing groups argue that something is irreparably lost when we permit the quality of our environment to decline. For these people, the fruits of industrialization, while valuable, cannot replace a clear mountain stream, a pristine forest, or a smogless view of the distant horizon. For people who hold this view, the unhindered application of technology will inevitably mean deterioration of our environment to the point where its beauty and untouched nature will be irretrievably lost.

Both sides of this debate attempt to offer objective facts to support their position. Yet, observing this argument from the interactionist perspective, the crucial point is that these opposing groups have different versions of reality; each group is talking about what it perceives to be valuable and what it believes to elevate the quality of life. The interactionist perspective sensitizes us to the fact that people's definitions of reality are not based solely on objective fact. Such definitions emerge from the interaction between objective reality, personal desires and interests, and our relationships with important people around us. Because of this, such beliefs cannot be changed simply through the presentation of facts—no matter how accurate they may be.

Environmental problems as they exist today are extremely complex. There are many positions that one might take on such issues, and there are a wide array of interest groups attempting to exert influence in this area. Full understanding of environmental problems and their solutions requires that we understand the arguments on each side of the issue. We now turn to a discussion of what groups are important, the positions they take, and the manner in which decisions concerning the environment occur.

INTEREST GROUPS AND THE ENVIRONMENT

Although it is something of an oversimplification, we can separate people into two camps on the environmental issue: those who place economic activity and the development of technology ahead of the preservation of the environment, and those whose priorities are precisely the reverse. First, we will discuss the groups relevant to the controversy and the resources available to them; then we will elaborate the arguments that each makes to support its position.

One consequence of emphasizing economic growth more than environmental quality is depicted in this example of strip mining near Butte, Montana.

Business and the Environment

The particular perception of reality that certain vested interest groups in the United States share is expressed in the sentiment attributed to Charles Wilson, Secretary of Defense in the Eisenhower administration: what's good for General Motors is good for the country. That is, business should be allowed to pursue its goals unimpeded, and the outcome would benefit the country as a whole. Business and industry have been in a unique position in relation to environmental issues because of the power and resources they possess with which to influence decisions. Power may be based on a wide variety of resources, but it usually rests on an economic foundation. **It is important to realize that economic resources can be used not only to influence economic decisions but also to acquire other forms of power, including political influence.** The resources on which power is based vary considerably from culture to culture. In Latin America, for example, the military and the Roman Catholic Church were two of the most important sources of power. On the other hand, the church and the military are less powerful in the United States; the economic sector is dominant in terms of decision making in this country.[10]

In the past, a somewhat oversimplified view of decision making held that the outcome of decisions could be predicted by assessing the economic clout of the different sides of the issue. However, the outcome of an issue is determined not only by the *amount* of resources (such as money) available to the participants but also by their *willingness to expend* these resources.[11] For example, if a steel factory and a local environmental group are both interested in influencing the outcome of a piece of legislation affecting environmental pollution, and if the steel factory contributes the equivalent of $200,000 in money and employee time to its effort while the environmental group contributes $500,000 raised from its constituency, the likelihood is that the environmental group will win. This will be true even though the steel factory may have additional resources totaling $10 million, whereas the environmental group's resources total only the relatively small amount it can raise from its followers. **Only those resources that a participant is willing to commit to an issue will be a factor in its outcome.**

In order to understand the way in which environmental issues are resolved, we must ask what leads groups to commit their resources to the resolution of issues. A group will commit its resources to a particular issue if it perceives the outcome of the issue as affecting its interests.[12] In simpler terms, **those most likely to be affected by a decision will try to influence the outcome and thus commit resources toward that end.**

Business, industry, some scientists, educators, and a few public officials are among those most likely to perceive their interests as being affected by environmental issues. The representatives of business and industry have tended to wield a disproportionate influence in most environmental decisions because of their vested interests and their control over resources. These resources could be used to finance protracted legal battles and candidates for elected office, to make available (or to withhold) jobs, to finance charities or other projects in the affected area, and to place economic pressure on individuals charged with making decisions. In the past, most other groups have not perceived the majority of environmental questions as directly affecting them and have, in any case, been without sufficient economic resources to make their will felt on such issues. Consequently, business and industry have generally prevailed in the resolution of these problems.

The Environmental Movement

While many people in American history have believed that the environment was there to be exploited, there has also been a long tradition of opposition to this ethic.[13] During the latter half of the nineteenth century, foresters like George Perkins Marsh and Gifford Pinchot advocated an end to uncontrolled consumption and an emphasis on the management of forest resources. One hundred years ago, Carl Schurz was perhaps the first Secretary of the Interior to interpret his primary obligation as that of preserving resources for the future rather than easing the way for their immediate

exploitation. At about the same time, surveyor John Wesley Powell preached the necessity of land-use planning for the dry lands in the west. Conservationist John Muir championed the development of Yosemite Valley as a park and was, in a sense, the father of our National Park System. Theodore Roosevelt used the powers of the presidency to implement some of the policies advocated by these early environmentalists.

The environmentalists of this era did have some effect on the course of events, but their efforts were for the most part fragmentary and only marginally successful. Three main reasons account for their limited success. First, the myth of superabundance still had wide acceptance. Second, each of these crusaders was concerned about only one aspect of the environment instead of a more comprehensive and coordinated program. Third, the environmentalists' efforts were in conflict with powerful economic interests that had a stake in the myth as it then existed.

During the first half of the twentieth century, new campaigns concerned with environmental issues emerged. A few governmental programs such as the Civilian Conservation Corps (CCC) of the Depression years were aimed at reclaiming environmentally damaged areas. However, these efforts were overshadowed by rapid economic expansion both before and after the Depression and by continued industrialization. As a result, the myth of superabundance, although modified, still exerted a tremendous influence on environmental policies. So throughout the first half of the twentieth century, the business of the country, as Calvin Coolidge once observed, remained *business*.

By the late 1950s, scientists and other interested persons were becoming increasingly concerned about the effect of economic policies on the environment—especially on the dwindling supply of certain natural resources. The launching of *Sputnik I* by the Soviets in the autumn of 1957 eclipsed environmental concerns, however, and focused the nation's attention on international issues and the need to be first in scientific and technological developments. This coincided with the need for increased industrial output at a time when the nation was slipping into an economic recession.

These events set the stage for new environmental writers of the 1960s, who challenged the old value of economic gain at any cost and helped to provide the American people with a new perspective on environmental issues. Perhaps the best known of the writers is Rachel Carson. In *Silent Spring,* Carson pointed out the dangers associated with the excessive use of insecticides and demonstrated some of the potential hazards in the wholesale elimination of insects.[14] Today, almost everyone is aware that DDT and other chemicals can create major, undesirable alterations of the ecosystem. However, at the time of the publication of Carson's book, these frightening prospects were unfamiliar to most Americans. Other writers of the 1960s came out with books supporting the new environmental ethic. For example, the then Secretary of the Interior, Stewart Udall, detailed a history of American mistreatment of the environment in his book *The Quiet Crisis.*[15] Raymond Dasmann, in *The Last Horizon* (1963), examined various environmental abuses from a world perspective and argued that unless they were checked, the earth would become far less habitable.[16] Other writers such as biologists Barry Commoner, in his *The Closing Circle* (1972), and Paul Ehrlich, in *Human Ecology* (1973), helped to bring an interest in environmental questions to college campuses.[17] As a result of this emerging popular concern, scientists and other citizens became more interested in the field of **human ecology—"the study of relations between human groups (or populations) and their environments."**[18] While this field of study was decades old in the 1960s, it emerged into greater prominence and focused more intensively on issues of environmental degradation.

The result of this activity of the 1960s was the development of a new social movement in the United States that became known as the *environmental movement,* which challenged the argument that continued environmental exploitation in support of business is essential to the nation's economic well-being. The supporters of this movement emphasized values relating to the quality of life as opposed to economic expansion.

Earth Day and the Environmental Movement

The environmental movement, expecially on college campuses, was only one of several activist movements during this period. It was influenced by the older civil rights and antiwar movements, which had already popularized such tactics as massive confrontations and sit-ins; these the environmentalists would also use. By 1968, a number of new organizations had been formed to protest and attempt to alter existing environmental policies. Two years later, these organizations, along with more traditional groups such as the Audubon Society and the Sierra Club, were united in working toward national environmental awareness and action. Much activity was still directed toward individual cases and regional concerns, but increasing effort was being directed toward national programs, which included concerted action by college students, environmental organizations, educators, and officials at all levels of government. For instance, more than 100 colleges and universities across the nation had developed environmental studies programs.

All of this activity was focused in what was to be the first annual observance of Earth Day on April 22, 1970. The day was set aside for appropriate programs, campaigns, discussions, and other actions aimed at developing an awareness of, and solutions to, environmental problems. Speeches, teach-ins, demonstrations and the development of educational programs were common activities across the country.

Despite all this activity, Earth Day did not represent a national consensus. Various groups began to raise questions concerning the environmental movement. For example, representatives of civil rights and poverty organizations argued that additional efforts and expenditures directed at the environment would divert attention from the plight of the poor and minorities in the United States. A *New York Times* survey conducted shortly after Earth Day found rising opposition to the environmental movement coming from a number of directions—from conservatives who felt that the problem was exaggerated, from blacks and liberals who saw the movement as diverting attention from other issues, and from consumers who were unwilling to stop buying goods whose production was associated with environmental problems. In addition, a number of scholars and many traditional environmentalists mistrusted the newcomers, especially the younger ones. They feared that their cause would become politicized—even be taken over by the radical left—and thus lose support from other segments of society. At the same time, American business and industry felt the pressure of the movement and began to fear the potential costs of implementing the changes advocated by environmentalists.[19] The necessity of economic growth for the maintenance of the American lifestyle continued to be one of the basic issues in the controversy.

This discussion of the emergence of the environmental movement demonstrates that the previous dominance of business and industry over decision making on environmental issues no longer exists. While business is still quite powerful, other interest groups have formed to moderate its influence. The ability of the environmental movement to achieve this was due to a number of factors. First, environmental groups encouraged public awareness that environmental problems affect all of us. Second, these groups had access to important intellectual and organizational resources with which they could bring about changes in the laws and in government policies relating to the environment. Third, environmental groups brought to public awareness the growing body of scientific research indicating that environmental alterations can have much more serious and long-range consequences than most people had previously believed.

Although the two sides of the environmental issue can be clearly delineated, the issues are considerably more complex than this. People do not fall neatly into "pro-environmentalist" and "anti-environmentalist" categories. In order to delve into the complexity of this issue, we will now elaborate on the arguments made in support of each position. The student should consider which of the arguments on each side he or she finds convincing.

The Modern Environmental Controversy: Economic Growth v. An Unchanging Environment

Economic Growth as the Highest Value

On one side of the environmental controversy are those people who advocate continued economic growth even if one consequence might be some degree of environmental degradation. Those who advocate this position do so for a number of different reasons.[20] First, some feel that there are still adequate resources in the world and that there is no need to hinder their exploitation. Second, some feel that resource shortage and other problems can be adequately dealt with only through the unhindered operation of the private enterprise system. Third, some groups, such as the industrial and financial community, have a vested interest in continued economic growth even though it might cause environmental damage. Finally, some pro-growth economists challenge the basic assumptions upon which the environmentalists base their arguments concerning the desirability of no economic growth. Because the arguments made by these economists are likely to have the greatest impact in the immediate future, we shall examine them more closely.

These pro-growth economists maintain that environmentalists base their position on value judgments: that no growth and an undisturbed environment is better than continued growth and greater material affluence, and that resources that might have been used for economic expansion could better be used to satisfy other human wants. The pro-growth economists make the following arguments to support their position that economic growth is *both desirable and necessary*. First, growth *in itself* is not related to environmental damage, since production does not necessarily damage the environment. Second, low rates of economic growth make it more difficult to solve social problems, such as those associated with poverty or the environment itself, since there is less revenue available to government and industry for dealing with these problems. Finally, these economists argue that only a growth economy can satisfy the wants associated with what has come to be defined as an adequate standard of living.

These economists realize that not all economic growth is desirable. For example, if resources are invested today in order to ensure growth tomorrow, they remain unavailable for other needs, such as the solution of environmental problems, the purchase of food and clothing, or the satisfaction of other wants.[21] However, the problem (pollution) that the public usually associates with growth is actually not a *growth* problem at all. Rather it in-

Water pollution exemplifies what economists term externalities —the public rather than the producers bears the clean-up costs. If clean-up efforts fail, then we may suffer the costs of permanently damaged water resources.

volves what economists called **externalities.** As economists use the term, an externality is a cost of production that the producer does not bear and therefore is not included in the cost of doing business. If, for example, the production of an item results in certain waste products, and if these are disposed of by dumping them in a river, then the general public, rather than the consumers of this particular item, may have to pay the high costs of cleaning up this pollution. If the costs of cleaning up environmental pollution become a part of the producer's cost of doing business, then they cease to be an externality. Consumers will then be required to pay the full cost of production—including the cost of cleaning up the waste products of the process—and they may decide that a particular item is not worth it, given the total costs. **Thus, these *pro-growth economists* argue that the pollution problem is not one of growth but rather one of incorporating all of the costs into the decisions about production and consumption.**[22]

The various interest groups opposed to the environmental movement base their opposition on a variety of grounds. Whatever the reason for their position, they generally agree that the activities of environmentalists should in some way be altered, for they assert that environmental problems are less serious than environmentalists believe. These pro-growth groups feel that the negative consequences of radical changes in our economy would be far greater than our "so-called" environmental problems.

An Unchanging Environment as the Highest Value

On the other side of the environmental controversy are those people who, for a number of reasons, place great value on maintaining the environment in a relatively undisturbed state. Economist John Kenneth Galbraith epitomizes the position of this "pro-environment" group on the issue of economic growth:

It is hard to suppose that penultimate Western Man, stalled in the ultimate traffic jam and slowly succumbing to carbon monoxide, will be especially enchanted to hear from the last survivor that in the preceding year the gross national product went up by a record amount.[23]

For these people, continuous growth is regarded as suspect or dangerous, and the maintenance of a cleaner, more healthful environment takes precedence over other economic goals.

As we have already seen, much of the impetus for this pro-environment position has resulted from the work of environmental writers and professional ecologists. *The thrust of the ecological argument is that the earth constitutes a more or less closed system containing finite resources. Any activity within the system affects, to a greater or lesser extent, the entire system.* An example in support of this argument is the construction of the Aswan high dam on the Nile River in Egypt, which had a number of ecological consequences. Since the Nile could no longer flood the adjoining farmland, the silt that had fertilized the land for thousands of years had to be replaced with commercial fertilizers. The silt meanwhile collects and builds up behind the dam, eventually rendering it useless. In addition, the irrigation canals expose large quantities of water to the sun, resulting in greater water loss through evaporation and a buildup of salts and other minerals in the soil. Because there is a continuous water supply, as opposed to the wet and dry cycles that preceded the construction of the dam, conditions are favorable for the survival of snails carrying schistosomiasis, a debilitating disease affecting an increasing number of Egyptians. Finally, since the nutrients formerly carried into the eastern Mediterranean are now held behind the dam, the sardine catch in the Mediterranean has been reduced by 97 percent.[24]

If this example is typical — and ecologists argue that it is — then any major alteration of the natural environment may have similarly far-reaching and often unforseen negative consequences. It is in this context that Boulding has used the phrase **spaceship earth** to suggest that the earth, like a spaceship, is a closed system with finite resources.[25] Despite differences between the planet earth and a spaceship (e.g. a spaceship would have a base to return to where it could presumably obtain additional resources), this analogy points up the care that must be taken in altering our environment in order to avoid the irretrievable loss of limited resources or irreparable damage to the ecosystem. In fact, the earth may be even more like a spaceship today than in the past because technology and economic growth have resulted in a much greater ability to alter vital environmental systems.[26]

Ecologists, environmentalists, and economists opposed to continuing growth (or at least to growth at current levels) use this spaceship view of the world as a closed system to make several arguments. First, they assert that **growth uses up limited resources.** In fact, they say, much growth is not really growth at all but merely replacement. In this view, real economic growth is the expansion of goods and services over and above those used for replacement of existing goods and services. Yet today, 70 percent of all clotheswashers, for example, are purchased to replace older washers. What we often refer to as *growth,* measured in terms of an increase in the gross national product, is actually only a measure of the rate of consumption. If growth or consumption is not slowed or checked by conscious design, a disastrous halt will result from the exhaustion of, or competition for, scarce resources.

A second argument of this pro-environment group is that **growth may result in increased pollution.** Often, the real costs of economic expansion are concealed. Boulding pointed out that the gross national product not only is an inaccurate measure of growth, but it does not include all the costs of economic production and expansion.[27] Externalities, such as pollution, must be included with the costs of growth in order to formulate realistic estimates of the amount of economic growth. So long as growth is expected and so long as economic decisions do not include the cost of externalities, pollution is inevitable.

A third argument of the opponents of growth is that **growth does not lead to a more equitable distribution of income** because producers use advertising to artificially generate more consumer wants, which in turn absorb any increases in incomes due to growth. Furthermore, without such advertising, the resources that are turned into consumer goods might be freed for alternatives, such as cleaning up the environment.

A final argument of the pro-environment group is that **the kind of technology associated with twentieth-century industrial growth often creates enormous problems.** For example, technological innovations are often used before their effects can be understood. The negative effects of nuclear testing, insecticides, and other chemicals are examples of the potential hazards associated with rapid technological innovations.[28] As Table 5.3 makes clear, the inclusion of certain chemicals into products that are important to our lifestyle can have widespread effects on the ecosystem and can affect the health of a large number of people. There is also the increasing danger that

technology will become so complex that its human creators cannot adequately control it. For instance, massive power failures, such as those of 1965, when most of the East Coast was without electricity, and 1977, when New York City experienced a blackout, illustrate the devastating consequences of even a minor failure in a complex system. The potential for accidental nuclear warfare resulting from technological failures poses another frightening potential.

As technology becomes more pervasive and complex, there arises an increasingly serious problem of decision making concerning the development and use of technology. Traditionally, such decisions have been based on profit-and-loss considerations with little regard for human or environmental concerns.[29] However, future decisions, if they are to be environmentally sound, must take human values

TABLE 5.3
NIOSH[a] Advisories Concerning Suspected Cancer-Causing Chemicals

SUBSTANCES	DATE OF NIOSH BULLETIN	USES	NUMBER OF WORKERS POTENTIALLY AT RISK	COMMENTS
Chloroprene	1/20/75	Production of synthetic rubber	2,500	
Trichloroethylene	6/6/75	Industrial solvent (dry cleaning, metal degreasing) extraction of caffeine from coffee, anesthetic	200,000	In June 1975, the Health Research Group petitioned FDA to ban decaffeinated coffee containing trichloroethylene (Petition No. 75P-0132, acknowledged June 27, 1975). CPSC is preparing a monograph on consumer exposure.
Ethylene dibromide (EDB)	7/7/75	Leaded gas additive.	650,000 service station personnel.	Limited sampling of EDB by an EPA contractor found low levels in air and water at gas stations and 2 manufacturing sites. EDB is believed not to accumulate in the environment but to degrade at moderate rates in soil and water. An EPA report concludes that these low levels do not represent a significant health risk, and that increased use of unleaded gas since 1975 will reduce any possible risk from EDB added to gasoline. The Environmental Defense Fund has petitioned EPA to investigate the possible health risk of EDB residues in fumigated grain, which have been detected at levels up to 6.10 ppm.
		Manufacture of dyes and pharmaceuticals	214 in manufacturing and merchandising	
		About 100 pesticide products	8,897 fumigators	

TABLE 5.3 *(continued)*
NIOSH[a] Advisories Concerning Suspected Cancer-Causing Chemicals

SUBSTANCES	DATE OF NIOSH BULLETIN	USES	NUMBER OF WORKERS POTEN-TiALLY AT RISK	COMMENTS
Asbestos	8/8/75	Brakes and clutch assemblies	833,535 auto workers 67,679 garage workers 6,657 manu-facturers	The asbestos alert supplements the current occupational standard which applies to all work places but was primarily aimed at fabrication facilities and the construction trades, by calling attention to new data concerning the special hazard from asbestos exposure among workers who service brakes and clutch assemblies. A review of scientific literature on mesothelioma, a cancer of the lining of the abdominal cavity that is associated with asbestos exposure, has revealed at least four cases of these otherwise rare tumors in persons who had worked in jobs involving brake servicing. To protect an estimated 908,000 auto mechanics, garage workers, and fabricators, NIOSH has recommended interim procedures to minimize their exposure while alternatives are studied.
Chromate compounds	8/22/75	Paints and anti-corrosives.	1,000 in production of pigments. 65,600 in paint manufacturing. 487,000 painters and persons using chro-mate paint primers.	An October 1975 U.S. steelworkers petition to OSHA for a zero exposure emergency temporary standard was denied on April 29,1976.[c] OSHA intends to begin a rule-making procedure to establish an occupational exposure standard for hexavalent chromium. NIOSH recommended an exposure standard not greater than 1 μg/m² for carcinogenic chromium compounds and 25 μg/m² for non-carcinogenic compounds (41 Fed. Reg. 18869-18870, May 7, 1976).
Hexamethyl phos-phoric triamide (HMPA)	10/24/75	Solvent used in re-search labs.	5,000	
Polychlorinated biphenyls	11/3/75	Coolants and insu-lators in heavy electric equipment; hydraulic fluids, pesticide extenders, inks, etc.	12,000	See text.
4, 4-Diamino-diphenyl methane (DDM)	1/30/76	Production of poly-urethane.	2,500	

TABLE 5.3 *(continued)*
NIOSH[a] Advisories Concerning Suspected Cancer-Causing Chemicals

SUBSTANCES	DATE OF NIOSH BULLETIN	USES	NUMBER OF WORKERS POTENTIALLY AT RISK	COMMENTS
Chloroform[b]	3/15/76	Production of fluorocarbons, general solvent in preparation of dyes, drugs, pesticides, etc. Used in pesticides, cough and cold preparations (mouth wash, toothpaste, etc.), as an anesthetic, and as common laboratory solvent.	40,000	On March 11, 1976, Nader's Public Citizens Health Research Group filed suit in the U.S. District Court of Appeals for the District of Columbia to order FDA to recall more than 2,000 drugs and cosmetic products containing chloroform. In April, FDA proposed two new regulations that would ban chloroform in these products. Regulations were finalized June 29 with July 29, 1976, as the effective date. The ban does not recall items already on the market (41 Fed. Reg. 12842).
*1,-2-Bis(ethylsulfonyl)-1,2-dichloroethylene	3/26/76	None	None	Eye irritant; considered as a possible substitute for mercurial fungicides.
Dimethyl carbamoyl chloride (NMCC)	4/15/76	Synthesis of pharmaceuticals, chemical research.	Less than 200	

[a] National Institute of Occupational Safety and Health.

SOURCE. U.S. Council on Environmental Quality, *Environmental Quality — 1976* (Washington, D.C.: U.S. Government Printing Office, 1976), pp. 38–39.

into account. Instead of leaving such decisions to businessmen, scientists, or engineers, all of us must participate in some way. It is the obligation of those with technical knowledge, such as the scientists, to make environmental information available to the public in a usable form. Udall carries this argument one step further when he advocates the formulation of a new value system for decisions concerning technology, economic growth, and the environment.[30] Udall says that **we must decide how clean we want our environment, and how much we are willing to pay to achieve it.** We must choose between polluted air and the high cost of antipollution devices. Every technological innovation includes some costs.[31] The Industrial Revolution, with all of its benefits, also brought us the sweatshop, child labor, urban crowding, environmental pollution, and all of the problems associated with the automobile.

The Modern Dilemma

We have seen what the dimensions of the environmental problem are and the positions taken on this issue by different groups in America today. Who is right? What can be done? As we have stressed throughout this book, answers to these questions depend partially upon the perspective one uses to analyze the problem. Thus, **from the functionalist perspective, the problem is that new elements — technology, economic growth, and a growing population — have disrupted the relationships that had existed in the past between human populations and their environments. The system must respond to this new element in such a way that some equilibrium is established.** However, it need not involve the elimination of technology or economic growth. In fact, these elements are now

TABLE 5.4
Hydrocarbon (HC) Emissions Reduction and Expected Improvements in Air Quality 1975–90

REGION	PERCENT HC REDUCTION	DAYS ABOVE 0.08 PPM STANDARD		PERCENT CHANGE IN DAYS
		1975	1990	
Baltimore	59	51	5	90
Boston	61	41	0	100
Chicago	48	33	2	94
Cincinnati	58	50	0	100
Denver	65	70	0	100
D.C. Metro	64	61	<1	99
Houston	48	75	9	88
N.Y., N.J. Conn.	61	77	4	95
Philadelphia	58	102	9	91
St. Louis	53	54	2	97
San Francisco	53	84	3	96
South coast basin				
Upland	59	247	40	84
Pasadena	59	195	25	87

SOURCE. U.S. Council on Environmental Quality, *Environmental Quality – 1977* (Washington, D.C.: U.S. Government Printing Office, 1977), p. 183.

such an integral part of our society that for the functionalist, their elimination would also be highly disruptive and therefore undesirable. So, the task is to incorporate technology and economic growth into society in such a manner that their benefits are made available while their environmental impact is reduced. Many have pointed to improvements in environmental quality — such as the improved quality of water in many lakes and rivers and the anticipated reductions in air pollution due to utilization of pollution control devices (see Table 5.4) — to support the contention that this can be achieved. From this perspective, the environment will probably never be returned to a pristine state. Technology and population growth must have their impact. Yet the extent of this impact can be kept to levels that do not interfere with the smooth functioning of the system.

From the conflict perspective, the environmental problem is essentially a matter of who benefits from technology and economic growth as opposed to who gains by reductions in environmental pollution and degradation. The issue is which interest group has the political, economic, and social resources with which to pursue those policies beneficial to it. Until recently (and many would argue that this is still the case), business and industrial in-

terests were able to ignore environmental problems that might interfere with their economic activities, because they were by far the most powerful groups in society. They had a vested interest in viewing the environment as something to be exploited for economic gain. Today, environmental groups have been able to gather some resources with which to pursue policies focusing on environmental preservation. Yet, their achievements have been limited for a number of reasons. Many Americans still lack an awareness of the potential dangers of environmental problems. Furthermore, Americans have become used to the comforts offered by technology and look askance at any policies that might even indirectly threaten those comforts. Finally, interest groups have emerged to battle with environmentalists over the uses to which land will be put. For example, producers and users of off-road vehicles (such as trail bikes, snowmobiles, and dune buggies) have organized to fight legislative efforts to restrict their use of public lands (see Table 5.5). So, from the conflict perspective, the outcome of the environmental controversy depends on which groups have sufficient resources with which to pursue policies beneficial to themselves.

From the interactionist perspective, the extent of the environmental problem and the degree to which we need to search for a

As American society grows and becomes more affluent, there is increased demand for use of limited outdoor recreational areas.

solution is a matter of interpretation. It is a question of which environmental conditions we define as compatible with our lifestyle. Many people are quite content to live with air pollution in return for having access to an automobile, living in an exciting and vibrant urban area, or having available the material comforts of technology. In fact, one charge lodged against the environmental movement is that it is made up of a small group of outdoor enthusiasts, backpackers, and nature freaks who happen to get great personal enjoyment from a clean environment and are thus trying to foist their values on all Americans. **From the interactionist perspective, conditions are considered environmental problems requiring solutions because some group has been able to convince a sufficient number of Americans to share this version of reality with them.** If this definition of reality becomes widely shared, then appropriate action will be taken.

So, the modern environmental dilemma is, in a sense, to be able to clearly define the extent of the problem in order to work toward a solution. Is there an environmental problem, or isn't there? There are divergent perspectives on this issue and, at least today, little consensus about how serious the problem is or how much change is necessary to achieve solutions. Armed with these different perspectives, the student should be able to unmask distortions in people's arguments about this issue and to solutions in terms of their feasibility and effectiveness. One way to see these different processes at work and to comprehend the complexity of environmental problems is to trace the history of a particular problem from its inception to its presumed resolution.

CASE STUDY: KEPONE[32]

As far as we know, we can live with Kepone as the problem exists now . . . but our lifestyle has become one where we are bombarded with one chemical after another—and unfortunately the cumulative effects of them are not known.
Dr. Max Risenberg.

The following description of Kepone pollution is typical of what happens when environmental problems emerge. In most cases of environmental pollution, we find that

TABLE 5.5
Motorcycle and Snowmobile Use on National Forest Lands, 1965 and 1972–76

	MOTORCYCLES			SNOWMOBILES		
YEAR	TOTAL VISITOR DAYS (THOU-SANDS)	PERCENT CHANGE FROM PREVIOUS YEAR	PERCENT CHANGE FROM 1965	TOTAL VISITOR DAYS (THOU-SANDS)	PERCENT CHANGE FROM PREVIOUS YEAR	PERCENT CHANGE FROM 1965
1965	1,478.8			515.6		
1972	2,910.2		+96.8	2.862.6		+455.2
1973	3,137.7	+7.8	+112.2	3,258.0	+13.8	+531.9
1974	3,580.3	+14.1	+142.1	3,022.5	−7.2	+486.2
1975	3,840.0	+7.3	+159.7	3,276.0	+8.4	+535.4
1976	4,140.4	+7.8	+177.5	3,340.9	+2.0	+548.0

SOURCE. U.S. Council on Environmental Quality, *Environmental Quality — 1977* (Washington, D.C.: U.S. Government Printing Office, December 1977), p. 82.

1. the condition develops gradually;
2. it is associated with economic activity;
3. the conditions that bring about environmental degradation are beneficial to some interest group;
4. the potential danger remains unrecognized until after much damage is done;
5. the fault is difficult to determine because it is spread among many persons and agencies;
6. many people not directly involved suffer because of this condition; and
7. a solution is difficult to achieve due to the lack of technical knowledge, political considerations, and complicated civil and criminal court proceedings.

By studying the Kepone case, we shall better understand the conditions that surround most environmental problems.

The Trouble Begins

On July 23, 1975 Virginia health official Dr. Robert Jackson made the eighteen-mile trip from Richmond to Hopewell, a James River community mainly known for its production of chemicals. His purpose: to inspect the facilities of the Life Science Products Company, a relatively new concern whose sole activity was the production of the chemical pesticide Kepone. While chemists are not in complete agreement about the classification of this agent, it is generally considered a hydrocarbon like DDT. Kepone had been used with some success against fire ants in the southern United States, the banana root borer in Central America, and in domestically sold ant and roach killers. At the time of Jackson's inspection, Life Science was producing the chemical under contract for Allied Chemical Corporation.

When Jackson reached the Life Science plant, he found working conditions appalling. The plant consisted of an abandoned filling station and a metal building. Gray powdery Kepone dust covered everything. It was in the air, throughout the working area, and in the surrounding soil. There were times when traffic on nearby streets was slowed by poor visibility caused by the blowing dust, which sometimes drove the neighbors indoors. The workers seldom used respirators or dust filters and carried the dust home on their clothes and bodies.

The "Kepone Shakes"

After his inspection, Jackson asked Life Science officials to have workers report to a nearby doctor's office where he set up temporary headquarters for examinations. The examinations showed that those who had worked at the plant for some time had a number of symptoms, the most common of which was what workers referred to as the "Kepone shakes." Subsequent investigations revealed workers who could not hold a cup of coffee and at least one case of a man whose head, placed against the examining physician's shoulder, caused the doctor's entire body to shake. Other symptoms among these workers included tension, difficulty in breathing, and—in extreme cases—psychological disorientation.

Twenty-four hours after this examination, the Life Science plant was closed (permanently, as it turned out), but this proved to be only the beginning of a series of events that have not yet run their course. Still to come were frightening disclosures, such as that Kepone causes cancer in rodents and possibly in humans; that it is associated with difficulties in reproduction among birds; that it can lead to death among both rodents and birds; that perhaps 100,000 pounds of it were loose in the ecosystem of the James River and possibly Chesapeake Bay; that the James would have to be closed to most kinds of fishing; and that the poison would appear in the Hopewell industrial water supply one mile up the Appomattox River.

The Hopewell Story

What kind of community was Hopewell where such massive environmental damage could go on for so long without being noticed? The answer is that Hopewell is similar to a great many small industrial communities. Because of the dependence on industry, these communities do not conform to the picture of the typical, quiet American small town. Industry, especially the chemical industry, was and is the lifeblood of Hopewell, as the residents are well aware. As one worker put it, "There would be a lot of starving sons of bitches in this town if them stacks weren't smoking." Another worker, apparently unimpressed with the revelations concerning Kepone, put it more succinctly: "Kepone truckin'."

Like many industrial communities, Hopewell has experienced periods of boom and bust, and the citizens understand just how critical the chemical industry is to their economy. In 1912, the geographic area destined to become Hopewell was a corn field. By the end of World War I, the community had grown to 45,000 residents, most of whom were either employed in wartime industry or busy separating the war workers from their money. Hopewell was a wide open town where workers and others

drank, gambled, whored, and fought. One reporter described it as a modern Dodge City. Once, conditions became so bad that martial law was declared. The town grew so rapidly that property values increased from $12 per acre to $100 per foot of street frontage. Living space was in such demand that beds were rented out for eight hours at a time in order to accommodate three shifts of workers a day. Growth was so rapid that only 32 people out of thousands of residents were eligible to vote in the 1916 city council election. The boom was almost entirely attributable to the demand for war matériel in both Europe and America during World War I. At the peak of this period, the DuPont plant produced 1.5 million pounds of gun cotton per day with a daily payroll of $75,000. When the Armistice was signed in 1918, Hopewell's economy collapsed. Within a week, DuPont had closed. Hopewell's population dropped from 45,000 to 1400. By 1925, there were only 23 citizens who had taxable incomes.

Like other communities, Hopewell was affected by the Depression of the 1930s. Indeed, it would have been completely dead had it not been for Allied Chemical Corporation, an amalgam of five companies organized in 1920 to compete with the German chemical industry. During the 1930s, Allied manufactured fertilizer in Hopewell. Later—during and after World War II—Hopewell again took on some of the characteristics of a boom town, in large part because of the expansion of Allied.

At the time of the discovery of the Kepone problem, Hopewell had 46,000 residents. Allied was the town's largest employer. The smoke and odors that pervaded the atmosphere were offensive to visitors but went more or less unnoticed by most permanent residents. It is not surprising that the dust—the most visible sign of Kepone—went largely without comment. As retired Hopewell newspaper editor Gus Robbins put it, "There would be no Hopewell, period, without these chemical plants. . . . They're our bread and butter. Almost everyone benefits in one way or another from the industry here. It's a way of life with us." It was in this setting that William Moore and Virgil Hundtofte, two former Allied employees, set up Life Science Products to produce Kepone for Allied.

Genesis of a Chemical

Kepone was first developed for Allied by chemist Silvio L. Giolito in 1950. The application for patent of the formula and its production process submitted by Giolito and his supervisor indicated that the chemical would be effective against a number of nocuous organisms, including vegetable fungus, army worms, and DDT-resistant houseflies. Among its most "desirable" qualities was its resistance to dry cleaning in clothing and the tendency of its residues to remain potent for long periods of time.

Beginning in 1966, Allied manufactured Kepone intermittently in Hopewell. Testimony before a Senate committee concerning Allied's production conditions is contradictory, although one fact later became clear. During the eight years in question, Allied periodically discharged waste Kepone through an unregistered drainage pipe into Gravelly Run, a tributary of the James River. With the establishment of a federal permit system in 1971, it became illegal to dump drainage from an unregistered pipe. Allied refused to register its pipes discharging Kepone and eventually pleaded guilty to 940 counts of illegal dumping. Subsequent to the recognition of Kepone as a hazard, oysters that were taken from the James River and frozen in 1968, as well as fin fish taken and frozen in 1970, revealed Kepone contamination.

In 1974, with increased demand from Western Europe, Allied subcontracted the manufacture of Kepone to Life Science Products, a company formed for that specific purpose. Under a *tolling* agreement — a standard arrangement in the chemical industry — Allied would supply equipment and materials for Kepone production while Moore and Hundtofte would sell all of their production to Allied at a predetermined rate. Subsequent testimony during various court proceedings revealed that Allied agreed to pay an additional amount to Life Science Products on some of the Kepone produced to cover the costs of equipment designed to control pollution. It also seems clear that Life Science spent these funds, as well as part of their profits, on antipollution equipment. Nevertheless, pollution did occur, and the company's co-owners — as well as Allied — were eventually held at least partially responsible by the courts.

There were several important differences between the manufacture of Kepone by Allied and the process at Life Science. First, whereas Allied turned out intermittent batches of from 1500 to 2500 pounds, Life Science began by producing 3000 pounds per day, which was raised to 4000; on peak days, the figure was 6000. A second difference was that Allied had dumped its Kepone waste into Gravelly Run in an untreated condition, while Life Science discharged its waste into the Hopewell city sewage plant — killing the bacteria essential to the digestion process that breaks down the solid waste. Since this condition went unremedied, the city of Hopewell was dumping its untreated sewage, along with the Kepone, into Bailey's Creek, which flows into the James River.

Telltale Signs

Like most environmental crises, many have asked why Kepone was not recognized as a danger before it appeared in the blood of more than 200 people or contaminated the lower James River. Also like most environmental crises, the danger signs were there. The Kepone case was loaded with communication breakdowns, buck passing, and just plain bumbling.

Animal Research

As it turns out, research on the pesticide had been conducted as early as 1958. For example, quail that had ingested Kepone had high death rates. Symptoms, such as tremors, seemed to implicate Kepone as a cause. Other research on pheasants, laying hens, pigeons, laboratory mice and rats, as well as other organisms, demonstrated a number of detrimental effects of Kepone — enlarged livers, weight loss, quivering extremities, general tremors, problems associated with ovulation, inhibited reproduction, and so on. Most of this information had been published in scientific journals and therefore was readily available to the chemical industry. These findings, of course, referred only to the short-term effects of Kepone exposure; the long-term results, such as the potential for cancer, were still unknown. Interestingly enough, Allied itself had data on dogs, rats, and rabbits suggesting that Kepone's effects were much like those of DDT. These effects included tremors, loss of weight, the tendency of Kepone to collect in fatty tissues, kidney lesions among females, and atrophy of the testes among males.

Did Life Science have access to these data? The answer appears to be that some of it was available to them. In testimony given after the plant closing, Hundtofte and Moore indicated that Allied had not furnished them with all of the data available to the company. However, they also admitted that they had not read all of the information that had been furnished.

Workers' Maladies

Assuming that the Life Science officials lacked complete or convincing data concerning the toxicity of Kepone, were there other signs that something was wrong? As it happens, there were. For example, there was the working environment at Life Science, with Kepone dust almost everywhere. There was the fact that most workers experienced a skin rash and the "Kepone shakes." There were workers sufficiently affected to require medical care. One, Don Fitzgerald, experienced the "Kepone shakes" and, after several visits to hospital emergency rooms and trips to a number of doctors, was sent to a psychiatrist. During the course of these examinations, nobody thought to check out his place of work. After a blood sample was sent to the Medical College of Virginia, it was determined that the sample contained a DDT-like substance. Still, the evidence was not linked to Kepone. There was the case of Del White, a supervisor at Life Science, who, upon complaining to Moore and Hundtofte of tension and other symptoms, was told to see a doctor. There are other examples of workers who suffered symptoms but who chose to stay on at Life Science because they could not find other work. Ironically, it was difficult for them to find other employment because the "shakes" and other symptoms were often taken by potential employers as signs of alcoholism or drug addiction. Finally, there is the fact that at least seventy-five workers exhibited some symptoms during the life of the company, and more than two dozen saw physicians about these symptoms.

It is difficult to understand why it took so long for anyone to realize what was happening. However, a few facts help to make the matter more understandable. First, there were the workers themselves: many of them needed their jobs, which paid well. Like other Hopewell workers, many regarded the dangerous working conditions as a kind of test of manhood. Further, there was no union protection. Most workers seemed to feel that governmental safety agencies would not allow truly hazardous conditions to persist. Second, Kepone and its effects were not well known or understood by either doctors or government officials. The symptoms resembled those of alcoholism or drug addiction. Company doctors are often untrained in occupational medicine and unacquainted with the production process.

Missed Signals and Oversights

If the doctors and the Life Science management were unaware of the Kepone danger, they were not alone. The Kepone story is characterized by missed signals and oversights. Chronologically, they go something like this. In late February or early March 1974, shortly after Kepone production began at Life Science Products, the Virginia Air Pollution Control Board discovered that the company had no discharge permit, and that their operations were emitting sulphur trioxide, a Kepone ingredient. The board collected data on the product's physical and chemical properties and on the production process but apparently never realized that the end product was toxic. During the time that Kepone was produced by Life Science, the same board checked a monitoring station one block from the plant for floating particulates of dangerous air pollutants. Since Kepone dust was not listed as a dangerous air pollutant in the regulations, the filters were not checked for it, even though dust conditions were often bad in the area near the plant. Later, when stored filters were checked, they revealed residues of Kepone. Air experts recommended that the plant install a heavy dust collector, but this was not done until October of that year.

As early as April 1974, the solid-waste digesters at the Hopewell sewage plant began to exhibit problems, and, according to trial testimony by one of Life Science's co-owners, Hopewell officials were aware of Kepone traces on air-station filters as much as sixteen miles away. It has been disclosed that from February through August 1974, Life Science was discharging Kepone into the environment at far greater levels than existing regulations permitted. By the fall of that year, the solid waste digesters in Hopewell's sewage treatment plant had ceased to function because Kepone had killed their operating bacteria. Now the city had a problem, since Kepone-contaminated solid waste was building up. Because the requirements for dumping effluents into the James could no longer be met, the city began to dump this solid waste into an open field but, at the same time, took no action against Life Science. The city also failed to notify state agencies of the problem with the digesters or of the existence of Kepone in the sludge.

After a routine inspection in October 1974, State Water Board inspectors determined that the digesters were not working and soon identified Kepone as the cause. The board decided that the discharge of Kepone would have to be drastically reduced for the sake of the James River and set a level of 1/200 pound per day, a miniscule amount in a river the size of the James. The state contacted the Federal Environmental Protection Agency (EPA) and requested guidelines for Kepone. Debate on this question continued for months while Life Science continued to operate, often dumping Kepone in excess of the prescribed levels. While a sanitary engineer employed by the city of Hopewell recommended that pretreatment equipment be installed at Life Science, the EPA did not think it necessary. Noting that even clean industry can dump a bad batch once in a while, the agency showed little interest in investigating the production process during this period.

Another agency missing the boat was the Federal Occupational Safety and Health Administration (OSHA). In September 1974, a former Life Science employee reported to OSHA's Richmond office that he had been fired for refusing to clean gears in the drawer of a machine while it was operating because dust was blowing in his face. On OSHA's report form, the worker answered "yes" to a question concerning whether the condition about which

the report was being filed was dangerous to health or life. OSHA wrote to Life Science about the incident and requested information concerning a witness that the employee had said was present. The witness could not be found, and Life Science denied the allegation. The inquiry was dropped.

In March 1975, an EPA inspector visited Life Science to determine whether the company should be registered with the agency as a pesticide producer. The inspector, who saw only the plant's office and not its production facilities, was referred to an Allied attorney who contended that Kepone was not a pesticide but rather only a pesticide *ingredient*. The EPA conducted a lengthy examination on this point of law, which was still continuing as Life Science was closed down. Interestingly, even after Life Science was closed, production did not stop. OSHA, being unaware of Kepone's potential danger, determined that chemicals already in the production pipeline could be used up if protective clothing and other equipment were utilized.

The inability to recognize Kepone as a problem appears to be a function of communication failure and of the fact that most experts were so highly specialized that general coordination of findings was difficult. Nevertheless, as of this writing, one governmental body—the city of Hopewell—has been charged with violating federal water pollution regulations and has pleaded no contest (in effect, an admission of guilt)!

The Judgment

Subsequent to the closing of Life Science, civil suits and criminal charges were filed against Life Science, Allied, officials of both firms, and the city of Hopewell. While the resulting court proceedings were both protracted and complex, they led to a number of fines and suspended prison sentences. Those fined include: the city of Hopewell, $10,000; bankrupt Life Science, $3.8 million; Moore and Hundtofte, $25,000 each; and Allied, a record $13.4 million. This latter fine has been reduced to $5 million, with Allied pledging another $8 million to the cleanup effort. By the end of 1978, Allied had paid a total of $20 million in fines, legal fees, and settlements, and there were some suits still pending against the company.

Counting the Costs

Thus far, our account has focused on the history of Kepone and its effects on those most closely associated with it, but is it really such a problem after all? Although any complete assessment of costs associated with Kepone contamination is not likely to be complete for some time, some of the more devastating effects are already known.

Business Failures

Governor Mills Godwin, Jr., was forced to close the lower James River to fishing in 1975 because of Kepone contamination. Tests revealed that fish there — especially the predatory bluefish, which accumulates Kepone through an extensive food chain — carried the substance in concentrations far above the federally permitted level of 100 parts per billion. As a consequence, many people who had made their living from fishing or the selling of seafood have been adversely affected. The Virginia fishing industry lost at least $10 million in 1976 alone. It is estimated that at least 3500 persons have had their livelihood affected by Kepone pollution. Seafood dealers are understandably bitter about the situation, especially since some species, for example catfish, appear either not to accumulate or else to quickly purge themselves of the chemical. Samples of other species tested by the state have, at times, shown either lower levels of the chemical than the federal action level or else no Kepone at all. Because of this, the fishing ban has been modified to allow fishermen to catch certain of these species. Despite these changes in policy, some dealers still feel that they are victims of publicity and that their businesses have unjustly suffered. At the same time, some Chesapeake Bay bluefish have been found to contain Kepone, and traces of the chemical have been found in fish caught as far away as North Carolina. It is not clear, however, where these fish picked up the substance, since bluefish are migratory.

The James River

Another major problem associated with Kepone contamination is the status of the James River as a navigable waterway. Ordinarily, the shipping channel in the James is maintained by dredging to offset the shoaling that takes place naturally. Because of the more than 100,000 pounds of Kepone thought to be a part of the bottom sediment, dredging has been halted, for it may release more of the deadly compound, sending it downstream or into Chesapeake Bay, one of the nation's major fisheries. Further, if dredged material is taken from the river, there is the question of what to do with it, since under ordinary circumstances Kepone is exceedingly slow to break down. Some test dredging is being considered, and studies are being done on a hydraulic model of the James using dyes to determine the effect of disturbing the river bottom. However, the results are uncertain.

Human Diseases

There are other costs. In addition to its other toxic effects, Kepone may cause cancer. Nobody really knows for sure, and the knowledge may be some time in coming, since the carcinogenic effect of Kepone may not appear for years. Part of this particular difficulty is that Kepone is bio-accumulative — the body retains all that it ingests rather than passing it off in wastes. So, while small amounts of Kepone may not be dangerous, a continuous exposure can accumulate to dangerous levels. Kepone does not readily break down — it is estimated to have a half-life (the time it requires to lose half of its potency) of twenty-five years. The matter is further complicated by the fact that nobody really knows for sure just how many people have ingested the chemical. Tests have shown that plant workers and their families (including at least one child conceived while the father was employed at Life Science), people in the neighborhood of the plant, steady consumers of James River fish, and perhaps others, have the pesticide in their systems. While medical researchers are working on ways of ridding them of the substance, at present their future is uncertain.

What of future costs? "Kepone is probably one of the most chronically toxic substances scientists have had to deal with in the environment," according to Dr. Robert Huggett of the Virginia Institute of Marine Science. Further, as Dr. Jack Blanchard, head of EPA's Kepone section, has pointed out,

Kepone may eventually spread throughout much of the marine life in Chesapeake Bay. It could very well be that we will have to live with small amounts of the substance in our bodies as we presently do with DDT, mercury, and other environmental contaminants. There is little comfort in such a prospect, but it may be inevitable. As Shirley Briggs, director of the Rachel Carson Trust Fund, has said, "Kepone is one of the five or six worst things like this we know of. . . . The Kepone story suggests this sort of thing can go on for a long time."

The Way Out

If Kepone contamination is a problem for Hopewell, the James River, surrounding residents, fishermen, seafood dealers, and perhaps many others, how can we deal with it? A number of solutions have been suggested. At present, none of these is completely satisfactory, although some seem promising.

Among the solutions that have been proposed are: banning the human consumption of fish from the affected areas; reducing the Kepone content of fish by removing the heads and fatty tissues before eating, by pouring off the residual oil, or by preparing fish through boiling or poaching; total or partial dredging of the affected areas of the James River; and burning the Kepone residue. Other efforts have been directed toward removing Kepone from the systems of those affected or otherwise checking its action. Research at the Medical College of Virginia has shown considerable promise in removing Kepone from the bodies of former Life Science employees through the use of various chemicals. In most of the cases treated, levels of Kepone were significantly reduced — in some instances, to a point at which they could not be detected by scientific instruments.

If enough material could be removed from the river bottom by dredging where much of the chemical remains, the contamination would be eliminated or greatly reduced. Dredging has been regularly carried out in the past by the Army Corps of Engineers in order to maintain the shipping channel. In this instance, however, the process may create nearly as many problems as solutions. First, there is the question *where* to dredge. If the river were dredged from Hopewell to its mouth, the costs would range between $100 million and $500 million. Second, assuming that only the "hot spots" (those sections of the river where Kepone is thought to collect) were dredged, it is possible that the dredging, by stirring up the bottom sediment, could cause more serious contamination in the river and the bay than now exists.

Even assuming that the entire affected portion of the river could be dredged with impunity, there is still the problem of what to do with the dredged material. It is estimated that dredging two inches deep from Hopewell to the river's mouth would create a mound 30 feet high and 20 miles square. It cannot be dumped in the ocean or any place else where the Kepone could affect human beings or food. If dumping were on land or in a landfill, there is great danger that the Kepone residues (with a half-life of 25 years) would again appear in some waterway. Some Kepone-contaminated material, including topsoil from the area around the Life Science plant, has been buried in a special sealed pit constructed on Allied Chemical property. The area containing the pit is fenced and under twenty-four-hour guard. In addition, more than 500 barrels of Kepone have been shipped to West Germany to be buried at the expense of Allied. Nevertheless most agree that the real solution involves the actual destruction of the chemical.

One suggestion for accomplishing this destruction is burning. This does not mean simple incineration but rather exposure to very high temperatures. The research institute of the University of Dayton has developed a technique that may be used to destroy Kepone. The process, developed through an EPA grant, involves vaporizing the chemical and then exposing it to a temperature of 1000 degrees centigrade for one second. However, by the end of 1978, burning as a solution had not been implemented. This lack of action was in part due to the politically controversial nature of the Kepone issue. For example, a plan to burn Kepone in an existing incinerator in Wales had to be dropped because of public opposition.

Meanwhile, there is still the river sediment, those people in marine occupations who are still unemployed, and the civil suits. It will no doubt be some time before questions concerning all of these elements of the Kepone disaster are resolved. Ominously, resolution of at least some of these issues may be affected by two developments announced late in 1976. First, it was revealed that tests have demonstrated that oysters can accumulate the chemical at levels thousands of times higher than those of the surrounding water even when the amounts in the water are so small as to be undetectable. Second, it now appears that present techniques may not be able to detect all the Kepone in animal tissues. Thus, fish or other products that these tests show to be below action levels may, in fact, be above those levels.

The Kepone story is not at an end. There will undoubtedly be developments, both legal and scientific, that will keep the story alive for many years. Hopefully, there will be some resolution to the problem that is satisfactory from the point of view of environmental degradation and of the people it has affected. Nevertheless, what has happened in the Kepone incident to this point serves as a good illustration of how environmental problems develop and why they are so difficult to solve. Like all social problems, the Kepone incident has demonstrated a need for great sensitivity to, and preparation for, the unanticipated. This is often difficult to achieve because the issues involved have political consequences and affect vested interest groups. Further, the long periods of time that bureaucrats and scientists need to complete their work are quite different from the rapid shifts in public opinion. It is therefore tempting for officials, especially those who seek reelection, to offer quick, often sensational, panaceas instead of real solutions. When this course is followed, it not only does not lead to real solutions but, worse, it often delays work on them.

FUTURE PROSPECTS

There should be little doubt in the student's mind at this point that environmental problems are extremely complex and that workable solutions—especially solutions that are satisfactory to many

groups—are hard to come by. The problem is a serious one. Even those groups who do not take an extremist position on the topic admit that we must be constantly vigilant lest some irreversible and devastating damage to the environment occur. It is to some degree a technological problem—we must develop the scientific and technical knowledge to reduce or eliminate pollution. Yet, the technological problems are, in a sense, much easier to solve than the other barriers we confront when attempting to solve environmental problems. The more difficult barriers are twofold: (1) mobilizing public action to solve environmental problems without at the same time creating more serious problems, and (2) reducing the resistance of interest groups that perceive themselves to be adversely affected by environmental actions. We will discuss each of these issues in turn and then suggest a program for dealing with them.

Public Action on Environmental Problems

It was not until the 1960s that awareness of environmental problems became widespread among Americans. The development of this awareness has led to increased concern and eventually to public action on the part of many groups. Ecologists and others concerned about the environment have attempted to establish programs whose goals are to ensure that environmental systems are restored to an adequate level of functioning and that future damage is minimized. The development and implementation of such programs depends on the ability of these groups to mobilize the public in support of their efforts to solve environmental problems, and this in turn depends on three factors.

Accurate and Adequate Information

Although both the amount and quality of information about the environment is increasing by leaps and bounds, there is still much that we do not know. Does Kepone cause cancer? Will fluorocarbon aerosol sprays deplete the ozone in our atmosphere? Are our rivers and streams becoming cleaner or more polluted? These are difficult issues about which there is legitimate disagreement even

Kepone illustrates the complex ways in which environmental problems emerge and the difficulties involved in solving them. The accident at the Three-Mile Island nuclear generating facility is another recent example.

among scientists who are knowledgeable about them. In an atmosphere of such uncertainty, it is difficult to mobilize public action toward any solution. It is essential that the public have available accurate and adequate information with which to make decisions. Without it, people will believe in things that fit their preconceptions and support their vested interests. Since most solutions to environmental problems involve economic losses and changes in lifestyle for at least some people, it is all too convenient to dismiss environmental concerns with some label such as "overreaction" or "crying wolf." Unfortunately, as the case of Kepone illustrates, a policy based on such perceptions can prove disastrous. Accurate and adequate information made available to the public reduces the likelihood of such an outcome.

Comprehensible Information

The problem of inadequate public awareness is further exacerbated by the complexity and scope of the information in question. Some of the data cannot be simplified for general comprehension without distorting their meaning. In addition, the sheer

volume of information poses a problem. Environmental information ranges from data on the microscopic ecosystem in a drop of liquid to data on ecosystems of worldwide dimensions. Within each ecosystem, it is important to have reliable information concerning population, growth, technology, social control, resource availability, and human aspirations. Problems of credibility and comprehensibility, in short, are built into the subject and are as much a part of the problem as the environmental damage itself.

Planning and the Mobilization of Resources

The mobilization of resources for action represents still another difficulty. Where public action is to be taken, all the implications must be considered. To understand the complexity of such a task, the following are some of the questions that must be considered in determining the ramifications of environmental problems: How serious is the problem? Who is being hurt and to what extent? What are the costs of the current condition and who bears them? Are there alternative solutions, and if so, what are their costs and ramifications? Who will be hurt by the proposed solutions? Will this solution lead to yet other problems, and if so, how serious are they? What will be the reaction of the vested interest groups and the public to the proposed solution? Does the solution conflict with some basic cultural value or belief? What will be the effect of doing nothing? Planning for the solution of environmental problems must include the consideration of such questions; only in this way shall we increase the probability of finding a workable solution. We need only consider the case of Kepone to see how some of these questions might apply. In that disaster, we have an environmental problem involving alternative solutions with varying costs and probabilities of success. We find a number of opposing interest groups aligned on different sides of the issue. In addition, cultural beliefs and values concerning such issues as work, free enterprise, and the role of government influence the positions people take on the issues. For any ecological response to be effective, then, it must include careful study and planning, a consideration of costs and alternatives, an assessment of subsidiary results, and an understanding of human values and reactions.

In the absence of such planning, we are in danger of exacerbating the environmental problems we confront. A solution that creates an even greater problem is not really a solution at all. If we are able to have totally clean air by putting most of the population out of work, most people would probably not consider clean air worth the cost. We must decide how clean an environment we want and what we are willing to pay for it. The decision, of course, must involve not only the slum resident or the person living downwind, downriver, or near an industrial plant, or next to the strip mine or the oil-soaked beach; in the long run, it must include us all.

Interest Groups in the Solution of Environmental Problems

There are only 6 percent of the people of the world living in the United States, and we use 30 percent of all the energy. That isn't bad; that is good. That means we are the richest, strongest people in the world, and that we have the highest standard of living in the world. That is why we need so much energy, and may it always be that way.—Richard M. Nixon, November, 1973.[33]

As President Nixon so pointedly suggested, all Americans have an interest in ensuring that we receive a large share of the energy reserves of the world, and this points to another difficulty in attacking environmental problems—any solution will adversely affect some group and that group is likely to resist any environmental policy it views as detrimental to its interests. The problem is complicated by the fact that in most environmental issues there are a large number of groups with competing interests. Any attack on environmental problems must attempt to bridge the gap between these competing interests. We now consider a few examples.

The Economy and the Environment

Earlier, we examined some of the economic factors relating to environmental questions. **We have seen that people take the position either that growth is *not* a problem and must continue, or that growth *is* a problem and must be curtailed or even halted.** Yet, given the number of interest groups involved in these issues, it is unrealistic to assume that either of these extreme positions will attract many supporters. Therefore, if we want to find feasible answers, we must look for compromise solutions that are attractive to many groups.

Udall and his associates develop a position that falls between these two extremes and hopefully will have some attraction to both.[34] They forge the link between economic production and energy consumption by pointing out that more than 40 percent of all U.S. energy is consumed by industry. Since energy has traditionally been a minor cost item, there has been little motivation for industry to use it efficiently. However, as energy becomes more expensive and we must increasingly rely on foreign energy supplies, energy consumption becomes a concern for everyone (see Fig. 5.2). Udall and his associates suggest that in order to achieve an energy savings (and, we might add, to achieve a

At present, oil is essential to our industrialized economy and affluent life style, yet accidents accompanying the production of oil adversely affect the ecosystem. When the United States-owned tanker, Amaco Cadiz, broke up off the coast of France in 1978, many birds and fish perished.

reduction in environmental pollution associated with energy production), industry will have to alter its notions that bigger is better and that cheap energy will continue to be available. Cheap energy, of course, is in the interest of any consumer of energy. However, if energy costs are increased (e.g. by charging higher rates to those who consume large quantities of energy), then it is in their interests to economize.

Under such incentives, business can accomplish remarkable feats. Raytheon, the giant East Coast electronics firm, cut its fuel bill by 30 percent through energy-efficiency engineering; Lockheed achieved a 26-percent saving. The E. I. DuPont Company, in part through the energy-saving design of its new facilities, has managed to increase its output by 50 percent while its energy consumption has increased by only 10 percent. Udall and his associates cite numerous additional examples of major energy savings that can be achieved when corporations see such efforts as in their own interests.[35] The thrust of this solution, then, is not to

shun technology and engineering but rather to develop laws and policies that encourage economic interests to use technology and our engineering knowledge to reduce the damage to the environment. In this compromise, both opponents and proponents of growth gain something.

Another advocate of energy saving is the late economist E. F. Schumacher.[36] He argued that the kind of large, complex industrial organization typical of Western society is inefficient and suggests that it be subdivided into small, semi-autonomous units with limited tasks. Consistent with his call for a change of scale in our economic lives are his proposals for economic activity and development in the Third World. These entail regional development and planning that would permit the creation of small, yet coordinated, units in the rural areas of underdeveloped nations. He proposes four guidelines: (1) workplaces should be created where people now live (in the village and rural areas); (2) workplaces should be cheap enough to construct in large numbers so that they are not beyond the eco-

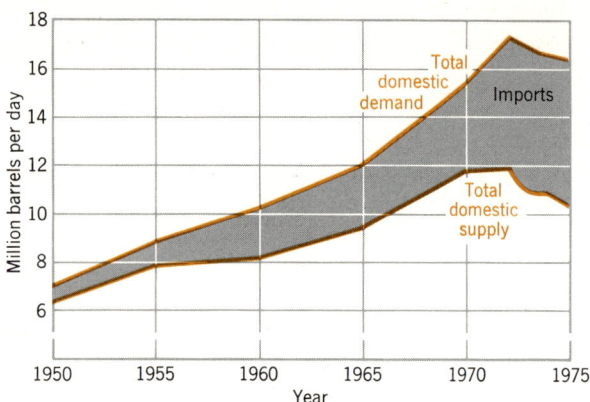

Figure 5.2 **U.S. Dependence on Imported Oil. U.S. Council on Environmental Quality,** *Environmental Quality—1976* **(Washington, D.C.: U.S. Government Printing Office, September 1976), p. 102.**

nomic capabilities of developing nations; (3) production methods should be simple (and somewhat labor-intensive—that is, maximizing the use of people instead of machines) so as not to require high levels of skill from the workers; (4) production processes should rely on local materials, and consumption should be primarily local.

These suggestions might be fruitful for the Third World if a form of "intermediate technology" were used. This technology would be low in capital costs but innovative rather than primitive; and it would not be a simple labor-intensive system. It would be possible for more advanced industrial societies to move into similar forms of organization if resources became limited and were unable to support the large-scale waste-producing systems currently employed. Schumacher's proposals are another effort to bridge the gap between the extremes of no-growth and growth-at-any-cost. Proponents of both positions have a stake in the outcome, and each of their interests must be considered in evaluating alternatives.

Vested Interests and the Environment

While those who support the pro-growth position have a vested interest in ignoring many environmental problems, there are also many other groups outside the economic sphere who have a similar vested interest. Their approach to solutions to environmental problems will depend on their interests, values, and knowledge. Whether such solutions are seen as beneficial will depend on how the group defines the situation. As the interactionist perspective suggests, it is a question of how reality is perceived and what is and is not defined as "real."

With some environmental solutions, such as closing a factory to stop pollution, the negative consequences of the action are obvious—people are thrown out of work—and one can weigh the different sides of the issue. In many instances, however, the consequences of different alternatives are not so clear-cut, and the interest groups affected are not always obvious. For example, not long ago, retired steelworker John Pahula and his mongrel dog, Pedro, were walking near Pahula's cabin in northern Minnesota when three large timber wolves appeared. They dragged Pedro into a nearby swamp and ate him. Timber wolves are increasing in northern Minnesota and are thought to number from 1200 to 1500. During the winter of 1976–77 they came into increasing contact with people and have apparently been responsible for the loss of livestock and pets. Since the Eastern Timber Wolf had been close to extinction in the continental United States, it was placed on the *endangered species list.* This means that the killing of a timber wolf is punishable by up to one year in prison and a fine of $20,000. While environmental groups have worked for rigorous enforcement of the law, some local officials have asked the Department of the Interior to change the wolf's classification to *threatened species,* a classification that allows for some killing of the animal. Some local citizens feel that this is not enough and have formed vigilante groups such as S.O.S. (Sportsman's Only Salvation). These groups have been hunting wolves and have dumped three carcasses at the doors of local government and newspaper offices. On one of the carcasses were sprayed the initials S.O.S.[37]

Predators in general, and the wolf in particular, are excellent examples of how perception and emotion enter into environmental decision making. Our folklore and children's literature are replete with stories and anecdotes that cast predators as "bad" because they kill. Although the ecologist understands that all life directly or indirectly subsists on other life, the act of killing for food conflicts with our norms and values (unless, of course, it is done by someone else, such as the butcher). Even when a predator has not killed pets, livestock, or people, it may be killed because of its reputation, even though from an ecological perspective the killing may be harmful to the environment.

In 1974, biologists from Northern Michigan University released into the woods of Michigan's Upper Peninsula four Eastern Timber Wolves imported from Minnesota. This was part of an experiment to determine whether the wolves could survive in their former habitat and whether they would mix with the few wolves still living in the area. The wolves were tracked from the air by means of radio-equipped collars. Within eight months, all four wolves were dead—one was killed by a car and three were shot. In some cases, the wolves may have been mistaken for coyotes on which there was a bounty, but in others, the killings appear to have been deliberate.[38] While the Michigan case is somewhat different from the situation in Minnesota, both illustrate how perceptions (whether or not they are accurate) and interests can influence a person's response to environmental problems. The interests of those opposed to predators such as the wolf are difficult for many people to comprehend because they are very subjective, deriving from the presumed threat of the predator to hunting or from a general hostility to predators. For most people, it is easier to empathize with a factory worker thrown out of a job. Yet, for those opposed to predators, their interest and concerns—whether they be comprehensible to others or not—are nonetheless real and serve as a basis for action.

While the groups discussed thus far have a vested interest in opposing some aspect of environmental preservation, many conservationists claim that all people have a vested interest in protecting the environment from certain kinds of changes. The Endangered Species Act of 1973 requires that government construction projects be halted if they threaten the existence of a species of plant or animal. In 1977, the $120-million Tellico Dam project on the Little Tennessee River was halted because the dam, when in operation, would destroy the only known habitat of an obscure species of fish, the three-inch-long snail darter. Environmentalists were able to defend this action successfully through the courts. Similar efforts have been attempted elsewhere. In Maine, a $700-million hydroelectric project threatened a little weed called the Furbish lousewort. Efforts were made to stop the project. Environmentalists forced the Forest Service to change its timber management plans in Texas in order to protect the red-cockaded woodpecker. The El Segundo blue butterfly, whose only habitat is unfortunately at the end of the runway of the Los Angeles airport, has managed to block the expansion of the airport. In all cases, environmentalists were able to use the Endangered Species Act to protect a species threatened with extinction against many other economic and social interests.[39]

Why would they do this? Why should we care about the El Segundo blue butterfly or the Furbish lousewort? Extinction, of course, is the eventual fate of all species. However, the rate of extinction appears to be increasing. In prehistoric times, the rate was one species extinct each 10,000 years; by the year 1600, species were becoming extinct at the rate of about one every 1000 years. Today, it is estimated that more than one species becomes extinct each year. The cause of this increase in the rate of extinction is the enormous impact that human beings, with our elaborate technology and industrial lifestyle, have on the environment. Some environmentalists argue that we should protect species because there is beauty in the diversity of species on earth or because the unthinking destruction of another life form is immoral if it can be avoided.[40]

However, a more common argument is based on the impact such loss may have on human life. As whole species are lost, the total gene pool of the earth is reduced, and we don't know what the consequences of such a loss are. We don't know what the value a lost species might have been. Penicillin, which has saved millions of lives, derives from bread mold; but who would have championed the cause of bread mold one hundred years ago? There are innumerable other minor, and seemingly "worthless," plants and animals that have proved extremely valuable to humans in areas such as medicine. Thus, environmentalists argue, we all have a vested interest in protecting other species because they may prove beneficial to ourselves or our offspring. However, many groups do not accept this argument. They contend that the remote possibility of some future benefit from a little-known species must be weighed against the immediate and measurable benefit that would accrue from a dam or a power plant. Thus, there are currently efforts being made to amend the Endangered Species Act to permit construction projects to continue under certain circumstances even though they might endanger the existence of some species.

A Strategy for Environmental Solutions

We have seen that mobilizing public action against environmental problems is an important but delicate task and that there are numerous interest groups whose concerns and desires must be taken into account. Given these difficulties, we might ask how we can ever hope to deal with environmental problems in ways that will be generally acceptable. In fact, it is probably impossible to satisfy everyone in most cases. We must reconcile ourselves to the fact that the solutions to most environmental problems will involve a delicate balance between a number of different interests. There will be no perfect solutions, nor is there necessarily *one single* solution that is the correct reaction to a particular problem. The choices are complex and difficult. William H. Matthews and his associates at the Massachusetts Institute of Technology have developed the outline of a general strategy for approaching environmental problems.[41] We can use their outline as a guide to approaching environmental problems.

Matthews and his associates point out that environmental problems are *general,* in the sense that they impact on a large number of systems—physiological, biological, political, economic, and social. It is therefore necessary to involve persons from many different areas—e.g. natural sciences,

social sciences, engineering, law, business, government—in the search for solutions. They outline a set of procedures for environmental management that can be applied to any particular environmental problem. These procedures summarize many of the issues already discussed.

Values and Perceptions

Matthews and his associates point out, as we have earlier indicated, that solutions cannot rely on technology alone but must take into account the *values, aspirations, and perceptions* of the people in question and how these are likely to change in the future. The cooperation of many groups is necessary to solve problems, and such cooperation would be difficult to obtain if the values and desires of the people were ignored.

Environmental Effects

It is necessary to acquire accurate and reasonably complete information about the ecology of the area in question. The problems resulting from a failure to follow this requirement are illustrated by the ecological problems, discussed earlier, associated with the construction of the Aswan high dam. In considering the need to assess the *environmental effects* of any action, several points are critical. First, effects are both direct and indirect. Second, because of the complexity of the ecosystem, a particular condition may be simultaneously a cause of certain environmental problems and an effect resulting from other conditions. Third, there are some instances where a clear-cut sequence of cause and effect is difficult to determine. Finally, it is necessary to have as complete a knowledge as possible of the situation in question to be able to sort out the various effects.

Environmental Indicators

For planners, policymakers, or the general public to be able to act rationally, they first must be aware of what is occurring and what the short- and long-range effects will be. *Environmental indicators* are measures of some physical, biological, or socioeconomic condition that relates to the environment;

they provide information about the state of the environment. Before any policies are implemented, all available environmental indicators should be used. At present, many environmental solutions are chosen not so much for their effectiveness as for the fact that they can be accomplished with our present technology. The lack of indicators is well illustrated in the case of Kepone, where there was so much delay and controversy in measuring the effects of Kepone on people and the environment.

Environmental Impact Methodology

Until recently, most decisions concerning the environment were made primarily on the basis of quantifiable, economic criteria—the costs of the decisions. Outcomes that were not easily quantifiable or expressed in terms of money tended to be ignored. For example, sociologist Delbert Miller found that, for leaders in the metropolitan region extending from Boston to Washington, issues of environmental quality had a relatively low priority in decision making.[42] However, as a healthy and livable environment has become more important to more people, this has begun to change. Now, environmental managers in both the private and the public sectors must devise and utilize an *environmental impact methodology*—a mechanism for determining both the economic and the noneconomic effects—whether quantifiable or not—of proposed activities on the environment. At present, the ability to assess *all* impacts has not been realized; however, attainment of this ability must continue to be a goal.

Growth and Its Implications

An area that all environmental planners and policymakers must consider is *economic growth and its implications for the future*. In recent times, the ideology of economic and industrial growth has been dominant in the world. Now, however, the impact of further growth raises serious questions concerning the environment, such as how much more growth can take place without undue environmental damage, how economic growth relates to population growth, and how growth patterns can be altered while at the same time allowing for needed improvements in the underdeveloped nations. The environmental manager is confronted with the task of questioning some long-standing assumptions about the relationship between economic growth and the quality of life.

Environmental Law

A relatively new area of concern for policymakers and planners is *environmental law*. Traditional legal conventions (such as common law and conceptions of private property and of trespass and negligence, to name only a few) are inadequate to deal with the new legal problems associated with environmental questions. As the earlier discussion of Kepone and its externalities demonstrates, our legal tradition has not had to cope with these types of issues in the past. Many of our current laws are inadequate and cumbersome. They often neither accomplish what their authors intended nor provide justice for those coming under their jurisdiction. Environmental managers must search for new developments in our legal system that will enable us to confront the novel situations created by modern environmental problems.

This set of procedures, outlined by Matthews and his associates, provides a means for attacking environmental problems in a rational and systematic manner. They are no panacea, but they do offer the guidance necessary to find solutions that will offer reasonably general benefits to many groups.

CONCLUSION

Problems of environmental pollution are possibly the most general, and at the same time the most all-encompassing, of the social problems we face. We have discussed the wilderness and the environmental practices of the first Americans. We have examined the role of economic development and the emergence of conflicting environmental values. We followed the development of the environmental movement as it challenged the proponents of continued economic growth. Reflecting on all of this makes certain conclusions stand out. For example, few would disagree with the position that a clean environment is preferable to a polluted environment. Yet, at the same time, we have learned that environmental issues do not exist in a vacuum—they must be considered within the context of other institutions, values, and expectations. It will be helpful to conclude our discussion of environmental problems by reviewing these issues in the light of the three theoretical perspectives.

The functionalist perspective leads us to an awareness of the interrelatedness of the various parts of any system. In terms of environmental issues, one fact of major importance is that we live in an industrial society and, barring some monumental catastrophe, it is unlikely that we will drastically change our lifestyle. Yet we must recognize that such an industrial lifestyle places great strains on the environment, and some of these stresses may have lethal consequences. It is unrealistic to expect such a lifestyle to leave the environment unblemished. We will probably have to reconcile ourselves to some level of environmental degradation. Yet it is clear, on the other hand, that we cannot simply ignore the problem of environmental degradation in the pursuit of industrial growth. As the Kepone case study illustrates, the economic and social costs of environmental pollution can be very high—so high that they become dysfunctional even if we place more value on economic growth than on environmental purity.

From the conflict perspective, environmental problems must be viewed in the context of who gets what share of what there is available. Inevitably, a decline in personal freedom will result—especially where that freedom involves the wasteful use of scarce and valued resources or where it infringes on the rights of others. If the industrialist uses the environment to promote economic growth, the environmentalist will be denied the use of that land for recreational or aesthetic purposes. If a hiker reserves the right to a certain area as a quiet retreat, then the snowmobiler is denied access to that land for recreation. Since making any choice involves forgoing some alternatives, there will always be some group that believes its interests have been threatened by a decision. The outcome of environmental problems, from this perspective, depends on the distribution of power and resources among the interests affected by the problem.

Rather than focusing on the characteristics of environmental systems or on the distribution of power and resources, the interactionist perspective emphasizes the importance of people's perceptions of reality in shaping their behavior. We realize that attempts to define environmental problems in an objective fashion (without reference to people's definitions of reality) will be futile. We must reconcile ourselves to the fact that beauty—in this case, acceptable environmental quality—is very much in the eye of the beholder. Furthermore, our experiences with pollution tend to shape our future perceptions of what is an acceptable amount of pollution. Many environmentalists fear that increasing pollution of our air, land, and water will in the future result in people's willingness to accept a higher level of pollution than they currently do because they will have come to view some degree of pollution as normal. Thus, in a sense the environmental problem could be "solved," from the interactionist perspective, if people came to view pollution as normal and acceptable—even though absolute levels of pollution might be quite high. So, we can expect increasing activity on the part of many groups to influence the perceptions of others in one direction or another in regard to pollution.

GLOSSARY TERMS

Bio-accumulation	Environmental indicators	Myth of superabundance
Ecosystem	Environmental Movement	Pro-growth economists
Endangered Species List	Externalities	Schistosomiasis
Environment	Industrialization	Spaceship Earth
Environmental ethic	Kepone	Threatened Species List

REFERENCES

[1] *Washington* (D.C.) *Star*, September 28, 1976.

[2] See Charles H. Southwick, *Ecology and the Quality of Our Environment* (New York: Van Nostrand Reinhold Co., 1972), pp. 104–105.

[3] Quoted in *Michigan Out-of-Doors* (February 1975), pp. 24–25.

[4] See Stewart L. Udall, *The Quiet Crisis* (New York: Holt, Rinehart, & Winston, 1963).

[5] See Udall, *The Quiet Crisis,* and Raymond F. Dasmann, *The Last Horizon* (New York: Macmillan, 1963).

[6] Udall, *The Quiet Crisis.*

[7] Udall, *The Quiet Crisis*, p. 54.

[8] President's Materials Policy Commission, *Resources For Freedom, A Report* (Washington, D.C.: U.S. Government Printing Office, June 1952), p. 1–5.

[9] Kenneth Boulding, "Fun and Games with the Gross National Product: The Role of Misleading Indicators in Social Policy," in Robert T. Roelofs, Joseph N. Crowley, and Donald L. Hardesty, eds., *Environment and Society* (Englewood Cliffs, N.J.: Prentice-Hall, 1974), pp. 126–136.

[10] See Delbert C. Miller, *International Community Power Structures* (Bloomington, Ind.: Indiana University Press, 1970).

[11] Terry Nichols Clark, *Community Power and Policy Outputs* (Beverly Hills, Calif.: Sage Publications, 1973).

[12] Miller, *International Community Power Structures.*

[13] See Udall, *The Quiet Crisis.*

[14] Rachel Carson, *Silent Spring* (New York: Houghton Mifflin, 1962).

[15] Udall, *The Quiet Crisis.*

[16] Dasmann, *The Last Horizon.*

[17] Barry Commoner, *The Closing Circle* (New York: Alfred A. Knopf, 1972), and Paul R. Ehrlich, Anne H. Ehrlich, and John P. Holdren, *Human Ecology* (San Francisco: W. H. Freeman and Co., 1973).

[18] Julius Gould and William L. Kolb, eds., *A Dictionary of the Social Sciences* (New York: The Free Press, 1964), p. 215.

[19] *New York Times* (May 4, 1970), p. 4, and *New York Times* (May 5, 1970), p. 1.

[20] See Wilfred Beckerman, *Two Cheers for the Affluent Society* (New York: St. Martin's Press, 1974), and Thomas D. Crocker and A. J. Rogers III, *Environmental Economics* (Hinsdale, Ill.: Dryden Press, 1971).

[21] Beckerman, *Two Cheers for the Affluent Society.*

[22] Ibid., and Crocker and Rogers, *Environmental Economics.*

[23] Quoted in David Lilienthal, "300 Million Americans Would Be Wrong." in Amos H. Hawley, ed., *Man and Environment* (New York: New York Times Co., 1975), p. 38.

[24] Garret Hardin, "To Trouble a Star: The Cost of Intervention in Nature," in Roelofs et al., *Environment and Society*, p. 120.

[25] Boulding, "Fun and Games with the Gross National Product," pp. 126–136.

[26] Lynton K. Caldwell, "The Coming Polity of Spaceship Earth," in Roelofs et al., *Environment and Society,* pp. 250–262.

[27] Boulding, "Fun and Games with the Gross National Product," pp. 126–136.

[28] Barry Commoner, "The Dual Crisis in Science and Society," in Roelofs, et al., *Environment and Society,* pp. 57–62.

[29] Robert Gomer, "The Tyranny of Progress," in Roelofs et

al., *Environment and Society,* pp. 63–71.

[30] Stewart Udall, "Introduction to *It's Your World,*" in Roelofs et al., *Environment and Society,* pp. 85–88.

[31] Gomer, "The Tyrrany of Progress."

[32] The following account is based on: Marvin H. Zim, "Allied Chemical's $20-Million Ordeal with Kepone," *Fortune* 98 (September 11, 1978), pp. 82–91, and articles appearing between August 3, 1976 and October 6, 1978 in the following: the *Washington Post,* the *Virginia-Pilot* (Norfolk), the *Times-Dispatch* (Richmond), the *Sun* (Baltimore), the *Daily News* (Dayton), the *Washington Star,* the *Milwaukee Journal,* and *Newsweek.*

[33] Quoted in Stewart Udall, Charles Conconi, and David Osterhout, *The Energy Balloon* (New York: McGraw-Hill, 1974), p. 249.

[34] Ibid.

[35] Ibid.

[36] E. F. Schumacher, *Small is Beautiful: Economics as if People Mattered* (New York: Harper & Row, 1973).

[37] "Wolves and Louseworts," *Newsweek* (February 21, 1977), p. 95.

[38] Thomas F. Weise, William L. Robinson, Richard A. Hook, and David L. Mech, *An Experimental Translocation of the Eastern Timber Wolf* (New York: National Audubon Society, 1975).

[39] See "Wolves and Louseworts," *Newsweek* (February 21, 1977), p. 95, and Philip Shabecoff, "New Battles Over Endangered Species," *The New York Times Magazine* (June 4, 1978), pp. 38–44.

[40] Ibid.

[41] William H. Matthews et al., *Resource Materials for Environmental Management and Education* (Cambridge, Mass.: The MIT Press, 1976).

[42] Delbert C. Miller, *Leadership and Power in the Bos-Wash Megalopolis* (New York: John Wiley & Sons, 1975).

SUGGESTED READINGS

Baxter, William F. *People or Penguins: The Case for Optimal Pollution.* New York: Columbia University Press, 1974. A good example of the traditional economic view of environmental questions. The author takes the position that decisions concerning the use of wildlife or other resources should be based on the greatest economic good for the most people.

Carson, Rachel. *Silent Spring.* New York: Houghton Mifflin, 1962. This is a modern environmental classic. It is one of the first books to consider the impact of the indiscriminate use of pesticides. It became a symbol for the environmental movement of the 1960s.

Crocker, Thomas D., and Rogers, A. J. III. *Environmental Economics.* Hinsdale, Ill.: Dryden Press, 1971. This is a cleverly written little book designed to painlessly introduce basic principles concerning environmental economics to the layman. The numerous humorous examples should help the reader recall the principles they illustrate.

Dasmann, Raymond. *The Last Horizon.* New York: Macmillan, 1963.

Like *The Quiet Crisis,* this is an example of one of the new environmentally oriented books of the 1960s. It differs from that book in that it emphasizes world problems and contains many examples of problems resulting from a lack of understanding of ecological principles.

Ehrlich, Paul R., et al. *Human Ecology.* San Francisco: W. H. Freeman and Co., 1973. A book that is often used as a text in courses oriented toward ecology. The author cites numerous examples of ecological problems and argues that we must develop a greater ecological awareness.

Matthews, William H. et. al. *Resource Materials for Environmental Management and Education.* Cambridge, Mass.: The MIT Press, 1976. A report of a recent conference on the problems of environmental management. The book is valuable because it suggests specific proposals for understanding and coping with environmental conditions and policy implementation concerning them.

Udall, Stewart L. et. al. *The Energy Balloon.* New York: McGraw-Hill, 1974.
A survey of energy use in the United States along with recommendations for conservation. The authors provide many concrete examples of how consumption can be reduced more or less painlessly. They also point out that Americans may have to accept what they call optimum levels of pollution — that is, a balance between some pollution and the cost of pollution abatement.

Udall, Stewart L. *The Quiet Crisis.* New York: Holt, Rinehart, & Winston, 1963.
A history of activity in the United States from colonial times to the 1960s. This was one of the first books emphasizing the fragility of the environment and the limited nature of resources. The author describes many historical and modern figures who have influenced the environmental issue.

Questions
for Discussion

1. Did the Native Americans have a conscious environmental ethic or values? In what ways did their views concerning the environment differ from those of the European settlers? In what ways did industrialization affect the environment and related views that concern it?

2. The functional perspective involves viewing environmental problems in essentially ecological terms. Explain this view and show how environmental questions can be defined as problems when using the functional approach.

3. The conflict perspective emphasizes that there are various interests competing over scarce resources. Is it possible for the different demands of the groups concerned with the environment to be reconciled? Will any such reconciliation be permanent or would it likely be only a temporary arrangement?

4. The interactionist perspective stresses the subjective nature of reality. How might a corporation utilize this perspective in coping with environmental questions? How might an environmental organization employ this perspective in coping with environmental questions? Compare and contrast.

5. Many economists along with owners and managers of industry take the view that economic growth is both necessary and desirable. What are the arguments supporting this position? Are they consistent with the best interests of the American people?

6. Ecologists and members of environmental organizations often take the view that economic growth must be limited or halted. Is this view consistent with the best interests of the American people? Why?

7. We have read about the problems facing the people of Hopewell, Virginia and the surrounding area in The Kepone Case. What does this case tell us about environmental problems? Is this an unusual incident or could it occur elsewhere? What steps might be taken in the future to forestall similar occurrences?

8. The text describes a number of approaches that can be used in attempting to solve or prevent environmental problems. Outline these steps and indicate whether you think any or all of them will work. In making this evaluation, consider each of them from the three theoretical perspectives.

CHAPTER 6

Wealth and Power in the Corporate State

CORPORATE AND GOVERNMENTAL POWER – A
BRIEF HISTORY

Corporate Growth. The Federal Government.

CORPORATIONS AND GOVERNMENT AS SOCIAL
PROBLEMS

The Functionalist Perspective. The Conflict Perspective.
The Interactionist Perspective.

THE CORPORATION IN MODERN SOCIETY

Power and Wealth. Corporate Power and the Individual
Consumer. Multinational Corporations.

GOVERNMENT

The Federal Government. The Interstate Commerce
Commission. Federal Government Expansion. The
Government and the Military.

WHO HAS POWER IN AMERICAN SOCIETY?

The Power Elite. Pluralism: An Alternate View of National
Power. Evaluation of the Models. The Power Elite and
Democratic Society.

FUTURE PROSPECTS

Government Reform. Citizens' Groups and People's
Lobbies.

CONCLUSION

Many of the largest business enterprises in the United States are financially stronger than the total economies of most countries. General Motors, one of America's largest industrial corporations in 1979, had total sales of over $54 billion and total assets of over $26 billion. G.M. reported earnings of over $3 billion. The direction of the American economy is largely determined by these industrial giants; in addition, there are complex interconnections between them, so that it is often difficult to separate the power of one company from that of another. For example, many companies are wholly owned subsidiaries of other companies. Many corporate directors sit on the boards of more than one corporation. These corporate giants are no longer limited to operating within the United States. Some of the largest American corporations—IBM, Uniroyal, Coca Cola, and others—derive at least 50 percent of their profits from overseas operations.[1] Along with this growth in industrial might, the size of government in America, especially at the federal level, has expanded enormously. The federal budget is now almost fifty times larger than it was just forty years ago.[2] Government now reaches into almost every aspect of our daily lives—it affects what we eat and what we sleep on, with whom we work or go to school, the type of gasoline we put in our cars, and the insurance we purchase.

In the first chapter, we considered the concept of power and observed that it is an extremely important ingredient in practically every social problem. The major issue in this chapter is not power as such, but the enormous concentration of power that has occurred in the United States. We will be concerned with determining what groups have acquired such ominous quantities of power and how they have done so. As we shall see, it is a relatively small number of people who share in this power. What is the impact on those who do not? How does this concentration of wealth and power affect the average American citizen? We will concentrate on the power accumulated by modern corporations and the federal government. We might have included other groups, such as labor unions, that certainly have substantial power and play a vital role in American society. However, corporations and government overshadow these other sources of power,

being by far the dominant institutions in determining the direction that our society will take. In order to understand the position of corporations and government today, it will be useful to see how they have developed in American society from rather small institutions to their current prominence.

CORPORATE AND GOVERNMENTAL POWER—A BRIEF HISTORY

Corporate Growth

The American economy before and during most of the eighteenth century was quite different from what it is today. Most business and manufacturing endeavors were oriented toward a local market; goods were produced in the same geographic location in which they were consumed. For example, a lumber mill found its market among community residents. Food was produced and consumed for the most part locally. Without efficient long-distance transportation, the widespread distribution of products, especially perishable items like food, was impossible.

Businesses or farms were usually owned by individuals or partners. The American economy consisted of many relatively small firms vying with one another in an atmosphere of often fierce competition. Individual entrepreneurs risked (and often lost) all their economic resources in the struggle with other business people. In such an economic environment, it was extremely difficult for one or a few individuals to concentrate substantial amounts of power in their own hands. Business enterprises were limited in scope—in terms of both size and geographic impact.

Toward the end of the nineteenth century, this situation changed dramatically. The fierce competition of the 1800s created a very unstable environment in which to do business. As one writer put it:

Improvements in technology were such that larger-sized plants were necessary to take advantage of the more efficient methods of production. Competition became so aggressive and destructive that small competitors were eliminated. Large competitors, facing mutual destruction, often combined in cartels, trusts, or mergers in order to ensure their mutual survival.[3]

In an attempt to make the business atmosphere more predictable and stable, business grew larger, buying out competing companies and attempting to control the whole production process.

Companies that conducted their business on a national and international level became much more common. Furthermore, the concentration of economic resources in the hands of a few massive companies proceeded apace. During this period, a new type of business enterprise, the corporation, become more prominent. One of the characteristics of **a *corporation* is that it is owned by stockholders who have only a limited liability—they risk only the money that they have spent on stocks, and they have no responsibility beyond that for the corporation's debts.** The result of these trends was the growth of businesses to a size unheard of before. The United States Steel Corporation, for example, had amassed a worth of close to $1.5 billion by the beginning of the twentieth century—an incredible concentration of economic resources for that period.[4]

While there were many advantages for business in such corporate growth and concentration, there was a public outcry over the actions of such giant industries as U.S. Steel and Standard Oil. Around the turn of the century, the federal government intervened with regulatory efforts aimed at controlling these giants. The Sherman Antitrust Act of 1890 and the Clayton Act of 1914 were two notable pieces of legislation in the government's effort to control the growth of business monopolies. Although the growth of business concentration has not been stopped, the government's actions have affected the shape and form of that growth. During the twentieth century, there has been continual give and take between business and government over the concentration of economic power. Partly as a result of its efforts to control corporate growth, the federal government itself has grown enormously.

The Federal Government

At the time of the founding of our nation, the federal government was, as it was intended to be, a rather small and weak body whose power was in many respects secondary to that of the individual states. America was founded on the basis of an antipathy toward a strong central government. The role of the federal government was generally limited to raising an army, providing a national currency, and promoting projects that benefited the common good. It employed few people (less than one hundred during George Washington's presidency) and for the most part only remotely affected the daily lives of most citizens.[5]

This limited role of the federal government has expanded beyond any bounds that the founders of our nation might have been able to imagine. There are a number of important reasons for the growth of government. First, there has been a trend for several centuries for the central government to take responsibility for the welfare of its citizens. Today, the state is viewed as responsible for helping the poor, the sick, and others who are unable or unwilling to care for themselves. This requires the enormous expansion of government programs and employees. Second, as we have noted, the growth of business has cast the government into the role of regulator of business enterprises and mediator between business and the citizenry. Originally, the government's role was limited to ensuring a free and unfettered competitive environment for business. Today the government works actively—through fiscal policy (such as taxation), monetary policy (changing the supply of money available), and the allocation of the incredibly large federal budget—to direct economic activity toward goals viewed as beneficial for all.

The final reason for the growth of governmental power has to do with the increasing complexity and interdependence within nations and between nations. It is no longer possible, as it once was, to view the different cities or regions of a nation as largely isolated units. Problems in one part of the country now have serious ramifications for other parts. It is no longer possible to allow cities, counties, or states to pursue their own goals with little concern for others. If one state pollutes a river, other states suffer. As a consequence of this interdependence, the government has taken the responsibility for coordinating the activities of the various parts of our society. Even though states still tenaciously resist intrusions by the federal government, the tendency has been for the government to take over more responsibility.

During the twentieth century, there were two major events that significantly boosted the growth of the federal bureaucracy. One was the Depression of the 1930s. In the hope of returning the nation to economic health, Franklin Roosevelt designed his "New Deal" so that government agencies could be expanded, providing for a new emphasis on planning and regulation at the federal level. Roosevelt accepted the advice of economists who argued that aggressive intervention and increased spending by the federal government would bring the nation out of the depths of the Depression. The Tennessee Valley Authority (TVA), the National Employment Service, and other agencies created by the National Industrial Recovery Act of 1933 are examples of this expansion of federal control.[6] Some of these agencies, such as TVA, are still powerful forces in the American economy.

The second important event of this century in terms of governmental expansion was World War II. The centralization of decision making and the need to control resources for this enormous military endeavor further enhanced the size and impact of the federal government. In comparison with Washington's handful of bureaucrats, the federal government today employs over 3 million people. As can be seen in Table 6.1, the federal budget has grown enormously. Today, federal authorities mandate the removal of additives from food, require automobile antipollution equipment, inspect meat, set rules for sewage treatment by communities, establish guidelines for the employment of minorities by any establishment receiving federal funds—and so on down an endless list of responsibilities.

Are these immense corporations and complex government bureaucracies a social problem? Using the above brief history as a foundation, we are now in a position to examine this issue as it exists today.

Why might these conditions be considered a social problem, and what are the dimensions of the problem?

CORPORATIONS AND GOVERNMENT AS SOCIAL PROBLEMS

The Functionalist Perspective

From the functionalist perspective, the various components of society—values, norms, institutions, and behavior—must be well integrated for society to function smoothly toward the achievement of desired goals. In American society, certain values are an important part of our heritage. For example, we place great value on the individual and individual self-reliance as being preferable to the domination of the individual by the group. We envision society composed ideally of individuals with equal rights and obligations, working toward common goals. In fact, the principles of individualism and equality are incorporated into our Constitution and the nation's legal system. All people are in principle equal before the law and should participate equally in the democratic process. Such values, when there

"MY PLAN IS THAT WE FORM A MERGER WITH AROUND 25 OF THE COUNTRY'S LARGEST CORPORATIONS, CREATE A JOINT EXECUTIVE COMMITTEE, AND TAKE OVER THE GOVERNMENT."

TABLE 6.1
The Federal Budget (in billions of dollars)

YEAR	RECEIPTS	OUTLAYS	OUTLAYS AS A PERCENTAGE OF THE GROSS NATIONAL PRODUCT
1940	6.4	9.5	10.0
1945	45.2	92.7	42.7
1950	39.5	42.6	16.1
1955	65.5	68.5	18.0
1960	92.5	92.2	18.5
1965	116.8	118.4	49.2
1970	193.7	196.6	39.9
1975	281.0	326.1	37.5
1977[a]	354.0	411.2	39.2

[a] estimate

SOURCE: U.S. Bureau of the Census, *Statistical Abstract of the United States: 1977* (Washington, D.C.: U.S. Government Printing Office, 1977).

is consensus about their importance, perform crucial functions — they serve as a guide on which people base their behavior, they serve to legitimize or justify existing social arrangements, and they motivate people to work toward societal goals.

According to this functionalist view, business is composed of individuals producing goods that are needed by members of society; the role of business is to provide the goods and services that make possible our way of life. Economic production and distribution in the United States is based on the value placed on the private ownership of property: private property is seen as the foundation of the private enterprise system, which is credited with our economic prosperity. Furthermore, private property is believed to serve as a source of power that can be used by individuals to ward off tyranny and preserve democratic institutions.

Given our heritage, many Americans tend to view a large government as almost inherently an evil one; this is summed up in the adage "That government is best which governs least." Americans place value in small government, which limits its activities to ensuring the existence of those conditions that aid the free production and distribution of goods and services. According to these beliefs, government should work to ensure that business activities serve the common good, but it is also believed that the common good is best served by the unfet-

tered operation of a market economy. **Thus, from the functionalist perspective, business and government should work together in harmony toward goals that are common to all Americans.** This is epitomized in Calvin Coolidge's statement "the business of the country is business." In theory, if business prospers, everyone benefits through increased employment, an abundance of consumer goods, and general prosperity.

However, the corporate and governmental structures that dominate American society today are in many respects inconsistent with American values of individualism, equality, and private property. Elaborate government bureaucracies and monstrous corporations now dwarf individuals. Decision making is far removed from the hands of most people. The concept of individualism becomes almost laughable when mammoth organizations shape and control each person's destiny. Equality becomes meaningless when some groups have almost infinite resources with which to pursue their goals while most individuals have almost none.

Yet, from the functionalist perspective, it is not the size or the power of corporations and government that make them a social problem. Rather, they are a social problem because they are no longer consistent with the values that underlie our society. When social institutions and values are in conflict, it becomes more difficult for people to guide their behavior on the basis of those values and there are fewer rewards for doing so. Why believe in equality and act on that belief when corporations and government agencies clearly dominate the lives of individuals? Why support any American institutions or values when they are so blatantly disregarded by others? With this incompatibility between institutions and values, it is more difficult to motivate people to work toward common goals, and the functioning of society may be threatened.

The Conflict Perspective

From the conflict perspective, there is no necessary harmony between corporations, government, and American citizens. Each constitutes an interest group (or, actually, a large number of interest

In the modern world, government and corporate bureaucracies become so immense that they dwarf the individual. People often feel that they have little control over these bureaucracies' actions.

groups) that pursues its own goals, whether or not they may be detrimental to the goals of others. There are groups that benefit from the actions of big business and big government, and there are others who suffer because of the same actions. In the past, many groups—the poor, the unemployed, minority groups, and the like—have experienced the negative consequences of the concentration of power and decision making in the hands of the few. **However, from the conflict perspective the concentration of power alone is not a social problem; nor is it a social problem because such concentration works to the detriment of some groups.** Recall that the conflict perspective assumes that there will always be some disharmony and lack of consensus and that a maldistribution of scarce resources is a normal state of affairs.

The concentration of power and decision making in the hands of big business and big government becomes a social problem when some influential group feels that it does not have a fair share of the decision-making power in the United States. Business and government become social problems when influential groups feel isolated from the centers of power and believe that they have lost their ability to direct their destiny and achieve their goals. Today, this feeling of powerlessness and impotence is widespread among the middle- and working-class groups who have the resources with which to make their discontent felt. Even among the poor and minority groups today, there is a greater awareness of how to make demands on business and government and a greater willingness to do so. Unlike the past, when subordinate groups either accepted their lowly state or felt helpless about changing their conditions, the emphasis on citizen advocacy and community organization today has convinced many groups that the monoliths of business and government can be made to work to their own advantage or that groups can at least stand up to these institutions with some hope of success. "Power to the people" has become the catchphrase for the newfound sentiment that any group should take action to control its own destiny. **So, from the conflict perspective, the unequal distribution of power is normal. This condition becomes a social problem when influential groups perceive it as working to their detriment and when they begin to take action to change that situation.**

The Interactionist Perspective

Since the role of corporations and government involves the major institutions in society, the functionalist and conflict perspectives are most helpful in understanding them. However, the interactionist perspective is also useful for the insights it provides on how the growth of corporations and government affects our daily lives and the ways in which we view ourselves and others. There was a time when it was more common than it is today for people to feel that they controlled those things that affected their lives; and those things beyond their control were either divinely regulated or the result of chance. Whether people actually had such control is less important, from the interactionist perspective, than their *perception* of such control. These perceptions had an effect on people's self-concepts—they often felt personally autonomous and powerful. To some degree this was a self-fulfilling prophecy: people felt that they had such power, and they acted on that basis. In so acting, they were able to direct and control their destiny. In a corporate world, however, things are quite different. People are more likely to feel (whether rightly or not) that they have very little control over their own destinies. They are more likely to feel that others determine the conditions of their life. These perceptions can lead to feelings of dependence, fatalism, and impotence.

The interactionist perspective emphasizes the importance of consensus and shared expectations as the foundation of social interaction. Without them, social interaction becomes difficult, if not impossible. The characteristics of the modern corporate and bureaucratic state make it far more difficult to achieve such an agreement. Because of experiences in our daily lives, we may grow to mistrust others. The extreme cynic becomes a folk hero. "Don't trust anybody" and "Look out for number one" epitomize this attitude. In such a situation, it is difficult, and perhaps foolish, to believe that we all share some common goals and values— that there is a consensus about "proper behavior." This cynical attitude offers no motivation for self-sacrifice and altruistic action.

The extent to which these attitudes of cynicism, mistrust, and powerlessness are dysfunctional for the system as a whole is a debatable point, however. In fact, one might argue that, among at least a portion of the populace, these attitudes might support the status quo by reducing the demands of these groups for a share of power and decision making. However, the interactionist perspective emphasizes the subjective nature of reality—a condition is a social problem because people define it and act toward it as such. As these attitudes become more widespread, larger segments of the population are defining them, and the social conditions that underlie them, as social problems. For most people, the feeling of being surrounded by persons that cannot be trusted and of living in institutions that cannot be controlled is unsettling and odious.

A person's perception and interpretation of reality is influenced by many things—values, interests, and past experiences. Both corporations and government spend enormous sums of money to alter those perceptions and interpretations in a fashion that is beneficial to them. Businesses, of course, advertise their products, but they also control information in order to encourage people to be more favorably inclined toward corporations and view them as benevolent institutions working for the good of society. For example, mining companies have been forced through legislation to include environmental concerns in their undertakings, but in their advertising the impression communicated is that they did this because it is in the long-term interests of America and because that is what the company is concerned about. Likewise, government is interested to see that its actions and policies are viewed in the best light possible. This ability to shape people's conceptions of the world is an important tool in creating a climate of opinion which enhances the likelihood that business and government will be able to pursue their own interests relatively unhindered.

THE CORPORATION IN MODERN SOCIETY

It is difficult to completely understand the impact on society of the growth of business and the emergence of corporations unless one is aware of the important role played by the economic organization of society. Karl Marx argued that the economic organization of society is the central institution. All other segments of society—government, the legal system, religion, education—are shaped by the form of the economy.[7] It is easy to recognize the importance of economic organization in terms of how it makes available the array of goods and services that are a part of our affluent lifestyle. However, economic arrangements have much more subtle and wide-ranging effects on the class structure of society, the distribution of power, and even on the way we think about and perceive the world. In this section, we will investigate some of these effects in present-day American society and the kinds of social problems that result.

Power and Wealth

According to Marx, the type of economic organization in society—the manner in which goods and services are produced and distributed—shapes the type of power and authority relationships that emerge and their distribution among groups.[8] As long as the American economy consisted of small, locally organized businesses and a large number of competitors, the power of the economic sector was decentralized, diffuse, and limited to local or regional levels. With such an economic organization, it was almost impossible for a business to accumulate a vast amount of power at the national level. Today, our economic organization is drastically different: the economy is highly centralized and is national, and even international, in scope. With such an economic organization, the possibilities for the concentration of power and wealth in the hands of a few are much greater.

The Corporation

An important part of the new economic organization is the prominence of the corporation as a legal and social entity. **A *corporation* is a legally created entity that is chartered to engage in business and that is considered a "person" before the law, with certain rights and privileges that apply to any individual.** The implications of the characteristics of corporations can best be understood by comparing them with individually owned businesses. The owner of a business is attached to it in certain legal ways. If the business goes into debt, the owner is legally liable, and all of the owner's possessions could be confiscated to ensure payment of the debt. If the owner dies, the business either ceases to exist or must be reorganized with a new owner.

The corporation is quite different from this. It provides an investor with limited liability. If the corporation goes into debt, those who own stock in it may lose only the money they have put into the venture, and they have no further responsibility for paying off the corporation's debts. In a corporation, ownership is separate from control. The stockholders own a part of the corporation, but they do not determine its day-to-day operating policies and activities and thus have only limited control over the corporation. This control is exercised by the corporate executives (who may also be stockholders). Corporations are also immortal in the sense that ownership is easily transferable. If a major stockholder dies, the corporation continues to function as before.

Because of its characteristics, the corporation is very attractive to investors. Capital can be accumulated and other resources amassed, with the potential for enormous profits with minimal risk to the individual stockholder. Some understanding of the immensity of corporations today can be gained from looking at the sales and profits of the twenty largest corporations in the United States (see Table 6.2).

The Concentration of Economic Power

The incredible financial power of corporations has been growing over a long period. In 1970, there were 200,000 separately owned industrial corporations in the United States. Of these, 100 controlled over 50 percent of all industrial assets—land, buildings, equipment, and the like used in manufacturing. Furthermore, the degree of concentration appears to be on the increase (see Fig. 6.1). It is important to understand the ways in which this concentration of economic power has occurred so that the dimensions of the problem and feasible solutions can be better comprehended.

In the late 1800s, one form of concentration

TABLE 6.2
The 20 Largest Industrial Corporations (ranked by sales), 1977

RANK '77	'76	COMPANY	SALES ($000)	ASSETS ($000)	RANK	NET INCOME ($000)	RANK
1	2	General Motors (Detroit)	54,961,300	26,658,300	2	3,337,500	1
2	1	Exxon (New York)	54,126,219	38,453,336	1	2,422,964	3
3	3	Ford Motor (Dearborn, Mich.)	37,841,500	19,241,300	4	1,672,800	4
4	5	Mobil (New York)	32,125,828	20,575,967	3	1,004,670	8
5	4	Texaco (White Plains, N.Y.)	27,920,499	18,926,026	6	930,789	9
6	6	Standard Oil of California (San Francisco)	20,917,331	14,822,347	7	1,016,360	6
7	8	International Business Machines (Armonk, N.Y.)	18,133,184	18,978,445	5	2,719,414	2
8	7	Gulf Oil (Pittsburgh)	17,840,000	14,225,000	8	752,000	10
9	9	General Electric (Fairfield, Conn.)	17,518,600	13,696,800	9	1,088,200	5
10	10	Chrysler (Highland Park, Mich.)	16,708,300	7,668,200	18	163,200	66
11	11	International Tel. & Tel. (New York)	13,145,664	12,285,522	11	550,667	15
12	12	Standard Oil (Ind.) (Chicago)	13,019,939	12,884,286	10	1,011,575	7
13	15	Atlantic Richfield (Los Angeles)	10,969,091	11,119,012	12	701,515	12
14	13	Shell Oil (Houston)	10,112,062	8,876,754	14	735,094	11
15	14	U.S. Steel (Pittsburgh)	9,609,900	9,914,400	13	137,900	84
16	16	E. I. du Pont de Nemours (Wilmington, Del.)	9,434,800	7,430,600	19	545,100	16
17	17	Continental Oil (Stamford, Conn.)	8,700,317	6,625,229	21	380,626	26
18	18	Western Electric (New York)	8,134,604	5,875,543	23	490,076	18
19	20	Tenneco (Houston)	7,440,300	8,278,300	15	426,900	21
20	19	Procter & Gamble (Cincinnati)	7,284,255	4,487,186	31	461,463	10

SOURCE. Reprinted from the 1978 *Fortune* Directory by special permission; © 1978 Time, Inc.

became prominent in the American economy. **Large firms were buying out their smaller competitors until they developed a** *monopoly —exclusive control of a product or service in a given area of industry.* These trusts—huge monopolistic corporations—were attacked by federal antitrust legislation beginning in the 1890s. In 1911, the government won an important battle and broke up the Standard Oil trust of John D. Rockefeller.

The government continues to monitor and regulate the formation of monopolies. Government intervention focuses on ensuring that competition exists in the various sectors of the economy. It is assumed that competition will guarantee products of high quality and relatively low prices. Recently, the government has filed suit against a number of large corporations, charging them with monopolistic practices—American Telephone and Telegraph Company in the communications field, International Business Machines in the computer field, and the four major producers of breakfast foods (General Mills, General Foods, Kellog's and Quaker Oats).[9]

However, the effectiveness of the monitoring today is not really known. These monolithic corporations have incredibly vast legal resources with which to battle the government—far greater legal resources than the Justice Department (which handles such cases for the government) can marshal. This illustrates one of the major problems that arise with such concentrations of power in corporations: is there any other source of power that can effectively control such economic monoliths? It is

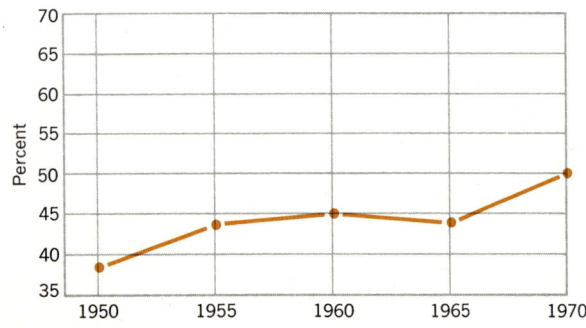

Figure 6.1 **Proportion of All Industrial Assets Controlled by the 100 Largest Corporations (expressed in percentage). Data from Thomas R. Dye,** *Who's Running America: Institutional Leadership in the United States* **(Englewood Cliffs, N.J.: Prentice-Hall, 1976), p. 20.**

debatable whether the government is really capable of doing so. If one could rest assured that corporations always acted with the best interests of the American public in mind, then concern would be uncalled for. However, since their primary concern is profits and growth, corporate interests can, and often do, diverge from those of many American citizens.

Another means of concentrating economic wealth and power is through *vertical expansion*— **the control or ownership of firms that operate at different stages in the development of a product.** For example, an automobile manufacturer might own iron mines and steel mills that produce the materials necessary for automobile production. At the distribution end of the manufacturing process, the automobile manufacturer might own transportation companies that move the vehicles to retail outlets and also own the distributorships where they are sold. The advantage of vertical expansion is that it ensures the smooth and uninterrupted flow of materials at a predictable price, permitting the central industry—automobile manufacturing—to operate in a stable and profitable fashion.

Another type of corporate expansion emerged during the 1950s: the conglomerate. **The *conglomerate* is a corporation that controls other companies in fields of production quite different from that of the parent company** (see Fig. 6.2). The advantage of this type of growth is economic stability, through diversity, for the parent company. If a given year is not financially lucrative for a particular industry, the profits from the other, unrelated industries help to prevent these losses from having a major impact on the

Figure 6.2 Conglomerate Holdings of Gulf and Western Inc. Gulf and Western Industries, Inc. 1978 Annual Report, In *Time* Magazine, Feb. 5th, 1979.

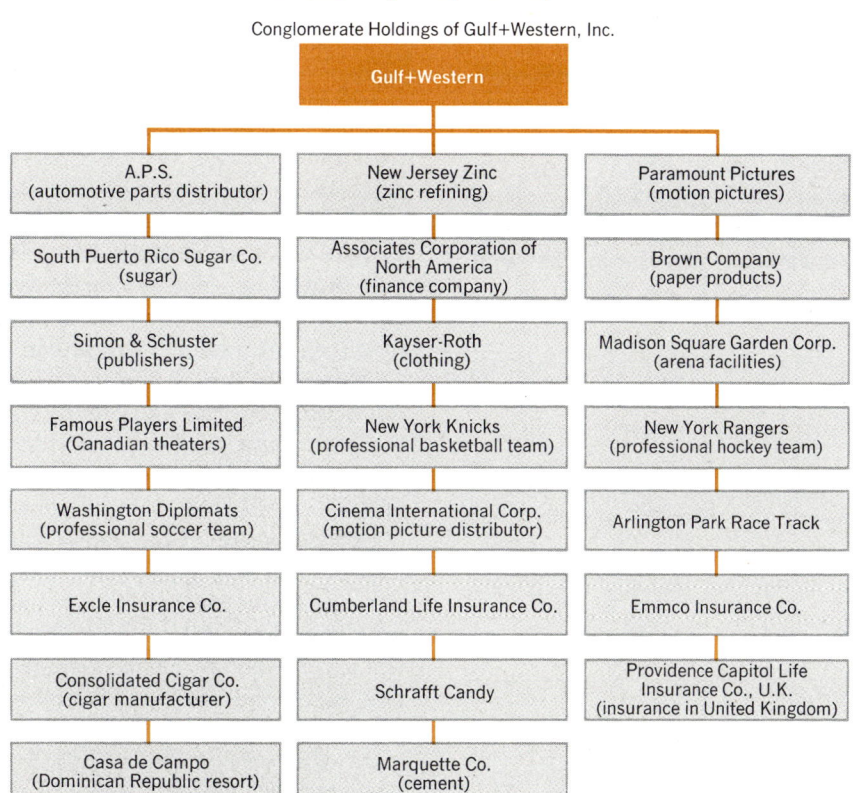

Conglomerate Holdings of Gulf+Western, Inc.

parent company.

Another means of concentrating power in the corporate world is through interlocking directorates. *Interlocking directorates* **refers to the linkage between corporations that results when a person serves on the board of directors of two different companies (a direct interlock) or when two companies each have a director on the board of a third company (an indirect interlock).**[10] The Clayton Act of 1914 made it illegal for a person to serve simultaneously as a corporate director of two companies that were in direct competition with one another. However, it is quite common to have interlocking directorates, especially indirect ones, among companies that are not competitors. For example, in 1976 American Telephone and Telegraph Company was indirectly interlocked with its closest rival, International Business Machines Corporation, through common membership on the boards of twenty-two other companies. In 1978, Exxon, the largest energy-related company and the second largest corporation in the United States, had two of its directors serving on the board of Citicorp, the largest banking firm. Along with them at Citicorp were directors from Mobil, Standard Oil of California, and a host of other energy-related firms, such as General Electric and Westinghouse.[11] In other words, there were substantial indirect interlocks between Exxon and other firms in the energy field through their common membership on the board of Citicorp.

The business community views these interlocking directorates as highly beneficial. Serving on more than one corporate board is seen as giving an executive a breadth of knowledge and experience that others do not have and that can be useful to the home company. The complete elimination of interlocking directorates, they argue, would considerably reduce the pool of highly skilled and experienced business executives from which a company might draw. However, regardless of the benefit to the companies involved, interlocking directorates are an important means by which power and decision making in the American economy are concentrated in the hands of a relatively few corporations and individuals.[12]

Corporate Power and the Individual Consumer

While the considerable concentration of power in the economic sphere is attractive to investors and beneficial to the corporation, it creates conditions that are considered social problems by others in society. When this tremendous amount of resources is concentrated among a very few firms or individuals, it creates conditions in which the power of the individual consumer is substantially reduced in comparison to the power held by the corporations. We now turn to two major issues that become important when there is such a massive concentration of power, and how they affect American citizens.

Failure of Competition

One result of this concentration is that the dominant corporations can produce fundamental changes in competitive conditions. For example, a conglomerate can subsidize its losses in one market with profits gained in another. To illustrate, a conglomerate could lower the prices on electronic calculators produced by one of its subsidiaries until the calculators sold at well below the cost of manufacturing. The losses that the calculator company incurred could be covered by the profits in another sector of the conglomerate. The effect of this underselling is the elimination of competitors who could not sell their products for less than the cost of producing them. Once competition is eliminated, the prices of the calculators could rise again and the profits restored to that sector of the conglomerate. In such a situation, pricing is determined not by production costs and market mechanisms but rather by the profit and growth needs of the conglomerate. In an economy based on open competition, inefficient companies marketing products of poor quality are more likely to be driven out of business because consumers will purchase the superior products of their competitors. In such an economy, the consumer has some control over business through decisions in the marketplace. However, in a noncompetitive environment, the individual consumer is at the mercy of the corporation in terms of product availability, quality, and pricing.

Some products have been identified by consumer groups as dangerous to the public. Numerous law suits were filed against the Ford Motor Corporation alleging that the gas tanks of their Pintos were likely to explode in rear-end collisions.

The enormous economic resources available to conglomerates also makes it possible for them to manipulate industrial buying and selling to their own advantage. The conglomerate can use its substantial and lucrative purchases of goods in some areas to persuade suppliers to purchase other products of the conglomerate. For example, an aircraft manufacturer could tell the manufacturer of aircraft seats that in order to retain its contract to supply seats to the aircraft manufacturer, it should buy its fabrics from a textile company that the conglomerate owns. Furthermore, the conglomerate-owned textile factor may, because its business is based on coercion rather than on market mechanisms, charge a higher-than-market price for its fabrics. Since this puts the passenger seat manufacturer in a profit squeeze, it is forced to compensate for this by charging higher prices to purchasers of its other products (who, in turn, pass *their* costs on to the consumer in the form of higher prices).

The end result is the restriction of the free play of market mechanisms and the continued concentra-tion of power and wealth as small firms disappear and a few giant firms control the bulk of the productive assets of the United States. As a consequence, the consumer pays high prices for poor-quality products. Traditionally, business was ultimately controlled by consumers through their decisions in the open marketplace. However, the extreme concentration of power threatens to remove this control from the hands of the consumers and leave them at the mercy of economic giants that are unresponsive to the regulation of the marketplace.

Lack of Social Responsibility

One central question concerning this massive concentration of economic power is, who determines how profits are to be used and toward what goals American economic power is to be directed? **In this regard, it is important to realize that *the primary motivation of corporations is to make profits and to ensure corporate growth.* They do not necessarily work for the common good of society.** Therefore, the actions of a corporation will be directed toward its own self-interest and will not necessarily reflect any sense of social responsibility.

There are few restrictions on how the great wealth of corporations is spent. As a result, corporations can influence beliefs, values, and lifestyles and shape the political and economic policies of our society. As one observer has noted,

Giant supercorporations become private governments, in the sense that their actions and policies govern the alternatives open to millions of people and thousands of communities. Prices, investment policy, product development, location of plants, wage and employment policies—the whole range of corporate policy—are decisions of national importance because of the size and significance of the organizations that make them. In that sense, much of our life is governed by the decisions made by a small group of men who are responsible only to themselves, who select their successors, and whose organizations continue for an indefinite time. A pattern of economic decision making has emerged that is only imperfectly controlled by market forces and which has questionable legitimacy and limited accountability.[13]

The impact of concentrating such power in the hands of a few corporations can be extremely subtle. In a report on interlocking directorates prepared by the staff of a Senate subcommittee, it was pointed out that the major problem was not of flagrant abuses of power but rather the ". . . danger of a business elite, an ingrown group, impervious to outside forces, intolerant of dissent, and protective of the status quo, charting the direction of production and investment . . ." in the United States.[14] Such a cooperative relationship among firms might result in economic policies beneficial to the growth of the corporations but detrimental to other segments of society. For example, decisions to build new manufacturing and retail outlets outside of the central city may be profitable for corporations because land is less expensive, taxes are often lower, and the residents are more affluent and highly skilled. However, partly because of this flight, our large cities are experiencing serious eco-

nomic and social problems that create a burden for all members of society because of resulting crime, disruption, and welfare and unemployment benefits. So economic decisions that make sense in terms of profits to corporations can lead to policies that are detrimental to other groups in society. While society may benefit from some of the actions of corporations, it is not certain that it always does.

Multinational Corporations

A recent development in the concentration of power and wealth in large, private corporations is the emergence of multinational corporations as prominent forces in the world economy. A *multinational corporation* is a corporation that has a large commitment of resources in international business, engages in production and manufacturing in a number of countries, and uses a worldwide perspective in its management and decision making. While foreign operations of business are by no means new, the number of companies that gain a significant amount of their income from abroad—from one-third to three-quarters of their total net income—increased dramatically in the past few decades.[15]

Some economists and business executives have taken a positive approach toward multinationals by looking at the benefits they provide. First, by operating on an international level, multinational corporations are able to produce a wide range of products as cheaply as possible by working in countries where the costs of operation (labor, taxes, land, and materials) are the lowest. This, they argue, benefits all through the wide availability of inexpensive consumer goods. Second, multinationals have brought modern products, techniques, and managerial skills to all parts of the globe, thus stimulating economic growth and the development of new industries. Third, supporters of multinationals argue that they serve as a stabilizing force in the world by establishing nonpolitical contacts between nations, which foster understanding and interdependence. In this way, the likelihood of international conflict is reduced.[16]

However, multinational corporations are viewed with suspicion by those concerned about the increasing concentration of power in the hands of a few corporations. This suspicion arises from certain aspects of the present-day organization of multinational corporations.

Allegiance

The primary (some would say, only) allegiance of the multinational corporation is to the maximization of profits. National loyalty, if it exists at all, is secondary. There is substantial potential for conflict between the goals of the multinational and the social, political, and economic goals of the nations in which it does business. A company could, for example, aim at maximizing its profits around the world on a long-term basis or it could seek a specific rate of return that would be stable over time. These goals might be achieved by a variety of actions — holding down profits in one country, shifting profits and jobs from one country to another when it seems profitable to do so, or accelerating production to exhaust some limited local resources before they can be used by competitors for other purposes.

Some, possibly all, of these actions might clash with the desires of the host country. The latter would undoubtedly desire to increase local production, to employ local workers instead of foreigners, and to ration certain scarce resources to ensure a future supply and to avoid dependence on other nations for those resources.[17] In other words, the goals of the multinational corporation and its host country do not always coincide. Nonetheless, the multinational's loyalty is to its own growth and profit maximization.

Unequal Resources

Multinationals are often far wealthier than the countries in which they do business and are thus in a position to expect or demand that these countries adopt policies beneficial to the multinational. Many nations find it difficult to pursue economic or political policies if these conflict with the goals of the multinational because the corporation has the resources to influence government decisions. For example, two multinationals, Anaconda and Kennecott, accounted for 20 percent of the domestic gross national product of Chile in the early 1970s.

The taxes paid by these two corporations to the Chilean government financed from 10 to 40 percent of all governmental expenditures. As a result, it was extremely difficult and costly for Chile to pursue policies contrary to the interests of these corporations.[18] If adverse governmental actions forced these corporations to leave Chile, the economic consequences would have been devastating.

Exploitation

In their quest to maximize profits, multinational corporations seek out countries in which labor costs are low. As a consequence, there is a tendency for corporations to move their manufacturing and production out of nations with relatively high labor costs, such as the United States and Western Europe, to areas of inexpensive labor, such as Asia and Mexico.[19] Yet it is precisely the high wages paid to American and European workers that has made possible the high standard of living and the stable political environment of these nations. Increasingly, workers are at the mercy of the decisions of the multinational. As businesses move abroad, serious social and economic problems are created in America: unemployment mounts; the importation of foreign goods increases, which results in a flow of dollars abroad; and as our balance of payments deficit increases, the value of the dollar declines relative to other currencies, which increases inflation and causes other economic problems.

Such multinational corporations, even though many are of American origin, show little concern about these dire economic consequences of their actions because their prime loyalty is, once again, to corporate profit and not to the American public. The exploitation of workers, then, with all the injury this may cause, is justified on the basis of corporate growth and profitability.

Intervention

Much of the influence of multinational corporations on their host nations is indirect and subtle — governments avoid political and economic policies that are not consistent with the interests of the multinationals operating within their borders. However, in a few cases, the influence is much more direct and dramatic, involving outright intervention in the domestic affairs of the host nation. The impact that such intervention can have is illustrated by the following case, in which the International Telephone and Telegraph Company (ITT), in collusion with some American government officials, played a role in the outcome of domestic elections in Chile.[20] ITT's approach illustrates the enormous influence that multinational corporations can have on their host nations.

In 1970, John McCone, a director of ITT and former head of the Central Intelligence Agency, offered the CIA a contribution of $1 million to finance an operation to interfere with the elections in Chile. ITT feared substantial corporate losses if Marxist candidate Allende won the presidency. When Allende won, in what most observers agree was a fair and democratic election, ITT drew up a plan to create economic chaos in Chile, which the corporation hoped would lead to Allende's overthrow.

> Jack D. Neal, an ITT employee with 35 years' experience in the State Department, had prepared an 18-point program designed to produce a coup d'etat. His methods included concerted economic pressure through the cutoff of credit and aid and the support of domestic antagonists of the regime. In time all his methods were employed.[21]

In 1973, President Allende was shot to death during a coup d'etat that resulted in the military overthrow of his democratically elected government. While it is not certain that ITT's campaign was the cause of the overthrow, the corporation's intent was clear. ITT benefited from the outcome, and found a sympathetic ear and some degree of support for its venture among some American government officials. While Americans might debate the role of ITT and the American government in this affair, their apparent complicity has done enormous harm to the image of the United States in Latin America. While such extreme ventures are rare as far as we know, this case does illustrate the lengths to which a corporation might go to protect its profits and the degree to which it can involve the American government in its actions.

Regulations

At present, the United States has no laws that regulate overseas operations of American firms effectively. The likelihood of the establishment of such laws and their rigorous enforcement is small because our government often either actively or passively cooperates with multinationals in their attempts to wield influence. Were there effective governmental regulation, it would still be possible for multinationals simply to move their home offices to more friendly nations without such restrictive laws. At this point, then, effective social and legal mechanisms to protect host nations from the possible abuse of power by multinational corporations simply do not exist.

In fact, some managers of multinational corporations argue that multinationals *should* transcend, and in a sense have equal status with, nations—independent of all countries and subservient to none. A recent chairman of the Dow Chemical Company expressed it thus:

> I have long dreamed of buying an island owned by no nation and of establishing the World Headquarters of the Dow company on the truly neutral ground of such an island, beholden to no nation or society. If we were located on such truly neutral ground we could then really operate in the United States as U.S. citizens, in Japan as Japanese citizens, and in Brazil as Brazilians rather than being governed in prime by the laws of the United States. . . . We could even pay any natives handsomely to move elsewhere.[22]

This would truly be a "corporate state," in which the profits of the corporation would be the only criterion for policy formulation and all regulations adverse to that goal could be removed.

Given the increasing political and economic interdependence of all people in the world today, some have argued that the sovereign nation-state, as we currently know it, is becoming an anachronism. As international organizations (such as the United Nations and the World Bank) and multinational corporations play an increasingly prominent role in the world, the nation-state will become less central and fade into a position secondary to these international groups.[23] Others maintain that powerful national governments will remain as a countervailing force to control the actions of the multinational corporations. In either case, national governments still play a crucial role, and it is to this topic—the role and power of government in America—that we now turn.

GOVERNMENT

Most people who have grown up in the United States have learned some of the key phrases in Abraham Lincoln's Gettysburg Address. Early supporters of democracy like Lincoln stressed proper representation for all and government "of the people, by the people, for the people." Political slogans like One Man, One Vote called attention to the belief that every voter's decision at the polls was important and highly valued. During the early years of American government, the issues were sufficiently limited so that most citizens could ponder the pros and cons of different political strategies. Indeed, Americans then felt, more than they do today, that they understood the issues and could make a significant contribution to governmental decision making. Government was small, and most people felt that it was responsive to the needs of citizens. Things certainly have changed over the past 150 years.

The poor, the aged, the undereducated, and the unemployed are groups whose members commonly feel powerless in affecting government decision making. Today, however, this feeling of powerlessness extends far beyond such underprivileged groups. The civil disorders and protests of the 1960s were, among other things, symptoms of a widespread dissatisfaction with what many viewed as almost total government control over issues like racial desegregation and the Vietnam war. The protestors were reacting to a phenomenon that has been developing since before the turn of the century —*the growth and concentration of power in government*. The explosive reaction to this phenomenon has been complicated by the emergence of a distinct lack of trust in government itself. The Watergate affair and Richard Nixon's ultimate resigna-

tion cultivated a deep feeling of skepticism among Americans about their government and about national leadership. One of the major thrusts of this chapter concerns the inordinate power of a small number of dominant institutions in our society. Government, particularly at the federal level, is one of these. During the early 1800s, government was relatively small and decentralized, and there were many groups—business, religious, and civic—that had sufficient power to influence, and possibly counteract, the actions of this rather weak government. Because there was no dominant power center, there was considerable compromise and give-and-take in the formulation of national policy. Many people feel that the situation has changed to such a degree that the average citizen today really has very little "say" in terms of national affairs. Even if the citizen of 1850 had limited influence on government decision making, he commonly *felt* more involved and important in this process. Today, a *power elite* has emerged, consisting of government as well as corporate and military sectors in our society. Let us now further examine the steady expansion and centralization of government.

The Federal Government

Although it may be difficult to envision, there was a time when the federal government of the United States seldom became directly involved in commercial affairs. Of course, government did take a national economic stand by creating a consistent currency system and by opposing trusts and monopolies, but there was a distinct absence of central and long-range planning for our country's economic future. Regions of the United States could be readily distinguished based on social, economic, and political policies. Today, the federal government has assumed a central position in the shaping of social and economic policy in the United States. Whatever else it may have been, Governor George Wallace's much publicized confrontation with federal officials over desegregation during the early 1960s in Alabama may be considered symbolic of the demise of states' rights. Today, the tentacles of government reach out in every direction and into every sphere of social life.

Figure 6.3 provides a partial table of organization for the government of the United States. In many ways, this chart oversimplifies the actual complexity of our political system. Consider that, if this diagram were extended, each and every independent office and establishment and every subestablishment at the bottom of the chart would have its own table of organization, with suborganizations possessing their own, and so on. This tremendous complexity has emerged in part because the government has become much more active in regulating both our public and our private affairs. This pro-liferation of governmental regulatory agencies began in the late 1800s. A consideration of one of these agencies will serve to illustrate the role that they play in our daily lives.

The Interstate Commerce Commission

The Interstate Commerce Commission (ICC) was created in 1887 to represent the public interest in opposition to highly organized transportation concerns such as the railroads. Its purpose was to ensure that all interests had access to dependable transportation at the most reasonable rates possi-

Figure 6.3 The Government of the United States. U.S. Bureau of the Census, *Statistical Abstract of the United States: 1977* (Washington, D.C.: U.S. Government Printing Office, 1977), p. 245.

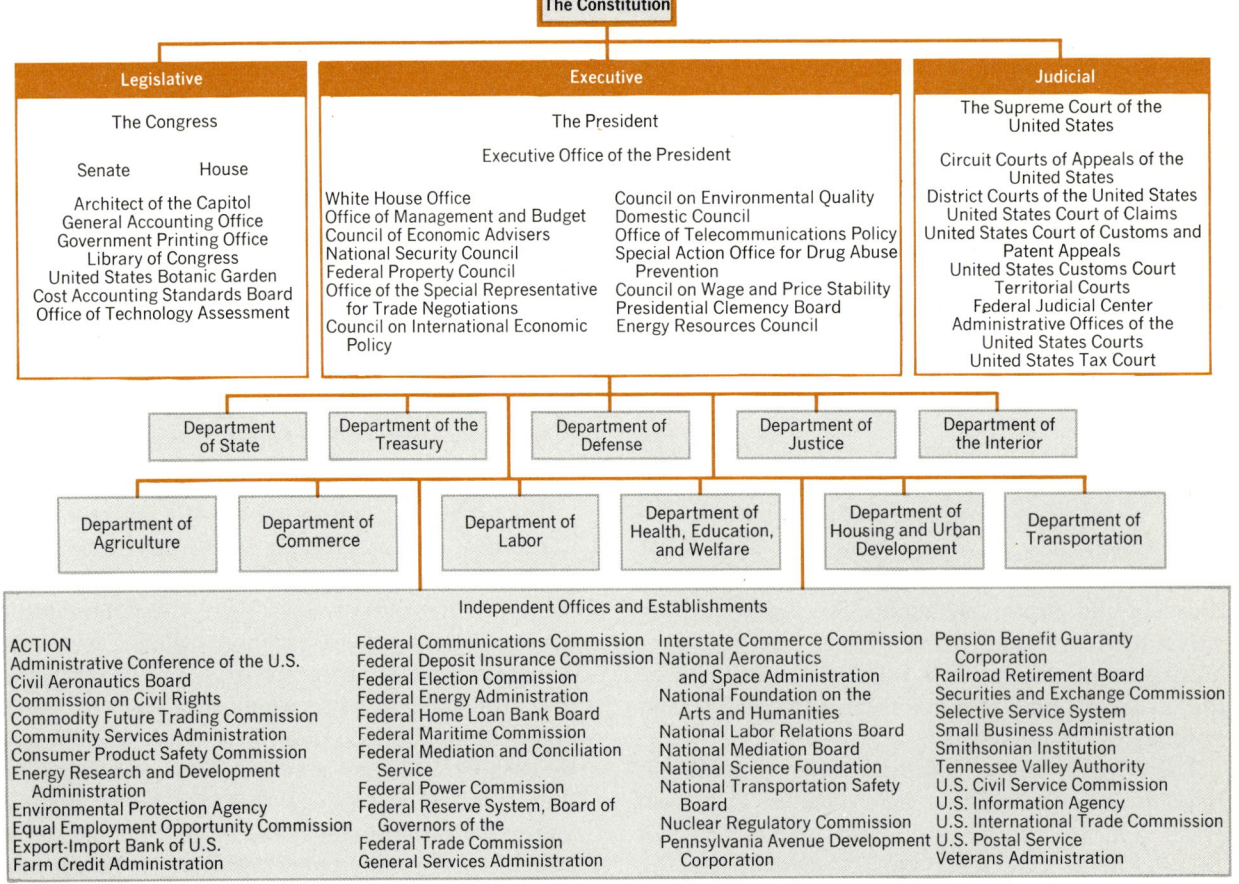

The Pentagon symbolizes the enormousness and complexity of modern government.

ble. Over the years, the ICC has encountered many difficulties that appear to stem ultimately from the commission's increasing cooperation with those it is supposed to regulate. Often, for example, staff appointments to the commission are cleared by high-ranking officials in industry before selections are finalized. The principles of checks and balances and of countervailing powers became lost in the shuffle. Powerful corporate interest groups like the American Trucking Association and the Association of American Railroads have essentially been able to hand-select their own "adversaries" on the ICC.[24]

The Interstate Commerce Commission was formed to protect the public from the abuse of power by large corporations. In fact, however, the commission has created regulations that favor organized transportation interests rather than those of the American public. According to one writer who has studied the ICC, rather than promoting competition, "ICC regulation has fostered the other extreme: rate collusion, price fixing, and absence of competition."[25]

The actions of the ICC and other government regulatory agencies have often led to increased costs and to overall economic inefficiency. Of course, these outcomes impact directly on the consumer in terms of elevated prices of retail goods. A short time ago, two expert commentators pointed out the extent of the difficulties surrounding the ICC:

> Nearly everyone agrees that the Interstate Commerce Commission (ICC) has failed. The disintegration of freight and passenger service; the dependence on highways; interstate trucking, and automobiles in the midst of a growing energy shortage and an ecology movement; the chaos of rates and regulations bearing little or no relation to costs all contribute to a massive transportation crisis that wastes billions of dollars annually.[26]

The problems confronting the ICC are not peculiar to that agency. Similar problems can be found in almost every government organization, and they stem from the same causes. First, these monolithic bureaucratic agencies become isolated from the American citizenry they are supposed to serve and thus lose sight of what would best suit the needs and desires of most Americans. With government so complex and far-removed from most people, there are few watchdogs that can guard against abuses by government bureaucrats. Second, powerful interest groups gain control of the offices and agencies and set policy that is in their own interest. For example, few people think about the ICC and the wisdom of its actions, yet the decisions of the ICC affect us all directly—it sets transportation rates, which become a factor in the prices of the products we buy; through its policies, it shapes the form of transportation, such as highway as against rail, that will be the dominant mode of travel in the United States. While the average citizen may ignore its daily activities, the interest groups affected by its policies work long and hard to ensure that policies beneficial to them are passed, even if such policies may be detrimental to society as a whole.

This discussion of the ICC points to one of the central problems that arise as government grows to enormous size—to what extent is such a government responsive to the desires of the citizen? Is such a government so controlled by a few interest groups that most citizens have essentially no input into the decision-making process? Answers to these questions will, of course, vary, depending on one's perspective. However, the mere fact that these questions are asked seriously indicates that many people today are deeply concerned about this issue. A related concern about which there is little debate is the enormous growth in the federal government's budget caused by the proliferation of its agencies and activities.

Federal Government Expansion

The Depression of the 1930s led to a number of significant changes in the scope and influence of American government. The Federal Reserve Board was created to control cash flow through the economy, and a host of agencies were formed to perform various functions, such as the Civilian Conservation Corps, which was to employ some of the jobless. As a consequence of Franklin Roosevelt's New Deal, the government bureaucracy became staffed with specialized personnel, with designated committees designed to handle isolated problems. During and after World War II, the federal government expanded to unprecedented proportions. Table 6.1 documents this growth between 1940 and 1975. As can be seen, government spending has swelled from a mere $9.5 billion in 1940 to over

$400 billion in 1977—that is, from 10 percent of the Gross National Product to nearly 40 percent!

After World War II, many new departments and agencies of the federal government were formed—Department of Transportation (DOT); Housing and Urban Development (HUD); Health, Education, and Welfare (HEW); the Office of Economic Opportunity (OEO); the Central Intelligence Agency (CIA), the Department of Defense (DOD), and a host of others. The creation of these organizations has led to the concentration of government power and to a massive increase in political complexity. The size of our federal bureaucracy makes it so bewildering at times that the average American often wonders what effect, if any, he or she can have on decision making or the country's direction.

The Government and the Military

We have seen that business and government in America have grown enormously in power. One aspect of this problem is the increased cooperation between government and corporations. This cooperation has been most intense in the area of military and defense spending. An examination of the federal budget illustrates the extent of our economic dependence on the Department of Defense. Figure 6.4 shows that, even if predictions that defense spending may decline as a proportion of the national budget come true, it would still represent a sizable share of the national budget. This is especially noticeable when we compare it to the relatively small 5 percent share for education and the 10 percent outlay for health.

The Military-Industrial Complex

In his final public address before leaving office, President Dwight D. Eisenhower coined the phrase "military-industrial complex" to refer to a problem of great concern to him. Eisenhower, himself a career military officer and Supreme Commander of the Allied forces during World War II, warned against what he viewed as an unhealthy relationship emerging between industry and the military:

Until the latest of our world conflicts, the United States had no armaments industry. American makers

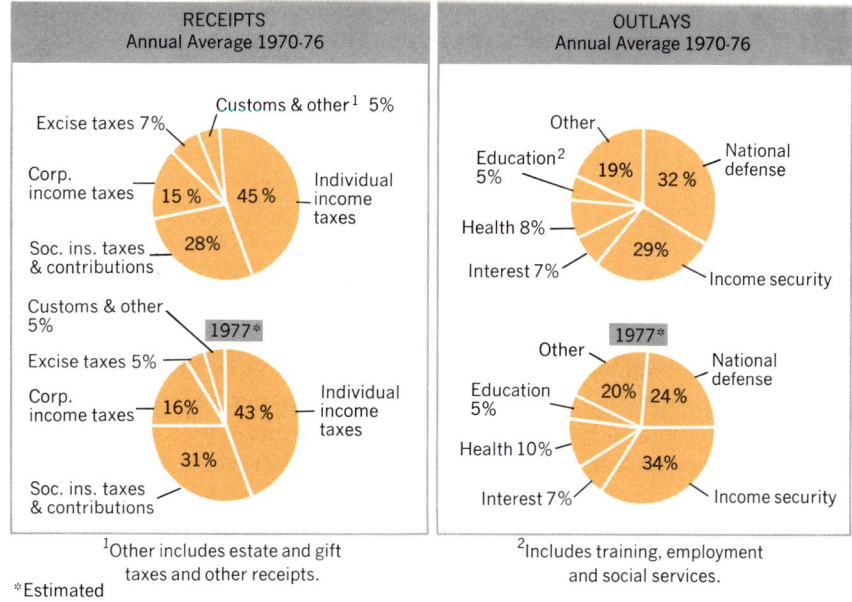

<mark>RECEIPTS</mark> Annual Average 1970-76

OUTLAYS Annual Average 1970-76

[1]Other includes estate and gift taxes and other receipts.

[2]Includes training, employment and social services.

*Estimated

Figure 6.4 **The Annual Federal Budget, 1970–1977. U.S. Bureau of the Census,** *Statistical Abstract of the United States: 1977* **(Washington, D.C.: U.S. Government Printing Office, 1977), p. 246.**

of ploughshares could, with time and as required, make swords as well. But now we can no longer risk emergency improvisation of national defense; we have been compelled to create a permanent armaments industry of vast proportions. . . . This conjunction of an immense Military Establishment and a large arms industry is new to the American experience. The total influence—economic, political, even spiritual—is felt in every city, every statehouse, every office of the Federal Government. . . . In the councils of government we must guard against the acquisition of unwarranted influence, whether sought or unsought, by the military-industrial complex. The potential for the disastrous rise of misplaced power exists and will persist.[27]

The term *military-industrial complex,* **then, refers to the relationship between the military, desiring to purchase weapons, and the corporations producing weapons. It is a relationship involving cooperation and the informal influencing of decision making about weapons systems.** Both the military and the cor-

porations benefit from a large military budget and policies favoring military solutions to international problems. In fact, as Eisenhower pointed out, some corporations are so dependent on defense contracts that a substantial reduction in defense spending would be a serious economic blow to them—they are essentially permanent manufacturers of weapons systems. (Table 6.3 lists the largest defense contractors in the United States.) The potential danger is that the development of weapons systems will be based on what is beneficial to these groups rather than on what is necessary for national security.

An important feature of the military-industrial complex is the interchange of personnel between the two spheres. During a three-year period in the 1970s, more than 2000 high-ranking Defense Department officials left their government jobs and accepted positions in corporations that were defense contractors.[28] By hiring former defense officials and high-ranking military officers, corporations gain considerable influence in the gov-

TABLE 6.3
Top Twenty Defense Department Research and Development Contractors, 1977

RANK & COMPANY	BREAKDOWN ($ THOUSANDS)	%/U.S. TOTAL
1. McDonnell Douglas Corp.	2,574,047	5.11
2. Lockheed Corp.	1,573,422	3.32
3. United Technologies Corp.	1,584,680	3.15
4. Boeing Co.	1,579,880	3.14
5. General Electric Co.	1,519,630	3.02
6. Rockwell International Corp.	1,479,798	2.94
7. Grumman Corp.	1,428,057	2.83
8. General Dynamics Corp.	1,371,504	2.72
9. Hughes Aircraft Co.	1,093,439	2.17
10. Northrop Corp.	1,046,669	2.08
11. Raytheon Co.	1,040,927	2.07
12. Westinghouse Electric Corp.	802,128	1.59
13. Tenneco, Inc.	744,868	1.48
14. Sperry Rand Corp.	651,492	1.29
15. Chrysler Corp.	619,930	1.23
16. Litton Industries, Inc.	609,287	1.21
17. Intl. Business Machines Co.	547,144	1.09
18. Todd Shipyards Corp.	468,402	.93
19. American Tel. & Tel. Co.	456,753	.91
20. Honeywell, Inc.	456,683	.91

SOURCE. *Aviation Week & Space Technology* 108 (May 1, 1978), p. 62.

ernmental policy-making process and in budget allocations. Because of their contacts, former government officials have informal access to important people and to information that has an impact on defense spending. Through such contacts, corporations hope to influence the development of weapons systems and to increase the likelihood of receiving defense contracts.

The coincidence of interests of industry and the military can lead to practices that have detrimental consequences for other groups in society. Defense proposals are sometimes not given the critical evaluation that they should receive in terms of their contribution to our overall defense posture. In addition, many government contracts are not awarded on the basis of competitive bidding. The Pentagon often permits corporations to make profits on defense contracts that are much larger than the average profit rate for industry. Finally, the real cost of defense contracts is sometimes hidden from both Congress and the public by allowing "cost overruns" in defense contracts—that is, the company involved is permitted to *increase* the cost of a

contract after it is granted to compensate for rises in production costs. While some of these increases are legitimate (because of inflation or design changes requested by the military after the contract has been awarded), cost overruns can mean that the full and final costs of a weapons system are not known to the public at the time the decision to adopt the system is made. In some cases, defense costs may be higher than necessary while not adding substantially to our defense capabilities.

Many of these problems are illustrated by one recent and very controversial defense project, the B-1 bomber.[29] Many policymakers in the Pentagon decided that the B-52—the primary bomber used by the Air Force—was obsolete and that a new bomber weapons system was needed. Rockwell International Corporation, a major defense contractor, had developed a new bomber model called the B-1, which it hoped the military would adopt. Rockwell and its subcontractors spent $500,000 in efforts to convince the Pentagon to replace the B-52 with the B-1. Rockwell's initial proposals placed the cost of a fleet of B-1 bombers in 1973 at $50 billion. The Pentagon supported the B-1 bomber as produced by Rockwell and exerted its influence on Congress and the executive branch of government to adopt the program and provide the necessary funds. By 1977, the estimate of the total cost of the B-1 project had risen to $90 billion—and it had yet to be approved. If the B-1 bomber (or some weapons system like it) is ultimately approved, any cost overruns beyond the expenses of the original contract must be added to the bill. Who pays for it?—the American taxpayer.

Defense contracts are very attractive to corporations because they are both lucrative (the Pentagon allows very large profits) and safe (if a weapons system does not perform as expected, the Pentagon won't ask for its money back). For example, the American public paid over $1.5 billion for the development of the B-70 airplane. However, it was such a poor piece of equipment that only two were ever built and neither of those is now in operation. There are many other examples, but the point is clear. The cozy relationship between the military and industry makes each reluctant to incur the wrath of the other. Each is also extremely dependent on the other. The industries need the military

Former President Dwight D. Eisenhower warned America about what he termed the Military-Industrial Complex—the coincidence of interest between industry and the military.

to keep the immense flow of defense funds coming their way. The military needs the defense industry to provide the expertise and technology from which new and more advanced weapons systems might emerge. However, this mutual dependence has created a situation in which checks against abuse — either by political leaders or in the operation of free market competition—often function inefficiently, if at all.

What should be the relationship between the various sectors—corporate, governmental, and military—of American society? Should there be cooperation or complete separation of decision making? The answer to these questions depends to some extent on the perspective one adopts. From the functionalist perspective, with the emphasis on the interdependence of the various segments of society, some degree of cooperation would be necessary in order to coordinate activities toward desirable societal goals. There would be danger, on the one hand, in too little cooperation because institutions might work at cross-purposes to one another. On the other hand, problems would arise from too extensive cooperation if it interfered with the achievement of other goals. In this view, one can talk about

a "national interest" that incorporates policies beneficial to all Americans— in a sense, "the greatest good for the greatest number." In essence, the system must achieve a balance that makes it possible for the various groups in society to receive some rewards and feel that their interests and values are supported.

From the conflict perspective, groups cooperate with one another if they feel it is in their interest to do so. In addition, some groups not participating in that cooperation will probably suffer from it. If these groups are relatively powerless, there is little that they will be able to do about the abuses resulting from such cooperation. For example, there has been cooperation between business and the military for a long time, but the groups concerned about it were neither respectable nor powerful. Once President Eisenhower addressed the issue, however, it became an acceptable topic of debate. The detrimental aspects of cooperation can be eliminated only when other groups exert what power they have to change the situation. Furthermore, these groups will do so only if they perceive that it is in their interests. From this perspective, there is no unified "national interest" toward which government or business should strive. Rather, each group has its own interests that may or may not coincide with the interests of others. The final policy decision emerges from the clash of these interest groups; the groups with the most power and resources will in all likelihood see their policies prevail.

WHO HAS POWER IN AMERICAN SOCIETY?

Thus far, we have discussed the two central institutions in modern American society—corporations and government—how their characteristics affect society, and the role they play both nationally and internationally. We have noted the awesome power that these institutions have amassed. Yet a number of questions are still unanswered. Who are the people who hold the important positions in these institutions? How do they gain these positions? How do they maintain their power? Social scientists have researched these questions intensively during the past two decades and learned much about the people who hold power in America. Basically, two quite different models of power in American society have emerged—the power-elite model and the pluralist model.

The Power Elite

In the 1950s, sociologist C. Wright Mills raised the issue of whether there was a small group of very powerful citizens who made all the important decisions in the United States.[30] He proposed a theory that he felt explained the exercise of power in American society and how it operated in international affairs. **His interpretation—which derives from the conflict perspective—is generally referred to as the theory of the** *power elite.*

The power elite is composed of men whose positions enable them to transcend the ordinary environment of ordinary men and women; they are in positions to make decisions having major consequences . . . they are in command of the major hierarchies and organizations of modern society. They rule the big corporations. They run the machinery of the state and claim its prerogatives. They direct the military establishment. They occupy the strategic command posts of the social structure, in which are now centered the effective means of the power and the wealth and the celebrity which they enjoy.[31]

While many sociologists do not accept all of Mills's assertions, there is considerable evidence to support many of his contentions. We will present those parts of his argument that are reasonably well founded and some of the recent evidence to support it.

Mills argued that three regions are the seats of power in American society: the giant corporations, the government, and the military. However, these sectors were not always the most influential ones. In an earlier period, when the economy consisted of many small companies competing with one another, they balanced out each other's influence and there was no dominant power elite. The political organization of our society consisted of a relatively loose collection of states and a weak central government. The military was a small and largely distrusted and decentralized establishment. Today, however, as we have seen, our economy is dominated by approximately one hundred giant corporations; the federal government has evolved into a monstrous bureaucracy, which has taken over many activities previously scattered among local and state governments; and the military has grown into one of our largest and most expensive bureaucracies, with an immense standing military force. Mills's argument that power has become increasingly concentrated in the hands of a few is supported by a recent estimate that between 5000 and 6000 of the top positions in business, government, and the military direct most of the nation's economic and social policy (see Table 6.4). That is a very small portion of the total American populace.

Who Are the Power Elite?

Mills argued that those persons who compose the power elite have many social characteristics in common and that these characteristics set them far apart from most other Americans. First, *members of the power elite*

Sectors of Power in American Society and Number of Top Positions in Each Sector

Corporate Sector	
Industrial corporations	1534
Utilities, communications, transportation	476
Banking	1200
Insurance	362
Total	3572
Governmental Sector	
U.S. Government	227
Legislative, executive, judicial, military	59
Total	286
Public Interest Sector	
Mass media	213
Education	656
Foundation	121
Law	176
Civic and cultural	392
Total	1558
Total	5416

SOURCE. Thomas R. Dye, *Who's Running America: Institutional Leadership in the United States.* © 1976, p. 14. Reprinted by permission of Prentice-Hall, Inc., Englewood Cliffs, N.J.

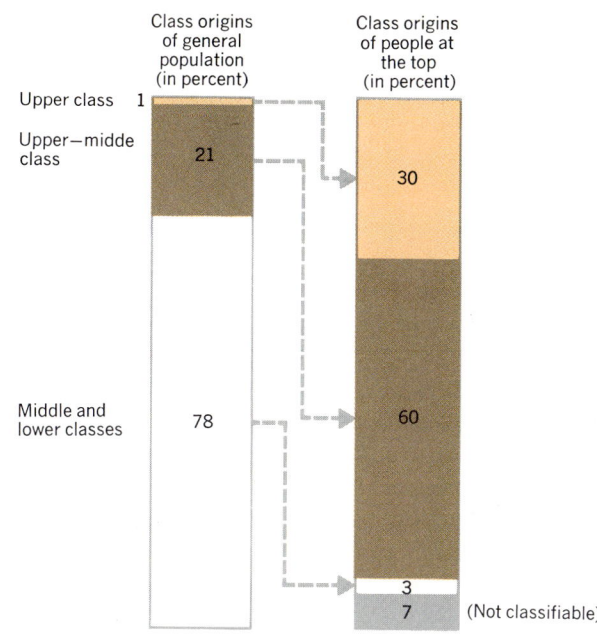

Figure 6.5 Social Class Recruitment of People at the Top. Thomas R. Dye, *Who's Running America: Institutional Leadership in the United States,* (c) 1976, p. 153. Reprinted by Permission of Prentice-Hall, Inc., Englewood Cliffs, N.J.

tend to come from the upper-middle and upper classes—families who have been wealthy for at least two generations (see Fig. 6.5). Because of this common background, they share an interest in either maintaining the status quo, which sustains the family fortune, or manipulating events to ensure an increase in the family holdings. Those who enter the power elite from a more modest background soon begin to share the elite's desire to maintain the status quo.

Second, *the offspring of the power elite attend private schools* **(such as St. Timothy's, Choate, Philips-Exeter, and other elite prep schools)** *and universities* **(such as Princeton, Yale, Harvard, Dartmouth, and Bryn Mawr),** *which support and reinforce an elitist outlook and in which social contacts are forged that will later prove beneficial.* The elitist viewpoint encouraged in these schools is based on a narrow philosophy that views the possession of power, privilege, and wealth by the elite as legitimate and

proper. These future leaders also learn that what is beneficial for the elite (prosperous businesses and increasing wealth) is also in the best interests of all Americans. In college, the elite join exclusive clubs and organizations where they meet other members of the elite and make friendships that will be maintained throughout life and that provide advantageous contacts during their careers.

Third, when these young members of the elite graduate and embark on their careers, *their careers and lifestyles are similar and crisscross over their lifetime.* They enter the large corporations, politics, or the military, and they move rapidly into positions of authority in these institutions. Since they typically begin their careers far from the bottom of the corporate ladder, the climb to powerful positions is neither arduous nor beset with disappointments. Within these huge bureaucracies—political, corporate, and military—they rise into the controlling directorate and begin to make decisions that influence the fate of their organizations and the direction of American society.

Fourth, *the social life of the power elite supports and maintains their dominant positions through informal social relationships.* They join exclusive social clubs where they renew friendships that originated in prep school or college, and they meet others with similar interests, values, and family backgrounds. Their other social activities also tend to be exclusive, revolving around other members of the power elite. This exclusivity, according to Mills, serves to reinforce their view of the world by helping them to avoid any dissident opinions and to form associations that will be beneficial in the world of business.

Interchangeability of the Elite

In order to understand the *power* **of the elite, it is crucial to recognize that its members occupy the upper echelons of the major bureaucratic organizations in the United States and that the functions of this directorate are quite similar regardless of the particular bureaucracy involved.** They all make policy decisions and coordinate the activities of their underlings. Thus, those in the upper echelons of the major bureaucracies are quite interchangeable with those in other bureaucracies. The extent of this interchangeability between the political and economic elites is shown in Table 6.5.

The ways in which this interchangeability occurs are diverse and complex. For example, Robert McNamara, a former president of the Ford Motor Company, became Secretary of Defense during the 1960s and later moved on to head the World Bank. Ford also happened to have many important contracts with the Defense Department. Another case is William E. Simon, secretary of the treasury under Presidents Nixon and Ford.[32] He was a wealthy bond trader on Wall Street before entering government service; when he left government in 1977, he joined a Wall Street brokerage firm and also became president of the John M. Olin Foundation, established and funded by the former chairman of the Olin Corporation. The foundation's purpose is to support research and scholarship that promote the philosophy of a laissez-faire, free enterprise econ-

TABLE 6.5

Percentage of Cabinet Members Who Were Members of the Business Elite before and/or after Cabinet Service

Member of business elite before *and* after cabinet service	41.0%
Member of business elite *only before* cabinet service	22.4
Member of business elite *only after* cabinet service	12.7
Lawyer whose business affiliation could not be determined (possible member of business elite)	11.7
Not a member of business elite	12.2
TOTAL	100% (205)

SOURCE. Peter J. Freitag, "The Cabinet and Big Business: A Study of Interlocks," *Social Problems* 23 (December 1975), p. 148. By permission of the Society for the Study of Social Problems.

omy. It has funded new schools of law and economics at universities, and centers for political and economic studies. The goal of the foundation is to shape the thinking of the American public so that it is more favorably disposed toward business and will support government policies beneficial to business. In this manner, the power elite uses its resources to persuade Americans to support the status quo, which in turn is advantageous to business.

As the men and women of the power elite move to other arenas in society, they continue to create a base for the close control of the political, military, and corporate spheres in society. Social activities typically bring together old acquaintances who all occupy elevated positions in the higher circles of control. These settings provide opportunities to discuss their problems, plans, and hopes; they suggest ways of helping out old friends; and in so doing they close the ranks of the power elite. The elite do not see these activities as a "conspiracy" on their part to maintain and enhance their positions, but rather as a normal part of their lifestyle. Furthermore, Mills was well aware that there were conflicts among the elite, and that they could not be viewed as a completely cohesive group. Yet, he maintained that there was a "coincidence of interests" among the power elite which makes their decisions appear to be conspiratorial, even though they may not actually be so.

The Power Elite and Foreign Policy

G. William Domhoff, who has undertaken extensive research on Mills's concept of the power elite, feels that the economic elite is dominant in the area of foreign policy, while the other two branches of the elite are subordinate. He characterizes the molding of foreign policy and the decision to wage war in these terms:

> American foreign policy is initiated, planned, and carried out by members and organizations of a power elite that is rooted in and serves the interests of an upper class of rich businessmen and their descendents. . . . public opinion is rarely felt and . . . Congress is usually bypassed. . . . the most important institutions in foreign policy decision-making are large corporations and banks, closely intertwined charitable foundations, two or three discussion and research associations financed by these corporations and foundations, and the National Security Council, State Department, Defense Department, and specially appointed committees of the federal government.[33]

There are many ways in which the power elite exerts its influence on foreign policy. One way is through the encouragement of a "military definition of reality" that enhances the interests of the power elite. Mills argued that "virtually all political and economic actions are now judged in terms of military definitions of reality."[34] According to such definitions, war or some military actions are important, and possibly inevitable, tools in foreign policy. In addition, a large military establishment is regarded as essential in conducting foreign affairs. The result is immense defense spending which is beneficial to both the economic and the military elite, and these components often devise policies that support this point of view.

A second way that the power elite exerts influence on American foreign policy is through the many groups that link private corporations and foundations with the important decision-making units in the federal government. For example, the Council on Foreign Relations (CFR) is a nonprofit, nonpartisan group whose ostensible goal is to inform people about foreign policy and to generate interest in international politics. However, beyond these goals, the CFR is one of the most influential nongovernmental groups working closely with the government to develop foreign policy by engaging in research, bringing new ideas to the government, lobbying for certain policies, and providing expert testimony.[35]

The primary sources of financing and leadership for the CFR are leading American corporations and foundations like the Chase Manhattan Bank and the Ford Motor Company. The CFR also promotes the selection of government appointees who will work for the interests of the power elite. For example, John J. McCloy, who has held numerous government positions over the past few decades, said that "Whenever we needed a man [for some government position], we thumbed through the roll of council [CFR] members and put through a call to [CFR headquarters in] New York."[36] When John Kennedy, newly elected to the presidency, was choosing officials to staff the State Department, a list of eighty-two names was prepared for him, at least sixty-three of which were Council members. Domhoff concludes from information such as this that members of the power elite, such as Kennedy or McCloy, feel reasonably certain that anyone on the rolls of the CFR will not threaten the interests of the power elite. In other words, the CFR, and the many other organizations like it, helps to filter candidates and select those who hold opinions and values that support elite policies.

Pluralism: An Alternate View of National Power

As he had hoped it would, Mills's power elite argument generated intense controversy that persists even today. Not all social scientists accept Mills's power elite interpretation of decision making and control in American society. The dispute over the accuracy of Mills's model has been heated but at the same time beneficial because it has led to much research on the exercise of power in America. Those who have challenged Mills's power elite concept contend that power in American society is *pluralistic* — spread over a large number of groups with divergent values, interests, and goals.

According to the pluralist view of power, government policy is shaped by the many interest groups in society. In the 1970s, members of many American farm organizations marched on Washington, D.C. in repeated attempts to affect the legislative process.

Interest Groups and Veto Groups

David Riesman, an early dissenter against Mills's position, proposed an alternative model based on **veto groups.**[37] Whereas clearcut leadership groups may have existed at one time, Riesman feels that

Today we have substituted for that leadership a series of groups, each of which has struggled for and finally attained a power to stop things conceivably inimical to its interests and, within far narrower limits, to start things.[38]

The nature of these groups puts them in a kind of middle-ground of power. As Riesman comments,

These veto groups are neither leader-groups nor led-groups. The only leaders of national scope left in the United States today are those who can placate the veto groups. The only followers left in the United States today are those unorganized and sometimes disorganized unfortunates who have not yet invented their group.[39]

According to Riesman's pluralistic model, then, *society is composed of a variety of interest groups who can muster veto power over decisions, and the exercise of power must be seen as a series of specific issues that can be resolved in a variety of ways.* For example, labor unions may have considerable influence over certain decisions regarding the economy, such as the level of unemployment benefits or the minimum wage laws; farmers may apply pressure to control the importation of food products; other veto groups will work on issues they perceive as relevant to their interests. There are a number of implications of this viewpoint.

First, not all groups have an interest in all issues. The farmers may have no interest in unemployment benefits, while the labor unions could not care less about how much beef is imported from Australia. Second, the various interest groups are not always in agreement with one another. Groups that sometimes align with one another on certain issues find themselves at loggerheads on others. For example, the insurance industry is in favor of mandatory automobile safety requirements, such as seat belts or passive restraints, because they result in fewer injuries and thus less cost to insurance companies; automobile companies, on the other hand, are vigorously opposed to such government intervention because it increases their costs of production. Third, there is no one dominant elite, but rather a number of different elites in the various decision-making spheres. The pluralist does not take the naive position that all interest groups have equal amounts of power. For example, one critic of Mills, although he views power as diffuse, recognizes that less than 1 percent of the population is involved in making decisions that affect the entire nation.[40] However, no one monolithic elite controls decision making in *all* spheres.

Policy Implementation

In evaluating the power elite and pluralist models of American society, it is important to consider the critical distinction between policy creation and policy implementation. *Policy creation* **is the development of guiding principles and ideas that will serve as the foundation for some course of action.** For example, in 1954 the United States Supreme Court ruled that separate but equal school facilities were unconstitutional and ordered school desegregation to begin. *Policy implementation* **is the manner in which the policy created is translated into some specific course of action.** Policy implementation often occurs at the hands of those subordinate to the leaders creating the policy and can have an important impact on the final outcome. For example, although the policy of school desegregation has been in force for more than twenty-five years, the manner in which it has been interpreted and acted upon at lower levels has delayed its complete implementation.

Thus, the exercise of power is more complex than it at first appears to be, because there are different levels of power, involving many different people. Which level is more important—policy creation or policy implementation? The answer to this depends on one's perspective. The power elite model would clearly give policy creation a more critical role

because this is the stage at which most of the major direction is given to the American economy. While agreeing that policy creation is sometimes more important than implementation, the pluralist would argue that the manner in which a policy is implemented can often impede or change the direction of the policy created.

Evaluation of the Models

Which model is a more accurate description of the exercise of power in the United States? As is often the case, reality undoubtedly lies somewhere between these two extremes. There is probably not a single power elite that dominates all or even most decision making. Furthermore, Mills probably overemphasized the degree to which the interests of the elite coincide. At a general level, there are certain goals that all members of the elite have in common—protection of the status quo and preservation of the economic and political advantages that give their families their stature and position in society. However, beyond these general goals, the interests of the different members of the elite often clash.

At the other extreme, a person taking the pluralist position is in danger of trivializing the unequal distribution of power among interest groups in the United States. Some groups are *far* more powerful than others. Given the evidence available today, it seems reasonable to conclude that in the areas of national policy and foreign affairs, there is a fairly small number of interest groups that possess a disproportionate share of the decision-making power in the United States. They do not operate unhindered, since other, less powerful interest groups can compete with them, on occasion successfully. They are also not completely cohesive and monolithic groups. Nevertheless, access to political and economic resources gives them an immense and often insurmountable advantage over the American public.

The Power Elite and Democratic Society

If there is a relatively small number of people in the economic, political, and military spheres who possess much of the power in American society, what kinds of problems does this pose for our society? From the functionalist perspective, one might argue that some degree of concentration of power in the hands of a few people is both necessary and desirable. Presumably, those who have gathered wealth and power to themselves possess certain desirable skills and qualities that made it possible for them to rise to positions of power—perhaps aggressiveness, intelligence, farsightedness, or managerial competence; they are equipped to head the critical businesses and institutions in American society. Not all people have the resources or skills to be leaders. Difficult and complex decisions are best left in the hands of those with such skill and expertise.

From the conflict perspective, the rise to power is seen quite differently. People gain power through struggling with whatever resources they can bring to bear. These resources include various intellectual and social skills, but they also include inherited wealth, privileged family background, racial or sexual characteristics, and other factors that can give one person an advantage in the struggle for power. A poor minority-group person simply cannot compete with the son of a wealthy business executive because the latter has an almost insurmountable head start in acquiring the resources that will lead to powerful positions in society. Because of the barriers placed in their way, some people have little opportunity of ever gaining these powerful positions.

Yet, even though power is concentrated in the hands of a select few, that immense power might be offset by other means. In fact, our democratic institutions are based on the assumption that elected leaders in government are beholden to the public and will protect them against the actions of such powerful interest groups. However, few members of the power elite—even those in the government sector—are elected. Who elects top military officials to their positions? Who elects the secretary of state, the secretary of defense, or other cabinet officials? Do these individuals serve the "national interest," or do they work for the interests of their respective bureaucracies? Furthermore, we have seen the collusion between government officials (both elected and appointed) and corporate leaders

that can result in policies that serve the interests of the power elite to the detriment of many other groups in society. The problem, then, is that vast amounts of power may be concentrated in the hands of a few, while at the same time no effective system exists to check or moderate that power with the interests of the public in mind.

A final issue along these lines concerns the beliefs that people have about what is proper and legitimate concerning who holds power and makes decisions. Recall that the interactionist perspective emphasizes the subjective nature of social reality. People act on the basis of what they believe is real rather than on the basis of objective reality. In this regard, powerful people are in a position to shape others' definitions of reality. Are multinational corporations beneficial? Does the power elite make decisions that favor the common interests of all Americans? Answers to these questions depend partly on what one believes. Both corporations and government spend enormous sums of money to convince the American public that their policies are beneficial. They also back research and educational efforts that are supportive of a private enterprise, corporate economy. Thus, power can be used to shape others' definitions of reality in a direction that is advantageous to the powerholder. If the public believes that those with power, and the economic system that supports their power, are the right and proper ones, then there is little dissent, and it is easier for the powerful to gain and retain their privileged positions.

FUTURE PROSPECTS

After reading this chapter, the student is hopefully more sensitive to one of the more frightening realities of modern America. Today, government and the corporate structure are so large, so broad in scope, so immersed in technical knowledge and language, and so immensely powerful, that the influence of most American citizens on decision making in the political and economic spheres seems to be overshadowed by forces beyond the control of the average citizen. We take pride in referring to

America as a participant democracy, where all people, including the elite, are publically accountable. Yet, it is in the interest of the power elite to maintain their influential positions and to expand their ability to make key decisions within arenas over which they have exclusive control. Many people feel that government and big business, along with the military, "run" the United States, with little input from most citizens, and that talk of democracy is practically nonsensical.

Indeed, the problems involved here extend beyond the almost total absence of *individual influence* in decision making. Large-scale organizations have become so powerful that *social mechanisms* that might control and regulate their activities are largely ineffective. Despite our government's regulatory agencies, designed to provide necessary checks and balances, multinational corporations, interlocking directorates, and elaborate agreements between government and the military are in abundance. The concentration of power in these areas continues to expand. What can be done about these problems? Is there any hope that the average citizen might regain some control over these goliaths? There are some developments that hold promise for the future.

Government Reform

Since the beginnings of the antitrust laws, critics have argued that we have the *potential* to control undesirable corporate growth by enacting legislation that would achieve this end. Yet many practices that increase the concentration of power, such as interlocking directorates, do not violate existing statutes. The regulatory agencies that are supposed to limit and control the actions of corporations often serve to enhance their power. Therefore some observers have suggested that we revise our laws and revamp our regulatory agency structure so that the public interest takes precedence over the interests of corporations. Laws can be designed to limit corporate growth and power. The composition of regulatory agencies can be structured so that some members of the agencies represent the public interest against efforts by those being regulated to use the agencies for their own ends.

If such laws can be devised, why has this not been done? One reason is that so many elected officials are beholden to powerful interest groups subject to the rulings of the regulatory agencies. First, through lobbying, these interests are able to gain the ear of lawmakers and convince them to pass legislation that is beneficial to the interest groups. Second, through campaign contributions, lawmakers are dependent on the rich and powerful for the resources to get elected and reelected. The result is that many elected officials come to serve the interests of those they should be controlling and regulating. What is necessary is some form of governmental reform that would avoid this problem.

One such effort was the Campaign Reform Act of 1974, which provided for a maximum expenditure of $20 million for a single presidential campaign, a limitation on individual donations to candidates for federal office to $1000, and a limit of $50,000 on spending by the immediate family of a candidate. In 1976, the Supreme Court ruled that the $20 million and $50,000 limitations were unconstitutional under the First Amendment. As a result, there are now almost no limits on the amount that may be spent on elections. Consequently, much of the original purpose of the Act was circumvented by the courts — wealthy candidates and those supported by rich interest groups or individuals have an obvious advantage in the political election process.

Nevertheless, the Campaign Reform Act represented a positive step and served to strip the mask of secrecy from financial campaign support maneuvers, opening them to public view. In addition, individual taxpayers may now donate $1 of their annual income tax to the presidential campaign fund, which is then divided between the candidates.

This reform effort shows that it is possible to change our laws such that the power of large groups is moderated. However, such reform will naturally be resisted by those groups that benefit from the status quo. The individual citizen standing alone clearly will have little effect against such groups. To that extent, traditional conceptions of individualism must be viewed as outmoded. Yet, individuals can *organize* and through *collective action* may initiate changes in those laws and regulations that are detrimental to their interests.

Citizens' Groups and People's Lobbies

In recent years, a number of citizens' groups have been organized to oversee the activities of government and corporations and to act in the public interest. Many believe that such groups hold great promise in terms of solving the problem of expanding government and business—by putting the power in the hands of the people. Some examples of such groups will illustrate the manner in which they can exert influence.

Environmental Groups

Environmental groups like the Sierra Club and the National Wildlife Federation have lobbied extensively for policies that will preserve and protect our natural environment. One result of such activities was the creation of the Environmental Protection Agency (EPA). The EPA sets standards for automobile engine emissions, industrial pollutants, and the like. Even though the EPA is a government organization, its activities are overseen by other public-interest groups, and as a consequence the standards are usually enforced. Of course, industrial concerns are generally opposed to EPA standards because they elevate production costs and lead to reduced sales and profits. Nevertheless, organizations like the EPA play an important role as a countervailing force to big business.

Some regulatory agencies, such as the EPA, have been surprisingly effective in enforcing legislation even though it results in policies violently opposed by very powerful interest groups. For example, enforcement of the Endangered Species Act of 1973 has often clashed with the interests of powerful groups. In 1967, construction was begun in Tennessee on the $120-million Tellico Dam. In 1978, the dam was nearly completed. Due to the efforts of numerous environmental groups, the federal government was informed that the dam would endanger the only known habitat for a small fish named the Snail Darter and that this would violate provisions of the Endangered Species Act. Finally, the dam's completion was halted by a United States Supreme Court ruling; in the words of the Justices, "The plain intent of Congress (in passing the Endangered Species Act) was to halt and reverse the trend toward species extinction, whatever the cost."[41] Even though halting the project was violently opposed by many powerful interests, such as the electrical utility industry, the laws favored the interests of the environmental groups, and they were able to prevail.

Consumer Protection Groups

In efforts to protect American consumers from poorly made or dangerous products, a broad range of organizations have been formed to alert both consumers and government officials to potential dangers or problems. Consumer's Research, Inc. was created in 1929, followed by the establishment in 1936 of Consumers Union, which publishes the popular magazine *Consumer Reports*. These concerns test products for quality and safety, publishing reports that highlight violations of safety standards by industrial producers.

Perhaps the best known of the consumer advocates is Ralph Nader. Nader emerged as a prominent national spokesperson for the consumer movement primarily as a consequence of his attack on the automobile industry's apparent indifference to public safety. In one particularly notable incident, he was able to demonstrate the dangers of a particular automobile manufactured by the nation's leading car manufacturer. As a result of his investigations, published in the book *Unsafe At Any Speed,* the manufacturer eventually discontinued production of what was an otherwise very popular car.

In 1968, a group known as Nader's Raiders launched an investigation of the Federal Trade Commission (FTC). The investigation exposed massive inefficiency and ineffectiveness by the FTC in meeting its assigned responsibilities. In 1969, President Nixon ordered an investigation of the FTC, to be conducted by the American Bar Association. The ABA agreed with the Nader group's findings and recommended a major overhaul of the commission.[42] Some other legislation attributed to Nader's activities include: the National Traffic and Vehicle Safety Act of 1966 (which established the Highway Traffic Safety Administration), the Wholesome Meat Act of 1967, the Natural Gas Pipeline Safety Act of 1968, the Coal Mine Health and Safety Act of 1968, and the Comprehensive Occupational Safety and Health Act of 1970.[43] Consumer groups such as Nader's Raiders have had a tremendous impact on America (as this legislation indicates) and have served to limit the ability of corporations to act without considering issues other than corporate profits.

Public Interest Advocates

Public interest advocates attempt to locate and rectify conditions in government and industry that do not benefit the public. Such groups do not limit their concerns to one area, such as consumer or environmental problems. Ralph Nader's investigation of the Federal Trade Commission and later of the Food and Drug Administration are examples of such activities. One of the best-known public advocate groups is Common Cause, founded by the former Secretary of Health, Education, and Welfare John W. Gardner.[44]

One of Common Cause's active areas of operation has involved election financing. Gardner's group maintained from the beginning that certain vested interest groups—such as the defense industry—were in effect bribing public officials by making large donations to election funds. While some legislation existed governing campaign contributions, abuses of these laws were seldom prosecuted. Between 1971 and 1975, Common Cause filed seven cases in federal court to enforce existing campaign laws. The results were impressive.

> More than any other group . . . Common Cause shaped current law regulating election finances. It managed to do so by developing and carrying out a craftsmanlike strategy which blended litigative, legislative, and publicist tactics into a coherent and mutually advantageous whole. Without litigation, the need for new laws might well not have become obvious. Without legislation, the court suits could have left campaign finance reform unconsummated. Together, they constituted an impressive example of a citizen lobby operating resourcefully and productively to benefit the public interest.[45]

Common Cause has been referred to as a middle-class activist group with most of its operation

depending on funds obtained through its members. In 1975, Common Cause had 320,000 members who paid $15 each in dues.[46] Using these resources and other donations, Common Cause considerably broadened its sphere of operation. In 1978 the members of this organization began to attack what they claimed to be deception on the part of industrial lobbyists. They charged that ineffective enforcement of federal lobbying disclosure regulations had led to increased influence over elections and the legislative process by industry. John Gardner has pointed out that, between 1974 and 1976, contributions to congressional candidates by special-interest groups had nearly doubled—from $12.5 million to $22.6 million. Furthermore, nine months before the 1978 congressional elections, special-interest committees had more money on hand than they had spent in the entire 1976 campaign.[47] By exposing to public scrutiny the extent of lobbying activity, Common Cause hopes that elected officials will feel pressure to be more careful about whose interests they serve.

Public Action

All of the groups discussed—environmental and consumer groups, public-interest advocates—take the public as their interest group, however broadly or narrowly they might define those public interests. They have achieved some success, however limited, in opposing certain government and corporate practices. These groups have been successful largely because they have been able to attract one of the primary resources necessary for the exercise of power—numbers of people—and have been able to organize those people to achieve their goals through collective action. Using strategic techniques of information dissemination, these public-action groups have been effective in informing the public of problems and potential solutions. Access to, and mastery of, the communication process is a critical factor in publication. As long as such groups are successful in informing the public, they will continue to have an important impact on the power of government and corporations.[48]

It is probably safe to assume that new groups paralleling the strategies of Nader's Raiders and

Concern about nuclear energy production provided one of the most recent examples of public outcry and collective action. Public action can be successful if it involves large numbers of people who are well organized.

Common Cause will continue to emerge on behalf of the public interest. As these groups grow more sophisticated in their use of the media and in their ability to obtain financial resources, they will probably increase their effectiveness in influencing regulatory agencies and legislative bodies. However, who is to be the final arbiter of what is truly in the public interest remains a perplexing question.

CONCLUSION

Power — the opportunity, within a social relationship, that allows one to carry out one's own will, even against resistance — operates at many levels and is held by diverse groups in society. It can be used to bring about either war or peace, to enact laws at all levels, to influence our fortunes and our outlook on life. Power relationships influence what we believe is right or wrong,

desirable or undesirable, and it is used to shape our interpretations of reality. The exercise of power is not always a blatant and obvious act, and since the subtlety of power does not detract from its importance, we must always be alert to the many forms that power takes.

Our special concern in this chapter has been with the increasing concentration of power in the hands of a few people who head the corporations and government of America. We have documented the extent of this concentration and the problems that it creates. Since most people today can do little personally in the realm of public decision making, they hand over to others the responsibility and authority for making those decisions that they cannot or will not make for themselves. However, there are consequences to placing such authority in the hands of others, and some of the consequences can be dysfunctional for society. The further removed and more isolated people become from decision making, the less we know about the *nature* of the decisions being made and *who* makes them. In our public political life, we vote for people we believe share our outlook and who are sensitive to our interests and needs. However, to assume that those elected representatives are the sole (or even the most important) decision makers not only is an error but also can be a dangerous misconception since it confers on those who wield power outside of the political spotlight an invisibility that makes them unaccountable to the public.

Some might say that the solution to these problems is to take the power away from people who use it improperly. However, from the functionalist perspective, this is not a feasible solution since power is a necessary mechanism in social relationships. A corporation could achieve nothing without the power made available to it through its economic resources and social contacts. Remember that the same corporation that abuses power also uses it in many beneficial ways that contribute to our high standard of living. A more realistic solution is to avoid the extreme concentration of power that enables one group to make decisions un-

checked by others. The question raised by functionalism is not should control exist, but rather at what point do specific forms of control become counterproductive and damaging to the well-being of society.

What has been emerging in American society with the advent of public-action groups and public-interest advocates is a state of affairs that is understandable from the conflict perspective. Corporations and government have grown powerful as interest groups pursuing policies that they perceive to be in their own interest. Recently other sources of power have begun to appear to oppose corporations and government: consumer groups, environmental groups, and the like. The distribution of power is still quite uneven, but corporations and government bureaucracies today find themselves considering the probable public reaction to policies they might embark on. Thus, we may be moving somewhat away from the elitist version of power and closer to the pluralist end of the spectrum. We can expect this struggle to continue. We will probably see shifting alliances and coalitions as each group tries to position itself in the most beneficial fashion.

GLOSSARY TERMS

Conglomerate

Corporation

Interlocking directorate

Military-industrial complex

Monopoly

Multinational corporation

Pluralism

Policy creation

Policy implementation

Power elite

Public-interest advocates

Vertical expansion

Veto groups

REFERENCES

[1] See "The 500 Largest Industrial Corporations," *Fortune* (May 8, 1978), p. 240, and Richard J. Barnet, Ronald E. Müller with Joseph Collins, "Global Corporations: Their Quest for Legitimacy," in Philip Brenner, Robert Borosage, and Bethany Weidner, eds., *Exploring Contradictions: Political Economy in the Corporate State* (New York: David McKay Company, 1974), p. 58.

[2] U.S. Bureau of the Census, *Statistical Abstract of the United States, 1977* (Washington, D.C.: U.S. Government Printing Office, 1977).

[3] E. K. Hunt, *Property and Prophets: The Evaluation of Economic Institutions and Ideologies* (New York: Harper & Row, 1972), p. 90.

[4] Martin L. Lindahl and William A. Carter, *Corporate Concentration and Public Policy,* 3d ed. (Englewood Cliffs, N.J.: Prentice-Hall, 1959).

[5] Ralph M. Goldman, *Behavioral Perspectives on American Politics* (Homewood, Ill.: Dorsey Press, 1973).

[6] Oscar Handlin, *The History of the United States* (New York: Holt, Rinehart, & Winston, 1968).

[7] Karl Marx, *Selected Writings in Sociology and Social Philosophy,* T. B. Bottomore, trans. (London: McGraw-Hill, 1964).

[8] Ibid.

[9] See Edward Cowan, "The Case Against the Big-4 Cereal Makers," *New York Times* (January 1, 1978), Section 3, p. 2.

[10] Judith Miller, "Interlocking Directorates Flourish," *New York Times* (April 23, 1978), Sec. 3, p. 2.

[11] Ibid., and Luther J. Carter, "Senate Staff Study Warns of Corporate Interlocks," *Science* 200 (May 5, 1978), p. 512.

[12] Thomas R. Dye, *Who's Running America: Institutional Leadership in the United States* (Englewood Cliffs, N.J.: Prentice-Hall, 1976), pp. 127–146.

[13] Daniel R. Fusfeld, "The Rise of the Corporate State in America," *Journal of Economic Issues* 6 (March 1972), p. 3.

[14] Carter, "Senate Staff Study Warns of Corporate Interlocks," p. 512.

[15] See David E. Apter and Louis Wolf Goodman, eds., *The Multinational Corporation and Social Change* (New York: Frederick A. Praeger, 1976), and Werner Sichel, ed., *The Economic Effects of Multinational Corporations* (Ann Arbor, Mich.: Michigan Business Papers, n. 61, 1975).

[16] Douglas A. Hellinger and Stephen H. Hellinger, *Unemployment and the Multinationals* (Port Washington, N.Y.: Kennikat Press, 1976).

[17] William A. Dymsza, *Multinational Business Strategy* (New York: McGraw-Hill, 1972).

[18] Theodore H. Moran, *Multinational Corporations and the Politics of Dependence: Copper in Chile* (Princeton, N.J.: Princeton University Press, 1974), p. 6.

[19] Hellinger and Hellinger, *Unemployment and the Multinationals,* pp. 89–105.

[20] See Richard J. Barnet and Ronald E. Muller, *Global Reach: The Power of the Multinational Corporations* (New York: Simon and Schuster, 1974), and Anthony Sampson, *The Sovereign State of ITT* (Greenwich, Conn.: Fawcett Crest, 1973).

[21] Barnet and Muller, *Global Reach,* p. 82.

[22] Quoted in Barnet, Muller, and Collins, "Global Corporations," pp. 57–58.

[23] R. J. Gilpin, *U.S. Power and the Multinational Corporation: The Political Economy of Foreign Direct Investment* (New York: Basic Books, 1975).

[24] See Robert C. Fellmeth, *The Interstate Commerce Omission: The Public Interest and the ICC* (New York: Grossman Publishers, 1970), and Ari Hoogenboom and Olive Hoogenboom, *A History of the ICC: From Panacea to Palliative* (New York: W. W. Norton, 1976).

[25] Fellmeth, *The Interstate Commerce Omission,* p. 126.

[26] Hoogenboom and Hoogenboom, *A History of the ICC,* p. ix.

[27] Quoted in Seymour Melman, *Pentagon Capitalism: The Political Economy of War* (New York: McGraw-Hill, 1970), p. 237.

[28] Michael Edwards, "Golden Threads to the Pentagon," *Nation* (March 15, 1977), pp. 306–308.

[29] See "Carter on the Big Bomber," *Newsweek* (June 20, 1977), pp. 30–33, and "Death of the B-1: The Events Behind Carter's Decision," *Science* (August 5, 1977), pp. 536–539.

[30] C. Wright Mills, *The Power Elite* (New York: Oxford University Press, 1959); for a recent analysis, see G. William Domhoff, *Who Really Rules?* (Santa Monica, Calif.: Goodyear Publishing Co., 1978).

[31] Ibid., pp. 4–5.

[32] "Simon: Preaching the Word for Olin," *New York Times* (July 16, 1978), section F, pp. 1, 9.

[33] G. William Domhoff, *The Higher Circles* (New York: Random House, 1970), pp. 111–112.

[34] Mills, *The Power Elite,* p. 235.

[35] Domhoff, *The Higher Circles.*

[36] Quoted in Domhoff, *The Higher Circles,* p. 117.

[37] David Riesman, *The Lonely Crowd* (New Haven, Conn.: Yale University Press, 1961).

[38] Ibid., p. 213.

[39] Ibid.

[40] Arnold M. Rose, *The Power Structure: Political Process in American Society* (New York: Oxford University Press, 1967).

[41] "Snail Darter Halts Dam—for Now," *Science News* 113 (June 24, 1978), p. 403.

[42] See Mark J. Green, Beverly C. Moore, Jr., and Bruce Wasserstein, *The Closed Enterprise System* (New York: Grossman Publishers, 1972).

[43] See Lucy Black Creighton, *Pretenders to the Throne: The Consumer Movement in the United States* (Lexington, Mass.: D. C. Heath, 1976).

[44] See Joel L. Fleishman and Carol S. Greenwald, "Public Interest and Political Finance Reform," *The Annals of the American Academy of Political and Social Science* 425 (May 1976), pp. 114–123.

[45] Ibid., p. 114.

[46] "The Rise of Middle Class Activism," *Saturday Review* 2 (March 8, 1975), pp. 12–16.

[47] John W. Gardner, "Of Bills and Coos," *New York Times* (June 1, 1978), Section A, p. 21.

[48] Fleishman and Greenwald, "Public Interest and Political Finance Reform," pp. 114–123.

SUGGESTED READINGS

Creighton, Lucy Black. *Pretenders to the Throne: The Consumer Movement in the United States.* Lexington, Mass.: D. C. Heath, 1976.

An account of the rise of the consumer protection movement, focusing on its aims and activities.

Domhoff, G. William. *Who Really Rules?* Santa Monica, Calif.: Goodyear Publishing Co., 1978.

A recent analysis of the concept of the power elite operating in the United States.

Mills, C. Wright. *The Power Elite.* New York: Oxford University Press, 1956.

One of the first sociological studies of the nature of the corporate state.

Mintz, Morton, and Cohen, Jerry S. *America, Inc.* New York: Dell Publishing Co., 1971.

A detailed account of the power and influence of America's major corporations.

Moran, Theodore H. *Multinational Corporations and the Politics of Dependence: Copper in Chile.* Princeton, N.J.: Princeton University Press, 1974.

A study of the effects of multinational corporations on the governments of foreign nations.

Questions
for Discussion

1. The growth of centralized government has affected decision making dramatically in our society. Is it possible to reverse the process and minimize the influence of the federal bureaucracy? What kind of answer to the question would be provided by a functionalist?

2. Would a conflict theorist view the power structure of our society as being abnormal? From the conflict perspective, what would be needed in order to make public-interest advocates a powerful force in the operation of our society?

3. One of the arguments against Mills's notion of the power elite is the existence of veto groups that can interfere with the elite's decisions. How effective do you believe veto groups are today? Can you think of any particular individuals who might be considered members of the power elite? Why do you consider them members of the power elite?

4. Multinational corporations exercise considerable power both here and abroad. Do you think that these corporations should be under tighter public control? If so, what kinds of control would you suggest? If not, why not?

5. Our society places a great deal of emphasis on the notion of democracy and the democratic decision making process. Given the discussion in this chapter, should we abandon this value system that seems to be contradicted by reality? Why or why not?

PART THREE

Social Institutions and the Life Cycle

CHAPTER 7

The Family

THE FAMILY: PAST AND PRESENT

The Family in Preindustrial Society. The Family and the
Industrial Revolution. Family in a Postindustrial Society.

THE FAMILY AS A SOCIAL PROBLEM

The Functionalist Perspective. The Conflict Perspective.
The Interactionist Perspective. What Is the Family?

CHANGING PATTERNS OF MARRIAGE AND FAMILY
LIFE

The Marital Bond. Oral Contraception and the Family.

DIVORCE

The Divorce Rate. Divorce and Social Class. Divorce and
the Law. The Future of Divorce.

ALTERNATIVE FAMILY FORMS

Open Marriage. Single Parenthood/The One-Parent
Family. Group Marriage. Serial Polygamy. Communes.
Parenthood: New Possibilities. Alternative Family Forms
and the Three Theoretical Perspectives.

THE FAMILY IN SEARCH OF A FUTURE

The Ideal and the Real. The Pluralistic Family.

CONCLUSION

Some of the social problems discussed in this book have not touched the lives of most of us in highly personal and direct ways and thus are less interesting to us than other problems. In sharp contrast, the problems related to marriage and family living have affected all of us — both the authors of the text and you who are reading it. Our definitions of a good marriage, our ideas on what brings about happiness within the family, our reactions when threatened with a loss of intimacy — these and other similar issues are central to an understanding and appreciation of marriage and family life in the modern world. In this chapter, we will analyze some of these questions and attempt to gain a better understanding of what is happening to marriage, the family, and related customs and practices in our modern society.

Since we spend most of our lives as part of some family unit, we think that we know quite a bit about "the family" and have a fairly clear idea of how to solve family-related problems. There is substantial disagreement, however, when it comes to the manner in which these problems may be approached. **Some social critics, including some social scientists, have argued that the family is in trouble and may even be collapsing.**[1] This view is representative of a school of thought referred to as the *social disorganization approach.* A pioneer of this approach, Carle C. Zimmerman, argued that the modern family (which he termed *atomistic,* meaning broken up and poorly integrated) is losing its capabilities to perform important social functions.[2] As a result, he said, individualism and hedonism had begun to run rampant, yielding higher divorce rates, childlessness, youth problems, and a general loss of confidence in the institutions of marriage and the family.

Is the family really collapsing? What information is available that might lend support to this suspicion? Some have focused on the climbing divorce rate. Between 1965 and 1977, the divorce rate in the United States more than doubled (see Fig. 7.1). This increase takes on more personal meaning when we realize that if current divorce rates persist, about 30 to 40 percent of women born between 1940 and 1944 will eventually be divorced.[3] In addition to divorces, other unsettling signs of the de-

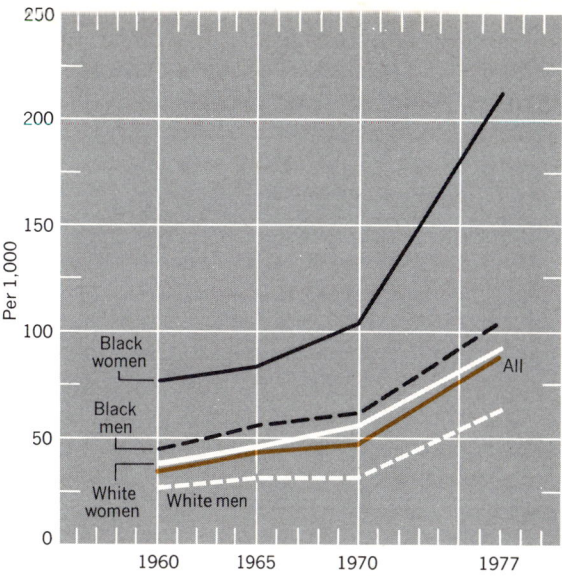

Figure 7.1 Divorced Persons per 1000 Married Persons with Spouse Present: 1960–1977. U.S. Bureau of the Census, *Current Population Reports,* Series P-20, No. 324, April 1978.

cline of the family are pointed to by those concerned about the state of the modern family. Although 95 out of every 100 adults marry eventually, there are more people today who remain single for longer periods of time (delaying marriage), and some are experimenting with some type of *consensual union* (in which the partners agree to some type of organized relationship, such as living together, but do not enter a legal contract like marriage).[4] Some feel that these divorce figures and experimental trends may spell the demise of marriage as it has been traditionally defined.

Over the past twenty years, the birth rate in the United States has declined. The drop in the birth rate was at first gradual — around 1958 — but picked up in the late 1960s (see Table 7.1). In addition to declines in the actual fertility rate, women today also expect to have fewer children than did women of two decades ago. However, in 1977 the total fertility went up 3 percent — the first increase of over 1 percent in a year since 1957 (the peak of the "baby boom"). While this trend may not continue, it is possible that it indicates the beginning of a coming increase in the number of births. Organizations

TABLE 7.1
Total Fertility Rate, 1920–1977

YEAR	RATE	PERIOD	RATE	PERIOD	RATE
1977	1815	1969	2465	1950–54	3337
1976	1768	1968	2477	1945–49	2985
1975	1799	1967	2573	1940–44	2523
1974	1857	1966	2736	1935–39	2235
1973	1896	1965	2928	1930–34	2376
1972	2022	1965–69	2636	1925–29	2840
1971	2275	1960–64	3459	1920–24	3248
1970	2480	1955–59	3690		

SOURCE. U.S. Bureau of the Census, *Current Population Reports*, Series P-20, No. 324 (April, 1978).

such as Planned Parenthood and Coalition For A National Population Policy that promote population control are familiar to most people. In 1971, the National Organization For Non-Parents (NON) was formed; its members (nearly 600 within a year or so) declared that they did not want twenty or more years of their lives occupied in a child-oriented existence.[5] What would happen to the family as an institution and to our society if the majority of people decided not to have children?

Among those who have children, many parents who divorce are delaying remarriage, and increasing numbers are deciding to raise their children without remarrying. At any given time in our society, approximately 3.5 million families with children have only one parent present; more than 7 million children live in these "one-parent families."[6] Some of the children live under such conditions for a very short time until the parent decides to remarry. Others, however, spend their entire youth living with parents who have no partner. In 1958, an organization called Parents Without *Partners* was formed; it has a wide following today, served by its own publication dealing with the problems of single parents. In light of these developments, we may ask, Is a *family* really a meaningful unit without *both* husband and wife—*both* mother and father? (This does not necessarily imply a *biological* father or mother, but simply whether a family in which children are present is complete without adults of both sexes present.)

In order to approach the perplexing issues that surround marriage and family as a social problem, it is helpful to acquire a historical perspective. Through an examination of the family's past and present forms in American society, we can begin to understand how the family has come to be viewed as a social problem today.

THE FAMILY: PAST AND PRESENT

The Family in Preindustrial Society

Our postindustrial social order has grown increasingly complex. It thus becomes more and more difficult for us to envision what family life was like in the "simpler times" prior to 1900. However, in order to understand family-related problems today, it is instructive to adopt a historical perspective.[7]

The Extended Family

During the nineteenth century, the United States experienced pronounced social change, generally referred to as the Industrial Revolution. Prior to this, the American economy was predominantly agricultural. The majority of people lived in rural areas, with families often isolated from one another on widely scattered farms. In preindustrial society, the family was more or less economically self-sufficient. Family life was organized around agricultural production, and most of what the family produced it also consumed. The home was the economic hub of activity, and all family members played specific roles. **The most common type of family was the *extended family*, which consisted of a married couple, their children, and a number of other relatives, all of whom shared a common domicile.** This type of family

The extended family of preindustrial society was usually large, emphasizing close kinship between blood relatives and "familism." The welfare of the family unit was a primary concern.

ranged in membership from very young children to the oldest grandparents or great-grandparents. The extended family was a socially cohesive and economically sound unit in which everyone had a specific role. This type of family was useful given the characteristics of preindustrial society. From a *functionalist* point of view, the extended family fit the needs of preindustrial society extremely well. Large, closely knit families were functional to the maintenance of social order.

Economic factors influenced a variety of family functions. Marriage was a desirable alliance for both economic and social reasons. In order to prosper in farming, it was useful for a man to have a robust and industrious wife and many children to help with the work; without them, he would not be able to compete with farmers who did have large families. Women were subject to extreme social criticism if they did not marry in their teens or very early twenties, and those who delayed marriage or did not marry at all were opprobriously labeled spinsters or old maids. There were few alternatives for women other than being wives and mothers— only in rare circumstances could a woman become a doctor or other professional—and unmarried women were considered burdens on their families.

Children were important economic assets in the preindustrial family. With more children, a farmer gained a larger and more effective labor force, and the family was thus able to bring more acreage under cultivation and thereby expand its economic base. Any such economic improvements were a benefit to the whole family. This economic interdependence fostered tightly knit family units. **The term** *familism* **describes the values regarding family life that were paramount in preindustrial society. Basic to familism was the belief that the individual was always secondary to the welfare of the family unit.** For example, in preindustrial America, if a husband and wife were trying to decide whether their eldest son should marry a particular woman, his individual preferences would be less important in the decision than the perceived welfare of the family as a unit.

Social roles in the extended family were relatively clear-cut and well defined; a distinct division of labor prevailed. The family was patriarchal: the father was the head of the family and made the important decisions; women and children were subordinate to him. In preindustrial society, there were clear advantages related to being male. Today, the persistent (although declining) desire of couples for a male infant as their first child is a vestigial carryover from the preindustrial era.

The Monolithic Code

The cultural beliefs that supported the extended family of preindustrial American society have been referred to as the *monolithic code*.[8] The edicts of this code, which were accepted by most people of this period, were as follows:

1. **The correct adult mode of life was marriage.**
2. **Marriages were "for keeps."** (While divorce was possible, it was rare and severely disapproved.)
3. **Sexual conduct was to be limited to the married state.** (While it was recognized that "the flesh was weak," especially among the young, the weakness could readily be atoned for by getting married at the earliest possible time.)
4. **Marriages should be fruitful.** (Children were not so much a privilege as an obligation, and the more of them the better. This precept was based on the biblical injunction "Be fruitful, and multiply").
5. **Parents should be responsible to their children at whatever cost,** and children should be obedient to their parents with a minimum of questioning and certainly no open challenge.
6. **Women's place was in the home.** (It was reluctantly granted that, under certain circumstances, such as the husband's illness or death, a woman might have to work, but the idea that she worked for self-expression or to enhance the family's standard of living was unthinkable.)
7. **There was a sharp division of labor between men and women both inside the home and out,** and the power to make and enforce decisions rested primarily, if not exclusively, with the husband.

These beliefs were strongly held by most people and were viewed as the morally appropriate way to lead one's life. To do otherwise, people felt, was to violate the dictates of both God and nature. For people in preindustrial society, this was the only possible family form.

Family Stability

One of the predominant characteristics of the preindustrial family was its stability. Geographic mobility, especially for individuals apart from their families, was less common than today. Such mobility was considered undesirable and possibly suspect unless overwhelming conditions demanded it. Any family that moved frequently from place to place was not highly regarded by neighbors. Residential stability was an important indicator of success. Vacations were not feasible because certain tasks necessary for optimal production had to be carried out on a daily basis — e.g. feeding animals and milking cows.

We can see, then, that the "extended" structure of the preindustrial family was consistent with the economic and social demands of that period. We shall now see how the social and economic demands of the industrial revolution brought about changes in this type of family organization.

The Family and the Industrial Revolution

As industrialization progressed in the United States, the economic and social base of American society changed.[9] The factory system and large-scale business organization began to replace family-centered modes of production. People moved from the rural areas to cities — sometimes in search of more attractive occupational opportunities in the city, other times because they were driven from the farm by economic considerations. Urbanization and industrialization went hand in hand. Products that had previously been made within the home or within small family shops were no longer competitive with goods mass-produced on the assembly line.

The Nuclear Family

The economic functions of the extended family steadily declined — it was no longer as necessary or desirable (or even possible) for family members to work together to produce the necessities of life. **The family became a more consumption-oriented unit** — buying what was needed from firms that sold goods produced in factories and from large, predominantly nonfamily farms. **The *nuclear family* began to dominate the scene — it usually consists of a husband, wife, and their immediate children.** Generally, fewer people were required to fill basic economic roles, which were now performed outside the family context. The times no longer demanded — or even rewarded to the same degree — an extended family structure.

Marriage became more a matter of personal choice than of economic necessity; the choice of a mate became more a matter of personal preference. Children were less likely to be economic assets and more often were liabilities — unproductive individuals who had to be fed, clothed, and sheltered. The practice in which a father brought his sons into the family farm or business continued, but on a limited basis. Sons more frequently became one partner among other partners rather than the sole heir of the business. The tightly knit economic organization of the extended family began to disintegrate. Family welfare per se became increasingly subordinate to individual desires. **The term *individualism* refers to this orientation, in which the desires of the individual take precedence over those of the family.**

Changes brought about by industrialization have had some dramatic effects on the role structure of the family. Conceptions of a man's or a woman's "proper place" in society began to change. An industrial economy calls for a highly specialized division of labor. Production exists largely outside the family. Formal occupational training is required in an increasing number of areas; and both men and women are encouraged to develop specialized skills. In addition, being female began to

The nuclear family of modern, industrial society tends to be small, emphasizing the relationships among husband, wife, and their immediate children and stressing individualism. The welfare of the individual often takes precedence.

take on a new meaning. Courtship and dating behavior have become increasingly liberalized. Sexuality is now more openly discussed, and the "double standard" of sexual morality—which required a different and more strict moral code of women than of men—has steadily diminished in importance. As women have entered the work force, they have been able to take part in a greater share of the decision making. Although patriarchalism has persisted throughout the industrial era, women are gradually asserting themselves by taking a greater role in making decisions affecting the family—and the society as well. During the industrial era, the nuclear family has been geographically mobile to an extent that would have been considered reprehensible in preindustrial times. Not only is it a requirement that members of nuclear families be prepared to move in order to maintain suitable employment, but it has also become socially desirable to be mobile.

The industrial family was "freed" from many of the obligations of the extended family; however, it has lost much of the economic security and social supports of the extended family. Despite these changes in the structure of the family and its role in society, many people still clung to the beliefs of the monolithic code. Even though the actual behavior of many people was at variance with these prescriptions, they remained very much a part of people's attitudes (as they still do today) and had some influence on their behavior. For example, men and women who remained single well past the expected age of marriage were perceived by some (especially by married people) as strange or odd. While divorced people began to enjoy increased freedom from stigma, many still felt that divorce implied personal inadequacy, fault, and an unsavory lifestyle. Premarital sex began, to some extent, to be taken for granted, yet for many it remained a sensitive issue that caused anxiety. Illegitimacy was still viewed with considerable stigmatization, and couples who were married for a long time and remained childless felt subtle pressure to have children (especially by people who had children). As these examples illustrate, although society and the

family had changed substantially, the monolithic code still exerted a powerful influence in shaping people's attitudes and their reactions to others' behavior.

The Functions of the Nuclear Family

We have noted that industrialization has been associated with a number of very important changes in family organization. In 1934, sociologist William F. Ogburn, as part of a report on social trends commissioned by President Hoover,[10] summarized the major changes brought about by advances in technology and industrialization:

1. **The family's *economic* function has changed.** (It is no longer a self-sufficient, productive unit. It has become consumption-oriented.)

2. **The family has by and large lost its *protective* function.** (Social institutions such as police, hospitals, insurance, and homes for the aged serve people when they are in need more frequently than do family members.)

3. **The family is less likely to serve as a center for *religious* activity.**

4. **The family has lost many of its *educational-socializing* functions.** (Schools, day-care centers, and the like have taken the place of family. Children leave the home earlier, both to attend school and to find jobs of their own.)

5. **The family has lost much of its *status-conferring* function.** (Individuals gain identity and status largely through their own achievements in formal organizations, such as higher education, occupations, etc., rather than from their family.)

6. **The family has lost much of its *recreational* function.** (Age-graded recreational activities outside the home have taken the place of family-centered recreation.)

7. **The family has retained its *affectional* function.** (Family members still regard each other as among the most important people in their lives and gain social and emotional satisfaction from this relationship).

Ogburn concluded:

> Prior to modern times the power and prestige of the family was due to the fact that it served these seven functions—the family was tied together by these functions. The dilemma of the modern family is caused by the loss of many of these functions in recent times—at least six of the seven family functions have been reduced as family activities in recent times, and it may be claimed that only one remains as vigorous and extensive as in prior eras (*affectional*).[11]

Professor Ogburn's observations were made in the 1930s—almost fifty years ago. What has happened to the institution of the family since then? Ogburn's assertion concerning the affectional function is important. Today, people appear to be placing even more emphasis on the importance of affection in family relationships.

Family in a Postindustrial Society

Some feel that America is developing into a *postindustrial* social organization. A ***postindustrial society*** has not left the industrial era—industrial production is still a central activity, but it constitutes a smaller part of the total output of the economy because service occupations (such as teaching and social work) expand. Computerized information and control systems increasingly replace human labor. What implications do such changes have for the family?

Futurist Alvin Toffler has referred to the postindustrial family as the *fractured family*. He has observed:

> The family has been called the "great shock absorber" of society—the place to which the bruised and battered individual returns after doing battle with the world, the one stable point in an increasingly flux-filled environment. As the super-industrial revolution unfolds, this "shock absorber" will come in for some shocks of its own. . . . Faced by rapid social change and the staggering implications of the scientific revolution, super-industrial man may be forced to experiment with novel family forms. Innovative minorities can be expected to try out a colorful variety of family arrangements. They will begin by tinkering with existing forms.[12]

During the industrial period, it was the nuclear family that appeared revolutionary compared with the extended family organization of a preindustrial society. **In postindustrial American society, equally revolutionary family forms may gain considerable popularity, such as the childless marriage, the consensual union (living together), and the group marriage.**

Irrespective of the particular form the family might take in a postindustrial society, the social and economic changes initiated by industrialization have precipitated a new and extremely important development—the emergence of a *pairist* orientation to the family. **In contrast to the familistic or the individualistic orientation, a *pairist* orientation emphasizes the quality of a couple's interpersonal relationship.** People are very much concerned about *themselves* in a postindustrial society (individualism); however, they also emphasize their *relationship* with their mate (pairism). Pairist associations can take many forms other than the traditional husband-wife unit, and one goal of this chapter is to explore some of these alternatives.

We now have a historical perspective on marriage and family, an idea of the changes that have taken place, and a glimpse of the implications of the changes. Before examining these issues in detail, we will now consider marriage and family as a social problem, utilizing the three theoretical perspectives: functionalism, conflict, and interactionism.

THE FAMILY AS A SOCIAL PROBLEM

The Functionalist Perspective

Functionalist theorists regard the nuclear family as the major supporting institution in an industrial society. They assume that it has existed in all human societies.[13] Similarly, they emphasize the functional importance of sex roles in society. Functionalists maintain that the needs of society shape the social roles and patterns of social relationships that emerge—at least to the extent of placing limits on the types of social arrangements that are possible. For example, male dominance and female subordination within the family in most cultures are seen as socially *functional* rather than as the result of conflicts and the exercise of power. Talcott Parsons, a prominent functionalist, has spelled out ways that sex role specialization is functional for society and how it benefits the nuclear family.[14] If husbands emphasize their instrumental, occupational roles and wives their expressive, homemaking roles, there is little chance of rivalry and subsequent marital dissolution. If women were as career-oriented as men, serious conflict between marital partners might threaten the equilibrium of the family.

The functionalists also argue that children should be socialized in traditional ways so that their behavior does not conflict with that of their parents and thus disrupt the harmony of the family. If such integrated and compatible social roles do not exist within the family, **the family becomes a social problem** *because its ability to perform important functions* **(such as providing a setting for child-rearing or offering emotional support to family members)** *is threatened.* So, the family takes the form it does because the needs of a particular society require it to be that way—it performs important functions that contribute to order and stability in that society.

A potentially serious difficulty emerges in the functionalist analysis of the family. Because of its emphasis on social stability, the functionalist perspective may discourage the examination of alternatives to the traditional (and allegedly stable) nuclear family model. To avoid this, it is important to be sensitive to the existence of *functional alternatives*—different family forms that can perform the same functions as the nuclear family. Otherwise, we may inadvertently ignore family types that may be functional in modern society.

The Conflict Perspective

The conflict perspective involves a very different approach to family analysis.[15] Conflict theorists argue that functionalists have a romantic view of society because they downplay the role of power, dissension, and conflict. They state that the func-

tionalist perspective implicitly justifies the status quo and that this inhibits social change that may be both necessary and desirable. For example, according to the conflict perspective, traditional socialization patterns are not necessarily in the interest of social order and equilibrium but rather may reflect the dominance of one group by another. Because sex role differences in the family exist does not mean that they are functional. They may persist because males have the power to resist changes that are not in their interests. **So, from the conflict view, social arrangements emerge out of the clash of interest groups with differing amounts of power rather than resulting from the needs of a particular society. The family takes the form it does because some powerful group benefits from such arrangements.**

For the conflict theorist, the family's cohesiveness is based on coercive interpersonal relationships, and some degree of conflict among family members is inevitable. Since the family must respond to change, the emergence of alternative family forms and socialization patterns is viewed as a necessary feature of a changing society. For example, sociologist Randall Collins has applied the conflict perspective to the analysis of sex role socialization.[16] Collins speaks of "sexual stratification" and asserts that males have traditionally dominated females because of their superior physical strength and because women have been restricted by their childbearing and rearing responsibilities. He points out, however, that when shifts in political and economic resources take place in society (such as those due to the Industrial Revolution), men and women come into conflict with each other. **So, from the conflict perspective, the family can be considered a social problem when groups with significant power feel that they are not gaining the rewards and satisfactions from the family that they feel they deserve.**

Considering the issues raised by both the conflict and functionalist perspectives, one might adopt a *reorganization approach* to the family—viewing the family as changing in response to new conditions and reorganizing into new forms. This contrasts with the *social disorganization* viewpoint

Conflict often characterizes the modern marriage and family. The conflict emerges from a struggle over scarce values and differences of opinion about their distribution.

discussed earlier. One proponent of the reorganization approach, family relations expert Clark Vincent, has proposed that the family is like a giant sponge—soaking up the effects of devastating social change, thereby serving an *adaptive* function by acting as a buffer between the individual and a changing society.[17] From this perspective, the family is an *adaptive institution* rather than a disorganized and deteriorating artifact of a bygone era. A high divorce rate, for instance, can be viewed as one of the necessary features of a society in which the primary function performed by the family is *affectional*—if a couple does not derive emotional satisfaction from a marriage, then it is essential for the couple to terminate that relationship and seek a more satisfactory alternative. Although there may be some disorganization present within the family, this does not imply that the family as a social institution is headed for destruction—only that the "face" of the family is changing.

The Interactionist Perspective

From the interactionist perspective, social order is made possible by the bonds of commonly shared definitions of social reality. If people define a situation as real, then it will be real in its consequences—people will behave as if that reality were true. Thus, reality is ultimately *subjective*. What is the best form of the family? This will depend on one's definition of reality. Prior to industrialization, there was considerable consensus about the "ideal family" in American society. Most people agreed that the family as summarized by the precepts of the monolithic code was how all family life should be. Even though specific families may in reality have deviated from this code, people still looked to the monolithic code as the ideal.

Today, the consensus regarding what the family should be like is not as solid as it once was. What is the "ideal family" today? How many members will it have? How long will it last? People's answers to these questions will differ because varying perceptions of what constitutes a good marriage and family are emerging. A person's convictions about what makes a "good family" are shaped by his own particular values, beliefs, and previous experiences. The beliefs of a large number of people are still affected by the many tenacious assumptions and prescriptions that have been carried over from the monolithic code. The outcome of all these factors is that **there is no longer the widespread consensus regarding proper family life that once existed.** In addition, there is often a lack of consistency between what people believe—the precepts of the monolithic code—and the family forms that exist—childless marriages, consensual unions, and the like. **From the interactionist perspective, it is this lack of consensus and this growing inconsistency that lead people to define the family as a social problem today.**

The commonly held beliefs about the ideal family emerge from the process of social interaction. From the interactionist perspective, social order is created from the social interaction of individuals. This can be illustrated by common occurrences in our daily lives. Recall, for a moment, the last time you were in a situation in which you felt compelled to be careful about what you said. Under these circumstances, weren't the things you said somewhat different from how you usually behaved? Consider the following examples. Joe and Sue are at a company party. Someone asks them how they feel about "swinging" (organized extramarital relations). Joe and Sue have been swinging for about a year, but they are afraid of what might happen if this information became known to company personnel. Both Joe and Sue feel compelled to affirm in public that swinging is undesirable and certainly isn't their bag. In another example, let us consider that you have asked a close friend why he or she got a divorce. The reply may be, "Oh, we had money problems—you know how it goes" or "We just couldn't get along—if she hadn't wanted to go back to school, maybe . . ." or "I thought he was ambitious at first, but he turned out to be lazy and a male chauvinist as well."

These hypothetical illustrations show how what people say gives others a *sense* of what society is like, even though that feeling may not be completely accurate. The concepts of *preachment, practice,* and *pretense* can help us understand the dynamics of such situations.[18] In a very general sense, when complex, sticky, and frustrating social circumstances (*pretense*) are involved—such as extramarital relationships, which have been traditionally defined as adultery, and which are often cloaked in secrecy, guilt, and fear—there may be gross inconsistencies between what people say (*preachments*) and what people do (*practices*). However, other people take the preachments—what people say—as the practices—what people actually do. Thus, people often *act* as though a certain form of the family were both desirable and common, and in so doing reinforce such beliefs. **Through interaction such as this, social reality is constructed, and certain beliefs about what the family ought to be like are reinforced.**

What Is The Family?

At this point, the student may feel no closer to an answer to the question What is the family? We have mentioned many types of relationships—from the extended family, to consensual unions, to cohabitation. We have analyzed the family from the viewpoint of each of our three theoretical perspectives. Given all of this, can we say what *the* family is? Because the family affects all of us personally and because we each have notions about what the family ought to be like, it is important to address this issue at the outset before encountering specific forms of the family problems in this chapter.

In American society, many people are socialized to believe that there is one *best* form of everything—the "good life," the successful career, the most stimulating recreation, the "happy family." At the same time, we also acquire knowledge (however biased) concerning what is undesirable in life. There is a tendency to learn to like what we know and to fear those things about which we are uninformed. For example, people have traditionally spoken of *the family* with the assurance that what constitutes a family is obvious. After all, everybody knows what the family is: it's your father and mother, and brothers and sisters, and grandparents; and when you grow up, your husband or wife and your own children, and then their children—your grandchildren. In preindustrial American society, this description of the family was reasonably factual. Today, however, it is no longer completely accurate.

Social change is an inexorable process by which customs and beliefs are altered. **We very com-**

monly become the victims of what Ogburn called *cultural lag*—that is, material culture (e.g. technology and its products) changes more rapidly than nonmaterial culture (e.g. values, beliefs, and expectations about human affairs).[19] As a consequence, beliefs and ideas about human affairs tend to persist—often far longer than they are applicable. For example, women in an industrial society give birth to considerably fewer children than did their ancestors, and their children spend much of their childhood years outside the home (e.g. in school). Thus, there is less need for such women to spend all of their adult lives rearing children. Yet, until recently, there has been vociferous, and sometimes ferocious, resistance to the notion that women might be more socially productive by joining the world of work on a permanent and full-time basis. Even today, many people still feel that the proper place for women is in the home, raising children and taking care of the family. Furthermore, technological advances, such as labor-saving devices and prepared foods, have released women from the necessity for being full-time homemakers and made it possible for them to have careers outside the home in addition to filling their traditional roles of wife and mother.

These innovations have produced dramatic alterations in the family as our forefathers knew it. Yet we still cling to many traditional ideas about what the family should be like. Many people lament the fact that mothers are not home all of the time, that family members spend less time together, or that the family seems to have lost its cohesiveness. They yearn for the type of family relationship that is graphically portrayed in television programs like *The Waltons* and *Little House on the Prairie*. Yet one must consider whether these attitudes reflect cultural lag—are they out of step with the type of society and level of technology that exists today?

This text takes the position that *the* family is a myth. No single form of the family is both acceptable to and useful for everyone in our modern society. Modern society is much less homogeneous—indeed it exhibits a sharply increasing diversity—when compared to preindustrial societies, and this is reflected in the structures and functions of the institutions of marriage and family.

As the popularity of television's *Little House on the Prairie* exemplifies, many Americans still cling to traditional or "romantic" ideas about what the family should be.

Social change can be devastating, particularly when it involves an institution, such as the family, that affects all of us. **However, changes in the family do *not* necessarily imply that the family is irretrievably deteriorating**—even though some authors have written about the "death" of the family.[20]

There is little disagreement among social scientists that the institutions of marriage and family are changing. New forms and configurations are continuously emerging, while at the same time the more traditional forms persist among some groups. If everyone agreed on what marriage and the family *should* be, *and* if nobody deviated from these norms, then there would be no social problem in these areas. The family *has* changed, however, and there are substantial differences of opinion on what the family should be like. In the remainder of this chapter we will analyze existing forms of the family, the problems they create, and their implications for the future.

CHANGING PATTERNS OF MARRIAGE AND FAMILY LIFE

The implications of social change for the family are very significant. People are understandably anxious about social changes when they feel that they might lead to the ultimate collapse of our society. The belief that "as the family goes, so goes the nation" is still a widespread and anxiety-provoking maxim. However, as we have cautioned, it is misleading to assume that any change is necessarily bad.

Let us now examine some of the marriage- and family-related issues that people are concerned about. The problems we will discuss are not exhaustive of those facing the family today but are representative of the primary concerns of most of us. Problems centered on marriage and the family are integrally related to many other social problems in our complex society—population problems, poverty, crime, juvenile delinquency, changing definitions of work, attitudes toward the aged, and health care problems. We can begin by looking at the marital relationship and some currently popular alternatives to it.

The Marital Bond

Marriage

For most people in the United States, married life is preferable to remaining single, and **the vast majority eventually do get married (more than 95 percent of the American people will be married at least once during their lives)**. Bernard Farber, a student of the American family, proposed what he termed a "permanent availability" model of dating, courtship, and marriage in our society.[21] According to this idea, Americans are always willing (and even eager) to consider the pos-

Despite the presence of many alternative life styles today, the majority of men and women eventually marry. Many have very traditional expectations about marriage.

sibilities in the marriage market. This tendency includes even those who have already been married at least once. The rate of first marriages has remained relatively stable, although it has declined somewhat since the early 1970s. The rates of second, third, and subsequent marriages in our society have also been high. The estimated number of remarriages in the United States increased sharply in the 1960s and peaked in the late 1960s, followed by a marked downward trend since then (see Fig. 7.2). In fact, approximately one out of four people marrying today has been married at least once before.

The median age at first marriage, which declined between 1900 and 1960, began to increase in the decade after 1960 (see Table 7.2). In addition, the

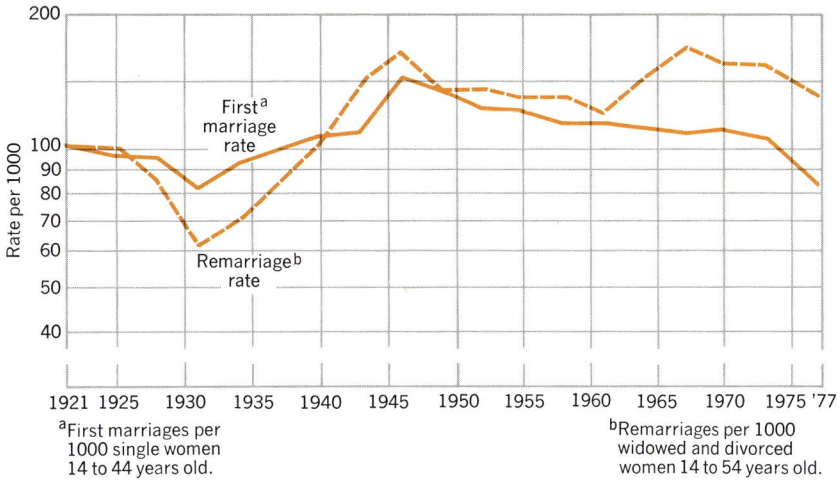

Figure 7.2 Rates of First Marriage and Remarriage for U.S. Women: 1921–1977. Paul C. Glick and Arthur J. Norton, "Marrying, Divorcing, and Living Together in the U.S. Today," *Population Bulletin, Vol. 32, No. 5* (Washington, D.C.: Population Reference Bureau, 1977), fig. 1.

first marriage rate plunged downward after 1972, with a 20-percent decline over a three-year period (see Fig. 7.2). This reflects the tendency of people to wait longer to get married and, perhaps, a tendency to postpone marriage through cohabitation.

Marriage appears to have many definite advantages over remaining single, including the possibility of two sources of income and the ability to satisfy parental desires for grandchildren. Some writers, however, feel that there are significant disadvantages to being married in modern society. One pessimistic view is that of social scientist Mervyn Cadwallader, who stated:

The truth as I see it is that contemporary marriage is a wretched institution. It spells the end of voluntary affection, of love freely given and joyously received. Beautiful romances are transmuted into dull marriages, and eventually the relationship becomes constrictive, corrosive, grinding, and destructive. The beautiful love affair becomes a bitter contract.[22]

Cadwallader argues that marriage was not designed to meet all the needs of the urban middle class. People in today's society possess heightened expectations about marriage—they expect the relationship to be honest, romantic, and trusting, in contrast with the outside world, which is viewed as phony and hypocritical. According to Cadwallader, this is a "painful paradox," because the marital institution simply cannot satisfy such expectations, and he believes that not much can be done to improve the situation. He ends on a sardonic note:

The braver and more critical among our teenagers and youthful adults will still ask, "But if the institution is so bad, why get married at all?" This is a tough one to deal with. . . .

How do you marry and yet live like gentle lovers, or at least like friendly roommates? Quite frankly, I do not know the answer to that question.[23]

The question that Cadwallader poses is interesting indeed. It is one that may not be readily answered but cannot be easily ignored. The voice coming from young people striving for intimacy seems to say, "I'm not sure that there *is* any style of life that is more satisfactory than marriage (including singlehood and cohabitation), but I'm willing to spend some time looking around for it."

TABLE 7.2

Median Age at First Marriage by Sex, 1890–1977

YEAR	MALE	FEMALE	YEAR	MALE	FEMALE
1977	24.0	21.6	1958	22.6	20.2
1976	23.8	21.3	1957	22.6	20.3
1975	23.5	21.1	1956	22.5	20.1
1974	23.1	21.1	1955	22.6	20.2
1973	23.2	21.0	1954	23.0	20.3
1972	23.3	20.9	1953	22.8	20.2
1971	23.1	20.9	1952	23.0	20.2
1970	23.2	20.8	1951	22.9	20.4
1969	23.2	20.8	1950	22.8	20.3
1968	23.1	20.8	1949	22.7	20.3
1967	23.1	20.6	1948	23.3	20.4
1966	22.8	20.5	1947	23.7	20.5
1965	22.8	20.6			
1964	23.1	20.5	1940	24.3	21.5
1963	22.8	20.5	1930	24.3	21.3
1962	22.7	20.3	1920	24.6	21.2
1961	22.8	20.3	1910	25.1	21.6
1960	22.8	20.3	1900	25.9	21.9
1959	22.5	20.2	1890	26.1	22.0

SOURCE. U.S. Bureau of the Census, *Current Population Reports*, Series P-20, no. 323 (Washington, D.C.: U.S. Government Printing Office, April 1978).

Singlehood

One alternative to marriage, growing in popularity, is to remain single. Today, more of the U.S. adult population than ever before—particularly young males and older females—are living by themselves or away from relatives. People who live alone have increased from about 3 percent of those aged 20–74 to nearly 10 percent. According to the Census Bureau, between 1970 and 1977, the number of men living alone went up 60 percent and the number of women living by themselves increased by 35 percent.[24] These findings do not necessarily demonstrate an enduring preference for a solitary lifestyle over marriage; however, they suggest a possible trend in this direction, one that seems to be limited to persons with certain social characteristics. Research findings have shown that among females, higher intelligence, more education, and higher levels of occupational status are related to singlehood, and that among males, poor interpersonal relationships with parents and siblings are associated with singlehood.[25]

There are some who favor voluntary singlehood as having definite advantages over marriage. One such person is social scientist Caroline Bird, who argues:

Marriage is no longer the only way to fulfill any basic need. It is still the most satisfactory as well as the easiest way to do a great many things, such as rearing children; but it is no longer the *only* way to make a success even of that. . . .

This is not to say marriage won't survive. . . . Many life styles will co-exist. . . . Traditional marriage will satisfy many men and women, but it will never again command the prestige of the "one right way" to live . . . it will never again confer the security it carried when traditional marriage was the only respectable choice.[26]

Cohabitation

Traditionally, marriage has been the most appropriate state of adult living—recall the prescriptions of the monolithic code. However, today the number of unmarried men and women living together in a single household is on the rise—it has more than doubled from 640,000 in 1970 to 1.3 million in 1977.[27] There are a number of factors that have encouraged this change. The acceptance of contraceptive procedures, liberalized abortion laws, human rights movements (especially for women), and more liberal premarital sexual standards—all have contributed to changes in our attitudes toward marriage. However, the increasing rate of remarriages reflects the continuing need for intimacy. Many still seek intimacy, within modified versions of the old monolithic code. It is as if these persons were searching for partners with whom they could enjoy both personal freedom and marital commitments, both independence and dependence. Some have turned to cohabitation as a solution to this dilemma.

Cohabitation **(or consensual union) refers to a couple's living together in a sexual and emotional relationship outside the legal bonds of marriage.** Such relationships may offer a number of opportunities that are restricted in the traditional marriage. For example, a cohabiting couple may feel more freedom to become sexually or emotionally involved with others than would a married couple. Should they decide to terminate their relationship, cohabitants are freed from the often punitive and adversary features of divorce that still prevail in many states.

Who are these cohabitants? Studies of cohabitation conclude that this arrangement has become increasingly common during courtship and that its popularity will probably increase in the future. One investigation of 1100 college undergraduates (of which one-third reported having cohabitated) concluded that cohabitants differ little from their non-cohabitating counterparts in terms of family and community background or level of intellectual and emotional functioning. These cohabitants appear to be interpersonally active and effective, and their experience is regarded by them as valuable and promotive of a more sustained and enduring relationship in the future.[28]

However, cohabitation does not always yield this bright picture of mutual enjoyment, for it has many built-in difficulties. For example, the couple is confronted first of all with a society that is geared to the customs of married people. When a married couple desires a divorce, the state will act as a mediator for property settlements, custody of offspring, and the like. Cohabitants, on the other hand, currently have little such legal recourse to impartial arbitration in the event that they decide to "split." While recent court cases, such as that of actor Lee Marvin, may result in changes in this area, it will probably be a long time before there is a coherent body of legal precedent dealing with the rights of cohabitants.

The findings of research studies conducted on cohabitation indicate a considerable lack of consensus between partners on the nature and probable consequences of their relationship. One such study found that cohabitant couples tended to disagree substantially about what the relationship really meant to them. For example, some females expected to get married, while the males did not.[29] In another study, a number of serious interpersonal and emotional problems emerged for cohabitants —emotional and sexual conflicts, disagreements with parents, and other types of internal and external strains related to cohabitation.[30] Nevertheless, some researchers conclude that the problems do not necessarily outweigh the potential benefits.[31]

It is evident that cohabitation can be a problem for the participants because we are living in a society "built for the married." Cohabitation is an example of an emerging alternative lifestyle that will probably continue. For example, Cathrina Bauby, an author in the field of human relations and interpersonal communication, has dedicated an entire book to the subject of people who either are considering, or have decided to cohabit.[32]

Currently, many cohabitants do not view such relationships as a permanent alternative to marriage. Whether cohabitation will ever replace marriage cannot be determined at this point. Some writers have viewed such alternatives to traditional marriage as indicators that the traditional family will eventually be replaced by other social arrangements. Cohabitation represents an effort to form an intimate and satisfying relationship outside the bonds of marriage. If cohabitation were to become very common in the future, marriage might come to be viewed as merely a legal or religious formality.

Oral Contraception and the Family

Perhaps the most significant *technological* development in terms of its implications for the family is the availability of oral contraceptives – the hormonal pills. With these contraceptives, couples can very effectively choose whether or not to have children. Today, this relatively inexpensive, reliable, and convenient method of birth control is taken for granted. Consider for a moment the tremendous impact that it and other modern means of birth control have had on couples' control over whether they will have children. Organizations like Planned Parenthood have encouraged married couples and cohabitants to be thoughtful and conscientious about having children; sexual activity does not have to be accompanied by parenthood. There have been dramatic changes in the contraceptive methods chosen by couples in the past two decades.[33] Between 1965 and 1970, there was a 10 percent increase in the number of couples using the pill. More recently, however, medical researchers have begun to question the safety of the pill. Research is beginning to implicate the contraceptive pill as an agent in a number of illnesses, such as cancer and thrombosis (blood clots). In addition, many women suffer side effects from the pill (e.g. weight gain and fluid retention). While the long-term effects of the pill are not yet known, some women have already reacted to the potential dangers by discontinuing its use. In the past few years, there has been a decline in the proportion of couples using the pill. However, other methods of contraception – sterilization, the IUD, and the diaphragm – are nearly as effective, or more so, although they are less convenient.

This increasing ability to choose whether to have children raises what, for many, is an unsettling question: What will hold the family together if not children? What will be the motivation for couples to establish enduring interpersonal relationships in the future if the trend toward childlessness continues? Some groups view childlessness as a threat to the very foundation of the family. For them, a family includes children. If an effective contraceptive technology had not been developed, it is possible that the future of the family would be quite different than the trends evident today – for example, childlessness might still be rare and frowned upon. In such a society, there might still be a consensus that the ideal family included children. Sterilization and abortion would be universally scorned because such practices violate these beliefs about the family. However, effective ways of preventing conception have developed, and couples can make the choice to have children or not. As a consequence, the values and beliefs of many have changed. Not all people today agree that the ideal family includes children. Sterilization and abortion are acceptable to some groups in society. **So, partly because of technological advances that make possible new alternatives, we find not *one ideal conception* of the family but rather *many different alternatives* regarding satisfactory family life.**

DIVORCE

One of the recurring and difficult questions concerning marriage and family life is, What is a successful marriage? There are many different ways to define marital success. For some people, a successful marriage is one in which the spouses share a special kind of intimate feeling; for others, it is the absence of interpersonal conflict; and in a few cases, marital success means little more than the absence of divorce. This last type of marriage may be considered stable because it persists, although it may not involve feelings of marital happiness. Traditionally, stable marriages were seen as desirable – especially when the alternative was divorce – even if the marital partners were unhappy. This was particularly true when a married couple had children.

How can we tell if a marriage is successful? Have you ever wondered whether some of the couples you know are really enjoying a happy, successful marriage? While some of our speculations about this may have been correct, we are often wrong because it is difficult to understand the complex mixture of attitudes, feelings, and relationships that make up a happy, successful, and enduring marriage. In our society, marital and family problems are regarded as extremely private. Individuals who are experiencing marital difficulties often mask their problems in the hope that others will view them as happily married. Because of these difficulties inherent in studying the happiness of a marriage, researchers turn to a clearly observable occurrence like divorce as a measure of the success of a marriage. **Many people view the high divorce rate as a serious problem and as a sign that the family is in trouble. Divorce is often viewed as symptomatic of the disintegration of the family.** It is to these issues that we now turn our attention.

The Divorce Rate

One must be careful in the analysis of divorce statistics because many methods of computing divorce rates have deficiencies. The traditional means of calculating the divorce rate is in terms of the proportion of marriages that end in divorce. However, this rate can be misleading because it does not differentiate between first, second, or subsequent divorces. For example, if during a given period there are 1000 marriages and 250 divorces, then the divorce rate is 1 out of 4. However, many of those 250 are divorcing for the second or third time within the period. A more meaningful rate is one based on the number of currently divorced men and women per 1000 married people.

The divorce rate has increased in the United States over the past century and continues to climb rapidly. As Figure 7.1 illustrates, the overall divorce rate has doubled between 1960 and 1977, and for some groups it has increased even more. It is significant that the rates are higher among black married men and women in view of our observations in chapters 11 and 12 concerning levels of social disorganization among racial minorities. These statistics might leave the impression that the family is indeed disorganized and rapidly deteriorating and that marriage may be on its way out. However, if this impression were true, we would not expect the rate of remarriages to be very high. Paul C. Glick, renowned demographer for the U.S. Bureau of the Census, has reported that: ". . . about four out of every five of those who obtain a divorce will eventually remarry."[34] In 1975, there were ap-

Drawing by Koren © 1973 The New Yorker Magazine, Inc.

Men and women today are more likely to divorce than ever before, and for those who do, their previous marriages are becoming more a matter of candid and public conversation than a source of guilt and shame.

proximately 9.1 million women between the ages of 14 and 75 who had been divorced after their first marriage. Sixty-six percent of these women were involved in a second marriage.[35] Expressing this in a different way, three of every four women 50 to 75 years old, whose first marriage ended in divorce, had remarried. In addition, there is some evidence that the second marriage is less likely to end in divorce than the first. Yet, the remarriage rate has leveled off since 1970 (see Fig. 7.2), and it is unclear whether people are postponing remarriage or deciding to opt out of marriage altogether.

If the high divorce rate does not signify a loss of confidence in the institution of marriage, then what does it mean? Many researchers interpret the high divorce rate to mean that people currently expect more from marriage and are less willing to accept a marital relationship that does not satsify these elevated expectations. (A hypothetical "formula" for marital success presented in the accompanying box is based on these ideas.) People today may be more willing to divorce and search for a more fulfilling relationship than to endure a marriage that does not provide personal or emotional gratification. In fact, this is consistent with the changing functions of the family already discussed. If the modern nuclear family performs only the affectional function, then a marriage that does not provide such affection is not functional. In a previous era, the extended family served many other economic and social functions; if it failed in the affectional area, it would probably still perform important functions in many other areas, and the dissolution of the family would be detrimental to society. If the nuclear family fails in its primary function (affectional), then would its dissolution not be functional for society? Many today feel that this is the case.

Another factor contributing to the rising divorce rate is that many of the barriers that discouraged people from divorcing in the past are less important today. There are substantial indications, for example, that the social stigma previously associated with divorce is less evident today. People are less willing to maintain an unsatisfactory marriage in order to avoid the threat divorce has traditionally posed to their personal or professional reputations. And findings quite contrary to the old supposition that parents should keep their marriages together "for the sake of the children" have indicated that an unhappy, "unbroken" home may be more harmful to the general welfare of the children than divorce.[36] In the 1970s, people who had been married for many years and who had grown, or nearly grown, children appeared to be more willing than their earlier counterparts to obtain divorces rather than continue to suffer the conflicts and unhappiness associated with marriages that had deteriorated to meaningless and distressful levels.[37] The pressures that once existed to encourage a couple to remain married are not nearly as strong today.

"Formula for Marital Happiness

$$\frac{\text{Marital}}{\text{Happiness}} = \frac{\text{Fulfillments}}{\text{Expectations}}$$

$$MH = \frac{F}{E}$$

Examples: If a couple has 50 expectations for marriage (e.g. "Our sex life will be wonderful and free from problems"; "We will see eye to eye in financial matters"; "Our interests will remain compatible"; "We want the same things for our children"; etc.) and actualizes 100 (twice as many as expected), the formula yields a positive factor of 2.

If on the other hand the couple has 100 expectations and realizes only 50, the formula yields a fractional quotient of 0.5.

In no way are we implying that a marital relationship's success can be determined by a mathematical formula. We are suggesting, however, that marital happiness is a function of the relationship between people's expectations and the degree to which those expectations are fulfilled. When expectations increase, fulfillments must do likewise in order to retain a given level of happiness.

SOURCE. Meyer F. Nimkoff, *Marriage and the Family* (New York: Houghton Mifflin, 1947), pp. 505–506.

Divorce and Social Class

United States census data have consistently indicated a positive correlation between socioeconomic position and marital stability. That is, people with higher educational levels, higher income, and professional occupational status are less likely to divorce than are those with lower educational levels, lower income, and nonprofessional occupational status. However, divorces among semiprofessional and professional people have increased sharply in the past few decades.[38] Figure 7.3 illustrates these findings. This does not mean that divorce is more common among the middle and upper classes than the lower classes, but it does suggest that **divorce may be viewed as socially acceptable by an increasing number of men and women in semiprofessional and professional positions.**

Divorce and the Law

The most capricious features of marriage and divorce in our society are the ambiguous laws and unpredictable decisions by judges. In many states, divorce proceedings are based on an *adversary* sys-

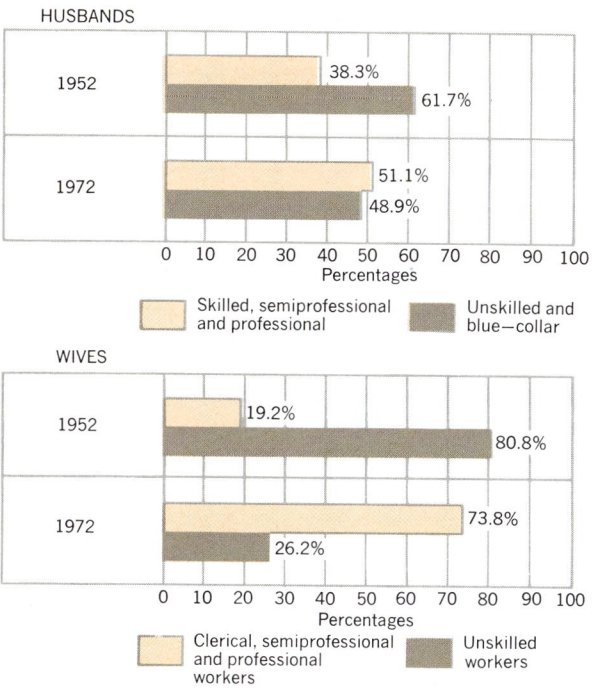

HUSBANDS

1952 — 38.3% | 61.7%

1972 — 51.1% | 48.9%

0 10 20 30 40 50 60 70 80 90 100
Percentages

☐ Skilled, semiprofessional and professional
■ Unskilled and blue—collar

WIVES

1952 — 19.2% | 80.8%

1972 — 73.8% | 26.2%

0 10 20 30 40 50 60 70 80 90 100
Percentages

☐ Clerical, semiprofessional and professional workers
■ Unskilled workers

Figure 7.3 Changes in Occupational Composition of Divorced People, 1952–1972 (expressed in percentages). Kenrick S. Thompson, "The Divorce Profile. Differential Social Correlates in 1952 and in 1972," *International Journal of Sociology of the Family* 6 (Autumn 1976), p. 261. Reprinted with permission from the International Journal of Sociology of the Family.

tem of justice — one person must act as the *plaintiff* (the person accusing the other of fault or blame) and the other as the *defendant* (the one accused of fault or blame). Unless *one* party has legal *grounds* (against the other) for divorce, then the marital contract cannot be legally broken. It is interesting to observe that under this adversary system, divorce is the only civil contract that cannot be terminated by mutual consent. If two people agree to sever a legal agreement involving the sale of a house, they need only tear up the contract to end the relationship legally. In the case of adversary divorce, this is tantamount to legal conspiracy. In addition, if both parties are found at fault, the divorce can not technically be granted.

In the present context of the women's movement and the continuing struggle for equal rights for the sexes, it is interesting to note that males remain the underdogs in divorce proceedings. Present divorce laws tend to be interpreted in ways that suggest that women are oppressed (plaintiffs) and that men are the oppressors (defendants). Sociologist Kenrick Thompson, who has studied divorce profiles, found that there was no significant decrease in the percentage of women acting as plaintiffs in divorce cases between 1952 and 1972 — nearly 85 percent of the cases he studied involved women serving in that capacity.[39] This would appear to indicate that lawyers and judges still believe that it is right and proper that men be the defendants in divorce proceedings, regardless of individual circumstances. In addition, most women may still traditionally view themselves as the "victim" — the plaintiff.

At the time of this writing, at least thirty states have adopted a divorce law (more frequently and legally described as a "dissolution" proceeding) that permits divorce on the basis of "marriage breakdown," so that it is not necessary to prove one of the traditional grounds for divorce, such as that one party is to blame (see Table 7.3). Some, but not all of these states refer to their divorce proceedings as *no fault* divorce. This kind of legal alteration reflects changing attitudes toward marriage, family, and divorce in our society.

The Future of Divorce

Given the trends in divorce rates, is divorce a social problem in the United States? If what we are witnessing now is a harbinger of the future, there is little chance of a foreseeable decline in the divorce rate. As early as the mid-1960s, some writers suggested that people might come to see first marriages as primarily experimental. Research on consensual unions indicates that cohabitants have the same kinds of interpersonal problems that married couples do and that the rate of dissolutions (albeit informal) is also extremely high for them. This tempts one to conclude that marital problems are an inevitable part of human relationships. Given this perspective, **divorce may be regarded not as a weak link in the marriage and family system, but rather as a necessary and even a desirable option for those people who do**

not experience success and happiness—which the family is expected to provide in American society.

Traditionally, marriage has been viewed as a permanent bond—something that we work hard to obtain and then strive equally vigorously to preserve. Today, we are becoming increasingly aware that marriage, like divorce, is a process. It is something that can, and typically does, change over time. It is important to place great value on working hard to preserve a marriage relationship—it is not something to be taken lightly. Yet, should we expect every marriage to remain rewarding for a lifetime? Given the diverse society in which we live, people change substantially during their lives. The successful businessman decides to give it all up for the more sedate life of the farmer; the middle-aged mother decides that her children can survive without her constant attention and returns to school to obtain a law degree. In many ways, people change during their lives, and it is not always possible for a spouse to make compatible changes. In such situations, **when a marriage is strained to provide the affection and emotional support that is its primary function, it may be more desirable that the couple separate and search out other fulfilling relationships. In other words, divorce may be an inevitable part of modern society.**

ALTERNATIVE FAMILY FORMS

As we have seen, many commentators who have studied the family during the past century believe that this social institution is in a state of disorganization—that it is deteriorating. There is a striking paradox in these observations, however. On the one hand, the family appears to be less stable—the divorce rate is higher than ever; increasing numbers of men and women, both young and old, are choosing to remain single longer or to cohabit with a partner outside of marriage; and traditional family norms involving kinship and cohesiveness seem to be less widespread. On the other hand, practically everyone gets married eventually; those who divorce usually marry again; and, in many respects,

more people are deliberately attempting to incorporate some traditional family norms back into their lives (for example, by vacationing together).

It is interesting, then, that although the family seems to be less stable, it displays no signs of disappearing. How might we understand such a situation? Certainly preindustrial extended-family organization has largely faded from view (although there are still some families that resemble it in some ways). Family *disorganization,* however, should be viewed in perspective. The appearance of alternatives to the traditional family might be viewed as a *normal* and *expected* response to social change rather than as indicative of the decline of the family as a social institution. As we have previously noted, if everyone agreed on the acceptability of alternative lifestyles, there would be no problem. However, because the family involves central norms and values and because it involves the sensitive areas of sexual and emotional relationships, there is intense controversy over the emergence of these alternative family forms. Some view them as repugnant aberrations that violate basic human values; others view them as amusing and probably harmless deviations limited to a small and somewhat strange group of people. For the student of social problems, our perspective must be somewhat more objective. These alternative family forms may survive or they may not; but in either event, they must be studied as responses to the changes in American society as we move into the postindustrial era.

In the previous sections, we have already seen a number of alternatives to marriage, such as remaining single or cohabitation. These lifestyles are not viewed as permanent for most people and therefore do not really represent "family forms." In the following sections, we will consider a number of alternatives to the traditional extended and nuclear family forms. These alternatives are regarded by those who adopt them as ongoing and potentially permanent relationships and thus can be considered as "family forms." It should be borne in mind throughout this discussion that these alternatives, should they survive, will probably not *replace* the traditional family forms but rather *supplement*

TABLE 7.3

Grounds for Divorce in the United States as of December 31, 1977

STATE OR OTHER JURISDICTION	RESIDENCE REQUIRED BEFORE FILING SUIT FOR DIVORCE	"NO FAULT" DIVORCE (a)			GROUNDS FOR ABSOLUTE DIVORCE					
		MARRIAGE BREAK-DOWN (b)	SEPA-RATION	PRIOR DECREE OF LIMITED DIVORCE	ADUL-TERY	MENTAL AND/OR PHYSICAL CRUELTY	DESER-TION	ALCO-HOLISM AND/OR DRUG ADDICTION	IMPO-TENCY	NON-SUPPORT BY HUSBAND
Alabama	6 mos.(c)	★	2 yrs.(d)	2 yrs.	★	..	1 yr.	★	★	★
Alaska	....	★	.....	.....	★	★	1 yr.	★	★	★
Arizona	90 days	★	.....	.....	..	..	......	..	..	..
Arkansas	60 days(g)	..	3 yrs.	.....	★	★	1 yr.	★	★	★(h)
California	(i)	★	.....	.....	..	..	......	..	..	..
Colorado	90 days	★	.....	.....	..	..	......	..	..	..
Connecticut	1 yr.(k)	★	18 mos.	.....	★	★	1 yr.	★	..	..
Delaware	3 mos.	★	.....	.....	..	..	......	..	..	..
Florida	6 mos.	★	.....	.....	..	..	......	..	..	..
Georgia	6 mos.	★	.....	.....	★	★	1 yr.	★	★	..
Hawaii	3 mos.	★	2 yrs.(d)	★(q)	..	..	......	..	..	..
Idaho	6 wks.	★	5 yrs.	.....	★	★	★	★	..	★
Illinois	90 days	..	.....	.....	★	★	1 yr.	2 yrs.	★	..
Indiana	6 mos.	★	.....	.....	..	..	......	..	★	..
Iowa	1 yr.	★	.....	.....	..	..	......	..	..	..
Kansas	60 days	★	.....	.....	★	★	1 yr.	★	..	★
Kentucky	180 days(t)	★	.....	.....	..	..	......	..	..	..
Louisiana	(u)	..	2 yrs.	★(v)	★	..	......	..	..	..
Maine	6 mos.(k)	★	.....	.....	★	★	3 yrs.	★	★	★
Maryland	(x)	..	(y)	.....	★	..	1 yr.	..	★	..
Massachusetts	30 days	★	.....	.....	★	★	1 yr.	★	★	★
Michigan	180 days(k)	★	.....	.....	..	..	......	..	..	..
Minnesota	1 yr.(k)	★	.....	.....	..	..	......	..	..	..
Mississippi	1 yr.	★	.....	.....	★	★	1 yr.	★	★	..
Missouri	90 days	★	.....	.....	..	..	......	..	..	..
Montana	90 days	★	.....	.....	..	..	......	..	..	..
Nebraska	1 yr.	★	.....	.....	..	..	......	..	..	..
Nevada	6 wks.(k)	★	1 yr.(p)	.....	..	..	......	..	..	..
New Hampshire	1 yr.(k)	★	.....	.....	★	★	2 yrs.	★	★	★
New Jersey	1 yr.	..	18 mos.	.....	★	★	1 yr.	★	..	..
New Mexico	6 mos.	★	.....	.....	★	★	★	..	..	..
New York	1 yr.(k)	..	1 yr.(d)	.....	★	★	1 yr.	..	(af)	(ag)
North Carolina	6 mos.	..	1 yr.	.....	★	..	......	..	★	..
North Dakota	1 yr.	★	.....	1 yr.	★	★	1 yr.	★	★	★(h)
Ohio	6 mos.	★(ah)	2 yrs.	.....	★	★	1 yr.	★	★	★(h)
Oklahoma	6 mos.(aj)	★	.....	.....	★	..	1 yr.	★	★	★(h)
Oregon	6 mos.	★	.....	.....	..	..	......	..	..	..

TABLE 7.3 *(continued)*
Grounds for Divorce in the United States as of December 31, 1977

IN-SANITY	PREG-NANCY AT MAR-RIAGE	BIG-AMY	UN-EXPLAINED AB-SENCE	FELONY CONVIC-TION OR IMPRISON-MENT	OTHER	PERIOD BEFORE PARTIES MAY REMARRY AFTER FINAL DECREE		STATE OR OTHER JURISDICTION
	GROUNDS FOR ABSOLUTE DIVORCE					PLAINTIFF	DEFENDANT	
5 yrs.	★	..	..	★	(e)	60 days(f)	60 days (f)	.... Alabama
18 mos.	..	..	..	★	....	....	....	.... Alaska
....	..	..	..	..	....	....	....	.........Arizona
3 yrs.	.·.	★	..	★	....	....	....	.... Arkansas
(j)	..	..	..	..	....	....	....	.........California
			..	..	....	....	....	.... Colorado
5 yrs.	..	..	7 yrs.	★	(l)	....	....	....Connecticut
....	..	..	..	..	....	....	....	...... Delaware
3 yrs.(m)	..	..	..	..	....	....	....	.... Florida
2 yrs.	★	..	..	★	(l,n,o)	(p)	(p)	.... Georgia
....	..	..	..	..	....	....	....	.... Hawaii
3 yrs.	..	..	..	★	....	....	....	.... Idaho
....	..	★	..	★	(r,s)	....	....	.... Illinois
2 yrs.	..	..	..	★	....	....	....	........Indiana
....	..	..	..	..	....	1 yr.(f)	1 yr.(f)	.... Iowa
3 yrs.	..	..	..	★	....	30 days	30 days	........Kansas
....	..	..	..	..	....	....	....	...... Kentucky
....	..	..	..	★	....	....	....	....Louisiana
....	..	..	..	..	....	....	....	.... Maine
3 yrs.	..	..	..	★	(z)	....	....	...... Maryland
....	..	..	..	★	....	....	....	.. Massachusetts
....	..	..	..	..	....	....	....	...... Michigan
....	..	..	..	..	....	6 mos.(f)	6 mos.(f)	...... Minnesota
3 yrs.	..	★	..	★	(n,aa)	....	(ab)	..... Mississippi
....	..	..	..	..	....	....	....	.......Missouri
....	..	..	..	..	....	....	....	.......Montana
....	..	..	..	..	....	....	....	......Nebraska
2 yrs.	..	..	..	..	....	....	....	.... Nevada
....	..	..	2 yrs.	★	(ac,ad)	....	....	. New Hampshire
2 yrs.	..	..	..	★	(ae)	....	....	..... New Jersey
....	..	..	..	..	....	....	....	...... New Mexico
5 yrs.(af)	..	..	..	★	....	....	....	...... New York
3 yrs.	★	..	..	..	(e)	....	....	.. North Carolina
5 yrs.	..	..	..	★	....	(p)	(p)	....North Dakota
4 yrs.	..	★	..	★	(l,ai)	....	....	.... Ohio
5 yrs.	★	..	..	★	(l, ai)	6 mos.	6 mos.	...... Oklahoma
....	..	..	..	..	....	60 days	60 days	........Oregon

TABLE 7.3 *(continued)*
Grounds for Divorce in the United States as of December 31, 1977

| STATE OR OTHER JURISDICTION | RESIDENCE REQUIRED BEFORE FILING SUIT FOR DIVORCE | "NO FAULT" DIVORCE (A) | | | GROUNDS FOR ABSOLUTE DIVORCE | | | | | |
		MARRIAGE BREAK-DOWN (B)	SEPA-RATION	PRIOR DECREE OF LIMITED DIVORCE	ADUL-TERY	MENTAL AND/OR PHYSICAL CRUELTY	DESER-TION	ALCO-HOLISM AND/OR DRUG ADDICTION	IMPO-TENCY	NON-SUPPORT BY HUSBAND
Pennsylvania . . .	1 yr.	..	......	......	★	★	2 yrs.	..	★	..
Rhode Island. . . .	2 yrs.	..	5 yrs.(p)	......	★	★	5 yrs.(am)	★	★	★
South Carolina . .	3 mos.(ap)	..	3 yrs.	......	★	★	1 yr.	★	..	..
South Dakota. . . .	....	..	......	......	★	★	1 yr.	★	..	★
Tennessee.	6 mos.	..	......	2 yrs.(p)	★	★	1 yr.	★	★	★
Texas	6 mos.	, ★	3 yrs.	......	★	★	1 yr.	..	..	..
Utah	3 mos.	..	3 yrs.(d)	......	★	★	1 yr.	★	★	★(h)
Vermont	6 mos.(as)	..	6 mos.	......	★	★	★	..	..	★(h)
Virginia	6 mos.	..	1 yr.	(at)	★	★	1 yr.	..	..	..
Washington.	....	★	......	......	..	..	..	..	..	..
West Virginia. . . .	1 yr.(k)	..	2 yrs.	......	★	★	1 yr.	★	..	..
Wisconsin	6 mos.	..	1 yr.	1 yr.	★	★	1 yr.	1 yr.	..	★
Wyoming	60 days(k)	..	2 yrs.(au)	......	★	★	1 yr.	★	★	★
Dist. of Columbia	6 mos.	..	6 mos.(ax)	★(ay)	..	..	......	..	..	..
Puerto Rico	1 yr.(k)	..	2 yrs.	......	★	★	1 yr.	★	★	..

*Prepared by the Women's Bureau, U.S. Department of Labor, with the assistance of the attorneys general of the states.

(a)　"No fault" includes all proceedings where it is not necessary to prove one of the traditional grounds for divorce. Not all states shown in this category refer to their proceedings as "no fault."

(b)　Expressed in statutes as irremediable or irretrievable breakdown of marriage relationship, irreconcilable differences, incompatibility, marriage unsupportable because of discord, etc.

(c)　Two years for wife filing on ground of nonsupport.

(d)　Under decree of separate maintenance and/or written separation agreement.

(e)　Crime against nature.

(f)　Except to each other. In Iowa, court can waive ban.

(g)　Three-month residency required before final judgment.

(h)　Ground available to husband, also.

(i)　No residency requirement before filing suit, but final decree cannot be entered until party is a resident for 6 months.

(j)　Incurable.

(k)　In some cases a lesser period of time may be allowed.

(l)　Fraud, force, or duress.

(m)　Mental incompetence.

(n)　Parties related by marriage or blood, contrary to statute.

(o)　Mental incapacity at time of marriage.

(p)　In the discretion of the court.

(q)　After expiration of term of separation decree.

(r)　Loathsome disease.

(s)　Attempt on life of spouse by poison or other means showing malice.

(t)　No decree until parties have lived apart for 60 days.

(u)　Must be domiciled in state and grounds occurred in state; 2 years separation need not have been in state.

(v)　Spouse who obtained separation from bed and board may obtain absolute divorce 1 year after decree of separation becomes final. Other party may obtain decree 1 year and 60 days from the date of the separation decree.

(w)　Attempt by either parent to corrupt son or prostitute daughter, or proposal by husband to prostitute wife.

(x)　One year if cause occurred out of state and 2 years if on grounds of insanity.

TABLE 7.3 *(continued)*

Grounds for Divorce in the United States as of December 31, 1977

GROUNDS FOR ABSOLUTE DIVORCE

IN-SANITY	PREG-NANCY AT MAR-RIAGE	BIG-AMY	UN-EXPLAINED AB-SENCE	FELONY CONVIC-TION OR IMPRISON-MENT	OTHER	PERIOD BEFORE PARTIES MAY REMARRY AFTER FINAL DECREE		STATE OR OTHER JURISDICTION
						PLAINTIFF	DEFENDANT	
3 yrs.	..	★	..	★	(l,n,ak)	....	(al)	... Pennsylvania
....	..	..	★	..	(am,ao)	6 mos.	6 mos.	....Rhode Island
....	•..	..	..	..	....	....	....	.. South Carolina
5 yrs.	..	..	..	★	....	....	....	...South Dakota
....	..	★	..	★	(s,aq)	....	....	......Tennessee
3 yrs.	..	..	..	★	....	30 days(f)...	....	.... Texas
(ar)	..	..	..	★	....	....	....	.... Utah
5 yrs.	..	..	..	•..	....	....	....	.... Vermont
....	..	..	..	★	....	....	....	.... Virginia
....	..	..	..	..	....	....	....	.....Washington
3 yrs.	..	..	..	★	....	....	....	....West Virginia
1 yr.	..	..	..	★	....	6 mos.	6 mos.	...... Wisconsin
2 yrs.	★	..	..	★	(av,aw)	....	....	.... Wyoming
....	..	..	..	..	....	....	....	Dist. of Columbia
7 yrs.	..	..	10 yrs.	★	(w)	....	301 days	..... Puerto Rico

(y)   Voluntary living apart for 1 year and no reasonable expectation of reconciliation, or living separate and apart without cohabitation or interruption for 3 years.

(z)   Any cause which renders marriage null and void from the beginning.

(aa)   Insanity or idiocy at time of marriage not known to other party.

(ab)   When divorce is granted on ground of adultery, court may prohibit remarriage. After 1 year, court may remove disability upon satisfactory evidence of reformation.

(ac)   Membership in religious sect disbelieving in marriage.

(ad)   Wife's absence out of state for 10 years without husband's consent.

(ae)   Deviant sexual conduct without consent of spouse.

(af)   Grounds for annulment.

(ag)   Grounds for separation.

(ah)   On petition of both spouses, accompanied by separation agreement executed and confirmed by both spouses in court appearance not less than 90 days after filing of petition.

(ai)   Defendant obtained divorce from plaintiff in another state.

(aj)   Five years if on grounds of insanity and insane spouse is in out-of-state institution.

(ak)   Remarriage after 2 years upon false but well-founded rumor of death of other spouse. (If first spouse reappears, he or she may seek divorce for bigamy within 6 months.)

(al)   If divorce is granted for adultery, the guilty party cannot marry the accomplice in adultery during lifetime of former spouse.

(am)   Or for shorter period in court's discretion.

(an)   Void or voidable marriage; in case party is deemed civilly dead from crime or other circumstances, party may be presumed dead.

(ao)   Gross misbehavior or wickedness.

(ap)   When both parties residents; 1 year when one is non-resident.

(aq)   Refusal by wife to move with husband to this state.

(ar)   Adjudication of permanent and incurable insanity.

(as)   Two years if grounds are insanity.

(at)   Limited divorce granted on the grounds of cruelty, reasonable apprehension of bodily hurt, willful desertion, or abandonment may be merged into an absolute divorce after 1 year.

(au)   Two years separation without material fault by plaintiff.

(av)   Husband guilty of conduct constituting vagrancy.

(aw)   Conviction of felony before marriage.

(ax)   Voluntary separation; involuntary separation, 1 yr.

(ay)   May be granted for voluntary separation of 6 months, separation for 1 year, adultery, or cruelty.

SOURCE. *The Book of the States, 1978–1979* (Lexington, Kentucky: The Council of State Governments, Volume 21), pp. 268–269.

them. In the future, one may have a choice among different forms of the family.

Open Marriage

One characteristic of traditional families in the United States is the "closed" quality of the husband-wife relationship. Each is viewed as having exclusive rights to the emotional and sexual attentions of the other. In a sense, each partner is expected to be all things — emotionally, personally, and sexually — to the other partner. In their book *Open Marriage,* George and Nena O'Neill, contemporary investigators of the family, conclude that such "closed marriages" are unrealistic because they place unreasonable demands on the two partners to be the sole source of gratification for each other.[40] The O'Neills suggest that the spouses should seek such gratifications outside the marital relationship, much as one might attempt to establish special friendships that meet particular needs. The result would be an *open marriage* — **one in which the partners are free to seek emotional, personal, and sexual gratification outside of the marriage relationship.**

Extramarital Sex

The pronounced experimental character of the O'Neills' alternative is brought forcefully home in the area of extramarital sexual activities. What kinds of potential problems are involved in seeking sexual fulfillment with an individual outside the usual marital relationship? On the one hand, the O'Neills ask whether any one individual can satisfy all of the intimate sexual and intrapersonal needs of another. On the other hand, we might respond, can any individual tolerate the emotional burdens (including jealousy, competition, and possessiveness)

that would seem inevitable in any attempt to maintain more than one intimate relationship at a time? Presently, these questions cannot be given a single answer that will be true of all (or even most) people. Some might be able to tolerate such relationships under certain conditions; others would not, or possibly could under different conditions.

The principles of sexual exclusivity and sexual possessiveness are deeply entrenched in the conception of marriage in American society — so much so, in fact, that much of the lay public regarded the O'Neills' book as intellectualized pornography and no more than a handbook on how to play "musical beds." Their proposal is unlikely to receive serious consideration as an alternative family form as long as such attitudes persist. The notion of one spouse "belonging" to the other and thus having an intimate relationship (including sexual exclusivity) with only that one person is persistent. The legal term for a married person's having sexual intercourse with someone other than his or her spouse is *adultery* — a relationship that is not only highly disapproved by most people in our society but that also has certain legal implications, including being grounds for divorce. In addition, it is forbidden by the major religions of the Western world. One of the Ten Commandments is "Thou shalt not commit adultery."

One has only to study the reaction to the Mormon experiment with *polygyny* to be impressed with the many ways that American society has responded to what are regarded as threats to monogamy. Moreover, one has only to review the resignations or dismissals of public officials who have been accused of committing adultery to appreciate the strength of public opinion in this regard. Seventy-three percent of adult men and women responding to a survey conducted in 1974 by the National Opinion Research Center stated that they regarded extramarital sex as "always" wrong. Despite this overwhelmingly negative opinion, it is generally conceded that large numbers of married men and women are engaging in extramarital sexual relations. Estimates concerning the proportion of marriages in which neither partner has at least one extramarital sexual episode place it at between 30 and 50 percent. Furthermore, while the rate of extramarital sexual activity among men does not seem to have increased, it has increased among women.[41] In addition, attitudes toward extramarital relations seem to be changing. For example, in 1976, Michigan politician Donald Reigle ran for the United States Senate and, despite confirmed allegations that he had had an extramarital affair while a member of the House of Representatives, he won the election.

Co-marital Sex

The term co-marital sex **has been employed to describe mate swapping, or other organized extramarital relations, in which both spouses agree to participate.**[42] Co-marital sex is distinctly different from a traditional extramarital affair, which is best characterized by its clandestine nature (i.e. one of the spouses is usually not aware of the other's extramarital relationship). Although the O'Neills' concept of open marriage need not involve the coordinated and organized activities of both parties that are found in co-marital sexual arrangements, these authors do emphasize that extramarital sexual activities should be acknowledged by both spouses in order for an "open marriage" to exist.

Are arrangements such as the O'Neills' open marriage and co-marital sexual activities viable alternatives to the family? Do they alleviate problems inherent in traditional marital relationships? Some research studies have suggested that such arrangements can create serious problems for the couples involved. For example, while some couples seem able to integrate co-marital agreements into their married lives successfully, others find their marriages disintegrating as a consequence.[43] Based on the reports of marriage counselors, one of the key reasons (reported in nearly 25 percent of the cases) why couples drop out of such co-marital relationships is jealousy.[44] Some marriages have been dissolved, presumably at least in part as a consequence of negative experiences. This does not imply, however, that there was a direct causal relationship between co-marital relationships and divorce. The couples who obtained divorces may have had unsatisfactory marriages prior to estab-

lishing co-marital agreements and may have discussed the possibilities of divorce long before their experimentation began. It seems clear that open marriage, with or without extramarital relationships, is at least a *perplexing* alternative within the contemporary marriage and family scene — a problem in large measure because it is an extreme divergence from traditional and persistent normative standards.

Single Parenthood/The One-Parent Family

In most people's minds, marriage and parenthood are seen as inevitably, and appropriately, going together. Yet, from their study of people's attitudes about children, family sociologists Letha Scanzoni and John Scanzoni conclude:

> Persons seem to fall into four categories when it comes to the matter of children. Traditionally, men and women have considered children as a major reward of marriage and thus have contemplated marriage with the "joys of parenthood" in mind. But in contrast to such couples, there are others who feel that the costs of children outnumber the rewards and thus remain voluntarily childless after marriage. A third category consists of single persons who have no desire for either marriage or children since they perceive the benefits of both to be outweighed by the disadvantages and costs. However, there is a fourth group . . . single persons who want children but who don't want marriage.[45]

There are a number of ways that one may become a **single parent.** First, it is possible in some states for unmarried people to adopt a child. This is somewhat revolutionary, since most people, including family and domestic-court judges, and many child psychologists and educators, cling to the belief that a child *needs* two parents — a mother and a father. Another way of becoming a single parent is for an unmarried, pregnant woman to refuse to marry and yet to keep her child after it is born. Traditionally, this has been a socially stigmatized state — the child is called a bastard or "love" child. Today, this negative stigma is not as strong as it once was, but it is still seriously frowned on by many.

Increased numbers of adults and children are living in single-parent families today. What are the implications of a "family" without a mother or a father?

A form of the family more common today than single-parenthood is the *one-parent family,* **in which a person divorces or legally separates and assumes custody of one or more children while choosing not to remarry.** While it has been traditionally the mother who was awarded custody of the children, today court officials (judges, referees, etc.) are more inclined to grant custody of children to the father. Moreover, according to recent investigations, men are more likely today to desire, and try to gain, custody of their children.[46]

Does the family without both parents pose a serious problem in American society? As in so many other issues, it is really premature to make a definitive judgment. It is clear, however, that such arrangements are becoming more commonplace. There are approximately 3.5 million one-parent families, with a total of about 7 million children.[47] With numbers of this order, we must assume that such family arrangements are now a part of the American scene. Although they violate traditional beliefs that a family should have two parents present, such one-parent families must be evaluated in the future in terms of their ability to perform those functions still important to the family.

Group Marriage

Of the new family forms that are emerging, one of the most unusual and controversial is *group marriage.* The characteristics of group marriage are often misunderstood or distorted. For example,

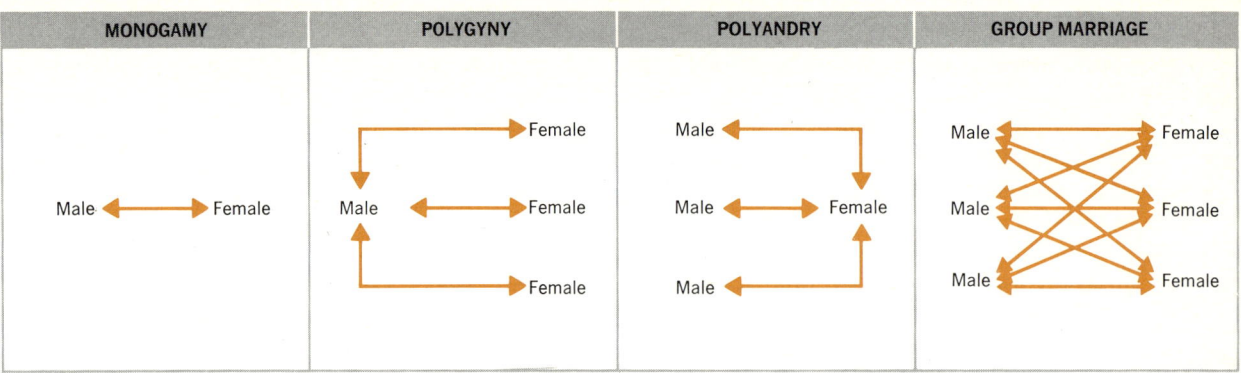

Figure 7.4 Relationships Involved in Different Forms of Marriage.

group marriages have often been confused with the cohabiting practices of some communes. However as we will see in the next section, communal groups emphasize cohabiting *pairs*. Members of a commune typically have economic sharing and brother-sister relationships in common, but not cohabitation. **In *group marriages*, on the other hand, the development of husband-wife-oriented ties between *all* adult members of the opposite sex is stressed.** The findings of recent research, although limited, suggest that group marriages are not usually practiced in contemporary communes. In addition, there is some evidence that people's attempts to incorporate the concept of group marriages into communal organizations have led to disorganization and disruption.[48]

James Ramey, of the Center for the Study of Innovative Life Styles, has concluded that **"Group marriage, which combines commitment to the group with multiple pair-bonding among the members of the group, is the most complex form of marriage."**[49] Group marriage is rare, not only in the United States, but all over the world. It is estimated that fewer than 1000 group marriages probably exist in our entire American society.[50]

Group marriage is extremely complex as well as rare. How it differs from other, better-known, deviations from monogamy is shown in Figure 7.4. *Polygamy* is a general term that describes a formal relationship involving one person with two or more spouses. Two variations of polygamy are *polygyny*, which refers to one husband with two or more wives, and *polyandry*, which describes a relationship involving one wife with two or more husbands. Group marriage is different from all of these, being a relationship in which two or more males are each married to the same two or more females. Each male is married to all the females in the group, and vice versa for females. Each individual loves all other members equally, and the group itself (rather than any particular individual in the group) is regarded as the center of their emotional and sexual involvement. The Constantines suggest the term *multilateral marriage* as more descriptive of these arrangements than the traditional term *group marriage*.[51]

Groups involved in multilateral marriage have many of the same problems that accompany extramarital relationships—sexual and emotional jealousies, possessiveness, anxieties about being wanted, and more. (Figure 7.4 illustrates how complex these entanglements can become, and the diagram is of a relatively small group—six people.) The fragility of such relationships is an obviously disturbing feature to highly dependent persons. According to the Constantine's research, the average lifespan of a group marriage is 6 to 12 months. On top of all these problems, this type of arrangement faces legal difficulties. At the present time, group marriage is not formally recognized by any state.

The Constantines have concluded that ". . . group marriage has the signal and unique advantage of providing for sexual variety for *both* men and women *within* a stable marital configuration."[52] At the same time, they have also predicted that only a very small minority of families will practice multilateral marriage in the foreseeable future. What, then, is the significance of this relatively infrequent variation for our consideration of social problems within marriage and family? **We can view such an unusual new family form as heralding the** *pluralistic* **nature of the family of the future. While the monolithic code said that there was only** *one* **proper form of marriage and family, pluralism implies that there is more than one acceptable model. Group marriage is one of the alternatives available.** Although it is chosen by few people, it may be an appropriate form of the family for people with particular needs or living in unusual circumstances.

Serial Polygamy

Monogamy, as practiced in American society today, is based on certain beliefs and has certain consequences that are important to consider in our analysis of the current marriage and family scene. As we have indicated, monogamy refers to a form of marriage where only one legal mate is permitted at any one time. However, it also carries with it the moral prescription (as set forth in the monolithic code) that the union is "till death do us part." Some writers in the marriage and family area have suggested that monogamy, as it is practiced today, is really a misnomer and most likely a myth.[53] Robert Francoeur, a physician who has written about the social implications of the family, has utilized the term *serial polygamy* as being more appropriate to describe modern marriage, since increasing numbers of people are married more than once in a lifetime, usually as a consequence of divorce.

There is considerable significance in Francoeur's suggestion for our study of the social problems related to marriage and family. One of the reasons that alternatives like group marriage appear to be so deviant and problematic is that we naturally assume monogamy to be the most acceptable form of marriage since it is presently the most widely practiced. However, when we realize that monogamy as practiced today by some is really serial polygamy, it makes us realize that we have to some extent moved away from the prescriptions of the monolithic code. For many people, the family as described in that code does not seem to perform the functions and provide the personal satisfactions that are important in the modern world. This makes us further consider the possibility that we should no longer use the monolithic code to judge the appropriateness of modern forms of the family. Thus, modern alternatives to the family—such as single parenthood or group marriage—must be viewed not in terms of the extent to which they are consistent with the monolithic code, but rather the extent to which they perform functions important in the modern world. While monogamy/serial polygamy will probably continue to be the choice of the majority at least in the near future, it may continue to be accompanied by a variety of alternatives as more and more people seek ways to cope with the struggle for intimacy.

Communes

In American society, some believe that the modern nuclear family is not the preferred institutional form and that a return to some type of extended family would be desirable. They lament the loss of many of the intimate kinship ties that appear to be a major consequence of our industrial and postindustrial society. **The** *commune* **is one kind of family arrangement that has some characteristics of the extended family. It is intentionally created and is usually designed to fulfill many functions that were once served by extended kinship networks in a preindustrial social order.**

A commune, a collective, a cooperative, an intentional community, and experimental community—each of these is an arrangement of three or more persons among whom the primary bond is some form of sharing rather than blood or legal ties. The degree of sharing is as varied as the arrangements made, ranging from perhaps simply owning land in common to holding all things in common.[54]

One of the confusing and depressing realities emerging from a postindustrial society is the sharp reduction in the number of intimate, personal relationships and the proliferation of impersonal relationships. In a preindustrial social order, an individual was generally a member of a closely knit kinship unit or "family clan." We have already noted that such folk societies were characterized by *familism:* a strong sense of closeness and a feeling of identity and belongingness among family members. In a communal setting, these feelings of togetherness are sought through the development of a common ideology rather than a common genealogy. In a sense, then, communes are in part rationally designed to meet some of the needs previously fulfilled by the kinship relations that have been hallmarks of extended families. However, one authority on communes, Benjamin Zablocki, has pointed out how communes can conflict with other aspects of American society:

It seems undeniable that community, which means bonds, obligations, and mutual interdependence, is fundamentally incompatible with individualism.[55]

Since individualism remains a predominant value in American society, communes (or any type of family) based on familistic bonds and values are always in danger of creating tensions between the individualistic tendencies and the familistic tendencies. In addition, the common ownership of property in communes contradicts the strongly held American value of private property.

Because they are viewed with suspicion in American society, communes face a multitude of personal, social, economic, and political problems. One of the principal difficulties is the reaction of other members of society, who often exhibit strong hostility toward members of the commune and reject the communal lifestyle. It is practically impossible for a relatively small group to live in a postindustrial society without depending on that society for many of the necessities of survival. Any attempt to maintain a completely independent way of life today would be futile. At the same time, the hostility of the larger society makes it difficult to develop and maintain ties, and the survival of the commune is often threatened.

There are numerous internal problems that communes must contend with, the most crucial of which is the establishment and maintenance of authority. Who has the legitimate right to make the decisions? How will differences of opinion within the commune be resolved? Today, many communards are attempting to incorporate pluralism rather than monism (that is, the monolithic code) into their communities and to establish democratic decision-making mechanisms. This may be a problem because group solidarity may fail to materialize without some degree of authoritarian leadership and ideology. Sociologist Rosabeth Moss Kanter has observed that during the nineteenth century successful communes possessed:

elaborate ideologies providing purpose and meaning for community life and an ultimate guide and justification for decisions. There tended to be strong central figures, charismatic figures, who symbolized the community's values and who made the final decisions for the community and set structural guidelines.[56]

In addition, communes face an array of other problems: ensuring survival, resolving sex role conflicts, allocating a workable division of labor, developing feasible plans for structuring sexual behavior, and resolving day-to-day interpersonal clashes.

Despite the problems, increasingly large numbers of people are attempting to adopt the communal lifestyle. In a recent series of newspaper articles, Associated Press writer Delores Barclay observed:

The commune, once the almost exclusive haven of the drug culture and social dropouts, is slowly re-emerging as a practical way of life for a wider cross-section of Americans. . . . There are plenty who see the commune as simply the only natural place for them to live.[57]

While the number of people who have chosen a communal family arrangement is relatively small, there has been, since 1960, a substantial increase in interest in communes among Americans.

Parenthood: New Possibilities

In our discussion of the monolithic code, we observed that traditionally a family is not considered complete unless children are present. Supporting this view of marriage and family is the related belief that women are not fulfilled until they have had children. This "maternal instinct" philosophy is reinforced by an elaborate system of formal—and to a greater extent informal—social pressures. Young married couples who do not have children are asked, "When are you two going to have a family?" It is interesting that people practically never ask, "Are you *planning* to have children?" The traditional assumption that married men and women without question want to be parents is still very prevalent.

There are still millions of pronatalists ("in favor of birth") in America; there are, however, also those who have taken a vocal stand that is frankly antinatalist. In *The Baby Trap,* Ellen Peck outlined the various social pressures that impinge on childless families.[58] Along with her husband, Ms. Peck founded a group called the National Organization of Non-Parents (NON). Among their mottos is "None is fun." The fact that increasing numbers of men and women are deciding not to have children does not imply that they are opposed to other couples becoming parents. Rather, people today seem to be examining their alternatives more closely. Instead of viewing childrearing as mandatory, more and more couples consider it as only one of the many options leading to a happy and successful marriage.

Parenthood involves *both* rewards and costs. Among the rewards are preservation of the family line and its traditions, the pleasures of playing with children, the joy of watching and helping another human being grow into adulthood, a sense of belongingness, and a sense of making sacrifices for someone else. Some of the costs include the financial responsibilities of feeding, clothing, educating, and protecting the health of children, increased potential conflicts between husband and wife over neglect of each other in deference to the demands of childrearing, and sacrifices of personal freedom. Contrary to what many believe, children do not necessarily bring spouses together. Despite these benefits and liabilities, the most important factor in a couple's decision concerning parenthood is the degree of choice. In preindustrial America, there was little deliberation—you simply had children because it was expected and appropriate. A woman who did not have children was often presumed to be incapable of doing so and was disparagingly referred to as "barren." Today this stigma is less likely to be attached to a woman who does not have children. Men and women now exercise their personal preferences to a far greater degree than they could before.

Alternative Family Forms and the Three Theoretical Perspectives

As we have seen, different social commentators have divergent views of alternatives to traditional family structure and the norms and values that accompany these "experimental lifestyles." Some observers are pessimistic and view emerging alternatives as a threat to family cohesiveness. A few of these critics even assert that the proliferation of nontraditional family forms may lead to the breakdown or demise of the institution itself. A substantial number of evaluations of alternative family forms are more optimistic, however. How might these alternatives be viewed from each of the theoretical perspectives?

According to the functionalist perspective, conditions in society that threaten social equilibrium may have undesirable consequences. **For the functionalist, experimental family forms or alternative lifestyles may upset the status quo and thus will be perceived as threats to traditional marriage and family practices.** For example, the open marriage philosophy does not censure sexual relationships outside of the marital unit, and this permissiveness must be analyzed in terms of whether it endangers a marriage and consequently places the family in jeopardy. As another example, the communal lifestyle is incompatible with certain aspects of American life, such as the nuclear family and the private ownership of property. For the functionalist, the key issue is whether this incompatibility is seriously disruptive to the operation of American society.

From the conflict perspective, no one form of the family will satisfy all the diverse and contradictory human needs. Alternative family forms may be beneficial to certain groups of people who cannot find gratification and fulfillment in traditional family arrangements. For example, an "open marriage" might generate conflict between particular husbands and wives, but this conflict might be beneficial in helping them establish a more successful marriage and consequent family situation. Indeed, it might also convince some couples that they could not find happiness with each other and that a divorce was the most reasonable alternative. For the conflict theorist, communes represent a different kind of family setting that may be more satisfying for some people than the more familiar family arrangements in our society.

Proponents of the interactionist perspective emphasize the importance of the relationship between self-concept and behavior. Many people may not be prepared to cope with the demands and changes in their self-concepts that result from exposure to alternative forms of marriage and family life. **For the interactionist, whether people find success and fulfillment in an alternative family form will depend on their individual relationships with others in society.** For example, this perspective can help us to understand how a person with a particular type of self-concept might find an "open marriage" to be less satisfying than would someone who had a quite different self-concept. A person who has been encouraged throughout life to share everything he or she has rather than having a feeling of owning things exclusively might be expected to find the communal lifestyle more acceptable and satisfying.

THE FAMILY IN SEARCH OF A FUTURE

We have discussed a number of changes that have occurred in the American family and analyzed some alternative forms of the family that exist today. Yet, what can we expect in the future? What will the family be like? Some sociologists believe that the family is moving toward disorganization and gradual deterioration. Carle Zimmerman, a *cyclical* theorist, expressed early pessimism about the future of the family.[59] According to *cyclical theory,* change occurs in large historical cycles and proceeds in a deterministic pattern. Social change occurs in blind fashion unless people come to understand its nature and take steps to control it. If people do not take control, argue cyclical theorists such as Zimmerman, change will occur nonetheless, but without the benefit of human guidance. After studying Western history from about 1500 B.C. to modern times, Zimmerman concluded that there is a very close relationship between the characteristics of family organization and the state of society in general. Zimmerman concluded that the family in an industrial society is *atomistic,* with an extreme emphasis on *individualism* (evidenced by feminist movements, childlessness, youth problems, etc.) and a deemphasis of *familism* (in which the family, as a unit, comes first). He called for a swing back to a *domestic family,* where interrelations within the family are so strong that they prevent the problems arising from individualism.

The most frequent criticism of Zimmerman's theory is that it cannot be adequately documented; we have never been able to demonstrate that history will repeat itself. Nevertheless, it is also obvious that Zimmerman cannot be proved wrong in his conclusions, at least at this point. **Today, most sociologists are not speculating whether the family will endure** *as an institution* **but rather whether it will survive** *in its present form.*

The Ideal and the Real

The well-known family sociologist John Cuber has suggested that a distinction should be made between the de jure and the de facto realms in relation to marriage and family institutions.[60] The *de jure* realm refers to the "thou shalts," the oughts, and the traditionally accepted appropriate behaviors. The *de facto* realm relates to what actually takes place and involves thinking and conduct that is frequently at odds with the de jure. Cuber concluded that today there is a considerable gap between the de jure and de facto conceptions and that as more and more of the de jure prescriptions for behavior become outmoded, many of the de facto arrangements will become acceptable. For example, the de jure conception of divorce is that it is undesirable and should be avoided (some would say at all costs). We know de facto, however, that more and more people are getting divorced. It seems probable that divorce, like so many other practices that are currently regarded as social problems, may be looked on as acceptable in the future.

Given the probability that people will continue to experiment with alternative lifestyles, it may be beneficial to adopt a more flexible stance toward family forms. There seems to be little doubt that the family can be different things to different people in a postindustrial society. Perhaps we should try to anticipate and be prepared for such social changes and the problems that they may occasion. In fact, we might influence the outcome of social change in order to avoid some of the problems.

The Pluralistic Family

While some people have predicted the death of the family, such predictions have little credibility among most sociologists. Family systems all over the world still serve several important functions and will undoubtedly continue to do so in the future. No society of record has had a family system that did not deal with such universal problems as mate selection, nurturance of the young, and formalized patterns of parenthood. Certainly, as Ogburn observed in the late 1930s, there have been a variety of changes in the manner in which many societal functions are met by the family in the United States, but not all functions have been eliminated. A British journalist with keen sociological insight, F. George Kay, has remarked:

> The human regard for the family is so fundamental that it has always evolved to meet the needs of its members. The family has never been rejected; it has merely changed in form.[61]

If the family is not dying, then, does it have a future? The answer is most assuredly *yes*. However, what may be emerging is a *pluralistic form of the family* in which a number of different types of family—from the extended family to group marriages—will exist side by side, each having an attraction for some segment of our populace. While the nuclear family will continue in something like its present form, one student of marriage and family in American society paints the following picture of what we might expect:

> What will the average American family be like by the turn of the century? It's not likely to consist of a working husband, a housewife, and their dependent children. Already this description of the traditional nuclear family accounts for only 37 percent of the people in this country. . . . The rest are divided among dual-career marriages, childless marriages, single-parent families, the once-married, the never-married, the group-married, the living-together, the homosexually paired, and other types of family units.
>
> We might also ask whether, despite a changing format, the family unit of the future will be bound together by traditional family values—loyalty, duty, self-sacrifice, sharing, lasting love. Already some observers worry that growing cultural emphasis on self-actualization, individual autonomy, and mobility is weakening family bonds and may eventually override them. However, this projection may be unnecessarily gloomy. Many of the changes we are seeing in family life have potential for enhancing the warmth, understanding, and supportiveness among members. By the year 2000, emotional ties within families may actually be stronger than they are now.[62]

This sentiment concerning the bright future of the institution of the family is echoed by many of the scholars who have studied the more radical and innovative forms of the family that have appeared on the scene. For example, the Constantines have concluded:

> We do not forecast the demise of the family, not even the passing of the family as most of us have known it. Far into the distant future we expect to see some families which even traditionalist would label traditional. Lifetime partnerships will become much less common, but even conventional sexually exclusive relationships will appeal to a sizeable minority. That will be possible through cultural pluralism. For people whose fulfillment lies in nontraditional settings, there will be an ever-growing system of family models.[63]

The family is alive, and well, and growing. It is a good bet that, for some, the family will change in the way it is structured. In many cases it will probably bear little resemblance to the traditional family of preindustrial times. It seems clear that we cannot return to the family of yesterday as the predominant family form. At the same time, it is most difficult, or even impossible with present knowledge, to envision a social order without some kind of family. It is, of course, impossible to describe the precise structures and functions that families will have in the future. To a great extent this will depend on the purposes served by the family and on future social conditions.

In attempting to see what the family of the future will be like, some point out that, in a sense, "the future is here today." It may be helpful to think about this for a moment. Imagine an alternative to the conventional family arrangement that has not already been tried or at least discussed by some group. We are approaching a time when it seems that every conceivable option has been experimented with. For example, sociologist Ira Reiss has stated:

> I believe Americans have opened up the range of possibilities but are not entering into an era wherein the rate of change will likely slow down, and we shall come to rank these alternative family forms and learn to choose life styles for ourselves. Most cultures have forced people to fit into a Procrustean bed and cut or stretched those who did not conform.

> We are in an era of unprecedented choice—a human experiment not tried by many societies in the entire history of mankind. All of us, young and old, traditional and nontraditional, are on the same voyage.[64]

Marriage

As for the future of marriage, its popularity will almost unquestionably endure. Men and women may wait longer to marry for the first time than in the past, but most will eventually marry. It appears likely that the number of couples that choose to form consensual unions will continue to increase as well. Although cohabitation is not legally recognized in most states, there are instances where courts have ruled that cohabiting couples who decided to dissolve their nonmarital living arrangements have certain legal obligations to one another quite similar to the obligations of a married couple. For example, in 1979 a California court judge ruled that Actor Lee Marvin must give $104,000 to a woman he cohabited with for six years.

Although organized swinging and multilateral marriage may persist in the future, these alternative lifestyles will probably be in the minority. At the same time, open marriage arrangements and homosexual marriages have gained limited acceptability among some groups in our society.

Family Forms

In terms of the family, there are some characteristics that appear to be fairly predictable. Most families will have fewer children than traditionally, and the responsibility for childrearing will rest less exclusively with the natural parents, especially the mother. In addition, there will be more single-parent families, including a higher incidence of never-married men and women who adopt children.

More family forms will probably continue to evolve in our society, but monogamy will be the norm. Some have argued that monogamy is outdated because it does not fit today's emphasis on individualism.[65] For example, it is already evident that today more people marry more than once during their lifetime (serial polygamy). Nevertheless, there are few people who are married to more than one person at any given time, and it is unlikely that our society will tolerate such polygamy.

Thus, the family of the future will be different from what has been traditional. In this regard, social scientist Leontine Young has commented:

> Whatever structure the family evolves into, it must, if it is to survive, answer certain basic human needs. It must protect the young and civilize them—a very complicated process. It is a personal, not a group process, and so long as human beings learn by identification, children will require close continuing contact with parents or parent substitutes. The family must provide personal security and refuge to its members, including its growing body of older people. It is the family that has taught loyalty, discipline, responsibility, and obligation, qualities that can be carried from the family to the larger society. They are all qualities essential in democracy; they are also qualities essential for a complete personality.[66]

The Search for Intimacy

Many social scientists have remarked that the family, in its pluralistic forms, is the last defense for the individual in postindustrial society. In such a society, some people are alienated because they feel that life is meaningless, that they have little control over events, that they are isolated from others and estranged from themselves.[67] The social world with which an increasing number of Americans must cope is empty, impersonal, dehumanized, and sometimes highly destructive. Today, an individual may feel that he is fighting a losing battle against forces and pressures of a mass society. The family can serve as the main resource that protects us from these alienating forces.

Impersonal relationships continue to proliferate in our modern society at the expense of intimate ones. Many of the personal relationships that were commonplace before the Industrial Revolution no longer exist. The family—in its many forms—still serves as a central locus for intimate interactions.

Increasingly we must turn to our own family (or some surrogate) for shelter from the depersonalization with which many must cope. The family can serve—and probably will continue to serve—as a very private setting where a feeling of belonging can survive and, one hopes, flourish.

CONCLUSION

On the basis of our examination of the family as a social problem, we have concluded that this institution does, indeed, have a future. There does not appear to be any convincing evidence that the family is dying or that it is destined to disappear. At the same time, recall what we said at the beginning of this chapter about *the* family as a myth—it is unreasonable to expect that one form of family can meet the complex and multifaceted needs of men and women in our modern, postindustrial society. Although some of the residuals of the monolithic code are still with us today, the family is increasingly a pluralistic institution that offers many alternatives to the traditional extended or nuclear family.

The functionalist perspective is helpful to us in understanding the changes in the family. As perplexing as some contemporary forms of family may be, the traditional extended family in preindustrial society simply does not fit the demands of our highly technological and industrialized society of the 1980s. Despite our tendencies to romanticize the past and to think that we would be better off if we could return to the seemingly more stable and rewarding family cohesiveness of a century ago, that kind of arrangement would not be functional today. Remember that many of the functions that the family used to perform have been taken over by other institutions in our society today. This does not, however, mean that the family is less functional now—only that it serves different functions in a postindustrial society than in a preindustrial one. From the functionalist perspective, the nature of social organization is determined by the demands of that organization at any given time. Today's social order is extremely heterogeneous and far more complex than in the past. In order for the institution of family to be functional, it must respond to this heterogeneity and complexity.

According to the conflict perspective, when certain desirable resources are in short supply, people will struggle for what they regard as their fair share of them. In addition, conflict theorists look on change as a normal state of affairs in society and consider that social change can even have positive consequences. As a result of the drastic alterations in our economic organization in American society, there have been equally dramatic shifts in our family structure. The family has been forced to reorganize in order to accommodate these other social changes. In the wake of this reorganization, considerable conflict has ensued, reflected in disquieting realities such as the rising divorce rate, the appearance of nontraditional lifestyles and alternative living arrangements, breakdowns in parent-child communication, and so on.

In our society today, alienation abounds, with men, women, and children being subjected to more social pressures to behave in particular ways than at any other time in our history. Although the "face" of the family has changed considerably over the past 100 years, the institution still acts as a huge emotional buffer for people's problems and concerns. From the conflict perspective, it is inevitable that the family will be viewed as a social problem under these conditions. At the same time, we can use conflict theory to advantage in understanding that while the family is in transition, it almost assuredly has a future because it is such a fundamental building-block in social organization. On the other hand, we can see that because of the ensuing conflict, the appearance of family may continue to change—even perhaps to the point where it could be unrecognizable to those of us living today.

As we observed early in this chapter, there are tremendous differences between what people say and what they do in actual practice. We also learned that the circumstances surrounding human behavior are crucial to our understanding of that behavior. From the interactionist perspective, people's individual definitions of the situation are very important in interpreting human activities. In addition, we can see that the family represents a complex network of interacting personalities. Whenever we confront such a network, there will be difficulties in terms of people communicating effectively with each other. Compounding these difficulties are the complexities elsewhere in society—in other social institutions. Men and women, and even young people, are being placed in situations where they are forced to play different roles—sometimes simultaneously. These circumstances make the already complex nature of human interaction even more complicated. Under these conditions, it is easier to understand the problems that confront the family in today's society.

GLOSSARY TERMS

Adultery
Atomistic family
Cohabitation
Co-marital sex
Commune
Consensual union
Cultural lag
Cyclical theory
Domestic family
Extended family

Familism
Group marriage
Individualism
Monolithic code
Multilateral marriage
Nuclear family
One-parent family
Open marriage
Pairism
Polyandry

Polygamy
Polygyny
Postindustrial society
Reorganization approach
Serial polygamy
Single-parent family
Social disorganization
   approach

REFERENCES

[1] See Carle C. Zimmerman, *Family and Civilization* (New York: Harper & Row, 1947), and David Cooper, *The Death of the Family* (New York: Pantheon Books, 1970).

[2] Zimmerman, *Family and Civilization.*

[3] A. J. Norton and P. C. Glick, "Marital Instability: Past, Present, and Future," *Journal of Social Issues* 32, pp. 5–20.

[4] U.S. Bureau of the Census, *Statistical Abstract of the United States: 1977* (Washington, D.C.: U.S. Government Printing Office, 1977), pp. 38, 40.

[5] Ellen Peck, *The Baby Trap* (New York: Bernard Geis, 1971).

[6] U.S. Bureau of the Census, *Current Population Reports,* Series P-20, no. 323 (April 1978), p. 26.

[7] See Arlene Skolnick, *The Intimate Environment: Exploring Marriage and the Family* (Boston: Little, Brown, 1978), pp. 90–116.

[8] John F. Cuber, Martha Tyler John, and Kenrick S. Thompson, "Should Traditional Sex Modes and Values Be Changed?" in Raymond H. Muessig, ed., *Controversial Issues in the Social Studies: A Contemporary Perspective* (Washington, D.C.: National Council for the Social Studies, 1975), pp. 87–121.

[9] Skolnick, *The Intimate Environment,* pp. 107–135.

[10] See William F. Ogburn, "The Changing Family," *The Family* 19 (July 1938), pp. 139–143.

[11] Ibid., pp. 139–143.

[12] Alvin Toffler, *Future Shock* (New York: Random House, 1970), pp. 238, 241.

[13] See Skolnick, *The Intimate Environment,* pp. 64–71.

[14] Talcott Parsons, "The American Family: Its Relations to Personality and to Social Structure," in Talcott Parsons and Robert F. Bales, eds., *Family, Socialization and Interaction Process* (Glencoe, Ill.: The Free Press, 1955), pp. 3–21.

[15] See Skolnick, *The Intimate Environment,* pp. 67–68.

[16] Randall Collins, "A Conflict Theory of Sexual Stratification," *Social Problems* 19 (Summer 1971), pp. 3–21.

[17] Clark Vincent, "Familia Spongia: The Adaptive Function," *Journal of Marriage and the Family* 28 (February 1966), pp. 29–36.

[18] John F. Cuber and Peggy B. Harroff, *Sex and the Significant Americans* (Baltimore: Penguin Books, 1965), pp. 19–42.

[19] William F. Ogburn, *Social Change With Respect to Culture and Original Nature* (New York: Viking Press, 1927).

[20] See Cooper, *The Death of the Family.*

[21] Bernard Farber, *Family: Organization and Interaction* (San Francisco: Chandler, 1964).

[22] Mervyn Cadwallader, "Marriage as a Wretched Institution," in J. Gipson Wells, ed., *Current Issues in Marriage and Family* (New York: Macmillan, 1975), p. 27.

[23] Ibid., p. 31.

[24] See Frances E. Kobrin, "The Primary Individual and the Family: Changes in Living Arrangements in the United States Since 1940," *Journal of Marriage and the Family* 38 (May 1976), pp. 233–239, and U.S. Bureau of the Census, *Current Population Reports,* Series P-20, no. 323 (April 1978), p. 6.

[25] Elmer Spreitzer and Lawrence E. Riley, "Factors Associated with Singlehood." *Journal of Marriage and the Family* 36 (August 1974), pp. 533–542.

[26] Caroline Bird, "Women Should Stay Single," in J. Gipson Wells, *Current Issues in Marriage and the Family,* pp. 39–40.

[27] Skolnick, *The Intimate Environment,* p. 374.

[28] See Eleanor D. Macklin, "Heterosexual Cohabitation among Unmarried College Students," *The Family Coordinator* 21 (October 1972), pp. 463–472, and Dan J. Peterman, Carl A. Ridley, and Scott M. Anderson, "A Comparison of Cohabiting and Noncohabiting College Students," *Journal of Marriage and the Family* 36 (May 1974), pp. 344–355.

[29] Judith L. Lyness, Milton E. Lipetz, and Keith E. Davis, "Living Together: An Alternative to Marriage," *Journal of Marriage and the Family* 34 (May 1972), pp. 305–311.

[30] Macklin, "Heterosexual Cohabitation Among Unmarried College Students," pp. 463–472.

[31] Ibid.

[32] Cathrina Bauby, *Between Consenting Adults: Dialogue For Intimate Living* (New York: Macmillan, 1973).

[33] See Charles F. Westoff, "The Modernization of U.S. Contraceptive Practice," *Family Planning Perspectives* 4 (July 1972), pp. 9–12, and "Surgery on Rise in Birth Control," *The Detroit Free Press* (August 23, 1978), p. 1b.

[34] Paul C. Glick, "Some Recent Changes in American Families," *Current Population Reports: Special Studies,* Series P-23, no. 52 (Washington, D.C.: U.S. Government Printing Office, 1975).

[35] U.S. Bureau of the Census, *Current Population Reports,* "Marriage, Divorce, Widowhood, and Remarriage by Family Characteristics, June, 1975," Series P-20, no. 312 (August 1977), p. 8.

[36] See Lee G. Burchinal, "Characteristics of Adolescents from Unbroken. Broken, and Reconstituted Families," *Journal of Marriage and the Family* 26 (February 1964), pp. 44–51; Judson T. Landis, "A Comparison of Children from Divorced and Nondivorced Unhappy Marriages," *Family Life Coordinator* 11 (July 1962), pp. 61–65; and Ivan F. Nye, "Child Adjustment in Broken and in Unhappy Unbroken Homes," *Marriage and Family Living* 19 (1957), pp. 356–361.

[37] Kenrick S. Thompson, "The Divorce Profile: Differential Social Correlates in 1952 and in 1972," *International*

Journal of Sociology of the Family 6 (Autumn 1976), pp. 253–263.

[38] Ibid.

[39] Ibid.

[40] Nena O'Neill and George O'Neill, *Open Marriage: A New Life Style for Couples* (New York: Evans, 1972).

[41] Skolnick, *The Intimate Environment,* p. 377.

[42] James Smith and Lynn Smith, "Co-marital Sex: The Incorporation of Extramarital Sex into the Marriage Relationship," in J. Smith and L. Smith, eds., *Beyond Monogamy* (Baltimore: Johns Hopkins University Press, 1974), pp. 84–102.

[43] See Brian Gilmartin and D. V. Kusisto, "Some Personal and Social Characteristics of Mate-Sharing Swingers," in R. Libby and R. Whitehurst, eds., *Renovating Marriage* (San Francisco: Consensus Publishers, 1973), pp. 146–166, and Brian Gilmartin, "Sexual Deviance and Social Networks," in Smith and Smith, eds., *Beyond Monogamy,* pp. 291–323.

[44] Duane Denfeld, "Dropouts From Swinging," *The Family Coordinator* 23 (January 1974), pp. 45–49.

[45] Letha Scanzoni and John Scanzoni, *Men, Women, and Change: A Sociology of Marriage and Family* (New York: McGraw-Hill, 1976), p. 157.

[46] Thompson, "The Divorce Profile," pp. 253–263.

[47] U.S. Bureau of the Census, *Current Population Reports,* Series P-20, no. 323 (April 1978), p. 26.

[48] See Larry Constantine and Joan Constantine, *Group Marriage: A Study of Contemporary Multilateral Marriage* (New York: Macmillan, 1973), and Albert Ellis, "Group Marriage: A Possible Alternative?" in Herbert Otto, ed., *The Family in Search of a Future* (New York: Appleton-Century-Crofts, 1970), pp. 85–97.

[49] James Ramey, "Emerging Patterns of Innovative Behavior in Marriage," *The Family Coordinator* 21 (October 1972), p. 440.

[50] Constantine and Constantine, *Group Marriage,* p. 32.

[51] Ibid.

[52] Ibid., p. 13.

[53] See Ibid., and Robert T. Francoeur, *Eve's New Rib: Twenty Faces of Sex, Marriage, and Family* (New York: Harcourt, Brace, Jovanovich, 1972).

[54] Richard Fairfield, *Communes U.S.A.: A Personal Tour* (Baltimore: Penguin Books, 1972), p. 1.

[55] Benjamin Zablocki, *The Joyful Community* (Baltimore: Penguin Books, 1971), p. 288.

[56] Rosabeth Moss Kanter, *Commitment and Community* (Cambridge, Mass.: Harvard University Press, 1972), p. 314.

[57] Delores Barclay, *News Series on Communes* (Associated Press, 1976).

[58] Peck, *The Baby Trap.*

[59] Zimmerman, *Family and Civilization.*

[60] John F. Cuber, "Alternate Models From the Perspective of Sociology," in Otto, *The Family in Search of a Future,* pp. 11–23.

[61] F. George Kay, *The Family in Transition: Its Past, Present, and Future Patterns* (Newton Abbot, England: David and Charles Publishers, 1972), pp. 7–8.

[62] Gilbert D. Nass, *Marriage and the Family* (Reading, Mass.: Addison-Wesley, 1978), p. 516.

[63] Constantine and Constantine, *Group Marriage,* p. 235.

[64] Ira L. Reiss, *Family Systems in America,* 2d ed. (Hinsdale, Ill.: Dryden Press, 1976), pp. 439–440.

[65] Rustum Roy and Della Roy, "Is Monogamy Outdated?" *Humanist* (March/April 1970), pp. 9–26.

[66] Leontine Young, *The Fractured Family* (New York: McGraw-Hill, 1973), p. 150.

[67] Robert Blauner, *Alienation and Freedom* (Chicago: The University of Chicago Press, 1964).

SUGGESTED READINGS

Bane, Mary Jo. *Here to Stay.* New York: Harper & Row, 1976.
An optimistic forecast concerning American families today.

Bernard, Jessie. *The Future of Marriage.* New York: Bantam Books, 1973.
An experienced sociologist's examination of the institution of marriage.

Cooper, David G. *The Death of the Family.* New York: Vintage Books, 1970.
A pessimistic statement by a philosopher on the future of the family.

Epstein, Joseph. *Divorced in America.* New York: Penguin Books, 1974.
A look at divorce by a writer with first-hand experience of this subject.

Hunt, Morton. *Sexual Behavior in the 1970s.* Chicago: Playboy Press, 1974.
A social scientist examines changes in attitudes concerning human sexuality from a layperson's point of view based on actual data from a national sample.

Libby, Roger W., and Whitehurst, Robert N., eds. *Marriage and Alternatives: Exploring Intimate Relationships.* Glenview, Ill.: Scott, Foresman, 1977.
A collection of articles on marriage and family today, with an emphasis on change and alternative lifestyles.

Otto, Herbert A., ed. *The Family in Search of a Future.* New York: Appleton-Century-Crofts, 1970.
A collection of articles on the changing nature of the American family, including an in-depth look at alternative family forms.

Toffler, Alvin. *Future Shock.* New York: Random House, 1970.
A journalist examines the implications of social change in America and how too much of it too quickly can affect the members of society.

Zablocki, Benjamin. "Communes in Retrospect—A Search for Family Ties." *American Psychological Association Monitor* 8:6, 1977, p. 9.
An up-to-date look at communal living written by a well-known sociological investigator of this topic.

Questions for Discussion

1. Discuss the history of the American family. Trace the changes in this institution that may be attributable to the Industrial Revolution. How do forms of family differ in preindustrial and industrial society?

2. Consider how a functionalist, a conflict theorist, and an interactionist would view the family as a social problem. What are the advantages of each perspective in better understanding the changes in the family since the Industrial Revolution?

3. What is the monolithic code? What are its precepts? How would representatives of the theoretical perspectives view the code? Discuss the significance of preachment, practice, and pretense for family as a social problem in contemporary society. Discuss the differences in behavior related to these terms and in conjunction with the code.

4. Discuss how the functions of family have changed over the past century. Do you find yourself aligning with the disorganization or reorganization viewpoint on family? Why?

5. Today, there are many alternatives to traditional family organization. Select two or three of them and discuss their contemporary significance. How did they emerge? How are they viewed today? What is their probable future?

6. Divorce is a very well known topic today. Why are there more divorces in today's society than in the past? Utilize the theoretical perspectives to examine marital dissolution. Can divorce be functional in modern society? Why or why not?

7. How will the position and attitudes of children in families in the year 2000 probably differ from those of children today? What are the likely trends in terms of parenthood, childrearing, or having children at all?

8. Discuss what the future of family might be. Does the family *have* a future or is it dying? Examine both positive and negative forecasts. Do you think that the ingredients that make family a social problem today will disappear, intensify, or remain the same? What might happen in each case?

CHAPTER 8

Health Care

HEALTH CARE IN AMERICA: A HISTORICAL
OVERVIEW

Early American Medicine. Emergence of Modern
Medicine. The Modern Scourge: Chronic Disease. The
State of Health in America.

HEALTH CARE AS A SOCIAL PROBLEM

The Functionalist Perspective. The Conflict Perspective.
The Interactionist Perspective.

SOCIAL FACTORS IN HEALTH AND ILLNESS

Social Class. Sex Roles. Occupational Status. Education.

MENTAL ILLNESS

The Nature of Mental Illness. The Treatment of Mental
Illness.

PROBLEMS IN THE HEALTH CARE DELIVERY
SYSTEM

Bureaucracy and Dehumanization. The High Cost of
Health Care.

FUTURE PROSPECTS: THE POLITICS OF HEALTH
CARE

New Programs and Health Practitioners. The Financing of
Health Care. Interest Groups in the Health Field.

CONCLUSION

In the 1950s, a commonly prescribed drug to prevent miscarriages was diethylstilbestrol, or DES. We have now learned through tragic experience that DES taken during pregnancy can cause vaginal cancer in the female offspring of the person taking the drug. Cancer of the uterus has increased dramatically in the 1970s, probably because of the use of estrogen to reduce the symptoms of menopause. Every year disease causes a tremendous financial drain and brings about incalculable human suffering for millions of Americans. In one recent year, over 26 million people suffered from heart and circulatory diseases and an additional 16 million from arthritis and rheumatic diseases. For every 1000 children born in the United States during 1978, 14 died before reaching the age of 1 year. Among nonwhites, 20 per thousand die at this young age. There are more Americans in mental hospitals and residential treatment centers than in all of our prisons, and, if present trends persist, this will be the case at least until 1985.[1]

These figures, as disturbing as they may be, are only a sampling of those that might have been chosen to illustrate the state of American health today. We face the paradoxical situation of being healthier than ever yet at the same time being more concerned about the extent of illness and suffering. There are a number of reasons for this. First, as we have become more affluent and technologically advanced, we have come to view *any* illness as undesirable and abnormal. Perfect health is viewed as the normal state of affairs. Illnesses that were once accepted as an inevitable accompaniment of life are now seen as conditions that can be avoided through proper health practices or alleviated by modern medical techniques.

A second reason for the paradox is that, while modern science has made considerable advances in providing the means of treating disease, the medical treatment process itself is sometimes harmful. For example, we now have a vast array of drugs—from aspirin to powerful chemicals for treating cancer—that are effective in treating human disease. However, our understanding of the complex effects of these drugs lags far behind our ability to produce vast quantities and types of these pharmaceutical remedies. As a consequence, they often have undesirable side effects that are not detected until the drugs have been widely used for several years. For these and other reasons, the illusory goal of a "healthy" population seems to recede further into the distance each time we try to approach it.

In this chapter we will investigate a variety of problems in the delivery of health care in the United States. What is the extent of both physical and mental illness in the United States, and which groups are especially prone to illness? What is the nature of mental illness? Are there some characteristics of health care organizations in the United States that create health problems? Why is health care increasing in cost in the United States? Such concerns are not new, although the form they take today is somewhat different from what it has been in the past. In order to understand the dimensions of problems in health care today, it is useful to understand how current conditions have emerged over the past few centuries.

HEALTH CARE IN AMERICA: A HISTORICAL OVERVIEW

Early American Medicine

Prior to the twentieth century, medicine was rather ineffective in the treatment of illness. All societies, even the most primitive, have some effective medical treatment, but until recently there was little accurate knowledge concerning the cause and treatment of most physical and mental illness.[2] While early American medical practitioners had largely rejected the religious explanations of disease that most primitive societies accept, the theories of disease that these early practitioners promoted were often inaccurate and in some cases harmful. A few illustrations should make clear the state of medicine in early America.

One group of physicians that rose to prominence during the late eighteenth and early nineteenth centuries were called *allopathic physicians*.[3] While allopathic physicians did not always agree among themselves concerning the causes of diseases, their treatments tended to be dramatic and often invasive. They placed great reliance on treatments such as cupping (drawing the patient's blood to a local area of the body so that it could be drained), blistering (in the belief that the pus forming around the resultant burns indicated that the disease was being drawn out of the patient), purging (inducing vomiting or bowel evacuation), and sweating. These physicians also prescribed large doses of drugs in their treatments. Most of these treatments were based on fallacious theories of disease. For example, Benjamin Rush, a famous physician during and after the American Revolution, felt that all disease, both physical and mental, was the result of excessive action and convulsive excitement in the walls of the blood vessels.[4] His treatment was to prevent or reduce this excited condition through bleeding and purging the patient. Furthermore, these treatments often did more harm than good. Patients who might have survived if left alone sometimes died from the abusive effects of the treatment.

Because such treatment by allopathic physicians was often unpleasant and largely ineffective, many alternative forms of medicine thrived during this period.[5] An approach called *Thomsonianism* (named after an itinerant herbal practitioner, Samuel Thomson) gained considerable popularity. According to this theory, disease had only one cause, cold, and only one cure, heat. Heat was applied to the body through both steambaths and certain "hot" botanical remedies, such as cayenne pepper. Another popular medical practice of this period was *Homeopathy*. This approach was originally developed by a German physician named Samuel Christian Hahnemann, who had become disillusioned with what he felt was abusive treatment and the excessive prescription of drugs for diseases (a problem that we tend to think of as modern in origin). Hahnemann developed two basic principles. First, like treats like. Thus, a fever is to be treated with a drug that also induces fever in the patient. Second, he felt that extremely small doses of a drug were effective in treating illness. Since his patients were given almost infinitesimal doses of drugs, their recovery was, for all practical purposes, left to nature. This remedy was often superior to the bleeding and purging treatments of the

allopathic physicians because, while the homeopaths' small doses may have done little good, they also did little harm.

These various forms of medical practice flourished because medical knowledge was in a rather primitive state. There was no consensus about what caused disease, and physicians were largely unaware how disease was transmitted from one person to another. As a consequence, access to physicians (of whatever variety) did not substantially increase one's likelihood of recovery because the treatments (such as bleeding and purging) often did more harm than good. Medical sociologist Rodney Coe points out the extent of such ignorance: "Physicians and surgeons generally ignored even the most rudimentary rules of sanitation when treating patients despite Semmelweis' discovery around 1847 that the medical staff was the cause of infecting newly delivered mothers with puerperal fever."[6] In other words, a physician with a germ-infested coat might have been more dangerous than no treatment at all!

Emergence of Modern Medicine

This rather bleak situation began to change dramatically during the nineteenth century because of a number of important events. Coe summarizes some of these developments:

> Biology moved from an organismic to a cellular level, and physiological and bacterial processes were being studied at that level. Eventually, the germ theory of disease was formulated, leading to the dominance of a unitary etiology and a search for specific disease agents. Surgery as a therapeutic technique made great strides following the development of anesthesia and asepsis.[7]

These changes, along with various technological developments, made it possible for medicine to treat illness and injury with greater success. Furthermore, the American Medical Association emerged in the middle of the nineteenth century as an important political force, with one of its goals being to develop legally enforced licensing procedures that would eliminate untrained practitioners of medicine. Because of the AMA's increasing effectiveness and its ability to pass legislation outlaw-

Leading Causes of Death in the United States,
1900 and 1978

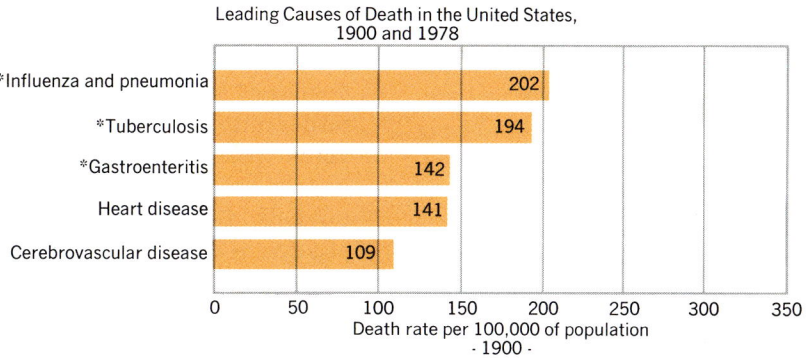

Death rate per 100,000 of population
- 1900 -

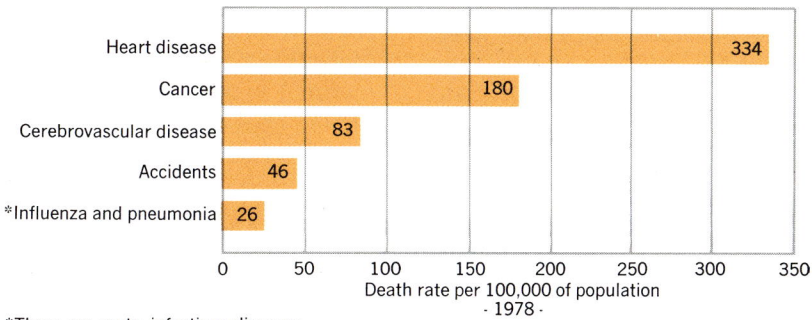

Death rate per 100,000 of population
- 1978 -

*These are acute, infectious diseases.

Figure 8.1 Leading Causes of Death in the U.S., 1900 and 1978. U.S. Bureau of the Census, *Vital Statistics Rates in the United States, 1900–1940* (Washington, D.C.: U.S. Government Printing Office, 1943), pp. 210–215, and National Center for Health Statistics, *Monthly Vital Statistics Report: Provisional Statistics* (June 16, 1978), p. 9.

ing other types of medical treatment, physicians began to emerge as the single group in society with legitimate authority to diagnose and treat illnesses.

These developments have resulted in dramatic changes in *morbidity* (rates of illness) and *mortality* (rates of death) among Americans over the past hundred years. A century ago, *acute,* infectious *diseases* (such as influenza, pneumonia, tuberculosis, etc.) were the most serious health problems and were the cause of most deaths (see Figure 8.1). Doctors did not have the medical knowledge to prevent these diseases effectively or to cure those who became ill from them.

In the past seventy years, however, substantial improvements in a number of areas have resulted

in the control of many of these diseases. For example, advances in the average American's standard of living have provided more people with the resources to live a healthy life and to avoid serious disease. More people can afford a balanced and nutritious diet; medical care is financially within the reach of most people, and modern education offers medical knowledge concerning disease prevention. During this period, very important medical advances have occurred. With improvements in physiology and bacteriology, medical science developed vaccines with which to combat disease. For example, the discovery of sulfa drugs in 1932 was an important step in the fight against infectious disease. Important developments were also occurring

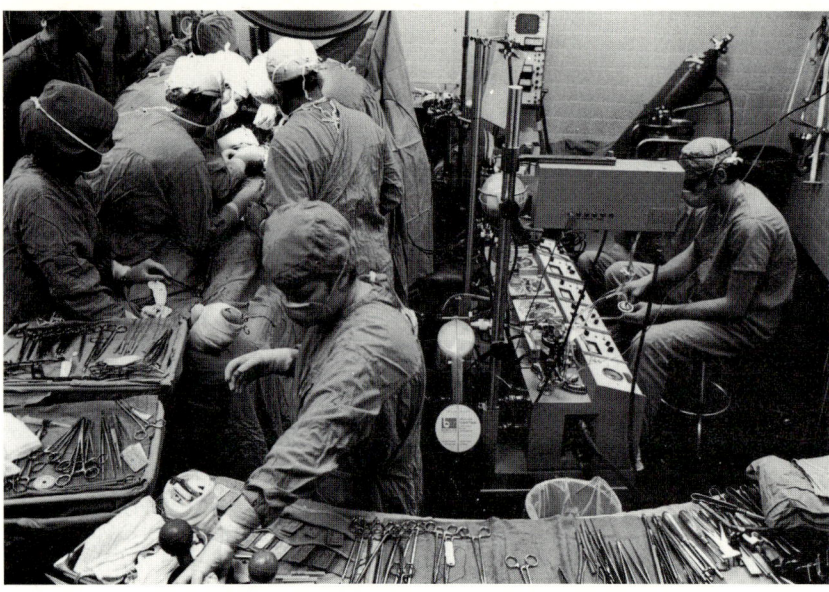

Modern medical technology has made impressive advances in treating disease, but American medicine still emphasizes "crisis" medicine more than preventive medicine.

in the field of public health. In particular, pressure was exerted on governments to ensure pure water for citizens, to dispose of sewage in a manner that would eliminate contamination, and to provide citizens with education in health care. As a result of these developments, the death rate for infectious diseases has fallen to a very low level.

The Modern Scourge: Chronic Disease

Despite these advances, the "grim reaper" still takes his toll. As can be seen in Figure 8.1, **the major causes of death today are chronic diseases: heart disease, cancer, cerebrovascular disease (such as strokes), diabetes, cirrhosis of the liver, bronchitis, and the like.** *Chronic diseases* progress over a long period of time and often persist during a considerable part of a person's life. Whereas the onset of acute disease is often dramatic and incapacitating, chronic diseases frequently exist long before we are aware of them because there are no symptoms in the early stages, or the early symptoms can be easily ignored. While some chronic conditions result from

the natural degenerative processes of the human body, social and environmental factors are important influences in the progression of these conditions. Coronary heart disease, for example, is known to be associated with a particular kind of lifestyle: a diet of highly saturated animal fats (beef, butter, and cheese), a sedentary life without consistent and vigorous exercise, heavy smoking, and stress.

In trying to combat these chronic conditions, the medical profession must use different methods than those that are effective in treating acute, infectious conditions. The treatment of many chronic diseases calls for continual, and in some cases lifelong, care that often requires that the patient change his or her lifestyle. In the previous example of coronary heart disease, patients must do such things as change their diet and stop smoking. Chemical or surgical intervention often only relieves the immediate symptoms of the problem while the underlying causes (natural degeneration, diet, and so forth) remain. The prevention of further deterioration may require that the patient permanently change his way of life. Furthermore, chronic diseases are best controlled through prevention, but **modern medicine is not organized around prevention; rather it is oriented toward** *crisis medicine:* **to treating people** *after they become ill.*[8] This strategy can be effective in coping with some types of disease, such as acute conditions. However, with chronic diseases, once the symptoms manifest themselves, much of the damage has already been done, and it is often too late to effect a complete cure. **In order to control chronic diseases, the health care delivery system should emphasize the prevention of illness before it occurs.** To date, such *preventive medicine,* while important, has had a lower priority—in terms of research funding, the construction of medical facilities, and the allocation of health care personnel—than has crisis-oriented medicine.

The State of Health in America

When we observe the bleeding and purging treatment techniques of the eighteenth century or the lack of consensus about the cause of disease in the nineteenth century, there is little doubt that we have made impressive advances in the field of medicine. Within this century alone, **the mortality rate in the United States has declined from 17 deaths per 1000 people in 1900 to under 9 deaths per 1000 in 1978, and most people project further, although not nearly as spectacular, declines in the future.**[9] What, then, is the problem in terms of health care in America?

First, health care is considered a social problem, despite the obvious advances, because people have come to expect so much more. Today, any illness is considered abnormal and unacceptable. **Second, health care is considered a problem because there is considerable evidence that Americans are not receiving all of the benefits that they might from the medical expertise available to us.** For example, in 1972, females born in the United States had a life expectancy of 75.2 years. However, in six other nations (Sweden, Norway, the Netherlands, France, Japan, and Denmark) female life expectancy exceeded this figure. American males compared even less favorably with males in

other nations: their life expectancy of 67.4 years was surpassed by that of males in eighteen other countries, including (in addition to the above) Greece, Italy, Ireland, Bulgaria, and Israel. Another important index of our nation's health is its **infant mortality**—deaths of children under one year of age. Despite our elaborate medical technology, in 1973 the United States had a higher infant mortality than 14 other nations.[10]

Mental illness is also a serious and costly problem for American society. In 1975, close to 6.5 million Americans were treated at some mental health facility. This compares with slightly over 1.5 million people treated in 1955[11]—a fourfold increase in the space of twenty years. And this figure does not include those treated by private psychiatrists and psychologists as well as those needing but not receiving mental health care. Although there is much disagreement about the nature of mental illness, it is something that vast numbers of Americans are confronting each year. This dramatic increase in treated mental disorders is not the result simply of more mental illness today than twenty years ago. An important part of this increase is the greater availability today of mental health facilities. Also, attitudes toward psychiatric care have become much more positive, and thus people are less ashamed to contact a psychiatrist or psychologist if they feel the need. As a result of this enormous increase, there is a tremendous expenditure of money and effort to cope with these problems.

So, while Americans today are much healthier in some respects than they were in the past, we still face important problems in the areas of physical and mental illness. We will address ourselves to the problems and the reasons behind them throughout this chapter. First, however, we need a clear conception of what health, illness, and disease are and in what ways illness and disease constitute a social problem.

HEALTH CARE AS A SOCIAL PROBLEM

Our conceptions of health and illness are so deeply ingrained that we rarely think it necessary to consider what health is and what illness is. However, conceptions of health and illness and the manner in which illness might constitute a social problem will vary, depending on the perspective one adopts.

The Functionalist Perspective

In order for any society to provide a socially acceptable standard of living for its members (and, in extreme circumstances, even survive), people must perform certain essential tasks and roles effectively. Parents must raise children; farmers must produce sufficient food; hunters must catch adequate amounts of game; carpenters must construct adequate housing for members of society. Disease, when it interferes with the accomplishment of these essential tasks, threatens the ability of the group to function at an adequate level and thus constitutes a social problem. **So, we can define *health*, from this perspective, as the ability to carry out those roles expected of one in society. *Illness* is a "deviant" status because the individual is no longer able to perform his normal and expected social roles.** This perspective does not deny the physical reality of disease and its effect on the human body. However, the functionalist is concerned with the impact of such disease on role performance.

From this perspective, definitions of health and illness will vary from one culture to another. For example, a paraplegic or a person who is blind in a hunting and gathering society would not be considered, from this functionalist perspective, healthy, because both afflictions seriously interfere with the ability to perform expected roles such as hunting or fishing. However, in an industrial society such as our own, these physical problems need not interfere with the performance of important tasks. People with such illnesses have filled many important positions in our culture. President Franklin Delano Roosevelt was confined to a wheelchair throughout World War II; Stevie Wonder and Ray Charles have been immensely successful as entertainers even though they are blind.

While it might be difficult to view a paraplegic as healthy, the student must keep in mind the perspective we are utilizing.[12] The sociological defini-

tion of health is quite different from the medical definition because each perspective has a different purpose. From a medical perspective, health is the absence of any abnormal biological or physiological condition or process. From this point of view, a blind person is not healthy, irrespective of his culture, because blindness is a deviation from perfect biological functioning. **The medical definition, then, refers to *disease* — a phenomenon that involves altered functioning of a person's body or mind. The sociological definition refers to *illness* — a phenomenon in which the person or those around him or her define the person as ill and accordingly alter their behavior toward that person.** So, our blind person has an altered bodily function that can be measured (a disease), but the person may not be treated any differently by people because of that condition (no illness).

The Conflict Perspective

Health, in whatever manner it is defined by a particular culture, is highly valued. All people prefer health to illness. However, one is better able to retain health if one has access to certain resources, such as money or knowledge about disease, and not all groups have equal access to these resources. So **health becomes a social problem from the conflict perspective for those groups in society that do not have access to the resources necessary to remain in good health and to ensure recovery if one does become ill.** A few decades ago, many groups, such as the American Medical Association, viewed medical care as a *privilege,* rather than a right — people should have access to health care only if they had the funds to purchase it.[13] Today, more people are beginning to view health care as a *right* to which all people are entitled. With this change in attitude, there has been some movement toward making health care more widely available. Nonetheless, with shortages of health care personnel and the high cost of medical care, there is still considerable disparity between the ability of different groups to gain access to medical care of high quality. Furthermore, as health care costs skyrocket, it takes a larger proportion of a family's income to purchase the same amount of health care. This necessitates the diversion of funds from other potential uses (such as leisure-time expenditures) to health care, and many affluent groups see this as a serious social problem because it threatens their ability to maintain their lifestyle.

The health care delivery system in the United States does more than make available the skills and expertise necessary to cure illness. From the conflict perspective, it must also be considered an arena in which various groups—doctors, nurses, social workers, and patients—use what power they have to struggle for the scarce resources available in health care institutions, which are a source of financial remuneration, prestige, and social power. The fact that the valued resources are unequally distributed among the groups, then, is a social problem for those groups not receiving what they feel is their fair share.

The Interactionist Perspective

What is considered an acceptable level of health in a particular culture depends on the values, the state of health care institutions, and the knowledge of disease in that culture.[14] In one South American tribe, dyschromic spirochetosis, a skin disorder caused by certain bacteria and characterized by variously colored spots on the skin, was so common that those without the condition were considered abnormal and even excluded from marriage. In our society, this disorder is considered a medical condition requiring treatment. In some cultures, an obese woman is viewed as highly desirable; ours considers obesity health-threatening, and we have medical clinics to treat such conditions. **Thus, according to the interactionist approach to health and illness, whether a person is considered healthy or ill depends on the social definition of that person by those around him or her.** Because of increasing technology and advances in our standard of living, we now define many health conditions as unacceptable, and thus a social problem, that previous generations accepted as one of the inevitable scourges of life. **Something is an illness because people de-fine it as such,** and this definition need not rest, as the functionalist view suggests, on an inability to perform important tasks. Many skin conditions for example, do not interfere with a person's ability to perform, yet they are defined as a disease and treated by a dermatologist.

A second important aspect of the interactionist approach to illness is that it is a social role into which a person is cast. As a social role, illness carries with it certain shared expectations and a particular self-concept. In other words, a person who is sick is expected to behave in certain socially approved ways and to act like a certain kind of person. In some societies, epileptics were viewed as invested with supernatural powers; in others, people so afflicted were treated with scorn, revulsion, and prejudice. Today, we define people who are ill as not being responsible for their condition and thus we avoid negative self-conceptions that might be attached to such roles. However, the institutions that have emerged to treat disease often treat sick people in a dehumanizing and impersonal fashion. When the sick are treated in this way, the result may be feelings of low self-esteem and a negative self-concept. **For this reason, according to the interactionist perspective, the manner in which health care is provided in the United States can be considered a social problem if it leads to socially devalued self-concepts on the part of those who must use the health care institutions.**

This discussion of health care as a social problem illustrates the diversity of conditions that might be so considered in our culture. In the remainder of this chapter, we will investigate some of the dimensions of this problem and some trends that are emerging in the health care delivery system.

SOCIAL FACTORS IN HEALTH AND ILLNESS

Many people view disease as simply a physical phenomenon that can affect anyone. However, in the preceding discussion, we have attempted to introduce some of the social dimensions of illness and disease. It is surprising the extent to which social

TABLE 8.1
Percentage of People with Some Limitation of Daily Activities Due to Illness

SELECTED CHARACTERISTICS	ALL PERSONS	WITH NO LIMITATION OF ACTIVITY	WITH LIMITATION, BUT NOT IN MAJOR ACTIVITY	WITH LIMITATION IN AMOUNT OR KIND OF MAJOR ACTIVITY	UNABLE TO CARRY ON MAJOR ACTIVITY
Population, all ages	100.0	88.3	2.6	6.2	2.9
Family income					
Less than $3,000	100.0	79.9	3.5	10.1	6.5
$3,000-$4,999	100.0	85.2	2.8	7.7	4.3
5,000-$6,999	100.0	88.6	2.5	6.2	2.7
$7,000-$9,999	100.0	89.9	2.5	5.5	2.4
$10,000-$14,000	100.0	90.7	2.5	4.9	1.8
$15,000 or more	100.0	91.5	2.5	4.3	1.6

SOURCE. National Center for Health Statistics, *Limitation of Activity Due to Chronic Conditions, 1969–1970*, Series 10, No. 80 (DHEW publication No. (HSM) 73–1506), 1973, p. 6.

factors can influence who becomes ill, what kind of disease she contracts, whether she receives medical treatment, and what kind of treatment she receives. In this section, we examine the impact of some of the more important social factors on physical and mental illness. Any attempt to reduce mortality and morbidity or to make health more available to people must take these factors into account.

Social Class

Social class is certainly one of the most important influences on our behavior. Research on illness and social class has led to one inescapable conclusion: **if you are poor in the United States, your chances of retaining the valued resource of good health are slimmer than if you are not poor.**[15] The poor are more likely to have high blood pressure, arthritis, and liver and stomach problems. They have eight times as many visual problems as the nonpoor. The incidence of heart disease, diabetes, and all forms of cancer are higher among the poor. The poor are more likely to have some degree of activity limitation due to illness (see Table 8.1). Even the youngest of the poor do not escape the social heritage of their birth. As Figure 8.2 illustrates, among the poor and nonwhites, infant mortality rates are substantially higher. Finally, lower-class people are more likely to have severe mental disorders, such as psycho-

ses, rather than the less severe disorders, such as neuroses (see Figure 8.3). In addition, studies have shown that lower-class people from socially unstable and disorganized communities are more likely

Figure 8.2 Infant Mortality Rates (Deaths per 1000 Live Births) by Race, Sex, and Income, 1964–1966. National Center for Health Statistics, *Infant Mortality Rates: Socioeconomic Factors*, Series 22. No. 14, (HEW publication No. (HSM) 72-1045, 1972), p. 12.

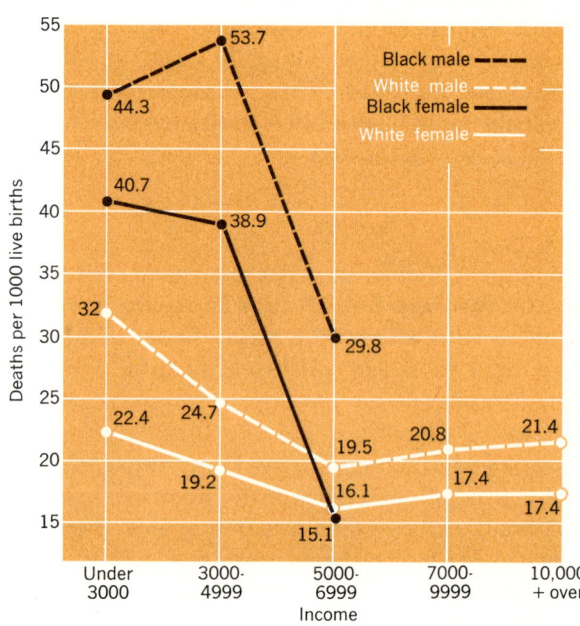

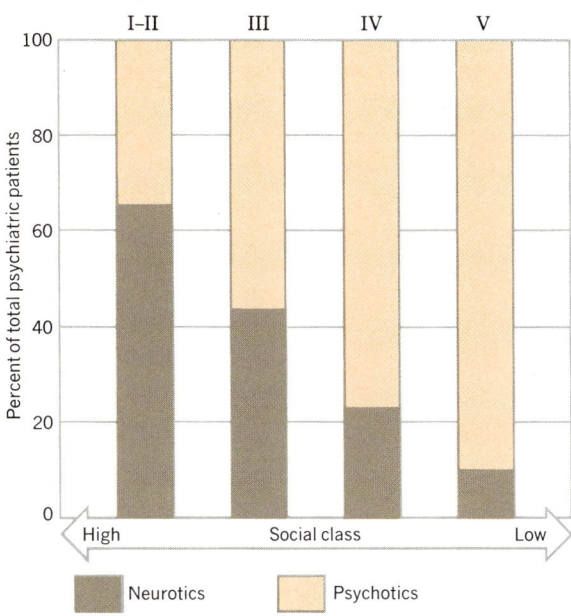

Percent of total psychiatric patients

High — Social class — Low

Neurotics   Psychotics

Figure 8.3 **Distribution of Neuroses and Psychoses by Social Class. A. Hollingshead and F. Redlich, *Social Class and Mental Illness: A Community Study* (New York: John Wiley & Sons, 1958), p. 223. Reprinted by permission.**

to have certain forms of mental illness, such as schizophrenia, while other disorders, such as manic depressive psychoses and organic conditions, are not found in unusually large proportions among such groups. This relationship between social class and health is not surprising once we understand the reasons for it.

The Economics of Health

In a number of different ways, it is expensive to stay healthy. **Modern health care is costly, and the poor cannot afford the same level of health care as can more affluent people.** Furthermore, the poor do not have the economic resources that make possible a lifestyle that reduces the danger of contracting disease. For example, the unsanitary living conditions of the poor increase the likelihood of spreading communicable diseases. Because the financial resources available to them are meager, the poor are more likely to decide to spend any surplus of funds on items other than health care.[16]

It would seem, then, that we could reduce the health gap between the rich and the poor by eliminating the financial restrictions on the poor. During the 1960s, government programs such as Medicare and Medicaid were established to eliminate the financial constraints that made medical care difficult for some to acquire. These programs, after a decade in operation, have come a long way in narrowing the gap in health status between Americans of different social classes; however, they have not eliminated the problem. We have become acutely aware that it is more than a lack of money that leads to low utilization of health care among the poor. The process of seeking health care is a complex social and psychological interchange, and, by understanding some of the noneconomic social factors that are central to this process, we can better grasp the reasons for different rates of health care utilization.

Recognizing Illness

In most cases, health care utilization begins with a person's recognizing that he or she has an illness that might be helped by medical treatment. This might seem to be an absurdly simple step, but consider the question: are you currently ill? In order to answer this in the affirmative, you must interpret certain physiological experiences as a health problem for which you might seek treatment. According to one investigator of this issue,

For the majority of [lower-class] Negroes . . . illness is primarily related to dysfunction in work and incapacitating symptoms; *symptoms which do not incapacitate are often ignored.* For . . . middle-class Negroes, like middle-class people everywhere, illness tends to relate more and more to conditions which do not incapacitate but simply, by their existence, call for medical attention.[17]

In other words, physiological experiences might be interpreted as something other than an illness that warrants medical intervention. Studies have found, for example, that middle-class people define lower back pain as a symptom of some ailment for which relief must be sought, while a lower-class person tends to define it as one of life's inevitable miseries that comes with increasing age. A study of a small

Although the poor receive more health care now than in the past, this treatment often occurs in crowded emergency rooms or out-patient clinics where the quality of care may suffer.

manufacturing community found that less than one-fourth of the lower-class people in the community defined the following as symptomatic of illness: loss of appetite, persistent coughing, joint and muscle pain, shortness of breath, and frequent headaches.[18] **So the very first step in acquiring health care—an awareness that you are ill—is not shaped solely by the availability of money; it is also very strongly influenced by the definitions of health and illness that exist among a particular group.**

Seeking Medical Care

Even though a person might recognize that he or she was ill, it does not immediately follow that scientific medical care will be sought out. How many of us have delayed contacting a doctor for a few days, weeks, or months out of fear, laziness, or faith in some home remedy? Suchman has found that people have different orientations toward medical care.[19] People with a **popular medical orientation** tend to have little knowledge about the causes, symptoms, and probable outcomes of various diseases; they are skeptical about what medicine can do for them and tend not to trust doctors or hospitals. Lower-class people are much more

likely to have this orientation than are members of any other social class. People with a popular medical orientation tend to delay seeking medical care from professionals, use folk remedies or self-medication, and seek care from lay people (e.g. family and friends). At the opposite extreme, those with a **scientific medical orientation** (common among the middle class) have relatively detailed medical knowledge, trust medical personnel, and at the first sign of illness tend to turn immediately to medical professionals. **So, even with the removal of economic barriers, the popular medical orientation of the poor still impedes their utilization of medical facilities.**

The Quality of Health Care

Once poor people do receive professional health care, the quality of that care is likely to be lower than the quality of the care received by the middle class. The poor are more likely to receive medical care in emergency rooms, outpatient departments, or health clinics. Middle-class people, on the other hand, are more likely to visit a private physician. The poor are less likely to have visited a doctor within the past two years or to have had the benefit of the services of a medical specialist, such as a pediatrician or obstetrician.[20] Even though the availability of health care for the poor may have expanded, differences resulting from social class still remain.

Preventing Illness

In avoiding chronic disease, good health can be achieved only if prevention is emphasized. The poor are considerably less likely to practice good preventive techniques such as visiting a physician or a dentist for a checkup (see Table 8.2). Especially with children, among whom treatments are more likely to be preventive, the poor make fewer visits to physicians or dentists each year and are less likely to have visited a physician within the past two years.[21]

TABLE 8.2
Percentage of Those Seeing a Dentist, by Income, Education, and Race, 1953, 1963, and 1970

CHARACTERISTIC	Percentage Seeing a Dentist		
	1953	1963	1970
Family income			
Under $2000	17	16	23
$2000–$3499	23	25	23 ⎫ 28
$3500–$4999	33		33 ⎭
$5000–$7499	44	40	35 ⎫ 40
$7500–$9999			44 ⎭
$10,000–$12,499	56	58	51 ⎫
$12,500–$14,999			50 ⎪ 55
$15,000–$17,499			53 ⎪
$17,500 and over			67 ⎭
Race			
White	—[a]	43	47
Nonwhite	—	20	24
Education of head			
8 years or less	—[a]	25	27
9–11 years	—	35	39
12 years	—	48	49
13 years or more	—	55	61
Total	34	38	45

[a] not available for 1953.

SOURCE. Ronald Andersen, Joanna Lion, and Odin Anderson, *Two Decades of Health Services* (Cambridge, Mass.: Ballinger Publishing Co., 1976), p. 60. Reprinted with permission.

In order to understand why the poor are less likely to avail themselves of preventive care, even when it is free, medical researchers Philip Moody and Robert Gray studied a polio immunization program.[22] They found that poor mothers were much less likely to have their children immunized than were more affluent mothers. However, the mothers who did not participate in the immunization program, whether poor or affluent, shared certain characteristics: they were less likely to participate in any community organizations such as the PTA or church groups, they felt alienated and powerless, and they felt isolated from other parts of American society. These findings suggest that the failure to utilize preventive health programs is part of a larger syndrome: a general lack of participation and involvement in the groups that make up American society. This lack of effective integration into the major groups and institutions is more commonly found among the poor. The poor lack the money, the social skills, the contacts, or the motivation to organize, and they find themselves at the mercy of large bureaucracies that they neither understand nor can cope with. This environment generates the feelings of social isolation and powerlessness that in turn reduce the probability of obtaining health care.

Mental Illness

The relationship between social class and illness is a complex one, and it is often difficult to determine the causal relationship between these two variables. This can be illustrated in current research findings on mental illness, which suggest that there are three possible explanations for the relationship between social class and mental illness.[23] The first is called the **social causation** hypothesis: according to this approach, the social and cultural environment in which poor people live (poverty, social isolation, social disorganization, and so on) is so stressful that it affects their mental health. The second hypothesis has been referred to as **downward drift,** according to which, when a person becomes severely mentally disturbed, he or she cannot fulfill normal duties and obligations (toward work, family, etc.); the person may lose job, friends, and family, and subsequently drift into a lower-class lifestyle. This lower-class lifestyle places fewer interpersonal or financial demands on the mentally ill person. The student will note that **the first approach suggests that social class causes mental illness, while the second argues that mental illness influences a person's class position.**

A third explanation for the relationship concerns the likelihood of receiving health care. The lower classes are less likely to define themselves as requiring psychiatric care, are less likely to seek out such care, and are less likely to continue a prolonged treatment program. Because of this, a lower-class person is less likely to receive adequate medical treatment, and a mild condition is more likely to become a severe one. Which of these hypotheses is correct? It is likely that all three processes are involved but that they occur under different conditions and with different people. This illustrates the complexity of the relationship between social class and illness. With this realization, one begins to understand the difficulties of finding workable solutions to these problems.

Sex Roles

In practically any way we wish to measure morbidity, the rate seems to be higher among women.[24] Women have more acute physical conditions, more days during which their activities are restricted because of illness, more visits to the doctor, more hospital visits, and the like. **Yet, at the same time, women have a longer life expectancy than men.** One explanation for this relies on the different socialization experiences of men and women. During the socialization process, women are encouraged to express their feelings and show weakness while men are taught to be strong, stoical, and unemotional. Thus, women are more likely to complain about symptoms and to report being ill because it is more acceptable for women to show weakness in the face of pain or disability than it is for men. If women complain more and thus receive more medical care, they would be more likely to prevent the onset of disease or to treat it at an early, and less debilitating, stage.

The higher mortality among men is also probably due to the fact that men are more likely than women to engage in activities injurious to health — smoking, drinking to excess, holding stressful occupations, and the like. All of these are related to poor health. As women begin to engage in more of these activities, they may have a deleterious effect on their health. In fact, we are already seeing a rise in the rates of lung cancer among women, presumably due to increased smoking. As women move into more stressful careers that had traditionally been reserved for males, we should observe an increase in stress-related illnesses among women.

There are also intriguing relationships between sex roles and mental illness. One sociologist found that married women have particularly high rates of mental disorders, and he attributed this to certain characteristics of the married female role — low status, low visibility, and the ambiguity of the expectations associated with that role.[25] Psychologist Phyllis Chesler found that the number of women under psychiatric care has drastically increased since 1964.[26] She thinks that this is related to the socialization experiences of the different sexes — men and women learn to cope with stress and tension differently. Chesler states that women learn to cope in ways that are symptomatic of certain mental disorders: depression, paranoia, a detachment from reality, and various neurotic tendencies. Men are more likely to turn to drugs or alcohol in stressful situations, whereas women are not encouraged to use these as means for coping with stress. A recent study of mental hospitalization found higher rates of mental illness among women than among men. However, men tend to be diagnosed at a younger age and to stay in the hospital longer.[27]

Occupational Status

Occupational status can have a dramatic impact on health. Most people are well aware that some jobs are more stressful than others and that stress is associated with the occurrence of many illnesses — coronary heart disease, cardiovascular disease, mental disorders, high blood pressure, and a host of others. Of course, occupation is not the only source of stress in a person's life. In fact, there is considerable research indicating that any change in a person's life situation—whether the person views it as desirable or not—may have negative health consequences. Yet, **for most adult Americans, their job is one of the most important statuses they hold, and job-related stress has a significant effect on health.**[28]

A person's occupation affects health in yet another way. In a technologically complex economy such as ours, there are many health-threatening conditions associated with the workplace. In chapter 5, we documented the detrimental health consequences of Kepone for workers in one particular factory. Yet, the problem goes far beyond a single work setting. For example, according to the National Institute on Occupational Safety and Health, almost 1 million auto and garage workers are exposed to potentially carcinogenic asbestos when they work on automobile brake and clutch assemblies. Over 0.5 million service station attendants are exposed to ethylene dibromide, which is an additive in leaded gas, and which also appears to cause cancer.[29] The list of such health-related occupational situations could be extended almost indefinitely. The point is that people who work in certain occupations are exposed to health risks that other Americans do not confront. In many cases, we do not know what the risks are or how serious they might be.

A final way in which occupational status can affect health is through unemployment.[30] Obviously, one reason people become unemployed is because of poor health, so we would expect unemployment to be related to illness. However, studies have shown that, when looking at a whole society (as opposed to individuals), increasing unemployment rates are strongly associated with rises in mortality, suicide, homicide, and automobile accident deaths.

Unemployment is also related to mental illness. M. Harvey Brenner conducted an exhaustive analysis of the relationship between mental illness and the state of the economy.[31] He compared fluctuations in the number of people in mental hospitals in New York with changes in the rates of employment. From 1841 to 1967, there was a substantial relationship between economic conditions and mental hospitalization. When unemployment was high, hospitalization increased; as unemployment

declined, the numbers of people hospitalized also declined. Since World War II, the impact of economic downturn has been especially dramatic on people between the ages of 15 and 34. In some cases, the loss of a job may push an already weak and unstable person over the edge. It may be the final straw that the person cannot endure. In other cases, unemployment may initiate a long sequence of events (family problems, health problems, downward mobility, and so on) that snowball into some mental disorder. In either case, it is clear that, in American society, occupation is an important determinant of a person's class position and of his or her feelings of importance and self-worth. Since we tend to define ourselves in terms of what we do, any change in occupational status may have implications for our mental health.

Education

Americans view education as the great equalizer; it is a commonly held belief that anyone can share in the best of American life if he or she can acquire the educational credentials that make possible self-advancement. In terms of health, education also has an important impact—more important, in some ways, than money. For example, death rates decline with higher levels of education—among both men and women and in all age categories. Especially among those with no more than an elementary school education, the death rates are quite high. People with high educational levels also have lower rates of infant mortality. Finally, people with higher educational levels are more likely to practice preventive medical care and to receive medical care when sick, and that care is likely to be of a higher quality.[32]

One might explain this relationship between health and education by pointing out that education and social class are related—people with more education also tend to have a higher social class standing. While this is true and does help us to understand the findings, there is also a somewhat more complex process at work here. After an extensive study of the relationships between poverty, education, and health, medical researcher Myron Lefcowitz concludes that "Health-related and health-oriented behaviors are primarily a function of valued lifestyles and . . . *education is a primary agent in the development of such tastes.*"[33] Part of the lifestyle referred to by Lefcowitz is, first, the exposure to and knowledge of information related to health and, second, the ranking of priorities such that expenditures for health care take precedence over other expenditures. In other words, he is suggesting that it is low education, not poverty, that leads to high rates of illness and low rates of health care utilization. Given the social programs available, a poor family can acquire good health care if its members have the information available to do so and if they make the decision to allocate their time and resources in that direction. Higher educational levels among people, even for the financially destitute, result in choices that are beneficial to health.

Health, illness, and the likelihood of receiving medical care are influenced by a variety of social factors; we have considered social class, race, occupational status, and a number of others. One point we have emphasized is that money, while important, is not the only key element, and in some ways it is less critical than it once was. The poor are less likely to have access to the resources other than money, such as education, that relate to health care. The gap between the kinds of health care available to different groups in America will be eliminated when these health-related resources are available to all groups. This involves a fundamental change in lifestyle. Spreading more money around and creating a more elaborate medical technology will not by itself solve this problem.

MENTAL ILLNESS

Mental illness, because it is not as well understood as physical illness, presents some unique concerns to the student of social problems. There is considerable disagreement among mental health professionals about what mental illness is and how it should be treated. They have achieved no real consensus on a theory of mental illness. Because of this, there is an additional issue, beyond those we treat in relation to both physical and mental illness,

that must be addressed when discussing mental illness: what is the nature of mental illness?

The Nature of Mental Illness

Mental illness can be found in one form or another in almost all societies. People have responded to the unusual, startling, and often frightening behavior of the mentally deranged by trying to understand what mental illness is and to develop treatments based on this understanding. During much of European history, the mentally ill were viewed as demon-possessed, sorcerers, or witches. Some communities drove them out, making them perpetual wanderers and vagabonds on the European landscape; others burned them at the stake or hanged them in order to eliminate the evil within them before others were so afflicted. At a later time, inaccurate theories about the cause of mental illness resulted in many bizarre treatments—burning and cauterizing the skin of manic patients, dunking them in cold water, or spinning them in a chair at a dizzying speed.[34]

In the eighteenth and nineteenth centuries, there was a long struggle toward more humane treatment of the mentally ill. For example, toward the end of the nineteenth century Sigmund Freud began to make popular the view that insanity had understandable and treatable psychological origins. During the twentieth century, many interest groups, such as the National Association for Mental Health, have formed to work for changes in the popular stereotypes of mental illness and to encourage legislative and governmental action favorable to a humanistic view of the treatment of mental illness.[35]

When we see the degrading, and sometimes painful, ways in which the mentally ill have been treated in the past, it is tempting to breathe a sigh of relief that we no longer perpetrate such barbaric practices. Yet while we like to consider ourselves an enlightened people, we still retain many negative stereotypes of the mentally ill. Consider the everyday terms that some people apply to those who are mentally ill: crazy, loony, bonkers, lost his marbles, lunatic, idiot, nuts, madman, squirrel. The list could be extended indefinitely, but the point is clear — **we have very ambivalent feelings toward those we classify as mentally ill.** Whatever sympathy we feel is mixed with a considerable degree of fear, loathing, and misunderstanding. To change these attitudes, we must understand the nature of mental illness. Unfortunately, students of the subject do not agree on this issue. Three different positions on the nature of mental illness have been taken: (1) some view it as a disease, (2) others view it as the performance of a social role based on normative expectations, and (3) still others view it as simply a problem that a person confronts in living a particular lifestyle.

Mental Illness as Disease

By far the most popular perspective on mental illness today is to view it as similar in nature to physical disease: the normal perceptual or personality processes of the individual are disrupted by some force or mechanism operating on the person.[36] The behavior of the mentally ill person is a symptom of this underlying disturbance. In other words, the medical definition of health and disease is applied to mental illness. Mental disturbances must be eliminated if the person is to get well. If left un-

French psychiatrist Dr. Philippe Pinel freed the insane from their chains and introduced a more gentle and humane treatment. This new treatment also became popular in nineteenth century America.

treated, the conditions will become progressively worse. As with physical illness, the "disease" of the mentally ill person is seen to exist irrespective of whether anyone recognizes it.

For the proponents of this position, there are many possible causes of mental derangement. It might be due to some disease-related organism that invades the body, to the failure to progress through certain essential stages of development, or to one's inability to integrate all of one's perceptions, experiences, and emotions into a consistent and positive view of oneself. While there are many such theories, they all share in common the assumption that mental illness can be viewed as a disease located in the person and that treatment must focus primarily on the individual. By making the patient aware of these underlying causes and by remedying the perceptual and personality processes that have become disturbed, the therapist hopes to restore the individual to a state that permits him or her to function without the tensions, anxieties, and bizarre behavioral manifestations that characterized the "illness."

Psychiatrists have been among the major proponents of the disease viewpoint on mental illness. However, it is also a very popular perspective among psychologists, nurses, social workers, and others who work in the field of mental health. It is certainly a more humane approach than the earlier views of mental illness as demon-possession, witchcraft, and the like. However, **there are potential shortcomings in viewing mental illness as a disease.** When we take this perspective, there is a tendency to restrict our focus to the individual and to ignore the extensive social environment in which the individual lives and the effect that social processes have on his or her behavior. The two remaining viewpoints on mental illness have arisen partially in reaction to these difficulties inherent in the disease-oriented approach.

Mental Illness as a Social Role

Some sociologists have pointed out that there is an important difference between engaging in occasional bizarre behavior that might be classified as symptomatic of mental illness and acting out the social role of a person who is mentally ill. The former might be the result of a variety of factors, but the latter is at least partially due to the reactions of other people to that person.

Thomas Scheff, a major proponent of this perspective, points out that everybody on occasion engages in behavior that might be classified as mental illness.[37] How often have you laughed inappropriately, responded in a way that another person could not understand, or gazed off vacantly into the distance (e.g. during a particularly boring lecture)? In most cases, those around you either failed to notice it or chose to ignore it.

How, then, do occasional lapses into unusual behavior emerge into a continuous and stable pattern of behavior? **Scheff argues that the crucial step is whether the person is labeled by others as mentally ill. For Scheff, there is a social role of mental illness — expectations shared by people concerning how persons with particular types of mental illness ought to behave.** Once a person is defined as mentally ill, we expect him or her to behave in ways appropriate to that role. If we believe the mentally ill are childlike, then we will not expect them to take on adult responsibilities, such as work or taking care of household finances. Their failure to perform well or at all in these areas is explained and justified as "part of their condition." It may become inconvenient, unrewarding, or sometimes impossible for the person so labeled to behave otherwise. For example, a person with a history of mental illness may be avoided, not given positions of trust, and so on. This communicates to the person (remember the *looking-glass self*) that others view her as dependent and untrustworthy. If people behave consistently toward her in this way, she most likely will begin to view herself as that type of person. This situation has all of the characteristics of a self-fulfilling prophecy: we treat a person as if she were mentally ill, and she subsequently begins to live up to our expectations.

Scheff readily admits that there are organic, biological, and psychological causes for disturbed behavior. However, he is arguing that some (possibly most) of the behavior of the mentally disturbed — once they are labeled mentally ill — is due to the reactions and expectations of other people rather than to the original source of their mental disturbance. He suggests that we shift our focus from the inner workings and mental derangements of the patient to the social relationship between the patient and those around him. He points out that you and I may help to create and intensify a person's bizarre behavior by the way we treat him or her. Furthermore, our mental institutions may help perpetuate mental illnesses by the way in which they treat patients. It would be more useful to focus on society at large rather than the individual in order to understand how mental illness develops and how to deal with it.

Mental Illness as Problems of Living

Even among psychiatrists there is not total agreement on the view that mental illness is a disease. Psychiatrist Thomas Szasz feels that this view is an incorrect and potentially dangerous myth because it defines a problem in our social relationships as medically based and thereby directs us toward inappropriate solutions.[38] Szasz agrees that organically based mental illness (such as that caused by advanced syphilis) should be viewed as a disease. However, any mental illness with no known organic cause must be treated differently. To treat these latter forms of mental illness as *disease* creates the hope that they can be cured through the application of medical techniques and directs our attention away from the more basic issues at hand:

> [It] . . . obscure[s] the everyday fact that life for most people is a continuous struggle, not for biological survival, but for "a place in the sun," "peace of mind," or some other meaning or value. Once the needs of preserving the body . . . are satisfied, man faces the problem of personal significance: What should he do with himself? For what should he live?[39]

Medicine cannot make your life meaningful and valuable — only you can do that. Furthermore, the myth of mental illness propagates the view that the normal state of human relationships is one of harmony, satisfaction, and comfort. Szasz claims, to the contrary, that human relationships are never completely harmonious: there is always a degree of stress, anxiety, and conflict inherent in our relationships with other people. **In other words, mental illness is not a** *disease***, according to Szasz, but a "problem of living" — it is the expression of the continuous struggle humanity confronts in determining how one should live one's life and how to relate to other human beings.** Categorizing the problems as *disease* and attempting to treat them as medical problems ignores these basic facts of social life.

Szasz argues that the traditional conception of mental illness as disease also ignores the moral and ethical aspects of human behavior. It absolves us of individual responsibility for our behavior. For example, if influenza hinders a person from performing her occupational duties, she is not blamed for failing to carry out her role — it is a result of the sickness over which she has no control. Likewise, if the child molester, the murderer, the parent who abuses his child, can attribute his behavior to "mental illness," he need not take personal responsibility for his actions. For Szasz, engaging in such behaviors should be considered ethical choices that an individual makes and should take responsibility for. By calling them symptoms of illness, we define them as practical problems whose solution only requires the choice of appropriate medical technology.

In summary, what is the nature of mental illness? Given the three viewpoints presented, we can see that this is a difficult question to answer. If we use the conflict perspective, then Szasz's idea that mental illness is the reflection of inevitable problems that we confront in human society would seem to be most accurate. Scheff, on the other hand, emphasizes the interactionist's concern with the social definition of reality and the importance of our relationships with others in constructing social reality. The idea that mental illness is a disease has similarities to the functionalist view of society because this position conceives of mental illness as an aberration or pathology that must be eliminated, while the absence of disease is the normal state of affairs. However, it is important to recall that all three perspectives are necessary in order to understand social life. So all three of these viewpoints on mental illness are important to a full comprehension of the problem. With this understanding of the nature of mental illness, we can turn to a discussion of the treatment of mental illness in American society.

The Treatment of Mental Illness

We seem to have come a long way in our understanding of mental illness since the dunkings, burnings, and rotations of the Middle Ages. Yet, have we? Do we know *that* much more about the treatment of mental illness now than we did then? In this section, we will look at three currently popular treatment approaches in terms of the basic assumptions and latent functions, or unintended consequences, that each performs.

Psychotherapy

The most common type of treatment for most forms of mental illness has been *psychotherapy.* In this treatment, a strong personal relationship is developed between the therapist and the patient. The therapist attempts to gain insight into the patient's problems and helps share in this understanding. The relationship serves as a safe and supportive environment in which the patient feels sufficiently secure to confront the reasons for his or her anxiety, discontent, or disturbing behavior. The relationship is crucial in the success of the treatment. There are many forms of psychotherapy based on different theories of the internal dynamics of the personality. However, they all focus on the *individual* and attempt to solve personal problems through a primary relationship with the therapist.

Does psychotherapy work? Studies by psychiatrists that compare patients before and after they have received treatment have shown psychotherapy to be quite successful in treating patients. However, for a number of reasons, we must be cautious in accepting these conclusions.[40] First, psychotherapists have a vested interest in the success of their therapy and this may easily influence their research. Second, patients who leave therapy before the treatment program is completed are not considered "failures" in many of these studies because it is assumed that these patients might have

improved if the treatment process had been allowed to continue to the end. Thus, many patients who show no improvement are dropped from the study, which introduces a bias toward finding psychotherapy successful. Third, some have suggested that giving a patient *any* personal attention and *any* explanation of his behavior will have some therapeutic value. Thus, Stuart presents studies showing that 2 out of 3 neurotic patients improve after therapy regardless of the type of therapy.[41] In other cultures, shamans, monks, or witch-doctors seem to have therapeutic value in alleviating personal problems. It is possible, then, that certain types of social relations and personal attention—whether from a therapist, a minister, or a friend—may have significant therapeutic value.

Where does this leave us? We must be very cautious in accepting the claims of either side of this argument. There are many forms of psychotherapy, many types of psychiatric conditions, and many different personal styles among therapists. At this point we do not know which combination of these will lead to the greatest success. Another important issue in evaluating the role of psychotherapy is the latent functions that it performs. Hurvitz argues that psychotherapy performs the latent function of preserving the status quo by fostering the view that failure and unhappiness are the result of individual inadequacies rather than being due to social factors, such as unequal opportunities, variations in the distribution of valued resources, and the like.[42] This might lead one to feel guilty about one's failure rather than anger at the societal barriers that contributed to the failure. As a consequence, psychotherapy encourages the person to change himself and adjust to social conditions rather than to change those conditions.

Behavior Therapy

This therapy (also called *behavior modification*) assumes that mental illness is learned; in other words, maladaptive or disruptive behavior patterns develop because they have been rewarded in the past.[43] This approach is based on well-known learning principles—rewarding a behavior increases the probability that it will be repeated; ignoring or punishing a behavior reduces the likelihood that it will occur again. A therapist may use this conditioning or learning process to replace disturbing behavior with desirable behavior.

This form of therapy can be illustrated by the case of a child who cannot adjust to school and who is disruptive in the classroom. The therapist looks for those aspects of the setting that reward disruption: it might be the attention of the teacher who lectures to the child on why he or she should not cause trouble, or possibly the reaction from other students in the class who laugh at the child's antics. Desirable behavior (paying attention, being quiet, raising your hand before speaking) may receive no reaction from the teacher. The therapist rearranges this reward structure in order to encourage desirable behavior; for example, the teacher is encouraged to ignore the child's disruptive behavior, comment on how good the student has been, praise her for good schoolwork, and call on her when she raises her hand. In this way the student learns that good classroom behavior is rewarding. **The goal of behavior therapy is to change specific and clearly defined behaviors. Psychotherapy, on the other hand, encourages the patient to achieve insight into his problem and thereby alter his own behavior.**

Behavior modification has become immensely popular because of its simplicity and its apparent effectiveness in dealing with a wide range of problems, such as alcoholism, childhood autism, and severe phobias.[44] However, we must be cautious about accepting this method as a universal treatment for mental disorders. Because it focuses on changing specific behaviors, it may be effective with well-defined symptoms of mental disturbance, such as tantrums, bed-wetting, and various phobias, but less successful with general disorders of perception and emotion (such as hallucinations or vague depressions and anxiety).

Despite the success of behavior modification in treating some conditions, there has been some concern regarding the potential latent functions of this type of therapy. For example, sociologist Alejandro Portes has argued that "Behaviorism has nothing at its core that prevents its practitioners from becoming behavior controllers at the service of whatever groups happen to have power in society . . . Behavior therapy is one of the therapeutic approaches most inclined to confuse mental health with conformity to social standards."[45] Is conformity to classroom routine the healthiest behavior for the disruptive child mentioned above? Disruption may be the result of boredom or a sign of extreme intelligence. Behavior therapy is very susceptible to viewing conformity to prevailing norms as "healthy." As with psychotherapy, the dominant group in society may use this therapy as a means of enforcing conformity to the status quo.

Community Mental Health

While community mental health (also called *social psychiatry* or *community psychology*) may utilize psychotherapy or behavior modification techniques, it is based on a different orientation toward mental illness.[46] It does not focus on the individual to the extent that the traditional treatment approaches do. **Rather, the community therapy approach assumes that the community (a total population or group of people) is its clientele.** For example, if a person is anxious and depressed, the psychotherapist would focus on that person's inner feelings and ability to adjust to his or her environment, while the behavior therapist would attempt to alter the reward structure in the situation. The community mental health worker, on the other hand, acknowledges that a patient's anxiety and depression might be the result of inability to find a job or provide the necessities of life for self and family. Counseling the patient to adjust to his or her plight might have a pacifying effect in the short run but does not really solve the problem. In order to do this, community mental health might establish job training programs, vocational placement, and compensatory education so that one can gain the skills that one needs to get a job. In other words, **community mental health tends to promote social change as well as individual adjustment—the emphasis is on changing the community as much as the individual.**

Proponents of this approach feel that the results of the community mental health effort have been impressive. They claim that their programs have reduced the number of people in state mental hospitals from 550,000 in 1955 to 191,000 in 1975.[47] The program has reached out to the aged, the poor, and the underprivileged who otherwise would not have received any psychiatric treatment. Demonstration projects have shown that community centers also have a dramatic impact on the attitudes of people toward health care.[48] In contrast to the previous two approaches, there seems to be more likelihood of social change rather than support of the status quo.

However, not all interested persons have accepted the movement with open arms. It has been pointed out that the decline in the number of patients in state mental hospitals began a full decade before community mental health centers were established in the mid-1960s and was largely due to the use of tranquilizing drugs that control violent behavior so that patients can live in the community. Others have argued that the maldistribution of mental health services has not been relieved by the program: community mental health centers are providing services in areas that already had many services. Finally, the basic philosophy of retaining the severely ill in the community has been questioned on the grounds that, since the community environment may be a partial cause of the mental disorder, keeping the patient in the community may simply compound the problem.[49]

There is considerable disagreement among professionals over the most effective treatment for mental illness. However, we have passed the stage at which it is easy to believe that one treatment approach can deal with all types of problems. The goal of the mental health field should be to provide a wide range of treatment alternatives and to ensure that some form of care is available to everyone. In the past, psychiatry provided care for the middle class but largely ignored the underprivileged. With the community mental health movement, more resources are being directed toward the care of the less privileged groups in society. There is also a growing awareness that any treatment for mental illness might inadvertently encourage conformity to and acceptance of the values of the status quo. In a diverse and heterogeneous society like America, any therapy must be sensitive to the cherished values of all groups.

PROBLEMS IN THE HEALTH CARE DELIVERY SYSTEM

In today's world, almost everybody will eventually confront the health care delivery system—visit a doctor, go to a health clinic, or be admitted to a hospital. Once this personal experience occurs, people become acutely aware of some of the problems that exist in the organization of our health care delivery system, and these problems are being discussed constantly by journalists and the public at large. While there are many such problems, we will focus on two central ones—the bureaucratic character of the health care delivery system and its effect on people, and the high cost of health care.

Bureaucracy and Dehumanization

How often have you done a "slow burn" as you waited in line for what seems like endless hours at a school, a government office, or some other large bureaucracy? Health care institutions, such as hospitals, outpatient clinics, and doctors' offices have many of the characteristics of these other bureaucracies, with many of the same consequences for people. However, the consequences in health care institutions are sometimes more serious. For example, the mother who must wait half a day to see a doctor about her child's headaches may not return once the symptoms disappear, even though her child may need follow-up care. What is it about these institutions that often makes our contact with them so unpleasant? Can they be made more humane?

Complexity and Specialization

Along with other parts of American society, the medical field has become increasingly complex and differentiated. A century ago, physicians with little specialization provided most medical treatment, while nurses (with little training) tried to keep patients comfortable, performed housekeeping chores, and assisted with the treatment. Today, medical knowledge has become too complex for any single physician to learn; in 1973, 78.5 percent of the active physicians in the United States were working in some speciality area.[50] Nursing now requires extensive education — often at the graduate level. In addition, no hospital can survive without licensed practical nurses, respiratory therapists, physical therapists, dieticians, and numerous other specialized personnel. Today, a bureaucratic form of organization serves to coordinate the behavior of all these interrelated roles.

Because of this elaborate division of labor, along with the need to operate health care institutions in an economically efficient fashion, patients are often treated in a standardized and impersonal fashion. The experience can be cold and dehumanizing. The patient is all too often treated as merely a physical entity with certain symptoms rather than as a complete person with beliefs, feelings, hopes, and desires. To illustrate this, we can compare these experiences with what often happens in a quite different context in our own culture. In many traditional Mexican American communities in the United States, the family might turn to a **curandera,** or folk-curer, when someone became ill. The curandera is usually a neighbor who knows the family well and is familiar with the local customs that will help put the patient at ease. For example, good manners require that the curandera sit and chat about recent events (weddings in the community, school affairs, the weather, etc.) before bringing up the topic of the patient's condition. The curandera is always attentive to the psychological and emotional needs of the patient and accepts the patient's cultural beliefs about the cause of his condition. If the patient thinks his illness is due to *mal ojo* (evil eye) or *susto* (fright), the curandera accepts this diagnosis and bases her treatment on it. Most care and treatment is done in the supportive environment of the home. Hospitalization is usually avoided because it is seen as a lonely, frightening, and not very useful experience.[51]

Compare all this with the experience that many middle-class Americans have had. Upon becoming ill, they go to the doctor's office (who remembers when doctors made house calls?) where they wait endlessly, reading old magazines. One nurse takes blood pressure and another leads the way to a barren examination room where muffled conversation from the next examination room can be heard. After another wait, the doctor conducts his or her examination for a few minutes and concludes that more tests will be necessary. Half a day may have been spent in this bureaucratic maze without getting any closer to learning what is wrong.

The Effect on the Patient

Yet, some would argue, if adequate medical care is dispensed, is it really important that the patient also feel *emotionally* satisfied with the experience? The results of research indicate that it does.[52] **Much evidence shows that satisfied patients are more likely to continue taking medication, return to the doctor for a follow-up appointment, and complete other treatments than are unsatisfied patients.** The patient's satisfaction depends, among other things, on personal treatment by health care personnel, clear and detailed explanations of the patient's condition, understandable instructions on how to carry out treatment, and a feeling that the health care providers know and care about the needs of the patient. The likelihood of receiving this level of personalized care in a large, crowded, and busy institution is, unfortunately, rather small. The consequence is that the patient is less likely to carry out the necessary treatment.

In addition to the inconvenience suffered by a patient, health care bureaucracies also have a dramatic impact on an individual's self-concept. For example, a person in a hospital loses considerable control over himself and what happens to him. He has a plastic identification bracelet on his wrist that, while helpful to the staff in identifying patients, may also convey to the patient the feeling that he is now the "property" of the hospital. He may be moved around in a wheelchair although he is quite capable of walking. He loses control over who has access to himself and his body. He may not even be permitted to close the door to his room. He must submit to the most intimate examinations by total strangers. He has little control over when and where things happen to him. He may be given little information about what is being done. Even the waste products of his body are inspected, weighed, and measured with intense concern.[53]

What is the impact of all this? From the point of view of the institution, all these procedures are essential, and hopefully the person will be a "good" patient: asking few questions, demanding little, and obeying the requests of the staff. However, the person's identity has been temporarily transformed: he used to think of himself as an autonomous, active individual who controlled his own destiny and surroundings. But now he feels that he has little control or autonomy. He feels dependent on others and helpless. In some cases, his life might be in the hands of the hospital staff. The institution and its staff treats him as a dependent and powerless person, and he begins to view himself as that kind of person.

In extreme cases, the treatment received in health care institutions can lead to *depersonalization:* the feeling of detachment from people or social groups that give life meaning and provide a sense of importance and self-worth. For example, Rosenhan found that the organization of mental hospitals and the attitudes and behavior of the staff encouraged these feelings.[54] The patients were ignored or treated like children who were not responsible for important matters. Physical examinations were conducted in semipublic rooms with little concern for the privacy of the patient. Attendants verbally, and on occasion physically, abused patients in the presence of other patients, but not in the presence of other staff members. Presumably, patients would not be treated as reliable witnesses in matters involving complaints of abuse. The staff had little contact with the patients and often ignored their questions. Daily contact with psychiatrists, psychologists, and physicians average 6.8 minutes—probably inadequate to establish a personal relationship of any therapeutic value. Here again we find that the patient's personal identity is greatly influenced by the institution. It often becomes a self-fulfilling prophecy: the patient becomes the kind of person the staff expects him or her to be. In other words, the attitude of the staff of the institution suppresses those characteristics of independence, autonomy, and self-control that are signs of a mentally healthy individual.

Why do institutions treat people in this dehumanizing fashion? Do they attract people who find pleasure in treating others in this way? Probably not. The members of the staff are as much a victim of the bureaucarcy as the patient because their behavior is shaped by many of the same organizational characteristics. For example, a lack of time or inadequate facilities make certain practices necessary. Humane treatment is difficult, time-consuming, and costly. Personnel are frequently overworked and underpaid, making it difficult to motivate them to perform these tasks. In many institutions, those having the most frequent contact with the patient—aides and orderlies—have the least training. A lack of adequate staffing makes it difficult for physicians, psychiatrists, or nurses to give the intensive, personal care that is necessary to overcome these problems. When health care facilities are understaffed, the employees must spend all their time on the essentials—feeding, clothing, and monitoring the patients. Little time is left to provide more humane treatment.

The High Cost of Health Care

The cost of health care has risen astronomically in the past few decades. In 1925, it cost about $3 for a one-day stay in the hospital. By 1964, the average daily cost of hospital care in the United States was $38. By 1977, the figure had grown again to nearly $225.[55] Per capita expenditures for health care have increased more than eightfold in the twenty-five years between 1950 and 1977 (see Table 8.3 and Fig. 8.4). Table 8.3 illustrates the increase in health care expenditures and how these are divided among various types of services. These rising costs have fallen more heavily on the low-income groups and the elderly who must survive on fixed incomes. Despite the various social welfare programs intended to ease the burden of health financing, the poor still pay a considerably larger proportion of their family income on health than do the more affluent members of society. In 1970, those with less than $2000 of yearly income paid 14.5 percent of

TABLE 8.3
National Health Expenditures in the U.S., Expressed in Percentages, 1940–1977

	1940	1950	1960	1970	1975	1977
Percentage of GNP		4.6	5.2	7.2	8.4	8.8
Per capita expenditures	$28.82	$78.35	$141.63	$333.57	$571.21	$736.92
Percentage spent for						
Hospital care	25.0	30.7	32.9	37.4	39.1	40.4
Physicians' services	24.4	22.4	21.6	19.4	19.3	19.8
Dentists' services	10.4	7.8	7.5	6.5	6.4	6.2
Other professional services	4.5	3.2	3.3	2.0	1.9	2.0
Drugs and drug sundries	16.0	13.7	13.9	10.3	8.4	7.7
Eyeglasses and appliances	4.6	3.9	2.9	2.6	1.4	1.3
Nursing-home care	.7	1.5	1.9	5.5	7.6	7.8
Other health services	2.4	3.3	4.0	3.2	2.8	2.7
Expense for prepayment and administration	4.1	3.6	3.9	3.6	4.7	4.7
Government public health activities	4.0	2.9	1.6	2.1	2.4	2.3
Research and medical-facilities construction	3.5	7.0	6.6	7.4	6.1	5.4

SOURCE. Robert M. Gibson and Charles R. Fisher, "National Health Expenditures, Fiscal Year 1977," *Social Security Bulletin*, 41 (July, 1978), p. 15.

their income for health care, while for those making more than $15,000 a year the equivalent proportion was 3.3 percent.[56] It is clear that, when a

Figure 8.4 National Health Expenditures and Percentage of Gross National Product, Selected Fiscal Years 1950–1977. Robert M. Gibson and Marjorie Smith Mueller, "National Health Expenditure, Fiscal Year 1976," *Social Security Bulletin* 40 (April 1977), pp. 3–22, and Robert M. Gibson and Charles R. Fisher, "National Health Expenditures, Fiscal Year 1977," *Social Security Bulletin* 41 (July 1978), p. 14.

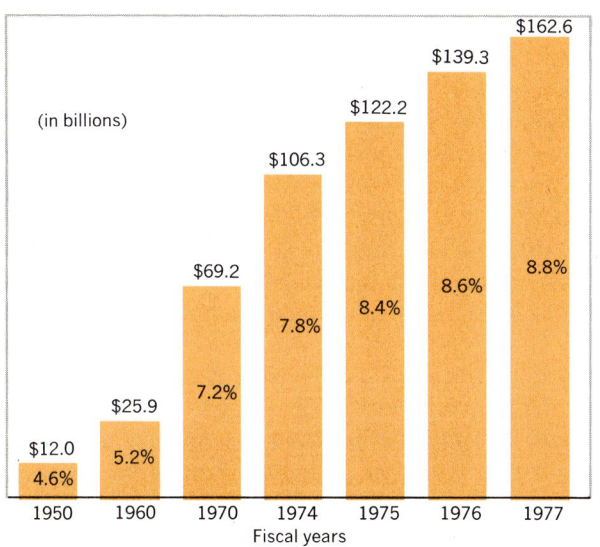

person becomes ill, it is more costly than ever before to regain his or her health.

Why have these costs risen so drastically? First, inflation has obviously been a factor. It is variously estimated that 40 to 50 percent of the increase in the cost of health services can be attributed to inflation in prices.[57] Second, a number of factors have increased the demand for health services substantially. Our population is larger and more affluent, which stretches the resources of the health care delivery system. Furthermore, the increased life expectancy of Americans means that a larger proportion of our population is old, and old people require more health care than young people. Another factor is increasing demand in the growing range of services available in many hospitals and health centers: psychiatric facilities, outpatient clinics, rehabilitation units, and laboratory facilities.

Third, costly diagnostic and treatment procedures that were unheard of a few decades ago are now commonplace. For example, today we spend tens of thousands of dollars on new intensive-care procedures to save newborn infants who would have died a decade ago when these techniques were not available. Fifteen years ago, we did not have such tremendously expensive medical innovations as cobalt machines, heart pacemakers, artificial heart valves, and microsurgical instruments that make it possible to perform surgery under a microscope.[58] Fourth, the many technically and professionally trained groups, such as nurses, therapists, and the like, are demanding salaries commensurate with their training and responsibilities. Physicians' salaries continue to rise at a substantially higher rate than the salaries of other occupations. Physicians continue to work in a largely noncompetitive setting and are thus able to set their fees without taking market considerations into account. Furthermore, physicians are in the somewhat unique position of being able to create the demand for their own services (because they determine what type of and how much treatment a patient should receive), and increasing demand leads to rising prices.

Finally, the widespread acceptance of health insurance has increased the cost of health care because physicians are more likely to recommend expensive diagnostic and surgical procedures if they feel it will not financially burden the patient. Furthermore, the increasing fear of malpractice suits encourages this excessive use of diagnostic procedures. Evidence is mounting that the increase in health care costs is partly due to the amount of unnecessary surgery performed in the United States. After reviewing many studies, journalism professor Spencer Klaw concludes that "at least one out of every five or six operations in the United States is medically unjustified."[59] Tonsillectomies, appendectomies, and hysterectomies are particularly susceptible to this alleged abuse. The number of hysterectomies (the removal of the uterus) has risen considerably in the United States in the past decade. Studies of some hospitals have shown that from 31 to 45 percent of the hysterectomies performed are medically unjustified.[60] Why do physicians perform surgery that is not medically necessary? In some cases, a surgeon who performs a particular operation hundreds of times a year may become skeptical of nonsurgical forms of treatment and almost habitually recommend surgery; in other cases, operations may be performed for practice by surgical residents recently graduated from medical schools. Finally, we cannot ignore the fact that the profits from such surgery will easily tempt the unscrupulous.

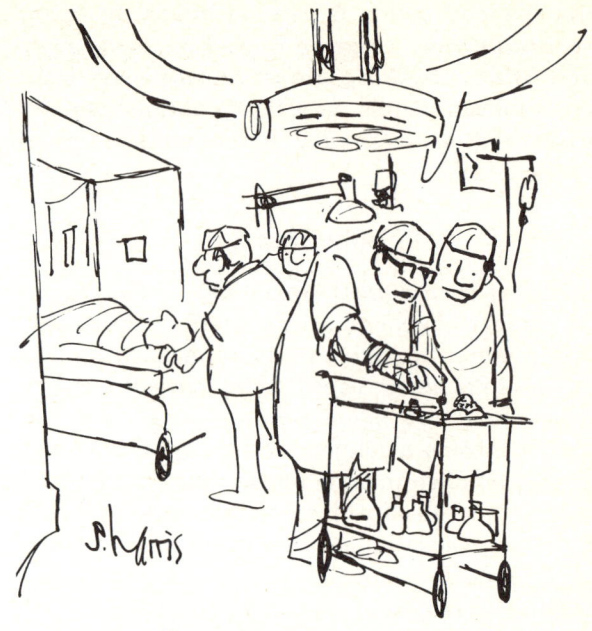

"THAT WASN'T BAD. I LOST MY SCALPEL, BUT I FOUND MELTON'S SPONGE."

FUTURE PROSPECTS: THE POLITICS OF HEALTH CARE

Some of the problems discussed in this chapter are not easily amenable to solutions in the short term. For example, clarification of the nature of mental illness will occur only after much research and analysis of the problem. However, in other areas, such as the dehumanization in health care institutions or the rising cost of health care, efforts at change are being made that could come to fruition quickly. In this regard, the health field today is the scene of rapid and, in some cases, fundamental developments that will alter the shape of health care in the future. We will now consider some of the more important changes.

New Programs and Health Practitioners

How can medical treatment and health care organizations be made more humane while at the same time the cost of health care is reduced? Increasing the size and the training of the staff would ease some problems at some institutions, but this would probably cost more. **A real solution to these problems may require a major reorganization of our thinking about health care delivery.** To illustrate this, we will look at three new programs that have been initiated recently in the United States.

Family Practice

There has been a great lament over the decline in the number of general practitioners — doctors with no specialty who take care of an individual's or a family's total health needs. In the days of the G.P., health care was often more personal, with the physician being a member of the neighborhood he served and often making house calls. It is unlikely that the house call will ever come back into style, but a new speciality has developed to fill some of these needs. An innovative training program called **Family Practice** was approved by the House of Delegates of the American Medical Association in 1968.[61] Family Practice is a medical specialty in which the physician, following medical school and a year of internship, goes through a residency program in which he receives advanced training in a broad range of medical areas so that he is better able to recognize a variety of health problems. (The general practitioner had no such advanced training in a residency program.)

A family physician is intended to be the first contact the patient has with the health care system. The family physician evaluates the patient's needs, provides the necessary care, and recommends a specialist's care if appropriate. In addition, the family physician should provide continuity of health care by coordinating and integrating the treatment of each specialist who cares for the patient. The family physician should ideally prevent the patient from becoming lost in the often impersonal maze of specialized health care.

Have family practitioners been able to eliminate dehumanization and reduce the shortage of medical personnel? It is too early to tell, since the program is so new. Because it is only a decade old, its role in providing health care has not yet totally evolved. There are still comparatively few family practice physicians, and the demand on those who do go into this field is great. Because of this, we may find that the offices of family practice physicians do not eliminate the conditions that lead to frustration and dehumanization: long waits, brusqueness and impersonality on the part of the staff, a primary concern with a single symptom, and little follow-up care. In some cases, family practice may simply add another medical bill prior to seeing a specialist.[62] However, the program has addressed some of the basic problems in the organization of health care and represents a departure from the increasing specialization that has led to segmentation of health care.

New Health Practitioners

A major problem facing health organizations is a shortage of personnel, especially physicians. This problem is compounded by the increasing demand for medical care. Furthermore, the distribution of physicians in the United States is very uneven. Rural areas are vastly undersupplied with doctors because the rewards of the medical profession (high income and prestige among colleagues) are more often found in the large cities.

One response to these problems is to provide some **New Health Practitioners** (NHPs) with the training and expertise to handle relatively simple medical problems and thereby make it possible for the physician to spend his or her time on more serious health problems.[63] The new roles of *physician's assistant* and *nurse practitioner* are intended for this purpose. The physician's assistant (or physician's associate) usually has two years of training beyond a college degree and can work only under the supervision of a physician. Nurse practitioners (or nurse clinicians) are registered nurses who have advanced training that may include achievement of the Master's degree. Their major task is to relieve the physician of those tasks that do not require the high level of training that physicians receive. For example, nurse practitioners conduct routine physical examinations, simple emergency care, prenatal care, and the like. They normally work under the guidance of a physician and may serve as the initial contact patients have with the health care system.

At this point, it is difficult to evaluate the outcome of these developments. As with family practice, these roles are still quite new, and there are relatively few NHPs. Many doctors have been reluctant to accept them fully, owing to the belief that only physicians are competent to provide the services that NHPs have begun to provide. However, most patients seem to have accepted these NHPs. Studies indicate that physician's assistants and nurse practitioners spend more time with patients and are less intolerant of minor symptoms than physicians. They provide care that is equivalent in quality to that provided by physicians, and patients are quite satisfied. Like the family practitioner program, the NHP plan may alleviate some important problems in the health field. These new practitioners can increase the number of health care providers at a considerably lower cost than training new physicians would entail. In addition, they can help relieve the problem of the maldistribution of health care workers by providing health care to small towns and rural areas.[64]

Community Health Centers

One way to reduce the bureaucratic impersonality that assails people in health care institutions is to reduce the size of health care facilities and make them a part of the communities they serve. Community health centers provide a wide range of therapeutic and preventive services for people who need not be hospitalized. They often take steps to establish a relaxed, more personal atmosphere, which large institutions seem unable to provide. In addition, many of these centers receive input from the community concerning the organization and operation of the center. All of this is oriented toward reducing the feelings of depersonalization and lack of control that arise in most bureaucratic structures.

These neighborhood centers have clearly been effective in bringing health care to more people and in changing their attitudes toward physicians and health care. For example, after one neighborhood health center was established, an evaluation of the program showed that community members received more medical care, made more preventive visits to the doctor, participated in more immunization programs, and were less likely to postpone receiving medical care than prior to the opening of the center.[65]

Other Developments

There are other programs that can help alleviate the problems that confront many health care bureaucracies today. For example, some hospitals have established patient **ombudsmen** whose purpose is to protect and fight for the interests of the patient. This is a reflection of a growing concern for rights of health care consumers and the value of bringing them into the decision-making process. In 1974, President Ford signed a bill establishing a network of Health Systems Agencies (HSAs) across the United States. The purpose of HSAs is to help decide how federal money for health care is to be spent, to coordinate the expenditure of health care funds to reduce overlap of services, to bring down the cost of health care, and to ensure the widest availablility of services. An important part of this law is that each HSA must have a consumer majority on its board—that is, people who are not involved in providing health care or teaching health care practitioners.[66] While developments such as ombudsmen and HSAs are certainly valuable, their impact cannot be fully appreciated until we consider one final topic—the cost of health care and the manner in which we organize and finance the overall health care delivery system.

The Financing of Health Care

Third-Party Medicine

The traditional organization of health care delivery involves the private physician in solo practice on a **fee-for-service-basis**. By the terms of this arrangement, the patient pays the doctor directly for each service or treatment he receives. In other words, it is a commercial relationship, in which the doctor is a person in business providing a product or service to the patient, who purchases it for a specified amount of money. One problem with such an arrangement is that many people are reluctant to view their doctor as a person in business trying to earn a dollar, and in fact the doctor-patient relationship is based on the assumption that the doctor will act solely in terms of the interests of the patient. We prefer to view doctors as people we can trust to make clinical decisions based on an interest in our physical well-being rather than in their financial gain. Another problem in the fee-for-service arrangement is that as health care costs have increased, few people have saved enough money to pay the thousands of dollars that even a minor illness might cost.

The fee-for-service arrangement has been largely replaced in the United States by *third-party medicine,* **in which the patient pays premiums into a fund and the doctor is paid from this fund when the patient receives treatment.** The "third party" might be either a private health insurance company or a government health program. In 1950, approximately 32 percent of all personal health expenditures were paid through some third-party arrangement. In 1974, that figure had more than doubled to about 65 percent.[67] By 1970, about three-quarters of the people in the United States had some sort of hospital and surgical-medical coverage. Higher-income groups are more likely to have such health insurance; however, low-income groups have made advances in the past few decades (see Fig. 8.5). Most of this third-party health care coverage involves private insurance companies, the best known being the various Blue Cross/Blue Shield programs.

Do these third-party arrangements solve the problems of financing health care? Do they make health care more available to people? A first problem with such financing arrangements is that they do not encourage efficiency and economy in the delivery of health care and thereby tend to increase its overall cost. Since the patient will not have to pay for costly diagnostic or treatment procedures, there is a tendency for physicians to recommend these more freely than if the patient had to pay for each service provided. As we have seen, surgery that is not really essential is sometimes performed. There is no incentive to encourage efficiency and economy. The physician is still a person in business who can make a greater profit if he or she provides more

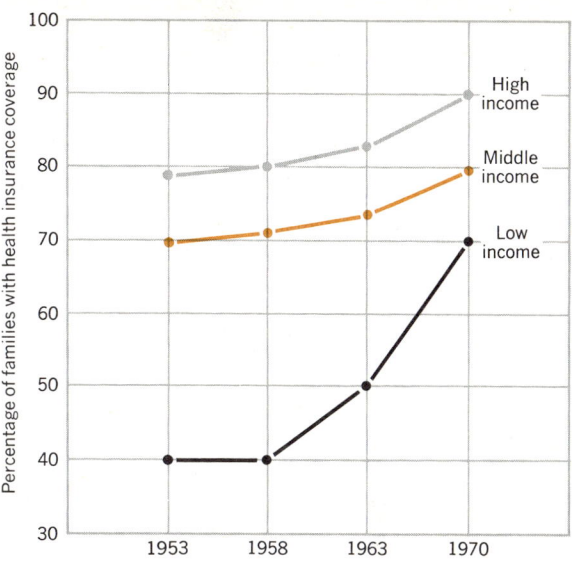

Figure 8.5 Social Class and Health Insurance Coverage, 1953–1970. Ronald Andersen, Joanna Lion, and Odlin Anderson, *Two Decades of Health Services* (Cambridge, Mass.: Ballinger, 1976), p. 124. Reprinted by permission.

services. In addition, the maximum fee schedule provided by the insurance company has become the standard fee for particular procedures.

A second problem with private health insurance is that it is not usually available to the poor, the aged, and the unemployed who cannot afford the premiums or do not have jobs where such insurance is available. The federal government made an effort to cope with this problem in the 1960s by establishing two programs now commonly known as Medicare and Medicaid. *Medicare* is intended for those over 65. It pays for some hospitalization or nursing-home care and makes available some low-cost government-financed health insurance that people can obtain voluntarily for a small fee. *Medicaid* is a joint federal-state program to provide medical care for low-income people of any age.

These programs are based on the belief that all people have a right to medical care, and they have certainly removed some of the economic barriers to health care. However, they are not free of problems. Fraud committed by both recipients and providers of health care has been commonplace. Phy-

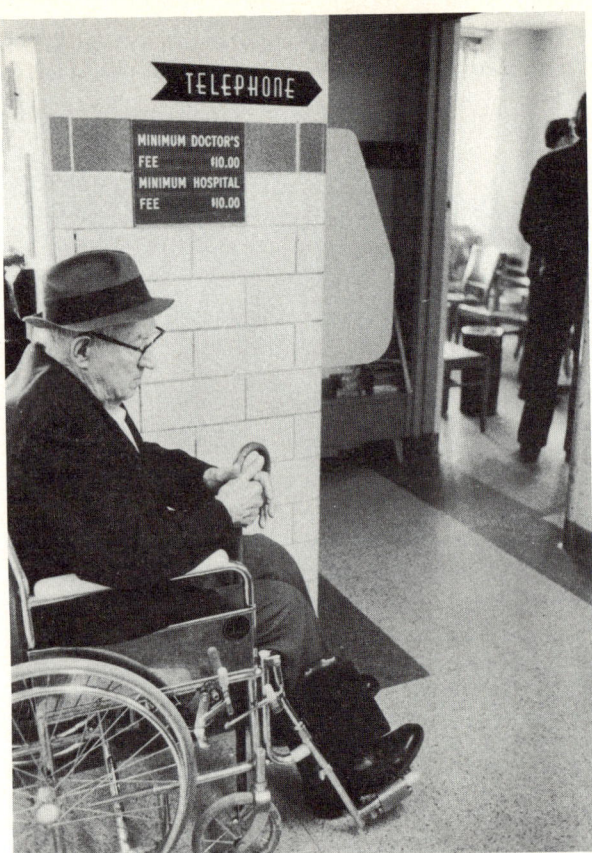

In the debate over the best method for financing health care, many are concerned with providing adequate services for all people, including the poor, while at the same time controlling the skyrocketing cost of medical treatment.

sicians have provided more treatment than is really necessary; medical laboratories have received payment for tests never performed. In such a large, cumbersome program, some abuse is inevitable, but it increases the cost of health care. In addition, these programs encourage inefficient utilization in the same way that private health insurance does—there is no mechanism in either approach to reward efficiency and economy.[68]

National Health Insurance

The United States has been moving in the direction of some form of *national health insurance*—**provided by the government to cover most, or all, American citizens.** If such a program is passed, it would be a move beyond the Medicare and Medicaid programs since national health insurance would not be limited to a small category of people. There are numerous proposals currently being considered. One plan was developed by the Nixon-Ford administration. It required that all employers offer some type of comprehensive private health insurance to their employees, while the government would continue to provide such insurance for the poor, the unemployed, and the elderly. Employees would share in the cost of the plan both through monthly premium payments and through a deductible charge on services. While this plan retains private health insurance companies as the mainstay of health financing, it is a departure from existing arrangements because of the requirement that all people have some coverage made available to them. In addition, the coverage required is broader than in most current health insurance plans (e.g. it includes dental coverage). A more comprehensive proposal under consideration is the Corman-Kennedy Bill, which would establish a single federal health insurance plan that would pay all the costs of health care for all people. Furthermore, it would call for complete financing through taxes—there would be no cost-sharing by the patient through a deductible charge on each service.[69]

There are a number of other proposals under consideration, and, although it is likely that some such policy will be adopted, it is impossible at this point to determine what its form will be. Because of this uncertainty, only general comments can be made. National health insurance would solve certain problems—it would further narrow the gap between income groups in terms of the financial availability of health care, and it would give the government a more direct means of controlling health care costs. However, national health insurance would still be a form of third-party medicine, and as such it would exhibit many of the same shortcomings that we considered in the preceding section. Thus, unless a program could be devised that would overcome these problems, national health insurance would be no panacea.[70]

Prepaid Group Plans

How do we reward the efficient and economic provision of health services? How do we encourage doctors and patients to more effectively utilize health facilities? One possible solution is a program of "comprehensive medical care" or *prepaid group plans* (also called health maintenance organizations or HMOs).[71] In this approach, an individual (or employer) pays a monthly premium and the health organization provides all of that person's health care needs. (Sometimes a nominal fee for each service is required.) Such prepaid group plans are "comprehensive" because they try to prevent disease as well as cure that which exists. Furthermore, many of these organizations employ all the health care personnel that provide care (although some of the smaller groups must contract with private physicians).

While there are still few people covered by such plans (see Table 8.4), there are many different types in existence. The Kaiser-Permanente Health Plan, originally begun in the 1930s by a private corporation to provide care for its employees, is no longer limited to employees of the corporation and is the largest and possibly most successful prepaid group plan. The Health Insurance Plan in New York is a community nonprofit organization. Some are organized by labor unions or local medical societies. In 1971, the United States Department of Health, Education, and Welfare listed the advantages of such organizations:

> They emphasize prevention and early care; they provide incentives for holding down costs and for increasing the productivity of resources; they offer opportunities for improving the quality of care; they provide a means for improving the geographic distribution of care; and by mobilizing private capital and managerial talent, they reduce the need for federal funds and direct control.[72]

Comprehensive health plans provide new ways of organizing the delivery of health care. The economic incentive to overutilize health care services is eliminated because the doctor is not paid for each service provided. When the doctor is paid for

TABLE 8.4

Percentage of Total Population Covered by Hospital Insurance, by Type of Enrollment and Type of Insurer, 1953, 1958, 1963, 1970

TYPE OF ENROLLMENT AND INSURER[a]	PERCENTAGE WITH HOSPITAL INSURANCE COVERAGE			
	1953	1958	1963	1970
Group				
Blue Cross	21	23	24	30
Private insurance	17	23	27	27
Prepaid group practices, other independents	5	6	5	6
CHAMPUS	—[c]	1	1	1
Medicare	—	—[c]	—[c]	10
Nongroup				
Blue Cross	6	8	7	7
Private insurance	12	9	10	8
Prepaid group practices, other independents	b	1	1	b
Total	57	65	68	77

[a] Individuals covered by two or more policies carried through different types of enrollment or underwritten by different types of insurers are counted twice in this table.

[b] Less than 0.5 percent.

[c] Program not yet in existence.

SOURCE. Ronald Andersen, Joanna Lion, and Odin Anderson, *Two Decades of Health Services* (Cambridge, Mass.: Ballinger Publishing Co., 1976), p. 130. Reprinted with permission.

each service provided, it is to his economic advantage to provide more services. When a member of a comprehensive health plan pays the same monthly premium whether sick or well, and pays no extra for treatment when sick, it is to the advatnage of the organization to make sure that the member stays well and to ensure that unnecessary care is not provided when he or she is sick. The more the member is sick, the more costly it is for the organization.

Does it work? Although many of these plans are relatively new, some findings point to their superiority over other modes of providing health care. For example, people in such prepaid group plans have a lower mortality rate, fewer premature births, lower rates of hospital admissions, and fewer surgical procedures than do people in private

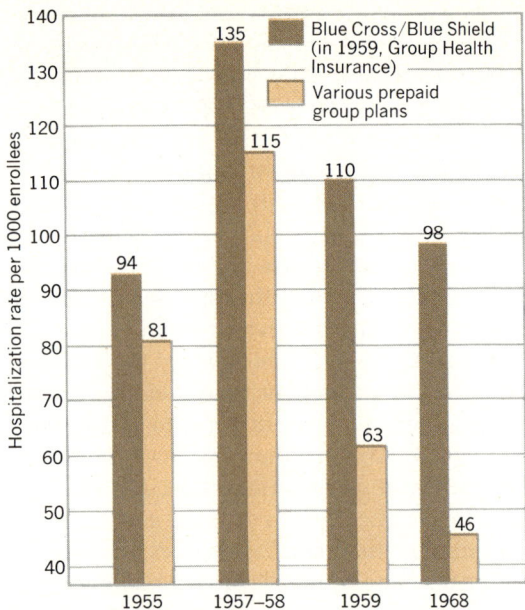

Figure 8.6 **Hospitalization Rates in Prepaid Group Plans (HMOs) and Third-Party Health Insurance Plans.** Duane F. Stroman, *The Medical Establishment and Social Responsibility* (Port Washington, N.Y.: Kennikat Press, 1976), p. 78.

health insurance plans (see Fig. 8.6). The prepaid group plans also have lower overall costs per participant. Whether these results are due to the better preventive care provided by the organization or to the fact that healthier people join such plans, we cannot yet say.[73] If they are the result of the better care provided by comprehensive prepaid group plans, then this is a strong argument in favor of choosing this method of financing our health care delivery system.

Interest Groups in the Health Field

From a conflict perspective, health care policy is developed as a result of the continuous clashing and give-and-take between interest groups with varying amounts of political resources. While the interest groups that vie for control of health care policy change over time, today four groups are especially significant in policy determination: physicians, the government, health practitioners other than physicians, and the health care consumer.

Physicians

A century ago, developments in chemistry, biology, and other sciences made it possible for physicians to deal effectively with sickness and disease. They were at the stage where they could successfully treat many conditions. In addition to their increasing technical competence, physicians began to organize in order to exert more political clout. In 1847, the many local and state medical societies in the United States were incorporated into the American Medical Association (AMA). The goals of the AMA included promotion of legislation favorable to the emerging profession, elimination of untrained and unlicensed practitioners of medicine, and the reduction of corruption among physicians. Because of their ability to effectively treat disease and their emergence as a strong political force, physicians have been the most powerful group in the determination of health care policy in the United States for the past century. Their position has been difficult to challenge because of their political power and their technical knowledge.

In many cases, the AMA has used its strong political position and its considerable resources to obstruct new health care policies viewed as detrimental to its members' interests. For example, there is developing support in the United States for some form of national health insurance; however, the AMA has been vehemently opposed to any such program. The AMA opposed the Medicare and Medicaid programs by arguing that they indicated a drift toward socialized medicine in the United States; although unsuccessful, the AMA spent hundreds of thousands of dollars in attempts to prevent their establishment. Through lobbying, campaign contributions, and the personal contacts of its members with politicians, the AMA has been able to impede, if not completely stop, other programs regarded as threatening to its own interests and values. For example, when the Nixon administration during the early 1970s promoted health maintenance organizations, the American Medical Political Action Committee—the political arm of the AMA—contributed $600,000 to the campaigns of senators and representatives in the hope (in this case correct) that the legislators could be influenced to oppose such developments.[74] Physicians are normally among the elite decision makers in local communities and thus have personal access to legislators. Among other things, this gives them an additional opportunity to influence decisions regarding health care policy.

The Government

For half a century, the government has become more involved in many parts of our lives — social security, welfare, safe food and drugs, air pollution, to name several. It is only natural that government would become more interested in the type of health care received by our citizens. The government has exerted its influence in the health field in a number of ways. It has stepped into areas that the medical profession finds unprofitable, such as public health. It has influenced the choice of medical specialties by medical students through selective distribution of federal funds to medical schools. It has encouraged the experimentation with HMOs by providing federal grants to groups that wish to start such organizations. As government interest in health care has developed, the medical profession has frequently been challenged because government officials have less of a vested interest in the medical status quo.

Other Health Practitioners

In addition to the government, a second challenge to the position of physicians comes from the other health professionals, especially the nursing profession. The traditional relationship between the physician and the nurse is one of superior and subordinate. However, as the training and skills of nurses have increased, they have begun to challenge, among other things, this traditional relationship through various organizations, such as the American Nurses Association and the National League for Nursing. They are attempting to use political resources — just as the physicians have done — to pursue their own interests.

Health Care Consumers

A third challenge to the status quo in the medical field comes from the health care consumer — that is, all of us who need medical care at some time. What rights does the patient have? Beginning in the 1960s, the traditionally powerless consumers began to organize to promote policies in their own interests. This occurred in the areas of auto design, food packaging, environmental pollution, and in the health field. Even though patients had always had certain legal rights, health care facilities did not commonly publicize the rights to which patients were entitled. In 1972 the American Hospital Association responded to pressure by accepting a "Patient's Bill of Rights," which listed the rights — not privileges — that a patient is entitled to. Among other things, these include the right to considerate and respectful treatment, the right to information about one's condition and treatment, the right to refuse treatment, the right to privacy, and the right to confidentiality in consultations, examinations, and treatments. The result of these consumer pressures has been to challenge the control of diagnosis, treatment, and health care policy that has traditionally rested with the physician.[75]

The traditional doctor-patient relationship is based on trust — the patient trusts the physician to make clinical decisions that are in the best interest of the patient, who has faith that the physician's only motive is the patient's welfare. However, the increasing cost of medical care, the rising incidence of unnecessary surgery, and the continuing dehumanization of health care institutions have created discontent, and this has encouraged more people to question the physician's privileged position. For example, activist women's groups are struggling for the right of women to be given all information concerning gynecological conditions and treatment so that a woman can decide what is best for her rather than trusting the "expert" opinion of the physician.[76]

CONCLUSION

At a time when Americans have access to better health care than in the past, there seems to be more concern over problems of health than ever before. Unacceptably high infant mortality rates, skyrocketing health care costs, bureaucratic dehumanization, increasing rates of mental illness — all of these issues have led Americans to scrutinize their health care delivery system. We have reviewed the dimensions of these problems in this chapter. We can conclude by utilizing our three theoretical perspectives to envision what might be in store in the field of health in the near future.

According to the functionalist perspective, any social institution—whether it is the family, the educational system, or the health care system—must be to some degree consistent with the values of the major groups in society and must be integrated with the other parts of society. In evaluating proposed solutions to problems in the health field, this functionalist position must be kept in mind. Thus, changes in the health care system cannot be totally inconsistent with our major values. We have only recently come to view health care as a right of all people, and we are only beginning to accept the idea that the government is obliged to ensure that all people receive health care. Furthermore, we still place great value on private enterprise, capitalism, private property, and individualism. There is a strong mistrust of government—especially the federal government. After the Watergate debacle, this became a major issue in the presidential campaign of 1976.

Given these values and beliefs, it is unlikely that the United States would turn at this time to a completely socialized medical system—one in which the government owned all medical facilities and in which medical personnel were employees of the government. The programs that are evolving in the United States today—prepaid comprehensive group plans (health maintenance organizations) and government-sponsored national health insurance—retain major aspects of the private enterprise dimension of our economy. Because they do not clash with our dominant values, while at the same time solving some of the important problems in the health field, they will probably become the backbone of our health care delivery system in the future.

We are clearly in the midst of a period of important and far-reaching social change in health care. The conflict perspective can be a useful aid in understanding this change. A number of different interest groups (physicians, nurses, technicians, and health care consumers) are competing for scarce valued resources in the medical field. Consumers want better and cheaper health care; physicians want to retain their position of dominance and control in health care decisions; nurses and technicians hope to improve their share of resources, both in terms of economic rewards and decision-making power. The final outcome will depend on the political resources that each group can bring to bear in the struggle. Physicians, for example, are certainly not on the way out. They will in all likelihood remain as one of the major groups in the health field. However, it appears that a rearrangement of valued resources may be occurring. Physicians may be forced to relinquish some of their exclusive control over health care decisions to consumers and other health professionals. They may have to share some of their prestige, and possibly some of their monetary rewards, with others in the field. In addition, because of rising costs and considerable dissatisfaction, the public is demanding more of health care institutions than they appear able to deliver—at least as currently organized. This pressure may also result in significant changes in the future.

Using the interactionist perspective, we can focus on shared expectations and people's definitions of reality. As medicine has become more successful at treating illness, people have grown to expect more —perhaps too much—from the health field. We tend to view any physical affliction or blemish as an illness requiring treatment. We expect medicine to be able to solve any physical problem, and when medicine fails, people are substantially dissatisfied. To some extent, this is the phenomenon of rising expectations: as conditions improve, people's expectations increase and they demand even more improvement. Yesterday's sought-after goal becomes today's taken-for-granted necessity. Given this phenomenon of rising expectations, we can expect people to put increasing demands on health care institutions in the future and to define health as a social problem if those demands are not met.

GLOSSARY TERMS

Acute disease
Allopathic physicians
Behavior therapy (Behavior
  modification)
Chronic disease
Community mental health
Crisis medicine
Curandera
Depersonalization
Downward drift hypothesis

Family practice medicine
Fee-for-service medicine
Homeopathy
Infant mortality
Morbidity
Mortality
Neurosis
New health practitioners
Ombudsmen

Prepaid group plans (health
  maintenance organizations)
Preventive medicine
Psychosis
Psychotherapy
Self-fulfilling prophecy
Social causation hypothesis
Third-party medicine
Thomsonianism

REFERENCES

[1] See William H. Glazier, "The Task of Medicine," *Scientific American* 228 (April 1973), pp. 13–17; National Institute of Mental Health, *Psychiatric Services and the Changing Institutional Scene, 1950–1985*, HEW Publication No. (ADM) 77-443 (Washington, D.C.: U.S. Government Printing Office, 1977); and National Center for Health Statistics, *Monthly Vital Statistics Report: Provisional Statistics* (June 16, 1978), p. 9.

[2] Rodney M. Coe, *Sociology of Medicine,* 2d ed. (New York: McGraw-Hill, 1978), pp. 129–171.

[3] Andrew C. Twaddle and Richard M. Hessler, *A Sociology of Health* (Saint Louis: C. V. Mosby Company, 1977), pp. 162–166.

[4] Benjamin Rush, *Medical Inquiries and Observations upon the Diseases of the Mind*, 5th ed. (Philadelphia, 1835).

[5] John Duffy, *The Healers: The Rise of the Medical Establishment* (New York: McGraw-Hill, 1976).

[6] Coe, *Sociology of Medicine*, p. 271.

[7] Ibid., p. 187.

[8] See Ronda Kotelchuck, "Government Cost Control Strategies," *Health/PAC Bulletin*, (March/April 1977), pp. 3–6, and Ivan Illich, *Medical Nemesis: The Expropriation of Health* (New York: Pantheon Books, 1976).

[9] Glazier, "The State of Medicine," pp. 13–17, and National Center for Health Statistics, *Monthly Vital Statistics Report* (June 1978), p. 9.

[10] National Center for Health Statistics, *Health: United States, 1975*, HEW Publication No. (HRA) 76-1232 (Washington, D.C. U.S. Government Printing Office, 1976), p. 349.

[11] National Center for Health Statistics, *Health: United States, 1975*, p. 321, and U.S. Bureau of the Census, *Statistical Abstract of the United States, 1977* (Washington, D.C.: U.S. Government Printing Office, 1977), p. 108.

[12] Coe, *Sociology of Medicine*.

[13] Duane F. Stroman, *The Medical Establishment and Social Responsibility* (Port Washington, N.Y.: Kennikat Press, 1976), p. 40.

[14] Rene Dubos, *Man Adapting* (New Haven: Yale University Press, 1965).

[15] Robert L. Kane, Josephine M. Kasteler, and Robert M. Gray, eds., *The Health Gap: Medical Services and the Poor* (New York: Springer, 1976); A. Hollingshead and F. Redlich, *Social Class and Mental Illness*, New York: John Wiley & Sons, 1958); and Robert E. L. Faris and H. Warren Dunham, *Mental Disorders in Urban Areas* (Chicago: University of Chicago Press, 1938).

[16] See Ralph H. Hines, "The Health Status of Black Americans," in E. Gartly Jaco, ed., *Patients, Physicians, and Illness*, 2d ed. (New York: The Free Press, 1972), pp. 40–50.

[17] Ibid., p. 41. Emphasis added.

[18] Earl L. Koos, *The Health of Regionville* (New York: Columbia University Press, 1954).

[19] Edward A. Suchman, "Social Patterns of Illness and Health Care," *Journal of Health and Human Behavior* 6 (Spring 1965), pp. 2–16.

[20] National Center for Health Statistics, *Health: United States, 1975*, pp. 289–293; Myron J. Lefcowitz, "Poverty and Health: A Reexamination," in Kane et al., *The Health Gap*, pp. 42–43; and Ronald Andersen, Joanna Lion, and Odin Anderson, *Two Decades of Health Services* (Cambridge, Mass.: Ballinger Publishing Co., 1976), pp. 29–64.

[21] National Center for Health Statistics, *Health: United States, 1975*, pp. 405–424.

[22] Philip M. Moody and Robert M. Gray, "Social Class, Social Integration, and the Use of Preventive Health Services," in Jaco, *Patients, Physicians, and Illness*, pp. 250–261.

[23] See H. Warren Dunham, "City Core and Suburban

Fringe: Distribution Patterns of Mental Illness," in Stanley C. Plog and Robert B. Edgerton, eds., *Changing Perspectives in Mental Illness* (New York: Holt, Rinehart, and Winston, 1969), pp. 337–363; Leo Levy and Louis Rowitz, *The Ecology of Mental Disorders* (New York: Behavioral Publications, 1973); and Enrico Jones, "Social Class and Psychotherapy: A Critical Review of Research," *Psychiatry* 37 (November 1974), pp. 307–320.

[24] Twaddle and Hessler, *A Sociology of Health,* pp. 59–85; and William C. Cockerham, *Medical Sociology* (Englewood Cliffs, N.J.: Prentice-Hall, 1978), pp. 66–67.

[25] Walter R. Gove, "The Relationship Between Sex Roles, Marital Status, and Mental Illness," *Social Forces* 51 (September 1972), pp. 34–44.

[26] Phyllis Chesler, *Women and Madness* (New York: Avon Books, 1972).

[27] William Tudor, Jeannette F. Tudor, and Walter R. Gove, "The Effect of Sex Role Differences on the Social Control of Mental Illness," *Journal of Health and Social Behavior* 18 (June 1977), pp. 98–111.

[28] See Saxon Graham and Leo Reeder, "Social Factors in the Chronic Illnesses," in Howard E. Freeman, Sol Levine, and Leo Reeder, eds., *Handbook of Medical Sociology,* 2d ed. (Englewood Cliffs, N.J.: Prentice-Hall, 1972), pp. 89–98.

[29] See the discussion in chapter 5, and Table 5.3.

[30] See M. Harvey Brenner. *Mental Illness and the Economy* (Cambridge, Mass.: Harvard University Press, 1973), and David Mechanic, *Medical Sociology,* 2d ed. (New York: The Free Press, 1978), pp. 169–170.

[31] Brenner, *Mental Illness and the Economy.*

[32] Twaddle and Hessler, *A Sociology of Health,* pp. 59–93, and Andersen, et al., *Two Decades of Health Services,* pp. 29–40.

[33] Lefcowitz, "Poverty and Health," p. 47.

[34] Michel Foucault, *Madness and Civilization* (New York: Random House, 1965).

[35] See Shirley S. Angrist, "The Mental Hospital: Its History and Destiny," in Stephen Spitzer and Norman Denzin, eds., *The Mental Patient* (New York: McGraw-Hill, 1968), pp. 298–304, and David Rothman, *The Discovery of the Asylum* (Boston: Little, Brown, 1971).

[36] See Miriam Siegler and Humphrey Osmond, *Models of Madness, Models of Medicine* (New York: Harper & Row, 1974).

[37] Thomas J. Scheff, *Labeling Madness* (Englewood Cliffs, N.J.: Prentice-Hall, 1975).

[38] Thomas S. Szasz, *Ideology and Insanity* (Garden City, N.Y.: Doubleday, 1970).

[39] Ibid., pp. 22–23.

[40] Richard B. Stuart, *Trick or Treatment: How and When Psychotherapy Fails* (Champaign, Ill.: Research Press, 1970).

[41] Ibid. See also Scheff, *Labeling Madness,* and Ari Kiev, *Magic, Faith, and Healing: Studies in Primitive Psychiatry* (New York: The Free Press, 1964).

[42] Nathan Hurvitz, "Psychotherapy as a Means of Social Control," *Journal of Consulting and Clinical Psychology* 40 (April 1973), pp. 232–239.

[43] David C. Rimm and John C. Masters, *Behavior Therapy: Techniques and Empirical Findings* (New York; Academic Press, 1974).

[44] Alejandro Portes, "On the Emergence of Behavior Therapy in Modern Society," *Journal of Consulting and Clinical Psychology* 36 (June 1971), pp. 303–313.

[45] Ibid., p. 305.

[46] Stuart E. Golann and Carl Eisdorfer, *Handbook of Community Mental Health* (New York: Appleton-Century-Crofts, 1972).

[47] See Franklin D. Chu and Sharland Trotter, *The Madness Establishment* (New York: Grossman Publishers, 1974), and Alcohol, Drug Abuse and Mental Health Administration, *Mental Health Statistical Note No. 146,* HEW Publication No. (ADM) 78-158 (Washington, D.C.: U.S. Government Printing Office, March 1978).

[48] Seymour S. Bellin and H. Jack Geiger, "The Impact of a Neighborhood Health Center on Patients' Behavior and Attitudes Relating to Health Care: A Study of a Low Income Housing Project," *Medical Care* 10 (May–June, 1972), pp. 224–239.

[49] For critiques of Community Mental Health, see Chu and Trotter, *The Madness Establishment,* Franklyn N. Arnhoff, "Social Consequences of Policy Toward Mental Illness," *Science* 188 (June 27, 1975), pp. 1277–1281; and Joseph L. Falkson, "Minor Skirmish in a Monumental Struggle: HEW's Analysis of Mental Health Services," *Policy Analysis* 2 (Winter 1976), pp. 93–120.

[50] National Center for Health Statistics, *Health: United States, 1975.*

[51] See Margaret Clark, *Health in the Mexican-American Culture* (Berkeley: University of California Press, 1959), and Arthur J. Rubel, "The Epidemiology of a Folk Illness: *Susto* in Hispanic America," in Ricardo Arguijo Martinez, ed., *Hispanic Culture and Health Care: Fact, Fiction, Folklore* (St. Lous: C. V. Mosby Company, 1978), pp. 75–91.

[52] David Mechanic, *The Growth of Bureaucratic Medicine* (New York: John Wiley & Sons, 1976).

[53] See Erving Goffman, *Asylums* (New York: Doubleday, 1961).

[54] David L. Rosenhan, "On Being Sane in Insane Places," *Science* 179 (January 19, 1973), pp. 250–258.

[55] See Spencer Klaw, *The Great American Medicine Show* (New York: Viking Press, 1975), and Cockerham, *Medical Sociology,* p. 191.

[56] Andersen et al., *Two Decades of Health Services.*

[57] National Center for Health Statistics, *Health: United States, 1975,* p. 11, and Stroman, *The Medical Establishment and Social Responsibility,* pp. 66–67.

[58] Klaw, *The Great American Medicine Show.*

[59] Ibid., p. 7.

[60] See Duane F. Stroman, *The Quick Knife: Unnecessary*

Surgery U.S.A. (Port Washington, N.Y.: Kennikat Press, 1978).

[61] Klaw, *The Great American Medicine Show*, and Twaddle and Hessler, *A Sociology of Health*, pp. 219–221.

[62] Joanne Lukomnik, "Family Practice: Teaching New Docs Old Tricks," *Health/PAC Bulletin* (January–February 1978), pp. 1–2, 25–31.

[63] See Klaw, *The Great American Medicine Show*, and Eugene Stewart Schneller, *The Physician's Assistant* (Lexington, Mass.: Lexington Books, 1978).

[64] Ibid.

[65] Bellin and Geiger, "The Impact of a Neighborhood Health Center on Patients' Behavior and Attitudes Relating to Health Care," pp. 224–239.

[66] Klaw, *The Great American Medicine Show*, and Darryl D. Enos and Paul Sultan, *The Sociology of Health Care: Social, Economic, and Political Perspectives* (New York: Frederick A. Praeger, 1977), pp. 268–279.

[67] National Center for Health Statistics, *Health: United States, 1975*, p. 41.

[68] Enos and Sultan, *The Sociology of Health Care.*

[69] Bridger M. Mitchell and William B. Schwartz, "The Financing of National Health Insurance," *Science* 192 (May 14, 1976), pp. 621–629.

[70] Cockerham, *Medical Sociology*, pp. 212–216.

[71] See David Kotelchuck, ed., *Prognosis Negative: Crisis in the Health Care System* (New York: Vintage Books, 1976), pp. 345–386.

[72] United States Department of Health, Education, and Welfare, *Toward a Comprehensive Health Policy for the 1970s: A White Paper* (Washington, D.C.: U.S. Government Printing Office, 1971), p. 31.

[73] Mechanic, *The Growth of Bureaucratic Medicine.*

[74] See Klaw, *The Great American Medicine Show*, and Twaddle and Hessler, *A Sociology of Health*, pp. 232–233.

[75] Enos and Sultan, *The Sociology of Health Care*, pp. 381–382.

[76] Barbara Seaman, *Free and Female* (New York: Coward, McCann, & Geoghegan, 1972), and Pauline Bart, "Women's Self-Help: A New Medical Concept," paper presented at the Annual Meeting of the North Central Sociological Association, 1974.

SUGGESTED READINGS

Brown, George W., and Harris, Tirril. *Social Origins of Depression: A Study of Psychiatric Disorder in Women.* New York: The Free Press, 1978.
A comprehensive study of the relationship between social environment and mental disorders. A good discussion of the complexity of social factors related to mental illness.

Chesler, Phyllis. *Women and Madness.* New York: Avon Books, 1972.
A very readable analysis of the reasons why women have higher rates of mental disorders than men and how women are treated by psychiatrists and others in the mental health field.

Corea, Gena. *The Hidden Malpractice: How American Medicine Mistreats Women.* New York: Harcourt, Brace, Jovanovich, Jove Books, 1977.
A tirade against the way in which women are treated by the health system in the United States. It includes a lengthy discussion of how women were gradually barred from healing roles by men during the nineteenth century.

Illich, Ivan. *Medical Nemesis: The Expropriation of Health.* New York: Bantam Books, 1976.
A scathing critique of the medical system in the United States today. The author argues that the health care delivery system is as detrimental to our health as it is beneficial.

Knowles, John H. *Doing Better and Feeling Worse: Health in the United States.* New York: W. W. Norton, 1977.
A collection of readings by physicians, psychiatrists, sociologists, and others knowledgeable about the health field. A reasoned and scholarly discussion of a wide range of problems in health care and possible solutions.

Kotelchuck, David, ed. *Prognosis Negative: Crisis in the Health Care System.* New York: Vintage Books, 1976.
An indictment of the health care system by the Health Policy Advisory Center. There is much emphasis on the problems of health care workers and an analysis of various ways of organizing health, such as HMOs.

Magaro, Peter A., Gripp, Robert, and McDowell, David J. *The Mental Health Industry: A Cultural Phenomenon.* New York: John Wiley & Sons, 1978.
An analysis of the provision of mental health within the context of cultural determinants and relevant vested interests. It evaluates the effectiveness of different types of treatment techniques.

Maxmen, Jerrold S. *The Post-Physician Era: Medicine in the 21st Century.* New York: John Wiley & Sons, 1976.
A radical approach to reorganizing health care delivery in the United States. It is argued that computers and television are two factors that will become extremely important and that will make physicians, as we know them, obsolete.

Szasz, Thomas S. *Ideology and Insanity: Essays on the Psychiatric Dehumanization of Man.* Garden City, N.Y.: Doubleday, Anchor Books, 1970.
A classic, unique, and stimulating approach to understanding mental illness and psychiatric treatment. The book argues that we must completely change our thinking about the nature of mental illness.

Questions
for Discussion

1. The functionalist approach emphasizes the smooth operation and survival of society. Under what conditions would a functionalist view illness—physical or mental—as a social problem? When would the interactionist do so?

2. From the conflict perspective, why is good health unequally distributed in society? How does this uneven distribution come about?

3. Which conception of the nature of mental illness is most compatible with the interactionist perspective? the conflict perspective? the functionalist perspective? Why?

4. What are the manifest and latent functions of the various types of treatment for mental illness?

5. The interactionist perspective emphasizes the importance of the interaction between self and others in creating social reality and in the development of a person's self-concept. From this point of view, how do health care institutions influence the individual? What important processes would the functionalist study in those same health care institutions? Why?

6. For the functionalist, any system must adapt to changing conditions that arise either within the system itself or from some external source. What changes are occurring within the health care system in response to concerns about dissatisfaction and dehumanization? Which of these changes seems likely to be effective?

7. From the conflict perspective, what are the mechanisms that have led to the increase in health costs in the United States?

8. From a functionalist perspective, health care programs must ensure that good health is available to enough people at an affordable cost so that people have adequate health to perform the essential tasks and roles in society. Which of the alternative programs available would best fit these requirements? Why? From a conflict perspective, health care programs result from the clash of competing interest groups with different amounts of resources. From this point of view, which of the alternative health care programs available is likely to become our primary means of financing health care in the future? Why?

CHAPTER 9

Work and Leisure

WORK AND LEISURE: A BRIEF HISTORY

The Emergence of a Leisure Class. The Emergence of
the Protestant Ethic. The Protestant Ethic and American
Values. Work and Leisure in Industrial Society.

WORK AND LEISURE AS SOCIAL PROBLEMS

The Functionalist Perspective. The Conflict Perspective.
The Interactionist Perspective. What Are Work and
Leisure?

WORK

The Multiple Dimensions of Work. The Decline of the
Work Ethic.

LEISURE

Reduced Work and Increased Leisure. Block Leisure
Time. Difficulties in Using Leisure Time. For Whom Is
Leisure a Problem?

THE FUTURE OF WORK AND LEISURE

The Decline of Individualism. The Reorganization of Work.
Leisure as Consumption. Scenarios of the Future.

CONCLUSION

William Faulkner once commented:

You can't eat for eight hours a day nor drink for eight hours a day nor make love for eight hours a day—all you can do for eight hours is work. Which is the reason why man makes himself and everybody else so miserable and unhappy.

More recently, George Allen, while he was head coach and general manager of the Washington Redskins, remarked:

If you enjoy your job, it isn't work. It's fun. If you detest going to work, then you're looking for ways to beat the clock. I'd rather come to the Redskin Park and do my thing, so-to-speak, than I would play golf. Golf is a fine sport, but it's too time-consuming. I don't have that time schedule.[1]

When we meet someone for the first time, one of the most important pieces of information we learn about that person is, what kind of work does he or she do? What is his or her occupation? We view a person's work as very important—it says a lot about that person. Yet, as the preceding comments illustrate, people have very different reactions to work and its related condition of leisure. Some view both very positively, while others see work as a curse, with leisure as the goal of life. There are even those who are at a loss when faced with the problem of filling up leisure time. Finally, work and leisure—central parts of our lives—are often misunderstood. One of the goals of this chapter is to clarify what work and leisure are and the role they play in our lives.

Most Americans place great value on work—it should be a satisfying and rewarding endeavor that makes some significant contribution to society. Ideally, one should have a sense of skill and pride in what one does. Work should provide fulfillment for the individual. Leisure-time activities are also important. Such sayings as "Work before play" and "All work and no play makes Jack a dull boy" imply that leisure plays a role in forming the complete individual. According to these values, leisure does not *replace* work but rather *complements and supports* it. In other words, leisure-time activities should, among other things, serve as a restorative that prepares one to resume one's work role better prepared to do a good job, and appropriate leisure activities make one into a well-rounded person. According to this view, then, work and leisure should be integrated to the extent that satisfaction in one realm makes more likely fulfillment in the other, and the individual gains in completeness and fulfillment by immersion in both realms.

To what extent is this conception of work realistic in today's world? In the remainder of this century, fewer people will need to work to produce the goods and services necessary to our lifestyle, and thus there may well be a "shortage of work"—especially of those jobs that are personally satisfying or intellectually rewarding.[2] Furthermore, many people today are dissatisfied with the monotonous and repetitive jobs they have, even though the jobs provide them with economic security. For these and other reasons that will be dealt with in this chapter, we must be concerned about whether work provides the fulfillment and satisfaction that people seek and about the consequences if work does not live up to people's expectations.

Because of industrialization and automation, we will all probably have to work less in the future. How will we then fill up that additional free time? **One of the unsettling paradoxes of our age is that, while we have achieved the technological capability to support ourselves while working less, there are many Americans who do not seem to know how to use their increased leisure time.** Some people, when faced with more free time, take a second job in order to make enough money to provide the material goods that will presumably usher in a satisfactory existence. Is this an appropriate use of leisure time? Many Americans fill their leisure time with activities revolving around material consumption. But does this serve the functions that leisure should serve?

These are the issues that we will analyze in this chapter. What is work and what is leisure, and what is their proper place in human life? What kind of problems arise in the modern world concerning work and leisure? What are the implications of these problems? In order to understand these issues, it is useful to have a glimpse of the way in which the realms of work and leisure have been viewed in our past, and how this has changed.

WORK AND LEISURE: A BRIEF HISTORY

Throughout most of human history, people had a clear recognition of the relationship between work and survival—one's survival depended on hard work. Physical exertion and long hours of work were necessary in order to eke out an existence. This does not mean that people in some societies did not have considerable free time. Those living in a plentiful physical environment could provide for themselves quite adequately with time left over for other, nonwork, pursuits. Yet they were still acutely aware that their work played a crucial role in the survival of the group. All gained a sense of importance and self-worth from the realization that their activities made a vital contribution to the success and survival of the group.

It is probably safe to say that the separation between work and leisure usually acknowledged by modern people made no sense to these preindustrial groups. The extreme efforts required for survival were inevitable and there were no alternatives. Of course, these people had to sleep and rest themselves in preparation for further toil. However, these nonwork activities were so *necessary* for their continued existence that preindustrial peoples were probably little concerned about the differences between work and leisure.

The Emergence of a Leisure Class

Modern American attitudes toward work and leisure are the product of particular historical developments in Western civilization. There have been very significant changes in Western society that have had direct implications for the realms of work and leisure. In particular, a more complex division of labor has emerged, due to the processes of urbanization and industrialization. The feudal society of medieval Europe did not encourage profit making, competition, or the pursuit of technological

progress. As a consequence, although there were a few people who had considerable wealth, most people were comparatively poor and there was little concentration of economic and political power. As modern capitalism and industrialism emerged, profit making and competition were encouraged, and concentrations of wealth and power in the hands of a few became more common. As these inequalities became more pronounced, elites emerged.

An elite is composed of those people who occupy the highest levels in a stratification system—they have gained the greatest control over scarce resources. The social structure and economic surplus in industrial society made it possible for a "leisure class" made up of elites to emerge. A functional interdependence developed between the elites and the various subordinate groups in society. In the late nineteenth century, well-known social scientist Thorsten Veblen pointed to the importance of property ownership in the emergence of a leisure class in modern industrial society: "In the sequence of cultural evolution the emergence of a leisure class coincides with the beginning of ownership. This is necessarily the case, for these two institutions result from the same set of economic forces."[3] Veblen pointed out that because of their ownership of, and consequent control over, scarce resources, members of the elite did not need to work as others did in order to support themselves. They were part of a propertied aristocracy, and they developed a distinct lifestyle that was regarded by most as highly desirable. Leisure time became a symbol of wealth and status.

The Emergence of the Protestant Ethic

Along with these structural changes in Western society resulting in the rise of a leisure class, there were also important changes in values that would have implications for both work and leisure. By the seventeenth century, the religious doctrine known as *Calvinism* began to exert influence on economic activity and attitudes toward work. According to Calvinist thinking, human fate is predestined—

people have been divinely selected for either salvation or damnation, and there is nothing people can do to alter their fate. Such beliefs reduce the role of the church and religious activity as a source of salvation. One's fate is predetermined and cannot be changed by religious activity on earth.

Although a person cannot know his fate until the judgment day, a common interpretation of Calvinist philosophy posits that indications of one's fate can be detected. Good deeds, hard work, and success at one's vocation (whether that vocation be religious or secular) were taken to be signs that one was destined for salvation. Thus, Calvinist theology encouraged the belief that secular activity, such as work, could have religious implications. Because of the uncertainty a person faced concerning his own salvation, and because hard work and success at one's vocation might be a sign of one's fate, hard work and frugality came to have great value for the Puritans. They considered this way of life desirable, and idleness or laziness sinful. They also developed a strong ascetic sense — the practice of strict self-denial as a means of religious discipline. Today we use the term *Protestant ethic* to refer to this constellation of values concerning hard work, frugality, and asceticism.

The Protestant Ethic and American Values

The implications of this protestant ethic for our attitudes toward work and leisure are clear. As the German sociologist Max Weber argued, the emergence of capitalism as an economic system was encouraged by the Protestant ethic:

In fact, the summum bonum of this ethic, (is) the earning of more and more money, combined with the strict avoidance of all spontaneous enjoyment of life. . . . It is thought of . . . so purely as an end in itself. . . . Man is dominated by the making of money, by acquisition as the ultimate purpose of his life.[4]

These attitudes were clearly expressed by the early American statesman Benjamin Franklin, who praised the values of making money and of working in the following delightful sayings: "time is

money"; "a penny saved is a penny earned"; "after industry and frugality, nothing contributes more to the raising of a young man than punctuality"; and "he who sits idle . . . throws away money." Nearly everyone has heard of *Poor Richard's Almanac,* and one of Poor Richard's admonitions was "waste neither time nor money; an hour lost is money lost."

The Protestant ethic represented a pervasive influence throughout nineteenth-century America, and was significant in the development of industrialization during the past two centuries. Even today, although most modern Americans no longer value the ascetic, frugal lifestyle of Puritanism that Weber described, we are still most assuredly influenced by an ethic of hard work.

The Protestant work ethic resulted in ambivalent attitudes about the use of free time. In fact, as one might guess, leisure was viewed with suspicion. The Puritan theology contained a built-in "detestation of idleness." Leisure was equated with idleness: "the idle brain is the devil's playground." Considering this early belief that time devoid of work was a dangerous thing, it is understandable that leisure was evaluated in a negative way.

People have always needed rest and relaxation, and the Puritans were no exception, emphasizing that the Sabbath was a day for rest and worship. However, leisure meant more than just enjoyment; it was defined as a means to an end. In fact, the word *recreation* implies a sense of refreshment from toil. The term is derived from the Latin *recreare* — to create anew, to restore, to refresh, the refreshment of strength and spirits after toil. Leisure properly used was preparation for further work.

Work and Leisure in Industrial Society

The Protestant ethic still exerts a pervasive influence on American life — we place great importance on work and still view leisure to some extent as a means to an end (a restorative for work). Yet, industrialization has led to profound changes in American society that have significant consequences for our perceptions of work and leisure. In the preindustrial and early industrial period, peo-

TABLE 9.1

Changes in America's Occupational Structure, Expressed in Percentages of Total Work Force

	1900	1910	1920	1930	1940	1950	1960	1970	1977
Both sexes									
White-collar workers	17.6	21.3	24.9	29.4	31 1	36.6	43.1	49.6	50.2
Manual and service workers	44.9	47.7	48.1	49.4	51.5	51.6	48.8	47.4	47.6
Farm workers	37.5	30.9	27.0	21.2	17.4	11.8	8.1	4.0	2.2
Males									
White-collar workers	17.6	20.2	21.4	25.2	26.6	30.5	37.3	41.1	42.1
Manual and service workers	40.8	45.1	48.2	50.0	51.7	54.6	52.8	53.4	53.8
Farm workers	41.7	34.7	30.4	24.8	21.7	14.9	9.9	5.5	4.1
Females									
White-collar workers	17.8	26.1	38.8	44.2	44.9	52.5	54.6	60.8	63.6
Manual and service workers	63.2	58.1	47.6	47.3	51.0	43.9	40.9	37.6	45.2
Farm workers	18.9	15.8	13.5	8.4	4.0	3.7	4.5	1.6	1.2

SOURCE. By permission from Carol A. B. Warren, *Sociology: Change and Continuity* (Homewood, Illinois: Dorsey Press, 1977), p. 169. Data for 1977 computed from U.S. Department of Commerce, Bureau of the Census. *Statistical Abstract of the United States, 1977* (Washington, D.C.: U.S. Government Printing Office, 1977).

ple had to work long hours to make a living. For both adults and children, it was not unusual to work ten or twelve hours a day, six days a week. Wages were low, and long hours were necessary to earn enough to support a family. As a consequence, while a few members of the elite had leisure time, most people had little free time. Work was something that had to be done to survive—personal enjoyment or fulfillment was not a concern for most people. Substantial leisure time was something that, while desirable, was rarely achieved.

Once America had become fully industrialized, the fruits of industrialization led to changes in what was possible in the areas of work and leisure. Living standards have risen; the average workweek has been shortened; and most of the time-consuming, exhaustive work has been transferred from people to machines. As a consequence, more time away from the job has become available to the masses. Previously, Americans were motivated by scarcity —the fear that there might not be enough food on the table. People in the United States today are confronted for the first time in history with a society of abundance. There were few surpluses in Benjamin Franklin's day; today, our productive capacity is so great that we are sometimes faced with the paradoxical situation of having to slow down production so that supply does not exceed demand.

As industrialization has progressed, the nature of work for most Americans has changed (see Table 9.1). A smaller number of workers are involved in primary occupations, such as farming and mining, in which resources are directly produced from the environment; a larger proportion of Americans are involved in secondary occupations, such as factory work, which involves the manufacture of goods from raw materials. Even more profound, there has been a dramatic rise in the number of Americans who work in tertiary or service occupations, such as teaching, nursing, or personnel work, which involve providing services. Furthermore, the proportion of Americans in white-collar occupations has almost tripled between 1900 and 1977. This means that, while many Americans still work with their hands producing or repairing some goods, we have become to a large extent a society of nonmanual laborers. Most Americans work with people rather than products. Most provide a service to other people rather than creating products that can be consumed.

All of the foregoing changes brought about by industrialization have had important effects on our attitudes about work and leisure. American society (notwithstanding the economic ups and downs of the 1970s) is characterized by affluence and more free time. Even though the Protestant ethic still influences the modern American value system, leisure is beginning to take on new meanings. It is somehow more than a restorative for work, and it has come to be regarded as activity that should be intrinsically satisfying—an end in itself. In the past, people spoke of *spending* their leisure time *profitably*. For example, a man or woman might "spend" his or her "free time" on Sunday afternoons repairing things around the house. Today, there are an increasing number who are less concerned about the utilitarian outcomes of using their free time. For example, one might buy a season ticket for the local professional football games—"I'm going to the game on Sunday afternoon and have a ball. To hell with the chores at home. I'll take care of those some other time." The goal is the sheer enjoyment of the activity.

Our attitudes toward work and leisure are changing dramatically. Despite these changes, modern feelings about work and nonwork are not clear-cut. People still disagree with each other and sometimes experience considerable personal strife over what should be gained from work or leisure time. This lack of consensus is a symptom of the unclear meaning of work and leisure in the modern world. In order to clarify what work and leisure are and how they may constitute social problems, we will examine them from the viewpoint of the theoretical perspectives.

WORK AND LEISURE AS SOCIAL PROBLEMS

As American society has grown more complex, work and leisure have emerged as more distinguishable ingredients in people's lives. Yet, at the same time, there is more confusion concerning precisely what work and leisure are, how they are related to each other, and what role they should play in the lives of individuals and in society as a whole. As we have seen with other issues relating to social problems, the answers to these questions depend on the perspective one utilizes.

The Functionalist Perspective

The functionalist perspective is concerned with the contribution made by each part of society to the operation of the whole system. In this regard, the role of work would seem fairly straightforward.

There are numerous jobs that must be done if society is to survive; work, and people's attitudes toward work, must be such that an adequate number of people are motivated to perform these essential tasks. The motivation to work may result from a number of things—intrinsic rewards of personal satisfaction and fulfillment, or external rewards of money or status. Leisure must also contribute to the functioning of the system. It can do this by serving as a restorative that prepares and motivates people for future work. **Work and leisure become social problems, from the functionalist perspective, when they no longer serve to motivate people to perform the tasks essential to the maintenance of society.** A major concern in this chapter is to determine the extent to which this is the case today.

While work and leisure can be dealt with as separate and distinct realms of a person's life, some sociologists have argued that, for certain people, the two spheres are integrated in the sense that there is no clear separation of work activities from leisure activities—they are like opposite sides of the same coin. Some argue that such integration is a desirable situation toward which all people should strive. This perspective is referred to as the *holist* or *integrationist* view of work and leisure.[5] An example of such integration might be poets or philosophers who so enjoy their work that they stop reading and writing only during sleep—there is no distinction between work activities and leisure activities.

However, some functionalists see a danger in such integration. They view work and leisure as essential, but separate, elements of social organization. This is referred to as the *segmentalist* or *differentiation* view.[6] The segmentation of work and leisure proposed by adherents to this perspective is consistent with the increasing fragmentation characteristic of modern industrial society. Some functionalists argue that this segmentation or fragmentation is beneficial in that problems in one realm of a person's life are less likely to interfere with performance in other realms. Thus, they argue, if work and leisure are integrated (the holist view), then failure to make adjustments or achieve satisfaction in one area, such as leisure activities, might lead to failure in the work sphere. These functionalists argue that a more workable arrangement, from the point of view of the whole system, is the compartmentalization of work and leisure so that failures or problems are limited in their effect on the whole society.

Functionalists, then, stress that work and leisure should be organized such that they serve to enhance the equilibrium of society. **Work and leisure can become social problems if there is a lack of segmentation or differentiation between the two spheres with the result that difficulties in one realm lead to reduced stability or equilibrium in the other realm.**

The Conflict Perspective

The conflict perspective emphasizes the fact that different groups in society have competing interests and that the desires of the group with the most power will most likely prevail. Work and leisure as social problems must be considered in terms of which groups benefit from existing social arrangements. We can approach this by first investigating the characteristics of *craftsmanship* as proposed by conflict theorist C. Wright Mills:

> Craftsmanship as a fully idealized model of work gratification involves six major features: [1] There is no ulterior motive in work other than the product being made and the processes of its creation. [2] The details of daily work are meaningful because they are not detached in the worker's mind from the product of the work. [3] The worker is free to control his own working action. [4] The craftsman is thus able to learn from his work; and to use and develop his capacities and skills in its prosecution. [5] There is no split of work and play, or work and culture. [6] The craftsman's way of livelihood determines and infuses his entire mode of living.[7]

Partly as a consequence of the emergence of industrial technology, it is to the advantage of some groups that craftsmanship declines while demeaning and repetitive work increases. With industri-

As our society becomes more industrialized, the role of the craftsman diminishes—replaced by more efficient, mechanical means of production. As craftsmanship disappears, what happens to work satisfaction?

alization, the sense of craftsmanship is largely removed from work because it is not the most economically efficient means of production. Karl Marx (an early conflict theorist)[8] and Mills have pointed out that industrialization separates people from the products of their labor—the product belongs to the owner of the factory rather than to the individual craftsman. Thus, the worker gains little intrinsic satisfaction from work because he or she is simply a tool of another person. However, the industrialist benefits because he can produce more products at a lower price with such a work organization. Craftsmanship, while it might be desirable in some respects to the worker, would lead to a loss of control and reduced profits for the industrialist. **From the conflict perspective, then, work and leisure have become social problems because some groups do not feel that they receive the rewards from either work or leisure to which they are entitled.**

It is important to note that one of Mills's characteristics of craftsmanship is that work and leisure are not separated but rather are intertwined. For the craftsman, work and leisure are one and the same. This points to similarities between some versions of the conflict perspective and the holist or integrationist approach to work and leisure. For conflict theorists like Marx, work is such a central part of one's life that it influences all other parts, including leisure. Furthermore, work in the form of craftsmanship is so rewarding and satisfying that it *is* leisure.

In our industrial society, a strong distinction exists between work and nonwork, between production and consumption. The production process under industrialism is alienating, demanding, and time-bound in terms of a nine-to-five schedule. Consumption, on the other hand, has involved a passive process that takes place "after hours." For example, most people work eight hours a day, five days a week, and most of their consumption-oriented activities take place outside of this forty-hour (or longer) period. These two processes have been traditionally in conflict and have failed to intermesh. **This failure, for conflict theorists, is a social problem because it means that some**

groups are destined to spend much of their time engaging in unsatisfying, demeaning, and alienating activities. Although some people argue that the distinction between work and leisure may vanish eventually, others feel that our society may become increasingly automated and machinelike, with an increased emphasis on consumption, and that this will interfere with the realization of the work-leisure integration ideal.[9] Indeed, some Marxian conflict theorists would argue that work and leisure will continue to be separated until a sense of craftsmanship is restored.

The Interactionist Perspective

For the interactionist, our subjective interpretations of what work and leisure imply are paramount. In fact, this subjectivity is one reason why work and leisure are such difficult concepts to define—they mean different things to different people living in different time periods. Traditionally, work and leisure have not been defined as social problems because only a small elite had significant free time; only they were concerned about how to use that time. Most people spent their time working to survive and had so little free time that the utilization of it was not an issue for them. Today, however, many people have a significant amount of free time, and thus the concern about the role of work and leisure is more widespread.

The interactionist perspective points to another important reason for the emergence of work and leisure as social problems. As basic-subsistence fears have subsided, people have come to expect more from work than merely survival—they also desire a feeling of personal satisfaction and fulfillment along with a positive sense of self-worth and importance. Individual self-worth is based on a shared consensus about what constitutes valued activities and important characteristics. During most of the nineteenth century, nonwork time was defined as idleness; free time was "rest time," or time to prepare for more work. The highly valued person was either working or preparing himself for work. Today, free time is not looked upon as idleness by many people, and there is less guilt associ-

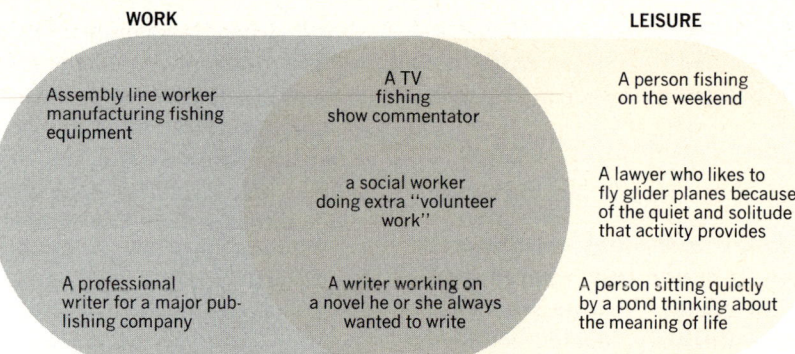

WORK   LEISURE

Assembly line worker
manufacturing fishing
equipment

A TV
fishing
show commentator

A person fishing
on the weekend

a social worker
doing extra "volunteer
work"

A lawyer who likes to
fly glider planes because
of the quiet and solitude
that activity provides

A professional
writer for a major pub-
lishing company

A writer working on
a novel he or she always
wanted to write

A person sitting quietly
by a pond thinking about
the meaning of life

Figure 9.1 The Realms of Work and Leisure and Their
Overlap.

ated with attempting to use this time for something other than work preparation. Nevertheless, we still retain a legacy from the past; some still feel that they must always be engaged in some type of productive activity—that leisure is somehow suspect. Thus there is not a strong consensus today about what is highly valued—whether work or leisure, or some combination of both, is the most desirable activity for a person.

Whether work and leisure should be integrated (the holist view) or separated (the segmentalist view) also depends, for the interactionist, on one's perspective. For one person, work may be drudgery and free time the only part of life looked forward to. Yet, the satisfactions provided by leisure may far outweigh the costs of work in this person's eyes. For another person, work may be a dominating feature of life—so much so that she works almost all the time; yet this need not mean that work is drudgery for her. Finally, for still others, work may be a satisfying part of their lives, with leisure as a related and very important component. The point is that work and leisure are perceived differently by people in different situations, and one goal of this chapter is to analyze the conditions under which one or both are perceived as social problems by certain groups. **So from the interactionist perspective, work and leisure are social problems according to our subjective perceptions of reality and people's different and unique life situations.**

What Are Work and Leisure?

As in many other areas of social life, problems of definition abound in the area of work and leisure. We have already seen that definitions depend to some extent on the perspective one adopts. This lack of precise definition reflects the varied nature of the phenomenon under study—in particular, the varied ways that work and leisure may overlap for different people. Figure 9.1 illustrates several dimensions of this interrelationship. Nevertheless, it is crucial that we develop some definitions to serve as a guide for our discussion. Although there is considerable difference of opinion on these issues, we propose the following definitions for the key concepts in this discussion.

Work

Work is the necessary means whereby people earn income required for survival. Work is subsistence time—time that is spent on the job. Most people in our society must work in order to survive. Few of us have the resources to permit us not to have to work at all. **Work, therefore, is obligated time,** and most people work at least partly because they have to.

Work-Related Time

Work-related time refers to activities that are closely related to, and necessary for, work, even though we are not actually on the

job. For example, traveling to and from the workplace is not really equivalent to being at work, but we are nevertheless obliged to travel in order to earn a living.

Existence Time and Nonwork Obligations

There are other hours in the day that represent *existence time* **because our bodies and our society demand certain things from us, e.g. eating, sleeping, bathing.** In addition, all of us have obligations that we consider to be mandatory, such as repairing our homes. These activities are not required in order to earn a living, but we feel obliged to do them nevertheless.

Leisure

Leisure is *chosen, discretionary time* **— it is activity that is non-obliged and free from requirements.** We can thus see why many have concluded that America is not really the "leisure society" that some have extolled. For many of us, comparatively little of our free time is actually spent in leisure, by this definition. The distinction between free time and leisure may be subtle and depend on individual definition, but it is nevertheless closely related to our understanding of work and leisure issues. What one person elects to do during free time may indeed represent leisure, while by another person this same activity would be regarded as work. In addition, some people elect to use their free time in more or less work-oriented or leisure-oriented ways. Consider this example:

John and Carol Jones are amateur photographers. So are Ed and Joann Smith. Both couples have approximately the same amount of free time available since each member has a career. John and Carol are interested in nature photography and have never sold any of their nature photos for profit. When they work on their nature photography, they do not feel constrained or pressured to meet deadlines, produce a given number of photos, or make photos that will satisfy others. The only constraints are self-imposed — how much time do they want to spend on their photography.

Ed and Joann began photographing weddings in their free time about a year ago and have found that they can make quite a bit of extra money doing so. Often when they use their "free time" in this manner, they are confronted with deadlines for the completion of wedding albums. Their free time has been transformed — it is not being used in a completely *discretionary fashion* and they are often *obliged* to use their free time in a particular way.

Is this activity leisure for Ed and Joann? They might claim that it is. And for some people their work might truly be their leisure. Nevertheless, these illustrations should help clarify the distinctiveness of leisure. Are you drawn to the activity because of its intrinsic enjoyment and fulfillment? Or are there external pressures and constraints that force you to engage in the activity? This is, to be sure, at least partly a matter of interpretation. Furthermore, the line between leisure and work is a fine one. Nevertheless, the distinctions between these concepts, while difficult to make, must be addressed. Figure 9.1 should now be reexamined in terms of the definitions presented.

Now that we have some understanding of what work and leisure are, it is time to turn to our primary concern — the problems of work and leisure in modern America.

WORK

Many dramatic occurrences — a worker shooting his foreman, high absentee rates among workers, heavy use of alcohol and drugs on the job — have focused attention on the world of work in the United States. There is rising concern about the alleged dissatisfaction of American workers with their jobs. During the 1960s, this concern was directed primarily toward people who held blue-collar occupations; some spoke of the "blue-collar blues," and the focus was on the alienation and monotony of factory work. There is considerable evidence to indicate that dissatisfaction among blue-collar workers is still common today.

However, there is developing concern that the same kind of work dissatisfaction has spread to white-collar occupations. For example, Pehr Gyllenhammar, the president of the Swedish automobile company Volvo, has remarked that al-

Some clerical and secretarial jobs—often classified as "white-collar"—are often thought to be as alienating and boring as factory or "blue-collar" work.

though we talk a great deal about blue-collar work and its problems, white-collar work is among the most deadly dull today. As our technology expands, more workers—both white-collar and blue-collar—will have routine, repetitive occupations. Increasingly, these people express their dislike for the things they do at work. Gyllenhammar wonders about the outcome:

> If the industrial society, with its intensive technological development, succeeds in putting people to one side, what will happen to them and, thus, to society itself? What kind of work will be available in the future as an alternative to the jobs that industry offers today?[10]

What precisely are the problems that exist in the world of work today? Let us now turn our attention to the specific social problems involving work.

The Multiple Dimensions of Work

Work is an activity that involves carrying out certain tasks that culminate in the provision of goods or services. Yet, work is much more than that. Work is also a central source of identity in our society, and some of our most important social con-

tacts take place at work. This means that problems arising at work can have wide-ranging ramifications. For example, on a modern assembly line there is little opportunity for people to develop satisfying relationships with one another; as a consequence, they often choose to associate with different people in their leisure time than they do at work. Even in white-collar occupations, it is sometimes undesirable to "make your colleagues your friends" because of the frequent competition that ensues among co-workers. Furthermore, on-the-job interaction with co-workers often affects the quality of our relationships with people outside the work setting. For example, a person who is having difficulties with his colleagues may become irritable and tense, and this attitude may be carried home and affect relationships with spouse and children.

Thus the problems arising at work are not necessarily limited to that setting—they can impact on many other parts of society. If people's interactions in terms of their work are not satisfying, their overall attitudes toward life may be adversely affected. Sociologist Lee Braude has pointed out that work looms so large in our lives that we tend not only to take it for granted but also to forget how frustrating it can be (or has become).[11] Braude views work as a multifaceted problem with many different aspects. Using the aspects identified by Braude as a guide, we can examine in detail four interrelated problems in the realm of work.

Specialization

As the division of labor expands, job skills become fragmented and work becomes more and more specialized. However, specialization may not necessarily mean an increase in how interesting a particular job will be. Even though there has been increased specialization in our industrial society, some studies have suggested that over 80 percent of all jobs are routinized and require few if any special skills. The remaining 20 percent are generally regarded as elite jobs that most people consider unattainable.[12] For most people, specialization has meant that their job is reduced to increasingly repetitive, disjointed, and boring tasks.

As the work process is divided into increasingly fragmented parts, there is a growing problem of ensuring that workers with suitable characteristics are placed in appropriate jobs. Social scientist Herbert Greenberg and his associates conducted interviews with nearly a quarter-million employees of 4000 firms over a fifteen-year period. He concluded that four of every five American workers are essentially "misemployed." In Greenberg's opinion, many people hold jobs for which they are unsuited. For example, he observes that about 20 percent of the nation's sales force is responsible for selling approximately *80* percent of products and services. The remaining salespeople are not really utilizing their training and hence are misemployed. One consequence is that they may become alienated from their work. He also reports that this alienation from work is high at the managerial level as well as among blue-collar jobs.[13]

Specialization has made work increasingly *depersonalized* for larger numbers of people. Workers do not feel that they have a personal stake in the product they help to manufacture or the services they assist in delivering. They often feel as though they were merely cogs in a huge bureaucratic machine.

This has also meant that today's worker, both white collar and blue collar, stands a much greater chance of feeling alienated from work than ever before.[14] Social scientists who have studied work have observed that it has always had a great deal to do with how people identify themselves and identify with others. As one such authority on problems of work has remarked: "It [work] is one of the major components of self-esteem and is a determinant of esteem by others. Work is also, sadly enough, one of the main areas of conflict."[15]

Work and Alienation

The concept of alienation is very important in understanding the problems associated with work. It illustrates the contribution that the conflict perspective can make to better our understanding of the effects of industrialization. Karl Marx predicted a growing conflict between members of the proletariat (the workers) and the bourgeoisie (the owners) culminating in a revolution that would bring about a new social and economic order. **According to Marx, this conflict is, in part, a consequence of *alienation* — the separation of workers from ownership of the means of production and from any control over the final product of their labor.** Marx commented on the essence of alienation:

> In what does this alienation consist? First, that work is external to the worker, that it is not part of his nature, that consequently he does not fulfill himself in his work but denies himself, has a feeling of misery, not well-being, does not develop freely a physical and mental energy, but is physically exhausted and mentally debased. . . . His work is not voluntary but imposed, *forced* labor. . . . Finally, the alienated character of work for the worker appears in the fact that it is not his work but work for someone else, that in work he does not belong to himself but to another person.[16]

Thus for Marx, alienation was a social condition — a situation in which a person was separated from the product of his labor and had little control over his work conditions. Modern research has shown that alienation also has important consequences for the subjective feelings of workers.[17] It leads to a feeling of *powerlessness* — a feeling that one has little control over the work process or more generally over any aspect of one's life. Alienation leads to a feeling of *meaninglessness* — the feeling that one does not understand the events occurring around one nor how one's personal contribution fits into these events. Alienation leads to feelings of *self-estrangement* — the feeling that one engages in activities for purely utilitarian reasons and with ulterior motives rather than for the intrinsic enjoyment of the activities. Finally, alienation leads to feelings of *social isolation* — the sense of exclusion or rejection from groups around one.

These, then, are the subjective experiences that alienated workers might have. In fact, many social scientists refer to these feelings as alienation — whether they arise from the social conditions that Marx described or from some other social factors. The important point is that many workers today find themselves in alienating circumstances and so experience these negative feelings. What are the consequences? One potential consequence is disruption of the industrial process or, in extreme cases, rebellion against the political and economic system that the alienated workers believe is the source of their plight. The proletarian revolution that Marx argued would be the consequence of alienation has not materialized in our society, but it might have were it not for a number of other societal developments. For example, Marx did not foresee the effectiveness of collective bargaining and developing technology in improving the conditions of workers during this century. However, while there has been no large-scale uprising by the common man to overthrow the bourgeoisie, alienation still has important consequences. For example, the ongoing conflict between management and unions serves as a constant reminder of workers' feelings about control over the conditions of their work. In addition, most commentators are convinced that alienation leads to many individual acts of disruption and rebellion by workers — in the form of theft or destruction of company property, work of poor quality, and high rates of absenteeism. While it is impossible to calculate the cost of all this, there is little doubt that alienation takes an enormous toll.

Although Marx's analysis of alienation was limited to industrial workers, we have begun to realize that alienation is not limited to that segment of the work force. Even within the professions, feelings of depersonalization are evident. For example, even though men and women in education are likely to be reasonably satisfied with their jobs, even they are not immune. Today's teachers are likely to feel increasingly like "interchangeable" cogs in the educational bureaucracy. They experience an increased sense of anonymity — a "warm body" in the classroom undifferentiated from the mass of other teachers. Their feelings are reinforced by the realization that they really do not participate in making important decisions about their work. Perhaps this explains, in part, the dramatic surge in unionization of public school teachers and, to an increasing degree, of college and university professors. When a worker feels that he or she can be readily replaced and that his or her skills and abilities may not be regarded as distinctly valuable, this person must be considered alienated from his or her work.

Automation

As we have seen, societal development and expansion in the division of labor led to greater complexity and specialization. **Another important change in the social organization of work has been automation.** Prior to the Industrial Revolution, work was frequently more intrinsically satisfying because a sense of craft was regarded as more important than the number of units that could be produced. The structure of work prior to industrialization often permitted workers to participate in most stages of the production process — from raw materials to finished product — and this allowed for the craftsman's being closely identified with his or her work.

With advancing technology, the social organization of work has changed drastically. Many craft-like occupational specialties such as cabinet making, gunsmithing, and shoemaking, have been largely eliminated by the emergence of production techniques that are more economically efficient—mechanization and automation. *Mechanization is a production process that utilizes machinery rather than human hands to produce goods. Automation is the production technique in which the whole system of production is controlled automatically by means of self-operating machinery.* An automobile assembly line is an example of both of these processes. There are a number of consequences of mechanization and automation. First, they can easily lead to the separation of workers from the fruits of their labor—alienation. Workers come to feel that they are cogs in the wheels of this monstrous and uncontrollable machinery. They increasingly feel that they have no personal control over the production process. They have no sense of accomplishment in the final product. In fact, the workers have little control in an automated setting. What automobile worker can stop an assembly line in order to tend to his own personal needs? Thus mechanization and automation by their very nature tend to result in alienation.

A second consequence of mechanization and automation is the effect these processes have on the jobs available to workers. When the assembly line concept was first introduced, there were about an equal number of men and machines on the job. Today, an automated plant can easily utilize ten people working at three or four machines and accomplish tasks that would have required thirty persons at thirty machines. Thus, automation displaces workers from their jobs.

As a result of our advanced technology, many people who previously had jobs have been replaced by computerized operations. For example, prior to the introduction of electronically controlled elevators, an operator was required for each one—at hotels, office buildings, and department stores across the country, which adds up to a lot of jobs. When Bell Telephone employed the direct-dial long distance system, thousands of operators were thrown out of work. At one time or another, each of these operators had to acquire certain skills, like learning how to use a PBX board. Direct dialing—a consequence of technology and an example of automation—essentially made their skills obsolete.

Of course, we have to give modern technology its due, since it *has* eliminated some of the monotony and routine from certain kinds of work. For example, because of automation, workers in some industries have been provided greater freedom and autonomy on the job. On the other hand, many other workers have simply become professional babysitters for machines. One researcher who conducted a study of workers at the Chevrolet Vega plant in Lordstown, Ohio reported that despite modern technology, worker alienation is still very high.[18] Another investigator studied office and factory workers and determined that the relationship between automation and alienation is a close one—workers are more alienated in automated settings—and that this is true among *both* white-collar and blue-collar workers.[19]

Worker Dissatisfaction

Work satisfaction has been shown to be directly related to the prestige level of the job, the degree of autonomy on the job, the social cohesiveness of the work group, the challenge and variety of work, working conditions, and job security. Some of these factors can be seen at work in the findings presented in Table 9.2 concerning the percentages of people in different occupational groups who would choose similar work again if given the chance. Note that about 43 percent of a cross section of white-collar workers said that they would stay in the same type of work—as against only 24 percent of a cross section of blue-collar workers. It is also instructive that 93 percent of urban university professors involved in this particular study affirmed their desire to pursue the same type of work again. This is probably the case because university professors have some measure of control over what they do—they are able to some extent to modify the conditions of their work as they see fit. In addition, there is an intrinsic reward to teaching that is not found in some other occupations. However, there are many jobs that have been rendered dull, repetitive, and meaningless by automation and technological progress.

One large-scale study conducted by the United States Department of Health, Education, and Wel-

Today's factory workers are often alienated from their jobs because of an automated, mechanized work setting, characterized by repetitive tasks.

TABLE 9.2

Percentages of People in Different Occupational Categories Who Would Choose Similar Work Again

PROFESSIONAL AND WHITE-COLLAR OCCUPATIONS		WORKING-CLASS OCCUPATIONS	
Urban university professors	93%	Skilled printers	52%
Mathematicians	91%	Paper workers	42%
Physicists	89%	Skilled autoworkers	41%
Biologists	89%	Skilled steelworkers	41%
Chemists	86%	Textile workers	31%
Firm lawyers	85%	Blue-collar workers (cross section)	24%
Lawyers	83%		
Journalists (Washington correspondents)	82%	Unskilled steelworkers	21%
		Unskilled autoworkers	16%
Church university professors	77%		
Solo lawyers	75%		
White-collar workers (cross section)	43%		

SOURCE. Table 5 from the *Human Meaning of Social Change*, Edited by Angus Campbell and Phillip E. Converse, p. 182, (C) 1972 by Russell Sage Foundation, New York.

fare (HEW) reported that many American workers in the 1970s are largely dissatisfied with their jobs.[20] The HEW investigation demonstrated that these feelings are present among workers from all occcupational levels, although they are not as severe within the more highly paid jobs. Other investigations, however, have documented that white-collar workers are increasingly affected by dissatisfaction because characteristics of factory work (impersonality, lack of control, etc.) are increasingly common within white-collar jobs.[21]

The HEW study also showed that there is a close connection between worker dissatisfaction and other social problems. For example, workers' physical and mental health are affected by their attitudes toward work. The incidence of alcoholism and drug addiction are higher among dissatisfied workers, as are divorce and violent behavior. Sociologist Lee Braude has pointed out that numerous studies conducted by universities and government agencies have determined that job dissatisfaction varies among different groups of

TABLE 9.3
Participation Rates of Black Men and Women in Certain Jobs, **1977 (Estimated)**

BLACK MALES	PERCENTAGE OF ALL MALES	BLACK FEMALES	PERCENTAGE OF ALL FEMALES
Total employed	8.7	Total employed	11.7
Longshore workers	30.8	Private housekeepers	53.3
Cement finishers	26.7	Chamber maids	38.8
Busdrivers	17.4	Postal clerks	28.0
Nursing aides	25.9	Nursing aides	24.9
Lumber workers	23.7	Dieticians	21.1
Cleaning service	24.0	Farm laborers	30.5
Taxidrivers	20.8	Cooks	21.9
Laundry–dry cleaning	23.4	Office machine operators	10.4

SOURCE. U.S. Bureau of the Census, *Statistical Abstract of the United States, 1977* (Washington, D.C.: U.S. Government Printing Office, 1977), pp. 407–410.

people.[22] Females, blacks, and those without college degrees tend to be more dissatisfied with their jobs than men, whites, and college graduates. One explanation for the elevated dissatisfaction among these people is found in the type of jobs that they typically hold. For example, Table 9.3 illustrates the types of jobs in which blacks are overly represented. The kinds of work shown are generally low paying and occupy a low status position in our society. These are jobs in which the worker has little control and in which there is often little intrinsic satisfaction. In addition, despite the movement for equality in our society, women earn about 50 percent of the pay of men.[23]

We have analyzed the problems of work in terms of the three components suggested by Braude—specialization, automation, and worker dissatisfaction. We have seen that these components are not separate from one another, but rather each has implications for the other two. There is yet another factor important in understanding the rise in job dissatisfaction that is crucial enough to warrant a separate discussion—that is, the decline that has taken place in our traditional devotion to work.

The Decline of the Work Ethic

As we have observed, the Protestant ethic was based on the belief that hard work is inherently good and that it leads to success—both in one's life on earth and in the hereafter. This ethic is responsible for many related beliefs and values in American society, such as the emphasis we place on "doing one's best." However, considerable change has taken place in this work ethic.

One cause of this change is technology, mechanization, and automation. We have seen that modern workers in our society experience less job satisfaction and feel more alienated about what they do for a living than workers before them. It is difficult to maintain a devotion to work as a valued activity under such conditions. However, another cause of this change is the increased levels of education and affluence of American workers. Today's young people entering the job market *expect* far more from their work. These modern workers are usually well paid and possess more job security than their predecessors. They are more selective about the kind of work to which they will devote themselves. They have begun to place more value on the *intrinsic* aspects of work than on the *extrinsic*.

Motivations For Work

Intrinsic **motivations for work relate to the rewards that come from the nature of the work itself.** For example, teachers are usually thought of as intrinsically involved in their profession. *Extrinsic* **motivation relates to rewards outside of the work context.** For example, a factory worker might think primarily in terms of a sizable paycheck rather than the "rewards" of working on an assembly line. Many of today's workers have obtained the economic benefits of higher-paying jobs and possess substantial job security. As a consequence, these extrinsic rewards are now seen largely as normal and commonplace. Workers now search for more intrinsic gratification from their work. With many jobs, however, such intrinsic rewards (like autonomy, craftsmanship, freedom, creativity, etc.) are not obtainable. For most workers, job dissatisfaction is partly a function of the lack of intrinsic gratification in what they do for a living. Management—those who control the means of production—has certainly recognized this and has tried to take remedial action, since it is in management's best interests to do so. Worker alienation and dissatisfaction threatens productivity and consequently affects profits.

One response of management has been to provide improved physical and social surroundings in an attempt to reduce worker alienation. For example, many companies have improved working conditions with better lighting, colorful décor, recreational facilities, snack bars, and the like. While these programs are often successful in maintaining work productivity, it has often been found difficult to restore real *value* and intrinsic meaning to depersonalized labor. Building a cheery employee lounge does not eliminate alienation or necessarily encourage a worker to feel a more valuable part of the total organization. Industrial relations experts have learned that they must be concerned about both extrinsic and intrinsic factors in order to enhance worker productivity. What follows illustrates the forms that such management activity can take.

In 1927, the Hawthorne Works of the Western Electric Company in Chicago began a series of studies designed to find out more about the effects of a wide range of working conditions on worker productivity.[24] The basic product of the Hawthorne Works was the telephone, and hence the plant operated on an assembly-line basis. The workers required no special skill other than speed in carrying out simple, repetitive tasks. They were not unionized, and management tended to be paternalistic in its attitude, being most concerned about the psychological well-being of the employees as it related to work efficiency. The Hawthorne studies were designed to determine what effects factors such as better lighting, rest breaks, changes in the wage structure, changes in the number of hours in the workday, improved food facilities, and the like had on the workers' productivity.

The results were contrary to expectations. Surprisingly, productivity continued to *rise* regardless of whether working conditions were improved or worsened. What could explain this? In their quest to unravel this unexpected finding, the investigators found that unintentionally, participation in the experiments had been made extremely attractive to workers. For example, those who participated were able to work in smaller groups, take part in decision making, and the like. As a consequence of (voluntarily) becoming a part of the studies, workers not only received considerable attention from key members of the plant's management (who sponsored the study) but they were also able to cultivate a strong sense of solidarity with their fellow-workers. The workers who participated apparently felt that they had been selected by the management for their individual abilities and so they worked harder, even in the face of less favorable conditions. The general conclusion reached by the Hawthorne investigators was that **morale and general attitudes toward work—intrinsic factors—determine work output to a greater extent than the physical conditions of the work setting—extrinsic factors.**

In another study, social scientist Lyman W. Porter argued that *behavior modification* techniques can be used in motivating the performance of "marginal workers"—individuals who fail to demonstrate consistent work attendance or fail to meet organizationally defined standards of acceptable performance. Porter suggests the implementation of certain rewards for the worker: better wages, more extensive fringe benefits, more recognition, greater social interaction on the job, more extensive participation in the complete production process (rather than just working on one cog in the process), more rewards for individual achievement and hard work, and the chance to acquire more skills and the opportunity for personal growth. Porter believes that by manipulating both extrinsic and intrinsic rewards, productivity can be increased.[25]

Work as a Central Life Interest

The Protestant ethic encouraged people to be devoted to their work, and many have argued that work should be the central aspect of a person's life (at least for males). Perhaps psychiatrist Erich

Fromm has best expressed the importance of a person's intrinsic sense of identity with his work:

> Is man, during the next few hundred years, to continue spending most of his energy on meaningless work, waiting for the time when work will hardly require any expenditure of energy? What will become of him in the meantime? Will he not become more and more alienated, and this just as much in his leisure hours as in his working time? Is the hope for effortless work not a daydream based on the fantasy of laziness and push-button power, and a rather unhealthy fantasy at that? Is not work such a fundamental part of man's existence that it cannot and should never be reduced to almost complete insignificance? Is not the mode of work in itself an essential element in forming a person's character? Does completely automatized work not lead to a completely automatized life?[26]

However, given the changes in the nature of work and the increased expectations of many workers, some have questioned whether work will continue to play the important role that it has in the past. In 1956, sociologist Robert Dubin argued that for factory workers, the job does not represent a "central life interest."[27] In other words, work and the workplace do not constitute important life concerns for industrial workers. Dubin implied that these types of jobs do not provide an adequate opportunity for realizing one's worth or value, and we therefore cannot expect to find a devotion to the work ethic among people in these occupations. In 1959, sociologist Louis Orzack conducted a companion study, concentrating on professionals instead of industrial workers. He found that work is more likely to be a central life interest for this group; for professionals, work represents a more significant source of self-identification.[28]

Most investigators agree that there is a far greater likelihood of deriving intrinsic reward from professional occupations than from unskilled or semiskilled jobs. It is important to remember, however, that twentieth-century America is moving further and further away from the work ethic. Sociological researchers have reported that there *has* been a decline in the traditional devotion to work. Satisfactions derived from the job have become less significant, and satisfactions from consumption and after-work activities are becoming more important.[29] We now turn our attention to the effects of this decline—the growing problem of leisure in our society.

LEISURE

Prior to the twentieth century, work was regarded as an intrinsically positive activity, with leisure viewed as a restorative that was needed in order to produce more work. In other words, leisure was treated as a means to an end. As we observed in the previous section, the problems involved in work grew out of the Industrial Revolution and the rise of technology. Prior to the emergence of technological society, the principle of scarcity prevailed. During those years, the "problem of work" involved how to do enough of it to survive. The "problem of leisure" was simple enough: people had to ensure that there was sufficient nonwork time to prepare and "recreate" themselves for more essential work.

Industrialization and the rise of technology brought significant changes in terms of American attitudes toward leisure. When productivity increases as a consequence of technology, there is usually also an increase in income and a sharp elevation in the standard of living. As these changes take place, working hours are sharply reduced.

With these social developments in mind, we can approach the "problem of leisure" in direct fashion. When the workweek (or time on the job) decreases, the amount of free time increases. Problems can emerge in relation to leisure when people work less and have more time away from work. How do they use that increased time? What effects does it have on other institutions in society? Does the average person have the knowledge and experience to deal with this additional nonwork time? Can the average person look upon the gain in free time as an increase in his or her leisure potential? For whom is increased leisure a problem? In order to answer these questions, we must first understand the dynamics of how the workweek has been shortened.

Today, men and women have more time away from their work and
select many different methods of utilizing their "free time."

Reduced Work and Increased Leisure

**An examination of labor statistics reveals
that the length of the average workweek has
been shortened from about 69.7 hours in
1850 to 35.9 hours in 1978 — an increase of
34.8 hours of free time per week.**[30] Work
and leisure researcher Sebastian DeGrazia estimates that paid vacations, sick leave, and holidays
add 2.5 additional hours of free time per week, for a
total of 37.3 hours.

These figures are impressive at first glance, but
they can be deceptive. They give us no indication
concerning what people do with their nonwork
time. Is it activity that could truly be called leisure
— enjoyable, freely undertaken, engaged in for its
own sake, and personally fulfilling and gratifying?
Or is it something quite different? Consider the
ways in which some people utilize this increased
free time: increased moonlighting (holding a second job); increased time spent commuting to and
from work (two hours a day is not uncommon in
urban areas); and an increased amount of time
spent on household chores. Once we add this time
to the number of hours worked each week, we end
up with a far more conservative estimate of our

gains in free time. In fact, it may be an overestima-
tion to assume that we have even ten to fifteen
more hours of free time per week than did our counterparts in 1850.

Even the remaining free time may, for many people, have only the appearance of leisure rather than
being the fulfilling and gratifying activity that we
have defined as leisure. Much of this free time
comes to be allocated to such matters as the removal of unwanted body hair, the fetish of smelling
fresh, or the maintenance of a boat or other recreational vehicle. These activities come to dominate
much of our free time because they must be done in
order to enjoy those brief flashes of leisure — those
couple of hours a month out on the boat. Yet, we
often derive little pleasurable leisure from these
maintenance activities. DeGrazia sums it up thus:
"The great and touted gains in free time since the
1850s, then, are largely myth."[31]

DeGrazia has devised an enlightening scheme
for estimating how the average American "spends"
a twenty-four hour day. He estimates that we are
occupied approximately 10 hours and 40 minutes a
day with work or work-related activities — job,
about 8 hours; journey to work, 1½ hours; house-

keeping, about 20 minutes; and do-it-yourself work like fixing the family car, about 50 minutes. DeGrazia further estimates that 10½ hours are encompassed by subsistence time—sleep, about 8½ hours; dressing, eating, cooking, and shopping, nearly 2 hours. He provides 20 additional minutes for activities like prayer, going to the barber, doing the laundry, and the like. Adding these categories, we arrive at a total of 21½ hours—leaving, on the average, only 2½ hours per day of so-called free time.

It appears that the gains men and women have made in leisure time are more wishful thinking than fact. In comparing Americans today with people in an earlier period, we appear to be working just as hard as they did. According to a recent study of workweek trends, employed American adults have made almost no gain in their time away from work over the past three decades. Table 9.4 illustrates this; in the opinion of economist John Owen, who conducted the investigation, if the rate of decline in time spent on the job prior to World War II had continued after the war, the workweek today would be more than one-half day shorter than it is.[32]

Block Leisure Time

Irrespective of how people use the free time available to them, we have nonetheless entered an era of *mass leisure*—leisure time is no longer limited to a small elite, but rather is available to a much larger number of people than ever before. This is due to the fact that we can produce the goods and services necessary to support our lifestyle with fewer people than before, so each of us can work fewer hours. An associated development that has important implications is the availability of *block leisure time*—free time of fairly long and continuous periods, such as days or weeks. It is helpful in understanding the problems associated with leisure to investigate the forms this block leisure time can take.

The 4/40 Week

The 4-day, 40-hour workweek is a very simple reallocation of work hours from 5 days to 4 days

TABLE 9.4

Hours of Work of Nonstudent Men Employed in Nonagricultural Industries, 1948–1975

YEAR	UNADJUSTED	ADJUSTED FOR GROWTH IN VACATIONS & HOLIDAYS
1948	42.7	41.6
1950	42.2	41.0
1953	42.5	41.4
1956	43.0	41.8
1959	42.0	40.7
1962	43.1	41.7
1966	43.5	42.1
1969	43.5	42.0
1972	42.9	41.4
1975	42.5	40.9

SOURCE. John D. Owen, "Workweeks and Leisure: An Analysis of Trends, 1948–1975," *Monthly Labor Review* (August 1976), p. 3.

that has been adopted in some form or another in over 1000 major companies throughout the United States.[33] The most popular variation in 4-day scheduling is the 4/10/40 in which employees work 10 hours per day for 4 days for a total of 40 hours. Among the employers that have experimented with the 4-day week are the city of Atlanta, the John Hancock Mutual Life Insurance Company, the Equitable Life Assurance Company, and the Samsonite Corporation. Although data concerning the success of the 4/40 are inconclusive, more than one survey has shown that the plan contributes to increased work production in many situations.

The 4/40 has a number of apparent advantages: among them, a 20-percent reduction in commuting time; a reduction in turnover rate and use of sick leave; a decline in absenteeism; an increase in job satisfaction; a rise in productivity; and last but not least, the three-day weekend, making travel and other extended leisure activities more practical. However there is considerable disagreement concerning whether the 4/40 workweek is completely positive. Some commentators have expressed concern about the additional free time it makes available because many people may not be prepared to cope with the increase in leisure time. If workers are bewildered about what to do with the increased leisure, then the 4/40 may even detract from on-the-job satisfaction. Some observers believe that the 4-day workweek will soon be widespread whether we like it or not, and they feel that it could be disastrous if we are ill-prepared.

It must be kept in mind that the 4/40 does not involve a decrease in the number of hours on the job. As Riva Poor, a well-known writer on the 4-day, 40-hour week, has observed, "Note that 4 days, 40 hours is not the 4 days, 32 hours that unions are beginning to talk about again, although it is possible that 4/40 could lead to 4/32, and will probably do so *in the long run*."[34] Despite Poor's optimism, government figures do not support the conclusion that the number of hours worked per week will decline. According to the Bureau of Labor Statistics, the 4-day week is not used extensively in any industry, and the practice has shown no substantial growth since 1973.[35] In addition, the same government information indicates that the number of workers on a 4-day week declined in mid-1976. Nevertheless, available information does reflect a long-term trend toward the reduction of our society's workweek, and experimentation with alternatives to the 5-day week will undoubtedly continue. For example, in 1976, the United Auto Workers initiated a unique holiday program. Despite management warnings that it represented a scheduling nightmare, the program seems to be running smoothly, and may represent a precursor to the 4-day workweek. The program is called "PPH" (paid personal holiday), and provides 7 personal holidays per year to all auto workers who have at least one year's seniority. The UAW hopes to increase that number over time until a regular 4-day week is achieved. Of course, this would obviously mean a significant increase in the number of personal holidays beyond the 7 originally provided for in the program.[36]

The 3-Day Workweek—A Possibility?

While most of us may view the possibility of a 3-day workweek as remote, there are others who have devoted considerable critical thought to this innovation. Among them is work and leisure investigator Millard C. Faught, who wrote an article entitled "The Three-Day Revolution to Come: 3-Day Workweek, 4-Day Weekend."[37] Faught believes that some workers will work 3 days, 12 hours a day each week, and machinery and other facilities will operate 6 days a week, 24 hours a day. This, he argues, will lead to increased efficiency of machinery in terms of eliminating much of the idle time of machines, the need for repeated stopping and starting, reheating, and other costly practices. The 3-day workweek also opens up opportunities for 2-month vacations, instead of 2 weeks. A few firms (among them, Mutual Life Insurance of New York and Anacomp, Inc. of Indianapolis) have already experimented with the 3-day workweek concept. However, there are no clearcut indications of its success or failure in terms of satisfaction among management and workers.

Earlier in this chapter it was suggested that in the future it may be a privilege to work at anything more than the most menial of tasks and that there may be insufficient desirable work to go around. The appearance of the 3-day workweek may be a sign of things to come, heralding a new era in terms of the balance between work and leisure activities in our society. It may also help alleviate the problem of work shortage by spreading existing jobs over a larger number of workers, each working for a shorter period of time. However, the question whether people will be able to use increased leisure effectively remains a puzzle.

Enforced Leisure

Those people with the most amount of block leisure time are, of course, those who do not work at all. It is hard to imagine people being "condemned" to a life of free time, but this is precisely the situation that some people find themselves in. Harold Wilensky has observed: "Those who have the most leisure are typically reluctant victims: (1) the involuntarily retired, (2) the intermittently unemployed, (3) the chronically unemployed."[38] In addition to not desiring such free time, people in these categories also have the fewest resources with which to make leisure enjoyable and meaningful; for them, it is often a condemnation to an unfulfilling life. (The problems facing these groups are dealt with in more detail in the chapters on poverty and aging.)

Difficulties in Using Leisure Time

A major concern in the study of leisure activities in the United States is to investigate the manner in which increased free time might be used. Will it be filled with voluntary, fulfilling activities? Or will it be filled with activities that provide little fulfillment or intrinsic reward? It is hard for some to imagine the problems that might emerge as people are afforded more leisure time. If anything, we can always envision ourselves "doing nothing." Yet, it has been suggested that the organization of work in the United States — and people's reactions to their work — can have very adverse consequences for how they spend their leisure time. Harold Wilensky points to two ways in which this might happen.[39]

Compensation

In some cases, leisure might serve as compensation for what work fails to provide: leisure activities become an effort to make up for the shortcomings and negative aspects of monotonous, routine, or unpleasant work. Sociologist Harold Wilensky creates a scenario that illustrates an extreme version of this compensatory mechanism:

> The Detroit auto-worker, for eight hours gripped bodily to the main line, doing repetitive, low-skilled, machine-paced work which is wholly ungratifying, comes rushing out of the plant gate, helling down the superhighway at 80 miles an hour in a second-hand Cadillac Eldorado, stops off for a beer and starts a barroom brawl, goes home and beats his wife, and in his spare time throws a rock at a Negro moving into the neighborhood. In short, his routine of leisure is an explosive compensation for the deadening rhythms of factory life.[40]

The compensation for work during leisure need not, of course, be so destructive. For example, a trial lawyer, longing for peace and quiet after a busy day in the courtroom, might fly a glider plane during his or her leisure time. The serenity provided by the sailplane compensates for the raucous and combative atmosphere in the courtroom. A major problem is to control the extent to which the effect of work on leisure is socially constructive rather than destructive.

"Run for your life! It's Boredom, spawned by technological advances and overabundance of leisure!"

Spillover

Leisure can also be affected by work to the extent that the attitudes, feelings, and perspectives that develop in the work setting are carried over into leisure activities—that is, the characteristics displayed at work "spill over" into nonwork time. Again, Wilensky provides an extreme, but instructive, scenario of this spillover mechanism:

> Another auto-worker goes quietly home, collapses on the couch, eats and drinks alone, belongs to nothing, reads nothing, knows nothing, votes for no one, hangs around home and the street, watches the "late-late" show, lets the TV programs shade into one another, too tired to lift himself off the couch for the act of selection, too bored to switch the dials. In short, he develops a spillover leisure routine in which alienation from life, the mental stultification produced by his labour, permeates his leisure.[41]

Once again, spillover can be positive. The inquisitive mind and intellectual attitude of teachers or scientists may come to characterize their orientation toward the world both on and off the job.

The main point of these considerations is that some people are encountering problems in using their leisure time in satisfying ways. Wilensky has identified two ways in which the social organization of work can contribute to this problem of using leisure. **In essence, our society has failed, as far as some people are concerned, to translate increases in free time into satisfying and fulfilling leisure.**

For Whom Is Leisure a Problem?

Social Class and Leisure

Increased leisure time does not necessarily create serious problems for all people. The results of one study demonstrate that expanded free time away from work is more of a problem for industrial than for business and professional workers.[42] The authors of this investigation explain that most business and professional people view their work as a *career* (that is, an activity that a person engages in

willingly) rather than a *job* and that they derive from their work many of the satisfactions and peaks of happiness in their lives. Their work is, in many respects, their leisure. The time that they utilize for leisure that is unrelated to work—which may involve fewer hours than it does for the industrial worker—may take on increased meaning because of the professionals' greater resources, both financial and educational.

There is substantial evidence, however, suggesting that many workers prefer more work-related activities when faced with larger amounts of free time. For example, one researcher asked a sample of autoworkers how they would utilize increased leisure if it were afforded them (see Table 9.5).[43] It is interesting to note that only 11 percent wanted to rest, relax, or loaf, while 97 percent preferred to work around the house. It appears that this preference for more work still prevails, with the appearance of the twin-income family, where both husband and wife work longer hours.[44]

TABLE 9.5

Responses by a Sample of Autoworkers Asked How They Would Use Increased Leisure Time (expressed in percentages)

	LEISURE-TIME ACTIVITIES
96.8	Would work around the house
76.8	Would spend more time with the family
53.6	Would travel
48.8	Would attend sports events
42.4	Would fish and hunt
25.6	Would engage in other hobbies
24.8	Would engage in some form of athletics
24.8	Would read more
19.2	Would go back to school or learn a trade
17.6	Would be more active in school boards, PTA
16.8	Would get another part-time job
15.2	Would join more social clubs
12.8	Would engage in more political action
11.2	Would rest, relax, loaf
4.8	Would swim, boat
2.4	Would work on car
1.6	Would engage in church activities

SOURCE. William A. Faunce, "Automation and Leisure," in H. B. Jacobson and J. S. Roucek, eds., *Automation and Society* (New York: Philosophical Library, 1959), Table 1, p. 304.

In a study of recreation problems among low-income urban dwellers in California, sociologist

TABLE 9.6

The Recreational Preferences of Low-Income Americans in Urban Areas of California (expressed in percentages)

RECREATIONAL PREFERENCE

53.0	Watching television
27.5	Reading
17.0	Sewing
15.0	Visiting friends or relatives
13.5	Going to local park
13.0	Going to movies
12.5	Swimming
11.8	Driving or traveling
11.0	Attending churches or clubs
9.5	Going to beach, lake, or mountains
9.5	Fishing or hunting
9.0	Gardening

SOURCE. William J. Emrie, *Recreation Problems in the Urban Impacted Areas of California* (Sacramento, Calif.: State of California Department of Parks and Recreation, 1970). Published by permission of California Department of Parks and Recreation.

William Emrie found that watching television is becoming an extremely popular form of leisure.[45] Table 9.6 presents his findings. It is interesting that well over 50 percent of the people in Emrie's study preferred watching television. This figure is comparable to current national averages concerning leisure preferences for lower-income groups.

Coping with increased leisure often involves dealing with unsatisfying work. That is, the kinds of jobs that provide the most free time are also the most alienating. Although some attempts are being made to incorporate more satisfaction into today's jobs, the typical factory worker not only faces a more alienated work situation but also appears to be the least equipped to cope with increased leisure in a meaningful fashion. While a "career person" is generally in a better position to redirect his or her energies into either more satisfying work-related activities or gratifying leisure, the industrial worker is more likely either to moonlight in an equally unsatisfying job or, as Emrie's study shows, to vegetate in front of the television set.

Passive v. Active Leisure

Not all uses of leisure time are the same. One distinction commonly made is between passive and active uses of leisure. ***Passive leisure repre-***

The individual's use of leisure, 1972

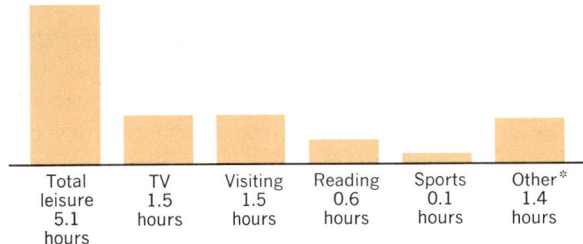

*Includes gardening, pet care, taking courses, and so on

Figure 9.2 The Individual's Use of Leisure, 1972 (in hours). Carol A. B. Warren, *Sociology: Continuity and Change* (Homewood, Ill.: Dorsey Press, 1977), p. 179. Reproduced with permission.

sents a category of activities in which people engage in more watching or listening than actual participation. Watching television is a prime example of passive leisure activity. ***Active leisure, on the other hand, involves activities in which people participate more and watch less,*** like camping, cycling, jogging, and fishing. While one type of leisure is not necessarily better than another, there has been a tendency for commentators on leisure usage to place more value on the active form; it is seen as more fulfilling, creative, and meaningful. Passive leisure, especially if overused, is viewed as a potentially stultifying experience that may be symptomatic of a person's alienation from those around him.

The amount of time devoted to watching television has increased steadily since 1950 for members of all social classes. Figure 9.2 illustrates the number of hours per day that are used for various leisure activities. It can be seen from the figure that much of people's leisure is passive. This is true despite tremendous increases in consumer expenditures for "active leisure accoutrements" like jogging shoes, tennis racquets, and camping equipment. Figure 9.3 shows the dramatic increases in the percentage of households with television sets; Figure 9.4 shows the rise in the number of hours per day of watching television.

Today, passive leisure activities like TV viewing are still more common among the lower classes—those with less education and income, and low oc-

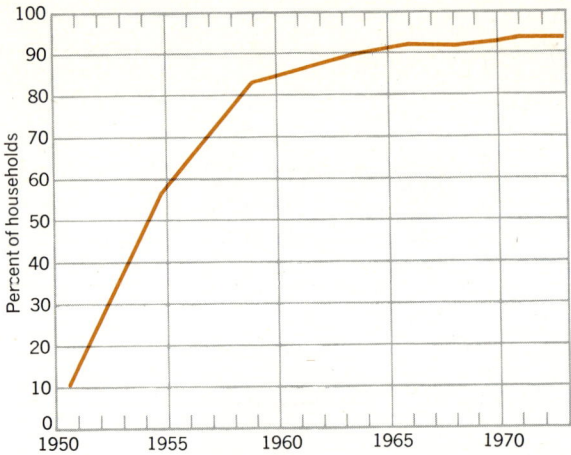

Figure 9.3 Households with Television Sets, 1950–1972 (in percentages). Office of the President, Office of Manpower and Budget, *Social Indicators, 1973: Selected Statistics on Social Conditions and Trends in the United States* (Washington, D.C.: U.S. Governnment Printing Office, 1973), p. 221.

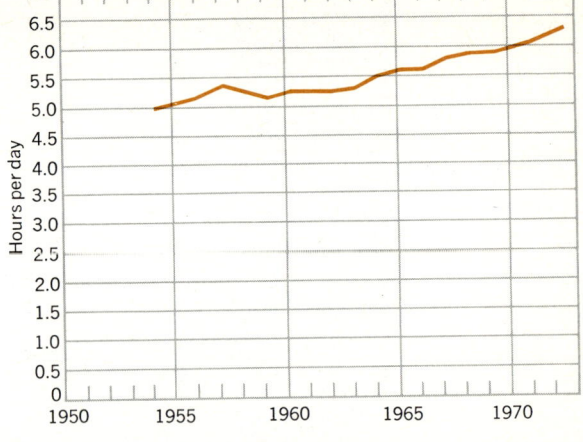

Figure 9.4 Television Viewing by Households, 1954–1972 (hours per day). Office of the President, Office of Manpower and Budget, *Social Indicators, 1973: Selected Statistics on Social Conditions and Trends in the United States* (Washington, D.C.: U.S. Government Printing Office, 1973), p. 221.

cupational prestige. Figure 9.5 shows that television viewing and income are inversely related; that is, as income goes up, the amount of television viewing decreases. It may be, as Wilensky suggests, that people who have the most free time today are also those who are the least equipped to use it in an active or meaningful way.

There are no clear-cut answers to the question of how people can better cope with increased leisure. In fact, it is difficult to define what constitutes

Figure 9.5 Television Viewing by Household Income and Sex: November 1970. Office of the President, Office of Manpower and Budget, *Social Indicators, 1973* (Washington, D.C.: U.S. Government Printing Office, 1973), p. 222.

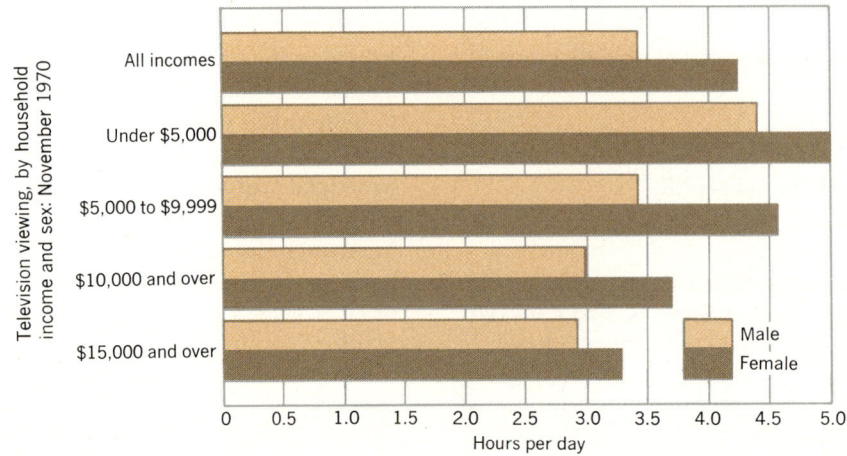

Watching television is one of the most popular "passive" leisure activities among members of lower socioeconomic groups. Sometimes, people who have the most free time may be in the least advantageous position to use it in an active and meaningful way.

meaningful leisure for a particular person because the type of activity that might perform the functions of leisure for one person might be perceived as work by another person. Some have argued that the view of active leisure as superior to passive leisure is simply a reflection of the values of one segment of society. Because of these difficulties, and because our society is in the midst of profound change in relation to these issues, the future of work and leisure is perhaps as uncertain as many other aspects of the postindustrial society in which we live. It is to the future that we now turn our attention.

THE FUTURE OF WORK AND LEISURE

Just as we encountered difficulties in defining the realms of work and leisure, there is also considerable uncertainty concerning what lies ahead in these realms for the United States. In order to analyze the implications of various possibilities, it is useful to return briefly to our theoretical perspec-

tives. From each perspective, how might we view the future of work and leisure?

As we observed earlier in this chapter, the separation of work and leisure is viewed as an important, and in some cases essential, condition for the functionalist. As society grows more complex and the balance between its constituent parts becomes more precarious, the maintenance of equilibrium is that much more essential. Should the effort to integrate people's work and leisure worlds fail, the resulting disharmony, on a mass scale, could contribute to the imbalance of the entire system. Thus, for the functionalist, many workers may well continue to make very basic distinctions between their work and their leisure, and this may be the most beneficial posture for society. Society must strive to make on-the-job hours more satisfying and less frustrating. In addition, it is important that people learn to take advantage of their leisure time and to use it in such a way that they feel refreshed and fulfilled.

Conflict theorists place more emphasis on the outcome of worker dissatisfaction and the use of leisure time as an escape from work. According to conflict theory, intrinsic satisfaction in one's work is becoming an even more scarce resource than how much one is paid for the work performed. As we have seen, even semiskilled workers today have many of the luxuries that were available only to members of the elite one hundred years ago. Conflict theorists point to the fact that money no longer seems to be sufficient as a major source of satisfaction in the work process. Labor disputes over working conditions, collective decision making, and the like point to the problems that most assuredly lie ahead, unless some major changes are made. In addition, if more workers continue to "flee into their leisure" only to ultimately return to unsatisfying work, this situation may breed more conflict that will affect the whole society. Adherents of the Marxist camp within conflict theory are likely to predict more major forms of confrontation between workers and managers in the future. For them, the only solution to the problem is a major reorganization of work in our society.

For the interactionist, the future of work and leisure depends on the shared feelings and expectations about these spheres of life among the members of society. If people aspire to work that is meaningful and stimulating, then their ability to achieve this will be a problem with severe consequences for our society. What if, as the data we have presented suggests, white-collar workers experience increased job dissatisfaction? Perhaps the enormous consumption levels by Americans on "leisure" reflects our growing desire to compensate for the alienating characteristics of the work environment. We have already noted how important work is as a source of identity in our society. Will this change? For the interactionist, the ways that people view themselves in their work roles are closely related to how they will feel about their leisure pursuits.

Armed with these ideas on how to analyze various future alternatives, let us turn to what lies ahead.

The Decline of Individualism

There are certain social trends related to work and leisure that are fairly clear and that will probably continue for the foreseeable future. For example, we can be reasonably certain that our society will remain highly industrialized and that our dependence on an elaborate technology will increase. As automation and mechanization become even more widespread than they are today, people will become, to an increasing extent, caretakers and operators of machines. In addition, our lives will probably become more dominated by monstrous bureaucracies that control our work and, increasingly, our leisure activities. The extent to which we might in the future be at the mercy of such bureaucracies during our leisure hours is brought dramatically home to anyone who has visited one of the new breed of vastly large and complex amusement parks, such as Disneyworld in Florida. Other leisure activities, such as hunting, fishing, or camping in a recreational vehicle, are hemmed in by government regulations concerning licensing, safety procedures, and the like.

Many modern social thinkers, such as C. Wright Mills, William H. Whyte, and Jacques Ellul, have called our attention to some of the consequences of increasing technology, automation, and bureaucratization.[46] As much as we might loathe the idea, these writers have argued that individualism is on the decline. David Riesman and his coauthors wrote about the "lonely crowd," theorizing that American society was becoming more **other-directed,** which means that people were becoming more concerned with how they appeared to others and with popularity rather than with living up to internalized moral standards.[47] Some critics have asserted that America is a "nation of sheep"—that we are so concerned about "keeping up with the times" that we permit other people to direct our lives. The psychologist B. F. Skinner claims that humankind is "beyond freedom and dignity"—that individual decision making is unrealistic.[48] In addition, critics have painted a grim and discouraging portrait of how human relationships are becoming depersonalized. While some of these ideas were first presented over twenty years ago, the social conditions to which they are attributed—automation, technology, and bureaucracy—continue to expand and influence our lives. There is not total agreement that individualism is on the wane; however, most people are in agreement that, at least potentially, these social conditions may have adverse consequences for modern society. It is unpleasant to realize the extent to which we have lost control over the decision-making processes that affect our future; it is discouraging to admit that oneself and one's fellow-citizens are probably led more often by the whims and desires of others than on the basis of one's own personal goals and values. Yet the picture is not totally bleak. Our awareness of these problems makes it possible for us to intervene to change conditions, and in the realms of both work and leisure there are efforts being made to ameliorate some of the problems.

The Reorganization of Work

We have seen that many Americans are dissatisfied with their work. Most factory workers would change jobs if given the opportunity. The dissatisfaction arises not from economic deprivation but from the inability of work to provide a satisfying and meaningful experience for the worker. Many social scientists and industrial-relations experts have responded to this by proposing that the very organization of the workplace be changed in order to overcome these shortcomings. Some companies have experimented with a variety of alternative working conditions in an attempt to compensate for the alienating character of repetitive factory work.

Job Enrichment Programs

Companies like Volvo and Saab in Sweden and Chrysler and General Electric in the United States have experimented with job enrichment or enlargement programs. The intent of such programs is to provide employees with more autonomy by allowing them to work on a project from start to finish, and to let them determine the pace of their work. It is hoped that such complete involvement in the whole production process will reduce alienation by giving the worker the feeling of contribution to the total production process—that the final product is at least partly the individual worker's. Pehr Gyllenhammar, the president of Volvo, has reported substantial success with such efforts.[49] However, the results of a Cornell University project funded by the

Ford Foundation casts considerable doubt on whether the plan would work in the United States.[50] Six Detroit engine plant employees spent four weeks at a Saab engine assembly plant in Sweden. At the Saab plant, teams of three or four workers built car engines at a rate of up to eight per hour. Team members decided among themselves who could work on what part of the engine.

The six American autoworkers reported that even this individualized style of factory work has its drawbacks. One felt as if his team were assembling "little toys." Another commented, "If I've got to bust my ass to be meaningful, forget it; I'd rather be monotonous." The workers found the entire Swedish system far too regimented and, although benevolent, they viewed it as unacceptably paternalistic. Perhaps American workers are now accustomed to the grass-roots unionism of Detroit; so much so that the Swedish plan might be unsuccessful here. Job enrichment efforts such as these will surely continue, at least on an experimental level, in the United States. However, whether they will play a permanent role is still unclear. They will certainly be no panacea.

Flexitime

In the late 1960s, a number of German companies introduced *flexitime*—a system of scheduling that allows employees to start and stop work earlier or later than traditional company working hours. The intent of this program was to ease alienation from work by making schedules more flexible. The basic idea is to have most workers present during traditional "core" hours when everyone works but to leave the remaining hours and days per week worked at the discretion of employees. For example, under some flexitime plans, workers choose their own starting and quitting times and then follow that schedule each day. In others, employees can come to work at different times each day. In addition, some workers can stay on the job for more than eight hours and possibly obtain a four-day week. Nearly 100,000 government employees are now on flexitime, including workers in the Department of Health, Education, and Welfare in several major cities. In addition, thousands at Control Data

Institute and Metropolitan Life Insurance are now on flexitime.[51]

In general, both managers and workers agree that the advantages and gains of flexitime far exceed the disadvantages and costs. Although supervisors complain that it is more difficult to coordinate the work of employees who begin at different times, they also report that productivity increases and absenteeism declines under flexitime. The words of an expert on flexitime, Barbara Fiss, may sum up the program's future: "No shop in the government has tried it and dropped it."[52]

Shared Decision Making

In Europe, some companies have experimented with a plan called *codetermination,* in which each worker is provided a voice in decision making. Employees are encouraged to become members of workers' councils that meet regularly with management officials. In addition, there are some firms that have worker representatives on their boards of directors. German coal and steel companies have used codetermination since the 1950s. Germany has been regarded as Europe's "leading industrial power and wealthiest nation," and worker democracy has not appeared to interfere with its success.[53] One Proctor & Gamble factory in Lima, Ohio introduced a democratic plan and experienced an increase in worker productivity and a decrease in production costs.[54] Presumably, such participation in the decision-making process should reduce feelings of alienation and powerlessness, which are one cause of job dissatisfaction. However, codetermination programs are still quite rare in the United States, and although they are successful in Europe, it is still unclear what role they will play in America in the future.

A Marxian View

Some of the experiments in work reorganization that we have examined seem to be fairly successful in that worker satisfaction has improved and productivity has increased. So far, however, most firms still adhere to the old ways and have done little to combat the depersonalization that so frequently accompanies repetitive types of work.

Some pessimists, including those who are inclined to the Marxian version of the conflict perspective, have argued that such minor changes in the organization of the workplace cannot possibly overcome the continuing trend toward alienation and dehumanization in industrial society. They point to the spreading dissatisfaction among white-collar workers to support their position. In 1964, Herbert Marcuse wrote *One-Dimensional Man: Studies in the Ideology of Advanced Industrial Society,* in which he provided a critical analysis of our technocratic society.[55] Marcuse asserted that we are living in a *one-dimensional* society: a postindustrial society in which peoples' lives are so routinized and controlled that they find it almost impossible to have ideas and aspirations that transcend the daily grind of work and survival and the conventionalized way in which they have been conditioned to view the world; the routines and material products of our society so indoctrinate us that we are unable to see alternative ways of organizing our lives. When people bemoan the fact that they are "locked into the system" or "unable to change the quality of their lives," they are pointing to characteristics of Marcuse's one-dimensional man. Within white-collar as well as blue-collar groups today there are many "ritualists"—people who are so committed to the bureaucratic rules of the game and conventionalized ways of thinking that they lose track of the aspirations that they once believed were important.

Marcuse sees modern technocratic society as having such a subtle, yet all-pervasive influence that we may be doomed to live with the consequences. Many have argued that we are approaching the point at which it will be more important than ever before to make qualitative and sweeping changes in the character of work in our society. Marxian social thinkers would argue that minor changes such as flexitime or codetermination will have little effect. For them, the ultimate culprit is a capitalist society based on profit making and individual greed in which it is to the benefit of one group to keep another subservient and alienated. Only when capitalist economic arrangements are swept away, they believe, will the negative aspects of modern work be eliminated.

TABLE 9.7
Where the Money Is Spent for Leisure, 1976

Recreation equipment, sporting goods, admissions, etc.	77 billion dollars
Vacations and travel — domestic	55 billion dollars
Foreign travel	11 billion dollars
Second or vacation homes, land, etc.	3 billion dollars
Total	146 billion

LEISURE GOODS AND ACTIVITIES	1967	1976
Recreation, sports equipment	9.5 billion	24.5 billion
Radios, TV sets, records, musical instruments	8.5 billion	17.5 billion
Books, magazines, newspapers	6.0 billion	11.5 billion
Admission to sports events, movies, theater	3.5 billion	9.0 billion
Clubs, fraternal organizations	1.0 billion	1.5 billion
Gardening materials	1.1 billion	3.8 billion
Race-track receipts	0.8 billion	2.0 billion
Other personal consumption activities	2.5 billion	6.8 billion

SOURCE. United States Department of Commerce, Bureau of the Census, *Statistical Abstract of the United States*, 1978 (Washington, D.C.: U.S. Government Printing Office, 1978), pp. 245, 251.

Whether the fundamental reorganization of work proposed by the Marxists would solve the modern problems of work is not currently known. The recent experiences in socialist societies is not heartening. They seem to have many of the same problems with worker dissatisfaction and alienation that occur in the United States. This has led many to argue that the culprit is *not capitalism but industrialism,* and as long as we have an industrial society we shall face these problems. Whether we can remain an industrial power while at the same time alleviating the problems we have discussed can be answered only after the various alternatives mentioned have been in practice for awhile.

Leisure as Consumption

What about leisure? Here, as in the case of work, the situation is filled with uncertainty. We have already observed that the so-called leisure boom in America has really been more a "consumption boom." Leisure is, as French sociologist Joffre Dumazedier prefers to term it, *discretionary time*.[56] The customary view that leisure is booming stems from the fact that consumer spending continues to rise at a record rate.

Merely in terms of dollars and cents, it is fascinating to examine our present romance with "leisure spending." In Table 9.7 the expenditures on various leisure-oriented activities and materials in 1976 are shown. In 1977, Americans spent about $160 billion on "leisure." In terms of expenditures on recreation and sports equipment alone, the figure approaches $26 billion.[57] In the United States today there are well over 5 million camping vehicles, over 0.5 million swimming pools, 20 million CB radios, nearly 6000 marinas (for storing, docking, and launching boats), in excess of 2 million vacation homes, and about 11,000 golf courses.

Considering the inflation rates and economic fluctuations during the middle 1970s, one might guess that this type of spending would decline. But this is absolutely not the case. America's spending boom has increased steadily since 1969 ($82.6 billion) to $105 billion in 1972, $125 billion in 1974, $146 billion in 1976, and by 1985 the figure is expected to climb to $300 billion![58] This dollar amount is much larger than national defense costs and also well exceeds total U.S. corporate profits after taxes.

Thus leisure consumption is big business and will almost certainly continue to grow in the future. However, as Americans buy more recreational vehicles, second homes, vacation property, and snowmobiles, the nagging question that some continue to ask is, do these activities perform the functions that leisure is intended for? Are these activities rewarding, fulfilling, and voluntary? Do our new possessions bring us greater leisure happiness or merely more burdensome responsibilities?

Some have referred to the "leisure boom" as the "consumption boom," as Americans extend their love affair with recreational equipment.

We spend more money on activities that we call "leisure" than ever before, but to what extent do we think about what leisure *should* be for each of us? A three- or four-day workweek and accompanying three- or four-day weekend may sound attractive, but what would we *do* with that extra discretionary time once we had it? It appears likely, on the basis of what is already known, that over two-thirds of this additional time would be redirected into more work (e.g. a second job) or work-related activities. Although there have been changes in the Protestant ethic, it is still alive for many Americans. It appears that much of the remaining free time available to people will be directed into consumer spending on recreational pursuits. Whether this will satisfactorily fulfill the purposes of leisure can be answered only in the future.

Scenarios of the Future

For the reasons we have cited, it is difficult to predict, with any certainty, exactly what is in store for the realms of work and leisure. Some things we can predict: more elaborate technology, increasing automation, and more bureaucracy. To these, fu-turist Alvin Toffler adds another probable trend: more social heterogeneity.[59] In fact, Toffler believes that this increasing diversity may be one of the major qualities that will enable us to survive because we will be in the best position to cope with inevitable change. Yet, this diversity at the same time makes it difficult to predict the precise direction of work and leisure in the future. Many alternatives have been suggested.

Some writers have predicted that economic affluence will continue to accelerate, but that traditional conceptions of work, achievement, and advancement-oriented values may be rejected.[60] Others, like work and leisure researcher Jacques Ellul, have confidently asserted that we will misuse our advanced technology and that human beings will become mere cogs in the machinery that provides our abundance.[61] Still others have optimistically predicted the "best of all possible worlds," suggesting that *Homo sapiens* has the ability to use technology in ways that are not only productive but self-fulfilling as well.[62]

Possibly the most useful way to summarize these divergent opinions is in terms of four scenarios of the future presented by Thomas Kando.[63]

Technocratic

In his first scenario, Kando predicts that we will see much more emphasis on technology in every sphere of life, with leisure continuing to be nothing more than material consumption. Work and leisure would become even more sharply separated. Every ten years, the average workweek would decline by four hours—to a twenty-hour week by the year 2000. There would be a "leisure explosion," but the emphasis would be on material consumption. The key to the technocratic scenario is "more of the same—more of what we are seeing today."

Neo-Marxian

The neo-Marxian prognosis, which Kando believes more likely, forecasts the gradual deterioration and ultimate demise of capitalism. As economic conditions worsen and as inflation and unemployment rise, the situation continues to deteriorate—the rich get richer and the poor get poorer. As a consequence, the luxuries of material extravagance will become less available and the quality of social life will slowly erode. Leisure becomes increasingly spectacle-oriented, with little focus on the arts and the humanities.

Neo-Malthusian

The neo-Malthusian script for the future is a kind of "ecological Armageddon" according to Kando. Here, the prophecy of doom is a bit different because the causes of civilization's collapse are regarded as primarily demographic and ecological. Under the conditions described in this scenario, creative participatory leisure like craft-oriented hobbies will disappear, as will spectator-oriented mass leisure events. Social and personal disorganization will run rampant, and society could ultimately perish.

Countercultural

The fourth scenario is Kando's favorite and, as he explains, it is an "extrapolation of many elements found in the counterculture."[64] (By *counterculture* he refers to the rejection by many young people during the late 1960s of the values and material trappings of American society.) The key word here is *integration*—work and play begin to interpenetrate; age, social class, and sex categories are increasingly blurred; cultural form and content merge. In this regard, Kando has observed:

> A distinction traditionally central to our culture has been that between work and nonwork, production and consumption. The production process has been alienating, demanding, and from eight-to-five. The consumption process has been the passive consumption of commodities or culture after hours. The two have not intermeshed. Today, however, an increasingly widely accepted tenet of the sociology of work and leisure is that *the solution to both problems of work—alienation—and problems of leisure—passivity—must be sought in their mutual integration.* The traditional active-passive dichotomy must fall.[65]

The quality of work and leisure in the year 2000 and beyond will depend on the extent to which these elements are integrated effectively. For this integration to occur, society must make available the occupational and leisure-time opportunities that make possible such integration. In addition, this integration will not occur by osmosis; an important variable will be people's responses to changes in the work-leisure environment—more specifically, their *willingness* to accept change.

CONCLUSION

Some of the social problems discussed in this book are relatively clear cut and easily identified. For example, most Americans would agree that crime is a problem. In terms of work and leisure, however, there is less agreement. In fact, some people in our society might say "Where's the problem? Everybody has to work to make a living and everyone likes to have fun, so what's problematic about it?" After reading this chapter, it is hoped that *you* are now more aware of how work and leisure pose a social problem in our society. The three theoretical perspectives will help us to summarize our discussion.

According to the functionalist perspective, the interrelated parts of any social organization must be in reasonable balance in order for the system to maintain itself. Changes in one institutional arrangement will affect others in society. As a consequence of industrialization and a wide range of technological advancements, the nature of work and our attitudes toward it have changed dramatically. Many people in our society are alienated from their work and experience substantial dissatisfaction in this part of their lives. At the same time, leisure is now a mass phenomenon that is available to nearly everyone. Yet, what many of us call leisure is little more than organized consumption.

From the functionalist perspective, the current lack of balance in both of these realms poses a threat to the ongoing maintenance of our social organization. What would happen if there were not a sufficient number of satisfying jobs to go around? What are the effects of worker alienation on economic productivity? Are there any *real* similarities between the lesson of Rome's excessive emphasis on passive leisure and the future for *our* society? For the functionalist, the answers to these questions hinge on how we choose to handle our work and leisure problems. It may be necessary to reincorporate a feeling of pride among American workers, and to provide them with meaningful, active leisure opportunities if we are to overcome the problems related to work and leisure.

According to the conflict perspective, social problems emerge over a struggle involving finite resources. In our highly technological society, there continue to be a decreasing number of jobs that involve craftsmanship and intrinsic rewards. As a consequence, how much workers are paid becomes the primary concern—as reflected in current union demands during negotiations. One question that many work and leisure investigators are asking is "How long will offers of increased wages be sufficient to satisfy workers in terms of their attitudes toward their work?" The future may involve a struggle over a seriously diminished resource: the feeling that one's work is worthwhile and of value. There are already some visible indicators of workers' feelings along these lines. Empty beer cans inside new automobile doors, iron filings in transmissions, and hosts of defects in all kinds of merchandise made in America are signs of dissatisfaction and boredom.

Another very important concern in terms of work and leisure as a problem is that there may be too few jobs to go around in the future. It has been suggested that it may even be a privilege to work in the twenty-first century. For example, as more women have joined the labor force, conflict has emerged between men and women over job opportunities. Should there be a shortage of jobs, more people will have more time on their hands. We may be able to avoid an increase in our unemployment rate by instituting programs such as the three-day work week. If this occurs, a pressing question is posed in terms of leisure: what will these men and women do with their spare time? Conflicts could emerge over a fair share of *both* leisure *and* work resources.

The interactionist perspective emphasizes the subjective nature of reality and how individuals' definitions of the situation vary considerably. There are few socially problematic issues that involve so many subjective components as work and leisure. As we have seen, Americans have many different perceptions of what work implies—for some it represents any type of obligated activity, while for others only laborious and physically demanding tasks represent work. This is also true for leisure, as the well-known phrase "one person's work is another's leisure" illustrates. For some people, sitting quietly by a small pond is leisure, while for others, this activity would be boring and unenjoyable.

Using the interactionist perspective, we can better understand how a person's dissatisfaction with work can affect his or her whole lifestyle. In particular, the degree of success that people have in relating with others effectively can depend on how well their work integrates with the rest of their lives. If men and women appreciate and enjoy their leisure time, their interactions with other family members are likely to be more rewarding. If people are stagnant in terms of their leisure, this condition will very likely be reflected in their interactions with others.

GLOSSARY TERMS

Active leisure
Alienation from work
Automation
Block leisure time
Calvinism
Codetermination
Craftsmanship
Discretionary time
Existence time–Nonwork

obligations
Extrinsic motivations for work
Flexitime
Holist (Integrationist) view
Intrinsic motivations for work
Leisure
Mass leisure
Mechanization
One-dimensional society

Other-directed
Passive leisure
Protestant ethic
Recreation
Segmentalist (Differentiation) view
Social isolation
Work
Work-related time

REFERENCES

[1] Studs Terkel, *Working* (New York: Avon, 1975), p. 507.

[2] See Thomas M. Kando, *Leisure and Popular Culture in Transition* (St. Louis: C. V. Mosby Company, 1975).

[3] Thorsten Veblen, *The Theory of the Leisure Class* (reprint of the original 1899 edition; New York: Viking Press, 1967), p. 22.

[4] Max Weber, *The Protestant Ethic and the Spirit of Capitalism* (New York: Charles Scribner's Sons, 1958), p. 53.

[5] See Sebastian DeGrazia, *Of Time, Work and Leisure* (New York: Anchor Books, 1964); Stanley Parker, *The Future of Work and Leisure* (New York: Praeger, 1971); and Kando, *Leisure and Popular Culture in Transition.*

[6] See Robert Dubin, "Industrial Workers' Worlds: A Study of the Central Life Interests of Industrial Workers," in Erwin O. Smigel, ed., *Work and Leisure—A Contemporary Social Problem* (New Haven: College and University Press, 1963), pp. 53–72, and Edward Gross, "A Functional Approach to Leisure Analysis," *Social Problems* 9 (Summer 1961), pp. 2–8.

[7] C. Wright Mills, *White Collar—The American Middle Class* (New York: Oxford University Press, 1951), p. 221.

[8] See Karl Marx, *Selected Writings in Sociology and Social Philosophy,* T. B. Bottomore, trans. (New York: McGraw-Hill, 1964).

[9] Kando, *Leisure and Popular Culture in Transition,* p. 275.

[10] Pehr G. Gyllenhammar, *People at Work* (Reading, Mass.: Addison-Wesley, 1977), p. 4.

[11] Lee Braude, *Work and Workers: A Sociological Analysis* (New York: Frederick A. Praeger, 1975).

[12] Briggitte Berger, "The Coming Age of People Work," *Change* 9 (May 1976), pp. 24–30.

[13] See Joseph Cassidy, "Research Firm Finds . . . 8 Americans in 10 are Unhappy and Frustrated in Their Jobs," *National Enquirer* (August 7, 1973).

[14] Judson Gooding, "The Fraying White Collar," *Fortune* (December 1970), and U.S. Department of Health, Education, and Welfare, *Work in America* (Washington, D.C.: U.S. Government Printing Office, 1973).

[15] Walter S. Neff, *Work and Human Behavior* (New York: Atherton Press, 1968), p. 16.

[16] Karl Marx, *Selected Writings,* pp. 85–86.

[17] Melvin Seeman, "Empirical Alienation Studies: An Overview," in R. Felix Geyer and David R. Schweitzer, eds., *Theories of Alienation* (Leiden: Martinus Nijhoff, 1976), pp. 265–305.

[18] Emma Rothschild, "Auto Production—Lordstown," in Jerome Skolnick and Elliott Currie, eds., *Crisis in American Institutions,* 3d ed. (Boston: Little, Brown, 1976), pp. 329–341.

[19] Jon Shepard, *Automation and Alienation: A Study of Office and Factory Workers* (Cambridge, Mass.: The MIT Press, 1971).

[20] U.S. Department of Health, Education, and Welfare, *Work in America* (Washington, D.C.: U.S. Government Printing Office, 1973).

[21] Barbara A. Kirsch and Joseph J. Lengermann, "An Empirical Test of Blauner's Ideas on Alienation in Work as Applied to Different Type Jobs in a White-Collar Setting," *Sociology and Social Research* (October 1971), pp. 180–194.

[22] Braude, *Work and Workers: A Sociological Analysis,* pp. 182–183.

[23] U.S. Department of Labor, Employment Standards Ad-

ministration, Women's Bureau, "Twenty Facts on Women Workers" (Washington, D.C.: U.S. Government Printing Office, June, 1978.

[24] Fritz J. Roethlisberger and William J. Dickson, *Management and the Worker* (Cambridge, Mass.: Harvard University Press, 1939).

[25] Lyman W. Porter, "Turning Work into Non-Work: The Rewarding Environment," in Marvin D. Dunnette, ed., *Work and Nonwork in the Year 2001* (Belmont, Calif.: Wadsworth, 1973), pp. 113–133.

[26] Erich Fromm, *The Sane Society* (New York: Rinehart, 1955), pp. 288–289.

[27] Dubin, "Industrial Worker's Worlds."

[28] Louis Orzack, "Work as a 'Central Life Interest' of Professionals," in Erwin O. Smigel, ed., *Work and Leisure—A Contemporary ·Social Problem* (New Haven: College and University Press, 1963), pp. 73–84.

[29] See Arthur Shostak, *Blue-Collar Life* (New York: Random House, 1969), and Ralph C. Deans, "Productivity and the New Work Ethic," in Hoyt Gimlin, ed., *American Work Ethic* (Washington, D.C.: Congressional Quarterly, 1973).

[30] DeGrazia, *Of Time, Work and Leisure*, and U.S. Bureau of the Census, *Statistical Abstract of the United States, 1978* (Washington, D.C.: U.S. Government Printing Office, 1978), p. 412.

[31] DeGrazia, *Of Time, Work and Leisure*, p. 79.

[32] John D. Owen, "Workweeks and Leisure: An Analysis of Trends, 1948–1975," *Monthly Labor Review* (August 1976), p. 3.

[33] *American Management Association*, 1972.

[34] Riva Poor, ed., *4 Days, 40 Hours: Reporting a Revolution in Work and Leisure* (Cambridge, Mass.: Bursk and Poor, 1970), p. 15.

[35] *Bureau of Labor Statistics*, 1977.

[36] "Detroit Inches Closer to a Four-Day Week," *Business Week* (February 13, 1978), pp. 85–86.

[37] Millard C. Faught, "The Three-Day Revolution to Come: 3-Day Workweek, 4-Day Weekend," in Riva Poor, ed., *4 Days, 40 Hours: Reporting a Revolution in Work and Leisure* (Cambridge, Mass.: Bursk and Poor, 1970), pp. 133–142.

[38] Harold L. Wilensky, "The Uneven Distribution of Leisure: The Impact of Economic Growth on 'Free Time,' " in Erwin O. Smigel, ed., *Work and Leisure—A Contemporary Social Problem* (New Haven: College and University Press, 1963), pp. 107–145.

[39] Harold L. Wilensky, "Work, Careers, and Social Integration," *International Social Science Journal* 12 (Fall 1960), pp. 543–560.

[40] Ibid., p. 548.

[41] Ibid., p. 548.

[42] Robert S. Weiss and David Riesman, "Some Issues in the Future of Leisure," *Social Problems* 9 (Summer 1961), pp. 78–85.

[43] William A. Faunce, "Automation and Leisure," in Smigel, ed., *Work and Leisure: A Contemporary Social Problem*, pp. 85–96.

[44] "The Upward Mobility Two Incomes Can Buy," *Business Week* (February 20, 1978), pp. 80–82.

[45] William J. Emrie, *Recreation Problems in the Urban Impacted Areas of California* (Sacramento, Calif.: State of California Department of Parks and Recreation, 1970).

[46] See Mills, *White Collar—The American Middle Class;* C. Wright Mills, *The Sociological Imagination* (New York: Oxford University Press, 1951); William H. Whyte, Jr., *The Organization Man* (New York: Simon and Schuster, 1956); and Jacques Ellul, *The Technological Society* (New York: Alfred A. Knopf, 1964).

[47] See David Riesman, with Nathan Glazer and Reuel Denney, *The Lonely Crowd: A Study of the Changing American Character* (New Haven: Yale University Press, 1961).

[48] See B. F. Skinner, *Beyond Freedom and Dignity* (New York: Bantam/Vintage Books, 1971).

[49] Gyllenhammar, *People at Work.*

[50] "Doubting Sweden's Ways," *Time* (March 10, 1975), p. 40.

[51] "Flexitime," *Time* (January 10, 1977).

[52] "The Flexitime Concept Gets a Wider Test," *Business Week* (May 24, 1976), p. 38.

[53] Paul Weaver, "When Workers Call the Tune in Management," *U.S. News and World Report* (May 10, 1976), pp. 83–85.

[54] David Jenkins, "Democracy in The Factory," *Atlantic* (April 1973), pp. 78–83.

[55] See Herbert Marcuse, *One-Dimensional Man: Studies in The Ideology of Advanced Industrial Society* (Boston: Beacon Press, 1964).

[56] See Joffre Dumazedier, *Toward a Society of Leisure* (New York: The Free Press, 1967) and *Sociology of Leisure* (New York: Elsevier, 1974).

[57] "The Boom in Leisure: Where Americans Spend $160 Billion," *U.S. News and World Report* (May 23, 1977), pp. 62–63.

[58] "People Are Shelling Out More than Ever for a Good Time." *U.S. News and World Report* (February 21, 1977), pp. 40–41.

[59] See Alvin Toffler, *Future Shock* (New York: Bantam Books, Inc., 1970).

[60] Herman Kahn and Anthony Wiener, "The Future Meanings of Work: Some 'Surprise-Free' Observations," in Fred Best, ed., *The Future of Work* (Englewood Cliffs, N.J.: Prentice-Hall, 1973), pp. 141–154.

[61] See Ellul, *The Technological Society*, 1964.

[62] Carolyn Symonds, "Technology and Utopia," in Best, ed., *The Future of Work*, pp. 175–179.

[63] See Kando, *Leisure and Popular Culture in Transition*, 1975.

[64] Ibid., p. 275.

[65] Ibid., p. 275.

SUGGESTED READINGS

Best, Fred, ed. *The Future of Work.* Englewood Cliffs, N.J.: Prentice-Hall, 1973.
A collection of articles, both classic and contemporary, that relate to the future of work in the United States.

Cheek, Neil H., Jr., and Burch, William R., Jr. *The Social Organization of Leisure in Human Society.* New York: Harper & Row, 1976.
A textbook approach to the study of leisure in society.

Dunnette, Marvin D., ed. *Work and Nonwork in the Year 2001.* Belmont, Calif.: Wadsworth, 1973.
A collection of articles by scholars from the disciplines of psychology, management, business, economics, and others on the future of work in our society.

Gyllenhammar, Pehr G. *People at Work.* Reading, Mass.: Addison-Wesley, 1977.
A detailed look at the philosophy of work at the Volvo automobile plant in Sweden, written by the company's president.

Haug, Marie R., and Dofny, Jacques, eds. *Work and Technology.* Beverly Hills, Calif.: Sage Publications, 1977.
A collection of articles on the relationship between work and technology in our society.

Kando, Thomas. *Leisure and Popular Culture in Transition.* Saint Louis: C. V. Mosby, 1975.
Probably the most popular textbook in the sociology of work and leisure — a good, overall survey of the problem.

Parker, Stanley. *The Future of Work and Leisure.* New York: Frederick A. Praeger, 1973.
An English social scientist reflects on the future of work and leisure — a good theoretical approach.

Terkel, Studs. *Working.* New York: Avon Books, 1975.
A popular writer talks to a variety of people with different occupations about their work and how they feel about it.

Questions
for Discussion

1. How does the history of work and leisure in our society relate to these issues as social problems today? Was there always a leisure class? What is the Protestant ethic and how has it influenced our values and attitudes toward work and leisure? Consider the impact of the Industrial Revolution and how it affected Americans' perceptions of these issues.

2. Consider work and leisure, utilizing the theoretical perspectives. How would a functionalist view work and leisure as a social problem? a conflict theorist? an interactionist?

3. What is the holist or integrationist view of work and leisure? How does it differ from the segmentalist or differentiation position? Try to take each stance yourself and then examine work and leisure as social problems today.

4. Definitions of work and leisure vary according to one's perspective. Compare and contrast the text's definition with your own ideas about what each one implies. Is every activity that one engages in a clear-cut example of work *or* leisure? Why or why not?

5. Many Americans do not enjoy their work and would prefer a different occupation if they were provided the chance. Consider the dimensions of work as examined in the text and explore the issue of work dissatisfaction. Are factory employees and people with processual, routine jobs the only ones who are not happy with their work? Why?

6. Discuss how the Protestant ethic has declined in America. What kind of worker is most likely to regard his or her job as a central life interest today? What changes have taken place in people's attitudes toward their work?

7. It is difficult to imagine how anyone would *not* know what to do with more "leisure time" if it were available. Nevertheless, it appears that many people use gains in free time for more work. Discuss the implications of mass leisure, including the 4/40 work week, the possibilities for a 3-day week, and Wilensky's spillover and compensation modes of adaptation.

8. What might the future of work and leisure in America be like? How are experiments with alternative work programs, like job enrichment and flexitime, affecting our attitudes toward work? Will leisure continue to represent consumption for most Americans? Use Kando's scenarios of the future of work and leisure in your examination.

CHAPTER 10

Aging

THE AGED IN HISTORICAL AND CROSS-
CULTURAL PERSPECTIVE

The Aged in Other Cultures. The Role of the Aged. The
Aged in American History.

AGING AS A SOCIAL PROBLEM

The Functionalist Perspective. The Conflict Perspective.
The Interactionist Perspective.

PROBLEMS OF THE AGED IN CONTEMPORARY
AMERICAN SOCIETY

Work and Retirement. Finances. Social Participation and
the Elderly. Aging and Health. Deviance and Aging.
Institutionalization and the Aged.

THE FUTURE OF THE AGED IN AMERICA

Providing for the Elderly. Communities for the Elderly.
The Institutionalization of Death. Political Action. Interest
Groups, and the Elderly.

CONCLUSION

Each student reading this book will one day, in all probability, be old. What do you have to look forward to? In 1970, almost one-half of all residents of custodial institutions (e.g. prisons, hospitals, nursing homes) were over age 65.[1] Horror stories abound about conditions in these institutions, and some of the stories are true. For example, in 1976, residents of a New York adult-care facility testified before the United States Senate Subcommittee on Long-Term Care that they lived in fear of beatings by the staff, that the conditions in the home were filthy and squalid, and that they were sometimes forced to pay bribes for their meals.[2]

These and other problems are intensified by the financial condition of the elderly. For example, in 1977, the median income of men over 70 was $5007, while the median income for women of the same age was $3108 (see p. 346). These meager incomes, hardly sufficient to offer a varied and dignified existence, were severely eroded by inflation. In 1976, the Social Security Administration announced that Medicare recipients (that is, the elderly) would be required to pay an additional 19 percent of their hospitalization and nursing home costs in order to cover increased health care costs. This followed a 13-percent increase over the previous two years.[3]

It is difficult for the young to imagine what it is like to be old—the problems, inconveniences, and even degradations that can result from living in a society that glorifies youth and is structured around the desires and capabilities of the young and healthy. The situations described above illustrate two of the problems that confront the elderly in modern society—the likelihood of spending one's declining years in an institution and the dire financial straits of some older people. For people who have worked long and hard all their adult life, the threat of such unpleasant conditions after retirement is frighteningly real. There is always the nagging fear that the rewards one hopes to reap will evaporate.

If the threat of these problems were confined to a small group of people, it is unlikely that they would be considered a major social problem. However, increasing numbers of people are aware that such conditions might personally affect them or some-

one close to them. With an increasing life expectancy, more and more people can expect to live into their 80s and even 90s. So the likelihood of being institutionalized is a real one for many people. While the dire conditions described above exist only in the worst institutions, even the remote possibility of experiencing such misery and degradation has led many people to define these conditions as a serious social problem facing our society.

So the "golden years" are tarnished for many people. Why is this the case? Why do we Americans—with our tremendous wealth and reputed concern for the individual—often disregard the needs of the elderly? Who among the elderly are most adversely affected by these conditions? In this chapter we will offer some answers to these questions. In addition, we will discuss the current status of the elderly in terms of housing conditions, finances, social participation, health, and institutionalization. We will also evaluate various attempts to alleviate these problems. First, however, we will study how other societies have treated their elderly in order to determine if there is a "natural" way for a society to treat old people. This will give us insight into the social mechanisms that are important in relation to the position of the elderly in society.

THE AGED IN HISTORICAL AND CROSS-CULTURAL PERSPECTIVE

The Aged in Other Cultures

What is the "natural" way for a society to treat its elderly? What are the "best" social arrangements for providing health and happiness to older citizens? By studying how other societies have dealt with such issues, we can see what social mechanisms are important in creating and solving problems in particular social institutions.

In the mountainous Caucasus region of southern Russia, between the Black Sea and the Caspian Sea, live people for whom old age takes on a completely different meaning than it does for us—a people who often live beyond 100 years of age.[4] While the precise ages of these people have been hotly debated, there is fair certainty that they live longer than do most Americans. Khfaf Lazuria, for example, was a small, slender woman who lived to be 140 and was still able to thread a needle without the aid of eyeglasses. She married four times during her life—the last at the age of 108! In this culture, a person gains in power and social standing within the community as he or she grows older. This is partially due to the value placed on the family—it is a central institution that envelopes a person in an elaborate web of supportive relationships. According to one investigator who has written about these

In the mountainous Caucasus region of Southern Russia, the elderly receive great respect in the community and wield considerable political and economic power.

people, "There is no identity for an individual outside of this intricate network."[5]

Traditionally, the elders have controlled both family business and village affairs. A person's prestige and very identity depend on extensive family ties and the fact that numerous relatives are concerned about that person's happiness and wellbeing. Therefore, the elderly, who have had more children than younger Caucasians, possess more of what these people value highly—relatives who honor and comfort them. In addition, life for the Caucasians is quite stable and harmonious because its fabric (e.g. work, diet, family) has changed little over the years. They need not fear getting old, because they know what to expect—a long and healthy life marked by increasing social prestige and the emotional support and physical security that only a large family can offer.

The cold and barren regions inhabited by some Eskimo could not be more different than the lush, mountainous environment of the Caucasus.[6] Traditional Eskimo life was a continuous search for fish and meat (mainly seal) and an effort to preserve what was found for times of scarcity. Neither food nor material possessions were plentiful. The eldest male was generally considered the head of the family as long as he retained his ability to hunt, provide leadership, and perform other tasks essential for the group's survival. Growing old was viewed as a continuous decline in strength, and few looked forward to it. With the onset of age and less ability to perform arduous physical tasks, the individual's contribution to the welfare of the household diminished, with a resulting loss of influence in making family decisions.[7]

Still, old people were respected and expected to contribute within their capacities. Old men trapped animals or served as lookouts for caribou herds. Old women gathered materials for the fire and sewed clothing for the family. However, as one student of Eskimo life put it, "Owing to the small margin of survival in which [many Eskimo] live, excessive attention to nonproductive or only nominally productive persons would lessen a household's and the community's chance to survive during a period of hunger or actual starvation."[8] The key word is *productive*. In the harsh and barren Arctic environment, the elderly—especially when they lose their physical abilities—can be supported during good times, but during scarcity the group must travel far and wide in search of caribou and other game. There are reports that, in stringent and dire circumstances, some Eskimo groups have abandoned their elderly knowing that they could not survive alone.[9]

A final illustration of the impact of culture on the treatment of the elderly is the Israeli collective settlements, or *kibbutzim*. The kibbutzim are based on the common ownership of almost all property; all are expected to contribute to the production of goods that are then allocated on an egalitarian basis; and the community is run as a single economic unit, very much like one large household.[10] The elderly enjoy economic security along with social honor within the community. The community takes care of them when they are sick and supports them in retirement. They retire gradually over a period of time, which reduces the negative impact of the sudden loss of occupational status.

The kibbutzim originally developed from a radical break between some youthful members of Israeli society and their more traditional countrymen. This had led to a strong value-emphasis on youthfulness, hard physical labor, and productivity. Aging was seen as a period of steady decline—both physically and in terms of contribution to the community. This often resulted in a decline in social status and self-respect because the aging person did not possess the physical stamina and skills that are highly valued in the community.

The Role of the Aged

Why do we find such wide variation in the treatment of the elderly in different cultures? Society is comprised of interrelated and interdependent parts, each tied in complex ways to the others. The status of the elderly must be integrated with the other aspects of each culture. While there are many factors that shape the position of the aged in society, the following three factors seem to be especially influential:

1. **Social status and prestige are associated, to a considerable degree, with a** person's ability to make *economic, political,* **and** *social contributions* **to society.** In rapidly changing, youth-oriented societies, one's contributions to the community tend to decline with age. For example, among the Eskimos and in the Israeli kibbutzim, the loss of such social power is associated with the decline of physical stamina and the obsolescence of crucial skills.

2. **The** *kinship relations* **in a culture affect the treatment of the elderly.** If the family is a central social and economic unit and the elderly play an important role in the family, then the elderly tend to be revered. In the Caucasus, for example, the family is an irreplaceable association for the individual, and the elderly play an important leadership role in the family.

3. **The status of the elderly is influenced by the extent to which** *socialization to the new identity* **of the "aged person" occurs.** This socialization should provide sufficient opportunity and incentive for the person to learn meaningful roles with clear expectations that integrate this new identity with other parts of the person's life. In the Israeli kibbutzim, for example, the retirement process is a gradual change involving progressively less work, rather than the abrupt and complete cessation that commonly occurs in the United States.

As we discuss the position of the elderly in American society, these three factors should be kept in mind—especially in terms of the feasibility of particular solutions.

The Aged in American History

Preindustrial America

Like most people, Americans have a tendency to romanticize their own past—to conceive of some previous time as an idyllic period in which harmony and satisfaction were the rule rather than the exception. One of the most persistent, and misleading, myths regarding the "typical" American family of the past is one that Goode referred to as "the classical family of Western nostalgia."[11] According to this legend, the most common type of household prior to America's industrialization at the turn of the twentieth century was one with three or more generations of relatives living together, usually on the family farm. The members lived and worked together harmoniously under the leadership of the elders, who were greatly loved, highly revered, and very productive members of the family. This certainly sounds like a desirable time to have lived—especially for the elderly! However, this conception of the status of the elderly is more apt to mislead than to enlighten. For example, there is much evidence to suggest that the most prevalent household type consisted only of the husband, wife, and children and that it was not much more common than it is today for elderly parents to live with their married children.[12]

Regardless which household type was most common, the economic, political, and social arrangements of preindustrial America supported the position of high status held by the elderly. During this period, fathers often exerted considerable control over their sons—until they reached middle age and even beyond, because the sons were economically dependent on their fathers.[13] Marrying and setting up a household required substantial economic resources, which were, for most young couples, available only from their parents or other relatives. The son often depended on inheriting the family property upon retirement or death of his father in order to support his own nuclear family.

Since the labor of each family member was often crucial for the economic viability of the family, it was essential that all members cooperate toward that common goal. Because of this economic and social interdependence, it was natural for the family members to place high value on, and express respect for, one another—especially for the elderly who possessed skills and knowledge important to community welfare, owned the means through which the family made a living, and held influential positions in the community and church. With such social and economic arrangements, the elderly could demand respect. Open conflict and dissension within the family were not tolerated by the powerful older members of the family.

This need for harmony and cooperation was incorporated into the values of the community and

was enforced by the authority of the family elders, by the force of community mores, and by the law itself. If one showed disrespect for one's elders, there were very strong negative sanctions—in the form of gossip, ridicule, ostracism, and even arrest. So even though the high status of the elderly may have been functional for the period, their dominant position was maintained through their ability to wield more economic, political, and social power. Respect for the elderly came not only from some idealized moral notion that the elderly deserved respect, but, more importantly, it was the result of the place of the elderly in the social structure and power relationships of the time.

Industrial America

A number of fundamental changes that have had profound consequences for the status of the elderly have taken place in American society over the past century.[14] The family farm and small family-centered business have given way to agribusiness (huge corporations owning thousands of acres of farmland worked by hired employees) and enormous corporations or conglomerates. The self-employed individual is no longer the backbone of our economy; most of us are destined to be salaried employees of large organizations. The economy is heavily based on mass production and automation. With continuous and sweeping developments in technology, the skills required to hold a job change rapidly.

What impact have these changes had on the elderly? In the first place, it means that older workers' skills are frequently outmoded even before they retire. According to one authority who has studied this problem: "Given a labor market characterized by a sustained high level of unemployment and little immediate prospect that the situation will change, there is little bidding for the services of elderly workers."[15] Second, children no longer learn their future trade or profession within the family context, where the elderly could play an important role. Such vocational and professional skills are now acquired independently in other institutions, quite apart from the family.

Third, sons and daughters are less economically dependent on their parents because they need no longer wait for an inheritance (of the family farm or business), which often did not occur until the parents were quite elderly. In our economy, the young acquire skills that permit them to begin accumulating their own economic wealth long before they might receive an inheritance from their parents. Fourth, whereas in the preindustrial period most of the elderly worked until they died or were too feeble to continue productive employment, most Americans today retire before their productive capacity has fully declined and while they are still quite physically capable of continuing work. Finally, industrialization and the growth of bureaucratic organization have resulted in considerable geographic mobility, most often for occupational reasons. This means that parents are commonly separated geographically from their children and grandchildren.

The outcome of all of this is that the social status of the elderly has declined because they no longer hold positions of economic power; their children are no longer dependent on them for their own livelihood; and they no longer perform tasks that are viewed as essential for the group's welfare. (Compare the position of the elderly in America with that of the elderly among the Caucasians, the Eskimo, and in the Israeli kibbutzim.) Because the economic links have declined and the social interdependency has lessened, relationships with grandparents, aunts, uncles, and other relatives, are less important than previously. People may still love and respect their parents and grandparents, but they are probably not living in as close proximity to them and are not as economically and socially dependent on them as in the past.

The Future

The problem of the position of the elderly in society may become more severe in the future. A declining birthrate along with an increasing life expectancy means that American society will "age." That is, if these trends continue, the elderly will constitute a larger proportion of our population than they do today. In 1900, people over 65 constituted 4 percent of the American population (3 million people); by 1976, they made up over 10 percent of our populace (22 million).[16] It is projected that by 2030 there will be more than 50 million people over 65 in the United States—about 17 percent of our populace (see Fig. 10.1). What kind of social problems do we face now and shall we face in the future because of this growing population of elderly people? In order to understand the ways in which aging might be a social problem, it is beneficial to view this issue from our three theoretical perspectives.

AGING AS A SOCIAL PROBLEM

The Functionalist Perspective

From the functionalist perspective, societies are well-integrated and relatively smooth-functioning systems, in which each part contributes to the maintenance of the whole. The status and power of each group in society depends primarily on the contribution of that group to the functioning of the whole system. The extent to which a certain group can make a significant contribution depends on whether they possess highly valued and functionally important skills or characteristics. Groups who cannot make such contributions become, in a sense, parasitic on the system—they use resources but contribute little that is important or essential. The elderly in industrial societies often find themselves in this situation. For a number of reasons, such as outdated occupational skills or declining physical capacities, the elderly are no longer seen to possess important skills and so are less likely to hold important positions or perform crucial functions. **Thus, the position of the elderly constitutes a social problem to the extent that they do not perform roles that are integrated with the other parts of society and that make an important contribution to the survival of the system. From the functionalist perspective, it is dysfunctional to have a large group depleting essential resources in society while not contributing to their production and distribution.**

In the same way that all the parts of the system should be integrated, the functionalist also argues that the different stages in a person's life should be integrated, rather than viewed as separate from, and independent of, one another. There should be a continuity to life, in which each stage has some meaning and importance in relation to the whole of life. One stage might be seen as preparation for a later one; a later stage might be conceived of as reward for activities undertaken at an earlier point. Such continuity serves to motivate individuals to perform well by making tasks at one stage understandable and meaningful in terms of their place in the whole cycle. Any stage in the lifecycle, includ-

ing old age, would be a social problem to the degree that it is not integrated with the other stages. Thus, a comfortable and secure old age might be viewed as a reward one receives after a long life of productive work and as a time of reflection and evaluation of one's life. If a society does not provide the elderly with the material, social, and spiritual rewards that they feel they deserve, then there is a discontinuity in the lifecycle that can be considered a social problem.

The Conflict Perspective

From the conflict perspective, societies are conflict-ridden arenas in which interest groups struggle

Figure 10.1 Projections for the Population 65 Years of Age and Older, 1976 to 2050. U.S. Bureau of the Census, *Statistical Abstract of the United States, 1977* (Washington, D.C.: U.S. Government Printing Office, 1977), pp. 6–7; U.S. Bureau of the Census, *Current Population Reports,* Series P-20, no. 307, "Population Profile of the United States: 1976" (Washington, D.C.: U.S. Government Printing Office, 1977), p. 12; and U.S. Bureau of the Census, *Current Population Reports,* Series P-25, no. 704, "Projections of the Population of the United States: 1977 to 2050" (Washington, D.C.: U.S. Government Printing Office, 1977), p. 86.

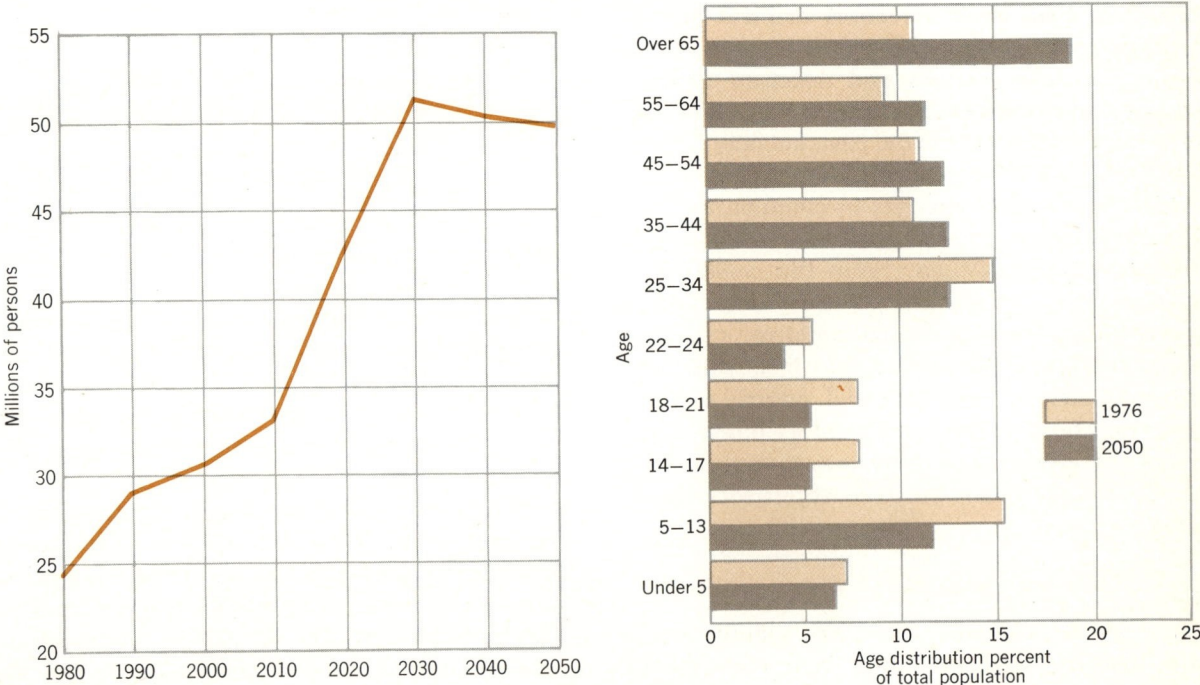

over scarce resources. A person's power and prestige flow, primarily, from possession of valued resources – not from his or her objective contribution to the well-being of the community. Those with power and prestige make laws and encourage the acceptance of customs that support and reinforce their dominant position. The elderly in preindustrial America held considerable power because they owned and controlled property and could enforce customs and laws that supported their position. Thus, the elderly had high status in the community because they controlled economic, political, and social sources of power.

The declining status of the elderly in industrial societies is a function of the limited access that the elderly have to these sources of power. They no longer control property, dominate families, or in other ways inhabit powerful positions in society. However, this loss of power is not the major fact that makes the condition of the elderly a social problem from the conflict perspective. From this perspective, a condition becomes a social problem when some powerful group believes that its interests are not being served. **The condition of the elderly is a social problem to the extent that they feel that their interests are not served and that they have the resources to make their demands known and listened to by a larger constituency.** There have been many dissatisfied elderly people in the past, but only recently have they begun to realize that old people as a group have certain interests in common and can exercise whatever power they have available to change these conditions. From the conflict perspective, it is not the inequitable distribution of power that creates a social problem; rather, a social problem arises when that inequitable distribution affects some powerful group – a group that can, through the exercise of its power, command the attention of other groups and possibly change the conditions which constitute social problems.

The Interactionist Perspective

From one point of view, the elderly can be considered quite well off today; they are in better health and more affluent than any previous generation of old people. Where, then, does the problem of the elderly lie? The interactionist perspective sensitizes us to the subjective nature of social reality – a condition is a social problem because important groups define it as a problem and act on the basis of that social definition. The affluent lifestyle of many Americans is now perceived as the only acceptable lifestyle. Anything less than that is defined as unacceptable. **Since the elderly often find it difficult to maintain such a lifestyle, their present conditions are now defined by many as a social problem.**

The interactionist perspective also sensitizes us to the social sources of a person's self-concept – our feelings of self-esteem and self-worth are the product of others' reactions to us and of our social position in society. **The condition of the aged becomes a social problem to the extent that their position in society and the treatment of them by other people make it difficult or impossible for them to maintain a positive self-concept.** Whether through forced retirement or a result of dehumanizing treatment in institutions, there are conditions in society that make the maintenance of a positive self-concept difficult for the elderly.

PROBLEMS OF THE AGED IN CONTEMPORARY AMERICAN SOCIETY

Work and Retirement

The United States is a work-oriented society. Work roles are not only the primary means by which Americans achieve economic rewards but are also a major source of social esteem and feelings of personal self-worth. People work not only to earn a living but also to enhance their social status, to maintain their range of interpersonal relationships, and to receive intrinsic satisfaction from on-the-job accomplishments.

While more people will reach old age than ever before, there has until recently been a trend toward establishing a mandatory retirement age of 65 years or, in some industries and government agencies, even younger. The mandatory retirement age for most workers was recently raised to 70. This means that the time span between retirement and

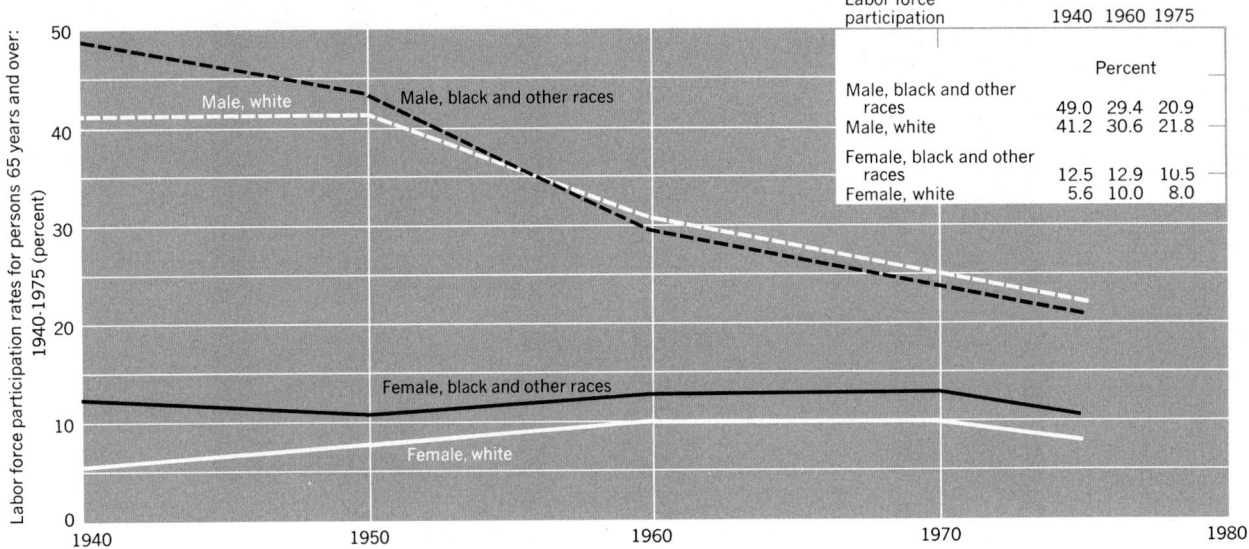

Labor force participation	1940	1960	1975
		Percent	
Male, black and other races	49.0	29.4	20.9
Male, white	41.2	30.6	21.8
Female, black and other races	12.5	12.9	10.5
Female, white	5.6	10.0	8.0

Figure 10.2 Labor Force Participation Rates for Persons 65 Years and Older, 1940–1975. U.S. Bureau of the Census, *Status: A Monthly Chartbook of Social and Economic Trends* (Washington, D.C.: U.S. Government Printing Office, 1976), p. 30.

death is much greater now than in the past because people live longer today and fewer people over 65 continue to work (see Fig. 10.2). In 1977, only 20 percent of those 65 and over were gainfully employed.[17] In addition, the number of men between the ages of 60 and 64 who remain in the labor force has declined from 83 percent in 1957 to 63 percent in 1977. However, as can be seen in Figure 10.2, participation in the labor force varies considerably by sex—elderly women are substantially less likely to be working than are elderly men. In other words, more than 80 percent of Americans 65 years of age and older are retired even though many are physically and intellectually capable of working. The recent increase in the mandatory retirement age is not expected to change this substantially.

The Decision to Retire

A decision to retire, like many other decisions, is the result of many factors impinging on the individual. Economic security is certainly an important factor. People are reluctant to retire if it means a substantially reduced standard of living. The atti-

tudes of people important to the potential retiree also play a role in the decision. Are they supportive of a retirement decision? Obviously, mandatory retirement is an important consideration—some workers simply have no choice. However, studies in which people were asked to state why they retired indicate that slightly more than half did so because of "poor health." Yet one must be cautious about accepting responses to questionnaire items or other such verbalizations of motives as causes per se. Factors other than health (e.g. having been shifted to a less desirable position by one's employer in order to ease the impact on the company) may play a greater role in the retirement process than the "poor health" to which the retiree attributes the retirement decision.[18]

The Effect of Retirement

Any dramatic transition in a person's life, such as retirement, must have widespread ramifications for the person. Retirement involves relinquishing the status of worker and accepting the ambiguous role of retiree. Some social gerontologists have used the

A controversial question in modern America is whether retirement should be voluntary or mandatory. Some argue than mandatory retirement is a waste of valuable resources and unfair to the elderly.

term *roleless role* to describe retirement because of the ambiguities of this status in our society. The role is simply less well defined than many other roles.[19] As a consequence, people react to this new status in varying ways. After retirement, some workers suffer a loss of morale and feelings of depression and anxiety, while others experience increased morale and feelings of contentment. When retirees do show a loss of morale and signs of emotional instability, this seems to be mainly a function of the general lifestyle of the retiree, and only incidentally is it the result of the retirement process. In other words, for most elderly people, retirement in and of itself is not the primary cause of their problems.[20]

However, retirement is often associated with other undesirable changes. For example, one common accompaniment of retirement is a substantial reduction in income. One investigator found that only a small number of those with moderate incomes missed their jobs. In other words, if one can maintain a retirement income that permits an acceptable lifestyle, not having a job is relatively unimportant. It is the sharp decrease in income and

the resulting change of lifestyle that contributes to a decline in morale and lack of contentment among some of the elderly.[21]

Retirement: Mandatory or Voluntary?

It is clear that few generalizations can be made about how people react to retirement. For some it is a joy, for others a curse. However, there is sufficient concern about mandatory retirement, and its consequences, to bring this issue up for public debate. In response to an outpouring of concern about these problems, in 1978 Congress raised the mandatory retirement age for most workers to 70. This was done partly to alleviate the financial drain on Social Security created by the growing number of retirees collecting benefits. However, there was strong pressure for raising the retirement age — or even eliminating mandatory retirement altogether — on humanistic and civil libertarian grounds. Many feel that a person's ability should be the sole criterion of whether he or she works. To do otherwise, these opponents of mandatory retirement argue, is to discriminate unfairly on the basis of age and to condemn older people to unwanted idleness and a reduced standard of living.

On the other side of this issue, proponents of mandatory retirement argue that a system of completely voluntary retirement has significant ramifications that might create new problems while solving others. First, the U.S. economy is geared to a labor force that is quite small when compared to the size of the total population. There are simply not enough jobs for the vast majority of young persons below 22 years of age and older citizens above 65. In addition, if mandatory retirement were eliminated, young workers would find promotions far less common because the better positions would be occupied for a longer period by older workers.

Second, the plight of the elderly person who wants to continue working is compounded by the rapid advances in technology that have made the skills of many workers obsolete even before they reach middle age. For example, the formal educational requirements necessary to hold most jobs above the level of unskilled laborer have increased dramatically over the past few years, often outstripping the older worker's level of educational attainment.[22] Whereas twenty-five years ago a person with an eighth-grade education would have little difficulty in finding a job, today one must have at least a high school education to obtain any but the most menial employment. In addition, a skilled worker trained twenty-five years ago would be unemployable today without a continual updating of skills to keep pace with technological advances.

Third, mandatory retirement has served as a socially acceptable means for employers to eliminate those older workers who, while able to continue working, might be less productive, aggressive, or innovative than some younger workers. Without this excuse, employers would be faced with the unpleasant task of firing an aging worker who is no longer productive.

Fourth, older workers, because of seniority and pay raises over the years, are generally more expensive laborers than young workers. In addition, the older workers place a heavier demand on other company resources, such as health care costs. The consequence of this is increased production costs to the company, which may force it to raise prices or employ fewer people in order to make an acceptable profit.

Finally, without a mandatory retirement age, a person with health problems whose condition might benefit from retirement might feel compelled to continue working rather than face a drop in income. With mandatory retirement, the decision is removed from his hands.

For these reasons, raising or eliminating the mandatory retirement age may have wide-ranging implications for American society. Although the final outcome is as yet unclear, the various interest groups are beginning to marshal their resources to pursue their goals on this issue. A potential compromise solution to this problem might be to institute a program of gradual retirement such as is found in the Israeli kibbutzim. That is, a person might continue to work as long as he or she was physically able, but for an ever decreasing period of time each week or month. This would provide jobs for large numbers of people while at the same time easing the transition to retired status.

Alternatives to Work

Some have argued that we should find activities other than work in which older people can find satisfaction and fulfillment. One alternative popular today is volunteer work in schools, hospitals, and other settings. In 1974, 22 percent of those over 65 did some type of volunteer work.[23] (Surprisingly, so did a larger number of people under 65: 35 percent.) Volunteering is greater among those with higher income and educational levels. A rather startling finding is the fact that a larger proportion of the employed people over 65 did volunteer work than those not employed. This suggests that volunteering may not simply replace employment but rather supplement it. However, many people hold negative attitudes about volunteering. For example, in a survey of a representative sample of Americans, almost three-quarters agreed that if work is valuable, the worker ought to be paid for performing it, and those over 65 agreed more strongly with this position than did those under 65. Thus in people's minds, volunteer work is not valuable and productive, because one does not get paid for it.

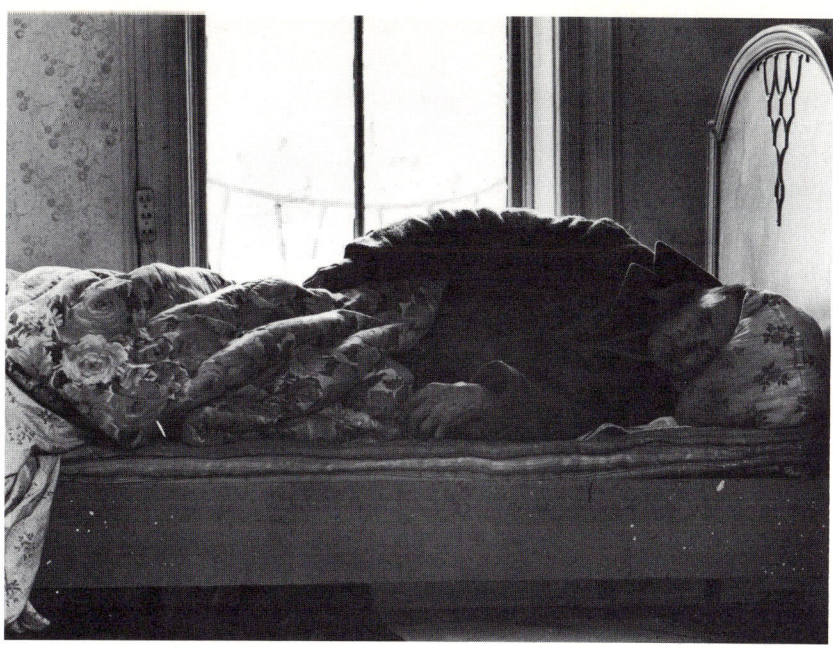

For some Americans, old age is a time of poverty, failing health, and loneliness—a tragic irony in an affluent country such as the United States.

Before nonwork activities such as volunteering can completely replace work as a core interest and central life task, Americans will have to change their attitudes. The American preoccupation with work and work-related roles is not universal; it is not found in all cultures or even in all groups within our own culture. People can and do gain satisfaction from activities outside the work setting.[24] Because of this, alternative solutions to the problems of the elderly may be more feasible than trying to bring them back into the work force. For example, improvements in the economic status of the elderly or in their use of leisure time may be more easily attained and less disruptive than the elimination of mandatory retirement. In addition, such nonwork solutions may be more acceptable to many of the elderly themselves than is their continued participation in the work force.

Finances

In the United States, one of the most affluent countries in the world, many of the elderly are economi-cally deprived. This does not simply mean that they cannot afford the transportation costs necessary to visit their children or that a winter vacation in Florida is out of their reach. The severely deprived elderly lack adequate food, essential drugs, and possibly a telephone in the house from which to make emergency calls. One 69-year-old man was arrested in Miami Beach for attempting to steal a twenty-five-cent can of soup from a grocery store. He had to survive on an income of $114 per month in 1971![25]

In 1977, the median income for American families headed by a person 65 or over was $9110, just over *half* the $16,000 income for American families headed by persons of all ages (see Fig. 10.3). For unrelated (widowed, divorced, single) aged persons, the median income (about $3829) was only about 75 percent of that ($5907) for all unrelated individuals.[26] **This means that many elderly must live on incomes that are below the nationally established poverty level.**

Income is one of two main sources of financial security; the other is personal assets.[27] Income flows

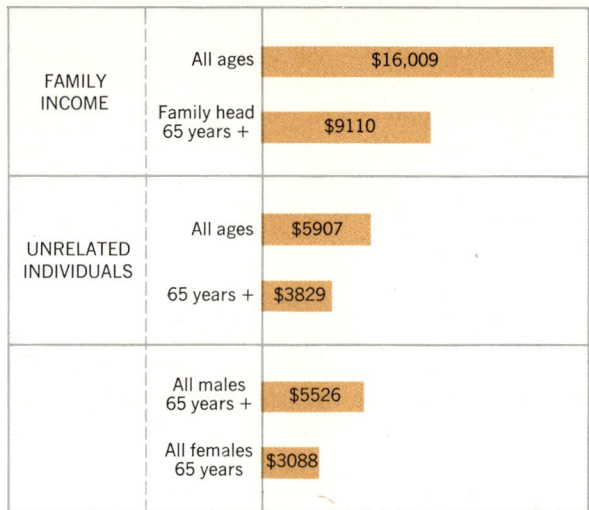

Figure 10.3 **Median Income of the Older Population, 1977. U.S. Bureau of the Census, *Current Population Reports*, Series P-60, no. 116, "Money Income and Poverty Status of Families in the United States: 1977," advance report (Washington, D.C.: U.S. Government Printing Office, 1978).**

from pensions, salaries and wages, rents, interest from savings and investments, and the repayment of loans by debtors. Social security, however, is the major source of income for the elderly who are retired. While social security has made an important contribution to providing a steady income for the elderly, the benefits are not adequate to continue a preretirement lifestyle or, in many cases, to maintain a decent standard of living. For example, if a worker's average yearly earnings after 1950 were $6000, the monthly benefit at age 65 is $323.40.[28]

Personal assets include ownership of, or equity in, a home and furnishings, other real estate, savings, securities such as stocks and bonds, and private insurance and annuity programs. However, in terms of assets, the situation of many elderly is bleak. More than half of the elderly own no equity in a home and few have other assets that are substantial enough to provide real economic security.[29] While some older people can use their personal assets to supplement their incomes, there are many who do not have sufficient assets to do so.

The financial difficulties of the elderly are compounded by additional factors that tend to have a more adverse effect on them than on younger people. For example, at least 86 percent of the elderly suffer from some chronic disease that results in an additional drain on their incomes. In addition, the elderly face high property taxes, either as homeowners or tenants (increased property tax is usually passed on to tenants in the form of higher rents), that outstrip their usually fixed incomes. Inflation is especially devastating to those on fixed incomes. Between 1967 and 1978, for example, food costs soared 114 percent according to the Consumer Price Index.[30] Low-income families, including a majority of the elderly, spend just over 70 percent of their income on food and housing combined, while higher-income groups pay 47 percent or less of their total incomes for these crucial items.[31]

Financial security affects one's entire lifestyle. It determines one's diet, ability to seek good health care, to visit relatives and friends, to maintain a suitable wardrobe, and to find or maintain adequate housing. One's financial resources, or lack of them, play a great part in finding recreation (going to movies, plays, playing bridge or bingo, etc.) and maintaining morale, feelings of independence, and a sense of self-esteem. In other words, if an older person has the financial resources to remain socially independent (having her own household and access to transportation and medical services), to continue contact with friends and relatives, and to maintain her preferred forms of recreation, she is going to feel a great deal better about herself and others than if she is deprived of her former style of life.

Social Participation and the Elderly

Agism

According to the interactionist perspective, social interaction and participation in groups have very important consequences for the individual. Recall the ***looking-glass*** *self*— we learn about ourselves through the reactions of other people to us. Through interaction and participation, we develop and maintain a self-concept based on the way others react to us. We gain a sense of personal importance and self-worth, a feeling that we have a place in the world and that others care about and depend upon us. We learn who we are and how highly we are valued by others. This interaction need not occur at a face-to-face level; rather, the elderly can become aware of society's attitudes about them through the portrayal and stereotyping of the elderly in the media and in advertising.

Today the reaction to the elderly, whether at a personal level or through the media, is often a negative one. **The term *agism* refers to "the negative or pejorative image of, and attitudes toward, an individual simply because he or she is old."**[32] **It is like racism or sexism because it involves discrimination and prejudice against all members of a particular social category.** Among many of the elderly, agism is viewed as an especially pernicious influence because it is often done with the best of intentions and with the good interests of the elderly in mind. For example, some argue that mandatory retirement—even if done for the good of the older worker—is agism because it discriminates against a person solely on the basis of age.

Some militant senior citizens have focused their wrath on the media, especially television, as the primary purveyors of negative stereotypes of the elderly.[33] *Media Watch* is a nationwide volunteer force created by the Gray Panthers to oversee the treatment of the elderly on TV. They are incensed by such characterizations as Johnny Carson's Aunt Blabby, who is presented as the ultimate silly old woman, and Carol Burnett's sourpuss old lady. The fear of such groups is that the negative and unrealistic portrayal of older people in the media will influence attitudes toward the elderly—Aunt Blabby will come to be seen as characteristic of most older women—and that social policy might be developed based on these false stereotypes. An equally important concern is that these portrayals provide nothing for the elderly viewer to feel proud of, to identify with, or to emulate. Society's reaction to the elderly person—as filtered through the media—is an overwhelmingly negative one.

Group Involvement

Because of agism, the social participation of the elderly in American society sometimes has negative consequences—the reactions of others are not supportive of a positive self-concept. However, are there other group involvements—with family, friends, or acquaintances—that might ease the impact of these negative encounters? What sort of transitions do the elderly experience in terms of group attachments? It is to these issues that we now turn.

It is a myth that most of the elderly in the United States live either alone or in an institution (see Fig. 10.4). In 1975, only 27 percent of the elderly lived alone, and 5 percent were residents of institutions. While the majority of older people live with friends or relatives, there are certain changes that must naturally occur as a person grows older, particularly in relation to the family. The elderly are less likely to have a living spouse than are younger adults. For example, a person over 65 is much more likely to be widowed or divorced than is a younger person—and elderly women are about 3.5 times as likely to be widowed or divorced as are elderly males (see Fig. 10.5). An increasing number of older people—especially women and those in advanced old age—live alone. Of course, a person who has lost a spouse and lives alone can still have an active social life with extensive and satisfying social relationships.

Despite these expected changes in group involvements, the individual has some freedom to shape how he or she responds to growing old. There have been a number of attempts to explain the experiences of the aged as they make the transition into their new status. One such attempt is the *social disengagement theory of old age*.[34] From this point of view, the transition to old age involves a mutual disengagement or withdrawal between the individual and society. It would be dysfunctional in our society—based as it is on efficiency, competition, and individual achievement—to assign necessary roles to that age group with the least physical stamina and the highest death rate. Such deaths would lead to very serious disruptions in society because of the many important leadership, occupational, and personal relationships that would be broken.

Traditionally this disengagement process has been viewed as a reduction in the number of roles

PERSONS 65 YEARS & OVER MARCH 1975

TOTAL 22,210,000		Thousands of persons
	Living with spouse	11,405
	Living alone	6,008
	Living with other relatives	3,217
	Inmates of institutions	1,088
	Living with non relatives	493

Figure 10.4 Living Arrangements of Persons 65 Years and Older. U.S. Bureau of the Census, *Status: A Monthly Chartbook of Social and Economic Trends* (Washington, D.C.: U.S. Government Printing Office, 1976), pp. 26, 33.

All persons over 65 years

Living alone **27%**
With other relatives **15%**
Inmates of institutions **5%**
Living with non relatives **2%**
Living with spouse **51%**

Persons 65 years and over, below the poverty level

Living with spouse **30%**
Living with relative(s) other than spouse **8%**
Living with nonrelative(s) only **6%**
Living alone **56%**

Figure 10.5 Marital Status of Persons 65 Years and Older, 1975. U.S. Bureau of the Census, *Status: A Monthly Chartbook of Social and Economic Trends* (Washington, D.C.: U.S. Government Printing Office, 1976), p. 27.

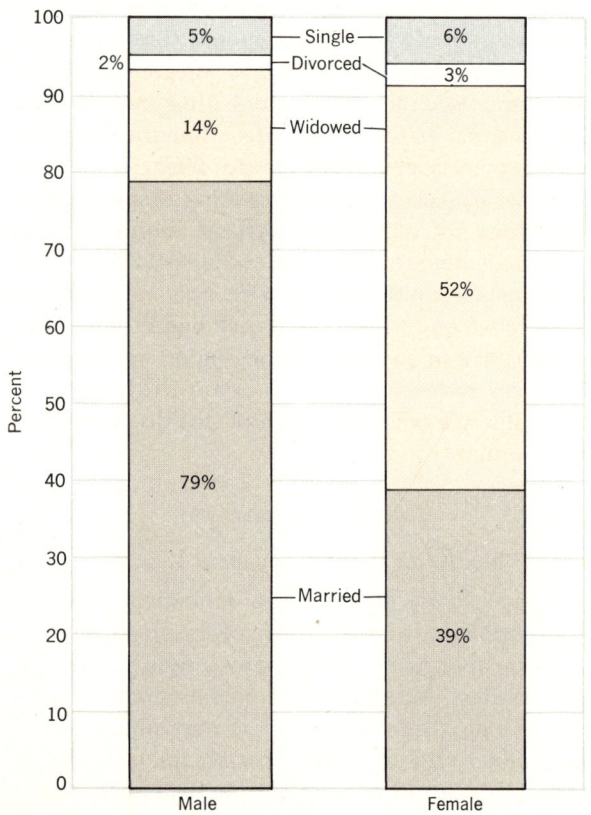

social relationships held by the elderly. The importance of occupational roles declines or is completely eliminated; kinship relationships become more important, but at the same time parents have less control over and contact with their offspring; because of deaths or physical limitations, the elderly have fewer contacts with friends and voluntary organizations. One expert refers to this as a "process of reduction and simplification" of social roles and social ties.[35] However, it may be more accurate to think of this not necessarily as a reduction in number of contacts but rather a change in *emphasis*. As gerontologist Elaine Cumming says, "The most crucial step in the disengagement process may lie in finding a *new set of rewards*."[36] For example, the self-esteem and feelings of self-worth that were attained because of personal achievement in one's occupation may have to be generated by some other activity—personal relationships with friends, leisure-time pursuits, and the like. In other words, the social activity of the elderly may not actually decline in quantity or quality, but rather a change of *emphasis* may occur as one makes the transition to elderly status.

How active are older people in our society? Contrary to disengagement theory (and many popular conceptions), most older people maintain relatively extensive group involvements and associations with friends and acquaintances. While it is less in some areas than among younger people, it is still substantial. There are certain variations in activities, depending on the characteristics of the older person. For example, those who are in advanced old age (more than 70 years old) are less likely to visit or have extensive associations with close friends. Friendship patterns are also associated with social class. The more affluent elderly have more friends and are more likely to visit them than are the less affluent. This does not seem to be a function of economics alone since some studies show that, within a particular class, a person's financial status makes little difference in the likelihood of his or her being isolated from friends. It seems that middle-class persons acquire certain social skills that make it easier for them to develop and maintain friendships, whereas lower-class persons find this more difficult to do.[37]

Work also provides an opportunity and a context in which to develop friendships. Sociologist Zena Blau found that people maintain their morale in old age, regardless of the extent of social participation, as long as they are married or working.[38] After widowhood or retirement, they are more likely to maintain their morale if their levels of social participation are fairly high.

As with friendship relations, older people also retain a fairly active involvement in various *voluntary associations* (unions, fraternal organizations, church groups, etc.). Such involvement declines with increasing age. It also declines very substantially among the working and lower classes. For example, one study found that over 83 percent of those over 65 in higher socioeconomic classes participated in some associations, while only 28 percent of those in the lower socioeconomic statuses did so.[39] It is clear that contentment and feelings of self-worth are greatly dependent on some form of social participation—whether this is achieved through work, marriage, leisure activities, or other means.

Adaptation to Aging

These studies of social participation among the elderly suggest that the disengagement explanation alone is too simple to describe the complex reality of the aging process. There are, in fact, numerous ways to respond to aging. Blau has taken Robert K. Merton's theory of how people respond to ambiguous, stressful, or unique situations and applied it to the experiences of the elderly.[40] According to Merton, one response to such situations is *retreatism* — the kind of withdrawal described by disengagement theory. However, others adapt to the aging process quite differently. Some people develop new interests, expand their circle of friends, join various clubs and guilds, and do volunteer work. These people enjoy life more after retiring than they did before. This response is referred to as *innovation*. A third mode of adaptation, *conformity,* is characterized by a tendency to adjust to the conditions of old age. The conformist does not lose interest in activities or relationships with others as the retreatist does; but neither does the conformist seek out new ways of enjoying old age. The conformist does not enjoy life more (or less) than he or she did before.

There are, then, at least three common modes of adaptation to old age. The response that a particular person is likely to exhibit is affected by many social and psychological factors. Most importantly, the evidence strongly indicates that those in the lower social classes are more likely to be retreatists. However, there is another response that Blau does not mention: *rebellion.* Some elderly, while accepting the fact that some social roles and relationships must change with age, refuse to be stereotyped and treated as if they had little to offer society. These people are beginning to marshal resources to force society to adapt to their needs and skills. We will hear more of this group later in the chapter.

Aging and Health

Medical Quackery and Fraud

Growing old is, of course, a biological process. Most people are acutely aware of the physical deterioration that often accompanies aging and that necessitates limitations and adjustments in one's life. As one grows older, one commonly becomes more concerned about the possible failure of faculties, such as sight or hearing, the decline in ability to take care of oneself, and the potential physical

While some people lower their horizons as they grow older, others prefer to remain active and vigorous. For some, old age is a time to expand one's interests and explore new activities.

pain and discomfort (see Table 10.1). **Because of these fears, and also because our society places such value on youthfulness, the elderly are especially susceptible to quackery that promises to rejuvenate them and reverse the inexorable movement toward death.** It is estimated that health frauds and medical quackery cost Americans upwards of $1 billion per year.[41] Large amounts of money are spent on cosmetics, hair dyes, and wrinkle removers that help maintain the outward appearance of youth.

Even more serious is the fraud perpetrated on the elderly that promises "magical" cures for such ailments as arthritis, which medical science cannot presently cure. The real tragedy is that these fraudulent cures may be attempted in place of treatment that is known to be effective in alleviating symptoms. In the case of diseases that modern medicine can cure, effective treatment may be postponed until the condition has become more severe. For example, Dr. Kaadt's Diabetic Remedy was sold for a time as a treatment for diabetes. It consisted of a combination of vinegar, saltpeter, resorcinol, and Takadiastase that was consumed along with digestive and laxative tablets. This treatment was espe-cially appealing to diabetic patients because all dietary restrictions were removed—no insulin injections were necessary and the patients could eat whatever they pleased. The perpetrators of this fraud took in $6 million before they were put out of business. The treatment has no curative value (there is no known medical cure for diabetes). Furthermore, the disease is controlled by insulin and diet, and those patients who went off this regimen while taking Dr. Kaadt's remedy often suffered such complications as gangrenous infection, diabetic coma, and damage to (or loss of) eyesight.[42]

While anyone can be taken in by medical quackery, the elderly are especially susceptible for a number of reasons: they often have painful, chronic, degenerative illnesses that cannot be cured; loneliness and isolation make them easy prey for a dynamic confidence man who promises not only a cure but also sympathy and companionship; the immediacy of death makes very appealing any treatment that is claimed to postpone it; finally, the ability to make judgments and evaluate claims for cures may deteriorate with the physiological changes of old age and is also reduced when a person is alone without help to evaluate such claims.

TABLE 10.1

Persons with Activity Limitation by Selected Chronic Conditions, by Age and Sex, 1976, Expressed in Percentages

CONDITION	BOTH SEXES		MALE				FEMALE			
	All ages	65 yr. and over	All ages	Under 45 yr.	45–64 yr.	65 yr. and over	All ages	Under 45 yr.	45–65 yr.	65 yr. and over
Percent limited by										
Heart conditions	15.7	23.4	16.7	3.6	22.2	25.3	14.8	5.0	15.9	22.0
Arthritis and rheumatism	16.8	24.9	11.4	3.7	14.9	16.3	21.7	7.4	24.2	31.6
Visual impairments	5.4	8.2	5.7	5.2	4.7	7.6	5.0	2.8	3.2	8.6
Hypertension without heart involvement	6.9	8.9	4.8	1.9	6.8	6.1	8.9	3.6	11.1	11.1
Mental and nervous conditions	4.9	3.0	4.4	6.2	4.7	2.0	5.4	6.1	6.6	3.8
Percent of all persons with										
No activity limitation	85.7	54.6	85.7	93.0	74.9	51.7	85.7	93.6	76.5	56.6
Activity limitation	14.3	45.4	14.3	7.0	25.1	48.3	14.3	6.4	23.5	43.4
In major activity[a]	10.8	39.4	10.8	4.1	20.0	43.7	10.7	3.9	18.2	36.4

[a] Major activity refers to ability to work, keep house, or engage in school or preschool activities.

SOURCE. U.S. Bureau of the Census, *Statistical Abstract of the United States, 1978* (Washington, D.C.: U.S. Government Printing Office, 1978), p. 120.

Health and the Quality of Life

It is difficult for those who are young and healthy to understand the subtle ways in which physical deterioration can affect the quality of a person's life as one grows old. For example, America is increasingly – in some regions exclusively – dependent on the automobile for daily work and leisure activities. However, many older people suffer from physiological changes that reduce their ability to use the automobile as freely as others do. Some elderly cannot see clearly at a distance; they find it more difficult to adapt to, and see in, darkness. There are clearly measurable hearing losses among the elderly. Reaction time declines with age, and there is a decline in the ability to coordinate complex sensorimotor activities. These changes in function make the operation of an automobile more difficult. In fact, some studies have shown that people over 70 have one of the highest accident rates of all age groups.[43]

It is easy to imagine the threat that the loss of a driver's license would pose to an older person. The car may be the only means of transportation to his or her job; in all probability it is the major link with social life. Loss of a driver's license threatens the person's ability to work, see friends and family, shop, go to church, attend the movies and sporting events. Imagine for a moment all that you would miss without your car! While some cities have public transportation, it is often not very efficient and in high-crime areas can be a real danger to an elderly person. While we have focused on the impact of declining health only in the area of automobile use, this illustrates the dramatic effect that one's health can have on the quality of one's life.

The Economics of Health

Even without the problems created by fraud and quackery, health care is an extremely costly business – and more so for the old than for the young. Because illness and disability are so much more common among the elderly, they are especially hard hit. They are more likely to suffer a loss of income because of an inability to work. Their heavy utilization of health care services means that rising health care costs are an immediate and constant concern for them. In addition, since they live on fixed incomes, they are especially susceptible to the effects of inflation. As a consequence of these factors, **the elderly pay substantially more per year for medicine than do those under 65.**[44]

In 1965, the Medicare Act became law, its major purpose to provide government assistance for some basic health services for those over 65.[45] Medicare is of two parts — hospital insurance and medical insurance. Under the hospital insurance (Part A), a person is entitled to 90 days of inpatient care. However, the patient must pay for the first $160 of the first 60 days' charge, $40 a day between 60 and 90 days, and $80 a day after that. One is also entitled to 100 days of care in a skilled nursing facility (the patient pays $20 per day after the first 20 days) and 100 home health visits after being released from the hospital or nursing facility. The hospital insurance covers such services as room and board, nursing services, blood transfusions, drugs, and equipment.

The medical insurance (Part B) can be obtained by paying a monthly premium. In January 1979, it was $8.50 per month. (This is 14 percent higher than 1977 — another example of the effect of inflation and increasing health care costs to the elderly.) The medical insurance covers physician's services wherever provided (including drugs and supplies the physician administers), outpatient hospital services, 100 home health visits under certain conditions, outpatient physical and speech therapy, diagnostic services (such as X rays), and some other services.

There is a $60 annual deductible on the medical insurance, and Medicare pays 80 percent of the charges thereafter. There are, however, services for which Medicare will not pay: the first three pints of blood, private-duty nurses, convenience items (such as a telephone or television in the room), custodial care (such as help in bathing, eating, or walking), routine physical checkups, eye examinations and glasses, dental work, hearing examinations and hearing aids, and some other services.

While Medicare certainly reduces the financial burden of sickness for the elderly, it is no panacea. In addition to the services not covered under Medicare, the premiums and deductibles can lead to considerable out-of-pocket costs for the elderly. In addition there are certain flaws in the program. First, Medicare will pay only for care that is "rea-

sonable and necessary." Each participating institution has a Utilization Review Committee that determines, for each particular condition or service, how much and what kinds of treatment are reasonable and necessary. If a person visits the doctor more than is normal for people with similar conditions or stays in the hospital longer than the Committee feels is necessary, Medicare will not pay for the "extras," which become another out-of-pocket cost for that person.

Second, Medicare will pay only "reasonable charges" for various services. These charges are determined by what is customarily charged for each service in a particular area. If a doctor charges more for a particular service, then the patient must pay the difference. Often the patient does not know whether the doctor's charges are reasonable until after treatment has been rendered and Medicare has refused to pay for some of them. At this point it is too late to refuse service or change doctors — the bill must be paid by the patient. So the elderly still pay substantially for health care. They pay a much larger proportion of their income for health services than do younger people.

Deviance and Aging

An unpleasant reality concerning the elderly is the high rates of various kinds of deviance — mental illness, substance abuse, crime, and suicide — among older citizens. Although there are many reasons for this, an important contributing factor is the poverty, loneliness, depression, and fear that plagues significant numbers of elderly. We will discuss four types of deviance in relation to the elderly.

Mental Illness

Rates of mental illness increase with age.[46] This is especially true for *psychoses* — ailments involving severe personality disorders with loss of contact with reality, sometimes characterized by delusions and hallucinations. One reason for this can be found in the physiology of aging. *Organic psychoses* are often the result of the degeneration of the central nervous system, hardening of the arteries, and other physiological changes that accompany aging and that can cause disturbances in thought, perception, and feeling. However, *functional psychoses* — conditions that have no demonstrable organic cause — are also more common among the elderly.

A second reason for the high rates of mental illness among the elderly relates to their living conditions. If one is cut off from the social supports of family, friends, and community involvement, this social isolation can contribute to mental illness. For example, among both males and females, those elderly who are still married have the lowest rates of mental disorders, while divorced and separated persons have the highest rates.

Substance Abuse

It has been estimated that there are a million alcoholics over the age of 55 in the United States. Alcoholism among the elderly is associated with the effects of social isolation — difficulty in relating to other persons and feelings of loneliness and lack of self-worth.[47] In addition, the problems of the elderly alcoholic often go unrecognized; as two social workers put it: "The elderly alcoholic is a social pariah. Unknown to the various groups and agencies designed to help the alcoholic, he is slowly drinking himself to death in the solitude of his own home."[48]

There is some evidence that the use of addictive drugs such as heroin is more common than usually thought among the elderly. Most people associate drug abuse with the young; professionals in the field of substance abuse have generally felt that addicts die long before they reach 60. However, a program in New York to substitute methadone for heroin found that 15 to 20 percent of the early applicants to the program were over 60 years of age.[49] Apparently, many of these people began using opiates in the 1920s and 1930s, before the Harrison Act of 1914 was rigorously enforced. It was not until 1951 that stiff federal penalties were placed on the possession of heroin. The lifestyle of elderly drug users is different from that of younger addicts — it is more self-protective and less conspicuous, so that they are less likely to come to the attention of the authorities of drug control programs.

Since it now appears that addicts do not always die before reaching old age, the tremendous increase in drug use among the young in the past two decades may presage an increasing drug problem among the elderly in the future.

Crime

The overall crime rate is lower among the elderly than among any other age group. The more aggressive crimes (murder, rape, assault, armed robbery) are committed by younger offenders, while the more sophisticated crimes (embezzlement, fraud), and crimes suggesting personal disorganization (drunkenness, disorderly conduct, vagrancy) tend to be characteristic of older offenders. For example, in 1977, over 44 percent of the arrests among the elderly were for drunkenness or some other conduct disorder, while only 16 percent of all arrests in the 15–24 age group were for such offenses. **The types of offenses for which the elderly are arrested seem to be a reflection of their overall living conditions and social status in society; these offenses tend to involve dissipation and social withdrawal.**[50]

Suicide

The final solution to a lonely and dissatisfying life is, of course, to engineer one's own demise. While suicide is an option at any age, the elderly make greater use of it than does any other age group.[51] However, this is more common for males than for females; suicide rates for males continue to increase with age while the female rate actually declines somewhat after age 60. This is a form of *egoistic suicide* which results when important social relationships, such as marriage or strong religious ties, do not exist to serve as social constraints that deter people from killing themselves. People with such important social bonds would be reluctant to commit suicide because self-destruction would sever the valued social ties. As we have seen, such social ties tend to decline among some of the elderly. When such ties do exist, suicide rates are lower. For example, married older people have the lowest suicide rates, divorced older people have the highest suicide rates, and the widowed and single fall in between. There are certainly many reasons for suicide among the elderly, one of the most important of which is undoubtedly relief from physical pain and discomfort. However, strong social relationships reduce the likelihood that one will respond to such factors through suicide.[52] If one's spouse is still alive, or close ties are maintained with friends and family, the physical discomfort is more easily endured. In addition, there is often the feeling of obligation to continue to provide emotional and possibly financial support to those close to you.

Institutionalization and the Aged

Much of the concern about the plight of the aged in our society focuses on those in some sort of institution—nursing homes, mental hospitals, extended care facilities, and the like. Most studies indicate that, at any given time, only about 4 or 5 percent of those over 65 live in such institutions.[53] However, a study in the Detroit metropolitan area showed that 20 percent of the deaths among those over 65 occurred in nursing homes, and another 4 percent occurred in other extended care facilities.[54] This means that close to one-quarter of the elderly reside in such institutions at some time in their lives. (The figure is conservative since some of the elderly who died in hospitals had undoubtedly been transferred there from nursing homes after becoming ill or injured.) If the experience in Detroit is common to the rest of the country, then institutionalization is a fate that will eventually befall a good number of elderly.

Who are the elderly that eventually end up in an institution? There are more women in these institutions than men. The institutionalized have fewer social ties than those who have remained in the community—they are less likely to have a living spouse or children and more likely to have lived alone prior to coming to the institution. Those who are institutionalized also have fewer financial resources and are more likely to be receiving some sort of public assistance.

We tend to assume that a person is institutionalized because of sickness. This is true in some cases, especially with mental patients. But people are often sent to nursing or old age homes not because they are especially ill but because they have lost the social and financial supports that had made it possible for them to live, even though infirm, outside an institution.[55] For example, many have lost their housing; in some cases persons who had taken care of them are no longer around (as when a spouse dies); for others, declining financial support meant that institutionalization was the only economically feasible alternative; or finally, the strain of caring for a person with declining capacities might create tension that could be relieved only by the person's being institutionalized. **It is when supports outside the institution become inadequate that the person is forced into some institutional arrangement.**

According to the interactionist perspective, the manner in which others treat a person is an important determinant of one's view of oneself. Once a person assumes a social role, people behave toward him or her on the basis of the expectations associated with that role. What sort of expectations do we have for elderly persons who are residents of a nursing home or an extended care facility? The patients (or "inmates" or "residents," to use the old and new euphemisms, respectively) typically play a passive role while the staff operates the organization and makes important decisions, including those relating to the most elementary activities, such as eating or brushing one's teeth. These institutions are authoritarian, often organized more for the convenience and efficiency of the staff rather than the needs of the patient. They are regimented, impersonal, and occasionally lack the most basic amenities of life.

The reality of the patients' lack of control over what is happening to them and what is going on around them can be brought home by considering some possibilities. Are the residents free to go out and have a beer? Can they order a hamburger from McDonalds? The answer to each of these questions, of course, is no. (You may recall the movie *One Flew Over the Cuckoo's Nest,* which illustrates some of these problems.) Patients' positions in the organization and the reactions of others to that position tell them that they are dependent, that they lack control over even the most rudimentary aspects of their personal life, that they are no longer autonomous and self-sufficient individuals. When others treat the institutionalized person in this way, the elderly residents may, and often do, begin to view themselves as dependent, helpless, and powerless. This situation has all the elements of the *self-fulfilling prophecy*—the patient becomes what others expect him to be. Given the high value that Americans place on mastery and control, these are certainly devastating feelings to have about oneself.

Depersonalization is the feeling of detachment from people or social groups that give life meaning and provide a sense of importance and self-worth. According to sociologist Rodney Coe, the more all-encompassing an institution is, the more depersonalization occurs.[56] Of the institutions he studied, nursing homes led to the most depersonalization—the residents tended not to think of themselves in terms of their role relationships with others, such as their occupational position or family status; they described themselves in such terms as "human being" or "person," which did not distinguish them from other people. The most common way that the nursing home patients responded to the institution was withdrawal—not responding to much of what was going on around them. Many gave up the possibility of reestablishing family, occupational, or other social roles. One of the patients in Coe's study put it this way: "I wish I was home to see my people more often, but my daughter don't want me. She never comes to see me here; she has forgot me."[57] In a few cases the patient may drift into a delusional world that represents an almost total break with reality. For example, they may carry on conversations with deceased friends or relatives as if those people were present in the room to respond to them.

Can this tendency toward depersonalization and withdrawal be reversed? In some cases, these changes are undoubtedly the result of physical degeneration, such as arteriosclerosis. However, in other cases it is the institution and the behavior of the staff that encourage the changes. Skilled nursing care in such institutions can *personalize* the care and reverse this trend.[58] Verbal and nonverbal stimulation of patients by the staff can reorient the patient toward the world and group life. Programs designed to provide personal care have brought about significant changes in patients. They become more interested in their surroundings, they show more interest in relating to others, and they begin (if permitted) to take more control over available resources. Programs to allow greater participation by nursing home residents in making the decisions that affect them should alleviate the feelings of powerlessness. While not all nursing homes and extended care facilities are as bleak as those described here, there are enough homes that fit the description to generate concern.

THE FUTURE OF THE AGED IN AMERICA

Providing for the Elderly

America's population is aging. In 1970 approximately 1 out of every 10 Americans was over 65; by the year 2030, if the current trend continues, there will be more than 50 million elderly—1 out of every 6 Americans. One of the most critical problems we face is how to provide the financial support of so many old people at a level they find acceptable. The following are the primary sources of financial support for the elderly.

Private Pensions

One common means for supporting the elderly is through private pension funds. However, a majority of older workers now nearing retirement are not covered by private pension benefits—only a small fraction of retired persons currently collect these. For example, only a quarter of the elderly who receive Social Security also draw funds from a private pension plan.[59] In addition, many private pension plans have folded because the employer has gone out of business without making provision for continued retirement coverage for former employees, and many plans still in effect are in serious financial straits. The major problem is their soaring cost.[60] For example, according to one report:

At General Motors Corporation . . . the bill for pensions has doubled in the last decade and will double again over the next ten to fifteen years. In 1967, General Motors had ten workers on its domestic payroll for each retiree drawing a pension. Today, the ratio of General Motors workers to pensioners—what demographers call the dependency ratio—is just 4 to 1. By the early 1990s, it may be close to 1 to 1.[61]

In other words, if this projection comes true, there will be one worker paying into the pension plan for each retiree drawing a pension from it!

In 1974, Congress passed the Employee Retirement Income Security Act to deal with problems common to private pension programs. This law seeks to protect people from losing their pension rights by placing federal control over the vesting and financing of private pension funds. However, the existing law does not require employers to provide private pensions; it does not guarantee that the employee can transfer his pension from one employer to another; and the machinery for dealing with violations of the act has not been fully tested as yet.[62] So while private pension plans may be one means of providing income for the elderly, they contribute very little today, and we may not be able to rely on them as a primary source of retirement income in the future.

Social Security

The technical name for Social Security is Old-Age, Survivors, Disability, and Health Insurance Program (OASDHI)—the single most important public income-maintenance and health care assistance program in the United States. It is designed to provide services not only for retired persons but also for disabled workers and their families, and for the survivors of deceased workers as well. Enacted by Congress in 1935, Social Security is a compulsory federal insurance program (all qualified workers and their employers must contribute to the fund) in which the employee and the employer each pay an equal share of the contribution. (Self-employed persons pay the entire contribution themselves at a slightly lower rate than the combined contribution of employee and employer.) At retirement, recipients of Social Security receive a monthly check based mainly on their total contribution to the program during their working years. However, need is taken into consideration, so that there is a minimum payment ($107.90 in 1976) for the participant regardless of the size of the participant's total contribution to the Social Security Program.

Has Social Security solved the problem of providing financial security for the aged? Has it guaranteed economic security and quality health care for our elderly citizens? The answer is clearly no. Over 80 percent of the older people in the United States collect OASDHI; for about *half* of them, it is their only source of income (see Table 10.2).

There are inequities in the Social Security Program that lead to special benefits for the wealthy. For example, income from savings, investments, pensions, insurance, or royalties does not affect the amount of one's monthly check from OASDHI. However, in 1979, if one's annual income from wages and salaries exceeded $3480 for a person between 62 and 65 years of age or $4500 for a person over 65, OASDHI withheld $1 in benefits for each $2 in earnings above that figure. What this means, of course, is that the elderly who choose to, or must, work throughout most of the year for a wage or salary to supplement their retirement incomes suffer a reduction in Social Security benefits, while the affluent with investment income in addition to OASDHI receive full benefits regardless of the amount of their additional income.

TABLE 10.2
Sources of Income for the Elderly, 1968

SOURCE	Percentage of total income
Social security payments	34
Wages and salaries	29
Income from assets	15
Private pension benefits	5
Public assistance	4
Other sources	14

SOURCE. Lenore E. Bixby, "Income of People Aged 65 and Older: Overview from 1968 Survey of the Aged," *Social Security Bulletin* 33 (April 1970), pp. 10–11.

TABLE 10.3
Number of Contributors and Beneficiaries to the Social Security System, 1940–1978

	RETIRED BENEFICIARIES[a]	SURVIVOR BENEFICIARIES	DISABILITY BENEFICIARIES[a]	CONTRIBUTORS	NUMBER OF CONTRIBU- TORS FOR EACH BENEFICIARY
1940	148,000	74,000	—	35,390,000	159.4
1945	691,000	597,000	—	46,390,000	36.0
1950	2,326,000	1,152,000	—	48,280,000	13.9
1955	5,788,000	2,172,000	—	65,200,000	8.2
1960	10,599,000	3,558,000	687,000	72,530,000	4.9
1965	14,175,000	4,953,000	1,739,000	80,680,000	3.9
1970	17,096,000	6,468,000	2,665,000	93,090,000	3.5
1975	20,364,000	7,368,000	4,352,000	100,400,000	3.1
1978	21,869,000	7,533,000	4,864,000	110,000,000	3.2

[a] Includes dependents

SOURCE. "Current Operating Statistics," *Social Security Bulletin* 41 (December 1978) p. 33, and "Quarterly Statistics," *Social Security Bulletin,* 41 (December 1978), p. 74.

Social Security is in serious financial straits. In 1977, the Social Security system took $965 a year from a person earning $16,500 or more. By 1981, people will pay social security contributions on all wages up to $29,700. Unless this amount continues to increase at a pace proportionate to that of the increasing costs of maintaining OASDHI, there will be a growing deficit in the Social Security fund. As with many private pension plans, the number of people receiving social security benefits is growing at a faster rate than the number of people contributing to it (see Table 10.3). In 1976, OASDHI paid out $3.2 billion more than it took in.[33] However, there may be limits to what people are willing to pay into Social Security. As economist Conrad Jamison told the editors of *Newsweek:* "There is a danger . . . that in the future workers will just say, 'We've had it. We will no longer support all these old people, these leeches.' "[64]

In summary, although Social Security has prevented many of our elderly citizens from falling into the worst depths of poverty, it has fallen short of being a total solution to the problem of providing economic security and quality health care for the aged. Unless there are rather dramatic changes in the future, Social Security will continue to be only one means of caring for the elderly in American society. The economic problems facing private pension plans and Social Security must be dealt with if the elderly are to have a financially secure future.

Communities for the Elderly

Traditionally, most of the elderly lived within their own household or that of a close relative—whether they were healthy or ill, and irrespective of how old they were. There were few alternative institutional arrangements for the elderly. While this is still the case in most nonindustrialized societies, the United States, with its elaborate division of labor, has developed specialized institutions to handle problems such as the care of the elderly. In this section we will discuss some of the current and emerging institutional arrangements for the elderly, their purposes, and their consequences.

Retirement Communities

The planned retirement community is a new development for those elderly who can afford to rent or buy a dwelling there and do not need the medical care of a nursing home. In the past two decades, such communities have been developed in a num-

"TOMORROW MORNING... 10 A.M... WE'RE MAKING A BREAK...PASS IT ON..."

ber of locations — Sun City in Arizona, Rossmor Leisure World in California, and others. These are usually new and totally planned by private development corporations; they are very appealing to those elderly who can afford to live in them. One can associate with others of the same age and stage of development; and children, which some elderly find to be a source of noise and irritation, are normally not permitted as residents. These planned communities also provide easily accessible shopping and other services and are designed to reduce the fear of crime.

However, there is much controversy over whether planned retirement communities are a desirable development in American society. Some feel that the developers have been exploitative — playing on the often unrealistic fears of crime and the racial and ethnic prejudices of the elderly in order to sell them a very expensive product. In 1973 it cost a minimum of $6000 a year for a single per-

son and $8000 a year for a married couple to live in a retirement community. Since this cost only covers housing and not the other necessities of life, it is far beyond the financial capabilities of most of the elderly; such a retirement community is within the financial means of only the affluent.

Some fear that these communities will create too much segregation between the elderly and other age groups in society — they may become enclaves of the elderly. Sociologist Arnold Rose has argued strongly that the aged can easily become an isolated subculture within American society.[65] As communication and social contact with other groups decline, stereotypes begin to develop on both sides, which can lead to prejudice and discrimination. In other words, in creating geographical and social isolation between the elderly and others — even though it is a voluntary isolation — we may be sowing the seeds of intergroup hostility and discrimination.

Communes

"Communes" usually arouse an image of young people with long hair and beards working in the fields—yet there are some communal arrangements among the elderly. These living arrangements usually arise out of practical or fortuitous circumstances rather than as the culmination of some ideological development. They are often the most realistic solution to the economic and physical limitations suffered by the aged. For example, one such commune in Winter Park, Florida—the Share Home Association—consists of twelve elderly people between the ages of 71 and 94. They live together in a large home and share both the expenses of running the household and the work that needs to be done. In another similar situation, the group has elected a manager—who happens to be younger—to organize the work roles, take care of the finances, and generally oversee the operation of the home. However, he serves at the pleasure of the residents and can be removed from the office at their will.[66]

Whether "senior communes" will be a common sight on the American landscape is difficult to say. There are several problems with such arrangements. Many elderly are simply unable to adjust to the very different lifestyle of communal living. A commune made up solely of the elderly may find it difficult to mount the physical strength or technical expertise necessary to develop the elaborate arrangements for coping with minor and major illnesses and disabilities. The anxieties associated with aging, especially death, may create tensions that are disruptive to the community effort. Yet, communes offer sensible and simple solutions to the financial crunch confronting some elderly. They can also provide continual social bonds that help overcome the emotional trauma, loneliness, and anxiety of losing one's spouse and close friends. Thus, while such arrangements may not become terribly common, they are certainly workable alternatives for some elderly.

Homes for the Aged

The term *homes for the aged* refers to non-profit, voluntary institutions run by religious groups, fraternal or benevolent organizations (such as labor unions), and trust organizations for the benefit of their members. Generally, these homes take only people who are reasonably healthy. Some medical and social services are offered, but a person who becomes seriously ill usually must move to a commercial nursing home. Because of problems in funding, the care and programs at these homes are quite variable—one cannot be assured of high-quality care in all homes for the aged. Some homes, such as those funded by some labor unions, have the resources and financial backing to provide excellent programs. Others must charge high prices and still find it difficult to provide such quality. There is growing pressure to divert more tax money into these homes; should this happen, they might well become an important source of care for the elderly in American society. Such institutions are undoubtedly a permanent fixture in our society and, as their quality improves, the elderly may be less hesitant to enter them and in many cases may look forward to them as an enjoyable environment in which to spend their final years.[67]

Nursing Homes

Most of the institutionalized elderly live in commercial nursing homes, or *proprietary homes* as the nursing home industry prefers to call them—institutions intended to make a profit for the owner. Some of these homes are very well organized and provide excellent care for their residents. However, the majority of the homes fall short of providing the service and comfort that many feel the elderly deserve. Robert N. Butler, recently the director of the National Institute on Aging, sums up his two decades of visiting commercial nursing homes in this way: "I have concluded that a nursing home is a facility that has few or no nurses and can hardly qualify as a home."[68] Over the years he has been visiting nursing homes, Butler has found patients lying in their own urine or feces, food that was so unappetizing that the residents refused to eat it, and boredom and apathy evident on the faces of patients as well as staff members. He also found poorly illuminated corridors and stairwells creating hazards that would be

The poor among the elderly are those most likely to spend their final years in nursing homes that provide little in terms of emotional fulfillment or personal satisfaction.

and degrading settings. Why do these conditions exist? Are the employees of such institutions insensitive and cruel people who are not disturbed by human suffering and degradation? Individuals are shaped in part by the social institutions of which they are a part. The social roles and expectations, along with the reward structure within any institution, encourage some types of behavior and discourage others. There is always a potential conflict between the profit motive of commercial nursing homes and the desire to provide adequate services for the residents. With only limited resources available, managers of nursing homes realize that providing new medical and recreational programs or hiring more highly qualified staff must have one of two consequences—a reduced profit margin for the owners or an increased monthly cost to the elderly. In too many cases, the owners place more value on a large profit margin than they do on the provision of more adequate services to the residents.

Securing and retaining qualified staff is one of the most difficult and costly problems confronting nursing homes.[70] There is a tendency to hire people with little or no training for low salaries. Many are people of lower socioeconomic status or high school students who could find no other job. They do not have the concern, involvement, professionalism, or expertise that might generate innovative programs and practices even in the absence of increased funds.

Because of the salary and working conditions, the turnover rate among skilled nursing personnel in nursing homes is extremely high. In 1973, the turnover rate for registered nurses was 73 percent! This continual influx of new staff means that the leadership necessary for continuity of programs and services is absent. High rates of absenteeism are another problem. Daily operation of the nursing home becomes difficult because supervisors cannot plan on adequate staffing for any given day. Programs and services must be dropped or performed quickly and inadequately in order to compensate for high daily absentee levels. This supervisory problem also contributes to the difficulty of retaining good supervisors—skilled registered nurses are likely to take other positions without these staffing problems.

disastrous in an emergency. Basic physical assistance and the fundamental human courtesies and amenities were often lacking. Medical care was often poor, and dental care scarce. Doctors sometimes make "gang visits," seeing large numbers of patients during a brief visit. For each patient seen or injection given, a bill can be submitted to Medicare. One doctor received $42,000 one year for giving 8275 injections to 149 patients![69]

Certainly, not all nursing homes are like this. The more affluent elderly have the resources necessary to live in good nursing homes. It is the less affluent who are more likely to end up in such disgusting

As such problems have become more apparent, the government has attempted to develop programs and regulatory mechanisms to eliminate the most serious abuses. For example, there are programs to train nursing home inspectors and more professional and paraprofessional nursing home personnel, as well as to place *ombudsmen* in nursing homes so that patients will have an interested party working for them. Yet, abuses continue.

What else can we do? Should we eliminate nursing homes? The answer may be both yes and no. The same functions can be performed, but in a considerably different manner than at present. The ideal nursing home should be truly like a "home" for the patient—pleasant, enjoyable surroundings in which lively involvement with others can be interspersed with quiet and solitude for those who desire it. The administrative and medical staff should be adequately trained in the care and problems of the aged. A whole range of medical and social services should be available to the residents. Rather than being devoted solely to inpatient care, the facility should perhaps be a number of multi-purpose centers that can handle the needs of inpatients and also of those elderly in the community who do not require institutionalization. For example, some facilities have developed day-care centers where the elderly who still live at home can come during the day for meals, medical and social services, and recreational activities. This is considerably cheaper than total institutionalization. Other centers have developed home care programs in which medical, social, and nutritional services are provided for the elderly who are house-bound.

These outreach programs avoid the high cost of institutionalization and the detrimental effects on personal identity that this can create. Such elderly are still independent, living at home, and able to exercise considerable control over their daily activities. Finally, it is clear that while federal financial support for such programs must continue, the duplication, inefficiency, and inconsistency that plague current programs must be eliminated. Going a step further, the federal government might create demonstration centers that would serve as a guide and showcase for commercial ventures.

The Institutionalization of Death

As our population becomes older and as the American family structure changes, the conditions attendant on death are seen by many as a social problem. Most people die in hospitals or nursing homes surrounded by strangers. Those who care for the sick are sometimes not psychologically prepared to cope with a dying patient because doctors and nurses are oriented toward saving and curing. Death is often viewed by members of the medical profession as a failure of their efforts. While a person can die at any age, the concern over how one will die is more immediate among the elderly because they know they will soon be experiencing it.[71]

Our modern technological capabilities have led to a profound clash in values. On the one hand, we value life and hope that our sophisticated medical technology can postpone our confrontation with the "grim reaper" indefinitely. On the other hand, there is an emerging concern with the consequences of this effort—in some cases, a prolonged life means only extended suffering and financial crisis, while in other cases vegetative bodies are maintained indefinitely with little hope of ever being conscious of their surroundings or socially involved with other people. The grim possibility of large warehouses of the elderly hooked up to machines that maintain their bodily functions, but who are either unconscious or unable to lead a meaningful life, is a frightening prospect—yet possible with today's technology. Of course, it is not easy to provide a satisfactory definition of a "meaningful life." However, for most people it would probably include a sense of accomplishment, involvement with others, and feelings of importance and self-worth. Many fear that technology will be used to prolong their life far beyond the point at which these things can be achieved. A major problem, then, is the degree of control that people have over the point at which medical efforts will be abandoned and they will be allowed to die.

Euthanasia and Living Wills

The term *euthanasia* refers to "a painless, peaceful death."[72] As it is used today, it means a death with dignity, a death with comfort, a death at the time a person chooses and is prepared to die. *Passive euthanasia refers to withholding medical treatment that might prolong life.* *Active euthanasia, or mercy killing, involves some overt act that brings about the person's death.* Legally, any person has the right to refuse medical treatment. However, the patient may be comatose, delirious, or in some other mental state that in the doctor's view renders him or her unfit to make decisions about the treatment. Still, the doctor does not have the legal right to make this decision for the patient. Who, then, shall decide when life-prolonging efforts should be halted? Some have proposed a "living will," which a person signs when of sound mind and body. This will specifies the conditions under which the person would prefer medical treatment to be discontinued (for example, one might specify seriously impaired movement, speech, or vision as such conditions). In most states, the living will has no legal standing. However, as of 1978, eight states had laws allowing living wills, and the legislatures of twenty-seven other states were considering such proposals. The living will is one attempt to grapple with this very difficult and emotion-laden problem.[73]

What if there is no living will? Who makes the decision about continued treatment for the patient? The courts might appoint a legal guardian to make such a decision. However, some have suggested that close relatives are too personally and emotionally involved with the dying person to make a decision that is truly in the best interests of the patient — for example, concern about doing all one can for the patient may lead to the prolongation of a helpless situation. Some have proposed the establishment of a committee of impartial experts to make these decisions. For example, in 1976 Massachusetts General Hospital established a committee of doctors, nurses, psychiatrists, lawyers and patients to determine the patient's probability of survival and whether therapy should be continued.[74]

Such programs are still experimental and will undoubtedly be modified as experience with them is gained. However, there are dangers in such arrangements. These presumably impartial experts can be unknowingly influenced in their decisions in ways that are not beneficial to the patient. For example, one investigator has shown that medical personnel more quickly consider a person beyond help if he is old, poor, or of low or stigmatized social status.[75] There is a real danger that such a committee might unknowingly be influenced by such factors. In any event, we are confronting the clash between the ability of our technology to keep people alive and the desire of people to die a dignified death when they are prepared to die.

Hospices

One means of providing a dignified death is the *hospice:* a home for the care of the dying.[76] Hospices have their origin among the European religious orders of the Middle Ages who welcomed travelers who were hungry, tired, or sick. The most famous today is St. Christopher's Hospice near London. **The goal of the hospice is to give loving and emotionally supportive care to the dying, while at the same time utilizing modern medical science to eliminate physical pain.** By being freed of pain and the fear that their last hours will be agonizing, the patient is able to live out his or her final days in relative comfort and peace of mind. Increasing doses of pain relievers are used to keep the patient one step ahead of pain.

Hospices sometimes have educational and entertainment programs; the children of the staff often come to work with their parents; and visitors are common. The mood of the hospice is surprisingly pleasant and cheerful. St. Christopher's also has a home care program in which patients are able to take their pain relievers home and often spend their final hours with their family. In England, hospice care is less expensive than hospital care. Furthermore, two-thirds of the hospice patients die at home, compared with only 2 percent of terminally ill patients in the United States. In 1975 the National Cancer Institute's Divison of Cancer Control and Rehabilitation began a program to set up experimental hospices in the United States for the care of terminally ill cancer patients.[77] The hospice, then, is one response to the problem of dying with dignity in an emotionally comforting surrounding.

Americans place great value on human dignity. Because of this, the plight of the elderly cannot be ignored, and most people feel that the conditions many elderly live in must be improved. But at what cost? Some of the alternatives, such as multipurpose centers for the elderly, will involve substantial increases in the proportion of our national wealth that will be spent in providing for the elderly. If financial resources are to be redirected in this fashion, other groups, mainly younger persons during their working years, are going to have to pay for these programs through higher taxes. While most Americans are reluctant to pay more taxes for any reason, the problems of the elderly cannot be simply ignored, owing to the political activism of groups representing the elderly.

Political Action, Interest Groups, and the Elderly

In New York's borough of the Bronx, a group of elderly residents, concerned that youthful criminals who prey on the aged are being given lenient treatment by the courts, have organized a "case watch": they are monitoring juvenile cases in the courts in the hopes of encouraging judges to treat such offenders more strictly.[78] **Older people are thus showing signs of political activism, and in some cases even radical militancy; these elderly rebel against traditional concepts of the elderly and policies for dealing with their problems.** Some of the elderly, especially the more affluent, have the financial and organizational resources to pursue their own interests in competition with other interest groups. These actions have proceeded along two lines. Some groups have been concerned with providing social programs, hobby activities, and the like to enrich the lives of the elderly, while other groups have focused on political action to encourage government programs favorable to the elderly and to ensure that government funds are channeled in that direction.

Two popular organizations are the American Association of Retired Persons (AARP) and its affiliated group, the National Retired Teachers Association.

The elderly constitute an interest group that has begun to organize to pursue policies beneficial to them. Older people are increasingly reluctant to allow conditions detrimental to their well-being to continue.

The AARP, membership in which is open to anyone over the age of 55, has over 5 million members in the United States and is one of the largest alliances of older people in America. This group offers a substantial number of programs and services to the elderly, such as courses in income tax preparation and programs to develop an impressive variation of skills (e.g. typing, sewing, stamp collecting, public speaking). AART/NRTA also serves as a lobbying group that presses the interests of the aged at the federal, state, and local levels of government.

Another sizable and influential group is the National Council of Senior Citizens (NCSC), which was first organized through the joint effort of labor leaders and the White House. It is open to people of all ages, charges no mandatory membership dues, and is a nonprofit organization. Much of the funding of the NCSC comes from labor unions, although its growth in membership (now over 3 million) has enabled it to reduce its dependence on this source of revenue. The NCSC offers a variety of services to its members, such as health insurance to supplement medicare, low-cost travel arrangements, a discount on drugs, and so on. Unlike the AARP/NRTA, the NCSC has attracted many of the nonaffluent elderly. The NCSC has also served as a lobbying group, but there is some conflict of interest in the organization because programs beneficial to the elderly may be detrimental to younger workers, and the NCSC obtains substantial backing from labor unions representing those workers. For example, NCSC has been reluctant to support increases in Social Security which, while beneficial to the elderly, would lead to increased payroll deductions for workers. The NCSC has also organized mass demonstrations in state capitals and in Washington to protest cuts in state and federal programs for the elderly.

While these organizations have been effective in many areas, they have limitations that may hinder their pursuit of the interests of the elderly. The NCSC is associated with labor unions and to some degree with Democratic party politics, which means that the cause of the elderly may be compromised for other goals. The AARP/NRTA is informally linked to the Republican party and thus may have similar problems. It is also subsidized by Colonial Penn Groups, a successful insurance company that has access to its membership lists and that may influence AARP/NRTA decisions.[79] Both organizations have tax-exempt status, which limits their ability to pursue aggressively the cause of the elderly in the political arena. Finally, women and minority groups are substantially underrepresented in both organizations; yet these are the groups among the elderly who are most severely affected by the problems we have been discussing.

A radical group that has caught the public eye is the "Gray Panthers," whose official name is Consultation of Older and Younger Adults.[80] Open to people of all ages, the Gray Panthers are definitely not a service organization but rather a social activist group that takes a distinctly radical and militant perspective on the problems of the aged. Members feel that the lobbying and political efforts of the other groups are piecemeal and do not attack the real issues at hand. They also argue that the problems of the aged stem from structural defects in American society. **The most fundamental flaw in our society, according to the Gray Panthers, is our emphasis on materialism and the consumption of goods and services rather than on improving the quality of life for all our citizens—including the elderly.** Old people, who are no longer permitted to be fully productive because of prejudice, discrimination, the obsolescence of their skills, or forced retirement, are seen as worthless and are abandoned— like worn-out automobiles.

The Gray Panthers hope to change our orientation toward people and to advance the goals of human dignity, human freedom, and self-development. They want to "liberate" people from what they perceive as an outmoded way of thinking and to encourage self-determination so that one can use one's time, experience, skills, and resources to pursue one's own goals and enhance those of the community and society. The tactics of the Gray Panthers are quite different from the more staid groups. As Margaret (Maggie) Kuhn, the 67-year-old founder of the group, put it, "We are not mellow, sweet old people. We have got to effect change and we have nothing to lose."[81]

While these groups representing the elderly differ in terms of their sponsorship and methods, they share the common goal of using political means to improve the conditions of the elderly. Whether others agree or not, the elderly will continue to struggle against those who would treat them as second-class citizens.

CONCLUSION

The position of the elderly in the United States has changed dramatically over the past several decades. In preindustrial America, older people generally held a great deal of power and prestige in the community. Today, the elderly are less powerful and are held in less esteem than in the past. In order to understand the current status and future prospects of the aged in our society, it is useful to employ the three sociological perspectives.

From the functionalist perspective, the power and prestige of any group flows from their functional importance in their society. With industrialization, the role of the elderly began to shift. No longer did they have the skills and knowledge that young people found useful and necessary to take their place in society. Because their roles were no longer essential for society's functioning, the elderly became "excess baggage" and younger people did not feel the compulsion to hold them in high regard. In addition, the functionalists point out that the position of the elderly in the United States is partially the result of cultural lag. Our society has industrialized and urbanized so quickly — with the resulting changes in employment patterns and family relations — that the elderly are only now beginning to find roles in today's society that are useful to the social system and rewarding to themselves.

From the conflict perspective, society is an arena in which various groups compete with one another over scarce resources. The elderly are not exempt from that competition. Conflict theorists state that the prestige of the elderly in preindustrial America was a direct result of their power in society. Industrialization resulted in a loss of power by the aged which led in a direct way to a subsequent loss of prestige in the community. In preindustrial society, the elderly owned the farms and businesses upon which the young depended for their means of subsistence. As a consequence, the elderly held sway over younger people. Conflict theorists emphasize that as the elderly in today's society become better organized and more militant in their demands for scarce resources, they will become more powerful and receive more respect from young people. The elderly will simply not permit themselves to be abandoned. They have learned — from the black power, brown power, and other movements — the efficacy of political organization. Militant groups are emerging to pursue the interests of the elderly. "Gray Power" may become a common refrain.

What can we expect in the future? Undoubtedly, the elderly will continue to emerge as an important and powerful interest group in the United States. The groundswell of outrage against past indignities has already developed, and it is likely that such abuses will not be permitted to continue for long in the future.

From the interactionist perspective, the way people view the elderly is the key to their future status in America. The elderly are often viewed as useless and over-the-hill. As the elderly become more active in community affairs and otherwise fight the negative stereotypes people hold of them, public definitions of the elderly will change in a more positive direction and the public esteem and power will be regained.

GLOSSARY TERMS

Active euthanasia
Agism
Conformity
Depersonalization
Egoistic suicide
Euthanasia
Functional psychoses

Innovation
Homes for the aged
Hospices
Kibbutzim
Organic psychoses
Passive euthanasia

Proprietary homes
Psychoses
Rebellion
Retreatism
Social disengagement
Voluntary associations

SUGGESTED READINGS

Robert C. Atchley, *The Social Forces in Later Life: An Introduction to Social Gerontology,* 2d ed. (Belmont, Calif.: Wadsworth Publishing Company, 1977).

A brief but comprehensive introduction to the subject of human aging. Particular emphasis is placed on the social and social-psychological aspects of the aging process.

Robert N. Butler, *Why Survive? Being Old in America* (New York: Harper & Row, 1975).

A readable and realistic account of what it means to be old in America today by a person who has been involved in attempts to improve social policy toward the elderly.

Jaber F. Gubrium, *Living and Dying at Murray Manor* (New York: St. Martin's Press, 1975).

A very personal account of daily life in a nursing home. This book presents the complexities of social life in a nursing home—the joys and accomplishments as well as the boredom and despair.

Anita S. Harbert and Leon H. Ginsberg, *Human Services for Older Adults: Concepts and Skills* (Belmont, Calif.: Wadsworth Publishing Company, 1979).

A practice-oriented combination text and anthology designed to provide educators and human-service workers with a reference source dealing with the fundamental principles of working with older adults. Problems of older people are addressed from a "how-to" perspective.

Jon Hendricks and C. Davis Hendricks, *Aging in Mass Society: Myths and Realities* (Cambridge, Mass.: Winthrop Publishers, 1977).

A comprehensive survey of the field of gerontology and the status and current problems of the elderly in America.

Cary S. Kart and Barbara B. Manard, eds., *Aging in America: Readings in Social Gerontology* (Port Washington, N.Y.: Alfred Publishing Co., 1976).

An anthology that provides an issue- or problem-oriented introduction to social gerontology. Included in the issues covered in the book are various theoretical approaches to aging, methodological issues in social gerontology, biological and psychological aspects of aging, and death and dying.

Elisabeth Kubler-Ross, *On Death and Dying* (New York: Macmillan, 1969).

A now-classic work that argues for a new and more positive attitude toward death and the process of dying. This book is essential reading for anyone interested in the areas of aging or death.

George E. Rejda, *Social Insurance and Economic Security* (Englewood Cliffs, N.J.: Prentice-Hall, 1976).

A comprehensive and sophisticated yet readable analysis of the financial problems of older Americans. The book focuses on the sources of these economic problems, their impact on the elderly, and the relative merits of alternative solutions.

REFERENCES

[1] Cary S. Kart and Barbara B. Manard, eds., *Aging in America: Readings in Social Gerontology* (Port Washington, N.Y.: Alfred Publishing Co., 1976).

[2] Nathaniel Sheppard, Jr., "Residents of City Adult Care Homes Tell of Abuses," *New York Times* (March 20, 1976), p. 17.

[3] Institute of Gerontology, *Information on Aging* (Wayne State University/University of Michigan, no. 10, October 1, 1976).

[4] Sula Benet, *How to Live to Be 100: The Life Style of the People of the Caucasus* (New York: Dial Press, 1976).

[5] Ibid., p. 121.

[6] Edward Moffat Weyer, *The Eskimos: Their Environment and Folkways* (Hamden, Conn.: Archon Books, 1969).

[7] Asen Balikci, *The Nitsilik Eskimo* (Garden City, N.Y.: Natural History Press, 1970).

[8] Nicholas J. Gubser, *The Nunamiut Eskimos: Hunters of Caribou* (New Haven: Yale University Press, 1965), p. 121.

[9] Weyer, *The Eskimos.*

[10] Leonard Weller, *Sociology in Israel* (Westport, Conn.: Greenwood Press, 1974).

[11] William J. Goode, *World Revolution and Family Patterns* (New York: The Free Press, 1963).

[12] Peter Laslett, "The Comparative History of Household and Family," in Michael Gordon, ed., *The American Family in Social-Historical Perspective* (New York: St. Martin's Press, 1973), pp. 19–33.

[13] Philip J. Greven, Jr., "Family Structure in Seventeenth Century Andover, Massachusetts," in Gordon, ed., *The American Family in Social-Historical Perspective,* pp. 77–99.

[14] Goode, *World Revolution and Family Patterns.*

[15] George L. Maddox, "Retirement as a Social Event in the United States," in John C. McKinney and Frank T. deVyver, eds., *Aging and Social Policy* (New York: Appleton-Century-Crofts, 1966), p. 120.

[16] Institute of Gerontology, *Information on Aging.*

[17] National Council on Aging, *The Myth and the Reality of Aging in America* (Washington, D.C.: National Council on the Aging, 1975), p. 80, and "A Sharp Increase in Retirements is Viewed as a Cause for Concern," *New York Times* (December 17, 1978), Section 1, p. 72.

[18] See Maddox, "Retirement as a Social Event in the United States," pp. 117–135; Robert C. Atchley, *The Social Forces in Later Life* (Belmont, Calif.: Wadsworth, 1977); and Jon Hendricks and C. Davis Hendricks, *Aging in Mass Society* (Cambridge, Mass.: Winthrop Publishers, 1977), pp. 235–238.

[19] Hendricks and Hendricks, *Aging in Mass Society,* p. 232.

[20] Atchley, *The Social Forces in Later Life.*

[21] Ibid.

[22] Matilda White Riley and Joan Waring, "Age and Aging," in Robert K. Merton and Robert Nisbet, eds., *Contemporary Social Problems,* 4th ed. (New York: Harcourt, Brace, Jovanovich, 1976), pp. 354–410.

[23] National Council on Aging, *The Myth and Reality of Aging in America.*

[24] Robert Dubin. "Industrial Worker's Worlds," *Social Problems* 3 (July 1955), pp. 131–142.

[25] Robert N. Butler, *Why Survive? Being Old in America* (New York: Harper & Row, 1975).

[26] Bureau of the Census, "Consumer Income," *Current Population Reports,* Series P-60, no. 116 (July 1978), p. 12.

[27] Atchley, *The Social Forces in Later Life.*

[28] Social Security Agency, *Your Social Security* (Washington, D.C.: U.S. Department of Health, Education, and Welfare, 1976), HEW Publication no. (SSA) 76-10035.

[29] Matilda White Riley and Anne E. Foner, *Aging and Society: Volume 1, An Inventory of Research Findings* (New York: Russell Sage Foundation, 1968).

[30] George E. Rejda, *Social Insurance and Economic Security* (Englewood Cliffs, N.J.: Prentice-Hall, 1976), and U.S. Department of Labor, Bureau of Labor Statistics, *CPI Detailed Report,* July 1978.

[31] Sidney Goldstein, *Consumption Patterns of the Aged* (Philadelphia: University of Pennsylvania Press, 1960).

[32] Hendricks and Hendricks, *Aging in Mass Society,* p. 416.

[33] Bill O'Hallaren, "Nobody (in TV) Loves You When You're Old and Gray," *New York Times* (July 24, 1977), Section D, p. 21.

[34] Elaine Cumming and W. E. Henry, *Growing Old: The Process of Disengagement* (New York: Basic Books, 1961), and Elaine Cumming, "Further Thoughts on the Theory of Disengagement," in Kart and Manard, eds., *Aging in America,* pp. 19–41.

[35] Cumming, "Further Thoughts on the Theory of Disengagement," p. 25.

[36] Ibid., p. 24. Emphasis added.

[37] Riley and Foner, *Aging and Society,* and National Council on Aging, *The Myth and Reality of Aging in America,* p. 57.

[38] Zena Blau, *Old Age in a Changing Society* (New York: New Viewpoints, 1973).

[39] Riley and Foner, *Aging and Society.*

[40] Blau, *Old Age in a Changing Society.*

[41] Herman J. Loether, *Problems of Aging* (Encino, Calif.: Dickenson Publishing Co., 1975).

[42] Warren E. Schaller and Charles R. Carroll, *Health, Quackery and the Consumer* (Philadelphia: W. B. Saunders, 1976).

[43] Riley and Foner, *Aging and Society,* p. 253.

[44] Ronald Andersen, Joanna Lion, and Odin W. Anderson, *Two Decades of Health Services: Social Survey Trends in Use and Expenditure* (Cambridge, Mass.: Ballinger Publishing Co., 1976).

[45] Department of Health, Education, and Welfare, *Your Medicare Handbook* (Washington, D.C.: U.S. Government Printing Office, 1976), HEW Publication no. (SSA) 76-10050.

[46] Riley and Foner, *Aging and Society.*

[47] National Institute on Alcohol Abuse and Alcoholism, *Newsletter* (March 3, 1977).

[48] G. L. Duckworth and Adylin Rosenblatt, "Helping the Elderly Alcoholic," *Social Casework* 57 (May 1976), p. 296.

[49] Emil Pascarelli, "Alcoholism and Drug Addiction in the Elderly," *Geriatric Focus* 11 (December 1972), pp. 1, 6–7.

[50] U.S. Department of Justice, "Crime in the United States, 1977," *FBI Uniform Crime Reports* (Washington, D.C.: U.S. Government Printing Office, 1978), pp. 180–181.

[51] See chapter 15.

[52] See Riley and Foner, *Aging and Society.*

[53] Ibid.

[54] Robert Kastenbaum and Sandra E. Candy, "The 4% Fallacy: A Methodological and Empirical Critique of Extended Care Facility Population Statistics," in Kart and Manard, eds., *Aging in America,* pp. 166–177.

[55] See Riley and Foner, *Aging and Society,* and Atchley, *Social Forces in Later Life.*

[56] Rodney M. Coe, *Sociology of Medicine,* 2d ed. (New York: McGraw-Hill, 1977), pp. 330–348.

[57] Ibid., p. 344.

[58] Ibid.

[59] Rejda, *Social Insurance and Economic Security.*

[60] Hendricks and Hendricks, *Aging in Mass Society,* pp. 231–255.

[61] "The Graying of America," *Newsweek* 89 (February 28, 1977), pp. 51–52.

[62] Atchley, *Social Forces in Later Life.*

[63] Edward Cowan, "Carter Will Seek to Add Billions in Social Security," *New York Times* (May 8, 1977), pp. 1, 15.

[64] "The Graying of America," p. 52.

[65] Arnold M. Rose and Warren A. Peterson, *Older People and Their Social World: The Subculture of the Aging* (Philadelphia: F. A. Davis, 1965).

[66] Arlie Russell Hochschild, "Communal Lifestyles for the Aged," in Kart and Manard, eds., *Aging in America,* pp. 367–384.

[67] See Butler, *Why Survive.*

[68] Ibid., p. 263.

[69] Ibid., p. 264.

[70] Ibid., p. 266.

[71] Elisabeth Kübler-Ross, *On Death and Dying* (New York: Macmillan, 1969).

[72] Victor Richards, "Death and Cancer," in Edwin S. Schneidman, ed., *Death: Current Perspectives* (Palo Alto, Calif.: Mayfield Publishers, 1976), p. 480.

[73] "New Laws Allowing Control Over Dying," *New York Times* (November 26, 1978), Section 1, p. 60.

[74] Barbara J. Culliton, "Helping the Dying Die: Two Harvard Hospitals Go Public With Policies," *Science* 193 (September 16, 1976), pp. 1105–1106.

[75] David Sudnow, *Passing On* (Englewood Cliffs, N.J.: Prentice-Hall, 1967).

[76] See Cicely Saunders, "St. Christopher's Hospice," in Schneidman, ed., *Death*, pp. 516–522, and Sandol Stoddard, *The Hospice Movement: A Better Way of Caring For the Dying* (New York, Stein & Day, 1978).

[77] Constance Holden, "Hospices: For the Dying, Relief From Pain and Fear," *Science* 193 (July 30, 1976), pp. 389–391.

[78] Judith Cummings, "Elderly in Bronx Monitor the Youth-Offender Cases," *New York Times* (March 27, 1977), p. 40.

[79] Morton Mintz and Jerry S. Cohen, *Power, Inc.: Public and Private Rulers and How to Make Them Accountable* (New York: Viking Press, 1976).

[80] Carol Offir, "Old People's Revolt—At 65, Work Becomes a Four Letter Word," *Psychology Today* 7 (March 1974), p. 40.

[81] Butler, *Why Survive*, p. 341.

Questions for Discussion

1. Describe the manner in which older people are treated in the Caucasus region of southern Russia, in the traditional Eskimo culture, and in the Israeli Kibbutzim. What does knowledge of these cultural practices teach us about the role of elderly in society?

2. What changes have occurred in America and American institutions over the past few centuries that have resulted in changes in the role of the elderly in American society? According to the functionalist perspective, why have these societal changes had implications for the elderly in our society?

3. From the conflict perspective, why has the position of the elderly in American society changed? What changes can we expect in the future position of the elderly in American society?

4. According to the interactionist perspective, a positive self concept is important in enabling people to lead a satisfying life and contribute to society. What aspects of modern American society reduce the likelihood that the elderly will find support for a positive conception of themselves? How might this situation be changed?

5. Work is an important part of a person's life. What are the advantages and disadvantages of mandatory retirement? What are the consequences of lowering the retirement age? What policies are likely to emerge in the future in relation to mandatory retirement?

6. What are the different ways by which the elderly adapt to their change in status? What social factors influence the mode of adaptation likely to be followed by a particular individual?

7. What methods are currently in use to provide financial support for the aged in America? What are the weaknesses of these methods? How might they be improved?

8. As our population has become older and the structure of the family has changed, there has been increasing concern about death and the conditions under which people die. What conditions are not perceived as social problems in relation to death and dying? What programs or practices have been developed to alleviate these problems? What more could we do?

CHAPTER 11

Poverty

POVERTY IN AMERICA: A BRIEF HISTORY

Industrialization and Poverty. The Poor in America. The
Development of Modern Poverty Programs.

POVERTY AS A SOCIAL PROBLEM

The Functionalist Perspective. The Conflict Perspective.
The Interactionist Perspective. What Is Poverty?

THE MANY FACES OF POVERTY

The Welfare Poor. The Marginal Poor. The Displaced
Homemaker. The Working Poor.

WHO ARE THE POOR?

Race. Rural Dwellers. The Elderly. The Young.

CAUSES OF POVERTY

Functionalism and the "Inevitability of Poverty." Poverty
as Conflict. Blocked Opportunity. The Culture of Poverty.
Interactionism, Societal Reaction, and Poverty. Welfare
and Poverty.

POVERTY IN AMERICA: PROSPECTS FOR THE
FUTURE

Interpersonal Involvement and Individual Worth. A New
War on Poverty. Full Employment. Training the Poor—A
Functionalist Approach. Self-Help and Community
Organization.

CONCLUSION

In describing his early life, novelist Richard Wright observed:

> Hunger stole upon me so slowly that at first I was not aware of what hunger really meant. Hunger had always been more or less at my elbow when I played, but now I began to wake up at night to find hunger standing at my bedside, staring at me gauntly. The hunger I had known before this had been no grim, hostile stranger; it had been a normal hunger that had made me beg constantly for bread, and when I ate a crust or two I was satisfied. But this new hunger baffled me, scared me, made me angry and insistent. Whenever I begged for food now my mother would pour me a cup of tea which would still the clamor in my stomach for a moment or two; but a little later I would feel hunger nudging my ribs, twisting my empty guts until they ached. I would grow dizzy and my vision would dim. I became less active in my play, and for the first time in my life I had to pause and think of what was happening to me.[1]

A mother from Baltimore describes what it is like to live on welfare:

> My daughter can't get up in the morning and eat cereal, I have to give her grits. She ought to be able to eat eggs.
>
> She is honor roll in school, but they're talking about giving her a zero because I can't afford to give her the things she needs for school.
>
> Everybody reads that social services is going up, and they say, damn, those welfare people are getting more again. But they don't print in the paper like it really is. It's hard.[2]

Both of these people are describing what it feels like to be poor — so poor that you do not even have enough to eat. Poverty can mean many things. It can mean not having enough to eat, wearing outdated and inadequate clothing, living in a place that is dangerous or undesirable, or receiving poor health care resulting in a shorter life expectancy. It can mean facing old age with a fixed income and an erosion of purchasing power due to inflation, or a childhood characterized by misery, degradation, and failure. Finally, and possibly most important, for many it means living a life of utter despair in which there is little hope for a better future.

In all likelihood, you will never personally confront the ugly face of poverty. Why, then, should you be concerned? Why is poverty considered a social problem? Public awareness of, and interest in, the poor has waxed and waned over the years. During the 1950s, there was (compared to other eras) relatively little public discussion of poverty. Many people believed that America was entering a period of plenty and that increasing economic production would take care of any poverty problem that existed. In the 1960s, government, the media, and citizen action groups turned the spotlight on poverty, and as a result public interest and concern rose substantially. More recently, the attention paid to the poor has again declined. People seem to have turned their attention to other issues. Possibly, with the recession of the 1970s and changes in the employment picture, people have become more concerned with securing their own affluence and find less time to worry about the plight of others.

Despite these fluctuations in public interest, poverty has continued over the years to attract the attention of students of social problems. Yet, we still might ask, Why should *you* concern *yourself* with poverty? Beyond humanitarian considerations, poverty can have serious and undesirable consequences for all of us. For example, the existence of poverty dramatizes the discrepancy between our cultural ideal of helping the less fortunate to help themselves and the reality that many people live permanently outside our affluent society; the cost of maintaining a large welfare system, especially its bureaucracy, is a burden to all; crime is linked to poverty and substandard living conditions; and perhaps most significant from a long-range view, one must seriously consider the possibility of political unrest or outright rebellion among the poor. Thus, poverty is a concern for all of us because it poses a threat to our way of life. In the following discussion we will amplify both the nature of poverty and its consequences. We will also identify the social characteristics of the poor. Finally, we will evaluate various alternative solutions to the poverty problem.

POVERTY IN AMERICA: A BRIEF HISTORY

Poverty is an age-old problem. It has been written that Jesus said to his disciples, "For you always have the poor with you . . ."[3] In fact, poverty as a human condition can be traced back to the point at which human societies were able to accumulate a surplus of food and material goods. With such surpluses, a more complex division of labor emerged; some people were freed from the task of food production and were able to devote their energies to other tasks. With surpluses of food and other materials, it was possible for some people to accumulate more goods than others. These changes ushered in a more elaborate system of *social stratification*—an arrangement in which some people, of higher rank, receive greater rewards than those below them. Whereas previously distinctions between people were based primarily on age and sex, it was possible to differentiate between people in terms of their role in the division of labor and their possession of valued material goods.

Thus, poverty as a social condition arises when a certain type of social organization exists. Poverty emerged not because people were deprived of food or other material goods—living at or near the level of subsistence has been the fate of most people throughout history. Rather, **poverty arises when a social organization is based on an uneven distribution of the resources available, resulting in some people accumulating more goods and resources than others.** For much of human history, poverty has been accepted by many as a state that is probably inevitable. With the development of *feudalism* in Western Europe, the perpetuation of poverty was virtually guaranteed by an elaborate set of norms, values, and legal statutes that bound serfs to their lords for succeeding generations.[4]

Industrialization and Poverty

Accompanying the Industrial Revolution were a number of significant changes in social organization that directly affected the poor.[5] First, the hereditary relationships underlying feudalism were replaced by contractual obligations—people were now free to sell their labor to anyone who could afford to purchase it. Second, there was a substantial migration of people into the growing commercial and industrial centers, and the ownership of farmland became a less important determinant of one's position in society. Third, with the decline of feudalism and the extended family, people were less able to depend on traditional sources of support, such as family or community, during times of hardship. Fourth, the technology and scientific knowledge that accompanied industrialization gave human beings substantially more control over their environment. Much that had previously been beyond the realm of human intervention was now amenable to some degree of control.

One consequence of these changes was that the differences between the lives of the poor and the nonpoor increased substantially. In the feudal era, people in all social classes suffered many of the same hardships—drafty houses, fatal or debilitating diseases, and, often, dangerous living conditions. Especially in the early feudal period, lords and serfs frequently lived and worked together with little noticeable distinction between their lifestyles. With the development of new technology, this situation changed drastically. The wealthy were able to avoid those unpleasant conditions that still afflicted the poor. The difference between being poor and not poor became increasingly visible and obvious to all.

A second consequence of these changes in social organization was that one's social position no longer depended on heredity—people were no longer permanently and immutably bound to the social class into which they were born. This opened up possibilities for improving one's lot in life. Upward social mobility, while admittedly open to only a few, became a real possibility. If you were poor, you could do something about it. In addition, this brought about subtle changes in attitudes toward poverty: with improvement possible, one might reason that people remain poor at least partially because they have not made sufficient efforts to change their lives. When social mobility is possible, it becomes easier to view poverty as a voluntary condition, or at least as due to individual inadequacies rather than social conditions.

A third consequence of these changes was the beginning of a great debate — still in progress today — concerning what should be done about poverty and what role the government should take in the matter. On one side of the debate were those who for a number of reasons — religious, humanitarian, and practical — argued that it was the government's responsibility to provide for the sick and the indigent when these people did not have other sources of support. In England during the eighteenth and nineteenth centuries, this sentiment led to such developments as state-run workhouses, which put the poor to work, and wage subsidies to ensure that people had sufficient funds to support themselves.

On the other side of this debate were those who argued that it would be better to leave the poor alone and let nature run its course. Government assistance for the poor, particularly in England, was opposed by Malthusians, who argued that any such efforts were useless and even inhumane because they would lead to even greater vice and misery. Such government support, they insisted, would encourage the poor to multiply far beyond their ability to support themselves. This would make it even more difficult for the poor to improve their lot. The situation was complex indeed, and the plight of the poor in England and much of Europe was a major factor in bringing about migration to the Western Hemisphere.

The Poor in America

Immigrants came to America for many reasons, but foremost was the hope of finding a better life. Many were trying to escape the poverty that intermittently plagued various parts of England and Europe. While the New World may have offered them another opportunity to improve their lot, treatment of the poor in the United States was quite similar to that in England and Europe. The poor, the physically ill, and the emotionally disturbed tended to be lumped together as paupers. During the 1700s and early 1800s, the poor were cared for primarily by family, friends, or neighborhood. The

workhouses and almshouses that did exist tended to be small and organized like a family. Poverty was viewed as an unavoidable and possibly inevitable condition, and most people saw no need for punishing the poor by institutionalizing them.[6]

During this period, working with the poor was seen by many as a Christian duty. The principal characteristics of those who worked with the poor were supposed to be neighborliness and a good moral character. During the 1800s, and especially following the Civil War, this charitable view toward poverty began to change. According to historian David Rothman:

> An acute sense of peril went together with the highest expectations. Observers feared that paupers were draining the nation's resources, demoralizing its labor force, and threatening its stability. . . . Yet, reformers also expected to be able to control and even to eliminate poverty in the new republic. The investigation into the nature of dependency . . . promised great rewards for success, and awful penalties for failure.[7]

One reason for this emerging fear was the increasing number of immigrants who filled the ranks of the poor. Previously, the poor had been unfortunate members of the community with values and an Anglo Saxon Protestant background that were quite similar to the nonpoor in the community. However, as the nineteenth century progressed, the immigrant poor were increasingly likely to have a different language, different values, and different religious beliefs. Poverty came to be associated with the foreign, the strange, and the alien. Another reason for this fear was the increasing concern that poverty could lead to social disruption — a view fostered by the fact that the foreigners who constituted many of the poor seemed to have little attachment to American beliefs and values.

The optimist's view that poverty could be eliminated derived from the increasing *secularization* of society — the rejection of the belief that God's will could explain all social conditions and that human nature is inherently wicked.[8] This optimism also derived from the conditions of life in America during this

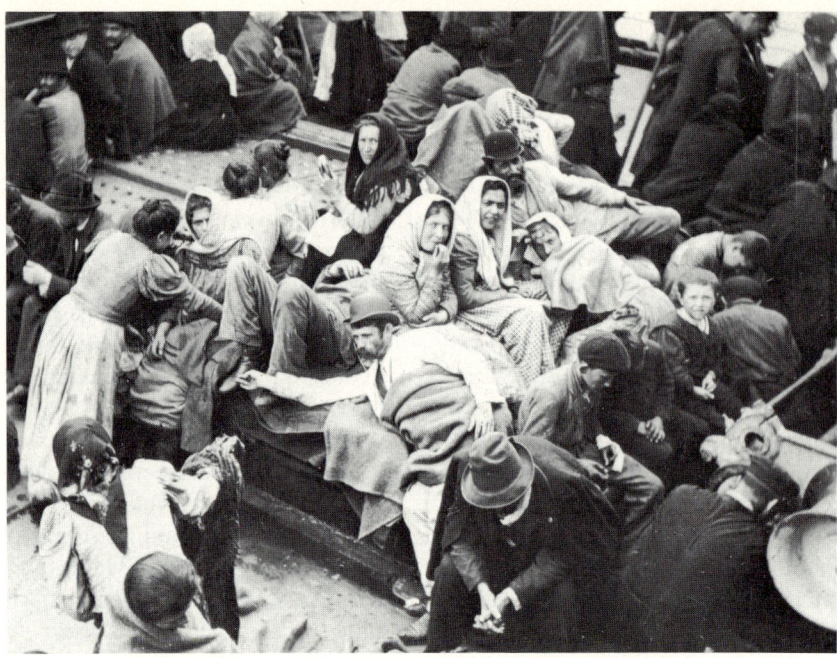

Many European immigrants viewed America as a land of promise, without the threat of poverty they experienced in their own countries. In reality, many of the immigrants did face considerable poverty in America.

period, especially the economic and industrial expansion and the opening of the West. To many people, it seemed that anything was possible. Why should poverty be inevitable? Why could Americans not conquer poverty in the same way that they did the immense American wilderness? **One common explanation of poverty during this period was that it resulted from individual failure.** It was assumed, because America was a land of such seeming plenty, that morally respectable, industrious citizens would be economically successful. There were still some who viewed social institutions as the cause of poverty, but the essential point is that many held the hopeful view that the problem of poverty could be attacked successfully.

During this period, many organizations were created to help the poor, to settle the new immigrants, and assist them in adapting to American life.[9] One effort was called the *Scientific Charity Movement,* which purported to apply the scientific method to the problem of poverty. Rather than giving relief indiscriminately to the poor, this group offered intensive investigations of each case to determine the best method of intervention, to evaluate the cause of the need, and to study the prospects of rehabilitation in each case.

The Development of Modern Poverty Programs

By the beginning of the twentieth century, many of these charitable organizations had been consolidated, and the emphasis had begun to change from sending out neighborly persons with good intentions to training professional social workers. The Great Depression of the 1930s had considerable impact on programs for the poor. Suddenly, millions of people were added to the ranks of poverty, jolting many into the realization that almost anybody could have the misfortune to be poor, and thus it was a problem for everybody. As a consequence, the federal government initiated massive programs to cope with the army of poor, and the current era—in which the poor are viewed as the responsibility of the federal government—was ushered in.

Beginning with the programs developed during the Depression, modern poverty programs have evolved as a three-pronged strategy.[10] First, some programs focus on *employment* by encouraging government policies that maintain high levels of employment in the economy and by providing educational and training opportunities to the poor who are capable of working. Second, some programs provide *social insurance,* which protects people from utter poverty if unemployment levels rise precipitously or if unemployment is temporary owing to illness or injury. Third, *public assistance* is offered to those who, because of disability or family obligations, are unable to work at all.

Since World War II, there have been fairly high levels of employment, widespread affluence, and considerable upward social mobility. Although there have been some setbacks, it has been a fairly optimistic period during which poverty has shrunk from the public view. Nevertheless, there has been, especially in the past two decades, considerable ferment over the issue of poverty. People are again concerned about finding the causes of poverty and developing programs that can solve the problem. During the course of this chapter we will be discussing these issues. From this brief historical discussion, the student should be aware that poverty as a social condition must be considered only within the context of a particular society, and that people's reactions to and attitudes toward poverty are by and large a product of the historical era of which they are a part. Before we look at poverty and poverty programs in modern America, we need to examine the divergent approaches toward poverty as a social problem that are used by sociologists.

POVERTY AS A SOCIAL PROBLEM

Given the variability in the forms that poverty can take, is it possible to define poverty in a precise fashion? **Any single definition of poverty—especially one that is designed for legal, administrative, or statistical purposes—will inevitably have many shortcomings. Most importantly, any definition will be limited to a particular time period, nation, or region within a nation. Being poor is a relative condition**—today's poor are typically better fed, housed, clothed, and healthier than the kings and rulers of past centuries. To be poor in the United States generally implies a far higher standard of living than being poor in India, Bangladesh, or even Mexico.

There are a host of other issues that any single definition of poverty might well fall short of resolving: Is the poverty voluntary and temporary (e.g. a college student making little money while preparing for a future career)? How long has the condition persisted? What chances does the person involved have of improving his or her situation? While no definition will be completely satisfactory, it is important to look at alternative ways of defining poverty because these guide our choice of solutions to the problem. Using the theoretical perspectives, we will examine definitions of poverty and the question why poverty is a social problem.

The Functionalist Perspective

From the functionalist perspective, society is a system in which all of the parts make some contribution to the functioning of the whole. In order to ensure that each part makes a positive contribution, there must exist corrective mechanisms that guide the behavior of the parts and penalize those who deviate.[11] This is the role that is played by systems of social stratification and the poverty that accompany them. In this view, poverty is a form of deviant behavior—the poor behave in ways that are not adaptive and functional for society. As a consequence, they are at the bottom of the stratification system and receive few of the material and social rewards available. This threat of being at the bottom of the heap serves to motivate people to perform their proper roles. **From the functionalist perspective, poverty becomes a social problem when it no longer performs this** function of motivating people to make productive contributions to society. **This might occur if there were large numbers of poor because the system was unable to reward all those who performed important tasks; or it might occur if, because of some inequities in the system, the performance of important tasks only carried a small likelihood of moving up in the stratification system.**

Some functionalists view poverty in a different way—they argue that the poor actually perform important functions for society.[12] In this view, there are poor people because the poor make a contribution to the functioning of the system. For example, the poor do all the difficult, demeaning, and low-paying jobs that are essential but that no one else wants to do. If this is so, then it is important that poor people adapt to their situation rather than pose a threat or serve as a source of disruption to society. Thus, a certain way of life—a culture of poverty—emerges with distinctive values and attitudes, which helps the poor adjust to their situation. For example, a lack of ambition or aspiration among the poor is functional for society because then the poor will not have goals that they cannot achieve. Their aspirations will be consistent with what it is possible for them to achieve. **Poverty becomes a social problem, from this perspective, when the poor are no longer able to adapt to their plight and thus pose a threat to the functioning of society.**

Irrespective of which particular view is emphasized, functionalists tend to see poverty as an objective condition—it grows out of the operation of particular social and economic systems. As such, poverty can be defined largely in economic terms—a person is poor if he or she is below a certain economic level defined as necessary to enjoy an acceptable standard of living.

The Conflict Perspective

Like the functionalists, conflict theorists posit that the seeds of poverty are inextricably related to the economic system of society. However, they do not see poverty as either essential or beneficial. Rather, poverty arises because some groups benefit from it—some groups gain access to greater material and social rewards if others are deprived of those rewards. Since there is only a finite amount of resources available, one group can gain more only if another has less. Through the exercise of power, one group will work to ensure that it receives a larger share of the goods available. **From the conflict perspective, poverty becomes a social problem when some group feels that the existing distribution of resources is unfair and unjust and that something can and should be done about it.**[13]

The conflict perspective also sheds a different light on the culture of poverty, which is now seen as a mechanism that makes it easier for the dominant groups to protect their position from inroads by the poor. The most effective means of controlling the poor is to convince them that they do not want to change their situation. In this view, the educational system or the welfare system actually encourages this culture of poverty because it does not work to raise the aspirations of the poor or to provide them with skills with which to compete with others. **For the conflict theorist, it is not the breakdown of the culture of poverty that constitutes a problem; rather the culture of poverty itself is a social problem because it inhibits the ability of the poor to struggle with other groups over scarce resources.**

For the conflict theorist, poverty can also be defined largely in economic terms. Poverty exists when a group has fewer economic assets when compared to other groups in society. The conflict theorist, however, might have a very different perception of where poverty begins than would the functionalist. For the functionalist, poverty motivates people to perform important tasks, so one might define poverty in some absolute sense—above a certain economic level, poverty would not exist because there would be no deprivation and thus no incentive to work. **For the conflict theorist, the emphasis is on more relative criteria. One is poor relative to what other groups have. Rather than establishing absolute cutoff points, one must think in terms of relative inequality.**

The Interactionist Perspective

The interactionist perspective emphasizes the subjective nature of reality. **In this context, poverty is considered a social problem because it is defined as such by influential groups.** There is no objective amount of deprivation that one can call poverty. In this sense, poverty is relative — it depends on what you compare it to. Poor Americans today are certainly far better off than many people in earlier historical periods who were not considered poor. Yet the point of comparison has changed — we compare them not with people of an earlier era (or even people in other countries today); rather we compare them with affluent Americans. Using this standard, the conditions of the poor today are undesirable and they can and should be changed. In fact, an intriguing issue is whether, from the interactionist perspective, poverty could ever be eliminated as long as inequality existed. Even if the poorest people were quite affluent and comfortable, might they still not define themselves as poor as long as others had much more than they had?

While to this point the interactionist definition of poverty bears similarities to the conflict definition, the interactionist is less concerned with establishing an economic cutoff point than with viewing poverty as a negative label that some members of society ascribe to others. **For interactionists, poverty is a matter of shared expectations — and the poor often share the negative definition of themselves that is held by others in society. Those who are the objects of such labeling are stigmatized and may begin to behave in accordance with those expectations. The interactionist emphasizes that poverty is not just a matter of economic deprivation, but involves the person's self-concept.** Sociologist David Matza identified those whom he called the *disreputable poor:* people who remained unemployed during periods of nearly full employment.[14] These are the poor most likely to accept the definition of the situation that others (the nonpoor) project on them. For the interactionist, a simple economic definition of poverty hides this complexity. Not all poor people view themselves in the same way. The third-generation welfare recipient undoubtedly views himself much differently (and much more negatively) than does a person working his way through college — even though both may have the same income. For the interactionist, definitions of poverty should take into account this complexity.

What Is Poverty?

It is impossible to provide a single definition of poverty that will be useful at all places and all times. Yet it is possible to develop definitions that are limited to specific times and purposes. For practical and administrative reasons, bureaucrats and planners develop definitions that will enable them to identify the poor. The two most commonly used definitions are *economic* and *cultural*.

Economic Definitions

Most people think of poverty primarily in terms of a person's financial or economic status. Economic definitions of poverty are useful because they are easily quantified, and the poor can thus be treated as a statistical category. **Economic definitions involve establishing an income level below which poverty is said to exist. Definitions of this type may be either *relative* (in which the poverty cut-off point is a proportion of the median family income of some group) or *absolute* (a fixed dollar cut-off point, as is currently used in the United States).** These poverty thresholds are sometimes arbitrarily established and can create some disturbing inequities. For example, a family classified as poor may actually receive more total assistance than a family whose income falls above the poverty line because the poor family receives, in addition to direct income assistance, goods and services through "nondollar" contributions, such as food stamps and Medicaid (see Table 11.1).

In order to overcome such problems, attempts have been made to construct a more complex definition of poverty based on income. In 1964, President Lyndon Johnson announced his "War on Poverty." This led to the passage of the Economic

TABLE 11.1

Hypothetical Comparison of Family Eligible for *Aid to Families with Dependent Children* (ADC) with a non-ADC Family.

	ADC FAMILY	NON-ADC FAMILY
Annual income	$4800	$5100
Food stamps	$ 792	0
Medicaid	$1500	0
Total income	$7092	$5100

SOURCE. Based in part on data supplied by the Department of Social Services, Marquette County, Michigan.

Opportunity Act and the establishment of the Office of Economic Opportunity (now the Community Services Administration). Also in 1964, a statistician with the Social Security Administration, Mollie **Orshansky** developed a **measure of poverty** that was subsequently adopted by the Office of Economic Opportunity and later, in 1969, by the Office of Management and Budget as the federal government's official measure of poverty. This definition is based on a series of indicators related to nutrition and purchasing power, taking into consideration such factors as family size, number of children, age and sex of the head of household, and farm versus nonfarm residence.[15] Using this definition, there are actually different income cutoffs for different family types, as shown in Table 11.2. Using this definition, in 1977, 24,720,000 (11.6 percent of the population of the United States) were poor.[16]

This definition of poverty, based on a series of income cutoffs, is more complex and takes into ac-

TABLE 11.2
1979 Poverty Income Cutoffs

SIZE OF FAMILY UNIT	NONFARM FAMILY	FARM FAMILY
1	$3400	$2910
2	4500	3840
3	5600	4770
4	6700	5600
5	7800	6630
6[a]	8900	7560

[a] For family units with more than 6 members, add $1100 for each additional member in a nonfarm and $930 for each additional member in a farm family. Alaska and Hawaii have different cutoffs.

SOURCE. *Federal Register* 44 (May 7, 1979), p. 26746.

count many relevant factors. Yet, it is still not perfect. For example, even with this definition, it is difficult to measure and compare different types of **in-kind income** (nonmoney income such as government health care assistance or home-grown food). Some people receive more of this in-kind income than do others. Furthermore, some groups of poor have special needs—families headed by women may face fewer employment opportunities; families with young children may have special school-related expenditures; and rural families must pay more for transportation to distant schools or shopping centers. Although we can recognize the shortcomings of these economic definitions, some definition is still necessary for legal and administrative purposes.

Cultural Definitions

If there are such problems with economic definitions of poverty, then it may be valuable to search for some very different way of defining poverty. We have discussed the interactionist objection to defining poverty solely in economic terms. **Along these lines, some have argued that we should define poverty as a cultural rather than economic condition. For example, L. F. Hayes has suggested that poverty should not be defined in terms of *how much* people have, but rather in terms of *why* they are at a particular economic level.**[17] Thus, poverty might be the result of unemployment, the piling up of unavoidable debts beyond a person's financial capacities, or the inability to budget one's income efficiently. Others have argued that something like the culture of poverty should be used to classify the poor. The poor are those who feel alienated, helpless, and hopeless about their condition. It is toward these people that poverty programs should be directed.

If we use any such cultural definition, the people classified as poor are likely to be those who will remain in poverty for a long period of time, often several generations. While this definition would include most people who would also be considered poor using purely economic criteria, the cultural definition tends to exclude the temporarily or circumstantially poor. The college student who undergoes temporary low income in order to gain a college degree is not considered among the poor. Proponents of this definition argue that the real problem of poverty lies with the chronic long-term poor people. For example, many were upset when the food stamp program was first initiated because college students—who were poor by the economic criteria—were often able to collect food stamps. It was felt that this drained funds away from the real problem—the permanent, hard-core poor. Thus, the cultural definition attempts to get around the rigidities of the economic definition in order to focus attention elsewhere.

THE MANY FACES OF POVERTY

No definition of poverty can bring home the reality of being poor—the misery, the degradation, the helplessness. We have seen that poverty means quite different things to different people. Those who are poor have quite a different view of poverty than do those who are not poor. In fact, a major obstacle in finding solutions to the problem of poverty is that many people are isolated from poverty. When was the last time you met, or talked at length with, someone who is poor? Among those who are not poor, reactions to the poor range from sympathy, through ambivalence, to outright hostility. John E. Tropman, a professor of social work at the University of Michigan, found that most Americans do not feel kindly toward the poor. Some common reactions that he encountered are:

They are like alcoholics—just wasting away their lives.
They generally don't care. Sometimes, it is lack of ambition.
They are too lazy to work.[18]

In order to grasp what poverty means to the people who must suffer it, we will examine the lives of some of America's poor today.[19] In doing so, we will see how varied the many faces of poverty are. We will also be able to evaluate how accurate the perceptions of Tropman's respondents are.

The Welfare Poor

Less than half of all Americans whose income falls below the poverty line receive any form of welfare. Nevertheless, it is usually the welfare poor who are the objects of our wrath when we are besieged by high taxes and frustrated at our inability to reduce them. It is all too easy to believe that a sensationalized incident of welfare abuse—the recipient who drives a new Cadillac or earns $15,000 a year —really represents the way most welfare recipients live. To better understand what it is like to be on welfare, let us meet some welfare recipients.

There is a 32-year-old woman from Dallas who has had eight major operations and may require a ninth. After her mother's death in 1965, she inherited the responsibility of supporting seven brothers and sisters. The departure of her husband only added to her troubles. She also has two children of her own with whom she lives in a dilapidated house. The children lack winter coats and shoes and usually live on cereal, macaroni, and other inexpensive foods. The $4-per-day allotment that she receives does not buy gourmet food or stylish clothing. If welfare is the easy, "free ride" that some critics say it is, this woman would rather get off. She has held a half-dozen jobs in the last twelve years, and none for very long. Each time, her chronic health problems forced her to quit. It is not surprising that mothers receiving assistance through Aid to Families with Dependent Children (AFDC) want to work. In 1977, the allotment in Dallas was $86 per month for a mother and one child and $185 for a mother and five children.

Even when the allotments are higher, the plight of recipients is not necessarily improved. Consider the case of a rural Grand Rapids, Michigan man whom we shall call Raymond. He has a wife and three children and receives $545 per month in Aid to Dependent Children Incapacitated (ADCI). During the harsh winter of 1976–1977, Raymond walked the roads near his home collecting twigs, scrap lumber, and other combustible material in order to heat his house. The family had an oil furnace, but in the bitter weather there was not enough money for fuel oil. Since oil dealers considered Raymond a poor credit risk, the furnace remained cold. On January 26, the Kent County Community Action Agency purchased a tank of fuel for Raymond's family and temporarily solved his problem. Raymond's case is typical of many poor families living in cold northern climates. Houses often lack insulation and storm windows. With increased fuel costs and a fixed welfare allotment, there is frequently not enough money during winter months for such necessities.

A final example, quite different from the preceding ones, clearly illustrates the diverse nature of poverty in our society. Some welfare recipients work but are referred to as *circumstantially poor,* or sometimes even as the *affluent poor.* Consider the situation of Kurt and his 35-year-old wife, Karen, who live in northwestern Indiana. Kurt is employed and earns $13,000 annually. Kurt's case can hardly be said to represent poverty—or can it? Karen developed multiple sclerosis, and treatment costs $1300 per month. In addition to the expenses associated with this treatment, Kurt and Karen have one child who also suffers from multiple sclerosis and another with brain damage. State welfare officials ruled that Karen could not receive assistance through Medicaid because of Kurt's salary and told the family that if Kurt would turn his salary checks over to the state, he would be allowed to keep $400 a month of the salary to support his family, and the state would then pay Karen's medical expenses. Yet that leaves the family—with two children still sick—only $4800 a year to live on. Ironically, there is another course that the family could have taken. If Kurt had divorced Karen, he could keep his full salary and make Karen eligible for Medicaid.

The Marginal Poor

Maggie, a woman from San Jose, supplemented her general-assistance payments by donating blood to an organization that paid a small sum for it. She did this in order to pay the rent on her small hotel room. Otherwise, she would be forced into the street to live with derelicts. There are many poor people—including the derelicts that Maggie so desperately worked to avoid—who are not a part of the welfare population because they do not receive

public assistance. This group includes not only drunks and vagrants, but also older men who lack jobs, homes, or family ties. The problems of these poor people can be illustrated by the problems surrounding the demise of a hotel that was home for such men in a community in northern Michigan.

The old hotel has certainly seen better days in its eighty-two years of existence. Nevertheless, it is home for nearly 40 low-income elderly men. It is not an elegant home to be sure, but when the alternative is no home at all, elegance is not a prime concern. As the owner said, "My old men come out of shacks . . . They're just glad to be warm."[20] Recently, the residents of the old hotel faced the alternative of no home at all. In July of 1977, the building was cited for numerous health and safety code violations. Although some of these problems have been corrected, others remain. The problems facing this hotel and its residents create a dilemma for the residents, the hotel owner, and city officials. On the one hand, city officials are reluctant to order the structure closed for the sake of the men who live there. On the other hand, conditions such as wiring and the age of the structure make it a prime target for fire. City officials feel that they must enforce the code since failure to do so would make them liable for any injury or damage that might occur. In short, humanitarian impulses incline city officials toward ignoring violations of the code, while practical and legal concerns force them to move toward strict adherence to the rules. The matter is complicated by the fact that room rates—$16.50 per week, or $4 per night—do not make it profitable for the owner to make major renovation. A group of local contractors have offered to assist in making some changes, but the fate of the building and of the old men who call it home remains far from certain.

The Displaced Homemaker

Partly as a consequence of the modern emphasis on women's rights, there is growing recognition of the problems facing a particular group of women— those who are widowed, divorced, or separated and who lack job skills that would enable them to support themselves at a satisfactory level. Such women are being referred to as *displaced home-makers.*

There is, for example, Cynthia, a 53-year-old woman from Detroit, divorced after thirty years of marriage. The divorce settlement required that Cynthia's husband make mortgage payments on their home and pay her $30 per week in alimony. Although Cynthia kept house and reared children over a thirty-year period, and even though her husband makes $19,000 a year, she has few options for supplementing the alimony payments. Homemaking skills are not readily translated into job skills. Though Cynthia had worked as a keypunch operator twenty-five years earlier, she was not able to find employment in this field. Perhaps the fact that she suffered from cancer and phlebitis contributed to her inability to get a job. Cynthia's case is like many others.

Because of this growing problem, two women, Tish Sommers and Laurie Shields, founded the Alliance for Displaced Homemakers in order to publicize the problem. The organization has concentrated on legislation at both the state and federal levels to establish training programs specifically designed for such women. The programs are viewed as necessary since these women not only lack training but also often experience age discrimination in the job market. Given the fact that more divorces are occurring after ten or more years of marriage, the displaced homemaker will probably continue to be represented among the American poor.

The Working Poor

There has been a great deal written about putting the able-bodied poor to work. Utah has such a program, and it has proven beneficial for most of those concerned. The real difficulty is that many persons — hard-working people who normally would not have such problems — are experiencing difficulty in finding employment. There are many reasons for this, including shifts in the types of skills in demand in the economy, a lack of job skills, and the movement of industry from one region of the country to another. The following cases, describing people who would be considered average Americans, illustrate this aspect of poverty.

A Virginia carpenter, who was unemployed throughout the harsh winter of 1976–77, had to live with his wife and four children on an unemployment check equal to about one-quarter his normal salary. The family was not eligible for AFDC because the father remained in the home. By the end of the winter, the carpenter was two months behind on his utility and car payments and a month behind on his rent. What little money there was went to purchase food stamps.

A somewhat different experience is that of Richard, a 49-year-old former rubber-worker living in Connecticut. After twenty-eight years in the industry, Richard had attained the position of supervisor and was making about $300 a week. Then the plant closed, leaving Richard and about 800 others jobless. Some found new jobs, but for many middle-aged workers, there were either no jobs or the jobs they found were at considerably lower wages. Richard's story is typical of many middle-aged workers. He learned his trade well but now cannot use his skills unless he leaves the area where he has spent his life. Even then, there is no guarantee of employment.

High levels of unemployment work a special hardship on young people. For example, a 19-year-old Los Angeles man lost his job with a plastics firm and was unemployed for a month and a half. He filled out many applications and went for repeated interviews, but to no avail. After six weeks, he was willing to accept jobs that paid far less than the plastics firm. His experience is typical not only of California, but of most of the nation. Young persons between the ages of 16 and 19 continue to have some of the highest unemployment rates of all groups. For black teenagers, the picture is especially grim, with the rate remaining at 35 percent through the first quarter of 1978.[21] Teenagers often find themselves in a kind of double-bind situation. Employers frequently require experience, but you cannot accumulate experience without being employed.

We see in the lives of all of these poor people the many sides that poverty has. Poverty may take the form of a welfare mother or a disabled father, a deserted housewife or an underemployed worker. Most of all, a poor person could be any one of us. It

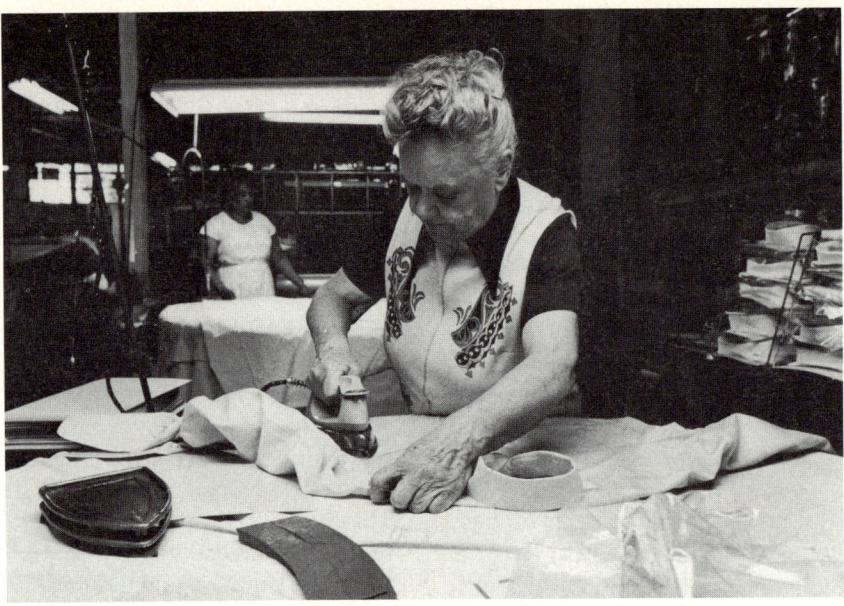

The stereotype of the poor is often that of a welfare recipient who is lazy and unwilling to work. In fact, many poor people work hard at jobs that are both difficult and low-paying.

is all too tempting to oversimplify the complex reality of poverty. As we investigate the dimensions of poverty today and evaluate various programs, we must keep in mind that poverty takes many forms, and there is probably no single solution to the diverse problems of poverty.

WHO ARE THE POOR?

In his book *The Other America,* which played an important role in mobilizing Americans to do something about poverty in the 1960s, Michael Harrington pointed out that poverty in the United States tends to be "invisible."[22] The places where we live and work are organized in such a way that people who are not poor do not have to come face to face with the ugly reality of poverty. We build freeways over, under, and around poor neighborhoods so that the affluent commuter is spared the confrontation with poverty. The police keep derelicts and panhandlers off the street—especially in those neighborhoods that the middle class and affluent are likely to frequent. Vigorous objection is often

made to any attempt to build low-cost housing for the poor in middle class communities.

Because of this invisibility, few affluent people have much first-hand experience with poverty, and thus there are many misconceptions about who is poor in the United States. Harrington argues that this invisibility is an important factor in perpetuating poverty because it is easy to ignore what you do not see. Furthermore, without accurate information on the characteristics of the poor, it is impossible to develop effective programs to deal with poverty. Who, then, are the poor in the United States?

Race

It is a common belief that most poor people in the United States today are nonwhite—mostly black. Practically every news story or documentary on poverty perpetuates this stereotype by devoting a predominance of their footage to blacks or other racial minorities. Yet it is a totally false stereotype. Blacks make up about 31 percent of the poor in the United States, and Hispanic-Americans 11 percent.

The majority of poor in the United States are whites.[23] **However, racial minorities do contribute a disproportionate share of people to the ranks of the poor.** In 1977, blacks constituted 12 percent of our population but made up 31 percent of the poor. Hispanic-Americans were 6 percent of our population, but made up 11 percent of the poor. The widespread poverty among racial minorities is reflected in the low levels of income among these groups (see Figs. 11.1 and 11.2).

Why are racial minorities so overrepresented among the poor? While we shall consider the causes of poverty in the next section, it is useful to look at the black experience in America in order to understand some of the special problems that these groups face.

The history of blacks in the United States has been radically different from that of whites. Most of the ancestors of the present black population were forcibly brought to the United States as slaves. While there is still some controversy over the precise effects of slavery, there is general agreement that the consequences were profound and long-lasting. The Africans were torn from their traditional African culture; then the remnants of their culture that survived the journey to America were systematically destroyed by slaveholders. One commentator has even suggested that slavery was analogous to conditions in Nazi concentration camps in terms of its destructive effects on the personality.[24]

One consequence of slavery that is especially important for our discussion was its effect on human initiative and ambition. Slaves were expected to be lazy, stupid, lack initiative, and to accept their plight. It was assumed that blacks wanted nothing more than this. Thus, slaveholders had little patience with slaves who wanted an education. In fact, it was illegal to teach a slave to read or write. Slaves who wanted to survive were well advised to show little or no ambition or motivation. Many of the slaves came to accept these expectations themselves.[25]

The social system that developed after slavery provided more personal freedom but few opportunities for blacks to succeed as other Americans were encouraged to do. Patterns of prejudice and discrimination still excluded blacks from any opportunities to advance themselves. The black family, which was largely *matriarchal* (i.e. female-headed), was less stable than the families of many immigrant groups and did not provide the solid encouragement for males to succeed through aggressiveness and determination.[26] In addition to the effects of slavery, there was the fact of visibility, or what sociologist Erving Goffman has called "the badge of color."[27] It was much easier for those of European ancestry to become less distinguishable from the general population by learning English and possibly by anglicizing their names. Black Americans usually remained visible and distinct regardless of what they did. Thus, the prejudice and discrimination that affected various European groups for perhaps one generation have continued to be the lot of most black Americans. Black Ameri-

Figure 11.1 Median Income by Race, 1977. U.S. Bureau of the Census, *Current Population Reports,* Series P-60, no. 116, "Money Income and Poverty Status of Families and Persons in the United States: 1977," advance report (Washington, D.C.: U.S. Government Printing Office, 1978), p. 1.

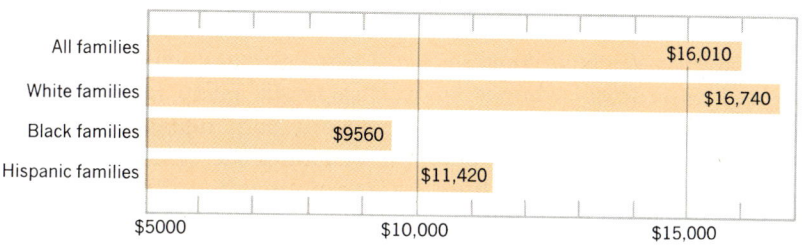

All families	$16,010
White families	$16,740
Black families	$9560
Hispanic families	$11,420

$5000 $10,000 $15,000

cans found difficulty blending into the great American "melting pot." This situation also led to feelings of both hopelessness and hostility on the part of many blacks. In view of the systematic discrimination in housing, education, employment, and almost every other aspect of social relations, the struggle to climb out of poverty has been understandably more difficult, more frustrating, and considerably less successful for blacks and other racial minorities than for white immigrants.

Rural Dwellers

Farm Families

There is a strong tendency in American history to glorify the farmer and the virtues of living close to the soil. However, today it is no idyllic existence; the farm family faces many difficult, and in some cases insurmountable, problems—problems that are even more serious for farmers trying to survive on poor, marginal acreage. In 1977, the farm popu-

Figure 11.2 Percentage of People in Various Groups below the Poverty Level, 1976. U.S. Bureau of the Census, *Current Population Reports,* Series P-60, no. 115 (Washington, D.C.: U.S. Government Printing Office, July 1978), pp. 37–38.

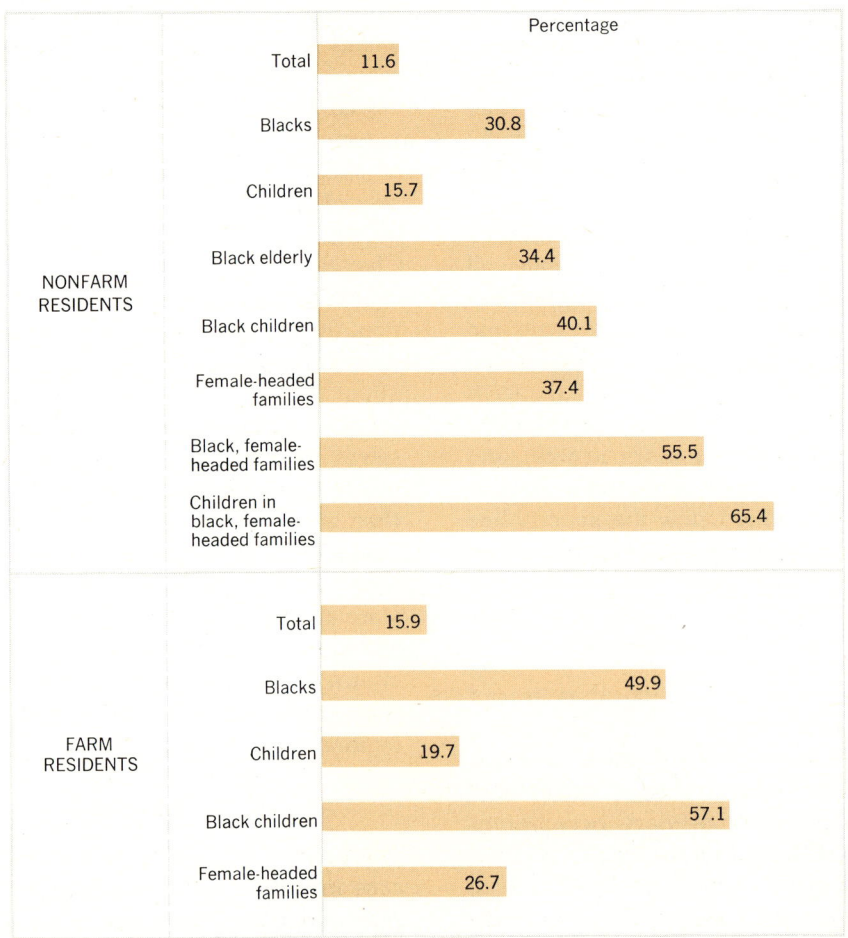

	Percentage
NONFARM RESIDENTS	
Total	11.6
Blacks	30.8
Children	15.7
Black elderly	34.4
Black children	40.1
Female-headed families	37.4
Black, female-headed families	55.5
Children in black, female-headed families	65.4
FARM RESIDENTS	
Total	15.9
Blacks	49.9
Children	19.7
Black children	57.1
Female-headed families	26.7

TABLE 11.3
Per Capita Income for Selected States and Rural Nonfarm Counties (1976)

STATE	PER CAPITA	COUNTY	PER CAPITA
Idaho	$4,417	Custer County	$3,643
Indiana	$4,673	Brown County	$3,944
Kentucky	$4,002	Harlan County	$3,442
Louisiana	$3,922	East Carroll Parish	$2,035
Michigan	$4,884	Keweenaw County	$3,143
Missouri	$4,571	Clark County	$3,092
Virginia	$4,954	Buckingham County	$2,968

SOURCE. U.S. Bureau of the Census, "Population Estimates and Projections," *Current Population Reports.* Series P-25 (Washington, D.C.: U.S. Government Printing Office, January 1979).

lation of the United States was a mere 4 percent of our total population, yet 17.1 percent were classified as poor (compared with 11.3 percent of the nonfarm population).[28] However, these figures do not tell the whole story since some groups are especially hard-hit. For example, almost one-half of the blacks living on farms are poor, and fully 57 percent of the black children on farms are poor (see Fig. 11.2).

While these figures describe disproportionate poverty among farm people, they cannot convey all of the special difficulties that make being poor in a rural area so trying. In rural areas, health care and social services are not as readily available as in urban areas; houses are less likely to have such modern amenities as indoor plumbing; employment opportunities are much more scarce; and transportation needs and costs are usually greater. Thus the farm family living below the poverty line may actually be worse off than its nonfarm counterpart.[29]

The Other Rural America

There is a large rural population that is not engaged in farming. In Appalachia, the Southwest, the Upper Great Lakes, and a number of other areas of the country, there are large numbers of rural, nonfarm poor. Their primary occupations vary with the region. Many have no regular occupation and little prospect of finding one. Some of these groups have received much attention in writings on rural poverty. For example, the miners,

would-be farmers, and unemployed in Appalachia have been described in works such as *Everything in Its Path*.[30] Other groups remain less visible. The woods workers of the Upper Great Lakes region, many of whom make a marginal living, have received little attention. Still others, such as the migrant workers in the western states, have come to public attention in large part because of their own efforts and those of labor organizations such as the United Farm Workers headed by Cesar Chavez.

Unlike the urban poor or the poor farm population, these groups tend not to be included in efforts by the federal government to collect information about the poor. Because of this lack of data, and because these groups are so different among themselves in terms of occupation and geographical location, we know less about rural nonfarm poor than we do about other categories of poor people. Table 11.3 illustrates that rural nonfarm counties tend to have lower per capita incomes than the state average. It is clear that there is substantially less income available in these areas. The desperate character of their plight is increased by the fact that there are few job opportunities in such regions.

The Elderly

The specter of poverty relentlessly stalks Americans into their "golden years." For those in poverty, reaching old age often means a worsening of their position. For others, their sixty-fifth birthday

" I'VE TRIED DOG FOOD, BUT BOTH THE CONSISTENCY AND TASTE ARE VERY UNPLEASANT. ALSO, THE INGREDIENTS ARE QUESTIONABLE. I PREFER CAT FOOD. "

Although this cartoon has a humorous vein, it has been documented that poor people have, on occasion, consumed pet food.

may mark the entrance into poverty. In 1977, 13 percent of persons over 65 had incomes below the poverty level. While this figure is high, some subgroups among the elderly are even worse off. In nonmetropolitan areas, for example, in 1976 the figure was 19.8 percent compared to 12.1 percent in metropolitan areas. Also, 17.9 percent of women over 65 were poor compared to 10.8 percent of men. Even more dramatic, 34.8 percent of blacks in this age group were poor compared to 13.2 percent of whites.[31]

The Young

The largest single group of poor in the United States is children under the age of 18. This group is significant not only because of its size but also because, as an old saying goes, "the child is father to the man." The experiences of children will have a substantial impact on how well they will perform as adults. The incidence of poverty among this group thus has far-reaching implications for the future. In 1976, over 10 million children under the age of 18 were classified as poor — 15.8 percent of all such children.[32] Considering the incidence of poverty in the general population, this figure is not surprising. However, a more detailed examination of the data leads to some shocking conclusions (see Fig. 11.3). **Children in black families and female-headed families are disproportionately represented among the poor.**

Children living in these kinds of families will have considerably fewer opportunities to succeed in the future, compared to nonpoor children. They are trapped in the vicious cycle of generation after generation of poverty. Sociologist Daniel Moynihan has argued that the female-headed black family is the major culprit in that it ill-prepares the young to succeed in our society.[33] Others have argued that racism more than family structure accounts for the disproportionate poverty among female-headed black families.[34] Yet the fact remains that the condition persists and may have significant repercussions in the future.

Because of the special ramifications of poverty among children, a number of programs have been established to offset its effects. Head Start and Title I of the Elementary and Secondary Education Act of 1965 were designed to make funds available to support special programs for low-income children in both public and private schools. In addition, school busing, which has been mainly directed at racial desegregation, is also intended to bring poor black children into greater contact with middle-class white children in the hope of alleviating the negative educational implications of poverty. Overall, dealing with poverty among children may prove most difficult and frustrating and yet most fruitful in terms of long-term consequences.

CAUSES OF POVERTY

Any program to alleviate the plight of the poor must be based on a solid understanding of why

		UNDER 18	UNDER 6
ALL PERSONS	All races	15.8	17.7
	White	11.3	13.0
	Black	40.4	41.9
PERSONS IN FAMILIES WITH MALE HEADS	All races	8.5	9.4
	White	7.1	8.1
	Black	19.4	18.3
PERSONS IN FAMILIES WITH FEMALE HEADS	All races	52.0	64.3
	White	42.7	59.2
	Black	65.6	70.4

Figure 11.3 Percentage of Children under 18 and under 6 Living below the Poverty Level, 1976. U.S. Bureau of the Census, *Current Population Reports,* Series P-60, no. 115 (Washington, D.C.: U.S. Government Printing Office, July 1978), p. 37.

The conditions under which many black youths live often serves to maintain the vicious circle that is characteristic of poverty in America.

poverty exists. There are many positions on this issue, and there is a considerable degree of controversy over the importance of each. Some approaches focus on those factors that bring about poverty, while others deal with social processes that help to perpetuate poverty once it exists. We will discuss both types of approaches. Although theories about the cause of poverty do not fit neatly into one theoretical perspective, our three perspectives serve as a guide to the various approaches. Regardless which one is used, it should become clear to the student that the poor are to a large extent victims of forces that they have had little role in creating.

Functionalism and the "Inevitability of Poverty"

The functionalist perspective has served as an important source of explanations for poverty. The conclusion that many functionalists arrive at—that poverty is inevitable—is rather unpalatable to many. Let us see how they arrive at that conclusion.

Poverty as Motivation

According to functionalists Kingsley Davis and Wilbert Moore, a person's position in the class structure of society depends on the importance of the contribution he or she makes to the functioning of the whole society.[35] The more important the contribution, the higher a person's position in the class structure will be and the greater the rewards, such as money or status, that person will receive. Furthermore, this differential allocation of rewards is necessary and functional because it serves to motivate people to take on, and perform well at, arduous and complex but essential tasks. The amount of rewards that are allocated for a particular task depend on (1) the importance of the task, (2) the scarcity of people with the talents and abilities to perform that task, and (3) the difficulty and length of training for the task. **According to this functionalist position, those people who perform tasks that are of little use to society or who perform no tasks at all should receive few, if any, rewards.** Thus, if the consequence of not

contributing to society is poverty, this will motivate people to strive for, and perform well at, the jobs important to society.

The functionalist position can be illustrated with sample occupations. Physicians receive high rewards because they perform a functionally important task and possess skills that are in relatively short supply. In addition, their training is long and arduous. It would be difficult, if not impossible, to motivate people to become physicians if this did not entail substantial rewards. A garbage collector, on the other hand, performs an important activity, but it requires relatively little training, and there is no shortage of people who can be garbage collectors. As a consequence the rewards, although adequate, are substantially lower than they are for physicians. From the functionalist view, poor people perform no important tasks, and they properly receive few rewards.

Study of the class structure in the United States provides some support for this functionalist view of poverty—there is a partial relationship between the contributions a person makes and the level of reward that person receives. However, this position has been criticized because there are so many exceptions—cases where people are rewarded but make little apparent essential contribution to society (e.g. musicians, professional athletes, and producers of nonessential items such as cotton candy). Likewise, there are many who make important contributions and whose skills are in short supply, such as nurses, who receive relatively small rewards. Despite these criticisms, it is clear that Davis and Moore have located some factors that must be considered in developing poverty programs.

The Positive Functions of Poverty

Davis and Moore point out that one important function of poverty is to motivate people to work. To them, poverty is functional for the system as a whole. However, poverty is also functional for particular groups in society. Sociologist Herbert Gans has argued that poverty is beneficial to some groups (such as social workers and penologists) while at the same time it is detrimental to another group (the poor).[36] Poverty continues to exist partly because it is functional for some groups.

According to Gans, the poor perform functions that are beneficial to various groups in society:

1. they are available to do the unpleasant jobs that no one else wants to do;
2. by their activities, they subsidize the more affluent;
3. jobs are established for those people, such as social workers, who provide services to the poor;
4. they purchase goods, such as those of poor quality, that otherwise could not be sold;
5. they serve as examples of deviance that are frowned on by the majority and that thereby support dominant norms;
6. they provide an opportunity for others to practice their "Christian duty" of helping the less fortunate;
7. they make mobility more likely for others because they are removed from the competition for a good education and good jobs;
8. they contribute to cultural activities by providing, for example, cheap labor for the construction of monuments and works of art;
9. they create cultural forms (e.g. jazz and the blues) that are often adopted by the affluent;
10. they serve as symbolic opponents for some political groups and as constituents for others;
11. they often absorb the costs of change (e.g. by being the victims of high levels of unemployment that result from technological advances).

There may, of course be *functional alternatives* to poverty — alternative social arrangements that could perform these same functions. However, the groups who benefit from the status quo would undoubtedly resist most of these alternatives since they would require some redistribution of wealth and power. Thus, Gans would argue, poverty may not be inevitable, but it is likely to continue as long as it performs these positive functions for groups.

From the functionalist perspective, we see that the poor are poor either because of functions they do not perform *or* because of functions they do perform. Since this situation is functional either for the system as a whole (the Davis and Moore argument) or for those groups within the system who have greater influence in determining its operation (the Gans argument), poverty will persist. There is yet a third functionalist argument for the persistence of poverty.

Poverty and the Economy

The Davis and Moore argument is that poverty will exist in any society because all societies must motivate people to fill important positions. Some have argued, however, that there are peculiar characteristics of the American economy (and possibly all industrial economies) that make some poverty inevitable, even though poverty need not exist in all societies.

In an economy such as ours, characterized by limited competition and an emphasis on achievement, there will be both "winners" and "losers." If rewards are based on competition between individuals, then there must always be some people who lose out in the competition and who are thus poor relative to others (although the degree of poverty may vary greatly).

A somewhat different, although related, argument has been advanced by professional economists. Many economists believe that productivity and employment are linked to the level of inflation.[37] As unemployment increases, people have less money to buy goods, and thus there is less competition for the goods available. Less competition for goods means stable or falling prices. With higher levels of employment, people have more money to spend. This increased demand leads to rising prices for goods — inflation.

As politicians and economists came to accept these conclusions, the United States government, beginning in 1946, attempted to regulate the American economy by controlling the money supply. In effect, this regulation has amounted to curbing inflation by allowing unemployment to increase. Those who are disproportionately affected by rising unemployment are, of course, the poor and the near-poor. So, proponents of this position argue, poverty is the price we must pay for regulating the economy and controlling the negative consequences of inflation.[38]

Poverty as Conflict

Some modern writers have taken exactly the opposite approach from that of the functionalists.[39] **Rather than viewing poverty as inevitable or functional, they argue that the poor are poor because they are exploited by more powerful groups who benefit from the existence of poverty.** Furthermore, these conflict theorists argue that the functionalist position has been used as a smoke screen by dominant groups to legitimize their own position. The so-called objective work of social scientists who take the functionalist perspective has actually served to justify the existing social order.

People are poor, in this conflict view, because they are exploited and powerless. Since, in this case, poverty is perpetuated because it benefits certain groups, it is the power of these groups that must be challenged in order to attack the problem. The conflict view is in sharp contrast to the view of those who rely on the initiative of the powerful (such as the federal government or philanthropic foundations) for a solution. It would be to the advantage of the powerful to *appear* to solve the poverty problem while actually changing nothing. For example, a January 1976 report of the Congressional Budget Office (CBO) argues that, if the in-kind contributions to the poor were added to their income (which is not currently done in computing annual income), the result would place about half of the present poverty population above the poverty line.[40] But this is merely statistical manipulation—the condition of the poor will not actually have changed. Yet the CBO argued that the status of the poor had improved, even though poor people were actually losing ground *relative to* the rest of the population. In evaluating this effort, Harrington dismisses the possibility that the report's conclusions might have been the result of a lack of information by citing Gunner Myrdal's contention that "ignorance is never random." Put another way, Harrington suggests that the CBO has selected figures that underestimate the amount of poverty and thus constitute a rationale for taking less action. It is to the government's benefit to appear to attack poverty even if little is actually done.

Blocked Opportunity

The *blocked opportunity* thesis, originally developed by Richard Cloward and Lloyd Ohlin to explain crime and delinquency, was eventually instrumental in shaping the War on Poverty.[41] **According to social scientists Cloward and Ohlin, people are prone to crime, delinquency, or poverty because they have few, if any, other opportunities available to them.** Their opportunities for success through the accepted channels—education and working at a legitimate occupation—are blocked. They do not have the education or the training to hold a job that will keep them out of poverty. According to this approach, people will pursue socially acceptable avenues of achievement if such opportunities are made available. However, when the opportunities are blocked, people either attempt to achieve success through illegitimate means such as crime or simply slide into poverty. Many federal poverty programs are designed to attack this problem by making available to people the training that will enable them to retain good jobs.

Although few would argue with the basic premise of the blocked opportunity thesis, there is intense controversy over its implications. Some functionalists would argue that the lack of skills and training among certain groups is a sign that the system is not fully integrated. It would be beneficial to society, then, to make training available so that all members of society—even the poor—can make a contribution. Conflict theorists, on the other hand, would point out that some groups benefit because the opportunity of others is blocked. Groups use whatever resources they have available—political power, discrimination, oppression—to ensure opportunities for themselves, even if that means blocking the path of some other group. The conflict theorist would not view blocked opportunities as simply a malfunction in the system. Rather, they are an inherent part of any system. It might take the form of racism or sexism or some other form of discrimination. The route to a solution to the poverty problem will be quite different depending on whether one views blocked opportunities from the functionalist or the conflict perspective.

The Culture of Poverty

We have already seen that poverty can be defined as a cultural phenomenon — a set of beliefs, attitudes, values, and behavior that are distinctive of the poor. The notion of the *culture of poverty* **was developed with this in mind.**[42] **Proponents of the culture of poverty point out that the long-term poor often share common cultural characteristics and values that separate them from other groups in society and that make it difficult for them to struggle out of poverty.** This culture of poverty is viewed as an adaptive response to the hopelessness, deprivation, and lack of opportunity that are the daily companions of the poor.

According to proponents of the culture-of-poverty theory, poor families are likely to be unstable, headed by females, and less able to respond to the needs of the children. There is considerable discontinuity in family life, with marriages dissolving and the makeup of the family changing. Such a family does not provide the supportive and stable environment that would enable the young to acquire the skills and motivation to work their way out of the cycle of poverty. In addition, the poor are isolated from the centers of decision making about their lives. They do not involve themselves in political activities or join groups that might exert political influence.

Because of these experiences, the poor feel cut off from the "system," from the sources of power in American society. They tend to give up and see little point in making any efforts to exert an influence. The poor tend to be fatalistic — they feel that they have little control over what happens to them and thus become resigned to the degrading and unpleasant conditions in which they live. The culture of poverty is also marked by a *present-time orientation* — a tendency to seek gratification in the present and not worry about the future. Long-range plans and goals are secondary to pleasurable pursuits in the present.

The proponents of this culture-of-poverty theory argue that the culture tends to be self-perpetuating. The poor raise their children with the values and attitudes common to this culture, and these attitudes and values make it extremely difficult for the children to get out of poverty. So they face a vicious cycle of poverty — one generation unintentionally bestowing upon its children precisely those characteristics that will condemn most of the new generation to continued poverty.

Criticisms of Culture-of-Poverty Theory

The notion that a culture of poverty exists has had important implications for social policy and in fact helped initiate the War on Poverty of the 1960s. Yet there has been considerable reservation about whether it is an accurate description of all, or even most, of the poor.[43] For example, one study of people receiving public assistance in California found that the characteristics described by the theory existed but that they were more common among Hispanic Americans than among whites or blacks. Furthermore, this was true for those receiving public assistance as well as for those who were not.[44] Other studies have shown that the traits usually associated with the culture of poverty can be found in less than one-half of the poor.[45] These findings suggest, first, that the characteristics of the culture of poverty are less common among the poor than the proponents of the theory have argued, and second, that these characteristics may be a part of the culture of certain groups in our society (e.g. Hispanic Americans) rather than simply the result of poverty.

Culture-of-poverty theory has also been faulted for taking the stance of "blaming the victim" for his condition.[46] People are poor, according to the theory, because they have certain characteristics that make success difficult, and they pass these characteristics on to their children. In a sense, then, individual inadequacy is at the core of this explanation of poverty. Such a stance ignores the lack of opportunity, the discrimination, and the prejudice that cause much poverty. To that extent, it absolves the social arrangements that protect the dominant groups from being charged with any fault in the process.

Interactionism, Societal Reaction and Poverty

The interactionist perspective is particularly useful in helping us understand some of the mechanisms operating to perpetuate poverty. *Societal reaction theory,* or **labeling theory,** is a version of the interactionist perspective. As such, it focuses on the manner in which people's behavior is shaped by learned expectations. This theory pays special attention to the way in which a self-concept and expectations are learned through interaction with others.

Howard S. Becker, a proponent of the interactionist perspective, argues that a member of a subculture learns the roles, rules, and general outlook of that subculture.[47] Unless the person has strong attachments to other groups, he or she is likely to begin to identify with the subculture and its members. Eventually, members of this subculture, as well as those who are part of the larger culture, may begin to define or label the individual as a member of the subculture. The person may in turn come to accept these labels and a self-definition as a member of the subculture. This process—which is important in learning to become a rock musician, a delinquent, a barber, or a doctor—involves a person's accepting a self-conception based on the way others perceive and react to him or her. It is important to realize that this process does not occur at a single moment but rather over a long period of time.

This labeling process can affect poor people as well. In our culture poor people are defined negatively, and numerous undesirable traits are attributed to them. They are characterized as lazy, stupid, immoral, and lacking in initiative and aggressiveness (recall the respondents in social worker Tropman's study). If these reactions from other people are consistent and continuous—and especially if they come from important individuals, such as family, friends, or teachers—then the individual (especially in childhood) is likely to accept this definition.

The labeling of poor persons as inadequate and the acceptance of the label by the poor themselves contributes to the perpetuation of poverty. This labeling process may take place in many different contexts and among different groups. In a study of a St. Louis housing project, one researcher found that mothers and other female relatives tended to label male children as irresponsible and unreli-

able.[48] Some males came to incorporate these labels as a part of their self-concept and to behave in accordance with the expectations associated with such a self-concept.

Of all the labeling that takes place, the most devastating may occur in the schools. Americans believe that hard work and an education will enable one to get ahead. Yet research has shown that low-socioeconomic-status (SES) children are far less likely to complete their education. The reasons for this failure are complex; but the attitudes of teachers is one important factor. Studies done over more than forty years have demonstrated that schools and schoolteachers tend to have a strong middle-class bias such that poor children begin school with a built-in disadvantage.[49] Middle-class children are rewarded for doing what they have learned at home and therefore have a head start; lower-class children have not learned these behaviors that teachers desire. In a 1968 study, social psychologists Robert Rosenthal and Lenore Jacobson demonstrated that, when teachers believe that children will perform at a high achievement level, the chances of this improvement occurring are greatly increased.[50] Although these writers' methodology has been subject to some criticism, it seems clear that the labeling of school children as successes or failures by their teachers has a considerable influence on their actual chances of success; furthermore, middle-class children are more likely to be labeled successful than are lower-class children. Whether it comes from parents or children, the consequence is the same—a negative self-concept that reduces the likelihood that the poor person will be able to change his or her station in society.

Welfare and Poverty

The number of people receiving welfare and the amount of money spent on welfare has increased by leaps and bounds over the past two decades (see Fig. 11.4). Most people consider welfare to be at least hopefully a part of the solution to the poverty problem. Yet there are some who believe that welfare may actually be a part of the problem itself because it helps to perpetuate poverty rather than eliminate it. For example, one writer argues that there is a **dual welfare system** in the United

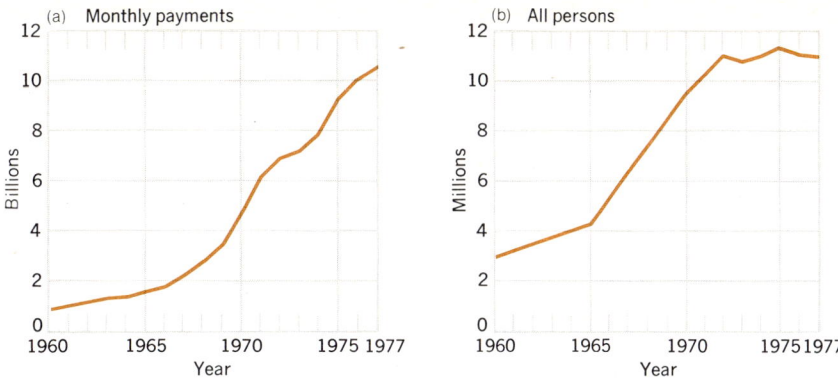

Figure 11.4 Aid to Families with Dependent Children, 1960–1977. "Current Operating Statistics," *Social Security Bulletin* 41 (December 1978), pp. 57–58.

States — one for the poor and one for the affluent.[51] The welfare system serving the affluent consists of the benefits from various types of government subsidies and the tax benefits available to the more affluent. An example of these benefits is the state and federal funding of colleges, universities, and the construction of highways, which tend to be more advantageous to the relatively affluent portions of the population. These benefits for the affluent also include subsidies to agriculture, shipping, railroads, and other special interests; one with widespread impact is the ability of homeowners to

Although public assistance programs such as food stamps are designed to assist the poor, participation in them often carries a stigma that can have negative consequences for the self concepts of poor people.

deduct interest on their home mortgages from their income tax. Many of these benefits are regressive — that is, they increase as income increases. For example, there are provisions of the federal tax law that make it possible for wealthy taxpayers to pay proportionately less tax than do the poor. The above-mentioned researcher pointed out that these subsidies to the affluent are similar to other programs that are considered welfare-based, but they are not usually thought of as welfare, and there is no stigma attached to accepting them.

The other welfare system — the one for the poor — is highly stigmatized. The poor who accept welfare are often defined as lazy, stupid, or incompetent. Some social scientists have observed that if society were to conclude that most poor people are poor because of circumstances beyond their own control, it would follow that others are affluent because of factors mainly unrelated to their own efforts — which would be in conflict with the American belief in individual achievement.

Because of the negative value placed on welfare for the poor, such programs are usually funded at a level considerably lower than that of the other welfare system. One investigator points out: "In Mississippi the average monthly Aid to Families with Dependent Children payment per recipient was only $14.39. In that same state, a corporate farm, Eastland, Inc., owned by the family of the U.S. Senator, received over $250,000 annually in various farm subsidies."[52] In fact, the economic position of the poor has actually declined relative to other parts of the population. As Figure 11.5 shows, the median income in the United States has risen at a considerably faster rate than the income cutoff for poverty. The gap between the nonpoor and the poor has grown larger.

The following account, although fictionalized, illustrates the tendency of people to view government payments to the poor as welfare while refusing to perceive government financial support for the affluent as welfare:

A young man lived . . . in Hamilton County. He attended public school, rode the free school bus, enjoyed the free lunch program.

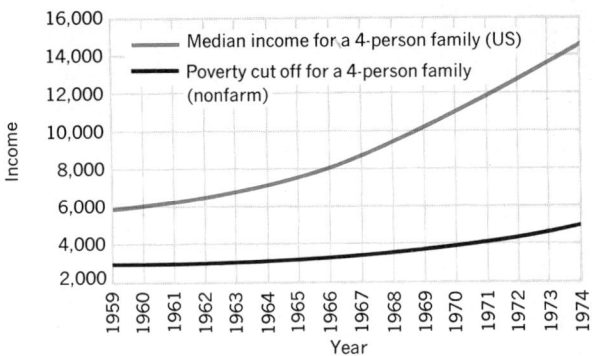

Figure 11.5 Comparison of Median Family Income and Official Poverty Cutoff for a Family of Four, 1959–1974. U.S. Department of Health, Education, and Welfare, *The Measure of Poverty* (Washington, D.C.: U.S. Government Printing Office, April 1976), p. 72.

Following graduation from high school, he entered the Army and upon discharge kept his National Service Life Insurance. He then enrolled in an Ohio university, receiving regularly his GI check. Upon graduation, he married a Public Health nurse, bought a farm in southern Ohio with an FHA loan.

Later going into the feed and hardware business in addition to farming, he secured help from the Small Business Administration when his business faltered. His first baby was born in the county hospital. This was built in part with Hill-Burton federal funds.

Then he put part of his land under the Eisenhower Soil Bank Program and used the payments for not growing crops to help pay his debts. His parents, elderly by now, were living comfortably in the smaller of his two farm houses, using their Social Security and the Old Age Assistance checks. Medicare covered most of their doctor and hospital bills. Lacking electricity at first, he got the Rural Electrification Administration to supply the lines. A loan from the Farmers Home Administration helped clear the land and secure the best from it. That agency suggested building a pond, and the government stocked it with fish.

The government guaranteed him a sale for his farm products. The county public library delivered books to his farm door. He, of course, banked his money in an institution which a federal agency had insured up to $15,000 for every depositor. As the community grew, he signed a petition to help the economy in his area. About that time, he purchased a business and real estate at the county seat, aided by an FHA loan. His children in college received financial assistance from the federal government, his son under the National Defense Student Loan Program and his daughter under the Nurse Training Act. Both lived in dormitories and studied in classrooms paid for with federal funds. He was elected to office in the local Chamber of Commerce. A little later it was rumored he joined a cell of the John Birch Society and also the Liberty Lobby, both right-wing extremist groups.

He wrote his Senators and Congressman denouncing excessive government spending, Medicare, big government, United Nations, high taxes, etc. and enclosed John Birch propaganda pamphlets, some containing outlandishly false statements. He wrote:

I believe in rugged individualism. People should stand on their own two feet. I oppose all those social trends you have been voting for and demand return to the free enterprise system of our forefathers.[53]

Not only are the two welfare systems defined and funded differently, but there are gradations in the system serving the poor. One writer points out that programs for the aged, blind, and permanently disabled, while small, still provide more aid than those serving the more highly stigmatized poor—Aid to Families with Dependent Children (AFDC) and general relief. Since persons served by these latter programs, especially general relief, are seen as having the least excuse for their condition, the programs are funded at the lowest levels. Furthermore, the benefits from these programs are highly variable in different parts of the country, as Figure 11.6 illustrates.

Another problem with the dual welfare system is that, given most welfare regulations, there are built-in disincentives for poor people to work. Because of this, it is very difficult for people to get out of poverty, and this is why some people view welfare as a part of the problem of poverty rather than a solution to it. For example, for each dollar earned through wages and salaries by the welfare recipient, the individual loses one dollar in aid—an effective tax rate of 100 percent. This does little to en-

courage people to seek out work—especially if the only job options are low-paying jobs. In this same context, the system as presently constituted creates great inequities. The person who is just above the poverty cutoff (commonly referred to as the "knotch") may actually receive less real income than a person just below the cutoff (see Table 11.1). One way of resolving this inequity, or at least reducing some of its more painful effects, would be to raise poverty cutoffs. However, this would be difficult because the number and type of local, state, and federal welfare programs is mind-boggling.

POVERTY IN AMERICA: PROSPECTS FOR THE FUTURE

Few people would balk at the statement that something should be done about poverty. Grandiose pontifications about how poverty will be attacked have been made by both government leaders and private philanthropists for many years. Yet, poverty is still with us. One reason for this intractable nature of poverty is that, to eliminate it, it would be necessary either to redistribute existing wealth or to locate new sources of wealth. Although there are some possibilities for generating new wealth, it is no easy task. The idea of redistributing wealth is extremely controversial. Indeed, as presidential candidate George McGovern found out in 1972 when he proposed a radically altered tax structure that favored the poor, even modest proposals for income redistribution prove unpopular with a majority of the electorate.

Assuming, however, that this resistance could be overcome, the meaning of poverty goes far beyond that of a mere lack of money. If there are to be effective remedies, they must come to grips with the nonmonetary aspects of poverty that we have examined.

Interpersonal Involvement and Individual Worth

In our discussion of labeling, we suggested that a major problem for poor people is their negative self-concept. If an individual is repeatedly labeled as a failure, he may accept this designation as a

Figure 11.6 Average Monthly Public Assistance Money Payment Per Recipient, December 1976. U.S. Department of Health, Education, and Welfare, Social and Rehabilitation Service, *Public Assistance Statistics, December 1976,* DHEW Publication no. (SRS) 77-03100 (Washington, D.C.: U.S. Government Printing Office, April 1977).

AVERAGE MONTHLY PUBLIC ASSISTANCE MONEY PAYMENT PER RECIPIENT, DECEMBER 1976

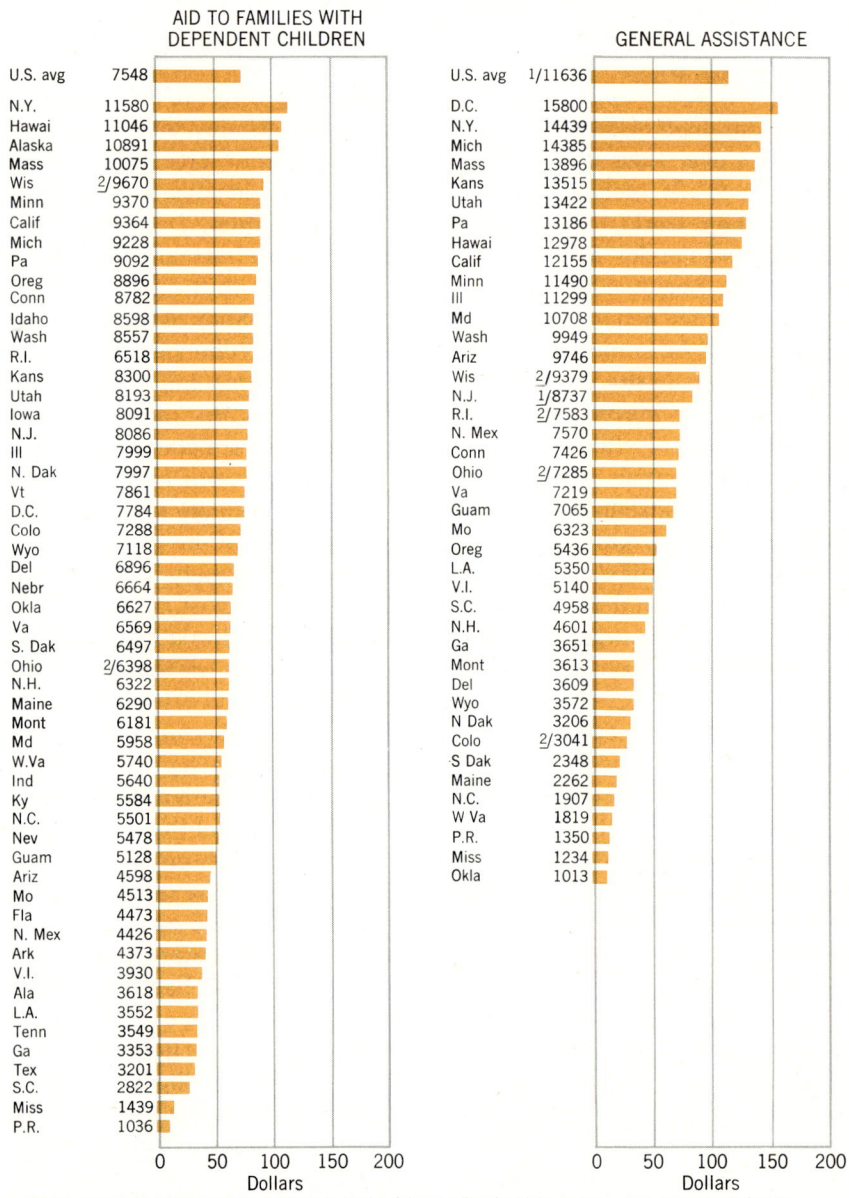

AID TO FAMILIES WITH DEPENDENT CHILDREN

U.S. avg	7548
N.Y.	11580
Hawai	11046
Alaska	10891
Mass	10075
Wis	2/9670
Minn	9370
Calif	9364
Mich	9228
Pa	9092
Oreg	8896
Conn	8782
Idaho	8598
Wash	8557
R.I.	6518
Kans	8300
Utah	8193
Iowa	8091
N.J.	8086
Ill	7999
N. Dak	7997
Vt	7861
D.C.	7784
Colo	7288
Wyo	7118
Del	6896
Nebr	6664
Okla	6627
Va	6569
S. Dak	6497
Ohio	2/6398
N.H.	6322
Maine	6290
Mont	6181
Md	5958
W.Va	5740
Ind	5640
Ky	5584
N.C.	5501
Nev	5478
Guam	5128
Ariz	4598
Mo	4513
Fla	4473
N. Mex	4426
Ark	4373
V.I.	3930
Ala	3618
L.A.	3552
Tenn	3549
Ga	3353
Tex	3201
S.C.	2822
Miss	1439
P.R.	1036

GENERAL ASSISTANCE

U.S. avg	1/11636
D.C.	15800
N.Y.	14439
Mich	14385
Mass	13896
Kans	13515
Utah	13422
Pa	13186
Hawai	12978
Calif	12155
Minn	11490
Ill	11299
Md	10708
Wash	9949
Ariz	9746
Wis	2/9379
N.J.	1/8737
R.I.	2/7583
N. Mex	7570
Conn	7426
Ohio	2/7285
Va	7219
Guam	7065
Mo	6323
Oreg	5436
L.A.	5350
V.I.	5140
S.C.	4958
N.H.	4601
Ga	3651
Mont	3613
Del	3609
Wyo	3572
N Dak	3206
Colo	2/3041
S Dak	2348
Maine	2262
N.C.	1907
W Va	1819
P.R.	1350
Miss	1234
Okla	1013

Dollars — 0 50 100 150 200

Dollars — 0 50 100 150 200

1/Base on data for 42 states. Does not include Alaska, Arkansas, Florida, Idaho, Indiana, Iowa, Kentucky, Nebraska, Nevada, Tennessee, Texas and Vermont; data not reported, not computed for Alabama. Fewer than 50 recipients. Data for New Jersey include assistance to the working poor program 2/Estimated

part of his self-concept. As we know from the interactionist perspective, what we believe to be real is, for all practical purposes, real in its consequences. It would seem, then, that poverty could be attacked by bringing about changes in the individual's self-concept so that he or she will be better able to do those things essential to getting out of poverty.

Changing the Poor

One way to change the ingrained belief of the poor that they have no control over their destiny is to give them the experience of successfully bringing about some change in their world or achieving some desired goal. One successful achievement can make inroads into the negative feeling that they cannot succeed. Once they begin to feel that success is possible, there will be some motivation and desire to make new efforts in the future. They will begin to feel some sense of mastery and control. Many attempts to organize the poor have utilized these principles. For example, in the 1960s the United Farm Workers Organizing Committee (UFWOC), led by Cesar Chavez, began an effort to organize the farm workers in California, most of whom were Mexican American and all of whom were bitterly deprived. In the early stages, the farm workers were extremely skeptical and very reluctant to flock to the ranks of UFWOC. However, as the fasts, strikes and boycotts organized by UFWOC showed some success—especially a very effective nationwide boycott of California grapes—the skepticism began to dwindle, and the previously docile farm workers began to realize that the right type of efforts could help them achieve their goals. Thus, success motivates one toward more effort, which in turn increases the likelihood of future success.

Efforts such as these, to change the self-concept of the poor, are not without their problems. History is strewn with numerous examples of programs that failed and simply reinforced the belief of the poor that they were basically powerless and ineffectual. A program must be designed to avoid this. A community organizer working with the poor should initially select target projects, not so much for their long-range impact on poverty, but rather for their short-range feasibility and likelihood of success. Since the poor are used to failure, subsequent failures will simply confirm their existing beliefs and discredit the organizer. Early successes are essential to creating a positive self-concept among the poor and enlisting their help for future actions.[54]

Head Start

If it were possible to intervene before such negative self-concepts develop, many problems would be much easier to solve. It is for this reason that much recent effort in poverty programs has been directed toward children. This emphasis is important because, as we have already seen, children have less experience with the culture of poverty and the negative socialization associated with it, and it is therefore easier to change their beliefs about the world. A program that has received the most attention, and at times the most criticism, is one directed primarily toward poor preschool children. This program, which came into being as a part of the Economic Opportunity Act of 1964, is *Head Start*.

Like many of the programs created by the Economic Opportunity Act, the rationale for Head Start was, at least in part, based on the "blocked opportunity" thesis discussed earlier. The proponents of the act felt that, if preschool children could be given the kind of positive experience and instruction that they presumably did not receive at home (but which was typical in middle-class families), they would be better able to perform in school and thus break out of the cycle of poverty.

Early research on the effects of Head Start was discouraging. The gains from participation in the program declined as children passed through the first three elementary grades.[55] However, research done since 1969 has been more positive.[56] There are benefits for poor children, their families, and the community. These benefits include cognitive development (intelligence), personal and social development, child health and nutrition, and a more positive attitude on the part of parents toward their children and their community. These findings would seem to indicate that Head Start does make a positive contribution—not only to the children who are its direct participants, but also to their families and indirectly to the community as a whole.

Head Start is not the only program that serves the poor, although it has been one of the most successful. While we might consider other efforts, it is clear from what we have seen that, if poverty is to be alleviated, the disadvantages associated with labeling and negative socialization experiences must be overcome. Furthermore, the efforts to accomplish this will be most fruitful among children, where there is the greatest probability of breaking the vicious circle of intergenerational poverty.

A New War on Poverty

Many efforts to alleviate poverty in the United States are based on the assumption that such a goal can be achieved only if there is substantial involvement by the federal government. In addition, it is felt that this can be done only if there is a commitment of resources that goes far beyond the original War on Poverty. In fact, some have called for a New War on Poverty that will marshal massive resources and hopefully be the death knell of poverty in the United States. In order to evaluate the feasibility of such an option, it is helpful to examine the original War on Poverty and what it achieved.

The Economic Opportunity Act of 1964 established the Office of Economic Opportunity (OEO) at the national level and the Community Action Agency (CAA) and its Community Action Program (CAP) at the local level.[57] The impetus for OEO and CAP grew out of community development work in the United States and in the developing countries. There was included in the Act a provision for the "maximum feasible participation of the poor." The implications of this provision were not imagined by the authors of the Act, and for a time there was much controversy over its interpretation. Essentially, *maximum feasible participation* came to mean that poor persons were to be involved in the activities of the local community action agencies, not only as staff members but also on policy-making boards.

Within a short time, CAAs were founded throughout the country. By 1966, more than 900

grants had been made for the planning of community action programs—all of the fifty largest cities in the country had CAPs, and programs were operating in more than a thousand counties.[58]

Despite this beginning, community action never achieved the goals that were expected of it. There are a number of reasons for this failure. First, groups with a vested interest in the status quo were unwilling to accept the kinds of changes that true "maximum feasible participation" on the part of the poor might have brought about. Many were unwilling to let the poor determine what was in their own best interests. Second, the radicalism of many middle-class people who functioned as leaders in local CAP programs tended to arouse opposition among the generally conservative local leaders. Third, resources that might have supported this "War on Poverty" were siphoned off to pay for the Vietnam war. Fourth, Congress became sufficiently aroused over these problems to pass an amendment (the Green Amendment) that severely limited participation of the poor in the administration of CAP programs.[59]

After Richard Nixon became president, government policy toward the war on poverty took the form of systematic attempts to dismantle OEO. Today, although the agency continues as the Community Services Administration, it has been greatly modified. Not only have most of the more radical individuals and programs been eliminated, but funding has been directed toward more politically acceptable programs such as Head Start.

Does this mean that all federal efforts to help the poor are doomed to failure? Not at all. There are a number of weaknesses in current welfare programs that will almost surely make it difficult for them to succeed. First, the financial support given to people is often too low to truly make possible an improvement in their lives. Second, support is often given or withheld for reasons other than financial. In some cases, welfare administrators make arbitrary and unjust decisions about who should receive aid. For some programs, aid cannot be provided if there is an able-bodied male in the house. Third, there is little incentive in most programs for the recipient to find work and get off welfare. In many cases, the working poor are excluded from benefits.[60]

If a welfare system could be designed that could overcome these difficulties, its chances of achieving its goals would be much greater. Some efforts have been made in this direction. *Income maintenance programs* (also called Negative Income Tax programs) have been devised in which a person does not lose welfare payments equal to the wages earned. In other words, the person might lose $1 of welfare payments for each $2 earned in wages, until some designated cutoff point. This provides an incentive for the person to work since a part of any wages earned are added to the welfare payments. These programs also provide assistance to the working poor by providing them with supplementary assistance to bring their income up to the designated level.[61]

One concern with such programs is that the worker might respond to this added income by working less — with the income supplement it would be possible for the person to work fewer hours and still receive the same income as before the supplements. Studies indicate that this may not be a serious problem.[62] In some studies, the labor force participation for men is unchanged — they continue to work as much after receiving supplementary funds as before. However, some groups, especially black women, do tend to reduce the amount they work after receiving funds. While this might be viewed as bad from the point of view of work incentive, it may be desirable on other grounds. If it allows women to spend more time with their families and create a more stable and orderly homelife, it may in the long run make it more possible for their children to get out of poverty.

The above discussion reveals several problems associated with any attempt to establish a new War on Poverty. Alleviating poverty involves institutional change, and a change of this kind involves inevitable conflict with vested interests. Such groups are unlikely to support programs that they define as contrary to their own interests. If, therefore, a new War on Poverty is to come into being, it will probably require the use of other sources of power, including the poor themselves.

Full Employment

Some have proposed that the poverty problem can be alleviated by changing the structure of the American economy. Some have argued for extreme alterations — such as the elimination of capitalism — while others opt for more modest ones, such as changes in the tax structure that would benefit the poor. We shall focus on one idea that has received much recent attention: *full employment.*

The notion of full employment — everyone who wants a job would have one — would not seem controversial. In fact, most politicians support it, at least in principle. The Full Employment Act of 1946 was intended to achieve this goal in part. More recently, the Full Employment and Balanced Growth Act of 1978 (popularly known as the Humphrey–Hawkins Act) requires that the president establish short-term goals that will lead to full employment (defined as an overall unemployment rate of 4 percent, and an adult unemployment rate of 3 percent). There is considerable disagreement over whether the Humphrey–Hawkins Act is a realistic approach to full employment or whether it is primarily a symbolic but ineffective measure that serves to appease certain interest groups. Despite the debate over this specific piece of legislation, most politicians support the concept of full employment.[63]

Despite their seeming desirability, there has been intense controversy over full employment programs. Some object because they do not believe full employment is possible; others are concerned about the effects of full employment on the American economy. It will be useful to review some of these issues.[64] First, many economists argue that full employment (or anything approaching it) will lead to substantial inflation. It is a trade-off, but many feel that the long-term effects of inflation are much more destructive than a certain amount of unemployment. In fact, economist Robert Lekachman has argued that inflation could be offset only by price regulation and possibly nationalization of parts of the private sector. This is the price for full employment that many are unwilling to pay.

Second, taxation and government subsidies tend to discourage full employment by encouraging investment that favors the use of machines over human beings. It is cheaper to invest in labor-saving machinery than to hire new workers because it is unnecessary to pay social security or health benefits for machines. Third, full employment is in conflict with the view of some economists that a shortage of jobs should always exist so that the jobs available are given to the most qualified applicants. Fourth, full employment per se would not necessarily eliminate poverty since many people might still hold jobs that do not pay above the poverty level.

Given these problems and possible implications, it is not surprising that full employment programs have been so controversial. Whether they can make a sizable dent in the poverty problem remains to be seen.

Training the Poor—
A Functionalist Approach

If, as the functionalists argue, poverty persists because it serves certain functions and because the poor lack skills that are useful and valuable to society, then it would seem that one approach to the problem of poverty would be to train the poor in some useful skills. Beginning with the concern over the "blocked opportunity" thesis in the days of the War on Poverty, a number of programs have been implemented to do this. While the programs are quite varied in form and intent, their basic goals are to provide the poor with skills that will make them employable in today's economy and thus enable them to get out of poverty. Two recent programs are the *Comprehensive Employment and Training Act* (CETA) and Preparation for Employment Program (PREP).[65]

CETA is designed to deal with high unemployment and to give the unemployed needed experience and training. A person may work in a CETA program for a maximum of one year. The reason for this restriction is that the program is intended to provide training and experience rather than permanent employment. It is assumed that after one year the person will be more employable because of the on-the-job experience and training gained. The program is intended as temporary employment focused on reintegrating the worker into the private sector.

PREP is a somewhat different approach to training the poor. It is directed toward welfare mothers and high school dropouts. While the program includes job training, much of the effort is directed

toward the development of self-confidence, a positive self-concept, and good work habits. The rationale is that these personal changes will give people the confidence and motivation to search out opportunities and thus break out of the cycle by which poverty, failure, and welfare dependency are perpetuated. Such efforts at training and educating the poor are tailored to the needs of each individual.

These job training programs have been an important part of our effort to cope with the problem of poverty; they directly attack one of its primary sources. However, they have not been the panacea

Although welfare programs are intended to assist the poor in improving their lot in life, there is considerable debate about the consequences of such assistance. Some have questioned whether welfare helps poor people or whether it perpetuates poverty.

that they were once touted as being, for these programs are based on a central assumption—if job training is provided, then most poor persons can be made employable.[66] Unfortunately, this view overlooks the fact that much poverty will be unaffected even if job skills are widely available. Children, the elderly, and women who are heads of households cannot compete for jobs even despite the availability of job training programs. This is a rather unpleasant conclusion to reach in a society that places great value on individual initiative and achievement. We like to believe that the Horatio Alger myth that hard work will lead to success applies to everyone. Yet the reality is that some categories of poor people will not be able to improve their condition even if the job training programs are available.

Self-Help and Community Organization

The programs we have considered so far are mostly initiated by people other than the poor and then imposed on them. The interests of those who shape and administer the programs do not necessarily coincide with the interests of the poor. In view of this, some have argued that the most effective long-range approach must be based on the poor helping themselves. Only in this way can the poor expect to ensure that programs will serve their needs.

Though self-help is not a new idea, it is more difficult to implement than it might at first appear. In a recent work on neighborhood organizations, social scientist David O'Brien points out that problems in organizing the poor are due not only to the social, cultural, or psychological characteristics of the poor. In addition, difficulties arise because the poor, like any interest group, must find a way to get people to pay—in terms of time, effort, and money —for those gains that will benefit the entire group.[67] O'Brien compares the problem of organizing the poor with the problem of organizing labor unions or any other interest groups. He contends that for organization to be effective, common interests must be identified and recognized. This involves C. Wright Mills's notion of translating "private troubles" into "public issues" (discussed in ch. 1). In addition, the organization must find a method of compelling its members to pay for the benefits that all will receive. Given the alienating and self-defeating experiences of the poor, one can grasp the difficulties of developing an organization such as this among the poor.

Despite these difficulties, some have maintained that it is time for the poor to take matters into their own hands. Strategies calling for a radical reorganization of the social order have been proposed on the grounds that the poor have little to lose and perhaps a great deal to gain. One such strategy was developed by social scientists Richard Cloward and Frances Fox Piven.[68] They recommend the alliance of militant civil rights organizations, antipoverty organizations, and the poor. It is their belief that a coordinated effort would be more productive than is the current situation, in which individual organizations pursue fragmented objectives. The goal of such a coalition would be the fomentation of a political and economic crisis of such proportions that Congress would be forced to enact legislation establishing a guaranteed annual income and thus an end to poverty.

Regardless of whether such legislation would eliminate poverty, we might ask if the Cloward and Piven strategy could possibly produce such a crisis. The answer cannot, at this time, be an unequivocal yes. According to Cloward and Piven, there is a vast discrepancy between the welfare benefits that people actually receive and those to which they are entitled under law. Furthermore, only about half of those eligible for welfare actually receive it. The discrepancy goes unrecognized in a society oriented toward getting people *off* the welfare rolls rather than ensuring that all eligible people are *on* the rolls. Cloward and Piven see this gap as an integral feature of the welfare system—a reflection of our view of the poor as undeserving. They contend that a massive drive, by the coalition of organizations mentioned above, to recruit eligible persons for welfare would create a massive fiscal and administrative crisis. Since the responsibility for many welfare programs has been scattered throughout local and state governments, the problem of coordinating a response to this crisis would be magnified. It is this turmoil, they believe, that would pressure Congress into action.

Obviously this kind of crisis, like others based on disrupting the system, involves certain dangers. Cloward and Piven point out that such strategies could lead to violence, might alienate members of the Democratic party, which has traditionally been supportive of aid to the poor, and could even drive working-class whites out of that party. Yet they argue that the poor have little choice since the Democratic party is no longer proposing realistic solutions to poverty and since existing conditions are as likely to lead to violence as the strategies that they propose.

Cloward and Piven's proposal is only one example, albeit an extreme one, of how the poor might organize to help themselves. Some efforts have been more within the traditional framework of actions taken by American interest groups, such as the organization of the migrant farm workers in California. In whatever form, they are based on the belief that the poor must help themselves, that they can make changes in their lives if they organize effectively, and that only the poor can work in their own best interests.

In this section we have considered a number of possible solutions to the problem of poverty. Each of these has some promise, but at the same time, each possesses deficiencies. In making any policy recommendations, an overriding consideration should be that any solution may affect the vested interests of some segment of society, and to just that extent, the implementation of the solution may be compromised.

CONCLUSION

According to the United States Bureau of the Census, poverty now affects more than 10 percent of our population. Indeed, if poverty were defined as some experts on the subject believe it should be, this figure would be over 25 percent.[69] Given the magnitude of this problem and the shortcomings inherent in proposed solutions, it is unfortunate but probable that poverty will be a feature of our society for a long time to come. We can evaluate some of the important factors in the future of poverty as a social problem in America by utilizing the three theoretical perspectives.

From the functionalist perspective, poverty plays an important role in society: it serves to motivate people to lead productive lives. If the alternative to working hard and contributing to society is poverty, then most people will choose to work. Thus, from this point of view, there are limits to what we might do to relieve the problem of poverty. If there were no sanctions for nonproductivity—for example, if economic resources were distributed somewhat evenly among all members of society—this would be detrimental to the whole system because some important tasks might not be accomplished, or might not be accomplished as effectively as they should be. The functionalist is not arguing that people must be so poor that they starve or experience some other dire consequences. That, too, would be detrimental to the system. However, there must be some differential distribution of rewards so that people find it desirable to take on important tasks. To achieve this, poverty programs should be designed to encourage people to seek productive employment rather than to make poverty itself a not unpleasant condition.

We have seen that poverty can be functional for certain people in society. The conflict theorist would argue that there will be resistance to altering the status quo by those who benefit from poverty, and that, so long as the poor accept their plight, poverty will probably persist. Let us illustrate: a very elaborate analysis of the attitudes and voting behavior of various groups in the United States shows that the American electorate is predominantly "unyoung, unpoor, and unblack."[70] Their values, attitudes, and consequent voting behavior are shaped not by poverty and the needs of the poor but by their own particular needs and social circumstances. In fact, they are likely to see the poor as a threat to their affluence and may not support programs to aid the poor. As a consequence, the majority of those who vote, and consequently those whom policymakers are most likely to heed, are middle-aged, middle-class, nonpoor white people. The government is unlikely to pursue programs that are directed toward the solution of poverty if they run counter to what most of the electorate perceives as their interests.

If those who make crucial political decisions are

most sensitive to "unpoor" people, the outcome is predictable. The original War on Poverty was predicated on the assumption that our economy would continue to grow and that inflation would be manageable. In actual fact, the 1970s have been less than satisfactory in regard to both of these hopes. Any *new* War on Poverty will be in competition for scarce dollars with other national programs. Since many of these programs serve interest groups that have far more power than the poor, the future of poverty programs may be dismal at best.

From the interactionist perspective, poverty is a matter of social definition: people are poor if we define them as such and behave toward them as if they are poor. There is no objectively definable state of poverty, from this viewpoint. This presents

an unsettling possibility when we consider solutions to the problem of poverty: will those groups with the lowest standard of living always be defined as poor even though their objective situation is comparatively comfortable and affluent? The poor in America today, although their condition understandably causes great concern, are much better off than the poor of previous generations. Yet, we have come to expect much more today. As our expectations continue to rise, what we define as poverty in the future may be, by today's standards, not poverty. Thus, from the interactionist perspective, proposed solutions for the problem of poverty will have to take into account this definitional aspect of the problem.

GLOSSARY TERMS

Absolute poverty
Blocked opportunity
Comprehensive Employment
 Training Act
Culture of poverty
Disreputable poor
Displaced homemakers
Dual welfare system

Feudalism
Full employment
Head Start
Income maintenance
 programs
In-kind income
Labeling theory
Maximum feasible

participation
Orshansky's measure of
 poverty
Present-time orientation
Relative poverty
Secularization
Social stratification

REFERENCES

[1] Richard Wright, *Black Boy* (New York: Harper & Row, 1945), p. 21.

[2] Newsbank, Welfare and Poverty, Microfiche Card 13 B9, "Grits But No Eggs" (Annapolis, Md.: *Evening Capital,* March 10, 1977).

[3] Matt. 26:11. (Rev. Standard Version.)

[4] Joan Huber, "Poverty, Stratification, and Ideology," in Joan Huber and H. Paul Chalfant, eds., *The Sociology of American Poverty* (Cambridge, Mass.: Schenkman Publishing Co., 1974), pp. 1–16.

[5] See E. K. Hunt, *Property and Prophets: The Evaluation of Economic Institutions and Ideologies* (New York: Harper & Row, 1972).

[6] Helen Crampton and Kenneth K. Keiser, *Social Welfare: Institution and Process* (New York: Random House, 1970).

[7] David J. Rothman, *The Discovery of the Asylum: Social Order and Disorder in the New Republic* (Boston: Little, Brown, 1971), p. 155.

[8] Ibid., pp. 155–179.

[9] Sidney E. Zimbalist, *Historic Themes and Landmarks in Social Welfare Research* (New York: Harper & Row, 1977), pp. 31–49.

[10] Robert Harris and Alair A. Townsend, "Poverty," in Robert Morris, ed., *Encyclopedia of Social Work*, vol. 2 (New York: National Association of Social Workers, 1971), pp. 896–906.

[11] See Kingsley Davis and Wilbert E. Moore, "Some Principles of Stratification," *American Sociological Review* 10 (April 1945), pp. 242–249, and Jack Roach, "Sociological Analysis and Poverty," *American Journal of Sociology* 71

(July 1965), pp. 68–75.

[12] Herbert J. Gans, "The Positive Functions of Poverty," *American Journal of Sociology* 78 (September 1972), pp. 275–288.

[13] See S. M. Miller and Pamela Roby, *The Future of Inequality* (New York: Basic Books, 1970), and Lee Rainwater, *What Money Buys* (New York: Basic Books, 1974).

[14] David Matza, "The Disreputable Poor," in Neil J. Smelser and Seymour Lipset, eds., *Social Structure and Mobility in Economic Development* (Chicago: Aldine, 1966), pp. 310–339.

[15] U.S. Department of Health, Education, and Welfare, *The Measure of Poverty—A Report to Congress As Mandated By the Education Amendments of 1974* (Washington, D.C.: U.S. Government Printing Office, April, 1976), p. xxi.

[16] U.S. Bureau of the Census, *Current Population Reports*, Series P-60, no. 116, "Money Income and Poverty Status of Families and Persons in the United States: 1977," advanced report (Washington, D.C.: U.S. Government Printing Office, 1978).

[17] L. F. Hayes, "Non-Economic Aspects of Poverty," *Australian Journal of Social Issues* 5 (February 1970), pp. 41–54.

[18] Newsbank, Welfare and Poverty, Microfiche Card 8 A10, "Bless the Poor? Not in America" (Detroit, Mich.: *Free Press*, February 18, 1977).

[19] These accounts were taken from articles appearing between January 23, 1977, and March 1, 1978, in the following newspapers: Dallas *Morning News;* Grand Rapids *Press;* San Jose *Mercury;* Gary *Post-Tribune;* Marquette (Mich.) *Mining Journal; Chicago Sun-Times;* Denver *Post; Detroit Free Press; Washington Post; Hartford Courant;* Rockford (Ill.) *Register-Star; Los Angeles Times.*

[20] Marquette (Mich.) *Mining Journal* (March 1, 1978), p. 21A.

[21] U. S. Department of Labor, Bureau of Labor and Statistics, *Employment and Earnings,* vol. 25, no. 11 (Washington, D.C.: U.S. Government Printing Office, November 1978), p. 25.

[22] Michael Harrington, *The Other America* (Baltimore: Penguin Books, 1962).

[23] U.S. Bureau of the Census, *Current Population Reports,* 1978, p. 3.

[24] Charles Silberman, *Crisis in Black and White* (New York: Random House, 1964).

[25] See Kenneth M. Stampp, *The Peculiar Institution: Slavery in the Ante-Bellum South* (New York: Alfred A. Knopf, 1956), and Julius Lester, *To Be A Slave* (New York: Dial Press, 1968).

[26] E. Franklin Frazier, *The Negro Family in the United States* (Chicago: University of Chicago Press, 1966).

[27] Erving Goffman, *Stigma: Notes on the Management of Spoiled Identity* (Englewood Cliffs, N.J.: Prentice-Hall, 1963).

[28] U.S. Bureau of the Census, *Current Population Reports,* 1978, p. 25.

[29] U.S. Department of Health, Education, and Welfare, *The Measure of Poverty: A Report to Congress as Mandated by the Education Amendments of 1974* (Washington, D.C.: U.S. Government Printing Office, 1976).

[30] Kai T. Erikson, *Everything in Its Path* (New York: Simon and Schuster, 1976).

[31] U.S. Bureau of the Census, *Current Population Reports,* 1978, pp. 3, 42–47, 52.

[32] Ibid., p. 37.

[33] Daniel P. Moynihan, "The Negro Family: The Case for National Action," in Lee Rainwater and William L. Yancy, eds., *The Moynihan Report and the Politics of Controversy* (Cambridge, Mass.: The MIT Press, 1967), pp. 39–124.

[34] Lee Rainwater and William L. Yancy, *The Moynihan Report and the Politics of Controversy* (Cambridge, Mass.: The MIT Press, 1967), and David A. Schulz, *Coming Up Black* (Englewood Cliffs, N.J.: Prentice-Hall, 1969).

[35] Davis and Moore, "Some Principles of Stratification," pp. 242–249.

[36] Gans, "The Positive Functions of Poverty," pp. 275–288.

[37] Paul A. Samuelson, *Economics,* 8th ed. (New York: McGraw-Hill, 1970), p. 810.

[38] See Michael J. Harrington, "Hiding the Other America," *The New Republic* (February 26, 1977), pp. 26–28.

[39] See Ralf Dahrendorf, *Class and Class Conflict in Industrial Society* (Stanford, Calif.: Stanford University Press, 1959); Alvin Gouldner, "Reciprocity and Autonomy in Functional Theory," in Llewellyn Gross, ed., *Symposium on Sociological Theory* (New York: Harper & Row, 1959), pp. 241–270; and Rainwater and Yancy, *The Moynihan Report.*

[40] See Harrington, "Hiding the Other America," p. 26.

[41] Richard A. Cloward and Lloyd E. Ohlin, *Delinquency and Opportunity: A Theory of Delinquent Gangs* (New York: The Free Press, 1960).

[42] See Oscar Lewis, "The Culture of Poverty," *Scientific American* (October 1966), p. 19–25; Walter Miller, "Lower Class Culture As a Generating Milieu of Gang Delinquency," *Journal of Social Issues* 14 (July 1958), p. 5–19; and Harrington, *The Other America.*

[43] For more detailed criticisms, see Eleanor Burke Leacock, ed., *The Culture of Poverty: A Critique* (New York: Simon and Schuster, 1971), and Charles A. Valentine, *Culture and Poverty: Critique and Counterproposals* (Chicago: University of Chicago Press, 1968).

[44] Lola M. Irelan, Oliver C. Moles, and Robert M. O'Shea, "Ethnicity, Poverty, and Selected Attitudes: A Test of the 'Culture of Poverty' Hypothesis," *Social Forces* 47 (June 1969), pp. 405–413.

[45] Barbara E. Coward, Joe R. Feagin, and J. Allen Williams, Jr., "The Culture of Poverty Debate: Some Additional Data," *Social Problems* 21 (June 1974), pp. 621–634.

[46] See William Ryan, *Blaming the Victim* (New York: Pantheon Books, 1971).

[47] Howard S. Becker, *Outsiders: Studies in the Sociology*

of Deviance (New York: The Free Press, 1963).

[48] Schulz, *Coming Up Black*.

[49] See W. Lloyd Warner, Robert J. Havighurst, and Martin B. Loeb, *Who Shall be Educated?* (New York: Harper & Row, 1944); August B. Hollingshead, *Elmstown's Youth* (New York: John Wiley & Sons, 1949); and James S. Coleman, "The Concept of Equality of Educational Opportunity," *Harvard Educational Review* 38 (Winter 1968), pp. 7–22.

[50] Robert Rosenthal and Lenore Jacobson, *Pygmalion in the Classroom* (New York: Holt, Rinehart, & Winston, 1968).

[51] A. Dale Tussing, "The Dual Welfare System," *Society* 11 (January/February 1974), pp.. 50–57.

[52] Ibid., p. 53.

[53] The Washington Post (July 15, 1968), p. B-1.

[54] Si Kahn, *How People Get Power* (New York: McGraw-Hill, 1970).

[55] Westinghouse Learning Corporation, *The Impact of Head Start: An Evaluation of the Effect of Head Start on Children's Cognitive and Affective Development*, volume 1 (Clearinghouse for Federal Scientific and Technical Information, 1969).

[56] Marian S. Stearns, *Report on Preschool Programs: The Effects of Preschool Programs on Disadvantaged Children and Their Families* (U.S. Department of Health, Education, and Welfare, Office of Child Development, 1971), and Ada Jo Mann, Adele Harrell, and Maure Hurt, Jr., *Work Draft: A Review of Head Start Research Since 1969* (Unpublished, 1977).

[57] Lillian B. Rubin, "Maximum Feasible Participation: The Origins, Implications, and Present Status," *The Annals of the American Academy of Political and Social Science* 385

(September 1969), pp. 14–29.

[58] Daniel P. Moynihan, *Maximum Feasible Misunderstanding* (New York: The Free Press, 1969).

[59] Ibid., and Rubin, "Maximum Feasible Participation."

[60] See Robert A. Levine, *The Poor Ye Need Not Have With You* (Cambridge, Mass.: The MIT Press, 1970), pp. 201–204, and Theodore R. Marmor, *Poverty Policy* (Chicago: Aldine-Atherton, 1971), pp. 33–34.

[61] See Levine, *The Poor Ye Need Not Have With You*.

[62] Institute for Research on Poverty, University of Wisconsin, *The Rural Income Maintenance Experiment: Summary Report* (Washington, D.C.: Department of Health, Education, and Welfare, November 1976).

[63] "Humphrey-Hawkins: The Day of Reckoning," *Fortune,* 99 (January 29, 1979), pp. 27–28.

[64] See the special issue of *The Annals of the American Academy of Political and Social Science* 418 (March 1975).

[65] Newsbank, Employment, Microfiche Card 66 C2, (Carson City) *Nevada Appeal,* August 28, 1977, "How CETA Jobs Work," and Newsbank, Employment, Microfiche Card 72 B8, *Atlanta* (Ga.) *Journal,* August 28, 1977, "Welfare Moms Try to Get Out."

[66] Garth L. Mangum, "The Why, How, and Whence of Manpower Programs." *The Annals of the American Academy of Political and Social Science* 385 (Sept. 1969), pp. 50–62.

terest Group Processes (Princeton, N.J.: Princeton University Press, 1975).

[68] Richard A. Cloward and Frances Fox Piven, *The Politics of Turmoil* (New York: Pantheon Books, 1974).

[69] Harrington, "Hiding the Other America."

[70] Richard M. Scammon and Ben J. Wattenberg, *The Real Majority* (New York: Coward-McCann, 1970).

SUGGESTED READINGS

James Baldwin, *Nobody Knows My Name: More Notes of a Native Son* (New York: Dial Press, 1969).
A series of descriptions of and reflections on the experiences of black people in America. Baldwin shows how activities such as the construction of housing projects have served to discriminate against blacks.

Kai T. Erikson, *Everything in its Path.* (New York: Simon and Schuster, 1977).
An account of the Buffalo Creek flood and the reactions of the people affected by it. With great sensitivity, Erikson probes the lives and problems faced by a group of people living in Appalachia.

Frank Gell, *The Black Badge: Confessions of a Caseworker.* First edition (New York: Harper & Row, 1969).
This somewhat unusual work by a New York City welfare caseworker writing under the pseudonym Frank Gell, describes the lives of a number of welfare recipients. Gell

shows that, contrary to the common stereotype, welfare recipients are as varied as are Americans in general. Perhaps the most important point made in this book is that the welfare system is designed to keep the poor out of sight rather than to provide them with real opportunities for independence and self improvement.

Michael Harrington, *The Other America.* (New York: Macmillan Co., 1962).
A modern classic which focuses on the poor. Harrington's account of the many different types of poverty pricked the conscience of Americans and was instrumental in bringing about some of the poverty programs of the 1960s.

Si Kahn, *How People Get Power.* (New York: McGraw-Hill, 1970).
A relatively brief presentation of tactics and strategies for organizing the poor and other relatively powerless groups. Kahn advocates, among other things, knowing the rules

under which government operates, knowing the limitations of one's adversary, and initially selecting projects which can be accomplished so that the group will develop confidence.

Daniel P. Moynihan, *Maximum Feasible Misunderstanding.* (New York, Free Press, 1969).

An account of the early phases of The War On Poverty. Moynihan argues that the authors of the Economic Opportunity Act of 1964 had little, if any, idea of the implications of the provision for maximum feasible participation of the poor. The eventual reaction of entrenched power groups in local communities along with some members of Congress led to modifications of The War On Poverty which effectively checked this participation.

David A. Schulz, *Coming Up Black.* (Englewood Cliffs, New Jersey: Prentice-Hall, 1969).

A description of life in the Pruitt-Igoe Housing Project in St. Louis. Schulz observed five "complete" and five "incomplete" black families. He points out that the male and female children had very different kinds of socialization which, in turn, affected their response to the environment in which they lived.

Studs Terkel, *Hard Times.* (New York: Random House, 1970).

This account of the Great Depression is based on the recollections of some of those who experienced it. Terkel contrasts this experience with the reactions of younger people born too late to have been directly affected. One major point made by the book is that being poor was not stigmatized since so many Americans were in this condition.

Questions for Discussion

1. From the functionalist perspective, poverty exists both because poor people do not perform important functions and because poverty itself makes a functional contribution to society. Does this explanation of poverty seem consistent with any or all of the cases described in The Many Faces of Poverty? Cite specific instances where this explanation does and does not apply.

2. From the conflict perspective, poverty exists because poor people lack the power to effectively compete for scarce resources. Using this perspective can you account for any or all of the cases described in The Many Faces of Poverty? Where appropriate show how the explanation can be used in specific cases.

3. From the interactionist perspective, a condition such as poverty is real because people define it as real. Are there examples from The Many Faces of Poverty where this perspective applies. Do any of the cases represent instances where definitions of reality have changed over time?

4. The text describes alternative definitions of poverty giving special emphasis to economic and cultural ones. Describe these definitions and show how they might apply to different groups of poor people, blacks, the

elderly, children, etc.

5. The text discusses a number of alternative explanations of the causes of poverty. Discuss these explanations and show how they fit with the three theoretical perspectives. Which if any, of these explanations seem plausible to you?

6. The text describes a number of programs designed to reduce or eliminate poverty, including Head Start, a new War on Poverty, and governmentally mandated full employment. What are prospects for each of these and how effective are they liable to be?

7. We have considered possible solutions to the problem of poverty from a functionalist and conflict perspective. Does the functionalist point of view offer any realistic solutions or is it simply a convenient way of avoiding the issue? Can conflict oriented solutions, such as those aimed at the poor really work or are they unrealistic?

8. What factors will be likely to affect our thinking about poverty in the future? Consider, here, such possibilities as, the attitudes of elected officials, the ability to finance new or existing programs, and the probable effects of doing nothing.

CHAPTER 12

Race and Ethnic Relations

RACE AND ETHNIC RELATIONS

Race. Ethnicity. Minority Group.

A HISTORY OF MINORITY GROUPS IN AMERICA

Blacks. Hispanic Americans. Native Americans.

INTERGROUP RELATIONS AS A SOCIAL PROBLEM

The Functionalist Perspective. The Conflict Perspective.
The Interactionist Perspective.

THE STATUS OF MINORITIES IN THE UNITED
STATES TODAY

Blacks. Hispanic Americans. Native Americans. The Costs
of Racism.

REACTIONS TO PREJUDICE AND DISCRIMINATION

Black Reactions. Mexican American Reactions. Native
American Reactions. Intergroup Relations.

SOURCES OF PREJUDICE AND DISCRIMINATION

Psychological Sources. Prejudice and Discrimination as
Learned. Prejudice, Discrimination, and the Social Order.

PROSPECTS FOR THE FUTURE

Programs to Reduce Individual Discrimination. Programs
to Reduce Institutionalized Discrimination. The Politics of
Equality.

CONCLUSION

One of the most fascinating and enriching aspects of life in America is the great physical and cultural diversity of the peoples who have settled here. This diversity has provided us with an extraordinary range of cuisines, art forms, and lifestyles. Many cities boast of their Chinatown, Greektown, Polish community, or Italian neighborhood. This same diversity, however, has been a major source of divisiveness and conflict within society. Groups with divergent traditions, values, and languages have struggled with one another over power, privileges, and prestige. More often than not, one group has tried to impose its own way of life on other groups. Epithets abound to document the hostility that has characterized American race and ethnic relations — *coon, wetback, honky, beaner, wop,* and innumerable others.

Intergroup conflict in America dates back to the Puritan founders of this country. For instance, diseases carried by white settlers killed many Native Americans shortly after the *Mayflower* landing. Cotton Mather, a prominent minister in New England and descendant of the *Mayflower* group, found this to be beneficial rather than bad: "The woods are almost cleared of those pernicious creatures, to make room for better growth."[1] Each immigrant group in its turn — the Irish, the Italian, the Polish, and the others — met hostility and discrimination in the United States, often in the form of exclusion from desirable jobs and neighborhoods, sometimes in the form of physical attacks. The history of clashes between blacks and whites in the United States can be traced far back in our history. During the middle to late 1800s, Chinese immigrants were commonly viewed by whites as disease-ridden opium smokers who need not be accorded the privilege of citizenship. In 1882 Congress passed the Chinese Exclusion Act, which barred further Chinese immigration into the United States. Those Chinese already in the country encountered continual discrimination and harassment, and even occasional lynchings.[2] During World War II, thousands of Japanese Americans were removed from their homes and held in prison camps because of their presumed threat to the security of the United States.

American reaction to racial and ethnic diversity has clearly been ambivalent — viewing the differences as a source of strength on the one hand, yet also showing considerable hostility and even fear of any group that is different. The antagonistic relationships between groups in the United States alone have at times represented a major social problem. In addition, intergroup conflict has contributed to other problems, such as poverty, crime, and substance abuse. In this chapter we will be concerned with why such intergroup hostility exists, the state of contemporary American intergroup relations, and what can be done about these problems. Because this is such a volatile and emotion-laden topic, it is important that we clearly define related concepts so that there is minimum misunderstanding.

Race

People use the term *race* quite freely and often with little understanding of its precise meaning — the "German race," the "Jewish race," and the "Chinese race," are not uncommon expressions. Certainly, there is considerable physical variation within the human species. People differ in height, weight, bone structure, musculature, amount and distribution of body fat, and a myriad of other external physical traits. However, only a few of these physical characteristics are used to distinguish between people. Skin color, hair texture, and the shape of the eyelid and nose are currently viewed as important traits that serve to distinguish between the races.

The term *race* is associated with the external physical differences between groups that are considered important. **A race is a large number of people who are considered a biological unity because they share genetically transmitted traits that are defined by influential groups as important.** The most widely accepted contemporary classification divides the human species into three major categories: *Caucasoids,* with light skin and straight or wavy hair; *Mongoloids,* with yellowish skin and a distinctive fold around the eyes; and *Negroids,* with dark skin and woolly hair. There are many groups that cannot be neatly fitted into one of these categories, however. For example, among the peoples classified as Caucasoids are groups as physically varied as the Laplanders of the Arctic region of Europe, with extremely fair skin and blond or light-brown hair, and the Indians of Asia, with Caucasoid features, but with skin that is often darker than that of many Negroid groups. The diversity among people classified as Caucasians is so great that the idea of biological unity among them is really meaningless. In addition, there are no known intellectual, behavioral, or cultural differences that result directly from physical differences between the races. Nevertheless, **we must consider race to be a *social category* because in America, as in other societies, racial distinctions are considered important, and we distinguish between people on the basis of them.**[3]

Racial distinctions are used not only to differentiate between groups of people, but also to explain and justify differences in the possession of wealth, power, and prestige.[4] The term *racism* is useful in understanding these differences. ***Racism* is an ideology or belief that justifies the domination and exploitation by one group of another group that is viewed as different and inferior because of that group's characteristics. Racism is a belief in the racial inferiority of others.** Black subordination in South Africa, for example, is justified by the racist ideology that blacks are inherently inferior to whites and that it is the "white man's burden" to make decisions on their behalf. This same ideology was used by white slaveholders in the United States to justify slavery.

Ethnicity

Groups that share distinctive cultural traits such as a common language, national origin, religion, or a sense of historical heritage have been a major source of diversity and change that has enriched American life. Mexican Americans, Greek Americans, Mormons, the Amish, and Jews are only a few of the many ethnic groups in the United States that have made significant contributions to our way of life. On the other hand, much of the tension, con-

flict, and violence that have been a part of our history—and that remain prominent aspects of American society today—have centered on ethnic differences.

An *ethnic group* is a large number of people who share a common historical and cultural heritage and sense of group identity and belongingness. Ethnicity is usually based on common national origins and/or religious heritage. Ethnicity is usually displayed in the traditions, values, beliefs, attitudes, customs, lifestyles, and personality types of individuals who identify with particular ethnic groups. The results of an inves-

These Hassidic Jews live and work in their own ethnic neighborhood in New York City. Ethnicity is still a vital part of American life and is displayed in the traditions, values, beliefs, attitudes, customs, lifestyles, and personality types of individual members of ethnic groups.

tigation of sources of ethnic identity among Finnish Americans conducted by sociologists Dale Spady and Kenrick Thompson illustrate this "display" of ethnicity:

> Through social networks especially created in this country (e.g., politics, language, and education), the Finnish immigrant has been able to retain and pass on to successive generations selected attitudes, beliefs, values, and ceremonial practices of the Finnish culture. Finnish Americans have come to realize that they have a special heritage that is not simply a facet of the broader American culture.[5]

Ethnic groups often comprise subsocieties within the larger society. Ethnicity can be a source of emotional and social support for the members of an ethnic group; ethnic differences, on the other hand, can be a source of divisiveness in society. For example, Spady and Thompson found that from the time that the first Finnish immigrants arrived in Michigan, Finnish Americans have had to contend with considerable hostility and that these feelings generated from "outsiders" create both a stronger sense of identity among the members of the ethnic group *and* a condition of conflict that can lead to divisiveness.[6]

Minority Group

What could a black resident of an urban ghetto, a Mexican American farm worker, and a white suburban homemaker possibly have in common? All three are representative of minority groups in our society, and because of this their members have a lesser chance of receiving substantial social and economic rewards that do members of a majority group. **A *majority group* consists of those people whose distinctive physical and/or cultural characteristics are considered superior in society and who thus have more power than other groups.** Note that this definition says nothing about numbers—a majority group may in fact be numerically quite small. **A *minority group* is a group that: (1) is subordinate in power to the majority; (2) can be distinguished on the basis of physical and/or cultural characteristics; (3) is collectively** **regarded as different and inferior; and (4) has fewer rights, privileges, and opportunities than the majority.** Let us look at each of these characteristics in turn.

Subordination

Minority groups are subordinate in power to the dominant majority group even though they might far outnumber them. For example, in the United States, women outnumber men; but, as a category, they have far less economic clout, political influence, and prestige than males. Blacks in South Africa are another example of a group that is subservient to a group that it far outnumbers. The white "majority" in South Africa has far more economic advantages, political rights, and social privileges than the subordinate black "minority." This dominance is often highly institutionalized and is sometimes legitimized through religious dogma and legal statutes.

Distinctiveness

Minorities are defined as different on the basis of physical and/or cultural traits that are thought to distinguish them from the majority. Blacks, women, Japanese Americans, and Puerto Ricans are easily identifiable in part because of their physical characteristics. Often, the physical and social characteristics selected to differentiate between people are thought to be innate. For example, many people believe that women are more emotional and unstable than men, that they are not effective at performing mechanical tasks, that they are not as rational and logical as men, and that they are not as interested in, or capable of, achievement as men—and that all of these characteristics derive from constitutional differences that may be explained genetically rather than as the result of socialization and the learning of sex roles.

Prejudice

Members of minority groups are generally considered inferior by the majority. *Prejudice* **is an attitude of hostility or rejection held about a group that is considered different and infe-**

rior. Minorities are the objects of prejudice. For example, the belief in the innate superiority of whites has provided a rationale for the subordination of blacks in American society.

Discrimination

Minorities are excluded from full participation in their society. They have fewer rights, immunities, and privileges than the majority and therefore have fewer opportunities to achieve the "good life." Whereas prejudice is an attitude, discrimination involves behavior. *Discrimination* **is the negative treatment of people because of their membership in a minority group rather than their individual ability or behavior.** Jews and other minorities in the United States, for example, have traditionally been discriminated against and denied the opportunities open to many Americans. Prior to the Civil Rights acts of the 1960s, many graduate and professional schools had strict quotas limiting the number of Jews and women admitted, regardless of their qualifications.

Even though all minority groups have something in common, no two groups have had precisely the same experiences. Each has been shaped by the particular historical background that is its heritage. All minority groups have gone through ordeals, although some have experienced more trying and degrading conditions than others. Yet, the problems we confront today in intergroup relations can be best understood if we are aware of the historical context from which the problems evolved. Our focus will be on three contemporary minority groups: blacks, Hispanic Americans, and Native Americans. There are other groups that we could examine, but these three represent the largest minority groups numerically and also face the most severe problems. They illustrate the range of problems faced by the members of American minority groups today.

A HISTORY OF MINORITY GROUPS IN AMERICA

Historically, the dominant ethnic group in American society was made up of Anglo-Saxon Americans (whites of predominantly British descent). The founders of the New England and Virginia settlements were Anglo-Saxons. Their culture and traditions — including religious beliefs and practices, conceptions of and attitudes toward family life, educational philosophy, economic arrangements, and legal principles — provided the foundation of the "American way of life." Prior to the 1830s and 1840s, Anglo-Saxons were very successful in compelling other groups to conform to their culture. The major exception was the Native American. However, after that period, large numbers of non-Anglo-Saxons began to immigrate to the United States. The first of these groups were Irish Catholics, who came primarily to work on the canals and railroads and to avoid the hardships associated with famine in Ireland. They posed a problem for the Anglo-Saxons, who viewed themselves as the only "true Americans." As a consequence, the Irish were the objects of considerable prejudice and discrimination. Many other groups had experiences similar to those of Irish Catholic immigrants. The Italians, the Poles, the Jews, the Finns, and many others were, in their time, viewed as minority groups and were the targets of the wrath of the dominant groups. These groups for the most part no longer face the prejudice and discrimination that they once did. Today, a number of groups find themselves on the bottom, and it is to them that we turn our attention.

Blacks

Blacks have been the object of considerable prejudice and discrimination throughout American history. In addition, because of their historical status as slaves, their lot has been particularly difficult. The first blacks from Africa arrived in Jamestown, Virginia in 1619. Originally, they had the same status as white indentured servants. They could gain their freedom after working for a specified number of years and upon conversion to Christianity. However, in 1661 the colonial legislature of Virginia passed a law making black servants slaves for life. They could not make legally binding contracts, could not marry, and were considered to be their master's property, the same as his barns, livestock, or farm implements. By 1790, well over 90 percent of the blacks in America were slaves.[7]

The impetus to enslave blacks was *not simply racism,* but a response to the economic need for cheap labor in the colonies. Many whites believed that it was to their economic advantage to have a stable, reliable, and cheap supply of labor. In fact, the Northern states began to outlaw slavery in 1780, but for the South, the belief that slavery was economically beneficial persisted. Between 1815 and 1861, cotton was the mainstay of agriculture in the South. Cotton growing was labor-intensive—it required a large labor force that should also ideally be cheap and docile. Black slaves were considered ideally suited for this purpose. They were imported in large numbers to work in the fields and mills.[8] Slavery, as practiced in the United States, had a profound influence on later relations between black and white Americans. Blacks were torn from their culture in Africa, transported across the ocean, and thrust into a society in which they had a totally subordinate position. Little heed was paid by whites to protecting and preserving the black family or other aspects of black social organization. Marriages among slaves were not recognized by the law, and slaves were commonly sold with little regard to effects on marital or family ties. Throughout the period of slavery and even beyond it, blacks were discouraged from demonstrating intelligence, ambition, or initiative. In fact, it was at one time illegal to teach blacks to read or write. Acting stupid and lazy were means of survival for most blacks under slavery. Throughout the centuries of slavery, the superior/subordinate relationship between blacks and whites became deeply imbedded in the legal structure, the norms and values, and the psyches of both blacks and whites.[9]

Not all blacks of this period were slaves—in 1860, there were almost a half-million free blacks in the United States, about half of these in the North. Yet they fared little better than their enslaved counterparts, and most were limited to lower-level occupations. This discrimination against free blacks provided the precedent for the unequal treatment of emancipated blacks after the Civil War.[10]

With the end of the Civil War, all blacks who were still held as slaves gained their freedom. Between 1865 and 1876, the nation witnessed the "radical reconstruction" of the South. During this period, many blacks participated in politics and enjoyed a degree of freedom that they would not experience again for many decades. However, by 1877 whites began to reassert their dominance, and the era of "white supremacy" was under way. The capstone of the Jim Crow era—the period of legalized white supremacy—was the decision of the United States Supreme Court in *Plessy* v. *Ferguson* (1896), which gave birth to the "separate but equal" doctrine that served as the legal basis for discrimination against blacks in schools, housing, and other areas for the next six decades. It was not until the Court's decision in *Brown* v. *Board of Education* (1954) that the "separate but equal" doctrine, which legalized segregation, was overruled and the Jim Crow era began to fade. This landmark decision ushered in two decades of increasingly violent conflict between blacks and whites which would lead to radical changes in the status of blacks in the United States.[11]

Even though blacks have been in America longer than many other minority groups, they still find themselves the object of prejudice and discrimination and they still face problems as severe as those confronting other minorities. This brief history gives some clues as to why. First, prejudice and discrimination against blacks is deeply imbedded in American history. As we have tried to tackle these problems, we have become aware of how entrenched prejudiced beliefs and discriminatory practices are in our society. Second, and more so than with other minorities, there has been a total disregard for those aspects of black culture that might have made it easier for blacks to improve their lot. For example, slavery had a detrimental impact on the black family, and even today welfare policies at times work against the cohesiveness of the family. Third, throughout the history of blacks in America, there have been few incentives for hard work, initiative, or ambition on the part of individual blacks. In fact, such qualities were most often discouraged, sometimes with force, by members of

This impoverished black family in the backwoods of Kentucky grouped around their wooden shack (circa 1892) illustrates the economic suffering of many blacks even after gaining their "freedom" with the end of the Civil War.

the white majority and by other blacks who shared the views of the dominant group.

Hispanic Americans

Hispanic Americans are Americans of Spanish origin (see Fig. 12.1). This broad categorization includes Mexican Americans (Chicanos), Cubans, Puerto Ricans, people from Central and South America, the West Indies, and others of Spanish origin. Hispanic Americans are a diverse group bound together by their culture, language, and ties to Roman Catholicism. We can touch on only some of their varied history here.

Mexican Americans

The largest Hispanic group in the United States is Mexican Americans. Many people are unaware of the long history of settlement that Mexican Americans have in this country. By the advent of Mexican

independence from Spain in 1821, there were isolated Spanish communities located throughout the

Figure 12.1 Percentage Distribution of Hispanic Americans by Type of Spanish Origin, 1976. U.S. Bureau of the Census, "Persons of Spanish Origin in the United States: March 1976," *Current Population Reports*, Series P-20, no. 310 (Washington, D.C.: U.S. Government Printing Office, 1977), p. 1.

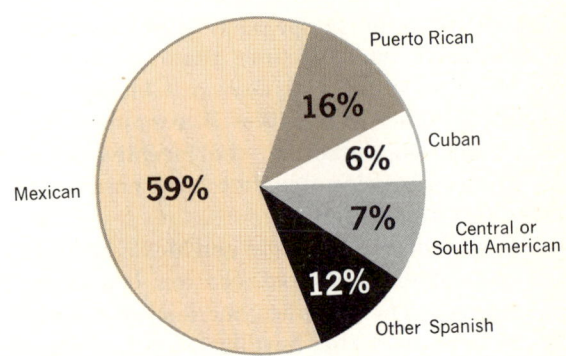

American Southwest. These early Mexican Americans were for the most part small landholders. After Mexican independence, large numbers of Anglos (white persons of non-Spanish descent) migrated into the area to take advantage of the land grants that were given to them by the Mexican government to encourage their settlement in the region. As more Anglos moved into these regions, competition for good land became fierce, and many Mexican Americans were displaced by large Anglo-owned cattle and agricultural interests. In 1836, the settlers (including many of Spanish descent) in Texas conducted a successful insurrection against the Mexican government, and in 1845 the Lone Star Republic was annexed to the United States. As a consequence, most of the descendants of the Spanish settlers became American citizens. However, this spelled the demise of these early settlers as a powerful group because, as the Anglo population in the Southwest grew, the economic prospects for all classes of Mexican Americans declined. They were forced off the land and out of the more influential positions in these states.

The Mexican Revolution that began in 1909 ended the slave-like status of hundreds of thousands of Mexican peasants, many of whom then migrated to the United States. There was much demand for cheap labor because of expanding agriculture and railroads in the Southwest. For many Mexican families, however, their status in the United States was peonage at a slightly higher standard of living than what they had known in Mexico. The depression of the 1930s resulted in a decline in farm work. Many were driven to the cities to seek employment and public relief. The first urban **barrios** (Spanish speaking quarters of U.S. cities that have often become ghettos) began to spring up in such cities as Denver, Chicago, and Los Angeles. When World War II armament production began in California, the incentive to go west to the Los Angeles area drew large numbers of Mexican Americans there.[12]

Relations between the Anglo and Mexican American communities would, on occasion, become vicious and ugly. The prejudice and fear on the part of the Anglos and the hostility and feelings of oppression on the part of the Mexican Americans

The largest Hispanic group in the United States is Mexican Americans. Mexican Americans and other Hispanics have retained, and taken pride in, a long cultural heritage that has served as a source of identity for them over the generations.

would erupt into a violent confrontation. One extreme example occurred in Los Angeles in 1943. Whites, particularly naval personnel, attacked and beat Mexican American youths on the street and in some cases forced them to disrobe. These "zoot-suit riots" (named after the distinctive mode of dress of the young Mexican Americans) started when Anglos became incensed over rumors that Mexican Americans were assaulting white women. Mexican American youths retaliated against unwary naval personnel—propelled by rumors of harassment of Mexican American women by sailors. Before the disturbances died down, some 600 Mexican Americans were arrested. While this incident was more violent and widespread than most, it was symptomatic of the underlying tension that has characterized the usually peaceful relationship between Anglo and Mexican American communities.

Since World War II, the status of Mexican Americans in the United States has changed substantially. First, their numbers have grown steadily. This has resulted from a continuing stream of migration from Mexico and a high birthrate among Mexican Americans. In sheer numbers alone, they have become a significant force in American society. Second, Mexican Americans have become much more forceful and militant in their stance toward the white majority. Over a half-million Mexican Americans served in World War II, and this exposed them to a broader world. The veterans began to revitalize old community organizations and to form new ones that were far more militant. The civil rights activities of blacks provided encouragement for this more militant stance. In addition, second- and third-generation Mexican Americans had fewer ties to Mexico than did their elders, and they oriented more toward the majority American culture in terms of aspirations and goals.[13]

Other Hispanic Groups

Puerto Ricans are the second largest Hispanic group in the United States. Unlike Mexicans, Puerto Ricans are citizens of the United States, having been granted this status in 1917. A small number of Puerto Ricans immigrated to the United States before World War II, mostly attracted by farm labor jobs, but a few came to work in factories in the east. Following World War II, this immigration increased dramatically. A number of factors drew Puerto Ricans to the mainland. First, the jobs available in the United States, while menial and low paying, were usually better than those available in the chronically depressed economy of Puerto Rico. Second, because they are citizens of the United States, there are no legal restrictions placed upon Puerto Rican travel to the United States. Finally, relatively cheap air travel between the island and the mainland made such movement possible for even poor Puerto Ricans. Puerto Ricans have tended to settle in the northeast; over half live in New York City and many others in Chicago.[14]

Cuban Americans are relatively recent migrants to the United States. Most are political refugees, having fled Cuba following the takeover by Fidel Castro in 1959. Prior to that, there were about 79,000 Cubans living in the United States. Their numbers grew to about three-quarters of a million people by 1976. Some of these refugees came to the United States before commercial flights between Cuba and the United States were discontinued. Later, many escaped in private planes, boats, or other vessels. The Cubans who have come to the United States tend to be different from many other Hispanics in that they are generally well educated, often from professional or managerial backgrounds. Large numbers of Cubans have settled in Southern Florida, particularly the Miami area.[15]

Although they share a language, a culture, and a religion, it would be a mistake to overemphasize the common heritage of Hispanic Americans. There is much diversity and conflict among Hispanics themselves. Many Cubans look down upon Mexican Americans, especially the Chicanos in low-paying occupations. Many Chicanos feel no affinity with Puerto Ricans. This diversity can be a stumbling block to coordinated action. Yet, in comparison with blacks, the experience of Hispanics has shown one notable difference—Hispanics have held onto, and taken pride in, a long cultural heritage that has served as a source of identity for them over the generations.

Native Americans

The period between 1519, when Cortez landed at Vera Cruz, and 1821, when Mexico won independence from Spain, was one of Spanish conquest over Native Americans. These Americans, who had only spears and bows and arrows and who were divided into hundreds of tribes and dozens of alliances, were no match for the Spanish, with their superior military technology and organizational unity. Thousands of Native Americans were killed or enslaved, their women taken as concubines, and their gold, silver, and art treasures expropriated by the Conquistadores.

Prior to the American Revolution, white contacts with Native Americans were highly varied. The first settlers in the New England colonies and in the Dutch and French settlements had, for the most part, harmonious and cooperative relationships with the natives. For example, the Iroquois and whites were involved in an elaborate fur trading network. However, as more whites immigrated from Europe and Great Britain, increasing the competition for land, their relations with the native population rapidly deteriorated—especially those between the colonists and the more settled agricultural and horticultural tribes, who occupied highly desirable land. These groups were not only driven from their lands and robbed of their cultural heritage, but they were often victims of attempts at outright genocide. *Genocide* **is the use of deliberate, systematic measures designed to exterminate an entire group or population.**

In 1789, the federal government was required, under the Constitution, to negotiate treaties with the several Native American groups that were treated as if they were separate nations. In 1824, the Bureau of Indian Affairs (BIA) was created by Congress as a division of the War Department in order to seek a military solution to what many congressmen referred to as the "Indian Problem." In 1830, Congress succumbed to pressures for opening up more Indian land to white settlement and ordered the BIA to relocate all Native Americans west of the Mississippi River. This allowed the Army to remove Cherokees, for instance, from their homes in North Carolina, Tennessee, and Georgia and to send them to the Oklahoma Territory.

Once this removal process was nearly completed, Congress enacted the Trade and Intercourse Act of 1834, which regulated access to tribal lands west of the Mississippi.

The pattern during the following sixty years, repeated again and again, was invasion of Indian land by whites, Indian resistance, and the "protective" action by the American Military which allowed the white settlers to consolidate and defend their holdings of Indian land.[16]

Two generations of Native Americans on a reservation in New Mexico illustrate the mixture of native and Anglo cultures. Many of those living on reservations suffer great poverty.

The policy of treaty negotiation with individual tribes continued until 1871, when Congress decided that no new treaties were to be made, although existing ones were to be honored. In 1887 the Indian Allotment Act (Dawes Act) had as its stated objective the making of Indians into farmers. Each family or individual was given from 40 to 160 acres. However, after each Native American received his or her allotment, excess property was opened for homesteading or purchase by whites.

It was not until 1924 that Congress passed the Indian Citizenship Act, granting citizenship to all Native Americans. In 1968, Congress enacted the Indian Civil Rights Act, which extended the basic human rights guaranteed by the Bill of Rights to persons living on tribal lands. While this undoubtedly had many positive benefits for Native Americans, it may have had negative consequences for tribes that possessed their own judicial systems based on tribal customs differing in some respects from federal statutes. The Indian Civil Rights Act may, in fact, have undermined tribal control and unity.[17]

All Native American groups had one thing in common: they were here before the white man came. Whites apparently did not perceive the Native Americans as useful to them. Blacks, at least, could serve as slaves. Native Americans were viewed simply as a hindrance—they tried to keep land that white civilization desperately needed for expansion. In wresting the land away from them, white civilization also had a very destructive impact on Native American culture. It took away from them those parts of their culture—such as the land, the buffalo hunt—that served as the core of their world and a source of identity. The devastating impact of this loss of culture is described in the words of one Native American, Standing Bear:

> When the Indian has forgotten the music of his forefathers, when the sound of the tomtom is no more, when noisy jazz has drowned the melody of the flute, he will be a dead Indian. When from him has been taken all that is his, all that he has visioned in nature, all that has come to him from infinite sources, he then, truly, will be a dead Indian. His spirit will be gone, and though he walk crowded streets, he will, in truth, be—dead![18]

While the history of each minority group is unique, there are certain common threads that can be found. In each case, some group gains social and economic benefits by depriving another group of an equal chance to acquire resources. In addition, the dominant group manipulates the legal system to its own advantage. Outbreaks of hostility and violence are more commonly initiated by the dominant group than by the subordinate group. Finally, the impact of such intergroup relations is widespread—it creeps into many spheres of life and has implications that few are aware of at the time. One goal of this chapter is to analyze precisely what problems such intergroup relations have

created for the United States. First, however, it will be helpful to inquire into the conditions under which, from each of our theoretical perspectives, intergroup relations might constitute a social problem.

INTERGROUP RELATIONS AS A SOCIAL PROBLEM

Prejudice, discrimination, race riots, ethnic slurs: when we read of such things in the newspaper, it seems obvious that contemporary intergroup relations pose a serious social problem. However, we want to know precisely how, why, and for whom these conditions are social problems, and the three sociological perspectives can be employed to help us achieve this understanding.

The Functionalist Perspective

From the functionalist perspective, any condition that threatens the effective operation and smooth functioning of society is a social problem. Those conditions that threaten the ability of the system to accomplish essential tasks are seen as the most threatening. **Prejudice and discrimination are a threat to the social system, and therefore a social problem when they contribute to mistrust, hostility, and conflict between groups, to the extent that concerted effort toward common goals is difficult.** When prejudice or discrimination lead to conflict and violence, it can seriously disrupt the performance of crucial tasks in society. For example, many of our major cities are suffering from such serious problems as deteriorating buildings and inadequate public services (e.g. police and fire protection, hospitals, and schools). Prejudice, mistrust, and hostility between groups make it difficult for people in authority to implement policies that require cooperation and mutual sacrifice. In addition, prejudice and discrimination can lead to violent confrontations, such as those witnessed during the urban riots of the 1960s, which can bring a city almost to a complete halt. The personal injury, deaths, and property damage resulting from such outbreaks is very costly and disruptive to the functioning of society. Resources must be spent on social control which might better be spent elsewhere.[19]

Prejudice and discrimination can also threaten the well-being of society when potentially useful people who could perform essential tasks cannot develop their talents because of barriers to their advancement. Inasmuch as discrimination is associated with other social problems—such as poverty, crime and delinquency, and substance abuse—it is disruptive of the smooth and efficient operation of the social system. People who feel the brunt of prejudice and discrimination often become alienated, apathetic, unproductive, and do not participate in important activities in their communities. They use vital resources but contribute little in return. For example, people of lower social status are less likely to vote and to participate in community affairs. It is very difficult for them to feel they are a part of the system and to be aware that they have a stake in crucial issues that affect us all.

The student should realize that **from the functionalist perspective, discrimination and prejudice are not, by themselves, a social problem.** In fact, one could argue that during part of the period of slavery in the United States, prejudice and discrimination against blacks were functional (at least for the dominant groups) because they helped to ensure a cheap and docile labor force that was essential at the time. For the functionalist, prejudice and discrimination become a social problem when they threaten the ability of society to achieve its goals.

The Conflict Perspective

While the functionalist perspective sensitizes us to how intergroup relations can be viewed as a problem at the community and societal levels, the conflict perspective helps us to understand how such relations can be defined as a social problem from the vantage point of particular groups. **From the conflict perspective, a condition will be defined as a social problem by a particular group when it feels that the condition deprives the group of its "fair share" of valued resources.** Conflict theory emphasizes the point that not all groups have the same interests. Conditions that benefit one group may work to the detriment of another. The critical issues in determining whether a social problem exists are whether a group has the power and resources to protect and enhance its own interests and feels that it is not receiving its equitable share of valued resources. The status of blacks and other minorities came to be viewed as a social problem when these groups felt deprived and when they were able to acquire the resources and power to force others to listen to their demands. Inequality alone does not necessarily create a social problem; you must also make others aware of, and sympathetic to, the problem.[20]

Conflict theorists emphasize that prejudice and discrimination should be viewed as social problems for the victims of these conditions. For those who are members of the dominant group, existing relationships between themselves and minority groups may be viewed as fair, equitable, just, and the way things ought to be. A white employer, for instance, might resist hiring Native Americans because of a belief that they are unreliable and lack initiative. The employer may be convinced that established policies are sound and just. For this person, state and federal laws prohibiting ethnic discrimination in hiring constitute a serious social problem. For the Native Americans in the community, on the other hand, not having access to a job in that employer's establishment is part of the social problem. Antidiscrimination laws are seen as vehicles by which the Native Americans can gain access to the positions to which their talents and skills entitle them. From the conflict perspective, it is normal for such groups with competing values and interests to struggle with one another over scarce resources. However, when the struggle results in the subordination of one group to another and the subordinated group feels this is unfair and can do something about it, then this condition represents a serious social problem.

The Interactionist Perspective

From the interactionist perspective, social order is based on a shared consensus about reality, including ideas about what is proper, fair, and just. When groups share similar views, harmonious and cooperative social interaction can be maintained. However, when consensus is lacking, intergroup relationships become uncooperative, hostile, and conflict-ridden. Interactionists view American society as basically pluralist—comprised of divergent subgroups with different traditions, values, beliefs, and competing interests. Prejudice and discrimination are for the most part by-products of pluralism.[21]

When divergent groups share the same general values and beliefs, effective communication and cooperation will take place. **From the interactionist perspective, prejudice and discrimination are not a social problem as long as all groups, including the subordinate groups, accept the same version of reality. However, they become social problems when groups have different perspectives on important issues, consensus is lacking, and mutual cooperation breaks down.** For example, as long as Anglos and Mexican Americans in a community share the view that the Mexican's "proper place" is one of subservience and compliance with the values of the dominant group, hostility and conflict will be minimized and no social problem exists. However, when Mexican Americans question the assumptions held by whites concerning the nature of social reality and attempt to assert themselves (e.g. by trying to preserve their cultural heritage or demanding better educations and jobs), then a social problem exists.

From the interactionist perspective, prejudice and discrimination have severe costs for their victims. It is very difficult for a person who is defined and treated as different and inferior to maintain a positive self-concept. People with low self-esteem are not as likely to develop their talents and to be happy and productive members of their society. They are likely to feel frustrated, apathetic, and alienated. This makes self-improvement extremely difficult. Prejudice and discrimination also have a negative impact on their perpetrators. People who discriminate against others often rob themselves of friendships and mutually beneficial relationships with others from whom they might otherwise gain a wider view of the human condition and appreciate the variety of diverse perspectives and lifestyles in our society.

THE STATUS OF MINORITIES IN THE UNITED STATES TODAY

Try to imagine the situation if a law were passed by any state legislature requiring blacks, Native Americans, or any other minority group to perform twice as well as white students in order to receive a high school diploma. There would be an outcry of protest that would probably not be stilled until the offending legal statute were removed from the books. Yet, conditions similar to this fable exist today insofar as minority group members often must struggle against social barriers that make it doubly difficult for them to achieve the same recognition as whites. Certainly there have been improvements in the past two decades—the turmoil, violence, and destruction of this period led to changes in the status of many minorities. Yet it is all too tempting to be complacent and assume that the problems of minority groups in the United States have been solved. How do the various racial and ethnic groups fare in the United States today? What barriers do they face? Instead of attempting a comprehensive review of all minority groups, we will focus on three important groups today—blacks, Hispanic Americans, and Native Americans.

Blacks

Blacks can be found in all economic positions and social statuses in the United States today. However, for many black Americans, life is best characterized by the despairing situation described by one 39-year-old man:

> How can you have any pride? I'm a part-time worker—a part-time husband. I guess I'm really a part-time man. I can't find enough to do to keep food on the table. Guess some people would think that I'm the sorriest man that ever wore out shoe leather. It ain't that I don't have no get-up, it's just that I can't find nothing to do. I had to leave home so the children

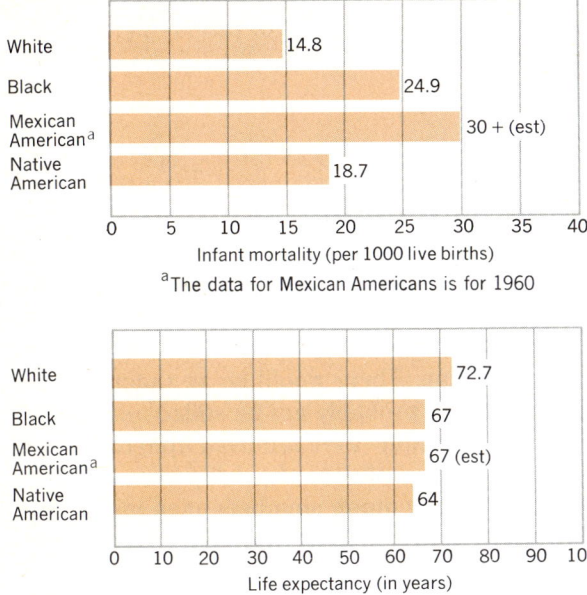

Figure 12.2 **The Health Status of Minority Groups, 1974.** U.S. Bureau of the Census, *Social Indicators 1976* (Washington, D.C.: U.S. Government Printing Office, 1977); Joan W. Moore, *Mexican Americans* (Englewood Cliffs, N.J.: Prentice-Hall, 1970), p. 73; Joseph Strauss, Bruce A. Chadwick, and Howard M. Bahr, "Indian Americans: The First Is Last," in Anthony G. Dworkin and Rosalind J. Dworkin, eds., *The Minority Report* (New York: Frederick A. Praeger, 1976), pp. 221–253; and Patricia D. Mail, "Hippocrates Was a Medicine Man: The Health Care of Native Americans in the Twentieth Century," *Annals of the American Academy of Political and Social Science* 436 (March 1978), pp. 40–49.

could eat. While I'm sitting here with you, they're out looking for me. That ain't so bad—what really hurts is that my wife is going to tell them people down at the welfare that some other man is the baby's daddy or else she thinks she can't get no aid. If they take her off the welfare she'll starve. So every time she has another baby she gives a different guy's name—excuse me for bawling, man, I just can't help it—but it sure ain't no justice when a man's got to make his own children bastards in order to feed them.[22]

Blacks constitute approximately **12** percent of our nation's population, a majority of whom live outside the South. Four out of five blacks reside in metropolitan areas, over half of them in the central cities. Furthermore, American cities are still racially segregated, with blacks living for the most part in predominantly black neighborhoods.[23] From the beginning of life, blacks fare less well than whites. The black infant mortality rate—the death rate during the first year of life—is more than 1.5 times greater than that for whites (see Fig. 12.2). High infant mortality rates result from poor nutrition, inadequate access to prenatal medical care, and limited knowledge about proper health practices (see ch. 8). These poor health practices and lack of utilization of health care facilities continue throughout life and, when added to the sress arising from years of reacting to discrimination and racial insults, reduce the life expectancy of blacks. The median life expectancy of blacks is 67 years, whereas for whites it is slightly less than 73 years—a difference of nearly 6 years (see Fig. 12.2). Contrary to the stereotype of blacks as poor but easygoing and basically content with their lot in life, health statistics show a high incidence of stress-related illnesses, such as heart attacks and strokes.[24]

Blacks fare little better in the economic sphere than they do in the area of health. Blacks are over-represented among our nation's poor (see ch. 11). Black families are three times as likely as white families to have incomes that fall below the federally established poverty level (see Fig. 12.3). Unemployment is a serious problem faced by many Americans, but the black unemployment rate has been about twice that for whites since the early 1950s. While unemployment is high among all young people, it is an especially pressing problem for black teenagers, whose rate of unemployment is about 35 percent, compared with approximately 15 percent for white youths.[25] Given this devastatingly high unemployment rate, it is understandable why many young blacks look with a great deal of skepticism on the American dream of achievement through hard work and initiative. From their perspective, it looks more like a myth.

The type of job a person has is very important to his or her self-esteem and lifestyle. Occupational status is closely related to income, prestige, job satisfaction, and a sense of control over one's work situation. We judge people, and ourselves, by the work we do. People employed in higher-level white-collar occupations have the highest incomes and

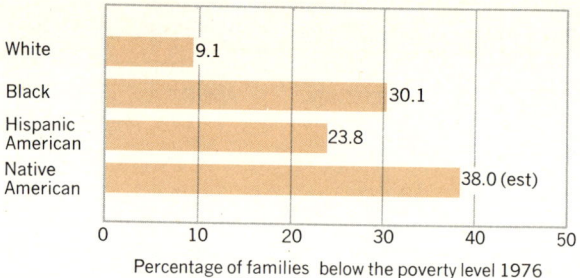

Percentage of families below the poverty level 1976

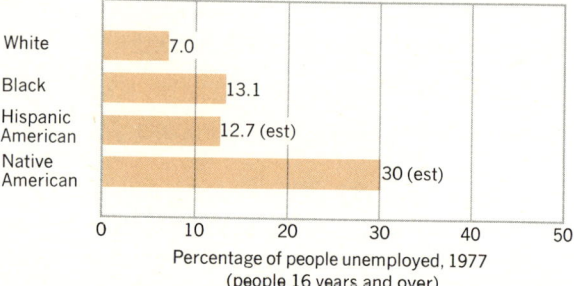

Percentage of people unemployed, 1977
(people 16 years and over)

Figure 12.3 The Economic Status of Minority Groups. U.S. Bureau of the Census, *Current Population Reports*, Series P-20, no. 292 (March 1975); U. S. Bureau of the Census, *Current Population Reports*, P-20, no. 292 (March 1976); U. S. Bureau of the Census, *Current Population Reports*, Series P-60, no. 15 (July 1978); and Alan L. Sorkin, "The Economic Basis of Indian Life," *Annals of the American Academy of Political and Social Science* 436 (March 1978), pp. 1–12.

prestige, and enjoy the greatest degree of job satisfaction, while unskilled blue-collar workers have the lowest incomes and prestige, and the lowest level of job satisfaction.[26] The economic and social opportunities available to family members are also closely associated with the occupational status of the head of household. Table 12.1 shows that a person's race or ethnic origin still has a very profound impact on the type of occupation, if any, he or she is likely to have. Blacks are concentrated in lower-level jobs, both at the white-collar and blue-collar levels. Whereas 24.9 percent of white heads of households were employed in higher-level white-collar jobs, only 7.2 percent of black family heads were so employed. In addition, whites are almost twice as likely to hold upper-level blue-collar jobs as are blacks. The largest concentration of black employees is in the lower blue-collar categories—37.1 percent of the black heads of household

are employed as operatives, laborers, or service workers. The low family income among blacks is a reflection of their position in the occupational hierarchy. The median family income for whites in 1977 was $16,740 while for blacks it was $9560—57 percent of that of white families (see Table 12.2). These income differences have been quite constant since the early 1950s, indicating that there has been little change in the financial status of blacks relative to whites over the past three decades.

Education is a very important resource in our society. People with more education are in a better position to obtain good jobs and to enjoy a high income. For example, Peter Blau and Otis Dudley Duncan, two prominent social scientists who conducted an extensive study of occupational mobility in America, found that the most important factor affecting whether a son moved to a higher social status than his father's was the amount of education that the son received.[27] A high school diploma is required for most jobs, and many employers require at least some college training. Educational attainment varies with race and ethnic origin. Whereas 27.3 percent of whites over 25 years of age had some college training in 1975, only 18.8 percent of blacks had attended college (see Table 12.3). In addition, the percentage who have not finished high school is much higher for blacks—54.6 percent compared to 36.4 percent for whites.

Hispanic Americans

There are about 12 million Hispanic Americans living in the United States, constituting about 5.5 percent of the population (see Fig. 12.1). In addition, there may be as many as 8 million Hispanics who are living and working illegally in the United States.[28] In the 1960 census, the Bureau of the Census defined as Hispanic anyone who was born in Spain, Central or South America, Puerto Rico, and other related countries, along with any U.S. residents with Spanish surnames. In the 1970 census, Hispanic was redefined to include the racial origin of respondents even if they had not been born in any of the above countries or did not have a Spanish surname. This resulted in a substantial increase in the number of people counted as His-

TABLE 12.1
Employment Status and Occupation of Head of Household, by Race or Ethnic Origin, 1975, Expressed in Percentages.

EMPLOYMENT STATUS OR OCCUPATION	WHITE	BLACK	HISPANIC AMERICAN	NATIVE AMERICAN (est.)
Unemployed or not in labor force	[24.2]	[37.6]	[29.2]	[45]
Higher white-collar (professional, technical: managers, officials, proprietors)	24.9	7.2	10.1	7.8
Lower white-collar (clerical; salesworkers)	10.6	8.4	7.8	4.5
Higher blue-collar (craftsmen, foremen)	15.9	8.0	14.2	12.2
Lower blue-collar (operatives, laborers, service workers)	20.6	37.1	37.2	29.3
Farmers and farm managers	2.3	1.1	0.2	1.3
Totals	(98.2)	(99.4)	(98.7)	(100.1)

SOURCE. U.S. Bureau of the Census, "Consumer Income," *Current Population Reports*, Series P-60, no. 105 (Washington, D.C.: U.S. Government Printing Office, 1977), and Alan L. Sorkin, "The Economic Basis of Indian Life," *Annals of the American Academy of Political and Social Science* 436 (March 1978), pp. 1–12.

panics. Census officials plan to be even more diligent in the 1980 census, and we will undoubtedly see even greater increases in the number of Hispanics. (Hispanics living in the United States illegally are not included in the government's statistics.)

The infant mortality rate for Hispanic Americans is at least twice that for whites and even higher than the black rate (see Fig. 12.2). The mean life expectancy for Hispanic Americans is about the same as for blacks. In 1976, about 24 percent of Hispanic families were living below the poverty level (see Fig. 12.3). However, not all Hispanic

TABLE 12.2
Median Family Income, by Race or Ethnic Origin, 1977

RACE OR ETHNIC ORIGIN	MEDIAN FAMILY INCOME (DOLLARS)	PERCENTAGE OF WHITE FAMILY INCOME
White	16,740	100
Black	9560	57
Hispanic American	11,420	68
Native American	8806 (est.)[a]	57 (est.)[a]

[a] The income for Native Americans and the white income used for comparison is for 1976.

SOURCE. U.S. Bureau of the Census, *Current Population Reports*, Series P-60, no. 116, "Money Income and Poverty Status of Families and Persons in the United States: 1977"; advance report (Washington, D.C.: U.S. Government Printing Office, 1978), p. 1; Alan L. Sorkin, "The Economic Basis of Indian Life." *Annals of the American Academy of Political and Social Science* 436 (March 1978), pp. 1–12; and Joseph Strauss, Bruce A. Chadwick and Howard M. Bahr, "Indian Americans: The First Is Last, in Anthony G. Dworkin and Rosalind J. Dworkin, eds., *The Minority Report* (New York: Frederick A. Praeger, 1976), pp. 221–253.

TABLE 12.3
Education, by Race or Ethnic Origin, 1975, (Expressed in Percentages of Persons over 25 Years of Age)

EDUCATION	WHITE	BLACK	HISPANIC AMERICAN
Less than 4 years of high school	36.4	54.6	64.4
4 years of high school	37.3	27.6	24.7
Some college	12.8	9.6	7.5
4 or more years of college	14.5	9.2	4.4

SOURCE. U.S. Bureau of the Census, *Current Population Reports*, Series P-20, no. 295, "Educational Attainment in the United States: March 1975" (Washington, D.C.: U.S. Government Printing Office, 1976), Table 1, pp. 9–16.

groups are struck equally hard by poverty. In 1975, Puerto Ricans were in the worst financial predicament, with 33.5 percent living in poverty; Mexican Americans were next with 26.5 percent, and Cubans had a relatively low 17 percent.[29] Unemployment among Hispanic Americans is high; and, while lower than for blacks, unemployment among Hispanics was almost twice as great as for whites (see Fig. 12.3). Like blacks, Hispanic American heads of household have jobs that are concentrated in the lower-level blue-collar segment of the occupational structure (see Table 12.1).

In 1977, the median income for Hispanic families was 68 percent of that for white families—slightly higher than for blacks (see Table 12.2). Again, Mexican Americans and Puerto Ricans had the lowest incomes among Hispanics.[30] In addition, Mexican American and Puerto Rican families have a lower per capita income because their families tend to be larger than white, black, or other Hispanic families. The percentage of Hispanic Americans finishing high school is low (64.4 percent do not complete four years of high school), and the proportion entering college is also very small. Overall, the situation faced by Mexican Americans in the United States today is as discouraging as, and possibly slightly worse than, that faced by blacks.

Native Americans

Today, there are about 800,000 Native Americans living in the United States. They constitute approximately four-tenths of 1 percent of our nation's population. Historically, Native Americans have been the most deprived ethnic minority in the United States. About two-thirds of them still live on reservations segregated from the rest of society; most Native Americans on reservations are poor. Over 90 percent of those not on reservations live in urban areas, however, and have roughly similar employment and income levels as blacks.[31]

The infant mortality rate for Native Americans has improved significantly in recent years. In 1955, it was an astounding 62.5 per 1000 live births—well over twice the national rate. By 1974 it was 18.7 (see Fig. 12.2)—a decrease of 70 percent over a

twenty-year period, and not far above the rate for whites. Improvements in general health status and living conditions among Native Americans account for this progress.[32] However, their life expectancy was approximately 64 years in 1974—nearly 9 years less than for whites (see Fig. 12.2).

Over one-third of all Native American families live below the poverty level (see Fig. 12.3). Native Americans on reservations are heavily dependent on government for jobs and income. For example, in 1972 nearly 40 percent of reservation earnings was accounted for by the federal government, with an additional 20 percent coming from tribal, state, and local government. In addition to earned income, about 20 percent of all families received welfare income, compared with about only 5 percent of the total United States population.[33]

The unemployment rate for Native Americans is about 30 percent (see Fig. 12.3). The biggest economic problem on reservations is unemployment, which has averaged 40 percent of the labor force for the past twenty years.[34] Those employed, both on and off reservations, have predominantly lower-level blue-collar jobs (see Table 12.1). The median family income for all Native American families—from all income sources—is about 57 percent of that for whites (see Table 12.2). Although income levels for Native Americans have improved substantially over the past twenty years, most of their families are still relatively poor.

The level of educational attainment among Native Americans has also improved greatly in recent years. There has been rapid growth in school and college enrollments of Native American youth together with tentative movements toward greater initiative and responsibility by Native American communities for the administration of their schools.[35] In 1978, about 90 percent of Native Americans aged 6–17 were enrolled in school. Only 38 percent of younger Native Americans had not completed high school in 1975 (see Table 12.3). Because of funds provided by the federal government and tribal councils, many Native Americans go on to postsecondary education—in 1970, 20 percent entered a university-level institution, and another 10 percent entered a postsecondary institution for vocational training.

However, some of these educational gains are sometimes more apparent than real because the education of many Native Americans is not on a par with that of other groups in society. For example on standard tests of school achievement, Native American students fall well below national averages.

> This relatively low academic achievement is not because [they] are less intelligent than white children. Several studies based on intelligence tests which do not require reading ability show [them] to be at or slightly above the level of white children.[36]

School achievement depends to a large extent on children's experience in the family and neighborhood. The lower level of reading skills of Native American children is due primarily to the fact that many adults in their families and communities do not speak or write English well, if at all. In addition, because of poverty, the children have not been exposed to experiences such as frequent visits to museums and libraries that enhance children's performances on standardized educational tests. The absence of these skills poses definite obstacles to social mobility for young Native Americans. Even though the life chances of Native Americans have improved, they still lag far behind those of whites.

The Costs of Racism

The picture that comes through from this recitation of facts and figures concerning blacks, Hispanic Americans, and Native Americans is very clear and rather unsettling. There have been gains over the past few decades; the gap between whites and minority groups has narrowed in the areas of health and education. Yet, the gaps persist, and in some cases they are substantial. Racism in America has very clear-cut and measurable costs for the groups who are its victims. There are additional costs that are difficult to quantify but that nevertheless have a profound influence on our society. These costs affect not only the victims of racism but its perpetrators as well. We all pay the price of prejudice and discrimination. Let us look at some of the costs.

Prejudice has a negative impact on the self-concepts and feelings of self-esteem of minority-group members. Cultural norms in our society equate goodness with lightness and badness with darkness. Young children, including black children, have a preference for light skin color over dark skin color. Preschool children express a high degree of general acceptance of other children as potential playmates; however, both black and white children accept white children more frequently than black children because of the cultural bias in favor of lighter-skinned people.[37] This early skin color bias may contribute to the development of true racial bias as the child learns the importance of race in our society and encounters the various cultural and familial messages that are associated with racial classifications.

There appears to be no clear relationship between the social prestige of groups and the self-esteem of their members. Parents who support, are interested in, and express feelings of warmth toward their children tend to generate high levels of self-esteem in them. Acceptance or rejection within the neighborhood may be more important than acceptance or rejection of a group by the larger society. However, many studies note that blacks and lower-class children have negative self-concepts when compared to middle-class whites. Although the family might overcome the detrimental effect of negative reactions from the larger society, it often does not.[38]

People who are the objects of prejudice and discrimination encounter barriers to developing their full potentials as human beings. For example, minority-group children are less successful in school, on the average, than are children from the dominant white group. Grades, scores on standardized tests of educational achievement, and the percentages completing high school are especially low for blacks, Hispanic Americans, and Native Americans. Although researchers differ concerning which social factors (e.g. segregated schools or family income and values) they believe cause these differences, there is considerable agreement among social scientists that minority-group children have less access to a quality education and the opportunities associated with it.[39]

Prejudice and discrimination impair intergroup communication and cooperation. Members of various ethnic groups frequently hold negative stereotypes of one another. This results in distrust, a lack of effective communication, and a high potential for negative encounters between persons from different racial or ethnic groups. Studies show for example, that encounters between blacks and white liberals—who presumably are not prejudiced—are frequently negative and emotionally tense. Apparently, communication between members of the two groups is impaired by a generally high level of distrust on the part of blacks toward whites.[40] When communication is ineffective, cooperation towards mutually beneficial goals is less likely to occur.

Discrimination is economically detrimental to most members of the majority group. For example, social scientist Albert Szymanski found that most whites today do not gain from economic discrimination directed at members of minority groups; on the contrary, white working people actually *lose* economically from such discrimination.[41] Szymanski argues that racism is a divisive force that undermines the economic and political strength of working people and acts to worsen the economic position of white workers in the most racist areas—where white workers have the lowest incomes and there is the greatest degree of economic inequality between white workers. Racism is a barrier to collective action that could be mutually rewarding—such as unionization—between white and black workers.

Racism and discrimination in the United States undermine many of our nation's political goals. For example, the expansion of human rights (such as political and religious freedom) in the world is very difficult when the most vocal advocate of such a stance—the United States—is plagued by racial and ethnic discrimination. Many nations view us as hypocritical when we seek economic sanctions against nations such as South Africa as a means of reducing racial discrimination there. We must be more serious about putting our own house in order if we are to make an effective argument for human rights on a worldwide scale.

Racism has costs for various segments of American society. This young, black Airman in an Atlanta rail terminal in 1956 seems to be confused by the sign indicating where the colored waiting room is and whether he is required to use it.

The effects of racism are widespread. It permeates all aspects of a society. We tend to ignore the impact it has on those who presumably benefit most from it. One of the legacies of our own racism that we must cope with is the lingering hostility, tension, and fear that is still noticeable today. To understand how these feelings have emerged, we will examine how minority groups in America have reacted to prejudice and discrimination.

REACTIONS TO PREJUDICE AND DISCRIMINATION

The ways in which minority groups in the United States have reacted to their subordinate status have left significant and indelible marks on our history. These reactions have ranged from resignation to social protest, and from rioting to (in a few cases) insurrection. This history has shaped the current relationships between dominant and subordinate groups, with effects on the possibilities for the future. For these reasons, it is important to understand what these reactions have been.

Black Reactions
Accommodation and Rebellion

Not all slaves in American history were docile; there was considerable turmoil in the history of American slavery.[42] The best-known and probably the bloodiest slave revolt occurred in Virginia in 1831. The insurrection was led by Nat Turner, a slave mystic who felt that he was divinely ordained to lead his people out of bondage. By the time Turner's poorly planned insurrection had been quelled, the rebels (who numbered about 60) had killed 55 whites. However, recognizing the futility of organized rebellion, most slaves remained apathetic or vented their hostilities through personal acts of vandalism of their masters' property or through individual attempts to escape.

Most blacks, both before and after the Emancipation Proclamation, adjusted, however reluctantly, to the demands of the dominant group and accepted their subordinate position. The major advocate of black accommodation to the white supremacy of the Jim Crow era was the black educator Booker T. Washington. In his "Atlanta Compromise" speech of 1877, Washington encouraged blacks to accept their relegation to a subordinate position in society and to adapt to their situation through individual self-improvement. William E. B. DuBois, who is regarded by many as the most productive black teacher and scholar in American history, was a contemporary of Washington's and a vigorous opponent of the accommodationist view. DuBois argued that this stance was a self-defeating sell-out by blacks to white domination over their lives. For most blacks, however, acquiescence and accommodation seemed to be the only feasible option. With a few exceptions, blacks simply had too little power to do anything else.

The Civil Rights Movement

When the civil rights movement started in the 1950s, it spelled the beginning of the end of such black acquiescence. In 1955 a black seamstress, Mrs. Rosa Parks, refused to surrender her seat on a public bus in Montgomery, Alabama to a white man. She was immediately arrested for this violation of the law, which was also viewed as an outrageous breach of the norms of racial etiquette. When word of her arrest spread through the black community, the Montgomery Bus Boycott — and the civil rights movement — was born. The bus boycott in Montgomery was followed by similar actions in other southern cities. The most influential civil rights group was the Southern Christian Leadership Conference headed by the Reverend Martin Luther King, Jr. The philosophy of nonviolent protest, through such means as passive resistance, became the hallmark of the newly emerged movement. A long series of similar protests began. For example, in 1960 four black college students who were refused service at a lunch counter in a nationally owned five-and-dime store staged the first "sit-in" by refusing to leave the store until they were served, even after it closed. "Freedom rides," antisegregation demonstrations, and voter registration campaigns became commonplace in the civil rights movement.

The movement also appealed to a large number of well-educated, middle- and upper-class whites who contributed money and time to such civil rights organizations as Dr. King's Southern Christian Leadership Conference. A few even participated in the demonstrations themselves. In fact, whatever successes the civil rights movement achieved can be partly attributed to blacks' forming coalitions with powerful white groups and individuals. However, because black expectations for greater civil rights and a better life outstripped their gains, the civil rights movement was, by the mid-1960s, in serious trouble. Its role as the major force in the quest for black rights really ended by 1965.[43]

Black Power

The Black Power movement first gained prominence in the spring of 1966 and continued as a potent force until the early 1970s. *Black Power begin as a call to black Americans to liberate themselves from oppression by assuming control over their lives economically, politically, and socially.*[44] The civil rights movement was basically reformist. It aimed at changing some of the structural aspects of American society that blatantly discriminated against blacks. The Black Power movement, at least in its earlier stages, went far beyond social reform—it demanded control by blacks of the economic, political, and social organizations that affect their lives. The most radical element in the Black Power movement was the black nationalist or black separatist component. The black nationalists were heavily Marxist in their orientation to the problem of black rights. It was their contention that blacks could never achieve equality within the framework of a white-dominated capitalist society. Black nationalists proposed that blacks set up their own separate communities, controlled entirely by themselves.

The Black Panthers are probably the best known of the more militant black power groups. In the mid-1960s, the Black Panther Party, whose leadership portrayed itself as machinegun-toting revolutionaries, called on all blacks to unite for a violent confrontation with oppressive white society. However, after massive attempts by the federal government to infiltrate their ranks and to arrest their leadership, the Black Panthers, having won very little support in the black community, changed their rhetoric and strategy. In all likelihood, their goals have also changed to the reform approach of the civil rights movement. For example, in 1973, Bobby Seale, Chairman of the Black Panther Party, wore a business suit and tie and ran for mayor of Oakland, California. In 1976, Eldridge Cleaver—who while in exile in Algiers headed the international section of the Black Panther Party—claimed to be a born-again Christian and reentered the United States to join the circuit of Christian evangelists. In 1977, Huey P. Newton (cofounder of the Black Panther Party) returned to the United States from self-imposed exile in Cuba. Meanwhile, as the Black Panthers waited for their former leaders to return, the party changed direction under the able leadership of Elaine Brown, who made it into a powerful and respectable element in California politics. For example, under Brown's guidance, the Black Panthers in Oakland operate an elementary school that has a reputation for educational excellence and a minimum of militant rhetoric; they have a special escort and transportation system to take senior citizens shopping without fear of street crime; and Brown herself has served as a delegate to the 1976 Democratic National Convention and as a member of several influential public commissions.[45]

While black groups such as the Black Panthers have adopted nonviolent means for achieving their goals, this does not necessarily mean that we have seen the end of violence. Blacks have made gains in some areas and have suffered losses in others. Some feel that a potential for violence still exists, because while many whites subscribe to the principle of equality, they are not willing to pay the price in tax dollars and social change that will be required to implement the goal of equality completely.[46]

Mexican American Reactions

Anglo dominance in the Southwest was achieved primarily through force of arms. However, before that dominance was complete, there was considerable Mexican resistance. For example, beginning in 1859 Juan Cortina led raids on Texas settlements for over a decade, urging Mexicans to join him and reclaim their lands from the "gringos."

Once whites had established themselves as the dominant force in the Southwest both physically and economically, the use of force or violence became a much less viable alternative for Mexican Americans. They adopted the accommodating stance of most blacks, although violence would occasionally flare up. In 1943, the widely publicized "zoot-suit riots" between young Chicanos and Anglos, mainly sailors, focused national attention on Mexican Americans as a significant minority. Although biased press coverage reported that it was Mexican youth gangs who attacked "defenseless" sailors, it appears on closer examination that it was the sailors who usually attacked the Mexican youths. "If they had not already known, . . . the

Cesar Chavez and his United Farm Workers Organizing Committee successfully boycotted major wineries in a militant and effective movement. Their efforts gained improved working conditions and wages for farm workers (most of them Hispanic) in California and across the United States.

Zoot-suit riots made it clear to California's Mexican population just how second class their citizenship was."[47] The fact that young Mexicans who were attacked by sailors were almost always arrested, while the Anglos were released, was a dramatic illustration to Mexicans that discrimination could take violent forms and that they could not count on legal authorities to protect their civil rights.

In reaction to what they defined as the dehumanizing, "culture-robbing" dominance of Anglo society, the student-inspired Chicano movement emerged in the late 1960s. The Chicano movement is based on a broad ideology that rejects accommodation to Anglo dominance and stresses unity in the struggle for Mexican American rights. Included in the Chicano movement are Reies Tijerina's violent uprising to reclaim territories lost earlier in northern New Mexico, the farm-labor protests of Cesar Chavez, and the protests of Chicano high school and college youths. The dual themes of unity and ethnic pride are the hallmarks of the Chicano movement.

The most highly publicized aspect of ethnic militancy in the Mexican American community was the formation of a separatist third party—La Raza Unida Party (LRU)—in 1970. The LRU was a response by Chicanos to the insensitivity of the Anglo-dominated political system to the problems of Mexican Americans. The LRU has had some noteworthy successes, the most notable of which was in Crystal City, Texas where LRU candidates gained control of the city council and board of education in the 1970 elections. However, since the LRU is comprised mostly of young Chicanos and has adopted radical positions on most issues—including a near split with Cesar Chavez over his endorsement of George McGovern in 1972, whom they considered too conservative—it appears to be no substantial threat to the Democratic and Republican parties. However, both major parties now realize that Mexican Americans are an important "swing" group that can affect elections. This portends improvements for the situation of Mexican Americans.[48]

Native American Reactions

In large measure because of their cultural diversity, the various Native American tribal groups have reacted differently to the white invasion of their lands and the disruption of their traditional way of life. For example, the Apache became raiders on horseback and sporadically attacked white settlers in a futile attempt to regain their lost lands. In contrast, the Cherokee organized into a series of close-knit farming communities that made up a federation, thereby giving them the economic and political strength to deal with the white man on the white man's terms.

Recent Native American reactions have been considerably more militant than Indian accommodation to the invasion of the white man that was characteristic of most groups in the past. In 1964, for example, two Native Americans claimed Alcatraz Island as Native American land under the Sioux treaty of 1868, which included a provision that surplus federal property be given to the Sioux. The claim was quickly rejected by the federal courts and the case was dropped. In 1969, as a method of attracting support for reconstruction of the San Francisco Indian Center that had burned down earlier that year, two hundred fifty Native Americans occupied Alcatraz. However, the federal government merely "waited out" the occupation force, until only twenty were left by the summer of 1971. Federal marshals surprised the remaining occupants and escorted them off the island.

The most dramatic of the recent Native American protests was the seventy-day occupation of Wounded Knee, South Dakota in 1973. Approximately three hundred Native Americans supported by the American Indian Movement (AIM) took eleven local residents as hostages and claimed that they represented the Sioux people, on whose reservation Wounded Knee is situated. They demanded that the tribal constitution and government, imposed on them by the Bureau of Indian Affairs

(BIA), be suspended, that the BIA police force be withdrawn from the reservation, and that there be an investigation of the loss of sovereign rights guaranteed by treaty.

The occupation received enormous coverage in the media. After nearly a month, serious negotiations to end the siege began, and a tentative settlement was announced but never reached. A government helicopter flying over Wounded Knee became involved in a shoot-out with protesters, and the occupation ended when one hundred fifty Native Americans surrendered themselves and their arms to the federal marshals.

Even though such Native American protests have not appeared to be very effective, there is evidence that Congress is taking its responsibilities to deal with Native American affairs more seriously. Recently, a Senate subcommittee has investigated violations of treaties with Native Americans; the subcommittee is responsible for formulating proposals that will allow Native Americans to redress their grievances. Meanwhile, some Native American groups have turned to the courts in order to receive compensation for land that they claim was illegally taken from them when treaty provisions were broken or laws ignored. As early as 1950, one tribe, the Colorado Ute, receive over $31 million in this fashion, and more such efforts were mounted in the 1970s.[49]

Intergroup Relations

The patterns of relationships that have existed between the dominant groups and minority groups in the United States are varied, but there are certain commonalities that exist. **The most common relationship has been _assimilation_, in which the minority group loses its separate identity and is absorbed into the dominant culture.** This has been the fate of most ethnic minorities of the past two centuries. The Irish, Italians, Poles, and many others tended to give up the trappings of their culture and become like the Anglo majority. There are two differing views on assimilation in America. First, sociologist Milton Gordon argues that assimilation in America has meant "Anglo conformity" – minority groups are expected to adopt Anglo customs, language, and institutions.[50] In other words, migrants were expected to become Anglos. Second, some argue that America is a "melting pot"—that American culture is a unique blending of all the different peoples and the accompanying cultural beliefs that have come to our shores. In this view, migrants do not become "Anglo," they become "American," and in so doing they add a little to American culture and change it slightly. There is probably some truth to each of these views of assimilation. Certainly, Anglo culture has been dominant in shaping what it means to be American. At the same time, the combined impact of such a large influx of immigrants has undoubtedly changed that Anglo influence.

For some groups, however, assimilation has been either impossible or undesirable. **Another pattern of intergroup relations is** *pluralism,* **in which a number of separate ethnic or racial groups coexist, each retaining a distinct identity and lifestyle, while also participating in the larger culture.** The reasons why a group would retain its own identity are many. In some cases, there is a strong consciousness of common heritage and pride in a particular identity. In other cases, the minority group is not allowed to assimilate, often because visible differences with the dominant group make such assimilation difficult. Blacks, Hispanic Americans, and Native Americans have to a large extent not been allowed by the white majority to assimilate. Because of this they have had to acquiesce in their subordinate position in society. However, in recent years these groups have begun to emphasize cultural pluralism as the preferred relationship with whites. They no longer want to assimilate but rather want to retain their identity and culture while still participating as equals in American society.

Another relationship often found between dominant and minority groups is *separatism,* **in which the minority group makes efforts to break away from the dominant culture and establish a separate society.** Such movements can be found among American minorities, but they have rarely gained many adherents. Successful separatism calls for much more power and access to resources than American minorities have had.

When we review the treatment of minority groups in the past and their status today, there may be a temptation to make comparisons between their treatment and the ideals of American society. In view of our heavy emphasis on the values of individualism and achievement, why is it not possible to simply treat each person as an individual and evaluate that person on the basis of what he or she can achieve? Why do we not live up to our ideals? Unfortunately, human behavior is much more complex than this. There are many influences on our behavior other than our ideals or values, and some of these other influences, although less tangible, can be very powerful. Before we can look to the future, we must investigate what the causes of prejudice and discrimination are and how they are perpetuated.

SOURCES OF PREJUDICE AND DISCRIMINATION

One of the primary goals of any investigation of problems in racial and ethnic group relations is to provide a more effective means for dealing with these difficulties. In the following pages we will discuss a number of theories concerning the causes of racism, minority group subordination, prejudice, and discrimination, how they originate, how they are perpetuated, and what can be done to deal with them effectively. However, as we have noted elsewhere in this text, there are no simple answers. No single theory provides a complete picture of these problems. By using a combination of approaches, however, the student will be better sensitized to their nature and sources.

Psychological Sources

Psychological approaches to intergroup relations view prejudiced attitudes as the main source of discrimination.[51] Prejudice is seen as characteristic of a particular personality type, supported and reinforced by the social environment in which the individual operates. There are a number of psychological theories to explain prejudice and discrimination.

The Authoritarian Personality

Social scientist T. W. Adorno and his associates concluded from their research on prejudice that some people have a distinct set of personality traits that together comprise what they termed the "authoritarian personality."[52] People who have an authoritarian personality have anti-intellectual and antiscientific attitudes; they view the world in very rigid and stereotyped terms such as win or lose, good or evil, and them versus us; they are highly conventional in their attitudes (if not in their behavior) and condemn, reject, and wish to punish those who violate conventional norms; they have a low level of tolerance for ambiguity, especially concerning sexual and religious matters; they are preoccupied with status and power relationships and are submissive to superiors and bullying to inferiors.

A prejudiced personality such as this develops within a home environment characterized by an atmosphere of negativism and rejection. The socialization process is characterized by discipline, dominance, and differences in status. Because an individual who experiences such socialization develops negative stereotypes of persons outside his or her own social sphere and because this person has a low level of self-esteem, he or she tends to project problems onto other people. **Projection is a psychological defense mechanism in which one attributes to others characteristics that one is unwilling to recognize in oneself.** For example, people who view blacks as lazy and preoccupied with sex may be projecting deepseated doubts about their own industriousness and their sexual fantasies onto another group.

A psychological mechanism closely associated with projection is scapegoating. **Scapegoating involves placing the blame for one's troubles on an individual or group incapable of offering effective resistance.** For example, a parent might blame the birth of a child as an obstacle to his or her occupational success. Thus the child becomes a scapegoat who is blamed for the parent's lack of success. By using the child as a scapegoat, the parent can avoid the painful experience of confronting himself with his own inadequacies. Another example of scapegoating involves poor and working-class whites who rationalize their own lack of worldly success by referring to alleged advantages of minority groups that are given jobs through affirmative action programs (programs by state and federal agencies—such as active attempts to locate and recruit minority-group members into educational institutions and professions—designed to compensate for generations of discrimination).

Frustration and Aggression

Another psychological approach to prejudice and discrimination is the *frustration-aggression hypothesis*, in which aggression is regarded as a logical and expected consequence of frustration.[53] If a person is frustrated in achieving a particular goal, tension develops within that person; aggression either removes or destroys the obstacle to goal attainment, or it can serve to release tension even if the obstacle is not removed. The frustration component of the ghetto riots of the late 1960s is described by psychologist Kenneth Clark:

> A central fact emerges from the murky background of the present urban eruptions: a society of affluence has raised the expectations and aspirations of the poor but has bypassed them, thereby increasing their frustration and anger, their bitterness, [and] hostility.[54]

In the case of the ghetto riots, the source of the frustration was *relative deprivation*—blacks believed that, compared to other groups in society, they were deprived of the economic rewards and social standing that they deserved. The targets for aggression were objects symbolizing the white racist society, which was perceived as the source of the frustration. According to this theory, aggressive actions such as rioting or burning, even though they may not remove the real source of frustration, nonetheless result from the buildup of tension due to frustration and serve to release that tension.

Because prejudices are learned and reinforced in particular types of social environments, however, psychological theories do not provide a complete understanding of the origins and perpetuation of prejudice and discrimination.[55] Approaches that focus on how prejudice and discrimination are learned and on characteristics of society that perpetuate them must also be considered.

Prejudice and Discrimination as Learned

The interactionist perspective focuses on the social processes through which prejudice and discrimination are learned and perpetuated. Our attitudes and to a large extent our behavior are the product of social interaction with others and a shared consensus about reality. **Rather than seeing prejudice and discrimination as personality traits, the interactionist sees them as emerging from the interaction of group members.**[56] **One important part of this process is *ethnocentrism*—the belief that your own group is different from, better than, and possibly superior to, other groups.** Ethnocentrism is normal in groups and develops when there is a strong sense of group identity and belongingness. However, it should be clear how feelings of ethnocentrism can develop into prejudice and discrimination. If your group is presumably superior, then it is a short step to viewing the qualities possessed by members of your group, such as race or ethnicity, as more desirable. Groups may begin to claim advantages and privileges based on these qualities and to become suspicious of, and often hostile to, other groups.

A person tends to adopt the attitudes, including the prejudicial and ethnocentric attitudes, of the group of which the person is a member or of the group that he or she wants to belong to.[57] Such groups are a primary means of social reinforcement for a person's attitudes and behavior; they are important in the formation and reinforcement of a person's self-concept. For example, a white person who identifies with white supremacist groups such as the Ku Klux Klan will view herself as superior to blacks and will be likely to discriminate against them. By the same token, a black person who identifies himself as a member of an inferior group may be quite receptive to the definition held by white su-

premacist groups. He may act like an "Uncle Tom" because obsequious behavior is consistent with his image of other blacks and his conception of himself.

Because prejudice and discrimination are learned behaviors, the definitions of intergroup relations held by people and groups that are important to us are a primary source of reinforcement for our attitudes and actions. For example, if we are surrounded by people who are prejudiced, we are more likely to be prejudiced ourselves. If, on the other hand, we have developed nonprejudiced self-conceptions that are reinforced by groups with which we identify, we shall be less likely to discriminate.

How are prejudices learned? How are they perpetuated? Learning prejudices involves the same processes as does the learning of any other attitude. Prejudices are learned through contact with prejudice rather than with the people about whom prejudices are held.[58] For example, a person from a predominantly white town might tell others, "I was not prejudiced until I went into the Army, but the way those black so-and-sos acted really changed my mind in a hurry." With all sincerity, he may defend his "newly acquired" view of blacks with a number of anecdotes that illustrate his unpleasant experiences with them. However, regardless of protestations to the contrary, negative contacts with blacks are more likely to be a result of prejudice than the source of it. If a person enters a situation with a positive attitude based on a favorable definition of the other participants, it is highly probable that a positive encounter will result. However, if a person enters a situation in which she interacts with persons toward whom she is prejudiced, she will exhibit cues that indicate her prejudice, and a negative encounter that confirms her prejudice will likely occur.[59]

Prejudice, Discrimination, and the Social Order

Opportunity

The social order is an important source of prejudice and discrimination in that it offers the opportunities for people to have prejudicial attitudes and engage in discriminatory actions. *Individual discrimination* **occurs when a prejudiced person acts out his or her prejudicial attitudes in his or her treatment of another person or group.** Certainly, if they are given the opportunity, prejudiced people are more likely to discriminate than unprejudiced people. However, the relationship between prejudice and discrimination is far more complex than that of a simple causal linkage in which prejudicial attitudes automatically result in discriminatory behavior. *Opportunity and social reinforcement* **are important factors in determining whether a person will discriminate against others, and the extent to which the social order provides these varies from one situation to the next.**

The functionalist perspective sensitizes us to the complex relationship between prejudice and individual discrimination. Sociologist Robert Merton proposed a model of the relationship between prejudice and discrimination that helps us to understand that complexity.[60] The model is based on four possible relationships between prejudice (an attitude) and discrimination (a behavior). The *unprejudiced nondiscriminator* accepts the formal values of American democracy and adheres to the ideal of equality in both theory and practice. Such a person is not prejudiced and does not discriminate against others because of their racial, ethnic, or minority group status. The *unprejudiced discriminator* has no personal prejudices but may discriminate when it is convenient to do so. For example, a white realtor may hold no personal prejudice against blacks. However, she may avoid showing black families houses in certain neighborhoods where she knows that they will not be welcome. In addition, she may be concerned about possible offense to future clients of her realty company. The *prejudiced discriminator* is the "true bigot" who is prejudiced and consistently discriminates on the basis of his or her prejudiced attitudes. The *prejudiced nondiscriminator* is prejudiced against other groups; but, because of social and legal pressures, this person is reluctant to translate his or her attitudes into action. For example, a white businessperson who dislikes blacks intensely but whose business is located in a predominantly

black neighborhood will more likely keep his or her prejudices private, at least while at work. This person will not openly discriminate against black customers because it is not good business practice and because it is now illegal to do so.

The two types in Merton's scheme that show a consistency between their attitudes and their behavior—the unprejudiced nondiscriminator and the prejudiced discriminator—may actually be less common than the other two because opportunity and social reinforcement are as important as a person's attitudes in determining that person's behavior. Thus the realtor and businessperson just described behave inconsistently with their attitudes because it was in some way to their benefit to do so. This illustrates the power of the social order in shaping our behavior. Because of the numerous social and legal pressures placed on individuals, it is difficult to be consistently bigoted or nonbigoted.

Economic Sources

Conflict theorists emphasize that discrimination is built into existing economic, political, and social arrangements in the United States. From the conflict perspective, the most important source of discrimination is institutionalized discrimination. *Institutionalized discrimination* **refers to inequalities that are rooted in the normal and impersonal operation of existing institutions in society.** Racial and ethnic group discrimination is an inherent part of our political, economic, educational, and religious organizations, and it serves to maintain and enhance the economic position of the dominant groups. How did institutionalized discrimination originate in our society? How is it perpetuated? We will look at some of the ways in which this occurs.

Sociologist James W. Vander Zanden argues that prejudice and discrimination result from competition between different groups for scarce and highly valued resources such as educational opportunities, good jobs, and desirable wages.[61] For intergroup conflict to arise, three essential conditions must be met: (1) there must be two or more social groups, identifiable by their visible physical characteristics or cultural practices; (2) there must be competition between the groups for valued resources, such as power, land, jobs, or prestige; and (3) these groups must be unequal in power, so that one of them is able to make its claim over scarce resources at the expense of other groups. For example, much of the racism in the southern United States arose from the situation in which lower socioeconomic status whites and blacks were pitted against each other as competitors for scarce resources like a good education or a good job.

One variation of this economic explanation of institutionalized discrimination is the notion of *internal colonialism*.[62] Just as colonialism refers to the domination of one country by another, *internal colonialism describes* **a situation in which a dominent group subordinates another group in its own country and exploits that group for its own economic gain.** This notion of internal colonialism emphasizes the fact that nonwhite migration to the United States was different from that of other ethnic groups and that this has had consequences for the place of these groups in the American stratification system. Nonwhite Americans often came to this country under economic and political pressure, and were frequently exploited — they were to do menial jobs that others refused to do. Examples of this are the Africans, who were brought to this country as slaves and Mexicans brought here to take difficult and low-paying jobs as migratory farm workers. The subsequent adaptation of nonwhite groups was along nonegalitarian lines, with continuing elements of coercion. The original colonial relationship between the dominant and subordinate groups results in discrimination being built into political, educational, and other institutions. This makes it especially hard for a subordinate group to achieve equal status.

Another approach that focuses on the economic origins of ethnic antagonism and conflict in the United States is the split labor market hypothesis. **A** *split labor market* **is an economic arena in which there is a large differential in the price of labor for the same occupation.**[63] Within split labor markets, conflict usually develops among three groups: business, higher-paid labor, and cheaper labor. It is in the interests of the upper classes, especially those in business, to secure as

cheap and docile a labor force as possible in order to compete effectively and to maximize profits. To do so, cheap labor is frequently imported, such as African slaves in the pre-Civil War South, the Irish and Chinese to work on the canals and railroads during the mid- and late-nineteenth century, and blacks from the rural South for Northern industry during and after World War I.

Cheap labor, however, tends to displace higher-paid labor. Thus higher-paid labor finds its interests threatened. Where cheap labor involves a different racial or ethnic membership, this class antagonism commonly takes the form of racial or ethnic conflict. What is basically class conflict, then, becomes translated into the rhetoric of racism. According to the split labor market hypothesis, it is in the interests of the upper classes to maintain racism, especially institutionalized discrimination, as a means of guaranteeing a large pool of cheap labor.

These two variants of the economic argument show us different faces of prejudice and discrimination. In the case of internal colonialism, prejudice and discrimination serve to keep the weaker group in subordinate status and thus ensure a cheap and docile source of labor. In the case of the split labor market, prejudice and discrimination serve as mechanism for higher-priced labor to exclude those willing to work for lower wages from competing for their jobs. In this case, the businessperson may not get the cheapest labor possible, and thus it may not be to his or her advantage. However, in either case, the focus is on the manner in which economic arrangements are the source of prejudice and discrimination.

Whether prejudice and discrimination emerge from psychological factors, from the learning process, or from some aspects of the social order, it is clear that there are very powerful mechanisms that underlie prejudice and discrimination. It would be naive to believe that these problems can be easily ameliorated. Yet, as we learn more about people as social beings, we are in an increasingly advantageous position to attack problems such as racism. In the next section, we will see what can be, and is being done to solve the problems of prejudice and discrimination in American society.

PROSPECTS FOR THE FUTURE

Without question there have been improvements in racial and ethnic relations in the United States. Overt hostility and violence in the form of lynchings and assaults are largely things of the past. The legal status of minority groups has improved considerably. Yet, as we have seen, some very serious problems still exist, and the gaps between dominant groups and minority groups are still present. Recent attempts to deal with this continuing legacy of racism have focused on reducing either individual discrimination or institutional discrimination. We will discuss each of these efforts.

Programs to Reduce Individual Discrimination

In order to reduce individual prejudice and discrimination, some people have focused on the importance of educating people about why prejudice and discrimination exist and their costs, in the hope that this information will motivate people to stop engaging in these practices. Others have placed faith in positive contact between members of groups in order to reduce prejudice and discrimination.

Educational Programs

For many years, organizations such as the National Association for the Advancement of Colored People (NAACP) and the National Council of Churches used means such as radio and television advertisements and special conferences in an attempt to inform the public about the negative aspects of prejudice. The net effect of these programs has not been very impressive, and they are usually ineffective in bringing about attitude change. Highly prejudiced persons are generally either unaware of their own prejudice or, if they are aware of it, unresponsive to such information — ignoring it as irrelevant to them or dismissing it as propaganda. There is substantial research evidence to show that it is difficult to change people's attitudes through such educational programs — especially if the attitudes are prominent and supported by other group values, which is usually the case with racial and ethnic prejudice.[64]

Programs for Intergroup Contact

If attitude-change efforts do not work, then perhaps contact between groups might — prejudiced persons could learn that their stereotypes are inaccurate and their fears unfounded. However, mere contact between groups does not automatically result in the emergence of positive feelings and harmonious future interaction. On the contrary, under certain circumstances, intergroup contact is quite likely to result in greater hostility. What, then, are the circumstances in which contact is likely to reduce prejudice and discrimination?

First, infrequent, involuntary, and tension-laden contact is likely to increase prejudice. For example, white and black prison inmates, who make their first contact on a personal, face-to-face basis with members of the other race, are quite likely to become more prejudiced while in prison — because they meet one another in an environment already fraught with mistrust, tension, and hostility.

Second, pleasant, equal-status contact of people from different groups, but who are from essentially the same social class, occupational and educational levels, is likely to reduce prejudice. For example, interaction between a wealthy white person and her black maid will probably have little effect on each person's opinion of the other group as a social category — even though the two women may develop a close and affectionate relationship. However, two women — one white, the other black — who are from wealthy and influential families and who have similar educations, are more likely to become less prejudiced with increased contact — a reduction in prejudice that is likely to be generalized beyond the specific individuals involved.

Third, "stereotype-breaking" contacts that show minority-group members in roles not usually associated with them is likely to reduce prejudice. For example, interaction between a prejudiced male and a waitress is not very likely to break down his stereotype of a "woman's place." On the other hand, contact between a "sexist" male and a female physician is more likely to reduce prejudice.

Fourth, contacts that bring minority and majority group members into mutually beneficial, cooperative, and interdependent activities tend to reduce prejudice. For example, while competition between Native Americans and whites over hunting rights on certain federal lands is likely to increase prejudice, cooperation between the two groups to get the government to improve the land so that both groups can use it more effectively is likely to reduce prejudice.[65] **In summary, then, intergroup contact, if it occurs under favorable conditions, can be effective in reducing prejudice and discrimination.**

Programs to Reduce Institutionalized Discrimination

Attempts to reduce institutionalized discrimination have taken two major forms: social protest and legal reform.

Social Protest

Protest has been a major means (during the past two decades) by which minority groups have attempted to call the public's attention to their plight in the hope that programs to reduce prejudice and discrimination would result. The outcomes of social protest have been mixed.[66] Nonviolent protest such as that typical of the civil rights movement was somewhat successful in achieving legal and economic gains for blacks. This was probably attributable to the fact that the movement had a great deal of support in the black community and that it helped many whites to become more keenly aware of the problems faced by blacks. However, more violent episodes of protest such as the 1967 riots in Newark, Detroit, and elsewhere (see ch. 14) seemed to alienate both blacks and whites who identified with the goals of the civil rights movement. The principal value of protest seems to be the stimulation of public awareness of particular problems. Continued protest past a certain (although indeterminate) point seems to have little additional positive effect.

Legal Reforms

The major attempts at legal reform in order to reduce institutionalized discrimination are civil rights legislation (especially the Civil Rights Acts of 1964 and 1965), busing to achieve racial balance in public schools, various affirmative-action programs, and other legal challenges of past inequities.

Civil Rights Legislation

Various pieces of legislation have been passed by state and federal governments to make institutionalized discrimination illegal. Voter-rights acts and laws prohibiting discrimination in jobs, housing, and public facilities were passed in the 1960s and early 1970s as a means of reducing discrimination that had been built into the normal day-to-day operations of major American institutions. The net results have been fairly impressive in reducing the more blatant forms of discrimination. For example, minority groups who were once openly prohibited from certain occupations and public facilities now enjoy a much greater freedom of movement than in the past. However, as we have noted, there is still a great deal of discrimination for which this legislation has been quite ineffective. For example, where jobs require certain minimal educational requirements before an applicant is seriously considered, educational discrimination must be overcome before many minority-group members will be able to take advantage of these opportunities.

Busing

In the late 1960s, the use of busing to achieve racial balance in the public schools was seen by many as a relatively simple means of reducing prejudice and discrimination in the long run and of providing greater educational opportunities for minority-group members in the short run. In the southern United States, busing was used traditionally to achieve racial segregation rather than integration.[67] In the beginning, blacks as well as whites went along with busing in the South. However, there have been vigorous and vocal protests against busing over the past few years (including an attempt by supporters of conservative candidate Ronald Reagan in the 1976 Republican Convention to incorporate an antibusing plank in the party's platform) by both white and black groups opposing it. In addition, some have argued that busing increases "white flight" from desegregated schools in city districts with high proportions of minority students surrounded by largely white suburbs.

Whether busing increases or decreases residential, and thus educational, segregation, is still very controversial.[68] Sociologist James Coleman, whose well-known "Coleman Report" advocated busing as one means of achieving racial integration, has recently stated that the use of busing to achieve that goal has fallen considerably short of what he had anticipated.[69] Busing remains a hotly contested issue and is considered by some to be a social problem by itself. It is difficult to project at this point whether its long-term effect will be beneficial or detrimental. However, it is increasingly clear that busing is no panacea for racial problems in our urban areas.

Affirmative-Action Programs

As we have mentioned at several points in this chapter, discrimination has been a tradition in American society. Up until the past few years (prior to civil rights legislation in the 1960s) blatant, open discrimination against minority-group members has been the rule. This means that these people were almost completely excluded from certain aspects of American life and that there were strict quotas with regard to their participation in others. For example, certain clubs, landlords, colleges, and public facilities barred blacks, Native Americans, women, Jews, Mexican Americans, and other minorities openly, and with the support of related state and federal laws such discrimination was, for all practical purposes, legal. Organizations such as colleges and universities that did not strictly prohibit minority-group members frequently had quotas that were rigidly enforced — regardless of the qualifications of minority-group members. As previously mentioned, many institutions of higher learning, including many law schools and medical schools, had strict quotas on how many women

and Jews would be admitted each year. In order to qualify under these quotas, then, a female or Jewish applicant would have to be among, say, the top 5 percent of the applicants in order to gain admission.

Prior to civil rights legislation and affirmative-action programs, employers were not required to advertise job openings in most states; where they were, there was little means of systematically enforcing that requirement. Job discrimination was rampant. Not only were minority-group members discriminated against, but whites without local connections were often excluded.

Under civil rights legislation, but prior to affirmative-action programs, employers could legally meet the demands for their cooperation in hiring minority-group members by merely asserting their willingness to do so. However such "voluntary" programs were quite ineffective because the only legal means for enforcing antidiscrimination laws was for the individual applicant to file suit — a costly, time-consuming, and generally ineffective means of dealing with job discrimination. To overcome these problems, the government has initiated affirmative-action programs.

Affirmative action has operated on four levels: (1) active efforts to locate and recruit qualified minority applicants (e.g. advertising in schools that have students who are predominantly minority-group members); (2) positive action to increase the pool of qualified minority applicants (e.g. special training programs designed to deal with particular needs and problems of minorities); (3) preferential hiring and admission requirements for minority applicants (e.g. systematically favoring minority applicants even though they may be less well qualified than many majority applicants); and (4) hard quotas, under which specific numbers of minority members must be accepted to fill vacant positions, regardless of their individual qualifications (e.g. a university requiring that half of its new faculty appointments be female).

Affirmative-action programs have faced several problems. Positive action and minority recruiting programs are difficult to enforce. Preferential hiring and quota programs involve **reverse discrimination** — that is, qualified majority-group members are often arbitrarily excluded.[70] This, of course, has infuriated those who have been excluded. Emotional appeals by members of the majority based on the fact that discrimination is traditional in America and that it is "their turn" somehow have not appeased many who have been rejected under affirmative action. There have been several successful lawsuits claiming reverse discrimination, and there will probably be more in the future. The best-known case so far is that of Allan Bakke, a white male who was initially denied admission to the medical school at the University of California at Davis.[71] He alleged reverse discrimination, since several minority students with lower grades and lower scores on the Medical College Admissions Test were accepted ahead of him under the university's minorities quota policy. In 1978, his claim was upheld by the U.S. Supreme Court in what is undoubtedly a historic decision. The Court ruled that strict racial quotas, such as those used by UC Davis, were unconstitutional. However, the Court did not rule out that race might be used as one among many criteria used in admissions decisions. Thus it is not at all clear whether the Bakke case will impede affirmative action or not. There will undoubtedly be many more court cases before a coherent policy emerges in this area.

What affirmative-action programs probably *have* accomplished is that the more flagrant forms of discrimination have been eliminated and minority applicants have been given a better chance of having their applications seriously considered. Since affirmative action applies only to job vacancies, it has had a limited impact in many sectors where seniority systems are in effect. People with seniority in an employing organization are not as likely to quit and take a new job, thus leaving a vacancy, as are newer employees. A corporation, for example, whose staff comprises a high percentage of employees with seniority is not going to be much affected by affirmative-action programs.

Other Legal Challenges

By the 1970s, there was a growing awareness among minority groups of the limitations of social protest as a means of redressing grievances. Many

people began to realize that the American legal system, if properly utilized, could be an important tool in the struggle for equality. Thus there has been increased activity in this realm. For example, Native American groups all across the country have begun to press claims to land, water, and mineral rights on the grounds that old laws and treaties were either illegally established or illegally enforced.[72] In 1977, the Passamaquoddy and Penobscot tribes went to court for the return of 5 million acres of the state of Maine, nearly one-third of the state. These Native Americans charged that their land had been bargained away in violation of the Nonintercourse Act of 1790, under which only Congress had the power to negotiate with Native American tribes. This case was settled out of court in 1978, with the two tribes receiving $25 million in cash, an additional $1.7 million a year for 15 years, and 300,000 acres of land at the phenomenally low cost of $5 an acre.

Other Native American groups have pushed, and will undoubtedly continue to push, such claims for the redress of past inequities. Many tribes have successfully petitioned the courts to guarantee them hunting and fishing rights based on treaties over a century old. Whether these efforts will enable such groups to narrow the social, economic, and health gap between themselves and the dominant groups is more difficult to say. It is possible that the economic boon resulting from these court settlements will enable Native Americans to greatly improve their lot in American society.

The Politics of Equality

We now return to a sentiment expressed earlier in this chapter: why do we not live up to our ideals of equality and treat everyone on the basis of their skills and abilities? Why not adopt and enforce those programs that will achieve such a goal? Reflecting back on the three theoretical perspectives, we can gain an understanding of some of the reasons why, even though it might be desirable, such a straightforward approach is unlikely to be adopted. From the conflict perspective, programs such as affirmative action and busing are attempts by groups to acquire what they see as their "fair share" of scarce and valuable resources. Inevitably, some vested interests will be adversely affected by any such change and particular groups will make efforts to prevent it. For example, in the case of Native American efforts to win the return of land through court action, economic interest groups currently benefiting from that land have struggled to keep it. In Maine, the fear of losing valuable timberland and property for commercial and residential development has led to substantial resistance to such moves. Many small landowners fear that they will lose their property in such cases. Thus, while many people may espouse belief in ideals of equality, the same people's behavior results from many forces, including whether they believe they will gain or lose by particular actions or policies.

The interactionist perspective makes us aware of the importance of different definitions of reality in the area of intergroup conflict. Many Anglo males tend to feel that discrimination has ended when legal barriers to jobs and education have been eliminated. Members of minority groups, on the other hand, are more inclined to believe that years of discrimination and subordinate status have left marks making it more difficult for minority-group members to compete with whites. Therefore they feel that special efforts, such as quotas, must be instituted to overcome the effects of past discrimination. With these differing versions of reality, it is unlikely that programs acceptable to all members of each group can be found. Thus, we can anticipate more disagreement and conflict over the road toward equality.

Finally, the functionalist perspective emphasizes the self-equilibrating tendency of societies. For example, dominance by Anglo-Saxon males in the preindustrial era may have been functional for that type of society. However, this type of dominance may be viewed as dysfunctional for a pluralistic, postindustrial society. Most of the intergroup conflict in the United States can be seen, then, as an effort by society to adapt to new and changing conditions. This conflict is one means by which society is moving toward a new and more functional state of equilibrium. Given the complexity of society and the diverse ways in which discrimination can work, it is understandable that many different kinds of efforts are necessary to make the changes that are called for. For the functionalist, then, no one program should be expected to solve the problem. Rather, programs must be designed to attack the problem in different sectors of society and as the problem affects different groups. Furthermore, the final outcome will represent an equilibrium or balance. The needs of the various groups and of society as a whole must be taken into account. Thus, no one group can expect to achieve all of its goals, but rather there must be some compromise in terms of the balance most beneficial to the system as a whole.

CONCLUSION

There have been improvements in racial and ethnic relations in recent years. Civil rights legislation has provided minority-group members with legal protections against many of the traditional forms of institutional discrimination. Affirmative-action programs have given some minorities direct access to the opportunity structures in education and employment. However, racism, prejudice, and discrimination still exist in American society. In addition, the struggle for equality has left a legacy of fear and hostility. There are competing proposals for public policies to deal with racism, prejudice, and discrimination. In evaluating these alternatives, it is important to analyze them from the point of view of the three theoretical perspectives.

From the functionalist perspective, racism, prejudice, and discrimination are not, of themselves, social problems. In fact they may serve to enhance the stability of the status quo. For example, a group that is the target of racism may be so subdued that it serves as an inexpensive labor force which then enhances the economic productivity of the whole system. Prejudice and discrimination become dysfunctional when they threaten the order and stability of the social system. Thus, the functionalist perspective makes us aware that prejudice and discrimination—and solutions to these problems—cannot be viewed in isolation. They must be considered within the context of other institutions and values.

From the conflict perspective, racism, prejudice and discrimination can serve the interests of dominant groups in society. Groups tend to resist policies and programs that they view as threatening to their interests. In addition, conflict theorists point out that one thing must be understood: there still are, and there will continue to be, struggles over scarce resources. Such programs as affirmative action have, in a sense, served to make this scarcity even more apparent. Some intergroup hostility is likely to continue in those realms in which opportunities are limited because of economic necessity or social policy. We must realize that, despite our most sincere desires to achieve equality, some of the sources of prejudice and discrimination remain with us. For example, economic competition is a fact of life and continues to lurk as a potential catalyst of discrimination. In this regard, we must be sensitive to any new groups that might become the focus of prejudice and discrimination. We have focused our discussion on blacks, Hispanics, Native Americans, and (in the next chapter) women. These groups are now relatively powerful interest groups and are in a much better position to struggle to protect their own rights. There are other racial and ethnic minorities, however, who are not yet as powerful. In addition, we must be sensitive to prejudice and discrimination based on grounds other than racial or ethnic membership. For example, many argue that there is widespread prejudice and discrimination in American society against welfare recipients, the handicapped, the mentally retarded, or some other disadvantaged minority.

From the interactionist perspective, people's definitions of social reality are more important than whether something is functional for them or is, in fact, contrary to their best interests. Racism, prejudice, and discrimination are, in most ways, genuinely threatening to the stability and longrun welfare of American society. However, public policies and programs designed to eliminate these problems will be met with resistance as long as groups perceive prejudice and discrimination as appropriate responses to minority groups.

Interactionists also point out that a particularly devastating consequence of prejudice and discrimination—an effect that is difficult to directly attack through legislation—are the feelings of inferiority and negative self concepts that its victims often experience. Programs to create more opportunities for minority groups can be effective only if the members of these groups are emotionally and psychologically prepared to avail themselves of existing opportunities. Means of boosting the self confidence and sense of control of minority-group members must be devised. One such effort has been initiated by the Reverend Jesse Jackson. Jackson has been traveling around the country preaching to black youths that self-discipline and hard work are essential in order to compete with other groups in America. While Jackson feels that compensatory programs, such as affirmative action, are necessary, he also believes that they will be phased out in the future and that minority groups will have to survive and compete by their own devices. Jackson views a stable and positive self concept as an important weapon in this battle.

GLOSSARY TERMS

Affirmative action
Assimilation
Authoritarian personality
Barrios
Black power
Discrimination
Ethnic group
Ethnocentrism
Frustration-aggression
  hypothesis
Genocide

Individual discrimination
Institutionalized
  discrimination
Internal colonialism
Majority group
Minority group
Pluralism
Prejudice
Prejudiced discriminator
Prejudiced nondiscriminator
Projection

Race
Racism
Relative deprivation
Reverse discrimination
Scapegoating
Separatism
Split labor market
Unprejudiced discriminator
Unprejudiced
  nondiscriminator

REFERENCES

[1] Quoted in Howard Zinn, "Violence and Social Change in America," in Thomas Rose, ed., *Violence in America: A Historical and Contemporary Reader* (New York: Vintage Books, 1969), p. 72.

[2] See Wen Lang Li, "Chinese Americans: Exclusion from the Melting Pot," in Anthony G. Dworkin and Rosalind J. Dworkin, eds., *The Minority Report: An Introduction to Racial, Ethnic, and Gender Relations* (New York: Frederick A. Praeger, 1976), pp. 297–324.

[3] Joe R. Feagin, *Racial and Ethnic Relations* (Englewood Cliffs, N.J.: Prentice-Hall, 1978).

[4] See Richard T. Schaefer, *Racial and Ethnic Groups* (Boston: Little, Brown, 1979), pp. 16–19.

[5] Dale R. Spady and Kenrick S. Thompson, "The Finnish-American: An Exploration of Ethnic Identity," *Siirtolaisuus Migration* 3 (Spring 1977), p. 20.

[6] Ibid., p. 19.

[7] Schaefer, *Racial and Ethnic Groups*, pp. 157–168.

[8] Samuel Eliot Morison et al., *A Concise History of the American Republic* (New York: Oxford University Press, 1977), and Schaefer, *Racial and Ethnic Groups*, pp. 163–164.

[9] See Kenneth M. Stampp, *The Peculiar Institution: Slavery in the Ante-Bellum South* (New York: Alfred A. Knopf, 1956), and Julius Lester, *To Be A Slave* (New York: Dial Press, 1968).

[10] Alphonso Pinkney, *Black Americans*, 2d ed. (Englewood Cliffs, N.J.: Prentice-Hall, 1975).

[11] Ibid.

[12] See Schaefer, *Racial and Ethnic Groups*, pp. 283–289.

[13] Joan W. Moore, *Mexican Americans* (Englewood Cliffs, N.J.: Prentice-Hall, 1976), p. 13.

[14] Schaefer, *Racial and Ethnic Groups*, pp. 303–318.

[15] Ibid., pp. 119–122.

[16] Joseph Strauss, Bruce A. Chadwick, and Howard M. Bahr, "Indian Americans: The First Is Last," in Dworkin and Dworkin, eds., *The Minority Report*, pp. 222–223.

[17] See Schaefer, *Racial and Ethnic Groups*, pp. 237–250.

[18] Quoted in Earl Shorris, *The Death of the Great Spirit: An Elegy for the American Indian* (New York: Simon and Schuster, 1971), p. 13.

[19] See Milton M. Gordon, *Human Nature, Class, and Ethnicity* (New York: Oxford University Press, 1978), pp. 97–210.

[20] See William J. Wilson, *Power, Racism, and Privilege* (New York: The Free Press, 1973).

[21] See Tamotsu Shibutani, *Society and Personality* (Englewood Cliffs, N.J.: Prentice-Hall, 1961), pp. 341–354.

[22] William Moore, Jr., *The Vertical Ghetto* (New York: Random House, 1969), p. 71.

[23] U.S. Bureau of the Census, "Social and Economic Characteristics of the Metropolitan and Nonmetropolitan Population: 1977 and 1970," *Current Population Reports*, P-23, no. 75 (Washington, D.C.: U.S. Government Printing Office, 1978), and Albert A. Simkus, "Residential Segregation by Occupation and Race in Ten Urbanized Areas, 1950–1970," *American Sociological Review* 43 (February 1978), pp. 81–93.

[24] See John D. Reid et al., "Trends in Black Health," *Phylon* 28 (Summer 1977), pp. 105–116.

[25] United States Department of Commerce, *Social Indicators, 1976* (Washington, D.C.: U.S. Government Printing Office, 1977).

[26] See U.S. Department of Health, Education, and Welfare, *Work in America* (Cambridge, Mass.: MIT Press, 1973).

[27] Peter M. Blau and Otis Dudley Duncan, *The American*

Occupational Structure (New York: John Wiley & Sons, 1967).

[28] See "It's Your Turn in the Sun," *Time* (October 16, 1978), p. 48.

[29] U.S. Bureau of the Census, "Persons of Spanish Origin in the United States: March 1976," *Current Population Reports*, Series P-20, no. 310 (Washington, D.C.: U.S. Government Printing Office, 1977).

[30] Ibid.

[31] Alan L. Sorkin, "The Economic Basis of Indian Life," *Annals of the American Academy of Political and Social Science* 436 (March 1978), pp. 1–12.

[32] Patricia D. Mail, "Hippocrates Was a Medicine Man: The Health Care of Native Americans in the Twentieth Century," *Annals of the American Academy of Political and Social Science* 436 (March 1978), pp. 40–49.

[33] Sorkin, "The Economic Basis of Indian Life," pp. 1–12.

[34] Ibid.

[35] Robert J. Havighurst, "Indian Education Since 1960," *Annals of the American Academy of Political and Social Science* 436 (March 1978), pp. 13–26.

[36] Ibid., p. 18.

[37] John E. Williams and J. Kenneth Morland, *Race, Color, and the Young Child* (Chapel Hill: University of North Carolina Press, 1976).

[38] Robert H. Lauer and Warren H. Handel, *Social Psychology: The Theory and Application of Symbolic Interaction* (Boston: Houghton Mifflin, 1977), pp. 191–193.

[39] See James S. Coleman et al., *Equality of Educational Opportunity* (Washington, D.C.: U.S. Government Printing Office, 1966), and Christopher Jencks et al., *Inequality: A Reassessment of the Effects of Schooling in America* (New York: Basic Books, 1972).

[40] Art Poskocil, "Encounters between Blacks and White Liberals: The Collision of Stereotypes," *Social Forces* 53 (March 1977), pp. 715–727.

[41] Albert Szymanski, "Racial Discrimination and White Gain," *American Sociological Review* 41 (June 1976), pp. 403–414.

[42] Herbert Aptheker, *American Negro Slave Revolts* (New York: International Publishers, 1963).

[43] See Martin Luther King, Jr., *Why We Can't Wait* (New York: Mentor, 1963), and Lewis M. Killian, *The Impossible Revolution, Phase 2: Black Power and the American Dream* (New York: Random House, 1975).

[44] Pinkney, *Black Americans.*

[45] See Robert Staples, *Introduction to Black Sociology* (New York: McGraw-Hill, 1976), and Ross K. Baker, "The Transformation of the Panthers," *The Washington Post* (February 13, 1972), Section B, pp. 1–2.

[46] See Killian, *The Impossible Revolution, Phase 2.*

[47] Harry T. Kitano, *Race Relations* (Englewood Cliffs, N.J.: Prentice-Hall, 1974), p. 245.

[48] Joan W. Moore, *Mexican Americans* (Englewood Cliffs, N.J.: Prentice-Hall, 1976).

[49] See Schaefer, *Racial and Ethnic Groups,* pp. 237–274, and Vincent N. Parrillo, *Strangers to These Shores* (Boston: Houghton Mifflin, 1979).

[50] Gordon, *Human Nature, Class, and Ethnicity,* pp. 181–208.

[51] See Gordon W. Allport, *The Nature of Prejudice* (Cambridge, Mass.: Addison-Wesley, 1954), and Jack Levin, *The Functions of Prejudice* (New York: Harper & Row, 1975).

[52] Theodore W. Adorno et al., *The Authoritarian Personality* (New York: W. W. Norton, 1950).

[53] Neal E. Miller and John Dollard, *Social Learning and Imitation* (New Haven, Conn.: Yale University Press, 1941), and Kenneth B. Clark, "Explosion in the Ghetto," *Psychology Today* 1 (September 1967), pp. 31–38, 62–64.

[54] Ibid., p. 31.

[55] Graham C. Kinloch, *The Dynamics of Race Relations: A Sociological Analysis* (New York: McGraw-Hill, 1974).

[56] Herbert Blumer, "Race Prejudice as a Sense of Group Position," *Pacific Sociological Review* 1 (Spring 1958), pp. 3–7, and Marilynn B. Brewer and Donald T. Campbell, *Ethnocentrism and Intergroup Attitudes: East African Evidence* (New York: Halstead Press, 1976).

[57] See Thomas F. Pettigrew, *Racially Separate or Together* (New York: McGraw-Hill, 1971).

[58] See Allport, *The Nature of Prejudice,* and Levin, *The Functions of Prejudice.*

[59] See Poskocil, "Encounters between Blacks and White Liberals," pp. 715–727.

[60] Robert K. Merton, "Discrimination and the American Creed," in Robert M. MacIver, ed., *Discrimination and National Welfare* (New York: Harper & Row, 1949), pp. 103–110.

[61] James W. Vander Zanden, *American Minority Relations: The Sociology of Racial and Ethnic Groups,* 3d ed. (New York: Ronald Press, 1972).

[62] See Oliver C. Cox, *Caste, Class, and Race* (Garden City, N.Y.: Doubleday, 1948); Robert Blauner, *Racial Oppression in America* (New York: Harper & Row, 1972); and Schaefer, *Racial and Ethnic Groups,* pp. 32–33.

[63] These ideas have been developed in three articles by Edna Bonacich: "A Theory of Ethnic Antagonism: The Split Labor Market," *American Sociological Review* 37 (October 1972), pp. 547–559; "Abolition, the Extension of Slavery, and the Position of Free Blacks: A Study of Split Labor Markets in the United States, 1830–1863," *American Journal of Sociology* 81 (November 1975), pp. 601–628; and "Advanced Capitalism and Black/White Race Relations in the United States: A Split Labor Market Interpretation," *American Sociological Review* 41 (February 1976), pp. 34–51.

[64] See Philip G. Zimbardo, Ebbe B. Ebbeson, and Christina Maslach, *Influencing Attitudes and Changing Behavior,* 2d ed. (Reading, Mass.: Addison-Wesley, 1977).

[65] George E. Simpson and J. Milton Yinger, *Racial and Cultural Minorities: An Analysis of Prejudice and Discrimination,* 4th ed. (New York: Harper & Row, 1972).

[66] *See* James W. Button, *Black Violence: Political Impact of the 1960s Riots* (Princeton, N.J.: Princeton University Press, 1978), pp. 156–179.

[67] Charles U. Smith, "Public School Desegregation and the Law," *Social Forces* 54 (December 1975), pp. 317–327.

[68] *See* Daniel U. Levine and Jeanie Keeny Meyer, "Level and Rate of Desegregation and White Enrollment Decline in a Big City School District," *Social Problems* 24 (April 1977), pp. 451–468, and Diane Ravitch, "The 'White Flight' Controversy," *The Public Interest* 51 (Spring 1978), pp. 135–149.

[69] Coleman, *Equality of Educational Opportunity.*

[70] Nathan Glazer, *Affirmative Discrimination: Ethnic Identity and Public Policy* (New York: Basic Books, 1976).

[71] *See* Allan P. Sindler, *Bakke, DeFunis, and Minority Admissions: The Quest for Equal Opportunity* (New York: Longman, Inc., 1978), and Robert L. Simon, "Preferential Treatment: For Groups or for Individuals," *Phi Kappa Phi Journal* 58 (Winter 1978), pp. 7–9.

[72] *See* Richard Boeth et al., "A Paleface Uprising," *Newsweek* (April 10, 1978), pp. 39–40, and Vincent N. Parrillo, *Strangers To These Shores* (Boston: Houghton Mifflin, 1979).

SUGGESTED READINGS

Milton M. Gordon, *Assimilation in American Life* (New York: Oxford University Press, Inc., 1964).
A lucid and comprehensive statement on the role of race, religion, and national origins in American society.

Lewis M. Killian, *The Impossible Revolution: Phase II Black Power and the American Dream* (New York: Random House, 1975).
A somewhat pessimistic outlook for blacks using totally peaceful means to resolve existing problems in race relations is voiced by Killian.

E. Digby Baltzell, *The Protestant Establishment: Aristocracy and Caste in America* (New York: Vintage Books, 1964).
An excellent analysis of the social and historical origins of prejudice and discrimination in the United States and their social costs.

Joe R. Feagin, *Racial and Ethnic Relations* (Englewood Cliffs, New Jersey: Prentice-Hall, 1978).
An excellent, recent text that provides an overview of the history and current status of major ethnic groups in the United States.

Robert Staples, *Introduction to Black Sociology* (New York: McGraw-Hill, 1976).
A readable and basic sociological analysis of the position of blacks in American society.

Joan W. Moore, *Mexican Americans.* Second edition (Englewood Cliffs, New Jersey: Prentice-Hall, 1976). An overview of the current status and historical experience of Mexican Americans in the United States.

Alan L. Sorkin, "The Economic Basis of Indian Life," Patricia Mail, "Hippocrates Was a Medicine Man: The Health Care of Native Americans in the Twentieth Century," and Robert J. Havighurst, "Indian Education Since 1960," *Annals of the American Academy of Political and Social Science.* 436 (March, 1978).
Together these articles provide an excellent view of the opportunities of Native Americans in the United States today.

Questions
for Discussion

1. Race, racism, and ethnic group are key concepts in the study of race and ethnic relations. What are the differences between groups distinguished on the basis of race and those based on ethnicity? Discuss racism as ideology.

2. From the functionalist perspective, racism, prejudice and discrimination constitute a social problem only under certain conditions. What are these conditions? When do racism, prejudice and discrimination constitute a social problem from the conflict perspective? From the interactionist perspective?

3. Compare the current status of blacks in American society with that of Hispanic Americans and Native Americans. How do their opportunities differ from those of whites?

4. What has been the history of black reactions to prejudice and discrimination? How have Hispanic Americans and Native Americans reacted to prejudice and discrimination?

5. What are some of the psychological theories of the sources of prejudice and discrimination? How do they differ from sociological theories?

6. Compare and contrast functionalist theories of the origins and perpetuation of prejudice and discrimination with conflict theories such as internal colonialism and the split-labor hypothesis.

7. Discuss the social costs associated with prejudice and discrimination.

8. How can prejudice and discrimination be reduced? Focus on policies and programs at both the individual and institutional levels.

CHAPTER 13
Sex Roles

THE HISTORY OF SEX ROLES

Hunting and Gathering Societies. Preindustrial America.
Industrial America. The Women's Rights Movement: The
Early Days. The Women's Rights Movement: A
Resurgence.

SEX ROLES AS A SOCIAL PROBLEM

The Functionalist Perspective. The Conflict Perspective.
The Interactionist Perspective.

MASCULINITY AND FEMININITY

Gender versus Sex Role. Growing up Male. Growing up
Female.

DISCRIMINATION AND INEQUALITY

Economic Discrimination. Other Types of Discrimination.

THE CHANGING MALE SEX ROLE

Men and Masculinity. Men's Liberation. Some Dimensions
of the "Liberation."

FUTURE PROSPECTS

Masculine, Feminine, or Human? The New Women's
Movement and the Quest for Human Rights. Recent
Developments.

CONCLUSION

"The lesson of history so far is that women cannot gain equality regardless of the methods used to obtain it."[1] This unequivocal statement was made by William O'Neill, a long-time observer of the human rights movement, in 1969. It is unlikely that such an unqualified assertion would be made about blacks, Hispanics, or other racial or ethnic groups that are the victims of prejudice and discrimination. Yet, this astute observer felt safe in making such a statement about women. Why would someone be drawn to make such a gloomy prediction? One purpose of this chapter is to find out.

When the topics of inequality and discrimination in the United States are discussed, racial and ethnic groups are usually the focus of the discussion. This was our concern in the previous chapter. Yet we would be remiss if we did not discuss another group that faces many of the same problems—women. Inequality between the sexes dates back to the beginning of recorded time. In almost every known society, women have been bound by more social restrictions than men, they have tolerated (although not always complacently) lower status than men in nearly every arena, and they have received a consistently smaller measure of recognition for their labors than have men. Men and women have been regarded as "different" in all societies—not only biologically but also psychologically, emotionally, and intellectually. The heritage of the fundamental inequality of men and women has a strong foothold in traditional religious teachings. Judeo-Christian thought, Hinduism, and Islam all provide support for the dictum that women should occupy inferior positions in society. Women did not even have the right to vote in most parts of the United States until 1920.

There are, of course, many women *and* men who would take serious issue with the implications of O'Neill's pessimistic statement that women can never gain equality. In addition, there is evidence that we are moving more rapidly toward sex role equality in our society today than in the past. For example, during the past thirty years, the proportion of women who are part of America's labor force has increased substantially. In 1950 women comprised only 30 percent of the work force, whereas in 1977 this figure rose to 41 percent.[2] In 1970, a Harris poll provided survey data indicating that only 42 percent of the American people approved of efforts to elevate the position of women in our society; by 1975, 63 percent of our population supported these efforts, including more than 50 percent of American males.[3]

Yet there is still a substantial gap between the way men and women are treated in our society. In this chapter, we will investigate the dimensions of that gap and the costs that it places on our society. We will also try to assess the accuracy of O'Neill's statement. Are we moving toward a condition of equality between the sexes, or is there a backlash developing that will leave most women as "not quite equal." Finally, what are the implications in all of this for men? What are the costs for men living in a society based on sex role inequality? In order to evaluate the state of affairs today, it is helpful to compare it with conditions in the past.

THE HISTORY OF SEX ROLES

Hunting and Gathering Societies

Hunting and gathering societies provide insight into the development of sex roles. In these societies, the food gathering technology was simple—they hunted game and gathered nuts, plants, and other foods. In these societies, the ability to acquire food supplies was related to social status. Men tended to be hunters—a prestigious activity. As a group, they were physically stronger and had greater stamina than females. Even though women often collected more food than men were able to procure through hunting, the males' hunting activities were regarded as more important.

Men were relatively free of childbearing and rearing responsibilities. Women were expected to bear as many childen as circumstances permitted—by choice, but also because birth control was generally unheard of. During much of their adult lives, they were usually either pregnant or in the process of nursing their infants.[4] Having a large number of children was important for these nonliterate societies because of their high death rate. Child bearing and rearing was considered a very valuable and essential contribution to the survival of the group. Women were usually involved in what may be termed "domestic activities," such as cooking, washing, and sewing. Men, on the other hand, engaged in pursuits focused outside the home and family—constructing vehicles for transportation and fabricating weapons for defending the group.

Given the level of technology in these societies, this sexual division of labor can be viewed as functional and indeed practical. Given the biological necessity for women to have and nurse children, it was possible for them to do domestic activities or gather food at the same time. It would be difficult for a woman with a nursing infant to wander far and wide hunting game. However, once these sex role distinctions had become firmly established as a part of the group's tradition, they were then supported by strong group norms that made these differentiations independent of their functional origins. They came to be seen as the "natural" and only ways for men and women to behave, rather than as practical means of achieving a goal.

These behavioral patterns (and the norms supporting them) were perpetuated through the socialization of the young. Children were taught that it is in the natural order of things that men do some tasks and women do others. This sex role socialization not only involved training males and females to perform different tasks, but also resulted in sex differences in attitudes or personality dispositions. Since men were to be the defenders of their group in case of attack by other tribes, they were reared to be aggressive and to be leaders. This may be regarded as a primitive version of "Big boys don't cry—you may have to defend your country some day." Women, on the other hand, could depend on the men in the tribe for protection and were taught to be more passive and dependent and to provide emotional support for their men.

Even though cultures vary in terms of the *kinds* of rights and obligations regarded as inherently masculine or feminine, all societies distinguish between the genders. In one way or another, sex role identity has been transferred consistently from generation to generation.

Preindustrial America

As we have observed elsewhere in this text, preindustrial society was in striking contrast to the industrial and postindustrial America of this country. Families were larger in preindustrial societies, authority tended to rest with the male, and family units were more economically self-sufficient. Each member contributed in some meaningful way to the economic survival of the family. Divorce was infrequent, and child rearing was a lifelong activity for most parents. **Most important in terms of our consideration here is that the sex role structure of preindustrial America was clear-cut and functional.** Men and women knew what was expected of them, and they could anticipate playing these same roles throughout life. Women were usually involved in what may be termed *domestic* activities; men, on the other hand, engaged in what were regarded at that time as more *productive* pursuits outside the home. Men and women were confident about where they belonged in society and what was expected of them through the various stages of their lives. As with hunting and gathering societies, this sex role socialization trained males and females to perform different tasks and also resulted in different attitudes and personality characteristics. The two old sayings "It's a man's world" and "A woman's place is in the home" capture the flavor of the differences between sexes during that era.

Industrial America

The *extended family* was well suited to a preindustrial, agrarian society. During the nineteenth century, the Industrial Revolution began seriously to affect how the traditional American family was structured. As industrialization progressed, the *nuclear family* emerged, and the traditional sex roles were affected in a variety of ways.

First, the importance of the family as an economic unit declined. Men were now more likely to go outside the family, to a factory or other setting, to provide the economic support of the family. Thus the basis of family cohesiveness changed, and some of the pressures on family members to conform to traditional roles declined. Traditionally, both men and women provided the economic support for the family; now the man alone performed that function, and the woman's role was simply to provide support for the male. Second, as urbanization and industrialization progressed, the size of the family declined. This meant that child-rearing activities—which lasted throughout most of the adult life of women during earlier periods—consumed less of a woman's time. In addition, the development of mass education meant that even young children spent a good part of their time outside the family. Third, technology eliminated the necessity for much of the activities that had consumed a woman's time prior to industrialization. Food preparation (e.g. baking bread, canning vegetables) are now done by factories rather than homemakers. Labor-saving devices have eliminated much of the time-consuming household work that women had to do.

The outcome of all these changes were revolutionary. First, the traditional activities of women—oriented around child-rearing and housework—have become less functionally essential to society. It is no longer necessary for all, or even most, women to do these things. Second, and related, the distinctions between the sexes—viewed throughout history as natural and inevitable—began to blur; sex roles became less clear-cut. As the traditional role of women changed, some women began to pursue activities that had traditionally been limited to men. This has almost inevitably led to a questioning of what it means to be male or to be female. Equally important, this blurring process has called attention to the inequities between men and women that had existed for so many years. Scientific advances and changes in laws during the early 1900s affected fertility patterns in important ways as well. More modern birth control procedures became available; through these advances women gained freedom from having and caring for children and were in a position to have occupations other than housewife or homemaker.

During World War II, large numbers of women joined the workforce, taking the places of men who had been inducted into the military. Between 1940 and 1945, the female labor force expanded by 5.5 million. At that time, over 38 percent of all women sixteen years of age and over were working.[5] When the war was over, there was a male backlash as returning servicemen competed with women for available jobs.[6] It was felt by many people, both men and women, that women had done their duty for the war effort, but that they should return to their homes and families so that the servicemen could have the jobs that were properly theirs. Even today, women who hold jobs that have been traditionally male-dominated sometimes report that some men will tell them: "Why the hell don't you go home where you belong so that some of my unemployed [male] friends can get jobs?"

The Women's Rights Movement: The Early Days

Most people today probably look to the 1960s as the beginning of the women's movement in the United States. However, the history of the struggle for women's rights in America began much earlier —even prior to the women's *suffrage* movement of the early 1900s. In 1848 two radical feminists, Elizabeth Cady Stanton and Susan B. Anthony (along with a few others), organized the first women's rights caucus at Seneca Falls, New York. These early leaders and their followers demanded the vote (*suffrage*) for women and the reform of many laws that were openly discriminatory against women. The Seneca Falls Convention was the beginning of a nearly seventy-five-year struggle for women's suffrage. During the 1900s, the militant efforts of early feminist leaders like Alice Paul and of others with more conservative interests finally resulted in the passage of the Nineteenth Amendment to the Constitution in 1920, giving all adult Americans the right to vote. Almost a century and a half after the American Revolution, women finally had the vote!

Anyone who has campaigned actively for something over a prolonged period of time is aware how elation over a single victory can cause one to lose sight of the "big picture." It appears that the victory of women's suffrage had this effect. Total sexual equality was so long viewed as going hand in hand with the right to vote that women regarded

By 1945, there were many women working in America—some held nontraditional occupations that had been vacated by men who fought in World War II.

During the early 1900s in America, women lobbied for, and finally gained, the right to vote—their efforts represent the beginnings of the modern womens' movement.

the suffrage victory as more significant than it really was. The "women's movement" essentially lay dormant for the next forty years.

The Women's Rights Movement: A Resurgence

It was not until the 1960s that interest in the issue of sex role inequality again became widespread. Before that, few people, including sociologists, defined sex roles or sex role inequality as a social problem. There were a number of reasons for the resurgence of concern in the late 1960s. More women were attending college, where they could learn about the problems of other women and communicate with women about these issues. As women moved into new occupational areas, they became more acutely aware of the extent of discrimination against women. Furthermore, the civil rights movement served as a model of how women might work to change conditions. Finally, there has been an explosion of scientific research on the relationship between gender and behavior that has been instrumental in defining sex roles as a social problem. A brief review of this research will illustrate how people have become aware that sex role differences actually represent a social problem.

In 1955, social scientists John Money, J. G. Hampson, and J. L. Hampson conducted a study of 110 hermaphrodites.[7] A *hermaphrodite* is a person born with both male and female sexual characteristics but who nonetheless is assigned to one sex at birth and who develops the gender identity of that sex.[8] The study provided early convincing evidence that "male" and "female" are not mutually exclusive categories. When hermaphrodites are born, they are almost always labeled male or female based on their external physical appearance. Money and his associates sought to determine whether there was a significant correlation between the hermaphrodites' own feelings about their sexual identities and their physical characteristics. There was none. In many cases, in fact, the hermaphrodites were living satisfactory lives as members of one gender, when practically all observable sex characteristics placed them in the other category. Money's investigation cast doubt on

many of the time-honored answers to the question, What does it *really* mean to be male or female?

Twenty years later, social scientists H. L. Rheingold and K. V. Cook published the results of a study that surveyed the contents of children's bedrooms as an index of parents' socialization behavior. Their findings showed pervasive differences in terms of how boys' and girls' rooms were furnished and what personal belongings were displayed. The study was conducted in a middle-income neighborhood of a university community where one might expect a less traditional approach to sex role socialization. Yet Rheingold and Cook reported:

> The rooms of boys contained more animal furnishings, more educational art materials, more spatial-temporal toys, more sports equipment, and more toy animals. The rooms of girls contained more dolls, more floral furnishings and more ruffles.[9]

Perhaps even more revealing is the fact that the 48 boys' rooms contained 375 vehicles (toys, models, etc.), whereas the 48 girls' rooms had only 17; 26 of the 48 girls displayed baby dolls in their rooms, but only 3 of the 48 boys had such playthings. A study of a Sears, Roebuck "Christmas Wish Book" (toy catalog) found that in illustrations of toys relating to marriage and parenthood, 84 percent pictured only *girls* and *none* pictured only boys. In contrast, for task-oriented toys (like construction sets), 75 percent of the Sears catalog's illustrations depicted only boys, while a very small 8 percent pictured only girls.[10]

Other studies documented that parents tend to interact with their sons differently from the way they do with their daughters.[11] For example, parents tend to interact more with male infants, hold and generally stimulate them more, and even look at them more often than at female infants.[12] During the first few months of life, boys are afforded more proximal stimulation (like rocking and handling) by their mothers, whereas girls receive more distal stimulation (like talking and looking). Fathers usually play rougher with their infants if they are male.[13] Another element in the perception of sex roles as a social problem is our recently expanded awareness of cultural differences in the

Although many changes are taking place, footballs, boxing gloves, and other sports-related equipment are still more likely to appear in boys' rooms rather than girls' rooms.

roles of women. For example, in some Middle East societies, men are sensitive and emotional while women tend to be more practical and impassive.[14] In Sweden, over 75 percent of heavy-machinery operators are women.[15] In the Soviet Union, women comprise well over one-half of the labor force and nearly three-quarters of the physicians.

The accumulation of scientific findings such as these has had an impact on how both scientists and laypersons have viewed sex role differences in the United States. What had traditionally been believed to be *inherent, biological* differences between men and women were now coming to be viewed as the result of socialization and *cultural learning*. Concern about this issue, while by no means unanimous, has caused considerable controversy and conflict in the United States. There is much disagreement concerning whether sex roles are a social problem, why they are a social problem, and what to do about it. Before we investigate the current dimensions of the problem, it would be helpful to see how sex roles can be considered a social problem from each of our theoretical perspectives.

SEX ROLES AS A SOCIAL PROBLEM

The Functionalist Perspective

The functionalist perspective can be very helpful in understanding how sex roles evolve in society. Sociologist Emile Durkheim pointed out that as social organization becomes more complex, the division of labor also increases in complexity.[16] In a preindustrial, agrarian social order like early nineteenth-century America, both the extended family and clear-cut sex roles facilitated the smooth functioning of society. Women *and* men "knew their place" during that period, and there was little doubt where they belonged or what they should be doing. Order was enhanced by these clear-cut distinctions; thus, traditional sex roles were functional to society at that time.

We should remember that, regardless of our individual biases in terms of the sex roles issue, *some* role differentiation is functional to society. If nobody knew his or her place in society, there would be no order. This does not imply that roles based upon one's sex are necessary, but simply that role assignments in terms of the division of labor are functional and contribute to social equilibrium. The important issue today is *what type* of role differentiation is functional for our society.

For the functionalist, sex role differentiation becomes a social problem when it threatens the smooth operation of society by creating some sort of imbalance. When men and women begin to feel dissatisfied or insecure about their respective roles, or unsure of what is proper behavior for a man or woman, then equilibrium and social order may be in jeopardy. Functionalists Talcott Parsons and Robert Bales argued that all human groups, if they are to survive, must satisfy what they called instrumental and expressive functions.[17] *Instrumental functions* refer to the goal-oriented activities of the group—the tasks that must be accomplished if it is to survive. Traditionally, the male has performed the instrumental functions for the family—activities such as working and house repairs. *Expressive functions* refer to activities focused on the relationships between people—maintaining happiness, harmony, and emotional stability. Traditionally, these have been the female's concerns, providing love and support within an emotionally satisfying climate.

Some functionalists argue that these tasks should still be sex-linked—that it is more beneficial for the family if the male engages in instrumental behavior and the female exhibits expressive characteristics. **For these functionalists, any breakdown of the traditional sex role differentiation would be a social problem because it would threaten the ability of the family to function.** However, we can take a broader view of the functionalist position by arguing that these instrumental and expressive functions must be performed *in some fashion,* although they need not be sex-linked. From this point of view, **sex roles are a social problem because they no longer serve as a guide to behavior and nothing has yet emerged to take their place.** In other words, there is a void in modern society: whereas one's sex served as a guide in the past, it no longer does, and people are left without direction. This does not mean that traditional sex role differentiation must return, or even that sex must necessarily be an important determinant of the division of labor. However, it does mean that *some differentiation* must arise to provide the direction that previously had resulted from sex differences.

The Conflict Perspective

From the conflict perspective, dominance and sub-ordination, inequality and discrimination, are normal parts of social life. Conflict emerges when groups compete for certain scarce and desirable resources. Conflict, subordination, and inequality are not necessarily social problems. **Sex role differentiation becomes a social problem when it leads some group to feel that it is not receiving its fair share of valuable resources and that group has the power to make its concerns a public issue.** The conflict relating to the sex roles issue in our society has been enhanced by the increasing awareness on the part of some women that their subservient position in the social order is a function of an essentially male-dominated society rather than due to the traditionally presumed inherent inferiority of women. When a group experiences a condition of relative deprivation, conflict in some form usually emerges; these group members, in quest of the desirable resources, will generally opt for change. The group controlling or dominating these resources will usually be reluctant to share them with others.

Men and women have, to some extent, cooperated with one another in order to reach their individual goals. As one sociologist points out, however, even in such a situation, conflict can take the form of *sexual bargaining,* in which men and women negotiate with one another (not always consciously) for various rewards in social exchange.[18] Cooperation occurs only if the members of each group feel that it is in their best interests to cooperate (see ch. 1). **Indeed, according to the conflict perspective, the sex roles issue has become a social problem because some female and male groups in our society believe that their interests are not being served by current sex role distinctions and that they are not receiving their share of scarce and desirable resources.**

Another source of conflict is represented by the backlash generated by members of groups opposed to sex role equality. Many males, for example, resent the fact that they must compete with women for occupational opportunities. In addition, the women's movement has encountered considerable opposition, and many women are not in favor of substantial changes in traditional sex role distinctions.

Phyllis Schlafly, for example, is a vociferous opponent of the Equal Rights Amendment and believes that women could actually *lose* certain important rights as a consequence. Schlafly also feels that women find their greatest fulfillment at home with the family. One might also consider the effects of Marabel Morgan's "total woman" program.[19] According to Mrs. Morgan, in order to achieve total happiness, a woman must strive to be everything that her husband desires—an efficient homemaker, a good mother, and an attractive sex partner. Morgan suggests, for example, that the total woman will do anything to please her man, including meeting him at the door in a sexy negligee at the end of his long day. Needless to say, among feminist supporters, Morgan's suggestions are viewed with considerable disgust. **Nevertheless, it is clear that, for some men and women, sex roles are a social problem because modern change threatens their ability to gain rewards and satisfaction from the traditional male-female relationships.** From all of the foregoing, it is clear that conflict concerning the sex roles issue emanates from different sources. The "problem" of sex roles displays a variety of dimensions—all of them complex and often difficult to understand.

The Interactionist Perspective

According to the interactionist perspective, human beings relate to one another on the basis of symbols that have meaning within a given culture. Early interactionist social thinkers like George Herbert Mead[20] and Charles Horton Cooley[21] asserted that through our interactions with people important to us (principally our parents and peers) we form our self-concepts, which Cooley called *looking glass selves*.

In addition, social structure, including sex roles, is based on sets of shared expectations, and it is through this sharing that interaction takes place smoothly. For example, in preindustrial society, when a father proclaimed that he had made a decision for the family, the other family members accepted the decision—they all shared the expectation that the father had the authority and legiti-

mate right to make decisions for the family. (Even though others, especially the mother, may have participated in the decision, the family acted *as if* the father were the sole decision maker.) The expectations that accompanied family life at that time made this arrangement appropriate and desirable.

In our modern industrial society, however, social structure and sex roles are changing—they are not as clear-cut and unambiguous as they once were. For example, the father today might not be in the best position to make certain decisions—at least not unilaterally. It is very likely that his wife is working, and she may even earn more money than he does. His children may also have more significant input, because of the contemporary ideology of democratic decision making in the family. In modern society, males are less likely than in the past to command a completely dominant position in family life.

In preindustrial society, the "proper" woman waited for the right man to make advances toward her rather than initiating them. The woman waited for "Mr. Right" to ask her for her hand in marriage; it was seldom the other way around. Today, a different set of expectations is emerging. For example, the decision to marry is often not so much a matter of the male's "popping the question" as it is an agreement that emerges out of mutual interaction. **For the interactionist, sex roles become a social problem when there is a lack of consensus and shared expectations about what it means to be male or female.** People's definitions of sex roles and expectations for each other's behavior are changing. This means that people's self-concepts in relation to their sexual status are more likely to be uncertain or ambiguous. In preindustrial societies, such ambiguity was uncommon—there was more consensus about what it meant to be male or female.

It should be emphasized that although there has been a great deal of change in sex roles, there is still a predominant version of how boys and girls and men and women should behave. Although sex roles are blurring, there still exist some very popular and influential ideas about masculinity and femininity. We now turn to a discussion of these ideas.

MASCULINITY AND FEMININITY

Of all the characteristics that you possess, the one that you probably question the least is your sex. Of course you may be concerned about whether you are *acting* sufficiently masculine or feminine, but you probably rarely wonder about whether you *are* male or female. We tend to think of masculinity and femininity as well-understood, objectively determined traits, like hair color or skin pigmentation. Yet, scientific research has shown that masculinity and femininity are ultimately based on the shared and subjective expectations that people have for males' and females' behavior. We are learning the extent to which our views of masculinity and femininity are based on stereotypes that often have little relation to reality.

Consider the traditional, and still quite common, view of athletic women as "unfeminine." We tend to think of athletes as competitive, aggressive, and strong, and these are qualities not commonly associated with women. Yet, there are women athletes —football players, boxers, and surfers—who are quite feminine and physically attractive. For example, women's surfing expert Laura Blears Ching is extremely athletic, yet is also sufficiently feminine and physically attractive to be chosen as one of *Playboy* magazine's playmates. The point is not that women should aspire to be playmates— in fact, many women today view this status as offensive, degrading, and not at all feminine. **The point is that masculinity and femininity are matters of definition, and we retain stereotypes about them that are sometimes false.**

It is very different, as we will see, to "grow up male" and to "grow up female" in our society. Although some of the differences have been reduced in the past few decades, much of the traditional thinking about appropriate sex-role-related behavior remains. Our collective judgments concerning the appropriate appearance and behavior of males and females from birth to death are the crux of what we broadly refer to as masculinity and femininity. Let us now explore these perceptual differences.

Gender versus Sex Role

There is a powerful tendency in our society for people to believe that being *born* male or female automatically implies specific behavioral differences. That is, if one emerges from the womb with a penis as opposed to a vagina, this sexual distinction will automatically result in differences in behavior on the child's part in the future. **Sociologically, however, there is a crucial difference between gender and sex role.** *Male* and *female* **are used as gender-related terms.** *Gender* **refers to the biological—the inherent—features of sexual identity.**[22] Human beings are normally born with a clearly identifiable gender (the hermaphrodite is an exception that occurs infrequently). *Masculine* **and** *feminine,* **on the other hand, are used as role-specific terms.** *Sex role* **refers to learned behavior in terms of how to function as males and females in society.** The important characteristics of *roles* are: (1) that the expectations associated with a particular role are defined in a reasonably precise fashion in society and are assumed to apply to everyone in a particular category, and (2) that they represent *learned* behavior. Even though roles are rather precisely defined, there is much variation in how the individual might meet the expectations attached to a role. Therefore, role behavior varies. The distinction between gender and sex role has often been ignored, and the result has been a distorted and inaccurate view of sexuality. One illustration will suffice to show how this can happen and what the consequences can be.

"Biology is Destiny"

Sigmund Freud's theories of psychosexual development have had a powerful and undeniable influence on modern thinking about human sexuality. While Freud certainly cannot be blamed for all current stereotypes about men and women, he serves as a good illustration of the pervasive influence that ideas can have once they are widely accepted. Freud argued that because males possess a larger (and according to his definition, superior) sexual organ, men must experience more pleasure in sexual relations than women. Until research by Masters and Johnson scientifically dispelled such ideas, Freud's assertions were widely accepted.[23] Consider as well his distinction between *vaginal* and *clitoral orgasm,* with the assumption that clitoral orgasmic response is inferior to vaginal sexual climax. Physiological research has proven this assertion incorrect. There is even some evidence that female sexual response is more versatile and intense than the male's.[24]

Social scientist Judd Marmor has described the most salient features of Freud's psychoanalytic position on women:

(1) *Anatomy is fate.* The basic nature of woman is determined by her anatomy, most importantly by her discovery that she does not possess a penis.

(2) *Penis envy.* All female children naturally envy males for having penises, and the desire for a penis is a universal fact of normal feminine psychology, only partially compensated for by giving birth to a male child.... Penis envy is a natural consequence of the fact that the clitoris actually is "an inferior organ" in terms of its capacity to provide libidinal gratification, as well as for its lack of "the forward thrusting, penetrating qualities of the penis."

(3) *Masochism and passivity.* These outgrowths of normal feminine developments are natural and essential components of healthy femininity.

(4) *Faulty superego development.* Due to the fact that the feminine castration complex (precipitated by the little girl's discovery that she has no penis) pushed the little girl *away* from her mother *into* an Oedipal attachment for her father, the little girl has greater difficulty than the boy in resolving the Oedipal complex. Consequently, she tends to develop a defective superego.... The result in women, according to Freud, is an inadequate sense of justice, a predisposition to envy, weaker social interests, and a smaller capacity for sublimation.[25]

The implication of Freudian theory is very simple — "biology is destiny." Freud ignored the distinction between gender (the biological) and sex role (the learned).[26] Freudian thought has occupied a position of considerable stature in the social scientific community over the years and has had a tremendous impact on popular thought. Even though most social scientists no longer accept much of Freudian theory, his thinking has been widely accepted by the public and is still quite influential.

In terms of gender, the distinction between male and female is biological and relatively simple — males are equipped with a penis, testicles, and the capability of producing sperm, and participate correspondingly in reproduction. Females have a vagina, a uterus, produce ova and serve their respective part in reproduction. The distinction between gender and sex roles or identity is more complex. The separation between gender and sexual identity is shown very clearly in the case of transsexuals, and a brief discussion of this condition will serve to further illustrate the fact that biology is *not* destiny.

Transsexuality

Transsexuality refers to the condition in which a person possesses a fundamental feeling that he or she is, or should be, a member of the opposite sex. It is important to distinguish between transsexualism, homosexuality, and transvestism. *Homosexuals* are sexually attracted to members of the same gender, and (usually) have no desire to *be* a member of the opposite sex. *Transvestites* have a predilection for dressing as members of the opposite sex, but do not feel any desire to undergo any genital transformation — that is, to transfer their biological identity to the opposite gender. Transvestites are typically *not* homosexuals, however, and by dressing as members of the opposite sex, they are not attempting to attract members of their own (biological) gender. *Transsexuals* usually exhibit certain features of both homosexuals and transvestites. In other words, the individual is sexually attracted to members of his or her *biological* sex and wants to dress as a member of the "opposite" sex. The crucial point here, however, is that the transsexual acts and dresses according to what he or she views as his or her *real* sexual identity — which, of course, happens to be different from the biological genitalia he or she possesses. Recently, tennis pro and transsexual Dr. Renée Richards attracted a great deal of public attention when she (Dr. Richards was born a biological male and underwent genital surgery and hormonal treatment to "become" a female) insisted that she be permitted to compete in women's professional tennis competition.

The importance of transsexuality for the problem of sex roles is illustrated by the work of Jan Morris (a transsexual). In her book *Conundrum,* Morris describes how she was born and reared as a male (James Morris) and how she desired to be female from an early age. Until age forty-six, Morris lived as a male, served in the military, married, and fathered children. Nevertheless, Morris felt that her male gender was incorrect. She comments:

> To me gender is not physical at all, but is altogether insubstantial. It is soul, perhaps, it is talent, it is taste, it is environment, it is how one feels, it is light and shade, it is inner music, it is a spring in one's step or an exchange of glances, it is more truly life and love than any combination of genitals, ovaries and hormones. It is the essentialness of oneself, the psyche, the fragment of unity. Male and female are sex, masculine and feminine are gender, and though the conceptions obviously overlap, they are far from synonymous.[27]

At age forty-six, James Morris underwent genital surgery wherein his penis and testicles were removed and replaced with an artificial vagina. Hormone injections discouraged the growth of facial hair and encouraged the development of breasts. Today she is Jan Morris, and to her, she is just as much a female and "feminine" as any other woman.

Although transsexuality remains much of a mystery, the condition suggests that there is far more to sex role identity than merely possessing a penis or a vagina. **Masculinity and femininity are examples of *learned behavior,* even though most of us continue to regard these traits as solely inborn, biological characteristics. This is not to suggest that biology is irrelevant, but that the interplay between social environment and biological conditions is crucial indeed.**

Growing up Male

The Stereotype

One of the longest running programs in the history of American television was "Gunsmoke." In every episode, as Marshall Matt Dillon journeyed into the streets of Dodge City to gun down the bad guy, millions of viewers were undoubtedly thinking to themselves, "Now *there* was a man!" Dillon never married, of course, because the heavy weight of the U.S. marshal's badge and the compassionate sense that he might be shot to death at any time compelled him to avoid the altar. Nevertheless, every viewer knew that Matt was sexually virile and that he and Miss Kitty had a "thing going" (he and his comical male sidekicks were friends, but nothing more).

Consider what image of masculinity the character Matt Dillon conveys. Different writers have discussed a variety of supposed masculine characteristics.[28] Among them are aggressiveness and sadistic qualities, protectiveness toward females, mechanical ability, athletic prowess, bravery, courage, violence, and a tendency to be overbearing. In a more recent assessment, social scientists Deborah David and Robert Brannon point out that the masculine man is frequently characterized as a person who is never depressed or vulnerable, never cries, is a tower of strength, is always aggressive, tough, confident, determined, and of course, *never feminine.*[29] These descriptions seem to fit old Matthew to a T, don't they? "Gunsmoke" is now a television rerun, but there are many other similar protrayals of males in the media today. A glance between the covers of women's magazines such as Mademoiselle, McCall's, Ladies' Home Journal, Cosmopolitan, Glamour, or Vogue will reveal a similarly stereotyped view of masculinity. Males are protrayed as husbands and providers, never as homemakers. Motion pictures also provide an equally stereotyped portrait. Consider who the most popular movie starts are today; what kinds of characteristics do they possess? Consider, for example, Paul Newman, Steve McQueen, Robert Redford, and Kris Kristoffersen. The stereotypes are still with us.

"Well, here comes the old masculine mystique."

Drawing by Stan Hunt © 1978 The New Yorker Magazine.

The Socialization Process

Our concern here is not with how desirable these qualities might be, but rather with how accurate the sterotype is and whether it is biologically linked to being male. From the interactionist perspective, we know that human interaction is essential to the development of personality. Both male and female infants generally form their first and strongest identification with their mother.[30] Female infants model their mother's behavior, are rewarded for it, and begin to internalize the expectations of the female role. The male infant experiences some initial difficulty, however. His mother punishes him for modeling much of her behavior, and his father often joins in this negative reinforcement process by admonishing his son not to be a "sissy" and to "act like a man." Studies have shown that little boys experience far more difficulty at first than little girls in terms of sex role identity, but later, boys have greater success than girls in internalizing appropriate sex role expectations.[31] The reason for this is that females are permitted to engage in "male-like" behavior until they approach adolescence, while males are consistently punished for behaving in a "female-like manner." For example, one study demonstrated that girls often display a fondness for the elevated prestige of the masculine role by becoming "tomboys."[32] "Tomboyism" is acceptable to a much greater extent than a little boy's being a "sissy." In fact, girls are more prominent in boy's games than boys are in girl's games—testament to the less negative reactions to "tomboys" than to "sissys." Another investigator discovered that boys play more competitive games than girls and that girls typically do not learn how to deal with direct competition.[33]

In school, little boys are usually encouraged to play with trucks and G.I. Joe toys, to climb ropes, and to get involved in contact sports. (There are a few schools in the United States, of course, where sex role specific learning is discouraged, and boys and girls learn the same behavior patterns.) Later, young men are usually rewarded for taking wood and metal shop courses and for developing interests in the sciences, engineering, law, and business.

Over time, a young person's self-concept can become a *self-fulfilling prophecy*—the person begins to behave in a fashion similar to what others expect of him or her because that is the most rewarded and accepted way to behave. Beyond a very early age, males are discouraged from engaging in overt affection—indeed, to be extremely affectionate is defined as "unmanly." Males are taught to look for material rewards such as money and are encouraged to respect and desire power, dominance, and prestige. In the marital relationship, one of the premium male rewards appears to be the impression that he is dominant.[34] In fact, research indicates that some females actually *fear* achievement and success because they have been taught to "play dumb" and to "boost the male ego."[35]

A significant part of the socialization process occurs in school. School systems are characteristically staffed in such a way that children's perceptions of masculinity and femininity are reinforced. Researchers have determined that nearly 90 percent of grade school teachers are female, while close to 90 percent of their principals are male. Thus, from the beginning of school, children see men in posi-

TABLE 13.1

Characteristics Assigned Males and Females by Grade-School Teachers, Expressed in Percentages

CHARACTERISTIC	BIOLOGICALLY INNATE TO:		NO DIFFERENCE	CULTURAL TRAIT OF:		TOTAL NUMBER OF TEACHERS[a]
	MALES	FEMALES		MALES	FEMALES	
Aggressive	40	6	26	26	1	147
Practical, objective	15	15	34	20	15	116
Compassionate, sentimental	3	39	26	1	30	148
Idealistic	3	19	48	5	25	151
Verbal ability	8	11	54	16	11	149
Follower	4	18	31	1	45	144
Moral, trustworthy	3	13	67	5	13	150
Intuitive	3	41	33	2	21	150
Abstract reasoning ability	16	10	47	20	6	152

[a] Totals vary because "no responses" were omitted.

SOURCE. Janet Saltzman Chafetz, *Masculine, Feminine, or Human: An Overview of the Sociology of Sex Roles*, (C) 1974, p. 89. Second edition (C) 1978. (Reproduced by permission of the publisher, F. E. Peacock Publishers, Inc., Itasca, Ill.)

tions of dominance and authority and women in subordinate positions.[36] In addition, female elementary school teachers tend to express numerous sex role stereotypes. Table 13.1 shows that 40 percent of the teachers in one study felt that aggression is an innate characteristic of males but not females, and many believed that males are more capable than females of abstract reasoning.[37] It is highly likely that these teachers, most often without realizing it, encouraged their students to behave in a fashion consistent with their own sex stereotype. Since young schoolchildren are at a very formative and impressionable stage in life, it is hard to underestimate the impact that these school experiences can have on children.

While the feminine character has been studied extensively for many years, studies concerning masculinity are a relatively recent innovation. Social scientist Marc F. Fasteau spoke of a "masculine mystique"—a set of stereotypes about men (men are strong, dominant, tough, unemotional, and the like).[38] **Fasteau's point is that socially imposed expectations concerning male behavior can be as limiting for men in our society as the well-known stereotypes involving females have been for women.** For example, men are expected to be "strong" in emotional situations and not to cry. Psychologically, crying is not only a normal human reaction, but it can be cathartic as well. Men are limited, then, in that they are expected to refrain from this form of catharsis.

Growing up Female

The Stereotype

Considering the amount of attention that women's rights and related issues have received in recent years, one might think that by now many of the stereotypes about females would have been nearly eliminated. Although substantial progress has been made in some areas toward this end, little girls are still raised to be mothers and homemakers (and, to a limited extent, for occupations outside the home). This training begins very early in life and may be both direct and indirect. The authors of this book, for example, grew up on a steady diet of "See Dick — See Jane" textbooks in elementary school, but they were obviously unaware of the implications at the time. In these books, as might be expected, Dick was always the "doer" and Jane the follower. Dick accomplished a great deal, while Jane watched with admiration and a sense of servitude. Dick was often portrayed as a budding physician while Jane served as a nurse or in some other position to act as Dick's assistant. "Sugar and spice and everything nice—that's what little girls are made of." We learned that newborn little boys are always dressed in blue and little girls in pink; young males are outgoing and aggressive, while young females are reserved and passive.

This sex role bias in education has changed somewhat since the 1940s, but not to the extent that supporters of the cause of women's rights have hoped or expected. Current surveys of preschool, elementary, junior high, and even high school textbooks demonstrate that the stereotypes are still prevalent. Female characters still appear far less often in these books than males and are typically portrayed as more passive and dependent than their male counterparts.[39]

In 1972, the National Organization of Women (NOW) published a survey of elementary school textbooks and found a heavy concentration of stories about boys, with males depicted in a variety of creative roles. Females, on the other hand, were almost always pictured as mothers and teachers. Other studies have found the same kinds of stereotypical depictions of males and females in picture books for preschool children.[40] Recently, women's groups in several states have pressured boards of education at different levels to take steps to monitor the content of textbooks to ensure that females are not depicted in subservient ways.

This stereotype of women surfaces in many different contexts, some of them rather surprising. For example, studies have shown that many contemporary theories in psychology present a view of women as naturally more passive, nurturing, and maternal.[41] The traits most often associated with women in psychological theory are described by one investigator as passivity, emotionality, lack of abstract interests, greater intensity of personal relationships, and an instinctive tenderness for babies.[42] It is also interesting that in recently published marriage manuals, there is *still* a tendency toward stressing the female's passive role in sexual relations.[43]

Even mental health clinicians are prone to stereotyping women in negative and sometimes destructive ways. In a study conducted about a decade ago, clinicians (psychiatrists, psychologists, and social workers) completed a questionnaire soliciting their views on the characteristics of healthy adult men, healthy adult women, and healthy adults in general (sex not specified). Psychologist Phyllis Chesler reports the following results:

> Clinicians had different standards of health for men and women. Their concepts of healthy mature men did not differ significantly from their concepts of healthy mature adults, but their concepts of healthy mature women did differ significantly from those for men and for adults. Clinicians were likely to suggest that women differ from healthy men by being more submissive, less independent, less adventurous, more easily influenced, less aggressive, less competitive, more excitable in minor crises, more easily hurt, more emotional, more conceited about their appearances, less objective, and less interested in math and science.[44]

Furthermore, the characteristics assigned to healthy adult males are those that are normally viewed as socially desirable in our culture, while those assigned to healthy adult women are generally regarded as less socially desirable. In addition, *women clinicians were in total agreement with their male counterparts on these issues!* It is important to realize that these clinicians are not reporting what healthy women in our culture *are* like— they are suggesting what healthy American women *should* be like. They are saying that healthy adult women in our culture should possess fewer socially desirable characteristics than men and should differ considerably from a "normal health adult"! The fact that this inaccurate stereotype prevails among some psychologists and mental health clinicians—people presumably knowledgeable about such issues—illustrates its subtle and pervasive character.

Sexism

With these stereotypes in mind, we are now in a position to examine some important issues in relation to sex roles in our society. **Sexism refers to the conglomerate of cultural values and social behaviors related to the belief that one sex is superior to the other and that makes it possible for one sex to dominate over the other.** We have seen how certain masculine characteristics have an implied sexism built in. Sometimes, many of us have the tendency to believe that sexism is a relatively new phenomenon. This is far from the truth. Sexist belief systems are firmly entrenched in Western philosophical, religious, and intellectual thought. For example, organized religion is dominated by *men* even though women attend church more often, pray more frequently, hold firmer religious beliefs, and contribute to church programs more often than men.[45] Modern Roman Catholicism is experiencing a number of conflicts related to changing sex role expectations—all the way from the average Catholic female using artificial birth-control devices to women attempting to become priests. Even today, devout Jewish men offer a daily prayer thanking God for not making them female!

It has been pointed out that there are many sexist implications built into the English language. When speaking of human beings, we invariably employ gender-linked terms (*he, she*), but the male-related expressions (like *he*) seem to be employed universally. In what may be regarded as an awkward solution to this problem, feminist writers Kate Millett and Casey Swift have suggested that "common gender" terms should replace the more traditional gender linked ones: *tey* would take the place of *he* and *she; ter* would be used instead of *his* and *her;* and *tem* would substitute for *him* and *her.*[46] The pressures that many of us have felt to utilize the word *person* rather than *man* is an excellent illustration. One extreme example is the suggestion that the newspaper *The Manchester Guardian* be renamed *The Personchester Guardian!* The authors of one study report that "many people who claim they are referring to both males and females when they use the word *he* switch to the feminine pronoun when they begin to speak of someone in a traditionally female occupation, such as homemaker or schoolteacher or nurse."[47] All of this may sound humorous and even absurd; however, it illustrates the emotional intensity that accompanies the sex roles issue today and the extent to which sexism invades all parts of our culture.

As with racism and agism, the discrimination that often results from sexism is most effective if the subordinate group cooperates in perpetuating the beliefs upon which sexism rests. Throughout history there has been, and to some extent there still is, a tendency for some women to behave in a fashion that reinforces the stereotype. For example, we have noted that young girls often participate vigorously in traditionally male-dominated pursuits such as football. However, such a "tomboy" is generally expected to relinquish her rugged, rough-and-tumble ways shortly after she enters puberty. She now learns that if boys are to be interested in her for reasons other than wanting her as a member of the sandlot baseball team, she must try to be "feminine." Even though she may know that there are many things she can do just as well as, or better than, boys, the expectation is to "play dumb"; don't be too eager to win." For example, females reading this might reflect how many times they felt compelled to "lose" a tennis match or similar athletic contest in order to accommodate the ego of the man they were playing with. Although they might have won had they played their best, they chose not to do so. This occurs in the intellectual arena as well. Now for the male readers: they can perhaps recall a situation where they felt that a woman was behaving in a particular way in order to accommodate their ego. Males may have sensed that a woman was "playing dumb" in order to suit them. Of course, they may have appreciated it at the time.

As yet, there is little evidence to suggest that most of these stereotypically male and female behaviors are the result of biological differences. Ultimately, masculinity and femininity are largely learned roles. Nevertheless, the sexism that results from these stereotypes is real. We now turn our attention to the consequences of this unequal treatment—the impact it has on women and society in general.

DISCRIMINATION AND INEQUALITY

Many Americans pride themselves on their fairness to all people, regardless of race, creed, or color. Yet not until recently has *sex* been considered one of the key factors in discrimination and inequality. In fact, the Civil Rights Act of 1964 – a landmark in the field of civil rights legislation – exempted federal, state, and local governments from the stipulations of the act prohibiting discrimination against women. This meant that discrimination against women could and did continue in many government jobs. As long as people accepted the biological stereotypes discussed previously, it was possible for people to justify such discrimination on the grounds that women were incapable of doing most of the things that men could do.

While women are a numerical majority in our society, they comprise a *minority group*. There are a number of important similarities between women and other minority groups (see ch. 12). Like blacks, they still have unequal access to valued resources and suffer discrimination on many fronts. For example, in America's labor force there are still characteristically male and female occupations. Women account for nearly 100 percent of the nation's secretaries but constitute only 3 percent of our country's engineers. In order to evaluate the extent to which sex roles are a social problem for American society, we will look at the discrimination and inequality that emerges from our stereotyped views of sex role identity.

Economic Discrimination

When a husband and wife squabble about who is to do the dishes or take out the trash, regardless of who eventually performs these tasks, the stakes are not very high. While it may be an important personal issue for that couple, it does not significantly affect their ability to support themselves at an acceptable economic level. However, much sex role discrimination has direct implications for the ability of women to support themselves. Recall that a person's position in the system of social stratification has important implications. Whether people regard themselves as successful or unsuccessful, happy or unhappy, depends a great deal on their socioeconomic status. The three widely accepted dimensions of socioeconomic status (SES) are education, occupation, and income.

Education

In the United States, education has long been a key channel of mobility, particularly for members of disadvantaged social groups. It is paradoxical, then, in a country that stresses equality for all, that there has been unequal access to educational opportunities in America. For example, the opportunity for higher education is *not* equally available to all in our society. Until about 1850, women were almost completely excluded from the "halls of ivy." In a preindustrial social order, it was assumed that women required less education since their career would be as homemakers and mothers. This assumption was translated into discriminatory policies whose effects are still evident. For example, until 1950, the Harvard Law School excluded women entirely. Prior to 1970, as unbelievable as it may seem, most professional schools placed quotas on the number of female students who were admitted.

Since 1950, more young people are graduating from high school than before, and increasing numbers of both sexes are attending college. The number of Americans 25 years and older with some college training almost tripled between 1950 and 1976.[48] Nevertheless, Table 13.2 illustrates that as the amount of education increases, the percentage of men with more education exceeds those of women. At the Ph.D. level, the statistics are particularly impressive – see Table 13.3. Although more women earned doctorates between 1972 and 1975 than between 1969 and 1972, the gains are not impressive. Thus, even though more women are pursuing a college education than ever before, men still predominate in this very important arena in our society.

TABLE 13.2

Percentage of Years of School Completed by Persons 25 Years Old and Over, by Sex, March 1977

YEARS OF SCHOOL COMPLETED	MALE	FEMALE
High School, 4 years	32.1	39.6
College, 1 to 3 years	14.2	12.7
College, 4 or more years	10.3	8.0

SOURCE. "Educational Attainment in the United States: 1977," *Current Population Reports*, Series P-20, no. 314, December 1977.

TABLE 13.3

Number of Doctorates Conferred on Majority Men, Majority Women, Minority Men, and Minority Women, 1969–1972 and 1972–1975

	1969–72	% OF TOTAL	1972–75	% OF TOTAL	% CHANGE
Majority men	43,768	(82.1)	39,773	(74.6)	−9
Majority women	7,781	(14.6)	10,451	(19.6)	+34
Minority men	1,332	(2.5)	2,139	(4.0)	+61
Minority women	414	(0.7)	964	(1.8)	+133

SOURCE, Table 2, p. 858 in J. L. McCarthy and D. Wolfe, "Doctorates Granted to Women and Minority Group Members," *Science* 189, no. 4206, 12 September 1975, pp. 856–859.

Occupation

Women are concentrated at the lower end of the occupational status hierarchy. Table 13.4 illustrates, for example, that women represent 99 percent of all secretaries, 85 percent of all file clerks, 71 percent of all school teachers, but only 9 percent of the nation's lawyers, 21 percent of our physicians, and only 11 percent of the sales managers. Even more surprising is the fact that less than 3 percent of America's engineers are women. As we observed in the previous section, more women are going to college today, representing over 45 percent of college students.[49] After graduation, however, more men than women are found in the most desirable occupational slots. Although about the same proportion of men and women occupy technical and professional positions in our society, women are typically employed as elementary and secondary-level teachers and as nurses, while men are concentrated in higher-status and more economically rewarding fields such as medicine and law. In another arena, female graduate students in the social sciences have superior academic records in comparison to their male counterparts,[50] yet female Ph.D.s are less likely than males to attain the rank of Full Professor and receive tenure.[51] This remains the case today, even though research demonstrates that female Ph.D.s are as productive in publishing research papers and books as their male counterparts.[52]

Despite the recent emphasis on equal employment opportunities for women, 99 percent of the nation's secretaries and 85 percent of all file clerks are women.

Even though affirmative action has been designed to discourage discrimination in hiring practices, the Equal Employment Opportunity Commission annually receives thousands of formal complaints involving sex discrimination. In one study of discriminatory employment practices, it was demonstrated that both men and women are "sex typed" for various jobs.[53] For example, males looking for jobs were often encouraged by prospective employers to apply for managerial posts, while women were encouraged to apply for lower-level positions. There are some who believe that in certain areas there is a kind of reverse discrimination in operation today — in the same fashion that members of certain ethnic groups are afforded job opportunities through affirmative action, females

TABLE 13.4
Employment Positions Held by Women

	TOTAL NUMBER OF WORKERS EMPLOYED	PROPORTION HELD BY WOMEN
Secretaries	3,421,000	99%
Child-care workers	443,000	98
Receptionists	531,000	97
Typists	1,006,000	96
Registered nurses	879,000	96
Hairdressers, cosmetologists	526,000	88
Bank tellers	408,000	90
Bookkeepers	1,726,000	90
Cashiers	1,326,000	87
Health service workers	1,747,000	89
File clerks	274,000	85
Librarians	208,000	80
Counter clerks (nonfood)	343,000	78
Office machine operators	759,000	74
School teachers	3,024,000	71
Food-service workers	4,095,000	69
Retail clerks	2,316,000	70
Social workers	444,000	60
Office managers	343,000	58
Real estate agents	502,000	44
Cleaning-service workers	680,000	34
Writers, artists, entertainers	1,141,000	36
College teachers	562,000	32
Accountants	868,000	27
Bank, financial officers	543,000	27
Sales managers	666,000	21
Physicians and dentists	724,000	11
Electrical and electronic engineering technicians	194,000	10
Protective service workers (police, etc.)	1,324,000	8
Lawyers and judges	462,000	9
Engineers	1,267,000	3
Construction craftsworkers	2,404,000	1

SOURCE. U.S. Bureau of the Census, *Statistical Abstract of the United States, 1978* (Washington D.C.: U.S. Government Printing Office, 1978), pp. 418–421.

may actually be preferred over males in some occupational situations.

Income

In 1977, the median income for American males working year-round and full time was $15,070. For females in the same category, the median income was $8814.[54] This is a difference of about $5300—a substantial amount of money. In other words, the average female income was only 59 percent of the average male income. When one examines related statistics, the differences in dollar amounts become even more significant. In 1976, 36 percent of those families headed by women were below the poverty level in comparison to only 3 percent of male-headed households.[55]

It is also interesting to examine the income levels of male and female workers in different occupational categories. Table 13.5 illustrates that overall, women earn less income than males in every job

TABLE 13.5
Yearly Income for Year-Round Full-time Male and Female Workers by Occupational Category, 1976

MAJOR OCCUPATIONAL GROUP	MALE MEDIAN INCOME (DOLLARS)[a]	FEMALE MEDIAN INCOME (DOLLARS)[a]
Professional, Technical & Kindred Workers	17,431	11,365
Managers and Administrators	17,351	10,069
Sales Workers	15,198	6,701
Clerical and Kindred Workers	13,323	8,369
Craft and Kindred Workers	13,962	8.026
Operatives including Transport Workers	11,807	6,865
Private Household Workers		3,005
Laborers, except Farm	10,310	7,728
Service Workers, except Private Household	10,560	6,111
Farmers and Farm Managers	7,052	
Farm Laborers and Supervisors	6,310	

[a] Figure not shown when category is based on fewer than 75,000 persons.

SOURCE. "Money Income in 1976 of Families and Persons in the United States." *Current Population Reports*, Series P-60, no. 114, (July 1978).

category. Even in the armed forces, where pay levels are standardized it is less likely that women will receive "combat pay," "flight pay," "jump pay" (for an active parachutist), or "hazardous duty pay." Among college professors, studies reveal significant salary differentials between male and female sociologists, and these discrepancies are observable in practically every academic discipline.[56]

Certainly, some of these differences in income are due to the fact that men have been working longer than women and thus have gained seniority and salary increases that have boosted their income. However, studies that have taken this into account still come to the conclusion that women have tended to receive less pay than men for doing the same job.

Considering the situation that women face in terms of education, occupation, and income—the key determinants of socioeconomic status (SES)—it is understandable how difficult their quest for equality and human rights has been. While the gaps between the rewards received by men and women have narrowed, it is too early to predict whether these inequities will eventually be eliminated. For many women, especially those who must overcome additional barriers resulting from poverty or minority group status, it is even

more difficult than it is for men to achieve the same level of economic affluence. Furthermore, blatant economic inequality is only one type of discrimination faced by women. While we do not have space to catalogue all the areas of discrimination, we will illustrate some of the varied ways in which women are placed at a disadvantage in our society.

Other Types of Discrimination

Our legal system has had built into it a great deal of discrimination against women. Consider, for example, the legal implications of the marriage contract in America. In many instances, the husband retains final decision-making power regarding the buying and selling of property (when one considers the sex composition of state legislatures over the years, this is easy to understand).

Until recently, there were many states whose laws prevented women from owning their own businesses and being the sole signatories on legal contracts. One recent change in this area involves credit references (including bank cards, loans, etc.) for married couples. If requested, credit reports must now be on file and available under the names of *both* the husband and the wife. Previously, a married woman had no official credit rating since all credit transactions were in her husband's name.

If widowed or divorced, she encountered considerable difficulty getting credit.[57] In many areas, women have had difficulty obtaining loans to purchase houses, cars, or other items. As the number of single and divorced women in the United States increases, these forms of discrimination create substantial barriers to their ability to support themselves and their families. While there have been substantial improvements recently, some discrimination of this nature still does occur.

Until recently, many state laws prohibited interschool athletic competition between female teams.[58] In addition, colleges and universities have traditionally provided substantially more support for male athletic programs than for female athletics. Even though the enforcement of Title IX (federal legislation prohibiting various types of discrimination on the basis of sex) has opened more opportunities to young girls, such as Little League baseball participation, there are many informal devices such as peer pressure, ridicule, and hostility that continue to discourage their participation. In addition, "boys' clubs" are under closer scrutiny since they have been traditionally restricted in membership to males. Furthermore, the enforcement of Title IX may soon lead to a significant redistribution of resources between male and female athletes at the college and university level.

In terms of family relationships, "growing up female" implies that a woman's primary role is that of homemaker and mother. In a recent article, sociologist Jessie Bernard pointed out that women experience greater dissatisfaction and more depression in marriage than men. In addition, she noted that because women feel that they have a greater stake in the stability of their marriages than their husbands do, they usually make most of the adjustments necessary to keep them intact.[59] So powerful is this identification with the domestic role that even today's middle-aged woman is very likely to suffer severe depression when many of her tasks as a mother and homemaker are phased out—especially if she does not have a job outside the home. One researcher feels that this depression occurs because these women feel that they no longer perform important functions rather than because of the related physiological effects of menopause.[60] Fi-

nally, it is interesting to note that research demonstrates rather consistently that employed wives are happier than full-time homemakers.[61]

Much of the emphasis in the field of sex roles is on women—stereotypes about women, discrimination against women, limitations placed on women. However, male and female roles are reciprocal, and changes in one role is likely to have implications for the other role. It is time that we look at the changes that have been brought about in the male role in our society.

THE CHANGING MALE SEX ROLE

The sex roles issue has been "female centered" for a long time. Much of the active campaigning for sex role equality and the clamoring for change has focused on women. We have emphasized, however, that sex roles can represent a social problem for both women *and* men. It is important to examine how males fit into the overall picture.

It was not long ago that very little material could be found concerning the male sex role. It seems that this topic has been viewed as so self-evident (or unimportant) as to deserve little formal attention. This neglect is probably due to the fact that our society has been dominated by males, and males have not been the targets of the prejudice and discrimination resulting from inequality between the sexes. More recently, a great deal of literature has been generated in this previously neglected area. Problems and limitations created by the male sex role sparked attention only after the feminist movement led many to question the traditional female sex role. From this initial awareness has arisen a new area of social concern. Let us consider some of its dimensions.

Men and Masculinity

Two sociologists writing on the social implications of masculinity have outlined what they regard as the core expectations of the male sex role in our society:[62]

(1) *No sissy stuff*—don't be like girls, don't be feminine, don't permit yourself to be open or vulnerable

["Get a grip on yourself"; "Pull yourself together, man"; "Keep a stiff upper lip, boy"].

The pervasiveness of this expectation and the consequences for a person if he violates it can be illustrated by the following incident:

A friend explained to me that he broke down and cried in front of a colleague at the office after some personal tragedies and office frustrations. He explained, "The news of my crying was all over the office in an hour. At first no one said anything. They just sort of looked. They couldn't handle the situation by talking about it. Before this only girls had cried. One of the guys did joke, 'Hear you and Sally been crying lately, eh?' I guess that was a jibe at my masculinity, but the 'knowing silence' of the others indicated the same doubts. What really hurt was that two years later, when I was doing very well and being considered for a promotion, it was brought up again. My manager was looking over my evaluations, read a paragraph to himself and said, 'What do you think about that crying incident?' You can bet that was the last time I let myself cry."[63]

In another incident, Senator Edmund Muskie "broke down and cried" in public in 1968 over accusations about his wife, and this public display of emotion was later cited as evidence that he did not have the emotional stability to be president of the United States. Clearly, violating the expectation that men should not express such emotions can have severe consequences.

(2) *The big wheel image* — be successful, wealthy, and famous if you can; get people to look up to you; be competent; be the breadwinner, the provider.

The comments of one psychiatrist illustrate these expectations:

In our culture money equals success. Does it also equal masculinity? Yes — to the extent that a man is too often measured by his money, by what he is "worth." Not by his worth as a human being, but what he is able to earn, how much he can command on the "open market."[64]

(3) *The sturdy oak* — display a manly air of toughness, confidence, and self reliance; be physically strong and athletic.

Research on American soldiers during World War II illustrates the extent to which men are pressured to conform to this expectation:

Combat posed a challenge for a man to prove himself and others. Combat was a dare. One never knew for sure that he could take it until he had demonstrated that he could. . . . To fail to measure up as a soldier in courage and endurance was to risk the charge of not being a man. ("Whatsa matter buddy — got lace in your drawers?")[65]

In Latin American culture, the "sturdy oak" image is expressed in terms of "machismo" — the expectation that males distinguish themselves partially through bravery and a willingness to be aggressive in situations that "require" it.

(4) *Give 'em Hell* — portray an aura of aggression, violence and daring.

Warren Farrell's vivid description of the yearly Super Bowl competition describes this characteristic:

The special team employed during every kickoff or punt is called the suicide squad. The comparison to war is made by Rich Saul, a lineman for the Los Angeles Rams who is notorious for his play on suicide squads. "If you compare football to war, then the special teams are the marines or the infantry. We're the first ones to get into the game, we initiate the hitting, we determine where the battle is going to be fought and on whose grounds." Saul, who says he enjoys his job, "slams into ball carriers with such intensity that he mangled five steel face masks on the front of his helmet."[66]

This vivid depiction of the male role in society (in stereotypical fashion, of course) is illustrative. The "model male" is supposed to be strong; he is never depressed, anxious, or vulnerable; he never cries or openly displays any feminine emotion; he is successful, ever confident, always aggressive, forceful, and brave; and he is always in a position to dominate any situation. According to the stereotype, these are the ideal masculine characteristics that every male is expected to live up to, and to fall short of them is considered to be a failing or weakness. The "Give 'em Hell" image is well illustrated

in terms of key figures in American government and the military—like President Harry S. Truman and the well-known Army general, George S. ("old blood and guts") Patton. In January 1979, well-known Ohio State University football coach Woodrow Wilson "Woody" Hayes was fired as coach after an incident that occurred at that year's Gator Bowl. During a tense moment, Mr. Hayes struck a member of the opposing team (Clemson University) with his fists. Although it is not completely clear why he did this, Woody Hayes had a national reputation of being a man who regarded winning as more important than anything else. In some cases, it would appear that adherence to the stereotypical masculine role can be costly indeed.

We know that in reality people do not and cannot realize all of the cultural prescriptions or proscriptions put before them. Nevertheless, males who fail to measure up to many of these expectations may face problems in our society. Consider this example: A man and woman are on a date and begin to be harrassed by a 16-year-old male who is about six feet tall, weighs about 200 pounds, and insults the man's date. Regardless of how large or small, physically capable or incapable, the man may be, he is expected to squelch the youngster's bantering in one way or another. His date could be "The Fabulous Moolah" (a professional woman wrestler), and he would still be expected to "have the guts to put a stop to this nonsense." This is a heavy burden to carry, and the costs of failure can, in some cases, be devastating to the individual's sense of himself as a desirable, worthwhile person.

Ironic, isn't it, that someone who is ill-suited to a particular task is still expected to perform it. In fact, from the functionalist perspective, one could argue that it is dysfunctional for society to assign tasks to people who are not equipped to carry them out. Tasks may not be accomplished, or accomplished as well, if they are assigned to people not capable of carrying them out. Many proponents of changes in traditional sex roles argue that one's sex is no longer the most useful criterion for allocating many tasks. Some females today are better equipped to be truckdrivers and construction workers than are many males; likewise, some males may be better able to perform as housekeepers and childraisers

than would some females. From this point of view, it would be more functional to allocate roles and expectations on the basis of individaul abilities, rather than on sexual status. This would open up many new opportunities for both men and women and would, in fact, broaden the horizons of each. Let us glance at some of the ways this is being experimented with.

Men's Liberation

In his book *The Liberated Man,* social scientist Warren Farrell discusses what behaviors are expected of men and also how some are "liberating themselves" by circumventing these expectations.[67] He has even suggested that women's liberation is supportive (in an indirect sense) of men's liberation. In a very real sense, "men's liberation" may eventually become as significant an issue in our society as its female counterpart. There is at least one common ingredient in the two movements: both involve a striving for personal opportunities that have been socially denied in the past. In terms of male liberation from stereotyped behavioral expectations, psychiatrist Robert Gould comments:

> I suspect we will have to give up the whole idea of "masculinity" and start trying to find out about the real male person. We may find that masculinity has more to do with a man's sensitivity, with the nature of his emotional capacity to respond to others, than it has to do with dominance, strength, or ability to "provide for" a woman materially—especially if she isn't pretending to be helpless anymore.
>
> Someday soon, virility may be the measure of how well a male relates to a woman as an equal, and masculinity will be equated not with moneymaking prowess but with a man's power to feel, express and give love. That might just possibly be worth more than money.[68]

Changing the male sex role creates many problems, of course. There will be conflict between men and women in terms of the "liberation" issue. On the other hand, many feel that both men and women will be benefactors when unnecessary sex role distinctions are eliminated in our society. A

Although there are still many social pressures that encourage men to live up to a "macho" image, an increasing number of men are occupying nontraditional male roles.

social order without some sex role distinctions is very difficult to imagine. As we have already observed, however, it appears that only in a society in which *unnecessary* sex role distinctions are eliminated will people be able to actualize their full potentials as human beings. As one writer has noted:

If men cannot play freely, neither can they freely cry, be gentle, nor show weakness — because these are "feminine," not "masculine." But a fuller concept of humanity recognizes that all men and women are potentially both strong and weak, both active and passive, and that these and other human characteristics are not the province of one sex.

The acceptance of sex role stereotypes not only limits the individual but also has bad effects on society generally.[69]

It is probably hard for the average person to believe that a change of this magnitude could be more helpful than damaging, but there is considerable support for these kinds of alterations in our sex role structure. In his book *Men's Liberation: A New Definition of Masculinity,* social scientist Jack Nichols comments:

Because of quick social evolution men, both young and old, are beginning to realize that the psychological baggage they have been carrying into office and home is far too heavy. They need a rest, and the old values, with their incessant demands for stiff deportment, are tiring. Taboos, restrictions, and constrictions are disappearing like bald eagles, but masculine rulings die hard. Many people are not willing to admit that by the standards of the fifties they are pinko queers, and most haven't discovered this amusing fact yet. At present, American males are experiencing guilts as they abandon old roles. The roles, after all, were once sanctified and revered.[70]

While not all males can identify with Nichols's observations, many do. It will be useful to illustrate briefly some of the specific changes such liberation might entail.

Some Dimensions of the "Liberation"

Nontraditional Male Occupations

One important development of the past few decades has been the movement of men into roles and occupations that have been typically occupied by women. For example, there are probably very few males who identify themselves occupationally as "househusbands." Nevertheless, it is becoming increasingly more common than it once was for men to accept equal responsibility with their partners for domestic tasks. There is even a quite small, but growing, number of men who are becoming full-time domestics — devoting the majority of their time to home-oriented activities.

In terms of professional careers, male nurses are now more common in our hospitals. Recently a few males have even entered the nursing specialty of midwifery (the practice of assisting women in childbirth). A man in this unconventional male role, like the male nurse of a few years ago, must be prepared for incredulous, negative, and sometimes abusive reactions from others — even to the point of wondering whether such a person is homosexual because he chooses an occupation that others have stereotyped as suited for females. The masculine stereotypes may be on the wane, but they are tenacious.

In a recent article concerning child care work, one researcher pointed out that more male teachers are wanted and needed in these facilities.[71] He explained that males working in child care centers encounter considerable difficulty in freeing themselves from sexually stereotyped behavior and bear special burdens in their work. In other words, the male child-care worker must train himself to "act feminine" in terms of some of his duties. The results of this study indicate that as a consequence, the male worker must be seriously interested in, and extremely capable of, working with children.

We must be cautious, however, about overemphasizing the magnitude and importance of these changes. It is unlikely that we will see a widespread reversal of the traditional sex roles, with males and females exchanging places in the division of labor. There are many indications that males are reluctant to give up their traditional prerogatives, although there is a willingness to share them. For example, the Institute for Social Research at the University of Michigan surveyed high school seniors concerning these issues in 1978. Fully 85 percent of the seniors rejected the idea that it was appropriate for the wife to work full time while the husband took care of domestic chores, and 64 percent did not accept the idea of the husband working part time while the wife held a full-time job. These high school students were quite accepting of a wife working part time or full time while the husband worked full time, and there was considerable consensus that childrearing and housework should be equally shared, especially if the wife worked. These findings indicate that there has been considerable change in attitudes toward sex roles, but there will probably not be a dramatic reversal in the near future.[72]

"Father Power"

One writer has observed that little research has been conducted on fatherhood and that the father role has been largely ignored by social scientists.[73] Everyone seems to be interested in the father's relationship to his children, but the importance of the father role has been played down.

In a book entitled *Father Power,* social scientists Henry Biller and Dennis Meredeth discuss the importance of the role that fathers play in raising their children.[74] The authors are not speaking of tyrannical or paternalistic power but emphasize that the role of father is as important as the mother role in terms of effective child socialization. One may hear it said that "a father can't really be a father to his children until they get older." In the past, and to some extent today, this belief has led fathers to play a backstage role in parenting until the youngster begins to "cut the apronstrings," Biller, Meredeth, and other writers have emphasized that this does not have to be the case, and that from the beginning of the childrearing process, fathers should be encouraged to play as integral a role in parenthood as mothers do.

Attitudes toward occupations, domesticity, and parenthood illustrate how males are influenced by the same powerful social forces as are women in relation to sex roles. **The stereotypical male role limits the opportunities open to men in terms of occupations, domestic activities, emotional expression, and relationships with children.** Of course, since we are (and have been since the beginning) living in a male-dominated society, the situation still remains lopsided—women feel more of the brunt of discrimination than do men. Despite this imbalance, the issue of men's liberation will probably become more important in coming years, and we will probably see more males moving into nontraditional roles in the same fashion as women have done over the past fifteen years.

FUTURE PROSPECTS

Masculine, Feminine, or Human?

We, as a society, must develop a set of humanistic and socially conscious values that embraces the best of both traditional masculinity and traditional femininity. And we must expect people, regardless of sex, to embrace them. Merely allowing males to get into the costly "bag" females have long been in, and vice versa is no solution. We must also unlearn some traits almost completely, while tempering others. It is the task of the future to come to grips with this problem; to develop and teach a viable definition of humanness and equality that will enable us to live in personally and collectively rewarding ways in postindustrial society. It is the task of all of us to decide whether our society is to be comprised of people who are masculine/feminine or human.[75]

What *will* the future be like in terms of sex roles? What are the likely dimensions of the sex roles issue in the years to come? We cannot assert, with any degree of certainty, what the future holds in these areas. However, given the changes that have already occurred, **it seems likely that any meaningful change in our sex role structure will involve some degree of redefinition of both masculinity and femininity.** In the years to come, it is likely that we will see significant shifts in the way children are socialized and revisions of our legal system that affect both men and women. The extent of the change that will occur is something that cannot yet be determined. We may find, after much study and experimentation, that human beings require—for reasons we might not understand—some sexual differentiation. People may demand a return to clear-cut differences between the sexes. However, at this point we do not know. We are in the midst of a very exciting era of experimentation. We have an opportunity to shape our destiny in this area. If people decide that sexual differences are important, this need not entail a return to the inequality, discrimination, and oppression that were common in the past and that still linger today. Rather, sexual differences can be based on a scientific determination of which differences are essential or beneficial. We are still a long way from reaching such a determination. There is much that we still do not know. Let us conclude by looking at some ways in which sex roles are changing today in order to get a glimpse at some of the prospects for the future.

The New Women's Movement and the Quest for Human Rights

The "Feminine Mystique"

There is general agreement that early feminist

Betty Friedan in her book *The Feminine Mystique* provided the principal ideological baseline for the new women's movement in our society.[76] As we have already seen, Friedan outlined how Americans have become "tuned in" to the discrimination issue regarding black people but emphasized that inequality for women had been ignored for some time. She pointed out that women confronted a problem that they had not clearly defined, and she provided a name for it. Friedan referred to the lack of direction, the negative self-concept, and the lack of feelings of self-worth among women as the "feminine mystique." Her book sold over 3 million copies and continues to sell well today more than fifteen years after its initial publication. This tremendous response to her message was instrumental in the establishment of the National Organization for Women (NOW) in 1966. Friedan founded this group and acted as its leader in the early years. Out of the NOW movement sprang the National Women's Political Caucus (NWPC), the First Women's Bank, and a host of similar organizations. Today NOW has over 60,000 members, making it the largest women's rights group in the country and an influential political force.

According to sociologist Jo Freeman, the modern women's liberation movement originated from two relatively separate forces.[77] The first of these, the National Organization for Women, she refers to as a reform-oriented group that interested older women already involved in political issues. The other faction is a younger, more radical group of women who believe that women's rights can emerge only after a complete reorganization of government and society has occurred. Freeman observes that the older, "reform" group has been better organized and more effective in manipulating the existing political structure to achieve its goals. The "radical" group, on the other hand, has provided the most innovative ideas, even though it has been characteristically disorganized. The active members of the women's movement represent a numerical minority of the total female population in our society, are usually well educated, and generally possess middle- or upper-middle-class socioeconomic status.

The Equal Rights Amendment (ERA) and Other Legislation

As we have already seen, the Civil Rights Act of 1964 (Title VII) prohibits discrimination on the basis of sex. Even so, state laws have persisted that involve social differentiation between men and women. The Equal Employment Opportunity Commission (EEOC) was established in part to enforce the Civil Rights Act, but in 1965, the EEOC ruled that state laws designed to "protect" women from physical injury were not discriminatory.

In 1972, the Equal Rights Amendment (ERA) received congressional approval, which meant that it would become the Twenty-Seventh Amendment to the Constitution of the United States upon ratification by three-fourths (thirty-eight) of the states within seven years. The ERA stipulates that: "Equality of rights under the law shall not be denied or abridged by the United States or any state on account of sex."

The progress of ERA toward ratification has been difficult and filled with controversy. As of this writing, the Amendment has not passed. In four states that had passed ERA, the legislature has since voted to rescind it—which action may or may not be legal. Congress voted to extend the time limit for ratification beyond the original seven years; however, the outlook is still very uncertain.

If ratified, the ERA would eliminate numerous state laws that involve discrimination against women. One interesting result would be that women would receive no preferential treatment in divorce actions and could lose any legal claims on their spouse's earnings. Labor laws would have to be revamped to comply with ERA. For example, there now exist statutes that limit the amount of weight women may lift on the job, and others provide for additional rest periods for female employees. These would be eliminated by the ERA. In the case of a couple where the partners decided that the *husband* would assume responsibility for the care of a newborn child, a "maternity leave" would have to be available for him. In terms of our criminal justice system, statutory rape laws that establish younger ages of consent for women than men would be abolished. Male prostitution would

Women still participate in traditional, stereotyped female role activities like beauty contests; however, growing numbers of women today are experimenting with traditional male roles.

be punished in the same fashion that female prostitutes are now dealt with. One very controversial feature of the ERA is that it would require equal treatment of men and women in terms of military conscription (the draft). In other words, women could be drafted and assigned to duties in the armed forces on the basis of their qualifications and the needs of the services, rather than on the basis of gender.

Some have taken the difficulties encountered in passing the ERA as an indication that changes in the sex roles had gone about as far as most Americans would accept and that people were reacting to stop further change. While this may be the case, we must also realize that, from the conflict perspective, this clash of interest groups is a normal part of social order and social change. In fact, as we have seen, the conflict perspective would view the whole sex roles issue as a struggle over access to resources by different groups. Groups such as NOW and efforts like the campaign for ERA make clear that some women have the power to make their concerns heard and to pursue their interests in the political arena. There is little reason to believe that they will not continue to do so in the future. As women gain access to more powerful political and economic positions, they will become an even more formidable force in this struggle. At the same time, some men and women will continue to oppose further change. The final outcome for our sex role structure will, from the conflict perspective, derive from this struggle.

Recent Developments

While it would be impossible to review all of the recent developments that bear on the issue of changing sex roles, we can consider a few such developments in order to see the direction in which we may be moving.

Women in Sports and Athletic Competition

If we examine Olympic track and field records for men and women over the past several decades, we find that performance levels are beginning to converge somewhat. Women's times in the 100-meter dash, for example, are significantly faster from year to year, while men's times are improving less substantially. This does not suggest that women will eventually equal or surpass men in athletic competition, even though there has been some professional speculation that women possess more potential in distance running than do males. What these statistics *do* imply is that women are becoming involved in athletics much more than they were in the past and that they are entering certain types of competition previously confined to males. For example, although few women have won major stock car races to date, there are increasing numbers participating. During a recent National Hot Rod Association Dragracing Championship, Shirley "Cha-Cha" Muldowney won the AA Fuel Dragster event by defeating the well-known "Big Daddy" Don Garlets.

Perhaps an even more striking example of sex role reversals in the area of athletics is found in weightlifting. Usually, "pumping iron" is associated with large-biceped "he-men" such as Arnold Schwarzenegger, and the thought of lifting weights seems to be totally "unfeminine." Much to the contrary, however, many women are now hefting the barbells: some in the interest of their figures (e.g. Lynda "Wonder Woman" Carter); some in training for other athletic events (the Olympic javelin-thrower Kate Schmidt can dead-lift 400 pounds); and a few in actual powerlifting competition (Natalie Kahn and Cyndy Groffman respectively 25 and 23 years of age can dead-lift over 240 pounds and bench press over 100). Shirley Patterson, a North Hollywood body-building club owner, may be one of the strongest women in the United States for her size, weighing only 112 pounds and able to bench press 125 pounds.[78] Although it is common for men in weight-training to lift two-and-one-half times their own weight, it is most unusual (so far) for women to lift their own weight. There are increasing numbers of women who are boxing professionally; and women's wrestling, previously regarded as a form of "sideshow" entertainment, now has a serious following.

Does all of this mean that women will eventually be bulging with muscles and out to defeat men in everything? According to the women who are presently engaged in these nontraditional activities, not at all. In the first place, these women admit that women cannot compete on an equal level with men in weightlifting and do not want to. What it does demonstrate is that women's increased participation in athletics—particularly in the nontraditional realms—is attracting the public eye and is consequently having a significant impact on changing sex roles in our society. It means that these women are challenging some of the limits that have traditionally been placed on what women are allowed to do and to achieve.

Although weightlifting is still considered "unfeminine" by many Americans, it is however becoming more common among female athletes and among women who want to increase their strength.

Women in the Military

There have been WACs (Women's Army Corps) and WAFs (Women's Air Force) for many years, but only recently have women taken a more prominent and equal role in the military. In 1968, only about 35,000 women were members of the United States Armed Forces — about 1 percent of the nation's military personnel. In fact, prior to 1969, there was a legal ceiling placed on the number of women who could enter the military — they could not constitute more than 2 percent of military personnel. When manpower shortages occurred during the Vietnam War, this ceiling was abolished. Today approximately 110,000 women are in uniform — almost 6 percent of the armed forces' 2 million members. Estimates are that by 1983, there will be close to 220,000 women in the military, or about 10 percent of the armed forces at that time.[79] In the various branches of the service, women now undergo what is essentially the same basic training as men; some train side by side with them. West Point recently capitulated in its long-standing tradition of training only male cadets to become "officers and gentlemen." Women now also attend Annapolis and the Air Force Academy.

If conscription (the draft) is ever instituted again in this country, there is a very good chance that women will be subject to its stipulations — perhaps not as combatants (even though female soldiers in Israel and other countries are combat-trained); but women may be required to serve in the military in times of war. Considering ancient traditions in military service, we can see that social change in this area is very significant in terms of the sex roles issue.

Androgyny

A few years ago, there was a great deal of publicity and considerable consternation over a "unisex" movement in the United States. The longer hair styles for men, masculine clothing fashions for women, men carrying shoulder bags, and the proliferation of male jewelry seemed to point toward declining differences between the sexes. Regardless how active such a movement may be at this time, it is clear that there are fewer and fewer distinctions today in the appearance of men and women. Many considered the increasing similarity between men and women in physical appearance to be a sign that many other differences between the sexes were disappearing. Some viewed this possibility with revulsion, others were uninterested, and still others saw it as the long-sought wave of the future. Yet, similarity in clothing does not necessarily translate into similarity in roles or self-concepts. As we have seen, the female sex role has traditionally gone hand in hand with femininity — implying expressiveness, tenderness, helplessness, softness, and the like. The male sex role, on the other hand, has been aligned with masculinity—implying a work orientation, toughness, independence, hardness, and the like. Recently, some social scientists and feminists have proposed that it is possible for people, both men and women, to explore a broad range of role playing possibilities in society and to choose emotions and behaviors without regard to gender role stereotypes.

This new idea is referred to as *androgyny* (from *andro,* "male"; *gyne,* "female"). From this view, males and females can be socialized to be flexible in their role playing and to express themselves as human beings rather than in traditionally masculine or feminine ways. People can choose roles or tasks at which they are most competent and express emotions or attitudes with which they feel most comfortable—all without regard to whether they are stereotypically male or female characteristics. One psychologist recently conducted research illustrating that men and women who adhere to either traditionally masculine or feminine roles are ineffectual in role playing that requires acting out the characteristics of the opposite sex.[80] For example, in one experiment, "masculine" men were competent in being assertive, but not nearly as effective (and sometimes failures) in roles requiring warmth and concern. "Feminine" women were able to be comforting to people around them, but lacked expertise in being assertive and independent. In contrast, men and women who adhered to androgynous role playing were far more flexible and able to respond emotionally to different situations as required.

This research supports the argument that sexism limits *both* men and women in terms of their behavior. **Traditional perceptions of what is masculine and feminine are restrictive for everyone and limit what all of us are born with—the potential of human resourcefulness.** The extent to which androgyny is a desirable solution to the sex roles problem depends on the perspective adopted. For the functionalist, androgyny may be positive to the extent that it ensures that people are able to utilize whatever skills and talents they have. Traditional sex role defini-

tions limit the activities people engage in, even if a person might be particularly suited to something that does not fit the stereotyped view of what a person of his or her sex might do. A critical issue in this regard is the extent to which men are particularly suited to instrumental tasks and women to expressive activities. Proponents of androgyny, of course, argue that these are not sex-linked. If not, then any person, whether male or female, should perform instrumental tasks, and likewise for the expressive. From the functionalist perspective, this would be most beneficial because it would ensure maximum uti ization of the human talents available. If a particular woman is especially suited to be a soldier, sailor, or athlete, then it is functional for society if she develops her talents and is allowed to achieve all of which she is capable.

From the interactionist perspective, the social problem of sex roles will be alleviated when there is some shared consensus about expectations for the sexes in America. This could be achieved by the reestablishment of traditional sex roles or by changing to something such as androgyny—as long as there was consensus about these expectations. However, there must be consistency between sex roles and the other roles that a person performs. We cannot expect women to exhibit a certain kind of self-concept as women—passive, dependent, less intelligent—and to have a different self-concept in some other role they play, such as student, soldier, or business executive. **As women and men move into nontraditional roles in society, their self-concepts and identities will be changed by their experiences in these new roles. Only the future will reveal to what extent these changes will alter the present fabric of sex roles in our society.**

CONCLUSION

As we have noted throughout this chapter, sex roles are a complex social problem. On the one hand, depending upon one's values and beliefs, sex roles may not even represent a problem. On the other hand, we have seen that there are sufficient numbers of people today who regard sex role inequality as an undesirable social condition. Hence, we have explored this issue in detail. Additional examination of the problem utilizing the three theoretical perspectives will help us to conclude our discussion.

From the functional perspective, sex role distinctions can contribute to the maintenance of a society. Recall from our earlier discussion that in primitive societies, females were less likely to occupy mobile, hunting types of roles because they were either pregnant or suckling their children most of the time. Males, on the other hand, were, in those settings, better suited to occupy the role positions just mentioned. In other words, the structure of society and the nature of the existing technology—rather than the structure of men and women—demanded that males and females occupy particular roles.

For the functionalist, then, depending upon the nature and the configuration of a social organization, boys and girls will be reared differently, and men and women will behave in conjunction with how they are socialized. As we have seen, our society reflects how these traditional role identities affect each and every one of us. It has only been recently that these traditional role expectations have been seriously challenged. As changes have occurred in the other institutional arrangements of our society—economy, family, politics, religion, education, and the like—so too have changes in our attitudes toward sex roles come about.

For the functionalist, sex roles represent a social problem today because changes in this area threaten the equilibrium of the social organization as a whole. It is important to remember, however, that what appears to be a *nontraditional* sex role orientation today may be best suited to our society in the years to come. The functional perspective helps us to see these changes in dramatic relief, and more important, to understand them.

According to the conflict perspective, social problems arise when people struggle over scarce and finite resources in society. In the case of the sex roles controversy, men and women are increasingly found in competitive positions with each other—for desirable occupations and for power and authority. For example, men's athletic programs at colleges and universities across the country have been affected—sometimes adversely in terms of finances—by federal legislation demanding equal opportunities for both women and men in collegiate athletics. At the same time, college women are now in a much better position to participate in athletic competition than in the past.

In other words, men and women come into conflict with each other because of other changes in society. For the conflict theoriest, this struggle is not undesirable and may eventuate in overall social improvements. For example, some conflict-oriented social scientists argue that out of the sex role struggle may emerge a more "human" perception of both men and women. In fact, according to this view, our respective potentials as human beings may be more fully realized as a consequence of the struggle over sex role equality.

From the interactionist perspective, sex roles are a social problem according to individual's definitions and perceptions of this issue. In fact, some people (Phyllis Schlafly, for example) view the Equal Rights Amendment as a threat. This is an interesting illustration of the subjective nature of reality. While supporters of the ERA view long standing inequalities between men and women (e.g., the draft, separate restrooms, etc.) as undesirable and socially problematic, others, like Schlafly, regard the removal of such distinctions as a potential social problem.

For the interactionist, understanding sex roles as a social problem requires that we pay close attention to how men and women relate to each other. The social setting for their interaction is also very important. In a sense, men and women are actors on a "stage" of society. The props on that stage will affect the quality of their interaction. How we see ourselves depends upon how others see us and how we interpret their reactions to our behavior. In our modern society, women *and* men are more likely to respond to non-traditional expectations for behavior. For example, more support exists today for women to become professional athletes. Men may find encouragement to become housekeepers rather than full-time careerists. For the interactionist, the subtle yet very important relationship between human interaction and the social setting in which it transpires represents the key to understanding sex roles as a social problem.

GLOSSARY TERMS

Androgyny

Clitoral orgasm

Expressive functions

Gender

Hermaphrodite

Instrumental functions

Oedipal complex

Self-fulfilling prophecy

Sexism

Sex role

Sexual bargaining

Suffrage

Transsexuality

Transvestite

Vaginal orgasm

REFERENCES

[1] William L. O'Neill, *Everyone Was Brave: The Rise and Fall of Feminism in America* (Chicago: Quadrangle Books, 1969), p. 358.

[2] United States Department of Labor, Bureau of Labor Statistics, *United States Working Women—A Data Book,* Bulletin 1977 (Washington, D.C.: United States Government Printing Office, 1977).

[3] *Time,* January 5, 1976, pp. 6–16.

[4] Clelan S. Ford, "Some Primitive Societies," in Georgene H. Seward and Robert C. Williamson, eds., *Sex Roles in Changing Society* (New York: Random House, 1970), pp. 25–43.

[5] Francine D. Blair, "Women in the Labor Force: An Overview," in Jo Freeman, ed., *Women: A Feminist Perspective* (Palo Alto, Calif.: Mayfield Publishing Co., 1979), p. 272.

[6] Judd Marmor, "Changing Patterns of Femininity," in Arlene S. Skolnick and Jerome H. Skolnick, eds., *Family in Transition* (Boston: Little, Brown, 1971), pp. 210–221.

[7] John Money, J. G. Hampson, and J. L. Hampson, "An Examination of Some Basic Sexual Concepts: The Evidence of Human Hermaphroditism," *Bulletin of the Johns Hopkins Hospital* 97 (1955), pp. 301–319.

[8] See Clarice Stasz Stoll, *Female and Male: Socialization, Social Roles, and Social Structure* (Dubuque, Iowa: William C. Brown Co., 1974).

[9] H. L. Rheingold and K. V. Cook, "The Contents of Boys' and Girls' Rooms as an Index of Parents' Behavior," *Child Development* 46 (June 1975), p. 461.

[10] Laurel Walum, *The Dynamics of Sex and Gender: A Sociological Perspective* (Chicago: Rand McNally, 1977), p. 49.

[11] H. A. Moss, "Early Sex Differences and Mother-Infant Interaction," in R. C. Friedman et al., eds., *Sex Differences and Behavior* (New York: John Wiley & Sons, 1974), pp. 149–164.

[12] M. Lewis and M. Weinraub, "Sex of Parent—Sex of Child: Socioemotional Development," in Friedman et al., eds., *Sex Differences and Behavior,* pp. 123–142.

[13] See Eleanor Maccoby and Carol Jacklin, *The Psychology of Sex Differences* (Stanford, Calif.: Stanford University Press, 1974).

[14] See Clarice Stasz Stoll, ed., *Sexism: Scientific Debates* (Reading, Mass.: Addison-Wesley, 1973).

[15] See Warren Farrell, *The Liberated Man* (New York: Random House, 1975).

[16] Emile Durkheim, *The Division of Labor in Society* (New York: Macmillan, 1933).

[17] Robert F. Bales, *Interaction Process Analysis* (Reading, Mass.: Addison-Wesley, 1950).

[18] See John Scanzoni, *Sexual Bargaining: Power Politics in the American Marriage* (Englewood Cliffs, N.J.: Prentice-Hall, 1972).

[19] See Marabel Morgan, *The Total Woman* (Old Tappan, N.J.: Fleming H. Revell, 1973) and *Total Joy* (Old Tappan, N.J.: Fleming H. Revell, 1976).

[20] George Herbert Mead, *Mind, Self, and Society* (Chicago: University of Chicago Press, 1934).

[21] Charles H. Cooley, *Social Organization* (New York: Charles Scribner's Sons, 1909).

[22] See Janet Saltzman Chafetz, *Masculine, Feminine or Human?* (Itasca, Ill.: Peacock Publishers, 1974).

[23] William Masters and Virginia Johnson, *Human Sexual Response* (Boston: Little, Brown, 1966).

[24] Mary Jane Sherfey, *The Nature and Evolution of Female Sexuality* (New York: Random House, 1972).

[25] Marmor, "Changing Patterns of Femininity," pp. 214–215.

[26] See Shirley Weitz, *Sex Roles: Biological, Psychological, and Social Foundations* (New York: Oxford University Press, 1977), pp. 67–76.

[27] Jan Morris, *Conundrum* (New York: New American Library, 1975), pp. 25–26.

[28] See Myron Brenton, *The American Male* (Greenwich, Conn.: Fawcett Publications, 1966).

[29] Deborah S. David and Robert Brannon, eds., *The Forty-Nine Percent Majority: The Male Sex Role* (Reading, Mass.: Addison-Wesley, 1976).

[30] See David B. Lynn, *Parental and Sex Role Identification* (Berkeley, Calif.: McCutchen, 1969).

[31] Ibid.

[32] See Letty Cottrin Progrebin, "Down With Sexist Upbringing," *Ms.* (Spring 1972).

[33] Janet Lever, "Sex Differences in the Games Children Play," *Social Problems* 23 (April 1976), pp. 478–487.

[34] Judith Long Laws, "A Feminist Review of Marital Adjustment Literature: The Rape of the Locke," *Journal of Marriage and the Family* 33 (August 1971), pp. 483–516.

[35] See Matina Horner, "Fail: Bright Women," *Psychology Today* 3 (November 1969), pp. 36–38, 62; Vivian Gornick, "Why Women Fear Success," *Ms.* (Spring 1972), pp. 50–53; and Carol Tarvis and Carole Offir, *The Longest War: Sex Differences in Perspective* (New York: Harcourt, Brace, Jovanovich, 1976), pp. 190–193.

[36] Marcia Guttentag and Helen Bray, "Teachers as Mediators of Sex Role Standards," in Alice Sargent, ed., *Beyond Sex Roles* (St. Paul: West Publishing Co., 1977), pp. 395–411, and Walum, *The Dynamics of Sex and Gender: A Sociological Perspective,* p. 57.

[37] Pam Maye and Sara McMillan, "Student Project," in Chafetz, *Masculine, Feminine or Human?,* pp. 88–90.

[38] Marc F. Fasteau, *The Male Machine* (New York: Mc-

Graw-Hill, 1974).

[39] See Marjorie B. U'ren, "The Image of Women in Textbooks," in Vivian Gornick and Barbara K. Moran, eds., *Women in Sexist Society* (New York: Basic Books, 1971), pp. 218–225; Aileen Pace Nielsen, "Women in Children's Literature," *College English* 32 (May 1971), pp. 918–926; Susan Racklin and Glenda Vogt, "Sex Roles as Presented to Children by Coloring Books," *Journal of Popular Culture* 8 (Winter 1974), pp. 549–556; Marsha Federbush, "The Sex Problems of School Math Books," in Judith Stacey et al., eds., *And Jill Came Tumbling After: Sexism in American Education* (New York: Dell Publishing Company, 1974); and Janice Trecker, "Women in United States History High School Textbooks," in Stacey et al., eds., *And Jill Came Tumbling After: Sexism in American Education.*

[40] Lenore Weitzman et al., "Sex Role Socialization in Picture Books for Preschool Children," *American Journal of Sociology* 72 (May 1972), pp. 1125–1150.

[41] See Naomi Weisstein, *Kinder, Kuche, and Kirche as Scientific Law: Psychology Constructs the Female* (Boston: New England Free Press, 1969).

[42] Viola Klein, *The Feminine Character: History of an Idealogy* (Urbana: University of Illinois Press, 1975).

[43] Michael Gordon and Penelope J. Shankweiler, "Different Equals Less; Female Sexuality in Recent Marriage Manuals," *Journal of Marriage and the Family* 33 (August 1971), pp. 459–466.

[44] Phyllis Chesler, *Women and Madness* (New York: Doubleday, 1972), p. 68.

[45] Joseph H. Fichter and Virginia K. Mills, "The Status of Women in American Churches," *Church and Society,* (September-October 1972).

[46] Kate Millett and Casey Swift, "Desexing the English Language," *Ms.,* (Spring, 1972).

[47] Nancy Henley and Barrie Thorne, "Womanspeak and Manspeak: Sex Differences and Sexism in Communication," in Sargent, ed., *Beyond Sex Roles,* p. 203.

[48] United States Bureau of the Census, *Current Population Reports,* Series P-20, no. 314, "Educational Attainment in the United States: March 1977 and 1976" (Washington, D.C.: U.S. Government Printing Office, 1977).

[49] Ibid.

[50] Alice Rossi, "Status of Women in Graduate Departments of Sociology, 1968–1969," *American Sociologist* 5 (1970), pp. 1–12.

[51] Rita James Simon et al., "The Woman Ph.D.: A Recent Profile," *Social Problems* 15 (Autumn 1967), pp. 221–236.

[52] Leigh Bienen et al., "Sex Discrimination in Universities," in Nona Glazer and Helen Waehrer, eds., *Women in a Man-Made World,* 2d ed. (Chicago: Rand McNally, 1977), pp. 370–377.

[53] Richard M. Levinson, "Sex Discrimination and Employment Practices: An Experiment With Unconventional Job Enquiries," *Social Problems* 22 (April 1975), pp. 533–543.

[54] United States Bureau of the Census, *Current Population Reports,* advanced report, Series P-60, no. 116, "Money Income and Poverty Status of Families and Persons in the United States: 1977" (Washington, D.C.: U.S. Government Printing Office, 1978).

[55] United States Bureau of the Census, *Current Population Reports,* Series P-60, no. 114, "Money Income in 1976 of Families and Persons in the United States" (Washington, D.C.: U. S. Government Printing Office, 1978).

[56] Michael A. La Sorte, "Sex Differences in Salary among Academic Sociology Teachers," *American Sociologist* 6 (November 1971), pp. 304–307.

[57] See Joan Krauskopf, "Partnership Marriage: Legal Reforms Needed," in Jane Chapman and Margaret Gates, eds., *Women into Wives: The Legal and Economic Impact of Marriage* (Beverly Hills, Calif.: Sage Publications, 1977), pp. 93–122.

[58] Alan Booth, "Sex and Social Participation," *American Sociological Review* 37 (April 1972), pp. 183–193.

[59] Jessie Bernard, "The Paradox of the Happy Marriage," in Gornick and Moran, eds., *Women in Sexist Society,* pp. 145–162.

[60] Pauline B. Bart, "Depression in Middle-Aged Women," in Gornick and Moran, eds., *Women in Sexist Society,* pp. 163–186.

[61] Tarvis and Offir, *The Longest War,* p. 223.

[62] David and Brannon, *The Forty-Nine Percent Majority,* pp. 13–19.

[63] Ibid., pp. 53–54.

[64] Ibid., p. 113.

[65] Ibid., p. 180.

[66] Ibid., p. 216.

[67] See Warren Farrell, *The Liberated Man.*

[68] Robert Gould, "Measuring Masculinity by the Size of a Paycheck," in David and Brannon, eds., *The Forty-Nine Percent Majority,* p. 118.

[69] Jack Sawyer, "On Male Liberation," in Joseph H. Pleck and Jack Sawyer, eds., *Men and Masculinity* (Englewood Cliffs, N.J.: Prentice-Hall, 1974), p. 172.

[70] Jack Nichols, *Men's Liberation: A New Definition of Masculinity* (New York: Penguin Books, 1975), p. 322.

[71] K. Seifert, "Some Problems of Men in Child Care Center Work," *Child Welfare* 102 (March 1973), pp. 167–171.

[72] "Today's High School Students Wary of Role Reversal," Marquette (Michigan) *The Mining Journal* (December 2, 1978), p. 8.

[73] See Henry Biller, *Child and Sex Role* (Lexington, Mass.: Lexington Books, 1971) and *Paternal Deprivation* (Lexington, Mass.: Lexington Books, 1974).

[74] See Henry Biller and Dennis Meredith, *Father Power* (New York: Anchor Press, 1975).

[75] Janet Saltzman Chafetz, *Masculine, Feminine, or Human?* (Itasca, Ill.: Peacock Publishers, 1978), p. 258.

[76] See Betty Friedan, *The Feminine Mystique* (New York: Dell Books, 1963).

[77] Jo Freeman, *Women: A Feminist Perspective,* 2d ed. (Palo Alto, Calif.: Mayfield Publishing Co., 1979).

[78] "A Thoroughly Uplifting Experience," *Sports Illustrated,* August 2, 1976, pp. 36–41.

[79] "Women May Yet Save the Army," *Time,* October 30, 1978, p. 37.

[80] Sandra L. Bem, "Sex Role Adaptability: One Consequence of Psychological Androgyny," *Journal of Personality and Social Psychology* 31 (April 1975), pp. 634–643.

SUGGESTED READINGS

Henry Biller and Dennis Meredith, *Father Power* (New York: Anchor Press/Doubleday, 1975).
An overview of the art of effective fathering and how, in the opinion of the authors, having the father as an integral part of the child rearing process can benefit everyone.

Janet Saltzman Chafetz, *Masculine, Feminine or Human?* second edition (Itasca, Illinois: F. E. Peacock, 1978).
An excellent and current overview of the sociology of gender roles.

Deborah David and Robert Brannon, eds., *The Forty-Nine Percent Majority: The Male Sex Role* (Reading, Massachusetts: Addison-Wesley Publishing Company, 1976).
A collection of recent articles written by different authors concerning the male sex role in our society.

Jo Freeman, ed., *Women: A Feminist Perspective,* second edition (Palo Alto, California: Mayfield Publishing Company, 1979).
A collection of very recent articles written by different authors concerning women and their position(s) in our society. Most of the pieces are written from a feminist point of view.

Kate Millett, *Sexual Politics* (Garden City, New York: Doubleday Publishing Company, 1970).
Written by a prominent and well known feminist author, this book deals with the political characteristics of man-woman interaction in our society. Millett also provides a dramatic portrayal of social obstacles to the women's movement.

Betty Friedan, *The Feminine Mystique* (New York: Dell Publishing, 1963).
Friedan, who was one of the pioneers of the modern women's movement, provides an outline of how our society distinguishes between the genders — to the disadvantage of women.

Laurel Walum, *The Dynamics of Sex and Gender: A Sociological Perspective* (Chicago: Rand McNally and Co., 1977).
An excellent overview of the sex roles issue from a sociological point of view.

Shirley Weitz, *Sex Roles: Biological, Psychological and Social Foundations* (New York: Oxford University Press, 1977).
An excellent look at the history of sex roles in our society.

Questions for Discussion

1. Discuss the history of sex role identity, beginning with primitive societies—proceeding to preindustrial America—then to industrialization and its effects on sex roles. How do sex roles contribute to order and stability in a social organization? Where do we stand today in postindustrial America?

2. How did the sex roles issue become a problem in the United States? Consider whether it was always problematic—if not, then what combination of ingredients accounts for sex roles becoming a problem?

3. Discuss the problem of sex roles in our society from the functionalist, conflict, and interactionist perspectives. How would sex roles be approached from each of them? What distinct advantages (or disadvantages) does each perspective possess in terms of understanding sex role identity?

4. In comparison to the biologically based terms *male* and *female,* what do *masculinity* and *femininity* imply for behavior in our society? Discuss what is involved in growing up male or growing up female in America. Try to identify what kinds of adaptations are required on the part of individuals—both male and female—in order to align themselves with societal expectations in terms of sex roles.

5. What does Janet Chafetz mean by "growing up human?" In terms of a possible solution to the problem of sex roles, what might be gained (or lost) by trying to rear children according to androgyny?

6. What are the major dimensions of sex role identity? What kinds of characteristics are attached to the "ideal male" and the "ideal female" in America today? Try to identify those social characteristics that still contribute to a traditional perception of sex roles for men and women.

7. Discuss the women's movement from its beginnings to the present time. How has the movement changed? Although women are not a statistical (or numerical) minority, why are they considered by sociologists to be representative of a minority group? Try to tie this discussion in with conflict theory.

8. Discuss the male sex role in America. What are some of the problems affiliated with being "masculine?" How do your opinions compare with traditional conceptions of masculinity? Why do you feel the way that you do? What changes do you see taking place in this arena?

9. Discuss the future of sex role equality. What are the problems? The prospects? Is equality really the answer—why or why not? Is it possible that men and women in the future may desire more guidance from sex roles—and if so, what kinds of guidelines might they demand from society?

CHAPTER 14

Intergroup Conflict, Violence, and War

THE HISTORY OF VIOLENCE IN AMERICA
Civil Disorder. Political Violence. War.

CONFLICT AND VIOLENCE AS SOCIAL PROBLEMS
The Functionalist Perspective. The Conflict Perspective.
The Interactionist Perspective.

SOURCES OF INTERGROUP CONFLICT
Biological Sources of Violence. Frustration, Deprivation,
and Violence. Violence as Learned Behavior. Social
Sources of Violence.

THE CONSEQUENCES OF INTERGROUP CONFLICT
AND VIOLENCE
The Social Functions of Conflict. The Consequences of
War: The Impact on American Society.

CONTROLLING VIOLENCE: PROSPECTS FOR THE
FUTURE
Controlling Violence. Preventing Conflict and Violence.
Preventing War.

CONCLUSION

Most Americans view themselves as peaceful, law-abiding citizens and believe that their society is a fairly tranquil and stable social order. Yet, certain events occasionally force us to question these beliefs. Extremely violent and destructive civil disorders swept through urban ghettos and college campuses in the 1960s. In Watts in 1965, 13,500 National Guardsmen were called in to quell a six-day riot in which thirty-four people were killed, thousands injured or arrested, and $40 million worth of property destroyed. Many other cities experienced similar disruptions: between 1963 and 1968, Cleveland had 6 riots, Philadelphia and Pittsburgh each had 5, Detroit had 6, Des Moines had 5—the list seems endless and few major cities were spared.[1]

Violence need not always take the form of riot and disorder. In 1977 in the United States, there were over 19,000 murders and non-negligent manslaughters, almost half of these involving a handgun. There was one murder every 27 minutes and one aggravated assault every minute! In the same year, 93 police officers were killed in the line of duty—59 percent of them with handguns.[2] In the international arena, the extent of carnage and destruction is equally startling. Since 1945, there have been a minimum of fifty-five wars of some size somewhere in the world. The costs of this international conflict are enormous. Since World War II, the total military expenditures of all the countries in the world have *exceeded $6000 billion!* In 1977 alone, the United States sold over $11 billion worth of weapons to other countries.[3]

As these examples illustrate, the world certainly seems to be a dangerous place. Murder, mayhem, and war are extremely common occurrences. In reaction to this violence, people often yearn for the "good old days"—an idyllic past when people lived together harmoniously and worked toward commonly agreed-upon goals. In this romanticized view of the past, conflict and violence are seen as aberrations that mar the smooth flow of human social interaction. In this chapter, we will question the validity of this myth as it applies to America. We shall see that people often suffer from "historical amnesia"—forgetting the unpleasant parts of our past and emphasizing the happier moments. We will

also discuss some of the sources of human conflict. Is it the result of some innate "human nature" over which we have little control? Or is it due to some aspect of human social arrangements that can be changed? An important part of our discussion will be an analysis of the consequences (both positive and negative) of social conflict and the effectiveness of various programs to reduce or control conflict.

The terms *conflict* and *violence* are often confused. **Conflict refers to a situation in which people or groups perceive themselves to be involved in a struggle over resources or values.** *Violence,* **on the other hand, involves the use of physical force that might potentially injure people or destroy property.**[4] **Thus, conflict can be either violent or nonviolent.** Our primary concern is to understand those instances of conflict that are violent or that have a high potential for becoming violent. We also focus primarily on *intergroup* conflict—the struggle between groups over resources. *Interpersonal* conflict, such as a marital spat or many forms of crime, although important issues, are not covered here (some are discussed in other chapters).

THE HISTORY OF VIOLENCE IN AMERICA

In order to understand the dimensions and nature of the problem, it is useful to glance briefly at some examples of conflict and violence throughout American history. For these purposes, we can categorize violent episodes as civil disorders, political violence, and wars.

Civil Disorder

Civil disorder refers to strife or turmoil that is relatively spontaneous and disorganized. The goal—if there is any explicit goal—is a fairly short-term change in some specific condition in society. While it is difficult to measure the frequency of disorders, we can gain an idea of the magnitude of such occurrences through psychologist Sheldon

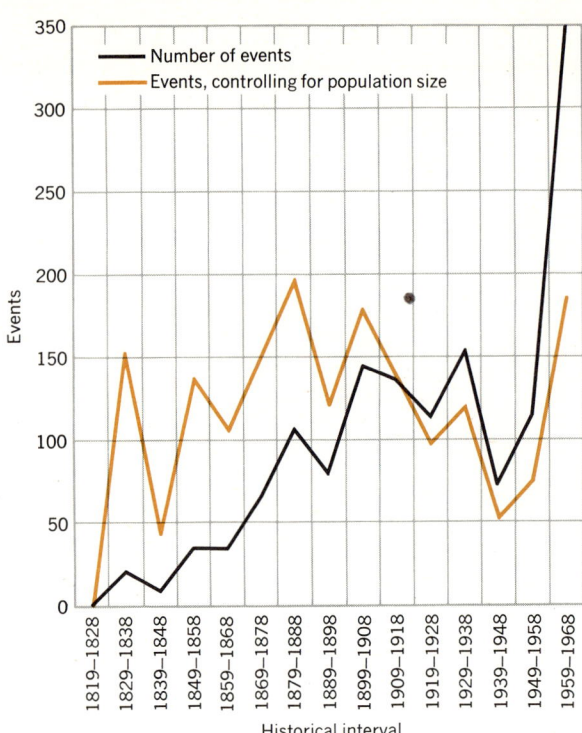

Figure 14.1 The Number of Politically Violent Events in the United States. Sheldon G. Levy, "A 150-Year Study of Political Violence in the United States," in Hugh Davis Graham and Ted Robert Gurr, eds., *The History of Violence in America* (New York: Frederick A. Praeger, 1969), p. 90.

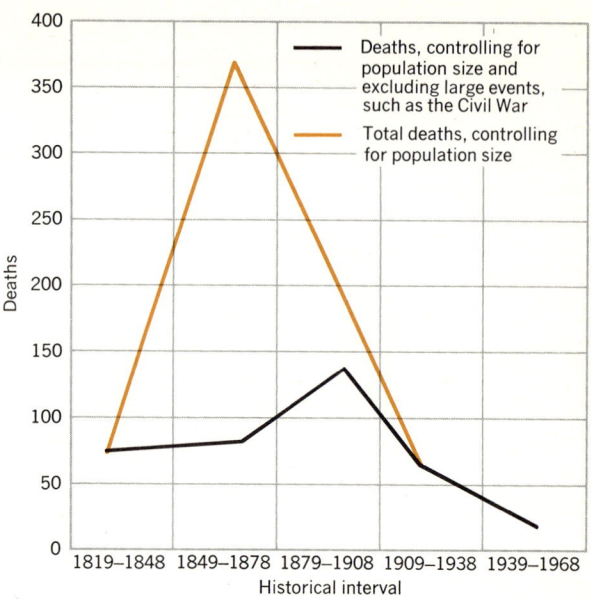

Figure 14.2 The Number of Deaths in Politically Violent Events in the United States. Sheldon G. Levy, "A 150-Year Study of Political Violence in the United States," in Hugh Davis Graham and Ted Robert Gurr, eds., *The History of Violence in America* (New York: Praeger, 1969), p. 91.

Levy's summary of politically violent events in America as shown in Figure 14.1. The number of such events has been rising very rapidly in the United States in the past 150 years. However, when one takes into account the increasing size of the American population, the pattern of violence is one of great variation but no apparent long-term increase or decrease. In fact, we see that the 1960s, which many viewed as an extremely violent period, were not terribly unusual—the 1880s had higher rates of disorders, and other periods in our history approach the 1960s in levels of violence. Furthermore, the number of deaths from such events is substantially lower in the past two decades than during prior periods (see Figure 14.2). Certain types of civil disorders have predominated on the American scene.

Racial Conflict

Racial conflict has a long and shameful history in the United States that most Americans would prefer to forget. As far back as the 1700s, white people's fears of a slave conspiracy to revolt resulted in violent clashes. For example, in New York City in the 1740s, such fears led white mobs to hang and burn scores of blacks and drive others from the city. With the end of slavery, groups such as the Ku Klux Klan emerged to intimidate not only blacks but also whites who opposed the reestablishment of white dominance in the South. Torture, whippings, burnings, and hangings were instruments of this intimidation process. Between 1882 and 1903, 1985 blacks were killed by Southern lynch mobs. Such mob violence, sometimes condoned by local authorities, was an important mechanism through which the dominant white group was able to exert social control and maintain the status quo.[5]

In the 1960s, most large, and many small, American cities experienced destructive race riots. Such civil disorders have occurred periodically throughout our history.

During the first half of this century, there were thirty-three major racial clashes in the United States. Especially violent conflicts occurred in East St. Louis (1917), Chicago (1919), Harlem (1935 and 1943), and Detroit (1943). **Racial disturbances of this period generally took the form of** *communal riots:* **they were clashes between blacks and whites over a previously all-white, but now racially contested, residential area of the city.**[6] The precipitating event of these disorders was usually the "intrusion" of blacks into some public place, such as a beach, that previously had been defined as all-white. Typically, whites were the aggressors in these disturbances, and the majority of casualties were blacks.

With the Harlem riot in 1943, however, a new form of race riot emerged on the American scene, the *commodity riot* — **a conflict over the inequitable distribution of resources and commodities in society.** These occur in a city with a high concentration of long-term residents in the black community. The riots begin within that community, rather than in an area undergoing a change in its racial composition. Furthermore, the major violence is not due to the clash between racial groups but rather to looting and burning by blacks of property and business establishments ("commodities"), usually those owned by whites who do not live in the community. Death and injuries usually result from clashes between blacks and the police or National Guard forces attempting to control the riot. The majority of racial conflicts that occurred throughout the 1960s were of this type (see Table 14.1).

Labor Conflict

Another frequent source of civil disorders in America has been the continuing effort of the American worker to improve his or her lot in life. The rudiments of labor organization can be traced to the colonial period, when impressment (forced labor) and economic difficulties led to rioting among sailors and longshoremen. However, it was not until the nineteenth century and the beginning

TABLE 14.1

Number and Severity of Race Riots in Selected American Cities, 1963–1968

	NUMBER OF RIOTS	OVERALL SEVERITY OF ALL RIOTS[a]
Birmingham, Ala.	4	5
Oakland, Cal.	3	1
New Haven, Conn.	2	5
Wilmington, Del.	3	8
Riviera Beach, Fla.	1	2
Tampa, Fla.	1	10
Alton, Ill.	1	0
Rockford, Ill.	1	1
Des Moines, Iowa	5	3
Wichita, Kansas	2	3
Cambridge. Md.	4	5
Detroit, Mich.	6	21
Flint, Mich.	1	1
Kalamazoo, Mich.	5	3
Mt. Clemens, Mich.	1	0
Pontiac, Mich.	1	5
Saginaw, Mich.	2	2
Ypsilanti, Mich.	1	0
Minneapolis, Minn.	3	2
Kansas City, Mo.	1	1
Omaha, Neb.	4	5
Englewood, N.J.	1	2
Newark, N.J.	2	20
Plainfield, N.J.	1	2
Albany, N.Y.	1	2
Buffalo, N.Y.	2	11
Lackawanna, N.Y.	1	0
Rochester, N.Y.	2	15
Syracuse, N.Y.	3	4
Wyandanch, N.Y.	1	1
Durham, N.C.	1	1
Cincinnati, Ohio	3	14
Cleveland, Ohio	6	25
Dayton, Ohio	3	3
Springfield, Ohio	1	1
Philadelphia, Pa.	5	19
Pittsburgh, Pa.	5	13
Nashville, Tenn.	2	4
Houston, Tex.	1	3
Milwaukee, Wis.	1	12

[a]A higher number indicates greater severity.

SOURCE. Excerpt from Table 1.1 in James W. Button, *Black Violence: Political Impact of the 1960s Riots* (Princeton, N.J.: Princeton University Press, 1978), pp. 18–19. Copyright © 1978 by Princeton University Press. Reprinted by permission of Princeton University Press.

of the Industrial Revolution that the labor movement emerged as a significant force in American society. The American labor movement has traditionally emphasized organization and collective bargaining—nonviolent mechanisms—as means of achieving economic goals; for the most part, it has not legitimized violence as an appropriate mechanism for reform and social change. Yet violence has been a pervasive element of the American labor scene. One of the most violent clashes occurred during a coal miners' strike in Colorado in 1913.[7]

When the Colorado coal industry refused to recognize the United Mine Workers of America, over 8000 miners went on strike against the Colorado Fuel and Iron Company in 1913. They moved their families from company-owned houses to a tent city at Ludlow that had been rented by the union. Sporadic violence between company guards and strikers occurred during the first five weeks of the strike, resulting in eighteen deaths. National Guard troops were brought in, but many of the Guardsmen and their commanding officers felt strong antagonism toward the strikers. (In fact, some had previously worked for the coal companies.) On April 20, 1914 the troops attacked the tent colony. Five men and a boy were killed by machine-gun fire; the militiamen then burned the tent colony. Eleven children and two women were suffocated to death in this holocaust that became known as the Ludlow Massacre. The strikers and their families dispersed into the countryside, and for ten days there were numerous clashes between workers and the militia. The final death toll from this strike and the resultant clashes was 74.

As unions have gained more acceptance, the amount of union-related violence has declined. Strong social pressures help to restrain the violent use of force on both sides of a strike. Considering the number of strikes each year and the number of employees going on strike, the present era is certainly more peaceful than previous periods. However, union violence is by no means a thing of the past. For example, in 1978 there was considerable violence during the coal strikes and intermittent violence—including some sniping—during a strike by independent truckers.[8] In addition, we should recognize that some of the violence and disorder of the past century has been one mechanism by which important social change has occurred—a certain amount of power has shifted from the owners and managers of business and industry to the employees.

Political Violence

America, especially in recent years, has been relatively free of serious threats to the stability and legitimacy of the central government in Washington. However, there have been, on occasion, episodes of political violence involving an attack on civil government in an effort to bring about fundamental changes in our political and economic system. Two forms that this violence has taken are insurrection and terrorism.

Insurrection

An *insurrection* is an organized attempt by some group to overthrow through violent means the existing government and replace it with alternative political arrangements and leadership. The United States as we know it today, of course, was born in the insurrection of 1776.[9] This revolution involved many forms of violence—clashes between insurrectionist groups and British soldiers; major clashes between the Continental and British armies; and violent and savage guerrilla forays against British troops and colonial Tories who opposed the revolutionary goal of separation from England. Concerning our whole revolutionary period, historian Richard Maxwell Brown concludes that:

> The meanest and most squalid sort of violence was from the very beginning to the very last put to the service of Revolutionary ideals and objectives. The operational philosophy that the end justifies the means became the keynote of revolutionary violence. Thus given sanctification by the Revolution, Americans have never been loathe to employ the most unremitting violence in the interest of any cause deemed to be a good one.[10]

Another important insurrection in our history was the bid by the Southern states to separate from the Union. The causes of the Civil War are still debated by scholars, but the consequences are evident—it was the greatest and most catastrophic military confrontation within the boundaries of the United States. In addition to the battlefield casualties and destruction of property, there was bitter guerrilla conflict and internecine warfare in both the North and the South. Renegades in both regions were attacked by loyalists, and the hostility to the war, especially in the North, resulted in violent confrontations in many cities. In New York City, for example, there were violent and destructive riots in opposition to the military draft. The unresolved tensions and conflicts that lingered after the war have been a continuing source of strain in American society.[11]

There have been some less well known attempts at insurrection in our history. For example, Dorr's Rebellion in 1842 was an attempt, eventually successful, by a group of dissidents in Rhode Island to gain universal male suffrage.[12] More recently, the ferment of the 1960s and 1970s has spawned a number of revolutionary groups. The best-known of these is undoubtedly the Symbionese Liberation Army (SLA)—the group of black ex-convicts and white radicals who captured the attention of the nation by kidnapping heiress Patricia Hearst in 1974. The SLA was devoted to the overthrow of the capitalist economic system and the redistribution of wealth in the United States. After fifteen months of sporadic violence, most members of the SLA were killed in a fiery police siege on their hideout in Los Angeles.[13]

Terrorism

In 1975, a bomb planted at LaGuardia Airport in New York City exploded killing eleven persons and injuring fifty-five. In 1977, a band of gunmen took over three buildings in Washington, D.C. and held dozens of people hostage. At least one person was killed before the episode was over. As these incidents make clear, terrorism is not alien to American life. To be sure, the number of terrorist acts has declined in recent years. In 1969 and 1970, there

There are many groups in American society that advocate political violence as a means of achieving goals. While these groups are small, they are potentially destructive, as this captured arsenal in St. Louis illustrates.

were 3000 bombings and 89 terrorist-related shootings in the United States; by 1976, there were only 65 bombings and 4 shootings.[14] Nevertheless, it would be deceptive to assume that this lull indicates the demise of terrorism on the American political scene.

As a form of political violence, terrorism has attracted a great deal of public attention in recent years. *Terrorism* **can be defined as "the selective use of fear, subjugation, and intimidation to disrupt the normal operations of a society."**[15] Modern terrorist activities have included skyjacking, bombing, extortion, assassination, and sabotage. Probably two of the best-known terrorist groups are the Palestine Liberation

Organization (PLO) and the Irish Republican Army (IRA). Because of their clandestine nature, it is difficult to identify many American terrorist groups, but some of those believed to be important by law enforcement officials in recent years are described in Table 14.2.

TABLE 14.2

Groups Suspected of Terrorist Activities in the United States

Armed Forces of National Liberation (FALN)

A group demanding independence for Puerto Rico. Claimed responsibility for bombings at two office buildings in New York in 1977. Has taken responsibility for 49 explosions since 1974, including one in 1975 that killed 4 people and injured 55.

The Armed Revolutionary Commandos of Independence (CRIA)

Also advocates independence for Puerto Rico. Based in New York, police credit it with 29 letter bombings since 1976.

The New World Liberation Front

A left-wing group that is believed to be an offspring of the Symbionese Liberation Army. Based in California, the NWLF claims responsibility for more than 40 bombings between 1975 and 1977.

The Weather Underground

A radical offshoot of some political activist groups of the 1960s, such as the Students for a Democratic Society. Claims to have taken part in 25 bombings since 1970. Some of its members have recently begun to "surface" from the underground.

Pragmatistas

Cuban terrorists opposed to the regime of Fidel Castro in Cuba. Focused mainly in southern Florida, they are believed by police to be responsible for more than 100 bombings between 1974 and 1977.

SOURCE. Dena Kleiman, "The Potential for Urban Terror is Always There," *New York Times* (March 13, 1977), Section E, p. 3.

Terrorism is not a new phenomenon. It has its roots in the activities of Maximilien Robespierre and his "Reign of Terror" during the French Revolution. Robespierre's motivations were political, and revolved around discontent concerning the leadership in France in the late eighteenth century. Today's terrorism is different from that during the French Revolution and generally appears in four distinct forms: criminal terrorism (e.g. Charles

Manson and his followers); terrorism for ethnic or national liberation (e.g. the PLO or the Armed Forces of National Liberation); state terrorism (e.g. the mistreatment of blacks by the Ku Klux Klan); and revolutionary terrorism (e.g. the Weather Underground).[16] Nevertheless, much of the terrorist activity that we are familiar with today has political beginnings and an origin in some kind of perceived injustice, the elimination of which is the terrorist's purpose.[17]

Terrorism is a particularly difficult form of violence to combat. Counter-terrorist measures can be helpful, but we are vulnerable at so many points in complex modern societies, and terrorist acts can take such diverse forms that anything like complete protection is probably impossible. It must be remembered that, in the words of one authority on these issues, terrorism has become "a method to establish claims to justice, to seek new societies, and to release frustrations that cannot be ameliorated through normal political channels."[18] Terrorism is part and parcel of the social system in which it takes place. Terrorists are making an effort to right perceived wrongs and feel that they have no other options than terrorism to achieve their goal. Terrorist activity in America, while not seriously disruptive at present, is symptomatic of tensions and strains among some groups and is another indication of the violence that lurks below the surface of an apparently tranquil American society.

War

Most people feel that peace is the normal state of affairs while war is an unpleasant interlude that must be tolerated. Few Americans consider our country a bellicose nation that initiates war for trivial reasons. However, social scientists J. David Singer and Melvin Small classify us among the more "war prone" nations of the world, calculating that between 1816 and 1965 the United States has been involved in six wars—not including the campaigns against the Indians and the Vietnam war.[19]

Americans are naturally most familiar with the most recent war in our history. The Vietnam war, in addition to resulting in over 50,000 deaths and many more injuries to American soldiers, gen-

erated much controversy over its legitimacy and has been seen as a contributing factor in other problems, such as inflation and the civil disorders of the 1960s.

In contrast to Vietnam, earlier wars of this century are remembered as less controversial and as having a moral purpose. For example, World War I, World War II, and the Korean War are seen as patriotic efforts to repel aggression and invasion. The threats seemed fairly obvious to most, and the costs of not doing battle seemed severe and unacceptable. The casualties of these wars were great, and civilian populations were often involved. In previous wars, the decimation of civilian populations was restricted by the limited technology available. Beginning with World War II, advances in weaponry made it possible to destroy the populations of whole cities. In the saturation aerial bombing of Dresden, for example, an estimated 135,000 civilians were killed, mainly by asphyxiation and burning. The first atomic bomb ever used in combat killed an estimated 70,000 and injured another 68,000 people in the city of Hiroshima in 1945. A few days later, another atomic bomb killed about 40,000 people in Nagasaki.[20]

What of the less well known wars in our history? One series of wars, which most Americans prefer to forget, are the Indian Wars—the brutal, unceasing, and inexorable drive by white society to remove the Native American as a hindrance to industrial and agricultural expansion. These wars began almost from the moment the first colonists landed in the new world and continued with only temporary interludes until the final massacre at Wounded Knee, South Dakota in 1890. Their costs are incalculable. One cost, of course, was the enormous number of lives lost on both sides. A second cost is the lingering impact of these brutal wars. Native Americans have still not been fully integrated into American society, and Red Power groups, such as the American Indian Movement, are demanding some reconciliation with our past.

What do we learn from this history of violence in America? There are three important "lessons" to be learned. First, our "historical amnesia" must respond to treatment by a good dose of history. We cannot maintain the myth that we are an especially peaceful people. While we are probably no more violent than most other societies, we have certainly had our share of conflict and turmoil. Second, if we are to understand human conflict, we must consider the theory that conflict, violence, and possibly even war, are inevitable accompaniments of human social life. An assumption of the functionalist perspective is that if some institution or practice continues to exist, it may be performing some important functions for society. Later in this chapter we will discuss the social functions that such conflict may perform.

Finally, one fact stands out—much of the violence that we have discussed was a part of some broader social change occurring in American society. Racial disorders foretold a newly emerging relationship between the races; labor conflict was a mechanism for establishing new distributions of power and resources between management and workers (and was also a part of societal adjustment to the change from an agricultural society of self-employed individuals to an industrial society of wage laborers). Conflict, and often violence, have played an important historical role in the development of American society. While an unpleasant experience, it may seem in some cases inevitable for the perpetuation of, and change in, human societies.

CONFLICT AND VIOLENCE AS SOCIAL PROBLEMS

While it would seem obvious that conflict and violence are important social problems about which we should concern ourselves, the three theoretical perspectives can be used to obtain a better understanding of the conditions under which they constitute social problems, and which groups they affect.

The Functionalist Perspective

From the functionalist perspective, conflict and violence are generally viewed as social problems because they are disruptive—they threaten the ability of the system to accom-

plish necessary tasks. In an extreme form, such as a nuclear holocaust, they may even threaten the very survival of the society. In less extreme form, conflict is seen to result from a lack of integration among the various parts of the system. The sources of this deficiency may be diverse. For example, through the socialization process, families and other agencies of socialization inculcate in the individual an acceptance of the dominant value system and a motivation to achieve the goals rewarded by that system. If this is not accomplished, those who do not accept the dominant values and goals may pursue disruptive alternatives—crime, rioting, or joining radical social movements.[21]

From the functionalist perspective, however, conflict is not necessarily a social problem. In addition to maintaining the existing society, any social system must be adaptive—it must respond to changes both from within itself and from the outside in order to continue to function in such a way that it can persist in a changing environment. Such an adaptation may involve a certain amount of conflict in achieving a new equilibrium. In our discussion of violence in American history, we pointed out that some instances of violence (such as race riots or labor conflict) were mechanisms through which social change occurred. **Conflict can also serve as a means of siphoning off hostilities in a way that is not threatening to the system as a whole.**[22] If some conflict, then, performs these latent functions, it would not be considered, from the functionalist perspective, a social problem for society.

The Conflict Perspective

While the functionalist perspective sensitizes us to the manner in which intergroup conflict can be defined as a social problem on a broad societal plane, the conflict perspective enables us to locate particular groups that view a certain source of conflict as a problem even though it might not be a problem for the whole of society. From this point of view, intergroup conflict or violence will be defined as a social problem by a group when that group feels that such conditions interfere with its ability to get its "fair share" of valued resources.[23]

Thus, conflict that might be functional for society may constitute a social problem for certain groups. Violence against slaves prior to emancipation and against free blacks afterward can be seen as functional for society because it protected existing social arrangements by controlling any destructive actions among subordinate groups. It also allowed the release of pent-up frustrations among lower-class whites in a fashion that was harmless to the status quo. Yet, for the victims of the violence, it is clearly a social problem because it impedes their ability to share in valued resources and to maintain an acceptable lifestyle. **This points to a clarification of the way in which conflict might be considered a social problem** — it is often not the existence of conflict, but rather its distribution, which leads it to be seen as a social problem by a particular group. Violence on the part of militant blacks would be defined as a social problem by the majority population because it threatens their ability to achieve their goals. For blacks, the social problem involves their inability to marshal sufficient resources to achieve their goals. If blacks controlled the means of utilizing violence effectively for the accomplishment of their ends, then it would not be, for them, a social problem.

The Interactionist Perspective

From the interactionist perspective, social order is based on a shared consensus about reality. It is only through such consensus that social interaction can be maintained. **Conflict (whether of a violent or nonviolent form) becomes a social problem when it threatens the ability of groups to achieve such a consensus.** One common consequence of intergroup conflict is a reduction in communication between the parties to the conflict.[24] Yet it is through communication that people become aware of the attitudes, interests, and perspectives of others and that shared meanings emerge through negotiation. To the extent that this communication breaks down, it becomes more difficult for people to agree — not only on issues directly related to the conflict, but also on unrelated issues. Not only do the two groups clash on the issue of controversy, but each also begins to question the actions and motives of its adversary in other areas, and the chances of cooperation in dealing with other issues is greatly reduced.

SOURCES OF INTERGROUP CONFLICT

One of the primary goals of an investigation of social conflict is to develop knowledge that will enable us to reduce the level of conflict — especially violent and destructive conflict — in the world. We shall be considering a number of theories concerning the causes of this conflict; however, a note of caution is warranted. There are no simple answers to help us understand complex and varied behavior, such as a race riot, a lynch mob, or a nuclear holocaust. No single explanation will account for all of this variability. In addition, any particular conflict is the result of a chain of multiple causation; many factors influence the final outcome. This should be kept in mind in reviewing each separate theory of intergroup conflict.

Biological Sources of Violence

Innate Sources of Aggression

Throughout history, many people have shared the belief that the biological nature of human beings somehow compels them toward violence. Much of the support for this position comes from research in the field of *ethology,* **which is the study of the instincts and behavior patterns of a species in its natural environment.** Pioneering ethologist Niko Tinbergen, for example, studied the territorial behavior of the stickleback fish. After the female fish deposits its eggs, the male fertilizes the eggs and then protects the nest territory from other male sticklebacks. The protective male will attack anything approaching the nest that looks like another male stickleback.[25]

The foregoing example suggests that one source of this innate response is the protection of territory — what student of ethology Robert Ardrey called the "territorial imperative."[26] According to this idea, it is an evolutionary necessity for a species to protect its territory from attack by others; otherwise, mating and procreation would be disturbed. Furthermore, this territoriality increases the likelihood of survival of the species by preventing overpopulation, which would occur if animals did not protect their habitat from invasion by others of their species. Another possible innate source of violent behavior rests on the evolutionary advantage to those members of the species who are especially aggressive. In the struggle over scarce food supplies, physical strength and prowess are definitely an advantage. It is "survival of the fittest"—the strongest and most aggressive members of the species are more likely to obtain adequate food, successfully compete for mates, and thus pass on these innate aggressive characteristics to their offspring. In the long run, their genes are more likely to dominate the gene pool of that species.

According to proponents of this biological approach, in the distant past the more aggressive and belligerent human beings were more likely to survive, and this biologically induced aggressiveness is still with us today (even though it may have little survival value). Thus, private property and patriotic nationalism are seen as expressions of the territorial instinct. Just as the stickleback fish is biologically motivated to protect the fertilized egg against predators, according to the biological approach, so too human beings have an innate tendency to protect their nation against attack from outsiders.

Sociobiology

A recent development in the study of the relationship between biology and social behavior is the discipline of sociobiology.[27] *Sociobiology* **is a mod-**

Because violence and war are so common in human history, some have concluded that these behaviors may be biologically determined. However, most social scientists take the position that social learning is more important than heredity in bringing about these behaviors.

ern effort to find a biological basis for human social behavior. A central thesis of sociobiology is that animals behave in a fashion that will maximize the survival of their genes. One form that this can take is to produce numerous offspring — the more children a person has increases the survival of that person's genes. Unlike Darwinian evolutionary tradition, which envisioned each animal struggling in order to protect and nurture itself, sociobiology proposes that animals work to save the genes of the species. This may, in some cases, require that they themselves die. Thus, a human being might endanger his own life to protect his children or other members of his group.

Sociobiologists argue that some animals other than humans engage in this sort of altruistic behavior: baboons, for example, will attack a prowling leopard and face almost certain death in order to allow other baboons to escape. The widespread occurrence of such behavior in many species is taken as evidence by sociobiologists that these behaviors are biologically linked. Through evolution, genes evolve that are the foundation of behavior, such as altruism, which increases the likelihood of survival of the genes of the species. For sociobiologists, violence or aggression may be biologically determined if it enhances the survival of the genes. However, in some cases, survival of the genes might be maximized if the person were nonviolent and passive. What evolves is not a genetic predisposition toward violence or aggression, but rather a tendency toward behaviors that will increase the survival value of the genes — in some contexts this might call for aggression and in another context, passivity.

Culture or Biology?

Are human beings ruled by such biological forces? Are we like other animals in this respect? The controversy over these issues is still quite intense and will probably not be settled until much more research is done. However, a few considerations are important to clarify some of the issues in this debate. First, it is important to realize that an instinct involves complex and automatic behavior. It is not something that one can choose to do or to ig-

nore — the concept of choice has no meaning when discussing instincts. Robert Ardrey points out that war and violent conflict are not instinctual but that they are biologically produced. He argues that aggression is a drive — a generalized tendency, rooted in the biological nature of human beings, to dominate others or to seek one's own ends at the expense of others' goals and desires. However, a drive does not tell the individual (as an instinct would) precisely how to go about satisfying this tendency. For example, hunger is a drive — we are motivated to do something about it — but the biological tension of hunger does not tell us what, when, and how to eat. Likewise, the biological drive of aggression does not determine the *form* that this aggression will take. It can be expressed in socially acceptable ways, such as athletic competition, or in socially destructive ways, such as war and rebellion. The *form* of aggression is socially determined.[28]

Whether in terms of instincts or drives, there are problems with this biological approach to human conflict. The interactionist approach sensitizes us to the fact that human beings are socialized into a particular culture and respond to a socially constructed reality — our behavior is based on a framework of shared meanings and values held in common with others in our group. In other words, people can be motivated by purely symbolic goals — such as freedom, dignity, religious principles, and the like. We also experience emotions that have no counterpart in other animals — pride, revenge, hate, spite. Are values, symbolic goals, and human emotions simply a rationalization to justify the satisfaction of man's presumed biological tendency toward aggression? Most social scientists reject this position and feel that these culturally created goals and human emotions can generate aggression, violence, and disruption irrespective of any hypothetical biological necessity for such behavior.

In addition, we must not ignore the extent to which human behavior is learned and shaped by social institutions and social processes. Even sociobiologists agree that the precise form of human social behavior is the result of two factors: the person's genetic makeup and the social, cultural, and physical environment in which that person exists.[29] Human beings are extremely variable—some are violent, others are not; we have both militarists and pacifists; some jealously guard their private property while others abandon personal belongings and live communally with others. Biological explanations alone cannot explain this variety. In the remainder of this section, we will investigate learning and social institutions as causes of human conflict.

Frustration, Deprivation, and Violence

We all have days when things just don't go as we had hoped. Our cars won't start; people don't meet us on time; the checkout line at the store moves too slowly, which results in missing a favorite TV show. Many people react to these occurrences with anger and hostility—they yell at people or make vicious remarks about them. These are illustrations of an important and complex process; frustration creates a tension within the individual that is often released through some type of aggressive behavior.[30] **Frustration is the inability to achieve some desired goal.** The release of this tension, however, does not necessarily have to be violent. Aggression can manifest itself through a variety of symbolic, but nonviolent, forms—insulting comments, derogatory rumors, ridiculing jokes or epithets. For example, in a situation where a frustrated group is powerless to directly attack a frustrating group, such covert types of aggression are common. Minority groups in the United States have typically responded in this way. Blacks have a host of pejorative terms (such as *honky*) and demeaning jokes that impugn the virility and common sense of whites.

According to the interactionist perspective, subjective social reality is more important in shaping human behavior than are objective conditions. Throughout history, human beings have lived in frustrating conditions of utter poverty, degradation, and deprivation without seeming to respond aggressively to these conditions. Why do people react to frustrating conditions with violence in one context and not in another? In order to understand this, we must consider *relative deprivation*—**the perceived discrepancy between the economic and social goals and values that people feel they deserve and the goals and values that they are actually able to achieve in their lives.**[31]

People experience conditions as frustrating relative to some standard that they establish for themselves, and that standard is constantly shifting. For example, workers in the United States have held continually changing beliefs concerning an acceptable standard of living and the level of economic return. While sixteen-hour workdays were acceptable in the early days of industrialization, working men and women have since come to feel that they should have more free time for leisure and to spend with their families. A century ago, few people saw anything inherently evil in ten-year-old children working for a living. We now feel that a person has a right to a more enjoyable childhood free from the limitations of such a life. So it is understandable that today a person working a forty-hour week might feel frustrated if he or she earned *only* $15,000 a year while a worker of a century ago, with considerably different standards, was content with less pay for longer hours.

This process has been described as a "revolution of rising expectations"—the tendency for people whose conditions are improving to expect even more improvement. This has often puzzled observers of group conflict. For example, many people were confused and angered by the black riots in the 1960s because the conditions of blacks in the United States seemed to have improved significantly as a result of civil rights activities in the previous decade and a half; some schools had been integrated, voting rights had been extended to many previously disenfranchised blacks, and significant inroads had been made against discrimination in transportation and housing. Yet, as these advances were made, blacks came to expect even more; *any* discrepancy between white achievements and black achievements came to be seen as a serious deprivation that required change. Violence and civil disorders can be understood only within the context of what people expect from a situation, not of what others feel that group deserves.[32]

Violence as Learned Behavior

Socialization and Modeling

Most social scientists today accept the proposition that the conditions under which human violence occurs and the forms that it takes are learned. Frustration and deprivation may be an underlying cause of violence, but people still learn when, how, and against whom to vent their frustrations. One of the fundamental learning processes among human beings involves rewards and punishments.[33] Rewarding a person for doing something increases the likelihood that he will repeat that behavior in the future. Similarly, ignoring or punishing a person for exhibiting a particular behavior reduces the probability that the person will repeat the behavior in the future. These rewards and punishments are called reinforcements. In our culture, there are many rewards for aggressive and violent behavior. Children playing with their friends are often rewarded for aggression—the child can force others to give him toys or let him play in a game. Adults often yield to a child's demands if the demands are backed by threats of violence, yelling, and general disruption associated with what we call a "temper tantrum." It is easier, in the short run, to give the child a toy or some candy than to have the child make a scene.

Our childrearing practices are an important source of violent and aggressive behavior. All parents think that they are knowledgeable about raising children and often resent the advice of persons trained in child development. Yet research on childhood socialization illustrates how parents may influence the development of aggression among their children. For example, one group of psychologists studied hundreds of families in New England and found that ". . . when the parents punish—particularly when they employ physical punishment—they are providing a living example of the use of aggression at the very moment they are trying to teach the child not to be aggressive."[34]

This learning process is referred to as *modeling:* by observing others' actions, a person can form an idea about how to do something. We tend to take as models those on whom we are dependent or with whom we identify. Most children both identify with, and are dependent on, their parents. So the parent who uses physical punishment is serving as a model for his child—the child learns that aggressive behavior can be used successfully in dealing with interpersonal problems. The subculture surrounding a person is also an important source of aggressive models. It is not surprising that aggressive behavior is more common in settings in which there are many such models.[35]

We have only touched on the various mechanisms through which people learn violence and aggression as ways of dealing with problems. Certainly, a person who modeled aggressive behavior as a child will not, as an adult, invariably go about punching or shooting people or taking any available opportunity to engage in mayhem or rebellion. However, that person will most likely have fewer inhibitions to aggression and violent behavior. If frustrated, he will be more likely to lash out violently at others— either physically or symbolically. These learning mechanisms are one important source of conflict and violence in American society.

The Mass Media

Television is certainly the most pervasive of the media. Ninety-six percent of all households in the United States have at least one TV set, and 30 percent have two or more sets. Many young children spend more hours watching television each week than they spend in the classroom (see Table 14.3). How have these technological developments affected our propensity toward violence or the extent of intergroup conflict in American society?

We have seen that children can learn appropriate behavior by utilizing other people as models. The characters that children see on televison—whether they be loving parents, studious youngsters, or aggressive fighters—can serve as such models. Television shows like "Starsky and Hutch" and "Baretta," and the "Dirty Harry" movies portray the ideal male as an individualistic "Lone Ranger"

TABLE 14.3

Proportions of Children Watching Different Amounts of TV Programs, Expressed in Percentages

NUMBER OF HOURS WATCHED PER WEEK	GRADE LEVEL		SOCIOECONOMIC STATUS		
	FOURTH	SIXTH	LOW	MIDDLE	HIGH
1–9	3	2	6	0	5
10–19	12	8	3	16	8
20–29	24	19	24	18	30
30–39	27	39	37	29	30
40–49	21	20	18	21	17
50–59	12	10	10	13	10
60–69	1	2	2	3	0

SOURCE. Clara P. Ferguson, *Preadolescent Children's Attitudes Toward Television Commercials* (Austin, Tex.: Bureau of Business Research, University of Texas, 1971), p. 24. Copyright 1975. Reprinted by permission from the Bureau of Business Research. University of Texas at Austin.

type who needs little support from others and solves problems with his fists or his gun. The so-called harmless "kiddie" programs commonly show characters using violence and aggression as solutions to problems. Even the educational television program "Sesame Street" has been accused of having too much violence.

Much indirect evidence on the relationship between viewing television violence and aggressive behavior is available, and it consistently supports the idea that a steady diet of TV violence does lead to aggressive behavior.[36] For example, those who watch a considerable amount of violence on TV are more likely to assume that others they observe are naturally aggressive, and they are more likely to be rated by their friends as aggressive. In controlled experimental settings, children who have viewed violent segments of films display more aggressive behavior toward human-like objects, such as rubber dolls and inflated balloons, than do those who have seen nonviolent films. They are also more likely to be aggressive toward playmates. The popularity of television as a form of leisure-time behavior is class-related — it is more popular among lower socioeconomic groups. Since these groups are also more likely to express themselves aggressively, the problem may be compounded by the confluence of these trends.

While these findings concerning the mass media are important, we must be careful about making too much of them. Watching a few shows on television or attending a few movies will not transform our children into bloodthirsty killers. It is normally only a small number of children who are significantly influenced by observing violence, and usually these are children who are already more likely to use aggression as a problem-solving technique. Furthermore, we do not know what the long-term effect of a steady barrage of such violence is on people's actual contacts with one another. Because a child punches a balloon more viciously after viewing violence does not mean that this child will later in life throw bricks through windows or support violent insurrections. In fact, a few studies find no relationship between *viewing* violence and *engaging in* violence.[37]

In addition to portraying violence and aggression, the mass media also serve as a forum for the dissemination of values, beliefs, and justifications for behavior. Television, newspapers, and magazines can spread beliefs about what type of behavior is acceptable and appropriate. In the 1960s, the term "riot culture" was used to refer to the emergence of a set of beliefs that supported aggressive confrontation, and possibly violence, as an appropriate and effective mechanism for dealing with social problems.[38] For example, through the various media, blacks learned of riots in other cities; they heard Stokely Carmichael and H. Rap Brown argue that centuries of racial oppression justified violence to bring about social change; they observed first-hand instances of police brutality in efforts to control demonstrations and protests. So the media can be a powerful means of spreading *ideas* that may transform intergroup conflict and confrontation into violent clashes.

Social Sources of Violence

Strain

Some sociological theories of violence focus on those aspects of American social structure that are the cause of violence.[39] According to this view, which leans heavily on the functionalist perspective, some groups in society do not have the opportunity to achieve success through legitimate means. The reasons for this are diverse. In some cases, racial or ethnic discrimination limits the opportunities available to the group. In other cases, poverty may hinder the person's ability to acquire the skills that aid one in achieving success. These groups are in a situation of structured strain in that the social organization of American society makes it difficult, or impossible, for them to be fully integrated into society. There are a number of ways that people react to such strain, and one common way is through participation in violent forms of behavior, such as crime or civil disorders.

These approaches to the problem of violence are similar to the frustration-deprivation hypothesis, but the emphasis here is on the fact that the ultimate source of individual frustration is to be found in the organization of society. Because there is poverty, prejudice, discrimination, and a lack of opportunity on the part of some groups, violence is almost an inevitable outcome. This directs our attention away from the individual as the source of the problem and forces us to investigate the failings in our social organization. From the functionalist perspective, such structured sources of strain might possibly be eliminated if the prejudice and discrimination at their source could be attacked. However, from the conflict perspective, such strain is the inevitable by-product of the struggle between groups over scarce resources. Some degree of strain will always result when one group is in a position subordinate to another.

Strain theories provide an important antidote to the tendency to view violence as a problem located in individuals. However, strain theories have their limitations. Not all people who experience strain react violently, and those who react violently do so only intermittently. Thus, strain theories locate an important condition of violence, but we must also consider learning processes and situational factors in order to develop a complete understanding of the sources of violence.

Subculture of Violence

In the 1960s, black activist H. Rap Brown justified violence in the fight against racial oppression by arguing that "Violence is as American as cherry pie."[40] Many others would agree with Brown that violence runs through the core of American society. In fact, it has been argued that there exists, at least among some groups, **a *subculture of violence* — a set of norms and values that condones and legitimizes the use of violence under certain conditions.** Thus, violence erupts because it is viewed as an acceptable way of dealing with a situation and in some cases may be seen as the preferred and "manly" response. In fact, it is argued, the ability to react quickly and courageously with violence when one is threatened or insulted can be a means of gaining status in the eyes of one's peers.[41]

While the subculture-of-violence theory has appealed to many people, recent research has cast doubt on its utility.[42] Rather than being widely approved in America, violence is actually disapproved by most Americans. Furthermore, while it is was long believed that the poor and nonwhites were most likely to engage in violence, we have learned that the relationships between race, poverty, and violent behavior are not nearly as strong as was originally thought. Some researchers also question the presumed regional variation in the propensity toward violence.

Even if there is no generalized subculture of violence, it still may be the case that groups will condone some kinds of violence under certain conditions. For example, following the quite violent actions of the Chicago police at the Democratic National Convention in 1968, one survey indicated that only 19 percent of the people thought that the police had used too much force while a quarter of the respondents felt that the police had used too little force.[43] This acceptance of violence on the part of much of the public was at least partly due to years of frustration over the inability of the police to control political and antiwar demonstrations. After an extensive study of attitudes toward violence, two social scientists concluded:

> We have not found any support for the proposition that police violence seriously violates American political norms. Extra-legal police actions directed against unpopular targets are unlikely to draw censure or even disapproval from those substantial segments of the American public for whom the police are the ' good guys."[44]

These attitudes may be more a reflection of the climate of the times in the 1960s rather than a generalized tendency of Americans to approve violence.

Stereotyping

Very commonly, we perceive people not as individuals but as members of some group or category — as whites or blacks, men or women. This often leads to the development of a *stereotype* — **a set of traits or attributes (both positive and negative) that one group generally believes are possessed by members of another group.** Such stereotypes can serve to summarize information about a person or group. However, they also often contain considerable inaccurate information. In addition, the traits that are a part of a stereotype are often perceived as the inherent qualities of members of that group (e.g. blacks are lazy), while in actuality the traits are often a reaction to the social situation to which the group must adapt (e.g. blacks were expected to be lazy and were not rewarded for showing initiative and aggressiveness).

The conflict between police and black demonstrators during the 1960s illustrates the importance of these stereotypes in generating intergroup violence.[45] Many blacks stereotyped police as vicious oppressors whose function was to keep them in the colonized and deprived ghetto. In 1962, black writer James Baldwin referred to the police as an

Stereotyping by one group of another group can intensify intergroup conflict because the stereotype often contains inaccurate or misleading information.

army of occupation. "Off the Pigs" (meaning to do away with the police) became a rallying cry for militant blacks. These negative stereotypes were reciprocated by the police. In one study, the unsolicited racial statements of police were recorded. In black precincts, 45 percent of police officers made statements such as "These scums aren't people; they're animals in a jungle" and "Hitler had the right idea — we oughta gas these niggers;" or they referred to blacks as "bastard savages," "maggots," "filthy pigs," and "buffaloes." For these police officers, blacks are degenerate, immoral, and less than human.

What are the consequences of these reciprocal stereotypes? Sociologist Rodney Stark summarized it very simply: ". . . blacks are filled with hatred of the police. The police are filled with hatred of . . . blacks. We mix them at our peril."[46] Each of these groups treats the other on the basis of its own stereotype. If blacks view police as "pig oppressors," this stereotype justifies ambushes and sniping attacks against the police. For their part, police reactions were also shaped by their stereotypes. If blacks are less than human, then one need not show the normal courtesy and moral restraint one would show toward humans. Given these reciprocal stereotypes, it is not surprising that the resulting conflicts were so violent and prolonged. It is clear that, whether true or false, such stereotypes shape the manner in which each side treats the other. Human beings respond not to the world as it is—but to the world as it appears to them.

THE CONSEQUENCES OF INTERGROUP CONFLICT AND VIOLENCE

The Social Functions of Conflict

As we suggested earlier in our discussion of violence in American history, conflict, even in its violent forms, can sometimes lead to positive outcomes and changes in society.[47] The functionalist approach sensitizes us to the possibility that a condition or practice that persists for a long time may be performing some important positive functions for some groups or society as a whole. What possible good can come from conflict?

Intergroup conflict can help to establish and maintain the boundaries between groups. It is important for any group to develop a sense of itself as possessing positive qualities and as being distinct from other groups, in order for it to pursue common goals and values through coordinated action. For example, during the tumultuous decade of the 1960s, conflict was important in the development of many groups. The violent clash between police and demonstrators in Selma and Birmingham, Alabama in 1963 clarified the division between civil rights groups and those opposing

them. Many people who had previously been apathetic about these issues began to identify strongly with one side or the other because the clash made the issues more immediate and dramatic.

Intergroup conflict can lead to an increased sense of self-worth among members of the group. Because a person's self-concept is an important determinant of his behavior, it is functional for society that members of groups view themselves in a positive way. A socially devalued personal identity can lead to dysfunctional behavior—a lack of aspiration, an unwillingness to work toward commonly accepted goals, and possibly criminal behavior. For example, the public image of blacks in the United States has historically been that they are weak, powerless, and lazy. This widespread public belief, along with the structural limitations placed on what blacks were able to achieve, has contributed to a low sense of self-worth among blacks themselves. However, violent confrontations with the police in the 1960s began to change this. Blacks could view themselves as more powerful, assertive, and self-assured people who had gained some mastery over their lives and could stand up to threatening situations. The gesture of raising a clenched fist and slogans such as "Black Power" were symbols of an emerging identity emphasizing power and mastery. Such changes in identity make it easier for a socially devalued minority group to become more effective in the struggle for a position of equality and contribution to society.

Intergroup conflict can serve as a safety valve to release pent-up hostilities, frustrations, and tensions that result from economic deprivation, racial discrimination, and the like. If feelings of rage and frustration were released through attacks on central economic and political institutions, the survival of the established order might be threatened. However, limited conflict focusing on less central issues or targets can serve as a safety valve that vents these actions in relatively harmless ways. For example, the lynching of blacks in the South in the late 1800s probably served as a release for the feelings of hostility and frustration among poor whites in a manner that did not threaten the dominant institutions. Of course, for the group that is the object of the aggression, such as the blacks being lynched, such actions were obviously dysfunctional.[48]

Intergroup conflict can also enhance group cohesion and feelings of solidarity among its members. If some external threat is to be overcome, a group must pull together and coordinate its actions. There are strong pressures to suspend dissenting views in favor of consensus over values and actions. Cohesion is also enhanced because differences within a group come to be seen as minor compared to the overwhelming external danger. There were many divergent opinions among the police in the 1960s concerning civil rights and student demonstrations. However, once the police felt directly threatened, as a result of sniping or other actions, they tended to coalesce behind a united front.

Finally, intergroup conflict can function as a mechanism of social change. Change is inevitable—all societies must respond and adapt to changing internal and external conditions. Conflict can serve as a catalyst and a vehicle for such change. The conflict between blacks and police in the 1960s served as a catalyst for many changes within the police forces in the United States. For instance, police were encouraged to recruit minority members in order to cope with some of the racial issues; more emphasis was placed on a better-educated police force as a means of dealing with difficult social issues; many police came to view themselves as not simply enforcing the law but also solving social problems, and this made it necessary for them to learn more about the social and psychological conditions underlying these problems and about the techniques to deal with them.[49]

It is difficult to accept the notion that conditions or events that are usually defined as wrong and destructive might be functional for society. Conflict and violence (along with poverty, deviance, and crime) are social conditions that, while normally viewed as undesirable, may be functional under certain circumstances. However, not all conflict is functional. In addition, we need not passively accept violence because it might have some positive outcomes for society. There may be nonviolent alternatives that can achieve the same outcomes. We need to understand what functions a particular type of violence performs before we will be in a position to suggest nonviolent substitutes. Even if conflict were an inevitable process in society, some of its more violent forms are so clearly destructive that most would consider them more dysfunctional than functional—they can indeed be considered social problems.

The Consequences of War: The Impact on American Society

For many people, war is a senseless, wasteful, and brutal occurrence. The human suffering and physical destruction that normally accompany war are seen as sufficient grounds to consider it a social problem. While these concerns are important, there is another side to the issue of war as a social problem that will hold our attention. From the functionalist perspective, any social system that is highly integrated and interdependent must be severely disturbed by the serious disruptions that accompany war. The need to mobilize men, material, and attitudes to support the war effort creates dislocations in many parts of society. In other words, war tends to create or intensify other social problems, such as violence, disruption, and crime. It is to these consequences of war that we now turn our attention.

Political Turmoil

More than one hundred fifty years ago, French historian Alexis deTocqueville made the following observation: "All those who seek to destroy the liberties of a democratic nation ought to know that war is the surest and shortest means to accomplish it."[50] DeTocqueville was referring to two conditions that are associated with wars. First, some wars result in a decline in the number of people viewing the government as legitimate—as a government that should be obeyed. This decline in legitimacy may manifest itself as a change in attitude toward the government, an unwillingness to support government agencies, or a willingness to engage in protest or rebellious actions.

The second condition threatening democracy is the increasing intolerance of dissenting opinions that often emerges during war. There is strong pressure toward consensus, and people are more willing to use repressive means to control dissent. As a consequence of both these conditions, most wars are associated with increasing levels of domestic violence.[51] In some cases, the violence is initiated by the government (e.g. harrassment and arrest of dissenters), while in other cases it is violence directed against the war or the status quo (e.g. antiwar protests or attempts to disrupt the war effort). In other words, deTocqueville is suggesting—and current research supports his opinion—that one of the victims of war may be the very political institutions and constitutional ideals that the war is intended to preserve! A brief discussion of domestic violence during some American wars will illustrate the magnitude of this problem.

The Civil War resulted in considerable violence beyond what occurred in military battle. While some clashes were between groups on opposing sides of the war, much strife was the outcome of antiwar sentiment. Thus, for three days in 1863, New York City was the scene of massive, almost uncontrolled antidraft riots. There were approximately 50,000 participants and 1300 deaths. Some of the violence was a reflection of class and ethnic animosity (poor Irish immigrants attacking blacks), but much of it was directed at the inequitable draft system (a person could buy his way out of the draft for $300—a sum of money available only to the affluent at that time).[52]

There was also considerable intergroup conflict generated during World War I because of opposition to the war. For example, in July 1917, 8000 Boston radicals and socialists marched in opposition to the war. The violence that accompanied antiwar protests during World War I was typically initiated by "patriotic" mobs attacking the demonstrators and pacifists (although it was usually the demonstrators who were arrested and charged with criminal offenses). Patriotic zeal also served as an excuse for attacks on radical groups. For example, the Industrial Workers of the World (the "Wobblies"), a revolutionary socialist labor group, were opposed to the war because they viewed it as a profit-making scheme of big business. Under the cover of patriotism, the enemies of the Wobblies set out to destroy them as an effective labor organizing group. Large numbers of Wobblies were jailed and beaten in Arizona, Montana, and other states.

The most recent war in our history, the Vietnam war, was also associated with considerable domestic violence. In the early part of the war, the violence was similar to that in previous wars—for the most part, nonviolent demonstrators were attacked by either the citizens or the police. For example, in 1965 a large group of demonstrators who had intended to close the Oakland Army Terminal were attacked by the Hell's Angels Motorcycle Gang while peacefully seated under the watchful eye of the police. However, beginning in 1967, the character of much of the violence associated with the war changed. The demonstrators began to initiate violence and to justify it as self-defense and actions against the "enemy." An increasingly radical wing of the antiwar movement came to see the war as due to fundamental problems in the structure of American capitalist society. For these people, the political system had lost its legitimacy so that they felt few restraints against the use of violence to achieve their goals. Attacks on police, ROTC installations, and other symbols of the war effort became more common.[53]

Some have argued that the violence in the 1960s that was unrelated to the Vietnam war, such as the ghetto riots, was intensified by the feelings aroused by the war. Studies show that people opposed to the war were much more willing to engage in aggressive actions—sometimes violent and rebellious—to stop the government from going about its business, even on issues unrelated to war. Another finding in support of deTocqueville's observations is that those who supported the Vietnam war expressed more willingness to use repressive measures against dissidents (such as police action to stop peaceful demonstrations).[54]

Economic Problems

Economic decisions involve costs and choices, and at the heart of the economist's concept of cost is the idea that any given use of resources has been

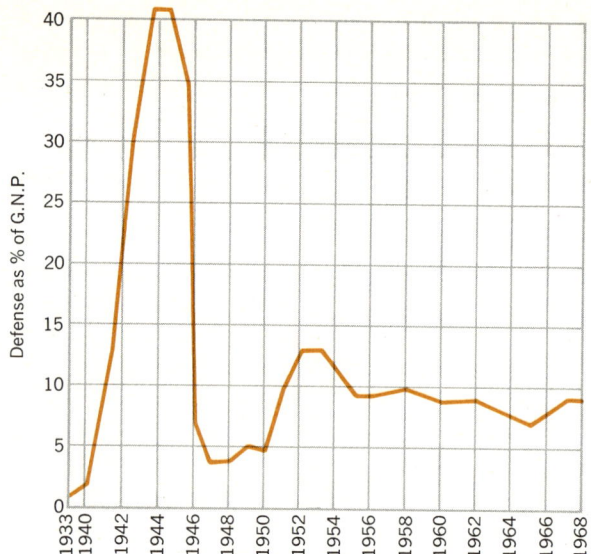

Figure 14.3   Defense Expenditures in the United States as a Percentage of the Gross National Product, 1939–1968. Bruce M. Russett, "Who Pays for Defense?," *American Political Science Review* 63 (June 1969), p. 413.

achieved *at the cost of* other possible uses to which these resources might have been put.[55]

Any limitation of a society's productive capability makes what is allocated to a war effort unavailable for alternative use. One way to examine the cost of war is to look at the proportion of the nation's resources spent on the war effort. An indicator of a nation's economic resources is its *gross national product* **(GNP) — the sum total of expenditures for personal consumption, investment or capital formation, government purchases of goods and services, and the extent to which exports exceed imports; it is the country's total output of goods and services.** As we can see in Figure 14.3, World War II was clearly the most costly of our recent wars; defense spending constituted almost half of the GNP. In these terms, both the Korean and Vietnam wars were considerably less costly.

However, the full economic impact of war cannot be measured simply in dollar figures or proportions of the GNP. It can also be calculated in terms of its overall effect on the economy and in the alternatives foregone in order to maintain the war effort.

World War II and the Korean war began during periods of considerable unemployment. This meant that the added stimulus of increased government spending for the war could be absorbed more easily and would have less of an inflationary impact. However, in 1965, on the eve of the major troop buildup in Vietnam, the American economy had reached a level of full employment, with continuous expansion and plants operating at 90 percent of capacity — an optimal economic situation that required no further economic stimulus. The increased defense spending for the war provided this added stimulus which led to increased demand for goods and brought about considerable price inflation. During both World War II and the Korean war, inflation was fought with wage and price controls. However, President Johnson and his close political advisers were convinced that the strong American economy could provide both guns and butter — that there was no need either for increased taxation to reduce demand or for wage-price controls to reduce inflation.[56]

Thus, one common economic consequence of war is inflation. Another serious problem is the manner in which economic resources are reallocated in order to accommodate defense spending.[57] Given a GNP of a certain size in a particular year, if more money is put into defense spending, there is less available for other areas. The personal consumption part of the GNP (the consumption of goods, such as automobiles, or of services, such as entertainment or transportation) is most drastically reduced when defense expenditures increase. In other words, the added money going to the construction of planes, guns, and the like comes at least partly from what people would normally have spent on such items as automobiles and television sets.

After an extensive study of the issue, one researcher summarized some of the less tangible economic consequences of the Vietnam war in the following way:

The results for the nation's economy of the Vietnam war . . . were the most virulent inflation in American history, the highest interest rates in history, a series of balance of payments crises worse than any that had gone before, an unnecessary recession in

1970–71, two serious declines in stock prices, . . . a collapse of the housing industry, . . . financial market distortions that bore extremely heavily on small business and that forced state and local governments to retrench on education and other vital services, and the eventual defeat of the most imaginative experimental approach to the problems of impacted poverty that had ever been tried.[58]

Not everyone would agree that the Vietnam war was the sole cause of all of these economic dislocations; yet it seems clear that it was an important contributing factor. Furthermore, some of these problems might have been avoided if political leadership had been more aware of potential consequences and had enacted economic and social policies to minimize their impact.

The Military and the Aftermath of War

The military establishment in the United States is limited by the Constitution to carrying out the goals of the civilian, political arm of our government. Nonetheless, it often bears much of the brunt of negative feelings about a war. Historically, people have commonly reacted to wars, especially to unpopular ones, through refusal to serve in the military. For example, the Vietnam war generated considerable effort to avoid military service. This was also the case during the Civil War (recall the New York City draft riots). There are even more severe consequences for the military. Civilian feelings about military service during the Vietnam war have resulted in a dramatic change in public policy. Political scientist Bruce Russett concludes that: "A special casualty [of the lack of military success in Vietnam] has been the popular respect and awe for the efficiency of the American professional military, which has resulted in a new willingness to cut military funds."[59] In 1973, the military draft was discontinued as a means of meeting manpower quotas. As a consequence, the military, especially the army, is finding it more difficult to maintain what it considers acceptable manpower levels. Furthermore, in order to maintain high levels of enlistment, it has been necessary to lower the minimum education requirements for entrance on active duty.

As a consequence, the military today consists of personnel who are less educated than in the past. There have also been an increasing number of disciplinary problems, including desertion.

Because of these trends, some argue that America may face two potentially sobering developments with serious consequences for our political structure. First, some fear that the all-volunteer army will become a "mercenary force"—a group of poor, uneducated individuals with few occupational options in civilian life who will be required to fight and die to save the political and economic fortunes of more affluent Americans. A related concern is whether a group with such a low level of education and evidencing some serious disciplinary problems will be able to function as a sophisticated military unit capable of making critical decisions and operating with technologically complex weapons systems.

A second danger that some envision is the emergence of a professional military elite that, socially and culturally, is isolated from the interests and values of the civilian population. Whatever disadvantages the draft may have had, it had one clear advantage—it meant that most of the men in uniform did not want to be there. They were civilians serving a short period in the military whose primary loyalties were to civilian authority. This serves as a constraint against the emergence of the military as a group that might use its monopoly over the means of violence to bring about political changes. Such use of military might against existing governments has been a common occurrence in many other countries. The United States has avoided this because, among other reasons, it has had a largely civilian military.

Crime and War

Many criminal acts occur during wars. Soldiers sometimes pillage and terrorize civilian populations over which they have control. Civilians often rob and steal in order to feed themselves or simply to take advantage of the disordered conditions that usually exist in combat zones. Soldiers occasionally exceed their orders and engage in inhumane actions, such as the massacre at My Lai in Vietnam.

These types of crimes resulting from war are a serious concern. Yet war also appears to have an effect on crimes that at first appear unrelated to the war.

One extensive study of homicide rates found a very consistent pattern: homicide rates increased substantially in the period immediately following wars.[60] The increase occurred following large wars as well as small; it occurred whether the nation experienced adverse economic conditions following the war or not; and it occurred among both men and women. The increase also occurred whether a nation won or lost, although it was more common among victorious nations, and nations with a large number of battle deaths were more susceptible to increases in homicide. The researchers concluded that "The war most likely to produce an increased homicide rate . . . is a war which is both deadly and won."[61]

This relationship between crime and war is not yet well understood. There is some indication that it may arise due to the legitimation of violence during wartime. Since violence, destruction, and killing are, in a sense, officially approved by the government during wartime, there are fewer inhibitions on the part of people to engage in such actions. We have already seen that a government itself often engages in violence during wartime in the suppression of dissension. This may create a climate in which violence is viewed as more acceptable and appropriate than at other times. However, there are other potential explanations of increases in crime following war, and further study is essential. What *is* clear is the subtle and pervasive effect of war on many other social problems in society.

CONTROLLING VIOLENCE: PROSPECTS FOR THE FUTURE

We have examined the diverse sources of conflict and violence and the many consequences, both obvious and subtle, that they have on society. Can violence and destruction be brought under some reasonable control? In order to address this question, it is helpful to return to the three theoretical perspectives. For the functionalist, as we have seen, some types of conflict have beneficial consequences for society. Any attempt to eliminate violence or reduce conflict must consider the impact of such actions on all parts of society. If violence or conflict does have positive functions, then workable alternatives to it would have to be located. In some instances, we might be willing to endure the negative consequences in order to enjoy the benefits of some actions. Thus, while wars generate much domestic conflict and violence, in some cases we might accept that as a bearable price for protecting desirable political and social institutions.

From the conflict perspective, conflict and violence can be mechanisms of subordination and oppression. However, we must be alert to the possibility that solutions to these problems might entail, whether wittingly or not, an attempt by some interest group to improve its position to the detriment of another group or by some vested interest to protect the status quo. For example, some have argued that increased federal spending in ghetto areas following riots does little to eliminate the basic causes of the riots but that it does appease ghetto residents sufficiently so that future riots are less likely. For conflict theorists, groups have different and conflicting interests, and it is unlikely that a solution to conflict and violence would serve the interests of all groups. It is critical, then, to examine who benefits and who loses from proposed alternatives.

From the interactionist perspective, we realize the crucial importance of the differing interpretations of social reality dominant in various groups. As our consideration of stereotyping made clear, these versions of reality, even when quite inaccurate, have profound influences on people's behavior. A great deal of misunderstanding occurs because of a lack of communication between groups. As conflict becomes more intense, communication becomes more stereotyped and narrowly focused. So, in evaluating the reactions of groups to proposed solutions, we must be sensitive to the possibility that the reactions are based on a definition of the situation that is stereotyped and distorted.

With these thoughts in mind, we can proceed to evaluate alternative proposals for controlling conflict and violence.

Controlling Violence

The problem of reducing the amount of violence in the United States might be approached by removing the means of perpetrating violence or by developing techniques to control it once it breaks out.

Gun Control

Recent American history has been marred repeatedly with assassination and attempts to assassinate important leaders by people wielding guns—John F. Kennedy, Robert F. Kennedy, Martin Luther King, George Wallace, Gerald Ford (twice). In addition, the majority of homicides are perpetrated with handguns; most police officers killed on duty are the victims of handguns; and the United States leads all other nations in the rate of homicides committed with guns. Opponents of handguns have used these and other facts to try to generate a groundswell of support for some form of gun control. Some propose registration and licensing of handguns; others feel that certain weapons, such as the cheap and easily purchased "Saturday Night Special," should be banned; more extreme opponents favor the banning of all handguns (and in a few cases, all guns, including rifles and shotguns). Their basic argument is that the availability of a handgun increases the likelihood that a family argument or lovers' quarrel will erupt into a shooting match. Without this availability such strife is much less likely to be lethal since guns are considerably more destructive than any other means likely to be available. Since most homicides and assaults are the result of impulse rather than preparation and planning, the impulse is likely to pass without lethal consequences if guns are not so readily available.

While there is not much research on the relationship between gun control and violence, what little there is does not support the opponents of handguns. For example, a study of the effect of state firearms laws shows that increasingly restrictive gun control laws do not reduce the rates of violence associated with firearms and do not reduce the rates of possession of handguns. Since no state has an outright ban on handguns, it is impossible

at this point to determine the impact of such a policy.[62]

There are strong vested interests that oppose the regulation of guns.[63] The most outspoken group is the National Rifle Association (NRA); with over 1 million members, it is able to mount influential campaigns to safeguard the interests of sportsmen and other gun enthusiasts. Since the NRA magazine, *American Rifleman,* is supported by the advertising of gun and ammunition manufacturers, the NRA has a strong vested interest in neutralizing any factors, such as restrictive governmental regulations, that threaten the sale of guns. While many sportsmen are in favor of some gun control legislation, the NRA has taken a strong position against any such controls. One reason for this is their feeling that minor controls will evolve into major controls and possibly a ban on certain kinds of weapons.

A second reason for the opposition to gun control legislation is based on the belief that Americans have a constitutionally guaranteed right to own weapons for their own use and protection. To support this, they cite the Second Amendment to the United States Constitution: "A well regulated militia being necessary to the security of a free state, the right of the people to keep and bear arms shall not be infringed." They feel that such a right is crucial to maintain a democratic society. However, proponents of gun control interpret this same amendment differently, emphasizing that "militia" and "people" *in the collective sense* are those with the right to keep and bear arms—not each and every individual citizen.

Many Americans retain a romantic and heroic notion of protecting their business, home, or family against robberies, burglaries and sexual assaults (see Table 14.4). Yet, the value of keeping a loaded gun in the house for these purposes has been questioned.[64] Despite the large number of guns in the United States, few home robbers or burglars are killed by their victims, and few business robberies are prevented by armed proprietors. In most such crimes, the victim is surprised and has little time to react. In too many cases, a victim with little skill with weapons is injured or killed by a frightened

The National Rifle Association is an interest group which zealously protects the right of Americans to own guns. They do so partly on the grounds that it is a constitutional right.

TABLE 14.4
Trends in Weapons Ownership in the United States, 1959–1977

	1959	1977	CHANGE
Percentage owning any weapon	49	50	+1
Percentage owning a rifle[a]	55	59	+4
Percentage owning a shotgun[a]	65	61	−4
Percentage owning a handgun[a]	32	41	+10

[a]This is expressed as a percentage of all those owning any weapon.

SOURCE. George H. Gallup, *The Gallup Poll: Public Opinion, 1935–1971* (New York: Random House, 1972). p. 1626, and National Opinion Research Center, *National Data Program for the Social Sciences, 1977 General Social Survey* (University of Chicago).

and attack him with it (for this reason, prison guards do not carry weapons when they mingle with prisoners). The police invariably warn against pulling a gun on a criminal because they have too often seen the consequences. Yet, the gun advocate would argue, if a person trained in the use of weapons can protect his home and family effectively, does he not have the right to do so? He should not, these advocates claim, be penalized because others are untrained in self-protection.

In determining the efficacy of a ban on guns as a means of controlling violence, another consideration is important. Would it be possible to ban handguns effectively? Experience with the prohibition of alcohol and the criminalization of marijuana has taught an important lesson: if some activity is widespread, supported by group values, and important to some significant interest group, it is very difficult to outlaw that activity effectively. As with alcohol and marijuana, a blackmarket would un-

criminal. Another danger is that an unarmed criminal might wrest the victim's gun away from him

doubtedly arise to support the inevitable demand for illegal weapons. Another difficulty in terms of regulation is to define precisely what a handgun is. With almost any legal definition, it might be possible to manufacture a "hand-sized weapon" that was small, easily concealable, and versatile but that was not a handgun according to the legal definition. One must weigh the costs of enforcement (such as the financial burden of additional police officers) and the potential infringement on other freedoms (such as the freedom from search and seizure) against the likely benefits of such laws.

Crowd Control

Much of the violence that we have examined in this chapter takes the form of street riots and other civil strife. Typically, the local police force, sometimes supported by the state militia or National Guard, is given the burden of bringing such disorders under control. However, until recently, few policemen have been given training in crowd containment and control nor have they had the equipment to do so. The major focus of their training and most of their actual work is dealing with individual criminals. This shortcoming became painfully clear during the 1960s when the police and the National Guard were woefully inadequate in controlling riots once they had begun. In fact, it became clear that the actions of the police would sometimes trigger a violent disturbance that might not have occurred otherwise, or intensify one that had already begun. In response to this situation, the police developed in two directions: first, enormous resources were expended in the development and stockpiling of exotic nonlethal weapons useful in controlling crowds — flicker lights that dazzle the eyes, Teflon confetti that makes the ground so slippery that rioters are unable to maintain their footing, high-volume foam generators that can cover 200 feet of street with 5 feet of foam in 10 minutes, thus making it extremely difficult for rioters to move, hot-air blowers to "sweat out" people participating in a sit-in.[65]

While many of these weapons have been, and will continue to be, useful in controlling crowds, more than technology is necessary. The second response of police to the disturbances of the 1960s was to train their personnel in strategies of crowd control. For example, police have learned how to interrupt communication within a crowd and how to enforce discipline among their own members so that they can engage in effective and coordinated action. (This was a major problem in the 1960s since the police, in their routine actions, are accustomed to acting individually or in pairs, rather than in large platoons.) The police have also learned to keep a low profile until the decision to suppress an incident has been made, and then to move quickly, using the minimal amount of force necessary. In many cases, police departments have combined these organizational and technological improvements in paramilitary groups called Special Weapons and Tactics, or SWAT. With these and other crowd-control strategies, police forces are much better equipped to deal with crowds.

Preventing Conflict and Violence

While it is essential to have the organizational and technological capability to stop violence once it breaks out, it is more efficient and less destructive if we are able to prevent such incidents from occurring in the first place — if we can eliminate some of the sources of conflict and violence.

Media Regulation

Since the portrayal of violence through the media seems to contribute to aggression and violence, it would seem reasonable to place some controls on the extent of violence permitted in the media. Yet, this task is not easily accomplished. Any governmental attempt to regulate such "entertainment" can interfere with First Amendment rights of freedom of speech and freedom of the press. A free and open media is the cornerstone of a democracy. Government censorship, even for the most altruistic of motives, might become a wedge for censorship of other materials. For example, the regulation of violence on dramatic shows could lead to a ban on reporting violent incidents on news shows. As with gun control, one must weigh the advantages to be gained from such censorship against the drawbacks in terms of a threat to liberty.

Another difficulty in controlling violence on the media is that *the violent shows are often the most popular ones!* For example, "Gunsmoke," which was the longest-running dramatic show in the history of television (it was on for 20 years and has recently gone into syndication), had its full share of shootings, stabbings, and fistfights in each show. More recently, the rash of police shows ("Hawaii Five-O," "Police Story," "Police Woman," "Starsky and Hutch") have been among the more popular shows that include a good dose of violence. They may have some harmful effects on children, but people certainly enjoy them. Networks are naturally reluctant to change shows that gain wide audiences.

The voluntary efforts introduced thus far have had some impact on reducing media violence, but there is no way as yet to determine its broader impact. The more violent shows carry warnings that some scenes may be disturbing to some members of the family and that parental discretion is advised. The networks have also instituted a "family hour" from 8 to 9 in the evening, during which programs available for the whole family are aired. After 9 P.M. there are presumably fewer children watching television. Clearly, more voluntary efforts can be made in this area. It is certainly possible to imaginatively design programs with less observable violence but that are still appealing to mass audiences. The popularity of shows that avoid overt physical violence, such as "All in the Family," illustrates the feasibility of this. However, it is easier for the producers to use gratuitous violence, rather than artistic creativity, as a formula for financial success.

Social Reform

Much of the conflict in American society springs from the frustration and deprivation experienced by groups who feel they possess an inequitable share of the social and economic resources. Many of the major disruptions in our history represent collective efforts to correct perceived wrongs—the draft riots of the Civil War, the race riots in the early part of this century, the ghetto riots of the 1960s, the student demonstrations of the 1960s, and the terrorism of the 1970s. Any program to deal effec-

tively with this conflict and violence must focus on efforts at social reform—changes in those social conditions that cause the violence.

For example, while it took much time and caused much pain and sorrow, labor strife in our country has been reduced by overcoming some of the major inequities. Workers' share of economic resources is greater today than it was before widespread collective bargaining. American workers have a lifestyle that is the envy of most other peoples of the world. Basic structural changes in the relationship between worker and employer were necessary for these improvements to occur. Through various changes, workers have gained greater control over working conditions and participate to some degree in the decision-making process. The ability to organize, bargain collectively, and legally strike are changes that an industrialist of a century ago would have viewed as presaging the impending downfall of the American economic order. Today, these have become institutionalized means of resolving conflict. While conflict still exists, the struggle over scarce resources takes a violent form much less frequently.

It would seem that any attempt to reduce conflict in America must deal with the discrimination, deprivation, and oppression that is frequently the basic cause of that strife. Unfortunately, there is a strong, and understandable, tendency to be primarily concerned with controlling the violence. If the violence is not controlled, of course, it may seriously disrupt society; yet, once controlled, any impetus for social reform (that is, the violence) is also gone! Money spent on equipment and personnel to cope with future riots siphons off funds that could be used instead to deal with the basic problems.

An important barrier to much social reform is the fact that the basic problem is often not something that can be approached with the infusion of large sums of money. For example, labor strife, while it certainly concerns economic issues, involves more basic values—the role of employer and worker in relation to one another and the issue of control over the conditions of work. Money alone would not solve this problem.

A final difficulty in dealing with these basic structural causes of social conflict is that we may not be aware of what they are, or there may be bitter controversy over their nature. For example, in analyzing the labor conflict or the ghetto riots, one who supports existing societal arrangements might see the core problem as a lack of access by individuals to the means of achieving an acceptable lifestyle. The most promising solution is to give workers, blacks, or any other deprived group access to the training or education necessary to improve themselves. If they fail, this defender of the status quo would argue, it is their own fault because they had been given the opportunity to succeed; the social and economic structure itself is basically equitable and sound.

At the other extreme, a radical might argue that such inequities are an inevitable part of a capitalist economic system which needs subordinate groups to serve as a cheap source of labor to support the affluent lifestyle of the wealthy. Inequities can be eliminated, the radical would argue, only if basic structural rearrangements are made — the elimination of a capitalist economic system and a significant redistribution of wealth to the poor. The student undoubtedly has his or her own ideas on these matters. However, these disagreements over the sources of conflict and effective solutions make it difficult to develop coordinated long-range programs to attack the causes of the problems.

Preventing War

Preventing wars would have a profound impact on social problems. Not only is war a social problem itself, but it can, as we have seen, be an important factor in creating many other social problems. What are the prospects for preventing war? The prevention of war is not a goal that one finally achieves; rather, it is a process that must be worked on continuously. The following are some ways in which nations today strive to avoid war.

Foreign Policy

The foreign policy of any nation is oriented toward the pursuit of the interests of that nation. In the nuclear age, one major goal of United States foreign policy has been to avoid a nuclear catastrophe while at the same time retaining our

"NOW, ALL THOSE IN FAVOR OF PEACE..."

position of military and political power in the world. A cornerstone of this effort has been former Secretary of State John Foster Dulles's policy of **massive retaliation** — the capability of inflicting debilitating damages on an enemy in response to their attack.[66] Dulles argued that aggression would be deterred if the aggressor were convinced that he would suffer damages far more costly than what he might expect to gain from his aggression. Dulles claimed that the existence of the *threat* would serve as an effective deterrent. If the threat were convincing (if the enemy believed it), then it would never have to be used. When two or more world powers develop extensive nuclear capabilities, as is the case today, this strategy takes a new form — each nation has the ability to destroy the other, but not before the attacked nation could retaliate sufficiently to destroy the aggressor. Many political and military leaders feel that this mutual destructive capacity serves as a **balance of power** — each side is restrained from attacking the other because of the costs involved — and so a major nuclear holocaust is avoided.

Our foreign policy has therefore been designed to prevent war *by being prepared for war*. Has it worked? Since there has not been a nuclear war, one might argue that it has. Yet we may have avoided nuclear war for other reasons. In addition, we have not prevented other wars, such as the limited conventional wars in Korea and Vietnam. While some have argued that these wars served as a safety valve that enabled us to avoid nuclear war by achieving our goals with a limited war, these conflicts, especially Vietnam, had within them the seeds of a nuclear holocaust. For example, there were strong pressures in the United States to use tactical nuclear weapons in the Vietnam conflict. If this had been done, the war might have escalated into a nuclear battle between the major powers. Another problem with a foreign policy based on the maintenance of a massive nuclear capability is the potential of accidentally unleashing a nuclear war. While the probability may be remote, it is real, and the destruction would be the same.

Arms Limitations and Disarmament

The leaders of the major nations extol the virtues of disarmament — but would accept disarmament only if they could feel secure that no other nation would take advantage of their lack of weaponry. This legitimate concern for the security of their nations has been one of the major stumbling blocks to disarmament or the limitation of arms. The progress of the world toward this goal has been meager — some would say nil. However, there has been some minor progress in the area of arms limitations. The Partial Nuclear Test Ban Treaty of 1963 bans the testing of nuclear weapons in the atmosphere, although underground testing is permitted. (Some nations, such as China and France, have continued atmospheric testing.) There has also been an agreement to prohibit nuclear testing in outer space and in the oceans. After years of negotiation, the Strategic Arms Limitation Talks (SALT) finally bore fruit, however meager, in 1972 and 1979 with agreement between the United States and the Soviet Union to limit the number of ballistic missiles and defensive antiballistic missiles in both countries. While hailed by our government as a major breakthrough, the SALT agreements

While many nations give verbal support to the goal of arms limitation, no nation is willing to divest itself of its weapons as long as another nation has the capability to attack it.

have not seriously hindered either nation's ability to continue stockpiling weapons.

If little has been achieved in terms of arms limitations, there has been no progress toward the larger goal of total disarmament. The major stumbling block, of course, is how to ensure that other nations have in fact divested themselves of their weapons. No mutually acceptable method of verification has been developed. Naturally, no nation will divest itself of its weapons until it is completely sure that no other nation has the capability to attack. The likelihood of developing some acceptable assurances in the foreseeable future seems small.

The United States and the Soviet Union, as the two major nuclear powers, have been the focal point of arms limitations talks. Some other nations have simply refused to participate. As nuclear weapons proliferate among smaller nations, arms limitation agreements between the major powers will be meaningless unless these others participate. Some smaller nations seem to be intent on stockpiling sophisticated weaponry as a means of protecting themselves from aggression and settling border disputes. It seems improbable that all these nations will participate in any worldwide arms limitation or disarmament program.

International Organization

Since the prospect of preventing war through the limitation or elimination of weapons seems rather bleak, what other options are available? Some have argued that, since individual nations will continue to view war as a means of pursuing their own national interests, the only alternative is some extra-national organization that takes into consideration the common long-term interests of all nations rather than simply the short-term goals of an individual nation.[67] There have been numerous attempts to establish international bodies to perform various functions. The League of Nations following World War I dealt effectively with a variety of social issues, such as world health, the narcotics trade, and agricultural improvements. However, it was almost totally ineffective in preventing international conflict.

The United Nations, established at the end of World War II, has also been quite successful in dealing with many social, environmental, and economic issues around the world. It has also helped settle some minor international conflicts and reduce tensions through its peacekeeping force. However, its overall success in preventing war is not much better than that of the older League. The major stumbling block to the effectiveness of any such organization is the willingness of nations to surrender any sovereignty—and especially their right to use force against another nation—to some international body. Nations insist on retaining these powers for themselves. In most cases, nations will support the UN if it is in their interests to do so and ignore it when the UN opposes their actions.

Whether nations will ever surrender their sovereignty to an international body is difficult to say. Proponents feel that such worldwide political bodies are the next stage in the evolution of human political structures that have already developed from family and clan-based organizations to larger units such as nation-states. Others feel that some current developments may lead nations to see it to their own advantage to give up at least some of their sovereignty. For example, as nuclear weapons are acquired by more and more nations, the danger of some nation initiating a nuclear holocaust increases. In such a situation, the control of these weapons by an international body may be viewed more positively. Opponents of international organizations feel that this is utopian wishful thinking that ignores a primary concern for self-interest. In either event, for the foreseeable future, it is unlikely that international organizations will be capable of preventing most wars.

CONCLUSION

Most people view conflict, especially in its violent forms, as undesirable. Yet, it seems to be an intractable problem that has been with us for much of human history. As we have seen, some have even proposed that human beings are naturally violent—that we have some biological drive toward violence or aggression. This is not a very optimistic view, but it is also a view that is strongly contested by many social scientists. We have presented throughout this chapter some of the social mechanisms which encourage or inhibit violence and conflict. It will be useful to conclude with a brief review of the problem from the theoretical perspectives.

From the functionalist perspective, social conflict can have important positive consequences for society. Yet, when considering solutions to the problem, we must consider the conditions under which the positive outcomes are preferable to its negative effects. Your position on this, of course, will depend on your position in society and the goals that you are trying to achieve. There will always be disagreement over the value of different manifestations of conflict. However, not all aspects of conflict situations are beyond our control. There are some conflict situations that we can influence. For example, we have discussed mechanisms, such as crowd control, that we can use to limit the *intensity* of violence. For conflict becomes seriously threatening to society only when it becomes very intense and destructive. Furthermore, we have seen attempts, such as the limitations of media violence, to eliminate some of the *sources* of conflict. While there is still much to be done, our developing knowledge of the causes of intergroup conflict should result in more successful efforts at such intervention in the future. Finally, we have examined efforts, such as arms limitation talks and labor union negotiations, that change the *form* of conflict. While conflict may be inevitable, violence against people and the destruction of property are not. Groups can struggle over the distribution of scarce resources within a framework that defines overt violence as illegitimate (or to be used only under extreme conditions). In this way, many of the socially threatening aspects of human conflict can be removed.

According to the conflict perspective, some degree of conflict is an inevitable accompaniment of human social arrangements. The discussion in this chapter has certainly provided substantiation for this position. However, even the conflict theorist makes distinctions regarding the extent and destructiveness of conflict. Conflict need not be violent, nor need it be destructive in terms of human life or property. Yet, we must recognize that the elimination of violence does not eliminate conflict. Thus, the lack of racial violence during some periods in our history did not signify a lack of conflict (although many people believed this to be the case). There was a struggle between racial groups over scarce resources, but it was largely nonviolent because blacks and other racial minorities had few resources with which to effectively wage a violent struggle. The ghetto riots of the 1960s should not be seen as newly-emerging conflict but rather as a continuing conflict that changed its form from nonviolent to violent. So, from the conflict perspective, we realize that conflict in some form may be inevitable. Because of this, we should evaluate solutions in terms of the extent to which they deal with the real source of conflict, rather than simply encouraging a change in form.

GLOSSARY TERMS

Balance of power
Civil disorder
Commodity riot
Communal riot
Conflict
Ethology

Frustration
Gross National Product (GNP)
Insurrection
Massive retaliation
Modeling
Relative deprivation

Sociobiology
Stereotype
Subculture of violence
Terrorism
Violence

REFERENCES

[1] See Robert Conot, *Rivers of Blood, Years of Darkness* (New York: Bantam Books, 1967), and James W. Button, *Black Violence: Political Impact of the 1960s Riots* (Princeton, N.J.: Princeton University Press, 1978).

[2] Federal Bureau of Investigation, *Uniform Crime Reports: 1977* (Washington, D. C.: U.S. Government Printing Office, 1978), pp. 6, 290, 292.

[3] See G. Thayer, *The War Business: The International Trade in Armaments* (New York: Simon and Schuster, 1969), and Jonathon Kandell, "European Arms Exports Growing," *New York Times* (April 4, 1978), Section 1, p. 1.

[4] James W. Vander Zanden, *Social Psychology* (New York: Random House, 1977), p. 247.

[5] See Richard Maxwell Brown, "Historical Patterns of Violence in America," in Hugh Davis Graham and Ted Robert Gurr, eds., *The History of Violence in America* (New York: Frederick A. Praeger, 1969), pp. 45–83.

[6] Morris Janowitz, "Patterns of Collective Racial Violence," in Graham and Gurr, eds., *The History of Violence in America*, pp. 412–443.

[7] Philip Taft and Philip Ross, "American Labor Violence: Its Causes, Character, and Outcome," in Graham and Gurr, eds., *The History of Violence in America*, pp. 281–395.

[8] See H. M. Caudill, "American Serfdom: The Backward Coal Industry," *Atlantic Monthly* 241 (June 1978), pp. 35–41, and W. Kroger, "Coal Strike: An Expensive Lesson," *Nation's Business* 66 (April 1978), pp. 48–49.

[9] Brown, "Historical Patterns of Violence in America," pp. 45–83.

[10] Ibid., p. 47.

[11] James C. Davies, "The J-Curve of Rising and Declining Satisfactions as a Cause of Some Great Revolutions and a Contained Rebellion," in Graham and Gurr, eds., *The History of Violence in America*, p. 554.

[12] James C. Davies, "Toward a Theory of Revolution," *American Sociological Review* 27 (February 1962), pp. 5–19.

[13] Les Payne and Tim Findley, *The Life and Death of the SLA* (New York: Ballantine Books, 1976).

[14] Dena Kleiman, "The Potential for Urban Terror Is Always There," *New York Times* (March 13, 1977), Section E, p. 3.

[15] Irving Louis Horowitz, "Transnational Terrorism, Civil Liberties, and Social Science," in Yonah Alexander and Seymour Maxwell Finger, eds., *Terrorism: Interdisciplinary Perspectives* (New York: The John Jay Press, 1977), p. 283.

[16] Robert A. Liston, *Terrorism* (New York: Thomas Nelson, 1977), p. 44.

[17] See Albert Perry, *Terrorism from Robespierre to Arafat* (New York: The Vanguard Press, 1976).

[18] Horowitz, "Transnational Terrorism, Civil Liberties, and Social Science," p. 296.

[19] J. David Singer and Melvin Small, *The Wages of War, 1816–1965: A Statistical Handbook* (New York: John Wiley & Sons, 1972).

[20] See Charles Bateson, *The War With Japan: A Concise History* (East Lansing, Mich.: Michigan State University Press, 1968), and A. J. Ryder, *Twentieth Century Germany: From Bismarck to Brandt* (New York: Columbia University Press, 1973).

[21] See Talcott Parsons et al., *Theories of Society,* vol. 1 (New York: The Free Press, 1961), and Neil J. Smelser, *Theory of Collective Behavior* (New York: The Free Press, 1963).

[22] Lewis Coser, *The Functions of Social Conflict* (New York: The Free Press, 1956), and Lewis Coser, *Continuities in the Study of Social Conflict* (New York: The Free Press, 1968).

[23] See Ralf Dahrendorf, *Class and Class Conflict in Industrial Society* (Stanford, Calif.: Stanford University Press, 1959), and Anthony Oberschall, *Social Conflict and Social Movements* (Englewood Cliffs, N.J.: Prentice-Hall, 1973), pp. 30–84.

[24] See Tamotsu Shibutani, *Society and Personality* (Englewood Cliffs, N.J.: Prentice-Hall, 1961), pp. 139–178.

[25] Niko Tinbergen, "The Curious Behavior in the Stickleback," in *Twentieth Century Bestiary* (New York: Simon and Schuster, 1955).

[26] Robert Ardrey, *The Territorial Imperative* (New York: Atheneum, 1967).

[27] See Edmund O. Wilson, *Sociobiology: The New Synthesis* (Cambridge, Mass.: Harvard University Press, 1975); David P. Barash, *Sociobiology and Behavior* (New York: Elsevier, 1977); and T. H. Clutton-Brock and Paul H. Harvey, eds., *Readings in Sociobiology* (San Francisco: W. H. Freeman and Co., 1978).

[28] Robert Ardrey, *The Social Contract* (New York: Atheneum, 1970).

[29] See Barash, *Sociobiology and Behavior,* pp. 35–69.

[30] John Dollard et al., *Frustration and Aggression* (New Haven: Yale University Press, 1939), and Klaus R. Scherer, Ronald P. Abeles, and Claude S. Fischer, *Human Aggression and Conflict* (Englewood Cliffs, N.J.: Prentice-Hall, 1975), pp. 56–63.

[31] See Robert K. Merton and Alice S. Kitt, "Contributions to the Theory of Reference Group Behavior," in Robert K. Merton and Paul F. Lazarsfeld, eds., *Continuities in Social Research* (New York: The Free Press, 1950), pp. 40–105; W. G. Runciman, *Relative Deprivation and Social Justice* (Berkeley: University of California Press, 1966); and Ted Robert Gurr, *Why Men Rebel* (Princeton, N.J.: Princeton University Press, 1970).

[32] See Leonard Berkowitz, "The Study of Urban Violence: Some Implications of Laboratory Studies of Frustration and

Aggression,'' in James Chowning Davies, ed., *When Men Revolt and Why* (New York: The Free Press, 1971), pp. 182–187.

[33] Albert Bandura, ''Social Learning Analysis of Aggression,'' in Emilio Ribes-Inesta and Albert Bandura, eds., *Analysis of Delinquency and Aggression* (New York: John Wiley & Sons, 1976), pp. 203–232.

[34] R. R. Sears, E. E. Maccoby, and H. Levin, *Patterns of Child Rearing* (New York: Harper & Row, 1957), p. 266.

[35] Bandura, ''Social Learning Analysis of Aggression.''

[36] See David L. Lange, Robert K. Baker, and Sandra J. Ball, *Mass Media and Violence: Report to the National Commission on the Causes and Prevention of Violence* (Washington, D.C.: U.S. Government Printing Office, 1969), and Dennis Howitt and Guy Cumberbatch, *Mass Media, Violence, and Society* (New York: John Wiley & Sons, 1975).

[37] S. Feshbach and R. Singer, *Television and Aggression: An Experimental Field Study* (San Francisco: Jossey-Bass, 1971).

[38] T. M. Tomlinson, ''The Development of a Riot Ideology Among Urban Negroes,'' *American Behavioral Scientist* 2 (March 1968), pp. 27–31.

[39] See Andrew F. Henry and James F. Short, Jr., *Suicide and Homicide* (New York: The Free Press, 1954); Smelser, *Theory of Collective Behavior*, pp. 47–67; and Robert K. Merton, *Social Theory and Social Structure*, rev. ed. (New York: The Free Press, 1957), pp. 131–160.

[40] Cited in St. Clair Drake, ''What is 'Natural' Today Need Not be Natural Tomorrow,'' *New York Times Magazine* (April 28, 1968), p. 24.

[41] Marvin E. Wolfgang and Franco Ferracuti, *The Subculture of Violence: Towards an Integrated Theory in Criminology* (London: Tavistock, 1967).

[42] See Sandra J. Ball-Rokeach, ''Values and Violence: A Test of the Subculture of Violence Thesis,'' *American Sociological Review* 38 (December 1973), pp. 736–749; Howard S. Erlanger, ''The Empirical Status of the Subculture of Violence Thesis,'' *Social Problems* 22 (December 1974), pp. 280–292; and James F. O'Connor and Alan Lizotte, ''The 'Southern Subculture of Violence' Thesis and Patterns of Gun Ownership,'' *Social Problems* 25 (April 1978), pp. 420–429.

[43] William A. Gamson and James McEvoy, ''Police Violence and Its Public Support,'' in James F. Short, Jr., and Marvin Wolfgang, eds., *Collective Violence* (Chicago: Aldine-Atherton, 1972), pp. 329–342.

[44] Ibid., p. 342.

[45] See Rodney Stark, *Police Riots* (Belmont, Calif.: Wadsworth, 1972).

[46] Ibid., p. 116.

[47] See Georg Simmel, *Conflict and the Web of Group Affiliations* (New York: The Free Press, 1955), and Coser, *The Functions of Social Conflict*.

[48] John C. Gunn, *Violence* (New York: Frederick A. Praeger, 1973).

[49] Gary A. Kreps, ''Change in Crisis-Relevant Organizations: Police Departments and Civil Disturbances,'' *American Behavioral Scientist* 16 (January-February 1973), pp. 356–357.

[50] Alexis deTocqueville, *Democracy in America,* vol. 2 (New York: Vintage Books, 1954), p. 294.

[51] Michael Stohl, *War and Domestic Political Violence: The American Capacity for Repression and Reaction* (Beverly Hills: Sage Publications, 1976).

[52] Robin Brooks, ''Domestic Violence and American Wars: A Historical Interpretation,'' in Graham and Gurr, *The History of Violence in America*, pp. 529–549.

[53] Ibid.

[54] See Robert B. Smith, ''Rebellion and Repression and the Vietnam War,'' in Short and Wolfgang, *Collective Violence*, pp. 224–235.

[55] Robert Warren Stevens, *Vain Hopes, Grim Realities: The Economic Consequences of the Vietnam War* (New York: New Viewpoints, 1976), p. 14.

[56] Ibid., and Bruce Russett, ''Who Pays for Defense?'' *American Political Science Review* 63 (June 1969), pp. 412–426.

[57] Ibid., and Jerry Hollenhorst and Gary Ault, ''An Alternative Answer to: Who Pays for Defense?'' *American Political Science Review* 65 (September 1971), pp. 760–763.

[58] Stevens, *Vain Hopes, Grim Realities*, p. 13.

[59] Bruce M. Russett, ''The Revolt of the Masses: Public Opinion on Military Expenditures,'' in John P. Lovell and Philip S. Kronenberg, eds., *New Civil-Military Relations: The Agonies of Adjustment to Post-Vietnam Realities* (New Brunswick, N.J.: TransAction Books, 1974), p. 83.

[60] Dane Archer and Rosemary Gartner, ''Violent Acts and Violent Times: A Comparative Approach to Postwar Homicide Rates,'' *American Sociological Review* 41 (December 1976), pp. 937–963.

[61] Ibid., p. 954.

[62] Douglas R. Murray, ''Handguns, Gun Control Laws and Firearm Violence,'' *Social Problems* 23 (October 1975), pp. 81–92.

[63] Robert Sherrill, *The Saturday Night Special* (New York: Penguin Books, 1973).

[64] National Commission on the Causes and Prevention of Violence, *Firearms and Violence in American Life* (Washington, D.C.: U.S. Government Printing Office, 1969).

[65] See Stark, *Police Riots*.

[66] John Foster Dulles, ''Police For Security and Peace,'' *Foreign Affairs* 32 (April 1954), pp. 353–364.

[67] See Donald A. Wells, *The War Myth* (New York: Pegasus, 1967).

SUGGESTED READINGS

Richard J. Barnet, *Roots of War* (Baltimore: Penguin Books, 1972).
An analysis of some of the reasons why America has been involved in various wars over the past few decades. The book focuses especially on how government bureaucracies and decision making lead to war.

Lewis Coser, *The Functions of Social Conflict* (New York: The Free Press, 1956).
A classic statement concerning the positive functions that conflict can perform for groups.

Alice Ross Gold et al., *Fists and Flowers: A Social Psychological Interpretation of Student Dissent* (New York: Academic Press, 1976).
A comprehensive investigation of one important source of intergroup conflict in America: the dissent among college students.

Hugh Davis Graham and Ted Robert Gurr, eds., *The History of Violence in America: Historical and Comparative Perspectives* (New York: Frederick A. Praeger, 1969).
A recent, and important, source of information about intergroup conflict throughout American history. This book offers an analysis of the nature and extent of violence in America.

Ted Robert Gurr, *Why Men Rebel* (Princeton, N.J.: Princeton University Press, 1970).
A presentation of the conditions under which people are likely to organize and support rebellion. This book focuses heavily on the role of relative deprivation in rebellion.

Rodney Stark, *Police Riots* (Belmont, Calif.: Wadsworth, 1972).
A very readable discussion of why police themselves in some cases engage in riots. This book offers a basis for understanding why confrontations between police and blacks or students in the 1960s often erupted into violence.

Robert Warren Stevens, *Vain Hopes, Grim Realities: The Economic Consequences of the Vietnam War* (New York: New Viewpoints, 1976). An eye-opening account of some of the costs of war that are not normally considered when the decision to wage war is made.

Surgeon General's Scientific Advisory Committee on Television and Social Behavior, *Television and Growing Up: The Impact of Televised Violence* (Washington, D.C.: U.S. Government Printing Office, 1972).
An important early summary of the research findings related to the effect of television on violence and aggression. This topic continues to be highly controversial.

Questions
for Discussion

1. America has had its share of conflict and violence. What major forms has this conflict taken? What implications has this conflict had for social change in America?

2. The functionalist perspective places heavy emphasis on order, stability, and continuity in society. Under what conditions, and in what ways, might conflict or violence enhance the achievement of an orderly and stable social system? When would conflict and violence become detrimental to the system?

3. Choose a particular form of conflict in American history (e.g. racial strife or labor conflict). From the conflict perspective, analyze that conflict in terms of which interest groups benefit from the conflict and for which groups the conflict is a social problem.

4. The interactionist perspective emphasizes the importance of shared meaning and social consensus. In what ways have particular examples of conflict in American history threatened the ability of groups to achieve shared meaning and consensus? How might this have been avoided?

5. Is violence and aggression on the part of human beings the result of cultural learning or biological inclination? How might these two disparate views of the source of human aggression be reconciled?

6. The functionalist perspective emphasizes the extent to which society is a system in which changes in one part affect other parts. What consequences does war have for American society in the area of political turmoil? Economic change? Criminal behavior? How might these detrimental consequences be avoided?

7. What efforts are currently being made in American society to prevent the onset of violent activities? Are they effective? How might they be made more effective?

8. Describe the current attempts by the world community to prevent the occurrence of war. How successful have these attempts been? What obstacles stand in the way of further gains in efforts to prevent wars?

PART FIVE

Deviant Behavior

CHAPTER 15
Deviant Behavior

DEVIANCE IN AMERICAN HISTORY
Absolutist. Legalist. Relativist.

DEVIANT BEHAVIOR AS A SOCIAL PROBLEM
The Functionalist Perspective. The Conflict Perspective.
The Interactionist Perspective.

SOURCES OF DEVIANT BEHAVIOR
Deviance and Social Structure. Deviance and Differential
Association. Deviance and Labeling.

HOMOSEXUALITY
Theories of Homosexuality. Patterns of Homosexuality.
Homosexuality as a Social Problem.

PROSTITUTION
The Extent of Prostitution. Becoming a Prostitute.
Functions of Prostitution. Problems and Exploitation.

PORNOGRAPHY
Pornography and the Law. The Scientific Evidence.

VIOLENCE IN THE FAMILY
Child Abuse. Spouse Abuse.

ABORTION
The Legal Status of Abortion. The Abortion Controversy.

SUICIDE
Explanations of Suicide. The Extent of Suicide. Suicide
Prevention.

CONCLUSION

The following five accounts illustrate some different faces of deviant behavior:

1. The voters of Dade County, Florida overwhelmingly (by a 69 to 31 percent margin) rejected an ordinance banning discrimination against homosexuals in housing and employment. Anita Bryant (founder of the Save Our Children organization) vowed that she was going to continue her efforts against a lifestyle that she considered *immoral:* "The more we let violence and homosexuality become the norm . . . the more we'll become such a sick nation that the Communists won't have to take us over—we'll just give up."[1]

2. Approximately 150 members of at least two large youth gangs carried out a well-organized attack on about 8000 people attending a rock concert in downtown Detroit. The youths freely robbed, raped, and beat concertgoers while the police, who were not prepared to handle such an attack, could do little to stop the violence.[2] The safety of the *property and person* of the concertgoers in Detroit was in danger.

3. For a few months, Professor Smith (chairman of the English department at a major university) exhibited fluctuations in mood that affected the performance of his duties and the morale of his department. At a faculty meeting, for example, he kept straying from the agenda and for no apparent reason dismissed the meeting with the closing remark that his authority was being "undermined by a bunch of paranoids preoccupied with political intrigue."[3] Professor Smith's behavior was highly *disruptive* of the normal day-to-day social interaction of his department and university.

4. "Some of these [alcoholics] are so loaded that they will fall and break their skull if you don't lock them up. Half of these guys have no place to stay except in a dingy heap. They are better off in jail . . ."[4] These norm violators are *harming themselves* more than they are anyone else.

5. In a clockwork guerrilla raid against three separate buildings in the nation's capital, 12 members of the small Hanafi Muslim sect took 134 hostages, shot one man to death, and stabbed or beat 19 others. Why? Apparently because they wanted to avenge the 1973 mass murder of seven of their members and to protest the movie *Muhammad*

Messenger of God, which they considered sacrilegious in its portrayal of Muhammad.[5] These terrorist activities not only threatened the property and lives of the hostages, but they *threatened the well-being of the community* and of the nation as well.

All of the foregoing are examples of *deviance—* socially disapproved behavior that exceeds the limits of community tolerance and for which, if detected, there is a high probability that the "deviant" will be punished. Acts defined as deviant are usually characterized as one or more of the following: *immoral* (e.g. homosexuality), *dangerous to people or property* (e.g. acts of interpersonal violence), *disruptive* of social interaction (e.g. bad manners or mental illness), *harmful to the deviant* (e.g. alcoholism or drug abuse), *harmful to the community* (e.g. political terrorism). Deviant behavior exists because people define it as such and, in many instances, because it is genuinely threatening to the well-being of the community and society as well as to particular individuals and groups.

In the remaining chapters of this book, we will be concerned with various forms of deviant behavior. In this chapter, we will focus on understanding the sources of deviant behavior as well as on certain types of deviance—prostitution, pornography, homosexuality, suicide, abortion, and violence in the family. In later chapters, we will turn our attention to crime, juvenile delinquency, various types of substance abuse, and some contemporary deviant lifestyles. First, however, we will investigate the views of deviant behavior that have figured prominently at different times in American society.

DEVIANCE IN AMERICAN HISTORY

It is often said of art and literature that "beauty is in the eye of the beholder"—each person judges for him- or herself whether something is beautiful. Similarly, when speaking of deviant behavior we might ask, Is deviance in the mind of the beholder? Is deviance what any person judges it to be? Or, are there specific types of behavior that are deviant? It is these issues that we will examine in this and the following section. We can begin by examining the different views of deviance that have played a prominent role in American history: the absolutist, the legalist, and the relativist views.[6]

Absolutist

The absolutist view of deviance can be traced back to the founding of our nation, and it is still quite popular today. **According to adherents of the *absolutist* school of thought, there are two clearly discernible categories into which human actions can be classified: good and evil.** Any behavior is either good or evil on the basis of universal standards that can be applied to all people at all times. Behavior is evil, and therefore deviant, because it violates these absolute standards. One example of absolutist standards that are important in our own history are the Ten Commandments of the Judeo-Christian tradition. Followers of this tradition believe that these commandments are principles that transcend time and place, person and circumstances. They are immutable laws given to mankind by God Himself.

The Puritans who settled the New England colonies during the early 1600s were moral absolutists. They believed that they possessed the absolute truth insofar as God had revealed it to man. According to historian David Rothman, American colonial society was founded on

the premise that the existing social order had divine approbation, that its form was not accidental or fortuitous, but providential. A higher design made some men rich, eminent, and powerful, and others low, mean, and in subjection.[7]

Deviant behavior was wrong because it contradicted this divinely approved social order. The Puritans came to the New World with the explicit goal of building the perfect social order — literally "heaven on earth" — based on the truth as stated in the Holy Bible. As a result of their moral absolutism, the Puritans were extremely intolerant of people whose moral principles and behavior differed from their own. They dealt rather harshly with "deviants" such as the Quakers, many of whom were tried for religious heresy and summarily imprisoned or hanged. In addition, the Puritans instituted a systematic program to exterminate some of the Native Americans who they were convinced

were "imps of the devil" and a threat to civilized man and God's own plan.[8]

Even though the colonists were repelled by many forms of deviant behavior, they were not optimistic that such behavior could be eliminated. Their sense of deviance as sin and their belief that corruption was a part of the imperfect nature of human beings led them to accept the inevitability of deviant behavior. They turned to family, church, and the network of community relationships as the bulwark against these evils. If these institutions were properly organized, deviant behavior would be reduced and a degree of stability might be achieved in a community. Because these early Puritan colonists and their descendants were an extremely influential group in American life, the moral absolutism of the Puritans has had a significant impact on contemporary views of deviance; their beliefs continue to pervade many of our mores and many of our legal principles as well.

Legalist

Legalists define deviance somewhat differently. Although an act may be a sin from the perspective of the Ten Commandments or from that of some other moral tradition, it is not considered a form of deviance requiring the application of social control by the state unless there is some secular law prohibiting it. In other words, **an act considered immoral may not necessarily be illegal.** For example, lying is forbidden by the Judeo-Christian commandments; however, lying in most contexts is not illegal.

The founders of the Constitution of the United States were legalists. They believed that justice and order should be maintained through the legal structure of the state. They were wary of the kinds of abuses of individual freedom that may arise when one takes an absolutist view — especially the tendency of one group to dominate society and thereby force members of other groups to adopt their values or, at least, to accept them passively. As a means of guaranteeing individual freedom and group diversity, certain legal protections were built into the Constitution: the Bill of Rights, the separation of powers between the three branches of the federal government, and the separation of states' rights from federal prerogatives.

Implicit in the legalist approach is the idea that passing a law prohibiting a deviant act and legal punishments for convicted deviants is the most effective means of deterring deviance. The legalist view has existed throughout American history, but in the past century it has come to dominate the official means of dealing with deviance. As a consequence, many people today view legal means as the most effective ways of solving social problems. We have witnessed a proliferation of laws in the United States covering almost every aspect of social life. Many deviant acts that were previously dealt with through informal mechanisms—such as family discipline, ostracism, or ridicule by one's peers—now fall within the purview of the law. In fact, many scholars and legal experts believe that we have initiated an era of *overlegalization*. **By *overlegalization* is meant the naive use, or misuse, of legal sanctions to deal with problems in cases in which other means, such as family socialization or community sanctions, would be more effective and appropriate.**[9] For example, behaviors such as drunkenness, truancy, or running away from home were once dealt with in an informal fashion—the culprit faced the wrath of friends and family or possibly public humiliation. Although these actions offended the absolutist's sense of morally appropriate behavior, there was little concern with whether a legal offense had been committed. We have tried to cope with these problems through the legal structure—by bringing the perpetrator before the law for punishment or rehabilitation. Many social scientists have begun to realize that some of these problems might more appropriately be dealt with informally rather than legally.

The absolutist and legalist views of deviance are not necessarily contradictory. In fact, a legalist view may simply incorporate absolutist standards into a set of laws. To a large extent, the American legal structure is based on our Judeo-Christian religious tradition. For example, legal prohibitions against homosexuality, prostitution, vagrancy, public drunkenness, and the like, reflect in part absolutist religious and moral principles that view these behaviors as inherently evil and reprehensible. One of the continuing tensions in the American legal structure is how to incorporate some moral principles into law while at the same time accommodating the extreme diversity in lifestyles that exists in America. Partly because of this tension, there has been a growing appreciation of the third, or relativist, view of deviance.

Relativist

From the *relativist* perspective, no human act can be judged unless it is first placed within the context of the culture or subculture in which it occurs. Whether an act is deviant must be evaluated not in terms of some allegedly universal criteria, but in terms of its meaning for the people for whom it has consequences and who define and enforce their group's norms. However, relativists do not imply that "anything goes." They are keenly aware that all groups have systems of norms that are taken very seriously by group members—regardless how incomprehensible they may seem to outsiders. For example, when an Eskimo family leaves an aging grandmother alone in the wilderness to die in order to preserve its dwindling food supply for the "productive" members of the group, this seemingly heartless act (according to our standards) is defined by the family as a necessary and, perhaps, honorable thing to do. From the perspective of the normative relativists, an act is neither intrinsically good nor inherently evil, but should be judged only within its cultural context. For the relativist, then, deviance is not an objective condition but a matter of social definition. It is a subjectively defined state that is a function of the values and interests of the group in which the act takes place.

Prior to this century, few people in America accepted this relativist view of deviance. People believed that an act could be determined to be deviant according to some objective (either absolute or legal) standards. The approach of cultural relativism to the study of deviant behavior is largely a product of twentieth-century social science, especially cultural anthropology. Through anthropo-

MORALITY...THEN

...AND NOW

CONCEIVED BY: MAX BRANDEL.   ARTIST: PAUL COKER, JR.

logical reports about other cultures, we have become aware of the wide range of human behaviors that are viewed as acceptable and desirable in other cultures. The moral and legal codes of societies other than our own are extremely difficult to understand from an absolutist or legalistic point of view.[10] Cultural relativism provides an approach that helps make sense out of the tremendous diversity of moral traditions and customs. This approach to deviance is predominant among social scientists today and clearly separates the view of the scientific community from adherents of the absolutist and legalistic approaches.

The three sociological perspectives used in this text are relativist in that they consider the cultural context to be important in the study of deviance. (The Marxian branch of the conflict perspective is an exception.) This strong emphasis on cultural relativity is one of the major factors differentiating

sociological analyses of deviance as a social problem from other approaches.

DEVIANT BEHAVIOR AS A SOCIAL PROBLEM

As you will recall, the functional, conflict, and interactionist perspectives view society and the nature of social bonds differently. This affects their definitions of social problems, including the problem of deviance, as well as the types of solutions that will be considered feasible by adherents of the perspectives. The major assumptions of each perspective regarding the law, deviance, and solutions to deviant behavior have been outlined in Table 15.1.

The Functionalist Perspective

From the functional perspective, society is a system made up of interdependent parts such as institutions, organizations, and groups. Something that affects one part of the system has implications for every other part. Social order is possible because the members of society share the same norms, values, and perspectives. Because people are dependent on one another, they tend to share fundamental interests. **From the functional perspective, deviant behavior results from structural flaws within the society and from the lack of adequate socialization or adequate opportunity to act in accord with socially approved norms.**[11]

In order to understand more clearly the functionalist perspective on deviance, it is important to differentiate between the terms *dysfunction* and *deviance*. A ***dysfunctional*** act or condition is one that actually threatens the well-being of the social order whether people recognize it or not. Such an act or condition may be inherently detrimental to the well-being of society and thereby entail a social problem yet not be defined as deviant by influential groups in that society. A deviant act, on the other hand, is deviant because a particular group defines it as such—irrespective of how dangerous it may be to the well-being of society. An act may be defined

TABLE 15.1
Sociological Perspectives on Deviant Behavior

	FUNCTIONALIST	CONFLICT	INTERACTIONIST
LAW	Codification of widely shared values for the protection of people and property and the maintenance of social order.	*Non-Marxian:* Codification of values essential to the repression of human selfishness and the preservation of social order. *Marxian:* Codification of powerful groups' values in order to enhance their own interests.	Codification of group values for a variety of purposes.
DEVIANCE	Behavior that violates widely shared social norms. Deviant behavior results from structural flaws in the society and from inadequate socialization and/or inadequate opportunity.	*Non-Marxian:* Behavior that violates the norms of powerful groups. Deviant behavior results from the selfish nature of human beings. *Marxian:* Behavior that violates the norms of powerful groups. Deviant behavior results from the objective life circumstances of a corrupt and conflict-ridden society.	Behavior that is defined by relevant groups as deviant. Deviant behavior results from inadequate socialization and the failure of the deviant to share the group's definition of appropriate behavior.
SOLUTIONS	No ultimate solutions. Social reforms to improve the social structure, better socialization, and improved opportunities for disadvantaged groups.	*Non-Marxian:* No ultimate solutions. More effective means to repress human nature and better surveillance and swifter and more certain punishment of deviants. *Marxian:* An ultimate solution. The radical restructuring of society so that institutions will be compatible with selfless human nature.	No ultimate solution. More effective means of socialization.

as deviant by a particular group even though it is not dysfunctional for that group; another act may be defined as quite normal, yet be extremely contrary to the basic interests of the group. Thus, some acts are both dysfunctional and deviant, while others are one but not the other.

An illustration will help make this distinction clear. Mass suicide by members of a group could be considered dysfunctional if it resulted in the annihilation of the group. If such suicide destroys the group, then it is obviously detrimental to that group's long-term interests. The mass suicide of the members of the People's Temple in Guyana in 1978 would be considered such a dysfunctional act, since it effectively brought about the demise of that group. Yet many members of the People's Temple probably did not consider such suicide deviant in the sense of a socially disapproved and stigmatized

act (although many certainly would have preferred that it had not taken place). On the contrary, many probably defined it as a necessary, although extreme, measure to protect themselves from reprisals against the People's Temple that they thought were imminent. A few may have even viewed the mass suicide as a courageous act that symbolized willingness to make the ultimate sacrifice for a cause. From the functionalist perspective, then, deviance is a socially constructed category that may have little or no relationship to the real interests and well-being of the defining group. Deviant behavior is any behavior that the members of a group define as threatening to the group.

From the functionalist perspective, deviance is a social problem because some types of deviance can threaten the well-being of society, and an excessively high rate

of deviance can threaten the smooth-functioning of society. In addition, the repression of actions that are defined as deviant, but that are in fact functional, entails a social problem. For example, blacks who participated in civil rights activities in the South in the 1950s were defined by most Southerners as deviant, if not totally subversive. Yet, we now realize that these civil rights activities were functional in that they represented one mechanism through which changes in race relations in the United States were occurring. Efforts to repress such civil rights activities were very costly in terms of destruction of property, injury to people, and the obstruction of social change.

The Conflict Perspective

From the conflict perspective, society is viewed as an arena in which groups struggle with one another over scarce resources. The social order is maintained by coercion and by alliances between interest groups. The law represents the codification of the values of powerful groups in society and is an instrument for the maintenance and enhancement of their own interests. **Deviant behavior is, therefore, behavior that violates the values of powerful groups that are codified into the legal structure and community mores. An act is defined as deviant if it threatens the interests of dominant groups in society. Deviance, therefore, is not an objective condition; it is a socially defined state—one defined by powerful groups.**[12]

The position of conflict theory can be illustrated by the variations in legal sanctions for different offenses. Thus, the severity of punishment applied to a crime is often influenced more by the social status of people who commonly commit those crimes than by the degree of danger that the offender's actions pose for the social order. For example, burglary is usually committed by people of lower social status who have little power in society; burglary often victimizes the more affluent and powerful. Burglary usually receives severe punishment, in the form of lengthy prison sentences, according to the conflict perspective, because of the threat burglary poses to powerful groups. On the other hand, price

fixing is always committed by the more affluent and powerful. Price fixing usually results in mild punishments, in the form of fines, because it victimizes the general public and it is committed by influential people in the community. In short, the powerful, who make the laws, ensure that crimes committed by people like themselves receive mild punishment while crimes committed by those of lower social standing (which crimes the affluent feel threatened by) receive severe punishment. It is clear that, from the conflict perspective, the law and other normative systems such as community mores are not universally applicable principles but are mechanisms whereby the powerful have transformed "might" into "right."

From the conflict perspective, deviant behavior is a social problem when it threatens the interests of the powerful groups in society or the interests of some group that is influential enough to make its concerns felt. Thus, burglars and robbers would be viewed by members of the dominant group as such a threat. However, the groups might also feel threatened by deviant behavior patterns that do not constitute such a direct attack on their material wealth. For example, if the children of influential members of society begin to join communes, run away with unconventional religious groups, or become involved in heavy drug use, these powerful groups will probably feel that their goal of passing on their lifestyle to succeeding generations is threatened. If these deviant patterns occur only among powerless or marginal groups, they are less likely to be defined as a social problem.

The Interactionist Perspective

While power, interests, and dominance/subordination are not an explicit part of the interactionist perspective (as they are in the other two perspectives), interactionism suggests a third approach to these issues. According to interactionists, society is analogous to neither an organism nor an arena for conflict. It is more like a jam session (see Table 1.4, p. 20) in that shared definitions of the situation by the various groups and individuals in society are the constraints that give a coherent pattern to social interaction. When people define social reality similarly, coordinated and predictable patterns of social interaction emerge. However, each interaction is somewhat unique because every person and group has a distinctive personality, values, and interests that leave their mark on each encounter.

From this perspective, deviant behavior has its origin in the relationship between the person and society.[13] **Groups define certain forms of action as deviant and then proceed to treat those who violate the group's norms as deviants—regardless of the degree to which the behavior is harmful or, possibly, helpful to any group's interests.** For example, from the interactionist perspective, the widespread American prohibition against marijuana smoking is not based on the fact that marijuana use is harmful to the individual user or dangerous to the well-being of the social order. Rather, it is based on the fact that people define marijuana use as harmful and dangerous and act in accord with their definition. **From the interactionist perspective, deviance becomes a social problem when groups define certain behavior as deviant and categorize individuals caught so behaving as deviants and treat them as such.**

Even though each sociological perspective views deviance as a social problem in a somewhat unique fashion, all three view deviance as a socially defined category—as socially disapproved behavior that exceeds the limits of community tolerance and for which, if detected, there is a high probability of active social control. With this understanding in hand, we can now turn to a consideration of the sources of deviant behavior.

SOURCES OF DEVIANT BEHAVIOR

Prostitution, drug abuse, alcoholism, pornography — it is often difficult for those who find such behavior offensive or immoral to comprehend how another person might engage in it. For many people, psychological explanations of such behaviors are appealing—deviant behavior results from flawed personalities or possibly chemical and hormonal disturbances in the body. While there may be some truth to these psychological explanations, sociologists have found them inadequate and incomplete. In this section, we will review some of the most important social factors that sociologists have found to be sources of deviant behavior.

Deviance and Social Structure

Anomie

Emile Durkheim, the founder of the functional perspective, made two major contributions to the study of deviant behavior.[14] First, he asserted that deviance is *sociologically normal* and often *functional*. It is normal because all groups define certain acts as deviant and all societies experience some forms of deviance. Deviance is functional because social norms are useless unless they are enforced. Deviance and punishment of the deviant serve to reaffirm the normative order in that they reinforce the boundaries of acceptable behavior and reaffirm the importance of behaving in conformity with the norms. Also, because all groups tend to be conservative—to resist new ideas and new ways of doing things—deviant behavior may in some cases represent innovations that are essential for the group's long-range well-being.

Durkheim's second contribution to the study of deviant behavior was the idea that *both the rates and the types of behaviors defined as deviant vary with social conditions.* For example, during periods of rapid social change (e.g. technological revolutions, economic depressions, and extreme prosperity), rates of deviance increase and the types of behavior defined as deviant tend to change. Durkheim coined the term **anomie** to refer to a state of "normlessness"—a condition in which the social norms are so inconsistent or changing so rapidly that people are unsure what is expected of them and find it difficult to tell the difference between right and wrong. People act erratically or even cynically because the "old" norms do not seem relevant to current social conditions and therefore provide no guide to appropriate behavior. Newly emerging norms are so ambiguous and poorly formulated that they do not serve as clear-cut and consistent guides to behavior. Under these conditions, argued Durkheim, some increase in the amount of deviant behavior is to be expected.

Modes of Adaptation

American sociologist Robert K. Merton extended Durkheim's anomie theory and applied it to the analysis of deviance in contemporary American society.[15] Merton argued that material success is a very important cultural goal in America, overshadowing many other goals. We are, he reasoned, a success-oriented society, in which the belief that all people have an equal opportunity to achieve worldly success is widespread. This success, as most Americans view it, is defined in terms of substantial wealth, political power, material privileges, and social status. Along with this success goal, there are certain culturally approved means of achieving success—inheritance, hard work in legitimate oc-

cupations, and the like. However, the harsh reality in American society is that there is great inequality. Many people do not have access to the culturally approved avenues to success. It is substantially more difficult, for example, for the poor and racial minorities to succeed than it is for other groups. Some people, through chance of birth, are socialized into a success orientation and have the talent, social skills, and connections necessary for achieving worldly success. Others do not have the opportunity to develop such skills and talents. For Merton, then, anomie is a condition of society in which some people cannot achieve the culturally approved goals by using the culturally approved means of attaining them.

According to Merton, there are five ways in which people might respond to this societal condition of anomie (see Table 15.2). *Conformists* are people who accept the cultural goal of worldly success and who use culturally approved means to achieve that goal. *Innovators* also accept the goal of success, sometimes with a vengeance, but use means that are not legally or morally acceptable to

TABLE 15.2
Modes of Individual Adaptation to a Societal Condition of Anomie

MODE	ACCEPTS CULTURALLY APPROVED GOALS	ACCEPTS THE CULTURALLY APPROVED MEANS	EXAMPLES
1. Conformity	+	+	Honest businessmen and professionals who acquire wealth and prestige.
2. Innovation	+	−	Organized criminals, professional criminals, and white-collar criminals.
3. Ritualism	−	+	Most Americans who have lowered their aspirations by the time they reach middle age.
4. Retreatism	−	−	Narcotics addicts and skid row alcoholics.
5. Rebellion	− +	− +	Revolutionary groups and some communes.

SOURCE. Robert K. Merton, "Social Structure and Anomie," *American Sociological Review* 3 (October 1938), p. 676.

accomplish their ends. The innovator feels that legitimate routes to success are closed to him or her and that illegitimate means are the only option open. *Ritualists* are people who have reduced or otherwise modified their aspirations for worldly success as defined in terms of power, privilege, and prestige, but who out of habit or because of their socialization continue to use culturally approved means. *Retreatists,* on the other hand, reject both conventional success goals and the culturally approved means for their acquisition—in other words, they simply drop out. *Rebels,* like retreatists, reject both the goal and the means. However rather than drop out, rebels attempt to change society by replacing socially acceptable means with their own—a response that is highly threatening to any established social order. It can be seen that three of the modes of adaptation described by Merton are associated with deviant behavior—innovation, retreatism, and rebellion. Merton concludes that the social structure of American society—in which people are taught to value success but then not given the opportunity to achieve it—is an important contributing factor in the high rates of deviance in our country.

Illegitimate Opportunities

Sociologists Richard A. Cloward and Lloyd E. Ohlin extended Merton's analysis to the study of opportunities provided for disadvantaged young people by the rackets.[16] They state that the emphasis on worldly success has an enormous impact on the youth of our inner-city slums who lack opportunities for success through legitimate channels. They point out that there are indeed success models from the rackets for the slum youth to emulate—the pimp with his string of girls and his $10,000 moneyroll, fancy clothes, and luxury cars; the loan shark who has hundreds of thousands of dollars on loan to "big people" uptown; and the people in the numbers racket who make more in one week than the governor of the state makes in a whole year. Cloward and Ohlin refer to this as the *illegitimate opportunity structure* and point out that, like its legitimate counterpart, these rackets are not an equal-opportunity employer—you have

Many people have limited access to culturally approved avenues to success. For them, some forms of crime, such as prostitution, may provide a means of achieving that sought-after success goal.

to have talent, guts, and connections to make it in the underworld. Consequently, only a few of the more skillful and well-sponsored youth really become successful in the rackets. The rest must make it in the legitimate world, become petty crooks who are in and out of prison, or become alcoholics or drug addicts.

Deviance and Differential Association

Durkheim pointed out that deviance is, from a sociological perspective, quite normal. Other sociologists have emphasized the similarities between the way in which deviant behavior emerges and the way in which other behavior emerges. **For example, criminologist Edwin H. Sutherland's theory of differential association emphasizes that deviant behavior is learned** through the same social and psychological processes that are involved in the acquisition of any learned behavior.[17] Deviant behavior is learned by exposure to attitudes, sentiments, values, and behaviors that define deviant behavior as more desirable in certain situations than nondeviant behavior.

Sutherland did not imply, however, that people become deviants simply because they directly imitate their deviant companions or that they are contaminated by a deviant environment as though by an infectious disease. The process of learning deviance is far more complicated. First, the person must learn to view deviance as more desirable than nondeviance. This occurs in association with other deviants who view that particular mode of behavior positively. Secondly, the person must learn the specific techniques and behaviors of a particular form of deviance: how illegal drugs are obtained, where one goes to make homosexual contacts, how weapons for use in a robbery are obtained. Unfamiliarity with these things makes it difficult to behave in a deviant fashion. People need strong reinforcement for deviant actions just as they do to maintain other types of behavior. For example, if a child's experience is of parents lying, cheating, and similarly cutting corners in achieving their goals, the child is likely to adopt these methods. If, however, they are not reinforced by companions and other significant people, the child will probably discontinue their use.

Deviance and Labeling

The theories discussed thus far focus on those conditions that lead up to, or bring about, deviant behavior. Some sociologists point out, however, that once a person commits a deviant act, some important social processes occur. **Labeling (or societal reaction) theory focuses on how the reactions of other people (including official agents of social control such as the police or mental health authorities) play an important role in shaping future deviant behavior.** It is the contention of labeling theorists (not all of whom agree on all issues) that these reactions can do more to perpetuate deviance than to deter it. Let us

review how this might occur.[18] (The process is outlined in Fig. 15.1.)

Labeling theorists point out that all of us engage in deviant behavior; at least occasionally, we all violate some of the normative standards of our groups. For example, most of us have committed some violations of the criminal law after reaching adulthood. However, few of us are caught and labeled — either by our friends or by official agencies — as criminals or deviants. What is the difference between so-called respectable people who commit occasional acts of deviance and the "hardcore" deviant? The terms *primary* and *secondary deviance* can help us draw this distinction. **Primary deviation refers to the violation of social norms in which a person is not caught and labeled as a deviant and in which there is no threat to the person's self-image as a nondeviant or to the community's image of the person as respectable.** There are many sources of primary deviance; however, the labeling theorist is not concerned with the source of primary deviance, but rather with what happens when the person is caught and labeled as a deviant.

Secondary deviance (or "career" deviance) is deviant behavior that a person adopts in response to the reaction of others to that person's primary deviance. In other words, the discovery of, and reaction to, primary deviation is a major means by which hard-core, secondary deviants develop. Let us illustrate how this might happen. Homosexual experimentation among males is fairly common, as we shall see. Imagine that a teenage boy, possibly out of curiosity or in reaction to social pressure, engages in a homosexual liaison. This would be primary deviance because there is no labeling and no change in the person's or the community's image of the boy. Suppose, however, that the boy's sexual activities were discovered by the police. The police might react with disgust, and the boy's parents might be horrified that their son is a "homosexual." At this point, the label "homosexual" is being attached to the boy by both police and parents. If knowledge of the boy's homosexual contact leaked out to his schoolmates, it is quite likely that they might taunt, harass, and possibly reject him.

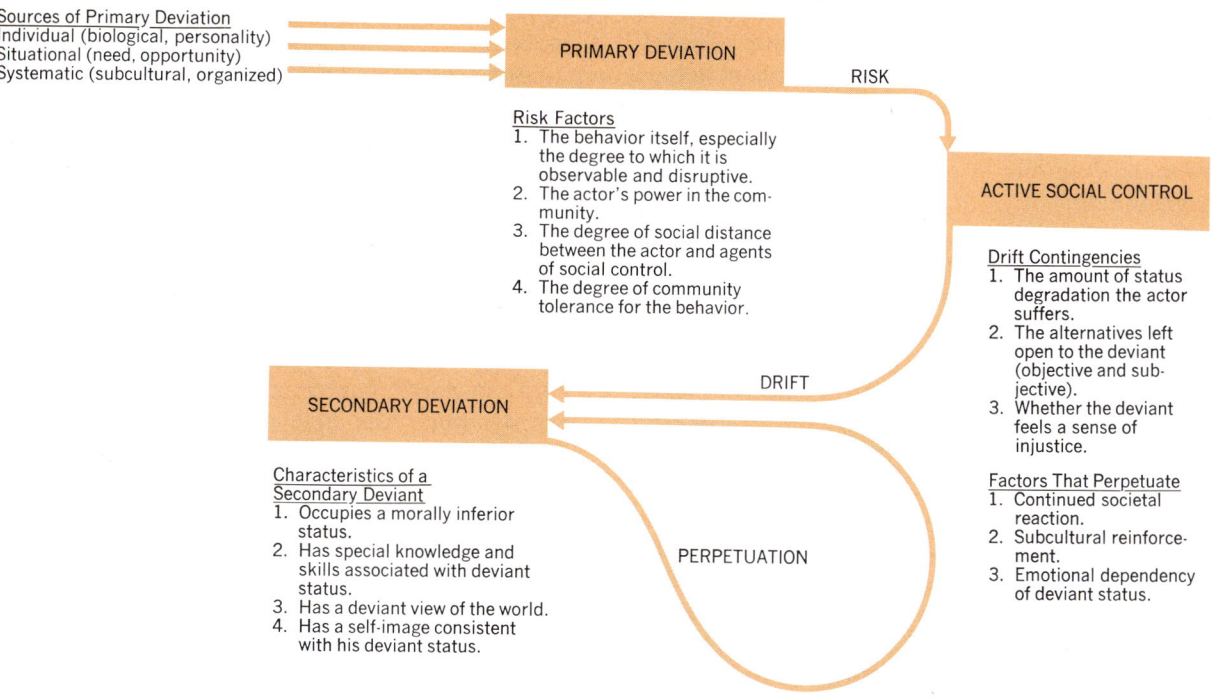

Figure 15.1   The Process of Becoming Labeled a Deviant.

One important consequence of this labeling is its effect on the boy's self-concept. Since the teenage years are formative ones in terms of sexual identity, the boy is likely to respond to others' reactions to him as a homosexual by accepting, at least in part, their judgment of him. If significant numbers of people think he is a homosexual (and he did, after all, engage in homosexual acts), then he is likely to accept that designation of himself. The boy may begin to think that he *is* homosexual — or at least that he has inclinations in that direction. A second important consequence of labeling is the effect it has on the boy's social relationships. If news of his arrest becomes widespread, some of his old friends may begin to shun him because of the perceived effect on their own reputations of associating with homosexuals. He may find it difficult to develop new friends, male or female, because of his past. However, he is likely to find acceptance among that deviant group of which he is accused of being a member — homosexuals. They are likely to accept him and treat him as a positive and worthwhile per-

son. Among them, there will be no negative stigma attached to his past. Thus, because of the labeling process, connections with the nondeviant world may be reduced, and contacts with other deviants increased.

As a result of both changes in self-concept and changes in social contacts, the likelihood that this boy will engage in future homosexual acts and develop a stable pattern of homosexuality is substantially increased. This is secondary deviance because it results from the boy's efforts to cope with the reactions of others to his primary deviation. Thus, instead of deterring primary deviance, labeling tends to perpetuate people's deviance because, once they are labeled, they have fewer alternatives — the self-fulfilling prophecy goes into effect. The person begins to view the world from the point of view of a deviant, and this is reinforced by society's and by his peers continued negative reaction.

One major caution concerning labeling theory is that it not be viewed in an overly deterministic fashion.[19] While labeling can and does have the consequences we have described, it is not inevitable that it will. Many other factors might reduce or eliminate the negative results of the label. If our imaginary teenager had had a strong perception of himself as a heterosexual, then the reactions of others would probably not have had such a powerful effect on his self-concept. If his parents and friends had reacted with concern and understanding rather than horror, the outcome might have been quite different. Thus, the labeling process should be considered as one among a number of processes that influence a person's behavior and affect whether or not that person will become deviant.

No one of these sociological theories represents a complete explanation of deviant behavior. Each one focuses on some of the important social sources of deviance. Furthermore, the forms that deviant behavior might take are extremely variable and thus we must approach each form of deviance individually in order to understand the specific dimensions of that particular problem. In the remainder of this chapter, we will review the contemporary status of six forms of deviance: homosexuality, prostitution, pornography, violence in the family, abortion, and suicide. A caution is in order here. **When sociologists refer to some pattern of behavior as deviant, there is absolutely no pejorative association attached to that term.** We are not arguing that homosexuality or prostitution is evil or immoral. To be sure, there are people who view these behaviors neutrally or positively. Behavior is deviant if it fits the definition of deviant behavior discussed earlier. From a sociological perspective, there is no evaluative connotation implied.

HOMOSEXUALITY

Homosexuality **involves sexual feelings, fantasies, or acts directed toward members of the same sex.** It is important to differentiate between homosexual thoughts and actions and a homosexual lifestyle. Many people have had at least one homosexual experience after reaching adolescence. However, only a small proportion of these people adopt a homosexual lifestyle. For ex-

ample, many people resort to homosexual relations as a means of coping with the deprivations of prison life but do not develop homosexual self-conceptions or become socially defined as homosexuals. **A** *homosexual lifestyle* **refers to frequent involvement in homosexual behavior, adopting a homosexual self-concept, and participating in the homosexual community.**[20]

In some cultures, homosexual liaisons are accepted as one of many normal sexual outlets.[21] Among the Siwans of North Africa, for instance, all males are expected to engage in homosexual activities throughout their lives. Homosexuality as a lifetime activity is rare, however. Usually homosexual relations are confined to a particular stage in the individual's life. For example, among the Aranda of Central Australia, there are long-term relationships between unmarried men and young boys, but the liaisons end at marriage. In ancient Greece, similar relationships existed between men and young boys, but the older man often had a wife as well. Young Greek boys were sometimes given a boy slave who could serve as a sexual partner until they were old enough to marry. Although in such societies there may be much homosexual behavior, many of these people are not *homosexuals* in the sense of people with an identity, lifestyle, and stable career pattern of homosexuality.

Theories of Homosexuality

Despite the fact that homosexuality is a highly disapproved form of sexual behavior that receives strong negative sanctions in our society, a large number of people engage in homosexual acts, and many of them adopt a homosexual lifestyle. Why is this? Are people born with homosexual tendencies? Do they learn the behavior while growing up? Although this is still a hotly contested issue, several theories have been proposed to explain processes by which people become involved in homosexuality.

Biological Determinism

Some scientists have taken the position that genetic, chromosomal, or hormonal factors predispose some people to homosexuality and others to heterosexuality. While some studies offer support for this view, others find no genetic or hormonal differences between homosexuals and heterosexuals.[22] Such biological explanations are insufficient to account for the variation in rates and patterns of homosexuality across cultures, at different time periods, and among different groups within our own society. If there is any legitimacy to biological explanations, it is probably that these factors may, in conjunction with social and environmental factors, predispose a person to homosexuality. Appropriate social or environmental factors would still be necessary for a person to engage in homosexual acts or take on a homosexual lifestyle.

Psychological Explanations

As with other forms of deviant behavior, homosexuality has been commonly explained on the basis of some presumed psychological maladjustment of the individual. Many psychological studies have concluded that disturbed family relations or pathological socialization experiences during childhood are at the core of homosexuality. According to some theories, the male who has a domineering and possessive mother and a hostile, weak, or absent father runs a much greater risk of becoming a homosexual. In such a situation, the male child does not have a positive masculine role model with which to identify. Similarly, female homosexuality is presumed to result from a broken home or a family situation in which the child strongly prefers one parent and feels hostility toward the other. In other cases, homosexuality may result from unconscious intrapsychic conflicts, such as an incest wish.[23]

Despite their popularity, there are many criticisms of these psychological explanations. First, many children raised under such conditions do not become homosexual. Second, many of the studies have been conducted on homosexuals undergoing psychiatric treatment. This is hardly a representative sample of all homosexuals. We would expect such psychiatric patients, whether homosexual or heterosexual, to exhibit high rates of psychological maladjustment. Third, some studies have found no

personality differences between homosexuals and nonhomosexuals.[24] Given these findings, we must conclude at this point that psychological factors might predispose a person to engage in homosexual fantasies or acts, but they are certainly not the total cause. In fact, in 1973, accepting these criticisms of psychological theories of homosexuality and recognizing the fact that many homosexuals do not consider their lifestyle pathological and do not want to change, the American Psychiatric Association removed homosexuality from its list of mental disorders.

Sociological Explanations

While not discounting the possible predisposing force of biological and psychological factors, sociologists have argued that some social or situational factors must be present before one will engage in homosexual acts and that certain social contingencies are essential before adopting a homosexual lifestyle. Many American males have engaged in homosexual acts without taking on a homosexual identity and lifestyle. Many—possibly most—of these contacts are casual or possibly the result of youthful experimentation. In other cases, these contacts occur in social situations in which homosexuality is viewed as acceptable. For example, sociologist Albert Reiss describes a group of adolescent male prostitutes who permitted their customers to perform fellatio for money. As long as they didn't seem to enjoy the experience or show any positive feeling toward the adult fellator, the delinquent males did not consider themselves homosexuals and continued to receive positive social support from their adolescent peers.[25]

Homosexuality is also very common in situations such as prisons, where there are no opportunities for heterosexual contacts.[26] In addition, sexual behavior in prisons often has social significance beyond mere sexual gratification—being dominant in sexual relations is a source (or symbol) of power, prestige, and self-esteem within the prison. For example, "wolves"— male inmates who are dominant in the sexual relationship—use homosexual acts as a substitute for heterosexual relations and as a means of asserting their power over more passive inmates. So there are a variety of situational factors that can result in the performance of homosexual acts. This does not mean, however, that a person who engages in homosexual acts under these situational pressures is then a *homosexual*— a person with an identity, lifestyle, and stable career pattern of homosexuality.

Whether a person takes on the identity and lifestyle of a homosexual depends on his perception and understanding of his own behavior and the reactions of other people to him. One of the primary ways that we learn about ourselves and who we are — about our attitudes, emotions, and characteristics — is by inferring them from our own behavior and the context in which this behavior occurs. In our culture, we define homosexuality and heterosexuality as mutually exclusive— a person is either one or the other— and we tend to believe that engaging in a single homosexual act makes one a homosexual. If a person engages in a homosexual act, what is he to infer (given these cultural beliefs) about himself? When and under what conditions does such a person begin to define himself as, or take on the identity of, a homosexual? Some sociological explanations of homosexuality focus on this process of self-definition as an important stage in developing a stable homosexual identity— anyone engaging in homosexual acts must be a *homosexual*.[27] Yet such an inference is not inevitable, since that act might have occurred in situations in which the person would deduce that the behavior was caused by other factors. For example, the adolescent male prostitutes define their homosexual behavior as caused by the money they receive; they still retain a strong heterosexual identity. So if there are plausible external or situational causes for the behavior, then a person is unlikely to develop a homosexual identity. However, if the behavior occurs in situations without such plausible reasons, then the emergence of a homosexual self-definition is more likely.

A person's self-definition as a homosexual can also be encouraged by the reactions of other people. According to labeling theory, a person labeled as homosexual by others is more likely to in-

ternalize that label as a part of his or her self-conception. This is especially true if those doing the labeling are important to that person, or if this labeling process occurs during a vulnerable period, such as adolescence, before the person has developed a stable sexual identity.

These are the major theories concerning homosexuality today. It is possible that some combination of theories is necessary to explain homosexuality (that is, predisposing factors in combination with situational factors resulting in homosexuality). For now, however, there is still much that we do not understand about the causes of homosexuality.

Patterns of Homosexuality

Male Homosexuality

It is difficult to make reliable estimates of the extent of male homosexuality in the United States. People are naturally reluctant to admit engaging in such stigmatized behavior. In addition, most studies have been based on unrepresentative samples. Nevertheless, these studies, if viewed cautiously, can give an indication of the extent of male homosexuality. The best of these estimates are summarized in Table 15.3. The investigations suggest that the bulk of homosexual experience occurs during adolescence and is not continued into adulthood. A recent estimate suggests that there are probably 30 million Americans who are exclusively or substantially homosexual, the majority being males.[28] Whichever estimate is accepted, homosexuality is considerably more widespread than is often realized.

There are many myths in American society concerning male homosexuals. One such myth is that they are effeminate, like to dress in women's clothes, and wish that they were women. Actually, homosexual males are no more likely to be effeminate than heterosexual males, and they are generally quite secure in their masculine identity. In addition, homosexuals do not show any more disturbed psychological characteristics or bizarre personality patterns than do heterosexuals, and most male homosexuals are as satisfied with their lives as are male heterosexuals.[29]

TABLE 15.3
Estimates of the Prevalence of Male Homosexuality in the United States

	KINSEY (1948)	GAGNON AND SIMON (1973)	HUNT (1974)	POMEROY (1972)	GEBHARD (1972)
Percentage of males with at least one homosexual contact	37	25–30	20–25	33	25–33
Percentage of males with homosexual experience since adolescence (or age 15)	25	5	10		
Percentage of males predominantly or exclusively homosexual	4	3	1–2		

SOURCES. Alfred C. Kinsey, Wardell B. Pomeroy, and Clyde E. Martin, *Sexual Behavior in the Human Male* (Philadelphia: W. B. Saunders, 1948); John H. Gagnon and William Simon, *Sexual Conduct: The Social Sources of Human Sexuality* (Chicago: Aldine, 1973); Morton Hunt, *Sexual Behavior in the 1970s* (New York: Playboy Press, 1974); Wardell Pomeroy, *Dr. Kinsey and the Institute for Sex Research* (New York: Harper & Row, 1972); and Paul H. Gebhard, "Incidence of Overt Homosexuality in the United States and Western Europe," *National Institute of Mental Health Task Force on Homosexuality: Final Report and Background Paper* (Washington, D.C.: U.S. Government Printing Office, 1972).

Female Homosexuality

Lesbians (female homosexuals) reflect the impact of their socialization as females. The female homosexual (like her heterosexual counterpart) tends to equate sex with love and is more likely to abstain from sex until the "right person" comes along. Lesbians also tend to be less assertive, even in their search for a mate in the homosexual community. Many lesbians pride themselves on being considerably less promiscuous than male homosexuals. Lesbian relationships are very much dependent on love and affection and tend to be more stable and enduring than male homosexual relationships. Although it is difficult to measure the extent of lesbianism, there is probably little reason to believe that the prevalence of female homosexuality is substantially less than that of male homosexuality.[30]

The first homosexual contact for women is infrequently the result of seduction. Most often, initial contacts are the result of a shared willingness to explore homosexuality.

Female homosexuals usually do not discover their homosexual feelings until very late in adolescence or in the years of young adulthood. The actual commencement of overt sexual behavior frequently comes as a late stage of an intense emotional involvement.[31]

A homosexual identity has often been formed before the first physical contact, and lesbians experiment with the dimensions of their sexual universe just as heterosexuals do. Most female homosexuals have had sexual relationships with men. "The female homosexual does not prefer sex with a woman because she has had no experience with a man; it is as likely that she has had such an experience as not."[32]

The Homosexual Community

Homosexual behavior is socially defined as deviant in our society—it is actually illegal in most states—and the homosexual lifestyle is still highly stigmatized. Homosexuals, like members of other deviant groups, have developed their own unique subculture and "community" within the boundaries of the larger society in order to cope with the problems associated with their stigmatized status. The homosexual "community" usually is not a community in the traditional sense of the term in that it lacks a territorial base with primary institutions serving a residential population. The ***homosexual commu-***

nity refers to a group of people engaging in common activities, sharing many common values and interests, and having a feeling of unity.[33]

> The homosexual community consists of persons tied together by friendship and sexual contacts. Along with a knowledge of one another, they share common interests, and the need to cooperate, if only to protect themselves from legal punishment and social condemnation.[34]

Because most homosexuals make every effort in their job situation to conceal their homosexuality from heterosexuals and also from many other homosexuals, community activities are largely leisure-time or recreational in nature. The homosexual community is an important mechanism whereby the individual with homosexual feelings and desires learns to cope with his or her situation. The phrase *coming out* refers to "that point in time when there is self-recognition by the individual of his identity as a homosexual and the first major exploration of the homosexual community."[35] The most important institution in the homosexual community is the "gay" bar that caters to the tastes and behavior of homosexual clientele. It provides a place where homosexuals can meet and express themselves freely with little fear of coming in contact with "straights"; it also serves as a focal point for social and emotional support for the homosexual identity and lifestyle. It is a dating marketplace and a major milieu of social interaction in the homosexual community.[36]

Homosexuality as a Social Problem

From a number of different viewpoints, homosexuality creates problems for contemporary American society. For homosexuals, the problem is the stigmatization and discrimination that they face in many spheres of their lives. Many people in the "straight" community fear homosexuality as a threat to their way of life. For society, the controversy over this deviant lifestyle has generated considerable tension and strife. A brief consideration of these problems is in order.

Traditionally, the major problem for homosexuals has been social exposure. Homosexuality was so frowned on in the past that most homosexuals were concerned about not letting their sexual preference become publicly known. Recently, however, there has been a change in mood within the homosexual community. Homosexuals have been taking steps toward making their lifestyle fully public; they are demanding equal treatment of homosexuals in all spheres of life. Some homosexual groups, such as the Mattachine Society and the Daughters of Bilitis, have been concerned for decades with the problems of homosexuals. The more recent groups, however, are often more vociferous, radical, and far-reaching than most earlier groups. The general term Gay Liberation Movement covers such groups as the Gay Liberation Front, the Gay Activists' Alliance, the National Gay Task Force (which is a coalition of many groups), and the International Union of Gay Athletes. These groups have taken legal steps to win civil rights and, if unsuccessful in the courts, have moved into the streets for demonstrations and protests. Because of this new-found militancy and openness, the problems surrounding homosexuals today have changed considerably.

One of the major areas of contention today is civil rights and equal opportunities for homosexuals. With some success, homosexual groups have been pushing for full acceptance of their lifestyle without any discrimination in housing, employment, and other areas. In this matter, the U.S. Civil Service Commission has ruled that homosexuals cannot be fired simply because of their sexual preference, and many large corporations have followed suit. Eighteen states have eliminated all laws prohibiting sexual acts between consenting adults, and forty cities and counties have passed ordinances banning discrimination against homosexuals.[37] While homosexuals have generally made advances in these areas, there have been recent setbacks. With the support of singer-entertainer Anita Bryant, a long campaign to overturn an ordinance in Dade County (Miami), Florida banning discrimination against homosexuals in housing, employment, and public accommodations was finally successful. This success has motivated other communities to mount similar antihomosexual campaigns. In 1977, the Washington State Supreme Court ruled that it was constitutional to fire

One of the major areas of contention today is over civil rights and equal occupational opportunities for homosexuals. Homosexuals have adopted a more militant stance in recent years to fight for their rights.

a teacher with homosexual preferences (even though no acts of overt homosexuality were proved) because this sexual orientation was considered immoral by conventional community standards and thus such people were ruled unfit to be teachers. Much of this opposition to homosexuality is based on religious grounds—it is often seen as immoral behavior that contravenes natural law.

Another issue that has arisen recently is the legal right of homosexuals to marry one another. Homosexuals feel that it is discriminatory to prohibit people of the same sex from forming legally binding marital relationships. Without such marriages, homosexuals are not permitted to achieve the personal gratification and financial advantages that are available to heterosexuals. Opponents of such marriages view them as a sacrilegious violation of the purpose of marriage and as a threat to the integrity of the family. A related issue concerns the right of homosexuals to have and keep their own children. There have been numerous court battles by lesbian mothers to retain custody of their children after divorce. Some have taken this deviant sexual preference alone as sufficient evidence that a

person is unfit to be a parent. In other cases, women have won custody of their children. Some states have passed laws prohibiting the adoption of children by homosexuals, while gay rights groups have argued that sexual preference should not be a consideration in adoption decisions. This would make it possible for an exclusively homosexual couple to have children. A primary issue in such decisions involving children is the effect on the child, especially on the child's sexual orientation, of being raised by a homosexual. Opponents feel strongly that homosexuals would simply pass on their preference to the child and thus perpetuate the problem. Yet, preliminary results of the research that is available indicate that such experiences have no impact on the child.[38]

The homosexual movement today is challenging American society on many fronts. Homosexuals have increasingly "gone public"; they have rejected the traditional definition of them as "sick" and in need of treatment; and they are organizing and utilizing the political resources they have available in order to enhance their position in society. However, it is difficult to predict the manner in which these various issues will be resolved because the opposition to homosexuality is also substantial and may become more vociferous in the future.

PROSTITUTION

Prostitution has often been referred to as the "world's oldest profession." Indeed, the sale of sexual favors is a practice found in the records of the Greek and other ancient cultures. Prostitution can be defined in two ways: social and legal. Jennifer James, a noted researcher on prostitution, proposes a social definition: *prostitution* is a sexual exchange in which the primary motivation and reward for the prostitute is neither sexual nor affectional.[39] However, such a definition would include as examples of prostitution employees who seek advancement through sexual means and even married persons who use sex as a means of manipulating their mates. Many people believe that such a social definition is excessively broad, and consequently the law provides a more customary basis for defining prostitution. Legal definitions focus on explicitly accepting money for sexual services.

The Extent of Prostitution

Laws exist throughout most of the United States defining prostitution as an illegal activity. Yet, despite longstanding attempts to abolish the practice, prostitution flourishes.[40] It is conservatively estimated that 500,000 prostitutes are plying their trade in this country. The major reason why prostitution endures is simple—there are demands for the service and there are people willing to supply it. It is estimated that American males spend between $7 billion and $9 billion a year on prostitution. In the landmark research by Kinsey and his associates, it was determined that 69 percent of the American white male population had had relations with prostitutes at least once.[41] The researchers also discovered that 15 to 20 percent visited prostitutes more than 3 times over a five-year period, and only 31 percent of the white male population had never had contact with a prostitute.

While prostitution is illegal in nearly all of the United States, one hundred nations—including Britain, France, Germany, Japan, and Italy—have decriminalized the sale of sex (although open solicitation, such as streetwalking, is often prohibited). In West Germany,

> prostitution is considered a social necessity, and the government actively supports the building of pimp-free prostitution hotels where prostitutes can live and work in comfortable rooms with access to shopping centers, bowling lanes, and tennis courts and where officials can easily perform mandatory medical inspections.[42]

Prostitution can be practiced in a variety of settings. American female prostitutes may be classified into the following types: streetwalkers, bar girls, "masseuses," studio models, escorts, stag-party workers, hotel prostitutes, convention prostitutes, call girls, Nevada house prostitutes, illegal house and apartment prostitutes, and circuit travelers (visiting lumber and other work camps).[43] Males also become prostitutes, but they usually provide commercial sex to other men rather than women. Homosexual males, transvestites, and boy (preteen) prostitutes may be found in many of the larger cities of America. Boy prostitution, for example, has existed in the United States at least since the late 1800s, when brothels were established to provide this special "service." Young males involved in prostitution today are usually runaways who have no other means of support and who are frequently taken in by a homosexual who makes them available for a fee.[44]

Becoming a Prostitute

How does a woman become a prostitute? While the specific situations vary considerably, one student of the subject describes the process in the following manner:

> It is the sexually active young woman who lives in a sexually exploitative environment, who is unskilled in other ways, who develops a "bad" reputation, who falls afoul of the juvenile court for being incorrigible, who is particularly at risk. The plans and values of these young women are quite conventional: they believe in marriage and hope for all of the same things

that other young women hope for; however, the forces of circumstance accumulate. Prostitution is not a career that is planned for; women are not volunteers, they are recruits or draftees. What women often do is move from a sexually active young adulthood into sexual activity for money. This transition can be abrupt (falling in with a pimp) or slow (taking money from a friend or having money left by a pickup).[45]

However, there is tremendous variation in the way people become prostitutes and the type of people to be found in "the world's oldest profession."[46] In recent years, police have noticed the appearance of "daytimers"—ex-models, jobless actresses, and bored housewives who are supplementing the family income. The New York City Police estimate that as many as 10 percent of the prostitutes in Times Square on a weekend are housewives from Long Island and New Jersey. Some women enter prostitution because of negative elements in their background—a broken home, parental promiscuity, or childhood traumas—that are conducive to such deviant activities. Others hope for a more attractive, exciting, and easier life than is available to them in more legitimate activities. Finally, for some women, it is economic pressure that serves as the inducement to take up prostitution. Given this variety, it would be deceptive to make generalizations concerning those who become prostitutes.

Functions of Prostitution

Why does prostitution exist on the scale found in the United States today? Sociologist Kingsley Davis observed that prostitutes are employed for a variety of reasons other than the simple desire for sexual gratification. He noted that,

The craving for variety, for perverse gratification, for mysterious and provocative surroundings, for intercourse free from entangling cares and civilized pretense, all play their part.[47]

In addition, Davis claimed that prostitution can be functional for society. Prostitutes provide sexual outlets for groups that might find such gratification difficult to obtain through socially acceptable

means. The groups to which he referred were military personnel, strangers in the community, persons whose sexual interests would be considered perversions by the norms of society, and those who are physically repulsive. For these groups the prostitute may be the only sexual outlet possible—no other institution exists to fill their needs. Davis also commented that pressures on families are reduced when a man seeks the services of a prostitute rather than pursuing another man's wife or pressing his own wife for sex if she does not desire it.

Problems and Exploitation

Despite the functional aspects of their trade, there are many serious problems associated with prostitution as it is practiced in the United States.[48] Prostitutes face substantial legal pressure in nearly every community. Approximately 30 percent of the population of women's jails are serving sentences for prostitution. In addition, there is much crime associated with prostitution. Many prostitutes rob their clients, especially if they feel that the customer will not report the crime for fear of public exposure. Some prostitutes are involved in heroin addiction, but in these cases they usually enter the profession to support an existing habit or that of a boyfriend. However, addiction to narcotics interferes with a prostitute's ability to practice her trade effectively, and therefore most streetwalkers avoid involvement with addictive drugs. Another difficulty—one that has attracted the attention of the feminist movement—is the economic exploitation of the female prostitute.

Most prostitutes who work the streets have a pimp—a paid male companion who typically has one or more prostitutes providing him with money. The pimp plays a multifaceted role in the life of the streetwalker.[49] He generally provides money for bail if she is arrested, he obtains legal services when needed, he protects her from abusive males, and he may also father her children. The pimp does, however, demand money from the woman, and, if she wants to maintain their relationship, she pays. A woman working the street will generally earn $1000 a week, but she is lucky if the pimp allows her to keep as much as $100 for herself.

The pimp plays a multi-faceted role in the life of the streetwalker —as protector, as lover, and possibly as the father of her children. Yet the relationship is basically exploitative—he takes the lion's share of her income.

In an effort to end this economic exploitation, some prostitutes have organized. On Mother's Day, 1972, a group of San Francisco prostitutes created COYOTE (Call Off Your Old Tired Ethics), an organization aimed at improving conditions for prostitutes. Today, COYOTE has over 8000 members, and similar organizations are emerging in other cities across the nation— including groups such as ASP (Associated Seattle Prostitutes), PONY (Prostitutes of New York), and a statewide group called CAT (California Association of Trollops). One of the more specific goals of these groups is the decriminalization of prostitution and the unionization of prostitutes. The feminist movement has supported the goals of these organizations, and the co-alition of prostitutes and feminists is beginning to make itself heard. To help publicize the views' of such groups, Kate Millet, a noted feminist writer, supported the goals of COYOTE by purchasing a printing press for the organization with some of the royalties from her book *The Prostitution Papers*. One factor that might provide motivation for the decriminalization movement is the high cost associated with the arrest of streetwalkers. In San Francisco, it costs the city approximately $1200 for each arrest, and the prostitute is usually back on the street after a relatively short period of time.[50]

***Decriminalization* involves the removal of criminal penalties attached to an act and changing it to a misdemeanor offense punishable by fines.** Would decriminalization of prostitution work, or would it create greater social problems? No definitive answer can be given to this question, but the experience of Nevada may provide some insight. Large areas of that state have decriminalized prostitution, and under a 1971 statute, 2 counties are legally permitted to license houses of prostitution. Proponents of legalization claim that through licensing, the problems often associated with prostitution will disappear. Licensed establishments are supervised by government agencies to protect both the prostitute and the patron. Medical examinations at regular intervals reduce the spread of venereal disease; managers of the houses are restricted to a certain percentage of the woman's earnings (in some Nevada establishments, prostitutes can earn over $30,000 a year); the establishments also ensure the patron's protection against robbery by the prostitute; and the use of drugs is strictly prohibited. Legal brothels in Nevada also provide daycare facilities for the prostitutes' children.[51]

The long-term effects of legalized prostitution are uncertain, but there seems to be no serious difficulties. In Winnemucca, Nevada (population 5000), there are five houses of prostitution. The local city attorney commented recently that he had heard no complaints in the past ten years.[52] While this is not evidence of a problem-free condition, Nevada provides the nation with an experimental situation that should be watched closely.

PORNOGRAPHY

Adult bookstores, ads for sexually explicit films, the display of erotic magazines on newstands, and similar phenomena have become a commonplace feature of many American communities. It is estimated that the market in pornography is a $500-million to $1-billion industry in the United States.[53]

Pornography and the Law

Perhaps the most difficult question to answer when considering sexually explicit materials is, what is pornography? To answer this question one must distinguish between legal erotic art and illegal pornography. The word **pornography** is derived from the Greek term *pornographos*—the writing of harlots.[54] Defining the modern use of the term pornography is not so simple. Few people have identical views of what constitutes pornography. Many are offended by simple nudity, while others consider anything short of bestiality perfectly acceptable and nonpornographic. This is a vivid example of the interactionist perspective in operation. As a result of these varied viewpoints, pornography has come to represent a legal distinction that is often applied inconsistently.

The first American conviction for pornography occurred under a Massachusetts law in 1821 when the book *Fanny Hill* was judged obscene. In 1865, the Federal Mail Act made it illegal to send obscene materials through the mails. It is noteworthy that under this law, birth control information and medical journals dealing with the treatment of unwed mothers were defined as obscene and therefore banned from the mails. Pornography became a major issue in 1957 when the Supreme Court delivered its verdict in *Roth v. United States*. The Court ruled that obscenity was *not* protected by the First Amendment of the Constitution, which guarantees freedom of speech. To provide guidelines for the application of its decision, the Court defined as obscene those materials that have a tendency to excite lustful thoughts and that have no redeeming social importance. These criteria have proved very difficult to apply in particular cases because the terms involved are vague and subjective.

In 1967, the United States Congress expressed its concern over the traffic in obscenity and pornography. To determine the harm done by obscene materials and to find ways of controlling pornography, Congress established the Commission on Obscenity and Pornography. In 1970, the commission released its report, in which it estimated that from 20 to 25 percent of the American male population has somewhat regular experience with explicit sexual materials often depicting heterosexual intercourse. After studying extensive research findings, the commission made its recommendation, which startled many lawmakers:

> In general outline, the commission recommends that federal, state, and local legislation should not seek to interfere with the right of adults who wish to do so to read, obtain, or view explicit sexual materials.[55]

Despite the data and conclusions of the commission, the Supreme Court ruled in 1973 that courts can *assume* sexually explicit material has negative effects and that this position need not be proved by scientific evidence. Furthermore, the Supreme Court offered fairly broad definitions of obscenity, saying that states could ban materials that were "prurient" or "patently offensive" to community standards and without any redeeming literary or artistic value. An important aspect of this decision was that it placed the final decision-making authority concerning obscenity within the local community, rather than establishing any national standards.[56] The impact of these rulings has been variable. In many places, pornography has flourished. Some cities have attempted to use zoning laws or harassment by legal authorities to control pornography when the local courts would not provide restrictive rulings.[57] At present, it is difficult to determine whether social policy will become more or less restrictive in the future. On the one hand, there is tremendous public concern and outrage over pornography; on the other, there is clearly a substantial demand for these materials. Such contradictory trends will undoubtedly result in considerable conflict over this issue in the future.

The Scientific Evidence

The recommendation of the Commission on Obscenity and Pornography ran contrary to the values of many members of Congress and to their expectations concerning the effects of obscene materials. Popular opinion regarding pornography has held that obscene materials lead to moral depravity, sex crimes, and other antisocial acts. Research conducted on the subject does not support these contentions. Consider, for example, the belief that pornography stimulates sex crimes. A study of the effects of liberalized pornography laws in Denmark showed that as pornography becomes increasingly available, there is a significant decrease in the number of sex offenses registered by the police. This decline was found to be especially notable in the area of child molestation. The study suggests that instead of increasing sexual crimes, the availability of pornography may have the opposite effect.[58]

Another study on the effects of pornography focused on the attitudes and behavior of persons exposed to large quantities of obscene material. A group of students were exposed to 90 minutes of pornographic films and photographs every day for 15 days. At the end of the test period, the attitudes and behavior of the students were examined. The researchers could determine no negative effects resulting from the exposure. In fact, massive exposure to sexually explicit material resulted in a lower interest in, and reduced physical response to, pornography. The investigators concluded that pornography is a harmless stimulus in which people quickly lose interest.[59]

There has been increasing public concern in recent years over perceived excesses in pornographic indulgence. In the mid-1970s there emerged a type of cinematic production sometimes referred to as a "snuff film." These films allegedly portray a man and a woman performing sex, fol-

Scientific evidence concerning the effects of pornography is not clear-cut. However, current studies indicate that pornography does not lead to moral depravity, sex crimes, or other anti-social acts.

lowed by the woman apparently being murdered and dismembered on the screen. Films of this type raise the question, even among the most avid civil libertarians, whether there should be limits to freedom of speech and expression. The answer of the majority, in certain cases, seems to be yes. For example, in many states there is legislation being enacted or already passed to control child pornography. The laws are aimed at protecting children by making it illegal to film them engaging in sexual activities; however, many of the laws do not yet prohibit the *viewing* of child pornography. As with "snuff films," there seems to be a distinction between viewing dramatizations of such acts on film and actually permitting real people to be harmed for the sake of an authentic film of actual rape, murder, or child molestation.

Even though pornography itself does not appear to be harmful to either the individual or society, many groups continue to view it as a problem. In an attempt to understand the basis for people's involvement in antipornography movements, sociologists Louis A. Zurcher and R. George Kirkpatrick studied participants in antipornography crusades.[60] They concluded that the typical participant is a person whose prestige in society is less than he expects it should be for someone committed to living a style of life normally associated with high prestige; therefore he joins with people who share that situation to maintain or raise the group's status. This is done by fighting an issue that symbolizes the forces that these people feel are at the root of their problem—in this case, pornography was that symbol. Whatever the basis for opposition may be, it is certain that pornography will continue to be a lively issue of debate in the future.

VIOLENCE IN THE FAMILY

People tend to view the family as a social institution in which love and gentleness abound—an arena where members receive affection, nurturance, and support from each other. In fact, the opposite is often true: violence is pervasive in American families. On the basis of officially compiled crime statis-

tics, approximately 20 percent of all murders in the United States take place within the family, and over one-half of these represent husband-wife homicides.[61] More police officers die as a result of answering domestic violence calls than in following any other avenue of their duty. Between 1973 and 1977, 599 police officers lost their lives in the performance of their duties. Of these, 121 were killed responding to disturbance calls, which include family quarrels. The facts surrounding family violence are often grisly as well. A well-known authority on child abuse has estimated that roughly 25 percent of all fractures seen in children under the age of two are caused by abuse from parents, and that 10 to 15 percent of all children under three years of age hospitalized for trauma have been abused, despite the protestations of their parents to the contrary.[62]

There are many misunderstandings and much misinformation concerning violence in the family. This is partly so because child abuse and spouse abuse—the latter usually in the form of wife beating—received minimal public attention and consequently very little investigation prior to the 1960s. In addition, it is extremely difficult to observe what goes on within American families. Traditionally, Americans have viewed the family as a sacred institution and private domain—what goes on within it is a personal concern and the responsibility of family members alone, not outsiders, including law enforcement authorities.

We have learned that conflict can be a fundamental and sometimes constructive component of social organization. In the case of the family, most people assume that conflict is detrimental, and that efforts must be made to protect family cohesiveness from the strains and tensions that accompany conflict. In doing so, however, the sources of conflict within the family are often covered up and ignored—in the interests of "family unity"—until they become more serious and difficult to solve. Many people persist in maintaining an idealized picture of harmony within family life in our society, and elaborate precautions are taken to strengthen and support it. While this mythology is quite functional in preserving confidence in the family, it can also hinder an objective analysis of violence within it.

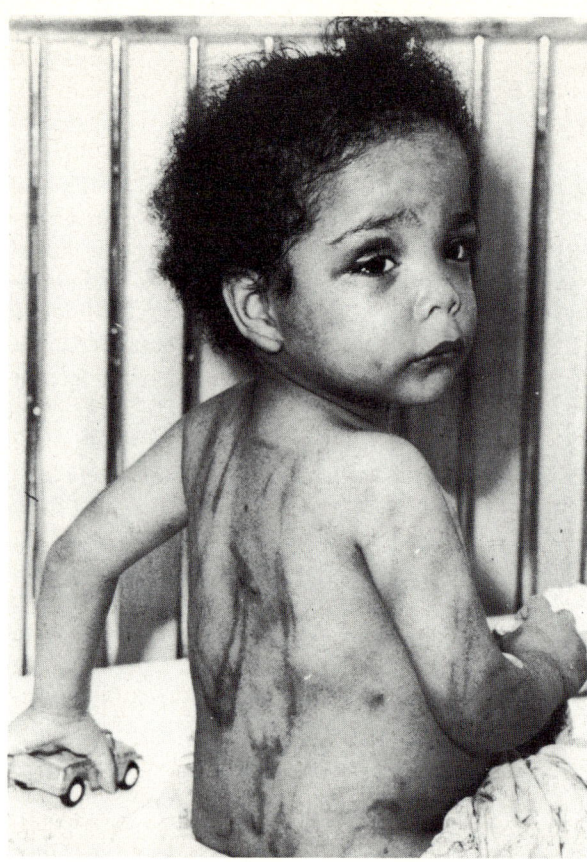

It is not easy to draw a clear line between child abuse and physical punishment that is beneficial to a child's development. However, few would disagree that actions that result in physical injury such as this boy received are child abuse.

Child Abuse

It has been estimated that the number of reports of child abuse is increasing at the rate of 30 percent a year and that between 1973 and 1982 there will be 1.5 million reports, 50,000 deaths, 300,000 permanent injuries. On the other hand, estimates concerning the actual incidence as opposed to reported cases of child abuse vary considerably.[63]

What Is Child Abuse?

Owing to increased public and professional attention recently directed toward child abuse, there is a tendency to conclude that it is a new social prob-

lem.[64] It is, however, neither new nor drastically increasing. In part, this is a result of the fact that child abuse has many definitions.[65] It has been narrowly defined to mean an occurrence in which a parent or caretaker injures a child not by accident but in anger and with deliberate intent. Others base their definition on a clinical condition (e.g. physical damage). There are other definitions of abuse that range from separated parents stealing children from their legal guardians to emotional mistreatment. However, it can be argued that there is *no* behavior that can automatically and objectively be recognized as child abuse.[66] This fact, of course, is a significant component of the social problem surrounding child abuse: Where is the line between physical punishment that may be beneficial to the socialization of the child and abusive physical punishment? The answer to this question is culture-bound; treatment of a child that one culture would define as abuse may be regarded as perfectly acceptable in another. Furthermore, these definitions will vary over time within a given culture.

Sociologist Richard J. Gelles, who has conducted extensive research on violence in the family, has proposed a social psychological model of the causes of child abuse (see Fig. 15.2) suggesting that the phenomenon is influenced by many variables — the social position of parents, class and community influences, socialization experiences, situational stress, psychological problems, and immediate precipitating situations.[67]

Who Are the Abusers?

The data on characteristics of abusive parents display considerable variablity.[6ʰ] Some studies indicate that the perpetrator of child abuse is more likely to be female than male, whereas others reflect an equal incidence of male and female abusers. Most abusers range in age from 20 to 40 — the typical childbearing, childrearing years. There is a general pattern of low socioeconomic status among parents involved in *reported* cases of child abuse. It is important to remember, however, that reported cases of abuse provide a misleading impression of the socioeconomic position of child abusers. Lower-class persons usually must go to

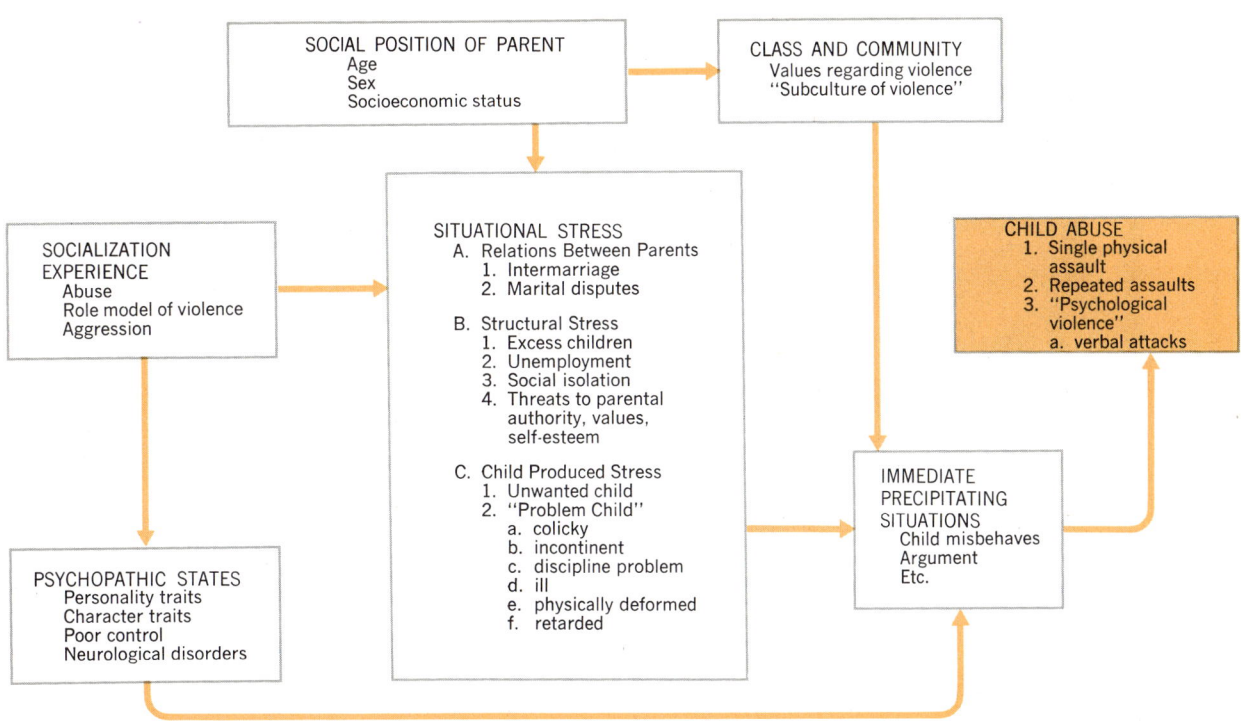

Figure 15.2 **A Social Psychological Model of the Causes of Child Abuse. Richard J. Gelles, "Child Abuse as Psychopathology: A Sociological Critique and Reformulation," *American Journal of Orthopsychiatry* 45 (July 1973), p. 619. Copyright © the American Orthopsychiatric Association, Inc. Reproduced by permission.**

public hospitals in order to seek treatment for their children, and these facilities are required to make reports. Upper-class parents are more likely to seek help from private physicians, who are sometimes willing to let the abuse go unreported.

Several investigators have found that abusing parents have experienced various forms of social deprivation during their own childhood (foster-home placement, hospitalization for mental illness, criminal records, etc.) if not actual physical abuse. The authors of one study found that 30 percent of the abusers had been severely beaten when disciplined as children. Indeed, it appears that being physically punished as a child can provide a training-ground for abuse.[69]

Since tension and conflict are always possible in families, the potential always exists for violence directed at children. One well-known researcher in the field suggests a method for reducing child abuse — the removal of positive approval and general acceptance in our society of physical punishment for disciplining children. In a conflict situation, then, a parent would be less likely to consider violence as an acceptable mode of resolution. This, one researcher on the subject suggests, could be accomplished through increasing public awareness of the potentially detrimental effects of verbally and physically aggressive methods of childrearing.[70]

Spouse Abuse

Our knowledge of physical aggression between husbands and wives is more limited than on child abuse. One of the more comprehensive studies has been conducted by Gelles.[71] He reports that over half (55 percent) of the families he studied had engaged in at least one incident of conjugal violence and that 26 percent of the sample practiced violence on a regular basis, ranging from 6 times yearly to every day. Husbands, Gelles found, are more violent than wives, but wives also participated in violence as perpetrators. There was a strong relationship between family violence and the use of alcohol. In addition, Gelles concluded that those families characterized by low education, low occupational status, and low income were more likely to experience such violence.

Spouse abuse is often *victim-precipitated*—that is, the recipient of physical abuse is the first to employ verbal or physical violence in the incident. In a recent court decision in Michigan, a woman was acquitted of murdering her husband (by setting their dwelling on fire as he slept) primarily because of convincing evidence presented by the defense that he had beaten her viciously and repeatedly over a long period of time. The jurors were apparently convinced that her actions were warranted as an act of "self defense." There are many implications of this decision. Historically, there has been a tendency for police officers to avoid interfering in wife-beating incidents, principally owing to feelings concerning the appropriateness of male dominance. In the opinion of some, women who have been beaten by their husbands must have deserved what they received. Today, these biases seem to be diminishing somewhat. For example, twenty-five years ago (or even less), the woman who killed her husband after she had been severely beaten would probably have been convicted. Some legal critics believe that the Michigan case may set a complex and contradictory precedent for the future.

Intrafamilial violence appears to be a product of a combination of frustration and a lack of resources. It also seems that those who use violence learn it from their parents. If one learns that violence is an acceptable response to frustration, then one may well respond in that way. The situational context is perceived by Gelles as a major intervening variable—some conditions are more conducive to violence than others.[72] Family violence is a multifaceted phenomenon and there is no easy answer to the question who the abusers are or under what circumstances violence takes place.

ABORTION

Abortion **is the termination of pregnancy before the fetus is capable of survival as an individual.** There are two types of abortion: (1) miscarriage, or the spontaneous expulsion of the fetus through natural causes, and (2) induced abortion. The abortion controversy revolves around the latter. Many people do not consider abortion a form of deviant behavior or a social problem. We consider it in this context because there are groups with significant influence who do define abortion as deviant and do consider it a social problem. Recall that behavior is deviant if it is defined by some influential social group (not necessarily all people) as socially disapproved.

The Legal Status of Abortion

Induced abortion, in various forms, has been practiced throughout much of human history. It was recognized, for example, as a form of population control among the Greeks and Romans. By the 1860s in America, a number of states had passed laws prohibiting induced abortion for any reason other than saving the life of the mother, and by 1873 a federal law had been passed removing from the mails "any literature, medicine, or article to do with contraception or abortion."[73]

From this time until the 1960s, the status of legal abortions remained almost unchanged in the United States. Despite the liberalization of abortion laws in the Scandinavian countries, Japan, and some of the Eastern European nations, laws in the United States have remained restrictive. It has been estimated that from 10 to 20 percent of pregnancies in the United States end in abortion, with the overwhelming majority of these being spontaneous.[74] Prior to court decisions that liberalized abortions, the illegal abortion "industry" was a major aspect of organized crime in the United States.

In the 1960s, the laws relating to abortion began to undergo considerable change. In 1967, three

Some people choose to deal with unwanted pregnancies by putting the child up for adoption. Others choose abortion, which is viewed by some interest groups as an undesirable alternative.

states – California, Colorado, and North Carolina – enacted laws based on a model proposed by the American Law Institute. This proposal made abortion allowable "if it is believed that there would be grave impairment to the physical or mental health of the mother, or that the child would be born with grave physical or mental defect, or that the pregnancy resulted from rape or incest."[75] By 1972, ten additional states had enacted such laws. While these laws led to an increase in legal abortions, their effect was minimal when compared to the impact of new laws enacted in Alaska, Hawaii, New York, and Washington. These laws essentially made legal abortion available upon request. In 1973, the Supreme Court ruled that extremely restrictive abortion laws were unconstitutional and thereby generally voided all restrictive abortion legislation. Although New York repealed its law in 1972, and despite continuing strong opposition to more liberalized abortion, legal abortions in this country have been increasing dramatically (see Table 15.4). It is estimated that by 1975, 1 million abortions were being performed in the United States, with about one-quarter occurring among low-income women on Medicaid.[76]

In addition to the fact that women who seek abortions are disproportionately poor, they are more likely to be young and members of minority groups. There are many reasons for having an abortion. For some women, it is a means of coping with an unwanted pregnancy that results from a lack of knowledge concerning contraception; for

TABLE 15.4

Incidence of Legal Abortion in the U.S., 1969–1974

	1969	1970	1971	1972	1973	1974
Total number of abortions	22,670	193,491	485,816	586,760	615,831	764,476
National abortion ratio (abortions per 1,000 live births)	6.3	52.0	136.0	180.1	195.1	242.0

SOURCE. U.S., Congress, House Committee on the Judiciary, *Proposed Constitutional Amendments on Abortion,* 94th Cong., 2d sess., 1976, Serial no. 46, pt. 1, p. 287.

others, it is a way of controlling family size; others feel unable to support another child; in some cases, the pregnancy has resulted from rape or incest. Some women who have abortions are married, although it appears that most are not. For example, in 1974, the percentages of married women having abortions ranged from a high of 45 percent in Mississippi to a low of 11 percent in Louisiana. In 1975, there were more illegitimate births than legitimate ones in Washington, D.C., and more abortions than the total number of births.[77]

The Abortion Controversy

The changing legislation, the Supreme Court ruling, and the increase in legally induced abortions are not isolated phenomena. They have occurred in the context of changing attitudes, values, and self-conceptions in American society. The abortion controversy has engulfed religious groups, the women's movement, the professions (especially medicine and law), and government, as well as the general public. One of these, the women's movement, is generally in favor of freedom of choice. One subgroup from the religious sector, the Roman Catholic clergy, is generally opposed to abortion on demand and has been active in the right-to-life movement. The arguments raised are both lengthy and complex and can be only briefly summarized here.

"Pro-Choice" Arguments

Karen Mulhauser, Executive Director of the National Abortion Rights Action League, argues that women should have control of their bodies and the right to seek abortion along with other forms of health care during pregnancy. In other words, women should have the right to make the choice whether they should have an abortion. Arguments concerning maternal health and fiscal responsibility have also been widely used by proponents of free choice.[78]

Proponents of choice also argue that prohibiting abortions increases the extent of child abuse, since the resulting children are unwanted and more likely to be victims of aggression. In addition, where abortion is restricted only to cases involving a threat to the mother's life, victims of rape and incest may be subject to unwarranted suffering. Finally, the "pro-choice" groups argue that restricting abortion serves no interest except to support the beliefs of some religious groups, and this is in violation of the First Amendment of the Constitution in that it imposes the beliefs of some religious groups on others.

"Pro-Life" Arguments

The anti-abortion position is based on a relatively simple assumption. Anti-abortion, or "pro-life," groups contend that abortion is murder because the termination of pregnancy takes a human life. Anti-abortion groups argue that by relaxing abortion laws, the government is sanctioning murder. They further contend that the availability of abortion on demand does not eliminate illegal abortions since some hospitals still report cases resulting from illegal abortion even though legal abortion is available. They also argue that restricting or eliminating the availability of abortion does not adversely affect maternal health. Finally, anti-abortion groups argue that no free society can truly remain free when it sanctions the murder of some of its members.

The arguments made by both sides are complex and confusing. Often they cite statistics and make interpretations of facts that are, at best, contradictory. It seems clear that anti-abortion groups will continue to work for the adoption of a constitutional amendment and other forms of restriction while pro-choice groups, especially members of the women's movement, will persist in working for enlarged opportunities for free choice. In any event, it seems clear that for the immediate future there will continue to be large numbers of people who do not understand or who do not use effective contraceptive methods.

If the 1973 Supreme Court decision remains in force, we may expect that in the early 1980s there will be approximately 500 abortions for every 1000 live births in the United States.[79] However, there is so much controversy and flux in this area that such predictions are extremely problematic. There is considerable support for an amendment to the Constitution that would allow abortions only to save the life of the mother. Some pro-life groups are pushing for a constitutional convention (it would be the first since 1787) in order to get such an amendment passed. If it were passed, studies indicate that the number of abortions in the United States would be substantially reduced. So, the extent of abortion in the future depends on social policies that cannot yet be predicted.

SUICIDE

Suicide has always been puzzling and frightening to many people. Most cultures define suicide as a deviant act — an act that violates important norms and values. Yet it is so common that it is found in one form or another in all cultures. Why would a person willingly take his own life? What are the factors that make suicide an acceptable alternative for some people?

Explanations of Suicide

The classic sociological study of suicide was conducted by Emile Durkheim and was first published in 1897.[80] Based on statistics of suicides in France,

he found that the crucial factor in suicide was the degree to which an individual was integrated into social groups. Durkheim concluded that there are three different types of suicide. *Egoistic suicide,* **which was the most common, occurs among people who lack ties to social groups that have important meaning for them.** They are not integrated into and involved with groups such as the family, church, or community. They do not see their behavior as having any consequences for some meaningful group. For example, the eccentric who associates with no one or the elderly person whose friends and relatives have died are prime candidates for egoistic suicide. Participation in some groups can serve as a constraint that inhibits a person from committing suicide because of the impact it would have on the group.

Anomic suicide **occurs in situations of confusion and contradiction, such as appear in periods of rapid social change, when there are no stable norms that guide and regulate one's behavior.** Without such regulation, stability and orderliness decline, and it is difficult for a person to develop a positive sense of identity and self-worth. For example, both the businessman who has lost his fortune and the rock singer who has acquired wealth beyond her wildest dreams are in an anomic situation in which previous norms regulating their behavior are no longer relevant. The person finds it difficult to adjust to the apparent surrounding disorder. Unless new norms are adopted to give order to and to regulate this new status, the person is a prime candidate for suicide.

Altruistic suicide **occurs in groups in which there is great emphasis placed on group identity and conformity and in which suicide is defined as an acceptable alternative.** The person places the furtherance of group goals and ideals ahead of his or her own life. Individual identity is so bound up with the group's survival that the person finds it difficult to separate the two. The soldier who sacrifices his life for his buddies and the Japanese committing hara kiri (a ritualistic form of suicide practiced by a person who has brought disgrace upon his family) are illustrations of altruistic suicide.

Other explanations of suicide include psycho-

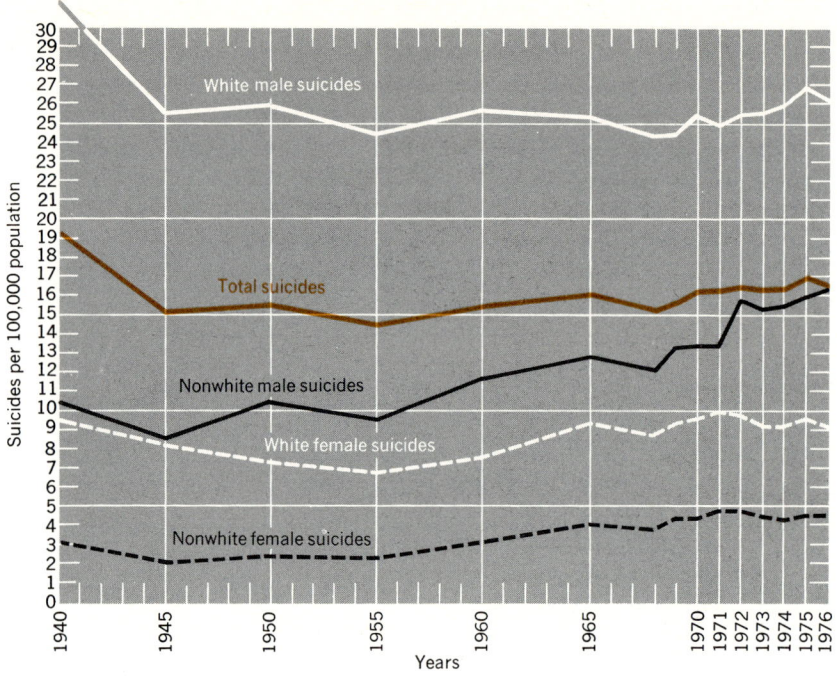

Figure 15.3 Suicide Rates by Sex and Race, 1940–1976.
U.S. Bureau of the Census, *Statistical Abstract of the United States, 1978* (Washington, D.C.: U.S. Government Printing Office, 1978), p. 182.

logical factors. Sociologists Andrew Henry and James Short view suicide as an aggressive response to frustration, but the aggression is focused inward against oneself, rather than outward against others (as would be the case in homicidal behavior).[81] One important source of frustration, they argue, is a person's failure to maintain a steady or rising position in the status hierarchy relative to other people. Such a situation might come about because of economic depressions. In fact, Henry and Short point out that "... about two-thirds of the variation in the suicide rate through time in the United States can be accounted for by economic fluctuations."[82]

The Extent of Suicide

According to official statistics, in 1976, 26,832 people committed suicide in the United States. However, for a number of reasons, there is considerable underreporting of the number of suicides. Because suicide is highly stigmatized in our culture, incidences of the act are sometimes recorded as being due to other causes in order to protect the reputation of the person and his family. In other cases, it is difficult to determine the actual cause of death. For example, it is assumed that many deaths in automobile accidents are actually suicides resulting from the deliberate actions of the driver. Taking into account this underreporting, suicidologists (scientists who study the cause and prevention of suicide) claim that the actual number of suicides is probably double the reported rate.[83]

While the suicide rate declined until the 1950s, it has been fairly stable over the past twenty years (although some groups, such as nonwhites, have shown considerable increase) (see Fig. 15.3). In 1975, it was the tenth most important cause of death. However, as Durkheim documented many years ago, suicide rates are still associated with specific social factors.

TABLE 15.5

Suicide Rates by Age, Sex, and Race, 1976 (rates per 100,000)

	5–14	15–24	25–34	35–44	45–54	55–64	65+ YEARS	ALL AGES
White Males	.7	19.2	23.7	23.6	27.7	31.6	39.7	19.8
Nonwhite Males	.3	14.7	22.8	16.8	13.5	12.3	14.5	11.0
White Females	.2	4.9	8.6	11.0	13.8	12.1	8.3	7.2
Nonwhite Females	.4	4.0	6.5	4.7	4.3	2.8	3.2	3.2

SOURCE. U.S. Bureau of the Census, *Statistical Abstract of the United States, 1978* (Washington, D.C.: U.S. Government Printing Office, 1978), p. 183.

Sex

Although women more often attempt suicide, the rate of successful suicides is substantially higher among men (see Fig. 15.3). This difference is partly due to the fact that males traditionally have held occupations that involve great stress, and these stressful situations can lead to anomic or egoistic suicide. The recent rise in the suicide rate among young females is undoubtedly related to the increasing numbers of women entering stressful and demanding occupations. In addition, sex role socialization has implications for suicidal behavior.[84] Females learn to respond to their negative and self-destructive feelings in a passive way, whereas males learn to respond more actively. Successful suicide attempts are more likely from a person with such an active orientation. American males are more likely to learn how to use, and to have access to, objects (such as firearms) that are effective means of killing oneself, whereas females have access to less effective means (such as pills), and the effect of these techniques is also more easily reversed.

Marital Status

Married people have the lowest rates of suicide, the divorced and widowed the highest, and single people fall in between.[85] The disruption of valued social relationships through divorce or widowhood, or the lack of such relationships among the single, leaves those people with fewer social constraints on their behavior—classic cases of Durkheim's egoistic suicide. However, among those 15 to 20 years old, the suicide rates of the married are higher than those of single people. This may be because these young people marry quickly and impulsively, based on a romantic notion of love and marriage rather than on a realistic notion of the requisites for sustaining a marriage and supporting a family.

Age

Suicide is relatively uncommon below the age of 15. After 15, age is related to both sex and race in determining suicide rates (see Table 15.5). Among white males, the suicide rate peaks in the highest age categories. This is probably the result of retirement and the attendant decline in social status and feelings of self-worth frequently occurring in this group. Among white females, middle age is the highest suicide period. This is in part due to the departure of grown children during this period of a woman's life and the resulting curtailment of the traditional female role of homemaker and mother. Among nonwhites, both male and female, the peak suicide period is young adulthood. This may be due to the stresses that many nonwhites in this age group experience because of unemployment, discrimination, and the failure to achieve success in American society.

Although the young have relatively low rates of suicide, these have been increasing in recent years, creating concern that some of the conditions that confront American youth today are responsible for this increase.[86] Some suicides among adolescents are associated with pressure from their parents to be successful. The parents strive diligently for success themselves, and they have similar expectations for their children. Such parental approval can be gained only through success (e.g. in school work, at the piano, on the playing field), and failure is experienced by the adolescent as intense humiliation. In addition, suicidal adolescents are typically unable to communicate their feelings—of unhappiness, frustration or love—to their parents. This serves to isolate them and to intensify feelings of failure.

The suicide rate among college students is very high and is related to their stressful situation. Many have moved away from home, family, and childhood friends for the first time in their lives and have not developed new social relationships to provide support and satisfaction. In addition, the college student is often confronted with many new, sometimes bizarre, ideas, values, and lifestyles. Finally, the intense pressure to attain high grades that are the key to financial and professional success places a great deal of stress on college students. The consequences of this stress and threatened failure are emotional problems, depression, and sometimes suicide. Next to accidents, suicide is the second most common cause of death among college students. One director of a university health service estimates that, for every 10,000 students, 1000 have severe emotional problems that require some professional help, 300–400 are at least temporarily handicapped by severe depression, 15–25 need treatment in a psychiatric hospital, 5–20 attempt suicide, and 1–3 are successful in that attempt.[87]

Race

The suicide rate for nonwhites in the United States is considerably lower than that for whites (see Fig. 15.3). However, there are some exceptions. For example, while the suicide rate among all Native Americans is about average, it is very high among their young people.[88] Males between the ages of 15 and 45 have a suicide rate that is four times the rate of non–Native Americans. The lack of educational and economic opportunities for young Native Americans is undoubtedly an important contributing factor to this situation.

Suicide Prevention

Considerable attention has been directed by many professional groups toward the prevention of suicide.[89] The more that is learned about the causes and dynamics of suicide, the better able people are to determine who is suicide-prone and how to intervene effectively. Many professional groups, such as physicians, nurses, and social workers, are being trained in the assessment of suicide risk, based on the characteristics of those likely to commit suicide (see Table 15.6). Intervention can take many forms, depending on the particular circumstances: establishing a close relationship with the person, reducing any immediate danger (removing lethal objects), giving medication if necessary to reduce feelings of stress and tension, and helping the person back into the network of social relationships and resources that will help reduce feelings of isolation and worthlessness.

Suicide prevention centers staffed by professionals and paraprofessionals have been established in many communities to reach people contemplating suicide. The staff can put a person in contact with other community agencies or resources that may be useful in coping with problems. While important steps have been made in attacking the problem of suicide, it is still on the rise. To be effective, a solution must involve those social conditions that give rise to suicide in the first place.

CONCLUSION

Deviant behavior is an extremely controversial, and at the same time decidedly fascinating, field of study. It rouses the emotions of people and engenders intense debate. We have tried to present the complexity of deviant behavior in modern America, and we have emphasized the importance of viewing deviant behavior from divergent perspectives. What is deviant for one group is conformity for another. In addition, there are competing proposals for public policies to deal with deviance. In evaluating these alternatives, some of which we have already discussed, it is important to analyze them from the points of view of the three theoretical perspectives. It will be useful to conclude this chapter with a brief discussion of alternatives in relation to these perspectives.

The various forms of sexual deviance are, and will undoubtedly remain, controversial issues. On

TABLE 15.6
Assessing the Degree of Suicidal Risk

BEHAVIOR OR SYMPTOM	INTENSITY OF RISK		
	LOW	MODERATE	HIGH
Anxiety	Mild	Moderate	High, or panic state
Depression	Mild	Moderate	Severe
Isolation/ withdrawal	Vague feelings of depression, no withdrawal	Some feelings of helplessness, hopelessness and withdrawal	Hopeless, helpless, withdrawn, and self-deprecating
Daily functioning	Fairly good in most activities	Moderately good in some activities	Not good in any activities
Resources	Several	Some	Few or none
Coping strategies/ devices being utilized	Generally constructive	Some that are constructive	Predominantly destructive
Significant others	Several who are available	Few or only one available	Only one, or none available
Psychiatric help in past	None, or positive attitude toward	Yes, and moderately satisfied with	Negative view of help received
Lifestyle	Stable	Moderately stable or unstable	Unstable
Alcohol/drug use	Infrequently to excess	Frequently to excess	Continual abuse
Previous suicide attempts	None, or of low lethality	None to one or more of moderate lethality	None to multiple attempts of high lethality
Disorientation/ disorganization	None	Some	Marked
Hostility	Little or none	Some	Marked
Suicidal plan	Vague, fleeting thoughts but no plan	Frequent thoughts, occasional ideas about a plan	Frequent or constant thought with a specific plan

SOURCE. Corrine Hatton, Sharon Valente, and Alice Rink. *Suicide: Assessment and Intervention,* 1977, p. 56. Courtesy of Appleton-Century-Crofts, publishing division of Prentice-Hall, Inc.

the one hand, some forms of sexual deviance do seem to perform important functions for society—they fill needs (although they are needs that some would prefer did not exist). For example, prostitution is a service that is in great demand in our society. Pornography, likewise, is a multimillion dollar business. For the functionalist, if there is great demand for such services or materials, then we must consider the possibility that they play a vital role in society. If they do, then their removal would create a void, and we must consider what would fill

that void. Would the elimination of pornography lead to an increase in sex crimes? We do not know the answer to this question. Yet if all the parts of society are integrated and interrelated, then we should expect a major change, such as the elimination of pornography, to have effects on other parts of society, and some of those effects might be worse than the original problem. However, the functional argument does not lead to the conclusion that no change is warranted, but rather that caution must be exercised in considering solutions to problems.

From the conflict perspective, sexual deviance is a matter of one group imposing its moral standards on another group. As such, solutions must be viewed in terms of which interest groups are concerned about the issue, the influence of these groups, and the resources they have available. Thus, as long as influential groups in American society (such as large and powerful religious groups) define homosexuality, prostitution, and pornography as immoral, decriminalization proposals and "gay rights" will confront substantial resistance. At the same time, activist groups among homosexuals and prostitutes will undoubtedly continue to demand the elimination of laws that restrict their right to do as they wish, and they have made considerable headway in bringing about changes in the law and in public attitudes. The conflict theorist views such struggle between groups as continuous and inevitable. The ability of a particular group to pursue its interests at a certain point in time depends on its effective exercise of power in relation to other groups.

Violence in the family has only recently been viewed by many people as a threatening form of deviant behavior. It is seen as dangerous to the safety of its victims, harmful to the abuser, and damaging to the order and well-being of the community and society. For the functionalist, the family is a central institution in society whose task it is to socialize children and to provide a source of emotional support and satisfaction for all. Violence in the family makes it more difficult for the family to achieve these goals, and thus such violence is both dysfunctional and deviant.

Some issues that are raised by the interactionist perspective are useful in evaluating solutions to the problem of violence in the family. One major issue is the separation of abusive violence from acceptable actions, and this in many respects is a matter of definition and subject to interpretation. Child abuse and spouse abuse are what we choose to define them. Some parents might argue that a few bruises will not permanently harm a child and that such corporal punishment is a useful tool in raising a child. Others would argue that any use of physical force is "abuse." A few would go so far as to classify childrearing practices that result in psychological disturbances in the child as a form of child abuse. Thus, as the interactionist perspective makes clear, social reality is subjective and depends on the interpretations and definitions that people bring to the scene.

The second issue that the interactionist perspective makes us sensitive to is the effect on the deviant of being labeled as different, especially if the label involves much negative stigmatization. In all likelihood, men and women who abuse their children do not define themselves as child abusers, and proposed solutions must be careful to avoid harmful labeling. Most programs—such as counseling programs and hotlines—make efforts to define the abuser as requiring medical or psychiatric care. However, in some cases, criminal charges must be made against the abuser, and it is then difficult to avoid the negative aspects of the labeling process. Nevertheless, the interactionist perspective makes us aware of the importance of the relationship between the deviant and society.

GLOSSARY TERMS

Absolutist
Abortion
Altruistic suicide
Anomic suicide
Anomie
Conformists
Decriminalization
Deviance

Dysfunction
Egoistic suicide
Homosexual community
Homosexuality
Homosexual lifestyle
Innovators
Legalist
Overlegalization

Primary deviance
Pornography
Prostitution
Rebels
Relativist
Retreatists
Ritualists
Secondary deviance

REFERENCES

[1] "A 'no' to the Gays," *Newsweek* (June 20, 1977), p. 30.

[2] "Detroit: Wild in the Streets," *Newsweek* (August 30, 1976), pp. 47–49.

[3] A hypothetical composite case based on the work of Edwin M. Lemert, *Human Deviance, Social Problems, and Social Control* (Englewood Cliffs, N.J.: Prentice-Hall, 1972).

[4] From Jacqueline P. Wiseman, "Court Treatment and Skid Row Alcoholics," in Earl Rubington and Martin S. Weinberg, eds., *Deviance: The Interactionist Perspective,* 2d ed. (New York: Macmillan, 1973), p. 210.

[5] "Seizing Hostages: Scourge of the '70s." *Newsweek* (March 21, 1977), pp. 16–27.

[6] See Marshall B. Clinard and Robert F. Meier, *Sociology of Deviant Behavior,* 5th ed. (New York: Holt, Rinehart and Winston, 1979), pp. 12–18.

[7] David J. Rothman, *The Discovery of the Asylum* (Boston: Little, Brown, 1971), p. 7.

[8] Kai T. Erikson, *Wayward Puritans: A Study in the Sociology of Deviance* (New York: John Wiley & Sons, 1966).

[9] Sanford H. Kadish, "The Crisis of Overcriminalization," *Annals of the American Academy of Political and Social Science* 374 (November 1967), pp. 157–170.

[10] See, for example, Bronislaw Malinowski, *Crime and Custom in Savage Society* (New York: Harcourt, Brace, 1932).

[11] See Emile Durkheim, *Division of Labor in Society* (New York: The Free Press, 1938), and William J. Chambliss, "Functional and Conflict Theories of Crime: The Heritage of Emile Durkheim and Karl Marx," in William J. Chambliss and Milton Mankoff, eds., *Whose Law? Whose Order? A Conflict Approach to Criminology* (New York: John Wiley & Sons, 1976), pp. 1–28.

[12] See Steven Spitzer, "Toward a Marxian Theory of Deviance," *Social Problems* 22 (June 1975), pp. 638–651, and Clinard and Meier, *Sociology of Deviant Behavior,* pp. 81–88.

[13] See Howard S. Becker, *Outsiders: Studies in the Sociology of Deviance,* enlarged edition (New York: The Free Press, 1973).

[14] See Durkheim, *Division of Labor in Society,* and Robert A. Nisbet, *The Sociology of Emile Durkheim* (New York: Oxford University Press, 1974).

[15] Robert K. Merton, *Social Theory and Social Structure* (New York: The Free Press, 1968).

[16] Richard A. Cloward and Lloyd E. Ohlin, *Delinquency and Opportunity* (New York: The Free Press, 1960).

[17] Edwin H. Sutherland and Donald R. Cressey, *Criminology,* 10th ed. (Philadelphia: Lippincott, 1978), ch. 4.

[18] See Becker, *Outsiders;* Erving Goffman, *Stigma: Notes on the Management of Spoiled Identity* (Englewood Cliffs,

N.J.: Prentice-Hall, 1963); Lemert, *Human Deviance, Social Problems, and Social Control;* David Matza, *Becoming Deviant* (Englewood Cliffs, N.J.: Prentice-Hall, 1969); and Thomas J. Scheff, *Being Mentally Ill* (Chicago: Aldine, 1963).

[19] See Milton Mankoff, "Societal Reaction and Career Deviance: A Critical Analysis," *Sociological Quarterly* 12 (Spring 1971), pp. 204–218.

[20] Barry M. Dank, "Coming Out in the Gay World," *Psychiatry* 3 (May 1971), pp. 180–197.

[21] See Mary McIntosh, "Societal Context and the Homosexual Role," *Social Problems* 16 (Fall 1968), pp. 182–192.

[22] See D. Rosenthal, *Genetic Theory and Abnormal Behavior* (New York: McGraw-Hill, 1970); G. Tourney et al., "Hormonal Relationships in Homosexual Men," *American Journal of Psychiatry* 132 (March 1975), pp. 288–290; and Richard C. Friedman, Flemming Wollesen, and Ruth Tendler, "Psychological Development and Blood Levels of Sex Steroids in Male Identical Twins of Divergent Sexual Orientation," *Journal of Nervous and Mental Disorders* 163 (October 1976), pp. 282–288.

[23] See Sigmund Freud, "Three Essays on the Theory of Sexuality," in J. Strachey, ed., *Standard Edition of the Complete Psychological Works of Sigmund Freud*, vol. 7 (London: Hogarth, 1953); Irving Bieber et al., *Homosexuality: A Psychoanalytic Study* (New York: Basic Books, 1962); and Jay S. Kwawer, "Male Homosexual Psychodynamics and the Rorschach Test," *Journal of Personality Assessment* 41 (February 1977), pp. 10–18.

[24] Evelyn Hooker, "Parental Relations and Male Homosexuality in Patient and Nonpatient Samples," *Journal of Consulting and Clinical Psychology* 33 (April 1969), pp. 140–142, and Alan P. Bell and Martin S. Weinberg, *Homosexualities: A Study of Diversity among Men and Women* (New York: Simon and Schuster, 1978).

[25] Albert J. Reiss, Jr., "The Social Integration of Queers and Peers," *Social Problems* 9 (Fall 1961), pp. 102–120.

[26] See Gresham M. Sykes, *The Society of Captives* (Princeton, N.J.: Princeton University Press, 1958); David A. Ward and Gene G. Kassenbaum, *Women's Prison: Sex and Social Structure* (Chicago: Aldine, 1965); Rose Giallombardo, *Society of Women* (New York: John Wiley & Sons, 1966); Alan J. Davis, "Sexual Assaults in the Philadelphia Prison System," *TransAction* 6 (December 1968), pp. 28–35; and Barbara Carter, "Race, Sex, and Gangs: Reform School Families," *TransAction* 11 (November–December 1973), pp. 36–43.

[27] Philip Blumstein and Pepper Schwartz, "The Acquisition of Sexual Identity: The Bisexual Case," paper presented at the annual meetings of the American Sociological Association, Montreal, 1974; Edward Sagarin, *Deviants and Deviance* (New York: Frederick A. Praeger, 1975); and Barbara Ponse, *Identities in the Lesbian World: The Social Construction of Self* (Westport, Conn.: Greenwood Press, 1978).

[28] "Battle Over Gay Rights," *Newsweek* (June 6, 1977), pp. 16–26.

[29] See Evelyn Hooker, "The Adjustment of the Male Overt Homosexual," *Journal of Projective Techniques* 21 (March 1957), pp. 18–31; Evelyn Hooker, "An Empirical Study of Some Relations Between Sexual Patterns and Gender Identity in Male Homosexuals," in John Money, ed., *Sex Research: New Developments* (New York: Holt, Rinehart, & Winston, 1965); and Bell and Weinberg, *Homosexualities.*

[30] See Jack H. Hedblom, "The Female Homosexual: Social and Attitudinal Dimensions," in Simon Dinitz, Russell R. Dynes, and Alfred C. Clarke, eds., *Deviance: Studies in Definition, Management, and Treatment*, 2d ed. (New York: Oxford University Press, 1975), pp. 235–259, and Ponse, *Identities in the Lesbian World.*

[31] William Simon and John A. Gagnon, "On Becoming a Lesbian," in Jack Douglas, ed., *Observations of Deviance* (New York: Random House, 1970), p. 108.

[32] Hedblom, "The Female Homosexual," p. 246.

[33] See Evelyn Hooker, "The Homosexual Community," in Douglas, ed., *Observations of Deviance*, pp. 115–128.

[34] Dinitz, Dynes, and Clarke, eds., *Deviance*, p. 215.

[35] William Simon and John A. Gagnon, "Homosexuality: The Formulation of a Sociological Perspective," *Journal of Health and Social Behavior* 8 (September 1967), p. 180.

[36] See Hooker, "The Homosexual Community," and Howard Brown, *Familiar Faces, Hidden Lives* (New York: Harcourt, Brace, Jovanovich, 1976).

[37] "Battle Over Gay Rights," *Newsweek* (June 6, 1977), pp. 16–26.

[38] Jane E. Brody, "Sex Research Has Earned Respectability," *New York Times* (January 8, 1978), Section 4, p. 20.

[39] Jennifer James, "Prostitutes and Prostitution," in Edward Sagarin and Fred Montanino, eds., *Deviants: Voluntary Actors in a Hostile World* (Morristown, N.J.: General Learning Press, 1977), pp. 368–428.

[40] See Charles Winick and Paul Kinsie, *The Lively Commerce: Prostitution in the United States* (New York: Quadrangle Books, 1971), and Alex Thio, *Deviant Behavior* (Boston: Houghton Mifflin, 1978), p. 169.

[41] Alfred C. Kinsey, Wardell B. Pomeroy, and Clyde E. Martin, *Sexual Behavior in the Human Male* (Philadelphia: W. B. Saunders, 1948).

[42] James, "Prostitutes and Prostitution," pp. 370–371.

[43] See Ibid., and Barbara S. Heyl, *The Madam as Entrepreneur: Political Economy of a House of Prostitution* (New Brunswich, N.J.: TransAction Books, 1971).

[44] Robin Lloyd, *For Love or Money: Boy Prostitution in America* (New York: Vanguard Press, 1976).

[45] John H. Gagnon, *Human Sexualities* (Glenview, Ill.): Scott, Foresman, 1977), p. 289.

[46] See Freda Adler, *Sisters in Crime* (New York: McGraw-Hill, 1975), p. 65, and Harry Benjamin and R. E. L. Mas-

ters, *Prostitution and Morality* (New York: Julian Press, 1964), pp. 90–91.

[47] Kingsley Davis, ''The Sociology of Prostitution,'' *American Sociological Review* 2 (October 1937), p. 753.

[48] James, ''Prostitutes and Prostitution,'' pp. 368–428.

[49] See John M. Murtagh and Sara Harris, *Cast the First Stone* (New York: McGraw-Hill, 1957), and Gail Sheehy, ''The Economics of Prostitution: Who Profits? Who Pays?'' in Erich Goode and Richard Troiden, eds., *Sexual Deviance and Sexual Deviants* (New York: William Morrow, 1974), pp. 110–123.

[50] ''Prostitutes Organize,'' *Newsweek* (July 8, 1974), pp. 65–66.

[51] Adler, *Sisters in Crime*, p. 227.

[52] Roger M. Williams, ''The Oldest Profession in Nevada and Elsewhere,'' *Saturday Review-World* (September 7, 1974), p. 9 et seq.

[53] Commission on Obscenity and Pornography, *The Report of the Commission on Obscenity and Pornography* (Washington, D.C.: U.S. Government Printing Office, 1970).

[54] Michael J. Goldstein and Harold Stanford Kant, *Pornography and Sexual Deviance* (Berkeley: University of California Press, 1973).

[55] Commission on Obscenity and Pornography, *The Report of the Commission on Obscenity and Pornography*, p. 51.

[56] See Paul J. McGeady, ''Obscenity Law and the Supreme Court,'' in Victor B. Cline, ed., *Where Do You Draw the Line?* (Provo, Utah: Brigham Young University Press, 1974), pp. 83–106, and Ray C. Rist, ''Pornography as a Social Problem: Reflections on the Relation of Morality and the Law,'' in Ray C. Rist, ed., *The Pornography Controversy: Changing Moral Standards in American Life* (New Brunswick, New Jeresy: TransAction Books, 1975), pp. 1–15.

[57] Fred Ferretti, ''Newest New York Commercial Sex Enterprise Is Opened on 53rd Street,'' *New York Times* (July 18, 1978), Section 2, p. 5, and ''Pornography Zones Proposed in State,'' *New York Times* (June 17, 1978), p. 51.

[58] Berl Kutchinsky, ''The Effect of East Availability of Pornography on the Incidence of Sex Crimes: The Danish Experience,'' *Journal of Social Issues* 29, no. 3 (1973), pp. 163–181.

[59] James L. Howard, Myron B. Liptzin, and Clifford B. Reiffler, ''Is Pornography a Problem?'' *Journal of Social Issues* 29, no. 3 (1973), pp. 133–145.

[60] Louis A. Zurcher and R. George Kirkpatrick, *Citizens for Decency: Antipornography Crusades as Status Defense* (Austin: University of Texas Press, 1976).

[61] Frederal Bureau of Investigation, *Crime in the United States: 1977* (Washington, D.C.: U.S. Government Printing Office, 1978), pp. 12, 291.

[62] C. Henry Kempe, ''Pediatric Implications of the Battered Baby Syndrome,'' *Archives of Disease in Childhood*

46 (1971), pp. 28–37.

[63] R. E. Helfer, *A Self-Instructional Program on Child Abuse and Neglect* (Denver: National Center for Prevention and Treatment of Child Abuse and Neglect, 1974).

[64] Richard J. Gelles, ''Demythologizing Child Abuse,'' *The Family Coordinator* 25 (April 1976), pp. 135–141.

[65] See David G. Gil, *Violence Against Children: Physical Abuse in the United States* (Cambridge, Mass.: Harvard University Press, 1970); and C. Henry Kempe et al., ''The Battered Child Syndrome,'' *Journal of the American Medical Association* 181 (July 1962), pp. 17–24.

[66] See Dexter M. Bullard et al., ''Failure to Thrive in the 'Neglected' Child,'' *American Journal of Orthopsychiatry*, 37 (1967), pp. 680–689; M. Morris et al., ''Toward Prevention of Child Abuse,'' *Children* (1964), pp. 55–60; and Richard J. Gelles, ''The Social Construction of Child Abuse,'' *American Journal of Orthopsychiatry* 45 (April 1975), pp. 363–371.

[67] Richard J. Gelles, ''Child Abuse as Psychopathology: A Sociological Critique and Reformulation,'' *American Journal of Orthopsychiatry* 43 (July 1973), pp. 611–621.

[68] See E. Bennie and A. Sclare, ''The Battered Child Syndrome,'' *American Journal of Psychiatry* 125 (1969), pp. 975–979; Gil, *Violence Against Children;* and S. Zalba, ''Battered Children,'' *TransAction* 8 (July–August, 1971), pp. 58–61.

[69] See Kempe, ''Pediatric Implications of the Battered Baby Syndrome''; Gil, *Violence Against Children;* and Blair Justice and Rita Justice, *The Abusing Family* (New York: Human Sciences Press, 1976).

[70] Suzanne K. Steinmetz, ''The Use of Force for Resolving Family Conflict: The Training Ground for Abuse,'' *The Family Coordinator* 28 (January 1977), pp. 19–26.

[71] Richard J. Gelles, *The Violent Home: The Study of Physical Aggression Between Husbands and Wives* (Beverly Hills, Calif.: Sage Publications, 1974).

[72] Ibid.

[73] Boston Women's Health Book Collective, *Our Bodies, Ourselves* (New York: Simon and Schuster, 1973), p. 140.

[74] See Warren S. Thompson and David T. Lewis, *Population Problems* (New York: McGraw-Hill, 1965), and William Petersen, *Population* (New York: Macmillan, 1975).

[75] U.S., Congress, House, Committee on the Judiciary, *Proposed Constitutional Amendments on Abortion*, 94th Cong., 2d sess., 1976, Serial no. 46, pt. 1.

[76] Ibid.

[77] Bureau of the Census, *Statistical Abstract of the United States, 1976* (Washington, D.C., 1976), p. 58, and *The Washington Post* (November 11, 1977).

[78] U.S., Congress, House, Committee on Appropriations, *Departments of Labor and Health, Education, and Welfare Appropriations for 1978*, 95th Cong., 1st sess., 1977.

[79] Carl W. Tyler, Jr. and Jan Schneider, ''The Logistics of Abortion Services in the Absence of Restrictive Criminal Legislation in the United States,'' *American Journal of Public*

Health 61 (March 1971), pp. 490–491.

[80] Emile Durkheim, *Suicide,* John Spaulding and George Simpson, trans. (New York: The Free Press, 1951).

[81] Andrew F. Henry and James Short, "Suicide and External Restraint," in Anthony Giddens, ed., *The Sociology of Suicide* (London: Frank Cass, 1971), pp. 58–66.

[82] Ibid., p. 63.

[83] Nancy Allen, "History and Background of Suicidology," in Corrine Hatton, Sharon Valente, and Alice Rink, eds., *Suicide: Assessment and Intervention* (New York: Appleton-Century-Crofts, 1977), pp. 1–19.

[84] A. Kay Clifton and Dorothy E. Lee, "Self Destructive Consequences of Sex Role Socialization," *Suicide and Life-Threatening Behavior* 6 (Spring 1976), pp. 11–22.

[85] Leonard L. Linden and Warren Breed, "The Demographic Epidemiology of Suicide," in Edwin S. Schneidman, ed., *Suicidology: Contemporary Developments* (New York: Grunne and Stratton, 1976), pp. 71–98.

[86] Michael Peck, "Adolescent Suicide," in Hatton, Valente, and Rink, eds., *Suicide,* pp. 165–175.

[87] Earl A. Grollman, *Suicide: Prevention, Intervention, Postvention* (Boston: Beacon Press, 1971).

[88] See William C. Cockerham, *Medical Sociology* (Englewood Cliffs, N.J.: Prentice-Hall, 1978), p. 37.

[89] See Hatton, Valente, and Rink, eds., *Suicide.*

SUGGESTED READINGS

Kai T. Erikson, *Wayward Puritans: A Study in the Sociology of Deviance* (New York: John Wiley and Sons, Inc., 1966).
An excellent combination of historical scholarship and contemporary sociological analysis. Viewing deviance in Puritan New England from the functionalist perspective, Erikson documents the effects of moral absolutism on defining and dealing with deviance.

Simon Dinitz, Russell R. Dynes, and Alfred C. Clarke, *Deviance: Studies in Definition, Management, and Treatment,* second edition (New York: Oxford University Press, 1975).
An excellent collection of essays that combines a large number of classical articles with current research on almost every major form of deviant behavior.

David J. Rothman, *The Discovery of the Asylum: Social Order and Disorder in the New Republic* (Boston: Little, Brown and Company, 1971).
A social and historical analysis of the emergence and changes in institutions such as mental hospitals, penitentiaries, and almshouses in nineteenth century America. In order to understand the structure and functioning of social service institutions today, Rothman's book is essential reading.

Alex Thio, *Deviant Behavior* (Boston: Houghton Mifflin Company, 1978).
A current and broad consideration of different issues in terms of deviant behavior. Thio provides an excellent overview of theoretical frames of reference, including functionalism, conflict, and interactionism.

Boston Women's Health Book Collective, *Our Bodies, Ourselves.* (New York: Simon and Schuster, 1973).
Describes social, emotional, and sexual problems of women in contemporary society, including a fairly comprehensive treatment of the abortion controversy in both contemporary and historical perspectives.

Martin S. Weinberg and Colin J. Williams, *Male Homosexuals.* (New York: Penguin Books, 1975).
An interesting social-psychological study of male homosexuals and the homosexual lifestyle.

Commission on Obscenity and Pornography, *The Report of the Commission on Obscenity and Pornography.* (Washington, D.C.: U.S. Government Printing Office, 1970).
A comprehensive report that provides an historical perspective on pornography and obscenity as well as summarizing most of the major research studies on the subject.

Kate Millet, *The Prostitution Papers: A Quartet for Female Voice.* (New York: Ballantine Books, 1976).

An overview of the impact of prostitution on the lives of the participants. Most of the information is derived from case studies and interviews of working prostitutes.

Corrine Hatton, Sharon Valente, and Alice Rink (eds.), *Suicide: Assessment and Prevention.* (New York: Appleton-Century-Crofts, 1977).

A brief, but very readable and informative, book of readings on suicide. It covers the gamut of topics on suicide from cause to assessment and treatment.

Suzanne K. Steinmetz and Murray A. Straus, eds., *Violence in the Family* (New York: Dodd, Mead and Company, 1974).

Steinmetz and Straus provide an excellent collection of readings on violence in the family, including child abuse, violence between spouses and kin, and a section on the family as a training ground for societal violence.

Questions
for Discussion

1. How does the text define deviant behavior? What kinds of behavior are defined as deviant in our society? Why are these actions considered deviant?

2. Different views of the nature of deviance have played a prominent role in American history. Define absolutism, legalism, and relativism. What implications does each viewpoint have for the types of behaviors that are defined as deviant and for the way deviants are dealt with officially?

3. How is deviance defined from the functional perspective? From the conflict perspective? From the interactionist perspective? Functionalists distinguish between the terms dysfunction and deviance. What is the difference between these two terms and why is the distinction important for the study of deviant behavior?

4. What are the differences between merely engaging in homosexual acts and adopting a homosexual lifestyle? Compare and contrast biological, psychological, and sociological theories of the origins of homosexuality. What are the differences between male and female homosexual lifestyles?

5. Define prostitution. From the functionalist perspective, what functions does prostitution perform in American society?

6. Define pornography. From the interactionist perspective, why is it difficult to define pornography? What are the effects of seeing pornographic films and pictures and reading pornographic materials according to recent scientific studies?

7. Violence in the family is not new. Why has violence in the family been recently discovered? What are the factors associated with violence in the family?

8. What is the difference between miscarriage and induced abortion? Has induced abortion always been illegal in the United States? Compare and contrast the positions on abortion taken by the ''Pro-Choice'' advocates and the ''Pro-Life'' advocates.

9. Why is suicide not an entirely individual decision? What are the different types of suicide according to Durkheim? Why do college students have a very high suicide rate?

CHAPTER 16

Crime and Delinquency

CRIME AND PUNISHMENT: A BRIEF HISTORY
Crime and Punishment in America. From Reform to Incarceration.

CRIME AND DELINQUENCY AS SOCIAL PROBLEMS
The Functionalist Perspective. The Conflict Perspective. The Interactionist Perspective.

CRIME AND CRIMINALS IN THE UNITED STATES
Measuring Crime. Characteristics of Criminals.

PATTERNS OF CRIMINAL BEHAVIOR
Criminal Assault and Homicide. Theft. Organized Crime. White-Collar Crime. Sex Offenses. Victimless Crimes.

THE SYSTEM OF CRIMINAL JUSTICE
Processing the Alleged Criminal.

JUVENILE DELINQUENCY
Measuring Delinquency. The Characteristics of Delinquents.

CRIME AND DELINQUENCY: FUTURE PROSPECTS
Punishment. Better Law Enforcement. Compensation of Victims. Bail Reform. Decriminalization and Legalization. Reforming the Offender. Reforming Juvenile Justice.

CONCLUSION

In 1977, according to the Federal Bureau of Investigation, there was one serious crime committed in the United States every 3 seconds of each day. It was also reported that one violent crime occurred every 31 seconds.[1] Authorities on crime agree that these are conservative estimates, since many offenses are not reported. The thousands upon thousands of murders, rapes, robberies, and assaults that occur every year take their toll on the quality of American life. A recent Gallup poll reported that residents of our large cities identified crime as the most serious problem in their communities. Crime was mentioned almost twice as often as the problem considered second in seriousness: unemployment.[2]

There are substantial costs—some obvious, others hidden—associated with crime. First of all, there are *economic* costs: loss of personal property; lost wages due to time missed from work as the result of physical injury or emotional trauma and from filling out police reports

and insurance claims; the expense of health and property insurance; the higher costs of goods and services that result when businesses raise their prices to cover losses due to theft or other crimes; the cost of maintaining residential and business security systems; and the cost of operating the criminal justice system.

There are also *physical* costs to victims of violent crimes—rape, assault, and armed robbery always involve the risk of serious physical injury. Victims of violent crimes are murdered, blinded, or crippled every day of the year. In some cases, permanent injury, such as paralysis, plagues the victims for the rest of their lives. **The *emotional* costs are also high.** Being victimized is always psychologically traumatic both to the people directly involved and the members of their families. This can lead to continuing anxiety, fear of additional physical and emotional injury, and reluctance to be on the streets after dark for fear of further victimization. Violent crimes also instill fear

According to the F.B.I., one serious crime is committed in the United States approximately every three seconds of each day, and one violent crime occurs every thirty-one seconds.

in the general public. Even property crimes such as burglary, auto theft, or fraud can be emotionally traumatic for the victim and for the victim's family and neighbors. Having one's car stolen or house broken into can result in feelings of personal violation. Being "conned" or swindled may result in loss of self-esteem, feelings of personal betrayal, and mistrust and cynicism about the motives and intentions of others.

Finally, the *social* **costs of crime are enormous.** Security measures such as posting a guard at one's apartment building or having to use a passkey are extremely inconvenient. People who fear crime lose much of their personal freedom by restricting their activities to avoid the risk of being victimized. For example, persons in high-crime areas may be virtual prisoners in their own homes because they fear what might happen to them should they leave their relative safety. Furthermore, fear of crime leads to mistrust of others and feelings of alienation toward strangers. Such mistrust impairs cooperative relationships and lowers the quality of life.

In this chapter, we are concerned only with crime, which is an act that violates the criminal law. **A** *criminal* **is a person convicted, in a criminal court proceeding, of a crime.** We are not concerned with other violations of social norms that do not violate the criminal statutes (some of these behaviors are analyzed in chs. 15 and 18). Prior to discussing the characteristics of crime and criminals in America, it will be useful to review briefly the historical roots of criminal law in the United States and how crime is viewed from the three sociological perspectives utilized in this text.

CRIME AND PUNISHMENT: A BRIEF HISTORY

In Europe and the British Isles prior to the Middle Ages (approximately A.D. 800–1400), crimes were not defined officially and there were no official actions by agents of the political state against people who violated norms of public decency or threatened the social order. Such acts were generally considered private matters between the offender and the victim. Individuals and their families who felt wronged by the actions of another person would seek retribution against the wrongdoer or his relatives. This notion of personal justice was quite common and functional in societies of this period. However, as societies became more complex and as the family structure of large, clanlike units began to change, private vengeance became difficult to enforce.[3]

With the advent of the political state, the king, who represented the state, defined acts that threatened the public order as offenses against the state — and thus against the king and all of his subjects. In this way, the state emerged as the provider of justice and retribution. The concept of **crime** evolved, and the king began to levy fines and impose other forms of punishment on *criminals*. These actions by the monarch became legal precedents, many of which were eventually enacted into legal statutes by parliamentary bodies.

Prior to the eighteenth century, the government and powerful groups in England viewed the primary functions of government (and its legal structure) as the protection of property rights and the maintenance of public order. Criminal law was conceived as an instrument to protect honest, respectable, and hard-working people from the "criminal class." Criminals were viewed as basically depraved and largely beyond reform. To control this menace, the English legal statutes called for rather crude intimidation through harsh punishments. Whipping, physical mutilation, and hanging were at that time believed to be the most effective means of discouraging criminals and controlling crime.[4]

Crime and Punishment in America

In colonial America, attitudes toward crime were somewhat similar to those existing in England. Historian David Rothman sums them up thus:

Although eighteenth-century Americans were . . . apprehensive about deviant behavior and adopted elaborate precautions and procedures to control it, they did not interpret its presence as symptomatic of a basic flaw in community structure or expect to eliminate it. They would combat the evil, warn, chastise, correct, banish, flog or execute the offender. But they saw no prospect of eliminating deviancy from their midst. Crime, like poverty, was endemic to society.[5]

In addition, colonial Americans tended to equate crime with sin, and the consequences were severe:

The identification of disorder with sin made it difficult for legislators and ministers to distinguish carefully between major and minor infractions. Both were testimony to the natural depravity of man and the power of the devil — sure signs that the offender was destined to be a public menace and a damned sinner. This attitude underlies the heavy-handedness of eighteenth-century codes, which set capital punishments for crimes as different as murder and arson, horse-stealing and children's disrespect for parents.[6]

Colonial criminal codes provided for a wide range of punishments: fines, whippings, the pillory, confinement in public stocks or cages, banishment, and the gallows. However, institutionalization was rarely used as a punishment. A person was kept in jail usually only during the period of determining what punishment was called for. Serving time in jail was yet to be widely used as a punishment.

In the early 1800s, attitudes toward crime began to change. Americans were being influenced by the Enlightenment philosophy of such social thinkers as Cesare Beccaria and Jeremy Bentham, which viewed human beings as pleasure-seeking and pain-avoiding creatures who possessed the capacity for reason and who could exercise free will. This was a considerable departure from earlier views of human nature that conceived of people as inherently evil and depraved. This Enlightenment view opened up the possibility that something could be done about crime — that it was not beyond the control of human intervention.[7]

The system of criminal justice in the United States began to show the influence of this new philosophy. Crime came to be equated with poverty, immorality, and corruption in society. Criminals were now seen as unfortunate victims of circumstance rather than as inherently depraved individuals. This made it possible to consider how individuals might be reformed. Attempts at change focused on those conditions thought to be at the core of the problem: a weakening of the institutions of church and family, and increasing corruption in the community. Institutions began to emerge to overcome these problems: almshouses for the poor, asylums for the insane, and penitentiaries for criminals. No longer were offenses against the law treated in an informal fashion; no longer were jails simply a place in which a person awaited punishment. The penitentiaries that burst on the American scene were conceived as positive efforts to remove the unfortunate from evil influences and to reform them into functioning members of society. Through the use of discipline, routine, and isolation, prisons were intended to remove the individual from temptations to evil and to provide a controlled regimen that was beneficial to society. The stakes were high, for, as Rothman put it, "Nothing less than the safety and future stability of the republic was at issue, the triumph of good over evil, or order over chaos."[8]

It was during this period that separate systems of justice for children and adolescents began to emerge. The notion that childhood was a separate social status and a special stage in the life cycle became prominent. Prior to the eighteenth century, children were seen in most societies as miniature adults — naive and less developed, but equally capable of, and inclined toward, evil. However, the Enlightenment ushered in a new era of thinking about childhood, and many treatises and manuals describing the ideal child were published in the seventeenth and eighteenth centuries as guides to parents. This new conception of childhood emphasized the following:

1. keeping a close watch over children;
2. disciplining children, rather than pampering them;
3. modesty as a virtue;
4. hard work and teaching the work ethic to children;
5. strict obedience to authority on the part of children.[9]

Juvenile misbehavior was seen to result from the same corrupting community influences that caused adult crime, and particularly from a lack of strong family discipline. It was assumed that juvenile delinquents would graduate to adult crimes if no efforts were made to remove them from evil environments and to reform them. The juvenile court emerged at the turn of the twentieth century as a result of this new view of childhood and as a means of saving children from sin and corruption. The juvenile court was based on the assumption that children should be treated differently than adults—that the juvenile justice system should serve more a parental role of guidance for the wayward child rather than as a punisher of the criminal offender.[10]

From Reform to Incarceration

The optimism about reform in the early part of the nineteenth century did not last. As the century progressed, prisons, hospitals, mental institutions, and training centers for delinquents came to be viewed less as centers of rehabilitation and more as places to incarcerate dangerous individuals who might prove threatening to the established order.[11] By the 1850s, almost every type of asylum was losing its special qualities as a place of reform, and by the 1870s, few traces remained of their original designs. In prisons, reform and rehabilitation gave way to goals of peace and security within the walls.

There are a number of reasons for this change of emphasis in prisons. First, the Civil War created more people who were dependent on the state because of the death or absence of a productive member of the family, while at the same time it drained off resources that states might have used to improve conditions in the prisons. Second, there was considerable public disappointment and disillusionment over the inability of prisons to eradicate crime and delinquency, and this drew public attention and support away from efforts to retain rehabilitation as the central goal of institutions. Third, the prison populations were increasingly composed of recent immigrants, such as the Irish, and this lent to prisons an alien and thus somewhat threatening and foreboding character in the minds of many Anglo-Saxon Protestant Americans. At the time of the Civil War, inmate populations in the New York penitentiaries were 44 percent foreign-born, in Illinois 46 percent.[12] For many people, this meant that prisons were no longer institutions designed to help unfortunate Americans who were led astray by corrupting influences in the community but rather were places to house and control evil and disruptive influences from foreign countries.

A final factor that changed the character of prisons was that mere incarceration was all too easily confused with the reform of the inmate. The rhetoric of reform remained a part of the public image of the institution while at the same time the superintendents were content to administer a custodial program.

Once begun, the decline from rehabilitation to custodianship took on a self-reinforcing quality. As the community increasingly utilized asylum facilities to confine the hardened criminal, the incurably insane, and the decrepit poor, the recently insane from comfortable households or the able-bodied poor in need of temporary relief avoided them as best they could. In turn, the chronic and the helpless filled the vacancies and the institutions became even less attractive to anyone else. Superintendents then more easily accommodated themselves to the tasks of custodianship, and the notion of reform became irrelevant to the daily routine.[13]

As long as the appearance of reform and rehabilitation existed, the public was largely content to leave the workings of the institutions to the superintendents. For the superintendents, it was easier and cheaper to focus on control and incarceration, with little concern for nobler goals.

This custodial emphasis in prisons and reformatories has persisted through much of this century. There have been periodic efforts to introduce new programs into the institutions, and some of these programs have been beneficial. However, we are still affected by the legacy of the nineteenth century. The primary function of institutions has remained to protect the public from criminals and delinquents rather than to provide a place of asylum for the offender where he can be protected from corrupting influences and rehabilitated to a virtuous life. Although we know much more today about the sources of criminality, we have to a large extent been no more successful in coping with the crime problem than were Americans during previous centuries. Before turning to some of the reasons why this is the case, we will look at the varied ways in which crime might be considered a social problem.

CRIME AND DELINQUENCY AS SOCIAL PROBLEMS

The Functionalist Perspective

Imagine what society would be like if there were no laws governing behavior. The consideration of such a possibility offers a special appreciation of the functionalist perspective on law and crime. From this view, law is a body of legal principles based on social norms that are widely shared by members of society. The primary purpose (or manifest function) of law is to preserve the social order by protecting people and their property, and preserving a valued way of life. **Crime and delinquency are social problems to the extent that they disrupt the smooth and efficient functioning of society and, in an extreme situation, threaten the very existence of society.** As we have seen, crime and delinquency are costly in economic, physical, social, and emotional grounds. If there were no laws and no police power to enforce them, social conditions would be chaotic—the rule of the most powerful, the shrewdest, or the most intelligent would prevail—and it would be impossible for society to achieve common goals.

From the functionalist perspective, crime and delinquency result from structural flaws in society. (The student should review the theories of deviant behavior discussed in the preceding chapter.) If people are properly socialized, they will share common values and goals and work through legitimate channels to achieve them. In addition, society must provide sufficient opportunities for individuals to achieve their goals through these channels. If there is failure at either level—individuals do not internalize important societal values and norms, or they are not given the opportunities to succeed—then crime and delinquency are likely to result. These problems do not result from individual inadequacies or personality deficiencies; the ultimate problem involves a flaw in the social system, resulting in some individuals not being fully integrated into society. The people involved are responding to the social conditions that they confront.[14]

Rather than naively assuming that all crime and delinquency are dysfunctional for society, functionalists are aware of the complexities of social reality: crime can be both beneficial and detrimental for society. For example, organized crime performs certain latent functions for our society that contribute to its overall operation. Syndicated criminal groups provide a number of products and services that the public demands—gambling, prostitution, illicit drugs, pornography, and the like. Organized crime in the United States is perpetuated, at least in part, because it performs certain functions that are not met by any legitimate institutions. For this reason we should expect organized crime to continue as an important part of our society until legal ways of performing these functions are developed. According to the functionalist perspective, if a social practice is widespread and continues over a long period of time, it may be performing important functions for society.

The impact of organized crime is not, of course, entirely positive. Some of the activities of organized criminal groups tend to be dysfunctional in that they undermine the well-being of American society. For example, organized crime often involves the corruption of public officials, which contributes to public cynicism about their honesty and their willingness to deal with the problems of crime. In evaluating the problem of crime and delinquency, it is essential to investigate all of the consequences—both positive and negative—before accepting possible solutions.

The Conflict Perspective

From the conflict perspective, crime and delinquency are not viewed as resulting from flaws in the system but rather are seen as normal parts of a social order in which different groups are struggling over scarce resources. There are not commonly shared values and goals, however, because what serves the interests of one group may work to the detriment of another.

For non-Marxian conflict theorists, the law is a set of rules for repressing human selfishness and maintaining order in society. The major purpose of law is to minimize conflict between competing interest groups by providing legal means for resolving issues and thus avoiding potential violent solutions. However, social conflict is viewed as an inevitable and normal part of a society in which there are differences in group values and interests. Interest groups might form temporary and shifting alliances with one another if they view such arrangements as beneficial, but they will be dissolved when they no longer serve those interests. According to non-Marxian conflict theory, crime and delinquency originate in human nature and in the competitive nature of society. In the struggle for dominance in society, some groups find it desirable to turn to criminal activities as a way of pursuing their interests.

One source of conflict between groups is the differences in social norms held by two groups who come in contact with one another. The dominant group attempts to incorporate its norms into law, and such legislation may make illegal behavior that is regarded as acceptable and appropriate by the other group.[15] For example, many immigrant groups brought with them to America values and customs that were divergent from those of the influential ethnic groups in the United States. The Italian custom of the vendetta — personal revenge for a wrongdoing committed against an individual or his family — clashed directly with the legal structure in America. **From the conflict perspective, crime and delinquency are social problems when they threaten the values and interests of some group with the power to make its concerns felt.**

The Marxian view of crime and delinquency is somewhat different. For Marxians, law is simply the codification of the values of the dominant groups in society. The primary purpose of law is to preserve and enhance the interests of these groups and ensure the subordination of other groups. Crime and delinquency have their origin in the nature of a social order that exploits and represses the non-powerful; they are a direct result of the social conditions under which the "have-nots" must live.

However, for the Marxians, social conflict can be eliminated if the social order is substantially changed: if the oppressive nature of capitalism is changed, then conflict — including crime and delinquency — can be reduced or eliminated. They also argue that some crime is tolerated because it serves the interests of the powerful and the privileged. Some Marxians would argue that organized crime, for example, continues without the threat of serious legal action because of its relationship to the political economy: it provides illegal services and products to business, government, and the public. In addition, it invests some of its profits from illegal activities into legitimate businesses in order to avoid prosecution and to gain the support of the business community by providing much needed capital.[16]

The Interactionist Perspective

The interactionist perspective emphasizes the importance of consensus about values and the role of social interaction and shared expectations in shaping behavior. Interactionists would agree that law is a set of formalized social norms that serve to preserve widely shared values. Crime and delinquency are learned behaviors that violate important societal norms. This learning occurs in social interaction and shapes not only the person's behavior but also his or her self-concept. **From this perspective, then, crime and delinquency are social problems to the extent that influential groups define them as such.** This has nothing to do with whether the behavior is functional or dysfunctional or whether some group feels that it is not receiving its fair share of resources. **For the interactionist, the critical factor is whether there is a consensus among the members of a particular group that a problem exists.**

The learning process by which a person becomes a criminal or delinquent is a long and complex one.[17] In some cases, he may be immersed in an environment that places great value on illegal behavior. He is encouraged by those around him to view such illegal activities positively. This does not mean that he will necessarily become a criminal or delinquent, but such influence certainly increases the likelihood of this outcome. In other cases, through the labeling process, people *expect* the person to engage in criminal behavior and thus increase the likelihood that he will do so. If there is a shared expectation of this person as a criminal, then he may begin to develop the self-concept of a criminal—he may begin to view himself as that kind of person.

Some forms of crime and delinquency are not, when considered objectively, a threat to American society. For example, in the previous chapter, evidence was offered that prostitution, pornography, and homosexuality do not constitute such a threat to American society today. Yet, many people view them as a problem and share a consensus that such activities should not be permitted to exist. For the interactionist, what is important is people's *definition* of reality, not objective reality. People act and develop social policy on the basis of their definitions of reality; so in order to understand their behavior, we must focus on those definitions. People may nevertheless be convinced by law enforcement agencies that there is a large rise in dangerous crime and may be willing to support policies (such as increasing minimum prison sentences for some offenses) as a way of combating this rise in crime. Thus, law enforcement officials might argue that there is a "crime wave" in order to obtain more funding for the police. Even though there may be little or no actual increase in crimes (or the increase might be among relatively nondangerous crimes such as auto theft), people who are convinced of the increase will support policies to attack the rising crime. **Thus, for the interactionist, people's definition of the situation is important in determining whether crime and delinquency are considered social problems.**

CRIME AND CRIMINALS IN THE UNITED STATES

Do you consider yourself a criminal? Before answering that question, think about whether you have ever committed a crime (a violation of the legal code). If you are like almost everyone else in the United States, you probably have committed some type of crime at one time or another. Studies have

shown that most Americans, by their own admission, have committed at least one crime.[18] However, very few have ever been arrested, and fewer still have been convicted of a criminal offense. Those who have been convicted are the proverbial "tip of the iceberg" of crime. Because only a fraction of total criminal activity is detected by or reported to law enforcement agencies, there are substantial difficulties in measuring the amount of crime that actually exists. Before we can consider the characteristics of *people who commit crimes,* it is essential to our understanding of the problem that we evaluate the different *sources of data about crime* that are available.

Measuring Crime

Official Sources of Data

The most widely used source of official statistics on crime in the United States is the Uniform Crime Reports (UCRs) that the Federal Bureau of Investigation publishes annually.[19] Monthly reports from more than 8000 cities and towns are collected by the FBI, providing information from areas inhabited by nearly 91 percent of the total population. Uniform Crime Report statistics include "crimes known to police" and "crimes cleared by arrest" for major offenses (Part I Offenses) and less serious offenses (Part II Offenses). (See Table 16.1.) The Crime Index (or official crime rate typically reported in the media) is based on the number of Part I offenses "known to the police" per 100,000 inhabitants. The FBI's Crime Index is the most widely used indicator of the actual amount and patterns (types of offenses and their distribution) of crime in the United States. However, there are serious flaws in the UCRs that make them of highly questionable *validity* and *reliability*.

The Uniform Crime Reports are gathered in a fragmented and uncoordinated manner. Although Congress has given the FBI responsibility for collecting national statistics on crime, the Bureau has no legal authority to compel state and local law enforcement agencies to report statistics. In addition, although the FBI provides each local

TABLE 16.1

Total Arrests of Persons by Age, Sex, and Race, 1977

OFFENSE CHARGED	GRAND TOTAL ALL AGES	UNDER 18	UNDER 25	PERCENT MALE	FEMALE	WHITE	NEGRO
TOTAL	9,029,335	24.0	56.4	84.0	16.0	71.7	25.7
Part I							
Criminal homicide:							
(a) Murder and nonnegligent manslaughter	17,163	9.7	43.5	85.5	14.5	45.9	51.0
(b) Manslaughter by negligence	2,933	11.1	51.3	88.8	11.2	78.5	19.2
Forcible rape	25,800	16.5	56.3	98.9	1.1	50.4	47.3
Robbery	122,514	32.0	74.4	92.6	7.4	40.8	57.0
Aggravated assault	221,329	16.3	49.0	87.2	12.8	59.1	38.8
Burglary	454,193	51.5	84.0	94.0	6.0	69.1	28.9
Larceny-theft	1,006,915	42.9	72.8	68.2	31.8	65.7	32.0
Motor vehicle theft	135,196	53.0	83.4	91.9	8.1	71.1	26.1
Violent crime[1]	386,806	21.0	57.3	89.6	10.4	52.2	45.7
Property crime[2]	1,596,304	46.2	76.9	77.6	22.4	67.1	30.6
Subtotal for above offenses	1,986,043	41.2	73.1	79.9	20.1	64.2	33.5
Part II							
Other assaults	399,854	19.1	52.1	86.2	13.8	64.1	33.5
Arson	16,525	49.8	73.0	88.7	11.3	76.8	21.3
Forgery and counterfeiting	67,984	12.8	53.8	70.9	29.1	67.0	31.8
Fraud	216,672	10.3	40.6	64.4	35.6	65.8	33.0
Embezzlement	6,607	11.8	45.1	77.3	22.7	77.1	21.7
Stolen property: buying, receiving, possessing	104,401	32.9	71.2	89.2	10.8	65.2	33.4
Vandalism	196,724	60.3	83.5	91.6	8.4	81.5	16.6
Weapons; carrying, possessing, etc.	136,214	16.0	51.2	92.0	8.0	60.0	39.4
Prostitution and commercialized vice	77,115	4.3	64.5	29.3	70.7	44.4	53.6
Sex offenses (except forcible rape and prostitution)	60,959	18.4	47.7	91.1	8.9	76.5	21.1
Drug abuse violations	569,293	23.2	73.9	86.1	13.9	76.8	21.7
Gambling	52,520	4.2	20.8	91.1	8.9	26.8	68.6
Offenses against family and children	53,385	5.9	36.5	89.7	10.3	66.0	32.5
Driving under the influence	1,104,132	2.2	31.0	91.7	8.3	84.3	13.0
Liquor laws	321,573	37.3	81.3	85.2	14.8	89.1	8.1
Drunkenness	1,208,525	4.1	28.2	92.8	7.2	78.6	17.9
Disorderly conduct	624,736	19.4	58.5	82.8	17.2	65.5	30.8
Vagrancy	44,172	12.7	56.5	65.4	34.6	60.1	37.6
All other offenses (except traffic)	1,487,133	20.8	55.8	84.6	15.4	68.2	28.9
Suspicion	23,305	26.5	69.7	85.7	14.3	67.1	30.9
Curfew and loitering law violations	86,013	100.0	100.0	78.1	21.9	73.8	24.4
Runaways	185,447	100.0	100.0	42.4	57.6	86.9	10.7

[1] *Violent crime* is offenses of murder, forcible rape, robbery, and aggravated assault.

[2] *Property crime* is offenses of burglary, larceny-theft, and motor vehicle theft.

SOURCE. U.S. Department of Justice, "Crime in the United States, 1977," *FBI Uniform Crime Reports* (Washington, D.C.: U.S. Government Printing Office, 1978), pp. 182–184.

TABLE 16.2
Comparison of NORC Survey and UCR Rates[a]

INDEX CRIMES	NORC SURVEY 1965–66	UCR RATE FOR INDIVIDUALS, 1965	UCR RATE FOR INDIVIDUALS AND ORGANIZATIONS, 1965
Willful homicide	3.0	5.1	5.1
Forcible rape	42.5	11.6	11.6
Robbery	94.0	61.4	61.4
Aggravated assault	218.3	106.6	106.6
Burglary	949.1	299.6	605.3
Larceny ($50 and over)	606.5	267.4	393.3
Motor vehicle theft	206.2	226.0	251.0
Total violence	357.8	184.7	184.7
Total property	1761.8	793.0	1249.6

[a]Rates per 100,000 population

SOURCE: The President's Commission on Law Enforcement and Administration of Justice, *The Challenge of Crime in a Free Society* (Washington, D.C.: U.S. Government Printing Office, 1967), pp. 21–22.

police department submitting information on crime with an elaborate instruction manual containing detailed illustrations of how to complete the reports, the Bureau has no systematic auditing program for checking the accuracy with which crime statistics are reported.

Crimes reported in the UCR are not representative of the actual amount and patterns of offenses. A great deal of criminal activity in America goes unrecorded, largely because it is not reported to the police. When the UCRs are compared with unofficial sources of information, such as the National Opinion Research Center (NORC) and the Law Enforcement Assistance Act (LEAA) studies, there is evidence that the UCRs underestimate the total number of Part I crimes by about half.[20] More recent data support these findings.[21] In addition, police investigate and officially record offenses reported by citizens only when the police believe the offense actually took place (see Table 16.2). Thus, the police make a judgment about the veracity of citizen reports.

The Crime Index is not comparable between jurisdictions and is not consistent from one year to the next within the same reporting unit. One reason for this is that there are fifty different states, each with its own criminal code. For example, an offense that is classified in one state as robbery may be classified as larceny or even burglary in another. What is considered forcible rape in one state may be defined as a less serious sex offense in another. The people responsible for filling out the UCRs are generally knowledgeable about the laws in their state and often fill out the reports based on local definitions of crime rather than following the instructions for the UCRs- an unintentional, but nevertheless serious, mistake in terms of the accuracy of the data. Another factor contributing to the lack of comparability between jurisdictions is that the overall crime index (based on the Part I offenses) does not provide an indication of the actual patterns of offenses. For example, Table 16.3 presents the crime index for two cities, with Kenosha, Wisconsin having a slightly higher rate of crime than Montgomery, Alabama. However, the patterns of offenses in the two cities differ considerably. Although one's property is in substantial danger in Kenosha (high rates of burglary, larceny, robbery, and motor vehicle theft), one's degree of personal safety is comparatively high because the rates of violent crimes (homicide, rape, and assault) are low. In Montgomery, on the other hand, there is more risk to personal safety, whereas property is comparatively secure. Problems of this sort tend to make the UCRs highly unreliable and difficult to interpret.

The Uniform Crime Reports are subject to manipulation and outright fraudulence. The

Crime Index for Two Standard Metropolitan Statistical Areas, 1977[a]

OFFENSE	CRIME RATE	
	KENOSHA WIS.	MONTGOMERY ALA.
Willful homicide	5.5	20.7
Forcible rape	26.1	41.7
Robbery	142.5	129.7
Aggravated assault	58.6	122.0
Burglary	1566.2	1613.6
Larceny ($50 and over)	4001.7	3285.7
Motor vehicle theft	734.0	311.7
Total rate of part I offenses	6534.6	5525.1

[a]Rate per 100,000 inhabitants

SOURCE: U.S. Department of Justice, "Crime in the United States, 1977," *FBI Uniform Crime Reports* (Washington, D.C.: U.S. Government Printing Office, 1978), pp. 62, 65.

UCRs are frequently used as indicators of organizational performance, and, as such, there is a built-in temptation for officials to use them to enhance their own and their organizations' image. For example, a crude indicator of police performance is the ratio of *offenses known to the police* to *offenses cleared by arrest* (that is, when some person is arrested, booked, and turned over to a lower court for an initial appearance for that offense). If there is a high proportion of arrests in relation to offenses, then it appears that the local police are doing their job and vigorously pursuing criminals. This makes it very tempting to clear many crimes by arresting "the usual suspects" (e.g. previously convicted offenders, youths, and others who find it difficult to defend themselves against this sort of harassment) in order to have a favorable ratio of arrests to "offenses known."[22] (Although "offenses cleared by conviction"—that is, someone is actually convicted of an offense known to the police—appears in the UCRs, they are rarely reported for public consumption.) These kinds of errors tend to invalidate the UCRs as indicators of the actual volume and patterns of crime.

Unofficial Sources of Data

Although the public is most familiar with the FBI data on crime, social scientists have developed other, unofficial sources of data in order to overcome some of the weaknesses of the Uniform Crime Reports and thus gain a more accurate picture of crime in America.

Observer-based **studies involve some kind of first-hand observation of criminal activity.** Sometimes this involves participant-observation—the observer participates in most of the group's activities except taking part in the actual crimes. For example, William F. Whyte became a member of a gang in order to study, among other things, their criminal behavior.[23] Observation studies face two major kinds of risks; one is legal, the other scientific. The legal problem relates to the fact that social scientists are not immune from legal prosecution if they keep confidential information regarding the illegal activities of a group they are observing; they can be legally cited for the criminal offense of withholding evidence. The scientific problem relates to objectivity. It is difficult to maintain a close relationship with the members of a group and still retain a purely scientific approach to their actions. This is especially difficult for a participant observer. He constantly runs the risk of "going native"—that is, becoming so much a part of the group he is studying that he begins to identify with them, takes on their perspective, and in the process loses his scientific objectivity.

Victim-based **studies of crime are the most important source of unofficial data.** As mentioned above, the NORC- and LEAA-sponsored research projects conducted large-scale studies with highly trained interviewers in which members of a representative sample of American households were asked if they or any member of their household had been a victim of a crime during the previous year. As mentioned above, these studies indicate that official statistics seem to greatly underestimate the total amount of crime. However, the ordering of offenses from least to most frequent is quite similar for the two indicators.

Self-report-based **measures of criminality involve anonymous questionnaires that ask people which offenses they have committed.** Such measures have been used on different target populations. Some are aimed at obtaining a representative sampling of adult Americans. Most, however, have focused on young people. For example, one study compared the unofficial, self-reported rates of delinquency with official, juvenile court, and police-report data sources.[24] The findings, which other self-report studies support, were that: (1) almost everyone, by his or her own admission, has broken some criminal law (often a serious offense), (2) the amount of hidden (unreported) crime is enormous, and (3) convicted offenders are highly unrepresentative of persons violating the criminal law. Those who are arrested and placed in prisons or juvenile training schools tend to be persons with limited resources and/or those who have committed serious offenses and done so frequently.

A comparison of official and unofficial indicators shows that serious offenses are more likely to be reported, and that the more persistent offenders—those who commit crimes frequently—are more likely to be arrested. Both official and unofficial data should be viewed with considerable caution. However, regardless of their flaws, they provide us with an estimate of crime in the United States. A combination of indicators provides us with a useful measure of the amount and patterns of crime in the United States. It is at the same time a measure that must be used with great care in making decisions about the criminal justice system.

Characteristics of Criminals

To be legally defined as a "criminal," a person must be convicted of a crime in a criminal court proceeding. However, since most people who commit crimes are not so convicted, we must cast a broader net in order to determine the social characteristics of those who commit crimes. The most widely used approach is to investigate the social characteristics of those arrested for Part I offenses—the more serious crimes. (Some crimes, such as embezzlement and prostitution, are, for obvious reasons, largely limited to that segment of the population having greater opportunity to commit such crimes.) The following social characteristics have been found to be important.

Age

While people under 25 years of age comprise about 40 percent of our population, they constitute fully three-quarters of the arrestees for Part I offenses (see Table 16.1). Young persons under the age of 18 also constitute the majority of persons arrested for arson, vandalism, auto theft, and violation of alcohol and drug laws. Certainly one reason for the overrepresentation of young people among arrestees is that they commit crimes at higher rates than do people in older age groups. Young people are less likely to have established social ties, such as marriage, or family and occupational commitments, that might restrain them from engaging in criminal acts. However, it is likely that young people are more prone to arrest because their crimes are more visible and they have fewer material resources that aid in avoiding arrest. The age variable is important in another respect. Since young people are more likely to commit crimes, and since this age category represents a growing proportion of our populace, then we can expect the crime rate to increase because of these demographic changes. In evaluating increases in crime rates, it is important to keep these factors in mind.

Sex

Sex is the most predictable factor in determining crime rates. Males commit far more Part I offenses than do females. While males comprise roughly half of our population, there are four males arrested for each female. (Obviously, some crimes, such as prostitution and abortion, are predominantly committed by females.) This predominance of males arrested for Part I crimes can be explained in part by sex-role expectations. The serious crimes, such as assault or homicide, are consistent with the characteristics of the traditional male sex role, with emphasis on activity, daring, and aggressiveness. Females are socialized to respond in a more passive and dependent fashion, and are likely to react to conditions differently than do males. Furthermore, females are less frequently arrested for criminal offenses than males. Finally, females have not committed serious offenses nearly as often as males. This appears to be changing, however—the rate of arrests among females for serious crimes such as robbery, assault, and larceny has been increasing at a much faster rate than for males. In the near future, there may be little difference between the rates and types of offenses among males and females.[25]

Race and Ethnicity

Traditionally, the racial or ethnic group that is on the bottom of the status hierarchy in the United States has exhibited the highest crime rates. In earlier times, it was the Irish or the Italians. Today, it is the blacks, Hispanic Americans, and Puerto Ricans. For example, blacks comprise about 12 percent of our population, but they account for 34 percent of the arrests for Part I offenses. Once again, there is undoubtedly a higher incidence of crimes committed by members of minority groups. However, this does not account for all the differences in arrest statistics. In addition, biases in the enforcement of law are undoubtedly a factor. **Racial prejudice, along with the fact that racial minorities are likely to have a low social standing in the community, increases**

People under 25 years of age constitute about three-quarters of all persons arrested for serious crimes. Blacks comprise about 12 percent of our nation's population, but they account for about 34 percent of the arrests for serious offenses. Poor people are more likely to be arrested than middle-income and affluent people.

the likelihood that members of these groups will be arrested for a crime. A respectable, middle-class white person is less likely to be arrested for the same offense.[26]

Socioeconomic Status

Studies conducted during the past four decades have documented the relationship between social class and crime: people with lower socioeconomic status are more likely to commit crimes. This finding is particularly pronounced when official sources of data (such as the FBI Uniform Crime Reports) are utilized. However, given the problems previously mentioned with official sources of data, many social scientists remained skeptical about this finding, and more recent studies have begun to cast doubt on the magnitude of the relationship. Studies based on self-reported information suggest that the amount of crime does not vary greatly *between* social classes, but that poor people are more likely to be arrested and convicted for their crimes, while "respectable" middle-class crimes are less often detected. Furthermore, the types of crime that a lower-class person is likely to commit (homicide, assault, robbery, and the like) are visible and more frequently reported to the police. The crimes that middle-class people are more likely to commit (such as fraud or embezzlement) are less often reported because of the embarrassment and chagrin of the victims. Thus, while the *types* of crimes committed may vary from one social class to another, there is a growing body of research demonstrating that the *amounts* of crime are not substantially different between social classes.[27]

PATTERNS OF CRIMINAL BEHAVIOR

Although we talk about "crime" as if it were a well-defined phenomenon, the word *crime* is actually a grab-bag term encompassing many diverse forms of behavior that have one thing in common: violation of criminal statutes. In order to understand the problems that crime creates for American society, it is essential to discuss the various types of crime separately, considering the nature of the offense

and the characteristics of people who are likely to commit such crimes. While we cannot consider all crimes, we will consider the more important ones and the ones that illustrate the range of effects that crime has on American citizens.

Criminal Assault and Homicide

Criminal assault **is the unlawful application of physical force to another person.** Such assaultive behavior is commonplace in American society. Well over one-half million people were arrested for some form of assault in 1977. It is especially common among those subcultural groups in which physical aggression (especially among males) is defined as a socially acceptable means of solving problems and viewed as a way of gaining status in the group.[28] Violence is usually learned in intimate contact with people who are important in the individual's life and is reinforced through observing role models on television and other media.[29]

Criminal homicide **refers to the unlawful killing of one person by another.** Close to 20,000 people were arrested for criminal homicide in 1977. Assaultive behavior and criminal homicide are closely associated in that most homicides are the *unintended* outcomes of physical assaults. Usually, violent situations that result in the victim's death are characterized by the intended or inadvertent angering of the offender by the victim's insult or ridicule, flirtation with the offender's lover or spouse, noncompliance with the offender's commands, and the like. The offender is often incensed by the victim's actions and retaliates. "Retaliation represents an offender's attempt to maintain face in response to challenge or degradation by a victim."[30] Assaultive behavior is only one form of retaliation and one that is highly associated with subcultural factors.

In contrast to the image presented in the media, a person actually has *more* to fear in terms of homicide and assault from *people he knows* than from total strangers. The vast majority of murders occur in the home or between persons who are acquaintances. For example, the President's Commission on Crime in the District of Columbia found that in 27 percent of all known homicides, the murderers were *known* to the victim as a spouse, in 10 percent as a relative, and in 40 percent as an acquaintance. In addition, homicides are typically "crimes of passion," occurring in the heat of an emotional situation. Homicide is also often associated with robbery. While both of the foregoing patterns have increased in frequency over the past few years, robbery-related homicide is increasing much more rapidly than the passionate pattern.[31]

Assault and homicide, by their very nature, are among the most feared crimes. They constitute a considerable threat to people's personal safety and well-being. They are costly in terms of physical injury to the victim, medical care for the victim, and the incarceration and prosecution of the apprehended offender. A far less tangible, but equally important, social cost of crime is the climate of fear that it creates in some areas of our cities. This fear of assault can lead a person to be cautious and distrustful of strangers (although, as we have seen, most of the danger comes from acquaintances) to the point that everyday social intercourse becomes strained and fraught with anxiety. However, people tend to *overestimate* their likelihood of being victimized. In fact, there is substantial evidence showing that the victim often plays a *precipitating* role in violence, and that violence is more likely to occur when both the victim and the offender (not just one of them) are prone to, and anticipate, violence. Victims often strike the first blow or are the first to engage in a show of force.[32]

Theft

Theft is the illegal taking away of another's property without the person's consent and with the intention of depriving the person of it. The term covers a broad range of property offenses, from such crude ones as burglary to such sophisticated forms as crimes involving multimillion-dollar swindles. Types of thieves vary from highly trained professional confidence men to service station attendants who pilfer tools from their employers or take candy and cigarettes without paying for them. Large-scale, organized theft is extremely profitable and involves relatively little risk of being caught and, if apprehended, of receiving a stiff penalty. Petty theft, on the other hand, is very risky and usually nets the offender little profit.[33]

The most successful thieves, and those most respected by their colleagues and law-enforcement authorities alike, are those whom sociologist Edwin Sutherland termed *professional thieves*.[34] Professional thieves must be good actors, likeable and trustworthy in appearance, to ply their trade effectively. Their crimes depend on their ability to convince others that they are somebody that they are not. Professional theft involves picking pockets, organized shoplifting, confidence games, forgery (including counterfeiting, passing illegal checks and money orders, and the like), sophisticated and well-organized burglaries and robberies, and extortion (e.g. blackmailing others who are engaging in illegal acts).[35]

Professional thieves use sophisticated, nonviolent techniques that usually involve manipulating the "mark" or victim. They steal as a regular business; their crimes are carefully planned; they are highly proficient in their trade; and they tend to associate primarily with others involved in the rackets, such as fences, and with those who profit from underworld activity, such as unscrupulous lawyers and corrupt policemen and other officials. They are members of the same subculture with a common language, code of conduct, and unique value system. They define themselves as thieves, and are so regarded by their associates. Professional thieves are generally rather conventional in their attitudes on most issues and respect people who are craftsmen like themselves — including honest and competent law-enforcement officers. However, they are rather contemptuous of their "inferiors" — the semiprofessional and amateur thieves.[36]

Semiprofessional thieves engage in strong-arm robberies, holdups, burglaries, and larcenies that do not involve much detailed planning or careful execution.[37] Many semiprofessional thieves work alone, such as in liquor store and service station holdups. Unlike professional thieves, who tend to come from all walks of life and social class backgrounds, semiprofessional thieves frequently get their start in crime as members of predatory street gangs in the inner-city slums. Adult semiprofessional thieves spend major portions of their lives in prison. They also tend to be *recidivists* — repeat offenders — who are returned to prison for the same kind of offense for which they were first committed. They tend to be "right guys" who get along fairly well in prison but who fail to stay out of trouble for very long on the outside, especially if they return to their old neighborhoods after release. They tend to define themselves as "crooks" who are victims of a corrupt and inequitable society, and are usually more hostile and antagonistic than their professional counterparts. They are, as a group, among the poorest parole risks.[38]

Amateur thieves are otherwise respectable persons who steal, or youthful offenders who commit criminal acts that are crude and unsophisticated. They define themselves as honest, law-abiding citizens. Typical of adult amateur theft is pilfering from an employer — a very costly crime that is estimated to amount to about $6 billion in merchandise and materials in 1979. Approximately 70 to 80 percent of thefts from businesses may be attributed to employee theft and shoplifting. Businesses and industries suffer substantial losses from thefts by customers who feel little guilt about stealing from them. For example, in her classic study of chronic shoplifters, Mary Cameron found that the offender was likely to be female, identified herself with respectable society, had no associations with known criminals, and was not a neurotic with some uncontrollable urge to steal.[39] However, Cameron's shoplifters did have special techniques and devices for stealing and had been systematically involved in similar thefts for some time.

Most violations of property laws committed by juveniles are amateur affairs in that they are unplanned, opportunistic, and highly unsophisticated. They include offenses such as stealing beer from a parked truck, stealing an unguarded bicycle, or slipping some jewelry into a purse. Even those serious offenses committed by juveniles, such as burglary and robbery, tend to be amateurish. For example, juvenile offenders, while burglarizing a house or apartment, will often ignore expensive items (such as electronic equipment or rare coins) because they are not aware of their value and are more likely to be attracted by familiar items (such as clothing, records, or alcohol).[40]

Organized Crime

Some forms of criminal activity are highly conducive to large-scale organization. For example, illegal gambling, prostitution, bootlegging, drug dealing, fencing (receiving and selling stolen goods), and extortion (in the form of selling protection) are especially amenable to *syndication* (large-scale, coordinated criminal operations involving several criminal groups). The high overhead costs in crimes like drug trafficking (the criminal must smuggle the goods into the country, pay off corrupt officials, and distribute the drugs) make small-scale operation more costly and less efficient than large-scale. In addition, the prospect of monopolistic prices, if only one or a handful of organizations control the market, favors syndication.[41] There is much confusion surrounding the use of the term "organized crime," and there are many myths and misconceptions regarding the structure and operation of organized criminal groups. Groups like the Cosa Nostra are large, bureaucratic, and organized to earn a profit through the supply of illegal goods and services. In comparison, a team of burglars, is usually a small, informally organized group, and provides no services to a public larger than its members and those (such as fences) supported by their own criminal activities. Because organized crime probably has the greatest impact on the public through both the sheer volume of crimes committed and their cost to the taxpayers, the following discussion will focus on large-scale, syndicated criminal organizations.

Because of the secretive nature of criminal syndicates, social scientists, law enforcement authorities, and the general public know very little about their structure and operation. Criminal syndicates are involved in a large number of illegal activities — too many, in fact, to be enumerated here. However, a few of the more important and better-documented activities of organized crime are outlined.

Organized crime is a prominent feature of American society, as was illustrated in the award winning film, *The Godfather.*

Drug Trafficking

The supply of illegal substances to a willing public is a major source of revenue for criminal syndicates. A $20 investment in a kilo (2.2 pounds) of opium in Mexico, Turkey, or Southeast Asia can net a street price of $500,000 in the United States.[42] The profits have to be divided several ways, of course, but the remaining profit margin is certainly large enough to tempt those who have the will and organizational skills necessary for this type of criminal enterprise. A conservative estimate of the number of heroin addicts alone in the United States is 600,000. At the current retail level, the purchase price of a year's supply of heroin for all of these addicts is over $5 billion. These figures do not include drug trafficking in cocaine, psychedelics, or marijuana, and the amounts involved are extremely difficult to estimate.[43]

Gambling

The profits from illegal gambling are enormous—accurate estimates of the profit to organized crime from illegal betting are difficult to make, but a conservative guess would place the figure at about $20 billion a year. According to one of America's most reputable pollsters, Elmo Roper, only the food, steel, auto, chemical, and machine-tool industries have a greater volume of business than does illegal gambling.[44]

Infiltrating Legitimate Businesses

Criminal syndicates have infiltrated a number of previously legitimate business operations including firms in advertising, the amusement industry, the automotive industry, banking, insurance, juke box distribution, linen supply outlets, restaurants, bars, hotels, garbage collection firms, real estate agencies, and scrap metal firms—to name but a few.

The control of [legitimate] business concerns is secured through (1) investing concealed profits acquired from gambling and other illegal activities, (2) accepting business interests in payment of the owner's gambling debts, (3) foreclosing on usurious loans, and (4) using various forms of extortions. A favorite operation is to place a concern [that organized crime] has acquired into fraudulent bankruptcy after milking its assets.[45]

Loan Sharking

The Shylock racket or *loan sharking*, as it is more widely known, is the lending of money at illegal, usurious rates. Customary rates of interest on a note from a loan shark will range between 1 and 150 percent, compounded on the unpaid balance each week. Much of the lending money comes from gambling operations. Loans are made to gamblers, drug users, politicians, and other persons who need money in a hurry to cover their unusual expenses or debts and to small businessmen whose legitimate channels of credit are closed.

Prostitution

Prostitutes offer a service much in demand in our society and very profitable for those who control their activities. Criminal syndicates have taken full advantage of this business opportunity. However, there is some evidence that syndicate involvement in prostitution is declining. On the other hand, profits from sex-related forms of crime are not. For example, a series of ambiguous court decisions have made the illegal distribution of pornographic magazines and films a highly profitable industry.

Racketeering

Racketeering **is the systematic extortion of money from persons or organizations such as businesses and labor unions.** An example of how racketeers operate is their infiltration of some labor unions. By controlling key positions in a union, racketeers can cheat employees by not paying them union wages or by misusing the union's welfare and pension funds. Racketeers can extort money from workers by forcing them to pay high union dues and fees in order to find and hold jobs. Furthermore, money can be extorted from employers by requiring them to make payoffs for union cooperation in avoiding strikes at particularly inopportune times.

How is syndicated crime organized? What makes it possible for syndicates to operate so successfully? What can be done about this type of organized crime? These questions are crucial to an understanding of syndicated crime; however, some are more easily answered than others. For example, the question regarding the internal organization of the syndicates cannot be answered because of the secret nature of these groups. There is a great deal of myth about the Mafia or Cosa Nostra. Evidence available to social scientists suggests that they are *not* international syndicates operated by groups outside the United States, nor is there a single syndicate controlling all (or even most) organized crime in this country. American syndicates are very much American in their goals and organization. For example, although many of the criminal organizations were patterned after similar groups in the homeland of syndicate founders (e.g. Italy or Sicily), they were very much affected by the new land, its pressures, its values, and its opportunities. In addition, just as there is competition between the giants in most legitimate business sectors, there is competition in drug dealing, illegal gambling, racketeering and the other financial ventures involving organized crime.

What forces perpetuate syndicated crime? The answer to this question is very complex. However, one fact is very clear – without respectable citizens who are willing to purchase the illegal goods and services offered by criminal syndicates, and without the cooperation of corrupt public officials who are willing to look the other way (or perhaps even become directly involved in organized crime themselves by patronizing syndicate business or by representing its interests), organized crime could not continue to operate. From the non-Marxian conflict perspective, organized crime and its toleration by the public have their roots in basic human selfishness and in competition over scarce resources. Marxian conflict theorists, on the other hand, emphasize that organized crime is a "natural" product of capitalist societies. They believe that all businesses are the same: basically corrupt. Some businesses are illegal because dominant groups who control the legal machinery have a vested interest in *defining* them as illegal. From the functionalist perspective, organized crime is a means by which certain groups have adapted to American society. For example, Merton refers to syndicated crime as a form of *innovation*. Organized crime is a means by which some members of subordinate ethnic groups, such as some Italians during the early part of this century, adapted to the lack of opportunity in the legitimate sectors of society and took advantage of opportunities in the rackets. Interactionists emphasize that America is composed of many subcultural groups with different values, social norms, and definitions of reality. Organized crime caters to the needs and desires of groups that cannot satisfy existing wants through legal means. Each of the theoretical perspectives contributes in a different way to a better understanding of the nature of organized crime in the United States.

Organized crime is harmful to society because it creates economic costs for victims, taxpayers, and consumers. It contributes to official corruption and public cynicism about the honesty of public officials. It breeds mistrust and often serves as a secret "government" undermining democratic decision making in business and labor as well as in government.

White-Collar Crime

White-collar crimes **are offenses committed by persons of respectability and high status in the course of their occupations.** Such crimes are widespread but rarely come to the attention of the police. White-collar criminals define themselves as basically honest and law-abiding. White-collar crimes are committed by organizations (or by groups within those organizations) or by individuals working alone (including offenses against the organization itself). The following illustrations of some types of white-collar crimes indicate how widespread—and costly—this type of criminal activity is.[46] '

Offenses against consumers are very prevalent white-collar crimes. Examples of business offenses against consumers include false advertising, violations of food and drug laws, violations of the Air Quality Act of 1967 (e.g. illegal emissions from industrial smokestacks or the release of industrial waste products into public waterways), and the insolvency of banks, businesses, or other financial agencies due to fraud or the negligence of officials. An example of consumer fraud on a large scale occurred in 1977. General Motors equipped medium-sized Oldsmobile automobiles with Chevrolet engines without informing the public and with the implicit understanding in their advertisements that the Oldsmobiles really had the larger, more powerful, and more expensive Oldsmobile engine. While precise estimates are impossible, consumer fraud probably costs the American public in excess of $20 billion annually.[47]

Antitrust violations **are business attempts to combine in restraint of trade or to monopolize a segment of the economy.** The biggest antitrust case in our history was the "Electrical Conspiracy" (ca. 1950–1960) that involved that nation's largest electrical equipment manufacturers. In all, 29 corporations (including General Electric and Westinghouse) and 45 individuals were involved in a conspiracy to rig prices and fix markets for heavy electrical machinery valued at $1,-700,000,000 annually. G.E. was fined $437,500; Westinghouse, $372,500. William Ginn, a high-ranking G.E. official who was allowed to continue in his $135,000 job as vice president of the Turbine Division until he went off to jail for his part in the conspiracy, received the biggest fine of all the defendants: $12,500. He and several other high-ranking officials also received thirty-day prison sentences.[48]

Embezzlement is a white-collar crime committed almost exclusively by trusted employees acting alone. **The embezzler is an employee who fraudulently converts some of the employer's funds to his or her own use through alteration of the employer's records.** Embezzlers who take large sums of money are usually respectable citizens in their communities and trusted employees in their work—characteristics essential to the person who commits this type of crime.

Persons in positions of financial trust become caught up in stealing from their employers when they experience financial problems that their regular income is insufficient to deal with.[49] Examples of these difficulties include gambling debts, demands — by a spouse or lover — that they feel they cannot refuse, and expensive medical care required by a sick relative. Embezzlers rationalize their theft by convincing themselves that they are merely "borrowing" the money, that their employers are really crooks who deserve to lose the money, or that the employers will not miss the lost funds.

Embezzlement is a costly crime (the annual financial loss from embezzlement is at least $3 billion), but it is a crime that rarely results in criminal prosecution because this action does not guarantee recovery of the stolen funds.[50] In fact, threat of prosecution is probably far less effective than an informal arrangement worked out between the thief and the former employer. In addition, financial institutions depend on public trust for their very existence, and a scandal involving employee dishonesty threatens the organization's public image.

White-collar crime is not only costly in economic terms, but it also has a corrupting influence on the organizations in which it occurs. Lower-level employees who observe their superiors engaging in illegal activities are provided with excellent role models for dishonesty and a rationalization for crimes that they themselves might commit. Why do people become involved in committing white-collar crimes? Crimes committed by corporations and groups of business or professional people are rooted in the capitalist order, according to Marxian conflict theorists. Breaking the law for business purposes becomes a logical extension of the profit motive. From the interactionist perspective, there is a great deal of pressure in some groups for their members to "cut corners." This includes violating the law if necessary. Such groups define the business and professional world as "cutthroat," and this definition helps to rationalize illegal behavior as a means of keeping up with the competition. From the functionalist perspective, such crimes may be viewed as "innovative" means of adapting to the pressures of a competitive, success-oriented society.

Sex Offenses

There are a number of different types of sex offenses in the United States.[51] ***Forcible rape* is an of-**

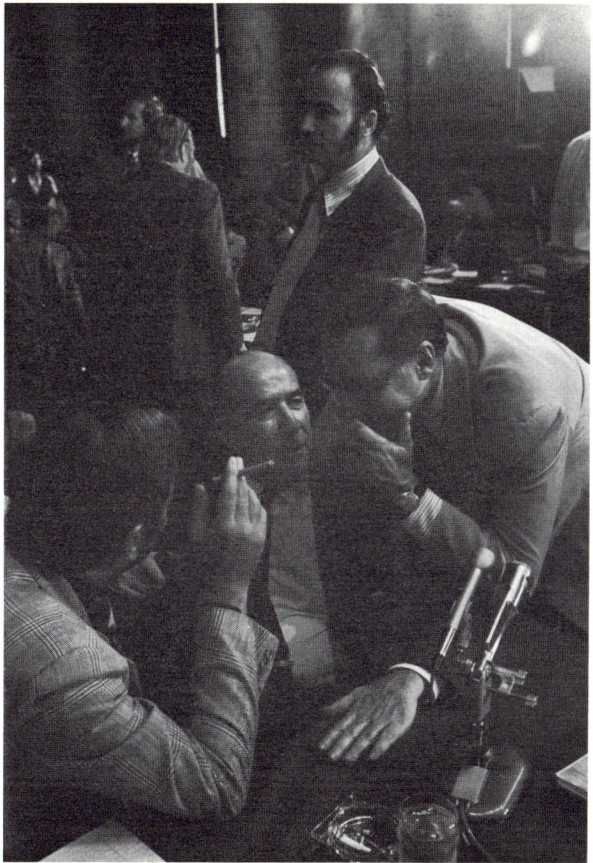

As this photograph of former Attorney General John Mitchell, taken at the Senate Watergate Hearings illustrates, white-collar crimes are offenses committed by persons of respectability and high status in the course of their occupations.

fense based on lack of consent — the offender makes sexual demands that the victim does not consent to. In most states, only males are legally liable for rape by force. In most cases, sexual intercourse does not have to occur for a rape to have taken place.

Forcible rape is a highly underreported crime. Comparisons between the Uniform Crime Reports and the NORC data (see Table 16.2) show that only about one-quarter of the victims report the rape to the police. Why? The answer is very complex, but a few factors seem to be particularly important. Some rape victims are women who have been previously arrested for sex offenses, such as prostitution, or who in some other way have acquired a "shady" reputation. Also, the accusation of rape can be used by a disappointed or angry woman to get revenge. Police who encounter these types of rape situations frequently tend to be quite cynical and unsympathetic toward women who report that they have been raped, including many who have been genuinely victimized. Victims, therefore, frequently refuse to report that they have been raped because of the possible humiliation in reporting the crime to unsympathetic law enforcement personnel.[52]

***Statutory rape* involves sexual contact between any male who is of a legally responsible age (usually seven years) and a female who is a willing and voluntary participant but who is below the legal age of consent (usually 16 years of age but in some states as high as 18).** In some states, sexual intercourse is not necessary for statutory rape. Females, under statutes in the vast majority of states, are not liable for the offense of statutory rape. Statutory rapists usually regard themselves as law-abiding citizens. "They . . . view themselves as unlucky persons who were simply doing what everyone else is doing, but go caught. There is, of course, considerable truth to that claim."[53]

Homosexual acts are another form of sex offense in many states. Male homosexual acts between consenting adults are illegal in the vast majority of states. In some states where male homosexuality is illegal, there are no laws prohibiting sexual acts between adult females. In some states, such as California, homosexual relations between consenting adults have been made legal.

***Incest* refers to sexual relations with a person too closely related for legal marriage.** In the United States, incest offenders who come to the attention of the police and courts are usually fathers who have been charged with having sexual intercourse with a daughter. Little is known about other types of incestuous relationships because they are so rarely reported. Father-daughter incest seems to follow a definite pattern. Acts of intercourse between father and daughter tend to develop in situations of physical and social isolation, where the daughter represents the only partner

available to the father. The daughter may be a relatively willing participant in sexual activity. "In some instances, the sexual activity between father and daughter is apparent to the mother, who tolerates the situation in order to avoid the sexual demands of the father."[54] Incest is generally reported by third parties, such as neighbors. Offenders usually receive stiff prison sentences because of the public abhorrence of this behavior.

Sex offenses are extremely emotional issues that often involve harsh punishments in the name of justice rather than programs to rehabilitate the offender and help the victims cope with their problems.

Victimless Offenses

***Victimless crimes* are offenses, such as gambling, homosexuality, substance abuse, and pornography, in which the "victims" are willing participants who consume highly demanded, but illegal, products or services.**[55] Many critics have suggested that these activities should be legalized, or at least decriminalized (removing the criminal penalties attached to these crimes and changing them to misdemeanor offenses punishable by fines), because the criminal penalties do more harm than good in society. For example, criminal penalties may damage the offender's self-concept as a respectable citizen. That is, if a person who prefers homosexual relationships is treated like a hardened criminal when he is caught, he may have a very difficult time regaining a positive self-concept. Criminal sanctions may also force the deviants to form a subculture in order to continue their illegal activity with greater safety. For example, drug users and homosexuals often form protective subcultures that serve to separate them even further from the mainstream of society.

Because the laws prohibiting victimless crimes are infrequently and inconsistently enforced, those who feel discriminated against may develop a disrespect for the law. For example, laws concerning gambling and drinking are enforced differently in the case of poor and young persons, thereby impairing their faith in the equity of the law. When highly desired goods and services are made illegal,

Figure 16.1 **A General View of the Criminal Justice System. The President's Commission on Law Enforcement and Administration of Justice,** *The Challenge of Crime in a Free* *Society* **(Washington, D.C.: U.S. Government Printing Office, 1967), pp. 8–9.**

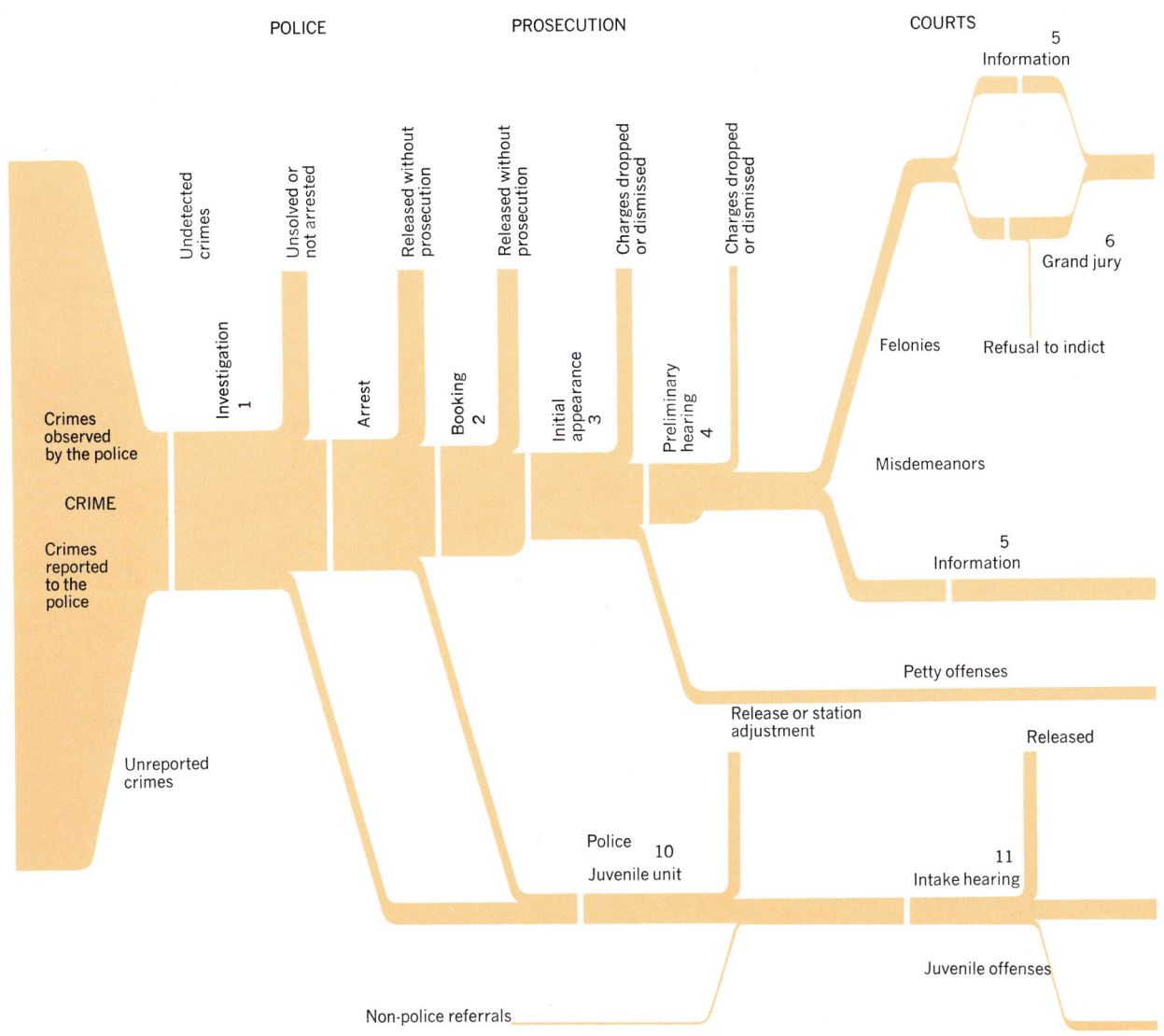

POLICE   PROSECUTION   COURTS

1. May continue until trial
2. Administrative record of arrest. First step at which temporary release on bail may be available

3. Before magistrate, commissioner or justice of peace. Formal notice of charge, advice of rights. Bail set. Summary trials for petty offenses usually conducted here without further processing
4. Preliminary testing of evidence against defendant. Charge may be reduced. No separate preliminary hearing for misdemeanors in some systems

5. Charge filed by prosecutor on basis of information submitted by police or citizens. Alternative to grand jury indictment, often used in felonies almost always in misdemeanors
6. Reviews whether or not government evidence sufficient to justify trial. Some states have no grand jury system, others seldom use it

Procedures in individual jurisdictions may vary from the pattern shown here. The differing weights of line indicate the relative volume of cases disposed of at various points in the system. But this is only suggestive since no nationwide data of this sort exist.

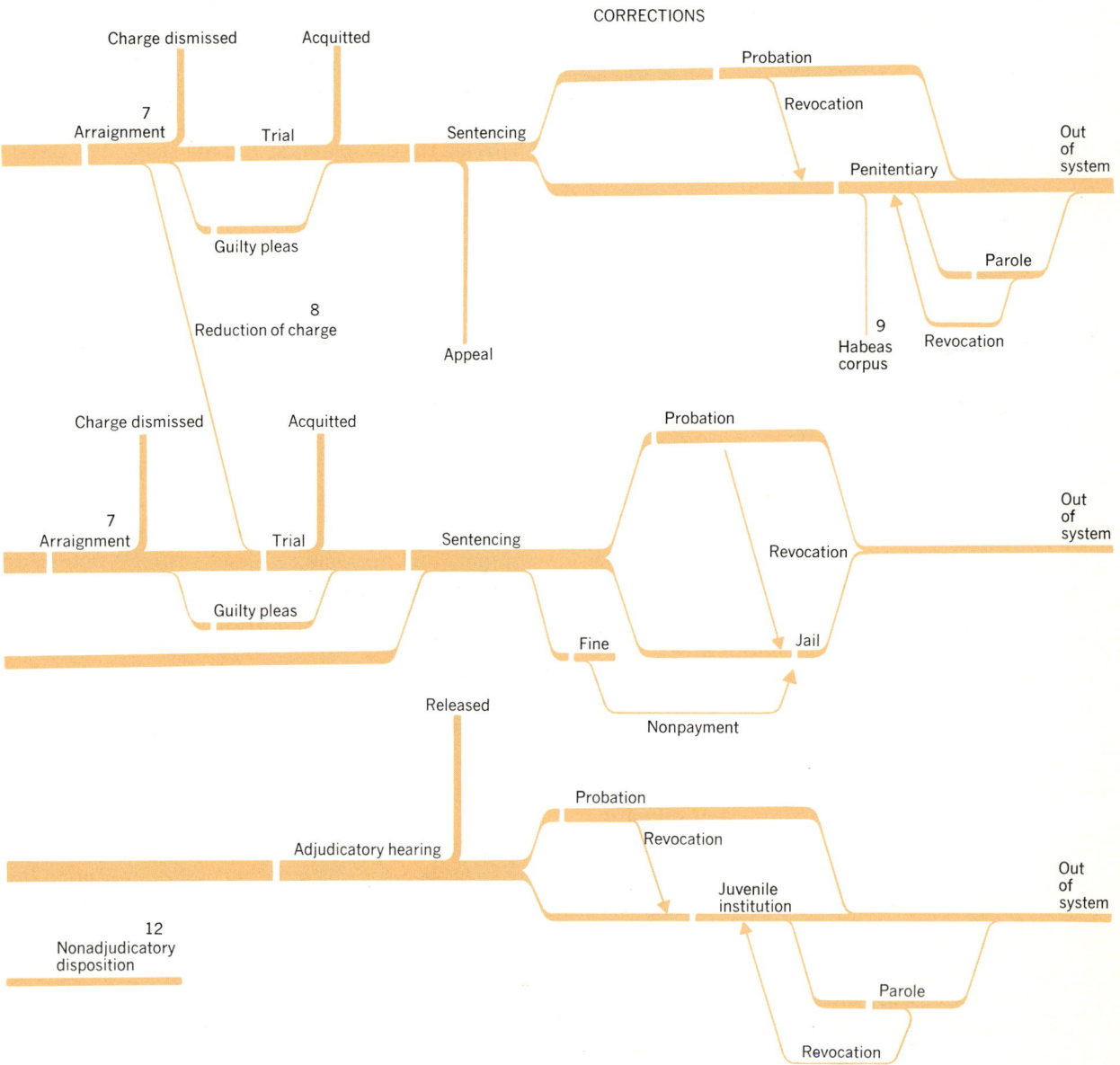

CORRECTIONS

7. Appearance for plea defendant elects trial by judge or jury (if available) counsel for indigent usually appointed here in felonies. Often not at all in other cases.
8. Charge may be reduced at any time prior to trial in return for plea of guilty or for other reasons

9. Challenge on constitutional grounds to legality of detention. May be sought at any point in process
10. Police often hold informal hearings, dismiss or adjust many cases without further processing

11. Probation officer decides desirability of further court action
12. Welfare agency, social services, counseling medical care, and so on, for cases where adjudicatory handling is not required

a black market involving organized criminal elements is almost certain to develop. Also, when the prices of illicit goods and services rise as a consequence of tighter law enforcement, consumers often have to steal, or steal more, in order to finance the continued purchase of these higher-priced items. Victimless crimes are related to police corruption (and other forms of public corruption as well) in that organized crime provides handsome financial rewards in the form of bribes for policemen and judges who cooperate with them. For these reasons, many have argued that making such offenses criminal acts does more harm than good, and that society would be served best by eliminating them from the criminal statutes.

THE SYSTEM OF CRIMINAL JUSTICE

In order to deal with the problem of crime, we no longer rely on such informal mechanisms as the personal vendetta. Instead, we have an elaborate bureaucratic organization—the criminal justice system—designed to protect the safety of people, secure their property, and preserve public order. However, there is considerable controversy today concerning how effectively the existing criminal justice system accomplishes these goals. Some have argued that its inefficient organization, its emphasis on incarceration, and its susceptibility to influence by powerful interest groups, have made it part of the problem of crime rather than its solution. In this section, some of the more important issues associated with our system of criminal justice are discussed.

Processing the Alleged Criminal

The system of criminal justice in the United States is an *adversary system,* **in which the accused (defendant) is assumed innocent until proven guilty in a court of law by the representative of the state (prosecutor).** The operation of this adversary system involves a number of complex steps—too many, in fact, to be included in a discussion here (see Fig. 16.1). We will focus on four especially important parts of that system: the police, the courts, bail, and plea bargaining.

The Police

The police are the citizen's first link with the system of criminal justice—and, probably, the most important one. When a crime occurs, the police are the first agents of the state to be involved. Police have a great deal of discretionary authority regarding the disposition of offenses reported to them in that they can use a broad range of means to deal with an incident—from an informally arranged agreement between the complainant and the suspect to arresting and booking the alleged offender. It is at this stage in the processing of an offender that the greatest amount of case attrition occurs—that is, only about one-half of the incidents known to the police move to the next stage of having a report filed concerning an incident (see Fig. 16.2).

For a number of reasons, the police are in a difficult and precarious position in American society. Because of the adversary system, they find themselves in a double-bind (a "damned if you do, damned if you don't" situation). The police are under constant pressure to repress crime, but at the same time they are expected to protect the constitutional and personal rights of suspects and other citizens. Ideally, both the repression of crime and due process of law (the legal proceedings of the adversary system established to protect the rights and liberties of the individual) are intended to be compatible. However, since the criminal justice system lacks the resources necessary for both the effective control of crime and the preservation of due process, justice has traditionally given way to expediency—crime has often been attacked at the expense of constitutional rights. Police often attempt to keep the peace by ignoring or circumventing the procedural rules that are supposed to govern their activities.

Because of the tremendous number of crimes and minor violations of the law that occur each day, the police must engage in selective and discretionary law enforcement, ignoring many violations while attending only to those that conflict with community mores.[56] Police are frequently asked to perform many "peace keeping" functions that are beyond their official duties and their professional competence. For example, law enforcement officers

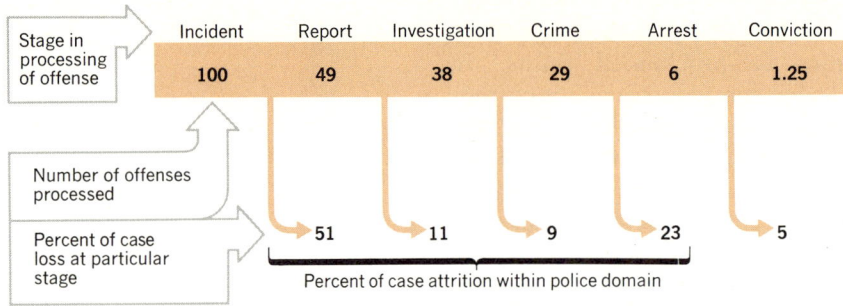

Stage in processing of offense	Incident	Report	Investigation	Crime	Arrest	Conviction
	100	49	38	29	6	1.25

Number of offenses processed

Percent of case loss at particular stage

	51	11	9	23	5

Percent of case attrition within police domain

Figure 16.2 Case Attrition in the System of Criminal Justice." Phillip H. Ennis, "Crime, Victims, and the Police." Publish by permission of Transaction, Inc., from *Transaction*, Vol. 4, No. 7, © (c) 1967 by Transaction, Inc.

are expected to provide emergency first aid to injured persons, to rescue trapped animals, and to keep an eye out for children and old people who are particularly prone to accidents. In addition, police are frequently asked to intervene in domestic disputes that do not involve a criminal offense, and to keep "undesirables" in their place. On top of all of this, they are, of course, expected to protect everyone from the criminal elements. All too frequently, however, police are provided with inadequate resources with which to do their job effectively.[57]

There has always been considerable public hostility toward the police among some segments of American society. The reasons for this sentiment are deeply rooted in the American experience. For example, Americans treasure their individual freedom and liberty, including many activities that are clearly illegal, such as the uncontrolled use of

The police are the citizen's first and most important link with the criminal justice system. As this picture of two police officers trying to deal with an emotionally distraught person illustrates, police are frequently asked to perform many "peace keeping" functions that go beyond their normal duties.

firearms, moonshining, and using marijuana. They tend to resent those who, like the police, attempt to deprive them of these self-proclaimed "rights." In addition there has been considerable police corruption in the United States over the years. This has been especially true of police departments in larger cities. Citizens often develop a rather cynical view of the police because of their experiences with this kind of corruption. In addition, at least prior to the Warren Supreme Court (1953–1969), police in some precincts were notorious for their use of questionable law enforcement techniques, such as the "third degree" (where suspects were questioned for several hours, sometimes for days, by teams of officers without proper nourishment or the provision of legal counsel) and harassment in the form of picking up a "troublemaker" on suspicion of a crime he clearly did not commit with the intention of releasing him after spending a night or two in jail to demonstrate "who's boss."[58]

The consequence of this precarious position of the police in America is that their job is made more difficult. Police feel, and often rightly so, that they receive little or no help and sympathy either from the criminals they hope to control or the respectable people they are supposed to protect.

The Court

As we have seen, the system of criminal justice in the United States is an adversary system. It is founded on the premise that citizens must be protected from the very same government that is designed to serve them. Under the adversary system, it is assumed that the power of government, if left unchecked, will be used by government officials to subjugate the citizenry. The procedural safeguards referred to as due process are designed to protect people from government encroachment on their rights.

There are four important positions in the court; the judge, the jury, the prosecuting attorney, and the attorney for the defense. Contrary to the impression that one might derive from watching television, juries are a relatively unimportant part of the processing of alleged criminals because of the widespread use of *plea bargaining* (an informal deal

"Well, this trial has provided us all with a lot of laughs, hasn't it? But, if I may be serious for a moment, I find you guilty as charged and sentence you to twenty years in the pen."

made between the prosecution and the defense). Plea bargaining accounts for over 90 percent of the convictions for both Part I (the serious offenses) and Part II offenses combined. Plea bargaining is involved in approximately 75 percent of the Part I offenses. Of the remaining 25 percent of the Part I cases, only three-fifths are tried before a jury. The remainder are tried at a bench proceeding before a judge.

Prosecuting Attorney

The office of prosecuting attorney is potentially the most powerful position in the system of criminal justice at the local level. Prosecuting attorneys have the discretionary authority to choose whether to seek a conviction in a given case and, if so, how vigorously they will prosecute the case. Prosecuting attorneys are political figures—they are either elected or appointed to office, and they must be reelected or reappointed periodically. Essential to any prosecuting attorney is a keen awareness of the values and interests of those who helped him or her gain office and of the mores of the community to be served.

In order to achieve these goals, prosecuting attorneys typically exert enormous pressure on the police, and this office is therefore more important than that of the chief of police or the police commissioner in the determination of police operations. For example, individual police officers, and police departments as well, are evaluated in terms of arrests that "stick"—that is, arrests that eventually result in convictions. Should the prosecuting attorney in a particular district feel that aggravated assaults are primarily "personal matters" that the court should avoid wasting time with, then the prosecutor's office may not vigorously seek convictions for this type of offense. The police, in turn, will soon take note and spend little time dealing with cases of this type. If, however, the same prosecuting attorney believes (or if influential supporters persuade him) that illegal drug use is a grave threat to the well-being of the community, the prosecutor's office may pursue convictions in drug-related cases more enthusiastically. As a consequence, the police soon learn that drug arrests are "good busts" and will alter their law enforcement patterns accordingly.[59] Thus, law enforcement efforts—which crimes will be pursued and how vigorously—are in part political issues that are determined by the needs and desires of influential groups. This situation can create cynicism and disrespect for the law among those groups that feel victimized by the police, who in turn are responding to political pressure.

Defense Attorney

Defense attorneys are supposed to represent their clients' interests before the criminal justice system. However, there are enormous pressures on them to place more emphasis on "negotiating justice" than in seeing to it that clients are provided with due process. For example, if the prosecution is enthusiastic about obtaining a conviction, it can use the vast resources of the state to secure evidence. On the other hand, only the most wealthy client can af-

ford an adequate defense under such circumstances. In these cases, plea bargaining is probably the most sensible (perhaps the only) alternative open to the client. Also, attorneys for the defense depend on the good opinion of their legal colleagues in the community to stay in practice. This includes judges and prosecuting attorneys. Often these considerations take precedence over the legal rights of the client.[60]

One means of trying to avoid these pitfalls in the system has been the use of court-appointed attorneys for impoverished defendants. However, this plan has generally worked very poorly, because court-appointed defense attorneys are usually young, inexperienced practitioners newly graduated from law school; older persons who are so incompetent that they must resort to this type of practice in order to survive professionally; or experienced and competent practitioners whose caseload is so large that they cannot devote sufficient time to properly defend indigent clients referred to them by the courts.[61] In any case, the client is usually poorly defended. On the other hand, the wealthy client, who can afford first-rate defense counsel along with private investigators and other such resources, stands a good chance of beating a conviction because of the limited resources available to the prosecution in all but the most highly publicized and politically important cases. Two additional problems relating to negotiated justice are bail and plea bargaining.

Bail

Bail **is money or credit deposited with the court in order to have an arrested person temporarily released on the assurance that he or she will appear for trial.** In the United States, the purpose of bail is to ensure the presence of a defendant at trial. However, bail is often used for preventive detention—that is, bail is denied a suspect or set at an amount beyond the suspect's financial capacity in order to keep a supposedly dangerous or politically controversial person confined until trial. Since the suspect who is free on bail is also free to commit crimes, there is great pressure in many cases to use preventive detention.[62]

There are other problems with the bail system in the United States. The decision whether to allow bail and how much it should be is made by a lower-court magistrate. However, if the accused cannot afford to post bail and does not have a friend or relative who can do so, then he or she must get it from a bail bondsman or else remain in jail. In most states, bail bondsmen are not officers of the court. They are businessmen, often with rather "shady" reputations themselves, who make their decision on the basis of financial considerations—is the suspect a good financial risk? Will he pay the interest charge on the bail note (usually about 10 percent of the bail amount, regardless of the duration of the loan or the outcome of the trial)? Bail usually involves collusion between police, courts, and bondsman inasmuch as they frequently cooperate in the bail decision—including whether the suspect should be granted bail and, if so, how much it should be. The interests of the suspect often get lost in the shuffle.[63]

Bail is prejudicial to the poor—those who cannot afford bail do not have access to it. The case of those not making bail is further prejudiced by their entrance into the courtroom in handcuffs (and, because of the poor facilities in most jails, they are not properly groomed for their court appearance), at the outset giving the judge or jury the impression that they are not to be trusted. Those not making bail may serve more time in jail prior to trial than after they are convicted, should they choose to plead guilty. Finally, failure to make bail means that the accused is being punished prior to a conviction—a violation of the basic principle of due process in the adversary system, which is based on the assumption that the alleged offender is innocent until proved guilty in a court of law.[64]

Plea Bargaining

The last aspect of the processing of criminal offenders that we will discuss is plea bargaining. **Plea bargaining is an informal deal between the defense, the prosecution, and the court that is not legally binding.** The police and prosecuting attorney can, once they get the suspect to confess, renege—leaving the suspect to fend for himself. As we observed earlier, plea bargaining is involved in over 90 percent of all convictions and is therefore a vital part of the American system of justice. For a plea of guilty, suspects may receive special considerations from the court. Some or all of the charges against them may be dropped; the judge may give the accused a more lenient sentence in exchange for a guilty plea for the offense(s) charged. If a suspect is willing to plead guilty to a lesser offense, then the judge may be more lenient at the time of sentencing. In addition, a suspect who pleads guilty to multiple charges may be sentenced to serve them concurrently.[65]

Plea bargaining is a problem since it is an informal means of dispensing "justice," allowing considerations such as local politics, community mores, and the perceived needs of criminal justice bureaucracies to take precedence over justice for the individual under due process of law.

JUVENILE DELINQUENCY

Juvenile delinquency is one of our most serious social problems. Juveniles are arrested for slightly over 40 percent of Part I crimes (see Table 16.1). Most of the vandalism, many of the burglaries and auto thefts, and a sizable proportion of the muggings are committed by juveniles. Large numbers of the young people involved in delinquency seem to have special problems that most other youths and even adult offenders do not face. A high proportion of delinquents have difficulties coping with the demands made on them in school, many come from homes in which there is family discord, and a large proportion are from lower socioeconomic groups and disadvantaged ethnic minorities. The juvenile court is designed to deal with these special problems.

Prior to this century in the United States, youthful offenders were dealt with by the criminal courts in pretty much the same fashion as their adult counterparts. Before the advent of the Juvenile Court in 1899, all persons over the age of seven years were defined as legally responsible for their actions under the laws of most states and were

"You boys shouldn't just hang around like juvenile delinquents. You should have plans, ambitions, objectives. How about joining the mob?"

treated accordingly by the judicial system. Children convicted of criminal offenses were sent to prison or otherwise punished, with very little regard for their age.[66]

Illinois instituted the first juvenile court in 1899, and other states followed by establishing similar specialized arrangements to deal with the problems of children. Wyoming, in the late 1940s, was the last state to organize a juvenile court system. While the primary function of the criminal court is to provide legal justice, the juvenile court espouses as its most important goal the treatment and rehabilitation of the offender. The major officially stated goal of the juvenile court is to protect the welfare of youth under the age of legal responsibility; protecting the community from the youtful offender is intended to be a secondary consideration. Because of this treatment philosophy, the state has assumed the responsibility to act as the "parent" of troubled children when, through neglect or inadequate resources, their own parents cannot assume a proper role. Because of its treatment orientation, the juvenile court traditionally has not been as concerned with due process as has the criminal court. Juvenile court officers have assumed that the treatment emphasis negates a need for the procedural safeguards of the criminal court. This assumption has often left the child almost entirely at the mercy of the juvenile court judge. The judge can make a range of dispositions concerning a juvenile believed to be in need of the court's supervision. For example, the child's parents may be instructed by the court to deal with the problem, psychological treatment may be ordered, or the child may be sentenced to a state reformatory.[67]

There are three categories of young persons who fall within the juvenile court's jurisdiction. First, **youthful offenders are persons below the age of majority and above the age of legal responsibility (usually ages 7 through 17 years, inclusively) who commit offenses for which, if they were adults, they could be tried in a criminal court.** However, because the primary responsibility of the juvenile court is to protect the child, rehabilitation rather than punishment is emphasized. Youthful offenders vary from children who commit larceny to those in their late teens who have long records of Part I offenses, often of a violent nature. The juvenile court was originally designed to deal with children who were not serious youthful offenders. This poses a serious problem for the courts today in many jurisdictions. Because of inadequate facilities to deal with youthful offenders, the court may release them to the custody of their parents or place them under the supervision of a probation officer. Youthful offenders may not be provided with needed help and may come to see the juvenile court as a "big joke." On the other hand, they may be sent to a jail that also houses adult offenders, with the consequent risk of exposure to negative influences.

Second, **status offenders are minors who commit acts that, while not in violation of the criminal code, represent breeches of the juvenile court code designed to protect them. Status offenses include truancy, curfew violations, running away from home, incorrigibility, and loitering.** Young people who commit these acts are offenders because of their age status—legally, they are minors. Under the protective function of the juvenile court, these acts are defined as contrary to the welfare of the child, and the court may intervene by taking appropriate remedial steps.

Third, *minors in need of care* **are children who are abused, neglected, or who in some other way require the care and supervision of the juvenile court.** This condition of need may result merely from the fact that the children's parents or others responsible for their care cannot provide an adequate home environment. The court has the duty to intervene on the child's behalf in cases of neglect, abuse, or inadequacy. The nature of the court's intervention may include assisting a child's family secure basic social services in the community or providing the child with temporary foster care until the responsible adults can make adequate arrangements. As a last resort the court may remove children from their natural parents' home and place them for adoption or confine them in a state institution.

One of the unfortunate circumstances that arise in the juvenile court is that the distinctions between the three categories of minors who fall within the court's jurisdiction are often ignored by the court in its disposition. Status offenders and children in need of care are about as likely to be institutionalized by many juvenile courts as are youthful offenders. There is also little effort to differentiate between these youngsters in terms of programs for intervention and treatment, and with regard to institutional living arrangements. For example, a study made by the Children's Bureau of the United States Department of Health, Education, and Welfare found that, of 1300 children in jail pending hearings, about 40 percent were either status offenders or children in need of care. Fifty percent of the children in detention homes were in these categories. In addition, status offenders who are institutionalized spend more time in institutions than do youthful offenders.[68]

Measuring Delinquency

The two main official sources of data on delinquency are the Uniform Crime Reports and infor-

mation provided by the juvenile courts. As we noted earlier, the Uniform Crime Reports are not extremely valid or very reliable indicators of the actual volume and patterns of crime. The same is true for their use as an index of delinquency. In addition, the UCRs include information only on minors arrested for criminal offenses (youthful offenders) and on two types of status offenders—curfew and loitering law violators and runaways (see Table 16.1).

Juvenile court data are based on cases referred to the court. A child is referred to the court through a petition initiated by any interested party seeking to invoke the court's jurisdiction. The interested party can be a policeman, the child's parents, his teacher or school principal, an officer of the court, or any other adult citizen. Approximately half the referrals are initiated by the police.

Unofficial data on delinquency are derived by the same means as those for crime—observer-based studies, victim-based studies, and self-reported behavior. As with the study of crime, a comparison of official and unofficial data sources indicates that young persons who commit serious acts of delinquency (youthful offenders) and engage in them frequently are more likely to be arrested by the police and referred to the court. So although the official statistics do not provide an accurate picture of the actual rates and patterns of violations of the juvenile code, they do offer an estimate of the more serious offenses and of the characteristics of the young people who commit them with some frequency.

The Characteristics of Delinquents

Juveniles comprise about one-quarter of the total arrestees for offenses cleared by arrest (see Table 16.1). As we have seen, they comprise over 40 percent of those arrested for serious crimes. Juvenile crimes tend to be opportunistic in that they are usually unplanned, spur-of-the-moment affairs. They are amateurish (as we observed in the section on theft), and they are often nonrational—that is, they do not make sense to most other people.[69] A number of important social characteristics distinguish delinquents from nondelinquents.

Sex

There are approximately four boys referred to the juvenile court for each girl referred. Boys are referred most often for theft and vandalism, girls for incorrigibility and running away from home (see Table 16.1). Boys tend to commit delinquent acts in groups, girls tend to act alone. Unofficial sources seem to indicate, however, that female delinquency, in terms of both the frequency and the type of offense, is becoming more similar to male delinquency patterns. Girls coming to the attention of the court are referred most often for conditions closely connected with their home life. For example, a referral for "incorrigibility" is likely to be related to alleged sexual misconduct.[70]

Socioeconomic Status

Lower-socioeconomic-status (SES) youngsters are overrepresented in the official statistics on delinquency. This is true for both arrests and referrals to the juvenile court. However, according to most unofficial reports, there is no significant difference of social class in the actual total volume of offenses.[71] On the other hand, the types of offenses do seem to differ significantly. For example, middle and upper SES youth commit more sophisticated offenses. These involve manipulating other people, as when four boys enter a clothing store at pretty much the same time and two of them distract the clerks by engaging them in conversation about the latest fashions. Meanwhile, the other two put on multiple layers of clothing in the dressing room. Lower SES youngsters tend to commit offenses that are less sophisticated. For example, a lower SES girl is much more likely to shoplift by merely placing articles into her purse than by using such manipulative techniques as those in the previous example. These different techniques are a reflection of class values — higher SES groups generally place greater value on manipulating others.

The severer types of offenses are more frequently committed by lower-class youth, consistent with their environment and class-related values. For example, the rate of violent acts, such as armed robbery and willful homicides, is much higher in lower SES juvenile groups. The class-related value on "toughness" encourages young persons, especially males, to take risks in terms of physical violence and to be prepared for "trouble" by carrying lethal weapons such as knives and handguns.[72]

Race and Ethnicity

Prior to 1930, over half of the referrals to the juvenile court were American-born children of foreign-born parents. However, as these immigrant groups have been assimilated into American society, their delinquency rates have dropped proportionately. **The most recent immigrants to the urban slums are blacks, Hispanics, and to a lesser extent, poor whites from the South. Arrest rates and court statistics reveal that the highest rates of juvenile delinquency in America today appear among these groups.** Children of these more recent migrants to urban areas now constitute a large proportion of delinquency cases.[73]

When unofficial statistics are compared with official data, the differences between ethnic groups in the total amount of delinquency are greatly reduced, however. One study, for example, compared delinquency statistics with responses to a questionnaire involving the self-reported delinquent behavior of white, black, and Japanese American boys.[74] According to official statistics, the black youngsters had a far higher rate of delinquency than did the white and Japanese boys; however, the self-reported rates indicated a fairly similar involvement in delinquency for all three groups. This can probably be attributed to three factors: (1) the biases of the official agencies, resulting in the greater likelihood of arrests for blacks; (2) the greater visibility of offenses committed by blacks; and (3) the demeanor of the youths when confronted with adult authority. Other studies have supported these conclusions.[75]

The Family

The family is the single most important socializing agency in society. It is involved in the transmission of culture from one genera-

tion to another, in the development of the child's self-concept, and in the establishment of the child's social identity. Because of these important tasks, there has been much concern about the role of the family as a cause of delinquent behavior. This has been especially true with regard to the role of the so-called broken home in the development of delinquency.[76]

Most studies report a high incidence of broken homes among delinquents. When divorce, desertion, death, or prolonged separation cause the absence of one or both parents, the child supposedly suffers some kind of deprivation—inadequate socialization, loss of affectional ties, or lack of proper supervision. The relationship between broken homes and delinquency, however, is far more complex than a clear-cut cause-and-effect relationship. There is a tendency for children from single-parent homes to be referred to the juvenile court in substantially greater numbers than children from homes in which both parents are present. The explanation is not that the child's behavior is more threatening to his own well-being or that of the community because he or she is from a broken home. Rather, it is because referral agents (whether they be police officers, school officials, or the child's parent) believe that the child with only one parent is in greater need of the services that the court is supposed to provide.[77] What is involved here is a self-fulfilling prophecy. Agents define reality in a certain way and then proceed to act on the basis of their definition. Because of this preferential referral practice, there are more official cases of youngsters from single-parent families appearing before the court. Then, when officers of the juvenile court see that youngsters from broken homes constitute the bulk of young people defined as delinquent, they consider the single-parent family to be a cause of delinquency. In addition, these officials continue with even greater confidence to preferentially refer children from broken homes—thereby perpetuating the myth.

Single-parent families tend to have lower incomes and are more likely to receive some kind of public assistance than two-parent families. They are therefore more susceptible to the scrutiny of of-ficial agents of the state. However, it appears that income level is more important than family composition in affecting referral for delinquency. Furthermore, there is evidence that the emotional climate and level of tension in a family is a more important factor in bringing about delinquency than is the presence of only one parent. For example, one study of delinquents and their families concluded that:

> Quarrelsome, neglecting families actually had a higher crime rate than homes in which a permanent separation had disrupted the family—conflict and neglect within the home predisposes a child to crime (even more so than broken homes).[78]

The School

Sociologist Albert Cohen suggests that delinquency on the part of lower-class boys is, in great part, a response to the unequal competition they encounter at school.[79] Lower SES boys are frustrated in their attempts to live up to middle-class standards imposed on them by their teachers and enforced by school administrators. They often become delinquent because of these expectations. As long as they stay in school, this frustration, and consequently their delinquency, will continue. In his research on juvenile delinquency, Delbert S. Elliot found that delinquent boys who drop out of school have a lower rate of referrals to the juvenile court because dropping out serves at least as a temporary solution to their problem of being measured by middle-class standards and failing in their attempts.[80]

Juvenile delinquency is very costly to society. The economic costs are extremely high; however, the social costs are even greater. The costs in terms of fear of victimization and the loss of freedom of movement as a consequence of that fear are incalculable. A more important cost, however, is the loss, as productive citizens, of many of the young people involved in delinquency. In addition, the costs associated with delinquency are borne by the delinquents themselves, and they often lead frustrated and unfulfilling lives as adults.

What are the roots of delinquency? What can be done in order to deal with this pressing social problem? To answer these questions, the three sociological perspectives will be applied.

Functionalists stress the pressures that are placed on youth in our society as an important factor in delinquency. These expectations pose an especially difficult problem for lower SES youngsters who are frequently measured by middle-class standards. Changes in basic institutions such as the family and the economy also have had an important impact on delinquency. To the degree that the family in America has lost many of its traditional functions, such as providing emotional support and stability to children, these changes in this institution contribute to delinquency. Young people's place in the economy has shifted from one of both producers and consumers to primarily that of consumers. Teenagers are less likely to gain the degree of independence and status that was once afforded them when they were fulltime participants in the world of work.

Interactionists emphasize that delinquency can be understood in the context of a particular group's values and expectations. Even serious acts of delinquency such as robberies and assaults, which may appear senseless to adults, may make sense when viewed from the perspective of a particular peer group's values and expectations. Since many young people do not have access to the types of activities that gain adults or many middle-class children high status, they often fabricate achievement out of the materials available in their environment. If a teenager can't make it as a sports hero or merit scholar, then demonstrating courage and physical prowess through committing illegal acts may secure status in the eyes of other delinquents.

From the Marxian conflict perspective, the primary purpose of the juvenile court is to impose the values of dominant groups on the lower classes through the legal structure. This is especially evident in status offenses. Rules that prohibit smoking or staying out late at night, for example, are based on ethnocentric biases of the upper and middle classes who control the juvenile court. Also from the Marxian perspective, serious delinquencies are concentrated among lower SES groups because of the harsh and brutal circumstances imposed on them by the dominant groups in society.

CRIME AND DELINQUENCY: FUTURE PROSPECTS

We considered theories of crime and deviant behavior in the previous chapter and the dimensions of the crime problem in this one. It should be clear by now that these are enormously complex problems, and because of this there are a number of ways to approach them. **There is, in fact, no single crime problem, but rather many different problems associated with crime in the United States. Each separate problem demands special attention and unique programs designed to cope with it.** We will consider some of the efforts being made today to grapple with these problems.

Punishment

To some extent, modern attitudes toward the crime problem are still heavily influenced by the Enlightenment view of human beings as pleasure-seeking and pain-avoiding creatures. Whenever a particularly scandalous and highly publicized crime occurs, there is usually a public outcry for the establishment of more severe punishments to cope with the crime problem. There is still a strong belief that severe punishment will serve as a deterrent to crime. There are two types of deterrence: specific and general. *Specific deterrence* **is the intimidation of individual offenders through punishment so that they will be fearful of committing crimes again.** For example, a speeder is caught, convicted, and given a heavy fine with the expectation that he will realize the negative consequences attached to speeding and refrain from that behavior in the future. *General deterrence* **is the intimidation of potential lawbreakers by the example of punishment directed at a specific offender.** For example, a person is found guilty of murder and put to death for this offense—not to deter him from future wrong doing, but to show others the negative consequences attached to murder. Scientific findings on the effects of punishment are far from complete. However, there are some generalizations that are supported by current research.

Punishment warns against committing specific deviant acts, but does not inform the deviant of what is acceptable behavior. For example, a youngster who habitually lies, cheats, and steals might be severely punished by his parents. But if the child is not instructed regarding appropriate behavior, the punishment is less likely to be an effective deterrent. Thus, punishment, to be most effective, should be associated with some positive direction for the offender.

The effectiveness of punishment as a general deterrent is reduced if it is not applied equally to all offenders, and in the United States it is not applied equally to all offenders. Women, older persons, persons from higher social classes, and whites are among the least likely to receive legal punishments for criminal offenses. This is especially evident in the administration of capital punishment.[81]

The widespread use of harsh punishment can also reduce its effectiveness and undermine public support for the system of criminal justice. For example, in England by the year 1780, there were approximately 350 offenses — including picking pockets — to which capital punishment was applied. The death penalty did not seem to provide a general deterrent (even though it is a foolproof specific deterrent), since public hangings were the favorite places of business for pickpockets. In addition, judges and juries were reluctant to convict all but the most publicly despised criminal suspects because of the harshness of the law.[82]

In addition to learning more about the conditions under which punishment is not an effective deterrent, we are beginning to understand how it can be used effectively. **Certainty and promptness of punishment seem to be more important than severity in achieving deterrence.** Punishment does not result in learning (or the deterrence of behavior) when there is a long interval between an act and the punishment or when there is little likelihood of being punished. An offender's awareness that there is considerable risk of detection and swift prosecution of a crime seems to be far more important as a deterrent than is the possibility of a long prison sentence or even the death penalty.[83]

The effective use of punishment also depends on the nature of the offense and the personality of the offender.[84] For example, capital punishment is probably an ineffective means of dealing with crimes of passion such as most criminal homicides. On the other hand, in the case of white-collar offenses that often involve the weighing of risks, swift and certain (but relatively mild) forms of punishment such as fines and short periods of incarceration seem to be more effective deterrents.

Better Law Enforcement

It is difficult to find someone who is not wholeheartedly in favor of better law enforcement, but there are greatly differing views of what better law enforcement entails. For the most part, attempts to achieve this goal have revolved around providing more policemen and supervisors, equipped with more technologically sophisticated law enforcement hardware (e.g. riot equipment, better radios, faster squad cars, more effective and accurate weapons), and training programs run primarily by experienced ex-policemen providing their expertise to new police officers.[85]

What *is* better law enforcement, then, if it is not better-equipped and more technically trained police officers? There is a criterion that defines better law enforcement in broader terms than equipment and technology and that is consistent with the American ideal of "equal justice under law." This criterion, or goal, is to control crime and at the same time to abide by the principle of due process. As noted earlier in this chapter, law enforcement agencies, from the police to correctional institutions, have few resources with which to implement this goal. One of the serious problems confronting those people who advocate better law enforcement is a lack of knowledge — about the causes of crime and about the workings of the criminal justice system. It would seem that basic research on the causes of crime and delinquency is essential for achieving the goal of better law enforcement. Another means of such achievement is through training programs that include instruction in the social and behavioral sciences. Educating the police in human motivation and the social and psychological causes of behavior will better equip them to respond to criminals and delinquents in a way that will help solve, rather than exacerbate, the problem. After all, the police are in many cases one of the few means that society has by which to change criminals.

Compensation of Victims

Although we seek legal justice against the offender in terms of some form of punitive action, the needs of the victim have usually been ignored by our system of criminal justice. Some state legislatures have proposed that victims of crime, especially those who suffer personal injury, should be compensated through general state revenues or through some type of restitution from the convicted offender. This has been attempted with some success concerning offenses like cashing bank checks with insufficient funds.[86] However, in cases involving large amounts of money or serious personal injury, the convicted offender is rarely in a position to repay the victim. In addition, most state funds are already seriously depleted without the extra burden of a victim-compensation program. It appears as though such programs, if instituted on a large scale, will have to be delayed.

Bail Reform

As we have seen, the current system of bail in most states involves a number of serious inequities. There have been several attempts to institute changes in bail procedures, probably the most liberal of which is the San Francisco plan, under which all noncapital offenders are eligible, and about 70 percent of those released on bail have been charged with felonies. This plan is supervised by a director and a social worker and assisted by a sociologist, a lawyer, law students, and volunteers. If the staff concludes that the accused should be released on his own recognizance (i.e. no monetary bail), that recommendation is passed on to the judge. In 85 percent of these cases, the judge has accepted the recommendation. Only 6 percent of those released on bail failed to appear for trial, and the city saved the large amounts of money it would have had to spend on keeping the suspect in jail while awaiting trial.[87]

There are some problems connected with this type of bail reform, however, the most important of which is that a potentially dangerous offender can be back out on the streets within hours of arrest. Of course, this can also be the case when bail is allowed but set at a very high rate; the accused person who is affluent can be on the street in a very short time. Bail reforms similar to the San Francisco plan allow the less affluent suspect, who is otherwise a good bail risk, to be freed prior to trial and to more adequately coordinate his defense.

Decriminalization and Legalization

To *legalize* an act is to make it no longer a violation of the law. To *decriminalize* an act is to remove the criminal penalties attached to it and change it to a misdemeanor offense punishable by fines. Legalization is a far more dramatic step than decriminalization. Many reformers have argued that legalization (or at least decriminalization) of the victimless crimes would be beneficial because it would release law enforcement personnel to attack more serious crimes. In addition, legalization would help to reduce the cynicism and mistrust of the criminal justice system that such crimes create. Some states have begun to do this. For example, homosexual relations between consenting adults have been legalized in California. Prostitution, though strictly controlled, is legal in some counties of Nevada. Michigan, Illinois, New York, and other states have legalized gambling by instituting a state-run lottery, and New Jersey residents have instituted legalized gambling in Atlantic City. However, most states have been reluctant to take these steps.

Organizations such as the National Organization for the Reform of Marijuana Laws (NORML) have lobbied for the decriminalization of "pot." This means that the possession of small amounts of marijuana, usually an ounce or less, would be a civil infraction—subject to a fine. The first-time offender would not be labeled with a criminal record. The reasoning behind this decriminalization movement is that marijuana is a relatively harmless substance that is widely used. Of course, this sentiment is subject to change as we gather more information about the drug. In addition, criminal laws prohibiting the possession of marijuana and its use place an unnecessary burden on the legal agencies that are expected to enforce an unpopular law. Opponents of decriminalization claim that lighter penalties will increase the use and abuse of pot and will lead to experiments with more dangerous drugs such as LSD and heroin (see ch. 17). However, despite the growing leniency of public attitudes toward marijuana, many states retain harsh penalties for simple possession. In Nevada, a state that has legalized both prostitution and gambling, for example, a first-time offender caught with an ounce of marijuana can be sentenced to six years in prison and a fine of $2000.[88]

Legalization or decriminalization of vice crimes and victimless offenses such as drug use, gambling, homosexuality, and prostitution, has another distinct benefit—it removes these goods and services from the black market and the clutches of organized crime. However, because there are so many groups that have some vested interest in their status as criminal offenses, we can expect continued resistance to attempts at decriminalization and legalization.

Reforming the Offender

Reformation, or rehabilitation as it is often called, has as its goal the modification of convicted offenders' behavior and attitudes so that the norms and values supporting law-abiding behavior will be internalized—and in the hope that they will conduct their lives accordingly. Prison systems based on the notion of reforming the criminal emerged as an American invention in the United States around 1820. They were initially based on the central principle that isolating inmates from the corrupting influences of the community (which the church and the family were unable to overcome) was essential to their own well-being and reformation.[89] However, by the turn of this century, the isolation of the inmate was redefined as essential to protect the community and respectable citizens from the evil influences of the criminal—a complete reversal of the logic of the original argument. Prisons still maintain the rhetoric of rehabilitation but much of

the substance of punishment. Today, prisons are primarily institutions for "warehousing" and punishing convicted law violators. There is little prospect of substantial change in that orientation in the foreseeable future.

Reforming Juvenile Justice

Children are often considered to be one of our most treasured resources and our "hope for the future." It is therefore disturbing to observe high rates of delinquency, especially when the juvenile justice system seems relatively ineffective in coping with the problem. This concern has led specialists on the problems of delinquency to focus their attention on developing reforms that might alleviate at least the worst of the problems. There are a number of proposals that are generating considerable optimism—and considerable controversy—in the field of juvenile justice.[90]

Elimination of Some Juvenile Offenses

Some experts have argued that it would be beneficial to remove from the juvenile court's code many behaviors that currently represent violations. For example, it has been suggested that status offenses (e.g. curfew violations, truancy, incorrigibility, and running away from home), which are illegal for juveniles but not adults, are prime candidates for such elimination. This, some have reasoned, would reduce the heavy case load facing many juvenile courts, leaving time for them to deal with more serious offenders and with abused and neglected children. It would also increase the likelihood that status offenders would be referred to community agencies that are better equipped than the courts to attack the problems these young people face. Finally, the elimination of status offenses would reduce the possibility that these offenders would be incarcerated with more serious youthful criminals who might serve as a negative influence.

There is not complete agreement about the benefits of this program. Opponents point out that in many communities, there are few agencies other than the juvenile court to provide guidance for these young people. In effect, if the juvenile court jurisdiction over these children is eliminated, they will be left unattended and uncared for, and their problems may become more serious. Furthermore, it is argued, the juvenile court currently has coercive power to force children, parents, and community agencies to confront these problems and seek solutions to them. If this coercion were eliminated, there would be no authority to force the issue, and many status offenders would probably receive little help.

Diversion

Diversion **refers to the effort to turn (divert) juveniles away from entry into the juvenile justice system and the traditional, and largely punitive, treatment programs.** The advocates of diversion argue that such a plan avoids the negative effects of the labeling process that can arise if the child is incarcerated in a reformatory or other institution (see ch. 15). The goal of diversion is to find sources of help outside of the machinery of the juvenile justice system whenever possible. Thus, when a juvenile comes to the attention of the police for committing an offense, he or she should be provided with counseling (by psychologists, social workers, or probation personnel), offered help with school work, extended occupational or recreational services, or directed toward any other agency that could provide assistance in personal, emotional, or family problems. Under such a program, the juvenile court and possible subsequent incarceration would be a last resort in dealing with delinquents who have committed repeated and serious offenses.

Critics of diversion point out that there is potential danger in leaving the decision whether to refer a youngster to juvenile court in the hands of untrained people. A schoolteacher or police officer may lack the necessary skills to assess a juvenile's problems adequately or to determine the degree of danger in a particular case. In addition, there is considerable room in such a program for personal bias that could influence the decisions of referral agents. Finally, there are often serious shortages of community agencies to cope with the juvenile's problems, and there is a considerable likelihood that youngsters will receive little or no help. For

these reasons, critics of diversion believe that the juvenile court should continue to play a central role in the administration of juvenile justice.

Due Process

Due process **of juveniles involves the protection of the constitutional rights of juveniles by making the juvenile court proceedings more like those of the criminal court.** Advocates of due process argue that juvenile courts, in their attempt to act as surrogate parents, have historically run roughshod over the rights of children and in fact have removed most of the constitutional guarantees (such as the right to a trial, the right to adequate legal representation, and the like) that are accorded adults. Many argue that this has worked to the detriment, rather than the benefit, of children. For example, in some cases youth are incarcerated for offenses (ostensibly for "their own good") for a much longer period than an adult would be for the same crime. For these reasons, due process advocates argue that the juvenile court procedures must be reformed in order to provide juveniles with due process.

Opponents of such changes point out that the juvenile court is intended to be different than the criminal court—the former is supposed to make decisions in the interests of the proper development of the child rather than simply determining guilt or innocence. To the extent that the juvenile court might begin to serve this latter, adjudicatory function (with the presence of defense and prosecuting attorneys and the other trappings of adult criminal court), it would become merely a criminal court for minors and would be unable to perform the special function of guidance and protection for the juvenile. For these reasons, they argue, due process, while desirable in some ways, would be detrimental to the juvenile.

Deinstitutionalization

Deinstitutionalization **refers to the elimination of most or all institutions for juveniles (such as jails, training schools, and clinical treatment centers) and replacing them with other modes of treatment.** The goal of such a program is to rid the treatment of juvenile offenders of the social isolation, the personal degradation, the rigid routines, and the severe punishments that often accompany institutionalization. Treatment and counseling, according to proponents of this view, could be provided in noninstitutional settings, such as community agencies. However, opponents point out that there often are no alternative programs to handle juveniles, and thus many of them would go without treatment.

The future of reform in the juvenile system is uncertain. Each of the suggestions mentioned is controversial and has many opponents. In addition, there is no clear evidence that these proposals would provide the benefits claimed by their advocates. One expert on the juvenile justice system has concluded: "There are many reasons to regard current reforms in juvenile justice as something less than a panacea."[91] Current reforms have done little to rectify the ambiguous position of children and juveniles in society and to deal effectively with some of the worst features of abuse, neglect, poverty, and ignorance. Whether all, or some combination, of the reforms mentioned could achieve these goals remains to be seen.

CONCLUSION

Crime, as we have seen, has many faces, and its effects reach all of us. The physical, economic, social, and emotional costs of crime are enormous. Juvenile delinquency is seen by many as an insidious scourge that attacks one of our most important resources. We have discussed the dimensions of these problems and some proposals for alleviating them. One rather unsettling conclusion that emerges from this discussion is that our effectiveness in coping with the problems of crime and delinquency seems to have increased very little over the years. This is disturbing because it suggests that there may be some fundamental processes involved in crime and delinquency that we do not yet fully understand. In concluding our discussion, it is useful to review the issues of crime and delinquency utilizing the three theoretical perspec-

tives in order to gain further insight into the difficulties we confront.

From the functionalist perspective, we should consider the possibility that, if a pattern of behavior persists over time, it is performing some positive function for society. Crime has certainly persisted for a long period of time. Is it in some way beneficial to society? Crimes such as gambling, drug trafficking, pornography, and prostitution provide an illicit, but much demanded, supply of goods and services to a willing public. Some types of theft, vice crimes, and organized crime serve as a means of employment for many people: the criminals themselves, people unsuccessful in securing legal occupations, fences, pimps, corrupt officials, law enforcement personnel, and corrections officials. Crime can also serve as a route to social mobility for some people, such as immigrants or members of minority groups, whose access to legitimate channels may seem blocked. In all these ways, crime performs positive functions for society. This does not mean, however, that we must content ourselves with the existence of crime, since these same functions might be performed in other, legal, ways. Nevertheless, this perspective does make us realize that the place of crime in American society is more complex than we first suspect and that, if we are to eliminate crime, we must develop alternative ways to satisfy these functions.

We have also seen that from the functionalist perspective, a certain amount of deviance, including criminal and delinquent offenses, may be an inherent feature of all societies. However, the more dysfunctional or threatening types of deviance can nonetheless be dealt with through the legal system. According to this perspective, deviance has its roots in certain structural flaws in the established order and in inadequate socialization or inadequate opportunity to behave consistently with widely shared social norms. With this in mind, programs for social reform provide the kinds of measures most likely to succeed according to the functionalist viewpoint.

There are numerous proposals for implementing changes to improve our means of dealing with criminals and deliquents, and some of them seem to make sense. However, as the conflict perspective helps us to realize, converting an idea into a well-organized and programmatic public policy is quite another matter. Criminologist Robert Rhodes summarizes some of the difficulties:

> Our inability to resolve the problems of crime is partly due to conflicts of interest in American society at large. Intellectuals (even between the disciplines of political science, sociology, law, economics, and psychology) have separate, competing paradigms [perspectives] over the issue. In addition, attorneys on and off the bench, police officers, probation and parole personnel, planners, and the bureaucracies accompanying these occupations have contending perspectives, not to mention the special-issue lobbyists for and against blue laws and victimless crimes, and the legislators themselves.[92]

The various interest groups and vested interest factions agree neither on the problems of crime and delinquency nor on the solutions.

The conflict perspective further suggests that crime and deviance may be inherent in *all* societies because it is basic to human nature. In this view, the most that any society can do is to *control* deviance. Programs of social reform are basically a waste of time and money from this perspective, because deviance is rooted primarily in the nature of societies in general and not in any particular social order. Public policies of deterrence are the only really feasible means of keeping deviant behavior in check, according to this perspective.

Because deviance and crime are socially defined categories from the interactionist perspective, all groups will define some behaviors as falling within that category. They are rooted in the diversity of American society and in inadequate or improper socialization—the failure of the individual to internalize the norms of groups of which he or she is a member. Programs for the effective socialization of young people and for the reinforcement of their elders to adhere to widely shared and crucial social norms are the most feasible means of dealing with the problem of deviance, according to the interactionist perspective. In addition, a greater appreciation of, and tolerance for, the divergent values and norms in our pluralistic society will help alleviate many of the problems associated with crime and delinquency by redefining many behaviors as no longer criminal. Many actions now defined as criminal (such as homosexuality among adults or status offenses among juveniles) might be redefined as divergence; that is, a number of value systems and lifestyles can coexist in relative harmony. Some programs of deterrence, educational programs that focus on socializing the young, and the legalization or decriminalization of many offenses are consistent with the interactionist perspective.

GLOSSARY TERMS

Adversary system

Amateur thieves

Antitrust violations

Bail

Criminal

Criminal assault

Criminal homicide

Decriminalization

Deinstitutionalization

Diversion

Due process

Embezzlement

Forcible rape

General deterrence

Incest

Legalization

Loan sharking

Minors in need of care

Plea bargaining

Professional thieves

Racketeering

Recidivists

Semiprofessional thieves

Specific deterrence

Status offenders

Statutory rape

Syndicated crime

Theft

Victimless crimes

White-collar crimes

Youthful offenders

REFERENCES

[1] United States Department of Justice, "Crime in the United States, 1977," *FBI Uniform Crime Reports* (Washington, D.C.: U.S. Government Printing Office, 1978).

[2] *New York Times* (July 28, 1975), p. 42, col. 8.

[3] See Herbert A. Bloch, *Man, Crime and Society* (New York: Random House, 1962).

[4] Leon Radzinowicz, *A History of English Criminal Law and Its Administration from 1750 (New York: Macmillan, 1948–1957).

[5] David J. Rothman, *The Discovery of the Asylum* (Boston: Little, Brown, 1971), p. 15.

[6] Ibid., p. 15.

[7] See Lamar T. Empey, *American Delinquency: Its Meaning and Construction* (Homewood, Ill.: Dorsey Press, 1978).

[8] Rothman, *The Discovery of the Asylum*, p. 85.

[9] Empey, *American Delinquency*.

[10] Anthony Platt, *The Child Savers* (Chicago: University of Chicago Press, 1969).

[11] Richard Quinney, *Criminology*, 2d ed. (Boston: Little, Brown, 1979).

[12] Rothman, *The Discovery of the Asylum*, p. 254.

[13] Ibid., p. 239.

[14] Robert K. Merton, *Social Theory and Social Structure* (New York: The Free Press, 1968).

[15] Thorsten Sellin, *Culture Conflict and Crime* (New York: Social Science Research Council, 1938).

[16] See Quinney, *Criminology*, and Jeffrey H. Reiman, *The Rich Get Richer and the Poor Get Prison* (New York: John Wiley & Sons, 1979).

[17] Edwin H. Sutherland and Donald R. Cressey, *Criminology*, 10th ed. (Philadelphia: Lippincott, 1978).

[18] See J. A. Wallerstein and C. J. Wyle, "Our Law-Abiding Lawbreakers," *Federal Probation* 25 (April 1947), pp. 107–112, and Gordon P. Waldo and Theodore G. Chiricos, "Perceived Penal Sanction and Self-Reported Criminality: A Neglected Approach to Deterrence Research," *Social Problems* 19 (Spring 1972), pp. 522–540.

[19] United States Department of Justice, "Crime in the United States, 1977."

[20] Phillip H. Ennis, "Crime, Victims, and the Police," *Trans-Action* 4 (June 1967), pp. 36–44, and National Criminal Justice Information and Statistics Service, Law Enforcement Assistance Administration, *Victimization Surveys in 13 American Cities* (Washington, D.C.: U.S. Department of Justice, 1975).

[21] Wesley G. Skogan, "Dimensions of the Dark Figure of Unreported Crime," *Crime and Delinquency* 23 (January 1977), pp. 41–50.

[22] Roland J. Chilton, "Persistent Problems of Crime Statistics," in Simon Dinitz and Walter C. Reckless, eds., *Critical Issues in the Study of Crime* (Boston: Little, Brown, 1968), pp. 89–96.

[23] William F. Whyte, *Street Corner Society* (Chicago: University of Chicago Press, 1943).

[24] Maynard L. Erickson and Lamar T. Empey, "Court Records, Undetected Delinquency and Decision-Making," *Journal of Criminal Law, Criminology and Police Science* 54 (December 1963), pp. 456–469.

[25] See Gail Armstrong, "Females under the Law — 'Protected' but Unequal," *Crime and Delinquency* 23 (April 1977), pp. 109–120, and Darrel J. Steffensmeier, "Crime and Contemporary Women: An Analysis of Changing Levels of Female Property Crime, 1960–75," *Social Forces* 57 (December 1978), pp. 566–584.

[26] See Edward Green, "Race, Social Status, and Criminal Arrest," *American Sociological Review* 35 (June 1970), pp. 476–490, and Michael J. Hindelang, "Race and Involvement in Common Law and Personal Crimes," *American Sociological Review* 43 (February 1978), pp. 93–109.

[27] See Charles R. Tittle et al., "The Myth of Social Class and Criminality," *American Sociological Review* 43 (October 1978), pp. 643–657, and Edwin H. Sutherland, *White Collar Crime* (New York: Dryden Press, 1949), pp. 3–13.

[28] See Walter B. Miller, "Lower Class Culture as a Generating Milieu of Gang Delinquency," *Journal of Social Issues* 4 (November 1958), pp. 5–19, and Hans Toch, *Violent Men* (Chicago: Aldine, 1969).

[29] See Alfred Bandura, *Analysis of Delinquency and Aggression* (New York: John Wiley & Sons, 1976).

[30] David F. Luckenbill and William B. Sanders, "Criminal Violence," in Edward Sagarin and Fred Montanino, eds., *Deviants: Voluntary Actors in a Hostile World* (New York: General Learning Press, 1977), p. 115.

[31] Elmer H. Johnson, *Crime, Correction, and Society*, 4th ed. (Homewood, Ill.: Dorsey Press, 1978), and Herbert A. Bloch, *Man, Crime, and Society* (New York: Random House, 1962).

[32] See Marvin Wolfgang, *Patterns in Criminal Homicide* (Philadelphia: University of Pennsylvania Press, 1958), p. 252, and David J. Pitman and William Handy, "Patterns in Criminal Aggravated Assault," *Journal of Criminal Law, Criminology, and Police Science* 55 (December 1964), p. 467.

[33] John E. Conklin, *Robbery and the Criminal Justice System* (Philadelphia: Lippincott, 1972).

[34] Edwin H. Sutherland, *The Professional Thief* (Chicago: University of Chicago Press, 1937).

[35] J. A. Mack, "The Able Criminal," *British Journal of Criminology* 12 (1972), pp. 44–54.

[36] See Sutherland, *The Professional Thief*, and Edwin M. Schur, "Sociological Analysis of Confidence Swindling," *Journal of Criminal Law, Criminology, and Police Science*, 48 (September-October 1957), pp. 296–304.

[37] Thomas A. Reppetto, *Residential Crime* (Cambridge,

Mass.: Ballinger, 1974).

[38] See Clarence C. Schrag, "A Preliminary Criminal Typology," *Pacific Sociological Review* 4 (Spring 1961), pp. 11–16; M. G. Neithercutt, "Parole Violations and Commitment Offense," *Journal of Research in Crime and Delinquency* 9 (July 1972), p. 87; and Marvin E. Wolfgang, Robert M. Figlio, and Thorsten Sellin, *Delinquency in a Birth Cohort* (Chicago: University of Chicago Press, 1972).

[39] Mary Owen Cameron, *The Booster and the Snitch* (New York: The Free Press, 1964).

[40] Ruth S. Cavan and Theodore N. Ferdinand, *Juvenile Delinquency,* 3d ed. (Philadelphia: Lippincott, 1975).

[41] See Edwin M. Schur, *Crimes Without Victims* (Englewood Cliffs, N.J.: Prentice-Hall, 1965), and Thomas C. Schelling, "Economics and Criminal Enterprise," in Marvin E. Wolfgang, Leonard Savitz, and Norman Johnston, eds., *The Sociology of Crime and Delinquency,* 2d ed. (New York: John Wiley & Sons, 1970), pp. 613–625.

[42] "Narcotics: The War Lords," *Newsweek* (October 11, 1976), p. 51.

[43] Martin R. Haskell and Lewis Yablonsky, *Juvenile Delinquency,* 3d ed. (Chicago: Rand McNally, 1978).

[44] Daniel Bell, "Crime as an American Way of Life," in Wolfgang, Savitz, and Johnston, eds., *The Sociology of Crime and Delinquency,* pp. 165–179, and Lowell L. Kuehn, "Syndicated Crime in America," in Sagarin and Montanino, eds., *Deviants,* pp. 157–219.

[45] Marshall B. Clinard and Richard Quinney, *Criminal Behavior Systems: A Typology,* 2d ed. (New York: Holt, Rinehart, & Winston, 1973), p. 227.

[46] Sutherland, *White Collar Crime.*

[47] See August Bequai, "Wanted: The White Collar Ring," *Student Lawyer* 5 (May 1977), pp. 45–46.

[48] Gilbert Geis, "The Heavy Electrical Equipment Antitrust Cases of 1961," in Gilbert Geis and Robert F. Meier, eds., *White Collar Crime: Offenses in Business, Politics, and the Professions* (New York: The Free Press, 1977), pp. 117–132.

[49] Donald R. Cressey, *Other People's Money* (New York: The Free Press, 1953).

[50] Bequai, "Wanted: The White Collar Ring," pp. 45–46.

[51] Stanton Wheeler, "Sex Offenses: A Sociological Critique," in Wolfgang, Savitz, and Johnston, eds., *The Sociology of Crime and Delinquency* 23 (April 1977), pp. 136–153.

[52] Gerald D. Robin, "Forcible Rape: Institutionalized Sexism in the Criminal Justice System," *Crime and Delinquency* 23 (April 1977), pp. 136–153.

[53] Don C. Gibbons, *Society, Crime, and Criminal Careers,* 3d ed. (Englewood Cliffs, N.J.: Prentice-Hall, 1977), p. 383.

[54] Ibid., p. 396.

[55] See Schur, *Crimes Without Victims.*

[56] See Rodney Stark, *Police Riots* (Belmont, Calif.: Wadsworth, 1972), and Jerome H. Skolnick, *Justice Without Trial* (New York: John Wley & Sons, 1975).

[57] Elaine Cumming, Ian Cumming, and Laura Edell, "Policemen as Philosopher, Guide, and Friend," *Social Problems* 12 (Winter 1965), pp. 276–286, and Egon Bittner, "The Police in Skid-Row: A Study of Peace-Keeping," *American Sociological Review* 32 (October 1967), pp. 699–715.

[58] See Lawrence Sherman, ed., *Police Corruption* (Garden City, N.Y.: Anchor Press, 1974); Julian B. Roebuck and Thomas Barker, "A Typology of Police Corruption," *Social Problems* 21 (Fall 1974), pp. 423–437; and Thomas Barker, "Peer Group Support for Police Occupational Deviance," *Criminology* 15 (November 1977), pp. 353–366.

[59] George F. Cole, "The Decision to Prosecute," *Law and Society Review* 4 (February 1970), pp. 331–343.

[60] Abraham S. Blumberg, *Criminal Justice* (Chicago: Quadrangle Books, 1967).

[61] Edwin M. Lemert, "Legislating Change in the Juvenile Court," *Wisconsin Law Review* (Spring 1967), pp. 442–443.

[62] Frederic Suffet, "Bail Setting: A Study of Courtroom Interaction," *Crime and Delinquency* 12 (October 1966), pp. 323–324.

[63] Caleb Foote, "The Bail System and Equal Justice," *Federal Probation* 23 (September 1959), pp. 43–48.

[64] Suffet, "Bail Setting," pp. 323–324.

[65] See Blumberg, *Criminal Justice;* Donald J. Newman, "Pleading Guilty for Considerations: A Study of Bargain Justice," in George F. Cole, ed., *Criminal Justice: Law and Politics* (North Scituate, Mass.: Duxbury Press, 1972), pp. 183–196; and John Barbara, June Morrison, and Horace Cunningham, "Plea Bargaining: Bargain Justice?" *Criminology* 14 (May 1976), pp. 55–64.

[66] Robert G. Caldwell, "The Juvenile Court: Its Development and Some Major Problems," in Rose Giallombardo, ed., *Juvenile Delinquency,* 3d ed. (New York: John Wiley & Sons, 1976), pp. 393–410.

[67] See Platt, *The Child Savers.*

[68] See Meda Chesney-Lind, "Judicial Paternalism and the Female Status Offender: Training Women to Know Their Place," *Crime and Delinquency* 23 (April 1977), pp. 121–130, and William H. Sheridan, "Juveniles Who Commit Noncriminal Acts: Why Treat in a Correctional System?" in Rose Giallombardo, ed., *Juvenile Delinquency,* pp. 599–605.

[69] See Cavan and Ferdinand, *Juvenile Delinquency.*

[70] See Gary J. Jensen and Raymond Eve, "Sex Differences in Delinquency: An Examination of Popular Sociological Explanations," *Criminology* 13 (February 1976), pp. 427–448, and Armstrong, "Females under the Law — 'protected' but Unequal," pp. 131–135.

[71] See Wolfgang, Figlio, and Sellin, *Delinquency in a Birth Cohort,* and Charles R. Tittle, Wayne J. Villemez, and Douglas A. Smith, "The Myth of Social Class and Criminality," *American Sociological Review* 43 (October 1978), pp. 643–656.

[72] Miller, ''Lower Class Culture as a Generating Milieu of Gang Delinquency.''

[73] Haskell and Yablonsky, *Juvenile Delinquency.*

[74] William J. Chambliss and R. H. Nagasawa, ''On the Validity of Official Statistics: A Comparative Study of White, Black, and Japanese High School Boys,'' *Journal of Research on Crime and Delinquency* 6 (January 1959), pp. 71–77.

[75] See Morris A. Forslund and Virginia A. Cranston, ''A Self-report Comparison of Indian and Anglo Delinquency in Wyoming,'' *Criminology* 13 (August 1975), pp. 193–198.

[76] Karen Wilkinson, ''The Broken Family and Juvenile Delinquency: Scientific Explanation or Ideology?'' *Social Problems* 21 (June 1974), pp. 726–739.

[77] Susan K. Datesman and Frank R. Scarpitti, ''Female Delinquency and Broken Homes: A Reassessment,'' *Criminology* 13 (May 1975), pp. 33–55.

[78] William McCord, Joan McCord, and Irving Zola, *Origins of Crime* (New York: Columbia University Press, 1959), p. 83. See also Roland J. Chilton and Gerald E. Markle, ''Family Disruption, Delinquent Conduct, and the Effect of Subclassification,'' *American Sociological Review* 37 (February 1972), pp. 93–99.

[79] Albert K. Cohen, *Delinquent Boys* (Glencoe, Ill.: The Free Press, 1955).

[80] Delbert S. Elliot, ''Delinquency, School Attendance and Dropout,'' *Social Problems* 13 (Winter 1966), pp. 307–314.

[81] Gerald W. Smith, ''The Value of Life: Arguments Against the Death Penalty: A Reply to Professor Lehtinen,'' *Crime and Delinquency* 23 (July 1977), 253–259.

[82] Radzinowicz, *A History of English Criminal Law.*

[83] See Charles R. Tittle and Charles H. Logan, ''Sanctions and Deviance: Evidence and Remaining Questions,'' *Law and Society Review* 7 (Spring 1973), pp. 371–392, and Gary F. Jensen, Maynard L. Erickson, and Jack P. Gibbs, ''Perceived Risk of Punishment and Self-Reported Delinquency,'' *Social Forces* 57 (September 1978), pp. 57–78.

[84] Maynard L. Erickson, Jack P. Gibbs, and Gary F. Jensen, ''The Deterrence Doctrine and the Perceived Certainty of Legal Punishments,'' *American Sociological Review* 42 (April 1977), pp. 305–317.

[85] Quinney, *Criminology.*

[86] Edwin M. Lemert, *Human Deviance, Social Problems, and Social Control,* 2d ed. (Englewood Cliffs, N.J.: Prentice-Hall, 1972).

[87] Sue Titus Reid, *Crime and Criminology,* 2d ed. (New York: Holt, Rinehart, & Winston, 1979), pp. 432–436.

[88] ''Easing the Pot Laws,'' *Newsweek,* March 28, 1977, p. 76.

[89] Rothman, *The Discovery of the Asylum.*

[90] See Empey, *American Delinquency,* and Clifford E. Simonsen and Marshall S. Gordon, III, *Juvenile Justice in America* (Encino, Calif.: Glencoe Publishing Co., 1979).

[91] Empey, *American Delinquency,* p. 598.

[92] Robert P. Rhodes, *The Insoluble Problems of Crime* (New York: John Wiley & Sons, 1977), p. 260.

SUGGESTED READINGS

Sue Titus Reid, *Crime and Criminology,* second edition (New York: Holt, Rinehart and Winston, 1979).
A sophisticated yet very readable text on crime and corrections. Reid combines sociological and legal analysis into a rare and successful brew that gives the reader the best of both approaches.

Lamar T. Empey, *American Delinquency: Its Meaning and Construction* (Homewood, Illinois: The Dorsey Press, 1978).
A current and comprehensive text on delinquency and the juvenile justice system. Empey traces the social construction of childhood as a unique stage in the life cycle and its impact on how delinquency is defined and dealt with.

Richard P. Rettig, Manual J. Torres, and Gerald R. Garrett, *Manny: A Criminal-Addict's Story* (Boston: Houghton Mifflin Company, 1977).
A sociological biography that traces the elaborate career of deviance of one of the coauthors. It begins with Manny's early experiences with gang life, then passes on through his involvement with gambling and heroin and his experiences with Synanon and with prison life.

William J. Chambliss and Harry King, *Box Man: A Professional Thief's Journey* (New York: Harper Torchbooks/ Harper and Row, Publishers, 1972).
The life story of Harry King, who from approximately 1910 until 1960 lived a life of crime as a professional safecracker. This is King's autobiography as told to Bill Chambliss, a prominent American criminologist.

Norman Johnston and Leonard D. Savitz (eds.), *Justice and Corrections* (New York: John Wiley & Sons, Inc., 1978).
A comprehensive collection of essays and articles on the criminal justice system. Included are sections on the police, the administration of justice, prisons, and treatment of offenders.

Leonard D. Savitz and Norman Johnston (eds.), *Crime in Society* (New York: John Wiley & Sons, Inc, 1978).
A comprehensive anthology that includes sections on criminological theory, the measurement of crime, and patterns of criminal offenses.

Don C. Gibbons, *The Criminological Enterprise: Theories and Perspectives* (Englewood Cliffs, New Jersey: Prentice-Hall, Inc., 1979).

Gibbons explores the major themes or theoretical perspectives that have guided criminologists over the past 75 years and discusses the future of criminological theory.

Jeffrey H. Reiman, *The Rich Get Richer and the Poor Get Prison: Ideology, Class, and Criminal Justice* (New York: John Wiley & Sons, Inc., 1979).

A readable little primer on the Marxian conflict perspective on crime and justice in the United States.

Robert P. Rhodes, *The Insoluble Problems of Crime* (New York: John Wiley & Sons, Inc., 1977).

A candid, policy-oriented book that analyzes the political conflicts of today's criminal justice system.

Questions for Discussion

1. There are substantial costs associated with crime. What are some of the economic costs of crime? Emotional costs? Social costs?

2. Reform and rehabilitation programs for dealing with adult and juvenile offenders are not new in the United States. What are some of the reasons that nineteenth century innovations in dealing with criminals and juvenile delinquents failed to be continued into the next century?

3. From the functionalist, conflict, and interactionist perspectives, the nature of crime and criminal law is viewed very differently. Compare and contrast each of the sociological perspectives in terms of the purposes of law and crime and delinquency as social problems.

4. The actual amount of crime in the United States is not known. Compare the relative merits of using the Uniform Crime Reports, self-report-based data, and victim-based information as indicators of the rate (amount) and patterns (types and distribution) of crime.

5. Syndicated crime is big business in the United States today. What kinds of criminal activities are criminal syndicates involved in and why are they so profitable?

6. What is white-collar crime? What are some of the various types of white-collar crime? Why are white-collar criminals generally given more lenient sentences than other property offenders such as robbers and burglars?

7. What is an adversary system of criminal justice? How do the informal relationships between police, judges, prosecuting attorneys, and defense attorneys promote justice in an adversary system? How do they undermine justice?

8. The traditional role of the juvenile court has been that of a substitute parent. What are some of the problems associated with that role? What kinds of programs outside the juvenile court can be used to effectively deal with juvenile offenders?

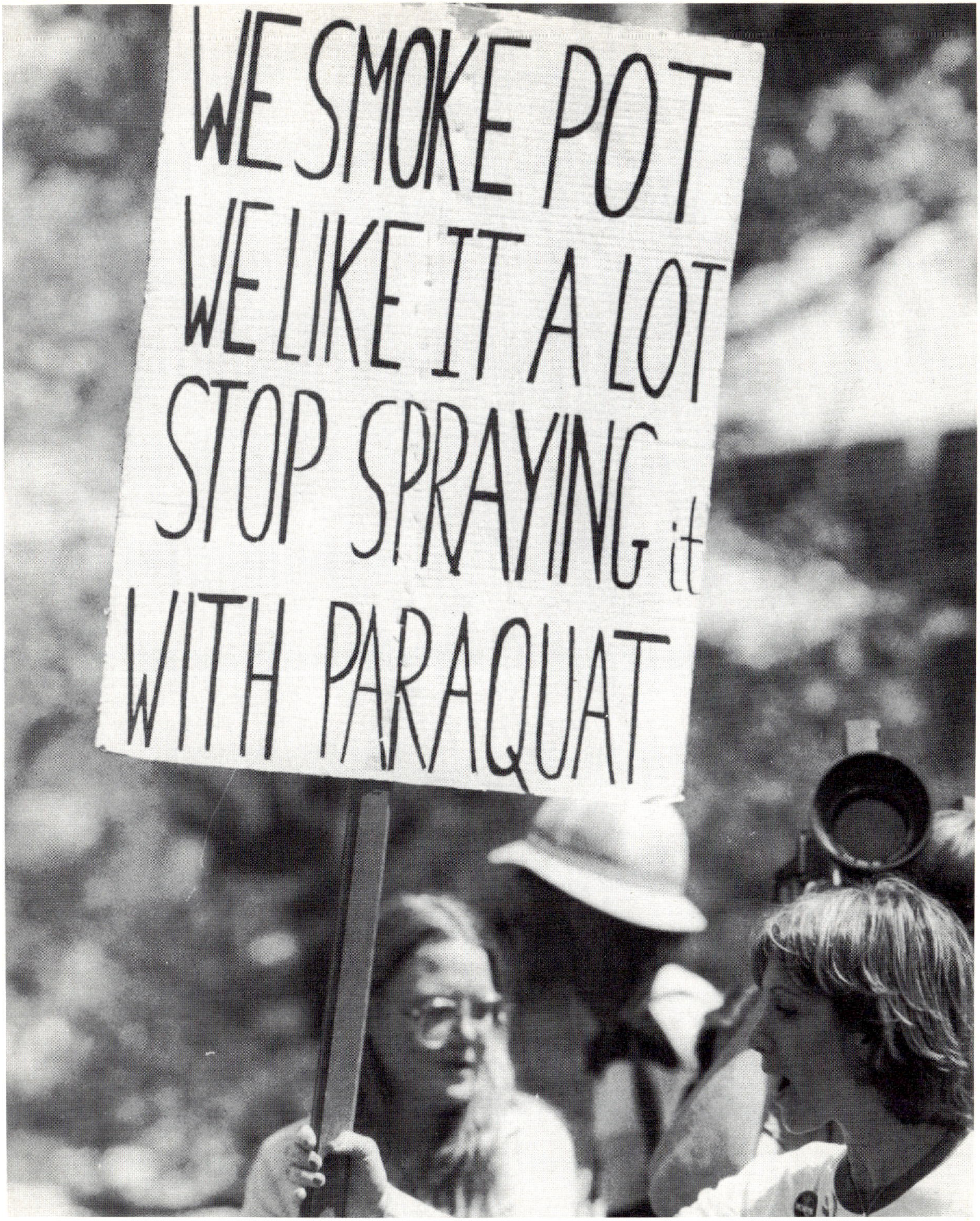
WE SMOKE POT
WE LIKE IT A LOT
STOP SPRAYING it
WITH PARAQUAT

CHAPTER 17
Drugs and Alcohol

ALCOHOL AND DRUG USE IN HISTORY

Drug Use: An Ancient Practice. Drugs and Alcohol in
America.

DRUGS AND ALCOHOL AS SOCIAL PROBLEMS

The Functionalist Perspective. The Conflict Perspective.
The Interactionist Perspective.

DRUGS, DRUG ABUSE, AND DRUG ADDICTION

Psychoactive Drugs. Drug Abuse. Drug Addiction.

STIMULANTS

Tobacco. Cocaine. Amphetamines.

DEPRESSANTS

Barbiturates. Tranquilizers.

HALLUCINOGENS

PCP.

MARIJUANA

Who Uses Marijuana? Marijuana as a Social Problem.

NARCOTICS

Who Uses Heroin? Heroin as a Social Problem.

ALCOHOL

Patterns of Alcohol Use. Theories of Alcoholism.

FUTURE PROSPECTS: DRUG USE IN AMERICA

The Treatment of Heroin Addiction. The Treatment of
Alcoholism.

CONCLUSION

The common pattern of effects described by users includes an "ozone stage" which occurs five to fifteen minutes after smoking PCP. In the ozone stage, which usually lasts from two to six hours, a person usually has a difficult time talking and walking, becomes confused, demonstrates repetitive behavior, and has a lack of attention. Things seem to slow down for a person on PCP. As one user described the drug, "it makes me not feel; I can put my mind in a box. It's not like getting high."[1]

The critical problem of polydrug abuse was brought to national attention . . . when former First Lady Betty Ford entered the Naval Hospital in Long Beach, California, to begin a special program to deal with her latest medical problem: dual addiction. "I am not only addicted to the medication I have been taking for my arthritis," she said, "but also to alcohol . . ." Steve Ford said his mother was fighting a battle against Valium and alcohol.[2]

It has only been within the past decade that phencyclidine (PCP) has emerged as an illicit street drug of major importance. Likewise, the number of men and women who, like Betty Ford, combine alcohol with other drugs has grown to considerable — some would say alarming — proportions in the past two decades. The reliance of Americans on alcohol and drugs (both legal and illegal) seems to have grown substantially and has emerged as one of our most costly social problems and one that is most difficult to control.

Why has the problem of drugs and alcohol become so serious in recent years? Many commentators have referred to the last few decades in America as a chemical age, in which people utilize a myriad of substances in order to cope with whatever problems they face: physical pain, emotional upsets, or blocked aspirations. Some have gone so far as to argue that America is a drug culture, and when we consider the enormous quantity and variety of drugs consumed by Americans each year (see Table 17.1), there may be some credence to this description. We are constantly bombarded with the message that there is a pill to solve every problem — major or minor, both physical and mental. In one

TABLE 17.1
The Use of Legal Drugs in the United States

DRUG	NUMBER OF PEOPLE WHO ARE REGULAR USERS
Barbiturates	4,500,000
Tranquilizers	5,000,000
Amphetamines (including diet pills)	2,250,000
OVER-THE-COUNTER DRUGS	REGULAR USERS
Sleep inducers (Nytol, etc.)	4,000,000
Stimulants (No-Doze, etc.)	3,000,000
Tranquilizers (Compoze, etc.)	2,500,000
Alcohol (average drinkers)	50,000,000
Alcohol (heavy drinkers)	14,000,000

SOURCE. Carl D. Chambers, James A. Inciardi, and Harvey A. Siegal, *Chemical Coping: A Report on Legal Drug Use in the United States* (New York: Spectrum Publications, Inc.), 1975.

indictment of our drug-oriented society, Senator Frank Moss of Utah commented:

The drug culture finds its fullest flowering in the portrait of American society which can be pieced together out of the hundreds of thousands of advertisements and commercials. It is advertising which mounts the message that pills turn rain to sunshine, gloom to joy, depression to euphoria, solve problems, and dispel doubt. Not just pills: cigarette and cigar ads; soft drinks, coffee, tea and beer ads — all portray the key to happiness as things to swallow, inhale, chew, drink, and eat.[3]

People have become increasingly alarmed over drug abuse in the United States because it seems to be such a growing problem. In the past two decades, the growth in the use of illicit drugs has been both rapid and massive (see Fig. 17.1). Furthermore, drug use is much more common among the young than it is among other age groups (see Fig. 17.2). Some people fear that such abuse of and dependence on drugs at an early age will make it more difficult for the young to become responsible and productive adults, and thus the costs of such drug use may plague us in the future. For many, this turning to drugs is difficult to understand — especially when it occurs among young and relatively affluent Americans. Recently, three social scientists provided an overly simplified, but nevertheless reasonable, explanation of some drug abuse: people use drugs to escape the stresses and

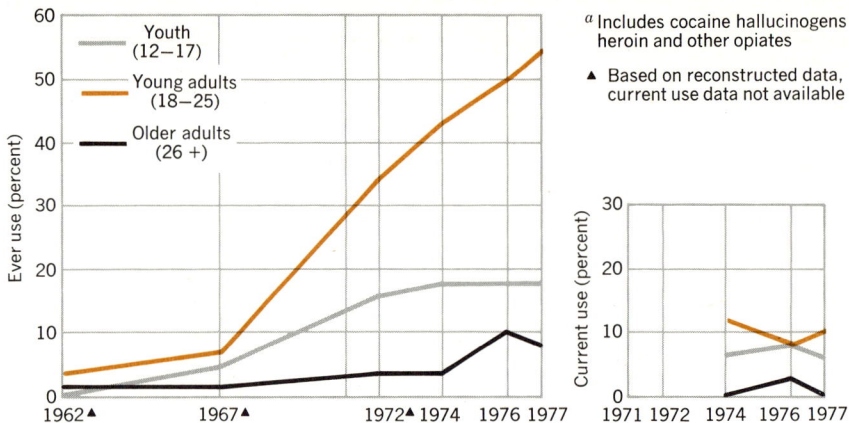

Figure 17.1 **Trends in Lifetime Experience with and Current Use of Stronger Drugs.**[a] **National Institute on Drug Abuse,** *Highlights from the National Survey on Drug Abuse: 1977* **(Washington, D.C.: U.S. Government Printing Office, 1978), p. 18.**

demands of everyday living and to seek enjoyment.[4] We will explore a number of reasons behind the rise in drug use in the United States, but first it is useful to examine the history of drugs and alcohol in the United States.

ALCOHOL AND DRUG USE IN HISTORY

Drug Use: An Ancient Practice

The drug problem that we face today centers on the use of many substances that are relatively new (e.g. tranquilizers such as Valium and Librium, hallucinogens such as LSD and PCP, and amphetamines such as Benzedrine and Dexedrine). Many of these chemicals are an outgrowth of our mounting knowledge in the fields of chemistry and biochemistry. Yet humankind has used drugs of one sort or another since the beginning of recorded history.[5]

The ancient Greeks and Egyptians knew about the opium poppy, and there is written evidence that opium was used prior to the birth of Jesus Christ. The Greek philosopher Aristotle and the Greek physician Hippocrates wrote about the poppy and its product, opium. In the centuries after Christ, the therapeutic and medical uses of the drug became

widely recognized. During this period, opium was regarded primarily as an analgesic (pain reliever). In the late 1600s, however, there are records of smoking opium for pleasure—beginning in the Far East, but spreading elsewhere. Between 1839 and 1842, China and Great Britain were involved in the Opium War, which was a dispute over the importation of opium into the British Isles. Shortly thereafter, Imperial China counted its drug addicts in the millions. The problem then began to affect many of the Asian countries, and by 1913 a number of nations formed the International Opium Commission in order to deal with opium addiction.

In the New World, European explorers found the Indians using a variety of plant drugs: jimsonweed, peyote, coca, certain types of mushrooms, and tobacco, to name just a few. The Indians used these plants for a variety of purposes: to relieve fatigue, to achieve a psychological uplift, and for religious purposes under the supervision of someone trained in their preparation and administration. In contrast to the experimentation that often characterizes drug use in modern America, the use of drugs by American Indians was usually undertaken with great caution and reverence. Drug use commonly had important religious or social significance. For example, some groups believed that, during the transition from youth to adulthood, a transforma-

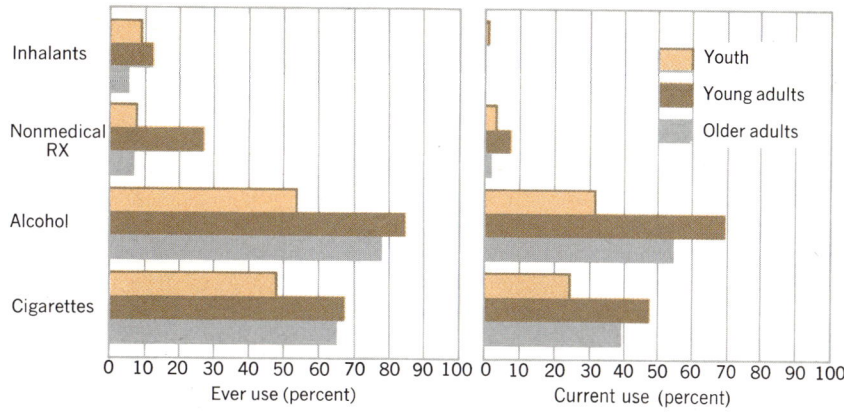

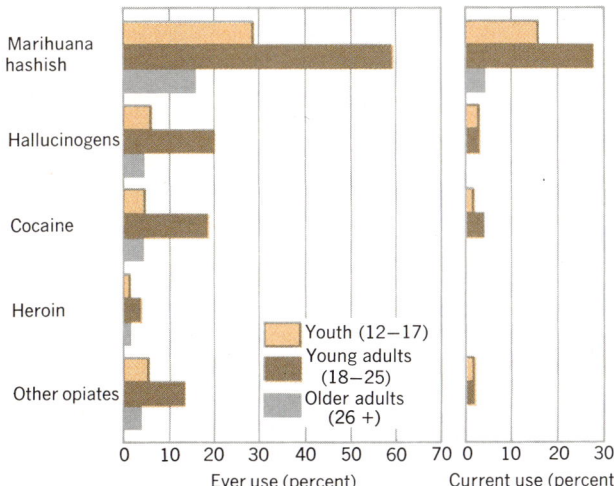

Figure 17.2   Lifetime Experience with and Current Use of Selected Drugs: 1977. National Institute on Drug Abuse, *Highlights from the National Survey on Drug Abuse: 1977* (Washington, D.C.: U.S. Government Printing Office, 1978), pp. 6, 8–9.

tive vision experienced by the young person was an important part of the transition. In some cases, the ingestion of a local drug was a part of achieving the necessary vision. In these societies, the use of drugs was often well-integrated into the belief system, the ceremonies, and other institutions.

Drugs and Alcohol in America

Narcotics

Prior to the Civil War, drug addiction was a relatively minor problem in the United States. Morphine, which is a concentrated derivative of opium, was isolated in the late 1700s. By 1810, it was being used in the practice of medicine, but its significance as a medical, and as an addictive, drug did

not emerge until the year 1856, when the hypodermic needle, which made for effective administration of the drug, was perfected. These developments, along with the use of morphine as an analgesic on the battlefield, led to addiction among many Civil War casualties. In 1874, heroin—a chemical derivative of morphine that is about four times as potent and produces fewer side effects—was first synthesized. It was first commercially produced by a German pharmaceutical company in 1898. At one time, heroin was thought to be a nonaddictive substitute for morphine. In fact, there were cases where heroin was actually used to *treat* morphine addiction. (This apparent medical naïveté can be placed in perspective by realizing that in our own era there was a general lack of concern about Valium's addictive potential after the drug was first introduced.)[6]

In time, the true addictive properties of heroin became recognized. By 1914, it has been estimated that there were close to 300,000 people in the United States addicted to narcotics—about 1 out of every 400 people.[7] Concern over this growing problem began to be translated into legislative action. In 1904, New York passed the Boyle Act to control the distribution of narcotics. Eventually, the federal government entered the scene, and in 1914 the Harrison Narcotics Act was passed and became the

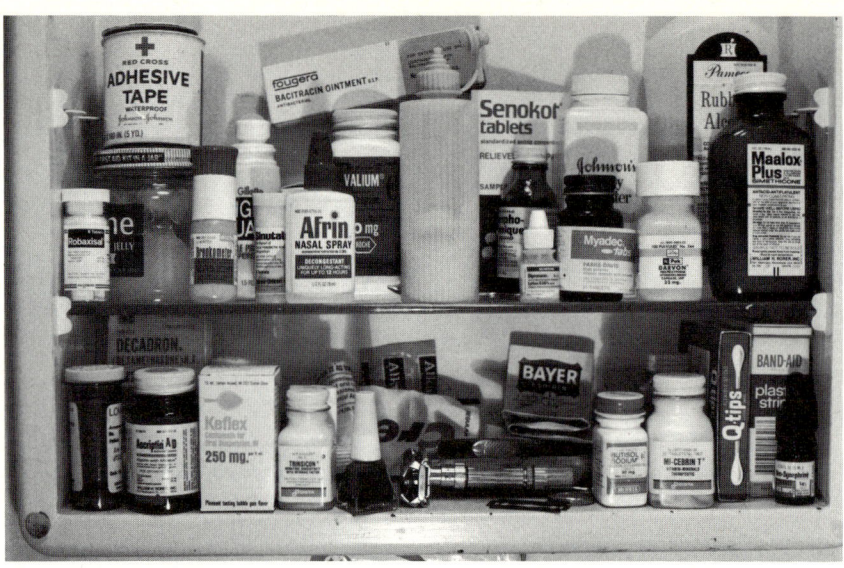

Medicine cabinets in many middle class homes today contain drugs that are both potentially addictive and dangerous if used indiscriminately. This explains, in part, why America has been characterized as a "drug culture."

basic antinarcotic legislation in the United States. The Harrison Act placed a federal excise tax on narcotics and required that they be dispensed only by registered physicians. For a while after passage of the legislation, physicians distributed narcotics quite widely to addicts, who were dependent on physicians to obtain their supply of drugs. However, the Federal Bureau of Narcotics remained concerned that narcotics were being prescribed to maintain the addict rather than for legitimate medical purposes, as required by the Harrison Act. Through a series of court decisions, the Bureau of Narcotics was able to halt the distribution of narcotics to addicts for the purpose of keeping them comfortable or of rehabilitating them. Thus, addicts were cut off from legal sources of narcotics and, in a pattern to be followed during the prohibition of alcohol, forced to rely on illegal sources to maintain their habit. A growing black market in narcotics, composed of newly formed criminal gangs, emerged to meet the demand for the illicit drugs.

The passage of legislation has important effects on people's attitudes toward narcotics. During the 1800s, when such narcotics were legal, people had a quiet understanding and sympathetic attitude toward users of morphine and heroin. It was often white, middle-class people, commonly women, who were addicted to these narcotics. Many of the syrupy tonics available to combat headaches, body aches, or depression contained a large dose of morphine. Since they could be obtained without a prescription and were considered to have medicinal value, they were widely used and easy to obtain.

The playwright Eugene O'Neill provided an intimate portrayal of early American attitudes toward drug addiction in his play *Long Day's Journey into Night*. O'Neill's sensitive drama about a mother's addiction to narcotics is based on fact and shows how addiction can arise out of unhappy family conditions and also make those problems more serious. There are important differences between his characterization and our negative views of drug abuse today. In O'Neill's play, it is clear that the most humane attitude toward drug addiction is one of sympathy and understanding rather than horror and rejection.

By 1914 and the passage of the Harrison Act, public sentiment was being aroused in the opposite direction. People who were addicted to drugs were no longer viewed as unfortunately ill but increasingly as practitioners of a socially disvalued vice. People who used the now-illegal substances were increasingly viewed as "addicts." Furthermore, the characteristics of those who used narcotics began to change. After 1914, more black, lower-class males were being identified as drug addicts and viewed as posing a threat to society. Reputable white people either discontinued their habits or were able to secure a supply of drugs through legitimate or semi-legitimate channels. Thus, more economically fortunate drug users were able to avoid detection, while narcotics use came to be increasingly associated with those of low social standing and minority group members.

Alcohol

The history of public attitudes toward alcohol, as well as of its social control, is somewhat reversed in comparison to the history of narcotics. During the 1800s and early 1900s, alcohol was legal, and organizations like the Womens' Christian Temperance Union (WCTU) were active in campaigning for its prohibition. According to the WCTU, alcohol was responsible for many social ills: crime, unemployment, the collapse of the family, and the like. Because immigrants and working- or lower-class males were the most visible consumers of alcohol (in taverns and in public), public attitudes associated alcohol consumption with these classes of people, and it was viewed negatively by groups of higher social standing. It was assumed that middle- and upper-class people did not use alcohol (or used it in acceptable moderation). Because alcohol use was associated in the public's mind with lower-class and marginal groups, it had a rather negative reputation.[8]

By 1920, a sufficient number of states had ratified the Eighteenth Amendment to the United States Constitution, which outlawed the sale of alcohol. Prohibition had begun. It soon became obvious that Prohibition was nearly unenforceable—people continued to drink in disregard of the law. In weak attempts to salvage Prohibition, some states stiffened the penalty for possession of alcohol. In Michigan, for example, the law was changed to

The speakeasy was one of the most common means of consuming alcohol by middle class people during the Prohibition era. Since alcohol was so popular among influential people, the repeal of the Eighteenth Amendment was not too far away.

specify that a fourth consecutive conviction for the possession of alcohol required a *mandatory* sentence of life in prison.[9]

Despite these efforts, Prohibition became one of the world's most recognized legal follies. It was a dismal failure. People continued to drink, and organized crime flourished as underworld groups competed with each other for the biggest share of the illegal liquor market. Nationally, Prohibition became a source of political embarrassment and a kind of laughing stock in judicial terms. In 1933, the Eighteenth Amendment was repealed. America learned an important lesson: the futility of attempting the legislative control over behavior that is widespread and that is seen by major groups in society as desirable. As the use of alcohol has become more widespread since Prohibition, and especially as it has become common among the middle and upper-middle classes, public attitudes toward alcohol have changed. It is no longer viewed by most as the scourge of society. While people recognize that it can cause problems, it is also viewed as a social amenity that is now part of our lives. Thus, while narcotics made the transition from respectability to disrepute in the past century, alcohol has made the opposite journey in the public's eye.

Marijuana

The hemp plant *Cannabis sativa* is the source of marijuana and hashish. It grows quite widely in temperate and tropical parts of the world. In America in the eighteenth and nineteenth centuries, marijuana plants were commonly grown and the plant fiber used to make rope, the seeds added to feed mixtures, and the oil used in the production of paint. However, few people realized that marijuana had psychoactive properties and thus there was little concern about it as a drug. Marijuana was used by some slaves in the South for its drug effect, but there was little public outcry against the drug and no effort to outlaw it.[10]

In the first decades of the twentieth century, concern over the use of marijuana began to emerge. Some people believed that marijuana caused crime, insanity, and moral depravity. By 1930, sixteen states had passed laws prohibiting the use of marijuana. (Marijuana was not classified as a narcotic and thus was not outlawed by the Harrison Act.) Yet, there was no consensus about the dangers of marijuana. In 1931, the Treasury Department, which was responsible for the enforcement of drug laws, reviewed the available facts and concluded that the growing concern over the use of marijuana was overstated and that marijuana was not a serious problem. Nevertheless, pressure to make the use of marijuana illegal continued. Some have argued that, despite the Treasury Department conclusion that marijuana was not a problem, some people within the Federal Bureau of Narcotics (a division of the Treasury Department), includ-

ing its director H. J. Anslinger, continued to campaign strongly against it. According to some sociologists, the Bureau was searching for some issue that it could control to compensate for its failure to make Prohibition effective.[11] However, there is no consensus about this interpretation. The Bureau did encourage uniform state legislation concerning marijuana, and by 1937 all states had outlawed the substance. In 1937, Congress passed the Marihuana Tax Act, which put marijuana in the same category as the narcotics controlled by the Harrison Act.[12]

The marijuana prohibition appeared to be fairly effective, mainly because very few people used the drug. However, in the 1960s marijuana use increased dramatically, and the prohibition lost its effectiveness. The states then reacted as they had during the final days of Prohibition — by enacting harsher penalties for sale and use. For example, in 1970 in Minnesota, a first offense of simple possession of marijuana had a penalty of 5 years to 20 years in prison. In Texas, first offenders could be given a sentence of life in prison. In Alabama, a second arrest for possession of marijuana drew a mandatory prison term of up to 40 years, with no suspended sentence or probation allowed.[13]

In recent years, there has emerged a greater understanding of drug abuse, and changes in public attitude toward the drug problem have resulted. These developments have been reflected in efforts to change the laws regarding drug use. In 1970, previous federal drug statutes (such as the Harrison Act) were replaced by the Comprehensive Drug Abuse Prevention and Control Act. This act reduced some penalties for possession of drugs (e.g. possession of marijuana has a maximum penalty of one year in prison and a fine of $5000); in addition, it makes it possible to send a first offender to a drug treatment program instead of to prison. While this federal legislation affects only those cases that fall under federal jurisdiction, such federal legislation often serves as a model for state legislatures to follow. At the state level, there have been a number of attempts to decriminalize marijuana and to view addiction to other drugs as a medical problem rather than a legal one. Before looking at the dimensions of the drug problem in America today, we will look at how drugs and alcohol are viewed as social problems.

DRUGS AND ALCOHOL AS SOCIAL PROBLEMS

The Functionalist Perspective

For the functionalist, social problems are created when there is disequilibrium that disrupts the smooth operation of society. It should be obvious that the use of certain drugs for established medical purposes can contribute to the maintenance of society. For example, when morphine is used as an analgesic, it contributes to our ability to control illness. Preliminary research has suggested that LSD and other hallucinogens may have substantial therapeutic value in helping terminally ill patients to cope psychologically with their impending death. The now well-known Brompton's Mix, which is used to ease the pain experienced by advanced cancer patients, is another example. This preparation contains morphine (or heroin, where legal), cocaine, and alcohol. If abused, it can be harmful and thus dysfunctional. In the context of treating the terminally ill, however, these drugs serve important positive functions.

From the functionalist perspective, then, the mere existence of drugs does not represent a social problem. Rather, it is the selective use of certain substances and the circumstances surrounding their use that pose difficulty to the smooth functioning of society. Thus, the use of drugs under certain conditions can disrupt the balance within society. The following are only a few examples: the use of euphoria-producing drugs while operating motor vehicles; the use of tobacco and its detrimental effects on health; and the addiction to heroin and other substances that may lead people to commit crimes in order to support their drug habit.

From the functionalist perspective, drug use becomes a social problem when its use interferes with the ability of people in society to contribute to the accomplishment of necessary tasks and the achievement of desired goals. In a technologically complex society such as the United States, people must be able to carry out tasks calling for either considerable manual dexterity or ample intellectual acumen. We must be clear-headed, rational, and able to coordinate our behavior with others. The heavy use of drugs, such as alcohol, amphetamines, or hallucinogens, can, and often does, interfere with these skills and abilities. For example, the heavy use of alcohol on the job among factory workers would undoubtedly have costly consequences for the whole production process. Thus, the extent to which drug use is a social problem for a particular society depends on the degree to which it interferes with the achievement of essential tasks and goals.

The Conflict Perspective

According to the conflict perspective, social problems involved a human struggle over desirable, but finite, resources. **Drug use becomes a social problem when some group feels that the use of drugs interferes with its ability to compete for scarce resources and achieve its goals.** Drugs can be a mechanism that serves to pacify subordinate groups so that they are not motivated to change the status quo. For example, according to the conflict perspective, the heavy use of alcohol and other drugs among poor people can make it exceedingly difficult for them to compete for scarce resources, such as desirable and well-paying jobs. This is beneficial to the dominant groups because it reduces the amount of competition over resources and reduces the likelihood that the poor will attempt to change the status quo to provide greater benefits for themselves.

Many minority groups have become aware of this aspect of the drug problem and realized that drug use is detrimental to the advancement of their group when it saps energies and resources that might be used to promote group goals. Black leaders such as Jesse Jackson have for this reason encouraged young blacks to avoid drugs and to work hard in school so that they can compete with others in the job market. **According to the conflict perspective, the extent to which drug use is defined as a social problem depends on which groups are affected.** When drug use was limited to poor people and marginal groups (minority groups, musicians, or beatniks), few considered it a serious social problem. As drug use spreads to more influential groups, it becomes defined as a problem by these groups.

The Interactionist Perspective

According to the interactionist perspective, the existence of social problems depends on people's definitions of certain conditions or behaviors as undesirable. If, for example, we view drug use as normal and expected human behavior, it would not be a problem. One excellent example of how definitions of certain substances change over time involves the use of tobacco during the early 1900s. Prior to the availability of medical evidence that smoking can lead to a number of illnesses, smoking was not regarded as a social problem. Many people smoked, and even those who did not smoke were more tolerant of those who did. As research data about the detrimental effects of smoking became more convincing, the use of tobacco came to be viewed increasingly as a social problem.

Another example of the varying definitions attached to the same drug has to do with peyote. The Native Americans who are members of the Native American Church have used peyote—whose chemical extract is mescaline—as a part of their religious ceremonies for hundreds of years. The use of peyote is considered a holy activity. After a long legal battle, the Native American Church has been permitted to use peyote as a part of their religious observances. Yet at the same time, people who are not members of the Church are engaging in illegal activities if they take peyote or mescaline and may risk jail sentences for doing so. **Thus, the social context in which a drug is used and the shared meanings attached to use of the drug result in very different attitudes and reactions toward use of particular substances.** The importance of the social context in determining our attitudes towards drugs is illustrated in the case of heroin and morphine. In chemical analysis, the differences between these two drugs are minimal. Heroin is generally much stronger than morphine, but when heroin is sold on the street it is usually diluted to the point where it is weaker than morphine. Sociologist Erich Goode has concluded,

By "objective" standards they are very nearly the same drug; they do more or less the same things to the tissues of the body. Nonetheless, heroin is declared to have no medical uses whatsoever. It is considered a menace, a killer. Morphine, on the other hand, is regarded a boon to mankind. It has the stamp of approval from the medical fraternity; it is a valuable therapeutic tool. And yet the roles and medical functions of the two drugs, and hence their social meanings, could easily be reversed.[14]

From the interactionist perspective, social interaction is based on shared consensus concerning social meanings and values. Drug use can threaten that consensus in a number of ways. The lack of predictability of behavior that is induced by many drugs can lead people to define them as a social problem. In other cases, the use of drugs may be perceived as interfering with the development and maintenance of this consensus. The drugs—especially illicit drugs—often lead to the emergence of drug subcultures with values and a definition of reality that is different from, and often incompatible with, the values and definitions of the dominant groups in society. Thus values such as hard work and respect for one's parents that underlie the lifestyle of the dominant groups may not be accepted among the subculture of marijuana or heroin users. The drug subculture becomes a focal point for the emergence of competing values and definitions of reality. Parents may fear that their children will become immersed in such subcultures and reject the values they hope to pass on to them.

DRUGS, DRUG ABUSE, AND DRUG ADDICTION

Psychoactive Drugs

When one tries to define what is meant by the term *drug*, difficulties arise immediately. Most Americans would agree that heroin and cocaine are drugs, but fewer people would apply that term to alcohol, and fewer still would call tobacco a drug. Yet from a purely medical point of view, all of these substances would be drugs. **From a medical standpoint, a drug can be defined as "any** substance other than food which, by its chemical nature, affects the structure or functioning of a living organism.''[15] This is an extremely broad definition that would encompass many substances not considered drugs in our society.

Our concern in this chapter is with *psychoactive drugs,* which are chemical sub-stances that affect the mind of the user.[16] Some psychoactive drugs are listed in Table 17.2. We will consider some of the dimensions and effects of particular psychoactive drugs, but it is useful first to make some general statements about these types of drugs.

Psychologist Oakley Ray has outlined four basic observations that are applicable to all psychoactive

TABLE 17.2
Controlled Substances: Uses and Effects

	DRUGS	OFTEN PRESCRIBED BRAND NAMES	MEDICAL USES	DEPENDENCE POTENTIAL: PHYSICAL	PSYCHOLOGICAL
NARCOTICS	Opium	Dover's Powder, Paregoric	Analgesic, antidiarrheal	High	High
	Morphine	Morphine	Analgesic	High	High
	Codeine	Codeine	Analgesic, antitussive	Moderate	Moderate
	Heroin	None	None	High	High
	Meperidine (Pethidine)	Demerol, Pethadol	Analgesic	High	High
	Methadone	Dolophine, Methadone Methadose	Analgesic, heroin substitute	High	High
	Other narcotics	Dilaudid, Leritine, Numorphan, Percodan	Analgesic, antidiarrheal antitussive	High	High
DEPRESSANTS	Chloral hydrate	Noctec, Somnos	Hypnotic	Moderate	Moderate
	Barbiturates	Amytal, Butisol, Nembutal, Phenobarbital, Seconal, Tuinal	Anesthetic, anti-convulsant, sedation, sleep	High	High
	Glutethimide	Doriden	Sedation, sleep	High	High
	Methaqualone	Optimil, Parest, Quaalude, Somnafac, Sopor	Sedation, sleep	High	High
	Tranquilizers	Equanil, Librium, Miltown Serax, Tranxene, Valium	Anti-anxiety, muscle relaxant, sedation	Moderate	Moderate
	Other depressants	Clonopin, Dalmane, Dormate, Noludar, Placydil, Valmid	Anti-anxiety, sedation, sleep	Possible	Possible
STIMULANTS	Cocaine†	Cocaine	Local anesthetic	Possible	High
	Amphetamines	Benzedrine, Biphetamine, Desoxyn, Dexedrine	Hyperkinesis, narcolepsy, weight control	Possible	High
	Phenmetrazine	Preludin	Weight control	Possible	High
	Methylphenidate	Ritalin	Hyperkinesis	Possible	High
	Other stimulants	Bacarate, Cylert, Didrex, Ionamin, Plegine, Pondimin, Pre-Sate, Sanorex, Voranil	Weight control	Possible	Possible
HALLUCINO-GENS	LSD	None	None	None	Degree unknown
	Mescaline	None	None	None	Degree unknown
	Psilocybin-Psilocyn	None	None	None	Degree unknown
	MDA	None	None	None	Degree unknown
	PCP‡	Sernylan	Veterinary anesthetic	None	Degree unknown
	Other hallucinogens	None	None	None	Degree unknown
CANNABIS	Marihuana Hashish Hashish oil	None	None	Degree unknown	Moderate

†Designated a narcotic under the Controlled Substances Act.
‡Designated a depressant under the Controlled Substances Act.

drugs.[17] First, there are no completely and inherently "bad" drugs. **When we speak of *drug abuse*, we are referring to our collective judgments about the ways that particular drugs are used.** For example, amphetamines are often used for medical purposes and are labeled as de-

sirable drugs in that context. During the early 1960s, many weight-conscious Americans took amphetamines by prescription from their physicians with the medically approved goal of losing weight. However, since amphetamines are very psychologically addictive, many people found they

TABLE 17.2

(continued)

TOLERANCE	DURATION OF EFFECTS (IN HOURS)	USUAL METHODS OF ADMINISTRATION	POSSIBLE EFFECTS	EFFECTS OF OVERDOSE	WITHDRAWAL SYNDROME
Yes	3 to 6	Oral, smoked	Euphoria, drowsiness, respiratory depression, constricted pupils, nausea	Slow and shallow breathing, clammy skin, convulsions, coma, possible death	Watery eyes, runny nose, yawning, loss of appetite, irritability, tremors, panic, chills and sweating, cramps, nausea
Yes	3 to 6	Injected, smoked			
Yes	3 to 6	Oral, injected			
Yes	3 to 6	Injected, sniffed			
Yes	3 to 6	Oral, injected			
Yes	12 to 24	Oral, injected			
Yes	3 to 6	Oral, injected			
Probable	5 to 8	Oral	Slurred speech, disorientation, drunken behavior without odor of alcohol	Shallow respiration, cold and clammy skin, dilated pupils, weak and rapid pulse, coma, possible death	Anxiety, insomnia, tremors, delirium, convulsions, possible death
Yes	1 to 16	Oral, injected			
Yes	4 to 8	Oral			
Yes	4 to 8	Oral			
Yes	4 to 8	Oral			
Yes	4 to 8	Oral			
Yes	2	Injected, sniffed	Increased alertness, excitation, euphoria, dilated pupils, increased pulse rate and blood pressure, insomnia, loss of appetite	Agitation, increase in body temperature, hallucinations, convulsions, possible death	Apathy, long periods of sleep, irritability, depression, disorientation
Yes	2 to 4	Oral, injected			
Yes	2 to 4	Oral			
Yes	2 to 4	Oral			
Yes	2 to 4	Oral			
Yes	Variable	Oral	Illusions and hallucinations (with exception of MDA); poor perception of time and distance	Longer, more intense "trip" episodes, psychosis, possible death	Withdrawal syndrome not reported
Yes	Variable	Oral, injected			
Yes	Variable	Oral			
Yes	Variable	Oral, injected, sniffed			
Yes	Variable	Oral, injected, smoked			
Yes	Variable	Oral, injected, sniffed			
Yes	2 to 4	Oral, smoked	Euphoria, relaxed inhibitions, increased appetite, disoriented behavior	Fatigue, paranoia, possible psychosis	Insomnia, hyperactivity, and decreased appetite reported in a limited number of individuals

SOURCE. U.S. Department of Justice, Drug Enforcement Administration, *Drugs of Abuse* (Washington, D.C.: U.S. Government Printing Office, n.d.).

had problems discontinuing use of the diet pills. In addition, amphetamines acquired a less than favorable reputation as young people began using them as "uppers." The "speed freak" (user of methamphetamine) emerged, and public attitudes concerning the use of this type of psychoactive drug changed.

A second observation concerning psychoactive drugs is that all of them have multiple effects. This is important because they can affect people's minds in many different ways and thus their outcome is not always predictable.

A third observation is that the effects of a particular psychoactive drug will depend on the amount that a user takes. This fact raises a number of issues. For one thing, increased dosages of psychoactive drugs can accentuate their effects. However, the effects of a particular drug may change substantially when the dosage is increased. Thus, users may increase a dose to accentuate a pleasurable experience, and the result may be a different, and possibly undesirable, experience.

A fourth observation regarding psychoactive drugs is that their effects can be influenced significantly by a particular user's past experience, expectations, and state of mind while using the drug. For example, sociologist Howard Becker, after much observation of people using marijuana, showed that the effects of marijuana are not only a function of the chemical action of the drug on the body. In addition, the person must be taught that certain physiological experiences (such as hunger or thirst) can be attributed to the drug, and the user must learn that these experiences are enjoyable.[18] Expectations also shape one's reaction to a drug. Studies of placebos have shown that, if one believes that there will be a certain reaction to a chemical, then the likelihood of having the reaction is increased.

Drug Abuse

There is no consensus today concerning what is the proper and acceptable use of drugs. Young adults, for example, often shake their heads when their parents use alcohol or tranquilizers but then light up a joint of marijuana in order to relax and enjoy some music. The parents, concerned about the use of drugs such as marijuana or hashish by their children, take a drink or a couple of Valium tablets to soothe their anxiety. Parents and offspring see each other as having a drug problem, while not recognizing that they themselves may be abusing drugs. When we begin to discuss the issue of when legitimate drug use ends and drug abuse begins, controversy is inevitable. Nevertheless, since the issue is crucial to our discussion, we will provide some guidelines.

The Medical Point of View

If we approach this issue from a medical frame of reference, drug abuse may be regarded as the regular or excessive use of a substance such that a person's health is damaged, relationships with other people are endangered, or society itself is jeopardized in the process. This definition poses a problem, however. While it includes many things that we would normally recognize as drug abuse, some activities that fall within the scope of this definition would not be so considered. For example, heavy use of tobacco is seriously harmful to one's health, yet few would call a heavy smoker a drug addict. At the other extreme, some people engage in frequent use of drugs such as heroin and cocaine over a long period of time, but suffer few health consequences and lead productive lives. Many Americans would consider these people drug abusers, yet there are no apparent detrimental physical or social consequences of their drug use. In short, the medical perspective, while helpful in defining drug abuse, does not provide a complete definition.

The Social Viewpoint

While medical considerations are important, they are only a part of our definition of drug abuse. We must also examine the social aspects of a definition of drug abuse. The interactionist perspective helps us to understand this crucial dimension of our definition. For example, during the 1930s, marijuana was thought to be a dangerous drug, and people who smoked it were regarded as abusers. The public, legislators, and law enforcement agencies

Drawing the line between the social use of alcohol and problem drinking is often difficult. Alcohol is a pervasive part of our culture, especially from the standpoint of young people.

were convinced that marijuana caused crime, insanity, and a host of other ills. The 1930s characterization of marijuana sounds a little unbelievable to most of us today. The major reason for the change in public sentiment about marijuana lies in people's definitions concerning its use. As marijuana has become more widely used, especially among middle- and upper-middle class groups, the image of its users has changed. Increasingly, marijuana use has taken on some of the same characteristics as the social use of alcohol.

It is important, then, to consider drug abuse within the context of a particular group's definition of that substance and its effects. **We can define** **drug abuse as the regular or excessive use of a substance when, as defined by a particular group, the consequences are detrimental to a person's health, endangers relationships with other people, or jeopardizes society itself.** This definition incorporates both medical and social viewpoints, and thus enables us to focus on those types of drug use that are considered abuse by many people in society.[19]

Drug Addiction

Much of the concern over drug abuse focuses on those who are addicted to drugs. There is also much misunderstanding of drug addiction. Drug addiction refers to an intense desire and craving for a drug.[20] There are two conditions that are of central importance in studying drug addiction: tolerance and dependency. (See Table 17.2 for an analysis of tolerance and dependence in relation to various drugs.) *Tolerance* **refers to the experience of reduced effects from a particular dosage of a drug.** With many drugs, the longer a person uses them, the higher dosage the person must take to achieve a given effect. Thus, a person addicted to a drug for which one can develop a tolerance will have to look forward to purchasing increasing quantities of the drug in the future in order to maintain the same effect. For expensive illegal drugs such as heroin, this can be a major problem for the addict.

Dependence **exists when distinct withdrawal symptoms, either physical or psychological, follow the discontinuance of the drug.** Physical withdrawal symptoms from such drugs as heroin include a running nose, sweating, nausea, vomiting, diarrhea, stomach cramps, and muscle spasms. Psychological withdrawal symptoms from drugs such as alcohol or cocaine might include depression or irritability. *Drug addiction* **is the result of dependence on a particular drug.**

We now have some understanding of what a drug is and what we mean by drug abuse and drug addiction. While there is still controversy over these issues, our definitions provide us with some guidelines that enable us to now turn to a discussion of particular drugs and the problems surrounding them.

STIMULANTS

Stimulants **refer to the broad range of drugs that stimulate the central nervous system.** Depending on the potency of the particular drug and the mindset of the user, a stimulant can provide relief from fatigue, increased alertness, elevate one's mood, and heighten one's sense of excitation and well-being. We will discuss the problems associated with some of the most widely used stimulants in American today.

Tobacco

Tobacco was first introduced into Europe by Spanish explorers in 1558. In 1561 the French ambassador to Lisbon, Jean Nicot, sent samples of the tobacco plant to his queen; the word *nicotine* is derived from his name. The tobacco plant was at one time believed to be a miraculous cure-all, but the acceptance of tobacco was short-lived. Once tobacco began to be smoked, consumed with wine or water, and eaten in large quantities, its intoxicating qualities became recognized, and there emerged a strong negative reaction against its use. George Sandys, who visited Constantinople in 1611, was told that a man convicted of smoking was sent through the streets riding backward on a donkey with a pipe forced through the cartilage of his nose. In 1628 two merchants in the Middle East had their noses and ears cut off for importing tobacco. In Iran, some twenty years later, merchants found smoking at an inn were punished by having molten lead poured down their throats. In Russia the death penalty was levied for habitual offenders of the law against selling tobacco.[21] While these reactions are extreme, they illustrate the intensity with which people reacted against tobacco when it was used as an intoxicant rather than a medicine.

Tobacco is one of the most widely used drugs in America today, yet few people consider it to be a drug. One reason that it is not classified with other drugs is that few people use it as a psychoactive drug. Indians in the New World at times used tobacco as a psychoactive drug; they smoked large quantities of very strong tobacco in the hope of inducing visions. In seventeenth-century Russia, tobacco was also smoked in a manner that enhanced its psychoactive properties. If tobacco is smoked in the same manner as marijuana—with deep puffs mixed with much air, protracted holding of the smoke in the lungs, and slow exhalation of the smoke—intoxication can result.[22]

Although tobacco is not viewed as a psychoactive drug in the United States, there is nonetheless considerable concern about its effects. Most of this concern focuses on the detrimental health effects of smoking tobacco: it has been associated with some forms of cancer, heart disease, emphysema, and many other serious health disorders. According to a recent report by the United States Surgeon General's Office, "smoking is the largest preventable cause of death in America."[23] According to the report, cigarette smoking is estimated to result in 80,000 deaths a year from lung cancer, 22,000 deaths from other forms of cancer, 225,000 deaths from cardiovascular disease, and 19,000 deaths from chronic pulmonary disease. In addition, the report noted that, given the numbers of women who currently smoke, lung cancer will in all likelihood overtake breast cancer in the number of deaths it causes among women.

It is clear that the toll in human lives and suffering from the use of tobacco is startlingly high—far higher than is the case with any other drug, with the possible exception of alcohol. Yet, until recently, there has not been the public outcry against tobacco that there has been against other drugs. Clearly, the use of tobacco is so deeply imbedded in our history and culture that we tend to ignore its negative side and are reluctant to take the steps necessary to reduce its detrimental impact on society. The government has controlled the advertising of cigarettes and required harsh warnings about tobacco's health effects on cigarette packages. Many states have passed laws either forbidding smoking in public areas or making non-smoking areas available in places such as restaurants and airplanes to those who do not smoke. Yet, despite these efforts to control smoking, the government still encourages the production of tobacco through federal subsidies to tobacco farmers, and there is no serious effort to outlaw smoking altogether. Because tobacco has been defined for so long in our culture as a socially acceptable and innocuous substance, it is unlikely that it will be outlawed in the near future.

Cocaine

Cocaine is one of the New World drugs derived from the leaves of the coca plant. It was and still is used by the Indians of the South American mountain regions to reduce fatigue. In the late 1800s, cocaine was used to flavor Coca-Cola. In fact when Coca-Cola was originally introduced in 1886, it was advertised as a patent medicine that would cure headaches, neuralgia, hysteria, and melancholy.[24] When cocaine was removed from the soft drink in 1906, caffeine was substituted so that a stimulant effect could be retained.

Cocaine remained a popular drug in the United States until the 1920s. The Cole Porter tune "I Get a Kick Out of You" originally contained the line "I get no kick from cocaine," subsequently changed to "I get no kick from champagne." Charlie Chaplin, in the film *Modern Times,* portrayed a character who took cocaine as a means of reducing fatigue and increasing his energy level.[25] Among the well-known fictional characters of Western literature, Sherlock Holmes, the archetypal private investigator, was also portrayed by Alfred Conan Doyle as being very fond of cocaine. These illustrations of the use of cocaine in popular literature and art indicate that during the late 1800s and early 1900s, cocaine was viewed as a socially acceptable drug, much as alcohol is today.

Who Uses Cocaine?

Cocaine is not as widely used today as it once was. This is in part due to its status as a controlled substance under the Harrison Act, but equally important in terms of its limited usage is its high cost. Because of its expense, it is often referred to as "the pimp's drug," the "champagne of drugs," or the

"society high." In 1977, cocaine cost from $60 to $100 per gram (about 1/30 of an ounce) in New York. The total revenue from the sale of cocaine has been estimated at about $20 billion a year.[26] In part due to its high cost, cocaine is more commonly used by people in the middle and upper classes than by other social classes.

The National Institute on Drug Abuse estimates that about 8 million Americans have tried cocaine.[27] A recent study found that, among high school students, over 10 percent of the 1977 senior class had tried cocaine at least once, and almost 3 percent had used it in the 30 days prior to being interviewed for the survey.[28] Cocaine users generally come to use the drug after having had experience with other drugs. One study of regular cocaine users found that, prior to using cocaine, 27 percent had tried other stimulants, 20 percent had tried barbiturates, 10 percent had used hallucinogens, and 2 percent had experience with opiates. In addition to having prior experience with drugs, cocaine users tend to be polydrug users — that is, users of more than one drug. Thus, 85 percent of this group of cocaine users also used alcohol, 66 percent used marijuana, 8 percent took amphetamines, and 5 percent used hallucinogens.[29]

The Effects of Cocaine

The effects of cocaine last for about two hours while, by contrast, the effects of heroin will last from four to six. The physical effects of cocaine are those of a stimulant and can be attained quickly when the powder is sniffed (snorted) into the nostrils. Under low doses there is increased motor activity, while higher doses can result in tremors, convulsive movements, shallow breathing, and even respiratory failure. However, few cases of death have been attributed to cocaine use.[30]

Cocaine gives users a sense of alertness and wakefulness (insomnia) and it can snap them out of low moods. It also makes users feel enormously powerful and causes them to overestimate their strength and abilities. One measure of the drug's appeal is its effect on laboratory animals that are given drug rewards for pushing levers. They will push levers up to

250 times in a row for caffeine, 4000 times for heroin, and 10,000 for cocaine.[31]

This experiment with laboratory animals may indicate the attractiveness of the drug to human users.

Experienced cocaine users rank it their first choice among recreational drugs because it produces euphoria, a sense of intense stimulation, and feelings of psychic and physical wellbeing accompanied by reduced fatigue. Another advantage, according to users, is that unlike LSD and heroin—which increase orientation toward self and one's internal processes—cocaine is a social drug that can facilitate social interaction. Another attraction to users is the belief that cocaine is relatively free from markedly undesirable side effects and is generally safe. This latter reputation, however, may be overstated, since it is based on low doses taken at infrequent intervals.[32] A common problem for long-term users who ingest cocaine by "snorting" is the permanent destruction of the mucous membranes in the nose, the development of breathing difficulties, and even the loss of the septum of the nose. Prolonged use can also result in sexual dysfunction and may lead to hypertension (high blood pressure).

The social attitudes surrounding the use of cocaine, especially when compared with tobacco, provide a good illustration of the difficulties of defining drugs and drug abuse. To date, evidence shows that physical damage from the use of cocaine is considerably less than the effects of some other drugs (such as alcohol and tobacco) that are legally available. Nevertheless, the possession or use of cocaine is illegal and carries considerable criminal penalties. In other words, many people believe it to be harmful, and it is therefore treated as a dangerous drug. Many of the problems that arise from cocaine use are primarily related to the fact that the drug is illegal: it must be smuggled into the United States, which means that organized crime is often involved and violence sometimes results from these activities. If cocaine were legal, many of these problems would probably disappear. On the other hand, we cannot ignore the possibility that long-term use of cocaine may have detrimental physical or psychological effects on the individ-

ual. Research into the effects of cocaine is very limited, and thus we have few data with which to come to definite conclusions in this regard.

Amphetamines

Amphetamines are mass-produced synthetic drugs with effects similar to cocaine: increased alertness and wakefulness, reduced fatigue, increased energy and motor activity, and heightened competence in motor skills.[33] Some of the more commonly known brand names under which amphetamines are distributed are Benzedrine ("bennies"), Dexedrine ("dexies"), and Methadrine ("meth" or "speed"). Amphetamines are widely prescribed by physicians for a number of purposes: to increase attention, to decrease appetite (for weight loss), and to enhance a person's mood.[34] There are two very different patterns of abuse of amphetamines, the quasi-legitimate use and the heavy use.

Quasi-Legitimate Amphetamine Users

The quasi-legitimate (but often illegal) use of amphetamines is by individuals who are not considered deviant and who often take amphetamines in order to enhance their ability to accomplish practical and socially acceptable tasks. Among this group would be the long-haul truckdriver who uses "bennies" to fight off exhaustion, the student who takes "dexies" in order to stay up all night cramming for an exam, and the housewife who wants to be in a better mood to carry out her duties for her family. For this group, the dosages are relatively small—2.5 to 15 milligrams per day. Since initial contact with amphetamines among this group often occurs through legal prescription, habitual use may develop while a person is taking them for weight reduction or other medically approved reasons. After the legal medical need for amphetamines is past, the person may for two reasons find it difficult to discontinue use of the drug. First, since tolerance to the drug can develop, the user may have increased the dosage to an addicting level during the legal use and find the withdrawal symptoms very unpleasant.

Second, amphetamines can be very addicting, especially psychologically. Thus, this form of amphetamine addiction is especially pernicious because the person is often unaware of the danger until the damage is done.

Another dimension of the social problems related to the legal use of amphetamines is their use in the treatment of behavior problems such as hyperactivity. Some amphetamines and other stimulants have a paradoxical effect when taken by children who are hyperactive. *Hyperactivity* (also known as hyperkinesis and minimal brain dysfunction) is characterized by excessive motor activity, a short attention span, restlessness, shifts in mood, and similar behavioral symptoms.[35] (Hyperactivity is an anomolous condition; little is known about its cause; and the condition, if untreated, disappears as the child matures.) Children exhibiting these symptoms can be extremely disruptive in school and at home. Stimulants, a popular one being Ritalin, can have a calming and soothing effect on such children; however much controversy has arisen over their use because of the considerable abuse that has occurred. While Ritalin has been widely prescribed for hyperactive children, the vague symptoms of hyperactivity have often resulted in the use of stimulants for many other unrelated behavior problems.

> Many of the children for whom Ritalin is prescribed are not really hyperactive to begin with. They are normal children who simply refuse to submit to what their teachers and parents consider orderly school and family routines. Categorizing children who are different as hyperactive often is a seductively convenient way to blame the victims of teachers' and parents' own shortcomings. Drugging these children, however, brands them as troublemakers and helps to further institutionalize drug use.[36]

While the abuse of such stimulants was a serious problem in the 1960s, it has since been considerably reduced, and much more caution is now used in diagnosing a child as hyperactive.[37] Nevertheless, our experience with Ritalin and hyperactivity stands as a lesson that great care must be taken even when stimulants are used for legitimate purposes.

Heavy Amphetamine Users

The massive and continual ingestion of amphetamines (particularly Methadrine) is engaged in by some people involved in the drug subculture. Much of their life revolves around taking "speed"; they take it to get high, rather than for any practical purpose; and the impact on their lives is much the same as for the heroin addict. The dosage for the "speed freak," when compared to that for the quasi-legitimate user, is enormous—possibly 500 to 1000 milligrams per day. Often, these heavy users of amphetamines follow a pattern of use called a "run" during which they stay awake for long periods of time (possibly 2 to 5 days) and take large doses of amphetamines either orally or through injection every 4 to 8 hours. The alertness that occurs when the drug takes effect can come on very rapidly, and some users equate this (called a "rush") with a sexual orgasm. The user will often take the drug for three or four days, sleeping and eating very little if at all. During this period, judgment may be seriously impaired, and the user may have feelings of overconfidence that lead to numerous accidents, both minor and serious. After several days of use the person will generally "crash"—sleeping for a long period (as much as 24 hours). Upon awakening, the heavy amphetamine user will likely repeat the process.[38]

The heavy amphetamine user is quite different from the quasi-legitimate user. Whereas the latter is typically a respectable member of society, the heavy user usually does not hold a permanent, full-time job and must resort to various illegal activities to support himself and his habit. Thus, he is deeply involved in a drug subculture and very often in a criminal subculture. Negative physical effects are commonly associated with heavy amphetamine use; some result from the euphoria created by the drug and the long periods of wakefulness and lack of food. Pneumonia is common among heavy users, along with tetanus and hepatitis. Some heavy users believe that they will not live more than two or three years—they see themselves living a high and fast life that will "burn them out." This is a dramatic exaggeration, but life expectancy is not enhanced by the self-neglect that can accompany use of this drug.

An area of concern commonly discussed in relation to amphetamine use is its effect on violence. While it is true that no drug will necessarily produce a *specific* form of behavior, violence is often associated with heavy amphetamine use. Compared to users of many other psychoactive drugs, heavy amphetamine users seem to commit an unusually high share of violent crimes.[39] Ellinwood explains one possible reason for this:

> Not infrequently the amphetamine abuser committing homicide is attacking his imagined assailant created in his paranoid, delusional thinking. The violent act may take place in a state of terror and panic, often secondary to misinterpretation of events or delusions. Perhaps equally important is the influence of amphetamines in creating (a) impulsive reactiveness and (b) a lability of mood, in which state the user abruptly vacillates from a warm congeniality to fiercely hostile moods for the most trivial of reasons. [40]

The lifestyle of the "speed freak" is a second possible reason that accounts for the connection between amphetamines and violence. The speed freak often lives through a series of high-risk, low-payoff hustles, such as male prostitution, strong-arm robbery, dealing in small amounts of speed, or "burning" (selling phony or highly adulterated substances as drugs). Since both he and his customers operate outside the protection of the law, the speed freak is vulnerable to many forms of coercion, especially violent ones. If she "burns" a customer, one resort of the customer to make restitution is violence. Since members of the drug subculture do not have access to legitimate forms of protection, they are likely to resort to illegitimate, and often violent, forms.

DEPRESSANTS

Depressants are psychoactive drugs that depress the central nervous system and result in drowsiness, sleep, and decreased alertness; most important from the viewpoint of abuse, they can lower inhibitions. There are three major classes of depressants: alcohol, barbiturates, and tranquilizers. Alcohol, due to the severity of the problems associated with its use, will be covered in a separate section of this chapter.

Barbiturates

Barbiturates, like the amphetamines, are found under a number of names among which are Seconal (reds), Luminal, Nembutal, Amytal, and Tuinal. Their use is quite widespread: there were about 18.5 million prescriptions for barbiturates in 1976.[41] Some experts estimate that the number of Americans addicted to barbiturates or tranquilizers easily exceeds one million. **Barbiturates are normally thought of as mild sedatives or sleeping pills, yet when abused they can be among the most dangerous drugs available —following tobacco and alcohol as a factor in drug-related deaths. Barbiturates can produce physical addiction, tolerance, and psychological dependency—the felt need or craving for the drug, even when no physical need is present.** The addiction traits of barbiturates are so severe that withdrawal from their addiction is more dangerous than withdrawal from heroin or the other narcotics; it is much more likely to result in death, and withdrawal, therefore, should take place in a hospital.[42]

The symptoms of withdrawal from the abuse of barbiturates involve nausea, cramps, headaches, sweating, uncontrollable convulsions, and occasionally coma and death.[43] Problems of barbiturate use among pregnant women are similar to those of narcotics addiction in that the child can be born addicted to barbiturates, and the prognosis for successful withdrawal of the infant is poor.

While barbiturates can have beneficial medical uses, they can also, especially if abused, have very deleterious consequences. Overdoses on barbiturates are common. One reason for this is that the user, while under the influence of the drug, forgets that one dose has been taken and takes another and repeats this until an overdose level has been reached. Overdoses of barbiturates can cause a slowing of vital bodily functions that eventually results in either a cessation of breathing or of heartbeat and thus causes death. The total number of overdoses per year is uncertain, but one study of 600 emergency rooms found that barbiturates were mentioned as the drug causing a medical emergency in over 10,000 cases in 1976. The same 600 emergency rooms reported that barbiturates were involved in the deaths of 1637 people during 1976.[44] Since barbiturates are readily available, they are also commonly used in suicide attempts. It has been estimated that of all drug-related suicides, barbiturates account for about 75 percent of the total.[45] Another serious problem in relation to barbiturates is combining their use with the consumption of alcohol: the combination can result in irreversible brain damage or death.

Most people who are addicted to barbiturates obtain their drugs through legitimate prescriptions from their physician rather than from some illegal source. If a physician becomes suspicious about a person's intake, it is relatively easy to obtain a prescription from a different physician. People who obtain barbiturates legally through prescription tend to be in the middle and upper socioeconomic classes and tend to come equally from all age groups.[46] People with respectable social standing usually have a good relationship with their physician and can thus obtain prescriptions with little difficulty. However, a black market in barbiturates does exist, and those who obtain drugs in this fashion tend to be mostly under 25 years of age. Older people are much less likely to be involved in this illegal market in barbiturates.

Tranquilizers

There are two classes of tranquilizers: major and minor.[47] *Major tranquilizers* **are generally used in the treatment of functional mental disorders, like schizophrenia and manic depression because they work to suppress the symptoms of these diseases. The most common of these antipsychotic drugs are the phenothiazines.** One fairly well-known substance within this broad classification is Thorazine (the most common brand name for chlorpromazine). *Minor tranquilizers* **are far more familiar to most people than the phenothiazines and are also more likely to be used and abused. Examples include Librium, Valium, Equamil, and Miltown.** These psychoactive drugs can yield some of the same effects as the barbiturates — a general feeling of relaxation and well-being and a reduction of tension. In high doses, tranquilizers can become addictive. Tolerance to these drugs can be developed, and their withdrawal symptoms resemble those from barbiturates and alcohol. As we observed early in this chapter, some of the most devastating consequences of the regular use of tranquilizers involve their interactive effects with alcohol.

In 1976, there were over 91 million prescriptions for tranquilizers in the United States.[48] Tranquilizers are normally thought of as being mild mood changers that can be used with impunity. Many users believe they are only taking a mild sleeping pill or harmless relaxant. However, that view is currently undergoing reevaluation. Some physicians and medical researchers are moving to the position that the differences between some tranquilizers and the barbiturates are practically nonexistent. Although they are not as potent as barbiturates, their addictive properties are now becoming recognized.[49]

The widespread use of tranquilizers in American society is in many respects not surprising. Our highly urbanized, industrialized, and intensely competitive society can be the occasion of an enormous amount of stress and anxiety. For the individual, this may mean irritability, depression, or an inability to sleep. Tranquilizers, with their ability to relax a person and reduce tension, are an obvious way to alleviate some of this tension and anxiety. Furthermore, the danger of serious side effects from tranquilizers is presently believed to be slight. For many people, the benefits are believed to far outweigh any potential risk. Unfortunately, most heavy users of tranquilizers are complacent in believing that they are running no risk at all.

HALLUCINOGENS

Hallucinogens— **sometimes referred to as psychedelic drugs—consist of both natural and synthetic substances that produce an alteration in the individual's perception of reality.** They can produce sensory illusions and hallucinations. Some of the more popular hallucinogens are: lysergic acid diethylamide (LSD), peyote, mescaline, STP, psilocybin, MDA, and phencyclidine (PCP). Of this group, the most commonly used drug is LSD. In the past, these drugs have been used for a variety of purposes. Morning glory seeds, which are closely related to the LSD compound, were used by the Aztecs to communicate with their gods; peyote was, and is, widely used by the 200,000 members of the Native American Church as a part of their religious services; and mushrooms with psychedelic properties were first used by the Mayans.[50] The religious function associated with the use of hallucinogens was carried over into the 1960s, when LSD became popular among many college students. Early "trips" on LSD were explained as a search for spiritual understanding and expanded consciousness. While the use of these drugs continues today, few users give the spiritual rationale of the past as the reason for their experimentation.

There is not the same pattern of prolonged use of hallucinogens that we observe with other psychoactive drugs. William H. McGlothlin explains this in the following manner,

> First, of course, there is no physiological dependence of the type resulting from opiates, barbiturates or long-term chronic use of alcohol. Second, at least for LSD and similar hallucinogens, the rapid buildup of tolerance precludes their use on a daily basis. A third reason why the hallucinogens appear unsuitable for chronic use is their lack of predictable effects. Habitual drug users seek to satisfy particular needs—e.g. escape, euphoria, anxiety relief, and relief from feelings of inadequacy. To qualify for chronic use, a drug must consistently produce the type of mood alteration desired. Hallucinogens are quite inconsistent in terms of mood alteration. The fourth and probably most important reason to expect persons to decrease rather than increase their use of hallucinogens over time is the diminishing utility of the experience as a function of continued use. The major attraction of these drugs is not mood change but the uniqueness of the experience. As the hallucinogen experience is repeated many times, what was initially unique becomes more commonplace; there is a process of diminishing returns. The effect of hallucinogens is indeed a "trip" and trips tend to lose their appeal when repeated too often.[51]

Much has been said about the potential physical and psychological damage that can result from the use of hallucinogens—especially LSD. According to most research findings, there is no conclusive evidence of either major or minor damage.[52] Some LSD-induced psychoses have been reported, but the conclusions drawn indicate that the drug aggravated an existing mental problem and did not produce it. Reports of LSD damage to human chromosomes have now been discounted; one knowledgeable researcher states that LSD has no effect on human chromosomes whatever.[53]

PCP

The emergence of phencyclidine (PCP) as an important hallucinogen in the past decade illustrates some of the difficulties in dealing with the drug problem in the United States.[54] PCP was first synthesized over fifty years ago, but it was not until the 1950s that it was recognized as having possible medical value as an anesthetic. However, it was found to produce very adverse side effects: agitation, delirium, hallucination, muscle rigidity, and seizure. Its use on human beings was therefore discontinued, but it continued to be used by veterinarians because it had no side effects among nonhuman primates. While there are legal sources of PCP, it is simple to synthesize with only a few chemicals and simple equipment, and thus it was a prime candidate for illegal production for human use. This is what has happened, beginning in 1967, when PCP began to appear on the illegal drug market. It acquired a number of slang names: Angel Dust, Hog, Killer Weed, Embalming Fluid, Cyclone, Zoom, and Horse Tranks. Some of these names reflect the ambivalent manner in which the drug culture seems to view PCP.

Based on a federal study of drug treatment programs, the typical PCP user is a white male between the ages of 10 and 29 who purchased the drug on the street for its psychic effects. In addition to the subjective reaction to PCP, which can be highly variable, PCP also causes dizziness, apathy, lack of coordination, double vision, nausea, vomiting, abdominal pain, jitteriness, insomnia, and feelings of paranoia. The effects of PCP differ from one person to another, and from one time to another. PCP users are often brought to emergency wards by family or friends who cannot cope with their agitated and often violent behavior. The user exhibits confusion, excitement, and a "blank stare" appearance. PCP poisoning can produce a mental state resembling schizophrenia. A characteristic that intensifies these problems is that PCP stays in the bloodstream for unusually long periods, and may even be recycled by the body. Thus the recovery from PCP poisoning is prolonged— sometimes for over two months— and future ingestion of PCP may result in intensified reactions because of the accumulation of the drug in the body. This makes the reaction to PCP, if one has used it in the recent past, even more unpredictable.

The history of PCP is common to that of other hallucinogens. In our efforts to utilize our knowledge of biochemistry to improve our health or standard of living, we produce drugs that have hallucinogenic properties that some people find desirable. Because these drugs are easily produced, they are rapidly disseminated to the black market even when they are outlawed. Because there is little laboratory research on them, we are often at a loss in terms of how to cope with adverse reactions to the drugs. Some hallucinogens, such as LSD, do not seem to be harmful, and this can easily lull people, especially the young, into the comforting conclusion that all hallucinogens are harmless. One of the serious drawbacks to the use of hallucinogens is the unpredictable nature of a person's reaction to them, which depends on many factors, including the individual's personality, mood while taking the drug, and the context in which it is taken.

MARIJUANA

Of all the drugs available today, probably the best known and most controversial is marijuana, which is the dried leaves and flowers of the plant *Cannabis sativa*. Over the past two decades, there has been enormous debate over whether marijuana should be legalized and whether it has any harmful effects. We will attempt to bring some information and clarity to these issues.

Who Uses Marijuana?

Because of its widespread use and popularity, we probably know more about the characteristics of marijuana users than is the case with most other drugs (see Fig. 17.3). According to a recent investigation, 24 percent of all adult Americans reported using marijuana at least once— 9 percent within the previous month.[55] With this many Americans using marijuana, it is clearly competing with alcohol and tobacco as the most popular psychoactive drug. In 1979, Americans consumed about 130,000 pounds of marijuana per day— four times the amount consumed 5 years earlier.[56] This translates into billions of cigarettes per year being smoked by Americans.

Who uses marijuana? Research indicates that marijuana today is much like alcohol in its patterns of use: it has spread across all social class, educational, sexual, racial, and ethnic divisions. It is found among practically all groups. Marijuana, like alcohol, has become pervasive in our society. Nevertheless, marijuana use is considerably more common among the young. Furthermore, most people tend to use it infrequently or to use it for awhile and then stop using it. Finally, and possibly most important, if a person knows others who use marijuana, it increases the likelihood that he or she will use it. In other words, having the opportunity to use marijuana is a critical factor in determining its use.[57]

Marijuana as a Social Problem

Marijuana, especially in the potency typically encountered in the United States, appears to be a very

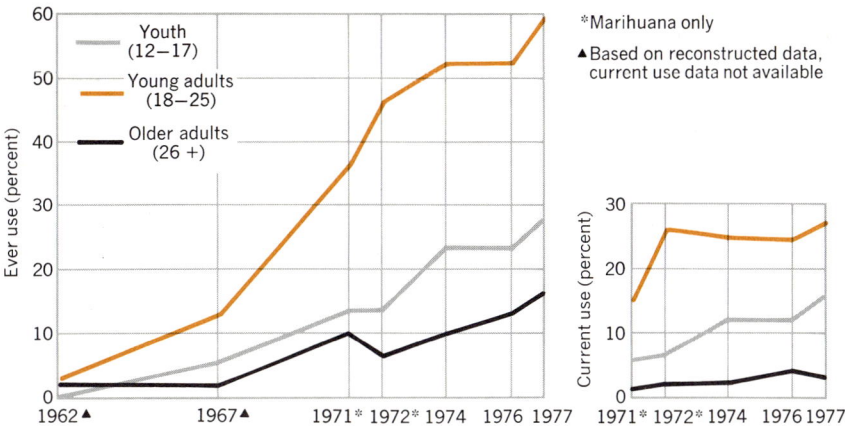

Figure 17.3 Trends in Lifetime Experience with and Current Use of Marijuana/Hashish. National Institute on Drug Abuse, *Highlights from the National Survey on Drug Abuse: 1977* (Washington, D.C.: U.S. Government Printing Office, 1978), p. 17.

mild drug. Like alcohol, the moderate use of marijuana can result in a pleasant euphoria and a feeling of well-being. These desirable effects, along with its use to ease the tension of social interaction, explain marijuana's growing popularity.[58] One recent Institute for Social Research study at the University of Michigan revealed that marijuana is fast becoming the drug of choice for recreational use among youth of high school age. One factor that has undoubtedly enhanced the popularity of marijuana is that it has not been shown to cause serious physical damage. In 1977 at an open hearing before the House Select Committee on Narcotics Abuse, which was investigating the possibility of removing federal penalties for marijuana use, Bertram S. Brown, the director of the National Institute for Mental Health, provided important testimony. He stated that over $20 million had been spent over the preceding five years on research into marijuana use. The conclusion reached was that no harmful effects had been clearly demonstrated.[59]

Given the increasing popularity of marijuana, it is important to evaluate the problems its use can lead to, and there are a number of identifiable factors that relate to marijuana use as a social problem. As was the case with tobacco use thirty years ago, the possible long-term health hazards of using marijuana are at present unknown. Research concerning the negative physiological and psychological effects of the drug are somewhat inconclusive at this time. It does appear, however, that lung damage similar to that produced by tobacco use may be one long-term effect for heavy marijuana users. Conclusive evidence on this will probably not be available for quite a few years. This is true in part because there are few people who have used marijuana extensively enough and for a sufficiently extended period of time to begin to manifest potentially longterm detrimental effects.

Another problematic feature of marijuana use is more subtle — its possible interference with the emotional development of adolescents and pre-adolescents. Adolescence represents a time of substantial change and psychological adjustment as people move from childhood to adulthood. This change can involve a great deal of stress, as the young person learns to cope with the trials and tribulations of social interaction, sexuality, and other responsibilities. The increased use of marijuana by young men and women of high school age may represent an attempt to avoid confrontation with the stresses sometimes associated with their changing status in society. If this is true, many young people who are using marijuana as an avoidance mecha-

The use of marijuana became so widespread during the 1960s and 70s that, like alcohol during the Prohibition era, influential citizens have continued to defy laws controlling the substance.

nism may not be developing the skills that are necessary to cope with problems.

Another problem associated with marijuana is the illegal and often violent business of supplying the drug to users. Because marijuana is illegal, the only source of supply is through persons or groups who employ illicit means to produce and import the drug. For example, in one Colombian city—Guajira —92 people were killed in various "drug wars" during a two month period.[60]

Reacting to the lack of proof that marijuana causes serious physical or psychological damage and to the problems associated with the drug's illegal status, several states have decriminalized the use and simple possession of marijuana—that is, they have made it a noncriminal offense punishable by a fine. However, no state has yet fully

legalized marijuana use. The legalization of marijuana—allowing public sale and use without any legal punishment whatsoever—is a very controversial issue. Proponents of legalization, such as the National Organization for the Reform of Marijuana Legislation (NORML), cite the research findings mentioned above and state that our government is exceeding its authority by restricting use and sale of a drug that a large segment of the population uses and finds relatively harmless. The fundamental issue raised by those who oppose legalization is well taken. They contend that we already have serious problems of legal drug abuse and do not need to compound the problem by permitting the use of another abusable drug. They assert that while a drug may not be harmful of itself, its use could be a problem. For example, we know that about 25,000 deaths and a half-million serious injuries per year result from automobile accidents in which the use of alcohol is involved. How many such accidents and fatalities will result from marijuana intoxication is unknown, but it is this uncertainty that has led some to be cautious about legalizing marijuana.[61]

NARCOTICS

The drugs that generate the greatest public fear and concern are probably the narcotics: opium and its derivatives (heroin, morphine, and codeine), and the synthetic narcotics (such as methadone, Demerol, and Percodan). **A *narcotic* is a drug that provides relief from pain and creates dependency in human beings; narcotics are among the most effective analgesics known.** (Cocaine and marijuana are also classified as narcotics under the Federal Controlled Substances Act, but they are not narcotics in terms of their effect on the human body.) Among the narcotics, heroin has probably received the most attention.[62] In the past decade, there have been periodic outcries over the "epidemic" of heroin use and over heroin flooding American schools. *Newsweek* magazine epitomized this concern when its issue entitled "The Heroin Plague" carried a picture on the cover of a young man sticking a needle into his arm—presumably "shooting up" with heroin.[63] Because of this public concern about heroin, we will focus this discussion of narcotics on the problems surrounding heroin use and abuse.

Who Uses Heroin?

The profile of the typical heroin addict in recent decades has shifted from white middle-class female to slum-dwelling minority-group male. For a person to be considered an addict, he or she must display certain traits—tolerance and dependency. However, not all heroin users are addicts; it is possible to use heroin on an infrequent basis without becoming addicted to it. This practice, sometimes referred to as "chipping," points out a myth usually associated with heroin use, namely, that one dose will

eventuate in addiction. Heroin can be a highly addictive drug, however it generally requires two to three weeks of regular use to produce tolerance and true physical dependence. But there is one more criterion that must be met before true addiction may be said to exist, and that is *craving*—an intense desire for heroin.[64] It is this craving that makes the treatment of heroin addicts so difficult. If tolerance and dependence were the only factors to contend with, treatment would simply require keeping the person away from the drug until the withdrawal symptoms were gone. It is the *desire* to take heroin that makes treatment a more difficult problem. The reason for craving is complex. Many addicts do not crave the drug for its psychoactive properties but to avoid withdrawal symptoms. Alfred R. Lindesmith, a prominent drug researcher, has explained it in the following manner,

> The hook in addiction arises, not from the euphoria which the drug initially produces, but from the beginner's realization that the discomfort and misery of withdrawal is caused by the absence of the drug and can be dispelled almost magically by another dose of it. The repetition of this experience functions as a conditioning process . . . which quickly establishes in the beginner the fatal craving for the drug.[65]

Lindesmith has also indicated two ways that people become addicts and the consequences of the path taken. The first way is through the therapeutic use of opiate-derivative drugs—generally from a doctor's prescription, but folk beliefs or popular custom may also be involved. The second path to addiction is through associating with persons who are heroin users and through situations in which the drug is used for recreational purposes. Lindesmith believes that the nature of drug laws tends to have an effect on which of these two paths is more common at a given time.

> When the policy is one of prohibition and punishment for addicts, the second pattern is ordinarily dominant and the number of addicts relatively large; when addicts are handled as patients and are given access to legal drugs, the number of addicts tends to be smaller and most of them have first used drugs for medical reasons.[66]

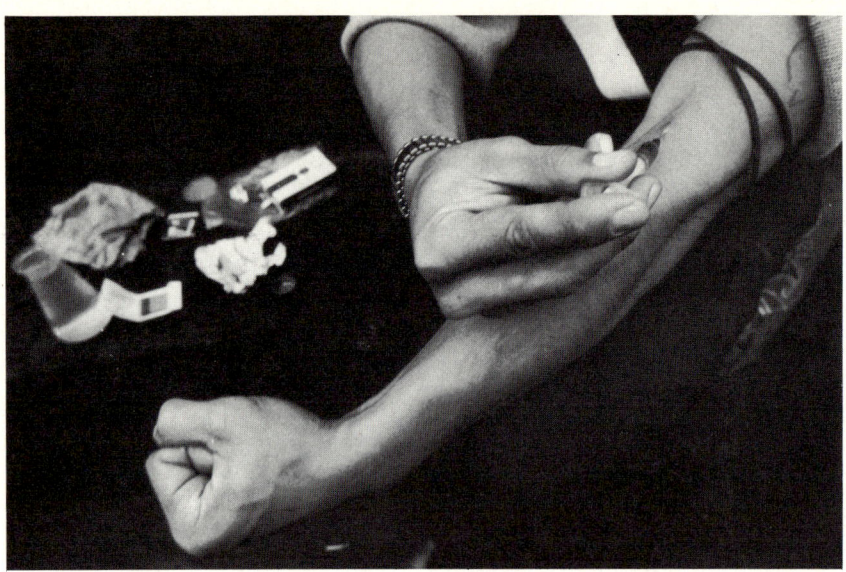

Tolerance, dependence, and craving can make "the needle" a
way of life for people who are addicted to narcotics.

Heroin as a Social Problem

Most people in our society consider heroin addiction a serious problem. We conjure up images in our minds of the depraved "dope fiend" committing the most heinous of crimes—an animal with no social conscience who is mercilessly driven to satisfy his or her need for the drug. Law enforcement authorities often support this view by pointing to the high percentage of crime committed to obtain drugs. Since addiction is expensive—$10 to $100 per day—the addict must obtain a large supply of money to support the habit, and crime is one typical source (see Table 17.3).

To determine the extent of criminal activity among heroin users, a study was conducted with a sample of addicts who were participating in a treatment program. The investigators found that of the sample of 38 males, 100 percent had performed criminal acts to support their habit, although only 79 percent had arrest records. Ninety-three percent of the crimes were property crimes, while only 7 percent were violent crimes. This predominance of property crimes is understandable in terms of the heroin addict's motive for committing crimes: nonviolent property crimes are an easier and more ef-

fective way to obtain money to purchase drugs. The female addicts tended to be less criminally involved; nearly two-thirds had never been arrested, but of those who had been, prostitution was the most frequent offense. One especially interesting finding of the study was that the male addicts averaged 23 crimes per month, and only 4 percent of their crimes were eventually reported in FBI statis-

TABLE 17.3
Estimates of the Sources of Funds of Heroin Addicts, 1970

SOURCES	PERCENT
Shoplifting	22.5
Burglary	19.0
Pickpocketing	5.4
Larceny	7.4
Robbery	3.4
Confidence games	4.7
Prostitution	30.7
Welfare	3.0
Other, legal sources	3.9
TOTAL	100.0

SOURCE. Adapted from Selma Mushkin, "Politics and Economics of Government Response to Drug Abuse," *The Annals of the American Academy of Political and Social Science* 417 (January 1975), p. 30.

tics.[67] This suggests that crime committed by heroin addicts is vastly underreported.

Some of the problems associated with heroin use have a direct effect on the user.[68] One such problem is the possibility of an overdose. Heroin overdose is difficult to control because it is directly related to the purity of the heroin taken, but heroin purchased through illegal channels is practically always of unknown purity. Heroin is generally cut or diluted many times before it is sold to the user. Normally, packets of heroin purchased illegally will vary from less than 1 percent to about 14 percent heroin, with the remainder being made up of substances like milk sugar or quinine. Thus, heroin addicts become accustomed to this dosage and may overdose if they unknowingly purchase and use heroin of greater purity. It is this unknown potency of the black market drug that makes heroin use such a dangerous practice. In one analysis of 110 packages of confiscated heroin, the concentration ran from about 1 to 77 percent pure heroin.[69] A user accustomed to 3 percent who "shoots up" with 77 percent will very likely overdose.

Aside from the issue of purity, there are other possible explanations for accidental overdose. They are:

> . . . injecting after not having abused heroin for a period of time (and subsequent loss of tolerance) of the previously used dosage; . . . the use by recently addicted addicts of the higher dose levels used by addicts who have developed a greater tolerance for the drug; . . . and the deliberate attempt by a pusher to induce a lethal overdose by providing purer heroin than usual.[70]

In 1974, about 1400 addicts died in New York City. The causes of death were as follows: 50 percent died from an adverse reaction to either heroin or methadone, 40 percent died violently (homicide), and 5 percent died from infection. The number of homicides was attributed to a shift toward a younger, more aggressive, and more antisocial addict population.[71] Infection is also a problem faced by addicts. Dirty equipment (such as an unsterile needle) passes on hepatitis and tetanus, and a lack of medical knowledge occasionally leads a novice to inject the drug into an artery instead of a vein, which results in gangrene.[72]

Some of the problems associated with heroin use are related to the fact that the drug is illegal. Physicians, who have easy access to drugs, have a narcotic addiction rate nearly double that of the general population, and they are sometimes addicted for 30 to 40 years without exhibiting problems typical of other addicts.[73] This is the case because physicians are able to obtain predictable doses of drugs and to adjust their tolerance levels according to pharmaceutical information. Furthermore, they are not exposed to unsterile conditions and equipment and are more likely than the addict to know how to inject drugs properly. Finally, they usually attend to nourishment and health care and avoid the physical deterioration of the addict. In considering ways to alleviate the problem of narcotics addiction, we must recognize that the problems come not from the drug itself but from the conditions under which it is currently used and the lifestyle of the user.

ALCOHOL

Alcohol abuse is, by any standard of measurement, the number-one drug problem in the United States today and is associated with many other social problems. Absenteeism from work due to hangover or intoxication is very common. It is estimated that about 5 percent of the employees in larger corporations are alcoholics and that this group has an absenteeism rate 2.5 times that of the other employees.[74] One out of every four patients in mental institutions in this country is or has been an alcoholic. Half of all traffic deaths—about 25,000 per year—are directly attributed to drunkenness. Approximately 60 percent of violent homicides involve drinking prior to the attack. In 40 percent of all male rapes of adult women, the offender was classified as being intoxicated. The toll in terms of broken families and lost employment is not exactly known but is assumed to be very high.[75] Given these statistics and others that illustrate the same point, there is little doubt that alcohol abuse is one of our most serious drug problems.

Patterns of Alcohol Use

Americans have always consumed a large volume of alcohol; beginning in 1790 there was a steady increase in per capita consumption, reaching a peak in 1830 when the amount used was about twice the present level.[76] Today, the per capita consumption of pure alcohol is about 3 gallons for all persons aged 15 years and older.[77] Of course, this figure includes many nondrinkers, but it is nevertheless an accurate index of the enormous amount of alcohol that is consumed each year.

Alcoholism

In 1974, surveys indicated that 68 percent of the adult population drank; the distribution by sex was 77 percent for males and 60 percent for females. More specifically, 42 percent of Americans 18 years of age and over either did not drink at all or drank only infrequently; 31 percent were light drinkers, taking about one drink per week; 18 percent were moderate drinkers, four or five drinks per week; and 9 percent were heavy drinkers, taking one or more drinks a day.[78]

The consumption of alcoholic beverages is not necessarily a serious social problem. In small amounts, alcohol may be beneficial in helping ease awkward social situations, relieving tension, relaxing inhibitions, and enhancing celebrations. However, the consumption of large amounts of alcohol can create problems for both the individual and society (see Table 17.4). **The term that is attached in our society to excessive drinking patterns is** *alcoholism.* One problem in arriving at an estimate of the numbers of alcoholics has been a lack of agreement concerning what constitutes an "alcoholic." **For our purposes, an** *alcoholic* **is a person who has become dependent on the drug alcohol, who drinks more alcohol than the socially accepted norm for our culture, and whose excess drinking has damaged his health, relations with family and friends, and his job performance.**[79] There is no set level of alcohol consumption that distinguishes between the social drinker and the alcoholic. **Alcoholics are those**

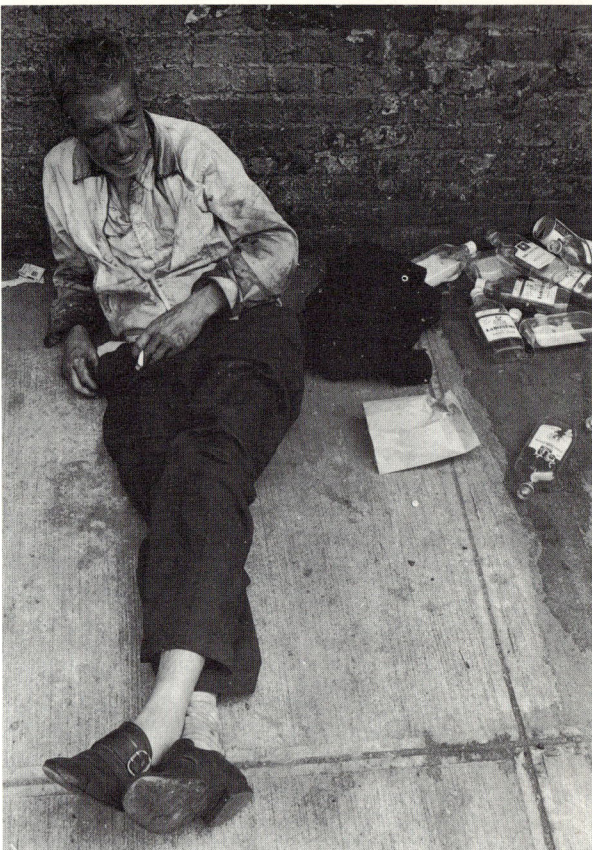

Alcoholism as a problem is usually a matter of degree. Influential people are better able to conceal the effects of their addiction than others.

TABLE 17.4
Percent of Alcohol in the Blood and Its Effects

PERCENTAGE OF ALCOHOL	EFFECTS
.05	Lowered alertness and a "high" feeling.
.10	Legally drunk in most states, decreased reactions, reduced coordination.
.20	Massive interference with senses and motor skills.
.30	Perceptions are nearly gone, understanding is nearly gone.
.40	Unconsciousness occurs.
.50	Death.

SOURCE. Adapted from Oakley S. Ray, *Drugs, Society, and Human Behavior* (St. Louis: C. V. Mosby Co., 1972), p. 86, and Erich Goode, *Drugs in American Society* (New York: Alfred A. Knopf, 1972), pp. 142–143.

who have lost control over their drinking. For some people, this may mean periodic episodes of intoxication, while for others it may be a nearly constant state of drunkenness.

Estimates of the number of alcoholics in the United States varies depending on how narrowly or broadly one defines alcoholism. Using the definition of alcoholism just presented, estimates place the number of alcoholics in the United States at about 6 million.[80] Who is likely to become an alcoholic? There are some observable variations in the social characteristics of those who are likely to have a problem with alcohol.

Sex

Males far outnumber females in the ranks of alcoholics. In fact, the rate of alcoholism among males is about 5.5 times higher than among females.[81] This difference is due in part to the varying expectations attached to sex roles in the United States. The use of alcohol is associated with the male role to a much greater extent than with the female role. It has traditionally been more acceptable for men to visit bars and consume substantial quantities of alcohol than it has been for women. Furthermore, it has been more socially approved for men to respond to stress or depression through the use of alcohol.

However, the sex-linked differences in alcohol use are declining. The proportions of women who consume alcohol has been increasing for the past three decades, as have rates of alcoholism and cirrhosis of the liver among women, and the gap between men and women has been narrowing. Why should there be such an increase in alcohol use among women? Much attention has been focused on changing sex roles as an explanation for these trends. There are a number of ways in which changing sex roles might lead to increased alcohol consumption among women. First, women are more likely to hold stressful and tension-filled jobs that previously had been held by males. Women can try to cope with this tension and anxiety as men often do, through increased alcohol consumption.[82] Thus, increased alcoholism may be one of the costs that some women may pay if they assume previously all-male jobs. Second, nontradi-

tional female roles are more likely to provide social support for drinking, whereas the traditional role of housewife and mother provided few such supports. It may prove difficult to abstain from alcohol in a social context in which there is encouragement to imbibe. Thus, in the workplace, women receive more encouragement to drink and it is viewed as more socially acceptable.

Third, alcoholism may derive from inconsistencies or conflicts in sex role orientation. For example, a woman who values femininity may find herself in a job that requires that she behave in a masculine fashion; likewise, a woman who values masculinity may be in a situation that calls for feminine characteristics. This incompatibility between values and behavior appears to be related to alcohol abuse. According to this argument, it is not the assumption of the male role per se that lends itself to alcoholism, but rather the fact that the role requires the person to behave inconsistently with her values.

Race

The relationship between race and drinking behavior is not a simple one. Thus, the drinking rates among black and white males is about equal. However, black females have a higher proportion of both abstainers *and* of heavy drinkers than do white females. Furthermore, blacks begin drinking at an earlier age than do whites.[83] Among Mexican Americans, drinking is largely a male prerogative. One study found that 72 percent of the Mexican-American males drank, but only 16 percent of the females used alcohol.[84]

Religion

Religion also exerts an important influence on patterns of alcohol consumption.[85] Thus, a large proportion of Jews consume alcohol (90 percent), but there are low rates of heavy drinking among Jews. Catholics also had a large number of drinkers (83 percent), and Catholics have higher rates of heavy drinking than Jews. Among Protestants, the figures for drinking varied considerably, with the more conservative denominations having the lowest proportion of drinkers (52 percent) and the more liberal groups having high proportions (90 percent).[86]

Age

Alcoholism is usually considered an adult problem — and most alcoholics are adults — but there is growing concern over alcohol consumption among young people. Recent studies have found an alarming increase in drinking among young people. About 70 percent of all high school students have tried alcohol, and the number who have become intoxicated has doubled over the past twenty years. In a study of New York City high schools, 80 percent of the boys and 75 percent of the girls drank on a irregular basis; but 12 percent drank enough to be considered abusers. According to the National Institute on Alcohol Abuse and Alcoholism, 1.3 million preteens and teenagers have serious drinking problems.[87]

We cannot state with certainty the reasons for the increase in alcohol consumption by grade school and high school students, but some contributing factors may be identified. Many of the young people who did not drink in the study cited above abstained because they said they did not like the smell or taste of alcoholic beverages. In recent years, however, we have seen the introduction of drinks that taste like chocolate milkshakes (Hereford's Cow), fruit drinks (Boone's Farm Wine), and soda pop (Ripple Wines). This removal of the "taste barrier" increases the likelihood of young people's experimenting with alcohol. Another factor in youth's wanting to drink is a permissive attitude on the part of parents. In a 1972 survey of teenage students in California, some typical responses to the question, "When did you first drink alcohol?" were

My aunt gave me my first can of beer when I was about fourteen and that started it.

At thirteen I was sent to live with an uncle in Nevada because my stepfather and I just couldn't get along. He felt that if, at an early age, you became aware of your capacity for booze, you wouldn't have any trouble with it later. So I had the freedom to drink anything in the house.

I started drinking when I was thirteen, the summer before seventh grade. My father drank beer and I wanted to be like him. He would give me tastes of his beer, and I developed a craving for it.[88]

With this earlier introduction to alcohol it is not unreasonable to expect that the alcoholics of the near future will be younger than the typical alcoholics of today.

Theories of Alcoholism

One of the most difficult questions to grapple with when discussing alcohol abuse is what causes alcoholism. Why are some people unable to control their drinking while others are able to? There is no simple answer to this question, and we will discuss three of the more prominent approaches to this issue.

Biological Approaches

Some researchers take the position that alcoholism is in some fashion related to the physical makeup of a person. One type of biological approach is *genetic theory,* which holds that alcoholism is an inherited biological trait or predisposition that is passed from one generation to the next. Support for this theory of alcoholism is found in the fact that alcoholism often runs in families — children of alcoholics are more likely to become alcoholics than are children of nonalcoholics.[89] However, caution must be exercised in accepting this theory because, first, the precise biological mechanism by which alcoholism is presumably transmitted has not been located. Some have proposed that there is an inherited fondness for the chemical properties of alcohol while others have suggested the existence of an inherited nutritional deficiency that can be corrected by the consumption of alcohol. Neither theory has been substantiated. Secondly, not all alcoholics come from families of alcoholics, and thus biological explanations are at best only partial explanations. Third, studies of the children of alcoholics who have been raised by others who were not alcoholics showed that these children were not more prone to alcoholism than were the children of nonalcoholics.[90] These findings suggest that psychological or environmental factors play an important role in causing alcoholism. Biological factors may create a disposition toward alcoholism that will be activated only by appropriate psychological or environmental factors.

Psychological Approaches

Psychological approaches are based on the assumption that alcoholism is a symptom of some mental problem or emotional need on the part of the individual.[91] Alcoholism is the person's way of coping with the tension or anxiety arising from psychological problems. One psychological approach is *social learning theory,* which posits that people are more likely to repeat behaviors that have rewarding or pleasant consequences and to avoid behaviors that have punishing or unpleasant consequences. Thus, an individual who is tense, anxious, or depressed may find that alcohol relaxes her and replaces her depression with euphoria. Given this pleasant outcome of alcohol consumption, she is likely to repeat it in the future when depressed or anxious. Eventually, a pattern of drinking to relieve stress may emerge, and drinking may become a routine part of the person's life. Social learning theory is undoubtedly important, but there are some limitations to it. For example, not all of the consequences of drinking are pleasant: the hangover, the social disapproval, and the marital problems that often arise are unpleasant but often do not deter the alcoholic. Thus, there is certainly more to alcoholism than social learning. If a person has been drinking heavily and continuously for some time, he may become physically addicted to alcohol, and this addiction would account for his continuing to drink even though many of the consequences were negative. Thus, heavy drinking may begin for one reason (social learning) but continue for quite a different reason (physical addiction).

Sociological Approaches

Sociological approaches to alcoholism focus on values, norms, and social organization as important causal factors.[92] One sociological approach is *normative theory,* which states that alcoholism emerges because it is condoned or even encouraged by the norms of a particular society or group. For example, among many Jewish Americans, alcohol consumption is viewed as having religious significance—it is a part of various sacred beliefs and practices. Sobriety is viewed as good

and drunkenness as bad. On the other hand, some Irish Americans drink not for religious or familial reasons, but rather for enjoyment or to meet crises and reduce tension. Drinking for these Irish-Americans is meant to enhance fellowship and to ease the tensions of social interaction. Thus, in the one culture alcohol consumption is encouraged but alcohol abuse is discouraged; in the other culture, there is little social censure for excessive drinking. According to normative theory, alcoholism is more likely to emerge when the social norms encourage excessive drinking or at least do not discourage it.

It would be satisfying if we could close this discussion of the causes of alcoholism with a simple and clear-cut statement as to what is the most important precursor. Unfortunately, the state of our knowledge in this field makes such a conclusion impossible. Alcoholism is a complex phenomenon, and all of the factors we have discussed—biological, psychological, and sociological—may be important at some level. Future research will hopefully clarify some of these issues. Despite our less than perfect knowledge of alcoholism, there *are* some things that can be done about the problem. We turn now to an analysis of some of the treatment programs currently in existence in the United States designed to cope with the problems of drug and alcohol abuse.

FUTURE PROSPECTS: DRUG USE IN AMERICA

Among our concerns for the future is the effectiveness of existing treatments for certain forms of drug abuse. In this section we will focus primarily on the treatment programs created for two addicting drugs—heroin and alcohol. What we learn from treating persons who are dependent on these highly addicting substances will help us to deal with other forms of addiction.

The Treatment of Heroin Addiction

Given a large addict population—estimates place the number between 3 and 5 million active users—we are faced with three primary choices:[93] first, to allow things to continue as they have in the past; second, to provide drugs for addicts; and finally, to provide some form of treatment. The first option is rejected by most people because to accept it would be to resign ourselves to living with the crime and loss of human potential that is associated with heroin addiction. Thus, we will turn our attention to the remaining two options.

The British Plan

In Great Britain, narcotics addicts are required to register with a government-based office in order to obtain treatment for their addiction from a physician. Through these doctors, addicts are given a maintenance dosage of the addictive drug in question. By reducing the dosage provided, these physicians attempt to control the user's degree of reliance on the drug and to eliminate the habit if possible. Addicts are not charged any medical fees and pay a moderate sum for the drugs themselves. Britain has instituted a network of clinics that are established to serve one hundred addicts each. The clinics are staffed with psychiatrists, nurses, and social workers who deal with the needs of the addict.[94] Perhaps the most important difference between American and British approaches is that the British consider addiction a problem for medicine and not one for law enforcement.

Interestingly enough, similar programs were in operation in some parts of the United States during the 1920s. Many large newspapers and influential individuals attacked these drug clinics and compared them to the opium dens of the Orient. Physicians became fearful of the effects of this publicity and sentiment on their reputations, and, for this and other reasons, these programs failed.

Over the past ten years, there have been a number of arguments in favor of the British plan—it has been pointed out that there are few addicts in Great Britain in comparison to America. In addition, it has been reported that heroin-related deaths, criminal acts associated with obtaining the drug, and other health problems are more limited than in America.[95] More recently, however, there have been indications that the number of addicts in Great Britain is increasing. In addition, there ap-

pears to have been an increase in the narcotics-related crime problem. Apparently, registered addicts often feel that their maintenance dose is insufficient, so they seek additional supplies from the black market. If this is true, of course, one might expect the crime rate to rise—in Britain or anywhere else, for that matter. Despite these criticisms, there are still many advocates of the British plan, and Great Britain still has a relatively small addiction problem in comparison to the United States. However, there is little serious political pressure currently to institute such a plan in the United States.

Methadone Maintenance

Treatment of heroin addiction in the United States has focused primarily on methadone maintenance. *Methadone* is a synthetic opiate (hydrochloride) that is prescribed for addicts who are enrolled in government-sponsored treatment programs. Methadone is itself a very addictive drug, and the addict will experience withdrawal symptoms if he stops using it. Methadone is taken orally on a daily basis —its effects last for about twenty-four hours, in comparison to six hours for heroin. It has some advantages over heroin in that patients on methadone maintenance seldom acquire a tolerance for the drug and therefore may continue to take the same daily dosage over time. If a sufficiently large dose is administered (called a "blocking dose"), the euphoric effects of heroin are blocked and such a dose is usually given in the beginning of the treatment program so that there is no incentive to use heroin at the same time. Later, a "maintenance dose" can be used, which is aimed at preventing physical withdrawal but leaves the addict in a mental condition to hold a job or engage in other productive activities.

Critics of the methadone maintenance program argue that most patients in methadone therapy return to heroin use after a short period of time.[96] In addition, some evaluations of these programs reveal a very high dropout rate.[97] In one treatment program that was studied, 15 percent of the patients had deliberately enrolled in more than one methadone program at the same time—thus doubling their daily supply of methadone. Forty-one percent of those enrolled indicated that they had utilized additional methadone obtained from illegal sources. In addition, 49 percent admitted to having sold or given away their weekend supplies of methadone to another person at least once.[98]

Proponents of methadone treatment argue that it does help some, although certainly not all, heroin addicts. Thus, in one large program based in New York City, over one-half of the patients enrolled were entirely free of drug habituation (including methadone) after two years of therapy.[99] Furthermore, some proponents point out that the goals of methadone maintenance should not be misunderstood. Dr. Vincent Dole and Dr. Marie Nyswander, who developed methadone treatment, believe that addiction to opiates creates a permanent biochemical change in the body and that methadone maintenance could be necessary for the life of the addict. They do not view the goal of methadone treatment as a cure but rather as the stabilizing of the lifestyles of addicts who cooperate in a treatment program so that they can lead productive lives.[100]

In addition, federal regulations require that methadone maintenance programs provide additional treatment such as group therapy, family counseling, vocational training, and social services. Thus the methadone program serves as a means of reaching out to the addict and providing a multipronged effort to control his problem.

Methadone maintenance programs are one important effort to control heroin addiction: this scene is from "The Tombs" prison in New York, where addicts receive daily doses of methadone.

Self-Help Programs

Self-help programs, such as Synanon, provide housing, counseling, and work for the addict. These programs are run by ex-addicts who seek to help others break their addiction. Programs tend to follow the model established by Synanon, and the treatment is sometimes harsh.

Each applicant is required to sever all former associations and contacts with relatives and friends for the first few months. This period of isolation is believed necessary to break the patterns of irresponsible behavior, avoid temptations and rationalizations, and to provide time to instill the Synanon philosophy. Once admitted, the addict immediately undergoes withdrawal "cold turkey," reinforced only by the emotional support the other members offer to mitigate the experience.

Once withdrawal is complete the individual is assigned work projects to occupy his daily life that are structured in a status hierarchy, in which the individual receives greater freedom, material benefits, and higher status as he becomes more mature. The small, highly structured community is authoritarian, demanding a high degree of conformity to its rules which is reinforced by group pressure. Transgressions are severely punished by public humiliation, reprimands and, in extreme cases, head-shaving as a public statement of how weak and irresponsible the transgressor has been.[101]

In recent years, a personality cult focused on Synanon's founder has caused considerable problems for Synanon and discredited it in the eyes of many people. Nevertheless, the mode of treatment in self-help groups such as Synanon remains successful for many addicts.

While self-help programs are often successful, they reach only an estimated 2 percent of the addict population, and about 75 percent of those who enter drop out within the first month.[102] Why such a small proportion of addicts remain in programs such as Synanon is not clear. The harsh authoritarian nature of the programs may be seen as unbearable by most heroin addicts. The lack of self-discipline is one factor that may be at the core of a person's addiction. Drugs may be seen by the individual as providing a simple and clear solution to problems that appear to be "closing in." By indulging in drug abuse, addicts can try to avoid the need for self-discipline or blame the addiction itself for their inability to face problems. Self-discipline is one of the traits that is needed to overcome drug addiction, so drug-treatment programs focus on building self-confidence and self-discipline so that the addict can muster the necessary self-control to make a lasting cure possible.

To provide effective treatment, it is likely that a variety of approaches will be needed. Maintenance, therapeutic communities, psychiatric counseling, community clinics, and other methods may provide some of the variety useful for reaching the different types of addicts. The first step to effective treatment may, however, be the recognition given to the problem by the British: that narcotics addiction is in large part a medical problem and not a problem for law enforcement.

The Treatment of Alcoholism

Nutrition Therapy

The genetic theory of alcoholism allows for only a limited number of treatment strategies. If the genetic problem is thought to be a function of the alcoholic's metabolism and nutritional needs, it is possible to prescribe a treatment program to supply the dietary necessities that are believed to be missing. There are a few programs that focus on nutrition as the only treatment mode. Of course, nutri-

tional concerns are a part of most treatment plans, but this is because most alcoholics do not observe a proper diet and, consequently, suffer from malnutrition. Because of this dietary imbalance, therapists first try to restore the patient to adequate physical health prior to beginning other forms of therapy.

Behavior Modification

The programs that subscribe to the psychological approach focus their energies on breaking the drinking patterns that have been created by the patient; usually this is accomplished through a process of *behavior modification*. If the alcoholic developed the drug dependency though finding alcohol use a means of avoiding unpleasant conditions, the therapy focuses on making alcohol consumption itself *more* unpleasant. This is usually called **aversion therapy,** and one of the methods used is electrical shock. Each time a patient attempts to obtain a drink, he or she receives an electrical shock. The theory is that the patient will associate alcohol consumption with unpleasantness or pain and will break the pattern of drinking.[103] One problem with this approach is that the person is aware of the presence of the apparatus and may avoid drinking only until discharged from the program. Upon release, the patient may resume drinking with the realization that alcohol consumption outside the context of the aversion therapy program will not lead to painful shocks.

A more widespread form of aversion therapy involves the use of a drug called antabuse. Antabuse produces a condition that makes it very unpleasant to consume alcohol; because nausea and vomiting are induced. The benefit of this technique is that the patient can be released from the hospital or clinic with a supply of the drug, and provided the drug is used after release, the patient can continue to avoid alcohol. One tablet will keep antabuse in the system for two days, so a momentary lapse of control may not affect the taking of the drug.[104]

LSD and Psychotherapy

Another mode of psychological treatment that is more controversial involves the use of LSD in conjunction with psychotherapy. Some of the earlier reports of LSD use in therapy have claimed up to 94 percent improvement—based on increased social stability and reduced drinking.[105] While the specific effects experienced by the patient are not completely clear, results indicate that the drug accelerates the psychotherapy process by helping bring the anxiety-producing experiences into conscious focus, where they may be worked on by the therapist. The treatment also seems to help increase the patient's tolerance of anxiety, to assist in removing emotional blocks, and to help intensify interaction between patient and therapist.

Therapeutic Communities

Within the area of treatment that emphasizes social factors as being a major cause of alcoholism, we find the use of therapeutic communities and groups such as Alcoholics Anonymous (AA). This treatment process is similar in nature to the operation of Synanon in that the staff consists of persons who have suffered from alcoholism themselves. In the AA system, the first step is that the patient must admit to being an alcoholic and to needing help from others. While this may seem a simple step, many alcoholics deny that they have a problem with alcohol because they fear the stigma that is attached to the label "alcoholic." The official steps and the underlying ideology in the Alcoholics Anonymous program outline what is expected of the member (see Table 17.5).

The half-million members of AA meet in small groups of about twenty-five persons one or two nights a week for discussion sessions, which resemble traditional group therapy meetings without the presence of a trained psychologist. In these meetings they discuss their problems, anxieties, and aspirations. Through the emotional support of the group, members are assisted in coming to grips with their problems. One interesting feature of the organization is that the alcoholic never loses the label. Even those who have not touched alcohol for many years are referred to as "recovering alcoholics"; in their view, there is no such thing as a permanently recovered alcoholic.

TABLE 17.5
Twelve Suggested Steps of Alcoholics Anonymous

1. We admitted we were powerless over alcohol—that our lives had become unmanageable.
2. Came to believe that a Power greater than ourselves could restore us to sanity.
3. Made a decision to turn our will and our lives over to the care of God as we understand Him.
4. Made a searching and fearless moral inventory of ourselves.
5. Admitted to God, to ourselves and to another human being the exact nature of our wrongs.
6. Were entirely ready to have God remove all these defects of character.
7. Humbly asked Him to remove our shortcomings.
8. Made a list of all persons we had harmed, and became willing to make amends to them all.
9. Made direct amends to people wherever possible, except when to do so would injure them or others.
10. Continued to take personal inventory and when we were wrong promptly admitted it.
11. Sought through prayer and meditation to improve our conscious contact with God as we understood Him, praying only for knowledge of His will for us and the power to carry that out.
12. Having had a spiritual awakening as the result of these steps, we tried to carry this message to alcoholics, and to practice these principles in all our affairs.

SOURCE. Alcoholics Anonymous.

In a survey of 11,355 members of Alcoholics Anonymous, it was found that about 38 percent had abstained from drinking for one year or less, 35 percent had abstained for 1 to 5 years, 13 percent had not used alcohol for 6 to 10 years, and 12 percent had abstained for between 11 to 20 years or more. Relapse—using alcohol—did occur among the members of AA, but the longer the person is a member of the group, the less likely a relapse is to occur.[106]

A Multi-Pronged Approach

In general, most of the treatment processes used in dealing with alcoholism utilize a multi-pronged approach. A given clinic may begin with aversion therapy, move on to psychotherapy, and finally shift to a group approach resembling Alcoholics Anonymous. The complexity of causal factors leading a person to alcohol abuse requires a variety of approaches to ensure meeting the needs of each patient. It is interesting to note that there is substantial disagreement among professionals concerning which type of treatment program is most effective.[107]

It is likely that problems of alcohol abuse will remain with us for some time. The use of alcohol in our society is approved and widespread, and we are constantly encouraged to continue to consume this psychoactive drug. About $250 million is spent each year simply advertising alcoholic products. It is not likely that we will see another attempt at Prohibition, owing to its disastrous failure in the past. The sale of alcohol, which realizes $27 billion per year in total receipts, will probably continue to prosper, and any attempts at renewal of Prohibition or some milder form of control would likely be opposed by this highly influential and wealthy interest group.

The emphasis in treating drug abuse problems has focused primarily on heroin and alcohol, while less attention has been devoted to the other drugs discussed in this chapter. Public service announcements appear on television that warn of the effects tobacco smoking has on health, but programs like AA have not emerged to combat its use—even though tobacco is associated with more deaths than heroin. Whatever the reason may be for deemphasizing concern over drugs such as tobacco, the amphetamines, or barbiturates, their abuse does have an impact on society, and, until some major attempt is made to resolve this problem, the prospects for the amelioration of drug abuse are not encouraging.

CONCLUSION

The use of drugs and alcohol in the United States has had a checkered history. Public opinion has shifted numerous times on the issue of which drugs are acceptable and which inappropriate. Heroin, once thought of as a useful drug for treating many physical maladies, is now considered one of the more dangerous menaces to our society. Marijuana, on the other hand, was once viewed with fear and loathing, but is today accepted as the drug of choice among many Americans. While public opinion concerning specific drugs has shifted over time, drugs of one variety or another have been a constant feature of our social landscape. In order to understand the ways in which people react to drugs and alcohol, it will be useful to review some issues related to substance abuse from the three theoretical perspectives.

From the functionalist perspective, the use of drugs and alcohol constitute a cultural practice that may be more or less well-integrated with other parts of society. To the extent that drug use continues in a fashion that does not support other social institutions, it is considered a social problem. Thus, excessive alcohol consumption may lead to absenteeism at work; addiction to heroin may lead to crime; smoking tobacco (and possibly marijuana) may lead to cancer and other health problems. For these reasons, excessive use of drugs and alcohol works to the detriment of important social institutions and threatens the smooth functioning of our social system. However, it is also very clear that the use of some drugs and alcohol is a cultural practice that is well entrenched in American society, and this leaves considerable room for pessimism over our ability to deal effectively with the abuse of drugs and alcohol. Our experience in attempting to prohibit the use of alcohol and our more recent effort to control the use of marijuana bring home forcefully the difficulty of banning a practice that is widely accepted in society. From the functionalist perspective, drugs and alcohol play an important role in some subcultures in American society, and this cannot be ignored when social policy is developed in this area. Thus, we are faced with the difficult problem of developing programs which permit the use of drugs and alcohol but at the same time discourage their abuse. As we have seen, our success at this up to now has been questionable.

From the conflict perspective, the use of drugs and alcohol can have strong political consequences in the sense that it has implications for the ability of groups to pursue their own interests. On the one hand, producers of alcoholic beverages and various legal drugs make economic gains from the consumption of their products. While no such major manufacturer would encourage the excessive use of their product, they do present their product in a fashion that will encourage people to use it. On the other hand, some groups, such as the poor, find it more difficult to improve their position in society because of the detrimental effects of drugs and alcohol on individual and family life. In fact, some poor communities have conducted citizens campaigns to rid their neighborhoods of drug dealers. Some have argued against the legalization of more drugs such as marijuana on the grounds that it would become more readily available and thus more susceptible to widespread abuse. In addition, there is a fear that the advertising that would accompany legalization would make the drug more attractive, especially to young people, and thus magnify the drug problem in the United States. Thus, from the conflict perspective, the use of drugs and alcohol works to the benefit of some groups and to the disadvantage of others. Unlike the functionalist perspective, the conflict approach does not posit any overall benefit or disadvantage to society as a whole. Thus, social policy in the area of drugs and alcohol will emerge out of the clash of competing interest groups.

For the interactionist, society is based on social consensus and shared expectations. In terms of drug and alcohol abuse, we can expect continued debate over the nature and social desirability of various drugs. Subcultural differences in what is defined as a drug will undoubtedly persist. We have reviewed the changing definitions of certain substances such as heroin and marijuana. The interactionist perspective leads us to believe that definitions will continue to shift and change in the future. Perhaps the most encouraging insight from the interactionist perspective is the importance of the shift in attitude toward the addicted drug user. In the past it was believed that anyone who used drugs to excess was of weak character or even evil in some respect. Today the addict is viewed with more compassion and his or her problem is recognized as a medical one that is capable of treatment. Viewing drug addiction as a medical problem tears away the stereotype of the depraved fiend lurking in the deteriorating sections of the community and allows us to see the addict as a person who has lost control over his actions, and, with the help of the community, can be returned to a reasonably normal life.

GLOSSARY TERMS

Alcoholic
Aversion therapy
Cannabis sativa
Dependence
Depressants

Drug abuse
Drug addiction
Hallucinogens
Methadone

Narcotic
Psychoactive drugs
Stimulants
Tolerance

REFERENCES

[1] United States Department of Health, Education and Welfare, Public Health Service, National Institute on Drug Abuse, "Phencyclidine—PCP," *Report Series 14,* no. 2 (March 1978), p. 5.

[2] William Stockton, "Dual Addiction," *The New York Times Magazine* (August 6, 1978), p. 10.

[3] Earle F. Barcus and Susan M. Jankowski, "Drugs and the Mass Media," *The Annals of The American Academy of Political and Social Science* 417 (1975), p. 89.

[4] See Ralph W. Hingson, Daryl Matthews, and Norman A. Scotch, "The Use and Abuse of Psychoactive Substances," in Howard E. Freeman et al., eds., *Handbook of Medical Sociology,* 3d ed. (Englewood Cliffs, N.J.: Prentice-Hall, 1979).

[5] John H. McGrath and Frank R. Scarpitti, *Youth and Drugs: Perspectives on a Social Problem* (Glenview, Ill.: Scott, Foresman and Co., 1970), pp. 1–2.

[6] United States Department of Justice, Drug Enforcement Administration, *Drugs of Abuse* (Washington, D.C.: U.S. Government Printing Office, n.d.).

[7] McGrath and Scarpitti, *Youth and Drugs: Perspectives on a Social Problem,* p. 2.

[8] Joseph Gusfield, *Symbolic Crusade: Status Politics and the American Temperance Movement* (Urbana, Ill.: University of Illinois Press, 1963), p. 50.

[9] See Brian Inglis, *The Forbidden Game* (New York: Charles Scribner's Sons, 1975), p. 150.

[10] Inglis, *The Forbidden Game,* p. 181, and U.S. Department of Justice, *Drugs of Abuse.*

[11] Alfred R. Lindesmith, *The Addict and the Law* (Bloomington: Indiana University Press, 1965), p. 228.

[12] John F. Galliher and Allyn Walker, "The Puzzle of the Social Origins of the Marihuana Tax Act of 1937," *Social Problems* 24 (February 1977), pp. 367–376.

[13] *The New York Times Index,* 1970, p. 554.

[14] Erich Goode, *Drugs in American Society* (New York: Alfred A. Knopf, 1972), p. 6.

[15] National Commission on Marijuana and Drug Abuse (Washington, D.C.: U.S. Government Printing Office, 1973), p. 9.

[16] Oakley S. Ray, *Drugs, Society, and Human Behavior* (St. Louis: C. V. Mosby Company, 1972), p. 3.

[17] Ibid., pp. 6–7.

[18] Howard S. Becker, *Outsiders: Studies in the Sociology of Deviance* (New York: The Free Press, 1963), pp. 41–54.

[19] Ray, *Drugs, Society, and Human Behavior,* p. 20.

[20] Alfred R. Lindesmith, *Addiction and Opiates* (Chicago: Aldine, 1968), p. 49.

[21] See Inglis, *The Forbidden Game,* and Walter L. Mendenhall, *Tobacco* (Cambridge: Harvard University Press, 1930), pp. 44–45.

[22] Goode, *Drugs in American Society,* p. 130.

[23] "Meaning of New Federal Report on Smoking," *U.S. News and World Report* (January 22, 1979), p. 68.

[24] See National Institute on Drug Abuse, *NIDA Research Monograph 13* (Rockville, Md.: U.S. Department of Health, Education, and Welfare, 1977).

[25] See Richard Ashley, *Cocaine: Its History, Uses, and Effects* (New York: St. Martin's Press, 1975).

[26] "The Columbian Connection," *Time* (January 29, 1979), p. 23.

[27] "Coke and Angel Dust," *Time* (July 18, 1977), pp. 49–50.

[28] See National Institute on Drug Abuse, *Research Monograph 14* (Rockville, Md.: U.S. Department of Health, Education, and Welfare, 1977).

[29] See National Institute on Drug Abuse, *NIDA R.M. 13* (1977).

[30] See Ashley, *Cocaine: Its History, Uses, and Effects,* 1975.

[31] Joel Fort and Christopher T. Cory, *American Drug Store* (Boston: Little, Brown, 1975), p. 39.

[32] See National Institute on Drug Abuse, *NIDA R.M. 13* (1977).

[33] Goode, *Drugs in American Society,* p. 125, and U.S. Department of Justice, *Drugs of Abuse.*

[34] Ibid.

[35] See Peter Conrad, *Identifying Hyperactive Children: The Medicalization of Deviant Behavior* (Lexington, Mass.: D.C. Heath, 1976).

[36] Fort and Cory, *American Drug Store,* p. 41.

[37] Carol K. Whalen and Barbara Henker, "The Pitfalls of Politicization: A Response to Conrad's 'The Discovery of Hyperkinesis: Notes on the Medicalization of Deviant Behavior,'" *Social Problems* 24 (June 1977), pp. 490–496.

[38] Goode, *Drugs in American Society,* pp. 138–142.

[39] W. C. Eckerman, J. D. Bates, J. V. Rachel, and W. K. Poole, *Drug Usage and Arrest Charges: A Study of Drug Usage and Arrest Charges Among Arrestees in Six Metropolitan Areas of the United States* (Washington, D.C.: U.S. Government Printing Office, 1971).

[40] Everett H. Ellinwood, Jr., "Amphetamine and Stimulant Drugs," in The Second Report of the National Commission on Marihuana and Drug Abuse, *Drug Use in America: Problem in Perspective,* Appendix, Vol. 2 (Washington, D.C.: U.S. Government Printing Office, 1973), p. 149. 1973), p. 149.

[41] National Institute on Drug Abuse, *Sedative-Hypnotic Drugs: Risks and Benefits* (Washington, D.C.: U.S. Government Printing Office, 1977), p. 60.

[42] Goode, *Drugs in American Society,* p. 153; Fort and Cory, *American Drug Store,* p. 41; and Donald R. Wesson and David E. Smith, "Barbiturate Toxicity and the Treatment of Barbiturate Dependence," in David E. Smith and Donald R. Wesson, eds., *Uppers and Downers* (Englewood Cliffs, N.J.: Prentice-Hall, 1973).

[43] Goode, *Drugs in American Society,* p. 153.

[44] National Institute On Drug Abuse, *Sedative-Hypnotic Drugs: Risks and Benefits,* pp. 71–72.

[45] Goode, *Drugs in American Society,* p. 153.

[46] See Wesson and Smith, *Uppers and Downers,* 1973.

[47] Hardin Jones and Helen Jones, *Sensual Drugs* (London: Cambridge University Press, 1977), p. 100.

[48] National Institute on Drug Abuse, *Sedative-Hypnotic Drugs: Risks and Benefits,* p. 63.

[49] Goode, *Drugs in American Society,* pp. 152–153.

[50] See Peter T. Furst, *Hallucinogens and Culture* (San Francisco: Chandler and Sharp, 1976).

[51] William H. McGlothlin, "The Epidemiology of Hallucinogenic Drug Use," in Eric Josephson and Eleanor E. Carroll, eds., *Drug Use: Epidemiological and Sociological Approaches* (New York: John Wiley & Sons, 1974), pp. 286–287.

[52] Goode, *Drugs in American Society,* p. 118.

[53] Ibid.

[54] See U.S. Department of Health, Education, and Welfare, *Report Series* 14 (1978).

[55] Robert Reinhold, "Smoking of Marijuana Wins Wider

[56] Exceptance," *The New York Times* (May 23, 1977), p. 29.

[56] "The Columbian Connection," *Time* (January 29, 1979), p. 22.

[57] National Institute on Drug Abuse, *Highlights From the National Survey on Drug Abuse: 1977* (Washington, D.C.: U.S. Government Printing Office, 1978), p. 25.

[58] Don H. Zimmerman and D. Lawrence Wieder, "You Can't Help But Get Stoned: Notes on the Social Organization of Marijuana Smoking," *Social Problems* 25 (December 1977), pp. 198–207.

[59] See Bertram S. Brown, "The Decriminalization of Marijuana," *Hearings of the House Select Committee on Narcotics Abuse* (March 14, 1977), First Session, 95th Congress.

[60] "The Columbian Connection," *Time* (January 29, 1979), pp. 22–29.

[61] National Institute on Drug Abuse, *NIDA R.M. 14* (1977).

[62] Kurt J. Guggenheimer, *Narcotics and Drug Abuse, vol. 3* (Queens Village, N.Y.: Social Service Publications, 1976), Secs. II-7, II-11.

[63] "The Heroin Plague" *Newsweek* (July 5, 1971), pp. 27–32.

[64] Alfred R. Lindesmith, *Addiction and Opiates* (Chicago: Aldine, 1968), pp. 73–74.

[65] Ibid.

[66] Lindesmith, *The Addict and the Law,* p. 129.

[67] James A. Inciardi and Carl D. Chambers, "Unreported Criminal Involvement of Narcotic Addicts," *Journal of Drug Issues* 2 (Spring 1972), pp. 57–64.

[68] Goode, *Drugs in American Society,* p. 163.

[69] Jerome J. Platt and Christina LaBate, *Heroin Addiction: Theory, Research, and Treatment* (New York: John Wiley & Sons, 1976), p. 84.

[70] Ibid., p. 84.

[71] See M. M. Baden, "Pathology of the Addictive States," in R. W. Richter, ed., *Medical Aspects of Drug Abuse* (Hagerstown, Md.: Medical Department, Harper & Row, 1975).

[72] Goode, *Drugs in American Society,* p. 163.

[73] Herbert C. Modlin and Alberto Montes, "Narcotics Addiction in Physicians," *The American Journal of Psychiatry* 121 (October 1964), pp. 358–365.

[74] See Mark Keller, "Drinking and Alcoholism Trends," mimeographed outline from *The Rutgers University Summer School of Alcohol Studies,* 1976.

[75] See U.S. Department of Health, Education, and Welfare, *First Report to the U.S. Congress on Alcohol and Health* (Washington, D.C.: U.S. Government Printing Office, 1971).

[76] W. J. Rorabaugh, "Estimated U.S. Alcoholic Beverage Consumption: 1790–1860," *Journal of Studies on Alcohol* 37 (1976), pp. 357–364.

[77] See Keller, "Drinking and Alcoholism Trends," 1976.

[78] U.S. Department of Health, Education, and Welfare,

Alcohol and Health (Rockville, Md.: Public Health Service, 1974), p. 7.

[79] See Ronald J. Catanzaro, "The Disease: Alcoholism," in R. J. Catanzaro, ed., *Alcoholism: The Total Treatment Approach* (Springfield, Ill.: Charles Thomas, 1968).

[80] U.S. Department of Commerce, Bureau of the Census, *Statistical Abstracts of the United States* (Washington, D.C.: U.S. Government Printing Office, 1978), p. 122.

[81] Ibid., p. 122.

[82] Thomas J. Keil, "Sex Role Variations and Women's Drinking," *Journal of Studies on Alcohol* 39 (May 1978), pp. 859–868; Joan Scida and Marsha Vannicelli, "Sex-Role Conflict and Women's Drinking," *Journal of Studies on Alcohol* 40 (January 1979), pp. 28–44; and Richard W. Wilsnack and Sharon C. Wilsnack, "Sex Roles and Drinking Among Adolescent Girls," *Journal of Studies on Alcohol* 39 (November 1978), pp. 1855–1874.

[83] Milton Argeriou and John Zinkowski, "Black Alcoholism," *Journal of Studies on Alcohol* 37 (July 1976), pp. 1003–1007.

[84] Herbert J. Paine, "Attitudes and Patterns of Alcohol Use Among Mexican-Americans," *Journal of Studies on Alcohol* 38 (March 1977), pp. 544–553.

[85] See C. R. Snyder, *Alcohol and the Jews: A Cultural Study of Drinking and Sobriety* (New York: The Free Press, 1958).

[86] See U.S. Department of Health, Education, and Welfare, *First Report.*

[87] "Teenage Drinking on the Rise," *New York Times* (March 27, 1977), p. 38.

[88] Jim Haskins, *Teenage Alcoholism* (New York: Hawthorn Books, 1976), p. 45.

[89] See Julian B. Roebuck and Raymond G. Kessler, *The Etiology of Alcoholism: Constitutional, Psychological, and Sociological Approaches* (Springfield, Ill.: Charles Thomas, 1972), Nancy S. Cotton, "The Familial Incidence of Alcoholism: A Review," *Journal of Studies on Alcohol* 40 (January 1979), pp. 89–116.

[90] See A. Roe, "Children of Alcoholic Parents Raised in Foster Homes," in *Alcohol, Science, and Society* (New Haven. Quarterly Journal on Studies of Alcohol, 1945), pp. 115–128.

[91] See Roebuck and Kessler, *The Etiology of Alcoholism*, and Albert Bandura, *Principles of Behavior Modification* (New York: Holt, Rinehart, & Winston, 1969), pp. 528–537.

[92] See Snyder, *Alcohol and the Jews*, and R. F. Bales,

"Cultural Differences in Rates of Alcoholism," *Quarterly Journal of Studies on Alcohol* 6 (March 1946), pp. 480–499.

[93] See Leon G. Hunt and Carl D. Chambers, *The Heroin Epidemic: A Study of Heroin Use in the United States* (New York: Spectrum Publications, 1976).

[94] Horace F. Judson, *Heroin Addiction in Britain* (New York: Harcourt, Brace, Jovanovich, 1974), p. 94.

[95] Zinberg and Robertson, *Drugs and the Public*, pp. 161–162.

[96] Gina S. Anderson and Richard W. Nutter, "Clients and Outcomes of a Methadone Treatment Program," *The International Journal of the Addictions* 10, no. 6 (1975), pp. 937–948.

[97] Judy Alsofrom, "Methadone Failures: Who Gets the Blame?" *American Medical News* (October 1976), pp. 15–17.

[98] Irving H. Soloway, "Methadone and the Culture of Addiction," *Journal of Psychedelic Drugs* 6 (January–March, 1974), pp. 91–99.

[99] Paula H. Kleinman, Irving F. Lukoff, and Barbara L. Karl, "The Magic Fix: A Critical Analysis of Methadone Maintenance Treatment," *Social Problems* 25 (December 1977), pp. 208–214.

[100] David F. Musto, *The American Disease: Origins of Narcotics Control* (New Haven: Yale University Press, 1973), pp. 237–238.

[101] Platt and LaBate, *Heroin Addiction: Theory, Research, and Treatment*, p. 210.

[102] National Clearinghouse for Drug Abuse Information, *Report Series* 34, no. 1 (April 1975), pp. 7–8.

[103] Roger E. Vogler, "Conditioning With Chronic Alcoholics," *Journal of Consulting and Clinical Psychology* 34 (June 1970), pp. 302–307.

[104] See Sanford L. Billet, "Antabuse Therapy," in Catanzaro, ed., *Alcoholism: The Total Treatment Approach*, 1968.

[105] Reginald Smart et al., *Lysergic Acid Diethylamide (LSD) in the Treatment of Alcoholism* (Toronto: University of Toronto Press, 1967), pp. 43–44.

[106] Barry Leach, "Does Alcoholics Anonymous Really Work?" in Peter G. Bourne and Ruth Fox, eds., *Alcoholism: Progress in Research and Treatment* (New York: Academic Press, 1973), p. 269.

[107] Melvin Kalb and Morton Propper, "The Future of Alcohology: Craft or Science?" *American Journal of Psychiatry* 133 (June 1976), pp. 641–645.

SUGGESTED READINGS

Peter T. Furst, *Hallucinogens and Culture.* (San Francisco: Chandler and Sharp Publishers, Inc., 1976).
This brief book analyzes how hallucinogenic drugs are integrated into the operation of cultures. It examines such issues as the use of drugs in religions, education, and recreation. Furst employs a clear and non-technical approach to the subject.

Erich Goode, *Drugs in American Society.* (New York: Alfred A. Knopf, 1972).
Goode provides a comprehensive examination of drugs and drug use from a sociological point of view. The interactionist perspective is clearly employed in discussions of the attitudes members of society have toward specific drugs, and how those attitudes came into being.

Jim Haskins, *Teenage Alcoholism.* (New York: Hawthorn Books, Inc., 1976).
This book examines the increasingly serious problem of alcoholism in teenagers. It provides several case studies to illustrate the development of alcohol dependence in young people, and it discusses a range of issues related to the treatment of teenage alcoholism.

Brian Inglis, *The Forbidden Game.* (New York: Charles Scribner's Sons, 1975).
Inglis has analyzed the historical data on drugs and drug use, and has produced a penetrating and comprehensive look at the use of drugs in the Western World. The book also provides an account of the developments of laws designed to suppress the use of various substances.

Horace F. Judson, *Heroin Addiction in Britain.* (New York: Harcourt, Brace and Jovanovich, 1974).
Judson studies the British approach to the treatment of heroin addiction from the historical system of heroin maintenance to the modern methadone clinics. He also compares and contrasts the American and the British methods of treatment.

Alfred R. Lindesmith, *Addiction and Opiates.* (Chicago: Aldine Publishing Company, 1968).
This book contains a thorough appraisal of the sociological and psychological elements of the addiction process. Something of a classic in the field.

Questions
for Discussion

1. All of the drugs which are abused today were at one time considered important in treating various illnesses. How do drugs become redefined as dangerous substances?

2. Although most experts agreed that marijuana use was not a serious problem in the 1930s, marijuana was classified as a narcotic. What effect did that classification have on the public perception of the drug, and how is the drug viewed today? What brought about the change?

3. From the functionalist perspective, what are the major differences for society between drugs such as heroin and marijuana? How are each viewed as problems from the functionalist perspective?

4. With respect to drug use, the conflict perspective views the problems created as being economic and political in nature. How can drug use be considered a political problem from the conflict point of view? How would a conflict theorist explain drug use in economic terms?

5. Many people do not consider tobacco and alcohol as being drugs. How would an interactionist explain that view?

6. How would an interactionist view the use of drugs as a serious problem for society? From that point of view how serious do you feel drug use could be?

7. There are many ways that drug use can be seen as drug *abuse*. What do you think the dividing line is between use and abuse? Why?

8. A number of modes of treatment for alcoholism are discussed in this chapter. Which form of treatment do you believe should be the most effective? Why?

9. There are many differences between the American and British methods of treating heroin addiction. What are the positive aspects of each approach? What are the negative aspects of each? Which of the two programs do you feel is the best to employ in this country? Why?

CHAPTER 18

Social Movements in a Changing America

SOCIAL MOVEMENTS IN AMERICAN HISTORY

Youth as a Subculture. Religious and Communal
Movements.

SOCIAL MOVEMENTS AS A SOCIAL PROBLEM

The Functionalist Perspective. The Conflict Perspective.
The Interactionist Perspective.

SOCIAL MOVEMENTS AS A RESPONSE TO SOCIAL
PROBLEMS

Social Movements and Social Change. Social Change in
America.

THE YOUTH MOVEMENT AND THE
COUNTERCULTURE

The Beliefs of the Youth Counterculture. Origins of the
Youth Counterculture. Who Joins the Youth Movement?
The Youth Movement as a Social Problem.

THE RISE OF UNCONVENTIONAL RELIGIOUS
MOVEMENTS

Krishna Consciousness. The Jesus Movement. The
Unification Church. Who Joins Unconventional Religious
Groups? The Unconventional Religions as a Social
Problem.

COMMUNES IN AMERICAN SOCIETY

Modern-Day Communes. The Ideology of Communes.
Who Joins Communes? Communes as a Social Problem.

FUTURE PROSPECTS

The Counterculture. The Unconventional Religions.
Communes.

CONCLUSION

————**After teaching philosophy at Harvard University for four years, Ron rejected that socially acceptable and prestigious lifestyle. He now supports himself by driving a Checker cab, while his primary activity is to work for the revolution that he believes will radically alter a materialistic America. He works hard to attract others to his ideas.**[1]

————**An intelligent young woman from a materially comfortable family graduated with honors from college and was accepted for graduate study in England. Instead, she joined a communal village in the mountains of California in her search for inner peace and satisfaction.**[2]

————**A young man from a wealthy family decides to forsake his background and join the Hare Krishna movement instead of a more conventional lifestyle. He, along with his coreligionists, adopts the shaved heads and flowing robes of the group, spends his days in long hours of prayer, selling newspapers on the street, and trying to convince others that his way of life is superior to the more materialistic ways of most Americans.**[3]

————**Parents of some of those who have joined unconventional religious groups have resorted to kidnapping their own adult children in order to "deprogram" them—eradicate what they believe to be a hypnotic hold that the religious group has over their wayward children and return them to a more acceptable path.**

If we consider for a moment the people we knew in high school or in college, most of us can recall someone whose life took on a pattern similar to one of those described above. For many different reasons, these people found themselves leading unconventional lifestyles—deviating rather substantially from the more socially acceptable adult pattern of marriage, family, and career within the confines of mainstream American society. Why should this be the case? Are groups such as these, that have emerged on the American scene in the past two decades, unique in American history? Are they aberrations, or do they fit into our historical development in some patterned and understandable way? These groups are referred to as *social movements:* fairly organized, unconventional, and nonin-

stitutionalized groups that persist over time and function to promote or resist change in society.[4] Because social movements have an impact on social change, they should be of concern to all of us because they may have direct effects on our lives. Cherished values and lifestyles may be threatened because the members of some social movement espouse the benefit, and work toward the establishment, of very different values and lifestyles.

The purpose of this chapter is to explore some of the major social movements in modern America. Our goals are threefold. First, we will investigate the extent to which such social movements constitute social problems. Second, we will study the ways in which such social movements emerge, with particular emphasis on the extent to which they might constitute responses to other social problems that confront American society. In order to understand these relationships fully, we will explore in some detail three recent social movements in America: the youth counterculture, recent unconventional religious movements (Krishna Consciousness, the Jesus People, and the Unification Church), and communes. Third, we will look at the future of these social movements and their possible consequences for American society. Will they contribute to significant and/or desirable social change in America?

One difficulty we confront in a topic such as this is defining what we mean by "unconventional." In chapter 15, we argued that behavior is deviant if groups so define it. The social movements considered in this chapter could certainly be considered deviant according to that definition. However, the term *unconventional* is even more restricted than this. In chapter 1, we described America as a *heterogeneous* society in which individuals and groups possess a wide range of different characteristics, beliefs, norms, and traditions. This tremendous diversity takes the form of many different ethnic groups, subcultures, interest groups, and the like. With so much diversity, is there anything that might be considered conventional? At the risk of oversimplification, there are certain values and practices that may be considered conventional or "mainstream" in America.[5] Some of these have been discussed in previous chapters:

1. Americans value hard work and productive activity (see the *Protestant Ethic*);
2. Americans emphasize success and achievement, particularly in the material realm;
3. American society is based on private ownership;
4. Americans value *individualism* and individual worth;
5. Americans place great importance on the sanctity of the family (see the *monolithic code*);
6. Americans tend to emphasize conformity, at least in regard to external appearances (see the forms of *deviant behavior*).

Is there consensus among all Americans on these values and practices? Certainly not. In fact, some of these (such as individualism and conformity) may come into some degree of conflict with one another. Nevertheless, these values come close to describing the dominant themes that give American life and behavior their shape and form. They can also serve as guidelines for defining unconventionality. **A social movement is *unconventional* to the extent that it deviates from these traditional values and practices.** Unconventional social movements are by no means limited to modern America, and the first step in understanding social movements and their relationship to social change is to investigate social movements in earlier American history.

SOCIAL MOVEMENTS IN AMERICAN HISTORY

Social movements of one sort or another have become a permanent feature of American society. Some people have argued that there are more unconventional movements today than in the past and that this is largely due to the increasing complexity and diversity of our industrial social order. There was certainly more consensus in preindustrial America about what was the proper way to lead one's life. However, it is important to keep in mind that unconventionality has always existed and that these social movements often played an important part in the process of social change.

Youth as a Subculture

Age is, of course, considered a biological phenomenon, but we often ignore the fact that it also has social implications. It is important to recognize that age is an important factor in determining the form of social relationships. Our social organization is shaped around the fact that certain things (work, marriage, education, and the like) begin or occur at particular ages in a person's life. Most of us marry at about 21 years of age, rather than 13 or 65; most of us begin fulltime work at 18 or 22, but usually not at 12; most of us become fully independent of our parents at 18 or 19, not 13 or 54. While there is some variation in precisely when individuals make these transitions, there is also generally a normal time, and there are unusual times, for making them.

The age at which such transitions occur is strongly influenced by the needs and demands of the society in which people live. Thus, what we think of as *youth* is a fairly recent development in human social history.[6] In most societies prior to the modern era, young people began to mix with adults and participate in adult activities as soon as they could do without the supervision of their mothers — sometimes as early as seven years old, but usually no later than twelve or thirteen. This did not mean they were regarded as full-fledged adults, but that they were becoming independent of their parents and beginning to immerse themselves in the adult world. Referring to preindustrial society, one authority on youth concluded:

> Beginning at what seems to us to be a very young age, children began to separate from their families and to go to live in other households. By 14, a great majority would be living in a state of semidependence, either as servants in households, apprentices living in their masters' homes, or students boarding away from their families.[7]

Thus, for preindustrial youth, detachment from the family occurred at a considerably younger age than it does in industrial society. People that we would today call teenagers were expected to support themselves and engage in some productive and responsible work.

Economic change—industrialization and an increasingly complex technology—has been the major reason for changes in the point at which one makes the transition to adulthood.[8] An industrial society requires that individuals possess more skills, greater literacy, and higher levels of education. Education and skill levels have increased in order to provide a trained workforce for an increasingly sophisticated and complex technology. In addition, our bureaucratic, paper-oriented society calls for literacy skills (the ability to read, write, and do simple arithmetic procedures) in practically all parts of our daily lives. The consequence of these changes is that we have prolonged the period of education and thus postponed the point at which young people take on adult responsibilities. At first, it was the sons and daughters of the well-to-do who stayed in school for a long time before taking positions of authority and responsibility in industry. However, increasingly—especially during this century—more education was expected of rank-and-file workers. Today, workers are expected to be able to read and write, and a high school education has come to be viewed as the minimum requirement for practically all jobs.

There is another important way in which economic developments have affected the position of young people in society. Industrialization and automation have made it possible to produce a sufficient supply of goods with a smaller workforce than in an agricultural economy. Preindustrial societies were labor intensive—most people had to work merely to survive. Even in the early stages of industrialization, people began working at a very early age—possibly as young as eight or nine years of age—and continued working until they were very old or had died. However, with the advancement of industrialization and automation, machines replaced people, and the young were one of the first groups to be relieved of the responsibility of supporting themselves. (As we have seen in ch. 10, the elderly were to follow suit.)

The consequences of these economic changes for young people have been both dramatic and fundamental. Over time, the average age at which young people enter the labor force as fully productive members of society has been postponed. For most young people, it is the late teenage years, and some will be in their mid-twenties before they do so. Thus, a new social category has emerged that is different from childhood or adolescence. **There is youth—those who are biologically mature (usually around age fifteen or sixteen) but who have not yet entered the adult world or the labor force as fulltime participants.**[9]

This transition has been a gradual one, to be sure, but it has had effects on the social world of young people. As sociologist Gerhard Lenski puts it: "In agrarian societies, young people were largely integrated into the adult world and separated from one another, while in advanced industrial society . . . young people tend to be cut off from the more inclusive adult world and thrown into a narrower world made up almost exclusively of their age peers."[10] **When a group is separated in this fashion and has some traits in common (such as age or social background), it may begin to form a *subculture*—a group with some norms, beliefs, and values that are distinct from those of the wider (in this case adult) culture.** Thus the prolongation of the period before young people become adults has within it the possibility that a youth subculture— with beliefs and values distinct from those of the adult world from which they are now isolated— might emerge.

For most of American history, the degree of separation between youth and adults was limited by the fact that most youth were incorporated into the adult world at a young age. However, the affluent among the young were the first to have the privilege of an extended period of youth, and it is among them, especially those who attended college, that we see a glimmering of the opposition to the adult world that would later characterize a youth counterculture.[11] For example, there has been a long history of student clashes with authority. There was an outbreak of student rebellion at Harvard University in 1790 that lasted for seven years and focused on the policies of the University administration. Other universities experienced similar outbursts at about the same time. Historian Samuel Eliot Morison characterized students of this period in the following way: "The typical student of the early seventeen-nineties was an atheist in religion, an experimentalist in morals, a rebel to authority."[12]

In 1823, half of the senior class at Harvard University was expelled for engaging in disruptive activities. In the 1830s and 1840s, clubs advocating the abolition of slavery appeared on many campuses. At the University of Michigan, a secret student organization worked to smuggle runaway slaves into Canada. During the antidraft riots of the Civil War (see ch. 14), students participated on the side of those opposed to conscription. Throughout our history, college students formed organizations espousing political activism of a sort that was distinctly repugnant to the conventional adult world. For example, the Intercollegiate Socialist Society, founded in 1905, was an early leftist student organization that advocated socialism and that, while largely educational, occasionally aroused the antipathy of the citizenry and precipitated crises of free speech by sponsoring radical speakers on college campuses. (The ISS counted among its members Upton Sinclair, Jack London, Clarence Darrow, and Walter Lippman — all of whom would rise to positions of prominence in American society.) During the 1920s and 1930s, a number of student groups espoused a socialist ideology. In the late 1930s, there was a small, but vocal, group of students espousing peace and disarmament who sponsored parades and demonstrations. This was largely limited, however, to a few colleges in metropolitan areas.[13]

When we review the activities of young people in American history, we realize that most of them led a rather conventional life and that there were no widespread movements toward unconventionality. However, among those young people with the affluence to attend college, there has been some opposition to adult values and political policies. Furthermore, the position of youth has changed drastically during this century — the prolonged period of youth and the separation from the adult world is no longer limited to a small elite but is now available to many, if not most, young people. It is this extension of youth to many young people today that holds within it the potential for a much larger and much more influential youth subculture than at any time in human history.

Religious and Communal Movements

Many people believe that the upsurge of unconventional religious groups and communal living arrangements in the 1960s and 1970s was a novel occurrence in America. Quite to the contrary, such religions and communes have existed, in one form or another, since America's beginning. People too quickly forget that Protestant sectarian movements were very important in the foundation of some of the American colonies.[14] The Pilgrims, who settled in Plymouth in 1620, and the Puritans, who settled in Massachusetts Bay in 1629, were fleeing from religious persecution in Europe. Between the 1720s and the 1740s, a religious revival, now referred to as the Great Awakening, swept through the colonies. It was a symptom of the dissatisfaction on the part of many Americans with the conditions of eighteenth-century life. For many who were caught up in it, the Great Awakening was a return to religious fervor and an intense involvement in religious activities. Through evangelical preaching and "glory shouting," the Great Awakening provided an expressive outlet, especially for the back-country population, which had been ignored by conventional religions. Many of the utopian movements of the 1800s were also religious movements with a theological justification for their attempts to establish a new social order.

The decades preceding the Civil War were a particularly fertile period for religious dissent and controversy. As professor of religion Clifton Olmstead put it:

> Where restlessness and dissatisfaction with the status quo were most pronounced there was most often a tendency to become identified with indigenous cults and movements which sprang up in fertile soil and offered escape from the stark realities of the work-a-day world to a dream land of perfection. This tendency was magnified by the rising tension over slavery, states rights, and nativism, which gripped the country during the three decades of unrest and upheaval antecedent to [the Civil] war.[15]

For example, the Mormons (Latter-Day Saints) emerged during this period and, under the tutelage of Joseph Smith and Brigham Young, made their trek westward and established themselves in Utah. Although the Mormons are now one of the established churches in the United States, they were considered during their formative years to be rather unconventional, and considerable hostility and vituperation was directed toward them. During this same period the Millerite movement (also called the Adventists) emerged and attracted a substantial following. The Millerites believed that the world was in the throes of moral deterioration and that the coming of Christ would usher in a millennium. (The extent and diversity of new religions during this period is illustrated in Table 18.1.)

It is clear that unconventional religious practices are not confined to the modern era. Periodically throughout American history, unconventional groups have risen to social prominence. Another unconventional lifestyle that can be found throughout our history is the communal society. Many of the unconventional religious groups were also communal in nature.

One of the peak periods of communal development occurred between 1780 and 1850 (see Table 18.2).[16] Many of the communes of this period represented a withdrawal from early industrial capitalism and from the values of competition and individ-

TABLE 18.1
New Religious Sects in America, 1820–1860

REGENERATIVE SECTS[a]	SCHISMATIC SECTS[b]	CULTIC SECTS[c]	QUASI-RELIGIOUS SECTS[d]
Old School	Missouri Synod (1847)	Mormon church	Owenism
Presbyterian old school	Norwegian Evangelical Synod (1853)	Spiritualism	(New Harmony, 1825)
Congregational old school	United Presbyterian Church of	Swedenborgianism	Fourierism
Antimission Baptist	North America (1858)	Mesmerism	(Brook Farm, 1841)
Anglo-Catholic Episcopal	Church of the United Brethren (1800)	phrenology	Oneida Society
Lutheran General Council	Evangelical Association (1803)	homeopathy	abolitionism
Mercersburg German Reformed	Cumberland Presbyterian church (1810)	Grahamism	agrarian reform
Quaker Hicksite	Methodist Protestant church (1830)	astrology	
	Free Methodist church (1860)		
New School	Free Synod (1827)		
Presbyterian new school	Disciples of Christ (1832)		
Congregational new school	Winebrunner Baptist (1823)		
American Baptist Home Mission Society	Millerites (1842)		
Low Church Episopal	(Former schismatic sects)		
Lutheran General Synod	Unitarian		
Methodist Episcopal Church	Universalist		
Quaker Guerneyite	Mennonite		
	Moravian		
	Shaker		
	Rappite		
	Seventh Day Baptist		
	Six Principle Baptist		
	Dunker Baptist		
	Free Will Baptist		
	Christian Connection		

[a]groups that attempt to modify traditional denominational beliefs and forms.

[b]groups advocating radical transformation in Christian beliefs, resulting in permanent separation from their former denominational affiliates.

[c]groups that substitute their own religious alternative for Christianity.

[d]groups that repudiate religion altogether and replace it with political beliefs and structures.

SOURCE. Linda K. Pritchard, "Religious Change in Nineteenth Century America," in Charles Y. Glock and Robert N. Bellah, eds., *The New Religious Consciousness* (Berkeley, Calif.: University of California Press, 1976), pp. 308–309.

TABLE 18.2

Better-Known American Communes, Their Starting Dates, and Longevity

COMMUNE	STARTING DATE	LONGEVITY IN YEARS
Snowhill	1800	70
Harmony	1804	100
Zoar	1817	81
Mormons	1836	current
Brook Farm	1841	6
Hopedale	1841	15
Northampton	1842	4
Amana	1843	90
North American Phalanx	1843	13
Bethel	1844	36
Oneida	1848	33
Shaker Villages	1774	180
Icaria	1848	30–50

SOURCE. Adapted from Rosabeth Moss Kanter, "Commitment and Social Organization: A Study of Commitment Mechanisms in Utopian Communities," *American Sociological Review* 33 (August 1968), pp. 499–517; William M. Kephart, *Extraordinary Groups: The Sociology of Unconventional Lifestyles* (New York: St. Martin's Press, 1976), p. 283; and Wayne Wheeler, et. al., "Icarian Communism," *International Review of Modern Sociology* 6 (Spring 1976), pp. 127–138.

ualism that were associated with it. For example, one commune called Brook Farm, established in 1841, was inspired by utopian planner Charles Fourier (1772–1837). He believed that happiness and fulfillment could be achieved only when individuals were released from the restraints of society. He proposed segmenting society into small units of about 1600 people, each of which would emphasize cooperative and united efforts toward common goals. Sharp distinctions of wealth were to be eliminated, and people would be free to move from one task to another as their interests dictated.

Other communal experiments of this period rested on religious foundations, especially fundamental Protestantism, including the Shakers, the Harmony and Amana colonies, and the Mormons. These communes were highly authoritarian and rigid structures, with little opportunity for the expression of individuality. Some communes imposed extremely austere lifestyles on their members. For example, the Shakers totally renounced sexual activities of any kind and went so far as to prohibit any type of physical contact between

Religious social movements, such as the Shakers, were a prominent feature of preindustrial American society. Some traditional groups continue to exist today, although their influence on society is less pronounced.

the sexes. They even proclaimed the "joys of celibacy." The Shakers rose early in the morning, worked hard, and prayed often. Much of their everyday life was circumscribed by the requirement that their behavior be highly ritualized. When eating, for example, good posture was absolutely essential; the elders were fed first; absolutely no food was to be left on one's plate; utensils were to be placed in precisely the appropriate position; and meat was always to be cut in squares.

Whatever their form, these early communal experiments were in part a reaction to the social problems that affected people in the early stages of industrialization in America.[17] They offered those individuals who were dissatisfied with the emerging industrial social order a means of escape into a cooperative experiment. They also preserved the belief for some people that alternative economic and social arrangements were possible—that increasing industrialization might not be inevitable, or at least that it could be avoided by some. However, these communal groups completely failed to alter the trend toward industrialization, technological sophistication, urbanization, and bureaucratization that has characterized our history since that time. If anything, communes encouraged these trends by serving as a safety valve: groups that were radically dissatisfied could find in communes a lifestyle and a cause that appeared to resist the emerging industrialism but that actually had little effect on it.

The previous review illustrates that social movements have existed throughout our history and at times have been quite common. Furthermore, we have learned that the movements arise in some cases as mechanisms by which individuals cope with social problems of the time—whether those problems be the isolation of people in the back country in the eighteenth century, the abolition of slavery in the nineteenth century, or the crowding and poverty associated with industrialization. Thus, it is essential to recognize that unconventional social movements are an integral part of the process of social change, either promoting such change or resisting it. At the same time, such social movements may constitute social problems themselves, and it is to this issue that we next direct our attention.

SOCIAL MOVEMENTS AS A SOCIAL PROBLEM

Social movements are not always social problems. In order to determine the conditions under which such movements become social problems, we will utilize the three sociological perspectives.

The Functionalist Perspective

According to the functionalist perspective, a social problem exists when some condition disrupts the smooth functioning of the social order. **Social movements, by their very nature, can disrupt the daily operation of society.** For example, the antiwar movement of the 1960s and early 1970s can be considered a social problem from this perspective, because the primary purpose of the movement was to interfere with the ability of the country to wage war. Attacks on ROTC installations and Selective Service Induction Centers clearly threatened the ability of the military to conduct the war effort. The youth counterculture, to the extent that it spawned support for antiwar activities or encouraged young people to challenge authority through attacks on institutions such as universities, also was disruptive and a threat to the social order. Whether the disruptions of the 1960s were sufficiently widespread to constitute a serious threat is a debatable issue; nevertheless, it would have been possible for such activities to threaten the social order if they had been able, for example, to close many universities in the United States.

Social movements may also constitute social problems from the functionalist perspective if they threaten the basic values and important institutions that serve as foundations for the established social order. Some revolutionary groups constitute this type of threat since their success would result in a new value system supported by new economic and political arrangements. The Russian Revolution of 1917 threatened, and finally eliminated, the political and economic power of the Russian aristocracy. Russian society was dramatically changed from a feudal one, in which power resided in the hands of the czarist aristocracy, to a society more congruent

Revolutionary groups, like the Weather Underground, would be considered a social problem from the functionalist perspective if they threaten the basic values and important institutions that serve as a foundation for the American social order.

with an industrial order in which political and economic power was more widely dispersed. In America during the past few decades, revolutionary groups, such as the Weather Underground and the Symbionese Liberation Army, would have basically restructured American society had they been able to achieve their goals.

Social movements can be revolutionary in a more subtle fashion. If a movement, for example, is able to interfere with the ability of conventional groups in society to raise their young to follow in their footsteps, then it might, over a long period of time, bring about dramatic changes in values and practices among those young. If, for example, young people can be convinced to adopt a communal lifestyle, then eventually the American values of private property and the nuclear family may be threatened.

The Conflict Perspective

In addition to being a general threat to some core values or lifestyle, a social movement might also represent an attempt by members of one group to gain access to specific scarce and valued resources, such as economic or political power, that are controlled by other groups. If such a social movement could mobilize sufficient resources to seriously threaten the ability of these groups to retain their power or resources, then that social movement would be defined as a social problem from the perspective of the threatened groups. For example, many people viewed the civil rights and Black Power movements as attempts by blacks to acquire some of the political and economic power that had traditionally been held by whites in American society. Many whites felt that the success of these movements would radically alter their position relative to traditionally subordinate groups; for them, such social movements were a serious social problem. Likewise, any revolutionary group, such as the Symbionese Liberation Army, would be a social problem from the conflict perspective because its primary goal is a redistribution of the political and economic resources in society.

From the conflict perspective, then, society is an arena in which people struggle over scarce resources, and social movements can be one party to this struggle. If certain groups, usually those with a vested interest in existing institutions and practices, feel that their position is threatened by these social movements, the movements will be defined as a social problem.

The Interactionist Perspective

All of us react in some way to social movements that we see emerging around us. We see some of them as rational and laudable efforts to change abhorrent conditions; others we view as humorous, but harmless, diversions that bring a little laughter into our day; still others we perceive as outrageous, threatening activities that should not be permitted to exist. It is the latter type of reaction that can lead to social movements being defined as social problems in society. **According to the interactionist perspective, some important groups in society may define a movement as a social problem and behave toward it as such, irrespective of whether it is objectively functional or dysfunctional. These subjective perceptions of threat are sufficient to constitute a social problem, because people respond to their perceptions of reality, not necessarily to objective conditions.**

People may perceive social movements as threatening a set of core values or a preciously held way of life. While no immediate or specific personal threat may be apparent, the mere appearance of an extremely divergent set of values can be seen as threatening. For example, many people viewed the political, moral, and sexual beliefs of the youth counterculture of the 1960s in this way, as illustrated by the diatribe of a policeman after the dispersal of a group of yippies (a group of antiwar activitists) from New York's Grand Central Station in 1968:

> Here's a bunch of animals who call themselves the next leaders of the country . . . I almost had to vomit . . . It's like dealing with any queer pervert, mother raper, or any of these other bedbugs we've got crawling around the [Greenwich] Village. As a normal human being, you feel like knocking every one of their teeth out. It's a normal reaction.[18]

This policeman's reaction does not seem to derive from any direct threat to his political or economic resources, but rather from his distress over the lifestyle and values of these yippies. The policeman's disgust results in part from *ethnocentrism* **— the belief in the superiority of one's own group and its way of life.** The core values that underpin a lifestyle define for members of the group what are desirable characteristics and socially approved behaviors. A person who has these characteristics or who behaves in the appropriate fashion

is viewed by members of the group as a valuable and worthwhile human being. The existence of values and lifestyles contradictory to one's own can threaten one's self-concept because they suggest that self-worth might derive from some source other than the values of one's group. This might shake one's faith in the superiority, righteousness, and perhaps even the adequacy of one's own way of life.

The extent to which an unconventional social movement can be perceived as threatening is illustrated by the violent reaction of many people to the religions that became popular during the 1970s. While many of these groups pose no immediate economic or political threat, they are in some respects departures from the religious, social, and cultural lifestyle that the majority of Americans have come to accept. This departure can involve both the doctrine (which sometimes derives from non-Western religions) and the forms (their seemingly fanatical passion and incessant proselytizing). Reverend Moon's Unification Church has probably generated the strongest and most intense negative reactions. Parents of the "Moonies" (followers of Moon) have been especially vociferous in charging that Moon is a threat to commonly held values and to core institutions, such as the American family. These parents believe that, if it were not for Moon's influence, they would be able to raise their children to accept more traditional religious beliefs and values. They have used legal channels, such as court trials, to have their children returned to them, and they have used illegal channels, such as kidnapping and deprogramming, to change their children's religious beliefs.[19]

SOCIAL MOVEMENTS AS A RESPONSE TO SOCIAL PROBLEMS

After reviewing the theoretical perspectives, it is clear that social movements in American society can, under the appropriate conditions, be seen as social problems. However, if we look no further than this, we will miss some of the fundamentally important characteristics of social movements. In addition to being social problems themselves, social movements can also be reactions to other social problems in society. In other words, the individuals who are attracted to social movements are often reacting to other social conditions in American society. Thus social movements play a role in the process of social change. Whether they play a big or small part depends on a variety of factors.

Social Movements and Social Change

At the height of the hippie phenomenon in the late 1960s, sociologist Fred Davis wrote an article subtitled, "Why All of Us May Be Hippies Some Day."[20] It shocked many people to think that a lifestyle they felt to be bizarre, if not immoral and repulsive, would one day be accepted by many or most people. However, Davis's point was that the hippie lifestyle offered one possible way of resolving current social problems. For example, it would be possible to reduce environmental pollution and slow down the depletion of natural resources if Americans adopted the hippie practice of sharing belongings and owning goods in common. Thus, the hippie lifestyle, while not acceptable to most Americans today, may be a harbinger of changes in the future. We will probably not all become hippies in order to solve environmental problems; but we may come to place greater value on sharing (e.g. through carpooling) in order to protect dwindling resources.

Davis was not acting as an evangelist for the hippie lifestyle, but he was pointing to an important aspect of the process of social change. When a society undergoes major structural change, the dislocations that result can lead to new, and in some cases unusual, developments in society that might eventually take the form of alternative lifestyles or social movements. Furthermore, there must be some vehicle or agent through which the change may occur. Thus, social movements can arise as a response to problems in some part of society and also serve as a vehicle for social change that is functional for society as a whole.

There are many illustrations of social movements that have played one or both of these roles. For example, traditional sex-role differentiation in American society could not change without the impetus of the various groups that have banded together under the rubric of the "women's movement" (see ch. 13). Likewise, the changing relationships between racial groups during the past few decades in the United States would not have occurred without the push for change by many social movement organizations, from the Southern Christian Leadership Conference to the Black Panther Party (see ch. 12).

This does not mean that every social movement that arises is a portent of what life will become. The relationship between social movements and social change is complex. Some movements serve as a safety valve through which certain groups, who are not content with existing social conditions, can be appeased in a way that is not threatening to the larger society. In addition, the social change that finally results is the outcome of the interaction among the various social movements themselves and between the movements and the dominant interest groups in society. The precise nature of the change that results depends on the power available to each group and the accommodations their members are willing to, or must, make.

Obviously, all of us have not become hippies—partly because the hippie lifestyle is too divergent from that of the dominant groups in our society. However, residues of the values and lifestyle of the hippies and the youth counterculture of the 1960s can be found as a part of American life today.[21] The acceptance and use of marijuana is certainly more widespread than in the past; there is evidence that automatic acceptance of authority and allegiance to one's country are less common than in the past; and the sexual values of the hippies and the counterculture may have contributed to the more liberalized attitudes toward sex today. Finally, hair and clothing styles for both men and women were influenced by the hippie movement. In other words, while the hippies as a separate and recognizable lifestyle may eventually disappear, they leave a subtle legacy that may combine with the changes brought about by other movements and be instrumental in changing America in the future. The change will probably not involve total conversion to the ways of the social movement; but, at the same time, society is usually not the same after having been influenced by an important social movement.

Our goal here is neither to advocate nor to reject the lifestyle and values of any particular social movement. Rather, we aim at understanding the role of social movements in the process of social change. Some movements are harbingers of things to come; others are extreme reactions that, at best, leave minor residues behind after their demise; while still others are dying outbursts of groups that have become anachronisms because they have been outpaced by social change. Whether we as individuals accept or reject the lifestyle of a particular group depends on our own personal values. The social scientist cannot resolve this basic question of values, because it is not one that can be verified by scientific observation. You cannot scientifically "prove" what is a better set of values or a superior lifestyle—this is a matter of individual preference and belief.

Social Change in America

Before discussing some current social movements, it is valuable to review some of the changing social conditions in American society that many scholars argue have contributed to the emergence of these movements. While there is not total consensus about the precise relationship between these changes and the movements considered in this chapter, there is little doubt that these alterations have had a profound effect on our lives and have made some contribution to the emergence of these lifestyles.

Industrialization and Technological Change

America has made the transition from a rural way of life to a highly industrialized, technologically complex society. There is an elaborate division of labor in which each worker, with a relatively high level of training and skill, contributes only one very specialized activity to the total work flow.[22] This has a number of consequences. First, each individual generally has less awareness of, and control over, the total production process. This conduces to some people's feeling alienated and separated from their work, and often from people around them.

Second, a smaller and smaller proportion of the population is needed to produce the goods and services necessary to support our affluent lifestyle.[23] This is partly the result of *automation*—the monitoring and control of the work process by machines. Currently, youth and the elderly are discouraged from working. For those under 18, we have advanced education; for those over 65, we have retirement. If current trends continue, we will need even fewer workers in the future, and our persistently high unemployment rates may be even higher. Thus, our industrial economy is organized such that some people are not encouraged to share productive work while others have jobs that are less than fulfilling.

From Scarcity to Abundance

In the past, the American economy relied heavily on entrepreneurial activity and was based on the notion of *laissez faire*—that business should be permitted to function independently of government regulation and interference.[24] There was competition between individuals and firms, and the entrepreneur took personal risks with his available resources in order to make a profit. An important driving force of the economy was scarcity, which led to an emphasis on saving, the accumulation of resources, and the postponement of gratification to ward off scarcity.

The American economy today is quite different. It is a corporate economy in which individual entrepreneurial activity is less highly rewarded.[25] The driving force is no longer the specter of scarcity; rather, it is the need to consume the immense volume of new products that the economic engine is capable of producing. While there is an abundance of food and material products that have traditionally been in short supply, there remains a sense of scarcity: we continually convince ourselves that we need other things. The central problem for the corporate economy is to encourage the consumer to purchase all that the system can produce.

Bureaucratization

The all-pervasive bureaucratic organizations that touch most areas of our lives have had significant consequences for American society.[26] Individualism, aggressiveness, and risk taking are not highly valued traits in bureaucracies. Instead, the goal is to learn to cooperate with others to achieve the ends of the bureaucracy, to please others that one must associate with, and to comply with the wishes of one's boss.[27] Bureaucracies are characterized by the diffusion of authority and responsibility, and they tend to be unresponsive to individual needs and desires. In some cases, it is a struggle for people to get what they want from a bureaucracy; learning how to cope successfully with it is a skill that some learn better than others. The social movements that we will discuss in this chapter have emerged partly as a reaction to the impersonality and unresponsiveness of bureaucracies.

At school, at work, and sometimes even at play, social relationships often tend to be superficial and impersonal. Many of our associates care little about us as complete human beings but are more concerned about specialized roles and tasks that we must perform.[28] This is due in part to the fact that the community to which we belong seems to have grown beyond individual control—we seem to have lost the sense that we are a part of a common effort over which we can have some control. People live in huge metropolitan areas, work in immense companies of which they, as individuals, are only a minuscule part, and eat at restaurants like McDonald's, which boasts having served over 23 billion hamburgers. Ties to family, friends, or neighborhood no longer seem as strong as they once were. The social and geographic mobility that is such an important part of modern America intensifies this isolation—old relationships must be broken up as a person moves to a new occupational or social setting. **The term *mass society* refers to such developments. In a mass society many individuals are unattached, isolated, with little control over important decisions that are made about their lives.** Many scholars have argued that individuals in a mass society are more susceptible to the appeals of unconventional social movements because they see them as possible solutions to the perceived inadequacies of conventional society.[29]

Sociocultural Values

As a part of the socialization process, members of society learn sociocultural values that help guide their behavior. If society is to continue functioning at a socially acceptable level, these values must encourage and reward behavior making it possible to achieve societal goals. Because of the changes we have considered—industrialization, increasing technology, bureaucratization—**America today faces the problem of *cultural lag*; our beliefs and values may not have changed to keep pace with changes in our technology (e.g. automation) and forms of social organization (e.g. bureaucracy).**[30] We can illustrate this cultural lag in the case of two sets of values—the Protestant ethic and individualism.

In chapter 9, we discussed a constellation of values referred to as the *Protestant ethic*—**the belief that hard work, frugality, and asceticism were desirable, while leisure and excessive consumption were immoral.**[31] This type of lifestyle was highly valued in the past and is still seen as desirable by many people today. While not all Americans accept every precept of the Protestant ethic, most feel that people should engage in some type of purposeful, goal-oriented activity. However, such a value system, at least if unqualified, is not totally consistent with the changes that have occurred in American society. Because of technological advances, many have argued, our society is geared toward increasing leisure time rather than unending hard work; we emphasize consumption and spending rather than production; our economic productivity depends as much on credit—each of us spending money we have not yet earned—as it does on frugality and saving. Practices that emphasize leisure time, consumption, and spending are, to some extent, inconsistent with the Protestant-ethic-related values that many Americans have internalized; thus, cultural lag exists. Since people assess their self-worth in terms of their ability to behave consistently with their values, some are likely to feel dissatisfied and unfulfilled. If they do not work hard and are not frugal, they may perceive themselves as inadequate and possibly worthless.[32]

The disparity between these Protestant ethic values and the options available in modern society can be clearly seen in the areas of welfare and unemployment. Unemployment is often a psychologically debilitating experience, especially when the unemployed believe that it is their own fault that they are without work. If only, they say, I had worked harder or acquired more training and education, I would have a job today. They feel that they *should* be working—that they are worthless, perhaps even immoral, because they are idle. Furthermore, many Americans (including some on welfare) believe that all those receiving welfare could find jobs if only they would work at it; they are on welfare because they are lazy and do not want to work. This illustrates our tendency to "blame the victim."[33] Our belief that hard work is desirable and will bring rewards overshadows the fact that there may be structural reasons for a relatively high level of unemployment.

Another value that has been an important part of the American tradition is *individualism.* Sociologist Robert Wuthnow defines *individualism* as

a form of consciousness in which the person occupies the position of authority. The individual himself is the agent responsible for governing his own destiny. Not God or some other force, but the individual's own choices determine the meaning and purpose he finds in life. His will power and effort determine whether he will succeed or fail.[34]

Although perhaps an unfounded belief, people in the past, more so than people today, felt that they could have significant control over the political and economic structures of society—that it was possible at least to shape one's small social world. This belief encouraged people to rely on themselves and their families. There were few governmental or bureaucratic organizations that one could turn to for help and sustenance.

Many modern thinkers believe that individualism is on the decline in American society.[35] New forces seem to be governing social reality. Tasks that were considered to be the responsibility of the individual or the family are now taken over by some large im-

personal organization, such as a school, a nursing home, or an insurance company. People seldom fabricate their own houses any longer; large construction firms now build thousands of houses at a time. Families seldom nurture the sick and infirm; they purchase health insurance and depend on that industry to pay their hospitalization when they are ill. It is no longer common for friends and family to rush to one's aid in times of unemployment or financial crisis; the government offers welfare and unemployment benefits.

Identity Crisis

While belief in the Protestant ethic and individualism is still strong among many Americans, the conditions of modern life make it more difficult to live up to such values. **The inability to behave in accordance with the values and expectations placed on oneself is one condition that can conduce to an** *identity crisis*—**a situation in which one finds it difficult to develop a coherent and consistent self-concept based on the reactions of important people in one's life.** It is difficult to define oneself as autonomous and self-reliant when one feels hemmed in by bureaucratic pressures and demands. Most employees of bureaucratic organizations face many conditions affecting their economic and occupational well-being over which they sense little or no control. For example, an employee might suppress certain political beliefs in order to please a superior who determines job promotion. It is difficult to reconcile this behavior with a belief in the value of individualism. **This is one form of** *alienation*—**a discrepancy between one's beliefs about how one should behave (based, for example, on the Protestant ethic or individualism) and one's actual behavior.** While there has always been some degree of alienation, many feel it is more common today. People experiencing feelings of alienation, isolation, and powerlessness may be more susceptible to the appeals of unconventional social movements, such as those discussed in this chapter. Such movements offer solutions to these personal problems through intense collective involvement.[36]

There is a second condition of modern postindustrial society that can lead to identity crisis.[37] Industrialization, the complex division of labor, the declining importance of work—these and other characteristics have created a society in which people must make many role transitions during their lives; in which they often perform more than one role at a time; and in which there are often no clear guidelines concerning the choices between alternative roles. Youth are particularly affected by this situation because they are in their formative years and must make choices concerning how they will lead their lives. In the past, the choice was much simpler; a boy followed in his father's footsteps while a girl modeled herself after her mother. Today, the decisions are much more complex. The sheer number of possible occupations confronting a young person today is staggering. In addition, the traditional separation of male and female roles is breaking down. A woman can be a nurse, a doctor, an astronaut, or a firefighter. A man can be a secretary, an airplane steward, or even a homemaker! The traditional guidelines based on sex or family background are less important today than they once were. A person who has an identity crisis is more likely to be attracted to a social movement as a means of finding a stable basis upon which to found an identity.

Crisis of Legitimacy

An important foundation of social order is tradition—the belief that certain customary and habitual forms of behavior are the proper and appropriate ways to lead one's life. In traditional societies, the major social institutions—family, church, and political arrangements—are accorded *legitimacy* by most people. That is, people think that it is right and proper that those institutions have authority over their daily lives (see ch. 1). However, **some social scientists feel that there has emerged in the past few decades a *crisis of legitimacy*—a massive erosion in the belief that the established institutions in America should properly be respected by, and have control over, the citizenry.**[38]

While this crisis of legitimacy appears to have been most prominent among the young, it is certainly widespread among much of the population. The ghetto and campus disturbances of the 1960s reflect this decline in legitimacy. The effort by many minority groups—women, blacks, Hispanic Americans, and others—to gain more control and a larger share of valued resources partially stems from this feeling that traditional beliefs and institutions need not be unquestioningly obeyed. Incidents such as the Watergate debacle have further debased the faith of the average citizen in the legitimacy of the government. As with changes in personal identity, this crisis in legitimacy results in considerable uncertainty, because cherished institutions no longer serve as sources of direction and social control. As a consequence, social movements may emerge as an attempt to develop institutional forms to replace the more traditional ones. And some may find these movements a satisfactory replacement for those institutions that have declined in legitimacy.

Many of the problems discussed in this section—alienation, identity crisis, crisis of legitimacy—are private in that they refer to personal feelings or attitudes. However, they become a social problem (or at least a part of a social problem) when the affected individuals come together into social movements that are disruptive of the social order or defined as a social problem by influential groups. According to the functionalist perspective, these private problems have emerged because America is currently undergoing fundamental social and economic change, and some parts of society have yet to change sufficiently to be consistent with changes that have occurred in other parts of society. This lack of integration can result in a certain proportion of the population feeling alienated, dissatisfied, confused, or unfulfilled, and some of these people will cope with their personal problems by joining social movements—possibly one of those discussed in this chapter. Thus, these social movements are, at least in part, a response to underlying changes in American society. In addition, however, they may also constitute social problems in their own right. As each social movement is discussed, the reader may find it instructive to consider which groups in society (depending on the theoretical perspective used) would view each social movement as a social problem.

THE YOUTH MOVEMENT AND THE COUNTERCULTURE

In all societies, broad age categories such as youth can serve as a subculture — a sharing of beliefs, values, and attitudes about themselves and their place in the world.[39] In some cases, an emerging youth movement is supportive of the dominant societal values. For example, Hitler's youth movement in Germany supported the values and goals of the Third Reich. **However, in the 1960s, a youth movement arose in the United States that took the form of a *counterculture* — a set of beliefs and values that were in opposition to some of the dominant values in society.**[40] Such a development was especially shocking and dismaying to some because it was not the underprivileged who were rejecting American values but rather the sons and daughters of the more privileged and affluent families in America.

The terms *youth movement* and *counterculture* are often used interchangeably to refer to certain trends among some young people that arose in the 1960s. *Youth movement* is an unfortunate term, because the trends being considered do not appear exclusively among the young; many who could by no means be considered young were often actively involved. Furthermore, these trends did not involve all, or even most, of the young. While it is impossible to state how many were involved, they were certainly never more than a clear minority of young people.

There were two major subgroups that constituted the counterculture of the 1960s and early 1970s: the hippies and the radical political activists.[41] Each left its mark on American history. The hippies gathered in large numbers in such places as New York's East Village and San Francisco's Haight-Ashbury. They gathered in parks, played rock music, and consumed an array of mind-altering drugs. Hippies were *colorful, unconventional* in ap-

pearance — and showed this in a wide variety of ways (clothing, artifacts, ornaments, adornments, footgear, headwear, etc.). They celebrated their values by *dramatizing* them in vestment (leather, used jeans, etc.) and accessories (money pouches, pot stashes, etc.). To most of conventional society, they seemed dirty, unkempt, and decidedly strange. The political radicals were intensely concerned about a number of social issues of the day — from the Vietnam War, to racial equality, to student control over universities. They supported their cause through massive rallies and marches, which occasionally ended in violence. They were out to change the institutions that they believed to be ineffective or corrupt.

The Beliefs of the Youth Counterculture

The youth counterculture does not espouse values that are only different from the values of the dominant groups; it has arisen mainly as a *reaction against* dominant values.[42] Certain common themes relate the disparate elements of the counterculture and can be understood as a reaction against some of the societal conditions discussed previously in this chapter. First, there is a desire to live in close fellowship and cooperation with others in a way that offers some sense of collective unity; it is a search for an intimate and comprehensible community to be involved in. The goal is to be immersed in a community of others similar to oneself rather than to be a fragmented individual. Second, there is the desire to join with others in controlling the conditions of one's life rather than being controlled by impersonal political, economic, or bureaucratic institutions. Third, there is the belief that personal relationships, ethical principles, or religious teachings are of greater value than material possessions. There is a tendency to reject the American emphasis on achievement, rationality, and hard work in favor of personal enjoyment of the present and the value of self-expression. Sociologist Richard Flacks, who has been concerned about these issues for many years at both a scientific and a personal level, summarizes some of the differences between the counterculture and more traditional American lifestyles in the following way:

Some members of the youth counterculture of the past two decades have been intensely concerned about social issues— from the Vietnam War, to racial equality, to student control in universities.

The [counterculture] that is struggling to be born stresses cooperation over competition, expression over success, communalism over individualism, being over doing, making art over making money, and autonomy over obedience.[43]

These themes can be found, in one form or another, in many of the types of social experimentation that emerged in the 1960s and 1970s.[44] For example, political experimentation has included a search for new governmental forms that represent a radical reorganization of existing political arrangements in society. The Students for a Democratic Society, the Black Panthers, the Weather Underground, and the Symbionese Liberation Army each espoused some version of anarchy or socialism. Economic experiments of the counterculture have involved efforts to develop new ways of producing and distributing goods. Communes, cooperatives, free clinics, and self-employed street artisans flourished in many parts of the country during the 1960s. The use of drugs, the long hair, the rock music, and the festivals of life (such as Wood-

stock) all expressed in some degree the distinctiveness of the youth counterculture and its opposition to dominant societal values. For example, one proponent of the counterculture defined the role and purpose of rock music in the following way:

Rock is a realistic, unabashed retreat from the rationally controlled, highly organized, unhappy technological world. Rock conjures up the primordial, the raw, the physical, the irrational, the mysterious, and the macabre, as touchstones to getting people back to themselves—back to inner sources of happiness and joy. The aim is the unexpected, unpremeditated joy of aesthetic, physical response. It is *play* —delight in the transformation of music, lyrics, and color . . . The emphasis on the visual and the ecstatic which is heightened by the volume of the music, the swirl of exploding lights and the distorted images—these, compounded with marijuana or psychedelic drugs and the dancing of groupies, consummate a collective tribal celebration of Dionysius. It is collective participation held up in contrast to

The youth counterculture was characterized by its opposition to the dominant values in American society. This opposition often took the form of "festivals of life" (such as the one in Woodstock, New York) in which youth expressed their separation from conventional society.

the abstracted representative participation which characterizes modern bureaucratic democracy.[45]

Thus, in its many forms the youth counterculture expressed its goal of offering something different and, its members believed, more desirable than the lifestyle offered by conventional society.

Origins of the Youth Counterculture

There are a number of arguments concerning why the counterculture emerged, but most approaches see it as arising in part as a response to the changes in American society discussed earlier in this chapter. Thus, historian Theodore Roszak, one of the early proponents of the idea of a counterculture, argues that the basic source of this movement is our advanced technology.[46] According to Roszak, the standardization, mechanization, and bureaucratic organization that are endemic to our technological society lead people to feel isolated and alienated. Furthermore, the extreme competitiveness in America, resulting from the Protestant ethic and fostered by our technology, can serve to separate people from one another. We lose feelings of interdependence and a sense of shared community if we are continually in competitive relationships with one another. Through advertising, individual desires may experience manipulation and a heightening so that there is an increased demand for the products of our technology. This further supports the development of our technology—thereby perpetuating these problems.

Flacks extends these ideas by suggesting that today's youth experience a clash between the values that they internalized during early socialization and the lifestyle that our economy and their position in society make possible.[47] While many young people are socialized to value Protestant-ethic-based principles of hard work and frugality, they are bombarded with encouragement to spend, use credit, get high, and the like. The emphasis is on consumption rather than production. Furthermore, since youth have not yet been permitted to fully join the adult workforce, they are in a situation of "enforced" leisure. They are not permitted to work hard as productive and useful members of society. This conflict can result in a crisis of identity; how do they establish a positive personal identity? If they cannot base their self-concepts on their work, which is the prime source of identity in American society, then what makes them useful and worthwhile members of society? It is this ambiguity and dissatisfaction, Flacks argues, that serves to lead some young people to find countercultural movements appealing.

Psychologist Kenneth Keniston has pointed to another source of countercultural aspiration in American society.[48] Young people who are biologically mature but not permitted to participate fully in adult life are encouraged to take up the highest ideals and values of American society. Many affluent middle-class parents raise their children in democratic, nonauthoritarian settings, and their children come to place great value on such relationships. They are encouraged to accept and try to implement democratic and equalitarian ideals. As Keniston put it:

> Somehow these parents communicated, often without saying outright, that human behavior was to be judged primarily in terms of general ethical principles: that right conduct was to be deduced from general maxims concerning human kindness, honesty, decency, and responsibility; that what mattered most was the ability to act in conformity with principles.[49]

Through the freedom provided by the educational system, especially at the university level, they are encouraged to look critically at American institutions and practices that do not live up to these high ideals. The system of higher education encourages social experimentation at the same time that students are released from parental supervision by going away to college. Furthermore, since many affluent college-age youth are supported by their families, they do not take great personal risk when

they dissent. They are free to criticize without threatening their livelihood or survival.

A final factor that is important in the emergence of the youth movement and the counterculture is that for youth in our industrial society there is no clear-cut transition to the status of adulthood. Many people are biologically mature long before they are accorded full adult status. This situation is more common among the affluent groups in society. For upper-middle-class youth who attend college, this not-quite-adult status may extend into the mid-twenties. These youth take on some of the characteristics of a minority group and may suffer status deprivation—being temporarily prevented from attaining positions of high status in society. This is one of the reasons that the youth movement was a predominantly middle-class phenomenon, especially in the early years. For many working- and lower-class youth, there were more clear-cut transitions to adulthood—either looking for a job upon leaving high school or marrying and having children. For the affluent youth suffering status deprivation, participation in the youth movement offered an alternative status system to that of the adult world.

So, in a sense, advanced industrial society has created its own critical counterculture out of these social forces: the potential alienation resulting from technology, the marginality of the young to the adult world, and the opportunity afforded the young to safely experiment and dissent. It is not surprising that it is youth who respond most dramatically to these changes because, in addition to having the opportunity to dissent, they are still in the formative years of establishing a coherent lifestyle and stable identity. They do not have a lifetime of previous choices and commitments that must be justified; they are still in the process of choosing.

The youth counterculture can be understood as a form of *rebellion*, one of the modes of adaptation to anomie proposed by Robert Merton (see ch. 15). In this way of adapting, the rebel rejects both the dominant cultural goals and values (such as material success) and the legitimate means of achieving those goals (such as hard work in a socially acceptable occupation). However, the rebel does not withdraw from society (as would be the case with some other modes of adaptation to anomie). Rather, he or she attempts to change those values, practices, or institutions that are found to be unacceptable.

Who Joins the Youth Movement?

Who among the young is attracted to the counterculture? This is a difficult question to answer since a counterculture is a general trend that can take many different forms, such as religious involvement, antiwar activity, radical political activity, and communal living. In fact, many people have some allegiance to countercultural beliefs even though they do not belong to any commonly recognized countercultural group. However, there is some support for the finding that countercultural values, in whatever specific form they take, are more common among the better-educated, more affluent, and more intellectually aware youth.[50]

The Youth Movement as a Social Problem

From the functionalist perspective, a social movement is considered a social problem if it threatens the core values and fundamental institutions that serve as the foundation of the social order. The youth movement of the past few decades, while it certainly attacked the established values and institutions, does not seem to have seriously threatened the survival of those values and institutions. While it may have brought about some minor changes (for example in hair or clothing styles), the central institutions and values appear to have emerged through the turmoil largely unscathed.[51]

According to the interactionist perspective, however, the youth movement certainly could be considered a social problem since it was perceived by many citizens as an attack on those institutions and values that they held dear and precious. Many viewed members of the counterculture as radicals and revolutionaries who threatened core American values and institutions such as the family and private property. These people often called for a return to traditional American values of family and

community (ironically, precisely what some members of the counterculture are searching for) and a respect for the authority of these institutions.

Some social scientists do not feel that the youth movement itself is necessarily a social problem at all. They view it as emerging out of the structural crisis in American society pointed to by Roszak, Flacks and Keniston. According to this view, we ignore the counterculture at our own peril because we thereby ignore serious problems in our society. In this view, a widespread social movement may be symptomatic of flaws in society, and we should search for those problems that give rise to such movements. Furthermore, such movements may be forerunners of important social change. Some, such as Flacks, feel that the youth movement is the vanguard of revolutionary changes that will occur as America makes the transition to a postindustrial society. A less extreme view is that some alternative structural and interpersonal relationships will be required in the future. What form these new arrangements will take is debatable; they may retain some characteristics of the counterculture while having a more traditional form. In either case, this view maintains that the counterculture is a signal of certain changes that will be necessary in the future as well as being a vehicle of those changes. Given the evidence available, the reader should evaluate the extent to which the youth counterculture has had, and will have, an effect on shaping the future direction of American society.

THE RISE OF UNCONVENTIONAL RELIGIOUS MOVEMENTS

In the late 1960s, many Americans were surprised, shocked, and even horrified by the emergence of intense, emotional, and cultish religious practices, predominantly among young people. Some of these movements were offshoots of fundamental Christianity (such as the Jesus People, and the Children of God), while others evolved from Eastern religions (such as the Krishna Consciousness movement and the Divine Light Mission of the Guru Maharaj Ji). While there is tremendous variation among these groups, they all share one thing in common: they provide a definite break, in one way or another, with traditional religious practices in the United States.[52] In order to understand why these groups emerged and to evaluate their impact on American society, we will discuss the origins, beliefs, and lifestyles of three such groups: the Krishna Consciousness movement, the Jesus People, and the Unification Church.

Krishna Consciousness

The Krishna Consciousness movement in the United States can be traced to the mid-1960s, when A. C. Bhaktivedanta Swami Prabhupada came to the United States from India and established the International Society for Krishna Consciousness (ISKCON) in 1966.[53] He chanted the names of Krishna (a name of God) in Tompkins Square Park in New York City and began to attract followers, many of them hippies. Many people are now familiar with their most important chant, the *mahamantra:*

> Hare Krishna, Hare Krishna,
> Krishna Krishna, Hare Hare,
> Hare Rama, Hare Rama,
> Rama, Rama, Hare Hare.

Repetitive chanting of this mantra is supposed to purify both the chanter and those who hear it. The chanter is considered to transcend the material plane. According to an ISKCON publication, "this meditation is the simplest and most sublime process for reviving God Consciousness in the current materialist age."[54] (*Hare* and *Rama* are other names for Krishna.) Swami Prabhupada was very successful in spreading his beliefs. As of 1974, he had 100 centers of Krishna Consciousness around the world, with 40 in the United States. They have a successful monthly magazine, *Back to Godhead,* and a thriving business in the manufacture and sale of incense. The Bhaktivedanta Book Trust, the publishing arm of ISKCON, has been very active, publishing millions of pieces of literature, including the works of Swami Prabhupada and many Indian spiritual works.

Beliefs

What do these disciples in flowing Indian robes and shaved heads believe in? According to an ISKCON publication, "The message of the *Vedas,* India's ancient spiritual and philosophical texts, is that the human form of life is meant for reviving our original God consciousness through the practice of spiritual discipline."[55] They believe in the emergence of a new consciousness—Krishna Consciousness—among millions of people. By practicing yogic discipline, a Krishna devotee can be eternally blissful and protected by Krishna. The material world, they believe, is illusion because, although real, it is a temporary manifestation. The Krishna devotee's present life is only a transitional stage to a higher spiritual reality and eventual reunion with Krishna. This higher spirituality can be achieved only by accepting the teachings of Krishna without question and by rejecting the material pleasures of the physical world. Otherwise, one is confronted with a descent to, and reincarnation as, a lower form of life.

Lifestyle

It is no easy life to follow the way of Krishna. The rigid code of behavior imposed on followers results in a rather ascetic and difficult life. Members are not permitted to eat meat, fish, or eggs, drink coffee or tea, gamble, or use alcohol or other drugs. Only married couples are permitted to engage in sexual relations—and then only once a month, following several hours of chanting to cleanse the mind. The organization of the movement is very authoritarian and hierarchical, and there are strong sanctions against deviation from the accepted teachings and beliefs. Converts to Krishna give themselves completely to the movement—they surrender both their material possessions and their previous identity (symbolized by such practices as shaving the heads of males and wearing the orange or yellow Hindu robes). Devotees arise early in the morning and spend a long day meditating, chanting, and selling the books printed by the Book Trust.

The Jesus Movement

The Jesus Movement or Jesus People (pejoratively, Jesus Freaks—although members use this term among themselves) is actually not one group, but rather a number of fundamentalist groups with common characteristics. *Fundamentalist religious groups are those that believe in a literal interpretation of the Bible.* The Jesus Movement is an outgrowth of the Pentecostal movement in the United States, which can be traced at least to the early part of this century.[56]

Beliefs

Pentecostal groups emphasize certain beliefs and practices—the experience of "being personally saved" or "touched" by Jesus or the Holy Spirit; a literal interpretation of the Bible; emotional religious services; healing by "laying on of hands"; and glossolalia, or "speaking in tongues." The Jesus Movement, while different in some ways from other pentecostal groups, shares these beliefs and practices. Many Jesus groups have an apocalyptic view—that the world will soon end and only those who accept the proper beliefs will be saved. Because it is an outgrowth of American Pentecostalism, the Jesus Movement is not the radical departure from American tradition that the Krishna Consciousness movement is.

Lifestyle

In outward appearance, the Jesus People often resemble hippies or members of the counterculture —long hair and a "hippie" mode of dress. But the similarity ends there. The Jesus People emphasize love of God, love of country, and obedience to authority. Like the Krishna Consciousness movement, the Jesus People eschew alcohol, drugs, and promiscuity. The leaders tend to be authoritarian (sometimes they are former Pentecostal preachers) and heavily emphasize proselytizing in order to gain new members, which they see as "saving" them. They value intense emotional religious ex-

pression and a thorough knowledge of the Bible. There are numerous other religious groups with a similar orientation. For example, the "charismatic" movement has become a popular form of religious expression. Charismatic religions emphasize intense religious expression, a direct and individual relationship with God, speaking in tongues, and other forms of emotional religion. There has also been a growing popularity among fundamentalist religions that emphasize the "born again" experience—the convert's "rebirth" through personal experience of the Holy Spirit. One such group that has been quite successful employs the slogan "I found it!" emphasizing the personal discovery of Jesus. This particular group has utilized modern advertising techniques effectively to spread their beliefs and gain converts.[57]

The Unification Church

One of the newest, and possibly most controversial, of the unconventional religions is the Unification Church founded by the Reverend Sun Myung Moon.[58] The Reverend Moon is a Korean evangelist who claims to have had a revelation in 1936 (when he was sixteen years old) in which Jesus told him that he was a prophet who was to restore the kingdom of heaven on earth and prepare the world for the return of Jesus. The Unification Church was founded in Korea in 1954, and developed a following in Japan, Taiwan, and Europe. However, there were only a small number of American followers until the early 1970s, when Reverend Moon declared that he had another revelation in which God informed him that he should go to America because ". . . the will of God is centered upon America."[59] In 1976, the Unification Church had about 30,000 followers in the United States and operated 120 communal centers.

Beliefs

The teachings of the Unification Church are a mixture of Christianity, anticommunism, and some novel beliefs. Moon feels that he is a divine instrument who must spread the word of God and unify Christianity in the world. He is to prepare the world for the restoration of the kingdom of heaven on earth. Communism is viewed as Satan's plan to subjugate humankind. According to Moon, Adam and Eve were supposed to give birth to perfect offspring who would then constitute a perfect God-centered family. This family would serve as a foundation for a perfect nation, perfect society, and perfect world. However, Lucifer's seduction of Eve interfered with this divine plan. Moon's church is intended to overcome man's fallen nature and bring mankind back into a God-centered family. Only then will a truly united and harmonious society be possible. By adopting the Unification principles, this strong and perfect family, which is the foundation of a moral society, can be achieved, and then man's true destiny of constituting God's perfect creation will have been fulfilled.

Lifestyle

As with the other new religions, the Unification Church requires its members to work hard, lead an ascetic life, forego premarital sexual relations, and eschew the use of drugs, including tobacco and alcohol. Most members engage in street proselytizing (or "witnessing," as they prefer to call it) to attract new adherents. In becoming a member, a person usually attends a series of workshops, which consist of highly regimented indoctrination efforts through the use of films, entertainment, prayer, meditations, calisthenics, communal meals, group discussions, clean-up chores, and other activities closely regulated and supervised.

After joining the Unification Church, the person generally gives up all financial belongings. The group lives communally, and their highly regimented days include "witnessing," giving and listening to lectures, and both communal and private prayer. However, there are whole families who join the Unification Church and who do not live communally.

The Unification Church has a substantial financial base—in 1976 it took in about $24 million—deriving primarily from private contributions and the street sale of candles, candy, flowers, and other items by its members. Unlike those of many other religious movements, the teachings and practices of the Unification Church have potential political consequences in that the Reverend Sun Myung Moon envisions America as an instrument of divine providence. He is avowedly anticommunist, and some people feel an eventual goal of the movement is to gain some political influence or power. The church has sponsored activities with political implications, such as protests against North Korean admission to the United Nations, prayer rallies in support of President Nixon during the Watergate period, and against pornography. The Unification Church has even entered the secular realm through the sponsorship of international conferences on the unity of the sciences.[60]

Who Joins Unconventional Religious Groups?

The Emergence of Sects

While it is difficult for many to understand why American youth would spurn traditional ways for such unusual philosophies, we must recognize that such religious groups are common in America, both today and in the past. One reason for this is that any religion will find it difficult to satisfy all of its members. As religions become more established, they commonly change their policies in order to attract new members and gain acceptance by powerful groups in society. Often these changes include the adoption of less expressive and personally involving forms of religious practice. As a consequence, these churches often do not provide the emotional fulfillment or the intense feeling of religious experience that some members are seeking. Staid religious services and abstract religious doctrines are insufficiently inspirational for some people. People who gain gratification from forms of religion neglected by these established churches will begin to look elsewhere. Dissatisfied church members may break away from the church and seek out or form a sect that provides such satisfaction. **A *sect* is a small religious group that emphasizes intense and spontaneous religious expression, individual participation, the use of laypeople rather than professional clergy, and membership through**

some type of conversion. So, some unconventional religious groups, such as the Jesus People, can be understood as sects that have emerged because the established churches do not provide the satisfaction some young members are seeking.[61]

Deprivation

In addition to this tendency for sects to split from established churches as a form of protest, Charles Y. Glock, a sociologist who has studied religion extensively, points out "that a necessary precondition for the rise of any organized social movement, whether it be religious or secular, is a situation of felt deprivation."[62] **Traditionally, social scientists have explained the emergence of religious sects as due to** *economic deprivation:* **intense religious involvement appeals to economically deprived groups because it provides an explanation for their plight and a source of gratification in their lives.** Throughout history, religious sects have been popular among economically deprived groups. However, with many modern religious movements, this does not seem to be the case; their membership is largely youth from the middle class. **More important for these modern groups is** *ethical deprivation* **— a failure to reconcile the ideals of society with those of some group or individual, or a discrepancy between societal ideals and actual achievements.**[63] They attack the "establishment" for perpetuating war, racism, environmental pollution, sexual promiscuity, and hypocritical religious practices. They have established high ethical standards, and American society is not seen as living up to them. For example, practically all of the members of one group believed that American society was in a state of moral decadence.[64] Thus, religious sects can be appealing to the young because they provide a new and more desirable set of ethical values.

Another important type of deprivation is *psychic deprivation* **— the perceived lack of a meaningful system of values by which to understand, organize, and guide one's life.** It may involve a form of anomie or alienation and sometimes manifests itself through a confused or ambiguous self-concept — an experienced inability to define oneself positively in relation to other people or groups. Those experiencing psychic deprivation often engage in a quest for meaning or identity; many drift from one "trip" to another — e.g. political activities, drugs — and they sometimes join religious or mystical groups as a part of this quest. For example, one study of the Catholic Charismatic Renewal found that 88 percent of the members claimed that the Renewal gave their life meaning, purpose and order, while 49 percent claimed that the Renewal was the major source of their identity — their sense of themselves as important and worthwhile people.[65] A study of some members of the Krishna Consciousness movement and the Unification Church concluded:

Notwithstanding the strong faith of some, one of the frequently observed characteristics of many persons who join these new religions is that they often change faiths, going from one movement to another. The majority of those surveyed in both the Hare Krishna movement and the Unification Church indicate that they had been following other spiritual paths than those of their parents before they joined either of these movements.[66]

Thus, unconventional religious groups offer a meaningful system of values that is simple and strongly supported by others in the group.[67]

A final form of deprivation is *social deprivation* **— the degree to which one does not receive the prestige and social acceptance that one desires.** A common theme among recruits to extreme religious movements is a search for belongingness — a close relationship with others in a supportive environment in which they can provide mutual support through shared experiences. Many cannot find this at home or in school. The new status system of the religious group offers high prestige for one's new identity at the same time that it legitimizes one's rejection of other societal values.

Recruitment

Deprivation, while important, is not the only factor conducive to a person's becoming involved in a particular religious movement. One must also learn that others share one's concerns, that there is no other way to overcome this deprivation, and that there is a particular religious group that has a possible solution to one's problems.[68] The proselytizing of the various groups is important in this respect because they actively seek out such people, and thus the person experiencing some form of deprivation is more likely to learn of their beliefs. Another important factor in conversion is that the potential convert is often at a crisis point in life—he is dissatisfied with his current life, possibly drugs have taken their physical and mental toll, his life is disrupted and disjointed. The convert is often at a point of decision—he has quit (or been expelled from) school or lost his job. At this point the meeting of the proselytizer and the convert is the beginning of induction into the movement. He may not stay; he may not find it satisfying or compatible with other parts of his personality. However, many do find it compatible and become highly committed members.

The Unconventional Religions as a Social Problem

American society has not greeted the emergence of these groups with open arms. While many people view them as simply strange and slightly comical, some influential groups perceive them as a serious social problem that calls for some corrective action. There was particularly intense concern, following the mass suicide by over 900 followers of the Reverend Jim Jones's People's Temple in 1978, that religious sects were dangerous and ultimately destructive to both society and the individual. The interactionist perspective sensitizes us to the importance of people's perceptions of reality. Some people find intense, open, expressive religious practice offensive and the active proselytizing an infringement of their right to be left alone. The normative structure in American society discourages such outward religious expression, and the violation of these norms is disconcerting to many individuals.

There is concern among some groups that the unconventional religions may either directly or indirectly threaten the American way of life. For ex-

The Unification Church of Rev. Sun Myung Moon has generated considerable opposition by parents who believe that the Church has hypnotic powers over its followers. Some parents have resorted to kidnapping and deprogramming their children in order to win them back.

ample, some feel that the leaders of movements such as the Unification Church have an almost hypnotic power over their followers and can "brainwash" their young recruits into rejecting not only traditional religious and social values but also their families. From the functionalist perspective, a group with such powers could seriously threaten the ability of the American family to raise its young in a fashion supportive of the dominant religious institutions and beliefs. The frustration and anguish of parents whose children have rejected their values and beliefs in favor of such groups is real and intense. Many parents have turned to "deprogrammers" to win back their children. *Deprogramming* is the intense effort—often carried out continually for days—to subject converts to harsh criticisms of their movement and to a barrage of traditional religious beliefs with the goal of returning the recruits to the fold of traditional religion and family. In some cases, parents have gained support from the courts for their deprogramming efforts by convincing the courts to make their children—even those over the age of twenty-one and thus legally adults—wards of their parents for the specified period of time. In this way, the parents hoped to win their children back to their previous way of life. Other parents have resorted to kidnapping their children in order to deprogram them.[69]

The conflict perspective emphasizes the struggle over scarce and valued resources, such as political and economic power. In the case of certain new religions, such as the Unification Church, some people fear that the Church has extraordinary powers to gain control over their followers that might result in a potent force in the struggle over resources. Many of these religious groups have demonstrated an ability to accumulate significant economic resources. The Unification Church has already engaged in some political activities, and there is speculation, based on some evidence, that the Church has been involved in lobbying and other political activities for the Korean government.[70] From the conflict perspective, then, these groups will be defined by some people as a social problem because they appear to threaten the political and economic resources of other groups in society.

However, there is another side to these religious movements that must be considered: the converts quite commonly lead hard-working, morally impeccable lives that represent a considerable transformation from their previous way of life.[71] For some converts, the religious group has instilled in them a sense of purpose and confidence that was lacking before. To the extent that this is the case, then we must consider the possibility that such religions perform an important social function—they are able to provide a meaningful and purposeful way of life for people who do not find this in conventional society. There is little question that converts to these religions are hard-working people and that

they do not contribute to other social problems such as crime or drug abuse.

COMMUNES IN AMERICAN SOCIETY

Modern-Day Communes

A *commune* is a social arrangement in which the primary bond is some form of common sharing (e.g. of property or possessions), rather than blood or legal ties; the degree of sharing can vary considerably between communes. While most of the nineteenth-century American communes died out, a few have managed to survive and prosper.[72] For example, in 1974, there were approximately 23,000 Hutterites scattered among 150 communities in North America. The Old Order Amish (the most conservative Amish group), who originally emigrated to America in the early 1700s, have in the past two decades begun fourteen new communities in Minnesota, Iowa, and Missouri. Despite these few continuing successes, communal societies declined after the Civil War, and by the turn of the century only a few were left. However, in the 1960s there was a resurgence of communal activity in the United States—in fact, the last two decades constitute the second peak period of communal development in the United States. It is difficult to estimate the number of communes in existence today. One estimate suggests that there were about 2000 communes in *urban* areas alone around 1970. Others place the number of rural and urban communes at several thousand. While there is disagreement over precise numbers, there is little debate that the number of communes has increased over the past two decades.[73]

The Ideology of Communes

There is tremendous variation among communes in terms of the ideology or belief system that holds them together and provides their raison d'être. In fact, the three religious social movements discussed earlier are communal in nature. In order to acquaint the student with the range of communal ideologies, we will discuss briefly three modern American communes. A common thread that runs through most modern communes is their expressed dissatisfaction with conventional American society, and this serves to connect them to the counterculture already discussed.

The Farm

The Farm is a Tennessee-based religious commune that is very clearly an offshoot of the youth counterculture of the 1960s.[74] The Farm has a membership of more than 1400 men, women, and children. It was inaugurated in the late 1960s by people who had been active in the hippie subculture of the Haight-Ashbury district in San Francisco. After becoming disgusted with the violence and heavy use of drugs among the hippies, Stephen Gaskin, the founder and current leader of The Farm, gathered some people together and began traveling around the country, finally settling in Tennessee. While seeming to be a drastic departure from traditional American lifestyle, The Farm actually places great importance on many traditional American values. For example, it emphasizes hard work and good deeds for acceptance by the community. Much of the permissiveness of the hippie culture has been denied in favor of rigid rules—there is a ban on adultery, and faith is placed in the unchallenged authority of Stephen.

All property is shared communally. Work and childrearing, in which all members of the group participate, are considered spiritual disciplines. The common good is placed above individual needs and desires. Personal ambition and egotism are considered destructive vestiges of the society they have left behind, and all traces of these "sins" must be eradicated. The Farm refuses to accept government welfare. There is a ban on artificial means of birth control, abortion, coffee, alcohol, and drugs other than marijuana. Marijuana is considered a sacrament in their religion, which is a mixture of Eastern religions and Christianity.

Unlike many communes, The Farm has prospered. Originally, there was intense conflict between the commune and the surrounding commu-

nity, because the lifestyle and values of the communards seemed to be such a drastic departure from traditional American values. However, this conflict has been allayed to a large degree as the commune has demonstrated its willingness to work hard and cooperate with the conventional community. In fact, the ability of some successful communes to cooperate with the surrounding community may be due to the similarities in basic values between the two groups even though their outward lifestyles seem so different.

Morningstar Ranch

Many modern communes were formed around the belief that human nature is basically good but that people are corrupted by the rules and restrictions placed on them by society. Thus, some communes have begun with an almost anarchist aversion to rules of any kind. Morningstar Ranch in California gave everyone free access to the land. Some of their principles were as follows:

> God is the sole owner of the land and we, as his children, are not meant to fight, quarrel and kill over the land, but rather to share this natural resource—to each according to his needs . . . The land itself selects the people. Those who do not work hard to build shelter and provide for their basic needs do not survive on the land.[75]

Presumably, this lack of rules and structure would be compensated for by the fact that these unhindered individuals would understand what needed to be done and would voluntarily cooperate toward its achievement. With a social structure that was small and comprehensible by all, these communards believed, self-interest would give way to cooperative effort toward common goals—in fact, self-interest and the common good would be inseparable.

The Twin Oaks Community

Many communes found that the utopian visions of harmonious social relations presumed by communes such as Morningstar Ranch were simply unrealistic (see Table 18.3). Experience seemed quickly to teach them that a stable social order is

TABLE 18.3
Problems Experienced in Urban Communes in Boston, 1972[a]

PROBLEMS	NUMBER OF COMMUNES MENTIONING EACH PROBLEM
Disagreement over housekeeping responsibilities	17
Money	2
"Organizational"	5
Located in slummy neighborhood	2
Personality clashes	18
Communication	5
Men-women problems	4
Different goals	7
Clashing opinions on the degree of closeness members should have	6
Members were too idealistic to begin with	3
Integrating new members into the house	3
People staying only for the summer	2
Relationships with people inside the house versus relationships with people outside it	3
Children in the house	3
Members did not share a common interest	2
Problems stemming from a member who owned the house	3
Members came from broken relationships	2
Couples	1
"Members weren't as close as they could have been"	4

[a] from a study of 63 communes.

SOURCE. Table on page 487, "Problems Experienced in Communal Living" by Ann Hershberger, in *Communes*, edited by Rosabeth Moss Kanter. Copyright © 1973 by Rosabeth Moss Kanter. Reprinted by permission of Harper & Row, Publishers, Inc.

impossible without some established structure of authority, including some degree of organization, hierarchy, and the ability to coerce recalcitrant members. The experiences of the members of the Twin Oaks Community in Virginia illustrate some of these problems.[76] Many new communes have a labor problem—people are either unwilling to put in the long hours of arduous work necessary to make a community survive, or they rely on a belief in individual freedom and an abhorrence of rigid hierarchy. Twin Oaks determined very early that many members, if left to their own whims and desires, would do little or no work and that essential tasks would be left undone. They solved this through a complex system whereby people must sign up for various tasks and receive labor credits for their work. Each member must accumulate a certain number of labor credits in order to remain a member in good standing. They found that strong positions often seemed necessary—some laggard members were told to either work or leave. Many communes hope to function with little or no government, on the assumption that formal structures corrupt the basic goodness of human nature. The members of Twin Oaks attempted this and immediately ran into problems (one member refused to attend their first meeting). After a number of attempts, they finally established a formally organized governmental structure that was authorized to sanction members' behavior.

Members of other communes have also realized the importance of formal structure for the group to achieve its goals. However, many such groups at the same time emphasize the equitable distribution of both work and rewards and a lack of status distinctions. For example, a commune in central Oregon had a formalized process in which *all* of the adults (and the children in some cases) participated in making decisions about the management of the commune. These communards also restrict membership by evaluating each potential member in terms of his or her seriousness and compatibility with the other members.[77]

Whatever the communal form, members of the communes of the 1960s had one thing in common — a general dissatisfaction and disillusionment with American society. As one member of a rural commune in Maryland put it:

Oceana may not be perfect, but it's sure an improvement over the way they live out there. Let's face it, society is all fouled up. In their hearts, most people know it, but they're afraid to do anything about it— except talk. It's grotesque! Ever notice how two strangers strike up a conversation? They begin by griping to each other, and if they can both gripe about the same thing, their egos are inflated and it makes them feel good.

Well, you won't find that nonsense here at Oceana. When you join here, you leave your complaints on the outside.[78]

These remarks illustrate a dissatisfaction that is not focused on any particular issue, such as crime or bureaucracy, but that rather generalizes to all the things that seem wrong with American society. It is a reaction to a societal state of *anomie*. As with earlier communes in American history, many of the communes of the 1960s had a faith in the *perfectibility of man*—although society may be corrupt, individuals who are unfettered by social constraints and given the proper setting and encouragement can realize a utopian community. They were fleeing many of the problems discussed earlier in this chapter, hoping to create a society free of the evils of technocratic, bureaucratic society.

Who Joins Communes?

Membership in communes is influenced by many of the factors mentioned previously in relation to the religious movements.[79] There is commonly some sort of felt deprivation along with the opportunity to learn about and participate in the commune. Of course, in the underground communication network of the counterculture, the existence of various communes is spread through word of mouth and by underground newspapers. In this manner, those who might be interested in joining can learn what various communes are like, how restricted or free they are, whether they admit new members, and the kind of person that is likely to be admitted.

While there are many different types of people in communes, sociologist William Kephart found that modern communes tend to be particularly attractive to certain types of people[80]: (1) **The Parent Haters**—many members harbor resentment and hostility toward their parents. Parents are a common topic of discussion in communes, and some members use their membership in the commune (and not informing their parents of their whereabouts) as a means of getting back at them. (2) **The Deep Feelers**—some members feel very strongly about certain problems in American society, whether or not they have been personally affected by them. Their intense feelings lead them to search out a setting, such as communal life, in which these problems can be attacked and resolved. (3) **The Noncompetitors**—some in Amer-

ican society find competition abhorrent, they see it as a destructive social relationship, in which someone must inevitably suffer. These people, who are often quiet and kindly, find the noncompetitive atmosphere of communes very appealing. (4) **The Borderliners**—some communes are attractive to drug addicts, alcoholics, or people with some personality disorder who find it difficult to function in the larger society. The commune is seen as a retreat or haven in which hostility from family members or from others cannot affect them. The openness and freedom of some communes make such an aberrant lifestyle acceptable.

Communes as a Social Problem

Communes appear to many people to represent a fundamental departure from traditional American values and lifestyle. According to the interactionist perspective, such a departure is at the core of defining a condition as a social problem. Some feel that communes generate disrespect for the family and for the larger society. Communes are sometimes joined as an expression of hostility toward one's family; many communes do not maintain the traditional nuclear family structure predominant in the United States. These practices lead many Americans to view communes as a threatening social condition that must be alleviated before detrimental consequences ensue.

Other critics view communes as encouraging and perpetuating behavior patterns that are detrimental to the American way of life. These critics argue that communes encourage laziness, substance abuse, and licentiousness. While in fact communes that permit such a lifestyle among its members find it difficult to survive, some people view such behavior as the standard for communes rather than the exception. A related criticism is that communes are simply a haven for the maladjusted and those who cannot fit into the mainstream. Finally, some people view communes as a problem because their members presumably use government services and receive welfare funds but pay few taxes. Clearly, a person who believes some or all of these things about communes must view them as a social problem and feel that American society could benefit by their eradication.

According to the functionalist perspective, a condition is a social problem if it poses a threat to society. Yet, modern communes do not seem to pose the dire threat that some have predicted. As with the communes of the early 1800s, the recent communes have not had a substantial impact on conventional American society. The family has not collapsed; private property is not about to be swept away by the tide of communal arrangements; and licentious lifestyles have not flooded the land. So, from the functionalist viewpoint, communes do not seem to be a social problem. In addition, there are certain positive functions performed by communes that help maintain the status quo. For example, as was true of the nineteenth-century communes, modern communes provide an alternative lifestyle for those who are dissatisfied with the bureaucracy, industrialization, and increasing technology of American society. The frustration and anger of dissident elements in society is siphoned off in ways that seem to be harmless to the dominant institutions. Rather than becoming revolutionaries, criminals, or dropouts, those who join communes often end up working hard and contributing to the social order through the production and consumption of goods. Communes can also provide a temporary (or in some cases permanent) respite for people unsure about the direction of their lives or for people with psychological problems that need to be worked out.

FUTURE PROSPECTS

English novelist Charles Dickens characterized life in eighteenth-century England by saying "It was the best of times, it was the worst of times."[81] In so doing, Dickens expressed the ambivalence that many of his contemporaries felt concerning the fundamental changes that were occurring in England as a result of the Industrial Revolution. The Industrial Revolution promised increased levels of economic productivity and new heights of economic affluence. At the same time, it meant severe social dislocations and a radical redistribution of power and resources.

Some view modern American society in a similarly ambivalent fashion. We have achieved levels of affluence unheard of in human history and still out of the reach of most human beings. Our technology has reduced the amount and drudgery of work we must do to provide for ourselves. Our understanding and control of physical and biological forces has reduced human misery caused by starvation and disease and increased the ease with which we lead our lives. Yet, despite these advances, America is faced with some very serious social problems—some of the most important of which have been discussed throughout this book. In addition, as we have seen in this chapter, there are social movements afoot in America which, to one degree or another, reject the conventional lifestyle of America. It is these contradictions—between the affluent lifestyle available in America on the one hand and the problems and dissatisfactions on the other—that might lead some to refer to our modern times in the words of Dickens: "It is the best of times, it is the worst of times."

What is in store for America? In each chapter of this book, we have analyzed the future prospects of the specific problems under discussion. In this chapter, we have argued that American society is undergoing some very fundamental social and economic changes and that modern social movements can be understood, in part, as a reaction to those changes. We can first look at the prospects for the three social movements discussed in detail in this chapter, and then we can consider social movements in more general terms in relation to American society.

The Counterculture

What is the future of the counterculture? It seems clear that its heyday is pretty much over. The wide appeal it had in the late 1960s and early 1970s seems to have declined as economic recession has led to a greater concern among young people over jobs and security. There is some evidence that as people grow older they tend to drop out of countercultural groups in favor of more traditional lifestyles. Nevertheless, while some groups have fallen by the wayside, others have consolidated and formed viable alternative institutions. For example, The Farm (the religious commune in Tennessee) is one of the largest working communes in the United States. It emerged out of the countercultural ferment of the late 1960s and is now quite successful and prosperous. Other counterculturalists have gone into occupations from which they hope to bring about some change in American society. Some have thus entered law, urban planning, or social work with the hope of advocating the cause of the disadvantaged and changing the orientation of our economic system to favor the consumer, the poor, and the have-nots. Ralph Nader's Center for Law in the Public Interest and Common Cause (the consumer lobbying organizations) are probably the best known of such groups.

The counterculture, although it may remain small, may play a role in twentieth-century America similar to communes of the early nineteenth century. Thus, countercultural lifestyles, which emphasize noncompetitiveness and belittle material accumulation, may provide an alternative status system and set of values for those who do not find an economically rewarding job in the changing occupational market of postindustrial society and for those who experience downward social mobility associated with shifts in the American occupational structure. It is also possible that the impact of the countercultural movement is far from spent. However, the changes that it engenders will probably have little relationship to the forms of the counterculture in the late 1960s, and these changes may not even be recognizable for decades.

The Unconventional Religions

What is the future of unconventional religious groups in America? Since the counterculture, from which so many of their converts came, is not nearly as extensive as it was a decade ago, it is possible that these groups will find it more difficult, in their present form, to attract sizable numbers of recruits. However, many of the conditions of deprivation we discussed are still widespread among American youth. The recent popularity of the Unifi-

cation Church may be a reflection of this. So, such religious groups will probably persist for some time in American society.

However, there is some evidence that some of these religions are beginning to make accommodations with other groups in American society. Some components of the Jesus Movement are beginning to develop rapport with established religious groups. Some segments of the Krishna Consciousness have begun to relax their rigid dress code by allowing members to wear traditional American garb and not shave their heads. This process of accommodation and institutionalization is common among social movements. In order to survive and recruit more members, it can become expedient to compromise with the beliefs and practices of conventional religions. In so doing, of course, some changes in the orientation of the movements are probably inevitable. However, this is truly a matter of compromise between the traditional church and the sect because the traditional church may also make changes in its practices in order to retain its appeal to a broad-based following. Thus, both the sect and the conventional church may be changed in the process. Some of today's new religions will undoubtedly continue to thrive and attract members. At the same time, the conventional religions in America may have to make some accommodations in order to retain their broad-based appeal.

Communes

What is the future of the communal movement in the United States? As we have seen, communes have existed throughout our history. While most have succumbed after a very short period, a few have managed to survive for a reasonably long time. Sociologist Rosabeth Moss Kanter has found certain characteristics in common among successful communes.[82] First, they have distinct membership practices—they are very selective about who is allowed to join, and they do not permit nonresident members. In this way, membership is restricted to those who are highly committed to the group and who have a large investment (in terms of time, energy, and emotion) in it. Second, successful communes hold regular rituals or ceremonies that encourage group contact and reinforce the values that hold the group together. While these rituals are often of a religious nature, decision-making sessions or regular meetings to discuss common concerns can perform the same function. Third, successful communes tend to isolate themselves to a greater extent from the society at large than do nonsuccessful communes. Fourth, a commune must be economically successful in order to survive. This does not mean that it need be prosperous but rather that it provides material goods at a level acceptable to the members. In the modern era, this commonly means making some accommodation with the surrounding community so that communal members can hold jobs in the community or sell their goods to the members of the community.

What is the likely outcome of the recent upsurge of communal arrangements? Kephart's summary seems to be a reasonable projection:

Many—probably most—of the present-day communes will succumb. After all, our society and our family system have much to offer. To survive, communes must be competitive: they must satisfy basic human needs as well as or better than the larger society. Many of them have not done this, hence their demise.

It is unlikely, however, that the communal movement will die. The more successful groups may not only survive but may actually provide a permanent supplement to our standardized way of life. Much

Some segments of the Krishna Consciousness have begun to relax the strict dress code imposed on its followers. This illustrates how some unconventional religious groups find it expedient to compromise their beliefs and practices in order to attract new members.

depends on the social organization, leadership, and commitment of the particular commune. These are the crucial elements, and only time will tell whether they can be made to work.

While the future of the American commune is thus speculative, one thing seems clear: the answer will be known within the lifetime of most readers.[83]

CONCLUSION

When a new lifestyle emerges in society—no matter how unconventional—it is essential to understand why and how it arose. There is little doubt that the social processes involved can be complex, and there is often much that we do not understand. We have attempted to shed some light on three contemporary social movements: the counterculture, unconventional religions, and communes. We will conclude with an evaluation of social movements in general from the three theoretical perspectives.

The functionalist perspective makes us aware that a new lifestyle may be performing some important functions for society. In earlier chapters, we have seen that activities viewed as undesirable by some—such as conflict, violence, and crime—often perform positive functions that help maintain the dominant values and institutions in society. In this chapter, we have seen that social movements may also perform such functions. There is little evidence at this point that they are seriously destructive of the dominant American value system and lifestyle. In fact, as Davis argues, these social movements may be an important mechanism of social change.[84] A wide variety of lifestyles can serve as a testing ground for various alternative ways of coping with problems in American society. They can alsso serve as a test to determine what changes will be acceptable to the influential groups in American society. Through the interaction between the dominant groups and the social movements, some type of accommodation will undoubtedly emerge. The precise form it will take is difficult to predict at this point.

Some social movements, rather than being harbingers of social change, are actually mechanisms by which members of groups that are unable to accept certain changes are accommodated. We have seen that communal movements have often performed this function. This, again, illustrates the fact that society is a complex mechanism of interrelated parts and that changes in one part of the system can bring about changes in other parts. Such major developments as industrialization and bureaucratization cannot occur without severe dislocations—many individuals and groups are negatively affected by such changes. Since these historical developments seem to be inevitable, some accommodation must be made for these dislocations.

From the conflict perspective, we realize that social movements may have different interests and values than do other groups in society. As we have seen, some conventional groups view these new lifestyles as a threat to their own way of life. Social movements often generate resistance and hostility that would seem out of proportion to their actual threat; however this strong reaction can be understood once we realize that the conventional groups perceive a threat to some of their basic values and institutions. The family, and its ability to pass on cherished values to offspring, is often one of the institutions seen as vulnerable to such social movements. While some might view the threat of such groups as minor, their influence and ability to survive should not be underestimated. If we look to history as a guide, we see that some social movements, which at their inception appeared rather weak and powerless, eventually gained considerable power and became one of the dominant groups in America. Thus, from the conflict perspective, we realize that there is a clash between dominant groups and newly emerging groups. In most cases, the dominant groups will prevail because they have considerably more resources with which to struggle. Howevever, on occasion, social movements will win out in the long run and make a significant impact on American society.

People have many personal reactions to unconventional social movements. Some we find acceptable; others we ignore; still others we find offensive. The interactionist perspective points out that groups base their beliefs and values on a shared consensus about what behavior is acceptable and what makes a person into a worthwhile human being. In other words, our conceptions of ourselves are tied to a consensus that exists in groups important to us. If other groups hold different beliefs and values—even if they are not a direct threat to our own—this can be unsettling because it suggests that our own beliefs and values are not the only one's that we might hold. In a diverse society such as our own, there will always be new social movements emerging, but the relationship between them and other groups in society will probably always be tentative: it is unlikely that such unconventional groups will be openly accepted. As the interactionist perspective points out, group membership is an important determinant of our own sense of self worth, and there will always be a tendency for people to view their own group as superior to other groups, especially new and unconventional ones.

GLOSSARY TERMS

Alienation
Automation
Commune
Crisis of legitimacy
Counterculture
Cultural lag

Deprogramming
Ethnocentrism
Fundamentalism
Identity crisis
Individualism
Laissez faire

Mass society
Protestant ethic
Sect
Social movement
Unconventional
Youth

REFERENCES

[1] Judith Hennessee, "Dropping Down: Is Lowering Your Career Expectations the Way to Raise Your Political Consciousness?" *Mother Jones* 2 (August 1977), p. 14.

[2] Ted A. Nordquist, *Ananda Cooperative Village: A Study in the Beliefs, Values, and Attitudes of a New Age Religious Community* (Uppsala: Borgstroms Tryckeri Ab, 1978), p. 94.

[3] J. Stillson Judah, *Hare Krishna and the Counterculture* (New York: John Wiley & Sons, 1974), pp. 112–113.

[4] See Joseph B. Perry, Jr. and M. D. Pugh, *Collective Behavior: Response to Social Stress* (St. Paul: West Publishing Co., 1978), pp. 221–222.

[5] See Robin M. Williams, Jr., *American Society: A Sociological Interpretation*, 3d ed. (New York: Alfred A. Knopf, 1970).

[6] Gerhard Lenski, *Power and Privilege: A Theory of Stratification* (New York: McGraw-Hill, 1966).

[7] John R. Gillis, *Youth and History: Tradition and Change in European Age Relations, 1770–Present* (New York: Academic Press, 1974), p. 2.

[8] Richard Flacks, *Youth and Social Change* (Chicago: Markham, 1971).

[9] Ibid., pp. 9–18, and John R. Howard, *The Cutting Edge: Social Movements and Social Change in America* (Philadelphia: Lippincott, 1974), pp. 163–165.

[10] Lenski, *Power and Privilege*, p. 407.

[11] See Seymour Martin Lipset, *Rebellion in the University* (Boston: Little, Brown, 1971), pp. 124–196.

[12] Quoted in Ibid., p. 128.

[13] See Philip G. Altbach and Patti M. Peterson, "Before Berkeley: Historical Perspectives on American Student Activism," in Philip G. Altbach and Robert S. Laufer, eds., *The New Pilgrims: Youth Protest in Transition* (New York: David McKay, 1972), pp. 13–31.

[14] See Roberta Ash Garner, *Social Movements in America*, 2d ed. (Chicago: Rand McNally, 1977), and John M. Mulder and John F. Wilson, eds., *Religion in American History: Interpretive Essays* (Englewood Cliffs, N.J.: Prentice-Hall, 1960), p. 335.

[15] Clifton E. Olmstead, *History of Religion in the United States* (Englewood Cliffs, N.J.: Prentice-Hall, 1960), p. 334.

[16] See William M. Kephart, *Extraordinary Groups: The Sociology of Unconventional Lifestyles* (New York: St. Martin's Press, 1976), and Garner, *Social Movements in America*.

[17] Ibid.

[18] Quoted in Rodney Stark, *Police Riots* (Belmont, Calif.: Wadsworth, 1972), p. 110.

[19] See Anson D. Shupe, Jr., Roger Spielmann, and Sam Stigall, "Deprogramming: The New Exorcism," *American Behavioral Scientist* 20 (July/August 1977), pp. 941–956.

[20] Fred Davis, "Focus on the Flower Children: Why All of Us May Be Hippies Some Day," in Jack D. Douglas, ed., *Observations of Deviance* (New York: Random House, 1970), pp. 327–340.

[21] Daniel Yankelovich, *The New Morality: A Profile of American Youth in the 1970s* (New York: McGraw-Hill, 1974).

[22] See Sigmund Nosow and William H. Form, eds., *Man, Work, and Society* (New York: Basic Books, 1962).

[23] Kenneth Keniston, *Youth and Dissent: The Rise of a New Opposition* (New York: Harcourt, Brace, Jovanovich, 1971).

[24] See E. K. Hunt, *Property and Prophets: The Evolution of Economic Institutions and Ideologies* (New York: Harper & Row, 1972).

[25] See Joseph Schumpeter, *Capitalism, Socialism, and Democracy* (New York: Harper & Row, 1972), and Flacks, *Youth and Social Change*.

[26] Peter Blau and Marshall W. Meyer, *Bureaucracy in Modern Society* (New York: Random House, 1971).

[27] David Riesman, *The Lonely Crowd* (New York: Doubleday-Anchor, 1953).

[28] Philip Slater, *The Pursuit of Loneliness* (Boston: Beacon, 1976).

[29] See William Kornhauser, *The Politics of Mass Society* (New York: The Free Press, 1959).

[30] William F. Ogburn, *Social Change* (New York: Viking

Press, 1950).

[31] See Max Weber, *The Protestant Ethic and the Spirit of Capitalism* (New York: Charles Scribners Sons, 1958).

[32] See Flacks, *Youth and Social Change.*

[33] William Ryan, *Blaming the Victim* (New York: Pantheon Books, 1971).

[34] Robert Wuthnow, *The Consciousness Reformation* (Berkeley, Calif.: University of California Press, 1976), p. 98.

[35] See Ibid., and Riesman, *The Lonely Crowd.*

[36] See Kornhauser, *The Politics of Mass Society,* and Melvin Seeman, "Empirical Alienation Studies: An Overview," in R. Felix Geyer and David R. Schweitzer, eds., *Theories of Alienation* (Leiden: Martinus Nijhoff, 1976), 265–305.

[37] See Flacks, *Youth and Social Change.*

[38] Robert N. Bellah, "New Religious Consciousness and the Crisis in Modernity," in Charles Y. Glock and Robert N. Bellah, eds., *The New Religious Consciousness* (Berkeley, Calif.: University of California Press, 1976), pp. 333–352.

[39] Milton Yinger, "Contraculture and Subculture," *American Sociological Review* 25 (October 1960), pp. 625–635.

[40] See Charles Reich, *The Greening of America* (New York: Random House, 1970), and Christopher Bone, *The Disinherited Children: A Study of the New Left and the Generation Gap* (New York: Schenkman, 1977).

[41] James L. Spates, "Counterculture and Dominant Culture Values: A Cross-National Analysis of the Underground Press and Dominant Culture Magazines," *American Sociological Review* 41 (October 1976), pp. 868–883.

[42] Ibid.

[43] Flacks, *Youth and Social Change,* p. 129.

[44] Wuthnow, *The Consciousness Reformation.*

[45] Bone, *The Disinherited Children,* p. 159.

[46] Theodore Roszak, *The Making of a Counterculture: Reflections on the Technocratic Society and Its Youthful Opposition* (New York: Doubleday, 1969).

[47] Flacks, *Youth and Social Change.*

[48] Kenneth Keniston, *Young Radicals* (New York: Harcourt, Brace, 1968).

[49] Ibid., p. 173.

[50] See Flacks, *Youth and Social Change,* and Wuthnow, *The Consciousness Reformation.*

[51] Spates, "Counterculture and Dominant Culture Values."

[52] See Glock and Bellah, eds., *The New Religious Consciousness;* Jacob Needleman and George Baker, eds., *Understanding the New Religions* (New York: Seabury Press, 1978); and Thomas Robbins, Dick Anthony, and James Richardson, "Theory and Research on Today's 'New' Religions," *Sociological Analysis* 39 (Summer 1978), pp. 95–122.

[53] See Judah, *Hare Krishna and the Counterculture.*

[54] *The Krishna Consciousness Movement is Authorized* (Bhaktivedanta Book Trust, 1975), p. 3.; see also Frederick Bird, "Charisma and Ritual in New Religious Movements," in Needleman and Baker, eds., *Understanding the New*

Religions, pp. 173–189.

[55] *The Krishna Consciousness Movement is Authorized,* p. 1; see also, Gregory Johnson, "The Hare Krishna in San Francisco," in Glock and Bellah, eds., *The New Religious Consciousness,* pp. 31–51; Howard, *The Cutting Edge,* pp. 205–207; and Bird, "Charisma and Ritual in New Religious Movements."

[56] See James T. Richardson, Mary W. Stewart, and Robert B. Simmonds, "Researching a Fundamentalist Commune," in Needleman and Baker, eds., *Understanding the New Religions,* pp. 235–251, and James T. Richardson and Rex Davis, "The Organization and Functioning of the Children of God," *Sociological Analysis* 37 (Winter 1976), pp. 321–339.

[57] See Frances R. Westley, "Searching for Surrender: A Catholic Charismatic Renewal Group's Attempt to Become Glossolalic," *American Behavioral Scientist* 20 (July–August 1977), pp. 925–940.

[58] See *Divine Principle* (Washington, D.C.: Holy Spirit Association for the Unification of World Christianity, 1974); Thomas Robbins, Dick Anthony, Madeline Doucas, and Thomas Curtis, "The Last Civil Religion: Reverend Moon and the Unification Church," *Sociological Analysis* 37 (1976), pp. 111–125; and Dick Anthony and Thomas L. Robbins, "The Effect of Detente on the Growth of New Religions: Reverend Moon and the Unification Church," in Needleman and Baker, eds., *Understanding the New Religions,* pp. 80–100; and Berkeley Rice, "Messiah From Korea: Honor Thy Father Moon," *Psychology Today* 9 (1976), pp. 36–47.

[59] Sun Myung Moon, *Christianity in Crisis, New Hope* (Washington, D.C.: Holy Spirit Association for the Unification of World Christianity, 1974), p. 65.

[60] See John Walsh, "Meeting on Unity of the Sciences: Reflections on the Reverend Moon," *Science* 189 (September 19, 1975), pp. 975–976; Robbins et al., "The Last Civil Religion"; and Anthony and Robbins, "The Effect of Détente on the Growth of New Religions."

[61] See Ronald L. Johnstone, *Religion and Society in Interaction* (Englewood Cliffs, N.J.: Prentice-Hall, 1975).

[62] Charles Y. Glock, "On the Origin and Evolution of Religious Groups," in Charles Y. Glock, ed., *Religion In Sociological Perspective* (Belmont, Calif.: Wadsworth, 1973), p. 212.

[63] See, for example, Westley, "Searching for Surrender," pp. 925–927, and Saul V. Levine and Nancy E. Sutter, "Youth and Contemporary Religious Movements: Psychosocial Findings," *Canadian Psychiatric Association Journal* 21 (October 1976), pp. 411–420.

[64] C. Lincoln Johnson and Andrew J. Weigert, "An Emerging Faithstyle: A Research Note on the Catholic Charismatic Renewal," *Sociological Analysis* 39 (Summer 1978), pp. 165–172.

[65] Ibid.

[66] J. Stillson Judah, "New Religions and Religious Lib-

erty," in Needleman and Baker, eds., *Understanding the New Religions,* pp. 206–207; see also Robert B. Simmonds, "Conversion or Addiction: Consequences of Joining a Jesus Movement Group," *American Behavioral Scientist* 20 (July–August 1977), pp. 909–924.

[67] See Ronald M. Enroth, Edward E. Erickson, and C. Breckinridge Peters, *The Jesus People: Old Time Religion in the Age of Aquarius* (Grand Rapids, Mich.: William B. Eerdsman, 1972).

[68] Glock, "On the Origin and Evolution of Religious Groups," and James T. Richardson and Mary Stewart, "Conversion Process Models and the Jesus Movement," *American Behavioral Scientist* 20 (July–August 1977), pp. 819–838.

[69] See Shupe et al., "Deprogramming," pp. 941–956, and Carroll Stoner and Jo Anne Parke, *All Gods Children: The Cult Experience – Salvation or Slavery?* (New York: Penguin Books, 1977).

[70] *The Detroit Free Press* (April 7, 1978), p. 9A.

[71] See Judah, "New Religions and Religious Liberty," pp. 201–208.

[72] See Richard Fairfield, *Communes, USA* (Baltimore, Md.: Penguin Books, 1971); John W. Bennett, "Frames of Reference for the Study of Hutterian Society," *International Review of Modern Sociology* 6 (Spring 1976), pp. 23–40; and Elmer Schwieder and Dorothy Schwieder, "The Paradox of Change in the Life Style of Iowa's Old Order Amish," *International Review of Modern Sociology* 6 (Spring 1976), pp. 65–75.

[73] Maren Lockwood Carden, "Communes and Protest Movements in the U.S., 1960–1974: An Analysis of Intellectual Roots," *International Review of Modern Sociology* 6 (Spring 1976), pp. 13–23, and Nordquist, *Ananda Cooperative Village.*

[74] Kate Wenner, "How They Keep Them Down on the Farm," *The New York Times Magazine* (May 8, 1977), p. 74ff.

[75] Quoted in Howard, *The Cutting Edge,* p. 201; see also Kenneth Lamott, "Doing Their Thing at Morningstar," in Rosabeth Moss Kanter, ed., *Communes: Creating and Managing the Collective Life* (New York: Harper & Row, 1973), pp. 133–141.

[76] Kathleen Kinkade, *A Walden Two Experiment: The First Five Years of Twin Oaks Community* (New York: William Morrow, 1973).

[77] Howard, *The Cutting Edge,* pp. 199–205.

[78] Quoted in Kephart, *Extraordinary Groups,* p. 284.

[79] See Andrew Rigby, *Alternative Realities: A Study of Communes and Their Members* (London: Routledge and Kegan Paul, 1974), pp. 176–227, and Nordquist, *Ananda Cooperative Village,* pp. 79–133.

[80] Kephart, *Extraordinary Groups,* pp. 287–292.

[81] Charles Dickens, *A Tale of Two Cities* (New York: Charles Scribners Sons, 1924), p. 1.

[82] Rosabeth Moss Kanter, "Commitment and Social Organization: A Study of Commitment Mechanisms in Utopian Communities," *American Sociological Review* 33 (August 1968), pp. 499–517.

[83] Kephart, *Extraordinary Groups,* p. 302.

[84] Davis, "Focus on the Flower Children," pp. 327–340.

SUGGESTED READINGS

Christopher Bone, *The Disinherited Children: A Study of the New Left and the Generation Gap* (Cambridge, Massachusetts: Schenckman Publishing Company, 1977).
A partisan view of the development of the youth counterculture of the 1960s and 1970s. It has a particularly detailed discussion of the ideology which fuels the counterculture.

Richard Flacks, *Youth and Social Change* (Chicago: Markham Publishing Company, 1971).
This book offers a detailed analysis of the role of youth and the effect of historical and sociocultural changes on the position of young people in modern America.

Roberta Ash Garner, *Social Movements in America,* 2d ed. (Chicago: Rand McNally Publishing Company, 1977).
An excellent analysis of social movements in America from the colonial period to the present. The author is particularly adept at relating the emergence of social movements to changes in the economic base of American society.

John R. Howard, *The Cutting Edge: Social Movements and Social Change in America* (Philadelphia: Lippincott, 1974).
The focus of this book is on contemporary American social movements. The discussion of each movement is brief, but informative.

Rosabeth Moss Kanter (ed.), *Communes: Creating and Managing the Collective Life* (New York: Harper & Row, 1973).
A comprehensive book of readings that covers a wide array of issues relating to communal life. It is especially good in analyzing the problems of survival that communes confront.

William M. Kephart, *Extraordinary Groups: The Sociology of Unconventional Lifestyles* (New York: St. Martin's Press, 1976).
A very readable and personalized account of a number of social movements, including the Amish, the Shakers, and modern communes.

Kathleen Kinkade, *A Walden Two Experiment: The First Five Years of Twin Oaks Community* (New York: William Morrow and Company, 1973).

A first-hand account of the beginning years of a commune that is still thriving. The author was one of the founders and provides many insights into the difficulties and pleasures of starting a commune.

Jacob Needleman and George Baker (eds.), *Understanding the New Religions* (New York: The Seabury Press, 1978).

A book of readings by sociologists, historians, theologians, and psychologists who are struggling to understand the resurging interest in unconventional religious practices among young Americans.

Questions
for Discussion

1. Social movements of many types have existed throughout American history. What role have these social movements played in society? How have they promoted or inhibited change in American society?

2. From the functionalist perspective, under what conditions would social movements be detrimental to society? When would they be beneficial?

3. From the conflict perspective, what groups in American society might view the social movements discussed in this chapter as a social problem? Why would they do so?

4. Using the interactionist perspective, what are the implications of the concept of ethnocentrism? How would ethnocentrism influence people's reactions to unconventional social movements? Would it be possible to overcome the influence of ethnocentrism on our attitudes and behavior?

5. In this chapter, a number of important changes in social and economic arrangements and in sociocultural values were discussed. What were these changes? How have these changes influenced the emergence of contemporary social movements?

6. What are the most likely explanations for the emergence of the youth counterculture? Modern communes? Unconventional religious movements?

7. What can we expect to happen to contemporary social movements in the near furture? Will they survive, prosper, or decline? Why? How have they influenced American society, and what influence will they likely exert in the future?

8. This chapter has argued that social movements and social change are related to one another. How are they related to one another? In what ways are social movements a catalyst of social change, and in what ways are they a reaction to social change?

Glossary

ABORTION Termination of pregnancy before the fetus is capable of survival as an individual. There are two types: (1) miscarriage, or the spontaneous expulsion of the fetus through natural causes, and (2) induced abortion, abortion through artificial means.

ABSOLUTE POVERTY A condition in which a family's income is below a fixed dollar cut-off point necessary for such basics as adequate food, shelter, transportation, and medical care.

ABSOLUTISM In the sociology of deviance, the belief that good and evil are two clearly discernible categories into which human actions can be classified.

ACTIVE EUTHANASIA "Mercy killing." Some overt act that brings death at a time a person chooses and is prepared to die.

ACTIVE LEISURE A category of leisure-time activities wherein those involved participate more and watch less.

ACUTE DISEASES Infectious diseases such as influenza and pneumonia, the major causes of death before this century, the onset of which is often dramatic and incapacitating.

ADULTERY A term (with legal implications) describing sexual intercourse by a married person with someone other than his or her spouse.

ADVERSARY SYSTEM A criminal justice system in which the accused (defendant) is presumed innocent until proven guilty in a court of law by the representative of the state (prosecutor).

AFFIRMATIVE ACTION Guidelines and programs provided by government departments to contractors and suppliers, recipients of government funds, and businesses engaged in interstate commerce as an attempt to overcome discrimination against minorities.

AGE-SPECIFIC BIRTH RATE The number of births per 1000 women in a specific age category.

AGISM The negative or pejorative image of, and attitude toward, an individual simply because he or she is old.

ALCOHOLIC A person who has become dependent on alcohol, who drinks more alcohol than the socially accepted norm for our culture, and whose excess drinking has damaged his or her health, relations with family and friends, and job performance.

ALIENATION A psychological state in which a person senses that he or she has no control over his or her social world, accompanied by the feeling of being an "alien" within that society. Symptomatic of alienation is a discrepancy between one's beliefs about how one should behave and his or her actual behavior.

ALIENATION FROM WORK A condition in which workers experience alienation because they are separated from ownership of the means of production and from control over the final product of their labor.

ALLOPATHIC PHYSICIANS A group of medical practitioners who rose to prominence during the late eighteenth and early nineteenth centuries and who advocated dramatic and invasive medical treatments.

ALTRUISTIC SUICIDE The type of suicide that most often occurs in groups in which great emphasis is placed on group identity and conformity and in which suicide is an acceptable alternative.

AMATEUR THIEVES Otherwise respectable persons who steal, or youthful offenders who commit crude and unsophisticated criminal acts.

ANDROGYNY The exploration of a broad range of role-playing possibilities in society to choose emotions and behaviors without regard to gender-role stereotypes.

ANOMIC SUICIDE The type of suicide that most often occurs in situations of confusion and contradiction such as periods of rapid social change, when there are no stable norms that guide and regulate individual behavior.

ANOMIE A state of "normlessness" in which the social norms are so inconsistent or changing so rapidly that people are unsure of what is expected of them and find it difficult to tell the difference between right and wrong.

ANTITRUST VIOLATIONS Business attempts to combine in the restraint of trade or to monopolize a segment of the economy.

AQUACULTURE The raising of fish and other aquatic food sources under artificial conditions.

ARITHMETIC MEAN An average calculated by dividing the sum of all values of a variable by the number of cases. The most widely used average, it is greatly affected by extreme cases.

ASSIMILATION The process by which a minority individual or group loses separate identity and is absorbed into the dominant culture.

ATOMISTIC FAMILY A term— used by sociologist Carle C. Zimmerman to describe the family in our industrial society—implying that the modern family is poorly integrated and losing its capabilities to perform important social functions.

AUTHORITARIAN PERSONALITY A set of personality traits characteristic of highly prejudiced people. Such persons have anti-intellectual attitudes, view the world in very rigid and stereotyped terms, are highly conventional in their attitudes, have a low level of tolerance for ambiguity, are preoccupied with power relationships, and are submissive to superiors but bullying to subordinates.

AUTHORITY Institutionalized power supported by the values of the group or society; power that is viewed as legitimate.

AUTOMATION The mode of production in which the whole system is controlled automatically by means of machinery.

AVERSION THERAPY A form of therapy that makes the taking of alcohol very unpleasant.

BAIL Money or credit deposited with the court in order to have an ar-

rested person released temporarily on the assurance that he or she will appear for trial.

BALANCE OF POWER A situation in which two nations are restrained from attacking one another because each knows that the other has the capability of destroying it.

BARRIO A Spanish word for a city district; widely used for Hispanic American ghettos.

BEHAVIOR THERAPY (BEHAVIOR MODIFICATION) A treatment of mental illness that assumes mental illness is learned. Behavior Therapy manipulates rewards and punishments in a setting in order to change behavior.

BIOACCUMULATIVE A characteristic of a substance such that an organism retains all it ingests rather than passing it off in wastes.

BLACK POWER A social movement based on an appeal to black Americans to liberate themselves from oppression by assuming control over their lives by controlling the economic, political, and social institutions that affect them.

BLOCK LEISURE TIME Free time of fairly long and continuous periods—days or weeks.

BLOCKED OPPORTUNITY thesis or hypothesis A theory, developed by Richard Cloward and Lloyd Ohlin to explain crime and delinquency, that maintains people are prone to crime, delinquency, or poverty when they have few, if any, other opportunities available to them.

CALVINISM A religious doctrine, stemming from the thinking of sixteenth-century theologian John Calvin, that is the origin of Puritan-based thought in America and, eventually,

the Protestant Ethic. Calvinism places emphasis on predestination and the philosophy that successful economic activity (work) is a desirable religious activity.

CANNIBIS SATIVA The scientific name for the marijuana plant.

CHARISMATIC TRUTH Knowledge allegedly possessed by someone with special powers; difficult to challenge effectively because people who possess it believe they have special insight others do not, either through their own charisma or that of a leader in whom they have great faith.

CHRONIC DISEASES Diseases that progress over a long period of time, often persist during a considerable part of a person's life, and frequently exist long before any symptoms are noticed.

CIVIL DISORDER Strife or turmoil that is relatively spontaneous and disorganized and whose goal is either not explicit or involves a fairly short-term change in some specific social condition.

CLASS CONSCIOUSNESS An awareness on the part of a social class that its members comprise a distinct group with common interests and goals.

CLITORAL ORGASM A term based on the Freudian distinction between clitoral and vaginal sexual climax. It is viewed as inferior to vaginal orgasm.

CODETERMINATION A plan instituted by some companies in Europe wherein workers are provided a voice in decision making by management.

COHABITATION A term sometimes used interchangeably with consensual union, applied to a couple living together in a sexual and emotional relationship outside marriage. The nonscientific phrase for cohabitation is usually "living together."

CO-MARITAL SEX A term employed to describe mate-swapping or other extramarital relations in which both spouses agree to participate.

COMMODITY RIOT A conflict over the inequitable distribution of resources and goods in society.

COMMUNAL RIOT A struggle between blacks and whites over a previously all-white, but now racially contested, residential area of a city.

COMMUNE A social arrangement in which the primary bond is some form of sharing (of property or possessions) rather than blood or legal ties. One kind of family arrangement that has some of the characteristics of the extended family, wherein a familylike group is intentionally created and designed to fulfill many functions once served by extended kinship networks in a preindustrial society.

COMMUNITY MENTAL HEALTH The treatment of mental illness that attempts to change the community or environment in which a person lives in order to improve individual functioning.

COMPREHENSIVE EMPLOYMENT AND TRAINING ACT (CETA) Legislation designed to deal with high unemployment and to give the unemployed needed experience and training.

CONFLICT A situation in which people or groups perceive themselves involved in a struggle over resources or values.

CONFLICT PERSPECTIVE A theoretical perspective on society which emphasizes that society is an arena where conflict over scarce but valued resources is a prominent fea-

ture of social life and a significant source of social change. From the conflict perspective, coercion and alliances between interest groups are the bonds that hold societies together.

CONFORMISM, conformity Adherence to rules. In the sociology of deviance, a mode of adaptation in which people accept the cultural goal of worldly success and use institutionally legitimate means to achieve that goal.

CONGLOMERATE A corporation that controls other companies in fields of production quite different from that of the parent company.

CONSENSUAL UNION An intimate relationship (usually between a male and female) wherein the partners involved agree to some type of organizational arrangement, such as living together, but do not enter a legal contract as in marriage.

CONTROLS Methods for excluding the likelihood that a third (or additional) variable or combination of variables might be influencing the relationship between two (or more) statistically correlated variables.

CORPORATION A legally created entity that is allowed to engage in business and is considered a "person" before the law, with certain rights and privileges that apply to any individual.

COUNTERCULTURE A set of beliefs and values in opposition to some of the dominant values in society.

CRAFTMANSHIP The feeling that stems from work when the person performing it receives a sense of intrinsic identity and reward from the final product; for the craftsman, there is no split of work and play, and the work determines and infuses his or her entire mode of living.

CRIMINAL A person convicted in a criminal court proceeding of a crime.

CRIMINAL ASSAULT The unlawful application of physical force to another person.

CRIMINAL HOMICIDE The unlawful killing of one person by another.

CRISIS OF LEGITIMACY An erosion in the belief that the established societal institutions should properly be respected by, and have control over, the citizenry.

CRISIS MEDICINE Treating people after they become ill, in contrast to preventive medicine, which emphasizes the prevention of illness.

CROWDING A person's perception that he or she has insufficient space. A subjective phenomenon in contrast to density, which can be measured objectively.

CRUDE BIRTH RATE The number of births occurring in a society in a given year per thousand people in that society.

Crude Birth Rate

$$= \frac{\text{births in a year}}{\text{midyear population}} \times 1000$$

CRUDE DEATH RATE The number of deaths occurring in a society in a given year per thousand people in that society.

Crude Death Rate

$$= \frac{\text{deaths in a year}}{\text{midyear population}} \times 1000$$

CULTURAL LAG A situation in which the beliefs and values of a group have not changed to keep pace with changes in technology or in forms of social organization.

CULTURAL RELATIVITY The approach to the study of cultures, societies, and social problems that assumes that no custom or convention is good or bad by itself, but must be viewed in terms of the whole culture within which it exists.

CULTURE OF POVERTY thesis or hypothesis The notion that the long-term poor often share common cultural characteristics and values that separate them from other groups in society and make it difficult for them to struggle out of poverty.

CURANDERA A traditional folk-healer in Mexican American communities.

CYCLICAL THEORY A theory according to which change occurs in large historical cycles and proceeds in a deterministic pattern.

DECENTRALIZATION People, business, and industry moving away from the city center and out beyond its political boundaries.

DECRIMINALIZATION Removing the criminal penalties attached to an act and making it a misdemeanor punishable by a fine.

DEFICIT FAMINE A food shortage in which there are no food supplies elsewhere to make up for local shortages.

DEFINITION OF THE SITUATION A perception and interpretation of a social encounter based on an individual's view of reality. If people define a situation in a certain way, that —for them—is reality and they will behave accordingly.

DEINSTITUTIONALIZATION The elimination of institutions for juveniles (or adult offenders) and their replacement with other modes of treatment.

DEMOGRAPHIC TRANSITION The changing patterns of birth and death rates brought about by industrialization. A theory that the growth rate

of a population tends to decrease and stabilize once a certain level of economic development has been achieved.

DENSITY Density is measured by the number of people in a given space. An objective phenomenon that is in contrast to crowding, which is subjective in nature.

DEPENDENCE The experience of distinct withdrawal symptoms, either physical or psychological, following the discontinuance of a drug.

DEPERSONALIZATION The feeling of detachment from people or social groups that gives life meaning and provides a sense of importance and self-worth.

DEPRESSANTS Drugs that depress the central nervous system and result in drowsiness, sleep, decreased alertness, and the lowering of inhibitions.

DEPROGRAMMING The process of subjecting converts to unconventional religions to harsh criticisms of their movement and to a barrage of traditional religious beliefs. The goal is to return the recruits to the fold of traditional religion and family.

DESALINIZATION The removal of salts and other minerals from sea water.

DESCRIPTIVE STATISTICS Attempts to condense and summarize numerical data in a clear and convenient form without attempting to derive broader generalizations from them. Averages are examples of descriptive statistics.

DESERTIFICATION The transition of previously nonarid land to deserts.

DEVIANCE Socially disapproved behavior that exceeds the limits of

community tolerance and for which, if detected, there is a high probability that the "deviant" will be punished.

DISCRETIONARY TIME A term used by French work and leisure expert Joffre Dumazedier to describe leisure.

DISCRIMINATION Negative treatment of people because of their membership in a minority group. Minorities traditionally have been discriminated against and denied the opportunities open to many other Americans.

DISPLACED HOMEMAKERS Women who are widowed, divorced, or separated and lack job skills that would enable them to support themselves at a satisfactory level.

DISREPUTABLE POOR A term used to refer to people who remain unemployed during periods of nearly full employment.

DISTRIBUTION FAMINE A food shortage that exists in a particular province or region although there is sufficient food elsewhere.

DIVERSION Efforts to turn juveniles away from entry into the juvenile justice system and traditional programs for dealing with them.

DIVISION OF LABOR Specialization by particular individuals or groups in particular economic activities.

DOMESTIC FAMILY A term used by sociologist Carle C. Zimmerman to describe the ideal form of family, where interrelationships between the members are so strong that they prevent the problems arising from an overemphasis on individualism as happens in the atomistic family.

DOWNWARD DRIFT HYPOTHESIS The theory that, when a person becomes severely mentally disturbed, he or she cannot fulfill normal duties and obligations (toward work, family, and the like) and thus may drift into a lower-class lifestyle that has fewer demands.

DRUG ABUSE The regular or excessive use of a substance to the extent that, as defined by a particular group, the consequences are detrimental to a person's health, endangers his or her relationships with other people, or jeopardizes society itself.

DRUG ADDICTION A condition in which a person has developed tolerance for, true physical dependence on, and an intense craving for a drug.

DUAL WELFARE SYSTEM The notion that two welfare systems exist in the United States—one for the poor and one for the affluent.

DUE PROCESS of Law Safeguards in our legal system designed to protect individual rights and liberties. In reference to the juvenile court, due process involves the protection of the constitutional rights of children by making the juvenile court proceedings more like those of the criminal court than has traditionally been the case.

DYSFUNCTION A consequence of some act or condition that threatens the well-being of the social order, whether people recognize it or not.

ECOSYSTEM An area in which living organisms and nonliving substances interact with one another to produce an exchange of materials between the living and nonliving parts of the system.

EGOISTIC SUICIDE A form of suicide that results when important social relationships, such as marriage

or strong religious ties, do not exist to serve as social supports and constraints.

EMBEZZLEMENT A crime in which an employee fraudulently converts some of the employer's funds to his or her own use through alteration of the employer's records.

EMIGRATION Leaving an area or nation.

ENDANGERED SPECIES LIST A list of species thought to be near extinction.

ENVIRONMENT All the conditions and circumstances that surround and affect an organism or group of organisms.

ENVIRONMENTAL ETHIC A perspective on the environment placing great value on preserving the natural order.

ENVIRONMENTAL INDICATORS Measures of some physical, biological, or socioeconomic condition that relates to the environment.

ENVIRONMENTAL MOVEMENT A social movement in the United States that challenged the argument that continued environmental exploitation in support of business is essential to the nation's economic well-being.

ETHNIC GROUP A large number of people who share a common cultural heritage and sense of group identity and belongingness. Ethnicity is usually displayed in the traditions, values, beliefs, attitudes, customs, lifestyles, and personalities of individuals who identify with particular groups.

ETHNOCENTRISM The tendency to view one's own culture and customs as "right" and "best" and to

judge other cultures by one's own standards.

ETHOLOGY The study of the instincts and behavior patterns of a species in its natural environment.

EUTHANASIA A painless, peaceful death, a death with comfort, a death at the time a person chooses and is prepared to die.

EUTROPHICATION The increase of nutrients in the water so that abnormal plant growth with an adverse effect on fish population is promoted.

EXISTENCE TIME (nonwork obligations) Hours in the day that are spent responding to things our society and bodies demand from us—sleeping, eating, bathing, etc.—activities not required to earn a living but that we nevertheless feel obligated to do.

EXPERIENTIAL TRUTH Knowledge based on personal observation and on firsthand experience. Since how we observe and experience things is affected greatly by our values, beliefs, interests, and backgrounds, experiential knowledge is not highly reliable.

EXPRESSIVE FUNCTIONS Activities focusing primarily on such relationships between people as maintaining happiness, harmony, and emotional stability.

EXTENDED FAMILY A type of family organization most characteristic of preindustrial societies, usually consisting of a married couple, their children, and a number of other relatives (kin) who were likely to share a common domicile.

EXTERNALITIES Costs of production that the producer does not bear and are therefore not included in the cost of doing business.

EXTRINSIC MOTIVATIONS FOR WORK When an individual seeks rewards primarily outside the work context (and relies on work only for a source of income), that person has an extrinsic identification with his or her work.

FACT Something that has been observed to occur in the world. Facts do not speak for themselves, they must be interpreted.

FAMILISM A term used to describe the values regarding family life that were paramount in preindustrial society, specifically that the individual was always secondary to the welfare of the family unit.

FAMILY PLANNING Programs designed to encourage and aid couples to have children when and if they are desired.

FAMILY PRACTICE MEDICINE A medical specialty in which the physician receives advanced training in a broad range of medical areas and then provides continuity of medical care by coordinating and integrating the treatment of various specialists.

FECUNDITY The biologically maximum number of children a given population can produce. (In contrast to fertility, the actual number of births.)

FEE-FOR-SERVICE MEDICINE An arrangement in which the patient pays the doctor directly for each service or treatment provided.

FERTILITY The number of children born; the *actual* number of births to the average woman of childbearing age in a given society. (In contrast to fecundity, the potential number of births.)

FEUDALISM A type of society characterized by an elaborate set of norms, values, and legal statutes that bound serfs to their lords for succeeding generations.

FLEXITIME A system of scheduling that allows employees to start and stop work earlier or later than traditional company working hours.

FORCIBLE RAPE A crime in which the offender makes sexual demands that the victim does not consent to.

FRUSTRATION The inability to achieve some desired goal.

FRUSTRATION–AGGRESSION HYPOTHESIS A theory that assumes aggression to be a logical and expected consequence of frustration. When a person is frustrated from achieving a particular goal, tension develops within the individual; aggression either removes or destroys the obstacle to goal attainment or can serve to release tension even if the obstacle is not removed.

FULL EMPLOYMENT The economic view that a job should be available to everyone who wants one.

FUNCTIONAL PSYCHOSES Mental ailments that have no demonstrable organic cause but result in disturbances in thought, perception, and feeling. Social isolation is thought to be one of the sources of functional psychoses.

FUNCTIONALIST PERSPECTIVE A theoretical perspective on society that emphasizes society as a system composed of interrelated and interdependent parts, each of which contributes to the operation of the entire system. From the functionalist perspective, consensus (agreement on values and norms) and mutual dependence (interdependence of parts) are the bonds that hold societies together.

FUNDAMENTALISM The view held by religious groups that believe in a literal interpretation of the Bible.

GATEKEEPING The ability of the mass media (sometimes through an agreement with the government) to withhold information from the public or channel and control what the public sees and hears.

GENDER The biologically inherent features of sexual identity; *male* and *female* are gender-related terms.

GENERAL DETERRENCE The intimidation of potential lawbreakers by the example of punishment directed at a specific offender.

GENOCIDE The use of deliberate, systematic measures designed to exterminate an entire group or population. Jews in Nazi Germany and many Native American groups in the United States were victims of genocide.

GHETTO A part of a city in which the members of some ethnic or racial group live or are restricted to.

GREEN REVOLUTION Technological developments and the resulting increase in agricultural production caused by attempts to increase crop yields.

GROSS NATIONAL PRODUCT (GNP) A country's total output of goods and services. Based on the sum total of expenditures in society for personal consumption, investment or capital formation, government purchases of goods and services, and the extent to which exports exceed imports.

GROUP MARRIAGE An alternative form of family where the development of husband-wife–oriented ties between *all* adult members of the opposite sex is stressed.

HALLUCINOGENS Substances that produce an alteration in the individual's perception of reality.

HEAD START A program designed to deal with poverty by focusing primarily on preschool children from poor families.

HERMAPHRODITE A person born with both male and female physical sexual characteristics. (Hermaphrodites are nevertheless assigned to one sex at birth and develop the gender identity of that sex.)

HETEROGENEOUS Differing in structure or kind. Descriptive of a group, community, or society characterized by a variety of people who hold a wide range of different values, beliefs, norms, customs, and traditions.

HOLIST or Integrationist Referring to a philosophy of work and leisure emphasizing the belief that work and leisure are integrated and there is no clear separation between the two.

HOMEOPATHY A nineteenth-century approach to medicine based on the belief that "like treats like" and that extremely small doses of a drug are effective in treating illness.

HOMES FOR THE AGED Nonprofit, voluntary institutions run by religious groups, fraternal or benevolent organizations, and trust organizations for the benefit of their members.

HOMOGENEOUS Similar in structure or kind. Descriptive of a group, community, or society characterized by people who hold very similar values, norms, beliefs, customs, and traditions.

HOMOSEXUAL COMMUNITY A group of homosexuals engaging in common activities, sharing common values and interests, and having a feeling of unity.

HOMOSEXUAL LIFESTYLE A style of life characterized by frequent involvement in homosexual behavior, adopting a homosexual self-concept, and participating in the homosexual community.

HOMOSEXUALITY Sexual feelings, fantasies, or acts directed toward members of the same sex; a condition in which a person is sexually attracted to others of the same gender.

HOSPICES Homes for the care of the dying, designed to provide an environment conducive to a painless and dignified death.

HUMAN ECOLOGY The study of relations between human groups or populations and their environments.

HYPOTHESIS A tentative statement relating variables or their characteristics to each other.

IDENTITY CRISIS A situation in which an individual finds it difficult to develop a coherent and consistent self-concept based on the reactions of important people in his or her life.

IMMIGRATION Movement into an area or nation.

INCEST A crime involving sexual relations with a relative too closely related to marry legally.

INCOME MAINTENANCE PROGRAMS Poverty programs in which a person does not lose welfare payments equal to the wages earned.

INDICATORS Devices that state in observable terms precisely how differences or changes in the variable under study will be measured. A thermometer, for example, is an indicator of differences or changes in temperature.

INDIVIDUAL DISCRIMINATION Discrimination that occurs when a single prejudiced person acts out individual prejudical attitudes in his or her treatment of another person or group.

INDIVIDUALISM A belief system that places the individual as the most important object and argues that the individual has the sole responsibility for his or her own destiny. In the sociology of the family, the belief that the desires of the individual take precedence over those of the family unit.

INDUSTRIAL REVOLUTION The changes in social and economic organization that resulted when human societies changed from using hand tools as the primary mode of production to using machines and power tools.

INDUSTRIALIZATION The development and use of technology in a factory system.

INFANT MORTALITY Deaths of individuals under one year of age.

IN-KIND INCOME Nonmoney income such as government health care assistance and home-grown food.

INNOVATION In the sociology of deviance, a mode of adaptation in which people accept the cultural goal of worldly success but resort to socially disapproved means of achieving it.

INSTITUTIONALIZED DISCRIMINATION The inequalities that are rooted in the normal and impersonal operation of existing institutions in society and serve to discriminate against people because of their membership in a minority group.

INSTRUMENTAL FUNCTIONS Goal-oriented activities of a group—the tasks that must be accomplished in order for the group to survive.

INSURRECTION An organized attempt by some group to overthrow through violent means the existing government and replace it with alternative political arrangements and leadership.

INTERACTIONIST PERSPECTIVE A theoretical perspective on society that focuses on face-to-face interaction between individuals. From the interactionist perspective, shared definitions of social reality are the bonds that hold societies together.

INTEREST GROUP Any group organized to support the distinctive and joint concerns of its members.

INTERLOCKING DIRECTORATE Persons serving on the board of directors of two or more different companies.

INTERNAL COLONIALISM A situation in which a dominant group subordinates members of another group in its own country and exploits them for its own economic gain.

INTERVENING VARIABLES Variables that come between the original variables in a causal sequence.

INTRINSIC MOTIVATIONS for work When an individual seeks rewards that come from the nature of the work he or she does, that person has an intrinsic identification with the work.

KEPONE A chemical pesticide generally classified as a hydrocarbon like DDT.

KIBBUTZIM Israeli collective settlements. The kibbutzim are based on the common ownership of almost all property; all members are expected to contribute to the production of goods, which are then allocated on an equali-

tarian basis; and the community is run as a single economic unit, very much like one household.

LABELING THEORY A theory that explains deviant behavior in terms of a process through which some people are labeled "deviant." It focuses on the manner in which people's behavior is shaped by learned expectations.

LAISSEZ FAIRE The economic position that states that business should be permitted to function independently of government regulation and interference.

LATENT FUNCTION A consequence of some element of the social system that was unexpected or unintended.

LEGALISM In the sociology of deviance, the approach that emphasizes that an act may be considered a sin by some moral traditions but that it is not considered a form of deviance requiring social control by the state unless there is a secular law prohibiting it.

LEGALIZATION Making a criminal act no longer a violation of the law.

LEISURE Chosen, discretionary time—activity that is nonobligated and free from requirements.

LOAN SHARKING The lending of money at illegal, usurious rates.

MAJORITY GROUP A large number of people whose distinctive physical and/or cultural characteristics are considered superior in society and who thus have more power than other groups. White Anglo-Saxon Protestants and males are examples of majority groups in the United States.

MANIFEST FUNCTION An intended consequence of some event or institution.

MASS LEISURE An expression relating to the modern development that leisure time is no longer limited to a small elite but is available to practically everyone in society.

MASS SOCIETY A society in which individuals are unattached and isolated, with little control over important decisions made about their lives.

MASSIVE RETALIATION A foreign policy position based on the idea that a nation must be capable of inflicting debilitating damages on an enemy.

MAXIMUM FEASIBLE PARTICIPATION A policy emphasizing that poor persons were to be involved in the activities of the local community poverty agencies, not only as staff members but also on policy-making boards.

MECHANIZATION A production process that utilizes machinery rather than human hands to produce goods.

MEDIAN The midpoint in a series of cases. There are just as many cases with values below the median as there are above.

METHADONE A synthetic opiate used by herion addicts in government-sponsored treatment programs.

METROPOLITAN COOPERATION A form of metropolitan government in which the various units discuss common problems and solutions without the decisions made being binding on the members.

METROPOLITAN FEDERATION A form of metropolitan government in which one governmental body makes legislation in areas that affect the whole region. In this situation decisions are binding on all members of the unit.

METROPOLITAN GOVERN-MENT Political institutions that have jurisdiction over the whole metropolitan area and consolidate competing and overlapping government services.

MILITARY-INDUSTRIAL COMPLEX An informal network of relationships between the military and corporations that influence decisions about weapons systems.

MINORITY GROUP A group that (1) is subordinate in power to the majority, (2) can be distinguished on the basis of physical and/or cultural characteristics, (3) is collectively regarded as different and inferior, and (4) has fewer rights, privileges, and opportunities than the majority. Blacks, Native Americans, Hispanic Americans, women, and the aged are examples of minority groups in the United States.

MINORS IN NEED OF CARE Minors who are abused, neglected, or who in some other way require the care and supervision of the juvenile court.

MODE The most frequently occurring value in a series of values.

MODELING A type of learning that occurs when a person forms an idea about how to do something by observing others' actions.

MONOLITHIC CODE of family life A set of cultural beliefs that supported the extended family of preindustrial America. The monolithic code emphasized, among other things, marriage, children, and a strict division of labor between mates.

MONOPOLY Exclusive control of a product or service in a given area of industry.

MORBIDITY Rates of illness.

MORTALITY Rates of death.

MULTILATERAL MARRIAGE A term used to describe group marriage — where two or more males are each married to the same two or more females, with each male being married to all of the females in the group, and vice versa for females.

MULTINATIONAL CORPORATION A corporation that has a large commitment of resources in international business, engages in production and manufacturing in a number of countries, and has a worldwide perspective in its management and decision making.

MYTH OF SUPERABUNDANCE The belief that our resources are inexhaustible, historically an assumption that made wise management of the land and provident husbandry superfluous.

NARCOTIC A drug that provides relief from pain and can create a state of dependency in the user.

NEUROSIS An emotional disorder, less severe than psychosis, in which the person is extremely anxious about something but is able to retain a grip on reality.

NEW HEALTH PRACTITIONERS Health personnel (such as physican's assistants and nurse practitioners) who have the training and expertise to handle relatively simple medical problems and thus can relieve some of the burden on the physican.

NORM, SOCIAL NORM An expected way of thinking, feeling, and behaving that a group defines as appropriate. A rule regulating social behavior.

NUCLEAR FAMILY A type of family organization most characteristic of industrial societies, consisting of a married couple and their immediate children.

OEDIPAL COMPLEX Sexual feelings in a child (especially a male) for the parent of the opposite sex, usually accompanied by hostility to the parent of the same sex (generally manifests itself first between ages three and five).

OMBUDSMAN A person appointed to receive and investigate complaints made by individuals against abuses or capricious acts of public officials. In the sociology of medicine, a person whose function it is to protect and fight for the interests of the patient in a medical setting.

ONE-DIMENSIONAL SOCIETY A term coined by Herbert Marcuse to describe the condition he identified in our postindustrial society in which people's lives become so routinized and controlled that individuals find it almost impossible to have ideas and aspirations that permit them to organize their lives effectively.

ONE-PARENT FAMILY In the sociology of the family, a situation in which a divorced or legally separated person assumes custody of one or more children while choosing not to remarry.

OPEN MARRIAGE A term used by anthropologists George and Nena O'Neill to describe a marital relationship in which the partners are free to seek emotional, personal, and sexual gratification outside of the marital union.

ORGANIC PSYCHOSES Mental ailments that are the result of physical disorders or impairment. They often are the result of degeneration of the central nervous system, hardening of the arteries, and other physiological changes that accompany aging.

ORSHANSKY'S MEASURE OF POVERTY A definition of poverty, developed by Mollie Orshansky, based on a series of indicators related to nutrition and purchasing power, taking into consideration such factors as family size, number of children, age and sex of the head of household, and farm versus nonfarm residence.

OTHER-DIRECTED A term used to describe a trend in America toward people's becoming more concerned with how they appear to others and with popularity rather than with living up to internalized moral standards.

OVERLEGALIZATION The naive use, or misuse, of legal sanctions to deal with problems in cases in which other means, such as family socialization or community sanctions, would be more effective and appropriate.

PAIRISM An orientation toward the family in which neither familism nor individualism is paramount, but rather emphasis on the quality of a couple's interpersonal relationship.

PASSIVE EUTHANASIA Withholding of medical treatment that might prolong life.

PASSIVE LEISURE A category of activities wherein the people involved engage more in watching than in direct participation.

PLEA BARGAINING An informal deal, such as a reduced sentence in trade for a confession of guilt, between the prosecution and the defense in a criminal trial.

PLURALISM A pattern of intergroup relations in which a number of separate ethnic or racial groups coexist in the same society, each retaining a distinct identity and lifestyle while also participating in the larger culture.

POLICY CREATION Development of guiding principles and ideas that will serve as the foundation for a course of action.

POLICY IMPLEMENTATION The translation of policy into a specific course of action.

POLYANDRY A variation of polygamy; the situation in which a wife has two or more husbands.

POLYGAMY A general term describing a formal relationship involving one person with two or more spouses.

POLYGYNY A variation of polygamy; the situation in which a husband has two or more wives.

POPULATION The total number of people inhabiting a country, town, or other area at a given point in time.

POPULATION DYNAMICS The factors (mortality, fertility, migration) that influence population size.

POSITIVE CHECKS on population Factors, proposed by Malthus, such as war, pestilence, and famine, that cause death and hence reduce the existing population.

POSTINDUSTRIAL SOCIETY A term used to describe modern American society, implying a continuation of industrial activity but with, in addition, an expansion of service occupations and an increased reliance on computerized information and control systems that replace human labor.

POWER The opportunity existing within a social relationship that permits one person to carry out his will, even against the resistance of others.

POWER ELITE thesis or hypothesis A small network of powerful and influential individuals who are alleged to make the most important political and economic decisions in American society. According to C. Wright Mills, the upper-class leaders of the executive branch of government, the military, and major corporations who influence American foreign policy.

PREJUDICE An attitude of hostility or rejection held about a group considered different and inferior.

PREJUDICED DISCRIMINATOR The "true bigot" who is prejudiced and consistently discriminates against others on the basis of his or her prejudices.

PREJUDICED NONDISCRIMINATOR A person who is prejudiced against other groups but, because of social and legal pressures, is reluctant to translate his or her attitudes into action.

PREPAID GROUP PLANS (HEALTH MAINTENANCE ORGANIZATIONS) An arrangement in which the individual pays a monthly premium to a health organization which then provides, with no extra charge, all of that person's health care.

PRESENT-TIME ORIENTATION A tendency to seek gratification in the present and not worry about the future, the opposite of deferred gratification.

PRESSURE GROUPS Interest groups that actively seek to enhance their own interests through economic and political pressure and by persuading the public of the righteousness of their cause.

PREVENTATIVE CHECKS on population Factors, proposed by

Malthus, such as late marriage and celibacy, that reduce the birth rate and hence check population growth.

PREVENTIVE MEDICINE An emphasis on using medical science in the prevention of illness before it occurs. (In contrast to crisis medicine, which emphasizes treating people after they become ill.)

PRIMARY DEVIANCE The violation of social norms in which the person is not caught and labeled as a deviant and in which there is no threat to the person's image of himself as a nondeviant or the community's image of him as a respectable person.

PORNOGRAPHY Writings, pictures, movies, and such material intended primarily to arouse sexual desire.

PROFESSIONAL THIEVES Highly skilled and successful property offenders who use sophisticated and usually nonviolent means to commit crime.

PROJECTION A psychological defense mechanism in which the individual attributes to others characteristics that he or she is unwilling to recognize in himself or herself.

PROPAGANDA Information designed to persuade people to adopt a particular viewpoint in order to further the interests of the propagandist or those he or she represents. Propagandists use several techniques to persuade the public. "Bandwagon" is a method in which the propagandist attempts to build support of a particular product, person, or idea by creating the impression that everyone else is lending support. "Card stacking" is a technique in which facts are selected and arranged in such a way that the only conclusion that seems logical is the one that supports the propagan-

dist's point of view. "Glittering generalities" is a method of surrounding a candidate, product, or policy with attractive and commonly accepted but rather vague and meaningless words or slogans. "Name calling" is a technique in which the propagandist attempts to attach an unfavorable label to something he or she opposes. "Plain folks" is a method of identifying the propagandist's product or ideas with the "common person." "Testimonial" is a technique of using famous and respected people to make public statements favoring or opposing something. "Transfer" is a method of seeking approval for something by associating it with something else that the audience views favorably.

PROPORTION A special type of ratio in which the denominator is the entire group. For example, if there are 1 Native American, 2 white, and 2 black families in a neighborhood, the proportion of white families is 2/5 or 40 percent.

PROPRIETARY HOMES Commercial nursing homes intended to make a profit for the owner.

PROSTITUTION The relatively indiscriminate exchange of sexual favors in which the primary motivation and reward is economic gain rather than sexual or emotional gratification.

PROTESTANT ETHIC The belief that hard work, frugality, and asceticism are desirable, while leisure and excessive consumption are immoral. In modern times, the belief that all people should engage in some productive activity.

PSYCHOACTIVE DRUGS Chemical substances that affect the mind of the user.

PSYCHOSES Mental ailments involving severe personality disorders with loss of contact with reality, sometimes characterized by delusion and hallucination.

PSYCHOTHERAPY The treatment of mental illness in which a strong personal relationship is developed between patient and therapist, with the therapist attempting to gain insight into the patient's problems.

PUBLIC INTEREST ADVOCATES Groups that attempt to identify and rectify conditions in government and industry that do not benefit the public.

QUALITATIVE METHODS Research techniques based on the assumption that social phenomena are not numerical in nature, or that information is lost or distorted by putting it in numerical form.

QUANTITATIVE METHODS Research techniques that codify social data in numerical form.

RACE A large number of people who are considered a biological unity because they share genetically transmitted traits that are defined as relevant by influential groups in society.

RACISM An ideology (or belief) that justifies the domination and exploitation by one group of another that is viewed as different and inferior because of that group's physical and, often, cultural characteristics. Racism is a belief in racial superiority.

RACKETEERING The systematic extortion of money from persons or organizations such as business and labor unions.

RATE A special type of ratio in which the numerator is the number of times a specified kind of event occurs during a particular time period and the denominator is the whole number of times that it might have occurred.

RATE OF NATURAL INCREASE The difference between the crude birth rate and the crude death rate.

RATIO The relation in size between two numbers. A ratio commonly used in the social sciences is the sex ratio measured as the number of males in a population per 100 females.

REBELLION In the sociology of conflict, an uprising against authority. In the sociology of deviance, a mode of adaptation in which people reject both approved cultural goals and socially approved means and substitute new, disapproved goals and means.

RECIDIVISTS Repeat offenders. Most recidivists are returned to prison for the kinds of offenses for which they were first committed.

RECREATION A term derived from the Latin *recreare,* meaning to create anew, restore, refresh, and the refreshment of strength and spirits after toil.

REDLINING The identification of a neighborhood by a bank or other lending institution as a high-risk area and the refusal of the bank to lend money for the purpose of buying or improving a building in that area.

RELIABILITY A characteristic of an indicator. A reliable indicator measures consistently over time and from one situation to the next.

RELATIVE DEPRIVATION Feelings of deprivation that are related to some other person or group. Depending upon whom one compares himself with, a person earning $50,000 a year may feel deprived (poor) or may feel well off earning $10,000 a year. The perceived discrepancy between the economic and

social goals and values people feel they deserve and the goals and values they are actually able to achieve in their lives.

RELATIVE POVERTY A condition in which a family's income is below a poverty cut-off point based on a proportion of the median family income of some group, such as families in the United States or in some state or region.

RELATIVIST APPROACH In the sociology of deviance, the approach that assumes that no human act can be judged good or bad unless it is first placed within the context of the culture or subculture in which it occurred.

REORGANIZATION APPROACH to the family A way of viewing the institution of family wherein it is assumed that the family is *not* disorganized and deteriorating, but rather adapting to a rapidly changing society, and acts as a buffer between the individual and social organization.

REPRESENTATIVE SAMPLE A sample from a population in which people with the various characteristics important to the study are included in the sample in the same proportion as they are found in the population to which one wishes to generalize.

RESEARCH DESIGN A plan for conducting a research project.

RETREATISM In the sociology of deviance, a mode of adaptation in which people reject both socially approved goals and the socially approved means of achieving them.

REVENUE SHARING A federal program that returns to state and local agencies tax dollars collected by the federal government.

REVERSE DISCRIMINATION The belief that affirmative action policies and guidelines arbitrarily exclude qualified majority-group members from positions to which they are entitled by merit.

RITUALISM In the sociology of deviance, a mode of adaptation in which people abandon the goal of considerable worldly success but compulsively continue to use legitimate means of achieving their lowered aspirations.

SAMPLING BIAS A feature of a sampling procedure that introduces an additional variable (or variables) that influences the relationship between the assumed cause and effect variables.

SCAPEGOATING Placing the blame for one's troubles on an individual or group incapable of offering effective resistance.

SCHISTOSOMIASIS A debilitating disease, predominantly in the region of the Nile River, carried by snails.

SCIENCE The general method (or set of characteristic methods) by which knowledge is obtained through systematic observation.

SECONDARY DEVIANCE (CAREER DEVIANCE) Deviant behavior that the person adopts in response to the reaction of others to his or her primary deviance. It is regular or habitual and is regarded as deviant by both the person and his or her community.

SECT A small religious group that emphasizes intense and spontaneous religious expression, individual participation, the use of lay people rather than professional clergy, and membership through some type of conversion experience.

SECULARIZATION of society
The process by which traditional religious beliefs and institutions lose their influence in society. The rejection of the belief that God's will could explain all social conditions and that human nature is inherently wicked.

SEGMENTALIST (OR DIFFERENTIATION) view of work and leisure A view that emphasizes that work and leisure should be viewed as two separate spheres of a person's life and of the organization of society.

SELF-FULFILLING PROPHECY
A prediction about some personal or social behavior that influences the actual behavior, so that the prediction (prophecy) is confirmed by the result it has caused. Specifically, if we treat someone as a certain kind of person, he or she will subsequently begin to live up to our expectations.

SEMIPROFESSIONAL THIEVES Property offenders who engage in strong-arm robberies, hold-ups, burglaries, and larcenies that involve little detailed planning or careful execution.

SEPARATISM A pattern of intergroup relations in which the minority group makes efforts to break away from the dominant culture and establish a separate society. An ideology advocating separation.

SERIAL POLYGAMY A term used to describe the situation where men and women are married to only one person at a time (monogamy), but can be expected to be married to more than one person in a lifetime (usually as a consequence of divorce).

SEX ROLE Learned behavior concerning how to function as males and females in society; *masculine* and *feminine* are sex-role-related terms.

SEXISM The conglomerate of cultural values and social behaviors related to the belief that one sex is superior to the other and that makes it possible for one sex to dominate the other. Sexism is an ideology (or belief) that justifies the domination and exploitation by one sex of the other.

SEXUAL BARGAINING The process whereby men and women negotiate with one another for various rewards in social exchange.

SINGLE-PARENT FAMILY A family with one parent present. In the sociology of the family, a situation where a person elects to assume responsibility for one or more children (either biologically, as in a women becoming impregnated, having a child, or through adoption) without ever having married.

SOCIAL CAUSATION HYPOTHESIS of mental illness The hypothesis that the social and cultural environment in which the poor live is so stressful that it has negative effects on their mental health.

SOCIAL DISORGANIZATION APPROACH to the family A way of viewing the institution of family wherein the assumption is that it is in trouble and may even be collapsing.

SOCIAL ISOLATION The feeling or sense of exclusion from or rejection by groups around a person.

SPACESHIP EARTH A phrase used to portray the fact that the earth, like a spaceship, is a closed system with finite resources that, if depleted or destroyed, cannot be replaced.

SPLIT LABOR MARKET An economic arena in which there is a large differential in the price of labor for the same occupation. Within split labor markets conflict usually develops between three groups: business, higher-paid labor, and cheaper labor.

SPURIOUSNESS A statistical correlation between two (or more) variables that stems, not from a connection between them, but from the fact that each is related to some third (or additional) variable or combination of variables that does not serve as a link in the process by which one of the correlated variables leads to the other.

SOCIAL DIFFERENTIATION
Differences between people and groups that develop out of social interaction.

SOCIAL DISENGAGEMENT hypothesis of aging The process by which people make the transition to old age through mutual disengagement or withdrawal from society. This process has been viewed as a reduction in the number of roles and social relationships held by the elderly.

SOCIAL MOVEMENT A fairly well-organized, unconventional, and noninstitutionalized group that persists over time and functions to promote or resist change in society.

SOCIAL PROBLEM A social condition that an influential group sees as threatening its values and that may be remedied by collective action.

SOCIAL STRATIFICATION The structural inequality of entire groups and categories of people who have different access to social rewards and life chances because of their status (position) in the social hierarchy. An arrangment in which people ranked more highly receive greater rewards than those below them.

SOCIOBIOLOGY The study of the relationship between biology and social behavior. Sociobiology's central thesis is that animals behave in a fashion that will maximize the survival of their genes.

SPECIFIC DETERRENCE Intimidating individual offenders through punishment so that they will be afraid to commit further crimes.

STATISTICAL CORRELATION Expresses the strength of a relationship between two (or more) variables in mathematical terms, usually as a number called a correlation coefficient. Correlations of 0.3 indicate a weak relationship between the variables. Correlations above 0.6 indicate a stronger relationship A correlation of 0.8 or higher is considered quite high.

STATISTICAL INFERENCE A research process concerned with making generalizations based on a limited sample of cases drawn from a population.

STATUS OFFENDERS Minors who commit acts, such as truancy, incorrigibility, and running away from home, that are violations of the juvenile court's rules but not violations of criminal law.

STATUTORY RAPE A crime involving sexual contact between a male who is of a legally responsible age and a female who is a willing and voluntary participant but who is below the legal age of consent.

STEREOTYPE A set of traits or attributes (both positive and negative) that one group generally agrees are possessed by members of another group.

STIMULANTS Drugs that stimulate the central nervous system.

SUBCULTURE A group with norms, beliefs, and values distinct from those of the wider culture.

SUBCULTURE OF VIOLENCE A set of norms and values that con-

dones and legitimizes the use of violence under certain conditions. A subculture in which violence is viewed as an appropriate problem-solving technique under certain circumstances.

SUFFRAGE The right to vote. The social movement of the late 1800s and early 1900s aimed at obtaining the right to vote for women.

SYNDICATED CRIME Crimes conducted by large, organized groups of criminals who operate in more or less clearly defined territories and maintain contacts with corrupt public and law-enforcement officials.

TERRORISM The use of fear and intimidation by a group in order to achieve its goals by disrupting the normal operations of society.

THEFT The illegal taking away of another person's property without that person's consent and with the intention of depriving him or her of it.

THEORY A statement about the relationship between two or more conditions. Theories attempt to explain and predict relationships between variables (or indicators of variables).

THIRD-PARTY MEDICINE An arrangement in which the patient pays premiums into a fund and the doctor is paid from this fund when the patient receives treatment.

THOMSONIANISM A nineteenth-century approach to disease based on the belief that disease was caused by cold and could be cured by heat.

THREATENED SPECIES LIST A classification that allows some killing of animals.

TOLERANCE The experience of reduced effects from a particular dosage of a drug.

TRADITIONAL TRUTH Knowledge based on a belief in the validity of custom and traditional authority. Because traditional truth is backed by custom and authority (including the law in many instances), it is extremely difficult to challenge effectively.

TRANSSEXUALITY A condition in which a person possesses a fundamental feeling that he or she is or should be a member of the opposite sex.

TRANSVESTITE A person with a predilection for dressing as a member of the opposite sex but who does not feel a desire to transfer his or her biological identity to that of the opposite gender.

UNCONVENTIONAL group A group or social movement whose behavior deviates significantly from traditional American values and practices.

UNPREJUDICED DISCRIMINATOR A person who has no personal prejudices but may discriminate when it is convenient to do so.

UNPREJUDICED NONDISCRIMINATOR A person who accepts the formal values of American democracy and adheres to the ideal of equality in both theory and practice. Such a person is not prejudiced and does not discriminate against others.

URBAN HOMESTEADING Programs that make housing available to the poor at little or no cost, with the provision that they live in and make certain specified improvements on the property.

URBAN PLACE An area with 2500 or more residents within it or an area that is incorporated.

URBAN RENEWAL A federally supported program originally aimed at rehabilitating slums and providing low-cost housing for the urban poor.

VAGINAL ORGASM Based on the Freudian distinction between vaginal sexual climax and clitoral climax, vaginal orgasm is considered genuinely satisfying to the female while clitoral response is viewed as inferior.

VALIDITY A characteristic of an indicator. A valid indicator measures what it claims to measure. For example, a yardstick is a valid indicator of length but an invalid indicator of temperature.

VALUES Socially shared ideas about what is good, right, and desirable. Standards shared by members of groups that specify desirable needs, wants, and attitudes.

VARIABLES Properties or characteristics whose value or form can vary. Age, sex, race, religious affiliation, and social-class standing are examples of important social variables.

VERTICAL EXPANSION The control or ownership of firms that operate at different stages in the development of a product.

VESTED INTEREST GROUP A group that benefits in some fashion from the status quo (existing social arrangements).

VETO GROUPS Interest groups that can muster veto power over specific decisions.

VICTIMLESS CRIMES Offenses such as gambling, homosexuality, prostitution, and dealing in pornography that involve the willing exchange, among adults, of strongly demanded but legally prohibited goods or services.

VIOLENCE Physical force that might potentially injure people or destroy property.

VOLUNTARY ASSOCIATIONS Organizations that a person joins primarily by individual choice. Fraternal organizations, church groups, and community service organizations, are examples of voluntary organizations.

WHITE-COLLAR CRIMES Crimes committed by "respectable" citizens of high status in the course of their occupations.

WORK The necessary means that enables people to earn income for survival — obligated time.

WORK-RELATED TIME Activities that are closely related to work, even though not time spent on the job, such as traveling to and from work.

YOUTH An age category in modern industrial societies that includes people who are biologically mature (usually around age fifteen or sixteen) but who have not yet entered the adult world or the labor force as full-time participants.

YOUTHFUL OFFENDERS Minors who commit offenses for which, if they were adults, they could be tried in a criminal court.

ZERO POPULATION GROWTH (ZPG) A situation in which population size remains stable over time. The number of girls born just replaces the number of mothers, and this situation must continue for at least fifty years before the population would actually stop growing.

Photo Credits

Chapter 1
Opener: Joe Monroe/Photo Researchers.
4:   Lorant Collection, Pennsylvania Division, Carnegie Library of Pittsburgh.
15:   Ellis Herwig/Stock, Boston.
18:   Peter Southwick/Stock, Boston.
22:   Sybil Shelton/Monkmeyer.
30:   Charles Gatewood.
31:   Sidney Harris.

Chapter 2
Opener: Stephen L. Feldman.
40:   UPI.
41:   UPI.
44:   Sidney Harris.
45:   Daniel S. Brody/Stock, Boston.
47:   Jean-Claude Lejeune/Stock, Boston.
58:   Donald Dietz/Stock, Boston.

Chapter 3
Opener: George Gerster/Rapho-Photo Researchers.
70:   Jean-Claude Lejeune/Stock, Boston.
72:   Sidney Harris.
78:   Camilla Smith.
80:   Ron Benvenisti/Magnum.
86:   (both) UPI.

Chapter 4
Opener: John Garrett/Woodfin Camp.
106:   David Mangurian/UNICEF.
107:   Owen Franken/Stock, Boston.
120:   Jason Laure/Woodfin Camp.
122:   Rockefeller Foundation.
129:   Bernard Pierre Wolff.

Chapter 5
Opener: Harvey Stein.
142:   Charles E. Glover.
145:   Peter Menzel.
149:   Anestis Diakopoulos/Stock, Boston.
155:   Bruce Davidson/Magnum.
164:   Bill Pierce/Contact-Camp.
166:   Alain Dejean/Sygma.

Chapter 6
Opener: Stephen L. Feldman.
180:   Sidney Harris.
182:   Ellis Herwig/Stock, Boston.
188:   UPI.
194:   Courtesy American Airlines.
198:   Leif Skoogfors/Woodfin Camp.
203:   Arthur Grace/Sygma.
209:   Victoria Rouse/Sygma.

Chapter 7
Opener: Peter Menzel.
220:   State Historical Society of Wisconsin, Van Schaick Collection.
222:   Freda Leinwand/Monkmeyer.
226:   John R. Maher/EKM-Nepenthe.
228:   Photo courtesy of The National Broadcasting Company, Inc.
229:   Jean-Claude Lejeune/Stock, Boston.
244:   Peter Vandermark/Stock, Boston.

Chapter 8
Opener: Vic Cox/Peter Arnold.
263:   Chris Maynard/Stock, Boston.
269:   Emilio Mercado/Jeroboam.
274:   Culver Pictures.
283:   Sidney Harris.
287:   J. Berndt/Stock, Boston.

Chapter 9
Opener: Ira Kirschenbaum/Stock, Boston.
303:   Vince Compagnone/Jeroboam.
307:   Ellis Herwig/Stock, Boston.
311:   Charles Harbutt/Magnum.
315:   Charles Gatewood.
322:   Burt Glinn/Magnum.
327:   Peeter Vilms/Jeroboam.

Chapter 10
Opener: Stephen L. Feldman.
337:   Eve Arnold/Magnum.
344:   Patricia Hollander Gross/Stock, Boston.
346:   Bruce Davidson/Magnum.
351:   Cary Wolinsky/Stock, Boston.
359:   Sidney Harris.
361:   Ian Berry/Magnum.
364:   Jim Anderson/Woodfin Camp.

Chapter 11
Opener: Shelly Rusten.
375:   Library of Congress.
383:   Arthur Grace/Stock, Boston.
387:   Sidney Harris.
388:   George Gardner.
394:   Sybil Shelton/Monkmeyer.
401:   Steve Hansen/Stock, Boston.

Chapter 12
Opener: Bob Adelman/Magnum.
411:   Henri Cartier-Bresson/Magnum.
415:   Bettmann Archive.
416:   Jean-Claude Lejeune/Stock, Boston.
418:   Nicholas Sapieha/Stock, Boston.
427:   UPI.
430:   Sam Sweezy/Stock, Boston.
440:   Sidney Harris.

Chapter 13
Opener: Paul Fortin/Stock, Boston.
453:   (top) Arthur Siegel/U.S. Office of War Information; (bottom) Buffalo and Erie County Historical Society.
455:   Camilla Smith.
466:   Jim Ritscher/Stock, Boston.
472:   (left) Anestis Diakopoulos/Stock, Boston; (right) Cary Wolinsky/Stock, Boston.
476:   (top) Maje Waldo/Stock, Boston; (bottom) Owen Franken/Stock, Boston.
478:   Cary Herz.

Chapter 14

Opener: Owen Franken/Stock, Boston.
490: UPI.
493: UPI.
503: Daniel S. Brody/Stock, Boston.
511: Jim Anderson/Woodfin Camp.
514: Sidney Harris.
515: Michel Artault/Gamma Liaison.

Chapter 15

Opener: Yan Lukas/Photo Researchers.
529: © 1974. Used with permission of E.C. Publications, Inc.
534: Charles Gatewood.
542: Ellis Herwig/Stock, Boston.
545: Bob Adelman/Magnum.
547: Jan Lukas/Photo Researchers.
549: UPI.
552: George Gerster/Photo Researchers.

Chapter 16

Opener: Owen Franken/Stock, Boston.
568: Donald McCully/Magnum.
579: Sygma.
583: Courtesy Paramount Pictures Corporation.
586: Mark Godfrey/Magnum.
591: Sepp Seitz/Woodfin Camp.
592: Drawing by Handelsman; © 1978 The New Yorker Magazine, Inc.
595: Reproduced by Special Permission by PLAYBOY Magazine; Copyright © 1966 by Playboy.

Chapter 17

Opener: Hawkins/Sygma.
615: Kathy Bendo.
617: Bettmann Archive.
623: Peter Manzel.
633: Hawkins/Sygma.

635: Nicholas Sapieha/Stock, Boston.
637: Jim Anderson/Woodfin Camp.
642: Gamma.

Chapter 18

Opener: Jeff Albertson/Stock, Boston.
659: Arthur Grace/Stock, Boston.
661: Harvey Stein.
669: Shelly Rusten.
670: Shelly Rusten.
677: Rhoda Galyn/Photo Researchers.
684: Shelly Rusten.

Name
Index

Aberle, D. F., 21n, 33n

Adler, Freda, 544n, 545n, 561n, 562n

Adorno, Theodore W., 433, 444n

Alinsky, Saul, 88, 98n

Allen, George, 298

Allen, Irving Lewis, 93, 98n

Allen, Nancy, 555n, 563n

Allport, Gordon W., 432n, 434n, 444n

Alsofrom, Judy, 641n, 649n

Altbach, Philip G., 657n, 687n

Andersen, Ronald, 292n, 353n, 368n

Anderson, Gina S., 641n, 649n

Anderson, Odin, 292n, 353n, 368n

Anderson, Scott M., 232n, 254n

Angrist, Shirley S., 273n, 293n

Anslinger, H. J., 617

Anthony, Dick, 674n, 688n

Anthony, Susan B., 452

Antonovsky, Aaron, 103n, 110n, 133n

Apter, David E., 189n, 211n

Aptheker, Herbert, 428n, 444n

Archer, Dane, 509n, 519n

Ardrey, Robert, 496, 498, 518n

Argeriou, Milton, 638n, 649n

Aristotle, 613

Armor, David, 82, 97n

Armstrong, Gail, 579n, 597n, 606n, 607n

Arnhoff, Franklyn N., 279n, 293n

Ashley, Richard, 625n, 647n

Atchley, Robert C., 343n, 355n, 368n

Ault, Gary, 507n, 519n

Babbie, Earl R., 48n, 60n

Bach, Victor, 91n, 98n

Baden, M. M., 636n, 648n

Bahr, Howard M., 418n, 443n

Bailey, Kenneth D., 46n, 60n

Baker, George, 673n, 688n

Baker, Ross K., 429n, 444n

Bakke, Allan, 440

Baldwin, James, 503

Bales, Robert, 24n, 456, 482n, 640n, 649n

Balikci, Asen, 337n, 367n

Ball-Rokeach, Sandra J., 502n, 519n

Bandura, Albert, 500n, 519n, 640n, 649n

Bandura, Alfred, 580n, 606n

Banfield, Edward C., 71n, 73n, 74n, 78n, 97n

Barash, David P., 497n, 518n

Barbara, John, 594n, 607n

Barclay, Delores, 247n, 255n

Barcus, Earle F., 612n, 647n

Barker, Thomas, 592n, 607n

Barnet, Richard J., 178n, 191n, 210n, 211n

Bart, Pauline, 290n, 294n, 469n, 483n

Bartlett, John, 133n

Bateson, Charles, 494n, 518n

Bauby, Cathrina, 232, 254n

Becker, Howard S., 393, 405-406n, 532n, 535n, 560n, 622, 647n

Beckerman, Wilfred, 148n, 149n, 172n

Behrens, William V., III, 116n, 135n

Bell, Alan P., 51n, 60n, 538n, 539n, 561n

Bell, Daniel, 583n, 607n

Bellah, Robert N., 667n, 688n

Bellin, Seymour S., 279n, 293n

Bem, Sandra L., 479n, 484n

Benet, Sula, 336n, 337n, 367n

Benjamin, Harry, 544n, 561n

Bennett, John W., 678n, 689n

Bennie, E., 549n, 562n

Bequai, August, 585n, 586n, 607n

Berg, Alan, 124n, 134n

Berger, Briggitte, 308n, 330n

Berger, Peter, 9, 26n, 33n

Berkowitz, Leonard, 500n, 518-519n

Bernard, Jessie, 469, 483n

Best, Fred, 469, 483n

Bieber, Irving, 538n, 561n

Bienan, Leigh, 466n, 483n

Bierstedt, Robert, 13, 14, 33n

Biller, Henry, 473-474, 483n

Billet, Sanford L., 643n, 649n

Bird, Caroline, 231, 254n

Bird, Frederick, 673n, 688n

Bittner, Egon, 591n, 607n

Blair, Francine D., 452n, 482n

Blake, Judith, 112n, 113n, 130n, 133n, 134n

Blanchard, Dr. Jack, 161

Blau, Peter, 423, 443-444n, 665n, 687n

Blau, Zena, 350, 368n

Blauner, Robert, 252n, 255n, 436n, 444n

Bloch, Herbert A., 569n, 581n, 606n

Blumberg, Abraham S., 593n, 594n, 607n

Blumer, Herbert G., 26, 33n, 434n, 444n

Blumstein, Philip, 539n, 561n

Boeth, Richard, 440n, 445n

Bonacich, Edna, 436n, 444n

Bone, Christopher, 668n, 669-670n, 688n

Booth, Alan, 469n, 483n

Boulding, Kenneth, 143n, 150, 172n

Bouvier, Leon, 131n, 134n

Brannon, Robert, 460, 482n, 483n

Braude, Lee, 308, 311-312, 330n

Bray, Helen, 462n, 482n

Breed, Warren, 556n, 563n

Brenner, M. Harvey, 272, 293n

Brenton, Myron, 460n, 482n

Brewer, Marilynn B., 434n, 444n

Briggs, Shirley, 162

Brody, Jane E., 542n, 561n

Brooks, Richard Oliver, 93n, 98n

Brooks, Robin, 506n, 519n

Brown, Bertram S., 632, 648n

Brown, Elaine, 429

Brown, Lester R., 119n, 120n, 121n, 134n

Brown, Richard Maxwell, 489n, 492, 518n

Bryant, Anita, 526

Bullard, Dexter M., 549n, 562n

Burchinal, Lee G., 235n, 254n

Burgess, Ernest W., 87n, 98n

Butler, Robert N., 346n, 360, 361n, 368n

Button, James W., 438n, 445n, 488n, 518n

Cadwallader, Mervyn, 230, 254n

Caldwell, Lynton K., 150n, 172n

Caldwell, Robert G., 595n, 607n

Calhoun, John B., 115, 134n

Cameron, Mary Owen, 582, 607n

Campbell, Donald T., 434n, 444n

Candy, Sandra E., 355n, 368n

Carden, Maren Lockwood, 678n, 689n

Carnegie, Andrew, 44

Carroll, Charles R., 351n, 368n

Carson, John, 348

Carson, Rachel, 147, 172n

Carter, Barbara, 538n, 561n

Carter, Luther J., 187n, 189n, 211n

Carter, William A., 179n, 211n

Cassen, Robert, 129n, 134n

Cassidy, Joseph, 308n, 330n

Catanzaro, Ronald J., 637n, 649n

Caudill, H. M., 492n, 518n

Cavan, Ruth S., 582n, 596n, 607n

Chadwick, Bruce A., 418n, 443n

Chafetz, Janet S., 458n, 474n, 482n, 483n

Chambers, Carl D., 636n, 640n, 648n, 649n

Chambliss, William J., 529n, 560n, 597n, 608n

Chaplin, Charlie, 625

Chapman, Jane, 469n, 483n

Chavez, Cesar, 386, 398, 430

Chesler, Phyllis, 271, 293n, 463, 483n

Chesney-Lind, Meda, 596n, 607n

Chilton, Roland J., 577n, 606n

Chiricos, Theodore G., 574n, 606n

Chu, Franklin D., 279n, 293n

Clark, Kenneth, 433, 444n

Clark, Margaret, 280n, 293n

Clark, Terry, 76n, 97n, 145n, 172n

Clarke, Alfred C., 540n, 541n, 561n

Clever, Eldridge, 429

Clifton, A. Kay, 556n, 563n

Clinard, Marshall B., 527n, 560n, 584n, 607n

Cloward, Richard, 391n, 402-403, 405n, 406n, 534, 560n

Cockerham, William C., 271n, 293n, 557n, 563n

Coe, Rodney, 39n, 60n, 260n, 261, 265n, 292n, 356, 368n

Cohen, Albert K., 598, 608n

Cohen, Joel E., 76n, 97n

Cohen, Morris R., 42n, 60n

Cole, George F., 593n, 594n, 607n

Coleman, James S., 81, 82, 97n, 393n, 406n, 426n, 439, 444n, 445n

Collins, Randall, 23n, 225, 254n

Commoner, Barry, 147, 151n, 172n

Comte, Auguste, 7, 19, 33n

Conconi, Charles, 165n, 166n, 173n

Conklin, John E., 581n, 606n

Conot, Robert, 488n, 518n

Conrad, Peter, 627n, 648n

Constantine, Joan M., 245-246, 251, 255n

Constantine, Larry L., 245-246, 251, 255n

Cook, K. V., 454, 482n

Cooley, Charles H., 26n, 33n, 457, 482n

Coolidge, Calvin, 146

Coons, John E., 81n, 97n

Cooper, David, 228n, 254n

Cornehls, James V., 90n, 98n

Cortina, Juan, 429

Cory, Christopher T., 626n, 627n, 647n, 648n

Coser, Lewis, 23n, 33n, 495n, 504n, 518n, 519n

Cotton, Nancy S., 639n, 649n

Cowan, Edward, 185n, 211n

Coward, Barbara E., 392n, 405n

Cox, Oliver C., 436n, 444n

Crampton, Helen, 374n, 404n

Cranston, Virginia, 597n, 608n

Creighton, Lucy Black, 208n, 211n

Cressey, Donald R., 43n, 60n, 535n, 560n, 573n, 585n, 606n, 607n

Crocker, Thomas D., 148n, 149n, 172n

Cuber, John F., 221n, 227n, 249-250, 254n, 255n

Cumming, Elaine, 348n, 349n, 368n, 591n, 607n

Cumming, Ian, 591n, 607n

Cunningham, Horace, 594n, 607n

Currie, Elliott, 310n, 330n

Cutright, Phillips, 114n, 133n

Dahrendorf, Ralf, 24n, 33n, 391n, 405n, 495n, 518n

Dank, Barry M., 537n, 561n

Darwin, Charles, 498

Das Gupta, Prithwis, 130n, 134n

Dasmann, Raymond, 147, 172n

Datesman, Susan K., 598n, 608n

David, Deborah, 460, 482n, 483n

David, Henry P., 127n, 134n

Davies, James C., 500n, 518-519n

Davis, Alan J., 538n, 561n

Davis, Fred, 663, 685n, 687n, 689n

Davis, Keith E., 232n, 254n

Davis, Kingsley, 104, 112n, 113n, 133n, 376n, 389, 390, 404n, 405n, 544, 562n

Davis, Rex, 674n, 688n

Deans, Ralph C., 314n, 331n

DeGrazia, Sebastian, 302n, 315-316, 330n, 331n

deLeuw, Frank, 84n, 97n

Denfeld, Duane, 243n, 255n

Denney, Reuel, 323n, 331n

deTocqueville, Alexis, 505, 519n

Dickens, Charles, 682, 689n

Dinitz, Simon, 540n, 541n, 561n

Dole, Vincent, 642

Dollard, John, 433n, 444n, 499n, 518n

Domhoff, William G., 202, 211n

Dorn, Harold, 108n, 110, 111n, 133n

Doyle, Alfred Conan, 625

Dubin, Robert, 302n, 314, 330n, 331n, 346n, 368n

DuBois, William E. B., 428

Dubos, Rene, 266n, 292n

Duckworth, G. L., 354n, 368n

Duffy, John, 261n, 292n

Dumazedier, Joffre, 326, 331n

Duncan, Otis Dudley, 423, 443-444n

Dunham, H. Warren, 267n, 270n, 292n, 293n

Durkheim, Emile, 7, 19, 33n, 72n, 97n, 445, 482n, 529n, 532-533, 554, 560n, 563n

Dye, Thomas, 211n

Dymsza, William A., 190n, 211n

Dynes, Russell R., 540n, 541n, 561n

Ebbeson, Ebbe B., 437n, 444n

Eckerman, W. C., 628n, 648n

Edell, Laura, 591n, 607n

Edwards, Michael, 196n, 211n

Ehrlich, Anne H., 172n

Ehrlich, Paul, 124n, 131, 134n, 147, 172n

Eisdorfer, Carl, 278n, 293n

Eisenhower, Dwight D., 195-196

Ellinwood, Everett, H., 628, 648n

Elliot, Delbert S., 598n, 608n

Ellul, Jacques, 323, 327, 331n

Empey, Lamar T., 570n, 578n, 602n, 604n, 606n, 608n

Emrie, William, 320, 331n

Ennis, Phillip H., 576n, 606n

Enos, Darryl D., 285n, 294n

Enroth, Ronald M., 676n, 689n

Erickson, Maynard L., 578n, 600n, 606n, 608n

Erikson, Kai T., 386n, 405n, 527n, 560n

Erlanger, Howard S., 502n, 519n

Eve, Raynomd, 597n, 607n

Fainstein, Susan S., 76n, 97n

Fairfield, Richard, 247n, 255n, 678n, 689n

Falkson, Joseph L., 279n, 293n

Farber, Bernard, 229, 254n

Faris, Robert E. L., 267n, 292n

Farrell, Warren, 455n, 470, 471, 482n, 483n

Fasteau, Marc F., 462, 482-483n

Faught, Millard C., 317, 331n

Faulkner, William, 298

Faunce, William A., 319n, 331n

Feagin, Joe R., 392n, 405n, 411n, 443n

Federbush, Marsha, 463n, 483n

Fellmeth, Robert C., 194n, 211n

Ferdinand, Theodore N., 582n, 596n, 607n

Ferracuti, Franco, 502n, 519n

Ferretti, Fred, 546n, 562n

Feshbach, S., 501n, 519n

Fichter, Joseph H., 464n, 483n

Figlio, Robert M., 582n, 607n

Findley, Tim, 492n, 518n

Firey, Walter, 88n, 98n

Fisher, Tadd, 123n, 134n

Fiske, Edward, 79n, 97n

Flacks, Richard, 656n, 664n, 669n, 670-671, 672, 687n, 688n

Fleishman, Joel L., 208n, 211n

Flink, James J., 89n, 98n

Foner, Anne E., 347n, 350n, 355n, 368n

Foote, Caleb, 594n, 607n

Ford, Clelan S., 450n, 482n

Form, William H., 664n, 687n

Forslund, Morris A., 597n, 608n

Fort, Joel, 626n, 627n, 647n, 648n

Foucault, Michel, 273n, 293n

Fourier, Charles, 659

Francœur, Robert, 246, 255n

Franklin, Benjamin, 300

Frazier, Franklin E., 384n, 405n

Freedman, Jonathan, 115-116, 134n

Freeman, Jo, 475, 482n, 484n

Freud, Sigmund, 273, 458-459, 538n, 561n

Fried, Joseph P., 84n, 97n

Friedan, Betty, 474-475, 484n

Friedman, Richard C., 454n, 482n, 538n, 561n

Frieland, Roger, 76n, 97n

Friskin, Francis, 94n, 98n

Fromm, Erich, 313-314, 331n

Furst, Peter T., 630n, 648n

Fusfeld, Daniel R., 189n, 211n

Gagnon, John A., 540n, 541n, 544n, 561n

Galbraith, John K., 149

Galileo, 40

Galliher, John F., 617n, 647n

Gamson, William A., 503n, 519n

Gans, Herbert, 377n, 389-390, 404n, 405n

Gardner, John W., 208

Garner, Roberta Ash, 657n, 687n

Gartner, Rosemary, 509n, 519n

Gates, Margaret, 469n, 483n

Geiger, H. Jack, 279n, 293n

Geis, Gilbert, 585n, 607n

Gelles, Richard J., 549, 551, 562n

Gerard, Karen, 75n, 97n

Geyer, R. Felix, 309n, 330n

Ghandi, Indira, 102, 128

Giallombardo, Rose, 538n, 561n, 607n

Gibbons, Don C., 587n, 607n

Gibbs, Jack P., 600n, 608n

Gil, David G., 549n, 562n

Giles, Michael, 82n, 97n

Gillis, John R., 655n, 687n

Gilmartin, Brian, 243n, 255n

Gilpin, R. J., 192n, 211n

Gimlin, Hoyt, 314n, 331n

Gioleto, Silvio L., 158

Glazer, Nathan, 243n, 255n, 440n, 445n

Glazer, Nona, 466n, 483n

Glazier, William H., 260n, 292n

Glick, Paul C., 218n, 234, 254n

Glock, Charles Y., 676, 677n, 688n, 689

Godwin, Mills, Jr., 161

Goffman, Erving, 281n, 293n, 384, 405n, 535n, 560n

Golann, Stuart E., 278n, 293n

Goldman, Ralph M., 179n, 211n

Goldstein, Michael J., 546n, 562n

Goldstein, Sidney, 347n, 368n

Gomer, Robert, 151n, 153n, 172n, 173n

Goode, Erich, 619, 624n, 626n, 627n, 636n, 647n, 648n

Goode, William J., 338n, 339n, 367n

Gooding, Judson, 308n, 330n

Gordon, George N., 57n, 60n

Gordon, Marshall S., III, 602n, 608n

Gordon, Michael, 463n, 483n

Gordon, Milton M., 420n, 432n, 443n, 444n

Gornick, Vivian, 463n, 482n, 483n

Gould, Julius, 133n, 147n, 172n

Gould, Robert, 471, 483n

Gouldner, Alvin, 391n, 405n

Gove, Walter R., 271n, 293n

Graglia, Lino A., 82n, 97n

Graham, Saxon, 272n, 293n

Gray, Robert, 267n, 270, 292n

Green, Edward, 580n, 606n

Green, Mark J., 207n, 211n

Greenberg, Herbert, 308

Greer, Scott, 58n, 97n

Greven, Philip J., Jr., 339n, 367n

Grollman, Earl A., 557n, 563n

Gross, Edward, 302n, 330n

Gubser, Nicholas J., 337, 367n

Guggenheimer, Kurt J., 634n, 648n

Gunn, John C., 505n, 519n

Gupte, Pranay, 81n, 97n

Gurr, Ted Robert, 499n, 518n

Gusfield, Joseph R., 15n, 33n, 616n, 647n

Guttentag, Marcia, 462n, 482n

Gyllenhammar, Pehr, 306-307, 324, 330n, 331n

Hahnemann, Samuel Christian, 261

Hamer, Andrew Marshall, 91n, 98n

Hampson, J. G., 454, 482n

Hampson, J. L., 454, 482n

Handel, Judith D., 52n, 60n

Handel, Warren H., 426n, 444n

Handlin, Oscar, 180n, 211n

Handy, William, 581n, 606n

Hardin, Garret, 150n, 172n

Harrell, Adele, 398, 406n

Harrington, Michael, 12, 13, 33n, 383, 390n, 391, 392n, 403n, 405n, 406n

Harris, Robert, 376n, 404n

Harris, Sara, 544n, 562n

Harroff, Peggy B., 227n, 254n

Harshbarger, Thad R., 55n, 60n

Haskell, Martin R., 583n, 597n, 607n, 608n

Haskins, Jim, 639n, 649n

Hatton, Corrine, 557n, 563n

Hauser, Philip, 104n, 108n, 111n, 133n

Havighurst, Robert J., 393n, 406n, 425n, 426n, 444n

Hawkins, Homer C., 84n, 97n

Hawley, Amos, 66n, 74n, 96n, 97n

Hayes, L. F., 379, 405n

Hedblom, Jack H., 540n, 541n, 561n

Helfer, R. E., 549n, 562n

Hellinger, Douglas A., 189n, 190n, 211n

Hendricks, C. Davis, 343n, 356n, 368n

Hendricks, Jon, 343n, 356n, 368n

Henker, Barbara, 627n, 648n

Henley, Nancy, 464n, 483n

Hennessee, Judith, 654n, 687n

Henry, Andrew F., 502n, 519n, 555, 563n

Henry, W. E., 348n, 368n

Hessler, Richard M., 260n, 292n

Heyl, Barbara S., 543n, 561n

Hindelang, Michael J., 580n, 606n

Hines, Ralph H., 268n, 292n

Hingson, Ralph W., 613n, 647n

Hirschi, Travis, 48n, 60n

Hitler, 40

Hochschild, Arlie Russell, 360n, 368n

Holdren, John P., 124n, 134n, 147n, 172n

Hollenhorst, Jerry, 507n, 519n

Hollingshead, A., 267n, 292n, 393n, 406n

Holt, Glen E., 68n, 97n

Hoogenboom, Ari, 194n, 211n

Hook, Richard A., 168n, 173n

Hooker, Evelyn, 51, 60n, 538n, 539n, 541n, 561n

Horner, Matina, 461n, 482n

Horowitz, Irving Louis, 493n, 518n

Hout, Michael, 114n, 133n

Howard, James L., 547n, 562n

Howard, John R., 656n, 687n

Huber, Joan, 373n, 404n

Huggett, Dr. Robert, 161

Hundtofte, Virgil, 157, 159, 160

Hunt, E. K., 179n, 211n, 373n, 664n, 687

Hunt, Leon G., 640n, 649n

Hurt, Maure, Jr., 398n, 406n

Hurvitz, Nathan, 277, 293n

Illich, Ivan, 264n, 292n

Inciardi, James A., 363n, 648n

Inglis, Brian, 616n, 624n, 647n

Irelan, Lola M., 392n, 405n

Jacklin, Carol, 454n, 482n

Jackson, Robert, 156

Jaco, E. Gartly, 292n

Jacobson, Lenore, 393, 406n

James, Jennifer, 543, 544n, 561n, 562n

Jamison, Conrad, 358

Jankowski, Susan M., 612n, 647n

Janowitz, Morris, 490n, 518n

Jenkins, David, 325n, 331n

Jensen, Gary F., 597n, 600n, 607n, 608n

Jesus, 40

John, Martha T., 221n, 254n

Johnson, David R., 114n, 133n

Johnson, Elmer H., 581n, 606n

Johnson, Gregory, 673n, 688n

Johnson, Lyndon, 378

Johnson, Virginia, 459, 482n

Johnstone, Ronald L., 676n, 688n

Jones, Enrico, 270n, 293n

Jones, Hardin, 629n, 648n

Jones, Helen, 629n, 648n

Jones, Rev. Jim, 677

Judah, J. Stillson, 654n, 673n, 676n, 687n, 688n

Judson, Horace F., 641n, 649n

Justice, Blair, 550n, 562n

Justice, Rita, 550n, 562n

Kadish, Sanford H., 528n, 560n

Kahn, Herman, 327n, 331n

Kahn, Si, 398n, 406n

Kalb, Melvin, 645n, 649n

Kammeyer, Kenneth C., 113n, 114n, 133n

Kando, Thomas, 298n, 327-328, 330n, 331n

Kane, Robert L., 50n, 60n, 267n, 292n

Kant, Harold Stanford, 546n, 562n

Kanter, Rosabeth Moss, 247, 255n, 683, 689n

Kart, Cary S., 336n, 367n

Kassenbaum, Gene G., 538n, 561n

Kasteler, Josephine M., 267n, 292n

Kastenbaum, Robert, 355n, 368n

Kay, F. George, 250, 255n

Keil, Thomas, 638n, 649n

Keiser, Kenneth K., 374n, 404n

Keller, Mark, 636n, 648n

Kempe, Henry C., 548n, 549n, 550n, 562n

Keniston, Kenneth, 664n, 671, 672, 687n, 688n

Kephart, William, 658n, 660n, 681, 684, 685n, 687n, 689n

Kessler, Raymond G., 639n, 649n

Keyfitz, Nathan, 116n, 134n

Keynes, John Maynard, 390

Kiev, Ari, 277n, 293n

Killian, Lewis M., 428n, 429n, 444n

King, Martin Luther, Jr., 428, 444n

Kinkade, Kathleen, 680n, 689n

Kinloch, Graham C., 434n, 444n

Kinsey, Alfred C., 543n, 561n

Kinsie, Paul, 543n, 561n

Kirkham, George L., 45n, 60n

Kirkpatrick, George R., 548, 562n

Kirsch, Barbara A., 311n, 330n

Kitano, Harry T., 430n, 444n

Kitt, Alice S., 499n, 518n

Klatzky, Sheila, 79n, 97n

Klaw, Spencer, 281n, 283, 284n, 293n, 294n

Klein, Viola, 463n, 483n

Kleinman, Paula H., 642n, 649n

Kobrin, Frances E., 231n, 254n

Kolb, William, 133n, 147n, 172n

Koos, Earl L., 269n, 292n

Kornhauser, William, 665n, 666n, 687n, 688n

Kotelchuck, David, 288n, 294n

Kotelchuck, Ronda, 264n, 292n

Krauskopf, Joan, 469n, 483n

Kreps, Gary A., 505n, 519n

Kubler-Ross, Elisabeth, 362n, 368n

Kuehn, Lowell L., 583n, 607n

Kuhn, Margaret (Maggie), 365

Kusisto, K. V., 243n, 255n

Kutchinsky, Berl, 547n, 562n

Kwawer, Jay S., 538n, 561n

LaBate, Christina, 636n, 648n

LaGreca, Anthony J., 80n, 97n

Landis, Judson T., 235n, 254n

Laslett, Peter, 339n, 367n

LaSorte, Michael A., 468n, 483n

Lauer, Robert H., 8n, 33n, 426n, 444n

Laws, Judith Long, 461n, 482n

Leach, Barry, 644n, 649n

Leacock, Eleanor Burke, 392n, 405n

Leavitt, Helen, 90n, 98n

Lee, Alfred McClung, 58n, 60n

Lee, Dorothy E., 556n, 563n

Lee, Elizabeth Briant, 58n, 60n

Lefcowitz, Myron, 270n, 292n

Lekachman, Robert, 400

Lemert, Edwin M., 526n, 535n, 560n, 561n, 593n, 601n, 607n, 608n

Lengermann, Joseph J., 311n, 330n

Lenski, Gerhard, 655n, 656, 687n

Lester, Julius, 384n, 405n, 414n, 443n

Lever, Janet, 461n, 482n

Levin, Daniel U., 79n, 97n, 439n, 445n

Levine, Robert A., 399n, 400n, 406n

Levinson, Richard M., 466n, 483n

Levy, Leo, 270n, 293n

Levy, Sheldon, 448-449

Lewis, David, 105n, 108n, 126n, 133n, 134n, 551n, 562n

Lewis, M., 454n, 482n

Lewis, Oscar, 392n, 405n

Li, Wen Lang, 410n, 443n

Libby, Roger, 243n, 255n

Lilienthal, David, 150n, 172n

Lindahl, Martin L., 179n, 211n

Linden, Leonard L., 556n, 563n

Lindesmith, Alfred R., 617n, 263n, 634, 647n, 648n

Lion, Joanna, 292n, 353n, 368n

Lipetz, Milton E., 232n, 254n

Lipset, Seymour Martin, 656n, 687n

Liptzin, Myron B., 547n, 562n

Liston, Robert A., 494n, 518n

Lizotte, Alan, 502n, 519n

Lloyd, Robin, 543n, 561n

Loeb, Martin B., 393n, 406n

Loether, Herman J., 351n, 368n

Logan, Charles H., 600n, 608n

Lombroso, Cesare, 43, 60n

Luckenbill, David F., 580n, 606n

Luckmann, Thomas, 26n, 33n

Lyness, Judith L., 232n, 254n

Lynn, David B., 461n, 482n

Maccoby, Eleanor, 454n, 482n

McCord, Joan, 598n, 608n

McCord, William, 598n, 608n

McEvoy, James, 503n, 519n

McGeady, Paul J., 546n, 562n

McGlothlin, William H., 630, 648n

McGovern, George, 396, 430

McGrath, John H., 613n, 614n, 647n

McIntosh, Mary, 537n, 561n

Mack, J. A., 581n, 606n

Macklin, Eleanor D., 232n, 254n

McMillan, Sara, 462n, 482n

Maddox, George L., 339n, 343n, 367n, 368n

Mail, Patricia D., 425n, 444n

Malinowski, Bronislaw, 529n, 560n

Malthus, Thomas Robert, 22, 107-108, 110, 111, 114, 133n

Manard, Barbara B., 336n, 367n

Mangum, Garth L., 402n, 406n

Mankoff, Milton, 536n, 560n, 561n

Mann, Ada Jo, 398n, 406n

Mannheim, Hermann, 43n, 60n

Manning, Peter K., 45n, 60n

Marcuse, Herbert, 325, 331n

Marmor, Judd, 134n, 452n, 459, 482n

Marmor, Theodore R., 399n, 406n

Marsh, George Perkins, 146

Martin, Clyde E., 543n, 561n

Marx, Karl, 7, 24, 33n, 97n, 108, 109, 133n, 211n, 304, 308-309, 330n

Maslach, Christina, 437n, 444n

Masters, R. E. L., 544n, 561n

Masters, William, 459, 482n

Matthews, William H., 169, 170, 173n

Matza, David, 378, 405n, 535n, 560-561n

Maye, Pam, 462n, 482n

Mead, George Herbert, 26n, 33n, 457, 482n

Meadows, Dennis L., 116n, 134n

Meadows, Donella, 116n, 134n

Mech, David L., 168n, 173n

Mechanic, David, 272n, 280n, 293n

Meier, Robert F., 527n, 560n, 585n, 607n

Melman, Seymour, 196n, 211n

Merideth, Dennis, 473-474, 483n

Merton, Robert, 21n, 33n, 350, 435n, 444n, 499n, 502n, 518n, 519n, 533, 534, 560n, 572n, 606n, 671

Mesarovic, Mehajlo, 117n, 134n

Meyer, Jeanie Keeny, 439n, 445n

Meyer, Marshall W., 665n, 687n

Miller, Delbert, 145n, 146n, 170, 172n, 173n

Miller, Judith, 211n

Miller, Neal E., 433n, 444n

Miller, S. M., 377n, 405n

Miller, Walter B., 392n, 405n, 580n, 606n, 608n

Millett, Kate, 464, 483n

Mills, C. Wright, 10, 33n, 38, 60n, 199-202, 211n, 303-304, 323, 330n, 331n, 402

Mills, Virginia K., 464n, 483n

Mitchell, John, 57

Modlin, Herbert C., 363n, 648n

Moles, Oliver C., 392n, 405n

Money, John, 454, 482n, 539n, 561n

Montes, Alberto, 636n, 648n

Moody, Philip, 270, 292n

Moon, Sun Myung, 40, 662, 674-675, 688n

Moore, Joan W., 417n, 431n, 443n, 444n

Moore, Wilbert, 367n, 389, 390, 404n, 405

Moore, William, 157, 159, 160, 422n, 443n

Moran, Barbara K., 483n

Moran, Theodore H., 190n, 211n

Morgan, Marabal, 457, 482n

Morison, Samuel Eliot, 414n, 443n, 656

Morland, Kenneth J., 426, 444n

Morris, Jan, 460, 482n

Morris, M., 549n, 562n

Morrison, June, 594n, 607n

Moss, Frank, 612

Moss, H. A., 454n, 482n

Moynihan, Daniel P., 387, 399n, 405n, 406n

Muir, John, 146

Muller, Ronald E., 191n, 211n

Murray, Douglas R., 510n, 519n

Murtagh, John M., 544n, 562n

Musto, David F., 642n, 649n

Myrdal Gunnar, 391

Nader, Ralph, 207-208, 683

Nagasawa, R. H., 597n, 608n

Nagel, Ernest, 42n, 60n

Nass, Gilbert D., 250n, 255n

Nathan, Richard P., 91n, 98n

Needleman, Jacob, 673n, 688n

Neff, Walter S., 308n, 330n

Neithercutt, M. G., 582n, 607n

Newton, Huey P., 429

Nichols, Jack, 472-473, 483n

Nicot, Jean, 624

Nielsen, Aileen P., 463n, 483n

Nisbet, Robert A., 33n, 532n, 560n

Nixon, Richard, 57, 165, 399

Nordquist, Ted A., 654n, 687n

Norton, A. J., 218n, 254n

Nosow, Sigmund, 664n, 687n

Nutter, Richard W., 641n, 649n

Nye, Ivan F., 235n, 254n

Nyswander, Marie, 642

Oberschall, Anthony, 495n, 518n

O'Brien, David, 402, 406n

O'Connor, James F., 502n, 519n

Offir, Carole, 461n, 469n, 482n, 483n

Ogburn, William F., 223-224, 228, 250, 254n, 665n, 687n

Ohlin, Lloyd E., 391, 405n, 534, 560n

Olexa, Carol, 80n, 97n

Olmstead, Clifton, 657

O'Neill, Eugene, 615

O'Neill, George, 242, 243, 255n

O'Neill, Nena, 242, 243, 255n

O'Neill, William, 450, 482n

Orenstein, Alan, 46n, 60n

Orshansky, Mollie, 379

Orzack, Louis, 314, 331n

O'Shea, Robert M., 392n, 405n

Osmond, Humphrey, 274n, 293n

Osterhout, David, 165n, 166n, 173n

Otto, Herbert, 245n, 255n

Owen, John, 316, 331n

Pai, Dr. D. N., 102

Paine, Hebert J., 638n, 649n

Palen, John J., 75n, 85n, 97n, 98n

Parke, Jo Anne, 678n, 689n

Parker, Stanley, 330n

Parks, Rosa, 428

Parrillo, Vincent N., 431n, 440n, 444n, 445n

Parsons, Talcott, 14n, 33n, 225, 254n, 456, 495n, 518n

Pascarelli, Emil, 354n, 368n

Paul, Alice, 452

Payne, Les, 492n, 518n

Peck, Ellen, 219n, 248, 254n, 255n

Peck, Michael, 556n, 563n

Perry, Albert, 494n, 518n

Perry, Joseph B., Jr., 654n, 687n

Pestel, Edward, 117n, 134n

Peterman, Dan J., 232n, 254n

Petersen, William, 102n, 103n, 104n, 105n, 111n, 112n, 114n, 117n, 133n, 134n, 551n, 562n

Peterson, Patti M., 657n, 687n

Peterson, Warren A., 359n, 368n

Pettigrew, Thomas F., 434n, 444n

Phillips, William R. F., 46n, 60n

Pinchot, Gifford, 146

Pinkney, Alphonso, 414n, 429n, 443n, 444n

Pitman, David J., 581n, 606n

Piven, Frances Fox, 97n, 402-403, 406n

Platt, Anthony, 571n, 595n, 606n, 607n

Platt, Jerome J., 636n, 648n

Pleck, Joseph H., 472n, 483n

Plissner, Martin, 57n, 60n

Polk, Kenneth, 80n, 97n

Pomeroy, Wardell B., 543n, 561n

Poor, Riva, 317n, 331n

Porter, Cole, 625

Porter, Lyman W., 313, 331n

Portes, Alejandro, 278n, 293n

Poskocil, Art, 427n, 434n, 444n

Powell, John Wesley, 146

Prabhupada, Bhaktivedanta Swami, 673

Progrebin, Letty C., 461n, 482n

Propper, Morton, 645n, 649n

Pugh, M. D., 654n, 687n

Quinney, Richard, 571n, 584n, 600n, 606n, 607n, 608n

Racklin, Susan, 463n, 483n

Radzinowicz, Leon, 569n, 600n, 606n, 608n

Rainwater, Lee, 85n, 98n, 134n, 377n, 387n, 405n

Ramey, James, 245, 255n

Randers, Jorgen, 116n, 134n

Ravitch, Diane, 82n, 97n, 439n, 445n

Ray, John B., 90n, 98n

Ray, Oakley, 620, 621n, 623n, 647n

Redlich, F., 267n, 292n

Reeder, Leo, 272n, 293n

Reich, Charles, 668n, 688n

Reid, John D., 442n, 443n

Reid, Sue Titus, 601n, 608n

Reiffler, Clifford B., 547n, 562n

Reiman, Jeffrey H., 573n, 606n

Reiss, Albert J., Jr., 538, 561n

Reiss, Ira L., 251, 255n

Rejda, George E., 347n, 356n, 368n

Reppetto, Thomas A., 581n, 606n

Rheingold, H. L., 454, 842n

Rhodes, Robert P., 605, 608n

Rice, Berkeley, 674n, 688n

Richards, Victor, 362n, 369n

Richardson, James, 674n, 677n, 688n, 699n

Ridley, Carl A., 232n, 254n

Riesman, David, 203, 211n, 323, 331n, 665n, 687n

Rigby, Andrew, 681n, 689n

Riley, Lawrence E., 231n, 254n

Riley, Matilda White, 345n, 347n, 350n, 355n, 368n

Rink, Alice, 557n, 563n

Risenberg, Max, 155

Rist, Ray C., 546n, 562n

Roach, Jack, 376n, 404-405n

Robbins, Thomas, 674n, 688n

Robespierre, Maximilien, 493

Robin, Gerald D., 587n, 607n

Robinson, H. F., 119n, 134n

Robinson, William L., 168n, 173n

Roby, Pamela, 377n, 405n

Roe, A., 639n, 649n

Roebuck, Julian B., 592n, 607n, 639n, 649n

Rogers, A. J., 148n, 149n, 172n

Roosevelt, Franklin, 180, 265

Roosevelt, Theodore, 146

Rorabaugh, W. J., 637n, 648n

Rose, Arnold M., 204n, 211n, 359, 368n

Rosenblatt, Adylin, 354n, 368n

Rosenhan, David L., 281, 293n

Rosenthal, D., 538n, 561n

Rosenthal, Robert, 393, 406n

Ross, Philip, 491n, 518n

Rossell, Christine H., 82n, 97n

Rossi, Alice, 466n, 483n

Roszak, Theodore, 670, 672, 688n

Rothman, David, 273n, 293n, 374, 404n, 527n, 560n, 569-570, 571n, 602n, 606n, 608n

Rothschild, Emma, 310n, 330n

Rowitz, Louis, 270n, 293n

Roy, Della, 251n, 255n

Roy, Rustum, 251n, 255n

Rubel, Arthur J., 280n, 293n

Rubington, Earl, 526n, 560n

Rubin, Lillian B., 399n, 406n

Runciman, W. G., 499n, 518n

Rush, Benjamin, 261, 292n

Russett, Bruce, 507n, 508n, 519n

Ryan, William, 392n, 405n, 666n, 688n

Ryder, A. J., 494n, 518n

Sagarin, Edward, 539n, 561n

Sampson, Anthony, 191n, 211n

Samuelson, Paul A., 390n, 405n

Sanders, William B., 580n, 606n

Sandys, George, 624

Sargent, Alice, 462n, 464n, 482n, 483n

Sawyer, Jack, 472n, 483n

Scammon, Richard M., 403n, 406n

Scanzoni, John, 243, 255n, 456n, 482n

Scarpitti, Frank R., 598n, 608n, 613n, 614n, 647n

Scanzoni, Letha, 243, 255n

Schaefer, Richard T., 411n, 414n, 416n, 417n, 419n, 431n, 443n, 444n

Schafer, Walter E., 80n, 97n

Schafly, Phyllis, 456-457

Schaller, Warren E., 351n, 368n

Scheff, Thomas J., 275-276, 277n, 293n, 535n, 560-561n

Schelling, Thomas C., 582n, 607n

Schneider, Jan, 554n, 562n

Schneller, Eugene Stewart, 284n, 294n

Schrag, Clarence C., 582n, 607n

Schulz, David A., 387n, 393n, 405n 406n

Schultz, Stanley K., 68n, 97n

Schumacher, E. F., 166, 167, 173n

Schumpeter, Joseph, 664n, 687n

Schurz, Carl, 146

Schwartz, Pepper, 539n, 561n

Schweitzer, David R., 309n, 330n

Schwieder, Dorothy, 678n, 689n

Schwieder, Elmer, 678n, 689n

Scida, Joan, 638n, 649n

Sclare, A., 549n, 562n

Seaman, Barbara, 290n, 294n

Seattle, Chief, 138

Seeman, Melvin, 309n, 330n, 666n, 688n

Seifert, K., 473n, 483n

Sellin, Thorsten, 573n, 582n, 597n, 606n, 607n

Selvin, Hanan C., 48n, 60n

Seward, Georgine H., 450n, 482n

Shabecoff, Philip, 54n, 60n, 168n, 173n

Shankweiler, Penelope, 463n, 483n

Sheehy, Gail, 544n, 562n

Shepard, Jon, 310n, 330n

Sheppard, Nathaniel, Jr., 336n, 367n

Sherfey, Mary Jane, 459n, 482n

Sheridan, William H., 596n, 607n

Sherman, Lawrence, 592n, 607n

Sherrill, Robert, 510n, 519n

Shibutani, Tamotsu, 421n, 443n, 496n, 518n

Shields, Laurie, 382

Shorris, Earl, 419n, 443n

Short, James F., Jr., 502n, 506n, 519n, 555n, 563n

Shostak, Arthur, 314n, 331n

Shupe, Anson D., Jr., 662n, 678n, 687n, 689n

Sichel, Werner, 189n, 211n

Siegler, Miriam, 274n, 293n

Silberman, Charles, 384n, 405n

Simkus, Albert A., 422n, 443n

Simmel, Georg, 72n, 73n, 97n, 504n, 519n

Simmonds, Robert B., 674n, 676n, 688-689n

Simon, Julian L., 42n, 48n, 60n

Simon, Rita James, 466n, 483n

Simon, Robert L., 440n, 445n

Simon, William, 540n, 541n, 561n

Simonsen, Clifford E., 602n, 608n

Simpson, George E., 438n, 444n

Sindler, Allan P., 440n, 445n

Singer, J. David, 494, 501n, 519n

Singer, R., 501n, 519n

Skinner, B. F., 323, 331n

Skogan, Wesley G., 576n, 606n

Skolnick, Arlene, 219n, 221n, 224n, 225n, 232n, 243n, 254n, 255n, 482n

Skolnick, Jerome H., 310n, 330n, 588n, 607n

Slater, Philip, 665n, 687n

Small, Melvin, 494, 518n

Smart, Reginald, 644n, 649n

Smelser, Neil J., 495n, 518n

Smigel, Erwin O., 302n, 330n, 331n

Smith, Charles U., 438n, 445n

Smith, David E., 628n, 648n

Smith, Douglas A., 597n, 607n

Smith, Gerald W., 600n, 608n

Smith, James, 243n, 255n

Smith, Lynn, 243n, 255n

Smith, Robert B., 506n, 519n

Snyder, C. R., 640n, 649n

Soloway, Irving H., 642n, 649n

Sommers, Tish, 382

Sorkin, Alan L., 425n, 444n

Southwick, Charles H., 138n, 172n

Spady, Dale R., 412n, 443n

Spates, James L., 668n, 672n, 688n

Spencer, Herbert, 44

Spitzer, Steven, 531n, 560n

Spreitzer, Elmer, 231n, 254n

Stacey, Judith, 463n, 483n

Stamp, Kenneth M., 384n, 405n, 414n, 443n

Stanton, Elizabeth Cady, 452

Staples, Robert, 429n, 444n

Stark, Rodney, 504, 519n, 588n, 607n, 662n, 687n

Sterns, Marian S., 398n, 406n

Steffensmeier, Darrel J., 579n, 606n

Steinmetz, Suzanne K., 550n, 562n

Stevens, Robert Warren, 507n, 519n

Stewart, Mary W., 674n, 677n, 688n, 699n

Stockton, William, 612n, 647n

Stohl, Michael, 506n, 519n

Stoll, Clarice S., 454n, 455n, 482n

Stoner, Carroll, 678n, 689n

Strauss, Joseph, 418n, 443n

Stroman, Duane F., 265n, 283n, 292n, 294n

Stuart, Richard B., 277n, 293n

Suchman, Edward A., 269, 292n

Suffet, Frederic, 593n, 594n, 607n

Sultan, Paul, 285n, 294n

Sutherland, Edwin, 43, 60n, 534-535, 560n, 573n, 581, 585n, 606n, 607n

Swift, Casey, 464, 483n

Sykes, Gresham M., 538n, 561n

Symonds, Carolyn, 326n, 331n

Szasz, Thomas, 276, 293n

Szymanski, Albert, 427, 444n

Taeuber, Conrad, 106n, 133n

Taeuber, Irene B., 106n, 133n

Taft, Philip, 491n, 518n

Tarvis, Carol, 461n, 469n, 482n, 483n

Taylor, George Rogers, 68n, 96n, 97n

Tendler, Ruth, 538n, 561n

Terkel, Studs, 298n, 330n

Thayer. G., 488n, 518n

Thio, Alex, 543n, 561n

Thomas, Dorothy, S., 12n, 33n

Thomas, William I., 12n, 33n

Thomlinson, Ralph, 103n, 133n

Thompson, Kenrick S., 221n, 235n, 236, 244n, 254n, 255n, 412n, 443n

Thompson, Warren S., 105n, 108n, 126n, 133n, 134n, 551n, 562n

Thomson, Samuel, 261

Thorne, Barrie, 464n, 483n

Tijerina, Reies, 430

Tinbergen, Niko, 496, 518n

Tittle, Charles R., 580n, 597n, 600n, 607n, 608n

Toch, Hans, 580n, 606n

Toffler, Alvin, 224, 254n, 327, 331n

Tomlinson, T. M., 501n, 519n

Tourney, G., 538n. 561n

Townsend, Alair A., 376n, 404n

Trecker, Janice, 463n, 483n

Tropman, John E., 380, 393

Trotter, Sharland, 279n, 293n

Tudor, Jeannette F., 271n, 293n

Tudor, William, 271n, 293n

Turner, Jonathan, 33n

Tussing, A. Dale, 394n, 395, 406n

Twaddle, Andrew C., 260n, 292n

Tyler, Carl W., 554n, 562n

Udall, Stewart, 139n, 140, 146n, 147, 153, 165, 166n, 172n, 173n

U'ren, Marjorie B., 463n, 483n

Valente, Sharon, 557n, 563n

Valentine, Charles A., 392n, 405n

Vander Zanden, James W., 73n, 97n, 435, 444n, 488n, 518n

Veblen, Thorsten, 299, 330n

Villemez, Wayne J., 597n, 607n

Vincent, Clark, 226, 254n

Vogler, Roger E., 644n, 649n

Vogt, Glenda, 463n, 483n

Waehrer, Helen, 466n, 483n

Waldo, Gordon P., 574n, 606n

Walker, Allyn, 617n, 647n

Wallerstein, James S., 574n, 606n

Walum, Laurel, 454n, 462n, 482n

Ward, David A., 538n, 561n

Ward, Lester Frank, 7-8, 33n

Waring, Joan, 345n, 368n

Warner, W. Lloyd, 393n, 406n

Washington, Booker T., 428

Wattenberg, Ben J., 403n, 406n

Weaver, Paul, 325n, 331n

Weber, Max, 14n, 33n, 300, 330n, 665n, 687-688n

Weinberg, Martin S., 51n, 60n, 538n, 526n, 539n, 560n, 561n

Weinraub, M., 454n, 482n

Weise, Thomas F., 168n, 173n

Weiss, Robert S., 319n, 331n

Weisstein, Naomi, 463n, 483n

Weitz, Shirley, 459n, 482n

Weitzman, Lenore, 463n, 483n

Weller, Leonard, 338n, 367n

Wells, Donald A., 516n, 519n

Wessen, Donald R., 628n, 648n

Westley, Frances R., 647n, 688n

Westoff, Charles F., 233n, 254n

Weyer, Edward Moffat, 337n, 367n

Whalen, Carol K., 627n, 648n

Wheeler, Stanton, 586n, 607n

Whitehurst, Robert, 243n, 255n

Whyte, William F., 577n, 606n

Whyte, William H., 323, 331n

Wiener, Anthony, 327, 331n

Wilder, D. Lawrence, 632n, 648n

Wilensky, Harold, 317, 319, 321, 331n

Wilkinson, Karen, 598n, 608n

Williams, J. Allen, 392n, 405n

Williams, John E., 426n, 444n

Williams, Robin M., Jr., 654n, 687n

Williams, Roger M., 545n, 562n

Williamson, Robert C., 450n, 482n

Wilsnack, Richard W., 638n, 649n

Wilson, Charles, 145

Wilson, Edmund O., 497n, 518n

Wilson, William H., 66n, 67n, 68n, 96n

Wilson, William J., 420n, 443n

Winick, Charles, 543n, 561n

Wirth, Louis, 72n, 97n

Wiseman, Jacqueline P., 526n, 560n

Wolfgang, Marvin E., 502n, 506n, 519n, 581n, 582n, 606n, 607n

Wollesen, Flemming, 538n, 561n

Wright, Richard, 372, 404n

Wuthnow, Robert, 666, 669n, 688n

Wyle, Clement J., 574n, 606n

Yablonsky, Lewis, 583n, 597n, 607n, 608n

Yancy, William L., 387n, 405n

Yankelovich, Daniel, 663n, 687n

Yinger, Milton J., 438n, 444n, 668n, 688n

Young, Leontine, 252, 255n

Zablocki, Benjamin, 247, 255n

Zalba, S., 549n, 562n

Zim, Marvin H., 173n

Zimbalist, Sidney., 375n, 404n

Zimbardo, Philip G., 436n, 444n

Zimmerman, Carle C., 218, 249, 254, 255n

Zimmerman, Don H., 632n, 648n

Zinberg, Norman E., 641n, 649n

Zinkowski, John, 638n, 649n

Zinn, Howard, 410n, 443n

Zinsser, Hans, 103n, 133n

Zola, Irving, 598n, 608n

Zurcher, Louis A., 548, 562n

Subject
Index

Abortion, definition of, 551
  history of issue, 551-553
  and law, 551-553
  pro-choice arguments, 553
  pro-life arguments, 553-554
Activists, political, 668
Adaptation, old age, 350
Addiction, drug, 623
Adversary system, definition, 588
Affirmative action, legal challenges
    to, 439-441
  and reverse discrimination, 439-
    440
  types of programs, 439
Age, crime rate by, 578
  and suicide, 556-557
  see also Aging; Elderly; Youth
Aggression, 496-499. *See also*
    Conflict; Violence
Aging, conflict perspective, 341-342,
    366
  functionalist perspective, 340-
    341, 366
  interactionist perspective, 342,
    347-348, 366
  see also Elderly
Agism, 347-348
Alcohol, 636-640
  American consumption, 637
  use of, history of, 616, 637
    prohibition of, 511-512
    and race, 638
    and religion, 638
    and sex, 638
    as social problem, 636
Alcoholic, and communes, 681
  defined, 637
Alcoholics Anonymous, 644-645
Alcoholism, 637-639
  among elderly, 354

treatment, aversion therapy, 643
  and behavior modification, 278
  LSD and psychotherapy, 643-
    644
  therapeutic communities, 644
Alienation, and preventive medi-
    cine, 270
  among youth, 666
American Association of Retired
    Persons, 364, 365
American Indian movement, 494
American Medical Association, 261,
    265, 284, 289-290
Amish, 678
Amphetamine abuse, 627-628
  and hyperactivity, 627
  and violence, 628
Amphetamines, 620-622, 626-628
Anglo Saxons (WASPs), 413
Anomie, and deviance, 532-533
  and suicide, 554
Antabuse treatment, 643
Arms limitation, 515-516
Assimilation, definition of, 431
  theory of ethnic relations, 431-
    432
Atomic bombs, 494
Authority, charismatic, 14
  as institutionalized power, 14
  legal-rational, 14
  sources of, 14
  traditional, 14
  see also Power
Automation, and social movements,
    664
  and youth, 656
  see also Work

Bail, reform in, 601
  system, 593-594

Balance of power, 514
Barbiturates, 628-629
  addiction, 628
  overdose, 628-629
Behavior modification, 277-278
Birth rates, 218-219
  age specific, 129
  crude, definition of, 105
Black Americans, educational at-
    tainment, 423
  health status of, 422
  history of, 413-415
  income, 422
  occupational status, 422-423
  population, 421
  status of, 421-423
  unemployment among, 422
  see also Race
Black Panthers, 663, 669
Black Power movement, 428-429,
    661
Boyle Act, 614
Brown *versus* Board of Education
    (1954), 414
Bureaucracy, and social move-
    ments, 664-665
Bureau of Indian Affairs (BIA), 431
Busing, and desegregation, 81-83
  and integration, 438-439

Calvinism, and work, 299-300
Catholic Charismatic Renewal, 676
Causation, *versus* correlation or as-
    sociation, 48
  criteria for inferring, 48-50
Chicano movement, 430-431
Cities, conflict perspective, 70-71,
    83
  functionalist perspective, 69-70,
    83

immigration, 66-67
interactionist perspective, 71
middle class flight, 75-76
migration to, 67-68
see also Urban
Citizen organizations, 207-208
Civil disorders, 488
definition of, 488
rates of, 488-489
and social strain, 502
see also Riots
Civil Rights, legislation, 438
Civil Rights movement, 428, 499, 661
Civil War, 492, 506, 508
Cocaine, 625-626
effects of, 625-626
user characteristics, 625
Cohabitation, 231-233
Colonialism, split labor market hypothesis, 436
theory of internal colonialism, 436
Common cause, 208
Communes, 246-248, 654, 669
in American history, 657-660
and elderly, 360
functionalist perspective, 682
in future, 683-685
ideology of, 678-679
interactionist perspective, 681
modern 678
and social change, 660
Community health centers, 285
Community mental health, 278-279
Competition, failure of, 187-188
Conflict, biological causes of, 496-499
conflict perspective, 495-496, 509, 517
definition of, 488
functionalist perspective, 495, 504-505, 509, 516-517
as inevitable, 494-495
interactionist perspective, 496, 498, 509
and social change, 495, 504-505

see also Violence
Conflict perspective, 23-25
Consensual union, 218. See also, Cohabitation
Consumer protection, 207-208
Contraception, oral, 233
Corporate state, conflict perspective, 181-182
functionalist perspective, 180-181
interactionist perspective, 183
Corporations, conglomerates, 186
definition of, 184
economic power, 188-189
growth, 178-179
interlocking directorates, 187
multinational, see Multinational corporations
vertical expansion, 186
Council on Foreign Relations, 202
Counterculture, 654
definition of, 668
and future, 682-683
see also Youth movement
Courts, 592
Crime, conflict perspective, 572-573
costs of, 568-569
definition of, 580
among elderly, 354
functionalist perspective, 572
history of, 569-572
interactionist perspective, 573-574
measuring, 574-578
rate, 576-580
types of, 580-588
and war, 508-509
Criminals, characteristics of, 578-588
decriminalization of crimes, 601-602
definition of, 569
types of, 580-588
Crowd control, see Riot control
Crowding, 115-116
Cultural lag, and elderly, 366
and individualism, 666
and protestant ethic, 665-666

Cultural relativity, definition of, 17
Culture-versus-biology debate, 498-499
Curandera (folk-curer), 280

Death, attitudes toward, 362-364
with dignity, 362-364
and education, 272-273
and elderly, 348-349, 355, 362-364
and prepaid group plans, 288-289
rate, 262-263, 264
crude, definition of, 105
and sex, 271
and unemployment, 272
Definition of the situation, 12-13
Demographic transition, 105-106
Demonstrations, 503, 504
antiwar, 503, 506
civil rights, 504
Dependence, drug, 623-624
Depressants, 628-629
Deprivation, relative, 499
and religious movements, 676
and violence, 499-500, 502, 504
Deprogramming, 654, 677-678
Deviance, absolutist view, 526-527
conflict perspective, 531
definition of, 526
and elderly, 353-355
examples of, 526
functionalist perspective, 529-531
interactionist perspective, 531-532
legalist view, 527-528
relativist view, 528-529
theories of, 532-537
types or patterns of, 537, 557-558
Differential association and deviance, 534-535
Disarmament, 515-516
Discrimination, Black reactions to, 428-429
conflict perspective, 420
costs of, 426-427
definition of, 413
elderly, 347-348, 359

functionalist perspective, 419-420

individual, 435

institutionalized, 435-436

interactionist perspective, 420-421

Mexican American reactions to, 429-431

native American reactions to, 431

programs to reduce individual, 437-438

sources of, 432-436

theories of, 432-436

see also Agism; Racism; Sexism

Disease, acute, 261-262

chronic, 263-264, 350-351

conflict perspective, 265-266, 291

and elderly, 350-353

functionalist perspective, 265, 291

heart, 263, 267

interactionist perspective, 266, 291

occupation and, 271-272

poverty and, 267-268, 273

race and, 268

self-concept and, 266

social class and, 267-271

unemployment and, 272

see also Health; Illness

Dissent, political, 505-506

Diversion, 603

Divorce, 233-237

future of, 236-237

grounds for, 236

law and, 235-236

rate of, 218, 234-235

social class, 235

Drug abuse, 621, 622-623

Drug addiction, and communes, 681

Drug use, conflict perspective, 618-619

functionalist perspective, 618

history of, 613-618

interactionist perspective, 619

Due process, 603

Education, financing, 79, 80-81

health and, 272-273

history of, 68-69

integration, 82-83

minorities, 81-82

poverty, 79-80

segregation, 81-82

solving social problems, 68-69, 78-79, 83

see also Busing

Elderly, deviance among, 353-355

finances of, 346-347, 350, 356-358

health of, 350-353

health costs and, 281-282, 286, 352-353

income of, 336, 344, 346-347, 357

and industrialization, 339-340

living arrangements among, 348, 355-356, 358-362

and media, 348

numbers of, 340, 356

occupational skills of, 345

in other cultures, 336-338

political action and, 364-365

self-concept of, 348, 355-356

social class and, 345

social status of, 388, 339

volunteer work among, 345-346

Employee Retirement Income Security Act, 357

Environment, and American Indians, 139

and business, 145-146

conflict perspective, 143-144, 154, 171

Earth Day, 147-148

and economic growth, 148-153

functionalist perspective, 143, 153, 171

future prospects, 163-170

interactionist perspective, 144, 154-155, 171

interest groups, 145-155

Kepone, 155-163

myth of superabundance, 140

and public action, 163-165

as social problem, 143-144

and solutions, 169-170

spaceship earth, 150

and vested interests, 167-169

Environmental movement, 146-148

Environmental problems, history of, 139-143

Equal Rights Amendment, 475-477

Ethnicity, definition of, 411

history of relations in U.S., 410

see also Race

Ethnocentrism, definition of, 17

and social movements, 662

Ethology, 496

Euthanasia, 362-363

Existence time, 306

Familism, and values in preindustrial society, 220-221, 247

Family, alternative forms, 237-249

atomistic, 218

conflict perspective, 225-226, 253

and cultural lag, 228

and delinquency, 597-598

extended, 219-221, 246

forms of, 251-252

functionalist perspective, 224-225, 252-253

industrial revolution, 219-223

interactionist perspective, 226-227, 253

nuclear, 222-223, 338-339

functions of, 223-224

one-parent, 219, 243-244

perceptions of, 249-250

pluralistic, 250-251

in postindustrial society, 224

preindustrial society, 219-221

reorganization, 225-226

as social problem, 224-229

stability, 221

Family planning, 128-130

Puerto Rico, 129

Family practice physicians, 284

Famine, 117-119

China, 104, 117

food distribution, 117

Ireland, 104

"Father-power," 473-474
Fecundity, defined, 112
Federal Bureau of Investigation, and crime statistics, 568
Federal Bureau of Narcotics, 615, 617
Fee-for-service medicine, 285-286
"Feminine mystique," 474-475
Fertility, 126-131
  beliefs and values, 113-114
  contraception, 127-128
  definition of, 112
  dynamics of, 112-114
  economic development, 130-131
  family structure, 112-113
  India, 112, 113
  institutional supports, 113
  Ireland, 113
  and machismo, 113
  and poverty, 125
  and religion, 114
  socioeconomic factors, 114
  status of women, 113
Flexitime, 324-325
Food, deficit famine, definition of, 117
  desertification, definition of, 119
  eutrophication, definition of, 120
  future prospects, 123-124, 125
  Green Revolution, 121-123
  land shortage, 119-120
  sea farming, 120-121
  shortages of, 117-124
Foreign policy, 514-515
Frustration, and violence, 499-500, 502
Functional alternatives, 21
Functionalist perspective, 19-23
Functional prerequisites, 21

Gatekeeping, definition of, 18
Genocide, 418
Germ theory of disease, 261
Glossolalia, 674
Government, growth, 179-180, 195
  organization, 193
  reform of, 206

Graphs, interpretation of, 55-56
Gray Panthers, 348, 365
Gross National Product (GNP), 507
Gun control, 510-512

Hallucinogens, 630-631
  history of, 630
Harrison Narcotics Act, 354, 614-615
Hawthorne effect, 313
Health, conflict perspective, 263-264, 291
  and education, 272-273
  among elderly, 343, 347
  functionalist perspective, 265, 291
  interactionist perspective, 266, 291
  see also Disease; Illness
Health care, bureaucracies in, 279-281
  costs of, 281-283, 285-289, 352-353
  dehumanization in, 279, 283-285
  depersonalization and, 281, 283-285, 356
  quality of, 269-270
  self-concept and, 280-281
Health care consumer, 290
Health insurance, and elderly, 353
  and health costs, 283
Health Insurance Plan of New York, 288
Health maintenance organizations, 288-289, 290, 291
Heroin, addiction process, 634
  and crime, 635
  among elderly, 354
  overdose death, 636
  as social problem, 635-636
Heterogeneity, 654
Hippies, 663-664, 668, 673, 679
Hispanic Americans, educational attainment, 425
  health status, 424
  history of, 415-417
  income of, 425

population characteristics, 423
  reactions to prejudice and discrimination, 429-431
  status of, 423-425
  see also Ethnicity
Homeopathy, 261
Homes for the aged, 360
Homicide, 580-581
Homosexuality, definition of, 537
  female, 540
  and homosexual community, 540-541
  and law, 541-543
  lifestyle, 537
  male, 539
  patterns of, 539-540
  theories of, 537-539
Hospices, 363-364
Housing, future needs, 84
  government programs, 85-87
  public, 85-87
  redlining, 87
Hutterites, 678
Hyperactivity, 627

Identity crisis, among youth, 666-667
Illness, and education, 272-273
  as social role, 266
  see also Disease; Health
Indian Wars, 494
Indicators, reliability of, 52
  validity of, 51-52
Individualism, 655, 666
  and communes, 658-659
  decline of, 323-324
  and values, 222
  and youth movement, 668
Industrialization, and communes, 660
  and conflict, 495
  effects of, 105-106
  and youth, 656, 667
Infant mortality, 260, 264
  education and, 272
Inflation, and war, 507
Information, problems of misinter-

pretation, 38

Institutionalization, and depersonalization, 356
among elderly, 355-356
and self-concept, 355-356
and sex, 355
and social class, 355
see also Nursing homes
Insurrection, 492
Interactionist perspective, 25-28
Interest group, definition of, 15
International organizations, 516
Interstate Commerce Commission,
193-195
Intimacy, the search for, 252

Jesus People, 654, 672, 676
beliefs of, 674
lifestyle of, 674, 683
Job enrichment, 324
Juvenile court, history of, 570-571
problems in, 596
Juvenile delinquency, measuring,
596
Juvenile delinquents, characteristics of, 596-599
types of, 595-596

Kaiser Permanente Health Plan, 288
Kepone, 155-163
Knowledge, types of, 38-44
Korean War, 494, 507, 515
Krishna Consciousness movement,
654, 673, 676
beliefs, 673
lifestyle, 673-674, 683
Ku Klux Klan, 489

Labeling, and deviance, 535-537
and homosexuality, 539
see also Poverty
Labor unions, and violence, 490-492
Latent function, 21
Lawyers, as defense attorneys, 593
as prosecutors, 592-593
League of Nations, 516
Learning, and violence, 500-502

Legalization, of criminal offenses,
601-602
Legitimacy, crisis of, 667-668
political, 505
of violence, 509
Leisure, 314-322
compensatory, 318
as consumption, 326-327
costs, 326-327
definition of, 306
enforced, 317
history of, 299-302
increases in, 315-316
integrationist view of, 302, 305
passive *versus* active, 320-322
segmentalist view of, 302-303,
305
social classes, 319-320
time blocks, 316
see also Work
Leisure class, emergence of, 299
Leisure time, difficulties in using,
318-319
Life expectancy, health costs and,
282
by sex, 264, 271
Living will, 362-363
Looking-glass self, 26
and elderly, 347-348
and mental illness, 275-276
LSD (lysergic acid diethylamide),
618, 630
alcoholism treatment, 643-644

Male occupations, nontraditional
types, 473
Male sex role, changing, 469-474
Manifest function, 21
Marijuana, 631-634
decriminalization of, 511-512,
633-634
history of use, 616-618
as social problem, 631-634
use in communes, 679
user characteristics, 631
Marijuana Tax Act, 617
Marital bond, 229-233

Marital happiness, "formula" for,
234-235
Marital status, and suicide, 556
Marriage, changing patterns, 229-
233
and family, 229-230
future of, 251
group, 244-246
open, 242-243
"Masculine mystique," 462
Massive retaliation, 514
Mass media, regulation of, 512-513
and social class, 501
and violence, 500-502
Mass society, 665
Media watch, 348
Medicaid, 269, 286-287, 289, 336
Medicare, 269, 286-287, 289, 336,
353, 361
Medicine, crisis, 264
early American, 260-261
knowledge of, 269
modern American, 261-263
preventive, 263-264, 270, 272,
285, 288-289
quackery in, 350-351
Men's liberation, 471-473
dimensions of, 473-474
Mental hospitals, and community
mental health movement,
278-279
and self-fulfilling prophecy, 281
Mental illness, 273-279
age and, 353-354
causes of, 275, 277
contemporary treatment of, 277-
279
as disease, 274-275, 276
downward drift, 270
increase in, 264
as problems of living, 276-277
sex roles and, 271
social causation, 270
and social class, 268, 270-271
as social role, 275-276
stereotyping of, 273-274
treatment in history, 273-274

unemployment and, 272

Methadone, 354

Metropolitan government, 93-95
  cooperation, 94-95
  federation, 94

Mexican Americans, *see* Hispanic
  Americans

Migration, dynamics of, 114-115
  Europe, 126
  Indonesia, 126
  United States, 126

Military-industrial complex, 195-
  199
  definition of, 196
  personnel transfer, 196-197
  and public interests, 197-198

Military and war, 508

Millerites, 658

Minority group, characteristics of,
  412-413
  definition of, 412
  history of in U.S., 413-419

Modeling, and aggression, 500

Monolithic code, 221

Monopolies, 185

Morbidity, *see* Disease

Mormons, 657-658

Morphine, 614, 619

Mortality, 110-112, 126
  Ceylon, 111
  developing nations, 111-112
  disease, 103-104
  industrial nations, 110-111
  infant, 103
  see also Death

Multinational corporations, benefits of, 189
  definition of, 189
  exploitation, 190
  politics, 190-191
  regulation of, 191-192

Murder, 488

Narcotic addiction, Civil War, 614
  and physicians, 636

Narcotics, 634-636
  definition of, 634

history of, 614-616

National Association for Mental
  health, 273

National Council of Senior Citizens,
  364-365

National health insurance, 283-285

National Organization for Non-
  Parents (NON), 219, 248

National Organization of Women,
  463, 475

National Retired Teachers Association, 364-365

National Rifle Association (NRA),
  510

Native Americans, educational attainment, 425-426
  health status of, 425
  history of, 417-419
  population characteristics, 425
  poverty among, 425
  reactions to prejudice and discrimination, 431
  status of, 425-426
  unemployment, 425

Natural increase, rate of, 105

Neurosis, 267

New health practitioners, 283-285

New towns, 93

Nuclear Test Ban Treaty, 515

Nurse practitioners, 284-285

Nurses, 280, 290
  health costs and, 283
  in nursing homes, 361

Nursing homes, 355, 356, 360-362

Obscenity, *see* Pornography and
  obscenity

Occupation, and health, 271-272

Ombudsmen, in hospitals, 285, 362

Organized crime, patterns of, 582-
  585

Overpopulation, consequences of,
  115-125

Pairism, 224

Parenthood, new possibilities, 248

PCP (phencyclidine), 630-631

effects of, 631

Pensions, 356-357

People's Temple, 677

Personal identity, *see* Self-concept

Personal troubles and public issues,
  10

Physicians, 261-262, 289-290
  allopathic, 260-261
  distribution of, 284-285
  family practice, 284
  and health costs, 283
  specialization of, 279-280, 284

Physicians' assistants, 284-285

Plea bargaining, forms of, 594

Plessy *versus* Ferguson (1896), 414

Pluralism, definition of, 432
  theory of ethnic relations, 432

Police, 502-504, 505
  and crowd control, 512
  and juvenile delinquents, 603
  and system of criminal justice,
  588-592

Policy creation, 204

Policy implementation, 204

Polyandry, 245

Polygamy, 245
  serial, 246

Polygyny, 242

Poor people, characteristics of, 383-
  387
  children, 387
  elderly, 386-387
  race, 383-385
  rural, 385-386

Popular medical orientation, 269

Population, conflict perspective,
  108-109, 132
  definition of, 102
  density, defined, 115
  dynamics of, 109-115
  functionalist perspective, 106-
  108, 132
  future prospects, 125-131
  growth, history of, 102-106
  India, 102
  interactionist perspective, 109,
  132

Malthusian view, 107-108
Marxian view, 108-109
as social problem, 106-109
Pornography and obscenity, Commission on Obscenity and Pornography, 546
effects of, 547-548
history of, 546
Supreme Court and, 546
Poverty, blocked opportunity, 391
community and self-help, 402-403
conflict perspective, 377, 391
cultural causes, 392
definition of, cultural, 379-380
economic, 378-379
dual welfare system, 393-394
among elderly, 336
functionalist perspective, 376-377, 389-390, 403
future prospects, 396-403
history of, 373-376
and immigrants, 374-375
and industrialization, 373-374
interactionist perspective, 378, 400
labeling theory, 393
marginal poor, 381
and modern poverty programs, 375-376
as social problem, 376-380
societal reaction to, 392-393
solutions to, changing self-conceptions, 396-398
Community Action Agencies (CAA), 399
Economic Opportunity Act, 399
Head Start, 398-399
income maintenance program, 400
training the poor, 401-402
welfare, 393-396
welfare poor, 380-381
working poor, 382-383
Power, and authority, 13-15
definition of, 13
exercise of, 13

and pluralism, 202-204
sources of, 13
Power elite, 199-202
characteristics of, 199-201
definition of, 199
and democracy, 204-205
foreign policy, 202
interchangeability, 201
Preachment, 227
Prejudice, Black reactions to, 428-429
conflict perspective, 420
costs of, 426
definition of, 412-413
against elderly, 348, 359
functionalist perspective, 419-420
interactionist perspective, 420-421
Mexican American reactions to, 429-431
native American reactions to, 431
sources of, 432-436
theories of, 432-436
Prepaid group plans, see Health maintenance organizations
Prohibition, 616, 617
Propaganda, versus education, 57
techniques or methods of, 58-59
Proprietary homes, see Homes for the aged
Prostitution, characteristics of, 543-544
decriminalization of, 545
definition of, 543
exploitation of prostitutes, 544-545
extent of, 543
functions of, 544
Protestant ethic, 655, 665-666, 670-671
decline of, 312
emergence of, 299-300
Psychoactive drugs, 619-622
Psychosis, 268
functional, 353-354
organic, 353-354
Psychotherapy, 277

in community mental health, 278
history and effects of, 599-600
Punishment, deinstitutionalization, 603-604

Race, characteristics of major categories, 410-411
definition of, 410
and ethnicity, crime rate by, 579-580
delinquency rate by, 597
and suicide, 557
Racial violence, 489-490
Racism, 348
costs of, 426-427
definition of, 411
Reality, subjective nature of, 12-13
Recreation, 300
Reform, of juvenile justice system, 602-603
of offender, 602
Reinforcement, 500
Relative deprivation, and violence, 499-500, 502, 504
Religious social movements, 654, 662
in American history, 657
conflict perspective, 678
and deprivation, 676
functionalist perspective, 677-678
and future, 683
interactionist perspective, 677
membership, 675-676
modern, 672-678
recruitment to, 676-677
Remarriage, rates of, 234
Resources, depletion of, 116-117
Retirement, 340, 342-346, 348
and financial insurance programs, 356-358
Retirement communities, 358-359
Revenue sharing, 92
Revolution, see Insurrection
Revolution of rising expectations, 499-500
Riot control, 512
Riots, commodity, 490

communal, 490
draft, 492, 506, 513
labor, 490-492, 495, 513
race, 489-490, 495, 499, 506, 513, 514
see also Civil disorders

Sampling, bias in, 50-51
representative sample, 51
Schools and delinquency, 598
Science, characteristic of the scientific method, 42-44
interest groups and objectivity, 44-45
and objectivity, 43-44
research process, 45-52
Scientific medical orientation, 269
Sects, religious, 675-676
Self-concept, and conflict, 504
of elderly, 338, 347-348
among youth, 671
see also Looking-glass self
Self-fulfilling prophecy, and elderly, 356
and mental hospitals, 281
and mental illness, 275-276
Separatism, definition of, 432
theory of ethnic relations, 432
Sex, co-marital, 243
crime rates by, 578-579
delinquency rates by, 596-597
extramarital, 242-243
and suicide, 556
Sexism, 854, 463-464
definition of, 463
Sex roles, androgeny and, 478-479
biology and, 458-459
characteristics assigned to, 462
conflict perspective, 456-457, 480
discrimination and inequality, 464-465
early women's rights movement, 452-454
economic discrimination, 465-468
education and, 462-463
and family structure, 451-452

female stereotype, 462-463
and femininity, 458, 460, 474
functionalist perspective, 455-456, 480
and gender, 458
and health, 271
hermaphrodites, 454
history of, 450-455
hunting and gathering societies, 450-451
industrial America, 451-452
inequality of, 452-455
interactionist perspective, 457, 480-481
language and, 464
and male socialization, 461-462
and masculinity, 458, 460, 469-471, 474
mental health clinics and, 463
preindustrial America, 451
self-fulfilling prophecy and, 461
as social problem, 445-458
Sex role differentiation, expressive functions and, 456
instrumental functions and, 456
Sex role discrimination, education and, 465-466
income and, 467-468
occupation and, 466-467
Sexual bargaining, 456
Sexual behavior
of Krishna Consciousness members, 673
of Shakers, 659-660
Sexual offenses, 586-587
Shakers, 659
Shared expectations, 27-28
Social class, health care expenditures and, 281-282
and illness, 267-271
and medical care, 269-270
see also Socioeconomic status
Social disengagement theory of aging, 348-350
Social movements, 654
in American history, 655-660
and bureaucratization, 664-665

conflict perspective, 661
functionalist perspective, 660-661
interactionist perspective, 661-662
radical, 495
and social change, 654, 663-664
and social problems, 654, 663-667
Social participation, among elderly, 347-350
and institutionalization, 355
and preventive medicine, 270
and social class, 350
Social problems, 9-12
in America, 12-19
basis for defining, 9-10
conflict perspective definition, 24-25
definition of 10-12
and democracy, 17-19
functionalist definition, 22
history of, 6-9
interactionist definition, 28
and norms, 12
and public interest, 8
and sociology, 6-7
solutions to, 29-31
and values, 9-10, 12-13
Social psychiatry, see Community mental health
Social reality, 26-27
Social Security, 344, 347, 356-358
Society, heterogeneous, 16
homogenous, 16
and subcultures, 16-17
Sociobiology, 497-499
Socioeconomic status, crime rates by, 580
delinquency rates by, 597
see also Social class
Southern Christian Leadership Conference, 663
Split labor market, 436
Statistics, correlation, 48
descriptive, 52-54
inference in, 52, 54-55
Stereotyping, of elderly, 347-348, 359

and violence, 503-504, 509

Stimulants, 624-628

Strategic Arms Limitation Treaty (SALT), 515

Stress, 263, 271-272

Students for a Democratic Society (SDS), 669

Subculture, American, 16-17
definition of, 26
of elderly, 359
of youth, 655-657, 668-672

Substance abuse, among elderly, 354

Suffrage, male, 492

Suicide, egoistic, 354
among elderly, 354-355
extent of, 555-557
and marital status, 354-355
mass, 677
prevention of, 557
and sex, 354
types of, 554-555
and unemployment, 272

Surgery, and health maintenance organization, 288
unnecessary, 283

Symbionese Liberation Army, 492, 661, 669

Technology, and youth movement, 670

Television, see Mass media

Territorial imperative, 496-497

Terrorism, 492-494, 513

Theft, 581-582

Theory, explanation of, 19

Third party medicine, 285-287

Thomsonianism, 261

Tobacco, 624-625
and United States Surgeon General Report, 624

Tolerance, drug, 623

Tranquilizers, 629

Transportation, 88-91
automobiles, 88-89
costs, 89-90
and decentralization, 75

history, 68
omnibus, 68
public, 89-91

Unconventional lifestyles, 654-655

Unemployment, and health, 272
and poverty, 4-6
and protestant ethic, 665
rates of, 4

Unification Church, 654, 662, 676
beliefs of, 674-675
finances of, 675
lifestyle, 675
as social problem, 677-678

United Nations, 516

Urban, block grant program, 91-92
complexity of life, 72
ghettoes, 84-85
housing, 83-87
impersonality, 73
individualism, 72-73
minority groups, 77-78
see also Cities

Urban economy, business, 75
decentralization, 73-75
New York crisis, 76-77

Urban land use, 87-88

Urban planning, 92-93

Urban renewal, 85-87

Value conflict, 10

Values, American, 654-655, 672

Vested interest group, definition of, 15

Veto groups, 203-204

Victimless offenses, 587-588

Victims, compensation of, 601

Vietnam War, 494, 506-508, 515, 668

Violence, and child abuse, 549-550
definition of, 488
and drug use, 628
frustration and deprivation, 499-500
and learning, 500-502
and modeling, 500
political, 492-494, 505-506

preventing, 510-514
and socialization, 500
social sources of, 502-504
and spouse abuse, 550-551
subculture of, 502-503
see also Conflict

Volstead Act, 10-11, 12, 1578 1579, 617

War, 488
American, 494-495
consequences of, 505-509
and crime, 508-509
and economic problems, 506-508
and instincts, 498
and military, 508
nuclear, 514-515
prevention of, 514-516

Watts, 488

Weather Underground, 661, 669

White-collar crime, 585-586

Women, in military, 478
in sports, 477
see also Sex roles

Women's Christian Temperance Union, 15-16, 616

Women's movement, 474-477
as social movement, 663

Work, 306-314
and alienation, 308-309
and automation, 309-310
as central life interest, 313-314
craftsmanship, 303-304
definition of, 305
and elderly, 342-346, 350
four-forty week, 316-317
history of, 299-302
integrationist view of, 302, 305
and leisure, conflict perspective, 303-304, 322-323, 325-326 329
functionalist perspective, 302-303, 322, 329
industrial society, 300-302
interactionist perspective, 304-305, 323, 329
as social problem, 302-306

and mechanization, 310
multiple dimensions of, 307-308
production and consumption, 304
reduction in, 315-316
reorganization of, 324-326
segmentalist view of, 302-303, 305
specialization and, 308
three-day workweek, 317
Workers, behavior modification and, 313

dissatisfaction of, 310-312
World War I, 494, 516
World War II, 494, 507, 516
Wounded Knee, 431

Youth definition of, 656
and education, 656, 671
in industrial society, 656, 671
in preindustrial society, 655-656
as subculture, 655-657, 668-672
Youth movement, 662, 668-672

and advanced technology, 670
beliefs of, 668-670
functionalist perspective, 672
interactionist perspective, 672
membership in, 672
origins of, 670-672
and social change, 672
see also Counterculture

Zero population growth, 131